SOMETHING ABOUT THE AUTHOR®

Something about
the Author *was named
an "Outstanding
Reference Source,"
the highest honor given
by the American
Library Association
Reference and Adult
Services Division.*

ISSN 0276-816X

SOMETHING ABOUT THE AUTHOR®

**Facts and Pictures about Authors
and Illustrators of Books for Young People**

volume 197

GALE
CENGAGE Learning™

Detroit • New York • San Francisco • New Haven, Conn • Waterville, Maine • London

GALE
CENGAGE Learning

Something about the Author, Volume 197

Project Editor: Lisa Kumar

Editorial: Dana Ferguson, Amy Elisabeth Fuller, Michelle Kazensky, Jennifer Mossman, Joseph Palmisano, Mary Ruby, Marie Toft

Permissions: Kelly Quin, Sara Teller, Robyn Young

Imaging and Multimedia: Leitha Etheridge-Sims, John Watkins

Composition and Electronic Capture: Amy Darga

Manufacturing: Drew Kalasky

Product Manager: Janet Witalec

For product information and technology assistance, contact us at
Gale Customer Support, 1-800-877-4253.
For permission to use material from this text or product,
submit all requests online at **www.cengage.com/permissions.**
Further permissions questions can be emailed to
permissionrequest@cengage.com

Gale
27500 Drake Rd.
Farmington Hills, MI, 48331-3535

LIBRARY OF CONGRESS CATALOG CARD NUMBER 62-52046

ISBN-13: 978-1-4144-2169-8
ISBN-10: 1-4144-2169-9

ISSN 0276-816X

This title is also available as an e-book.
ISBN-13: 978-1-4144-5743-7
ISBN-10: 1-4144-5743-X
Contact your Gale, Cengage Learning sales representative for ordering information.

Printed in the United States of America
1 2 3 4 5 6 7 13 12 11 10 09

Contents

Authors in Forthcoming Volumes vii

Introduction ix

SATA Product Advisory Board xi

Illustrations Index 195

Author Index 227

A

Ábalos, Rafael 1956- 1

Anderson, John David 2

Asher, Bridget
   See Baggott, Julianna 3

B

Baggott, Julianna 1969- 3

Banks, Merry 5

Bateson, Catherine 1960- 5

Beck, Scott 7

Bell, Hilari 1958- 8

Bode, N.E.
   See Baggott, Julianna 3

Bonner, Hannah 13

Brock, Delia
   See Ephron, Delia 64

Brooks, Kevin 1959- 14

Brooks, Kevin M.
   See Brooks, Kevin 14

C

Call, Greg 18

Carman, Patrick 1966- 19

Carruth, Hayden 1921-2008
   Obituary Notice 22

Chapman, Lynne 1960- 23

Cneut, Carll 1969- 25

Colfer, Eoin 1965- 27

Coman, Carolyn 32

Covert, Ralph 1968- 36

D

Darling, Sandra Louise Woodward
   See Day, Alexandra 39

Day, Alexandra 1941- 39
   Autobiography Feature 44

Decker, Timothy 1974- 57

Del Negro, Janice M. 58

E

Eason, Alethea 1957- 61

Elliott, Laura Malone 1957- 62

Elliott, L.M.
   See Elliott, Laura Malone 62

Ephron, Delia 1944- 64

F

Ferri, Giuliano 1965- 67

Fine, Anne 1947- 68

Foster, Mark 1961- 76

Fried, Janice 76

G

Gaiman, Neil 1960- 78

Giblin, James Cross 1933- 87

Gordon, Amy 1949- 91

Gott, Barry 94

Gunnella 1956- 97

H

Hanft, Josh 1956- 98

Hanft, Joshua E.
   See Hanft, Josh 98

Hawking, Lucy 1969- 100

Hughes, Pat 101

J

Journet, Mireille
  See Marokvia, Mireille 115

K

Kemly, Kathleen 1958- 104

King, Daren 1972- 104

Knowles, Jo 1970- 106

Knowles, Johanna Beth
  See Knowles, Jo 106

L

Lafrance, Marie 1955- 108

Lawson, Amy
  See Gordon, Amy 91

Leffler, Silke 110

Locke, Gary 1963- 111

M

MacPhail, Catherine 1946- 112

Mandabach, Brian 1962(?)- 114

Marokvia, Mireille 1908-2008
  Obituary Notice 115

Marokvia, Mireille Journet
  See Marokvia, Mireille 115

Mayr, Diane 1949- 116

McKean, Dave 1963- 116

McKean, David Jeff
  See McKean, Dave 116

Mohammed, Khadra 119

N

Nelson, R.A. 121

Neri, G. 123

Neri, Greg
  See Neri, G. 123

Neri, Gregory
  See Neri, G. 123

Noble, Trinka Hakes 124

Ólafsdóttir, Gudrún Elin
  See Gunnella 97

O

Oliver, Narelle 1960- 128

Olten, Manuela 1970- 131

Orback, Craig 131

P

Parsons, Garry 134

Patterson, James 1947- 136

Patterson, James B.
  See Patterson, James 136

Paz, Natalia Toledo
  See Toledo, Natalia 181

Pedler, Caroline 139

Peters, Julie Anne 1952- 140

Porfirio, Guy 1958- 144

R

Rader, Laura 146

Reinhart, Matthew 1971- 148

Reynolds, Aaron 1970- 150

Robertson, Mark
  See Robertson, M.P. 152

Robertson, M.P. 1965- 152

Robinson, Sharon 1950- 154

Ryan, Pam Muñoz 156

S

Sage, Angie 1952- 162

Sandin, Joan 1942- 165

Schmatz, Pat 169

Schy, Yael 170

Sedgwick, Marcus 1968- 171

Smallman, Steve 176

Sneider, Marian 1932-2005 176

T

Tallec, Olivier 1970- 178

Thomas, Jan 1958- 179

Toledo, Natalia 1967- 181

V

Vere, Ed 183

W

Walker, David 1965- 184

Weaver, Tess 185

Wild, Margaret 1948- 186

Authors in Forthcoming Volumes

Below are some of the authors and illustrators that will be featured in upcoming volumes of *SATA*. These include new entries on the swiftly rising stars of the field, as well as completely revised and updated entries (indicated with *) on some of the most notable and best-loved creators of books for children.

*Melvin Burgess ▌ Described as the "godfather" of young-adult fiction in the United Kingdom, Burgess combines fantasy with gritty realism in a series of novels that have been called both unsettling and controversial. In his books, which include *The Cry of the Wolf, Junk, Doing It,* and *Sara's Face,* Burgess showcases his creative and unique views on teen life. A winner of the prestigious Carnegie Medal, Burgess has earned critical acclaim on both sides of the Atlantic.

Emily McLachlan Charest ▌ Charest is the daughter of Newbery Medal-winning author Patricia MacLachlan, and she has joined her mother in creating several engaging picture books for young readers. The first collaboration between mother and daughter, *Painting the Wind,* is one of several joint projects, all of which are noted for their engaging artwork.

Julian Fellowes ▌ An actor in television and film, Fellowes added writing to his repertoire with the 1994 Emmy Award-winning television miniseries *Little Lord Fauntleroy.* While also writing the screenplays for the period dramas *Gosford Park* and *Vanity Fair,* Fellowes teamed up with illustrator S.D. Schindler to produce the nostalgic-themed picture book *The Curious Adventures of the Abandoned Toys.*

Joanne Fitzgerald ▌ Fitzgerald is an illustrator whose use of bright colors and detail have made her self-illustrated picture books popular in her native Canada and elsewhere. Her contributions to picture books by other writers have also earned Fitzgerald several awards: she won the coveted Governor General's Award for her artwork in *Doctor Kiss Says Yes* by Teddy Jam, and her illustrations for Celia Barker Lottridge's folk-tale adaptation *The Little Rooster and the Diamond Button* were honored with Canada's Mr. Christie's Book Award.

Max Grafe ▌ A printmaker and painter, Grafe joined the world of children's books by providing the illustrations to the English translation of French writer Daniel Pennac's story *Eye of the Wolf.* His evocative pictures, which are known for their textured, impressionistic effect, have also appeared in Nancy Wood's poignant *Old Wolf* and Laura Amy Schlitz's *The Bearskinner.*

*Grace Lin ▌ Boston-based illustrator and author Lin shares her Asian-American heritage in the colorful artwork she creates for original picture-book stories such as *Robert's Snow, Bringing in the New Year,* and *The Red Thread* as well as texts by other writers. In addition, Lin has written several novels that echo her picture-book themes, among them *The Year of the Dog, The Year of the Rat,* and *Where the Mountains Meet the Moon.* With their round-edged shapes, flat primary colors, and heavy black edges, Lin's artwork gives her picture books a timeless, folktale quality.

Gemma Malley ▌ Malley worked as a journalist for several major British publications, as well as taking a civil-service job, before turning to a career as a novelist. Her futuristic novels *The Declaration* and *The Resistance* are set in a future world in which ageing no longer exists and young people must be warehoused due to lack of space. Within this grim setting, Malley sets about exploring what would happen if modern science was able to cure the many infirmities of old age and mankind achieved its goal of eternal life.

*Phillip Pullman ▌ A writer of great range, depth, and imagination, Pullman is recognized as one of the most talented creators of children's literature of his generation. Best known for the "Sally Lockhart" and "His Dark Materials" books, he packs his complex stories with humor and high drama. An epic fantasy set in an Arctic-like region, "His Dark Materials" includes *The Golden Compass,* a novel that was adapted as a feature film and released in 2007.

*Matt Tavares ▌ Although Tavares had no intention of becoming a children's book writer and illustrator, an introduction to the genre proved inspirational. His first picture book, the award-winning *Zachary's Ball,* has been followed by several more boy-friendly stories—including *Oliver's Game, Mudball,* and *Henry Aaron's Dream*—all of which combine a love of baseball with Tavares' detailed paintings.

*Audrey Wood ▌ A prolific author who is known for her sense of whimsy, Wood has created the self-illustrated picture books *The Princess and the Dragon, Silly Sally, The Red Racer,* and *A Dog Needs a Bone.* She is also the member of an artistic family: she teams with her artist husband, Don Wood, in books such as *Heckedy Peg, The Napping House,* and *King Bidgood's in the Bathtub,* while *Alphabet Adventure* features illustrations by her son, Bruce Wood.

Introduction

Something about the Author (*SATA*) is an ongoing reference series that examines the lives and works of authors and illustrators of books for children. *SATA* includes not only well-known writers and artists but also less prominent individuals whose works are just coming to be recognized. This series is often the only readily available information source on emerging authors and illustrators. You'll find *SATA* informative and entertaining, whether you are a student, a librarian, an English teacher, a parent, or simply an adult who enjoys children's literature.

What's Inside *SATA*

SATA provides detailed information about authors and illustrators who span the full time range of children's literature, from early figures like John Newbery and L. Frank Baum to contemporary figures like Judy Blume and Richard Peck. Authors in the series represent primarily English-speaking countries, particularly the United States, Canada, and the United Kingdom. Also included, however, are authors from around the world whose works are available in English translation. The writings represented in *SATA* include those created intentionally for children and young adults as well as those written for a general audience and known to interest younger readers. These writings cover the entire spectrum of children's literature, including picture books, humor, folk and fairy tales, animal stories, mystery and adventure, science fiction and fantasy, historical fiction, poetry and nonsense verse, drama, biography, and nonfiction. Obituaries are also included in *SATA* and are intended not only as death notices but also as concise overviews of people's lives and work. Additionally, each edition features newly revised and updated entries for a selection of *SATA* listees who remain of interest to today's readers and who have been active enough to require extensive revisions of their earlier biographies.

Autobiography Feature

Beginning with Volume 103, many volumes of *SATA* feature one or more specially commissioned autobiographical essays. These unique essays, averaging about ten thousand words in length and illustrated with an abundance of personal photos, present an entertaining and informative first-person perspective on the lives and careers of prominent authors and illustrators profiled in *SATA*.

Two Convenient Indexes

In response to suggestions from librarians, *SATA* indexes no longer appear in every volume but are included in alternate (odd-numbered) volumes of the series, beginning with Volume 57.

SATA continues to include two indexes that cumulate with each alternate volume: the Illustrations Index, arranged by the name of the illustrator, gives the number of the volume and page where the illustrator's work appears in the current volume as well as all preceding volumes in the series; the Author Index gives the number of the volume in which a person's biographical sketch, autobiographical essay, or obituary appears in the current volume as well as all preceding volumes in the series.

These indexes also include references to authors and illustrators who appear in *Gale's Yesterday's Authors of Books for Children, Children's Literature Review,* and *Something about the Author Autobiography Series.*

Easy-to-Use Entry Format

Whether you're already familiar with the *SATA* series or just getting acquainted, you will want to be aware of the kind of information that an entry provides. In every *SATA* entry the editors attempt to give as complete a picture of the person's life and work as possible. A typical entry in *SATA* includes the following clearly labeled information sections:

PERSONAL: date and place of birth and death, parents' names and occupations, name of spouse, date of marriage, names of children, educational institutions attended, degrees received, religious and political affiliations, hobbies and other interests.

ADDRESSES: complete home, office, electronic mail, and agent addresses, whenever available.

CAREER: name of employer, position, and dates for each career post; art exhibitions; military service; memberships and offices held in professional and civic organizations.

MEMBER: professional, civic, and other association memberships and any official posts held.

AWARDS, HONORS: literary and professional awards received.

WRITINGS: title-by-title chronological bibliography of books written and/or illustrated, listed by genre when known; lists of other notable publications, such as plays, screenplays, and periodical contributions.

ADAPTATIONS: a list of films, television programs, plays, CD-ROMs, recordings, and other media presentations that have been adapted from the author's work.

WORK IN PROGRESS: description of projects in progress.

SIDELIGHTS: a biographical portrait of the author or illustrator's development, either directly from the biographee—and often written specifically for the *SATA* entry—or gathered from diaries, letters, interviews, or other published sources.

BIOGRAPHICAL AND CRITICAL SOURCES: cites sources quoted in "Sidelights" along with references for further reading.

EXTENSIVE ILLUSTRATIONS: photographs, movie stills, book illustrations, and other interesting visual materials supplement the text.

How a *SATA* Entry Is Compiled

SATA editors examine a wide variety of published sources to gather information for an entry. Biographical and bibliographic sources are consulted, as are book reviews, feature articles, published interviews, and material sometimes obtained from the biographee's family, publishers, agent, or other associates. Whenever possible, the author or illustrator is sent a copy of the entry to check for accuracy and completeness.

Entries that have not been verified by the biographees or their representatives are marked with an asterisk (*).

Contact the Editor

We encourage our readers to examine the entire *SATA* series. Please write and tell us if we can make *SATA* even more helpful to you. Give your comments and suggestions to the editor:

Editor
Something about the Author
Gale, Cengage Learning
27500 Drake Rd.
Farmington Hills MI 48331-3535

Toll-free: 800-877-GALE
Fax: 248-699-8070

Something about the Author Product Advisory Board

The editors of *Something about the Author* are dedicated to maintaining a high standard of excellence by publishing comprehensive, accurate, and highly readable entries on a wide array of writers for children and young adults. In addition to the quality of the content, the editors take pride in the graphic design of the series, which is intended to be orderly yet inviting, allowing readers to utilize the pages of *SATA* easily and with efficiency. Despite the longevity of the *SATA* print series, and the success of its format, we are mindful that the vitality of a literary reference product is dependent on its ability to serve its users over time. As literature, and attitudes about literature, constantly evolve, so do the reference needs of students, teachers, scholars, journalists, researchers, and book club members. To be certain that we continue to keep pace with the expectations of our customers, the editors of *SATA* listen carefully to their comments regarding the value, utility, and quality of the series. Librarians, who have firsthand knowledge of the needs of library users, are a valuable resource for us. The *Something about the Author* Product Advisory Board, made up of school, public, and academic librarians, is a forum to promote focused feedback about *SATA* on a regular basis. The nine-member advisory board includes the following individuals, whom the editors wish to thank for sharing their expertise:

Eva M. Davis
Director,
Canton Public Library,
Canton, Michigan

Joan B. Eisenberg
Lower School Librarian,
Milton Academy,
Milton, Massachusetts

Francisca Goldsmith
Teen Services Librarian,
Berkeley Public Library,
Berkeley, California

Susan Dove Lempke
Children's Services Supervisor,
Niles Public Library District,
Niles, Illinois

Robyn Lupa
Head of Children's Services,
Jefferson County Public Library,
Lakewood, Colorado

Victor L. Schill
Assistant Branch Librarian/Children's Librarian,
Harris County Public Library/Fairbanks Branch,
Houston, Texas

Caryn Sipos
Community Librarian,
Three Creeks Community Library,
Vancouver, Washington

Steven Weiner
Director,
Maynard Public Library,
Maynard, Massachusetts

something about the author

ÁBALOS, Rafael 1956-

Personal

Born 1956, in Spain.

Addresses

Home and office—Southern Spain.

Career

Lawyer. Writer of fantasy novels for children.

Writings

Bufo Soñador en la galaxia de la tristeza, Editorial Debate (Madrid, Spain), 2000.

Mago del mundo, illustrated by Patricia Losada, Universidad de Málaga (Málaga, Spain), 2001.

El visitante del laberinto, Debate (Madrid, Spain), 2001.

Grimpow: El camino invisible, Montena (Barcelona, Spain), 2005, translated by Noël Baca Castex as *Grimpow: The Invisible Road,* Delacorte (New York, NY), 2007.

Grimpow: El secreto de los sabios, Círculo de Lectores (Barcelona, Spain), 2005.

Kot, Montena (Barcelona, Spain), 2007.

Adaptations

Grimpow: The Invisible Road was adapted as an audiobook, Books on Tape, 2007.

Sidelights

Spanish lawyer Rafael Ábalos loved reading adventure stories as a child. When he discovered that he both enjoyed and had a knack for writing, Ábalos began his second career writing fantasy adventures for children. He is best known for his novel *Grimpow: El camino invisible,* a story that has been published in twenty-seven countries and released in an English-language version under the title *Grimpow: The Invisible Road.*

Grimpow is a peasant boy living during the middle ages. Discovering the body of a fallen knight and taking the knight's talisman, Grimpow realizes he has actually found the philosopher's stone, and he takes up the knight's secret quest. The Inquisitors are also seeking the stone, however, and Grimpow must keep two steps ahead of these emissaries from the Catholic Church in order to complete the knight's mission. Describing the novel as a cross between J.R.R. Tolkien's epic "Lord of the Rings" fantasy saga and Dan Brown's hit thriller *The Da Vinci Code,* a *Publishers Weekly* critic wrote that Ábalos "proves himself adept at moving the multiple story lines of the labyrinthine plot at a fast pace." The critic added that *Grimpow* should appeal to both teens and adults, although some reviewers cautioned that the multi-faceted tale might be too complex for younger readers. A *Kirkus Reviews* contributor referred to the novel as "exposition-laden," and Sharon Grover wrote in *School Library Journal* that Ábalos's "plodding story line . . . weaves in too many threads."

Cover of Spanish writer Rafael Ábalos's middle-grade fantasy novel Grimpow: The Invisible Road, *featuring artwork by David Argemi.* (Illustration by David Argemi. Photograph copyright © Photonica. Used by permission of Random House Children's Books, a division of Random House, Inc.)

Biographical and Critical Sources

PERIODICALS

Bookseller, July 8, 2005, "Random House Exchange Scheme Bears Fruit," p. 9.
Bulletin of the Center for Children's Books, February, 2008, April Spisak, review of *Grimpow: The Invisible Road,* p. 240.
Kirkus Reviews, September 15, 2007, review of *Grimpow: The Invisibile Road.*
Publishers Weekly, October 29, 2007, review of *Grimpow: The Invisible Road,* p. 57.
School Library Journal, May, 2008, Sharon Grover, review of *Grimpow: The Invisible Road,* p. 119.

ONLINE

Fantastic Fiction Web site, http://www.fantasticfiction.co.uk/ (February 18, 2009), "Rafael Ábalos."
Author Tree Web site, http://authortree.com/ (February 18, 2009), "Rafael Ábalos."*

ANDERSON, John David 1967-

Personal
Born 1967; married; children: two.

Addresses
Home—Noblesville, IN.

Career
Writer.

Writings

Standard Hero Behavior, Clarion (New York, NY), 2007.

Sidelights
John David Anderson lives with his wife and young twins in Noblesville, Indiana. His first novel, *Standard Hero Behavior,* follows a young bard, Mason, and Mason's best friend Cowel, a merchant who sells plumes for helmets. Mason and Cowel's village, Highsmith, has a resident hero, Duke Dirk Dalinger, who has protected Highsmith since all the other heroes—including Mason's father—left years ago on a quest from which they never returned. Mason discovers that Dalinger is in fact a fraud who has been raising taxes to come up with the money to buy off the orcs and goblins that threaten the town. Dalinger is now out of money, and needs some real heroes. Mason and Cowel start off to find the town's saviors, following the advice found in *Quayle's Guide to Adventures for the Unadventurous,* and just maybe find Mason's father along the way.

Kathleen Isaacs, reviewing the novel in *Booklist,* wrote that in *Standard Hero Behavior* "Anderson manages the difficult task of constructing a satisfying story while poking large fun at all genre traditions." Walter Minkel, writing in *School Library Journal,* found flaws in the narrative, writing that "Anderson's first novel is witty, but far too talky" because it lacks an action-driven plot. Paula Rohrlick commented in *Kliatt* that Anderson's "amusing fantasy adventure features a sardonic sense of humor and two winning, if bumbling, protagonists."

Biographical and Critical Sources

PERIODICALS

Booklist, October 15, 2007, Kathleen Isaacs, review of *Standard Hero Behavior,* p. 47.
Kirkus Reviews, October 1, 2007, review of *Standard Hero Behavior.*
Kliatt, November, 2007, Paula Rohrlick, review of *Standard Hero Behavior,* p. 6.

School Library Journal, January, 2008, Walter Minkel, review of *Standard Hero Behavior,* p. 114.*

*   *   *

ASHER, Bridget
See BAGGOTT, Julianna

*   *   *

BAGGOTT, Julianna 1969-
(Bridget Asher, N.E. Bode)

Personal

Born 1969; married David G.W. Scott (a writer); children: four. *Education:* University of North Carolina, Greensboro, M.F.A.

Addresses

Home—FL. *E-mail*—jcbaggott@aol.com.

Career

Novelist and poet. Florida State University, associate director of creative-writing program; Kids in Need—Books in Deed, co-founder.

Writings

FOR ADULTS

Girl Talk, Pocket (New York, NY), 2001.
This Country of Mothers, Southern Illinois University Press (Carbondale, IL), 2001.
The Miss America Family, Pocket (New York, NY), 2002.
The Madam, Atria (New York, NY), 2003.
Lizzie Borden in Love: Poems in Women's Voices, Southern Illinois University Press (Carbondale, IL), 2006.
(With Steve Almond) *Which Brings Me to You: A Novel in Confessions,* Algonquin (Chapel Hill, NC), 2006.
Compulsions of Silkworms and Bees (poetry), Pleiades (Warrensburg, MO), 2007.

ADULT FICTION; UNDER NAME BRIDGET ASHER

My Husband's Sweethearts, Delacorte (New York, NY), 2008.
The Pretend Wife, Bantam (New York, NY), 2009.

"ANYBODIES" TRILOGY; FOR CHILDREN; UNDER NAME N.E. BODE

The Anybodies, illustrated by Peter Ferguson, HarperCollins (New York, NY), 2004.

The Nobodies, illustrated by Peter Ferguson, HarperCollins (New York, NY), 2005.
The Somebodies, illustrated by Peter Ferguson, HarperCollins (New York, NY), 2006.

FOR CHILDREN; UNDER NAME N.E. BODE

(Under name N.E. Bode) *The Slippery Map,* illustrated by Brandon Dorman, HarperCollins (New York, NY), 2007.
The Prince of Fenway Park, HarperCollins (New York, NY), 2009.

Adaptations

The Anybodies was optioned for film by Paramount Pictures/Nickelodeon Movies.

Sidelights

Since Julianna Baggott had her first novel published at age twenty-two, she has continued to produce books under her own name as well as under the pseudonyms N.E. Bode and Bridget Asher. Baggott is known primarily for her adult novels, many of which center around women whose family relationships are troubled and dysfunctional. Her first novel, *Girl Talk,* focuses on a mother-daughter relationship and opens as the daughter muses while preparing to give birth to her first child as a single mother. In her poetry, Baggott often concentrates on similar themes; her verse collection *This Country of Mothers,* for example, also focuses on the relationships between mothers and daughters.

Baggott turns her attention to younger readers in her books written under the pen name N.E. Bode, a persona who is also a regular guest on XM radio. Her novel *The Anybodies* introduces readers to Fern Drudger, a girl who discovers that her very normal and very boring parents are not, in fact, the parents she was born to. Fern is actually the daughter of Bone, and both of them are "Anybodies," people who can take the shape of any other person or thing. Problematically, Bone is not very good at shape shifting, but he is attempting to further develop his abilities by studying a manual titled *The Art of Being Anybody,* which once belonged to Fern's mother. The manual is highly desired by Miser, an evil magician who hopes to use the powers of the book for his own dastardly plans. A *Publishers Weekly* critic described the book as "engaging in places," but also "overly precious." Mara Alpert writing in *School Library Journal,* compared *The Anybodies* to Lemony Snicket's fantasy series, as well as to Cornelia Funke's *Inkheart,* writing that "there's laugh-out-loud humor, fantasy, mystery, real-life family drama, and the potential for a sequel." Jennifer Mattson predicted in *Booklist* that "the loony goings-on will entice young bibliophiles back for future installments."

In *The Nobodies* Fern's adventures continue, this time alongside those of Howard, the real son of the Drudgers. The pair attends a camp that focuses on training

Anybodies to use and control their shape-shifting abilities. At camp, Fern begins receiving messages in soda-pop bottles that explain that she has to save someone. When she discovers that the camp counselors have become trapped in animal form overnight. Fern must unravel the mystery before it is too late. A *Kirkus Reviews* critic found the novel to be "rich in mystery, action and self discovery."

In *The Somebodies,* the scope of Fern's adventure expands: she is now a royal Anybody, and she must inherit her grandmother's abilities to keep the evil Blue Queen from destroying the city of the Anybodies, under Manhattan. Howard continues to be a part of the story as Fern's best friend, a foil for Fern's adventurous bravery. The pace "will keep kids turning pages through an imaginative kaleidoscope of transformations," wrote Quinby Frank in *School Library Journal.* Critics noted that all three books in the series reference other well-known children's books, such as bottles labeled "Drink Me" that evoke *Alice in Wonderland* and trips in glass elevators, à la Roald Dahl's "Charlie" adventures. "The series remains a delight for better-read audiences," wrote a contributor to *Kirkus Reviews.*

Cover of Julianna Baggott's pseudonymously published middle-grade fantasy novel The Anybodies, *featuring artwork by Peter Ferguson.* (Illustration copyright © 2004 by Peter Ferguson. All rights reserved. Used by permission of HarperCollins Publishers.)

Also writing for children under her Bode pseudonym, Baggott produced *The Slippery Map.* Here ten-year-old orphan Oyster wishes to be the victim of a mysterious temporary disappearance, like several other children in his Baltimore neighborhood. Then he discovers that these strange disappearances have actually been aimed at him. In fact, Oyster is the child of the creators of Boneland, an imaginary world that has taken on a life of its own. His parents are still alive in Boneland, captured by evil Dark Mouth, and only Oyster can save them. Oyster "comes to understand the power of unleashed imagination and discovers the true meaning of family," Kim Dare summarized in *School Library Journal,* the critic adding that *The Slippery Map* contains less whimsy than *The Anybodies.* A *Kirkus Reviews* contributor found the novel to be "inventive and an awful lot of fun," and Jennifer Hubert wrote in *Booklist* that "readers will be tickled by the punny dialogue." A *Publishers Weekly* critic concluded of *The Slippery Map* that Baggott "effortlessly renders an expansive, entertainingly quirky cast . . . [in] snappy prose."

Biographical and Critical Sources

PERIODICALS

Antioch Review, fall, 2007, Malinda Markham, review of *Compulsions of Silkworms and Bees,* p. 766.
Booklist, November 15, 2000, Michelle Kaske, review of *Girl Talk,* p. 621; February 15, 2002, Carolyn Kubisz, review of *The Miss America Family,* p. 990; August, 2003, Donna Seaman, review of *The Madam,* p. 1950; July, 2004, Jennifer Mattson, review of *The Anybodies,* p. 1841; June 1, 2005, Chris Sherman, review of *The Nobodies,* p. 1806; April 1, 2006, Debi Lewis, review of *Which Brings Me to You: A Novel in Confessions,* p. 16; November 1, 2007, Jennifer Hubert, review of *The Slippery Map,* p. 47.
Kirkus Reviews, January 15, 2002, review of *The Miss America Family,* p. 63; May 15, 2004, review of *The Anybodies,* p. 487; May 15, 2005, review of *The Nobodies,* p. 584; February 15, 2006, review of *Which Brings Me to You,* p. 143; August 1, 2006, review of *The Somebodies,* p. 781; August 15, 2007, review of *The Slippery Map;* July 1, 2008, review of *My Husband's Sweethearts.*
Library Journal, March 1, 2006, Beth Gibbs, review of *Which Brings Me to You,* p. 76.
New York Times Book Review, April 1, 2001, Elizabeth Judd, review of *Girl Talk,* p. 16.
Prairie Schooner, summer, 2008, Carrie Shipers, review of *Lizzie Borden in Love: Poems in Women's Voices,* p. 170.
Publishers Weekly, November 20, 2000, review of *Girl Talk,* p. 43; April 1, 2003, review of *The Miss America Family,* p. 53; June 30, 2003, review of *The Madam,* p. 51; May 24, 2004, review of *The Anybodies,* p. 63; February 6, 2006, review of *Which Brings Me to You,* p. 40; September 24, 2007, review of *The Slippery Map,* p. 71.

School Library Journal, July, 2004, Mara Alpert, review of *The Anybodies,* p. 98; July, 2005, B. Allison Gray, review of *The Nobodies,* p. 96; September, 2006, Quinby Frank, review of *The Somebodies,* p. 200; December, 2007, Kim Dare, review of *The Slippery Map,* p. 120.

ONLINE

Julianna Baggott Home Page, http://www.juliannabaggott. com (February 14, 2009).*

* * *

BANKS, Merry

Personal
Female.

Addresses
Home—Alameda, CA.

Career
Children's book writer and publishing executive. Chronicle Books, San Francisco, CA, executive.

Writings

Animals of the Night, illustrated by Ronald Himler, Scribner (New York, NY), 1990.
Come and See!, Silver Burdett (Saddle River, NJ), 1996.
Firefighters!, Houghton Mifflin (Boston, MA), 1996.
Oh, John the Rabbit! Houghton Mifflin (Boston, MA), 1996.
(With Susan Middleton Elya) *N Is for Navidad,* illustrated by Joe Cepeda, Chronicle Books (San Francisco, CA), 2007.

Biographical and Critical Sources

PERIODICALS

Booklist, November 1, 2007, Hazel Rochman, review of *N Is for Navidad,* p. 55.
Bulletin of the Center for Children's Books, June, 1990, review of *Animals of the Night,* p. 232.
Horn Book, March-April, 1990, Carolyn K. Jenks, review of *Animals of the Night,* p. 218; November-December, 2007, Jennifer M. Brabander, review of *N Is for Navidad,* p. 628.
School Library Journal, May, 1990, Barbara B. Murphy, review of *Animals of the Night,* p. 94.*

BATESON, Catherine 1960-

Personal
Born 1960; married; children: two. *Education:* University of Queensland, B.A. (art history).

Addresses
Home—Dandenong Ranges, Victoria, Australia.

Career
Creative-writing teacher and writer. Central Gippsland Institute of TAFE, Gippsland, Victoria, Australia, instructor in creative writing. La Mama Poetica (poetry festival), organizer until 1999. Presenter at poetry readings and on television.

Awards, Honors
Book of the Year designation, Children's Book Council of Australia (CBCA), for *Rain May and Captain Daniel;* CBCA Honour Book for Older Readers designation, and Australian Family Therapists' Award, both 2003, both for *Painted Love Letters;* New South Wales Premier's Literary Award, and Queensland Premier's Literary Award, both 2003, both for *Painted Love Letters,* and *Rain May and Captain Daniel;* John Shaw Neilson Award; CCBC Book of the Year shortlist, 2005, for *Millie and the Night Heron;* CCBC Notable Book for Older Readers, 2007, for *His Name in Fire;* CCBC Book of the Year for Younger Readers, Australian Family Therapists' Award, and Queensland Premier's Literary Award, all 2007, all for *Being Bee.*

Writings

FOR YOUNG ADULTS

A Dangerous Girl, University of Queensland Press (St. Lucia, Queensland, Australia), 2000.
The Year It All Happened, University of Queensland Press (St. Lucia, Queensland, Australia), 2001.
Painted Love Letters, University of Queensland Press (St. Lucia, Queensland, Australia), 2002.
Rain May and Captain Daniel, University of Queensland Press (St. Lucia, Queensland, Australia), 2002, published as *Stranded in Boringsville,* Holiday House (New York, NY), 2005.
The Airdancer of Glass, University of Queensland Press (St. Lucia, Queensland, Australia), 2004.
Millie and the Night Heron, University of Queensland Press (St. Lucia, Queensland, Australia), 2005, published as *The Boyfriend Rules of Good Behavior,* Holiday House (New York, NY), 2006.
Being Bee, University of Queensland Press (St. Lucia, Queensland, Australia), 2006, Holiday House (New York, NY), 2007.

His Name in Fire, University of Queensland Press (St. Lucia, Queensland, Australia), 2006.

The Wish Pony, University of Queensland Press (St. Lucia, Queensland, Australia), 2008.

OTHER

Pomegranates from the Underworld (poetry), Pariah Press (Kew, Victoria, Australia), 1990.

The Vigilant Heart (poetry), University of Queenland Press (St. Lucia, Queensland, Australia), 1998.

Also author of short fiction.

Sidelights

Award-winning Australian author Catherine Bateson credits a childhood spent in a used bookstore with sparking her career as a poet and author of young-adult fiction. Bateson made the transition from poetry to longer works with *A Dangerous Girl* and its sequel, *The Year It All Happened.* These verse novels, together with *His Name in Fire,* reflect the concerns and speech of modern Australian teens, while her middle-grade prose

Cover of Catherine Bateson's middle-grade novel Being Bee, *featuring artwork by Eric Brace.* (Illustration copyright © 2007 by Eric Brace. Reproduced by permission of Holiday House, Inc.)

novels *Stranded in Boringsville* and *Being Bee* address bullying, broken families, and budding romance. Bateson also turns to prose in *Painted Love Letters,* as teenager Chrissie must deal with the death of her mother to lung cancer and the tragedy's effect on other family members.

In *Rain May and Captain Daniel*—published in the United States as *Stranded in Boringsville*—an inner-city single mom and her twelve-year-old daughter learn to adapt to platypus, fruit bats, and other quirks of life in rural Australia after a move from cosmopolitan Melbourne to a small town in Central Victoria. While Rain's mom, whose husband has abandoned the family, now enjoys the slow pace of their new life, the preteen misses the bustle and friends she left behind in the city. However, a relationship with next-door-neighbor Daniel, a very smart but geeky boy with heart problems, helps the girl learn the importance of relationships. In *Booklist* Chris Sherman described *Stranded in Boringsville* as a novel featuring characters "whose conflicted feelings seem all to real," and in *School Library Journal* Debbie Stewart praised Bateson's novel for its "enjoyable and quirky story." "Giving people—and places—a closer look is the exceptionally handled theme of this Australian import," stated Jennifer M. Brabander in her *Horn Book* review of *Stranded in Boringsville.*

Preteens are also the intended audience of Bateson's *The Boyfriend Rules of Good Behavior,* a book originally published in Australia as *Millie and the Night Heron.* Here middle-grader Millie Childes and her free-spirited artist mother Kate live with Kate's best friend Sheri and Sheri's son Mitchell. When the group moves to a new town, Millie's home life—and her mother-daughter relationship—is complicated by the romantic choices the adult women make. Bateson's quiet coming-of-age story is salted with Australianisms, noted *School Library Journal* contributor Suzanne Gordon, the critic also predicting that "fans of mild realistic fiction" will enjoy witnessing "Millie's quiet challenges and triumphs." In *Kirkus Reviews* a critic praised the novel's "dialogue-filled narrative," calling *The Boyfriend Rules of Good Behavior* "a tender-hearted view of maturation from a blossoming young girl's perspective."

Bateson introduces a ten year old whose feelings are confused by her widowed father's new girlfriend in *Being Bee.* Jazzi takes charge almost as soon as she moves into Bee's laid-back home, and Bee resents the fact that her soon-to-be stepmother now takes up most of Bee's father's time. Venting her hurt and resentments in letters to her two Guinea pigs, Bee finds comfort, especially when she receives letters back that she assumes are from her dad. However, the girl's viewpoint changes when it turns out that someone else has been privy to Bee's inner feelings. Noting that Bee's "matter-of-fact, self-absorbed" perspective is portrayed effectively in the novel, *Booklist* contributor Suzanne Harold described *Being Bee* as "bitingly frank" in its portrait of the difficulties of children adjusting to a reconfigured

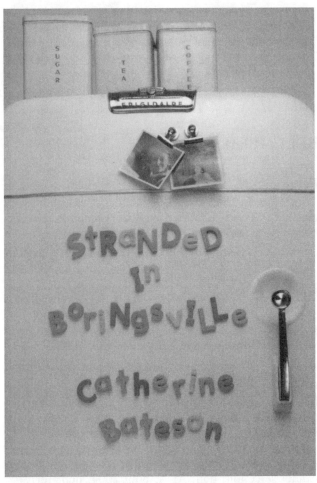

Cover of Aussie author Bateson's novel Stranded in Boringsville, *featuring artwork by Marc Tauss.* (Holiday House, 2002. Jacket photograph copyright © 2005 by Marc Tauss. Reproduced by permission.)

family. "Bateson deftly describes family and friendship strains in ways that are both touching and humorous," wrote a *Kirkus Reviews* writer, also in praise of the family-oriented novel.

Biographical and Critical Sources

PERIODICALS

Booklist, December 1, 2005, Chris Sherman, review of *Stranded in Boringsville,* p. 45; October 1, 2007, Suzanne Harold, review of *Being Bee,* p. 51.

Bulletin of the Center for Children's Books, November, 2006, Deborah Stevenson, review of *The Boyfriend Rules of Good Behavior,* p. 113.

Horn Book, January-February, 2006, Jennifer M. Brabander, review of *Stranded in Boringsville,* p. 73; November-December, 2007, Jennifer M. Brabander, review of *Being Bee,* p. 674.

Kirkus Reviews, October 15, 2005, review of *Stranded in Boringsville,* p. 1134; October 1, 2006, review of *The Boyfriend Rules of Good Behavior,* p. 1010; September 1, 2007, review of *Being Bee.*

School Library Journal, February, 2006, Debbie Stewart, review of *Stranded in Boringsville,* p. 128; November, 2006, Suzanne Gordon, review of *The Boyfriend Rules of Good Behavior,* p. 129.

Voice of Youth Advocates, February, 2006, Julie Watkins, review of *Stranded in Boringsville,* p. 481.

ONLINE

Catherine Bateson Web site, http://www.catherine-bateson. com (January 20, 2009).

University of Queensland Press Web site, http://www.uqp. edu.au/ (January 20, 2009), "Catherine Bateson."*

*   *   *

BECK, Scott

Personal
Married; children: two.

Addresses
Home and office—Montclair, NJ.

Career
Textile designer and children's author and illustrator.

Writings

SELF-ILLUSTRATED

Pepito the Brave, Dutton (New York, NY), 2001.

A Mud Pie for Mother, Dutton (New York, NY), 2003.

Little House, Little Town, Harry N. Abrams (New York, NY), 2004.

Happy Birthday, Monster!, Harry N. Abrams (New York, NY), 2007.

Sidelights

Author-illustrator Scott Beck began his career in art as a textile designer. His picture books for young readers feature an assortment of animal characters as well as monsters and real people. In Beck's first book, *Pepito the Brave,* he introduces Pepito, a small red bird who is afraid to fly. Encouraged by other animals, Pepito runs, hops, burrows, and even swims in order to reach the new nest where his siblings have flown. When he arrives, his siblings are so impressed with his bravery in trying all of these different modes of travel that they convince Pepito that he must be brave enough to fly. "Beck creates a genuine poster-bird for pluckiness," wrote a contributor to *Publishers Weekly,* and Rosalyn Pierini wrote in *School Library Journal* that the simple art in *Pepito the Brave* is a "perfect complement to [Beck's] . . . modest yet utterly satisfying tale."

In *A Mud Pie for Mother* a young pig struggles to fig- ure out what he should get his mother for Mother's Day. When the piglet hopes to pick a flower for Mom, a bee dissuades him, explaining that the flower is the bee's favorite. When the piglet attempts to make a mud pie, a farmer's wife claims that the mud is actually part of her garden. When he tries to take some hay, a cow protests that the hay is her bed. After the little pig wan- ders away from each of his ideas, however, those whose wishes he has respected come to his rescue: the bee of- fers honey, the cow offers milk, and the farmer's wife gives him bread. "Beck neatly and completely teaches a simple lesson," wrote Karin Snelson in *Booklist,* while a *Publishers Weekly* contributor cited the nostalgic- styled art in *A Mud Pie for Mother* for incorporating "crisp, simple shapes and [a] bold ochre, rusty red and spring-green palette." Sheilah Kosco noted in her *School Library Journal* review that "each picture is outlined in blue crayon, giving the illusion of having been drawn by a child."

Little House, Little Town features a more ordinary cast of characters. Told from the point of view of a young child observing his small town, Beck's story describes a sleepy day when neighbors in a small town go about their everyday tasks. "This sweet story told in rhyme is accompanied by simple acrylic illustrations," wrote Linda L. Walkins in a review of the book for *School Li- brary Journal.* A *Publishers Weekly* critic described *Little House, Little Town* as a "soothing look at the people and events of an infant's world."

A young demon and its dragon friend are the stars of *Happy Birthday, Monster!* When Ben the demon de- cides to throw a surprise party for Doris the dragon, a whole host of monsters arrives for the celebration. The book's cartoon-style illustrations are filled with visual jokes and speech-bubble commentary from the charac- ters. "Beck's monsters make an unintimidating crowd with their joyous smiles and wide-open eyes," wrote Jayne Damron in *School Library Journal,* and a *Kirkus Reviews* contributor called *Happy Birthday, Monster!* "completely non-threatening monster and birthday fun."

Biographical and Critical Sources

PERIODICALS

Booklist, February 15, 2003, Karin Snelson, review of *A Mud Pie for Mother,* p. 1072.
Kirkus Reviews, January 1, 2003, review of *A Mud Pie for Mother,* p. 140; September 15, 2004, review of *Little House, Little Town,* p. 910; September 15, 2007, re- view of *Happy Birthday, Monster!*
Publishers Weekly, December 18, 2000, review of *Pepito the Brave,* p. 77; December 23, 2002, review of *A Mud Pie for Mother,* p. 68; December 13, 2004, re- view of *Little House, Little Town,* p. 66.
School Library Journal, February, 2001, Rosalyn Pierini, review of *Pepito the Brave,* p. 92; April, 2003, Sheilah Kosco, review of *A Mud Pie for Mother,* p. 116; De- cember, 2004, Linda L. Walkins, review of *Little House, Little Town,* p. 98; November, 2007, Jayne Damron, review of *Happy Birthday, Monster!,* p. 86.
Tribune Books (Chicago, IL), April 8, 2001, review of *Pepito the Brave,* p. 8.*

* * *

BELL, Hilari 1958-

Personal

Born 1958, in Denver, CO. *Education:* Graduated from college. *Hobbies and other interests:* Camping, reading, board and fantasy gaming.

Addresses

Home—Denver, CO.

Career

Writer. Part-time reference librarian, until 2005.

Awards, Honors

Best Books for Young Adults selection, American Li- brary Association (ALA), and Best Book for the Teen Age selection, New York Public Library, both 2002, both for *A Matter of Profit;* Best Books for Young Adults selection, and Popular Paperbacks for Young Adults selection, both ALA, both 2004, both for *The Goblin Wood;* Best Books for Young Adults selection, ALA, 2009, for *The Last Knight.*

Writings

NOVELS

Navohar, New American Library (New York, NY), 2000.
Songs of Power, Hyperion (New York, NY), 2000.
A Matter of Profit, HarperCollins (New York, NY), 2001.
The Goblin Wood, HarperCollins (New York, NY), 2003.
The Wizard Test, Eos (New York, NY), 2005.
The Prophecy, Eos (New York, NY), 2006.

"FARSALA" NOVEL TRILOGY

Flame, Simon & Schuster (New York, NY), 2003, pub- lished as *Fall of a Kingdom,* 2004.
Rise of a Hero, Simon & Schuster (New York, NY), 2005.
Forging the Sword, Simon & Schuster (New York, NY), 2006.

"SHIELD, SWORD, AND CROWN" NOVEL TRILOGY

Shield of Stars, Simon & Schuster (New York, NY), 2007.

Hilari Bell (Photograph by Sandy Stone. Reproduced by permission.)

Sword of Waters, Simon & Schuster (New York, NY), 2008.

"KNIGHT AND ROGUE" NOVEL SERIES

The Last Knight, Eos (New York, NY), 2007.
Rogue's Home, Eos (New York, NY), 2008.

Sidelights

Hilari Bell has written a number of highly regarded science fiction and fantasy novels, including *The Goblin Wood The Prophecy,* and the works in the "Farsala" trilogy. In contrast to many books in those genres, Bell's tales are notable for their absence of clear heroes and villains; her characters and societies are drawn with distinct shades of gray and are often motivated by political considerations rather than honor or duty. Bell is "a master at crafting distinctive societies and characters," Sally Estes wrote in *Booklist.* Bell's books frequently feature multiple, well-developed cultures, including goblin, alien, and even whale societies.

Born in 1958 in Denver, Colorado, Bell developed an interest in literature at an early age. "The first chapter book I ever read was the *Book of Three,* by Lloyd Alexander," the author stated in an interview on the Harper-Collins Web site. "I was in first grade when I read it, and I spent the next few years living more in Prydain than I did in Denver, Colorado. Fantasy has been a favorite genre ever since. I got into science fiction when I read Anne McCaffrey's *The Ship Who Sang.* But I also read a lot of mysteries, and some historical fiction as well—if my first favorite book had been a mystery, I might be a mystery writer today." Bell began writing seriously after college, but it took seventeen years before she sold her first novel. "I'm the poster child for persistence," she remarked on her home page.

Bell's first published novel, *Navohar,* was written for an adult audience. The book is set in the future, after humans have successfully prevented an alien invasion of Earth with the help of a genetically engineered virus. However, this triumph turns out to be Pyrrhic: the virus has also infected the human population, causing millions of children to be born with altered genes that lead them to develop a fatal, incurable disease. One such child is Irene Olsen's nephew, Mark. These two are among the astronauts traveling the universe, searching for human populations who have not been exposed to the virus. Thus far, most of the formerly colonized planets where their crew has landed no longer have living human inhabitants, the colonizers having been wiped out by various alien diseases. However, when they land on Navohar, they discover a group of nomadic humans that has been driven out of their former colony by the Kong aliens, now lives in the deserts where the Kong do not like to go. A cure for the virus does seem to exist on Navohar, but the descendants of the colonists worry about what will happen to their planet if millions of Earth's children come there seeking it. "The story moves briskly," commented T.M. Wagner in *SF Reviews.net,* and "Bell's writing . . . is most amiable." This "easygoing, accessible writing style," the reviewer explained, "gives the book a certain degree of light-reading appeal." Plus, as Fred Cleaver wrote in the *Denver Post,* "the desert society and the interesting aliens are a delight."

Bell's first novel for young readers, *Songs of Power,* combines science-fiction and fantasy. The story is set in a technologically advanced future, but it is the main character's ability to do magic that drives the plot. Imina was taught some spiritual talents by her great-grandmother, an Inuit shaman, but the woman passed away when Imina was still a child. Now the girl lives with her parents in a research station at the bottom of the sea. Terrorists have released a virus that is rapidly destroying all land-based plants, so "technocrats" are working on developing a way to grow food in the oceans. The research station is plagued by technical problems, which the technocrats blame on sabotage by the terrorists, but Imina recognizes these problems as magical. Eventually, with the help of a skeptical classmate, she discovers that whales are using their magic to try to prevent humans from encroaching on their territory. "Bell's depiction of life in the habitat and her feisty main character, Imina, make for a suspenseful read," a reviewer commented in *Publishers Weekly,* and *School Library Journal* contributor John Peters called *Songs of Power* "a whale of a debut."

Bell's novels *A Matter of Profit* and *The Goblin Wood* offer an inclusive message about treating other sentient species as equals and being open to receiving their wisdom. In the first book, Ahvren is a young warrior who is sickened by the battles he has seen. Hoping to serve the emperor in other ways, Ahvren is tasked with getting to the bottom of an alleged plot on the emperor's life. To do this, he must understand the way of thinking

of the T'Chin Confederation, whose forty planets recently surrendered without firing a shot when Ahvren's Vivitare race came to conquer them. A bibliogoth, an exceptionally wise member of the T'Chin who is scholar and happens to look something like an ant, helps Ahvren understand why the T'Chin surrendered: their philosophy is always to maximize profit, and it was more profitable to come into the Vivitare Empire than to resist it. "Both the bibliogoth's wise mentorship and Ahvren's gradual and believable conversion to the T'Chin way of thinking are distinctively and engagingly handled," Anita L. Burkam wrote in *Horn Book. School Library Journal* contributor Mara Alpert praised the book as "well-written, thought-provoking, and exciting," further commenting: "It's got cool weapons and weird aliens, but it's also got some meat to it." Similarly, *Infinity Plus* reviewer John Grant found it "highly praiseworthy" that in *A Matter of Profit* "some pretty tough issues are tackled head-on in a way not normally associated with novels for this age-group." Noting Bell's ability to create believable characters and alien cultures, Estes dubbed *A Matter of Profit* "one of the best youth sf tales to come along in many years."

In *The Goblin Wood* Bell "illuminates the sometimes spider-thin lines that prevent cultures from living together in peace," wrote a *Publishers Weekly* reviewer. Makenna, the heroine of the tale, learns to respect goblins when both she and they are caught up in a decision to ban certain forms of magic. Makenna's mother, a hedgewitch, is executed, and Makenna flees into the woods. There, she allies herself with the goblins, whom the Hierarch is also trying to wipe out. For five years, these allies resist the Hierarch together, until a knight named Tobin is sent to eliminate Makenna. Instead of capturing or killing the young woman, Tobin falls in love with her, and the two work together to try to make the world safe for both humans and goblins. Several reviewers praised Bell for giving the Hierarch realistic, sympathetic reasons for cracking down on magic so harshly: he is only trying to stop an invasion of his realms. "The addition of political motivations to a genre mostly dominated by a good/evil dichotomy is a pleasing surprise," Burkam commented in *Horn Book,* while *School Library Journal* contributor Sharon Grover noted that Bell's exploration of "the gray areas . . . makes for some interesting and thought-provoking reading." As Hilary Williamson noted in *BookLoons.com, The Goblin Wood* is also "great fun."

The "sweeping fantasy" of Bell's "Farsala" trilogy "draws its underpinnings from ancient Persian poetry . . . and the relentless march of the Roman army," Sharon Grover explained in a *School Library Journal* review of the first book in the series, *Flame.* More-recently retitled *Fall of a Kingdom,* the novel finds the Persian side of the conflict represented by the country of Farsala, which is attempting to repulse an invasion by the Hrum. The tale is told through the interlocking stories of three young Farsalans: Soraya, the fifteen-year-old daughter of the Farsalan army commander;

Jiann, the illegitimate, half-peasant son of the same commander; and Kavi, a traveling peddler who is being blackmailed into spying for both sides. As in Bell's earlier books, "the cast is fully formed: the bad guys aren't entirely bad, the good guys not entirely good," commented a *Publishers Weekly* reviewer. Although the Hrum are bent on world domination, they treat their conquered subjects as citizens with full rights, while Farsala society maintains a sharp distinction between the noble deghans and the oppressed peasants. A *Kirkus Reviews* contributor praised Bell's treatment of these issues of class and culture, commenting that they "are interwoven so well with adventure and archetypal resonance that depth arrives unannounced."

In *Rise of a Hero,* the second entry in the "Farsala" trilogy, Soraya, Jiann, and Kavi work to expel the occupying Hrum army. While Soraya disguises herself as a servant to gain access to the Hrum camp, Jiann takes command of his father's remaining forces, and Kavi ignites a guerrilla resistance movement. "The characters maintain their distinctive identities here," remarked Estes, who also noted the "palpable sense of danger" in the narrative. "The details of military strategy and the clever, Scarlet Pimpernel-style ruses of the resistance

Cover of Bell's novel Flame, ***featuring artwork by Greg Newbold.*** (Jacket illustration copyright © 2003 by Greg Newbold, www.gregnewbold.com. Reproduced by permission.)

make for entertaining reading," Burkam stated. *Forging the Sword* brings the trilogy to a conclusion. Knowing that the Hrum army will withdraw if Farsala can resist the onslaught for a year, the three protagonists evoke the memory of Sorahb, a legendary Farsalan hero, to rally the citizens of the nation. Estes described the work as "an edge-of-the-seat finale," and a critic in *Kirkus Reviews* found *Forging the Sword* to be "memorable for its individual characters and extensively detailed cultures."

Bell explores themes of loyalty and honor in *The Wizard Test.* Set in the walled city of Tharn, the work concerns Dayven, a warrior in training who discovers that he possesses magical powers. Raised in a society that distrusts wizardry, Dayven is apprenticed to Reddick, an apparently buffoonish master, and later recruited by Lord Enar to spy on both the wizards and the neighboring Cenzars. The apprentice soon learns, however, that the motives of his own people may not be entirely honorable. In *The Wizard Test,* remarked *Kliatt* reviewer Paula Rohrlick, Bell "asks readers to consider issues from different viewpoints, and this gives the story added depth and appeal." Writing in *School Library Journal,* Sharon Grover remarked that "hard questions are asked and answered in a . . . book that will find a wide audience and spark much discussion."

In *The Prophecy,* scholarly Prince Perryn uncovers an ancient scroll that describes how to slay the black dragon that ravages his kingdom. According to prophecy, Perryn must locate a true bard, a unicorn, and a magical sword to restore peace to the land, but the prince's efforts are hindered by the king's advisor, a traitor to the crown. Bell "layers the breathtaking action with a cast of fully realized magical creatures and universal coming-of-age questions," observed *Booklist* contributor Gillian Engberg, and Rohrlick stated that the author "blends humor and adventure effectively in this brief, fast-moving, and entertaining coming-of-age tale."

Shield of Stars, the first book in Bell's "Shield, Sword, and Crown" trilogy, concerns fourteen-year-old Weasel, a former pickpocket who now clerks for the respected Justice Holis. When his employer is arrested for plotting to overthrow a corrupt regent, Weasel joins forces with Arisa, a girl with surprising talents, to search for the Falcon, an outlaw freedom fighter. "Bell's trademark shades of gray help shift readers' perceptions of the characters and their motivations," observed *School Library Journal* contributor Beth L. Meister.

In *Sword of Waters,* the second work in the trilogy, Arisa helps her mother, a powerful military commander who shares power with Holis, maneuver through troubled political waters. Along with Weasel and young Prince Edoran, Arisa uncovers a dangerous conspiracy that threatens the fragile peace that exists in Deorthas, their kingdom. "This middle installment picks up speed and delicious suspense," noted a contributor in *Kirkus Reviews.*

Cover of Bell's novel Shield of Stars, *the first volume in her "Shield, Sword, and Crown" fantasy series.* (Jacket illustration copyright © 2007 by Gene Mollica. Reproduced by permission of author.)

The exploits of a knight errant and a con artist are the subject of *The Last Knight,* the debut title in Bell's "Knight and Rogue" series. After Sir Michael and his reluctant squire, Fisk, rescue a damsel in distress—only to learn she is suspected of murder—they must survive a number of hair-raising adventures to recapture the prisoner. "Bell's plot is nicely inventive, and she writes with a robust cheer and peppery sense of irony," Deirdre F. Baker stated in *Horn Book,* and *Kliatt* reviewer Claire Rosser deemed the work an "intricate, intelligent story, told for amusement."

In *Rogue's Home* Fisk must help his family reclaim its honor after a mysterious villain ruins the reputation of the squire's brother-in-law. The novel "has the appeal of a dashing mystery-adventure," Baker observed, "but the deeper elements of friendship and family loyalty give it substance." A contributor in *Kirkus Reviews* also praised the work, stating that Bell's "writing is great: lots of humor, likable people, mystery and suspense aplenty."

As Bell stated on the HarperCollins Web site, "I'm not sure this is a life motto, but it's what I say to myself

Cover of Bell's fantasy novel Rogue's Home, *featuring artwork by* **Larry Rostant.** (Jacket art copyright © 2008 by Larry Rostant. Used by permission of HarperCollins Publishers.)

when I tackle a novel and am contemplating how much work writing all those hundreds of pages actually entails: *If you keep pushing it, it will fall over.*"

Biographical and Critical Sources

PERIODICALS

Analog Science Fiction and Fact, February, 2001, Tom Easton, review of *Navohar,* p. 133.

Booklist, August, 2001, Sally Estes, review of *A Matter of Profit,* p. 2116; June 1, 2003, Sally Estes, review of *The Goblin Wood,* p. 1758; September 1, 2003, Sally Estes, review of *Flame,* p. 122; February 1, 2005, Jennifer Mattson, review of *The Wizard Test,* p. 957; July, 2005, Sally Estes, review of *Rise of a Hero,* p. 1922; June 1, 2006, Gillian Engberg, review of *The Prophecy,* p. 58; December 15, 2006, Sally Estes, review of *Forging the Sword,* p. 48; May 15, 2007, Jennifer Mattson, review of *Shield of Stars,* p. 62; October 1, 2007, Carolyn Phelan, review of *The Last Knight,* p. 46; August 1, 2008, Carolyn Phelan, review of *Rogue's Home,* p. 61.

Denver Post, June 25, 2000, Fred Cleaver, review of *Navohar* and *Songs of Power,* p. G2.

Horn Book, January-February, 2002, Anita L. Burkam, review of *A Matter of Profit,* p. 76; May-June, 2003, Anita L. Burkam, review of *The Goblin Wood,* p. 339; September-October, 2003, Anita L. Burkam, review of *Flame,* p. 607; July-August, 2005, Anita L. Burkam, review of *Rise of a Hero,* p. 464; July-August, Anita L. Burkam, review of *The Prophecy,* p. 435; September-October, 2007, Deirdre F. Baker, review of *The Last Knight,* p. 566; September-October, 2008, Deirdre F. Baker, review of *Rogue's Home,* p. 577.

Kirkus Reviews, September 15, 2003, review of *Flame,* p. 1171; January 15, 2005, review of *The Wizard Test,* p. 116; May 1, 2005, review of *Rise of a Hero,* p. 534; November 1, 2006, review of *Forging the Sword,* p. 1121; March 1, 2007, review of *Shield of Stars,* p. 217; August 15, 2008, review of *Rogue's Home;* October 15, 2008, review of *Sword of Waters.*

Kliatt, May, 2003, Paula Rohrlick, review of *A Matter of Profit,* p. 23; September, 2003, Paula Rohrlick, review of *Flame,* p. 6; September, 2004, Samatha Musher, review of *The Goblin Wood,* p. 27; March, 2005, Paula Rohrlick, review of *The Wizard Test,* p. 6; May, 2005, Paula Rohrlick, review of *Rise of a Hero,* p. 6; July, 2006, review of *The Prophecy,* p. 7; November, 2006, Paula Rohrlick, review of *Forging the Sword,* p. 6; July, 2007, Claire Rosser, review of *The Last Knight,* p. 8.

Publishers Weekly, June 12, 2000, review of *Songs of Power,* p. 74; March 24, 2003, review of *The Goblin Wood,* p. 76; October 27, 2003, review of *Flame,* p. 70; March 7, 2005, review of *The Wizard Test,* p. 68; March 19, 2007, review of *Shield of Stars,* p. 63; September 24, 2007, review of *The Last Knight,* p. 74.

School Library Journal, May, 2000, John Peters, review of *Songs of Power,* p. 166; October, 2001, Mara Alpert, review of *A Matter of Profit,* p. 148; July, 2003, Sharon Grover, review of *The Goblin Wood,* p. 123; November, 2003, Grover, review of *Flame,* p. 134; March, 2005, Sharon Grover, review of *The Wizard Test,* p. 206; October, 2006, Sharon Grover, review of *The Prophecy,* p. 148; March, 2007, Sharon Grover, review of *Forging the Sword,* p. 203; May, 2007, Beth L. Meister, review of *Shield of Stars,* p. 129; December, 2008, Genevieve Gallagher, review of *Sword of Waters,* p. 119.

Teacher Librarian, February, 2004, Ruth Cox, "Grief and Acceptance," review of *The Goblin Wood,* p. 37.

Voice of Youth Advocates, April, 2004, review of *Flame,* p. 20.

ONLINE

BookLoons.com, http://www.bookloons.com/ (October 3, 2004), Hilary Williamson, review of *The Goblin Wood.*

HarperCollins Web site, http://www.harpercollins.com/ (November 1, 2007), "Hilari Bell."

Hilari Bell Web site, http://www.sfwa.org/members/bell/ (February 1, 2009).

Infinity Plus Web site, http://www.infinityplus.co.uk/ (August 4, 2001), John Grant, review of *A Matter of Profit.*

SF Reviews.net, http://www.sfreviews.net/ (November 1, 2007), T.M. Wagner, review of *Navohar.**

*   *   *

BODE, N.E.
See BAGGOTT, Julianna

*   *   *

BONNER, Hannah

Personal

Female. *Hobbies and other interests:* Tai Chi.

Addresses

Home—Spain. *E-mail*—hb@hannahbonner.com.

Career

Author and illustrator.

Writings

SELF-ILLUSTRATED

When Bugs Were Big, Plants Were Strange, and Tetrapods Stalked the Earth: A Cartoon Prehistory of Life before Dinosaurs, National Geographic (Washington, DC), 2003.
When Fish Got Feet, Sharks Got Teeth, and Bugs Began to Swarm: A Cartoon Prehistory of Life Long before Dinosaurs, National Geographic (Washington, DC), 2007.

ILLUSTRATOR

Melvin Berger, *Scholastic Science Dictionary,* Scholastic Reference (New York, NY), 2000.

Contributor of illustrations to numerous educational materials.

Sidelights

Although she has amassed credits as both a writer and an illustrator, Hannah Bonner primarily considers herself an artist due to her lifelong passion for illustration. Bonner began her career illustrating scientific topics during high school, when she was asked by her father to illustrate a book he had written about plants native to the Spanish island of Mallorca. "I've been drawing non-stop since I was a toddler, and have worked as an illustrator for many years," Bonner told Cynthia Leitich Smith for *Cynsations* online. "I've illustrated all sorts

of things—early readers, science-oriented educational materials, Majorcan folk tales, images for cookie packages, sea birds, fish, you name it. Over the years, I have been able to shift more and more into drawing only what I love, which is biology, paleontology, and the natural world in general."

Bonner's first self-illustrated title, *When Bugs Were Big, Plants Were Strange, and Tetrapods Stalked the Earth: A Cartoon Prehistory of Life before Dinosaurs,* came about as a joint idea between Bonner and an editor at *National Geographic* and focuses on the giant insects that lived before the dinosaurs. Balancing research, writing, and illustrating, "Bonner surrounds a lively, specific narrative . . . with a gallery of simply drawn, precisely detailed land and sea life," according to a *Kirkus Reviews* contributor. Calling *When Bugs Were Big, Plants Were Strange, and Tetrapods Stalked the Earth* "an exemplary curriculum support resource," Francisca Goldsmith added in *Booklist* that "kids who dig dinosaurs will read the book purely for pleasure." Describing both text and illustrations, Steven Engelfried wrote in *School Library Journal* that "the facts and the fun work well together, and it's always clear which is which."

A "prequel" of sorts to *When Bugs Were Big, Plants Were Strange, and Tetrapods Stalked the Earth, When Fish Got Feet, Sharks Got Teeth, and Bugs Began to Swarm: A Cartoon Prehistory of Life Long before Dinosaurs* covers the development in the Silurian and Devo-

Hannah Bonner begins her colorful guide to the roots of life on Earth in When Bugs Were Big, Plants Were Strange, and Tetrapods Stalked the Earth. (Copyright © 2004 by Hannah Bonner. Reproduced by permission.)

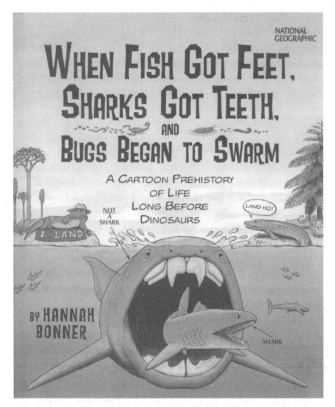

Cover of Bonner's self-illustrated natural history **When Fish Got Feet, Sharks Got Teeth, and Bugs Began to Swarm.** (Copyright © 2007 by Hannah Bonner. Reproduced by permission.)

nian periods, the eras where life on Earth moved from the oceans to dry land. "Bonner serves up a second heaping course of science that will both stick to the ribs and tickle them," wrote a *Kirkus Reviews* contributor. Noting that Bonner gears her text to upper elementary and middle-school readers, Danielle J. Ford wrote in *Horn Book* that the author/illustrator's "friendly and engaging writing enlivens a comprehensive explanation of conceptually challenging biology." Todd Morning, reviewing the natural-history title for *Booklist,* explained that Bonner's illustrated time line "manages to be funny" while also helping students "put each time period into context."

Biographical and Critical Sources

PERIODICALS

Booklist, February 15, 2004, Francisca Goldsmith, review of *When Bugs Were Big, Plants Were Strange, and Tetrapods Stalked the Earth: A Cartoon Prehistory of Life before Dinosaurs,* p. 1056; July 1, 2007, Todd Morning, review of *When Fish Got Feet, Sharks Got Teeth, and Bugs Began to Swarm: A Cartoon Prehistory of Life Long before Dinosaurs,* p. 59.

Bulletin of the Center for Children's Books, November, 2007, Elizabeth Bush, review of *When Fish Got Feet, Sharks Got Teeth, and Bugs Began to Swarm,* p. 131.

Horn Book, January-February, 2008, Danielle J. Ford, review of *When Fish Got Feet, Sharks Got Teeth, and Bugs Began to Swarm,* p. 106.

Kirkus Reviews, January 15, 2004, review of *When Bugs Were Big, Plants Were Strange, and Tetrapods Stalked the Earth,* p. 80; September 15, 2007, review of *When Fish Got Feet, Sharks Got Teeth, and Bugs Began to Swarm.*

Library Media Connection, April-May, 2004, review of *When Bugs Were Big, Plants Were Strange, and Tetrapods Stalked the Earth,* p. 77.

School Library Journal, February, 2001, John Peters, review of *Scholastic Science Dictionary,* p. 77; February, 2004, Steven Engelfried, review of *When Bugs Were Big, Plants Were Strange, and Tetrapods Stalked the Earth,* p. 126.

Science Teacher, January, 2005, review of *When Bugs Were Big, Plants Were Strange, and Tetrapods Stalked the Earth,* p. 66.

ONLINE

Cynsations Blog, http://cynthialeitichsmith.blogspot.com/ (February 7, 2008), Cynthia Leitich Smith, interview with Bonner.

Guild of Natural Science Illustrators Web site, http://gnsi.science-art.com/ (January 13, 2009), "Hannah Bonner."

*   *   *

BROCK, Delia
See EPHRON, Delia

*   *   *

BROOKS, Kevin 1959-
(Kevin M. Brooks)

Personal

Born March 30, 1959, in Exeter, England; married; wife's name Susan (an editor). *Education:* Attended Aston University, 1980; North East London Polytechnic, B.A., 1983.

Addresses

Home—Yorkshire, England.

Career

Writer. Formerly worked performing and recording music. Worked various jobs in England, including musician, gasoline station attendant, crematorium handyman, civil service clerk, hot dog vendor at the London Zoo, post office clerk, and railway ticket office clerk.

Awards, Honors

White Raven Award, Branford Boase Award, Sheffield Children's Book Award, Lancashire Children's Book Award, South Lanarkshire Book Award, and Carnegie

Kevin Brooks (Photo courtesy of Kevin Brooks. Reproduced by permission.)

Medal shortlist, all 2003, and Salford Children's Book Award, 2004, for *Martyn Pig;* London *Guardian* Children's Book Award shortlist, and Teenage Booktrust Prize shortlist, 2003, and North East Book Award, 2004, all for *Lucas.*

Writings

YOUNG-ADULT NOVELS

Martyn Pig, Scholastic (New York, NY), 2002.
Lucas, Scholastic (New York, NY), 2003.
Kissing the Rain, Scholastic (New York, NY), 2004.
Bloodline, Barrington Stoke (Edinburgh, Scotland), 2004.
(With Catherine Forde) *I See You Baby,* Barrington Stoke (Edinburgh, Scotland), 2005.
Candy, Scholastic (New York, NY), 2005.
The Road of the Dead, Chicken House (New York, NY), 2006.
Being, Penguin (London, England), 2007, Scholastic (New York, NY), 2008.
Black Rabbit Summer, Scholastic (New York, NY), 2008.

"JOHNNY DELGADO" NOVEL SERIES

Like Father, like Son, Barrington Stoke (Edinburgh, Scotland), 2006.
Private Detective, Barrington Stoke (Edinburgh, Scotland), 2006.

Sidelights

A poet and musician as well as an author, Kevin Brooks has earned praise for his young-adult novels that extends well beyond his native England. While Brooks pays careful attention to his prose, he also crafts tight-

knit plots that owe much to the dark themes of hard-boiled detective fiction. Brooks won Britain's prestigious Branford Boase Award for his first novel, *Martyn Pig,* and his more-recent novels, such as *Kissing the Rain, Being,* and *Black Rabbit Summer,* continue to draw the attention of critics and readers alike. In an interview for the Push Web site, Brooks remarked: "Being a writer is absolutely wonderful. I love writing, it's what I DO—thinking, writing, creating new worlds, it's fantastic."

While casting about for a career direction following college, Brooks wrote poetry and read widely, especially enjoying American detective novels by Raymond Chandler and Lawrence Block. He also worked in prose; In fact, *Martyn Pig* was actually his third completed novel. For the hero of Brooks's first novel, Martyn faces more than just the dilemma of going through life with a ghastly name. During the Christmas holiday, he witnesses the accidental death of his alcoholic, abusive father. Hoping to keep the man's death secret, Martyn seeks help from a would-be girlfriend named Alex, and together they craft a plan to dispose of the corpse. Despite its grisly subject matter, *Martyn Pig* abounds in humor, as the young narrator tries to come to terms with the strange twists his life takes. According to *School Library Journal* correspondent Connie Tyrrell Burns, Brooks's novel has "tremendous teen appeal" due to its unconventional subject matter and Martyn's "distinctive voice," and a *Publishers Weekly* critic praised the writer's "self-assured debut" as "at once hard-boiled . . . and . . . laugh-aloud funny."

Brooks's second novel, *Lucas,* is set on fictitious Hale Island, a small community separated from the mainland by a causeway that sometimes floods at high tide. The story's narrator, Caitlin McCann, recalls a previous summer when a strange, almost mystical loner named Lucas wandered onto the island. As Adèle Geras described the boy in London's *Guardian:* "He is wild. He is gifted. He is enigmatic. Also, he is deeply hated by the boorish, drug-fuelled, bored and jealous oafs in the community and their unpleasant and sinister female sidekicks." Unjustly accused of assaulting a girl, Lucas becomes the victim of vigilante justice, even as Caitlin falls in love with his inner goodness. Reviewing *Lucas,* a *Publishers Weekly* contributor predicted that the "powerful combination of big ideas and forthright narrative make this novel likely to linger in readers' minds." In *Booklist* Ilene Cooper cited the "purity" of the novel's prose, calling Brooks's narrative "by turns sweet, taut, and terrifying," while *School Library Journal* contributor Sharon Rawlins dubbed *Lucas* "extraordinarily lyrical" and "a powerful book to be savored."

A shy and overweight fifteen year old is the focus of Brooks's novel *Kissing the Rain.* Because of his passivity, Moo Nelson is bullied by his fellow students, but things go from bad to worse when he witnesses a car chase and violence that ends in tragedy. Another teen learns about life on the streets in *Candy,* Brooks's novel

about a fifteen-year-old Londoner named Joe Beck who finds help in an unusual place when he meets and falls in love with a young drug addict. Comparing *Kissing in the Rain* to J.D. Salinger's coming-of-age classic *Catcher in the Rye, Kirkus Reviews* writer dubbed Brooks's novel "effectively oppressive" and attractive to reluctant readers, while in *Booklist* Jennifer Mattson described *Candy* as "provocative" and "suspenseful." While describing Joe's first-person narrative as overly self-absorbed, *School Library Journal* contributor Johanna Lewis nonetheless found that "Brooks's plotting is masterful, and the action [in *Candy*] twists and builds to a frenzied and violent climax."

Gypsy brothers Ruben and Cole leave London after their father winds up in prison in *The Road of the Dead,* another novel that mixes suspense with coming-of-age themes. In the wake of the tragic death of their older sister, the brothers travel to remote Dartmoor, determined to track down Rachel's murderer. Brooks draws readers into the mystery of Rachel's rape-murder while also weaving in urban gang violence, police corruption, and ESP. *The Road of the Dead* is "an adventure story with atmosphere and interesting character development," wrote *Kliatt* critic Myrna Marler, while a *Kirkus Reviews* writer praised the book for its "thrilling, gritty

Cover of Brooks's highly praised teen novel **Martyn Pig,** *featuring photography by Tony Stone.* (Photograph copyright © 2002 by Tony Stone. Reproduced by permission of Scholastic, Inc.)

story and . . . memorable, heart-breaking characters." "Brooks's feel for mood and setting is as masterful here as in his taut, noir *Martyn Pig,* concluded Johanna Lewis in her *School Library Journal* review, the critic dubbing *The Road of the Dead* "a haunting, tense drama."

In *Being* Brooks "wraps high-speed, adrenaline-laced adventure around a thought-provoking exploration of the very nature of identity and existence," according to a *Publishers Weekly* contributor. In the novel, Robert Smith is undergoing a routine medical procedure when doctors discover that the abdomen of the sixteen year old is filled with metal and plastic machinery. Fleeing from the hospital with the help of a stolen gun, Robert must now discover the key to his identity before he is apprehended by those who wish him harm. The *Publishers Weekly* critic cited Brooks's "tantalizingly open-ended conclusion" while *Kliatt* critic Paula Rohrlick wrote of *Being* that "there's no lack of suspense in [this] . . . gritty, exciting thriller." Brooks's "poetic descriptions" of the teen's robot-like components "are terrifying and beautiful," wrote Claire E. Gross in *Horn Book,* the critic adding that *Being* is shadowed by the troubled teen's "tense self-loathing."

The disappearance of two small-town teens is the focus of Brooks's young-adult novel *Black Rabbit Summer.* After haughty Stella Ross and troubled, lower-class Raymond disappear during an end-of-summer carnival, Raymond's friend Pete attempts to solve the mystery. Citing the "hallucinogenic imagery and inexorable pacing" of the novel's "intricately constructed" plot, Gross explained that *Black Rabbit Summer* serves up biting social commentary in its thrilling storyline. "Brooks is a fine writer," noted Cooper, "and he knows how to keep the tension high" in his fiction. Describing novel's plot as "sinister yet seductive," a *Publishers Weekly* contributor dubbed *Black Rabbit Summer* characteristic Brooks due to its author's "painful awareness of teenage alienation . . . and a marked taste for ambiguity."

In an online interview with Nikki Gamble for *Write Away!,* Brooks explained: "I am interested in asking the questions which we think about a lot as kids, but get so used to when we grow up that we stop asking them. As adults we forget about the sky, and where we come from, and time, and pain, and all of those things; we just accept them. . . . Sometimes I get problems with American publishers who say they don't want to include this kind of thing because children aren't used to it or they won't understand it. But if you just keep avoiding difficult questions children won't learn to understand them."

Biographical and Critical Sources

PERIODICALS

Booklist, May 1, 2003, Ilene Cooper, review of *Lucas,* p. 1595; February 15, 2004, Ilene Cooper, review of

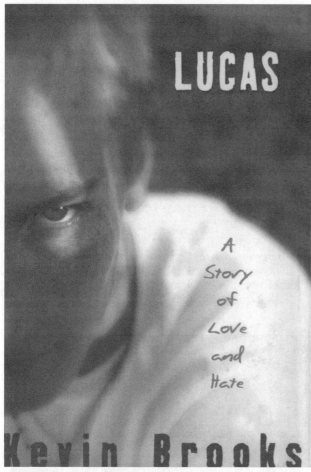

Cover of Brooks's young-adult novel Lucas, *featuring photography by* Tony Stone. (Photograph copyright © 2003 by Tony Stone. Reproduced by permission of Scholastic, Inc.)

Kissing the Rain, p. 1053; February 1, 2005, Jennifer Mattson, review of *Candy,* p. 954; January 1, 2006, Ilene Cooper, review of *The Road of the Dead,* p. 81; May 1, 2008, Ilene Cooper, review of *Black Rabbit Summer,* p. 46.

Bulletin of the Center for Children's Books, February, 2004, Deborah Stevenson, review of *Kissing the Rain,* p. 221; February, 2005, Deborah Stevenson, review of *Candy,* p. 245; April, 2006, Deborah Stevenson, review of *The Road of the Dead,* p. 344; February, 2007, Deborah Stevenson, review of *Being,* p. 60; September, 2008, Deborah Stevenson, review of *Black Rabbit Summer,* p. 7.

Guardian (London, England), January 11, 2003, Adèle Geras, "Stand and Deliver."

Horn Book, March-April, 2003, Lauren Adams, review of *Lucas,* p. 210; May-June, 2006, Timothy Capehart, re-

view of *The Road of the Dead,* p. 310; January-February, 2007, Clarie E. Gross, review of *Being,* p. 63; September-October, 2008, Claire E. Gross, review of *Black Rabbit Summer,* p. 578.

Kirkus Reviews, January 1, 2004, review of *Kissing the Rain,* p. 34; January 15, 2005, review of *Candy,* p. 117; February 1, 2006, review of *The Road of the Dead,* p. 128; June 15, 2008, review of *Black Rabbit Summer.*

Kliatt, May, 2003, Paula Rohrlick, review of *Martyn Pig,* p. 15; March, 2005, Paula Rohrlick, review of *Candy,* p. 6; March, 2006, Myrna Marler, review of *The Road of the Dead,* p. 6; January, 2007, Paula Rohrlick, review of *Being,* p. 10; July, 2008, Paula Rohrlick, review of *Black Rabbit Summer,* p. 8.

Publishers Weekly, May 27, 2002, review of *Martyn Pig,* p. 61; June 24, 2002, "Flying Starts," p. 27; February 10, 2003, review of *Lucas,* p. 188; January 31, 2005, review of *Candy,* p. 69; February 27, 2006, review of *The Road of the Dead,* p. 62; December 18, 2006, review of *Being,* p. 64; July 21, 2008, review of *Black Rabbit Summer,* p. 161.

School Library Journal, May, 2002, Connie Tyrrell Burns, review of *Martyn Pig,* p. 147; May, 2003, Sharon Rawlins, review of *Lucas,* p. 148; March, 2004, Jeffrey Hastings, review of *Kissing the Rain,* p. 203; March, 2005, Johanna Lewis, review of *Candy,* p. 210; April, 2006, Johanna Lewis, review of *The Road of the Dead,* p. 134; February, 2007, Kathy Lehman, review of *Being,* p. 116; August, 2008, Geri Diorio, review of *Black Rabbit Summer,* p. 116.

Voice of Youth Advocates, April, 2004, review of *Kissing the Rain,* p. 41; April, 2005, Sophie Brookover, review of *Candy,* p. 36; April, 2006, Beth E. Anderson, review of *The Road of the Dead,* p. 38; October, 2008, Joyce Doyle, review of *Black Rabbit Summer,* p. 330.

ONLINE

Guardian Online, http://books.guardian.co.uk/ (June 26, 2003), interview with Brooks.

Jubilee Books Web site, http://www.jubileebooks.co.uk/ (December 3, 2003), interview with Brooks.

Push Web site, http://www.thisispush.com/ (June 3, 2004), interview with Brooks.

Write Away Web site, http://www.writeaway.org.uk/ (January 20, 2009), Nikki Gamble, interview with Brooks.

*   *   *

BROOKS, Kevin M.
See BROOKS, Kevin

C

CALL, Greg

Personal
Born in CO; married; children: two. *Education:* Colorado Institute of Art, graduated 1983; Art Center College of Design, graduated 1988.

Addresses
Home—MT.

Career
Illustrator. Colorado Institute of Art, former art director.

Awards, Honors
Addy Award; awards from Society of Illustrators.

Illustrator
Doreen Rappaport and Joan Verniero, *Victory or Death! Stories of the American Revolution,* HarperCollins (New York, NY), 2003.

Dave Barry and Ridley Pearson, *Peter and the Starcatchers,* Hyperion (New York, NY), 2004.

Tony Abbott, *Kringle,* Scholastic (New York, NY), 2005.

Dave Barry and Ridley Pearson, *Peter and the Shadow Thieves,* Hyperion (New York, NY), 2006.

Candice Ransom, *Secret in the Tower,* Mirrorstone (Renton, WA), 2006.

Candice Ransom, *Bones in the Badlands,* Mirrorstone (Renton, WA), 2006.

Dave Barry and Ridley Pearson, *Escape from the Carnivale,* Hyperion (New York, NY), 2006.

Candice Ransom, *Horses in the Wind,* Mirrorstone (Renton, WA), 2007.

Candice Ransom, *Rider in the Night: A Tale of Sleepy Hollow,* Mirrorstone (Renton, WA), 2007.

Candice Ransom, *Signals in the Sky,* Mirrorstone (Renton, WA), 2007.

Dave Barry and Ridley Pearson, *Peter and the Secret of Rundoon,* Hyperion (New York, NY), 2007.

Dave Barry and Ridley Pearson, *Cave of the Dark Wind,* Hyperion (New York, NY), 2007.

Candice Ransom, *Gold in the Hills: A Tale of the Klondike Gold Rush,* Mirrorstone (Renton, WA), 2008.

Greg Call has created art for numerous book covers, among them Dorothy and Thomas Hoobler's novel In Darkness, Death. (Jacket art copyright © 2004 by Greg Call. All rights reserved. Used by permission of Penguin Group (USA) Inc.)

Laurel Snyder, *Up and Down the Scratchy Mountains; or, The Search for a Suitable Princess,* Random House (New York, NY), 2008.

Candice Ransom, *Message in the Mountain: A Tale of Mount Rushmore,* Mirrorstone (Renton, WA), 2008.

Candice Ransom, *Flames in the City: A Tale of the War of 1812,* Mirrorstone (Renton, WA), 2008.

Dan Elish, *The Attack of the Frozen Woodchucks,* Harper-Collins (New York, NY), 2008.

Ridley Pearson, *Kingdom Keepers II: Disney at Dawn,* Disney Editions (New York, NY), 2008.

Dave Barry and Ridley Pearson, *Blood Tide,* Hyperion (New York, NY), 2008.

Sidelights

Artist and illustrator Greg Call has degrees from the Colorado Institute of Art and from the Art Center College of Design in Pasadena, California. His freelance work has been sought after in a variety of industries, including publishing, video games, music, sports, and film. Both as a painter and a sculptor, Call's talent for conceptual work has provided the visual starting point for many of his clients' projects. He displays his paintings and sculptures in fine-art venues, in addition to producing commercial work and creating illustrations for a number of books.

Call has collaborated with the writing team of David Barry and Ridley Pearson to create the art for "Never Land" books such as *Peter and the Starcatchers, Peter and the Shadow Thieves,* and *Escape from the Carnivale.* These books include images of the fantastic, including flying carpets, mermaids, and Peter Pan and the Lost Boys in flight. Call's work includes color and black-and-white illustrations, and a frequent subject is the diabolical Captain Hook.

For the "Time Spies" fantasy novels by Candice Ransom, Call's artwork brings to life a group of children traveling through time with the aid of a magic spyglass. His illustrations for these books depict scenes from U.S. history, including the Revolutionary War, the War of 1812, and the fossil-hunting Bone Wars of the late 1800s.

Biographical and Critical Sources

PERIODICALS

Booklist, September 1, 2004, Ilene Cooper, review of *Peter and the Starcatchers,* p. 121; October 15, 2005, Ilene Cooper, review of *Kringle,* p. 48; June 1, 2006, GraceAnne A DeCandido, review of *Peter and the Shadow Thieves,* p. 66; November 15, 2007, Kathleen Isaacs, review of *Peter and the Secret of Rundoon,* p. 44; February 15, 2008, Carolyn Phelan, review of *The Attack of the Frozen Woodchucks,* p. 78.

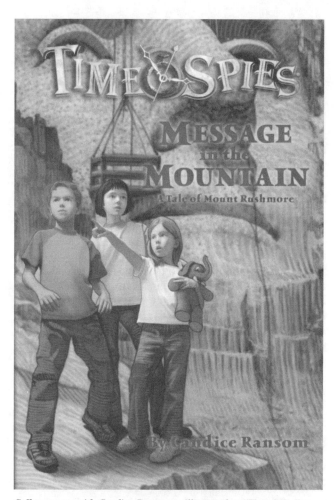

Call teams up with Candice Ransom to illustrate her "Time Spies" novels, among them **Message in the Mountain.** (Copyright © 2008 by Wizards of the Coast, Inc. Reproduced by permission.)

Kirkus Reviews, April 1, 2003, review of *Victory or Death!: Stories of the American Revolution,* p. 539.

Publishers Weekly, August 23, 2004, review of *Peter and the Starcatchers,* p. 55.

School Library Journal, June, 2003, Jean Gaffney, review of *Victory or Death!,* p. 168; August, 2006, Eva Mitnick, review of *Peter and the Shadow Thieves,* p. 113; February, 2007, Elaine E. Knight, review of *Bones in the Badlands,* p. 94.

ONLINE

Shannon Associates Web site, http://www.shannon associates.com/ (February 23, 2009), "Greg Call."*

*   *   *

CARMAN, Patrick 1966-

Personal

Born February 27, 1966; son of an entrepreneur; married; wife's name Karen; children: Reece, Sierra (daughters). *Education:* Willamette University, B.S. (econom-

ics). *Hobbies and other interests:* Mountain biking, fly fishing, crossword puzzles, basketball, reading, spending time with family.

Addresses

Home—WA. *E-mail*—fanmail@patrickcarman.com.

Career

Writer and entrepreneur. Founded four businesses, including an advertising agency. Volunteer on behalf of literacy campaigns.

Awards, Honors

iParenting Media Award, and Cochecho Readers Award, both 2005, National Lamplighter Award, 2007, and numerous state book award nominations, all for *The Dark Hills Divide;* National Lamplighter Award, 2008, for *Beyond the Valley of Thorns;* E.B. White Award nomination, 2008, and Truman Award nomination, 2009, both for *Atherton;* Kids Wings Award, Texas Bluebonnet Award shortlist, Oregon Battle of the Books listee, and E.B. White Award nomination, all 2008, all for *House of Power.*

Writings

Skeleton Creek, Scholastic Press (New York, NY), 2009.

"LAND OF ELYON" SERIES

The Dark Hills Divide, Orchard Books (New York, NY), 2005.
Beyond the Valley of Thorns, Orchard Books (New York, NY), 2005.
The Tenth City, Orchard Books (New York, NY), 2006.
Into the Mist (prequel), Orchard Books (New York, NY), 2007.
Stargazer, Scholastic Press (New York, NY), 2008.

"ATHERTON" SERIES

The House of Power, Little, Brown (New York, NY), 2007.
Rivers of Fire, Little, Brown (New York, NY), 2008.

"ELLIOT'S PARK" SERIES

Saving Mister Nibbles, Orchard Books (New York, NY), 2008.
Haunted Hike, Orchard Books (New York, NY), 2008.
The Walnut Cup, illustrated by Steve James, Orchard Books (New York, NY), 2009.

Author's novels have been translated into several languages.

Adaptations

Many of Carman's novels have been adapted as audiobooks by Brilliance Audio.

Sidelights

Patrick Carman is the author of several fantasy novels for middle-grade readers, including the "Land of Elyon" stories and the "Atherton" series, which mixes fantasy with ecological science fiction. His "Elliot's Park" books, which focus on a squirrel and his friends, are geared for younger readers and feature illustrations by Steve James, while the standalone novel *Skeleton Creek* attracts reluctant readers through its adventurous, fast-moving storyline and "multi-platform" format in which readers are guided to a special Web site that fleshes out the story.

A second-generation entrepreneur, Carman successfully launched four businesses—including an advertising agency—prior to turning to children's book writing full-time. Deciding that it was time to indulge his creative side, Carman penned a fantasy novel for young readers that was inspired by his daughters Reece and Sierra. Completing the book in nine months, he decided to publish the novel himself after failing to find a pub-

Cover of Patrick Carman's The Dark Hills Divide, *featuring artwork by Brad Weinman.* (Cover illustration copyright © 2005 by Scholastic, Inc. Reproduced by permission.)

lisher. *The Dark Hills Divide* became a local hit in western Washington, where Carman lives, and a representative from Scholastic publishers eventually discovered the book at a well-known Seattle book store. Soon, Carman had a contract for several more novels in his "Land of Elyon" series.

Twelve-year-old Alexa Daley, the heroine of *The Dark Hills Divide,* has grown up in a city surrounded by high walls, and she feels increasingly claustrophobic and longing for escape. One day she finds a tunnel that allows her to leave the shelter of her protected city and venture out into the unknown, where she comes across a magical stone that enables her to communicate with animals. From these creatures Alexa learns that her home fortress has actually been penetrated by a spy who seeks to destroy the city. It is up to her to return to the city to identify this spy and eradicate the opposed threat to her friends and loved ones.

Calling *The Dark Hills Divide* an "entertaining, accessible fantasy" that features a "highly cinematic" text, *School Library Journal* contributor Beth Wright noted that Carman's inclusion of "double identities, mysterious codes, and Alexa's magical gift of speaking with animals" creates an entertaining plot. "The most endearing parts of the story are the relationships Alexa forms with animals who help her," commented Claire Rosser in a *Kliatt* review of the novel, while a *Kirkus* reviewer praised Alexa as a girl who, "with her brains courage and grit, proves to be an appealingly strong female hero." "Readers of all ages will gain much from this tale," concluded a *Publishers Weekly* contributor, praising Carman for creating a "plucky, convincingly curious heroine" who "follows her passion" despite her fears.

The "Land of Elyon" series continues in *Beyond the Valley of Thorns,* the first of several sequels following Alexa's adventures. Joined by several unusual friends, including a squirrel, a wolf, a hawk, a giant, and a midget named Yipes, the girl hopes to vanquish the evil ogre Abaddon from the land. To do so she must do battle with a swarm of poisonous bats as well as with Abaddon's ogre army. In *The Tenth City* the origin of Elyon are revealed, Yipes is kidnaped by Grindall, a powerful lord beholden to Abaddon, and the battle with the supernatural ogre and his army continues. In *School Library Journal* Jessi Platt described Carman's text in *Beyond the Valley of Thorns* as "poetic, full of childlike wonder, and well written," although the critic cautioned that the vocabulary of the fantasy adventure might be too complex for reluctant readers.

In *Into the Mist* Carman starts a second series of "Land of Elyon" novels, as Alexa and Yipes join Captain Roland Warvold on a voyage leading to a pivotal face-off against Lord Grindall. On the way, readers as well as Alexa learn the history of their land and the reason for the kingdom's great divide. Abaddon shows his power as a shapechanger in *Stargazer,* and in his guise as a

Carman turns to younger readers in his squirrel-centered "Elliot's Park" series, featuring artwork by Jim Madsen. (Illustration copyright © 2008 by James Madsen. All rights reserved. Reproduced by permission of Orchard Books, an imprint of Scholastic, Inc.)

terrifying sea monster the creature follows Alexa and company to a refuge called the Five Stone Pillars. Citing the "nonstop action" of *Into the Mist,* a *Kirkus Reviews* writer added that the story propels readers "from crisis to crisis and ends on a classic Carman cliffhanger."

Carman's "Atherton" series draws readers into another fantasy world. In Atherton the richest citizens live in the Highlands while the lower flatlands, known as the Tabletop, serve as home to the peasant classes. Everything changes, however, when an earthquake causes the lands of Atherton to resolve into a level plane, and social and political chaos is the result. In *House of Power,* twelve-year-old orphaned Edgar goes in search of a secret book said to contain Atherton's secrets, and the boy's quest leads him to discover the land's actual creator and learn the genesis of his world following Earth's ecological meltdown. Edgar's adventures continue in *Rivers of Fire,* as he and friends Samuel and Isabel attempt to restore water to their parched and ecologically damaged land.

Reviewing the first "Atherton" novel, *Booklist* contributor Jennifer Mattson predicted that Carman's intended

middle-grade readership "will be caught up in the accessible, sf premise, extended with [the author's] evocative illustrations." While admitting that *House of Power* has a typical science-fiction premise, a *Kirkus Reviews* contributor noted that Carman's technique of seeding his plot with "frequently surprises," making the dystopian novel "a humdinger of a cliff-hanger [that] will leave even reluctant readers demanding more." Equally "fast-paced and suspenseful," according to another *Kirkus Reviews* critic, *Rivers of Fire* continues to draw fans into a saga in which "danger abounds, science seems to have run amok and a neat . . . ending ties up most of the loose ends."

In an interview for *Scholastic.com*, Carman reflected on his first novel and why he wrote it. "The walls in the book [*The Dark Hills Divide*] are very much like the emotional walls that kids build around themselves to cope with all the peer pressure. They feel they have to dress a certain way, to act a certain way, to talk to only certain people, and all of that. That's not what being a kid should have to be about. You should be able to just be yourself and be with the kids you want to be with and dress the way you want to dress and, . . . have a good experience with school. But so many kids are

afraid. And they lose themselves and they lost the opportunity of meeting the kids they probably should have met—of being the kid they really should have been."

Biographical and Critical Sources

PERIODICALS

Booklist, March 1, 2005, Sally Estes, review of *The Dark Hills Divide,* p. 1193; May 15, 2007, Jennifer Mattson, review of *The House of Power,* p. 60; May 15, 2008, Jennifer Mattson, review of *Rivers of Fire,* p. 56; June 1, 2008, Kay Weisman, review of *Saving Mister Nibbles,* p. 92; December 1, 2008, Stephanie Zvirin, review of *Skeleton Creek,* p. 52.

Bulletin of the Center for Children's Books, January, 2005, Timnah Card, review of *The Dark Hills Divide,* p. 202; July-August, 2007, review of *The House of Power,* p. 455.

Kirkus Reviews, February 1, 2005, review of *The Dark Hills Divide,* p. 174; September 1, 2005, review of *Beyond the Valley of Thorns,* p. 969; May 1, 2007, review of *The House of Power;* September 1, 2007, review of *Into the Mist;* March 15, 2008, review of *Saving Mister Nibbles!;* April 15, 2008, review of *Rivers of Fire;* December 1, 2008, review of *Skeleton Creek.*

Kliatt, January, 2005, Claire Rosser, review of *The Dark Hills Divide,* p. 6.

Publishers Weekly, December 13, 2004, John F. Baker, "Big Push for Self-published Kids' Author," p. 12; February 21, 2005, review of *The Dark Hills Divide,* p. 176; March 12, 2007, review of *The House of Power,* p. 58; December 15, 2008, review of *Skeleton Creek,* p. 55.

School Library Journal, April, 2005, Beth Wright, review of *The Dark Hills Divide,* p. 129; October, 2005, Jessi Platt, review of *Beyond the Valley of Thorns,* p. 154; August, 2006, Elizabeth Bird, review of *The Tenth City,* p. 117.

Seattle Post-Intelligencer, March 19, 2004, Cecelia Goodnow, "For Authors with Drive and a Good Story, Self-Publishing Can Be the Ticket."

Voice of Youth Advocates, April, 2005, Ann Welton, review of *The Dark Hills Divide,* p. 53.

ONLINE

Patrick Carman Home Page, http://www.patrickcarman. com (January 26, 2009).

Scholastic Web site, http://www.scholastic.com/ (January 29, 2009), "Patrick Carman."

Trades-Entertainment Industry Analysis Web site, http:// www.the-trades.com/ (December 5, 2004), Howard Price, interview with Carman.

*   *   *

Carman's second fantasy series, "Atherton," includes **The House of Power,** *a novel featuring artwork by Phillip Straub.* (Little, Brown & Company, 2007. Cover artwork copyright © 2007 by Philip Straub. All rights reserved. Reproduced by permission.)

CARRUTH, Hayden 1921-2008

OBITUARY NOTICE—

See index for *SATA* sketch: Born August 3, 1921, in Waterbury, CT; died September 29, 2008, in Munns-

ville, NY. Poet, publisher, magazine editor, educator, and author. Carruth's poetry enabled the reclusive author to offer to others a glimpse of the world as he saw it through the only means possible for him: the written word. For much of his life Carruth was unable to interact with society in a direct manner. A brief period as the editor of the magazine *Poetry* and an associate editor for the University of Chicago Press was followed by a nervous breakdown that confined him to a mental hospital for nearly two years. For the next twenty years, several of which he spent living in his parents' attic, Carruth's life played out through his solitary writings. They emerged quietly at the rate of approximately one book per year, usually in the form of a poetry collection. He then moved from Illinois to a remote farm in northern Vermont, where manual labor sustained his spirit and the pace of the natural world inspired his muse. In the 1970s Carruth emerged from his self-imposed exile and began a series of teaching appointments throughout his home state. He then taught at Syracuse University from 1979 to 1991 and founded a small publishing enterprise, Crow's Mark Press. Carruth never conquered his social diffidence, however, he once noted that he thought of "the whole human race," including himself, as "fundamentally alien." Carruth believed that the state of tension that permeated his life also improved his poetry. Carruth was a prolific poet, with dozens of collections of varying size published between 1959 and 2006, but critical acclaim came later in life. He won the poetry award of the National Book Critics Circle in 1992 for *Collected Shorter Poems, 1946-1991* and received a National Book Award in 1996 for *Scrambled Eggs and Whiskey.* Carruth's poetry revealed a stunning intellect, his critics claimed, energetically exploring—or attacking—a sprawling array of topics in language that is verbally restrained and charged with passion at the same time. His earliest work was published in *The Crow and the Heart, 1946-1959* (1959), his latest in *Toward the Distant Islands: New and Selected Poems* (2006). Carruth published miscellaneous nonfiction as well, including the memoir *Reluctantly: Autobiographical Essays* (1998).

OBITUARIES AND OTHER SOURCES:

BOOKS

Carruth, Hayden, *Reluctantly: Autobiographical Essays,* Copper Canyon Press (Port Townsend, WA), 1998.
Contemporary Poets, 7th edition, St. James Press (Detroit, MI), 1981.

PERIODICALS

Chicago Tribune, October 1, 2008, sec. 1, p. 35.
Los Angeles Times, October 3, 2008, p. B8.
New York Times, October 1, 2008, p. A29; October 2, 2008, p. A4.

CHAPMAN, Lynne 1960-

Personal

Born 1960, in London, England; married. *Hobbies and other interests:* Jiving, sketching, reading novels walking, films, travel.

Addresses

Home—Sheffield, England. *E-mail*—contact@lynne chapman.co.uk.

Career

Illustrator and author of children's books. Presenter of workshops, talks, and storytellings to schools, libraries, and festivals. Formerly worked as an editorial illustrator. Sheffield College, Sheffield, England, former lecturer in illustration and electronic imaging; Need to Read (young people's literacy project), former tutor.

Writings

SELF-ILLUSTRATED

When You're Not Looking!, Gullane Children's Books (London, England), 2004, Gingham Dog Press (Columbus, OH), 2007.
An ABC of Nursery Rhymes, Chicken House (London, England), 2008.

ILLUSTRATOR

Helen Paiba, compiler, *Funny Stories for Nine Year Olds,* Macmillan (London, England), 1999.
Ann Jungman, *Broomstick Rescues,* Scholastic (London, England), 1999.
Jemma Beeke, *The Show at Rickety Barn,* David & Charles (London, England), 2000, published as *The Rickety Barn Show,* Doubleday Book for Young Readers (New York, NY), 2001.
Helen Paiba, compiler, *Funny Stories for Eight Year Olds,* Macmillan (London, England), 2001.
Miriam Moss, *Smudge's Grumpy Day,* Gullane Children's Books (London, England), 2001.
Miriam Moss, *A New House for Smudge,* Gullane Children's Books (London, England), 2001.
Miriam Moss, *I'll Be Your Friend, Smudge,* Gullane Children's Books (London, England), 2001.
Miriam Moss, *It's My Turn, Smudge!,* Gullane Children's Books (London, England), 2001.
Simon Puttock, *Big Bad Wolf Is Good,* Gullane Children's Books (London, England), 2001, Sterling (New York, NY), 2002.
Terry Deary, *Into the Lion's Den,* A. & C. Black (London, England), 2002.
Miriam Moss, *Bad Hare Day,* Bloomsbury Children's Books (New York, NY), 2003.

Lynne Chapman (Courtesy of Lynne Chapman.)

Sue Purkiss, *Spook School,* A. & C. Black (London, England), 2003.

Jamie Rix, *Giddy Goat,* Orchard (London, England), 2003, Gingham Dog Press (Columbus, OH), 2004.

Julia Jarman, *Kangaroo's Cancan Café,* Orchard (London, England), 2004.

Tom Barber, *Open Wide!,* Chrysalis (London, England), 2004.

Pamela Love, *Two Feet up, Two Feet Down,* Children's Press (New York, NY), 2004.

Damian Harvey, *An Itch to Scratch,* Gullane Children's Books (London, England), 2005, published as *Just the Thing!,* Gingham Dog Press (Columbus, OH), 2005.

Dori Chaconas, *When Cows Come Home for Christmas,* Albert Whitman (Morton Grove, IL), 2005.

Hiawyn Oram, *Mr Strongmouse and the Baby,* Orchard (London, England), 2005.

Jamie Rix, *Giddy the Great,* Orchard (London, England), 2006.

Greg Gormley, *Rocky and the Lamb,* Barrons Educational (Happauge, NY), 2006.

Julia Jarman, *Class Two at the Zoo,* Carolrhoda Books (Minneapolis, MN), 2007.

S. Purkiss, *Ghosts Away,* Stone Arch Books (Minneapolis, MN), 2007.

S. Purkiss, *Ghost School,* Stone Arch Books (Minneapolis, MN), 2007.

Julia Rawlinson, *Mule School,* Gullane Children's Books (London, England), 2007, Good Books (Intercourse, PA), 2008.

Julia Jarman, *Class Three at Sea,* Carolrhoda Books (Minneapolis, MN), 2008.

Tony Mitton, *Gnash, Gnaw, Dinosaur!,* Kingfisher (London, England), 2009.

Susannah Corbett, *Dragon's Dinner,* Hodder (London, England), 2009.

Sidelights

Born in London, England, Lynne Chapman is a children's book illustrator whose work appears in dozens of picture books and beginning readers. In addition to her original self-illustrated picture book *When You're Not Looking!,* Chapman's pastel art, with its wide-eyed characters, has brought to life child-friendly stories by writers ranging from Julia Jarman and Simon Puttock to Hiawyn Oram and Miriam Moss. Praising her work for Damian Harvey's *Just the Thing!,* for example, Rosalyn Pierini wrote in *School Library Journal* that Chapman's "wonderful comic illustrations . . . highlighted by vibrant coloration add significantly to the humor and sweetness" of Harvey's picture-book tale.

While all of Chapman's books have been published in her native England, U.S. readers have also become familiar with her artistry through books such as Moss's *Bad Hare Day* and Dori Chaconas's *When Cows Come Home for Christmas.* In a review of *Bad Hare Day,* in which a young rabbit takes over coiffure-ing duties at her uncle Herbert's beauty salon, a *Publishers Weekly* critic concluded that Chapman contributes . . . more [visual] humor and characterization to the proceedings than the stolid text," while *School Library Journal* critic Martha Topol cited the artist's "vibrant and expressive" pastel drawings. In her collaboration with Chaconas, the illustrator "gives barnyard bovines a homey, humorous look," according to *Booklist* critic Connie Fletcher.

"I have always preferred drawing to painting," Chapman told *SATA.* "I love the hands-on messiness of pastels and their vibrant but subtle colours." She most enjoys illustrating humorous stories. "I have great fun creating funny, naughty or evil animal characters," the author/illustrator explained, "but it's not always easy. The very first drawings for a new book are always a bit scary. I often find excuses to put off getting going on that first day. I need to 'warm up' and the initial drawings can be pretty rubbish. Even after all these years, I always worry that I'll never be able to do it right, and then, like magic, on the next day it is fine!"

When it comes to writing, Chapman added, "People often ask where I get my ideas. Ideas come from ordinary, everyday things that are happening all the time all around you. The trick is to notice them."

When she travels, Chapman takes along a sketchbook, and she records people and places she sees, building visual diaries. These sketch books are among her most precious possessions; as she explained: "Each drawing is irreplaceable. It is not just a visual record, but forever imbued with all the smells, sounds and small happenings of the period it took to draw."

Biographical and Critical Sources

PERIODICALS

Booklist, February 1, 2001, Connie Fletcher, review of *The Rickety Barn Show,* p. 1055; April 15, 2003, Connie Fletcher, review of *Bad Hare Day,* p. 1479; October 15, 2005, Connie Fletcher, review of *When Cows Come Home for Christmas,* p. 55.

Kirkus Reviews, September 1, 2002, review of *Big Bad Wolf Is Good,* p. 1318; March 15, 2003, review of *Bad Hare Day,* p. 474; November 1, 2005, review of *When Cows Come Home for Christmas,* p. 1191; August 1, 2006, review of *Rocky and the Lamb,* p. 786; August 15, 2007, review of *Class Two at the Zoo.*

Publishers Weekly, January 8, 2001, review of *The Rickety Barn Show,* p. 65; March 24, 2003, review of *Bad Hare Day,* p. 75; September 1, 2003, review of *Giddy Goat,* p. 87; September 26, 2005, review of *When Cows Come Home for Christmas,* p. 89.

School Library Journal, April, 2001, Anne Parker, review of *The Rickety Barn Show,* p. 98; August, 2002, Anne Knickerbocker, reviews of *It's My Turn, Smudge* and *I'll Be Your Friend, Smudge!,* p. 161, and Kathleen Simonetta, review of *Big Bad Wolf Is Good,* p. 164; April, 2003, Martha Topol, review of *Bad Hare Day,* p. 133; December, 2003, Joy Fleishhacker, review of *Giddy Goat,* p. 124; January, 2006, Rosalyn Pierini, review of *Just the Thing!,* p. 103; September, 2007, review of *Class Two at the Zoo,* p. 166; August, 2008, Catherine Threadgill, review of *Mule School,* p. 100.

ONLINE

Lynne Chapman Home Page, http://www.lynnechapman. co.uk (January 10, 2009).

Lynne Chapman Web log, http://lynnechapman.blogspot. com (January 15, 2009).

*   *   *

CNEUT, Carll 1969-

Personal

Born August 1, 1969, in Belgium. *Education:* Attended Saint-Lucas Arts School (Ghent, Belgium), degree (graphic design).

Addresses

Home and office—Ghent, Belgium.

Career

Illustrator, writer, and costume designer. Previously worked as an art director for a publicity agency.

Awards, Honors

Honorable mention, Book Peacock award, 1998, for *Straatje zonder eind;* selection Gigant Fiaminghi, for *Varkentjes van Marsepein;* Jonge Gouden Uil longlist, 2000, and Children's and Youth Jury shortlist, Prix Octogones nomination, and Flemish Children and Youth Jury shortlist, all 2001, all for *Heksenfee;* honorable mention, Bologna Ragazzi awards, 2001, for *Woeste Mie;* Boekenpauw award, 2000, and Prix Enfantaisie shortlist, 2002, both for *Willy;* Prix Octogones, and Bookfeather award, both 2002, and Children's and Youth Jury shortlist, 2003, all for *Roodgeelzwartwit;* Jonge Gouden Uil longlist, 2003, for *The Amazing Love Story of Mr. Morf.*

Writings

SELF-ILLUSTRATED

Het ongeloofijk liefesverhaal van Heer Morf, De Eenhoorn (Belgium), 2002, translated as *The Amazing Love Story of Mr. Morf,* Clarion (New York, NY), 2003.

ILLUSTRATOR

Geert De Kockere, *Varkentjes van Marsepein,* [Belgium], 1996.

Chapman's whimsical art adds a humorous note to Jemma Beeke's picture book **The Rickety Barn Show.** (Illustration copyright © 2000 by Lynne Chapman. Used by permission of Random House Children's Books, a division of Random House, Inc.)

Brigitte Minne, *Heksenfee* (title means "Witchfairy"), De Eenhoorn (Belgium), 1999.

Geert De Kockere, *Willy,* De Eenhoorn (Belgium), 1999.

Geert De Kockere, *Woeste Mie,* De Eenhoorn (Belgium), 2000.

Brigitte Minne, *Roodgeelzwartwit* (title means "Redyellowblackwhite"), Dee Eenhoorn (Belgium), 2001.

Malachy Doyle, *Antonio on the Other Side of the World, Getting Smaller,* Candlewick (Cambridge, MA), 2003.

Carl Norac, *Un sécret pour Grandir,* Pastel (Paris, France), 2003.

Sam Swope, *Jack and the Seven Deadly Giants,* Farrar, Straus & Giroux (New York, NY), 2004.

Carl Norac, *Coeur de papier* (title means "A Paper Heart"), Pastel (Paris, France), 2004.

Carl Norac, *O monster, eet me niet op,* De Eenhoorn (Belgium), 2006, translated as *Monster, Don't Eat Me!,* Groundwood (New York, NY), 2007.

Marilyn Singer, *City Lullaby,* Clarion (New York, NY), 2007.

Illustrator of several books published in Belgium.

Sidelights

Belgian illustrator Carll Cneut grew up in a small village on the border of France and Belgium. From an early age, Cneut knew he wanted to be an artist, and one of his goals after graduating from the Saint-Lucas Arts School in Ghent, Belgium, was to see his art reproduced in a children's book published in the United States. Beginning his career as art director for an advertising agency, he did his first book illustration project in 1996. *Varkenjes van Marsepein,* a collaboration with Flemish writer Geert De Kockere, proved popular and marked the start of Cneut's illustration career. Cneut and De Kockere gained further recognition with *Willy,* which won the Boekenpauw award in 2000.

Before Cneut decided on a career in illustration, he considered becoming a circus artist, and his first original, self-illustrated picture book features a circus theme.

Carll Cneut creates the humorous illustrations for Carl Norac's picture book Monster, Don't Eat Me! (Groundwood Books, 2006. Reproduced by permission.)

First published in Belgium in 2002, *The Amazing Love Story of Mr. Morf* is the tale of a circus dog searching for a soul mate. The high-wire terrier cannot seem to find a good match, although he tries to make friends with a cat, an owl, a swallow, and a wolf. Ultimately, it is a flea that is able to keep the dog good company. "It is the delightfully offbeat acrylic-and-pastel illustrations that distinguish this picture book," wrote Teri Markson and Stephen Samuel in a *School Library Journal* review of the book. Several other critics deemed Cneut's artwork stronger than his story. The "densely textured acrylic-and-pastel illustrations outshine the wordy exposition," wrote a contributor to *Publishers Weekly,* in a review of *The Amazing Love Story of Mr. Morf,* and a *Kirkus Reviews* contributor wrote that "what makes this unique is the style of illustration." In contrast, Gillian Engberg commented in *Booklist* on the author/illustrator's "brief, simple language."

Other picture books featuring Cneut's illustration include *Antonio on the Other Side of the World,* a book by Malachy Doyle that reveals "a world filled with circus-like energy and whimsy," according to a *Publishers Weekly* critic. Abby Nolan wrote in *Booklist* that the illustrations here "offer up delectable details and a playful sense of scale." In *Jack and the Seven Deadly Giants,* "Cneut's wild illustrations . . . have the same off-kilter spirit" as his work in *Antonio on the Other Side of the World,* according to Nolan, while his work for Carl Norac's *Monster, Don't Eat Me!* includes illustrations described by *Resource Links* critic Michelle Gowans as "imaginative and expressive and filled with detail that elevates the book's overall appeal." Linda L. Walkins wrote in her *School Library Journal* review of *Monster, Don't Eat Me!* that the juxtaposition of deep tones against grayish background give the images "an oddly appealing sophistication."

Biographical and Critical Sources

PERIODICALS

Booklist, April 1, 2003, Gillian Engberg, review of *The Amazing Love Story of Mr. Morf,* p. 1400; October, 2003, Abby Nolan, review of *Antonio on the Other Side of the World, Getting Smaller,* p. 417; May 15, 2004, Abby Nolan, review of *Jack and the Seven Deadly Giants,* p. 1622; October 15, 2007, Gillian Engberg, review of *City Lullaby,* p. 51.

Horn Book, May-June, 2004, Christine M. Heppermann, review of *Jack and the Seven Deadly Giants,* p. 336; January-February, 2008, Sarah Ellis, review of *City Lullaby,* p. 79.

Kirkus Reviews, February 15, 2003, review of *The Amazing Love Story of Mr. Morf,* p. 302; October 1, 2007, review of *City Lullaby.*

Publishers Weekly, January 27, 2003, review of *The Amazing Love Story of Mr. Morf,* p. 258; September 29, 2003, review of *Antonio on the Other Side of the World,* p. 64; May 17, 2004, review of *Jack and the Seven Deadly Giants,* p. 50; November 12, 2007, review of *City Lullaby,* p. 54.

Resource Links, June, 2007, Michelle Gowans, review of *Monster, Don't Eat Me!,* p. 5.

School Library Journal, August, 2003, Teri Markson and Stephen Samuel Wise, review of *The Amazing Love Story of Mr. Morf,* p. 124; December, 2003, Catherine Threadgill, review of *Antonio on the Other Side of the World, Getting Smaller,* p. 112; May, 2004, Maria B. Salvadore, review of *Jack and the Seven Deadly Giants,* p. 125; August, 2007, Linda L. Walkins, review of *Monster, Don't Eat Me!,* p. 86.

ONLINE

Carll Cneut Home Page, http://users.telenet.be/carllcneut (February 14, 2009).

Children's Literature Web site, http://www.childrenslit.com/childrenslit/ (Feburary 23, 2009), "Carl Cneut."*

*   *   *

COLFER, Eoin 1965-

Personal

First name pronounced "Ow-en"; born May 14, 1965, in Wexford, Ireland; son of Billy (a primary school teacher, artist, and historian) and Noreen (a drama teacher, actress, and writer) Colfer; married 1991; wife's name Jackie (a teacher); children: Finn, Seán. *Education:* Carysfort College, education diploma, 1986. *Hobbies and other interests:* Reading, theater, parachuting.

Addresses

Home—Wexford, Ireland.

Career

Writer, 2001—. Primary school teacher in Coolcots, Ireland, 1987-92 and 1996-2001; worked in Saudi Arabia, Tunisia, and Italy, 1992-96.

Awards, Honors

White Raven Award, 1998, for *Benny and Omar;* Bisto Children's Book of the Year nomination, 2000, for *Benny and Babe;* Bisto Children's Book of the Year Merit Award, 2001, for *The Wish List;* Whitbread Children's Book of the Year shortlist, and Children's Book of the Year, British Book Awards, both 2001, Bisto Children's Book of the Year nomination, and Children's Book of the Year designation, W.H. Smith Book Awards, both 2002, all for *Artemis Fowl;* Irish World Literary Award, 2003; German Children's Book of the Year, 2004.

Writings

Benny and Omar, O'Brien Press (Dublin, Ireland), 1998, Hyperion (New York, NY), 2007.

Benny and Babe, O'Brien Press (Dublin, Ireland), 1999, Hyperion (New York, NY), 2007.

The Wish List, O'Brien Press (Dublin, Ireland), 2000, Hyperion (New York, NY), 2003.

The Legend of Spud Murphy, illustrated by Glenn McCoy, Hyperion (New York, NY), 2004.

The Supernaturalist, Hyperion (New York, NY), 2004.

The Legend of Captain Crow's Teeth, illustrated by Glenn McCoy, Hyperion (New York, NY), 2005.

Half Moon Investigations, Hyperion (New York, NY), 2006.

The Legend of the Worst Boy in the World, illustrated by Glenn McCoy, Hyperion (New York, NY), 2007.

Airman, Hyperion (New York, NY), 2008.

Contributor to *Click* (collaborative novel), Scholastic (New York, NY), 2007.

"ARTEMIS FOWL" NOVEL SERIES

Artemis Fowl, Hyperion (New York, NY), 2001.

The Arctic Incident, Hyperion (New York, NY), 2002.

The Eternity Code, Hyperion (New York, NY), 2003.

The Seventh Dwarf (story written for the Irish World Book Day celebration), Puffin (London, England), 2004.

The Artemis Fowl Files, Hyperion (New York, NY), 2004.

The Opal Deception, Hyperion (New York, NY), 2005.

The Lost Colony, Hyperion (New York, NY), 2006.

(Adaptor, with Andrew Donkin) *Artemis Fowl: The Graphic Novel* (based on the novel *Artemis Fowl,*), illustrated by Giovanni Rigano and Paolo Lamanna, Hyperion (New York, NY), 2007.

The Time Paradox, Hyperion (New York, NY), 2008.

Author's work has been translated into Danish, Dutch, French, German, Italian, Portuguese, and Spanish.

"O'BRIEN FLYERS" SERIES

Going Potty, O'Brien Press (Dublin, Ireland), 1999.

Ed's Funny Feet, O'Brien Press (Dublin, Ireland), 2000.

Ed's Bed, O'Brien Press (Dublin, Ireland), 2001.

Adaptations

Half Moon Investigations was adapted as a television series, British Broadcasting Corporation, 2009; *Artemis Fowl* was optioned for film.

Sidelights

Described by its author as *"Die Hard* with fairies," the middle-grade novel *Artemis Fowl* burst onto the book scene in 2001, and made its creator, Irish schoolteacher Eoin Colfer, the new wunderkind of children's literature. Colfer's humorous, high-tech fantasy about a twelve-year-old criminal mastermind started a bidding war among publishers and became the first in a series of immensely popular works about young Mr. Fowl. Since his breakthrough, Colfer has written such critically acclaimed books as *Half Moon Investigations* and

Airman. "It's just like a dream," Colfer told Heather Vogel in a *Publishers Weekly* interview. "[A] fellow from a small town gets a big break. You never think it's going to happen to you."

The second of five sons born to school teachers, Colfer grew up in Wexford, in the southeast of Ireland. His mother, Noreen, was a drama teacher and actress while his father taught primary school and was an artist and historian. "Understandably," Colfer wrote on his home page, "there was never a shortage of discussions, projects, artistic pursuits, or stimuli for the Colfer boys." They spent memorable summer holidays at the seaside village of Slade where Colfer's father was born. Young Colfer attended the grammar school where his father taught and early on developed a love of writing and of illustrating the stories he penned.

In secondary school, Colfer continued with his writing and began to read widely, enjoying especially the thrillers of Robert Ludlum and Jack Higgins. At a dance at a local girls' school, he met his future wife, Jackie. Inspired by his parents, Colfer decided to go into teaching, entering a three-year degree course in Dublin to qualify as a primary school teacher. In 1986, he returned to his native Wexford to teach, writing by night, both stories and plays, many of which were performed by a local dramatic group. He also wrote a novel which he sent to publishers "with visions of black sedans pulling up to the house the next day," as he told Jeff Chu in *Time Atlantic.* "I thought I was the best writer on the planet." However, the publishers did not quite agree. Colfer's breakthrough was put on hold.

In 1991, Colfer and Jackie married, and the couple left Ireland for four years, teaching in Saudi Arabia, Italy, and Tunisia. When they returned to Ireland in the mid-1990s, Colfer and his wife settled once again in Wexford, and he resumed teaching, squeezing in writing after school. A son was born in 1997, by which time Colfer had begun processing some of the experiences of his four years abroad and saw how they might very well fit into a juvenile novel, an obvious fit for this teacher who was familiar with the reading habits of the young.

The result of Colfer's labors was his first published novel, *Benny and Omar,* brought out by Dublin's O'Brien Press in 1998. The novel recounts the madcap adventures of a young Irish boy and his Tunisian friend in North Africa. Benny Shaw is a champion athlete at Saint Jerome's school in Wexford, Ireland, and is quite content with his life. Then his parents tell him they have decided to move to Tunisia where the locals have never heard of his sport, hurling. The village school where Benny ends up "is taught by feel-good hippies and filled with students actually bent on learning," according to Linda Bindner in *School Library Journal.* Benny is miserable until he meets up with Omar, a street-smart kid who lives by his wits and takes Benny under his wing. Benny at first loves the thrill of the

havoc they cause, going from one scrape to the next. Then he meets Omar's younger sister, a drug addict in a local institution, and suddenly understands the tragedy in Omar's life.

Bindner wrote of *Benny and Omar* that Colfer does a "masterful job of mixing humor and tragedy" in this "funny, fast-paced read . . . that takes a wonderful glimpse into some very non-American worlds." A reviewer for *Publishers Weekly* similarly found that Colfer "smoothly layers adventure, moments of poignancy and subtle social commentary, and his comic timing is pitch-perfect." *Booklist* contributor Frances Bradburn also had praise for this first novel, which became a best-seller in Ireland, and called it "an interesting and eye-opening study in contrasts" and a "comic adventure" that "likely will spawn a sequel."

In *Benny and Babe* Colfer's irrepressible protagonist is back in Ireland and visiting his grandfather in the country for the summer holiday. Benny is considered a "Townie" by the local kids and he has trouble finding a buddy until he meets up with the village tomboy, Babe, who has proven herself with the tough boys of the area. Babe and Benny hit it off, working together in Babe's business of finding lost fishing lures and flies and then reselling them. Things are going great for the friends until the bully Furty Howlin decides he wants part of their business. "Humor, sensitivity, and candor underscore this coming-of-age story that features incredibly well-drawn characters," wrote Renee Steinberg in a *School Library Journal* review of *Benny and Babe*. Steinberg went on to note that Colfer's second novel "has it all—an absorbing story, vibrant characters with whom readers will surely identify, and an on-target narrative voice." *Benny and Babe* was nominated for Ireland's prestigious Bisto Children's Book of the Year Award.

Next, Colfer turned his hand to a series for young readers aged five to seven. Ed Cooper is the character that figures in each of the titles: *Going Potty, Ed's Funny Feet,* and *Ed's Bed.* These tales find Ed alternately learning how to use a strange new toilet, having to wear corrective shoes, and dealing with a bed-wetting incident. In *The Wish List* the author spins a somewhat bizarre tale of "life, death and an unexpected hereafter," as Colfer himself described the novel on his home page. Winner of a Bisto Merit award, the book tells the story of an angry adolescent girl, Meg Finn, who sets out on a short-lived career of crime. Killed in the first chapter, Meg is given the rest of the novel as a chance to redeem herself; a moral tug of war ensues as the forces of good and evil battle for her soul. *School Library Journal* critic Janet Hilbun found *The Wish List* "an entertaining and compelling read," while *Booklist* critic Ilene Cooper called the work "surprisingly thought-provoking."

Dealing with fantasy of a sort for *The Wish List,* Colfer was encouraged to try more of the same, but this time with more humor and with the possibility of reaching a larger audience. As Colfer noted on his home page, "every child Eoin Colfer has ever taught will testify to his love of traditional magical Irish legends. They will also attest to his innate ability to make these legends come alive for them on a daily basis. It was in this genre he found his inspiration, but then took a unique slant on this well known underworld civilisation." Colfer blended this world of fairies and leprechauns with another constant interest, the *Die Hard* movies of Bruce Willis. "I really liked . . . [the film's] self-deprecating humor," Colfer told Vogel in *Publishers Weekly.* "They were big-budget action movies, but very much tongue-in-cheek, and I wanted to create an adventure with one foot in the comedy zone." So Colfer sat down to see how he could put these two genres together and knew that he had to do so employing a protagonist "original and different enough to make his mark and not just be the latest in line of clean-cut heroes," as he remarked to Vogel. He decided on a "a bit of a villain," and set the character to kidnap a leprechaun and demand a ransom in gold. "The twist being that these weren't the fairies you were used to reading about, but were actually quite futuristic," he explained. "It all fell into place after that." Colfer admitted to Vogel that he did not consciously set out to write a book that would appeal to both kids and adults, but he did "make a conscious effort to engage clever kids. The book doesn't talk down to them."

The finished manuscript, *Artemis Fowl,* ultimately proceeded to publication. Anti-hero Artemis is something of a boy genius and the last in a long line of a famous crime family who have lately fallen on hard times. Enlisting the help of his bodyguard, Butler, Artemis determines to restore the Fowl family wealth by capturing a fairy and then holding her ransom for all of the legendary fairy gold. He kidnaps Captain Holly Short, a leprechaun from LEPrecon, a branch of the Lower Elements Police and absolutely the wrong mark for Artemis to choose. He is set upon by a "wisecracking team of satyrs, trolls, dwarfs and fellow fairies," according to a reviewer for *Publishers Weekly,* who want to rescue Holly. These rescuers employ a good deal of elfin technology in their pursuit, while Artemis has to translate the arcana of the fairy folk's sacred book, employing a computer.

Reviewers made the inevitable comparisons to J.K. Rowling's "Harry Potter" books, as both have twelve-year-old protagonists and both employ types of magic. However, there the similarity ends. Colfer, in fact, had not read the "Harry Potter" novels before writing *Artemis Fowl.* Critical response was as varied as the plot of the book itself. Some found the novel less than successful. A *Horn Book* reviewer, for example, felt that Colfer's "revisioning of the fairy world as a sort of wisecracking police force . . . steal[s] focus from the one truly intriguing character, Artemis himself." The same reviewer noted that there is "a lot of invention here, but it's not used enough in service to the story, and may be deployed to better effect in the feature film." Daniel Fi-

erman, writing in *Entertainment Weekly,* felt that things turn "leaden" in the final "Die Hard-style standoff," and also found comparisons to J.K. Rowling's work specious, concluding that this demonstrates the difference "between a great children's book and a simply good one." Andrea Sachs, reviewing the novel in *Time,* wrote that "parents who might be worried about their children's reading a book glorifying extortion don't know the half of what's wrong with *Artemis Fowl.*" Sachs felt that the writing "is abysmal." Writing in *School Library Journal,* Eva Mitnick found Artemis to be "too stiff and enigmatic to be interesting," while the contributor for *Publishers Weekly* concluded that "the series is no classic in the making."

Other critics found more to like in the novel. *Library Journal* reviewer Jennifer Baker commented that the "quirky characters and delightful humor . . . will undoubtedly delight American readers." Baker further described *Artemis Fowl* as "fun to read" and "full of good humor." *Family Life* contributor Sara Nelson similarly called the book "action-packed" and "perfect for long, lazy summer days." Yvonne Zipp noted in the *Christian Science Monitor* that, after a slow first chapter, "the action kicks into high gear and never stops." *Time International* critic Elinor Shields added to the chorus of praise, describing *Artemis Fowl* as "pacy, playful and very funny, an inventive mix of myth and modernity, magic and crime," and Kate Kellaway, writing in the *London Observer,* dubbed Colfer's novel "a smart, amusing one-off" with "flashes of hi-tech invention."

Artemis Fowl goes into action for a second time in *The Arctic Incident,* in which the brilliant criminal teen returns to wander Colfer's magical underground world of fairies, trolls, satyrs, and gnomes. These creatures usually find themselves on the other side of the fence metaphorically from the "Mud People," or humans, who chased them underground. In the first installment, Artemis thought he had lost his beloved father, but via a video e-mail he sees a man who looks like his father sitting in the Arctic wasteland of Russia. Artemis wants to rescue this man, but not before he turns to his former enemies for some magical assistance. Meanwhile, below ground things are in a state of chaos after someone arms a band of trolls who wreaks havoc on the citizenry. Certain clues lead Captain Holly Short to Artemis, and in a turnaround from the first adventure, she kidnaps him in hopes of stopping the chaos. When she discovers Artemis is not responsible, the two former enemies join forces to fight both battles. Colfer's gun-toting, motorized fairies are back in action. "Once again," noted a reviewer for *Publishers Weekly* of this second installment, "the roller coaster of a plot introduces a host of high jinks and high-tech weaponry as Colfer blends derring-do with snappy prose." Writing in *School Library Journal,* Steven Engelfried found "the action . . . brisk, with fiendish plots, ingenious escapes, and lively battle scenes."

A year older, Artemis Fowl returns for a third adventure in *The Eternity Code.* This time, the teenager vies with

a dangerous businessman over the supercomputer Artemis built using technology stolen from the fairy world. Hoping to earn a few dollars before destroying the C Cube machine, Fowl's plan to deceive the millionaire Jon Spiro crumbles as the businessman double-crosses Artemis, threatening the existence of the fairy world. Calling again for help from his underground friends, the young trickster battles Spiro in a tale filled with "agile prose . . ., rapid fire dialogue, and wise-acre humor," according to a *Publishers Weekly* critic. Writing in *Booklist,* Sally Estes favorably compared *The Eternity Code* to the two previous books, claiming that "the action is fast and furious, the humor is abundant, [and the] characterizations are zany."

After the release of *The Artemis Fowl Files,* a collection of short stories, games, and puzzles, Colfer wrote *The Opal Deception,* which pits the now-fourteen-year-old criminal against his archenemy, Opal Koboi, a pixie who plans to destroy the fairy world. According to Estes, Colfer's fourth novel in the series "has plenty of action as well as great humor and clever plot manipulations." In *The Lost Colony,* the protagonist battles demonic imps who journey to Earth via a time tunnel. Kay Weisman, writing in *Booklist,* praised the "witty wordplay and dialogue" in the fifth series installment. Artemis travels into his own past in an effort to undo a terrible wrong that could save his mother's life in *The Time Paradox,* which inspired *School Library Journal* critic Robyn Gioia to observe: "Colfer's love of science shines through in the story's inventions and clever use of engineering."

The success of the "Artemis Fowl" series allowed Colfer to become a full-time writer, and he has gone on to produce several other books for children and young adults. *The Legend of Spud Murphy,* a humorous chapter book, focuses on Will and Marty, a pair of rambunctious brothers who must spend their summer afternoons at the library. There they encounter Mrs. "Spud" Murphy, a no-nonsense librarian who is rumored to possess a gas-powered potato gun to keep unruly patrons in check. Young readers "will laugh out loud at this clever book," Christine McGinty remarked in *School Library Journal.* Will and Marty also appear in *The Legend of Captain Crow's Teeth* and *The Legend of the Worst Boy in the World.*

The Supernaturalist, Colfer's dystopian science-fiction novel, centers on Cosmo Hill, a teenager who escapes from an orphanage that subjects its residents to medical experiments. After Cosmo is attacked by a Parasite—a creature that appears to feed off the dying—he is rescued by the Supernaturalists, a rebel group devoted to vanquishing the Parasites. The knowledge they gain on their missions, however, forces Cosmo and the Supernaturalists to question their objectives. "The action rarely lets up," Paula Rohrlick observed in *Kliatt,* and Saleena L. Davidson, writing in *School Library Journal,* remarked of *The Supernaturalist* that "the plot's twists and turns will keep readers totally engrossed until the last page."

A twelve-year-old detective is the focus of *Half Moon Investigations,* a "fast-paced romp," in the words of a *Kirkus Reviews* contributor. Fletcher Moon, a precocious crime-solver, is hired by classmate April Devereux to locate a lock of a pop star's hair that she bought online. Fletcher joins forces with Red Sharkey, the chief suspect in the case, to solve the crime. Set in the late nineteenth century, *Airman* concerns the adventures of Conor Broekhart, a teenager from the Saltee Islands who was born in the basket of an air balloon. When Conor witnesses the murder of King Nicholas, he is framed for the crime and imprisoned in the nightmarish world of the diamond mines. "Grippingly written, this is a fast-paced, highly entertaining tale of flying machines, criminals, martial arts, swordplay, princesses, poisons, and evil villains," stated Connie Tyrell Burns in *School Library Journal.*

Colfer's works have been praised for their complex, creative plots and fully developed characters. Discussing the source of his ideas, the author remarked on the Puffin Books Web site: "Inspiration comes from experience. My imagination is like a cauldron bubbling with all the things I've seen and places I've visited. My brain mixes them all up and regurgitates them in a way I hope is original."

Biographical and Critical Sources

BOOKS

Colfer, Eoin, *Artemis Fowl,* Hyperion (New York, NY), 2001.

PERIODICALS

Booklist, August, 2001, Frances Bradburn, review of *Benny and Omar,* p. 2118; May 1, 2002, Sally Estes, review of *The Arctic Incident,* p. 1518; June 1, 2003, Sally Estes, review of *The Eternity Code,* p. 1759; October 1, 2003, Ilene Cooper, review of *The Wish List,* p. 330; May 15, 2005, Sally Estes, review of *The Opal Deception,* p. 1651; November 1, 2006, Kay Weisman, review of *The Lost Colony,* p. 50; November 15, 2007, Francisca Goldsmith, review of *Artemis Fowl: The Graphic Novel,* p. 43; February 1, 2008, Stephanie Zvirin, review of *Airman,* p. 38.

Christian Science Monitor, March 22, 2001, Yvonne Zipp, "The Un-Potter at the Rainbow's End," p. 20.

Entertainment Weekly, July 20, 2001, Daniel Fierman, review of *Artemis Fowl,* p. 62.

Family Life, June 1, 2001, Sara Nelson, "Summer Reads," p. 70.

Hollywood Reporter, May 29, 2001, Matthew Dorman, "Storybook Beginnings," pp. 14-15.

Horn Book, July-August, 2001, review of *Artemis Fowl,* p. 449; January-February, 2002, Patty Campbell, "YA Scorecard 2001," p. 117.

Journal of Adolescent and Adult Literacy, September, 2008, James Blasingame, review of *Artemis Fowl: The Graphic Novel,* p. 87.

Kirkus Reviews, May 1, 2004, review of *The Supernaturalist,* p. 440; March 1, 2006, review of *Half Moon Investigations,* p. 227.

Kliatt, May, 2004, Paula Rohrlick, review of *The Supernaturalist,* p. 8.

Library Journal, June 15, 2001, Jennifer Baker, review of *Artemis Fowl,* p. 102; November 1, 2001, Nancy Pearl, "Not Just for Kids," p. 160.

New York Times Book Review, June 17, 2001, Gregory Maguire, review of *Artemis Fowl,* p. 24.

Observer (London, England), May 13, 2001, Kate Kellaway, "Elf and Happiness."

Publishers Weekly, April 9, 2001, review of *Artemis Fowl,* p. 75; April 23, 2001, Heather Vogel, "'Die Hard' with Fairies," pp. 25-26; July 9, 2001, review of *Benny and Omar,* p. 68; April 15, 2002, review of *The Arctic Incident,* p. 65; March 31, 2003, review of *The Eternity Code,* p. 68; October 13, 2003, review of *The Wish List,* p. 81; September 13, 2004, review of *The Legend of Spud Murphy,* p. 79; January 30, 2006, review of *Half Moon Investigations,* p. 70; November 12, 2007, review of *Airman,* p. 56.

School Library Journal, May, 2001, Eva Mitnick, review of *Artemis Fowl,* p. 148; December, 2001, Linda Bindner, review of *Benny and Omar,* pp. 132-133; March, 2002, Renee Steinberg, review of *Benny and Babe,* p. 226; July, 2002, Steven Engelfried, review of *The Arctic Incident,* p. 118; July, 2003, Tim Wadham, review of *The Eternity Code,* p. 128; December, 2003, Janet Hilbun, review of *The Wish List,* p. 148; July, 2004, Saleena L. Davidson, review of *The Supernaturalist,* p. 102; October, 2004, Christine McGinty, review of *The Legend of Spud Murphy,* p. 110; December, 2004, Saleena L. Davidson, review of *The Artemis Fowl Files,* p. 144; July, 2005, Farida S. Dowler, review of *The Opal Deception,* p. 100; January, 2008, Connie Tyrell Burns, review of *Airman,* p. 116, and Dawn Rutherford, review of *Artemis Fowl: The Graphic Novel,* p. 150; October, 2008, Robyn Gioia, review of *The Time Paradox,* p. 142.

Time, April 30, 2001, Andrea Sachs, "A Case of Fowl Play," p. 76.

Time Atlantic, May 7, 2001, Jeff Chu, "Legends of the Fowl," p. 56.

Time for Kids, August 6, 2008, Hannah Spicijaric, "A Backstage Chat with Eoin Colfer."

Time International, May 7, 2001, Elinor Shields, "A Magical Myth," p. 56.

Times Educational Supplement, May 11, 2001, Jan Mark, review of *Artemis Fowl.*

ONLINE

Artemis Fowl Web Site, http://www.artemisfowl.com (February 1, 2009).

BookPage Web Site, http://www.bookpage.com/ (February 1, 2009), Heidi Henneman, "*Artemis Fowl* Author Turns to Crime."

Eoin Colfer Home Page, http://www.eoincolfer.com (February 1, 2009).
Eoin Colfer Web Log, http://eoincolfer.com/news (February 1, 2009).
Puffin Books Web Site, http://www.puffin.co.uk/ (February 1, 2009), "Eoin Colfer."*

* * *

COMAN, Carolyn 1951-

Personal

Born 1951, in Evanston, IL; married Stephen Roxburgh (a editor and publisher); children: Anna, David. *Education:* Hampshire College, degree; studied bookbinding with Arno Werner.

Addresses

Home—PA.

Career

Writer. Bookbinder in partnership with Nancy Southworth, 1975-84; former editor for Heinemann (educational publisher). Writing instructor at Harvard Extension and Harvard Summer School, Cambridge, MA; Vermont College M.F.A. Writing for Children Program, 1998—; Hamline College M.F.A. in Writing for Children and Young Adults; and Whole Novel Workshops.

Awards, Honors

Newbery Honor Award, and National Book Award finalist, both 1996, Dorothy Canfield Fisher Children's Book Award nominee, 1997, and Iowa Teen Award nominee, 1999, all for *What Jamie Saw;* National Book Award finalist, *School Library Journal* Best Books of the Year citation, *Book Links* Lasting Connections citation, and *Booklist* Top of the List citation, all 2000, and Michael L. Printz Honor Book designation, and Best Book for Young Adults selection, ALA Young Adult Library Services Association, both 2001, all for *Many Stones.*

Writings

(With Judy Dater) *Body and Soul: Ten American Women,* photographs by Judy Dater, Hill & Co. (Boston, MA), 1988.
Losing Things at Mr. Mudd's, illustrated by Lance Hidy, Farrar, Straus (New York, NY), 1992.
Tell Me Everything, Farrar, Straus (New York, NY), 1993.
What Jamie Saw, Front Street (Asheville, NC), 1995.
Bee and Jacky, Front Street (Asheville, NC), 1998.
Many Stones, Front Street (Asheville, NC), 2000.
The Big House, illustrated by Rob Shepperson, Front Street (Asheville, NC), 2004.

Sneaking Suspicions (sequel to *The Big House*), illustrated by Rob Shepperson, Front Street (Asheville, NC), 2007.

Sidelights

The author of young-adult novels that include *What Jamie Saw* and *Bee and Jacky,* as well as of middle-grade fiction, Carolyn Coman is known for her distinctive voice and resilient protagonists. Honored with a National Book Award nomination and Newbery Honor Book designation, among other honors, she explores the darker side of growing up: dealing with a parent's abandonment through death in *Tell Me Everything,* abuse by a stepparent in *What Jamie Saw,* sibling incest in *Bee and Jacky,* and a political-inspired tragedy in *Many Stones.* Coman's characters are sometimes damaged; some have been the victims of abuse or neglect, while others, driven by their inner demons, inflict abuse on those they love. "As with the people in my life," Coman explained on the Front Street Books Web site, "some characters are easier to know and love than others. It's necessary for me to love them because as a writer I am often called upon to look at and say hard things. And the only way to do that without being cruel or disdainful is to have an understanding of and compassion for the wide range of what it means to be a human being."

Cover of Carolyn Coman's young-adult novel Bee and Jacky, *featuring artwork by Robert Day.* (Front Street, an imprint of Boyds Mills Press, 1998. Reproduced by permission of Boyds Mills Press, Inc.)

Coman was born in Evanston, Illinois, and attended Douglass College of Rutgers University before transferring to Hampshire College in Amherst, Massachusetts, where she majored in writing. After college, she apprenticed with master bookbinder Arno Werner and worked as a bookbinder for almost a decade, eventually supplementing this with a job as an editor at an educational publishing house. As Coman admitted to *Teenreads.com* contributor Tammy Currier, "I chose bookbinding because it kept me close to books and gave me a way of earning my living on more or less my own terms. I tried to believe that making books would somehow satisfy my desire to write them, but of course it didn't. Eventually I had to face up to the fact that nothing would do but writing."

Like many writers for younger readers, Coman did not set out to write juvenile or young-adult literature. She had written several stories and a novel before she realized that she was writing about children and often from the point of view of a child. Her first book, *Body and Soul: Ten American Women,* is cowritten with photographer Judy Dater and examines the diverse lives of ten American women. The subjects range from a Utah homemaker whose husband was killed in a battle with police because of his refusal to send his children to a public school, to a poverty-stricken Massachusetts woman who has worked to overcome a history of sexual abuse. "Although their personal circumstances differ," explained a *Publishers Weekly* contributor in a review of *Body and Soul,* "these individuals all demonstrate notable integrity."

Coman's second work was the picture book *Losing Things at Mr. Mudd's,* and it marked her first work for children. Intended for children under the age of ten, the book finds six-year-old Lucy meeting with continual frustration while visiting the museum-like home of her relative Mr. Mudd. She cannot even sit in the antique chairs in Mr. Mudd's house for fear of damaging them. As a *Publishers Weekly* critic explained, "a ruby ring and a 'lost' tooth prove the catalysts for a confrontation between the girl and her host . . . that brings greater tolerance and understanding to both participants."

With *Tell Me Everything* Coman begins exploring the problems and potentials of teenaged life. The novel's protagonist, twelve-year-old Roz Jacoby, has had a difficult life. Recently orphaned, she is a child of rape who never knew her father, and she has grown up socially isolated due to her mom's unorthodox religious beliefs. Roz's mom was killed in an accident while trying to rescue a boy who had lost his way, and now Roz lives with her Vietnam-veteran uncle, a man suffering from post-traumatic stress disorder. Hoping to come to terms with her loss and create a normal life, Roz begins to obsess about the boy her mother died trying to save. In *Tell Me Everything* "Coman's narrative skills are made bold by the unimpeachable truths of grief," declared a *Publishers Weekly* reviewer, "and she distills the process of accepting death into an act of discovery."

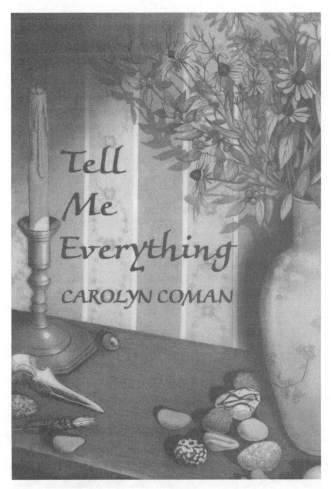

Cover of Coman's young-adult novel Tell Me Everything, *featuring artwork by Mary Teichman.* (Jacket design copyright © 1993 by Mary Teichman. Reproduced by permission of Farrar, Straus & Giroux, LLC.)

Coman's Newbery Honor Book, *What Jamie Saw,* also focuses on the issue of character, both in its development and in its realization. The novel begins with a direct, vivid image of child abuse. Nine-year-old Jamie watches as his stepfather, Van, picks up his baby sister Nin, and throws her across the room. Fortunately, Nin is rescued by her mother Patty, and soon Jamie, Patty, and Nin are fleeing into the night, ultimately finding refuge in New Hampshire with Patty's friend Earl. Now Jamie stops attending third grade and Patty gives up her job as a grocery bagger. The two of them only begin to turn their lives around through the intervention of Jamie's teacher, Mrs. Desrochers. The author "depicts with visceral clarity the reactions of both Jamie and his mother," Susan Dove Lempke observed in a *Booklist* assessment, "capturing their jitteriness and the love that carries them through the moments when they take their fear out on each other." According to a *Publishers Weekly* critic, Coman "so deftly slips into the skin of her main character that [Jamie] . . . seems almost to be dictating to her." "I don't create characters so much as I make room inside my mind and heart for them to come and get me . . . ," the novelist explained in her Front Street Books essay. "When they are finally willing to speak to me, I listen carefully to the sounds of their voices, and to what they are trying to say."

Coman tackles a provocative subject in **What Jamie Saw,** *featuring artwork by Brock Cole.* (Front Street, an imprint of Boyds Mills Press, 1995. Reprinted with the permission of Boyds Mills Press, Inc.)

In *Bee and Jacky* Coman tackles another difficult subject: serial sexual abuse between brother and sister. When thirteen-year-old Bee and seventeen-year-old-Jacky are left alone at home on Memorial Day weekend, they take the opportunity to reenact a game they began playing years before. The original game was distilled from their father's wartime service in Vietnam and their mother's inability to deal with her husband's mental and physical scars; it began with Jacky's "search-and-rescue" of Bee and ended with him attacking and raping his sister. The reenactment of the game now awakens Bee's suppressed memories, causing her to lose control of herself: she hallucinates, propositions her older brother, and removes her clothes before she goes outside.

As they had with *What Jamie Saw,* critics commented on Coman's capacity to create and maintain understanding for all her characters, perpetrators as well as victims, in *Bee and Jacky* According to a *Kirkus Reviews* writer, "Bee sees, and makes readers see too, that Jacky is no monster, just a soul tortured by fear," while *Booklist* contributor Stephanie Zvirin celebrated the author's "remarkable ability to elicit sympathy for all the characters—even Jacky, vicious and angry on the one

hand, yet clearly horrified at what he's done to his vulnerable sister." A *Publishers Weekly* critic called *Bee and Jacky* "the literary equivalent of a Diane Arbus photograph: it presents a sharp, shocking picture of pathology, but leaves it to the audience to imagine the world beyond the frame."

Many Stones was inspired by the murder of Amy Biehl, a Fulbright scholarship recipient working in South Africa. Here Coman confronts an overtly political issue—the killing of an American girl working in racially segregated South Africa—in the context of a damaged family relationship. Laura Morgan was working as a volunteer at a school near Cape Town when she was murdered in an apparently senseless act of violence. A year later, Laura's younger sister Berry and Berry's estranged father come to South Africa to view the unveiling of a monument constructed in Laura's honor. Berry has resented her father ever since he divorced her mother years before and began associating with a series of other women. In order to make sense of Laura's death and finally connect with her dad, Berry must come to understand both the dark and bloody history of apartheid in South Africa and the family dynamics that have brought her to her present state of mind. In *Many Stones* "Coman makes no slick parallels between the political reconciliation and Berry's personal struggle with her fa-

Cover of Coman's elementary-grade chapter book Sneaking Suspicions, *featuring artwork by Rob Shepperson.* (Illustration copyright © 2007 by Rob Shepperson. Reproduced by permission of Boyds Mills Press, Inc.)

ther," stated Hazel Rochman in *Booklist,* "except, perhaps, to show that both are difficult, incomplete." "Part coming-of-age, part tragedy, this realistic novel is not a light read," concluded *School Library Journal* critic Angela J. Reynolds, the reviewer going on to call *Many Stones* "a solid and powerful exploration into the mind of a grieving teen." "In the simplest words, as hard as stones," commented Rochman in her *New York Times Book Review* appraisal of the novel, "Coman connects a white American family's anguish with a nation's struggle to come to terms with its savage past."

With the middle-grade novels *The Big House* and *Sneaking Suspicions,* Coman turns from the darker themes that populate her work for teens. Inspired by childhood memories of her late brother, and the games they shared as children, these stories mix humor with a nostalgia-tinged text. "A lot of the dialogue came from my father's voice in my head," Coman explained to *Teaching PreK-8* online interviewer Jessica Rae Patton. "He was someone who used a lot of old-fashioned expressions he loved." In *The Big House* readers meet Ivy and Ray, siblings who are being trained in their parents' grifter lifestyle. When Mom and Dad are jailed and charged with embezzling funds from a children's charity, the children are sent to live with Marietta and Lionel Noland, the couple responsible for the arrest of Ivy and Ray's parents. Determined to clear their parents of the crime, the siblings begin snooping around the Noland's lavish mansion home and in the process discover a series of bizarre and sometimes startling clues. Ivy and Ray return in *Sneaking Suspicions,* as they join their now-released parents on a trip to the Florida Everglades to seek out a distant cousin who may have a valuable family relic. Reviewing *The Big House,* which features artwork by Rob Shepperson, *Horn Book* reviewer Christine M. Hepperman dubbed Coman's setting "comically gloomy" and recommended the novel to fans of Lemony Snicket. In *Publishers Weekly,* a reviewer wrote that "Coman . . . displays her versatility, with this sly comedy," and *School Library Journal* critic B. Allison Gray dubbed *The Big House* "an enjoyable romp of a mystery." In the "pleasantly rambling" *Sneaking Suspicions,* the siblings' further adventures are enlivened by "Ivy's constant attempts to decipher the world," according to a *Kirkus Reviews* writer. In *Booklist* Rochman maintained that Shepperson's pen-and-ink drawings "feed the slapstick" of Coman's tale.

"I'm happy to be writing books that are considered young adult," Coman explained in an interview posted on the Penguin Putnam Web site. "I've written enough now to know that I come back over and over to childhood and adolescent issues. It's something that really interests and concerns me, so when I get an idea for a story, I just go with it. I couldn't have been more graciously and more warmly received, and if all my books end up being in that genre, wonderful."

Cover of Coman's adventure-filled **The Big House,** *featuring artwork by Brandon Dorman.* (Cover illustration copyright © 2006 Brandon Dorman. Reproduced by permission of Puffin Books, a division of Penguin Putnam Books for Young Readers.)

Biographical and Critical Sources

PERIODICALS

Booklist, September 15, 1993, Jeanne Triner, review of *Tell Me Everything,* p. 150; December 15, 1995, Susan Dove Lempke, review of *What Jamie Saw,* p. 703; October 1, 1998, Stephanie Zvirin, review of *Bee and Jacky,* p. 324; April 1, 1999, p. 1383; December 1, 2000, Stephanie Zvirin, review of *Many Stones,* p. 692; January 1, 2001, Hazel Rochman, interview with Coman, pp. 938-939; September 15, 2004, Ilene Cooper, review of *The Big House,* p. 242; September 15, 2007, Hazel Rochman, review of *Sneaking Suspicions,* p. 66.

Book Report, May-June, 1994, Margaret Zinz Jantzen, review of *Tell Me Everything,* pp. 42-43.

English Journal, September, 1994, Lois Stover, review of *Tell Me Everything,* p. 87.

Horn Book, January-February, 1994, Nancy Vasilakis, review of *Tell Me Everything,* p. 72; March-April, 1996, Nancy Vasilakis, review of *What Jamie Saw,* p. 194; November, 1998, Susan P. Bloom, review of *Bee and*

Jacky, p. 726; January, 2001, review of *Many Stones,* p. 89; January-February, 2005, Christine M. Heppermann, review of *The Big House,* p. 91.

Kirkus Reviews, September 15, 1998, review of *Bee and Jacky,* pp. 1381-1382; September 1, 2004, review of *The Big House,* p. 862; September 1, 2007, review of *Sneaking Suspicions.*

New York Times Book Review, January 16, 1994, Erin Kelly, review of *Tell Me Everything;* February 11, 1996, Janet Bode, review of *What Jamie Saw,* p. 25; November 19, 2000, Hazel Rochman, "Truth and Reconciliation."

Publishers Weekly, March 11, 1988, review of *Body and Soul: Ten American Women,* pp. 92-93; June 15, 1992, review of *Losing Things at Mr. Mudd's,* p. 101; September 20, 1993, review of *Tell Me Everything,* p. 73; August 28, 1995, review of *What Jamie Saw,* p. 114; August 31, 1998, review of *Bee and Jacky,* p. 77; October 30, 2000, review of *Many Stones,* p. 76; September 6, 2004, review of *The Big House,* p. 63.

Riverbank Review, spring, 2001, Jenny Sawyer, review of *Many Stones,* p. 44.

School Library Journal, September, 1988, Dorcas Hand, review of *Body and Soul,* p. 212; November, 1998, Miriam Lang Budin, review of *Bee and Jacky,* p. 119; November, 2000, Angela J. Reynolds, review of *Many Stones,* p. 150; October, 2003, Jennifer Ralston, review of *What Jamie Saw,* p. 98; November, 2004, B. Allison Gray, review of *The Big House,* p. 138.

Times Educational Supplement, December 6, 1996, Geraldine Brennan, "Tulip the Battered Flower," p. 17.

Voice of Youth Advocates, December, 1998, Cynthia L. Blinn, review of *Bee and Jacky,* p. 353.

ONLINE

Front Street Books Web site, http://www.frontstreetbooks. com/ (December 1, 2000), "Carolyn Coman on Character."

Penguin Putnam Web site, http://www.penguinputnam. com/ (December 1, 2000), interview with Coman.

Teaching PreK-8 Online, http://www.teachingk-8.com/ (January 23, 2009), Jessica Rae Patton, 2005 interview with Coman.

Teenreads.com, http://www.teenreads.com/ (October 19, 2001), Tammy Currier, interview with Coman.

*   *   *

COVERT, Ralph 1968-

Personal

Born May 25, 1968, in SD; son of Richard (a genealogist and college professor) and Jean (a ceramist) Covert; married (divorced); married; second wife's name Rebecca; children: (first marriage) Fiona Grey Schenkelberg. *Education:* University of Iowa, degree, 1984.

Addresses

Home and office—329 W. 18th St., Apt. 313, Chicago, IL 60616. *Agent*—Leora Rosenberg, William Morris

Ralph Covert (Photo copyright © by Peter Thompson.)

Agency, 1325 Avenue of the Americas, New York, NY 10019. *E-mail*—waterdog@waterdogmusic.com.

Career

Musician, entertainer, and writer. Solo performer in Chicago, IL, 1984-87; formed pop/rock band the Bad Examples, 1987; founder (with Jay Whitehouse), Waterdog Records, 1991; *Bad Is Beautiful,* 1991; Recordings include *Meat: The Bad Examples,* 1987; *Cheap Beer Night,* 1992; *Eat at Godot's,* 1993; and *Ralph's World,* 2001. Producer of "5,000 Days" concert, Chicago, 2000. National Academy of Recording Arts and Sciences, regional governor and former member of national education and grants committees.

Awards, Honors

(With the Bad Examples) Band of the Year designation, WXRT Radio, 1989; (with the Bad Examples) Columbia College Brightest Stars on Chicago Club Scene citation, 1989; (with G. Riley Mills) Joseph Jefferson Award for Best New Work, 1988, for play *Sawdust and Spangles;* (with Rik Vrijman) De Grote prijs for best lyrics (Netherlands), 1997; *Billboard* and *Parents* magazines, Best Children's Album of 2001 designation, for *Ralph's World;* (with Mills) Joseph Jefferson Award for

Best New Work, 2001, for *Streeterville*; *Parenting* magazine Video of the Year designation, 2003, for "Say Hello!" (*Ralph's World* video).

Writings

(With G. Riley Mills) *Sawdust and Spangles* (play; also see below), produced 1997.

Ralph's World: Say Hello! (video recording), Mini Fresh, 2003.

(With G. Riley Mills) *Sawdust and Spangles: The Amazing Life of W.C. Coup,* illustrated by Giselle Potter, Harry Abrams (New York, NY), 2007.

Ralph's World Rocks!, illustrated by Charise Mericle Harper, Henry Holt (New York, NY), 2008.

(With G. Riley Mills) *A Very Nutty Nutcracker Christmas,* illustrated by Wilson Swain, Chronicle (San Francisco, CA), 2009.

LYRICIST; SOUND RECORDINGS

Ralph's World, Mini Fresh, 2001.

Ralph's World: Happy Lemons, Mini Fresh, 2002.

Ralph's World: At the Bottom of the Sea, Mini Fresh, 2002.

Ralph's World: Peggy's Pie Parlor, Mini Fresh, 2003.

Ralph's World: The Amazing Adventures of Kid Astro, Walt Disney Records, 2004.

Ralph's World: Green Gorilla Monster and Me, Walt Disney Records, 2005.

Welcome to Ralph's World, Walt Disney Records, 2006.

Ralph's World: Rhyming Circus, Walt Disney Records, 2008.

Sidelights

Part of a Chicago-area pop band called the Bad Examples during the 1980s and 1990s, singer and songwriter Ralph Covert began performing for children with his new band, Ralph's World, in 2001. As a children's entertainer, Covert has produced CDs and video recordings of his performances, as well as picture books for young audiences.

The multi-talented and very busy Covert has also composed music for the Shedd Aquarium, the Hedwig Dances dance troupe, and created the score of a film titled *The Reunion.* He has acted professionally both on stage in Chicago in shows such as *The Interview* and in industrial commercials. Part of the team that created the "Box of Fun" music video for Rice Krispies, Covert also served as an advisor for Kellogg's Operation Spark parenting group. He also has served as regional governor for the National Academy of Recording Arts and Sciences, the organization that sponsors the Grammy awards, and has served on their national education and grants committees.

Born in South Dakota, Covert began writing stories, poetry, and plays at a young age. He learned to play guitar in high school, and during college he wrote the score for an independent film. After graduating, Covert moved to Chicago, where he performed both as a solo artist and with the Bad Examples. It was not until he became a father that Covert became involved performing for children. While teaching "Wiggleworms," a music class for children, he performed traditional children's songs such as "Itsy Bitsy Spider" and "Old MacDonald," the last in which he added a verse about spiders. As Covert later recalled in *Billboard,* he then launched into "Ziggy Stardust," a tune by David Bowie. The next day, his boss approached him and commented on Covert's unusual performance. When he acknowledged that he had included rock music in the program, she told him: "Excellent—that's why I hired you. Keep it up." Covert soon began writing original material for the class, and in 2001, he recorded his first children's album, *Ralph's World.* "It's the rare musician who can both write and perform for adults and children, but Ralph Covert has done just that," wrote Kirsten Martindale in a *School Library Journal* review of the recording. In *Billboard,* Moira McCormick called *Ralph's World* "one of the finest kids' audio releases of this or any year."

In the years since, Covert has produced several more albums, as well as a video for young listeners. In *School Library Journal,* Beverly Bixler wrote of *Ralph's World: At the Bottom of the Sea* that "kids will get a kick out of listening to and singing along." In her review of Covert's video recording *Ralph's World: Say Hello!, School Library Journal* critic Kirsten Martindale wrote that, "lively and silly," the work "will provide hours of fun." Reviewing *Green Gorilla Monster and Me,* also for *School Library Journal,* Martindale predicted that "Covert will have listeners dancing and singing along."

Along with his musical works, Covert collaborated with G. Riley Mills on the play *Sawdust and Spangles,* a work the two have also adapted as the picture book *Sawdust and Spangles: The Amazing Life of W.C. Coup.* The book describes the life of a legendary circus leader who was once a partner of P.T. Barnum. While calling the biographical aspects of the title "sketchy," a *Kirkus Reviews* critic concluded that *Sawdust and Spangles* "captures the fascination with spectacle that drove" Coup throughout his life.

Another book by Covert, *Ralph's World Rocks!,* is a picture book based on the lyrics of his children's songs. While writing that some of the music is better heard that read from a page, a *Kirkus Reviews* contributor concluded of *Ralph's World Rocks!* that Covert's "clever wordplay is endearing."

Biographical and Critical Sources

PERIODICALS

Billboard, July 5, 1997, Craig Rosen, "'Birthday' May Boost Covert," p. 6; July 29, 2000, Moira McCor-

mick, "Covert Is Good Example on Mini Fresh," p. 55; February 10, 2001, Moira McCormick, "Minty Fresh Promoting *Ralph's World* with Borders Concerts," p. 65.

Kirkus Reviews, August 1, 2007, review of *Sawdust and Spangles: The Amazing Life of W.C. Coup*; July 15, 2008, review of *Ralph's World Rocks!*

Publishers Weekly, October 21, 2002, review of *Happy Lemons,* p. 32.

School Library Journal, September, 2002, Beverly Bixler, review of *Ralph's World: At the Bottom of the Sea,* p. 80, Kirsten Martindale, review of *Ralph's World,* p. 82; January, 2003, Kirsten Martindale, review of *Ralph's World: Happy Lemons,* p. 79; January, 2004, Kirsten Martindale, review of *Ralph's World: Say Hello!,* p. 59; January, 2006, Kirsten Martindale, review of *Ralph's World: Green Gorilla Monster and Me,* p. 84.

ONLINE

Ralph Covert Home Page, http://www.ralphcovert.com (September 13, 2009).

D

DARLING, Sandra Louise Woodward
See DAY, Alexandra

*   *   *

DAY, Alexandra 1941-
(Sandra Louise Woodward Darling)

Personal
Born September 7, 1941, in Cincinnati, OH; daughter of Charles Lawson (an artist) and Esther Grace (a homemaker) Woodward; married Harold Darling (a cinema/ bookstore owner and publisher), 1967; children: Sacheverell Austen, Rabindranath Tagore, Lafcadio Hearn, Christina Rossetti. *Education:* Swarthmore College, B.A., 1963; trained as an artist at Art Students' League (New York, NY), 1963-64. *Religion:* Episcopalian. *Hobbies and other interests:* Fashion design and dressmaking.

Addresses
Office—Blue Lantern Studio, 4649 Sunnyside Ave. N., Seattle, WA 98103-6900. *E-mail*—aday@gooddogcarl. com.

Career
Fine artist, writer, illustrator, and book publisher. Freelance artist, 1965—; Green Tiger Press, San Diego, CA, founder and owner with husband, Harold Darling, and note cards and stationery designer, 1969-86; children's author and illustrator, 1983—; Blue Lantern Studio, San Diego, CA (after 1993 Seattle, WA), owner with H. Darling, 1986—, Laughing Elephant Publishing (gift-book and paper goods manufacturer), Seattle, cofounder, 1992—, creator of Darling & Co. imprint, 1999, reacquisition of Green Tiger Press from Simon & Schuster, 2004—. Young Men's Hebrew Association, New York, NY, former crafts teacher. *Exhibitions:* Work exhibited at Every Picture Tells a Story, Los Angeles,

Alexandra Day (Courtesy of Sandra Darling.)

CA; Art of Illustration, Seattle, WA; Frye Art Museum, Seattle; Mazza Museum, OH; and Society of Illustrators, New York, NY.

Awards, Honors
Special mention, Children's Jury, Bologna Book Fair, and Children's Choice Award, International Reading Association/Children's Book Council, 1984, both for *The Teddy Bears' Picnic;* Parents' Choice Award for Illustration, 1984, for *The Blue Faience Hippopotamus.*

Writings

SELF-ILLUSTRATED; "CARL" SERIES

Good Dog, Carl, Green Tiger Press (San Diego, CA), 1985.

Carl Goes Shopping (also see below), Farrar, Straus (New York, NY), 1989.

Carl's Christmas, Farrar, Straus (New York, NY), 1990.

Carl's Afternoon in the Park (also see below), Farrar, Straus (New York, NY), 1991.

Carl's Masquerade (also see below), Farrar, Straus (New York, NY), 1992.

Carl Goes to Daycare (also see below), Farrar, Straus (New York, NY), 1993.

Carl Makes a Scrapbook, Farrar, Straus (New York, NY), 1994.

Carl Pops Up, includes illustrations by Vicki Teague Cooper, Simon & Schuster (New York, NY), 1994.

Carl's Birthday (also see below), Farrar, Straus (New York, NY), 1995.

Carl's Baby Journal, Farrar, Straus (New York, NY), 1996.

Follow Carl! (also see below), Farrar, Straus (New York, NY), 1998.

Carl's Sleepy Afternoon, Farrar, Straus (New York, NY), 2005.

You're a Good Dog, Carl (includes *Carl Goes Shopping, Carl's Afternoon in the Park, Carl's Masquerade, Carl Goes to Daycare, Carl's Birthday,* and *Follow Carl!*), Square Fish (New York, NY), 2007.

Carl Goes on Vacation, Farrar, Straus (New York, NY), 2008.

The "Carl" books have been translated into Spanish, Japanese, and French.

SELF-ILLUSTRATED

Frank and Ernest, Scholastic (New York, NY), 1988.

Paddy's Pay-Day, Viking (New York, NY), 1989.

Frank and Ernest Play Ball, Scholastic (New York, NY), 1990.

River Parade, Viking (New York, NY), 1990.

Frank and Ernest on the Road, Scholastic (New York, NY), 1994.

A Bouquet, Blue Lantern Studio (San Diego, CA), 1996.

(With Cooper Edens) *The Christmas We Moved to the Barn,* HarperCollins (New York, NY), 1997.

Boswell Wide Awake, Farrar, Straus (New York, NY), 1999.

(With Cooper Edens) *Darby, the Special Order Pup,* Penguin Putnam (New York, NY), 2000.

(With Cooper Edens) *Special Deliveries,* HarperCollins Children's Books (New York, NY), 2001.

Puppy Trouble (pop-up book), Farrar, Straus (New York, NY), 2002.

The Flight of a Dove, Farrar, Straus (New York, NY), 2004.

Not Forgotten: A Consolation for the Loss of an Animal Friend, Laughing Elephant (Seattle, WA), 2004.

Also author and illustrator of *My Puppy's Record Book,* Farrar, Straus (New York, NY).

ILLUSTRATOR

Jimmy Kennedy, *The Teddy Bears' Picnic* (book and record set), Green Tiger Press (San Diego, CA), 1983.

Joan Marshall Grant, *The Blue Faience Hippopotamus,* Green Tiger Press (San Diego, CA), 1984.

Cooper Edens, *Children of Wonder,* Volume 1: *Helping the Sun,* Volume 2: *Helping the Animals,* Volume 3: *Helping the Flowers & Trees,* Volume 4: *Helping the Night,* Green Tiger Press (San Diego, CA), 1987.

Ned Washington, *When You Wish upon a Star,* Green Tiger Press (San Diego, CA), 1987.

Abigail Darling, *Teddy Bears' Picnic Cookbook,* Puffin Books (New York, NY), 1993.

Christina Darling, *Mirror,* Farrar, Straus (New York, NY), 1997.

OTHER

(Editor with Cooper Edens and Welleran Poltarnees) *Children from the Golden Age, 1880-1930,* Green Tiger Press (San Diego, CA), 1987.

(Editor with Welleran Poltarnees) *A.B.C. of Fashionable Animals,* Green Tiger Press (San Diego, CA), 1989.

Adaptations

The "Carl" characters have been adapted for several books, including *My Puppy's Record Book,* Farrar, Straus, 1994; and *Carl's Baby Book,* Farrar, Straus, 1996.

Sidelights

Best known for introducing readers to a lovable rottweiler named Carl, author and artist Alexandra Day is the pen name of Sandra Darling. As Day, she is the creator of the picture-book classic *Good Dog, Carl* and its many sequels, as well as the author and/or illustrator of several other books. As Darling, she had become well-known in publishing circles as the cofounder, with husband Harold Darling, of the historic Green Tiger Press in 1969, as well as of the more-recently established Laughing Elephant Publishing and Blue Lantern Studio, both located in Seattle, Washington.

As the granddaughter of an architect and the daughter of a painter, Day grew up in a family where art was viewed as important. After attending Swarthmore College, where she majored in English literature, she moved to New York City and worked at the Young Men's Hebrew Association as a crafts teacher. She also took classes in figure drawing and painting at the Art Students' League and from Will Barnet. On a trip to California, she met Harold Darling, who owned a cinema and book store (housed in the same building), and they were married in 1967. Harold had three children from a

previous marriage, and during the next seven years the couple had four more children, each named after lesser-known authors the bookish couple admired.

Drawing on the vast collection of antique children's books Day and Darling collected, in 1969, the couple founded Green Tiger Press. The business, located in San Diego, California, originally published postcards, notecards and bookmarks featuring artwork from such talents as Arthur Rackham, L. Frank Baum, and others. Three years later they published their first book, *All Mirrors Are Magic Mirrors,* written by Harold Darling, and sold 50,000 copies by mail order. As Day recalled, the company grew, hired staff, and expanded its publications; then, after a dozen years a quandary pushed her into a new phase of her career. Needing an illustration for an old song, "The Teddy Bears' Picnic," and not having an appropriate image, she decided to create the art herself. The book was a success, and Day soon found herself illustrating other books published by Green Tiger Press.

On a trip in Zurich, Switzerland, the Darlings discovered an antique German broadsheet titled "Der brave Karo," about a poodle and a baby who played together while the baby should have been napping. Charmed by the story, the Darlings decided to create a similar work, casting the family rottweiler Toby in the poodle's role and Day's granddaughter Madeleine as the baby. *Good Dog, Carl,* published in 1985, became phenomenally popular among young readers. Since 1989, when the loveable Carl made his second picture-book appearance in *Carl Goes Shopping,* Day has produced several more "Carl" books, each characterized by a brief text and her engaging illustrations.

In *Good Dog, Carl,* a child's mother tells the family dog to watch the baby while she leaves the room; her words of praise upon her return are "Good dog, Carl!" Because the text is so brief, Day's illustrations, tell the story; rendered in what a *People* contributor described as "lustrous oils," Day's art is "a handsome counterpoint to the whimsy of the narrative." One of the last books to be published by Green Tiger Press prior to its sale to Simon & Schuster, the book sold over a half-million copies during its first five years. In addition to sparking a publishing phenomenon due to its small-press origins, the book also had another surprising effect. As Kelli Pryor explained in *Entertainment Weekly* as the "Carl" series took shape: "The warmth Day put into her realistically rendered oil paintings has earned the books so much adoration that it's not farfetched to speculate that Carl is partly responsible for boosting rottweilers . . . into the top five of the American Kennel Club's most-popular breeds list." While, over time, the models for Carl have changed as the Darlings' beloved family dogs have successively passed on, the personality of the original Toby shines through in each of the "Carl" books.

In *Carl Goes Shopping* Carl watches over a toddler and carries her into various departments in the store. Call-

ing the book a "thoroughly enjoyable adventure," a reviewer in *Horn Book* suggested that Day offers "the most pinchable baby and pettable dog of the season." After wreaking havoc everywhere they go, toddler and pup return before Mother does. The third book in the series, *Carl's Christmas,* in the words of a *Publishers Weekly* critic, is "imbued with enough 'good will towards man' to warm a whole town." Carl takes care of a puppy and a baby in *Carl's Afternoon in the Park,* published in 1991. In this book "the dogs are as charmingly true to life as ever," according to a *Kirkus Reviews* critic.

Carl and his toddler charge continue to charm young readers in *Carl's Masquerade, Carl Goes to Daycare, Carl's Sleepy Afternoon,* and *Carl Goes on Vacation,* among others. When toddler Madeleine follows her parents to a costume party, the loyal rottweiler comes to her rescue in *Carl's Masquerade.* According to Roger Sutton, writing in the *Bulletin of the Center for Children's Books,* the picture book's setting "allows Day free rein for her deliberately *outré,* painterly style and whimsical turn of imagination." In *Carl Goes to Daycare* the resourceful pup takes charge of Madeleine's preschool class when the teacher is accidentally locked outside. Ellen Mandel asserted in *Booklist* that this book "is sure to be a favorite in a deservedly popular series."

A *Publishers Weekly* critic wrote that "everyone's favorite rottweiler is back in top form" in *Carl's Birthday,* in which Carl and Madeleine secretly aid Mother's party preparations, while in *Follow Carl!* Carl leads the neighborhood children in a game of Follow the Leader. As a reviewer in *Publishers Weekly* noted, "the combination of grassy settings, friendly village shops and, of course, tender companionship" in *Follow Carl!* "adds up to an excursion virtually any reader would enjoy."

In *Carl's Sleepy Afternoon* the pup decides that an afternoon on his own would be better spent out and about than sleeping at home in the sun. When Madeleine and Mother go to town on errands, Carl is not far behind, catching a ride on a passing van. Spotting Madeleine in a bakery, the pup sneaks in and is given a cookie; helpful visits to a nearby druggist and a burning garage where he rescues a litter of stranded puppies round out Carl's day, and the two unsuspecting shoppers find him sleeping in the sun upon their return home. Noting that *Carl's Sleepy Afternoon* marks more than two decades of "Carl" books, a *Publishers Weekly* writer added that the rottweiler "has lost none of his appeal—or his spunk." "Day's stunningly realistic, brightly hued illustrations are as timeless and endearing as the plot," the critic added. Finding *Carl's Summer Vacation* a "charming addition to a whimsical series," Lisa Gangemi Kropp concluded in *School Library Journal* that Day's simple story about Carl and Madeleine's outdoor adventures near the family's summer cabin features Day's "richly detailed and beautifully hued illustrations."

In addition to the "Carl" books, Day has also written and illustrated a number of other highly praised chil-

dren's books, including a short series featuring a bear named Frank and an elephant named Ernest. In the first book, *Frank and Ernest,* the watercolor-illustrated pair runs a '50s-style diner, their story told in amusing diner dialogue explained in a glossary. Trev Jones, writing in *School Library Journal,* concluded that the book is "bound to become standard fare for story hour specials." *Frank and Ernest Play Ball* finds the pair managing a baseball team and using a dictionary to understand their job, while *Frank and Ernest on the Road* follows the duo as they find work as truckers, mastering Citizen's Band (CB) radio jargon along with readers. "Fans of the dynamic duo's previous adventures will appreciate this exploration of a new linguistic frontier," wrote Zena Sutherland in the *Bulletin of the Center for Children's Books,* referencing Day's inclusion of a glossary of CB terms.

In the picture book *Boswell Wide Awake* Day tells the story of a little bear who gets up in the middle of the night and does work around the house that was left undone at bedtime. "Day turns the plot into something of a tour de force," noted a reviewer in *Publishers Weekly,* "bringing to her visual storytelling the same extraordinary tenderness and seamless blend of fantasy and realism that characterize her Carl books." Other picture books by Day include *Puppy Trouble,* a pop-up book in which a young, rambunctious pup gets into a series of small, harmless scrapes with trouble, and *The Flight of a Dove.* In the latter book, based on a true story, Day focuses on a preschooler named Betsy who has autism and lives in a very lonely world due to her condition. Betsy's first experience at a new school is a frightening one, until an interaction with the class dog, and her experience watching a beautiful dove flutter around the room makes Betsy feel more comfortable with her surroundings and results in her first spoken word. While noting the story's somber theme, *School Library Journal* contributor Linda Beck praised Day's illustrations, writing that "the beautiful artwork effectively highlights [Betsy's] . . . sense of isolation and [ultimate] happiness," while in *Booklist* Linda Perkins explained that "the lush watercolor art . . . brings the story to life" and "demonstrates the miraculous therapeutic power of animals."

Day has also worked with fellow illustration aficionado and artist Cooper Edens on several picture books, among them *The Christmas We Moved the Barn, Darby, the Special Order Pup,* and *Special Deliveries.* Of *Darby, the Special-Order Pup,* Lucinda Snyder Whitehurst in the *School Library Journal* wrote that Day has "created another canine that children will love" as much as they have her famous Carl the rottweiler. Peter F. Neumeyer, in a review for the *Boston Sunday Globe,* called *Darby, the Special-Order Pup* "that rare, sophisticated specimen—a picture storybook in which the illustrations tell their own story and play off their own jokes in counterpoint to the written text." *Special Deliveries* was called an "imaginative, funny book" that "is alive with great pictures" by reviewer Ellen Mandel in *Booklist.*

A family business, Blue Lantern Studio publishes gift books and other paper products under the Green Tiger Press and Darling & Company imprints. While Day and her husband continue to oversee the company's direction, their children serve in design, production, and business capacities. Several book projects have resulted from this creative collaboration: Day has illustrated the *Teddy Bears' Picnic Cookbook,* a cookery book written by her stepdaughter, Abigail Darling, and *Mirror,* a fantasy storybook written by her youngest daughter, Christina Darling. Discussing their publishing philosophy on the *Laughing Elephant Web site,* the Darlings explain: "All of our imprints reflect our belief that values and ideals are enduring, and that the insights of past times are still valuable."

Biographical and Critical Sources

BOOKS

Children's Literature Review, Volume 22, Gale (Detroit, MI), 1991.
Silvey, Anita, editor, *Children's Books and Their Creators,* Houghton Mifflin (Boston, MA), 1995.

PERIODICALS

Booklist, February 1, 1993, Ellen Mandel, review of *Carl's Masquerade,* p. 986; December 15, 1993, Hazel Rochman, review of *Frank and Ernest on the Road,* p. 750, and Ellen Mandel, review of *Carl Goes to Daycare,* p. 763; November 15, 1994, Ellen Mandel, review of *Carl Makes a Scrapbook,* p. 610; January 1, 1996, Ellen Mandel, review of *Carl's Birthday,* p. 843; March 1, 1997, Carolyn Phelan, review of *Mirror,* p. 1170; September 1, 1997, Shelley Townsend-Hudson, review of *The Christmas We Moved to the Barn,* p. 138; November 1, 2000, Ellen Mandel, review of *Darby, the Special-Order Pup,* p. 547; May 1, 2001, Ellen Mandel, review of *Special Deliveries,* p. 1688; May 1, 2001, Ellen Mandel, review of *Special Deliveries,* p. 1688; November 15, 2004, Linda Perkins, review of *The Flight of a Dove,* p. 580; September 1, 2005, John Peters, review of *Carl's Sleepy Afternoon,* p. 143.
Boston Sunday Globe, September 3, 2000, Peter F. Neumeyer, "Strong Animal Tales, from Then and Now," p. M3.
Bulletin of the Center for Children's Books, December, 1992, Roger Sutton, review of *Carl's Masquerade,* p. 109; March, 1994, Zena Sutherland, review of *Frank and Ernest on the Road,* p. 219; November, 1994, review of *Carl Makes a Scrapbook,* p. 85; July, 1997, review of *Mirror,* p. 391.
Horn Book, January-February, 1990, review of *Carl Goes Shopping,* p. 50.
Entertainment Weekly, September 27, 1991, Kelli Pryor, "Day's Dog."

Kirkus Reviews, September 15, 1991, review of *Carl's Afternoon in the Park,* p. 1230; October 15, 1994, review of *Carl Makes a Scrapbook,* p. 1406; May 15, 2008, review of *Carl's Summer Vacation.*

People, September 23, 1991, "Top Dog," p. 83.

Publishers Weekly, September 14, 1990, review of *Carl's Christmas,* p. 123; October 17, 1994, review of *Carl Makes a Scrapbook,* p. 83; October 23, 1995, review of *Carl's Birthday,* p. 67; January 13, 1997, review of *Mirror,* p. 75; June 29, 1998, review of *Follow Carl!,* p. 57; November 8, 1999, review of *Boswell Wide Awake,* p. 66; June 4, 2001, review of *Special Deliveries,* p. 79; October 28, 2002, review of *Puppy Trouble,* p. 74; September 13, 2004, review of *The Flight of a Dove,* p. 78; August 22, 2005, review of *Carl's Sleepy Afternoon,* p. 62.

School Library Journal, August, 1988, Trev Jones, review of *Frank and Ernest,* p. 80; October, 2000, Lucinda Snyder Whitehurst, review of *Darby, the Special-Order Pup,* p. 120; May, 2001, Holly Belli, review of *Special Deliveries,* p. 114; September, 2004, Linda Beck, review of *The Flight of a Dove,* p. 157; October, 2005, Lynn K. Vanca, review of *Carl's Sleepy Afternoon,* p. 110; May, 2008, Lisa Gangemi Kropp, review of *Carl's Summer Vacation,* p. 94.

ONLINE

Farrar, Straus & Giroux Kids Web site, http://www.fsgkidsbooks.com/ (December 1, 2005), "Alexandra Day."

Good Dog Carl Web site, http://www.gooddogcarl.com (April 12, 2006).

Laughing Elephant Web site, http://www.laughingelephant.com/ (December 3, 2005), "A Little History of the Laughing Elephant."

Autobiography Feature

Alexandra Day

Darling contributed the following autobiographical essay to *SATA* in 2008:

Alexandra Day is my pen name. My real name is Sandra Louise Woodward Darling. I was born in 1941. My father was Charles Lawson Woodward; my mother's maiden name was Esther Arabella Claflin. My father's family was descended in America from John and Priscilla Alden. His branch of the family had long been in Cincinnati, Ohio, where I was born and raised.

My father's family was large and close. I grew up surrounded by aunts, uncles, and cousins. This led to a sense of security, of knowing where one stood in the larger world. Many of these relative were inclined to the arts. Among my father's brothers and first cousins, one earned his living as a painter and illustrator, one taught art at Wayne University, one was a conductor and professor of music, and two were architects. Painting was a very popular family recreation, and almost every excursion included one or more easels and a variety of sketch pads, chalks, paints, and pencils. My grandfather was an architect who designed many public and private buildings in Cincinnati, including the high school that I attended.

My mother's mother named among her ancestors Hannah Dustin, the pioneer woman who, with her newborn babe and nurse, was carried off by Indians. She, the nurse, and a captive English boy fought their way to freedom, and a monument to her still stands in Haverhill, Massachusetts.

My mother's father was a printer, and it is from this Irish strand of the family that my pseudonymous last name, Day, derives. (The first name, Alexandra, was the name my grandmother thought I should have been named, rather than the shortened Sandra.) My mother was raised in Oak Park, Illinois, a suburb of Chicago. My mother and father met at the University of Wisconsin. They were married in 1932 and came to live in Cincinnati. I was the first of three daughters. My sister Patricia, four years younger than I am, is a watercolorist who regularly exhibits in galleries in Canada, where she lives. Shawn is eight years younger than I am, and it is with her that I have always shared a love of animals.

My father attended the Cincinnati Art Academy after college and loved to paint landscapes in watercolor. I remember him having commissions to paint the homes of people in the Cincinnati area and occasionally accompanying him to the sites. One memorable afternoon we were in a field adjoining a farm he was painting, and I fell asleep. I was awakened by chewing noises and there, in a semicircle behind my father and me, were at least a dozen cows, chewing their cud and curiously looking on. He had been so absorbed that he hadn't noticed their approach. He did portraits of Mr. Proctor and Mr. Gamble which still hang in their headquarters. One of his favorite commissions was a series of paintings done for the Ohio River Steamboat Company, of the last of the paddle wheelers on the Ohio River.

Sadly, however, these commissions were not enough to support a family, and, like many artists, he was forced to take jobs in commercial art. One of these was for the

Parents, Charles Lawson and Esther Claflin Woodward, 1938 (Courtesy of Sandra Darling.)

Gibson card company, and I remember, at the age of about eight or nine, being taken to the print shop and getting my first lesson in how four-color printing was done.

My father worked at home from the time I was nine until I was thirteen years old. This was important because I could watch paintings grow from the first sketches to their finished reality. I particularly enjoyed arising in the morning and discovering how much my father's work in the night had changed from what had been there when I went to bed. My father encouraged my early painting efforts and offered, as well, practical advice upon which I still lean. My father taught me the power of images. When a beloved horse of mine died, he made me a portrait of her, and I was comforted by this memorial of her presence. I remember a beautiful mask of a fox which he painted me for a school play.

In my home, imagination was encouraged to flower. My father enjoyed L. Frank Baum's "Oz" books and frequently read them to us. He also referred to them in daily conversation. One Halloween he made himself a giant papier-mâché; head and attended a party as Jack Pumpkinhead. I saw how life and art reflected each other.

Another encouragement to the play-life of my mind was the gift to us, by a family friend, of a trunk full of costumes. For many years this allowed us to change character, to play in other times, and to realize, in a small way, our dreams.

My mother excelled in the arts of the home. She cooked and baked, and taught me to do so. She taught well so that I could follow a cookbook with understanding and precision or, when circumstances demanded, make a recipe to fit the circumstances. All my life this has benefited me, for I need not depend either on restaurants or commercially prepared food products for culinary adventure. She also taught me to sew, and again this has changed my life, for I have always been able to design and make my own clothes, which as a young woman encouraged my self-esteem, for I could dress with a style and individuality far beyond my purse. I also learned from my mother gardening, canning, cleaning, and many other things—all of which added up to a repertoire of devices by which one could achieve beautiful and orderly surroundings. Well into her eighties she still baked her own bread because she said that store-bought just wasn't the same.

Through the good efforts of both my parents, my home was always well supplied with those things necessary for creation, repair, and transformation—pencils, chalk, paint, brushes, paper, tools, wire, nails, glue, and so on. My sisters and I were always made to feel that these materials were there to be freely used. Even more significant was the assumption in our family that if you wanted something, whether it was a kite, a strawberry

With her mother, 1942 (Courtesy of Sandra Darling.)

pie, a prom dress, or a tree house, with a little ingenuity and application (and help, if necessary) you could make it.

We spent many of our summers at a vacation cottage on an island in Georgian Bay, a part of Lake Huron in the Canadian province of Ontario. This cottage was owned by my father's parents. It was rustic, had no telephone or electricity, and could only be reached by boat. We used an ice box and cooked and lighted with kerosene. On other islands in the area other branches of my father's family also vacationed. In the brief and brilliant summers I saw much of aunts and uncles, and played regularly with cousins, deepening my awareness of a large and comfortable family.

In Georgian Bay the woods and waters were the primary reality. Raccoons attacked our trash cans. Porcupines were backyard visitors, and our dogs had to be taught to leave them alone. Beavers built dams in inconvenient places, and we needed to dismantle them. Red squirrels went up and down every tree and raced along the porch railings. Because water was all around us we all became practiced swimmers and skilled in the use of canoes, rowboats, and small sailing craft.

The lack of electricity made us dependent on the sun, and in the evening we, like the animals, grew quiet and

retreated to our nests—in our case to pop corn and play games under lamplight. The omnipresence of the lake made us similarly dependent on the weather, and when the weather turned we fled to land much as the birds sought the trees.

For four years we lived on a hundred-acre farm in Kentucky. The space invited roaming, and the animals became my friends. Here I grew especially fond of horses, training and riding. It was a half a mile to our nearest neighbor, and this made me dependent on myself and my family. As with many country children, nature was a very important companion. I spent long periods playing in streams and fruitlessly attempting to redirect them. My grandmother Woodward was a very educated woman and had been a schoolteacher before her marriage. She taught me that "plants, animals, and birds are our friends. We must respect them, and learn their names, as we do our human friends." I am told she was proud of my learning to identify and say "Philadelphia fleabane" at the age of three. Here in Kentucky I put this knowledge to good use, and what had been before mere nodding acquaintances became close friends.

Living in the country led to lots of time for reading. My father had art books—I remember Rockwell Kent, Lynd Ward, Winslow Homer, Russell Flint, and Edward

At age six (Courtesy of Sandra Darling.)

Hopper, particularly. We had in our basement a run of *National Geographic* magazines from 1901 to current (with indexes) from which questions about Tibet or polar bears or the Okefenokee Swamp got answered. There were also my father's own children's books: *St. Nicholas* magazine, *Struwwelpeter* (which we all thought hysterically funny), the "Oz" books, *The Wind in the Willows,* and the "Winnie-the-Pooh" books (my mother's favorite, which she read aloud, with sound effects which we loved). My mother inherited, from her father, a beautiful set of books by Dickens, which had been read to her as a child and which she in turn read to us.

Another aspect of my strong feeling about the interconnection of spirit and matter is the importance which Christianity has had for me, especially since 1975. My father's family was Episcopalian and my mother Presbyterian, but we only attended church sporadically in my childhood. When our children were ready for school, my husband, Harold, and I heard about a school run by the All Saints Episcopal Church in San Diego. Through this wonderful school we discovered the church itself, and both Harold and I have been inspired and sustained by the traditional Anglo-Catholic spirituality which we found magnificently manifested there.

I remember being an avid reader of fairy tales; I also read Nancy Drew, the "Black Stallion" books, Laura Ingalls Wilder, E. Nesbit, and wept with *Black Beauty* and *Little Women.* I remember being tremendously impressed with George Macdonald's *At the Back of the North Wind.* This, I think, was no accident, as I have always been particularly attracted to stories which attempt to describe the relation between the material, tangible world and the spiritual. For this reason, George Macdonald has remained a favorite author of mine, along with C.S. Lewis, C.K. Chesterton, J.R.R. Tolkien, and Charles Williams. I think that one of the reasons my illustrations have appealed to people is that they can sense my sincerity. I have no trouble at all in believing that dogs can read, stuffed-animals come alive, or a bear and an elephant run a business. I know that marvels exist which are just outside our ordinary experience, but that at any moment we may turn a corner and encounter one of them. Children also believe this, and because they and I have this conviction in common, we, as creator and audience, make good partners.

I was living in Kentucky when I finished the sixth grade. My parents decided to make the considerable sacrifice of driving me each weekday into Cincinnati (forty-five miles away) so that I could attend Walnut Hills, a six-year, college-preparatory high school. It was an excellent school, and their effort did help me to a better education.

My father died when I was fourteen. Aside from the psychological blow to all of us, it changed things practically. My mother, who had always stayed home with us, now had to work. I, the oldest daughter, found myself assuming unfamiliar responsibilities. My father's

Age sixteen (Courtesy of Sandra Darling.)

death had tumbled me from the nest of childhood to the hard ground of practical necessity. Fortunately, my mother's lessons in domestic skills prepared me for a good portion of the new challenges.

In high school several remarkable instructors made good impressions on me. An art teacher encouraged me to believe that my talent was worth further development. He also taught me that the best approach to an artistic problem was the exploratory sketch. He was in charge of design for the school's drama department, and I found the experience of helping to paint sets liberating and instructive. Other excellent professors were one in physics, who started me thinking about the vastness, complexity, and order of matter, and one in French, who made me realize the goodness of single-minded devotion to an intellectual pursuit. I had always enjoyed reading books, and this affection led to a study of literature and my appointment as editor of the school literary magazine.

When it came time to attend college I decided that I wanted to attend a small liberal-arts institution. I had the opportunity to attend several colleges, and I visited their campuses. After visiting I found it easy to decide on Swarthmore College. The old stone buildings were set in a park-like setting surrounded by an arboretum. It

was a Quaker college, not far from Philadelphia, and the simplicity and friendliness of its heritage made it an ideal choice.

I had a major in English literature. I probably would have profited from studies in art, but Swarthmore, being an old-fashioned liberal-arts institution, eschewed the practical in all areas of study. Literature did prove a fruitful choice because it took me, an enthusiastic but untrained reader, and taught me that distinction, analysis, and background can greatly enrich one's enjoyment of books. In my last two years I was part of the honors program, in which it was assumed that the student was a mature scholar ready for research and self-direction. Seminars were held once a week, and in them the emphasis was on the writing of papers and discussion in the small group. We were expected to do research and present a clear and, if possible, somewhat individual presentation of the subject we had chosen that week. Though Swarthmore may have been too optimistic about the skills of a still relatively untrained student, their approach did encourage independence and responsibility, and did push me to raise my levels of performance and confidence.

Swarthmore had a strong sense of community. All students lived in dormitories, ate together in a dining hall, and adhered to clear, and rather strict, codes of behavior. Far beyond many colleges, Swarthmore valued intellectual achievement. Scholarship and creativity here were esteemed more than social facility or athletic accomplishment. My college proved to be, for me, an excellent choice. Its heritage of individual dignity, moral order, and idealistic striving are with me still.

After college I went to work for the Young Men's Hebrew Association in New York City. I had worked for this organization while I was in college, acting as a counselor in their summer camp for girls in Maine. In New York I taught crafts, primarily silversmithing, which I had learned as an extracurricular activity at Swarthmore. While in New York I took classes at the Art Students' League. I took figure drawing, and I am very glad to have this in my background for I believe that accurate observation should underlie all painting, no matter how idiosyncratic. I also took courses on painting from Will Barnet. At that time Barnet was an abstract painter, and in his classes he emphasized composition and the juxtaposition of shapes. His teaching has been valuable for me, for, being a realistic illustrator, there is always the temptation to surrender to the demands of narrative, forgetting the fact that each illustration should succeed as a painting if the book as a whole is to achieve its highest artistic potential.

While visiting a friend in California I heard that La Jolla was home to an excellent school of art. I went there to investigate, and though the school proved disappointing, I did meet my future husband, Harold Darling. He was the owner of a very unusual business: the Unicorn Cinema and Mithras Bookstore. The cinema

was small and featured remarkable programming. It was eclectic in the extreme, mixing foreign, Hollywood, experimental, short, and silent films in nearly equal measure. The bookstore, which sold a highly personal selection of new and used books, was the entry to the cinema and stayed open until the last film had concluded. As a consequence it had two lives: in the daytime it was a quiet bookstore, and in the evenings it pulsed with the life of the cinema. The theater tickets were dispensed from a counter in the store, and the cinemagoers waited for the change of films while browsing the shelves.

In 1967 Harold and I were married, and these two remarkable institutions became a part of my life. The cinema changed me in several ways. My mother and father were not moviegoers, and as a result I was a relatively unsophisticated film viewer. The immersion in moving images that the Unicorn offered somewhat moved me from the concept of an image as a fixed and individual thing to the idea of an image as part of a continuum. This helped prepare me for illustration when the opportunity offered itself.

The Unicorn issued seasonal brochures which described and pictured their future programs. I took on the task of designing these. I was thus moved from the world of fine art to that of commercial art. Typesetting and the practical and economic problems of paper and printing became familiar. So, too, did the underlying challenge, which was to gracefully combine the printed word and picture.

The Mithras Bookstore also had its impact on my life and thinking. Since it carried both new and used books, both of these two rather different worlds had to be attended to in order to keep the store running. Even though I had been a lifelong reader and had majored in English literature, I had had no idea of the width and depth of the ocean of books. Like most people, only those books that impinged on my life had significant re-

In 1968 (Courtesy of Sandra Darling.)

ality. What I discovered was that books are like the sands of the seashore; that every subject in the world has inspired a book, or more likely, a library of books; that behind every one of the numberless volumes there is a mind; that most books sink unremembered; that nothing is new under the sun; and that those few books that are remembered have something remarkable about them. All of these lessons were useful for a future maker of books, and they affect everything I do in my career as an illustrator.

Harold brought three children—Harold, Jr., Abigail, and Benjamin—to our marriage, and in 1969 our first son was born. We named him Sacheverell, after the English writer Sacheverell Sitwell. In 1971 Rabindranath Tagore was born, named after the Bengali poet of the same name. In 1972 Lafcadio Hearn was born, named after the American writer who is best known for his writings on Japan. In 1973 Christina was born. She was named after the English poet Christina Rossetti. We selected these names for a number of reasons. We chose only the names of authors, and we wished in our naming to pay tribute to the world of books. Further, they were not the best known of literary figures, and we wished to emphasize that excellence does not belong alone to the leviathans. We also liked the sound of each name. Finally, we hoped to encourage individuality in our children by giving them very different first names. I cannot be sure how this last intention was fulfilled, for the growth of character is a process too mysterious to chart, but all of the children have very individual characters, and all have come to be fond of their strange names.

We continued for some years in the cinema and bookstore business, but we realized that these businesses, both characteristically difficult to make profitable, were insufficient to support our rapidly enlarging family, and so we searched our minds for an activity that would fit our needs. We wanted to be in business for ourselves. We wanted it to proceed out of our enthusiasms, to draw equally on Harold and myself, and to utilize our knowledge and skills. We needed it so organized that a good portion of the necessary work could be accomplished at home, for our children were small and needed our presence.

Publishing was our answer, and the Green Tiger Press its manifestation. We founded it in 1970. In the beginning it published only postcards, but soon we were making notecards, calendars, posters, bookmarks, and so on. Our aim was to rescue from the pages of old children's and illustrated books images too good to be forgotten. Arthur Rackham was our first success, and he was soon followed by Edmund Dulac and Kay Nielsen. Harold had long been a collector of old books, and it was in his library that our pictures were found. My natural roles were design and art director, and I found these agreeable, though increasingly demanding. The business grew, in not too many months, too large for our home. Also we needed more hands than our own,

and employees were hired. Soon all the problems of a growing business surfaced, but the rightness of publishing was so great that the difficulties were worth bearing.

In 1972 we published our first book, *All Mirrors Are Magic Mirrors* by Welleran Poltarnees. It was a series of essays on the pictures in old children's books, a natural outgrowth of our interests. It proved to be a modest success, and our fate was sealed. Though stationery products were profitable and a marvelous vehicle for our trove of images, and though we continue to this day to publish them, books are, for both Harold and me, one of civilization's supreme achievements, and the opportunity to participate in their creation is a joy beyond our expectations.

All Mirrors Are Magic Mirrors had its colored illustrations tipped (glued) onto their pages. In doing this we were echoing a practice followed by the publishers of many of the book artists whose images we were publishing. We shortly thereafter began to produce our notecards in this fashion. We did this because we were determined to link our efforts to the efforts of our predecessors. In looking back I realize that our choice of old children's books as a focus of our business lives had deeper roots that we had realized. We were, in an age of confusion, determined to connect ourselves with timeless goodness and truth. Paul Hazard, in his *Books, Children, and Men,* said of these pictures we loved, "Children lead us back to the fountainhead. We are blasé; we have seen too many strange things. They call, inviting us to look at and admire, pictures that owe their strength to their simplicity." We wanted a stable and idealistic climate, and the world of myths, folklore, and children's stories is such a world. One of our catalogs put this clearly:

> Our company started by reproducing pictures from old children's books, and though we have since pursued a variety of other enthusiasms this origin says a great deal about us. We stress those qualities which the child exemplifies—the freshness of vision, the spontaneity, the hunger for mystery and adventure. Francis Thompson in his essay on Shelley said that to be a child was "to believe in love, to believe in loveliness, to believe in belief." We hold these as our ideals, and we select all that we print to their support and encouragement.

As Green Tiger Press published more and more, we grew increasingly discontent with the quality of work we were receiving from our printers. In 1975 we purchased our own printing press. This became my area of expertise and taught me much that has been valuable in my work as an illustrator. The more one knows about the creation of a book, the better one is able to conceive it correctly.

Some of the most valuable lessons I learned from Green Tiger Press came from reviewing unsolicited submissions sent to us to consider for publication. Harold and

I and a variety of employees shared the task of reviewing the thousands of manuscripts and portfolios that arrived each year. We discovered several valuable truths from this work. First, we found that very few were publishable by anyone (probably less than one percent). Second, though most of the submissions were picture-book texts, very few of the creators showed that they had ever studied the nature and demands of the genre. Third, many of the writers and artists of these many stories seemed to imagine that, since children's books were short and simple, their creation would be a short, simple task open to anyone who could write; that any jottings about children or animals was potential for publication.

It was apparently widely imagined that children were a simple people, satisfied with almost anything. The origin of these ideas seems to lie in the fact that one's own children are so glad for parental attention that they do welcome any attempt at a story. In truth, writing for children is a challenge akin to writing poetry, where every word must count and be in the right place. Fourth, most submitters seem to believe that children are more different from adults than they are; that they need to be talked down to and need cute language. Fifth, illustration, like story, was apparently thought to require little talent; probably deduced from the fact that children themselves have only primitive artistic skills. Sixth, too many people submitted books because they wished to be published, not because they had a story to tell or a vision to show. There were always drifts of manuscripts about whatever subject or character was fashionable at the moment. Those few that did proceed out of a real impulse at communication could achieve goodness, even if their makers were inexperienced and untalented. Genuineness is the one essential ingredient in a children's book. Lastly, storytellers were commonly heavily didactic, which was unfortunate since most editors, librarians, and children resent too-obvious moral instruction.

One of the best things about publishing is the nice people one meets, for the making of books draws decent and interesting people as honey draws bees. I was particularly interested in what the various illustrators had to teach and to learn. We worked with many artists who had not illustrated a book before, and no matter how accomplished they were at painting or drawing they did need to adapt their style to the necessities of reproduction. Some of the illustrators whose first books we published, and who continued into notable careers either at Green Tiger or elsewhere, were Don Wood, Michele Clise, Katie Thamer, Michael Hague, Jasper Tomkins, Dan Lane, and Cooper Edens.

Of all the friendships that arose out of our publishing activities the one that developed between ourselves and author/illustrator Cooper Edens was the most remarkable. We received, in the torrent of unsolicited submissions, his text for *If You're Afraid of the Dark, Remember the Night Rainbow* in 1976. We liked it and wanted

Watercolor study for a "Carl" book (Courtesy of Sandra Darling.)

to publish it, but we were cautious about letting Cooper illustrate it because his paintings for it were unique and somewhat naive. He, however, convinced us to let him do it. This book, which is a series of poetic solutions to common problems, went on to become one of the most successful we have ever published. It appealed to both children and adults, and continues to be popular, having sold more than a million copies.

This dual appeal is one of the things that characterizes Cooper's work and Green Tiger Press as well. We believe that adults and children are not as different as is commonly imagined; that they share the same needs for story, fantasy, and laughter; and that books occupying this common ground need not define their audiences. I believe all of our books, and my books as well, have been affected by this belief. Cooper became not merely one of our finest creators, but a friend and compatriot in many aspects of our publishing efforts. His enthusiasm for the pictures from old children's books became as great as our own, and the *Magic Spectacles Calendar,* which we published annually from 1981 to 1992, and again from 2004 to 2007, was his joint inspiration and responsibility. It was an engagement calendar and featured an abundance of antique illustration in both line and full color. Each month was organized around a theme, and each year's set of themes was different. For example, we had "A June of Solitude," "An August of Bubbles," "An October of Clowns," and "A March of Tigers." Quotations were added which illuminated each of our visual essays. Each year's choices involved hundreds of hours of image searching, which Harold and I and Cooper shared.

Another marvelous educational opportunity that our publishing house gave me was our frequent attendance

at the annual children's book fair in Bologna, Italy. Here the publishers of the world assemble each spring to show their new children's books to publishers from other countries, hoping they will wish to publish them in their own lands. Each is, of course, looking for foreign books to make their own. Here also come many illustrators, hoping to find commissions. The breadth of this experience gives one a better view of contemporary children's illustration than anything else I know. We secured for Green Tiger publication of many fine works. We were the first American publishers of several notable illustrators: Monique Felix (*A Little Mouse Trapped in a Book*), Mario Mariotti (*Hanimals and Humands*), and Frederic Clement (*Animals Ball*). We commissioned several European illustrators with pleasant results: Sophie Kniffice (*The Sunny Hours*), Louise Jalbert (*The Diverting Tale of the Radish and the Shoe*), Reinhard Michl (*Mr. Death and the Redheaded Woman*), and Alberto Pratelli (*Soup Pot*). The last two artists, the first German, the second Bolognese, became friends, and to them we owe a wider view of the art of illustration. Also at Bologna we met and came to know Paola Pallotino, a professor and expert on Italian children's books, and she helped broaden our understanding of this rich field.

It is strange to look back and realize that we had been publishers for twelve years and that it had never occurred to me to illustrate a book. It seemed as if my artistic time was fully utilized in designing books and helping illustrators find the best way to bring manuscripts to life. I had painted the occasional isolated illustration, but a book seemed out of my way. A customer of Green Tiger Press wrote us several times saying that we should make a book out of the old song "The Teddy Bears' Picnic." The music had been written in 1907, by John Bratton, and the words added in 1932 by Jimmy Kennedy. We searched our minds to discover who among the illustrators we knew would be right for the project, and, finding no one, I eventually wondered if I might not be the one. I had plentiful reasons for thinking it difficult. I had small children to raise and an important job to do at Green Tiger Press. We at that time lived in the mountains about forty-five miles east of San Diego. We arranged that I would stay home a couple days a week and paint on the book. I started work in 1982 and finished in about a year.

I was attracted to this project for several reasons. First, I liked teddy bears and had a small collection of beloved ones. I also borrowed bears from my son Rabindranath and a friend. Second, the words stimulated my imagination, offering hints and possibilities as to what took place and who attended that famous picnic, but not really specifying the answers. A key statement for me was "If you go down to the woods today you'd better go in disguise." What I decided, and what I pictured, was that the song was addressed to human children, and that this was advice to allow them to witness this remarkable picnic. Thus, in my book, human children put on bear suits, which allow them to attend unnoticed and

to mingle with teddies. The real teddy bears wear human costumes of human roles such as Indian chief, medicine man, and soldier. We accompanied each book with a phonograph record which contained two versions of the song, one sung by Bing Crosby and the other one sung by a local klezmer band, which we renamed the Bearcats.

The Teddy Bears' Picnic sold very well—in fact it continues to sell. Everyone seemed pleased with my work; it won an award from the children's jury at the Bologna Book Fair and was selected by the Children's Book Council as one of their choices for 1984. 1 thoroughly enjoyed the whole process, and so I determined to continue as an illustrator.

My second book was based on a short story published in 1942 by Joan Grant that we believed would make a good picture book. *The Blue Faience Hippopotamus* was published in 1984. It is set in ancient Egypt and tells the story of a river hippopotamus who falls in love with a human princess whom he sees while she is bathing. His love leads to sacrifice and a beautiful kind of fulfillment. I was attracted not only by the touching story but also by my love of animals and by what I perceived as the opportunity to emulate the Egyptian's love of flat patterns in my book design. I have always been fond of borders, and this opportunity to create them in the spirit of ancient Egypt was welcome.

We were visiting Zurich, Switzerland, in 1983 and found in a second-hand bookstore a volume of old German picture sheets. These were originally single sheets, intended to be sold individually on the streets, at a low cost, and were usually humorous in content. The volume was quite expensive, so we didn't buy it, but we did see a picture story about a poodle that played with a baby who was supposed to be napping. On the air flight home we talked about making a children's picture story on the same idea, but using our rottweiler in place of the poodle. The original had been farcical, cartoonish, and we decided that we wanted our book to be serious and lovely in approach. The rottweiler was a deliberate, not circumstantial, choice. We owned two other breeds of dog. We liked the apparent fierceness of our hero to contrast with his gentle care. The rottweiler, as a breed, does have considerable tenderness and sensitivity underneath his aggressive demeanor. In our story, titled *Good Dog, Carl,* the dog hero helps the baby out of bed, and they enjoy together a series of household adventures. When the mother returns she finds the baby back in her crib, all the disorder having been put to rights, and she mistakenly imagines that Carl has been a silent and trusty guardian. She closes the book by praising him with the phrase which is the book's title.

I went to work on the book in 1984. A book in our collection called *Our Hospital ABC,* illustrated by Joyce Dennys, inspired me to create my illustrations on gray paper. We realized that, since neither the baby nor Carl could talk, we were in a good position to avoid words, and thus the book has only a few words at the beginning and at the conclusion. This dependence on pictures to tell the story focused me on the narration, which drives the irrelevant out of the frame. Further, because the story rushes wordlessly forward, I pictured some of the episodes by showing only small pieces of the action as floating vignettes. This sketched quality was intended to convey to the reader that there was insufficient time to finish the paintings because the events were so fast moving. Molly Myers, the daughter of an employee, was my model for the baby girl.

Good Dog, Carl, published in 1985, was an even larger success than *The Teddy Bears' Picnic.* It and its sequels continue to sell enormously, and I have to fight off the pressure to make a career of babies and dogs.

The next project I turned to was, as my first book, based on a song: "When You Wish upon a Star," written for Walt Disney's *Pinocchio* in 1940. The words were by Ned Washington, the music by Leigh Harline. As before, we included a phonograph record. On one side was the voice of Jimmy Cricket (Cliff Edwards), and on the other a version by Louis Armstrong.

I chose a song again because I like the challenge of extending the reality that familiar songs have achieved in our minds. We remember Pinocchio's yearning when Jimmy Cricket sings "When You Wish upon a Star,"

Illustration from **Frank and Ernest Play Ball** (Courtesy of Sandra Darling.)

***Illustration from* River Parade** (Courtesy of Sandra Darling.)

and it was my desire to listen closely to the words. This I did, and this time applied them not specifically to Pinocchio's situation, but to the similar striving in all conscious creatures. In this work I carried further than I have ever done the impulse to work the words of a picture book into the pictures. Here they are painted on fences, appear as embroidered samplers, stand on the steps of a staircase and on the shelves of a bookcase, appear on a passing truck, and so on. No one comments on this aspect of *When You Wish upon a Star,* but I am pleased to have attempted so complete an integration.

When You Wish upon a Star was not a great popular success, and I think I know why. I have always tried to select stories of interest to both children and adults, for I believe that the best children's books manage to appeal to human traits that we all have in common. I failed to realize that the longing which is the core of this song, and my book, is not a feeling present in any strength in the child, who is occupied too fully by the present moment. I had selected for a children's picture book a theme of limited interest to children.

In 1986 we sold the Green Tiger Press, and thus *When You Wish upon a Star*—which was released shortly after the sale—was the last book of mine published by the company we had founded.

We sold the press because the financial and practical details had overwhelmed us. We now wanted to find a way to concentrate on the creative parts of bookmaking and get rid of the financial and administrative tasks

which we found unrewarding. To this end we founded the Blue Lantern Studio. Here we developed books for other publishers, an activity which has continued. Some of these are *Cracker Jack, The Ultimate Alice in Wonderland, Bon Voyage, A Christmas Alphabet, Child's Garden of Verses, Cakes Men Like, Favorite Fairy Tales, Three Princesses, Glorious Mother Goose,* and *Tips for Teens.* We now also have an ever-increasing number of the images from our library on Corbis.

The first book I illustrated for anyone except my own publishing house was *Frank and Ernest,* published by Scholastic in 1988. It is the story of a humanized elephant and bear who are in the business of taking care of other people's business enterprises for short periods, while they are away. In my book they take care of a diner and are faced with the challenge of learning the language used by waiters to relay their orders to the cook.

The origins of *Frank and Ernest* are complex. I chose an elephant and bear as partners because of my fondness for a book called *Martin et Tommy,* published in Switzerland in 1920. The characters are an elephant and a bear, and they act like human beings, though, unlike mine, they do not wear clothing. Ours were named Frank and Ernest because these names fit their personalities. We also remembered an old radio program in which a man named Frank asked a man named Ernest Bible questions. An interest in trade vocabularies was the spark from which the whole project started. The terms used in diners is called Hash House Greek, and Harold's desire to find a way to use this in a children's book started the thinking which led to Frank and Ernest. The biggest problem I had with this book was how to show animals, particularly an elephant, who has very clumsy feet, doing intricate human tasks. Fortunately, elephants' trunks are marvelously adroit.

Something which needs to be said is that the books of Alexandra Day are often written, sometimes conceived, by my husband, Harold. When I sign my pen name it is with the understanding that it includes both of our contributions.

Frank and Ernest was successful, and two more books featuring this helpful pair have been published by Scholastic: *Frank and Ernest Play Ball* (1990), in which they manage a minor-league baseball team and need to learn the Vocabulary, and *Frank and Ernest on the Road* (1994), in which they load and deliver a truckful of freight and learn the language of CB radio.

In the beginning, for *The Teddy Bears' Picnic,* I started my work in watercolor, but I was dissatisfied with the results, and so I used a combination of egg tempera and watercolor. The advantage of egg tempera is that it, unlike watercolor, allows one to build layers of paint, and this painterly technique was what I desired. I have used this method in many of my books. I was not entirely happy with the watercolor, egg, and body color method

I used for *Good Dog, Carl* because I found it too hard to render Carl's shiny black fur in that medium. So for *Carl Goes Shopping* I changed to oil on canvas. I used this for *Carl's Christmas* and *Carl's Afternoon in the Park* as well, but, particularly with the last of these three, we had trouble with color separation. I concluded that the laser scanner was picking up dark canvas, or the oil medium was causing a darkening and diffusion of the colors which was untrue to the feeling I wanted to achieve. Therefore, I changed medium again and now use either all watercolor, occasionally adding egg, or watercolor with certain areas (for example, Carl) overpainted in oil. This seems to separate more satisfactorily while giving me more range of effects where I need it.

Another book I illustrated was *Paddy's Pay-Day,* published by Viking in 1989. This is based on the character of our beloved Irish terrier, Padraic. He was graceful, clever, independent, adaptable, and friendly, and we wanted a book which manifested these traits. In the book he is the assistant for a lady acrobat. He receives his pay, as a small bag of coins, and we follow as he walks to town by himself, spends his wages on a variety of pleasures, and returns home under the moonlight. It is one of my favorite works, and though Paddy hasn't achieved Carl's fame, I get many letters from fans who love him.

One obvious theme that runs through my books is the interrelationship between humans and animals: Frank and Ernest are animals who mix with and act as humans, Carl and the baby have a close and sympathetic relationship, Paddy moves intelligently and comfortably in the world of people, and the blue faience hippopotamus is actually transformed through its empathy with a human. I myself feel this connection very strongly. I have been a vegetarian most of my adult life because I cannot be a party to killing animals. I think that this theme is one to which many people respond. There is an essential loneliness in the human condition, and we long for a sympathetic communion with the "other." Religious people believe this is a hunger for God, for the lost harmony of paradise; Jungians talk about connection with unconscious; and so on. There is a thrill which ravishes us at a deep level when we experience the gap being bridged—it can happen in romantic love, or as when the German and Allied troops in the First World War came out of their trenches on Christmas Eve and sang carols together. People dream of it between us and beings from other planets, and are moved to tears when someone gives his life for another.

Animals are manifestly "other" than we are, but most people feel that at least some communication with them is possible. They are therefore a natural manifestation and symbol for me of the "other" with whom we long to be at one.

With Arambarri (rottweiler) and Sprocket (Irish terrier), 1992 (Courtesy of Sandra Darling.)

Seattle weather influence (Courtesy of Sandra Darling.)

In 1989 Farrar, Straus & Giroux published my second "Carl" book, *Carl Goes Shopping*. In it, Carl and the baby (whom we named Madeleine, after our first grandchild) are supposed to wait in a designated area while the mother is shopping in a department store, but they leave and explore the book department, the toy and pet departments, and so on. Again, Carl was very popular, and the public's enthusiasm has led to a series of sequels, all published by Farrar, Straus & Giroux. *Carl's Christmas* (1990) chronicles a variety of Christmas Eve adventures, including a meeting with Santa Claus. *Carl's Afternoon in the Park* (1991) shows the variety of adventures a baby and dog can find in a large public park. *Carl's Masquerade* (1992) involves the two of them attending a masquerade party and avoiding the parents, who are attending as guests. In *Carl Goes to Daycare* the teacher is accidentally locked out of the class room, and Carl has to supervise the group in her absence.

River Parade, published by Viking in 1990, was a book that grew out of my many vacations at Georgian Bay, which began in childhood and still continue. It is the story of a little boy on vacation at a lake who is afraid of the water and who finds a way to conquer that fear. I painted this book at Georgian Bay, and it is, for me, a distillation of memories and a lovely memory in itself.

Teddy Bears' Picnic Cookbook (published by Viking in 1991 and reissued by Laughing Elephant in 2004), written by my daughter Abigail, was for me an opportunity to create vignette illustrations and decorative devices, both of which I particularly enjoy.

Carl's Afternoon in the Park has a rottweiler puppy that joins Carl and the baby on their adventures. This came about because our original rottweiler, Toby, who had been the model for Carl, died of old age just after *Carl's Christmas* was completed. To assuage our grief at losing him, we got a rottweiler puppy who was so appealing that I couldn't resist putting him into the book on which I was then working. Because we have long been enthusiastic fans of the Basque ball game of jai alai, a family vote named the new puppy Arambarri, after a favorite player. When he grew up I used him as a model for Carl. He was wonderfully athletic and would jump, carry, pose, etc., with a will. He loved children and was happy to have babies pose on his back.

He unfortunately died young, and was followed by a wonderful dog named Zabala. Zabala added a new dimension to "Carl" when he became a therapy and service dog and traveled with me to children's medical and educational facilities, as well as to bookstores, in many parts of the United States and Canada. He even had a bronze statue modeled after him which stands in the Meridian Park in Seattle and has grown shiny from the thousands of children who have ridden him. After Zabala died, we were able to get his half brother, Zubiaga, who has a similarly wonderful personality and who, like his brother, visits hospitals, schools, conventions, and bookstores. Both Zabala and Zubiaga have ridden in antique convertibles in the famous Adolphus Christmas Parade in Dallas.

I try to make Carl always look the same, but each of the dogs adds a little of itself to the portrayal. The same thing is true to an even greater extent with the baby in the "Carl" books, since I must change models with almost every book because the babies keep growing up.

For *Carl's Masquerade* I made much use of the Blue Lantern library, from which I got a wide variety of costume ideas from sources ranging from French magazines of the 1910s and 1920s, and nineteenth-century German costume catalogs, to fancy-dress fashion plates from the 1800s to the middle of the twentieth century. (I also used a couple of kids who came to the door on Hallowe'en.)

For *Carl goes to Daycare* a wonderful pre-school teacher at my children's school made costumes and props for the children and Arambarri (the "Carl" of the time) enacted many of the scenes which appeared in the book.

After finishing *Carl Goes to Daycare*, the Blue Lantern began to demand much of my time. After some years in the making of books for other publishers, we found ourselves missing being publishers ourselves, especially the rich variety of challenges and the fact that one had complete control over the form of each book.

In 1992 we started Blue Lantern Books and the Laughing Elephant, which was the note card and stationery arm of our enterprise. We reproduce, as we did in the beginning, pictures from our library of old children's books and ephemera. As before, they are popular. People enjoy the unfamiliar images that remind them of the timeless realm of childhood. We have published at this writing (2008) almost a hundred books and hundreds of cards, as well as other paper gift products such as notebooks, decorative labels, paper dolls, and calendars. We make gift books, because here fine design and rich imagery find a ready audience. We, of course, are involved with children's books. We have published many reprints of old picture books and will continue to reproduce old favorites. We have also created several anthologies which show many illustrators' approach to Mother Goose, alphabet books, children's poetry, and fairy tales. We will continue this program and additionally plan to commission new children's books by living authors and artists. We also create books that draw upon the fertile minds of our children and our associates, illustrator/author Cooper Edens, and graphic artist and retired university professor Richard Kehl.

In 1993 we moved from San Diego to Seattle, Washington. We chose Seattle because we like the seasons, the moisture, the lively cultural atmosphere (especially the classical music), and the fact that two of our best artistic collaborators—Cooper and Richard—reside there. With the help of Jan Gobel, a man who had been with us from our bookstore, theater, and Green Tiger days, we began to concentrate on our own publishing. Since 1993 we have added a trade book imprint called Darling & Co. and a children's book imprint for which we have revived the name Green Tiger.

At the heart of the Blue Lantern Studio, which is responsible for conceptual, editorial, and design aspects of the company, is our library. It now contains about 20,000 picture books and uncounted kinds and categories of ephemera. What makes it remarkable is that which makes any private library unique; it is the embodiment of our ideas and enthusiasms.

Our major enthusiasm is illustrated children's books, but we also have fair-sized collections of art, photography, design, natural history, fashion, typography, and Shakespearean books. Within the children's books we favor volumes published earlier than the 1940s and prefer fiction to fact. We naturally have a special fondness for particular artists and collect them fully. A few among

Sacheverell in the Blue Lantern Library (Courtesy of Sandra Darling.)

Christina at work (Courtesy of Sandra Darling.)

these are Charles Robinson, L. Leslie Brooke, Honor Appleton, Beatrix Potter, Arthur Rackham, Walter Crane, Edward Ardizzone, W. Heath Robinson, Peter Newell, Cecil Aldin, Ilse Wenz-Vietor, N.C. Wyeth, Ludwig Richter, John R. Neill, and Jessie Willcox Smith. We have subject specialties as well; for example, object books, primers, and readers; art instruction for children; baby record books; annuals and other children's periodicals; and books about elephants, dogs, and St. Nicholas. We also have a substantial reference library to help us understand the books and things we collect. Our collection of ephemera includes post and greeting cards, calendars, prints, labels, magazines, advertisements, and much more. Again these have been collected because of their imagery. Sometimes we know why, often we don't.

The Blue Lantern Studio, including our library, is now located in a wonderful Seattle building. It is called the Good Shepherd Center. It was built in 1902 as a nunnery but has been owned since 1906 by Historic Seattle. It is the home to a variety of nonprofit institutions and a few businesses such as a yoga center and ourselves. It is a large and comfortable old building, located in an eight-acre park. Our library, which had been crammed into an old house in San Diego, is now comfortably housed on shelves and in cabinets, which makes its use easy and pleasant. We have many large tables where we spread the materials for each book on which we are working. There are large windows all along three sides of our premises. From one side we look out into a small park with many old trees, including an eccentric and aged monkeypod tree. From another side we look over a larger park and the city and sound to the Olympic mountain range. From the third side we see across Lake Union to downtown Seattle and beyond that the snow-capped bulk of Mt. Rainier. This is a place where creativity seems the natural order of life.

Harold's three children, our four children, and our foster child, Jack, are a close and harmonious family. Many of them are involved in the business. Benjamin is in charge of trade shows and assists with marketing, Sacheverell is our designer; Abigail and Christina handle the library and do research, editorial, and secretarial jobs; Christina's husband, Jason, has taken over as business manager from our son Rabindranath, who now has his own business here in Seattle; and Jack is in our shipping department. Lafcadio is an attorney in Seattle, and Harold, Jr., lives in San Francisco and is a legal assistant. Our several grandchildren get called on regularly to model for me.

Perhaps influenced by the sense of adventure that the move to Seattle created in us, we decided to try a very different kind of "Carl" book. In *Carl Makes a Scrapbook* (1994) we attempted something unusual. Carl and the baby, who are supposed to be napping, pull out the mother's scrapbook and on blank pages imitate her work. Hers is organized around headings, for example: Friends, Vacations, Family, and Milestones. Carl understands what she has done and puts things on the facing page that are his dog equivalent. Madeleine does not understand exactly what is going on but sees it instead as an occasion to select and paste anything she finds colorful and appealing. Her contributions are placed every which way on the pages, sometimes even covering Carl's items.

The strangest thing about *Carl Makes a Scrapbook* is that, whereas the world of Carl has hitherto been a painted, entirely fictive world, now we are shown real things, actual photos of the characters and events we have come to know. All of the scrapbook's pages on which Carl and the baby are seen to be working are real pages with real things pasted onto them. In actuality it is only a counterfeit reality. The mother's photographs are either photographs of my models (the mother is my daughter, Christina, for example), their friends and relations, or unrelated photos from our collection. The things she includes (postcards, invitations, patches, greeting cards, and so on) are from our collection of

ephemera. The whole is a diverse accumulation, partially rooted in reality. We hope that we have fused all of these elements into an artistic reality.

Carl's Birthday (1995) was the first book in which the backgrounds start to reflect our move to the Pacific Northwest: lots of evergreens and flowers that don't grow in San Diego. For *Follow Carl* (1998) I rounded up the children on my street and used a local park and shopping area as venues. *Carl's Sleepy Afternoon* (2005), in honor of it being Carl's 20th anniversary, had eight more pages than usual, and I used many local stores, a local firehouse (and fireman) and even our veterinarian. *Carl's Summer Vacation* (2008) uses Lake Washington and a local cabin in the Oregon woods.

There have been a number of Carl-related books, calendars, puzzles, and coloring books. In 1994 Farrar published a baby book for puppies called *My Puppy's Record Book,* which included a medal for the puppy's neck. Farrar also published *Carl's Baby Book* for human babies in 1996. Two pop-up books were also made; *Carl Pops Up* (Simon & Schuster, 1994) and *Puppy Trouble* (Farrar, 2002). There were also calendars for 1998 and 1999.

In 1997 I decided that I again wanted to make books other than "Carl" books. Farrar published *The Mirror,* for which my daughter Christina wrote the text. I also made a book that year with Cooper Edens for Harper-Collins, titled *The Christmas We Moved to the Barn,* about a family that has to move at the last minute on Christmas Eve. I love painting snow! The family in that book has another adventure in *Special Deliveries* (HarperCollins, 2001). Cooper and I also did a book about his parents' troublesome bull terrier, titled *Darby, the Special-Order Pup* (Dial, 2000).

Farrar has published two other non-"Carl" books for me. *Boswell Wide Awake* (1999) is about a little bear who wanders around his house in the moonlight, eating pie, playing, giving the cat an outing, and finally kissing his parents goodnight. *The Flight of a Dove* (2004) is not exactly a children's book. I read an account of an autistic child in France who was eventually brought out of her isolation by a dove at a school where animals were part of the "curriculum." Since I have had personal experience of how animals can help children in pain or distress, I wanted to try to convey the inspiration I felt from this story.

Since the books we have so far published ourselves have used existing art for their illustration, most of them are created by my husband, Harold, usually with input from our children and me, but there are some that I have developed from the library (with input by the others, of course): *A Bouquet,* a book about the language of flowers illustrated with Victorian scraps; *Not Forgotten* (2004), a consolation for the death of a pet; *Hooray for Dogs* (2008), a celebration of all the ways dogs enrich our lives; and *Bridal Memories* (2008), a bride's record book decorated with beautiful old flowers and illustrations from our collection.

When people ask me my age (children have a great interest in this!), I always have to figure it out. This year is 2008, so I figure I'll be sixty-seven. That means I illustrated my first book twenty-five years ago. It's true I need glasses for close work these days, and my back objects to too much sitting or too much gardening, but on the other hand, my paintbrush obeys my desires more readily with each passing year, and ideas seem to be like love: the more one pours out, the bigger the pool from which one has to draw. I'm excited about all the things to do and think up and paint. I look forward to the rest of today and tomorrow and tomorrow.

*   *   *

DECKER, Timothy 1974-

Personal

Born 1974, in Camp Hill, PA; married. *Education:* Kutztown University, B.F.A., 1997.

Addresses

Home and office—Jersey City, NJ.

Career

Writer and illustrator. Literacy advocate and teacher of creative writing, 2004—.

Writings

SELF-ILLUSTRATED

The Letter Home, Front Street (Asheville, NC), 2005.
Run Far, Run Fast, Front Street (Asheville, NC), 2007.

Sidelights

A car accident suffered while he was working as a professional photographer inspired Timothy Decker to make some changes in his life. Tapping into his childhood love of art and writing, Decker began writing and sketching what would become his first book, *The Letter Home.*

A picture book for older readers, *The Letter Home* is set during World War I, and is the story of a soldier writing home to his family. The narrator describes his war experience in Europe to his son, who, at the end of the book, is clutching the letter as his father arrives home. Decker's "descriptions are brief but emotion-filled," Lucinda Snyder wrote in her *School Library Journal* re-

view, noting that the pictures contain details that flesh out the book's spare text. According to a *Kirkus Reviews* contributor, Decker's "delicately etched, black-and-white, pen-and-ink drawings, each framed on lovely cream-colored paper, are spare and beautiful." In *Publishers Weekly,* a critic commented on the complexity of the ideas in Decker's tale, concluding that "the retrospective 'letter,' which alludes to death while remaining nonjudgmental, implies the painful realities that adults try to withhold from children."

Decker's second book, *Run Far, Run Fast,* combines aspects of both the picture book and the graphic novel by combining traditional text layouts and a story told through illustrations. A young girl is told to leave home to avoid catching the Black Death in 1348. As the story progresses, the girl sees the effects of the plague, but does not understand everything that is happening around her. Eventually, she is taken in by a doctor who, although unable to stop the plague from spreading, does his best to help people suffer less. "Striking pen-and-ink illustrations tell more of the story than the spare text," wrote Robin L. Gibson in her *School Library Journal* review of *Run Far, Run Fast,* the critic calling the book "intriguing." Jesse Karp, writing in *Booklist,* noted that, like *The Letter Home,* Decker's "profound tale best suits advanced readers prepared for its subtle, potent message." Although a *Publishers Weekly* contributor noted that some of the drawings of people seem "awkward," the critic also assessed the "pen-and-ink panels [as] notable for their architectural renderings."

Along with his own writing and drawing, Decker is an advocacy for children's literature, and he teaches creative writing to young students. The author/illustrator described his philosophy about writing and art on his home page, noting: "In my world, writing is easier than drawing. A picture is worth 100,000 words, if not more. I'd rather rewrite an entire story than redraw a single image."

Biographical and Critical Sources

PERIODICALS

Booklist, September 15, 2007, Jesse Karp, review of *Run Far, Run Fast,* p. 60.
Kirkus Reviews, November 15, 2005, review of *The Letter Home,* p. 1231; September 15, 2007, review of *Run Far, Run Fast.*
Publishers Weekly, October 31, 2005, review of *The Letter Home,* p. 55; November 5, 2007, review of *Run Far, Run Fast,* p. 63.
School Library Journal, February, 2006, Lucinda Snyder, review of *The Letter Home,* p. 130; January, 2008, Robin L. Gibson, review of *Run Far, Run Fast,* p. 116.

Voice of Youth Advocates, December, 2007, Stacey Hayman, review of *Run Far, Run Fast,* p. 425.

ONLINE

Boyds Mills Press Web site, http://www.boydsmillspress.com/ (February 24, 2009), profile of Decker.
Timothy Decker Home Page, http://timothydecker.com (February 18, 2009).*

* * *

DEL NEGRO, Janice M.

Personal

Married; children: two daughters. *Education:* Hunter College, B.A.; State University of New York, Geneseo, M.L.S.; University of Illinois, Urbana-Champaign, Ph.D.

Addresses

Home—IL. *Office*—Crown 323, 7900 W. Division St., River Forest, IL 60305. *E-mail*—jdelnegro@dom.edu.

Career

Librarian and storyteller. Dominican University, River Forest, IL, assistant professor of library and information science. Former director of Center for Children's Books; editor of *Bulletin of the Center for Children's Books.*

Awards, Honors

Anne Izard Storytelling Award for *Lucy Dove;* Notable Children's Book designation, Association for Library Service to Children, American Library Association, Cooperative Children's Book Center Choice designation, and Irma Simonton Black and James H. Black Award for Excellence in Children's Literature Honor Book designation, Bank Street College of Education, all 2006, all for *Willa and the Wind.*

Writings

Lucy Dove, illustrated by Leonid Gore, Dorling Kindersley (New York, NY), 1998.
(Reteller) *Romantic Wonders: Tales of Love and Magic* (sound recording), 1999.
(Reteller) *Willa and the Wind,* illustrated by Heather Solomon, Marshall Cavendish (New York, NY), 2005.
(Reteller) *Passion and Poison: Tales of Shape-Shifters, Ghosts, and Spirited Women,* Marshall Cavendish (New York, NY), 2007.

Sidelights

An educator with a focus on youth services in public libraries as well as an accomplished storyteller, Janice M. Del Negro is actively involved with children's books as

a reviewer as well as a writer. Her folktale retellings have been recorded for audio and have also been adapted into print, and she is also the author of picture books such as *Lucy Dove* and *Willa and the Wind,* as well as a collection of supernatural tales for young adults titled *Passion and Poison: Tales of Shape-Shifters, Ghosts, and Spirited Women.*

In *Lucy Dove,* Del Negro draws from several versions of a traditional Scottish folk story in which brave seamstress Lucy Dove sews a pair of trousers in a haunted graveyard in order to win a prize from a local lord. When the ghosts and monsters of the place try to frighten Lucy away, the young woman refuses to succumb to fear. "Del Negro adeptly balances the scariness of the bogle (or monster) with the big laughs," wrote Susan Dove Lempke in *Booklist.* Mary M. Burns, reviewing *Lucy Dove* in *Horn Book,* noted "how skillfully the teller has polished her story to a mirror-like reflection of her sources."

In *Willa and the Wind* Del Negro retells a Norwegian folk story featuring a strong young heroine who is determined to get back the cornmeal Old Windy has blown off of her family's table. Willa accepts a magic handkerchief that provides food in exchange for the stolen cornmeal, but when her reward is switched for a regular handkerchief, the girl angrily marches back to Old Windy. The process continues until a magic whistle reveals the actual thief: the local innkeeper who has been keeping Willa's magic items for himself. "Willa's sassy, outspoken, courageous nature shines through in her actions and in the folksy dialogue," wrote Shelle Rosenfeld in her *Booklist* review of *Willa and the Wind,* and in *School Library Journal* Kathy Weizner recommended Del Negro's tale as "great for telling or reading aloud."

Passion and Poison offers seven stories filled with strong and determined heroines and frightening spirits. Along with the stories, which are written to be read aloud, Del Negro included notes on the folklore motifs that appear in each Gothic tale. "The language is cadenced and carefully chosen," wrote a *Kirkus Reviews* contributor in reviewing Del Negro's collection, while in *School Library Journal* Shawn Brommer described the author's narrative voice as "perfectly pitched; her conversational tone initially sets readers at ease and then delightfully startles them with perfect, sometimes shocking, conclusions." The "mesmerizing storytelling begs to be shared aloud," concluded Joanna Rudge Long in her *Horn Book* review of *Passion and Poison.*

"I am passionate about retelling folk tales," Del Negro told *SATA.* "I am passionate about excavating old tales, tales that have already survived for centuries, for emotional truths that resonate with contemporary listeners. There is no definitive version of a folktale, no 'original'; we can point to the earliest remembered, written, or preserved version, but not to an 'original.'

Vince Natale created evocative art to bring to life Janice M. Del Negro's short-story collection Passion and Poison. (Illustration copyright © 2007 by Marshall Cavendish. Reproduced by permission.)

Folk tales change over time in order to survive, and retelling folk tales for present-day listeners is a contemporary offshoot of what is popularly understood as the oral tradition.

"Tales come to us differently today than in the past. A handful of contemporary American storytellers can say they heard folk tales from family or friends, tales that were handed down orally, from mouth to ear, but many of us who retell folk tales first meet the tales on the page. Sometimes the tales work just as we find them; sometimes they resonate oddly, indicating currents beneath the surface. Those currents offer an opportunity to retell from where the teller stands now, instead of from where the story stood then.

"My stand includes my gender. I am a woman. I am fascinated by the women in folk tales, not just the women characters, but the women storytellers. Many of the tales we have were collected by men operating within the social mores of their times. The stories these good men chose to collect and the manner in which they collected them were filters through which the sto-

ries traveled, affecting the tale's content and presentation. I look at a folktale so collected and I want to know: what isn't there? What would the stories be like if the women were telling them to each other in the kitchen, while the collector was making notes on the polite version in the parlor? Those are the stories I want to tell, and since no one collected them in quite that way, I make my own. Filtered through my own experiences, I try and make an old tale new.

"Stories may be static on the physical or virtual page, but for as long as the storyteller is telling, the story has blood and breath. Every retelling of a folktale, imbued with the individual blood and breath of the storyteller, is unique. The storytelling community recognizes this in a practical and concrete way: there are many popular conference and festival programs in which several tellers elect to retell the same folktale, just to show what is possible.

"I am enormously interested in the fact that many female storytellers choose to retell traditional tales from points of view not always represented in collected or anthologized versions of folk tales. Milbre Burch, Elizabeth Ellis, Susan Klein, Barbara Schutz-Gruber, Megan Wells, my own students (and too many others to name) approach folk tales through their own artistic processes. I cannot speak to the specifics of anyone's process but my own, and even my process is malleable; the process changes with every story, because every story speaks differently to every teller."

Biographical and Critical Sources

PERIODICALS

Booklist, September 1, 1998, Susan Dove Lempke, review of *Lucy Dove,* p. 120; September 1, 2005, Shelle Rosenfeld, review of *Willa and the Wind,* p. 143; September 1, 2007, Shelle Rosenfeld, review of *Passion and Poison: Tales of Shape-Shifters, Ghosts, and Spirited Women,* p. 114.

Horn Book, September-October, 1998, Mary M. Burns, review of *Lucy Dove,* p. 615; November-December, 2007, Joanna Rudge Long, review of *Passion and Poison,* p. 678.

Kirkus Reviews, August 15, 2005, review of *Willa and the Wind,* p. 912; August 1, 2007, review of *Passion and Poison.*

Publishers Weekly, November 2, 1998, review of *Lucy Dove,* p. 50; November 7, 2005, review of *Willa and the Wind,* p. 73.

School Library Journal, December, 2005, Kathie Meizner, review of *Willa and the Wind,* p. 110; December, 2007, Shawn Brommer, review of *Passion and Poison,* p. 150.

ONLINE

Dominican University Web site, http://www.dom.edu/ (January 15, 2009), "Janice M. Del Negro."

Marshall Cavendish Web site, http://www.marshall cavendish.us/ (January 16, 2009), "Janice M. Del Negro."

E

EASON, Alethea 1957-

Personal

Born 1957. *Education:* University of Redlands, B.A. (English and religion), 1974; Sonoma State University, multiple-subject teaching credential, 1986; Chico State University, reading and language-arts credential, 1991.

Addresses

Home and office—Concon, Chile. *E-mail*—alethea eason1@yahoo.com.

Career

Writer and educator. Middletown Unified School District, Middletown, CA, teacher.

Awards, Honors

Eugene Ruggles Poetry Prize; "What's the Story" Contest winner, SRA/McGraw Hill Imagine It! Reading series, for "Turtle Soup."

Writings

Hungry, Eos (New York, NY), 2007.

Contributor of stories to anthologies, including *A Glory of Unicorns, Bruce Coville's Strange Worlds,* and *Bruce Coville's Alien Visitors.*

Sidelights

As a teacher of English in California, as well as in Chile, where she instructs Spanish speakers in the English language, Alethea Eason hopes to encourage her students by sharing her own writing life with them. "I bring drafts of my work to show my students when I want to reinforce the need to rewrite," Eason explained

Alethea Eason (Photograph by William Eason. Courtesy of Alethea Eason.)

on her home page. "I think some of the kids are more willing to take chances at expressing themselves because they know me as a writer as well as a teacher."

Eason contributed short fiction to several middle-grade anthologies before producing her first novel, *Hungry. Hungry* grew out of the short story "Deborah's Choice," which first appeared in *Bruce Coville's Alien Visitors.* The novel introduced Deborah, a young alien living on Earth disguised as a human. Deborah's quandary is an unusual one: she must decide whether she can fulfill her duties to her home world by eating her best friend. Preparing for an invasion of earth, Deborah and her family have to feed on human beings every year on Halloween. The girl accepts that this is part of being an average alien until her parents insist that her best friend, Willy, be their latest victim. When Deborah now starts to question what she knows about her home world, she discovers that other people from her planet would rather have a peaceful coexistence with the inhabitants of

Earth instead of continuing their quiet but violent invasion. Noting the parallels between Deborah's development and universal coming-of-age issues, Danielle M. Margarida wrote in *School Library Journal* that "Deborah's story has promise—after all, what 11-year-old doesn't feel like an alien at times?"

Biographical and Critical Sources

PERIODICALS

Bulletin of the Center for Children's Books, November, 2007, Katrina Bromann, review of *Hungry,* p. 137.
Kliatt, September 15, 2007, review of *Hungry.*
School Library Journal, December, 2007, Danielle M. Margarida, review of *Hungry,* p. 124.

ONLINE

Alethea Eason Home Page, http://www.aletheaeason.com (January 13, 2009).
SFReview Web site, http://www.sfrevu.com/ (January 29, 2009), "Alethea Eason."
Suite 101 Web site, http://teen-science-fiction.suite101.com/ (December 4, 2008), interview with Eason.

*   *   *

ELLIOTT, Laura Malone 1957-
(L.M. Elliott)

Personal

Born 1957; married; children: two. *Education:* Wake Forest University, B.A.; University of North Carolina, M.A.

Addresses

Home and office—VA.

Career

Writer.

Awards, Honors

International Reading Association (IRA) Teacher's Choice Award, and New York Public Library Book for the Teen Age selection, both for *Annie, between the States*; IRA/Children's Book Council Children's Choice selection, for *Hunter's Best Friend at School*; two-time finalist for National Magazine Award.

Writings

(With Charlotte Fedders) *Shattered Dreams: The Story of Charlotte Fedders,* Harper & Row (New York, NY), 1987.

(With others) *A to Z Guide to Your Child's Behavior: A Parent's Easy and Authoritative Reference to Hundreds of Everyday Problems and Concerns from Birth to Twelve Years,* Putnam (New York, NY), 1993.
(As L.M. Elliott) *Under a War-torn Sky,* Hyperion (New York, NY), 2001.
Hunter's Best Friend at School, illustrated by Lynn Munsinger, HarperCollins (New York, NY), 2002.
(As L.M. Elliott) *Flying South,* HarperCollins (New York, NY), 2003.
(As L.M. Elliott) *Annie, between the States,* Katherine Tegen (New York, NY), 2004.
Hunter and Stripe and the Soccer Showdown, illustrated by Lynn Munsinger, Katherine Tegen (New York, NY), 2005.
(As L.M. Elliott) *Give Me Liberty,* Katherine Tegen (New York, NY), 2006.
Hunter's Big Sister, illustrated by Lynn Munsinger, Katherine Tegen (New York, NY), 2007.

Contributor to *Washingtonian.*

Sidelights

Writing under the name L.M. Elliott, Laura Malone Elliott is the author of several books for young readers that draw on the history of the early United States. She has drawn on her background as a journalist in undertaking her research, gathering information on original accounts of historic events that a relevant to each story. "History took me by the hand, led me to my computer and whispered in my ear as I wrote," she described of writing one of these novels, *Give Me Liberty,* on the HarperCollins Web site. "Words alone aren't necessarily that exciting," she added. "But seeing how abstract ideals can completely alter the lives of ordinary boys—frighten, endanger, or liberate them—now there's a story!"

In Elliott's historical novel *Under the War-torn Sky,* Henry Forester is a teen pilot serving in the American Air Force during World War II. Shot down during a mission over Europe, Henry finds help from the French Resistance after they smuggle him over the border to safety. "Elliott paints a picture of war that we don't often see, one that is away from the battles, showing life and death in a war-ravaged land," wrote *Kliatt* critic Erin Lukens Darr. According to Connie Fletcher, writing in *Booklist, Under a War-torn Sky* is "packed with action, intrigue, and suspense," creating a story that "celebrates acts of kindness and heroism without glorifying war." Bruce Anne Shook wrote in *School Library Journal* that "Hank is a smart, strong, and courageous character who survives under the worst of conditions."

Set in 1968, *Flying South* finds Alice coping with her recently widowed mother's attempt to marry a local politician. Spending most of her time with Edna, the housekeeper, and Doc, the gardener, Alice learns about gardening and life while tending the roses with Doc. She tries to be patient with her mother, and eventually,

the woman recognizes Alice's strength of character. *Flying South* "is both a poignant mother-daughter story and a comforting tale of the affection between a lonely young girl and an irascible but devoted old man," wrote Gerry Larson in *School Library Journal,* while Hazel Rochman noted in *Booklist* that "Elliott creates a strong sense of the time and place" through Alice's narrative. Although observing that Elliott's use of some teen slang from the 1960s does not gel with the rest of the text, a *Kirkus Reviews* contributor felt that the characters' "dialogue is right on target."

Annie, between the States is, like *Flying South,* set in Virginia, but Annie's Virginia is one torn by the U.S. Civil War. Managing the family home in Virginia while her brothers are off fighting, the teenager falls in love with a Yankee officer, and this relationship makes Annie question everything she formerly thought was right. "Fiery, intelligent Annie remains a heroine to relish," wrote Jennifer Mattson in *Booklist,* while *School Library Journal* contributor Jane G. Connor called the teen a "strong and memorable heroine." According to a *Kirkus Reviews* critic, "Elliott does an admirable job of balancing the human story and the historical context."

The American Revolution serves as the backdrop for *Give Me Liberty,* Elliott's story of Nathaniel Dunn. Arriving in Virginia as an indentured servant and taken under the wing of a local schoolmaster, Nathaniel is apprenticed to a loyalist carriage maker. He must wade through the opposing ideals of the loyalists who want to stay a British colony and the patriots who want freedom yet support indentured servitude and condone slavery. "Elliott's engaging and highly readable novel is well researched and sprinkled liberally with renowned patriots of the period," wrote Kim Dare in her review of the novel for *School Library Journal.* The author "packs a great deal of historical detail into a novel already filled with action," wrote Carolyn Phelan in her *Booklist* review of *Give Me Liberty.*

Along with her historical fiction, Elliott is also the author of a series of books about Hunter, a young raccoon who struggles with peer pressure and sibling rivalry in various stories geared for young readers. In *Hunter's Best Friend at School,* Hunter goes along with best friend Stripes's plans to get into trouble, even though he feels guilty. After giving in and destroying an art project he was really proud of, Hunter realizes that he should listen to his feelings instead of going along with the crowd. "Elliott does a remarkable job portraying how difficult it is for Hunter," wrote a *Kirkus Reviews* contributor. Melina Piehler, writing in *School Library Journal,* described the book's characters "appealing" and considered *Hunter's Best Friend at School* "a solid choice, filling a need for stories about friendship and peer pressure."

Hunter and Stripe face off against each other in *Hunter and Stripe and the Soccer Showdown,* when the two play for competing teams during a soccer tournament.

Shelle Rosenfeld, writing in *Booklist,* observed that the tale involves "activities and situations kids will easily recognize and relate to." Blair Christolon noted in *School Library Journal* that *Hunter and Stripe and the Soccer Showdown* contains a "subtle, yet humorous, message that even parents can enjoy." In *Hunter's Big Sister,* Hunter loves playing with his sister, but she sometimes ignores him. He pesters her to get her attention, accidentally putting her in danger. Mary Elam, writing in *School Library Journal,* called *Hunter's Big Sister* "a must-read for families with siblings."

Biographical and Critical Sources

PERIODICALS

Booklist, October 1, 2001, Connie Fletcher, review of *Under a War-torn Sky,* p. 312; October 1, 2002, Stephanie Zvirin, review of *Hunter's Best Friend at School,* p. 334; August, 2003, Hazel Rochman, review of *Flying South,* p. 1982; December 1, 2004, Jennifer Mattson, review of *Annie, between the States,* p. 646; September 1, 2005, Shelle Rosenfeld, review of *Hunter and Stripe and the Soccer Showdown,* p. 119; October 1, 2006, Carolyn Phelan, review of *Give Me Liberty,* p. 51.

Bulletin of the Center for Children's Books, January, 2002, review of *Under a War-torn Sky,* p. 170.

Kirkus Reviews, June 15, 2002, review of *Hunter's Best Friend at School,* p. 879; May 1, 2003, review of *Flying South,* p. 675; October 15, 2004, review of *Annie, between the States,* p. 1005; July 1, 2005, review of *Hunter and Stripe and the Soccer Showdown,* p. 734; August 1, 2006, review of *Give Me Liberty,* p. 785; August 1, 2007, review of *Hunter's Big Sister.*

Kliatt, March, 2004, Erin Lukens Darr, review of *Under a War-torn Sky,* p. 19; May, 2006, Maureen Griffin, review of *Annie, between the States,* p. 18; May, 2008, Paula Rohrlick, review of *Give Me Liberty,* p. 20.

Publishers Weekly, July 1, 2002, review of *Hunter's Best Friend at School,* p. 78.

School Library Journal, October, 2001, Bruce Ann Shook, review of *Under a War-torn Sky,* p. 154; September, 2002, Melinda Piehler, review of *Hunter's Best Friend at School,* p. 190; May, 2003, Gerry Larson, review of *Flying South,* p. 150; November, 2004, Jane G. Connor, review of *Annie, between the States,* p. 142; August, 2005, Blair Christolon, review of *Under a War-torn Sky,* p. 50; September, 2005, Blair Christolon, review of *Hunter and Stripe and the Soccer Showdown,* p. 169; September, 2006, Kim Dare, review of *Give Me Liberty,* p. 204; September, 2007, Mary Elam, review of *Hunter's Big Sister,* p. 164.

Tribune Books (Chicago, IL), July 28, 2002, review of *Hunter's Best Friend at School,* p. 4.

Voice of Youth Advocates, December, 2001, review of *Under a War-torn Sky,* p. 356; August, 2003, review of *Flying South,* p. 223; February, 2005, Delia Culberson, review of *Annie, between the States,* p. 471.

HarperCollins Web site, http://www.harpercollins.com/ (January 15, 2009), interview with Elliott.

Laura Malone Elliott Home Page, http://www.lmelliott. com (January 15, 2009).*

*   *   *

ELLIOTT, L.M.
See ELLIOTT, Laura Malone

*   *   *

EPHRON, Delia 1944-
(Delia Brock)

Personal

Born July 12, 1944, in Los Angeles, CA; daughter of Henry (a writer) and Phoebe (a writer) Ephron; married Dan Brock (divorced, 1975); married Jerome Kass (a screenwriter), May 21, 1982; children: Julie, Adam (stepchildren). *Education:* Barnard College, B.A., 1966.

Addresses

Home—New York, NY. *E-mail*—Frannieinpieces@aol. com.

Career

Writer and film producer. *New York* magazine, New York, NY, writer, 1975-78.

Writings

(With Lorraine Bodger, under name Delia Brock) *The Adventurous Crocheter,* Simon & Schuster (New York, NY), 1972.

(With Lorraine Bodger, under name Delia Brock) *Gladrags: Redesigning, Remaking, Refitting All Your Old Clothes,* Simon & Schuster (New York, NY), 1975.

How to Eat like a Child, and Other Lessons in Not Being a Grown-up (also see below), Viking (New York, NY), 1978.

(With Lorraine Bodger) *Crafts for All Seasons,* Universe Books (New York, NY), 1980.

Teenage Romance; or, How to Die of Embarrassment, Viking (New York, NY), 1981.

Santa and Alex, Little, Brown (Boston, MA), 1983.

Funny Sauce: Us, the Ex, the Ex's New Mate, the New Mate's Ex, and the Kids, Viking (New York, NY), 1986.

(With John Forster and Judith Kahan) *How to Eat like a Child, and Other Lessons in Not Being a Grown-up* (musical; based on Ephron's book), Samuel French (New York, NY), 1986.

"Do I Have to Say Hello?": Aunt Delia's Manners Quiz for Kids and Their Grownups, Viking (New York, NY), 1989.

The Girl Who Changed the World, Ticknor & Fields (New York, NY), 1993.

Hanging Up (also see below), Putnam (New York, NY), 1995.

Big City Eyes, Putnam (New York, NY), 2000.

Frannie in Pieces, illustrated by Chad W. Beckerman, Laura Geringer Books (New York, NY), 2007.

Contributor to magazines, including *Vogue, Esquire, Glamour, Redbook, Cosmopolitan, House and Garden, Savvy, California, New York Times Magazine,* and *New York.*

SCREENPLAYS

(With sister, Nora Ephron) *This Is My Life* (based on the novel by Meg Wolitzer), Twentieth Century-Fox, 1992.

(With Nora Ephron; and executive producer) *Mixed Nuts,* TriStar, 1994.

(With Nora Ephron, Pete Dexter, and Jim Quinlan; and executive producer) *Michael,* New Line Cinema, 1996.

(With Nora Ephron; and executive producer) *You've Got Mail,* Warner Brothers, 1998.

(With Nora Ephron; and executive producer) *Hanging Up* (based on Ephron's novel), Columbia Tristar, 2000.

(With Nora Ephron) *Bewitched,* Columbia Pictures, 2005.

(With Elizabeth Chandler) *The Sisterhood of the Traveling Pants* (based on the novel by Ann Brashares), Columbia Pictures, 2005.

Adaptations

How to Eat like a Child was adapted for television by the National Broadcasting Corp. (NBC), 1982.

Sidelights

Novelist and screenwriter Delia Ephron is the author of numerous works of fiction and nonfiction for adults and children, including *How to Eat like a Child, and Other Lessons in Not Being a Grown-up, Big City Eyes,* and *Frannie in Pieces.* "I just love great storytellers," Ephron stated in an interview on the Random House Web site. "When I was a child I remember sitting in a chair with a plate of chocolate-chip cookies and reading *Anne of Green Gables* by L.M. Montgomery. I was swept away. As an adult, I want to pass on that feeling—of spending an afternoon someplace else. I want to keep you in the chair eating chocolate-chip cookies."

Ephron is best known for her collaborations with her sister, Nora Ephron, on such films as *Michael, You've Got Mail,* and *Bewitched.* While Nora is perhaps the more famous of the two, both sisters concede that it is Delia whose humor and ability with one-liners enlivens the scripts that the two produce together. According to London *Times* correspondent Martyn Palmer, the Ephron sisters "know how to exploit a winning formula" to produce "box-office gold."

Ephron calls screenwriting the "family business." Her parents, Henry and Phoebe Ephron, were collaborators whose screen credits include the musicals *Carousel, There's No Business like Show Business,* and *Daddy Long Legs.* Dinner-table conversations often included contests to see who could tell the funniest story, and the girls learned to leaven serious situations with a touch of irony as well. "Our mother was fond of telling us that 'no matter what happens, it's all copy'," Delia recalled to Martyn Palmer in the London *Times.* This sage advice has applied to Delia Ephron's career as both a print and a screen writer.

In the late 1980s Ephron began working with her sister on film projects, and she has been involved in one way or another with most of Nora Ephron's movies. By the mid-1990s the two were collaborating in earnest, living as neighbors in a Manhattan apartment complex and creating scripts in Nora's home office. The Ephron sisters' most successful movies include *Michael, You've Got Mail,* and *Bewitched,* all of which were directed by Nora.

Based on the bestselling novel by Ann Brashares, *The Sisterhood of the Traveling Pants* was adapted for the screen by Ephron and Elizabeth Chandler. The film centers on a quartet of teenage girls who make an unusual discovery while shopping at a thrift store. The girls find a pair of jeans that remarkably fits all four of them perfectly, despite their very different body types, and they decide that the pants must be magical. Since the lifelong friends will be spending their first vacations apart that summer, they agree to share the jeans, sending them around the globe. *The Sisterhood of the Traveling Pants* earned strong critical praise. Ephron and Chandler "capture the intense bonding that teenage girls have a gift for—calling your three best friends to breathlessly report every detail of your day; talking comfortably about sex even when you're spreading misinformation; being there 24/7 for one another," Ruthe Stein wrote in the *San Francisco Chronicle.* According to *Variety* reviewer Dennis Harvey, "This sentimental-in-a-good-way chronicle . . . mixes satisfying dollops of fun, tears, travel, romance and lesson-learning in a handsome package whose two hours pass faster than many a grownup entertainment."

Before becoming known for her films, Ephron wrote several humorous nonfiction books that appeal to both young people and adults. In *How to Eat like a Child, and Other Lessons in Not Being a Grown-up,* she covers such topics as birthdays, Christmas, sibling torture, car rides, school, and pets. Her *Teenage Romance; or, How to Die of Embarrassment* offers wry advice for the insecure teenager on dating, hiding pimples and other social embarrassments. *"Do I Have to Say Hello?": Aunt Delia's Manners Quiz for Kids and Their Grown-ups* is an overview of manners for children that lists obviously inappropriate behavior choices in quiz fashion, allowing the reader to choose which answer is best.

Funny Sauce: Us, the Ex, the Ex's New Mate, the New Mate's Ex, and the Kids wrings comedy from the phenomenon of blended families and is based on Ephron's own experience of helping to raise two stepchildren. In a *New York Times Book Review* appraisal of the book, Cyra McFadden concluded: "Whether she's firing off one-liners or writing in a quieter, more thoughtful voice, Delia Ephron's book is engaging. The new extended family is indeed a 'funny sauce.' This brief treatise on the subject manages to be both funny and wise." A *Publishers Weekly* critic likewise remarked that readers "will laugh loudly, but probably wince too as they recognize their households."

Having honed her ability to create characters and plots in movies, Ephron turned to novel-writing with some success. Her first adult novel, *Hanging Up,* applies her humor to a more serious topic, a middle-aged woman's relationship with her dying father. Eve Mozell, the heroine of the story, finds her already challenging life complicated still more when her difficult father begins "dwindling." Eve cannot call upon her sisters for help, and she finds herself spending more and more time talking to her father on the telephone. In the *Chicago Tribune,* Tananarive Due praised Ephron's "gift for the particulars and nuances of dialogue" which "keeps *Hanging Up* near its goal as a weighty work with a quirky sense of humor." "Among the many pleasures of *Hanging Up* is the way grave and ludicrous events ricochet off one another, scattering sentiment and anger and hilarity in all directions," wrote Eric Kraft in the *New York Times Book Review.* The critic added that the novel "is honest and deeply felt, and Ms. Ephron's comic timing is flawless. Eve is a likable, even admirable character, perplexed by life but equal to it." Ephron also wrote the screenplay for the film version of *Hanging Up.*

Ephron's novel *Big City Eyes* offers a humorous take on the family dynamic of a single parent raising an adolescent child. Journalist Lily Davis buys a house in a small Long Island town in order to remove her son from dangerous influences in Manhattan. At first the neurotic Lily finds her new surroundings comforting, but life intrudes—her son's new girlfriend speaks only in Klingon (a *Star Trek* language), she becomes attracted to a married man, and perhaps she has also witnessed a murder. "As a narrator, Lily is good company, and Ephron's always readable prose moves nicely between observant, wisecracking humor and an atmospheric creepiness," declared Maria Russo in the *New York Times Book Review.* In *Booklist,* Danise Hoover called *Big City Eyes* an "entertaining, if slightly silly, novel that reads like a movie concept," and a *Kirkus Reviews* contributor deemed the tale "good, clean, lighthearted fun with a moral ending."

Ephron turns to young-adult fiction in *Frannie in Pieces,* which focuses on a sensitive teenager dealing with the sudden, unexpected death of her artistic father. While searching through her dad's effects, Frannie discovers an elaborate jigsaw puzzle he created for her. After she

assembles the puzzle, Frannie appears to enter the image, where she reconnects with her father and learns valuable life lessons. Though some reviewers found the blend of fantasy and reality confusing, several complimented the work. "Ephron tells her story leisurely," noted a contributor in *Kirkus Reviews,* and Myrna Marler, writing in *Kliatt,* stated that the author's "characterizations are sly, and the messiness of human relationships, the process of grief, and the theme of changing perspectives are all examined in the novel."

Biographical and Critical Sources

PERIODICALS

Booklist, February 15, 2000, Danise Hoover, review of *Big City Eyes,* p. 1050; November 1, 2007, Ilene Cooper review of *Frannie in Pieces,* p. 40.

Chicago Tribune, August 11, 1995, Tananarive Due, review of *Hanging Up,* p. 3.

Houston Chronicle, December 31, 1998, Barry Koltnow, "Along with 'Mail,' Film's Writers Got Ryan, Hanks," p. 3.

Kirkus Reviews, July, 2000, review of *Big City Eyes,* p. 321; September 1, 2007, review of *Frannie in Pieces.*

Kliatt, September, 2007, Myrna Marler, review of *Frannie in Pieces,* p. 11.

Los Angeles Times, June 1, 2005, Carino Chocano, review of *The Sisterhood of the Traveling Pants.*

New York Times Book Review, October 12, 1986, Cyra McFadden, "Sharper than Lots of Serpents' Teeth," p. 13; July 23, 1995, Eric Kraft, "Daddy Dearest," p. 8; May 21, 2000, Maria Russo, review of *Big City Eyes.*

People, December 21, 1998, review of *You've Got Mail,* p. 31.

Publishers Weekly, March 6, 2000, review of *Big City Eyes,* p. 79; September 24, 2007, review of *Frannie in Pieces,* p. 73.

Time, February 28, 2000, Richard Schickel, review of *Hanging Up* (film), p. 94.

Times (London, England), February 13, 1999, Martyn Palmer, "Dream Team," p. 42.

Variety, December 14, 1998, Lael Loewenstein, review of *You've Got Mail,* p. 130; May 30, 2005, Dennis Harvey, review of *The Sisterhood of the Traveling Pants;* June 17, 2005, Brian Lowry, review of *Bewitched.*

ONLINE

Delia Ephron Home Page, http://www.deliaephron.com (February 1, 2009).

Random House Web site, http://www.randomhouse.com/ (February 1, 2009), "A Conversation with Delia Ephron."*

F

FERRI, Giuliano 1965-

Personal

Born 1965, in Pesaro, Italy; married Francesca Bosca. *Education:* Instituto d'Arte di Urbino (Italy), degree (animation).

Addresses

Home—Pesaro, Italy.

Career

Illustrator and fine artist. *Exhibitions:* Works exhibited at galleries and museums, including Pompidou Center, Paris, France; and Itabashi Art Museum, Tokyo, Japan.

Writings

SELF-ILLUSTRATED

Paul Quappe, Minedition (Bargteheide, Germany), 2007, translation adapted by Charise Myngheer as *Little Tad Grows Up,* Minedition (New York, NY), 2007.

ILLUSTRATOR

Francesca Bosca, *Cammina, Cammina,* Edizioni Aan Paolo, 1991, translated by Philip Hawthorn as *Caspar and the Star,* Lion Publishing (Oxford, England), 1991.

Martha Whitmore Hickman, *And God Created Squash: How the World Began,* Albert Whitman (Morton Grove, IL), 1993.

Martha Whitmore Hickman, *A Baby Born in Bethlehem,* Albert Whitman (Morton Grove, IL), 1999.

Michael McCarthy, reteller, *The Story of Noah and the Ark,* Barefoot Books (New York, NY), 2001.

Francesca Bosca, *The Apple King,* translated by J. Alison James, North-South Books (New York, NY), 2001.

Francesca Bosca, *Christmas Cakes,* translated by J. Alison James, North-South Books (New York, NY), 2003.

K.T. Hao, *One Pizza, One Penny,* translated by Roxanne Hsu Feldman, Cricket Books (Chicago, IL), 2003.

Michael McCarthy, reteller, *The Story of Daniel in the Lions' Den,* Barefoot Books (New York, NY), 2003.

Anne Marie Sullivan, *Albert Einstein,* Mason Crest (Philadelphia, PA), 2003.

K.T. Hao, *Little Stone Buddha,* Purple Bear Books (New York, NY), 2005.

K.T. Hao and Byung-Gyu Kim, *The 100th Customer,* Purple Bear Books (New York, NY), 2005.

Francesca Bosca, *The Three Grasshoppers,* Purple Bear Books (New York, NY), 2006.

Rachel W.N. Brown, *Small Camel Follows the Star,* Albert Whitman (Morton Grove, IL), 2007.

Biographical and Critical Sources

PERIODICALS

Booklist, March 15, 1993, Julie Corsaro, review of *And God Created Squash: How the World Began,* p. 1359; September 1, 1999, Susan Dove Lempke, review of *A Baby Born in Bethlehem,* p. 148; April 1, 2001, John Peters, review of *The Apple King,* p. 1476; October 1, 2001, Ellen Mandel, review of *The Story of Noah and the Ark,* p. 338; June 1, 2003, Ilene Cooper, review of *The Story of Daniel in the Lions' Den,* p. 1782; October 15, 2005, Gillian Engberg, review of *Little Stone Buddha,* p. 57; May 15, 2006, Gillian Engberg, review of *The Three Grasshoppers,* p. 48.

Bulletin of the Center for Children's Books, December, 1991, review of *Caspar and the Star,* p. 85; November, 1999, review of *A Baby Born in Bethlehem,* p. 95.

Kirkus Reviews, August 1, 2001, review of *The Story of Noah and the Ark,* p. 1128.

Publishers Weekly, March 15, 1993, review of *And God Created Squash,* p. 85; September 27, 1999, review of *A Baby Born in Bethlehem,* p. 62; March 19, 2001, re-

view of *The Apple King,* p. 98; November 24, 2003, review of *One Pizza, One Penny,* p. 63; October 22, 2007, review of *Small Camel Follows the Star,* p. 54.

School Library Journal, May, 1993, Patricia Dooley, review of *And God Created Squash,* p. 85; July, 2001, Sheryl L. Shipley, review of *The Apple King,* p. 73; November, 2001, Kathy Piehl, review of *The Story of Noah and the Ark,* p. 147; May, 2003, Linda Beck, review of *The Story of Daniel in the Lions' Den,* p. 138; March, 2006, Coop Renner, review of *Little Stone Buddha,* p. 190; August, 2006, Elaine Lesh Morgan, review of *The Three Grasshoppers,* p. 74; September 15, 2007, Gillian Engberg, review of *Small Camel Follows the Star,* p. 69.

ONLINE

Giuliano Ferri Home Page, http://www.giulianoferri.com (January 15, 2009).*

* * *

FINE, Anne 1947-

Personal

Born December 7, 1947, in Leicester, England; daughter of Brian (a chief scientific experimental officer) and Mary Laker; married Kit Fine (a university professor), 1968 (divorced, 1988); children: Ione, Cordelia. *Education:* University of Warwick, B.A. (with honors), 1968.

Addresses

Home—County Durham, England. *Agent*—David Higham Associates, Ltd., 5-8 Lower John St., Golden Square, London W1R 4HA, England.

Career

Writer. English teacher at Cardinal Wiseman Girls' Secondary School, 1968-70; Oxford Committee for Famine Relief, Oxford, England, assistant information officer, 1970-71; Saughton Jail, Edinburgh, Scotland, teacher, 1971-72; freelance writer, 1973—. Volunteer for Amnesty International.

Awards, Honors

London *Guardian*/Kestrel Award nominations, 1978, for *The Summer-House Loon,* 1983, for *The Granny Project,* and 1987, for *Madame Doubtfire;* Scottish Arts Council Book Award, 1986, for *The Killjoy; Observer* Prize for Teenage Fiction nomination, 1987, for *Madame Doubtfire;* Parents' Choice award, 1988, for *Alias Madame Doubtfire;* Smarties (6-8) Award, and Carnegie Highly Commended designation, both 1990, both for *Bill's New Frock;* Carnegie Medal, 1989, and *Guardian* Award for Children's Fiction, 1990, both for *Goggle-eyes; Publishing News* Children's Author of the Year designation, British Book Awards, 1990, 1993, runner-

Anne Fine (Reproduced by permission.)

up, 1991; Notable Book designation, American Library Association (ALA), and International Reading Association Young-Adult Choice citation, both 1991, both for *My War with Goggle-eyes;* Carnegie Medal, 1992, and Whitbread Children's Novel award, 1993, both for *Flour Babies;* Whitbread Children's Book of the Year, 1996, and ALA Notable Book designation, and *Booklist* Award for Youth Fiction, both 1997, all for *The Tulip Touch;* Hans Christian Andersen Award British nominee, 1998; named children's laureate of Great Britain, 2001-03; Carnegie Medal highly commended citation, 2002, for *Up on Cloud Nine; Boston Globe/Horn Book* Award, 2003, for *The Jamie and Angus Stories;* Royal Society of Literature, fellow, 2003; named to Order of the British Empire, 2003; D.Litt., University of Warwick, 2005; Carnegie Medal shortlist, 2007, for *The Road of Bones;* Nestlé Children's Book Award Silver Medal, 2007, for *Ivan the Terrible;* D.Let., University of Teesside, 2007.

Writings

JUVENILE FICTION

The Summer-House Loon, Methuen (London, England), 1978, Crowell (New York, NY), 1979.

The Other, Darker Ned, Methuen (London, England), 1979.

The Stone Menagerie, Methuen (London, England), 1980.

Round behind the Ice-House, Methuen (London, England), 1981.

The Granny Project, Farrar, Straus & Giroux (New York, NY), 1983.

Scaredy-Cat, illustrated by Vanessa Julian-Ottie, Heinemann (London, England), 1985, new edition, illustrated by Nick Ward, Egmont (London, England), 2002.

Anneli the Art Hater, Methuen (London, England), 1986.

Madame Doubtfire, Hamish Hamilton (London, England), 1987, published as *Alias Madame Doubtfire,* Little, Brown (Boston, MA), 1988.

Crummy Mummy and Me, illustrated by David Higham, Deutsch (London, England), 1988.

A Pack of Liars, Hamish Hamilton (London, England), 1988.

My War with Goggle-eyes, Little, Brown (Boston, MA), 1989, published as *Goggle eyes,* Hamish Hamilton (London, England), 1989.

Stranger Danger?, illustrated by Jean Baylis, Hamish Hamilton (London, England), 1989.

Bill's New Frock, illustrated by Philippe Dupasquier, Methuen (London, England), 1989.

A Sudden Puff of Glittering Smoke (also see below), illustrated by Adriano Gon, Picadilly Press (London, England), 1989.

Only a Show, illustrated by Valerie Littlewood, Hamish Hamilton (London, England), 1990.

A Sudden Swirl of Icy Wind (also see below), illustrated by David Higham, Picadilly Press (London, England), 1990.

The Country Pancake, illustrated by Philippe Dupasquier, Methuen (London, England), 1990, new edition published as *Saving Miss Mirabelle,* Egmont (London, England), 2007.

Poor Monty, illustrated by Clara Vulliamy, Clarion Books (New York, NY), 1991, new edition, illustrated by Kevin Evans, Egmont (London, England), 2002.

A Sudden Glow of Gold (also see below), Picadilly Press (London, England), 1991.

The Worst Child I Ever Had, illustrated by Clara Vulliamy, Hamish Hamilton (London, England), 1991.

Design-a-Pram, Heinemann (London, England), 1991.

The Book of the Banshee, Hamish Hamilton (London, England), 1991, Joy Street (Boston, MA), 1992.

The Same Old Story Every Year, Hamish Hamilton (London, England), 1992.

The Genie Trilogy (contains *A Sudden Puff of Glittering Smoke, A Sudden Swirl of Icy Wind,* and *A Sudden Glow of Gold*), Mammoth (London, England), 1992.

The Angel of Nitshill Road, illustrated by K. Aldous, Methuen (London, England), 1992.

The Haunting of Pip Parker, Walker (New York, NY), 1992.

Flour Babies, Hamish Hamilton (London, England), 1992, Little, Brown (Boston, MA), 1994.

Chicken Gave It to Me, illustrated by Philippe Dupasquier, Methuen (London, England), 1993, published as *The Chicken Gave It to Me,* illustrated by Cynthia Fisher, Joy Street (Boston, MA), 1993.

The Diary of a Killer Cat, illustrated by Steve Cox, Puffin (London, England), 1994, Farrar, Straus, & Giroux (New York, NY), 2006.

Press Play, Picadilly Press (London, England), 1994.

Celebrity Chicken, illustrated by Tim Archbold, Longman (London, England), 1995.

Step by Wicked Step, Hamish Hamilton (London, England), 1995, Little, Brown (Boston, MA), 1996.

Jennifer's Diary, illustrated by Kate Aldous, 1996, Farrar, Straus & Giroux (New York, NY), 2007.

Keep It in the Family, Penguin (New York, NY), 1996.

Countdown, illustrated by David Higham, Heinemann (London, England), 1996, new edition, illustrated by Tony Trimmer, Egmont (London, England), 2001.

How to Write Really Badly, illustrated by Philippe Dupasquier, Methuen (London, England), 1996.

Care of Henry, illustrated by Paul Howard, Walker (New York, NY), 1997.

The Tulip Touch, Little, Brown (Boston, MA), 1997.

Loudmouth Louis, illustrated by Kate Aldous, Puffin (New York, NY), 1998.

(Reteller) *The Twelve Dancing Princesses,* illustrated by Debi Gliori, Scholastic (London, England), 1998.

Ruggles, Mammoth (London, England), 1998.

Charm School, illustrated by Ros Asquith, Doubleday (New York, NY), 1999.

Roll over, Roly, illustrated by Phillippe Dupasquier, Puffin (New York, NY), 1999.

Telling Liddy: A Sour Comedy, Black Swab (London, England), 1999.

Bad Dreams, illustrated by Susan Winter, Doubleday (New York, NY), 2000.

Notso Hotso, Hamish Hamilton (London, England), 2001, Farrar, Straus & Giroux (New York, NY), 2006.

Very Different and Other Stories, Mammoth (London, England), 2001.

The Jamie and Angus Stories, illustrated by Peggy Dale, Candlewick Press (Cambridge, MA), 2002.

Up on Cloud Nine, Delacorte (New York, NY), 2002.

How to Cross the Road and Not Turn into a Pizza, Walker (New York, NY), 2002.

The True Story of Christmas, Delacorte (New York, NY), 2003, published as *The More the Merrier,* Doubleday (London, England), 2003.

Nag Club, Walker (London, England), 2004.

Frozen Billy, illustrated by Georgina McBain, Doubleday (London, England), 2004, Farrar, Straus & Giroux (New York, NY), 2006.

The Road of Bones, Doubleday (London, England), 2006, Farrar, Straus & Giroux (New York, NY), 2008.

Ivan the Terrible, illustrated by Philippe Dupasquier, Puffin (New York, NY), 2007.

Jamie and Angus Together, illustrated by Peggy Dale, Candlewick Press (Cambridge, MA), 2007.

The Return of the Killer Cat, illustrated by Steve Cox, Farrar, Straus & Giroux (New York, NY), 2007.

Fine's books have been translated into over twenty-five languages.

OTHER

The Killjoy (adult novel), Bantam (London, England), 1986, Mysterious Press (New York, NY), 1987.

Taking the Devil's Advice (adult novel), Viking (New York, NY), 1990.

In Cold Domain (adult novel), Black Swan (London, England), 1994.

Telling Liddy (adult novel), Black Swan (London, England), 1998.

Telling Tales (interview/autobiography), Mammoth (London, England), 1999.

All Bones and Lies (adult novel), Bantam (New York, NY), 2001.

(Editor) *A Shame to Miss 1* (poetry), Corgi (London, England), 2002.

(Editor) *A Shame to Miss 2* (poetry), Corgi (London, England), 2002.

(Editor) *A Shame to Miss 3* (poetry), Corgi (London, England), 2002.

Raking the Ashes (adult novel), Bantam (New York, NY), 2005.

Fly in the Ointment (adult novel), Bantam (New York, NY), 2008.

Also author of radio play *The Captain's Court Case,* 1987. Author of plays based on her books, including *Bill's New Frock, The Angel of Nitshill Road, The Granny Project, Goggle-eyes, Stranger Danger?, Flour Babies,* and *The Tulip Touch.* Contributor of short stories to periodicals.

Adaptations

Goggle-eyes was produced on cassette by Chivers Sound & Vision, 1992, and adapted as a British television series; *Alias Madame Doubtfire* was adapted as a motion picture starring Robin Williams, Sally Field, and Pierce Brosnan, Twentieth Century-Fox, 1993.

Sidelights

In such popular children's books as *Alias Madame Doubtfire, The Tulip Touch,* and *My War with Goggle-eyes,* novelist Anne Fine brings her keen comic insight to bear on family problems, particularly those caused by divorce. "I was brought up in the country, in a family of five girls, including one set of triplets," Fine once told *SATA.* "Family relationships have always interested me and it is with the close members of their families that the characters in my books are either getting, or not getting, along."

A multi-award-winning writer, Fine received one of the highest honors of her career in 2001 when she was named the United Kingdom's children's laureate for her outstanding achievement in children's literature. During her tenure, she established the Home Library Project, a Web site that offers scores of freshly designed and freely downloadable modern bookplates for children of all ages to encourage book collecting, and also published

Cover of Fine's award-winning middle-grade novel My War with Goggle-eyes, *featuring artwork by Rick Mujica.* (Copyright © 1989 by Anne Fine. All rights reserved. Reproduced by permission.)

three volumes of poetry during her three-year tenure. In 2003 Fine received yet another of her country's top honors when she was named to the Order of the British Empire.

St. James Guide to Children's Writers essayist Anthea Bell characterized Fine's style as "trenchantly witty," and called her books "20th-century comedies of manners, offering stylish entertainment to older children with a certain amount of sophistication." In addition to her books for both children and young adults, Fine is the author of several adult novels, including *Taking the Devil's Advice, In Cold Domain,* and *Raking the Ashes.*

Born in 1947, in Leicester, England, Fine exhibited a love of books and reading at an early age. Although reading and writing were enjoyable activities that came easily to her, she had no ambitions to be an author. In fact, Fine did not take writing seriously until after she had graduated from college, married, and begun to raise her family.

In her first published book, *The Summer-House Loon,* Fine presents Ione Muffet, the teenage daughter of a blind college professor who is sometimes oblivious to

his offspring. The novel portrays a single, farcical day in Ione's life as she attempts to match her father's secretary with an intelligent yet fumbling graduate student. Calling the novel "original and engaging . . . mischievous, inventive and very funny," *Times Literary Supplement* writer Peter Hollindale praised Fine's "fine emotional delicacy" as a characteristic that "sensitively captures, among all the comic upheaval, the passionate solitude of adolescence." *The Summer-House Loon* is "not just a funny book, although it is certainly that," Marcus Crouch likewise commented in *Junior Bookshelf.* "Here is a book with deep understanding, wisdom and compassion" that "tosses the reader between laughter and tears with expert dexterity."

A sequel to *The Summer-House Loon, The Other, Darker Ned* finds Ione organizing a charity benefit for famine victims. "Through [Ione's] observations of other people" in both these works, Margery Fisher noted in *Growing Point,* "we have that delighted sense of recognition which comes in reading novels whose characters burst noisily and eccentrically out of the pages." While noting that Fine's first two novels require "a certain amount of sophistication," Anthea Bell asserted in *Twentieth-Century Children's Writers* that for readers "in command of that sophistication they are stylishly lighthearted entertainment."

Reflecting Fine's concern over social issues are several novels that examine such issues as homelessness and care of the elderly. *The Stone Menagerie,* in which a boy discovers that a couple is living on the grounds of a mental hospital, is "devised with a strict economy of words, an acute sense of personality and a shrewd, ironic humour that once more shows Anne Fine to be one of the sharpest and humorous observers of the human condition writing today for the young," Fisher wrote in *Growing Point.* Using humor while "tackling the aged and infirm," *The Granny Project* "contrives to be both audacious and heart-warming," as Charles Fox remarked in *New Statesman.* The story of four siblings who conspire to keep their grandmother out of a nursing home by making her care a school assignment, *The Granny Project* is "mordantly funny, ruthlessly honest, yet compassionate in its concern," Nancy C. Hammond noted in *Horn Book.*

Alias Madame Doubtfire shines a farcical light on a serious theme: the break-up of a family. To gain more time with his children, out-of-work actor Daniel poses as Madame Doubtfire, a supremely capable housekeeper, and gets a job in his ex-wife Miranda's household. Miranda remains blind to her housekeeper's identity while the couple's children quickly catch on, leading to several amusing incidents. "Beneath the farce, the story deals with a serious subject," Mark Geller explained in his appraisal of *Alias Madame Doubtfire* for the *New York Times Book Review:* "the pain children experience when their parents divorce and then keep on battling." "The comedy of disguise allows the author to skate over the sexual hates and impulses inherent in the

situation without lessening the candour of her insights into the irreconcilable feelings of both adults and children," Margery Fisher concluded in her *Growing Point* review. "Readers of the teenage novel, weary of perfunctory blue-prints of reality, should be thankful to Anne Fine for giving them such nourishing food for thought within an entertaining piece of fiction."

For Fine, the "prime intent" of *Crummy Mummy and Me* and *A Pack of Liars* "is to make young people laugh," noted Chris Powling in the *Times Educational Supplement.* "Both exploit the standard comic techniques of taking a familiar situation, turning it on its head, and shaking it vigorously to see what giggles and insights fall into the reader's lap." *A Pack of Liars* recounts how a school assignment to write to a pen pal turns into a mystery of sorts, while *Crummy Mummy and Me* presents a role-reversal in the relationship between an irresponsible mother and her capable daughter. While Anthea Bell noted in her *Twentieth-Century Children's Writers* essay that "details of the plots . . . may sometimes seem a little farfetched in the abstract," the critic added that "the sheer comic verve" of Fine's text "carries them off." Powling agreed, commenting

Fine's novel **Alias Madame Doubtfire** *was adapted as a feature film starring Sally Field and Robin Williams.* (Copyright © 1988 by Anne Fine. All rights reserved. Reproduced by permission.)

that "once again the narrative shamelessly favours inge-nuity over plausibility on the pretty safe assumption that a reader can't complain effectively while grinning broadly." Both books, the critic concluded, "offer wel-come confirmation that humour is closer to humanity than apostles of high seriousness care to admit."

In *My War with Goggle-eyes,* Fine offers yet another "comic yet perceptive look at life after marriage," as Il-ene Cooper stated in *Booklist.* From the novel's open-ing, in which young Kitty relates to a schoolmate how her mother's boyfriend "Goggle-eyes" came into her life, "to the happy-ever-after-maybe ending, Fine con-veys a story about relationships filled with humor that does not ridicule and sensitivity that is not cloying," Susan Schuller commented in *School Library Journal.* In showing how Kitty gradually learns to accept her mother's new relationship, "Fine writes some of the funniest—and truest—family fight scenes to be found," Roger Sutton observed in the *Bulletin of the Center for Children's Books.* The resulting novel is "thoroughly delightful to read," Schuller concluded.

Step by Wicked Step also focuses on divorce and shift-ing family relationships. The novel is narrated by a suc-cession of high school-age classmates, each beginning his or her portion of the story where another has left off. Claudia, Pixie, Colin, Ralph, and Rob are on an overnight field trip and spend a stormy night in a creaky, nineteenth-century house. While exploring the house, the students find a diary written by a previous resident more than a hundred years ago. A reading of the dia-rist's entries, which describe the gradual destruction of his family due to the controlling personality of a strict stepfather, sparks a discussion of step-parents and other elements of modern family life. Each of the teens de-scribes his or her experiences of life after divorce and feels frustration, fear, and sadness. "Each storyteller has learned that those who shatter families are sometimes not good at fixing them, and that someone has to try to get along, 'step by wicked step,'" according to Jamie S. Hansen in her summary of the novel for *Voice of Youth Advocates.* Praising *Step by Wicked Step* as a "surefire success," *School Library Journal* contributor Julie Cum-mins noted that Fine's protagonists "are genuine, their stories are poignant, and the book as a whole is affect-ing without being maudlin, didactic, or biblio therapeu-tic."

In *The Book of the Banshee,* Estelle Flowers has be-come a teenager, and the Flowers home has become a war zone, according to brother Will, who narrates the middle-grade novel. With his parents distraught over Estelle's constant histrionics, Will fends for himself, re-counting a saga that *Horn Book* contributor Hanna B. Zeiger maintained "will bring many a laugh to the reader." "Estelle's adolescent angst and injuries" are handled capably, wrote *Bulletin of the Center for Chil-dren's Books* contributor Roger Strong, and "when it comes to family fights," Fine always provides her read-ers with "the best seat in the house." In the opinion of

School Library Journal contributor Connie Tyrrell Burns, *The Book of the Banshee* "has some of the fun-niest fight scenes in YA literature," while also operating as "a well-crafted work with layers of meaning and se-rious themes richly interwoven with the more comic ones."

Winner of several awards, including the prestigious Carnegie Medal, Fine's young-adult novel *Flour Babies* examines the flip-side of the parent-child relationship. Inspired by a magazine article describing a class project to make teens appreciate the hard work involved in par-enthood, the book finds underachieving teen Simon Martin and the rest of his class of troublemakers each assigned to care for a six-pound sack of flour as if it was a live infant. Along with the rest of his class, Si-mon ridicules the idea at first, but gradually begins to transfer the caring behavior he was never given as a child to his flour-sack "baby." As an essayist noted in *Children's Books and Their Creators,* Fine's "hulking teenage protagonist . . . reaches new levels of self-awareness and is perhaps the most appealing character to be found in any of the author's books." While imbu-ing *Flour Babies* with her characteristic humor, Fine also "takes a down-to-earth scenario and, like her pro-tagonist, turns it into an extraordinary adventure in liv-ing and learning," in the opinion of a *Publishers Weekly* contributor.

The Tulip Touch finds its author navigating "new terri-tory," according to Anthea Bell in her *St. James Guide to Children's Writers* essay on Fine. "Gone is the wry humour, although the sharp detailed observation of hu-man behavior remains." In this highly praised work, Fine tells the story of Natalie, who lives in rural England where her family manages a grand hotel called the Palace which caters to well-heeled out-of-towners. With companions her age at a premium, Natalie is ea-ger to become friends with Tulip, a local farm girl whose eccentric behavior eventually reveals a bitter, dark side to her personality. Only gradually does self-effacing Natalie realize she has lost confidence in her-self, as a result of her participation in the increasingly dangerous games initiated by her unusual and strong-willed new friend. "This complex and compelling book hits hard at a society which is aware of child abuse that is just within the limits of the law and so, feeling pow-erless to act, does nothing about it," explained *Magpies* reviewer Joan Zahnleiter, the critic describing Tulip as a victim of a "sadistic father," "neglected and deeply disturbed with a need to possess and humiliate." Noting that Fine only hints at the state of affairs that brought Tulip to her current emotional state, *Booklist* reviewer Hazel Rochman wrote that, "with thrilling intensity, she dramatizes the attraction the good girl feels for the dan-gerous outsider. . . . [Fine's] message grows right out of an action-packed story that not only humanizes the bully but also reveals the ugly secrets of the respect-able." Concluding her laudatory review of *The Tulip Touch* in the *Bulletin of the Center for Children's Books,* Deborah Stevenson noted that "while many children's

Fine's middle-grade novel The Tulip Touch, *featuring artwork by Joe Baker.* (Laurel-Leaf Books, 1999. Used by permission of Random House Children's Books, a division of Random House, Inc.)

books underestimate the intensity of youthful friendship and the seriousness of its repercussions, this one goes right to the heart of the matter."

Described by *Horn Book* contributor Vicky Smith as "a piece of Edwardiana with just a touch of the macabre," Fine's middle-grade novel *Frozen Billy* introduces readers to siblings Clarrie and Will. Since their father left for Australia to find his fortune, and their mother was wrongfully arrested in Ireland, the two have been living with Uncle Len. A well-meaning man who earns his living as a ventriloquist, Len is also an alcoholic with a penchant for gambling. When he discovers young Will's knack for imitating voices, Len hits upon a fraudulent scheme wherein the boy pretends to be a second dummy and performs onstage. As Will becomes increasingly caught up in his stage persona, older sister Clarrie finds her surreal family situation disturbing, and looks for help in regaining a stable family. *Frozen Billy* "paints an effective picture of a family on the edge," noted Smith, and "As usual," concluded *School Library Jour-*

nal contributor B. Allison Gray, "Fine creates fascinating characters, an intense impression of time and place, and a fast-paced plot."

Fine takes readers to the Soviet Union under the government of Josef Stalin in the young-adult novel *The Road of Bones*. In its first few decades, communism has progressed through several generations, and now ten-year-old Yuri sees that the corrupt single-leader government has begun engaging in widespread purges. When he speaks out, Yuri attracts unwanted attention that forces him to flee north to the inhospitable Russian steppe, and he is eventually sentenced to work in a Siberian mining camp. Writing that the novel successfully depicts the "desolation, cold, hunger, and hardship" of life under totalitarianism, Cara von Wrangel Kinsley added in *School Library Journal* that *The Road of Bones* provides "a good segue into discussions of both historical Communist Russia and modern society." Praising Fine's ability to create a compelling protagonist in Yuri, a *Kirkus Reviews* writer added that "the crushing atmosphere of Stalinist Russia is brilliantly evoked" in the author's "dark, intelligent novel." "Although the rise of movements against the government at first appear to offer Yuri hope," observed a *Publishers Weekly,* Fine's conclusion in *The Road of Bones* "underscores the notion that history repeats itself."

Named a Carnegie Medal highly commended book, *Up on Cloud Nine* focuses on the relationship between Stolly and Ian, two very different teenage boys. The book opens as Stolly lies unconscious in the hospital, his body bruised and broken after a fall from an upper-story window. His best friend, Ian, suspects the fall was no accident, however, and he begins to sort through his memories in an effort to determine if his friend attempted suicide. "The narrative shifts smoothly between past and present as it pieces together anecdotes of the boys' shared time," noted a critic in *Publishers Weekly;* readers learn of Stolly's penchant for Ouija boards, his uncanny ability to invent stories, and his distrust of authority. The teen's "philosophical viewpoint and way of life are the antithesis of Ian's solid practicality, and he expresses feelings that others are afraid to say," observed Carol A. Edwards in *School Library Journal.* When Stolly finally awakens, a *Kirkus Reviews* critic explained, "the author has brought readers so close to him and to those who love him that the question of whether he fell by accident or not has become, not irrelevant, but unimportant." According to *Horn Book* contributor Peter D. Sieruta, "Fine outdoes herself here, creating a truly singular character—a wildly imaginative boy with outsized emotions and manic enthusiasms who also happens to have a self-destructive streak."

In addition to more-serious fiction, Fine has written many illustrated stories for younger children. Here she focuses primarily on "that period during which the stability of childhood, when almost all decisions are made by others, is giving way to a wider world," as she once explained to *SATA.* "A sense of the need for a sort of

personal elbow-room is developing, and people outside the family seem to be showing other ways to go. Growing through to a full autonomy is, for anyone, a long and doggy business, and for some more sabotaged than others by their nature or upbringing, it can seem impossible. I try to show that the battle through the chaos and confusions is worthwhile and can, at times, be seen as very funny."

In both *The Jamie and Angus Stories* and *Jamie and Angus Together* Fine introduces a young boy and his stuffed toy bull Angus. As soon as Jamie spots Angus in the window of a toy store in *The Jamie and Angus Stories,* he knows he has found the perfect companion. The pair becomes inseparable; Jamie builds a farm from fabric and Popsicle sticks for his new friend and clings to Angus even after a washing machine accident turns the toy from silky white to scruffy gray. Further adventures, recounted in the sequel, find Jamie guarding Angus from a playmate who treats toys roughly, but also learning to detach from his special toy friend in favor of human company. "The breezy, often humorous repartee between the lad and the adults in his life, plus the authentic interplay of boy and toy, keep the narrative

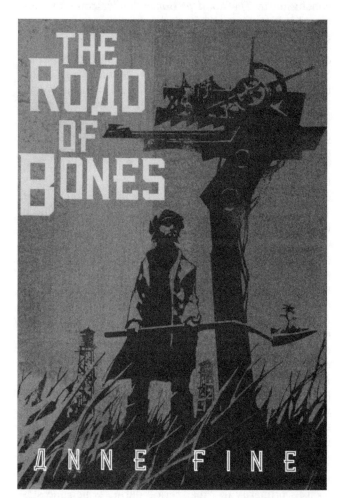

Fine turns to recent history in her novel **The Road of Bones,** *featuring artwork by Daniel Zezelj.* (Jacket design copyright © 2008 by Jay Colvin. Jacket art copyright © 2008 by Daniel Zezelj. Used by permission of Farrar, Straus & Giroux, LLC.)

moving at a sprightly clip," noted a *Publishers Weekly* contributor in describing *The Jamie and Angus Stories,* and *Horn Book* critic Susan P. Bloom commented that Fine "addresses young children in a natural read-aloud voice and is sentimental in only the right ways." Noting the similar accomplishment of *Jamie and Angus Together,* Susan Dove Lempke noted in the same periodical that "Fine always maintains Jamie's complete believability, conveying his perceptiveness and empathy side-by-side with his limited perspective."

Two other humorous chapter books created by Fine for early elementary readers are *The Diary of a Killer Cat* and *The Return of the Killer Cat. The Diary of a Killer Cat* contains the self-satisfied scriblings of a housecat named Tuffy, who stands accused of killing not only a bird and a field mouse, but also Thumper, the pet rabbit from next door. When his family places him in the care of a neighboring vicar in *The Return of the Killer Cat,* Tuffy the tabby cat hides at the neighbor's house but must endure the most terrible humiliation of all: being dressed up in baby clothes. In *School Library Journal* Diane Eddington cited the source of the cat's off-kilter wittiness as Tuffy's honest "confusion about reactions to his natural behavior," confusions that give rise to humor in "his defensive narrative." Both *The Diary of a Killer Cat* and *The Return of the Killer Cat* are highlighted by amusing line drawings by Steve Cox, resulting in "the same delicious wickedness" Fine exhibited in *Alias Madame Doubtfire,* according to Rochman in *Booklist.* Reviewing *The Return of the Killer Cat,* Ilene Cooper wrote in the same periodical that Fine's engaging tale will "resonate with kids who also like to have their own way."

In an essay she contributed to the *Something about the Author Autobiography Series,* Fine summarized her feelings about the power of fiction: "It changes people, and it changes lives. When we are young, we read about the miller's daughter spinning her straw to gold. And that, I believe, is the writer's great privilege. We only gain from letting our childhoods echo down the years, and we're allowed to spend our lifetimes spinning straw."

Biographical and Critical Sources

BOOKS

An Interview with Anne Fine, Mammoth (London, England), 1999.
Children's Books and Their Creators, Houghton (Boston, MA), 1995.
Children's Literature Review, Volume 25, Gale (Detroit, MI), 1991.
St. James Guide to Children's Writers, fifth edition, St. James Press (Detroit, MI), 1999.
Something about the Author Autobiography Series, Volume 15, Gale (Detroit, MI), 1993.

Fine turns to a younger audience in **The Jamie and Angus Stories,** *featuring artwork by Penny Dale.* (Illustration copyright © 2002 by Penny Dale. Reproduced by permission of the publisher, Candlewick Press, Inc., Somerville, MA, on behalf of Walker Books Ltd., London.)

PERIODICALS

Booklist, April 15, 1989, Ilene Cooper, review of *My War with Goggle-eyes,* p. 1465; September 15, 1997, Hazel Rochman, review of *The Tulip Touch,* p. 230; January 1, 1998, Hazel Rochman, "British Author Wins *Booklist,* Award for Youth Fiction," pp. 810-811; May 1, 2001, Stephanie Zvirin, review of *The Tulip Touch,* p. 1610; June 1, 2002, Ilene Cooper, review of *Up on Cloud Nine,* p. 1716; November 15, 2002, Julie Cummins, review of *The Jamie and Angus Stories,* pp. 609-610; September 1, 2003, Ilene Cooper, review of *The True Story of Christmas,* p. 133; May 1, 2004, Carolyn Phelan, review of *Ruggles,* pp. 1562-1563; January 1, 2006, Hazel Rochman, review of *The Diary of a Killer Cat,* p. 111; September 1, 2006, Michael Cart, review of *Frozen Billy,* p. 125; March 15, 2007, Ilene Cooper, review of *The Return of the Killer Cat,* p. 47; June 1, 2007, Suzanne Harold, review of *Jamie and Angus Together,* p. 81; June 1, 2008, Jennifer Mattson, review of *The Road of Bones,* p. 67.

Bulletin of the Center for Children's Books, April, 1988, Roger Sutton, review of *Alias Madame Doubtfire,* p. 155; May, 1989, Roger Sutton, review of *My War with Goggle-eyes,* p. 222; September, 1997, Deborah Stevenson, review of *The Tulip Touch,* pp. 3-4; October, 2002, review of *The Jamie and Angus Stories,* p. 55; April, 2006, Deborah Stevenson, review of *The Diary of a Killer Cat,* p. 351; December, 2006, Elizabeth Bush, review of *Frozen Billy,* p. 169.

Growing Point, September, 1980, Margery Fisher, review of *The Stone Menagerie,* p. 3756; September, 1987, Margery Fisher, review of *Madame Doubtfire,* p. 4858; May, 1990, Margery Fisher, review of *The Summer-House Loon* and *The Other, Darker Ned,* pp. 5343-5344.

Horn Book, October, 1983, Nancy C. Hammond, review of *The Granny Project,* p. 573; March-April, 1992, Hanna B. Zeiger, review of *The Book of the Banshee,* p. 209; July-August, 2002, Peter D. Sieruta, review of *Up on Cloud Nine,* pp. 459-460; January-February, 2003, Susan P. Bloom, review of *The Jamie and Angus Stories,* pp. 71-72; November-December, 2003, Martha V. Parravano, review of *The True Story of Christmas,* p. 743; January-February, 2004, transcript of Fine's *Boston Globe/Horn Book* acceptance speech, pp. 27-31; November-December, 2006, Vicky Smith, review of *Frozen Billy,* p. 708; September-October, 2007, Susan Dove Lempke, review of *Jamie and Angus Together,* p. 574.

Junior Bookshelf, August, 1978, Marcus Crouch, review of *The Summer-House Loon,* pp. 202-203.

Kirkus Reviews, May 15, 2002, review of *Up on Cloud Nine,* p. 732; August 1, 2002, review of *The Jamie and Angus Stories,* p. 1128; November 1, 2003, review of *The True Story of Christmas,* p. 1316; March 15, 2004, review of *Ruggles,* p. 268; January 1, 2006, review of *The Diary of a Killer Cat,* p. 40; November 1, 2006, review of *Frozen Billy,* p. 1122; April 1, 2007, review of *The Return of the Killer Cat;* June 1, 2007, review of *Jamie and Angus Together;* April 1, 2008, review of *The Road of Bones.*

Magpies, March, 1997, Joan Zahnleiter, review of *The Tulip Touch,* p. 36.

New Statesman, December 2, 1983, Charles Fox, "Beyond Tact," p. 26.

New York Times Book Review, May 1, 1988, Mark Geller, review of *Alias Madame Doubtfire,* p. 34.

Publishers Weekly, March 21, 1994, review of *Flour Babies,* p. 73; June 17, 2002, review of *Up on Cloud Nine,* pp. 65-66; July 29, 2002, review of *The Jamie and Angus Stories,* p. 72; September 22, 2003, review of *The True Story of Christmas,* p. 72; February 20, 2006, review of *The Diary of a Killer Cat,* p. 157; November 27, 2006, review of *Frozen Billy,* p. 51; May 12, 2008, review of *The Road of Bones,* p. 55.

School Library Journal, May 1989, Susan Schuller, review of *My War with Goggle-eyes,* p. 104; December, 1991, Connie Tyrrell Burns, review of *The Book of the Banshee,* pp. 135-136; June, 1996, Julie Cummins, review of *Step by Wicked Step,* pp. 121-122; July, 2001, June, 2002, Carol A. Edwards, review of *Up on Cloud Nine,* pp. 137-138; September, 2002, Cathie Bashaw Mor-

ton, review of *The Jamie and Angus Stories,* p. 190; October, 2003, Susan Patron, review of *The True Story of Christmas,* p. 63; February, 2006, Diane Eddington, review of *The Diary of a Killer Cat,* p. 97; November, 2006, B. Allison Gray, review of *Frozen Billy,* p. 134; February, 2007, Debbie Stewart Hoskins, review of *The Return of the Killer Cat,* p. 86; August, 2007, Sadie Mattox, review of *Jennifer's Diary,* and Donna Atmur, review of *Jamie and Angus Together,* both p. 80; June, 2008, Cara von Wrangel Kinsey, review of *The Road of Bones,* p. 138.

Times Educational Supplement, June 3, 1988, Chris Powling, "Relative Values," p. 49.

Times Literary Supplement, July 7, 1978, Peter Hollindale, "Teenage Tensions," p. 767.

Voice of Youth Advocates, August, 1996, Jamie S. Hansen, review of *Step by Wicked Step,* p. 156; August, 2002, review of *Up on Cloud Nine,* p. 191; August, 2008, Amy Sisson, review of *The Road of Bones,* p. 239.

ONLINE

Anne Fine Home Page, http://www.annefine.co.uk (January 26, 2009).

Children's Laureate Web site, http://www.childrenslaureate. org/ (April 25, 2005), "The Second Laureate."

My Home Library Web site, http://www.myhomelibrary.org (July 15, 2005).*

*   *   *

FOSTER, Mark 1961-

Personal

Born 1961, in Orlando, FL; son of Gerald Foster (an illustrator). *Education:* University of Massachusetts—Amherst, B.A.; attended Harvard Extension School. *Hobbies and other interests:* History, especially American social history, early industry, mills, whaling; the outdoors and the environment; Iyengar yoga.

Addresses

Home—Somerville, MA. *E-mail*—mark@fosterartand books.com.

Career

Works in museum exhibit design and architecture.

Writings

Whale Port: A History of Tuckanucket, illustrated by father, Gerald Foster, Houghton Mifflin (Boston, MA), 2007.

Sidelights

Mark Foster is a museum exhibit designer who has worked on exhibits for the National Trust and Chesterwood Museum, the Martin Guitar Museum, and for the Smithsonian Institute. A graduate of the University of Massachusetts—Amherst, Foster has an abiding interest in U.S. history and has been fascinated by the whaling industry since he was a child. The coast of New England is dotted with whaling museums, and as a child Mark toured them with his father, illustrator Gerald Foster. He shares all that he has learned about this early American industry in the children's book *Whale Port: A History of Tuckanucket.*

Tuckanucket is a fictional coastal town that was founded in 1683 by colonists who realized that the sea and whaling had more to offer than did farming the hardscrabble New England coastal lands. *Whale Port* follows the history of Tuckanucket in a timeline format, from 1683 through the boom years of the whaling industry until the present day. Tuckanucket survives the American Revolution, destructive fires, and the rise of petroleum in the early 1900s that displaced the country's need for whale oil.

Lynne Mattern, writing in *School Library Journal,* called *Whale Port* "an excellent choice for both curricular and recreational use," while a *Kirkus Reviews* writer noted that the book "blends large-scale colorful art and an abundance of information." *Horn Book* reviewer Roger Sutton noted that "the Fosters . . . have elegantly synthesized a tremendous amount of information into a beguiling format." *Whale Port* was described as "a fascinating testament to the ingenuity and perseverance of the country's North Atlantic communities" by Kristin McKulski in her *Booklist* review.

Biographical and Critical Sources

PERIODICALS

Booklist, December 1, 2007, Kristen McKulski, *Whale Port: A History of Tuckanucket,* p. 38.

Horn Book, November-December, 2007, Roger Sutton, review of *Whale Port,* p. 696.

Kirkus Reviews, September 1, 2007, review of *Whale Port.*

School Library Journal, November, 2007, Lynne Mattern, review of *Whale Port,* p. 146.

ONLINE

Foster Art and Books Web site, http://www.fosterartand books.com (February 19, 2009).*

*   *   *

FRIED, Janice

Personal

Female.

Addresses

Home—Metuchen, NJ.

Career

Illustrator.

Awards, Honors

Sydney Taylor Honor Book for Young Readers, 2008, for *A Mezuzah on the Door.*

Illustrator

Eden A. Delcher, compiler, *Animal Rhymes,* Allan Publishers (Baltimore, MD), 1992.

Eden A. Delcher, compiler, *Counting Rhymes,* Allan Publishers (Baltimore, MD), 1992.

Eden A. Delcher, compiler, *Favorite Rhymes,* Allan Publishers (Baltimore, MD), 1992.

Eden A. Delcher, compiler, *Rhymes about Children,* Allan Publishers (Baltimore, MD), 1992.

Amy Meltzer, *A Mezuzah on the Door,* Kar-Ben Publishing (Minneapolis, MN), 2007.

Contributor of illustrations to newspapers and magazines, including *YM, Highlights for Children, Pulse, American Lawyer, New York Times,* and *Newsday.*

Biographical and Critical Sources

PERIODICALS

Booklist, November 1, 2007, Kay Weisman, review of *A Mezuzah on the Door,* p. 55.
Kirkus Reviews, September 1, 2007, review of *A Mezuzah on the Door.*

ONLINE

Janice Fried Home Page, http://www.janicefried.com (February 1, 2009).*

G-H

GAIMAN, Neil 1960-

Personal

Born November 10, 1960, in Portchester, England; son of David Bernard (a company director) and Sheila (a pharmacist) Gaiman; married Mary Therese McGrath, March 14, 1985; children: Michael Richard, Holly Miranda, Madeleine Rose Elvira. *Education:* Attended Ardingly College, 1970-74, and Whitgift School, 1974-77. *Politics:* "Wooly." *Religion:* Jewish. *Hobbies and other interests:* "Finding more bookshelf space."

Addresses

Home—MN. *Agent*—(literary) Merilee Heifetz, Writer's House, 21 W. 26th St., New York, NY 10010; (film) Jon Levin, Creative Artists Agency, 9830 Wilshire Blvd., Beverly Hills, CA 90212-1825.

Career

Fiction writer, screenwriter, poet, essayist, and journalist. Freelance journalist, 1983-87; full-time writer, 1987—. Director of *A Short Film about John Bolton,* Ska Films, 2004. Songwriter for bands The Flash Girls and One Ring Zero.

Member

Comic Book Legal Defense Fund (member of board of directors), International Museum of Cartoon Art (member of advisory board), Science Fiction Foundation (committee member), Society of Strip Illustrators (chair, 1988-90), British Fantasy Society.

Awards, Honors

Mekon Award, Society of Strip Illustrators, and Eagle Award for Best Graphic Novel, both 1988, both for *Violent Cases;* Eagle Award for Best Writer of American Comics, 1990; Harvey Award for Best Writer, 1990, 1991; Will Eisner Comic Industry Award for Best Writer and Best Graphic Album (Reprint), 1991; World Fan-

Neil Gaiman (AP Images.)

tasy Award for Best Short Story, 1991, for "A Midsummer Night's Dream"; Will Eisner Comics Industry Award for Best Writer, 1992; Harvey Award for Best Continuing Series, 1992; Will Eisner Comics Industry Award for Best Writer and Best Graphic Album (New), 1993; Gem Award, Diamond Distributors, 1993; Will Eisner Comics Industry Award for Best Writer, 1994; Guild Award, International Horror Critics, and World Fantasy Award nomination, both 1994, both for *Angels and Visitations* and short story "Troll Bridge"; SONY

Radio Award, for script *Signal to Noise*; GLAAD Award for Best Comic, 1996, for *Death: The Time of Your Life;* Eagle Award for Best Comic, 1996; Lucca Best Writer Prize, 1997; *Newsweek* Best Children's Books listee, 1997, for *The Day I Swapped My Dad for Two Goldfish;* Defender of Liberty Award, Comic Book Legal Defense Fund, 1997; MacMillan Silver Pen Award, 1999, for *Smoke and Mirrors;* Hugo Award nomination, 1999, for *Sandman: The Dream Hunters;* Mythopoeic Award for Best Novel for Adults, 1999, for *Stardust;* Nebula Award nomination, 1999, for screenplay *Princess Mononoke;* Hugo Award for Best Science Fiction/Fantasy Novel, Bram Stoker Award for Best Novel, Horror Writers Association, and British Science Fiction Association (BSFA) Award nomination, all 2002, all for *American Gods;* BSFA Award for Best Short Fiction, Elizabeth Burr/Worzalla Award, Bram Stoker Award, Hugo Award for Best Novella, and Prix Tam Tam Award, all 2003, all for *Coraline;* World Fantasy Award for Best Short Story, 2003, for "October in the Chair"; BSFA Award for Best Short Fiction, 2004, for *The Wolves in the Walls;* Hugo Award for Best Short Story, 2004, for "A Study in Emerald"; Bram Stoker Award for Best Illustrative Narrative, 2004, for *The Sandman: Endless Nights;* Geffen Award, 2004, for *Smoke and Mirrors;* Locus Award for Best Short Story, 2004, for "Closing Time"; August Derleth Award, and Best Books for Young Adults selection, American Library Association (ALA), both 2006, both for *Anansi Boys;* Locus Award for Best Short Story, 2007, for "How to Talk to Girls at Parties"; Locus Award for Best Collection, 2007, for *Fragile Things;* John Newbery Medal for outstanding contribution to children's literature, ALA, 2009, for *The Graveyard Book;* international awards from Austria, Brazil, Canada, Finland, France, Germany, Italy, and Spain.

Writings

JUVENILE FICTION

The Day I Swapped My Dad for Two Goldfish, illustrated by Dave McKean, Borealis/White Wolf (Clarkson, GA), 1997.

Coraline (also see below), illustrated by Dave McKean, HarperCollins (New York, NY), 2002.

The Wolves in the Walls, illustrated by Dave McKean, HarperCollins (New York, NY), 2003.

Mirrormask (special children's edition; based on the film of the same title; also see below), illustrated by Dave McKean, HarperCollins (New York, NY), 2005.

(With Michael Reaves) *Interworld,* Eos (New York, NY), 2005.

M Is for Magic, illustrated by Teddy Kristiansen, HarperCollins (New York, NY), 2007.

The Graveyard Book, illustrated by Dave McKean, HarperCollins (New York, NY), 2008.

The Dangerous Alphabet, illustrated by Gris Grimly, HarperCollins (New York, NY), 2008.

Blueberry Girl, illustrated by Charles Vess, HarperCollins (New York, NY), 2008.

Crazy Hair, illustrated by Dave McKean, HarperCollins (New York, NY), 2009.

Also author of *Odd and the Frost Giants.*

GRAPHIC NOVELS AND COMIC BOOKS

(With others) *Jael and Sisera: Outrageous Tales from the Old Testament,* illustrated by Julie Hollings, Knockabout (London, England), 1987.

Violent Cases (originally published in comic-book format, 1987), illustrated by Dave McKean, Titan (London, England), 1987, Tundra (Northampton, MA), 1991, third edition, Kitchen Sink Press (Northampton, MA), 1997.

Black Orchid (originally published in comic-book form, 1989), illustrated by Dave McKean, DC Comics (New York, NY), 1991.

Miracleman, Book 4: The Golden Age, illustrated by Mark Buckingham, Eclipse (Forestville, CA), 1992.

Signal to Noise (also see below), illustrated by Dave McKean, Dark Horse Comics (Milwaukie, OR), 1992.

The Books of Magic (originally published in comic-book form), four volumes, illustrated by John Bolton and others, DC Comics (New York, NY), 1993.

The Tragical Comedy, or Comical Tragedy, of Mr. Punch: A Romance, illustrated by Dave McKean, VG Graphics (London, England), 1994, Vertigo/DC Comics (New York, NY), 1995.

(Author of text, with Alice Cooper) *The Compleat Alice Cooper: Incorporating the Three Acts of Alice Cooper's The Last Temptation,* illustrated by Michael Zulli, Marvel Comics (New York, NY), 1995, published as *The Last Temptation,* Dark Horse Comics (Milwaukie, OR), 2000.

Angela, illustrated by Greg Capullo and Mark Pennington, Image (Anaheim, CA), 1995, published as *Spawn: Angela's Hunt,* 2000.

Stardust: Being a Romance within the Realms of Faerie, illustrated by Charles Vess, DC Comics (New York, NY), 1998, text published as *Stardust,* Spike (New York, NY), 1999.

(Author of text, with Matt Wagner) *Neil Gaiman's Midnight Days,* DC Comics (New York, NY), 1999.

Green Lantern/Superman: Legend of the Green Flame, DC Comics (New York, NY), 2000.

Harlequin Valentine, illustrated by John Bolton, Dark Horse Comics (Milwaukie, OR), 2001.

Murder Mysteries (based on play of the same title, also see below), illustrated by P. Craig Russell, Dark Horse Comics (Milwaukie, OR), 2002.

1602 (originally published comic-book form as *1602,* volumes 1-8), Marvel Comics (New York, NY), 2004.

The Eternals, illustrated by John Romita, Jr., Marvel Comics (New York, NY), 2007.

The Facts in the Case of the Departure of Miss Finch, illustrated by Michael Zulli, Dark Horse Comics (Milwaukie, OR), 2008.

Coraline (graphic novel; based on the children's book of the same title), illustrated by P. Craig Russell, HarperCollins (New York, NY), 2008.

Also author of *Creatures of the Night,* illustrated by Michael Zulli. Contributor of comics, including *Babycakes* and *The Wheel,* to anthologies. Creator of characters for comic books, including Lady Justice, Wheel of Worlds, Mr. Hero, Newmatic Man, Teknophage, and Lucifer. Co-editor of *The Utterly Comic Relief Comic,* UK Comic Relief Charity, 1991.

"SANDMAN" GRAPHIC-NOVEL SERIES

Sandman: The Doll's House (originally published in comic-book form), illustrated by Mike Dringenberg and Malcolm Jones III, DC Comics (New York, NY), 1990.

Sandman: Preludes and Nocturnes (originally published in comic-book form as *Sandman,* volumes 1-8), illustrated by Sam Keith, Mike Dringenberg, and Malcolm Jones III, DC Comics (New York, NY), 1991.

Sandman: Dream Country (originally published in comic-book form as *Sandman,* volumes 17-20; contains *"A Midsummer's Night's Dream"*), illustrated by Kelley Jones, Charles Vess, Colleen Doran, and Malcolm Jones III, DC Comics (New York, NY), 1991.

Sandman: Season of Mists (originally published in comic-book form as *Sandman,* volumes 21-28), illustrated by Kelley Jones, Malcolm Jones III, Mike Dringenberg, and others, DC Comics (New York, NY), 1992.

Sandman: A Game of You (originally published in comic-book form as *Sandman,* volumes 32-37), illustrated by Shawn McManus and others, DC Comics (New York, NY), 1993.

Sandman: Fables and Reflections (originally published in comic-book form as *Sandman,* volumes 29-31, 38-40, 50), illustrated by Bryan Talbot, DC Comics (New York, NY), 1994.

Death: The High Cost of Living (originally published in comic-book form in three volumes), illustrated by Dave McKean, Mark Buckingham, and others, DC Comics (New York, NY), 1994.

Sandman: Brief Lives (originally published in comic-book form as *Sandman,* volumes 41-49), illustrated by Jill Thompson, Dick Giordano, and Vince Locke, DC Comics (New York, NY), 1994.

Sandman: World's End (originally published in comic-book form as *Sandman,* volumes 51-56), illustrated by Dave McKean, Mark Buckingham, Dick Giordano, and others, DC Comics (New York, NY), 1994.

(Author of text, with Matt Wagner) *Sandman: Midnight Theatre,* illustrated by Teddy Kristiansen, DC Comics (New York, NY), 1995.

(Editor, with Edward E. Kramer) *The Sandman: Book of Dreams,* HarperPrism (New York, NY), 1996.

Sandman: The Kindly Ones (originally published in comic-book form as *Sandman,* volumes 57-69), illustrated by Marc Hempel, Richard Case, and others, DC Comics (New York, NY), 1996.

Death: The Time of Your Life, illustrated by Mark Buckingham and others, DC Comics (New York, NY), 1997.

(Author of commentary and a story) *Dustcovers: The Collected Sandman Covers, 1989-1997,* illustrated by Dave McKean, DC Comics (New York, NY), 1997, published as *The Collected Sandman Covers, 1989-1997,* Watson-Guptill (New York, NY), 1997.

Sandman: The Wake, (originally published in comic-book form as *Sandman,* volumes 70-75), illustrated by Michael Zulli, Charles Vess, and others, DC Comics (New York, NY), 1997.

(Reteller) *Sandman: The Dream Hunters,* illustrated by Yoshitaka Amano, DC Comics (New York, NY), 1999.

The Quotable Sandman: Memorable Lines from the Acclaimed Series, DC Comics (New York, NY), 2000.

The Sandman: Endless Nights, illustrated by P. Craig Russell, Milo Manara, and others, DC Comics (New York, NY), 2003.

The Absolute Sandman, Volume One, DC Comics (New York, NY), 2006.

The Absolute Sandman, Volume Two, DC Comics (New York, NY), 2007.

The Absolute Sandman, Volume Three, DC Comics (New York, NY), 2008.

Contributor to *The Sandman Companion,* DC Comics (New York, NY), 1999.

FICTION

(With Terry Pratchett) *Good Omens: The Nice and Accurate Prophecies of Agnes Nutter, Witch* (novel), Gollancz (London, England), 1990, revised edition, Workman (New York, NY), 1990.

(With Mary Gentle) *Villains!* (short stories), edited by Mary Gentle and Roz Kaveney, ROC (London, England), 1992.

(With Mary Gentle and Roz Kaveney) *The Weerde: Book One* (short stories), ROC (London, England), 1992.

(With Mary Gentle and Roz Kaveney) *The Weerde: Book Two: The Book of the Ancients* (short stories), ROC (London, England), 1992.

Angels and Visitations: A Miscellany (short stories), illustrated by Steve Bissette and others, DreamHaven Books and Art (Minneapolis, MN), 1993.

Neverwhere (novel), BBC Books (London, England), 1996, Avon (New York, NY), 1997.

Smoke and Mirrors: Short Fictions and Illusions (short stories), Avon (New York, NY), 1998.

American Gods (novel), William Morrow (New York, NY), 2001.

(Reteller) *Snow Glass Apples,* illustrated by George Walker, Biting Dog Press (Duluth, GA), 2003.

Anansi Boys, Morrow (New York, NY), 2005.

Mirrormask (illustrated film script; based on the film of the same title; also see below), illustrated by Dave McKean, HarperCollins (New York, NY), 2005.

Fragile Things: Short Fictions and Wonders, Morrow (New York, NY), 2006.

EDITOR

(With Kim Newman) *Ghastly beyond Belief,* Arrow (London, England), 1985.

(With Stephen Jones) *Now We Are Sick: A Sampler,* privately published, 1986, published as *Now We Are Sick: An Anthology of Nasty Verse,* DreamHaven (Minneapolis, MN), 1991.

(With Alex Stewart) *Temps,* ROC (London, England), 1991.

(With Alex Stewart) *Euro Temps,* ROC (London, England), 1992.

SCREENPLAYS

(With Lenny Henry) *Neverwhere,* BBC2 (London, England), 1996.

Signal to Noise, BBC Radio 3 (London, England), 1996.

Day of the Dead: An Annotated Babylon 5 Script (episode of television series *Babylon 5,* 1998), DreamHaven (Minneapolis, MN), 1998.

Princess Mononoke (English translation of Japanese-language screenplay by Hayao Miyazak), Miramax (New York, NY), 1999.

(And director) *A Short Film about John Bolton,* Ska Films, 2002.

MirrorMask (based on the children's book of the same title), Samuel Goldwyn, 2005.

(With Roger Avary) *Beowulf,* Paramount Pictures, 2007.

Author of scripts for films *Avalon, The Confessions of William Henry Ireland, The Fermata, Modesty Blaise,* and others.

OTHER

Duran Duran: The First Four Years of the Fab Five (biography), Proteus (New York, NY), 1984.

Don't Panic: The Official Hitch-Hiker's Guide to the Galaxy Companion, Pocket Books (New York, NY), 1988, revised edition with additional material by David K. Dickson as *Don't Panic: Douglas Adams and the Hitchhiker's Guide to the Galaxy,* Titan (London, England), 1993.

Warning: Contains Language (readings; compact disc), music by Dave McKean and the Flash Girls, DreamHaven (Minneapolis, MN), 1995.

(Co-illustrator) *The Dreaming: Beyond the Shores of Night,* DC Comics (New York, NY), 1997.

(Co-illustrator) *The Dreaming: Through the Gates of Horn and Ivory,* DC Comics (New York, NY), 1998.

Neil Gaiman: Live at the Aladdin (videotape), Comic Book Legal Defense Fund (Northampton, MA), 2001.

(With Gene Wolfe) *A Walking Tour of the Shambles* (nonfiction), American Fantasy Press (Woodstock, IL), 2001.

Murder Mysteries (play), illustrated by George Walker, Biting Dog Press (Duluth, GA), 2001.

Adventures in the Dream Trade (nonfiction and fiction), edited by Tony Lewis and Priscilla Olson, NESFA Press (Framingham, MA), 2002.

Gaiman's works, including the short story "Troll Bridge," have been represented in numerous anthologies. Contributor of prefaces and introductions to sev-

eral books. Contributor to newspapers and magazines, including *Knave, Punch,* London *Observer,* London *Sunday Times, Wired, New York Times Book Review, Washington Post Book World,* and *Time Out.*

Gaiman's books have been translated into other languages, including Bulgarian, Danish, Dutch, Finnish, French, German, Greek, Hungarian, Italian, Japanese, Norwegian, Spanish, and Swedish.

Adaptations

The Books of Magic was adapted into novel form by Carla Jablonski and others, individual titles include *The Invitation, The Blindings,* and *The Children's Crusade,* HarperCollins (New York, NY). Several of Gaiman's works have been released as audiobooks, including *Neverwhere,* HighBridge Audio, 1997, *American Gods,* Harper Audio, 2001, *Coraline* (read by the author), HarperAudio, 2002, and *Two Plays for Voices* (includes *Snow Glass Apples* and *Murder Mysteries*), Harper Audio, 2003. *Signal to Noise* was adapted as a stage play by NOWtheater (Chicago, IL). *Stardust* was adapted as a major motion picture, Paramount, 2007; *Coraline* was adapted as a major motion picture, Focus Features, 2009. Several of Gaiman's works have been optioned for film, including *Sandman, The Books of Magic, Death: The High Cost of Living, Good Omens,* and *Chivalry.*

Sidelights

An author of comic books, graphic novels, prose novels, children's books, short fiction, nonfiction, and screenplays, Neil Gaiman is a best-selling writer who is considered perhaps the most accomplished and influential figure in modern comics as well as one of the most gifted of contemporary fantasists. Characteristically drawing from mythology, history, literature, and popular culture to create his works, Gaiman blends the everyday, the fantastic, the frightening, and the humorous to present his stories. His writing reveals the mysteries that lie just outside of reality as well as the insights that come from experiencing these mysteries. In the *St. James Guide to Horror, Ghost, and Gothic Writers,* a contributor noted that when Gaiman "is on form (which is most of the time), he is without peer. . . . His blending of poetic prose, marvelous inventions, and artistic vision has assured him of his place in the vanguard of modern-day dark fantasists."

Gaiman refers to the plots and characters of classical literature and myth—most notably fairy tales, horror stories, science fiction, and traditional romances—while adding fresh, modern dimensions. In fact, he is credited with developing a new mythology with his works, which address themes such as what it means to be human; the importance of the relationship between humanity and art; humanity's desire for dreams and for attaining what they show; and the passage from childish ways of thinking to more mature understanding. Al-

Cover of Good Omens, *a lighthearted look at the apocalypse coauthored by Gaiman and Terry Pratchett.* (Copyright © 1990, 1992 by Neil Gaiman and Terry Pratchett. Used by permission of Penguin Group (USA), Inc.)

though most of the author's works are not addressed to children, Gaiman has written a number of titles for young readers, including *Coraline,* an international bestseller, and *The Graveyard Book,* winner of the 2009 John Newbery Medal.

Gaiman, who has developed a huge cult-like following as well as celebrity status, is perhaps best known as the creator of the comic-book and graphic-novel series about the Sandman. This character, which is based loosely on a crime-fighting superhero that first appeared in DC Comics in the 1930s and 1940s, is the protagonist of an epic series of dark fantasies that spanned several years and ran for seventy-five monthly issues. Among his other works, Gaiman has co-written a satiric fantasy about the end of the world with English novelist Terry Pratchett; comic books about Todd MacFarlane's popular character Spawn; and screenplays for film, television, and radio, both original scripts and adaptations of his own works. Throughout his career, he has worked with a number of talented artists in the field of comic books and fantasy, including John Bolton, Michael Zulli, Yoshitaka Amaro, Charles Vess, and longtime collaborator Dave McKean.

As a prose stylist, Gaiman is known for writing clearly and strongly, using memorable characters and striking images to build his dreamlike worlds. Although his books and screenplays can range from somber to creepy to horrifying, he is commended for underscoring them with optimism and sensitivity and for balancing their darkness with humor and wit. Reviewers have praised Gaiman for setting new standards for comic books as literature and for helping to bring increased popularity to graphic fiction. Although the author occasionally has been accused of being ponderous and self-indulgent, he generally is considered a phenomenon, a brilliant writer and storyteller whose works reflect his inventiveness, originality, and wisdom. According to London *Times* contributor Amanda Craig, "his richly imaginative, dark fantasies have the classic element of appealing to the adult in children and the child in adults." Referring to Gaiman's graphic novels, Frank McConnell stated in *Commonweal* that the author "may just be the most gifted and important storyteller in English" and called him "our best and most bound-to-be-remembered writer of fantasy."

Born in Portchester, England, Gaiman was brought up in an upper-middle-class home. A voracious reader, he recalled in an interview with Ray Olson of *Booklist* that he first read *Alice in Wonderland* "when I was five, maybe, and always kept it around as default reading between the ages of five and twelve, and occasionally picked up and reread since. There are things Lewis Carroll did in *Alice* that are etched onto my circuitry." When he was about fourteen years old, Gaiman began his secondary education at Whitgift School, and by 1977, he felt that he was ready to become a professional writer. That same year, Gaiman left Whitgift School.

After receiving a number of rejections for short stories that he had written, Gaiman decided to become a freelance journalist so that he could learn about the world of publishing from the inside. In 1983, he discovered the work of English comic-strip writer Alan Moore, whose *Swamp Thing* quickly became a special favorite. As Gaiman told an interviewer in *Authors and Artists for Young Adults,* "Moore's work convinced me that you really could do work in comics that had the same amount of intelligence, the same amount of passion, the same amount of quality that you could put in any other medium." In 1984 Gaiman produced his first book, *Duran Duran: The First Four Years of the Fab Five.* Once he had established his credibility as a writer, Gaiman was able to sell the short stories that he had completed earlier in his career, and he decided that he was ready to concentrate on fiction. In addition, the comics industry was experiencing a new influx of talent, which inspired Gaiman to consider becoming a contributor to that medium.

In 1986 Gaiman met art student McKean; their first collaboration was the comic book *Violent Cases.* Around the same time, Gaiman contributed to *Jael and Sisera:*

Outrageous Tales from the Old Testament, which is credited with giving him almost instant notoriety in the comic-book community. Gaiman teamed with McKean again to do a limited-run comic series, *Black Orchid,* the first of the author's works to be released by DC Comics. Gaiman then was offered his choice of inactive DC characters to rework from the Golden Age of Comics (the 1930s and 1940s); he chose the Sandman. As originally presented, millionaire Wesley Dodds, a.k.a. the Sandman, hunted criminals by night wearing a fedora, cape, and a gas mask. When Gaiman began the series in 1988, he changed the whole scope of the character. The Sandman, who is also called Dream, Morpheus, Oneiros, Lord Shaper, Master of Story, and God of Sleep, became a thin, enigmatic figure with a pale face, dark eyes, and a shock of black hair. The Sandman is one of the Endless, immortals in charge of individual realms of the human psyche. The Sandman's brothers and sisters in the Endless are (in birth order) Destiny, Death, Destruction, the twins Desire and Despair, and Delirium (formerly Delight). Dream (the Sandman) falls between Death and Destruction.

In one of many collaborations, Dave McKean teams up with Gaiman to create the artwork for the popular middle-grade novel **Coraline.** (Illustration copyright © 2002 by Dave McKean. All rights reserved. Used by permission of HarperCollins Publishers.)

In *Preludes and Nocturnes,* Gaiman introduces the Sandman, the ageless lord of dreams, who has just returned home after being captured by a coven of wizards and held in an asylum for the criminally insane for seventy-two years. Dream finds that his home is in ruins, that his powers are diminished, and that his three tools—a helmet, a pouch of sand, and a ruby stone—have been stolen. Dream comes to realize that his captivity has affected him: he has become humanized, and he understands that he eventually will have to die.

In *The Doll's House,* Dream travels across the United States searching for the Arcana, the stray dreams and nightmares of the twentieth century that have taken on human form. *Dream Country* centers on Calliope, a muse and the mother of Dream's son, Orpheus. (In 1991, "A Midsummer's Night's Dream," a tale from *Dream Country,* won the World Fantasy Award for best short story, the first time that a comic book had won a prize that was not related to its own medium.) In *Season of Mists,* Dream meets Lucifer, who has stepped down from his position as ruler of Hell and has left the choice of his successor to Dream.

A Game of You features Barbara (nicknamed Barbie), a character who had appeared in *The Doll's House.* Barbie is drawn back into the dream realm that she ruled as a child in order to save it from the evil Cuckoo, who plans to destroy it. *Fables and Reflections,* a collection of stories featuring the characters from the series, includes Gaiman's retelling of the Greek myth of Orpheus. *Brief Lives* finds Dream and Delirium on a quest to find Destruction, who exiled himself on Earth over three hundred years ago. *World's End* includes a collection of tales told by a group of travelers who are waiting out a storm in an inn. In *The Kindly Ones* Hippolyta takes revenge upon Dream for the disappearance of her son with the assistance of the title characters, mythological beings also known as the Furies. In the final chapter of the series, *The Wake,* the Endless attend a ceremony to mark the passing of Dream.

Assessing the "Sandman" series, McConnell stated that what Gaiman has done "is to establish the fact that a comic book can be a work of high and very serious art—a story that other storytellers, in whatever medium they work, will have to take into account as an exploration of what stories can do and what stories are for." The critic concluded, "I know of nothing quite like it, and I don't expect there will be anything like it for some time." In the *Dictionary of Literary Biography,* Joe Sanders noted: "*The Sandman* is an example of how a serious writer can utilize the comics medium. Gaiman used the delay between issues to control his readers' absorption of details, especially in the long, methodically paced series of catastrophes leading to Morpheus's death in *The Kindly Ones.*" In addition to using different artists to vary the mood of his works, Sanders wrote that Gaiman "utilized the cheeky looseness of comics to bring together an astonishing range of

images; *The Sandman* considers, with equal sympathy and assurance, the personal and professional life of Shakespeare and the interpersonal dynamics of a convention of serial killers."

Although the "Sandman" series ended in 1996, DC Comics has since re-released the comics in a series of deluxe editions. The "Sandman" stories have also inspired related volumes, such as a book of quotations from the series, and merchandise such as action figures, stuffed toys, trading cards, jewelry, and watches. Discussing the success of his franchise in an interview on the Powell's Books Web site, Gaiman told John Bolton: "What I feel proudest of, honestly, is the fact that you're looking at a series of comics that I began to write seventeen years ago, that finished a decade ago, that is still in print right now, and selling more than it ever has."

Throughout his career, Gaiman has frequently featured young people as main characters in his works. *The Books of Magic* a collection of four comics that predates J.K. Rowling's "Harry Potter" series, features a thirteen-year-old boy, Tim Hunter, who is told that he has the capabilities to be the greatest wizard in the world. Tim, a boy from urban London who wears oversized glasses, is taken by the Trenchcoat Brigade—sorcerers with names like The Mysterious Phantom Stranger, the Incorrigible Hellblazer, and the Enigmatic Dr. Occult—on a tour of the universe to learn its magical history. Tim travels to Hell, to the land of Faerie, and to America, among other places, each of them showing him a different aspect of the world of magic. He also searches for his girlfriend Molly, who has been abducted into the fantasy realms; after he finds her, the two of them face a series of dangers as they struggle to return to their own world. At the end of the story, Tim must make a decision to embrace or reject his talents as a wizard. *The Books of Magic* also includes cameos by the Sandman and his sister Death. Writing in *Locus,* Carolyn Cushman said, "It's a fascinating look at magic, its benefits and burdens, all dramatically illustrated [by John Bolton, Scott Hampton, Charles Vess, and Paul Johnson], and with a healthy helping of humor."

Stardust tells a love story of seventeen-year-old Tristran Thorn who journeys to the fanciful land of Faerie on a quest to fetch a fallen star far from his village of Wall. He has promised his love, Victoria, this star, and on his journey he has to deal with others more powerful and ruthless who also seek the fallen star. Finally, Tristran's journey brings him back to a faerie market near his village where all secrets about his parentage are revealed. Set in nineteenth-century England, the tale "evokes the crisp style of the Brothers Grimm fairy tales," according to Kurt Lancaster writing in the *Christian Science Monitor.* Susan Salpini, reviewing *Stardust* for *School Library Journal,* called it an "old-fashioned fairy tale of mythic images, magic, and lyrical passages." Salpini further commented, "While the bones of the story—the hero, the quest, the maiden—are traditional, Gaiman of-

fers a role that is fresh and original." A contributor to *Publishers Weekly* noted that the author "employs exquisitely rich language, natural wisdom, good humor and a dash of darkness to conjure up a fairy tale in the grand tradition."

In 1996 Gaiman and McKean produced their first work for children: the picture book *The Day I Swapped My Dad for Two Goldfish.* In this tale, a little boy trades his father for two of his neighbor's goldfish while his little sister stares, horrified. When their mother finds out what has happened, she is furious. She makes the children go and get back their father who, unfortunately, has already been traded for an electric guitar. While on their quest to find him, the siblings decide that their father is a very good daddy after all. The children finally retrieve their father, who has been reading a newspaper all during his adventure. At home, their mother makes the children promise not to swap their dad any more. Writing in *Bloomsbury Review,* Anji Keating called *The Day I Swapped My Dad for Two Goldfish* "fabulously funny" and dubbed the protagonists' journey to fetch their father "delightful." Malcolm Jones, writing in *Newsweek,* predicted that Gaiman and McKean "may shock a few grandparents . . . but in fact the most shocking thing they've done in this droll story is to take the illegible look of cutting-edge magazines like Raygun and somehow make it readable."

In 2003 Gaiman and McKean completed a second picture book, *The Wolves in the Walls.* In this work, young Lucy hears wolves living in the walls of the old house where she and her family live; of course, no one believes her. When the wolves emerge to take over the house, Lucy and her family flee. However, Lucy wants her house back, and she also wants the beloved pig-puppet that she left behind. She talks her family into going back into the house, where they move into the walls that had been vacated by the wolves. Lucy and her family then frighten the sharp-clawed usurpers, who are wearing their clothes and eating their food. The wolves scatter, and everything seems to go back to normal until Lucy hears another noise in the walls; this time, it sounds like elephants. In her *Booklist* review of *The Wolves in the Walls,* Francisca Goldsmith found the book "visually and emotionally sophisticated, accessible, and inspired by both literary and popular themes and imagery." Writing in *School Library Journal,* Marian Creamer commented that "Gaiman and McKean deftly pair text and illustration to convey a strange, vivid story," and predicted that "children will delight in the 'scary, creepy tone.'"

Gaiman's first story for middle-graders, *Coraline,* outlines how the title character, a young girl who feels that she is being ignored by her preoccupied parents, enters a terrifying, malevolent alternate reality to save them after they are kidnapped. The story begins when Coraline and her parents move into their new house, which is divided into apartments. Left to her own devices, the

bored girl explores the house and finds a door in the empty flat next door that leads her to a world that is a twisted version of her own. There, Coraline meets two odd-looking individuals who call themselves her "other mother" and "other father." The Other Mother, a woman who looks like Coraline's mom except for her black-button eyes and stiletto fingernails, wants Coraline to stay with her and her husband. Tempted by good food and interesting toys, Coraline considers the offer. However, when the girl returns home, she finds that her parents have disappeared. Coraline discovers that they are trapped in the other world, and she sets out to save them. The Other Mother, who turns out to be a soul-sucking harpy, enters into a deadly game of hide-and-seek with Coraline, and the girl ultimately discovers new qualities of bravery and resolve within herself.

After its publication, *Coraline* became a subject of dispute. Some adult observers saw it as too frightening for young readers. However, other observers noted that children of their acquaintance considered it exciting rather than overly frightening. A reviewer in *Publishers Weekly* wrote that Gaiman and illustrator McKean "spin an electrifyingly creepy tale likely to haunt young readers for many moons. . . . Gaiman twines his tale with a menacing tone and crisp prose fraught with memorable imagery . . ., yet keeps the narrative just this side of terrifying." Writing in *School Library Journal,* Bruce Anne Shook commented that "the story is odd, strange, even slightly bizarre, but kids will hang on every word. . . . This is just right for all those requests for a scary book." A critic in *Kirkus Reviews* wrote of the book that, "for stouthearted kids who love a brush with the sinister, *Coraline* is spot on." *Coraline* has won several major fantasy awards and was adapted as a graphic novel and a major motion picture.

M Is for Magic, a collection of stories aimed at a young adult audience, features a number of tales from Gaiman's hard-to-find *Angels and Visitations: A Miscellany.* According to a critic in *Publishers Weekly,* the "volume is an excellent reminder of his considerable talent for short-form prose." *Interworld,* a science-fiction novel coauthored by Gaiman and Michael Reaves, centers on Joey Harker, an ordinary youngster who discovers that he has the ability to travel between dimensions. Once inside the Altiverse, which contains an infinite series of alternate Earths, Joey learns that he is at the center of an epic confrontation pitting the forces of science against the forces of magic. "Filled with bizarre imagery, innovative world-building, and breathless action, *Interworld* is equal parts survival escapade and David-and-Goliath epic," noted *Kliatt* reviewer Claire E. Gross, and John Peters, writing in *Booklist,* described the novel as a "fast-paced, compulsively readable tale."

Illustrated by Gris Grimly, *The Dangerous Alphabet* is Gaiman's take on the familiar alphabet book, with an eerie twist. In the work, a pair of Victorian children sneaks away from their father and, accompanied by their pet gazelle, journeys to an underworld where hidden treasure awaits. Along the way, however, the girl is captured by evil-doers and her brother must battle pirates, monsters, and trolls to rescue her. The children's story is told through thirteen rhyming couplets which incorporate the twenty-six letters. "Skillful narrative and visual storytelling combine to present a complex adventure that unravels through multilayered text and illustrations," Susannah Richards observed in *School Library Journal,* and *Booklist* contributor Thom Barthelmess reported that the author and illustrator of *The Dangerous Alphabet* "have combined forces to produce an acrid, gothic confection that bubbles with vitriol and wit."

The Graveyard Book, a reimagining of Rudyard Kipling's *The Jungle Book,* was inspired by Gaiman's trips to the cemetery with his then two-year-old son and took more than two decades to write. While his family is being murdered, a toddler slips away and finds refuge in a nearby graveyard, where he is cared for by the ghoulish inhabitants. Renamed Nobody Owens, or "Bod" for short, the youngster eventually rejoins the human world, where he encounters the mysterious killer from his past. *The Graveyard Book* earned rave reviews; Patrick Ness, writing in the London *Guardian,* praised "the outrageous riches of Gaiman's imagination." In the *Scotsman,* Charlie Fletcher called the work "a robust, big-hearted fantasy, tinged with darkness and lit with humour and surprise, and deeper than its genre surface might hint at." As Fletcher added, "the novel certainly has depth, along with its wide-ranging playfulness, and it has a sureness of tone in terms of precisely what aspects of the dark and macabre to omit, and what to leave in." According to Gross, "Gaiman's assured plotting is as bittersweet as it is action-filled . . . and makes this ghost-story-cum-coming-of-age-novel as readable as it is accomplished."

The mainstream success of *Stardust,* as well as the book and film versions of *Coraline,* and *The Graveyard Book,* "has changed Gaiman's place in the world from cult comic writer to respected author and highly sought-after creator of film, television and radio content," a contributor observed in the London *Independent.* As Gaiman stated in the same article, "I'm being taken seriously on a level that would have been inconceivable for someone who wrote comics, children's stories and fantasies to have been taken seriously 15 years ago." That kind of recognition is long overdue, Fletcher declared, adding his hopes that one day Gaiman will "no longer merely be seen as one of the brightest lights of the fantasy section in the increasingly ghettoised bookstores of the world. People will be saying he's one of the great British writers. Period."

Biographical and Critical Sources

BOOKS

Authors and Artists for Young Adults, Gale (Detroit, MI), Volume 19, 1996, Volume 42, 2002.

Artist Gris Grimly joins Gaiman in creating the humorously macabre picture book **The Dangerous Alphabet.** (Illustration copyright © 2008 by Gris Grimley.

Dictionary of Literary Biography, Volume 261: *British Fantasy and Science Fiction Writers since 1960,* Gale (Detroit, MI), 2002.

Kwitney, Alisa, *The Sandman: King of Dreams,* introduction by Neil Gaiman, Chronicle Books (San Francisco, CA), 2003.

Neil Gaiman on His Work and Career: A Conversation with Bill Baker, Rosen (New York, NY), 2008.

St. James Guide to Horror, Ghost, and Gothic Writers, St. James Press (Detroit, MI), 1998.

PERIODICALS

Bloomsbury Review, July-August, 1997, Anji Keating, review of *The Day I Swapped My Dad for Two Goldfish,* p. 21.

Booklist, August, 2002, Ray Olson, interview with Gaiman, p. 19, and Stephanie Zvirin, review of *Coraline,* p. 1948; August, 2003, Francisca Goldsmith, review of *The Wolves in the Walls,* p. 1989; August, 2005, Ray Olson, review of *Anansi Boys,* p. 1952; September 1, 2007, John Peters, review of *InterWorld,* p. 114; March 1, 2008, Thom Barthelmess, review of *The Dangerous Alphabet,* p. 72; May 15, 2008, Ray Olson, review of *The Facts in the Case of the Departure of Miss Finch,* p. 27.

Christian Science Monitor, February 18, 1999, Kurt Lancaster, review of *Stardust,* p. 19.

Commonweal, December 2, 1994, Frank McConnell, review of *Mister Punch,* p. 27; October 20, 1995, Frank McConnell, review of *Sandman,* p. 21; June 19, 1998, Frank McConnell, review of *Neverwhere,* p. 21.

Entertainment Weekly, June 24, 1994, Ken Tucker, review of *Sandman,* pp. 228-229; September 23, 2005, Jennifer Reese, "Lost 'Boys': Neil Gaiman Goes on a Madcap, Tangential Whirl in *Anansi Boys,*" p. 93.

Guardian (London, England), July 14, 1999, Nick Hasted, "The Illustrated Man," p. 12; October 25, 2008, Patrick Ness, review of *The Graveyard Book,* p. 11.

Hollywood Reporter, September 14, 2005, Gina McIntyre, "Cheap Thrills: Fantasy Author Neil Gaiman Finds Reality a Special Effect, p. 57; July 24, 2007, Noel Murray, "Dialogue with Neil Gaiman," p. 1.

Horn Book, September-October, 2007, Claire E. Gross, review of *InterWorld,* p. 575; November-December, 2008, Claire E. Gross, review of *The Graveyard Book,* p. 703.

Independent (London, England), October 22, 2007, interview with Gaiman, p. 10.

Kirkus Reviews, June 15, 2002, review of *Coraline,* p. 88; July 15, 2006, review of *Fragile Things: Short Fictions and Wonders,* p. 691; April 1, 2008, review of *The Dangerous Alphabet;* January 15, 2009, review of *Blueberry Girl.*

Kliatt, July, 2008, George Galuschak, review of *The Facts in the Case of the Departure of Miss Finch,* p. 32;

September, 2008, Paula Rohrlick, review of *The Graveyard Book,* p. 10, and George Galuschak, review of *Coraline,* p. 32.

Library Journal, September 15, 1990, Keith R.A. DeCandido, review of *The Golden Age,* p. 104.

Locus, April, 1993, Carolyn Cushman, review of *The Books of Magic,* p. 29.

Los Angeles Times, December 29, 2008, Geoff Boucher, interview with Gaiman.

Newsweek, December 1, 1997, Malcolm Jones, review of *The Day I Swapped My Dad for Two Goldfish,* p. 77.

New York Times, January 27, 2009, Motoko Rich, "*The Graveyard Book* Wins Newbery Medal," p. C1.

New York Times Book Review, November 9, 2008, Becca Zerkin, review of *The Dangerous Alphabet,* p. 2.

Publishers Weekly, November 23, 1998, review of *Stardust,* p. 63; June 24, 2002, review of *Coraline,* p. 57; July 18, 2005, review of *Anansi Boys,* p. 180; July 17, 2006, review of *Fragile Things,* p. 131; July 9, 2007, review of *M Is for Magic,* p. 54; December 15, 2008, review of *Blueberry Girl,* p. 52.

School Library Journal, February, 1999, Susan Salpini, review of *Stardust,* p. 142; August, 2002, Bruce Anne Shook, review of *Coraline,* p. 184; September, 2003, Marian Creamer, review of *The Wolves in the Walls,* p. 178; August, 2007, Beth Wright, review of *M Is for Magic,* p. 116; May, 2008, Susannah Richards, review of *The Dangerous Alphabet,* p. 98; October, 2008, Megan Honig, review of *The Graveyard Book,* p. 144.

Scotsman (Edinburgh, Scotland), November 8, 2008, Charlie Fletcher, interview with Gaiman.

Star Tribune (Minneapolis, MN), November 16, 2007, Colin Covert, "Gaiman's Take on *Beowulf:* Beyond Heroics," p. 13F.

Sunday Times (London, England), July 15, 1990, Nicolette Jones, review of *Violent Cases;* November 2, 2008, Nicolette Jones, review of *The Graveyard Book,* p. 57.

Times (London, England), November 1, 2008, Amanda Craig, interview with Gaiman, p. 8.

USA Today, July 31, 2007), Anthony Breznican, "Storyteller Gaiman Wishes upon a Star," p. 1D.

Washington Post Book World, April 7, 2002, Michael Swanwick, "Reel Worlds," p. 3.

ONLINE

Neil Gaiman Home Page, http://www.neilgaiman.com (February 15, 2009).

Neil Gaiman Web log, http://journal.neilgaiman.com (February 15, 2009).

Powell's Books Web site, http://www.powells.com/ (August, 2005), Chris Bolton, interview with Gaiman.

Time Online, http://www.time.com/ (September 25, 2005), Lev Grossman, "Interview: Neil Gaiman and Joss Whedon."*

*   *   *

GIBLIN, James Cross 1933-

Personal

Surname is pronounced with a hard "g"; born July 8, 1933, in Cleveland, OH; son of Edward Kelley (a law-

James Cross Giblin (Photograph by Sarah Hoe Sterling. Reproduced by permission.)

yer) and Anna (a teacher) Giblin. *Education:* Attended Northwestern University, 1951; Western Reserve University (now Case Western Reserve University), B.A., 1954; Columbia University, M.F.A., 1955.

Addresses

Home—New York, NY.

Career

Writer and editor. Freelance writer, 1955—. worked as a typist and at the British Book Centre, 1955-59; Criterion Books, Inc., New York, NY, assistant editor, 1959-62; Lothrop, Lee & Shepard Co., New York, NY, associate editor, 1962-65, editor, 1965-67; Seabury Press, Inc., New York, NY, editor-in-chief of Clarion Books (for children), 1967-79, vice president, 1975-79; Houghton Mifflin Company, New York, NY, editor and publisher of Clarion Books, 1979-89, contributing editor, beginning 1989. Adjunct professor at Graduate Center of the City University of New York, 1979-83.

Member

Society of Children's Book Writers and Illustrators (member of board of directors), Authors Guild, Children's Book Council (president, 1976).

Awards, Honors

American Library Association (ALA) Notable Children's Book citations, 1980, for *The Scarecrow Book,* 1981, for *The Skyscraper Book,* 1982, for *Chimney Sweeps,* 1985, for *The Truth about Santa Claus,* 1986, for *Milk,* 1987, for *From Hand to Mouth,* 1988, for *Let There Be Light,* 1990, for *The Riddle of the Rosetta Stone,* 1991, for *The Truth about Unicorns,* 1993, for *Be Seated,* 1995, for *When Plague Strikes,* 1997, for *Charles A. Lindbergh,* 2000, for *The Amazing Life of Benjamin Franklin*; Golden Kite Award for nonfiction, Society of Children's Book Writers and Illustrators, 1982, and American Book Award for Children's Nonfiction, 1983, both for *Chimney Sweeps;* Golden Kite Award for nonfiction, 1984, for *Walls,* and 1989, for *Let*

There Be Light; Boston Globe/Horn Book Nonfiction Honor Book designation, 1986, for *The Truth about Santa Claus;* Orbis Pictus Award for Nonfiction Honor Book designation, National Council of Teachers of English, 1998, for *Charles A. Lindbergh,* and 2001, for *The Amazing Life of Benjamin Franklin; Washington Post/*Children's Book Guild Award for Nonfiction, for body of work.

Writings

NONFICTION; FOR CHILDREN

(With Dale Ferguson) *The Scarecrow Book,* Crown (New York, NY), 1980.

The Skyscraper Book, illustrated by Anthony Kramer, photographs by David Anderson, Crowell (New York, NY), 1981.

Chimney Sweeps: Yesterday and Today, illustrated by Margot Tomes, Crowell (New York, NY), 1981.

Fireworks, Picnics, and Flags: The Story of the Fourth of July Symbols, illustrated by Ursula Arndt, Clarion Books (New York, NY), 1983.

Walls: Defenses throughout History, Little, Brown (Boston, MA), 1984.

The Truth about Santa Claus, Crowell (New York, NY), 1985.

Milk: The Fight for Purity, Crowell (New York, NY), 1986.

From Hand to Mouth; or, How We Invented Knives, Forks, Spoons, and Chopsticks and the Table Manners to Go with Them, Crowell (New York, NY), 1987.

Let There Be Light: A Book about Windows, Crowell (New York, NY), 1988.

The Riddle of the Rosetta Stone: Key to Ancient Egypt, Crowell (New York, NY), 1990.

The Truth about Unicorns, illustrated by Michael McDermott, Harper (New York, NY), 1991.

Edith Wilson: The Woman Who Ran the United States, illustrated by Michele Laporte, Viking (New York, NY), 1992.

George Washington: A Picture Book Biography, illustrated by Michael Dooling, Scholastic (New York, NY), 1992.

Be Seated: A Book about Chairs, HarperCollins (New York, NY), 1993.

When Plague Strikes: The Black Death, Smallpox, and AIDS, illustrated by David Frampton, HarperCollins (New York, NY), 1995.

Charles A. Lindbergh: A Human Hero, Clarion (New York, NY), 1997.

The Mystery of the Mammoth Bones, and How It Was Solved, HarperCollins (New York, NY), 1999.

The Amazing Life of Benjamin Franklin, illustrated by Michael Dooling, Scholastic (New York, NY), 2000.

(Editor and author of introduction) *The Century That Was: Reflections on the Last One Hundred Years,* Atheneum (New York, NY), 2000.

The Life and Death of Adolf Hitler, Clarion (New York, NY), 2002.

Secret of the Sphinx, illustrated by Bagram Ibatoulline, Scholastic (New York, NY), 2004.

Good Brother, Bad Brother: The Story of Edwin Booth and John Wilkes Booth, Clarion Books (New York, NY), 2005.

The Boy Who Saved Cleveland: Base on a True Story, illustrated by Michael Dooling, Henry Holt (New York, NY), 2006.

The Many Rides of Paul Revere, Scholastic (New York, NY), 2007.

Did Fleming Rescue Churchill?: A Research Puzzle, illustrated by Erik Brooks, Henry Holt (New York, NY), 2008.

FICTION; FOR CHILDREN

(Reteller) *The Dwarf, the Giant, and the Unicorn: A Tale of King Arthur,* illustrated by Claire Ewart, Clarion (New York, NY), 1996.

OTHER

My Bus Is Always Late (one-act play; produced in Cleveland, OH, 1953), Dramatic Publishing (New York, NY), 1954.

Writing Books for Young People (adult nonfiction), The Writer, Inc., 1990.

Also author of a play based on William Styron's novel *Lie down in Darkness.* Contributor of original short stories to anthologies *Am I Blue? Coming out of the Silence,* edited by Marion Dane Bauer, HarperCollins, 1994; and *Tomorrowland: Stories about the Future,* edited by Michael Cart, Scholastic, 1999. Contributor of articles and stories for children to *Cobblestone, Cricket,* and *Highlights for Children,* and of articles for adults to *Children's Literature in Education, Horn Book, Publishers Weekly, School Library Journal, Washington Post, Writer,* and *Writer's Digest.*

Sidelights

James Cross Giblin has been a major figure in the field of children's book publishing since the 1970s. Not only did he edit the work of many writers during his years at Clarion Books, but Giblin has also authored many original nonfiction books for young readers. His highly praised children's books include *Chimney Sweeps: Yesterday and Today, The Truth about Santa Claus, Let There Be Light: A Book about Windows,* and *Good Brother, Bad Brother: The Story of Edwin Booth and John Wilkes Booth.* As Giblin once explained, "Nonfiction books for children aged eight to twelve [give] me the opportunity to pursue my research interests, meet interesting and stimulating experts in various fields, and share my enthusiasms with a young audience. I try to write books that I would have enjoyed reading when I was the age of my readers."

A shy, bookish child, Giblin grew up in nearby Painesville, Ohio. As a boy, he enjoyed the comic strip "Blondie," and, with his mother's help, he began draw-

ing his own strips. Giblin also enjoyed going to the cinema as a youngster, especially melodramas and spy movies involving Nazi-era ne'er-do-wells such as *Casablanca.* In junior high, he worked on the school newspaper, which helped him overcome some of his shyness.

Giblin discovered a new interest during his high-school years: acting. His first role was in a community theater production of the play *Outward Bound.* After graduation, he studied drama at Northwestern University. However, he was unhappy there, and after one semester he transferred to Western Reserve University (now Case Western Reserve University), located near his parents' home. In addition to starring in many stage productions at Western Reserve, Giblin won a contest to costar in a radio drama in New York City with actress Nina Foch. As he gained experience on the stage, his ambitions changed. An experience with an old woman on a bus inspired him to write his first play, *My Bus Is Always Late,* which was produced locally and published by the Dramatic Publishing Company in 1954.

After earning a master's degree in playwriting at Columbia University, Giblin remained in New York City to write, supporting himself by working as a temporary office employee. He became involved in efforts to adapt William Styron's novel *Lie Down in Darkness* for the stage, but the project fell through for various reasons. This failure deeply affected Giblin, who had invested a year of work in the adaptation. After a recuperative visit home to Painesville, he returned to the city in hopes of finding a more dependable career. He started out as a special-order clerk at the British Book Centre, then joined the staff of Criterion Books in 1959, first as a publicity director, and later as an editor. He enjoyed the work, especially when given the opportunity to edit books for young readers. Deciding to concentrate solely on works for children, he moved to the editorial department of Lothrop, Lee & Shepard in 1962.

At Lothrop, Giblin began to think about writing his own books. but his first effort was rejected by a local publisher. In the late 1960s, he went to work for Seabury Press, where he was instrumental in developing the company's children's division, Clarion Books. In the 1970s, a trip to China inspired Giblin to attempt another book project of his own: an anthology of writings about the everyday lives of Chinese teens since 1949's Communist Revolution. When this project was judged too political, Giblin turned to writing articles about children's books to periodicals and lecturing at conferences of children's book writers and librarians.

In 1980, Giblin collaborated with Dale Ferguson on his first children's book, *The Scarecrow Book.* Since then, he has produced nonfiction titles on a wide range of subjects, among them biographies, general histories, and focused historical studies such as *Walls: Defenses throughout History* and *The Mystery of the Mammoth Bones, and How It Was Solved.* In 1989, Giblin retired

Giblin introduces young readers to one of the founders of American democracy in **Thomas Jefferson,** *a picture-book biography featuring artwork by Michael Dooling.* (Illustration copyright © 1994 by Michael Dooling. All rights reserved. Reproduced by permission of Scholastic, Inc.)

from his position as editor-in-chief of Clarion Books. Becoming a contributing editor at Clarion, he also embarked on a full-time writing career.

Ranging far afield in his focus, Giblin has explored such topics as milk pasteurization, Fourth of July celebrations, eating utensils, chairs, plagues, and the lives of pivotal historical figures, among many others. Reviewers frequently praise his ability to tell complex stories in a way that is simple, understandable, and entertaining. Elizabeth S. Watson, in her *Horn Book* review of *The Riddle of the Rosetta Stone: Key to Ancient Egypt,* stated that "the author has done a masterful job of distilling information, citing the highlights, and fitting it all together." *New York Times Book Review* contributor Philip M. Isaacson lauded Giblin's writing skills in *Let There Be Light,* noting that the author "has condensed a daunting body of material to provide young readers with a great deal of information about the evolution and technology of windows."

Giblin's texts, in addition to being easy to understand, are also loaded with valuable factual details. His "relaxed, affable manner belies the amount of information he offers," wrote Amy L. Cohn in a *School Library Journal* review of Giblin's *Chimney Sweeps.* Other critics have observed that this wealth of information is de-

rived from the author's painstaking research. "Giblin has such a flair for historic detail and research that he translates hordes of tales into a singular creation of Santa Claus," proclaimed a *School Library Journal* reviewer about *The Truth about Santa Claus*. An evaluation of the same book in the *Bulletin of the Center for Children's Books* lauded the author for his command of his subject, stating that Giblin has done "his usual good job of research and well-organized presentation." Reviewing Giblin's *The Mystery of the Mammoth Bones, and How It Was Solved,* a *Publishers Weekly* critic praised the author for having "the pacing of an ace detective [as he] unveils the painstaking steps in artist and naturalist Charles Willson Peale's 1801 discovery of mammoth bones."

Giblin's biographies include books on such historical figures as founding fathers George Washington, Thomas Jefferson, and Benjamin Franklin, colonial patriot Paul Revere, aviator Charles Lindbergh, and German chancellor Adolf Hitler. Assessing *The Amazing Life of Benjamin Franklin,* Ilene Cooper wrote in *Booklist* that Giblin's "writing is lively, and he wisely uses the story of Franklin's estrangement from his only living son, a Royalist, to heighten dramatic tension." In *Horn Book* Mary M. Burns wrote of the same biography that "Giblin demonstrates his mastery of the historical-biographical genre—he knows how to define a theme, develop a narrative, and maintain his focus to the last sentence."

Several of Giblin's biographies focus on what he calls "bad boys": Aldolf Hitler, presidential assassin John Wilkes Booth, and Nazi sympathizer and aviator Charles Lindbergh. As he explained in an essay for the Children's Book Council online, "in today's complex and often confusing world, I believe there's . . . room for biographies of people . . . whose destructive actions had such a devastating effect on human history. Youngsters need to know about them and their ilk—where they came from, and why they did what they did—if only to be on guard against the rise of similarly dangerous individuals in the future." In *The Life and Death of Adolf Hitler* Giblin begins his profile of the Nazi leader by depicting Hitler's normal childhood. According to *School Library Journal* critic Andrew Medlar, the book "maintains focus on the life of its subject—including his pets and love life" rather than "stray[ing] into areas belonging to books specifically on the Holocaust or World War II. Consequently, according to Medlar, *The Life and Death of Adolf Hitler* ranks as "the most complete and successful biography of the Fuhrer available for" middle-grade readers."

A uniquely American villain is the subject of *Good Brother, Bad Brother,* which contrasts the life of nineteenth-century stage actor Edwin Booth with that of his brother, John Wilkes, the man who murdered U.S. President Abraham Lincoln. Enriched by numerous period photographs and other images, the book also includes a "bibliography and discussion of sources opens

a wealth of avenues for further reading," according to *Horn Book* contributor Betty Carter. Asserting that "Giblin never forgets the 'story' part of history," GraceAnne A. DeCandido deemed *Good Brother, Bad Brother* an "absorbing narrative" in her *Booklist* appraisal, and in *School Library Journal* Jennifer Ralston wrote that Giblin's "writing is engaging and eminently readable, and presents history in a manner that is, in essence, consummate storytelling."

While Giblin's biographies focus on individuals whose stories are well known, he recognizes that the lives of people from all walks of life are part of the tapestry of history. His novel *The Boy Who Saved Cleveland: Based on a True Story* takes place in 1798, in the tiny settlement of Cleveland, Ohio. Having moved here from New England, Seth Doan is now ten years old. He must take on all the responsibilities for the family after his parents and other family members come down with the malaria fever. In addition to keeping his family fed by working the farm and grinding corn for food during the outbreak, the boy also cares for his neighbors when the disease spreads. "Crisply and succinctly told," according to a *Publishers Weekly* contributor, Giblin's "engaging tale featur[es] . . . a real-life peer and a generous number of atmospheric drawings" by Michael Dooling. Predicting that older readers "will admire the themes of perseverance, education, and responsibility" in Giblin's book, Pat Peach added in *School Library Journal* that "the clear writing and plot-driven pace" in *The Boy Who Saved Cleveland* will attract younger history buffs. Noting that Giblin devotes the same attention to detail that characterizes his nonfiction work, *Booklist* contributor Kay Weisman added that "the background research is still clearly evident, but added to that are some finely nuanced, believable characters."

Giblin's edited work, *The Century That Was: Reflections on the Last One Hundred Years,* serves as a natural extension of his former work as an editor. The volume contains thematic essays by eleven noted children's writers, each one looking back at a different aspect of life in the United States of America in the twentieth century. In *Booklist,* Hazel Rochman pointed out that while Giblin makes no effort to produce a "comprehensive" history, "the individual approaches, both personal and historical, will stimulate young people to look back and also forward to where we're going next." A *Horn Book* reviewer voiced a similar opinion, stating that "one of the older formulas of outstanding nonfiction . . . is the essay. It's back, and in fine fettle for a new generation of readers."

The work of a nonfiction writer involves a great deal of research, and Giblin illustrates how this important task is accomplished in his chapter book *Did Fleming Rescue Churchill?: A Research Puzzle.* Here readers meet ten-year-old Jason, a boy who has been assigned to write a school report on scientist Alexander Fleming, the man who discovered penicillin. When he turns to the Internet to complete his social-studies assignment,

Jason finds that some of the "facts" he finds contradict each other. His research also gives rise to questions and provokes the curiosity that inspires the boy to dig deeper: in this case into the relationship between Fleming and British Prime Minister Winston Churchill. *Did Fleming Rescue Churchill?* was described by *School Library Journal* contributor Jennifer Cogan as "the perfect story to impress upon young researchers the value of accuracy and the enjoyment of fact-finding." Phelan praised the "expressive pen drawings" contributed by illustrator Erik Brooks, and asserted that in this "unique" work for elementary graders the author "turns a potentially dull subject into a good story."

As a writer of historical nonfiction, Giblin enjoys investigating the factual details of his subjects and recognizes how important this task is to his work. "I love research," he admitted to *Publishers Weekly* interviewer Wendy Smith. "I love going down to Washington[, DC,] on a vacation week and using the Library of Congress. I enjoy making things clear for readers—maybe 'clear' is a unifying word in my work as an author and editor."

Biographical and Critical Sources

BOOKS

Children's Literature Review, Volume 29, Gale (Detroit, MI), 1993.
Something about the Author Autobiography Series, Volume 12, Gale (Detroit, MI), 1991.

PERIODICALS

Booklist, December 1, 1996, Carolyn Phelan, review of *The Dwarf, the Giant, and the Unicorn: A Tale of King Arthur,* pp. 666-667; February 15, 2000, Ilene Cooper, review of *The Amazing Life of Benjamin Franklin,* p. 1105; March 1, 2000, Hazel Rochman, review of *The Century That Was: Reflections on the Last One Hundred Years,* p. 1235; April 1, 2002, Todd Morning, review of *The Life and Death of Adolf Hitler,* p. 1336; September 15, 2004, Hazel Rochman, review of *Secrets of the Sphinx,* p. 240; May 1, 2005, GraceAnne A. DeCandido, review of *Good Brother, Bad Brother: The Story of Edwin Booth and John Wilkes Booth,* p. 1586; April 15, 2996, Kay Weisman, review of *The Boy Who Saved Cleveland: Based on a True Story,* p. 58; September 1, 2007, Carolyn Phelan, review of *The Many Rides of Paul Revere,* p. 116; March 15, 2008, Carolyn Phelan, review of *Did Fleming Rescue Churchill?: A Research Puzzle,* p. 50.
Bulletin of the Center for Children's Books, September, 1985, review of *The Truth about Santa Claus;* April, 2000, review of *The Century That Was,* p. 281; June, 2002, review of *The Life and Death of Adolf Hitler,* p. 364.
Horn Book, November-December, 1990, Elizabeth S. Watson, review of *The Riddle of the Rosetta Stone: Key to Ancient Egypt,* p. 758; March, 2000, review of *The Century That Was,* p. 211; May-June, 2000, Mary M. Burns, review of *The Amazing Life of Benjamin Franklin,* p. 333; May-June, 2002, Peter D. Sieruta, review of *The Life and Death of Adolf Hitler,* p. 346; May-June, 2005, Betty Carter, review of *Good Brother, Bad Brother,* p. 349; November-December, 2007, Tanya D. Auger, review of *The Many Rides of Paul Revere,* p. 697.
New York Times Book Review, March 12, 1989, Philip M. Isaacson, review of *Let There Be Light: A Book about Windows,* p. 35; May 20, 1990, Ann M. Martin, review of *From Hand to Mouth; or, How We Invented Knives, Forks, Spoons, and Chopsticks and the Table Manners to Go with Them,* p. 46.
Publishers Weekly, July 26, 1985, Wendy Smith, interview with Giblin, p. 169; November 11, 1996, review of *The Dwarf, the Giant, and the Unicorn,* p. 75; January 25, 1999, review of *The Mystery of the Mammoth Bones, and How It Was Solved,* p. 97; May 8, 2000, review of *The Century That Was,* p. 222; April 17, 2006, review of *The Boy Who Saved Cleveland,* p. 187.
School Library Journal, January, 1983, Amy L. Cohn, review of *Chimney Sweeps: Yesterday and Today,* p. 75; October, 1985, review of *The Truth about Santa Claus,* p. 192; March, 2000, Barbara Chatton, review of *The Amazing Life of Benjamin Franklin,* p. 224; July, 2000, Ginny Gustin, review of *The Century That Was,* p. 116; May, 2002, Andrew Medlar, review of *The Life and Death of Adolf Hitler,* p. 170; May, 2005, Jennifer Ralston, review of *Good Brother, Bad Brother,* p. 150; August, 2005, Blair Christolon, review of *The Amazing Life of Benjamin Franklin,* p. 48; May, 2006, Pat Peach, review of *The Boy Who Saved Cleveland,* p. 88; November, 2007, Carole Phillips, review of *The Many Rides of Paul Revere,* p. 146; April, 2008, Jennifer Cogan, review of *Did Fleming Rescue Churchill?,* p. 108.
Voice of Youth Advocates, February, 1998, review of *Charles A. Lindbergh: A Human Hero,* p. 364; October, 2000, Leah J. Sparks, review of *The Century That Was,* p. 285; June, 2002, review of *The Life and Death of Adolf Hitler,* p. 134; August, 2005, Marian Rafal, review of *Good Brother, Bad Brother,* p. 245; October, 2007, Roxy Ekstrom, review of *The Many Rides of Paul Revere,* p. 364.

ONLINE

Children's Book Council Web site, http://www.chcbooks.org/cbcmagaine/ (January 27, 2009), "James Cross Giblin: Portraying the 'Bad Boys' of History."*

*   *   *

GORDON, Amy 1949-
(Amy Lawson)

Personal

Born January 22, 1949, in Boston, MA; daughter of Lincoln (a professor, diplomat, and economist) and Al-

lison (an artist, writer, and mother) Gordon; married Richard Lawson (divorced 1995); children: Nicholas Lawson, Hugh Lawson. *Education:* Bard College, graduate, 1972. *Politics:* "Eclectic." *Religion:* "Eclectic." *Hobbies and other interests:* "Writing, reading, mountain climbing, sailing, spending time with people I like, traveling."

Addresses

Home—Montague, MA. *E-mail*—agordon49@gmail.com.

Career

Bement School (K-9 boarding school), Deerfield, MA, drama teacher and director, chair of fine-arts program, 1980—.

Awards, Honors

Texas Blue Bonnet Award nomination, 2004, and Missouri Association of Librarians award, both for *The Gorillas of Gill Park.*

Writings

(Under name Amy Lawson) *The Talking Bird and the Story Pouch,* illustrated by Craig McFarland Brown, Harper (New York, NY), 1983.
(Under name Amy Lawson) *Star Baby,* illustrated by Margot Apple, Harcourt Brace Jovanovich (San Diego, CA), 1991.
Midnight Magic, illustrated by Judy Clifford, BridgeWater (Mahwah, NJ), 1995.
When JFK Was My Father, Houghton Mifflin (Boston, MA), 1999.
The Gorillas of Gill Park, Holiday House (New York, NY), 2003.
The Secret Life of a Boarding School Brat, Holiday House (New York, NY), 2004.
Return to Gill Park, Holiday House (New York, NY), 2006.
Magic by Heart, illustrated by Adam Gustavson, Holiday House (New York, NY), 2007.

Sidelights

Amy Gordon's works for young people reflect the author's belief in the power of imagination. While her chapter book *Midnight Magic* extols the value and fun of imagination to beginning readers, Gordon's teen novel *When JFK Was My Father* asserts the benefits of a fantasy life for adolescents. In other books, such as *The Gorillas of Gill Park* and its sequel, *Return to Gill Park,* Gordon depicts a host of eccentric characters who band together to energize their neighborhood.

A native of Massachusetts, Gordon was born and raised in the Boston area. As a young adult, she moved to Rio de Janeiro, Brazil, with her family; after two years she

returned to the United States and was educated at a girls' boarding school. Gordon attended Bard College during the late 1960s and early 1970s. "During those years, I discovered I could get people to pay attention to me through the written word," she recalled on her home page. After graduating from Bard in 1972, Gordon was not sure what to do with her life, but she eventually became a teacher. As she noted, "I was a camp counselor for many years and knew that I loved working with kids. Now I teach drama and put on plays with kids and write as much as I can between teaching and raising my two sons."

Midnight Magic finds Uncle Harry babysitting Jake and Sam during a weekend of crises: Sam has lost a tooth and Jake's pet hamsters are missing. Uncle Harry distracts the children by enacting their favorite story, "Puss in Boots," and when they wake up on Saturday morning, Sam finds a golden key left under his pillow by the Tooth Fairy. When Sam and Jake begin a search for the evil ogre of the "Puss in Boots" story, hoping to return the golden key to him, they somehow end up on the hamster's trail. *School Library Journal* reviewer Mary Jo Drungil singled out Gordon's "utterly realistic" por-

Cover of Amy Gordon's teen novel The Secret Life of a Boarding School Brat, *featuring photography by Marc Tauss.* (Holiday House, 2004. Reproduced by permission.)

trait of two likeable young boys, as well as their "ideal" uncle, for special praise, and predicted that *Midnight Magic* is "certain to be appreciated by young fairy-tale fans."

Geared for middle-grade readers, *The Gorillas of Gill Park* is a humorous novel that focuses on Willy, a lonely middle-schooler who finds a world of new friends while spending the summer with his widowed aunt. The practical-minded Willy is instantly set at ease by his quirky Aunt Bridget, whose job as a costume designer now keeps her busy sewing gorilla costumes in her small urban apartment. Nearby, Willy discovers a small park run by an equally eccentric wealthy musician, Otto Pettingill, and when the park is threatened by land developers the boy's practical sense helps win the day. In *Booklist* Gillian Engberg praised *The Gorillas of Gill Park* as a "suspenseful, winning story" in which "delicious words, clever dialogue, and endearing characters" retain reader attention. Noting that Gordon draws her cast of characters from among "folk of varying degrees of eccentricity," a *Publishers Weekly* critic added that the young protagonist's "gradual discovery of his own worth is satisfying" and the storyline is "often funny."

In *Return to Gill Park,* Willy decides to move in with Aunt Bridget so he can attend an alternative school in her neighborhood and keep an eye on the park, which he inherited from Mr. Pettingill. When Willy learns that the park has been damaged by a group of vandals led by Dillon Deronda, he determines to stop them. There is only one hitch: Mr. Pettingill has left clues to a treasure, and Willy must work with Dillon to solve the mystery. Reviewing *Return to Gill Park* in *Booklist,* Todd Morning praised "the sheer goofiness and exuberance of the story," and *School Library Journal* contributor Elizabeth Bird observed that the work exhibits the "same good-natured flair exhibited in the earlier title." "Intriguing, idiosyncratic and fun to read," was the description a *Kirkus Reviews* critic bestowed on *Return to Gill Park.*

Taking place in the 1960s, Gordon's novel *When JFK Was My Father* centers on fourteen-year-old Georgia Hughes, a girl who lives in Brazil with her emotionally remote parents. When her parents get divorced, Georgia and her mother move back to the United States, and the teen is deposited in a boarding school. The highly inventive Georgia feels abandoned by both parents, particularly her father, and she compensates for her loneliness as she did in Brazil: by pretending that recently assassinated U.S. president John F. Kennedy is her real father. When Tim, a friend from Brazil who has run away from his boarding school, invites Georgia to hit the road with him, she suddenly realizes that her school, and the friends she has made there, may have filled an important void in her life. "Georgia's account of her virtual abandonment at school by her parents and her barely conscious search for a home is both poignant and gently funny," contended Lauren Adams in her review of *When JFK Was My Father* for *Horn Book.*

Cover of Gordon's humorous middle-grade novel The Gorillas of Gill Park, *featuring artwork by Matthew Cordell.* (Illustration copyright © 2003 by Matthew Cordell. Reproduced by permission of Holiday House, Inc.)

Praising Gordon's novel as "well paced with moments of dramatic tension," the critic added that "Georgia's refreshing narrative" ably reveals the cast of interesting secondary characters. "Gordon writes in a vivid, defining style that allows Georgia to emerge as a fresh, fully realized character," attested Ilene Cooper in *Booklist,* while Connie Tyrrell Burns wrote in *School Library Journal* that the success of *When JFK Was My Father* rests on Gordon's creation of a "likable and well-drawn character" with whom readers can identify.

The gift of a diary by her grandmother proves to be the salvation of th protagonist in *The Secret Life of a Boarding School Brat,* a book that had its basis in the author's own experiences. Also taking place in the 1960s, the novel follows Lydia Rice, a seventh grader who feels isolated, not only because of her parents' divorce and their decision to ship her off to boarding school, but also because of the recent death of her beloved grandmother. Written in the form of the diary Lydia starts while at Miss Pocket's Boarding School, the novel follows the girl's efforts to solve a puzzle from the past, a task put to the lonely girl by the school's kind-hearted maintenance man. Noting the novel's "lively pacing

Cover of Gordon's picture book **Magic by Heart,** *featuring artwork by* ***Adam Gustavson.*** (Illustration copyright © 2007 by Adam Gustavson. All rights reserved. Reproduced by permission of Holiday House, Inc.)

and appealing if improbable . . . characters," a *Publishers Weekly* contributor predicted that "many readers will be caught up in the mystery" like Lydia. In *Horn Book* Susan Dove Lempke had special praise for the young protagonist's "lively personality" and Gordon's depiction of "the intergenerational friendship she forms" with the school handyman, while a *Kirkus Reviews* critic dubbed *The Secret Life of a Boarding School Brat* a "pleasant read."

In *Magic by Heart,* a picture book by Gordon, a special girl helps others recognize their worth. After Belle and Sam, a childless couple, follow the unusual advice of magical Silvia, they are rewarded with the birth of their beautiful daughter Arietta. The youngster possesses a wonderful ability to see into people's hearts, and she can also fly when she dons a cloak made from artichoke leaves. After Arietta is kidnapped by Silvia's brother, Hector, a forlorn magician, a group of magical friends—both human and animal—must come to her rescue. "This eccentric fantasy is full of quirky characters," Carole Phillips remarked in *School Library Journal,* and a contributor in *Kirkus Reviews* stated that readers who enjoy complex fantasy narratives "will find enough to appreciate" in the story.

Gordon once told *SATA:* "When I was young, I was a shy person in a verbal, intellectual, talkative family. I discovered that if I *wrote* entertaining stories as Christ-

mas presents, then I could get the entire family to stop talking and pay attention to me. The written word allowed me to have a voice.

"I loved to read when I was young, and spent quite a lot of time pretending. I loved the world of childhood and left it reluctantly. In my adult life, I am very lucky to have a career (teaching drama and directing plays with 6th-9th graders) which allows me to encourage pretending. The creative problem-solving involved in teaching helps my writing, and the kids I teach, also, of course, inspire me. I am a lot less shy now, but I still feel the written word is my best tool for expressing and sharing my real self."

Biographical and Critical Sources

PERIODICALS

Booklist, June 1, 1999, Ilene Cooper, review of *When JFK Was My Father,* p. 1813; June 1, 2003, Gillian Engberg, review of *The Gorillas of Gill Park,* p. 1776; May 15, 2006, Todd Morning, review of *Return to Gill Park,* p. 45.

Horn Book, July-August, 1999, Lauren Adams, review of *When JFK Was My Father,* pp. 463-464; July-August, 2004, Susan Dove Lempke, review of *The Secret Life of a Boarding School Brat,* p. 452.

Kirkus Reviews, April 15, 2004, review of *The Secret Life of a Boarding School Brat,* p. 394; March 15, 2006, review of *Return to Gill Park,* p. 290; August 1, 2007, review of *Magic by Heart.*

New York Times Book Review, October 17, 1999, Patricia McCormick, review of *When JFK Was My Father,* p. 31.

Publishers Weekly, May 26, 2003, review of *The Gorillas of Gill Park,* p. 70; March 22, 2004, review of *The Secret Life of a Boarding School Brat,* p. 86.

School Library Journal, December, 1995, Mary Jo Drungil, review of *Midnight Magic,* pp. 80-81; April, 1999, Connie Tyrrell Burns, review of *When JFK Was My Father,* p. 134; April, 2006, Elizabeth Bird, review of *Return to Gill Park,* p. 140; November, 2007, Carole Phillips, review of *Magic by Heart,* p. 92.

PERIODICALS

Amy Gordon Home Page, http://www.amyagordon.com (February 1, 2009).*

*   *   *

GOTT, Barry

Personal

Married; children: two. *Education:* Bowling Green State University, B.F.A., 1994.

Addresses

Home and office—Cleveland, OH. *E-mail*—bgott@sbc global.net.

Career

Illustrator and author of children's books.

Writings

SELF-ILLUSTRATED

Class Pets, Sterling (New York, NY), 2005.

ILLUSTRATOR

Steven Kroll, *Patches Lost and Found,* Winslow Press (Delray Beach, FL), 2001.

Kelli Chipponeri, *Ouch!: Bye Bye, Boo-Boos,* Little Simon (New York, NY), 2001.

Betty Schwartz, *Knock, Knock, It's Halloween!,* Little Simon (New York, NY), 2002.

Jennifer Dussling, *The Rainbow Mystery,* Kane (New York, NY), 2002.

Lawrence David, *Horace Splattly: The Cupcaked Crusader,* Dutton (New York, NY), 2002.

Lawrence David, *When Second Graders Attack,* Dutton (New York, NY), 2002.

Barbara Bottner, *Be Brown!,* Grosset & Dunlap (New York, NY), 2002.

Lawrence David, *The Terror of the Pink Dodo Balloons,* Dutton (New York, NY), 2003.

Dan Danko and Tom Mason, *Operation Squish!,* Little, Brown (New York, NY), 2003.

Dan Danko and Tom Mason, *Sidekicks,* Little, Brown (New York, NY), 2003.

Cathy Goldberg Fishman, *Car Wash Kid,* Children's Press (New York, NY), 2003.

Barry Gott's illustration projects include creating art for Steve Kroll's picture book **Patches Lost and Found.** (Illustration copyright © 2001 by Barry Gott. All rights reserved. Reproduced by permission. To further explore the theme of this book through activities, games and links all over the world, please go to: www.readandclick.com. For educators: This book has been included in the Read&Click&Learn Curriculum Learning System's virtual library.)

Lawrence David, *To Catch a Clownosaurus,* Puffin (New York, NY), 2003.

Henry Barker, *It Came from Outer Space,* Kane (New York, NY), 2003.

Harriet Ziefert, *Hey, Irma!: This Is Halloween,* Blue Apple (Maplewood, NJ), 2003.

Dandi Daley Mackall, *It Must Be Halloween,* Little Simon (New York, NY), 2003.

James Solheim, *Santa's Secrets Revealed: All Your Questions Answered about Santa's Super Sleigh, His Flying Reindeer, and Other Wonders,* Carolrhoda (Minneapolis, MN), 2004.

Harriet Ziefert, *Hey, Irma!: It's a Contest,* Blue Apple (Maplewood, NJ), 2004.

Dan Danko and Tom Mason, *Attack of the Mole Master,* Little, Brown (New York, NY), 2004.

Harriet Ziefert, *Hey, Irma!: It's Mother's Day,* Blue Apple (Maplewood, NJ), 2004.

Kirsten Hall, *My New School,* Children's Press (New York, NY), 2004.

Dan Danko and Tom Mason, *The Candy Man Cometh,* Little, Brown (New York, NY), 2004.

Lawrence David, *The Invasion of the Shag Carpet Creature,* Puffin (New York, NY), 2004.

Lawrence David, *The Most Evil, Friendly Villain Ever,* Dutton (New York, NY), 2004.

Dan Danko and Tom Mason, *The Brotherhood of Rotten Baby-Sitters,* Little, Brown (New York, NY), 2005.

Laura Driscoll, *Super Specs,* Kane (New York, NY), 2005.

Sheila Bair, *Rock, Brock, and the Savings Shock,* Albert Whitman (Morton Grove, IL), 2006.

(With Mike Morris) Sarah Durkee, *Flushed Away: Movie Storybook,* Scholastic (New York, NY), 2006.

(With Mike Morris) Sarah Durkee, *Plumbing Problems* (based on the movie *Flushed Away*), Scholastic (New York, NY), 2006.

Michelle Knudsen, *A Moldy Mystery,* Kane (New York, NY), 2006.

Anne Bowen, *What Do Teachers Do (After You Leave School)?,* Carolrhoda (Minneapolis, MN), 2006.

Eleanor May, *The Real Me,* Kane (New York, NY), 2006.

Traci N. Todd, adapter, *Head, Shoulders, Knees, and Toes,* Kindermusik (Greensboro, NC), 2006.

Harriet Ziefert, *No! Yes!,* Sterling (New York, NY), 2006.

Ginger M. Churchill, *Carmen's Sticky Scab,* Tanglewood (Terre Haute, IN), 2007.

Nan Walker, *The Midnight Kid,* Kane (New York, NY), 2007.

Lisa Wheeler, *Dino-Hockey,* Carolrhoda (Minneapolis, MN), 2007.

Harriet Ziefert, *Class Worms,* Sterling (New York, NY), 2007.

Eleanor May, *The Great Shape-up,* Kane (New York, NY), 2007.

Kirsten Larsen, *Whoa! UFO!,* Kane (New York, NY), 2009.

Sidelights

Barry Gott is an illustrator, not only for children's picture books, but also for "greeting cards, magazine spots, and just about anything else that's remotely fun," as he noted on his home page. In addition to appearing in his original self-illustrated picture book *Class Pets,* Gott's digital art has captivated fans of two children's book series about super kids: the "Horace Splatly" series by Lawrence David, and the "Sidekicks" books coauthored by Dan Danko and Tom Mason.

For the "Splatly" books, "Gott's pop-eyed, rubbery-looking figures capture the general sense of goofiness perfectly," according to a *Kirkus Reviews* contributor. Sharon R. Pearce, writing a review of the second entry in the series, *When Second Graders Attack,* for *School Library Journal,* concluded that the story is "enhanced" by the artist's cartoon illustrations. Gott's "black-and-white sketches underscore the cartoonish aspects of the story," concluded Pat Leach in her *School Library Journal* review of a more-recent title, *To Catch a Clownosaurus.* Also writing for *School Library Journal,* Christina F. Renaud dubbed Gott's "Horace Splatly" illustrations "humorous."

In addition to his art for series fiction, Gott has also illustrated a number of single titles for a variety of authors. *Patches Lost and Found,* Steve Kroll's story about a lost hamster, "finds apt expression in Gott's digital artwork, which has the appearance of cut-paper collage," wrote Carolyn Phelan in a *Booklist* review of the book. According to Barbara Buckley, writing in *School Library Journal,* Gott's illustrations are "perfect for the story." Jane Marino noted in *School Library Journal* that Barbara Bottner's text for *Be Brown* allows Gott's "uncluttered, expressive illustrations to expand on the story," and a *Publishers Weekly* critic cited the illustrator's "hilarious animated" contributions to Bottner's tale.

Gott's illustrations for James Solheim's *Santa's Secrets Revealed: All Your Questions Answered about Santa's Super Sleigh, His Flying Reindeer, and Other Wonders* "contain oodles of humorous touches," according to a *Publishers Weekly* contributor, while Phelan concluded that the artist offers "bold colors in a cartoonlike style" in his art for Laura Driscoll's *Super Specs.* Mary Hazelton, a contributor to *School Library Journal,* described Gott's images for Ann Bowen's *What Do Teachers Do (After You Leave School)?* as "energetic and colorful with lots of whooshy movement and splashy action."

For Lisa Wheeler's *Dino-Hockey,* Gott contributes "action-filled paintings" of dinosaurs playing hockey and wearing "comically exaggerated expressions," according to *Booklist* critic Gillian Engberg. A *Kirkus Reviews* contributor, writing about the same title, commented on the artist's "high-energy scenes." Reviewing *The Great Shape Up* for *School Library Journal,* Linda R. Walkins concluded that Gott's "cheerful cartoon illustrations enhance the lessons" offered in Eleanor May's entertaining text.

Biographical and Critical Sources

PERIODICALS

Booklist, March 1, 2001, Carolyn Phelan, review of *Patches Lost and Found,* p. 1277; May, 2001, Barbara

Buckley, review of *Patches Lost and Found,* p. 126; September 15, 2002, Carolyn Phelan, review of *Rainbow Mystery,* p. 239; August, 2005, Carolyn Phelan, review of *Super Specs,* p. 2034; April 15, 2006, Hazel Rochman, review of *A Moldy Mystery,* p. 52; September 1, 2007, Gillian Engberg, review of *Dino-Hockey,* p. 137.

Kirkus Reviews, December 15, 2001, review of *Be Brown!,* p. 1754; April 15, 2002, review of *Horace Splattly: The Cupcaked Crusader,* p. 565; December 1, 2002, review of *The Terror of the Pink Dodo Balloons,* p. 1767; September 1, 2007, review of *Dino-Hockey.*

Publishers Weekly, January 7, 2002, review of *Be Brown!,* p. 63; September 27, 2004, review of *Santa's Secrets Revealed: All Your Questions Answered about Santa's Super Sleigh, His Flying Reindeer, and Other Wonders,* p. 63.

School Library Journal, October, 2001, Christina F. Renaud, review of *Horace Splattly,* p. 113; February, 2002, Jane Marino, review of *Be Brown!,* p. 96; July, 2002, Sharon R. Pearce, review of *When Second Graders Attack,* p. 88; February, 2003, review of *The Terror of the Pink Dodo Balloons,* p. 104; October, 2003, Lee Bock, review of *It Came from Outer Space,* p. 114; November, 2003, review of *Sidekicks,* p. 138; January, 2004, Pat Leach, review of *To Catch a Clownosaurus,* p. 96; December, 2004, Sandra Welzenbach, review of *The Big Game,* p. 109; November, 2006, Mary Hazelton, review of *What Do Teachers Do (After You Leave School?),* p. 84; May, 2007, Anne L. Tormohlen, review of *The Midnight Kid,* p. 110; September, 2007, Linda L. Walkins, review of *The Great Shape Up,* p. 172; December, 2007, Julie Roach, review of *Dino-Hockey,* p. 102.

ONLINE

Barry Gott Home Page, http://www.barrygott.com (January 13, 2009).

Herman Agency Web site, http://www.hermanagencyinc.com/ (January 13, 2009), "Barry Gott."*

*   *   *

GUNNELLA 1956-
[A pseudonym]
(Gudrún Elin Ólafsdóttir)

Personal

Born July 6, 1956, in Reykjavík, Iceland; married; children: one son. *Education:* Commercial College of Iceland, degree, 1974; College of Art and Craft (Iceland), degree (serigraphy), 1986. *Hobbies and other interests:* Gardening.

Addresses

Home—Garôaboer, Iceland. *E-mail*—gunnella1@gmail.com.

Career

Painter and graphic artist. Established graphics studio, c. 1986. *Exhibitions:* Work exhibited in solo and group exhibits in Reykjavík, Iceland.

Awards, Honors

Ten Best Illustrated Children's Books of the Year designation, 2005, for *The Problem with Chickens* by Bruce McMillan.

Illustrator

Bruce McMillan, *The Problem with Chickens,* Houghton Mifflin (Boston, MA), 2005.
Bruce McMillan, *How the Ladies Stopped the Wind,* Houghton Mifflin (Boston, MA), 2007.

Sidelights

Gunnella is a painter and illustrator who lives in Garôaboer, a small town hear Reykjavík, Iceland. A well-known artist, she entered a new phase of her creative career when she met Bruce McMillan, an American photographer and writer during an exhibition of her work. McMillan was visiting Iceland, a country to which he has returned to photograph many times, and when he discovered Gunnella's primitive-style paintings he recognized their potential. As the artist recalled on her home page, McMillan "saw my paintings . . . and asked me if he could write a story from them. He then took photos of many paintings, lined them up, and wrote a story around them." The story became *The Problem with Chickens,* a picture book that was listed among the *New York Times'* ten best illustrated children's books of 2005.

In *The Problem with Chickens* a group of women import several laying hens to their rugged rural Icelandic village, hoping to ensure a constant supply of fresh eggs for baking cakes. Unfortunately, the chickens soon decide to mimic the ways of humans and no eggs are laid, until the resourceful women engineer a unique solution to their perplexing problem. While noting that McMillan's story is "tenuous," *Horn Book* contributor Martha V. Parravano added that Gunnella's "distinctive" brightly colored paintings "have verve, vibrancy, and humor." Noting the "childlike humor" in the book's brightly colored images, Mary Hazelton added in *School Library Journal* that Gunnella is able to "convey emotion and absurdity with seemingly simple lines and expressive body language."

The stocky, apron-clad ladies from Gunnella's Icelandic village return in another adventure in McMillan's *How the Ladies Stopped the Wind.* Hoping to block the constant gusts of wind near their homes, the women decide to plant trees. While the egg-laying chickens help by producing fertilizer for the young saplings, the village sheep nibble away all the tender buds and leaves from the future forest, presenting a problem requiring the ladies to devise yet another clever solution. "The droll

humor of Gunnella's flat oil paintings is a perfect match for [McMillan's] . . . wry, economical text," wrote Lauren Adams in her *Horn Book* review of *How the Ladies Stopped the Wind,* while in *Kirkus Reviews* a critic praised the "humor and quirky characterization" in the artist's folk-style artwork. With their "round faces, stubby legs, patterned aprons, and colorful babushkas," Gunnella's hardy Icelandic ladies "are as comforting as they are clever," concluded *Booklist* critic Julie Cummins.

Gunnella gets her inspiration from the Icelandic landscape and its folk-art traditions. "Our roots are very important for we Icelanders, the old houses, our grandmothers with aprons on and of course the Icelandic nature," she explained to a writer for *Hús og Híbýli.* "All this seems to go into my paintings in one way or the other. Sometimes I drive around and take photos of old houses that I later on use in my paintings." She also draws from her memories of family and friends, what she calls "the photo-album of my mind." "The Saga of the Icelandic people is quite amazing," Gunnella added. "It was so very difficult to survive here. . . . My grandparents told stories of their primitive living from their growing-up years. . . . I tell stories of the old-time-living but in my own way, [incorporating] . . . spices like flowers and trees from my garden and the powerful Snæfellsnes glacier."

Biographical and Critical Sources

PERIODICALS

Booklist, September 15, 2005, Diane Foote, review of *The Problem with Chickens,* p. 74; October 1, 2007, Julie Cummins, review of *How the Ladies Stopped the Wind,* p. 64.
Horn Book, November-December, 2005, Martha V. Parravano, review of *The Problem with Chickens,* p. 708; January-February, 2008, Lauren Adams, review of *How the Ladies Stopped the Wind,* p. 76.
Hús og Híbýli (in Icelandic), July, 2008, "Sumarhús Gunnellu" (profile of Gunnella), pp. 42-44.
Kirkus Reviews, September 1, 2005, review of *The Problem with Chickens,* p. 978; September 1, 2007, review of *How the Ladies Stopped the Wind.*
Kliatt,.
Publishers Weekly, August 29, 2005, review of *The Problem with Chickens,* p. 55; July 23, 2007, review of *How the Ladies Stopped the Wind,* p. 67.
School Library Journal, September, 2005, Mary Hazelton, review of *The Problem of Chickens,* p. 177; December, 2007, Marian Drabkin, review of *How the Ladies Stopped the Wind,* p. 94.

ONLINE

Gunnella Home Page, http://www.gunnella.info (January 15, 2009).*

HANFT, Josh 1956-
(Joshua E. Hanft)

Personal

Born 1956; married; children: three sons. *Religion:* Jewish.

Addresses

Home—New York, NY. *E-mail*—josh.hanft@ansche chesed.org.

Career

Freelance editor and writer. Has also served as vice president of new product development at Golden Books Family Entertainment, as vice president and publisher at Dalmatian Press, and as director of licensed publishing at Scholastic. Congregation Ansche Chesed, New York, NY, executive director.

Writings

The Miracles of Passover, illustrated by Seymour Chwast, Blue Apple Books (Maplewood, NJ), 2007.
Miracles of the Bible, illustrated by Seymour Chwast, Blue Apple Books (Maplewood, NJ), 2007.

AS JOSHUA E. HANFT

(Adaptor) Howard Pyle, *King Arthur and the Knights of the Round Table,* illustrated by Pablo Marcos, Abdo Publishing (Edina, MN), 2002.
Jackie Robinson, illustrated by Pablo Marcos, Abdo Publishing (Edina, MN), 2005.

Sidelights

Josh Hanft, the executive director at Congregation Ansche Chesed in New York City, is the author of the well-received picture books *The Miracles of Passover* and *Miracles of the Bible.* In the former, Hanft tells the history of the Jewish holiday, relating the story of Moses, the plagues, and the parting of the Red Sea and also describing the traditional aspects of the Seder. A critic in *Publishers Weekly* complimented the "inviting, straightforward text" in *The Miracles of Passover.* A number of reviewers also offered praise for illustrator Seymour Chwast's inventive book design, which incorporates a lift-the-flap format.

Hanft and Chwast have also collaborated on *Miracles of the Bible,* a companion volume to *The Miracles of*

Josh Hanft's picture book **Miracles of the Bible** *features brightly colored artwork by Seymour Chwast.* (Illustration copyright © 2007 by Seymour Chwast. All rights reserved. Reproduced by permission.)

Passover. Here Hanft retells a dozen familiar tales from the Old Testament, such as Noah's ark, David and Goliath, Daniel in the lion's den, Jonah and the whale, the birth of Adam, and Samson and Delilah. "Each story is succinctly told in one page of simply written text with a short, relevant Bible verse," a contributor in *Kirkus Reviews* noted, and Ilene Cooper, writing in *Booklist,* observed that Hanft's prose is "both understandable and suitably dignified." Citing the combination of the author's "dramatic" vignettes and Chwast's gatefold illustrations, remarked a *Publishers Weekly* reviewer, predicting that young readers "will likely flock to this hands-on reading experience."

Biographical and Critical Sources

PERIODICALS

Booklist, May 1, 2007, Hazel Rochman, review of *The Miracles of Passover,* p. 92; October 1, 2007, Ilene Cooper, review of *Miracles of the Bible,* p. 72.

Kirkus Reviews, October 1, 2007, review of *Miracles of the Bible.*

Publishers Weekly, February 26, 2007, review of *The Miracles of Passover,* p. 94; August 27, 2007, review of *Miracles of the Bible,* p. 94.

School Library Journal, April, 2007, Lisa Silverman, review of *The Miracles of Passover,* p. 122; November, 2007, Rachel Kamin, review of *Miracles of the Bible,* p. 108.

*   *   *

HANFT, Joshua E.
See HANFT, Josh

*   *   *

HAWKING, Lucy 1969-

Personal

Born November 2, 1969, in England; daughter of Stephen (a physicist) and Jane Hawking; married Alex Mackenzie Smith, 1998 (separated); children: William. *Education:* Graduated from Oxford University.

Addresses

Home and office—London, England.

Career

Journalist. Autism Research Centre, University of Cambridge, Cambridge, England, administrative staff member. Writer for *New York* magazine, London *Daily Mail,* London *Telegraph,* London *Times,* and London *Evening Standard.* Has also worked as a radio journalist.

Writings

Jaded (novel for adults), Headline (London, England), 2004.
Run for Your Life (novel for adults), Plume (New York, NY), 2006.
(With father, Stephen Hawking) *George's Secret Key to the Universe,* illustrated by Garry Parsons, Simon & Schuster (New York, NY), 2007.

Sidelights

Journalist and novelist Lucy Hawking spent several years writing for adults, in newspapers an on the radio, before working with her father, physicist Stephen Hawking, on their first book for children. Part of an intended trilogy, *George's Secret Key to the Universe* is the story of George and Annie's trip through the universe when Annie's father, a scientist, uses a computer to a doorway to any point in the known universe. The book is an adventure story, but also designed to introduce concepts of physics and the far reaches of the universe to a young audience.

George and Annie embark on a series of sometimes dangerous adventures, and soon they discover that a competing scientist wants to steal the computer, called Cosmos, for himself. Not only do Annie and George have their hands full learning about space, the solar system, black holes, and Hawking radiation (named after the noted physicist and coauthor), but the pair must make sure that Cosmos does not fall into the wrong hands—and rescue Annie's father from his competitors. "The authors handily explore a range of themes, among them, the moral responsibilities of science, global warming and space colonization," explained a *Publishers Weekly* contributor. Noting that Stephen Hawking provides sidebars with science facts throughout the book, Debbie Carton wrote in *Booklist* that the notes are presented "in very comprehensible terms, but they don't compete with or overwhelm the fast-paced story." *School Library Journal* critic Steven Engelfried, on the other hand, found the novel to be "a well-intentioned attempt to combine the drama of fiction with the excitement of scientific inquiry," but ultimately, not strong enough as a story to draw in readers. Although a *Kirkus Reviews* critic was concerned that science facts were set aside for the convenience of the plot, in *Internet Bookwatch* a contributor called *George's Secret Key to the Universe* a "gripping adventure."

"Writing this book with my dad, Stephen Hawking was a lot of fun for both of us," Hawking wrote on the *George's Secret Key to the Universe* Web site. She explained to Caroline Horn of the *Bookseller* that she wanted primarily to tell an exciting adventure story, but she also wanted to show readers that "science is not boring and hard to understand. It's relevant to the world around them and exciting." To make sure that all the science was accurate, Hawking enlisted not only her father, but Ph.D. student Christophe Galfard to help her make sure that all aspects of the story were scientifically accurate and also held together in an entertaining fashion. "We didn't want people reading it and thinking: 'Oh, here comes the science,'" she told Horn. "The science and the story drove each other."

Biographical and Critical Sources

PERIODICALS

Booklist, December 1, 2007, Debbie Carton, review of *George's Secret Key to the Universe,* p. 40.
Bookseller, July 14, 2006, "Hawking for Kids," p. 9; June 29, 2007, Caroline Horn, "A Child of Science," p. 27; August 17, 2007, review of *George's Secret Key to the Universe,* p. S5.
Internet Bookwatch, March, 2008, review of *George's Secret Key to the Universe.*
Internet Wire, June 8, 2007, "Daughter of Professor Stephen Hawking Follows His Dream to Experience Weightlessness aboard Zero-G Father's Day Flight."
Kirkus Reviews, October 1, 2007, review of *George's Secret Key to the Universe.*
Magpies, March, 2008, Lyn Linning, "The Word Spy," p. 34.

Publishers Weekly, October 1, 2007, review of *George's Secret Key to the Universe,* p. 57.

School Library Journal, December, 2007, Steven Engelfried, review of *George's Secret Key to the Universe,* p. 132.

Sunday Times (London, England), August 1, 1999, "Stardust Memories," p. N4.

Time (International), October 8, 2007, Eben Harrell, "The Playful Genius," p. 56.

ONLINE

George's Secret Key to the Universe Web site, http://www.georgessecretkey.com/ (February 19, 2009), "Lucy Hawking."*

*   *   *

HUGHES, Pat

Personal

Born in Hamden, CT; daughter of Pat and Gloria Raccio; married Sam Hughes; children: two sons. *Education:* University of Connecticut, B.A. (psychology), M.A. (American literature).

Addresses

Home—Philadelphia, PA. *Agent*—Scott Treimel, 434 Lafayette St., New York, NY 10003. *E-mail*—pathughesbooks@gmail.com.

Career

Writer. Has also worked for the *Philadelphia Inquirer* and *Hartford Courant.*

Awards, Honors

Best Children's Book designation, Bank Street College of Education, 2004, for *Guerrilla Season;* Notable Trade Book in the Field of Social Studies designation, National Council on Social Studies (NCSS)/Children's Book Council (CBC), 2005, for *The Breaker Boys;* Best Children's Book designation, Bank Street College of Education, and Notable Trade Book in the Field of Social Studies designation, NCSS/CBC, both 2008, both for *Seeing the Elephant.*

Writings

Guerrilla Season, Farrar, Straus & Giroux (New York, NY), 2003.

The Breaker Boys, Farrar, Straus & Giroux (New York, NY), 2004.

Open Ice, Wendy Lamb Books (New York, NY), 2005.

Seeing the Elephant: A Story of the Civil War, illustrated by Ken Stark, Farrar, Straus & Giroux (New York, NY), 2007.

Sidelights

In her works of historical fiction, such as *Guerrilla Season* and *The Breaker Boys,* Pat Hughes focuses on young men who are forced to enter an often harsh adult world due to circumstances beyond their control. Hughes, who began writing on her own when she was in the third grade, earned a master's degree in American literature from the University of Connecticut. "My favorite person in that place was Professor J.D. O'Hara, who taught me all the important things about being a writer," she stated on her home page. "Most important, for me, was that writing is easy; rewriting is hard."

Cover of Pat Hughes' young-adult novel **Open Ice,** *which finds a teen hockey star reconstructing his life following a serious on-ice injury.* (Cover photograph copyright © 2005 by Paul Viant/Getty Images. All rights reserved. Used by permission of Wendy Lamb Books, an imprint of Random House Children's Books, a division of Random House, Inc.)

Ken Stark contributes detailed art to Hughes' history-themed picture book in **Seeing the Elephant.** (Illustration copyright © 2007 by Ken Stark. All rights reserved. Used by permission of Farrar, Straus & Giroux, LLC.)

Set in Northwest Missouri during the U.S. Civil War, *Guerrilla Season* concerns Matt Howard, a fifteen year old who runs his family's farm after the death of his father. Matt wishes to remain neutral in the conflict raging around him, but both Federal and Confederate soldiers threaten his community and question Matt's loyalties. Delivering lifelike characters and a stimulating plot, *Guerrilla Season* presents a good history of the turmoil surrounding war-torn Missouri," observed Kimberly Monaghan in her review for *School Library Journal.* In *Publishers Weekly* a contributor remarked that Hughes "gives readers an unbiased, unromanticized glimpse of war as she slowly but surely relays a compelling story about courage and sacrifice."

Seeing the Elephant: A Story of the Civil War, Hughes' debut picture book, is loosely based on an historical metaphor. Ten-year-old Israel longs to join his two older brothers, who have enlisted in the Union Army to "see the elephant," a phrase used to describe combat. After one of his brothers returns home, angry because he has missed battle due to two bouts of typhoid, Israel begins to learn more about what war is really like. The boy has a total change of heart when his aunt Bell, a nurse, takes him to visit a dying Confederate soldier in Washington, DC. According to a contributor in *Kirkus Reviews,* Hughes' story "will leave readers with the in-

sight that no side in a conflict has a lock on right or wrong." Grace Oliff stated in a *School Library Journal* review that in *Seeing the Elephant* the author "keeps her focus not on action, but on the impact of historical events on the personal lives and relationships of her characters."

The Breaker Boys, set in the late nineteenth century, examines the coal-mining industry. After he is expelled from school, twelve-year-old Nate Tanner returns to his family's Pennsylvania estate. There he makes friends with Johnny, an immigrant "breaker boy" who sorts coal in the mines owned by Nate's father. When the miners protest their conditions and a strike turns violent, however, Nate must choose sides. *School Library Journal* critic Elizabeth M. Reardon praised the novel, stating that in *The Breaker Boys* "Hughes has created a complex protagonist who's likable even when acting 'ugly'" A *Kirkus Reviews* contributor deemed the work "a strong story of family and friendship" that is "rooted in a fascinating period of American history."

With *Open Ice,* Hughes turns her focus to modern times. This young-adult novel focuses on hockey star Nick Taglio, an aggressive, hard-hitting sixteen year old who is advised to give up the sport after suffering yet another in a series of concussions. A frustrated Nick, whose life revolved around hockey, has difficulty coping with his situation, and he begins acting out in school and with his parents. In *School Library Journal,* Jeffrey Hastings complimented the novel, noting the author's "attention to detail in terms of both head injuries and the sport." *Booklist* contributor Bill Ott observed that, while Nick's many problems threaten to overwhelm the narrative, in *Open Ice* "Hughes feints left and skates right, confounding our expectations with a subtle twist of character that draws us deeper into the story."

Biographical and Critical Sources

PERIODICALS

Booklist, August, 2003, Hazel Rochman, review of *Guerrilla Season,* p. 1971; September 15, 2004, Hazel Rochman, review of *The Breaker Boys,* p. 233; November 1, 2005, Bill Ott, review of *Open Ice,* p. 40.

Kirkus Reviews, July 15, 2003, review of *Guerrilla Season,* p. 964; August 1, 2004, review of *The Breaker Boys,* p. 743; October 15, 2005, review of *Open Ice,* p. 1139; September 1, 2007, review of *Seeing the Elephant: A Story of the Civil War.*

Kliatt, November, 2005, Paula Rohrlick, review of *Open Ice,* p. 6.

Publishers Weekly, August 11, 2003, review of *Guerrilla Season,* p. 281.

School Library Journal, November, 2003, Kimberly Monaghan, review of *Guerrilla Season,* p. 140; November, 2004, Elizabeth M. Reardon, review of *The Breaker Boys,* p. 145; December, 2005, Jeffrey Hastings, review of *Open Ice,* p. 148; November, 2007, Grace Oliff, review of *Seeing the Elephant,* p. 93.

USA Today, November 14, 2006, Ashley Bleimes, "Blogging Now Begins Young."

ONLINE

Pat Hughes Home Page, http://www.pathughesbooks.com (January 20, 2009).

Guerilla Season Web log, http://guerrillaseason2008.blogspot.com/ (January 20, 2009).

School Library Journal Web site, http://www.schoollibraryjournal.com/ (December 1, 2006), Eric Langhorst, "The Dixie Clicks: How a Blog about the Civil War Turned into a Runaway Hit."

J-K

JOURNET, Mireille
See MAROKVIA, Mireille

*   *   *

KEMLY, Kathleen 1958-

Personal
Born 1958, in MI; married, husband's name Brian; children: two sons. *Education:* Attended Parsons School of Design.

Addresses
Home—Montague, MA. *Agent*—Melissa Turk, The Artist Network, 9 Babbling Brook Ln., Suffern, NY 10901.

Career
Illustrator. Worked as toy packaging designer in New York, NY; artist-in-residence for middle school students.

Member
Society of Children's Book Writers and Illustrators.

Awards, Honors
Seattle Arts Council arts in education grant.

Illustrator
Jeannie St. John Taylor, *What Do You See When You See Me?,* Faith Kids/Cook Communications (Colorado Springs, CO), 2002.
Dawn Bentley, *Kelly's Great Day,* HandPrint Books (Brooklyn, NY), 2005.
Charles Lehmann, *God Made It for You!: The Story of Creation,* Concordia Publishing House (St. Louis, MO), 2006.
Rae McDonald, *A Fishing Surprise,* NorthWord Books (Minneapolis, MN), 2007.
Kimberly Wagner Klier, *You Can't Do That, Amelia!,* Calkins Creek (Honesdale, PA), 2008.
Sean Callahan, *Shannon and the World's Tallest Leprechaun,* Albert Whitman (Morton Grove, IL), 2008.
Anna Egan Smucker, *Golden Delicious: A Cinderella Apple Story,* Albert Whitman (Morton Grove, IL), 2008.

Contributor to periodicals, including *Highlights for Children* and *Cricket.*

Biographical and Critical Sources

PERIODICALS

Kirkus Reviews, September 15, 2007, review of *A Fishing Surprise.*
Publishers Weekly, February 26, 2007, review of *God Made It for You!: The Story of Creation,* p. 94.
School Library Journal, May, 2008, Joy Fleishhacker, review of *Shannon and the World's Tallest Leprechaun,* p. 92.

ONLINE

Picture Book Web site, http://picture-book.com/ (February 1, 2009), "Kathleen Kemly."*

*   *   *

KING, Daren 1972-

Personal
Born 1972, in Harlow, Essex, England. *Education:* Attended Bath Spa University.

Addresses
Home—England. *E-mail*—hello@darenking.co.uk.

Career

Writer.

Awards, Honors

Guardian First Book Award shortlist, and Booker Prize longlist, both for *Boxy and Star*; Nestlé Smarties Children's Book Prize, for *Mouse Noses on Toast*.

Writings

FOR CHILDREN

Smally the Mouse and Friends (Who Don't Like Him) in: Smally's Party, Bloomsbury (London, England), 2005.
Mouse Noses on Toast, illustrated by David Roberts, G.P. Putnam's (New York, NY), 2006.
Sensible Hare and the Case of Carrots, Faber (London, England), 2007, G.P. Putnam's (New York, NY), 2009.
Peter the Penguin Pioneer, Quercus (London, England), 2008.
The Frightfully Friendly Ghosts, Quercus (London, England), 2009.

FOR ADULTS

Boxy and Star, Abacus (London, England), 1999.
Jim Giraffe: A Ghost Story about a Ghost Giraffe, Jonathan Cape (London, England), 2004.
Tom Boler, Jonathan Cape (London, England), 2005.
Manual, Faber (London, England), 2008.

Contributor to magazines and anthologies, including *All Hail the New Puritans, Piece of Flesh, New Writing 13, Cool Britannia, The Edgier Waters, To Hell Journal A,* and *The Flash.*

Sidelights

Daren King knew early on that he wanted to make his career as a writer. "Writing was something I could do," King told Katy Guest for the London *Independent.* "It was the only way I knew that I had a chance to become wealthy." King impressed the British literary world with his first novel for adults, *Boxy and Star,* which was shortlisted for the London *Guardian* First Book award. Along with his novels, King is also the author of several books for children, among them *Peter the Penguin Pioneer* and the quirkily titled *Mouse Noses on Toast.*

In *Mouse Noses on Toast,* Paul the mouse and his friends Sandra, a Christmas-tree angel, and Tinby, a metal monster, are horrified to discover that a local restauranteur is serving up mouse noses as a delicacy. Along with trying to undermine the humans who are promoting this new dish, Paul must conquer his allergy to cheese; the staple in a mouse's diet makes him look ridiculous after he eats it. "The story is suspenseful,

Daren King spins a quirky story about a frustrated rodent in **Mouse Noses on Toast,** *featuring artwork by David Roberts.* (Illustration copyright © 2006 by David Roberts. All rights reserved. Reproduced by permission of G.P. Putnam's Sons, a division of Penguin Putnam Books for Young Readers.)

witty and engaging, and the mild bathroom jokes will provide many a giggle," wrote a contributor to *Kirkus Reviews.* Kay Weisman, reviewing *Mouse Noses on Toast* for *Booklist,* wrote that the book's "short episodes, quirky characters, and humor that focuses on bodily functions will make this a popular choice."

Also for children, King's novel *Sensible Hare and the Case of Carrots* features a crime-solving rabbit and a beautiful bunny woman with a case for him to solve. Her case of carrots has been stolen, and she is counting on Sensible to get it back. Not all is as it seems, however, and Sensible has to deal with ghosts, secret passages, crooks, and strangers before getting to the bottom of things. "*Sensible Hare and the Case of Carrots* is every bit as accomplished, witty and inventive as its predecessor," declared Neville Hawcock in the London *Financial Times.*

In *Peter the Penguin Pioneer,* King turned from sleuthing to adventure stories, using the same sense of humor and ridiculous action to appeal to his audiences. In the book penguins Peter, an explorer, and Punky, his co-pilot, decide to go on a grand adventure in order to reclaim their ice-skating rink, which has been taken over by some strange penguins. On the way, they encounter angry polar bears, talking snowmen, flying fish, and other dangers of the Arctic.

Katy Guest wrote in the London *Independent* that her biggest surprise upon meeting King was that his writing does not come without effort. Rather, his "free-associating prose that reads like an uninhibited expression of the sheer joy of putting words on paper is in fact the result of very focused perfectionism."

Biographical and Critical Sources

PERIODICALS

Booklist, December 1, 2007, Kay Weisman, review of *Mouse Noses on Toast*, p. 42.
Bookseller, February 4, 2005, review of *Tom Boler*, p. 30.
Bulletin of the Center for Children's Books, January, 2008, Jeannette Hulick, review of *Mouse Noses on Toast*, p. 214.
Financial Times (London, England), September 15, 2007, Neville Hawcock, review of *Sensible Hare and the Case of Carrots*, p. 41.
Independent (London, England), June 13, 2008, Katy Guest, "Daren King: The Author Who Dances."
Kirkus Reviews, December 15, 2007, review of *Mouse Noses on Toast*.
Magpies, September, 2007, Helen Purdie, review of *Mouse Noses on Toast*, p. 36.
New Statesman, July 28, 2008, Charles Hill, "Enthralling Flatness," p. 50.
School Librarian, winter, 2007, Andrea Rayner, review of *Sensible Hare and the Case of Carrots*, p. 202.

ONLINE

Daren King Home Page, http://www.darenking.co.uk (February 24, 2009).*

*   *   *

KNOWLES, Jo 1970-
(Johanna Beth Knowles)

Personal
Born 1970; married; children: one son. *Education:* Simmons College, M.A. (children's literature).

Addresses
Home—VT. *E-mail*—jo@joknowles.com.

Career
Writer. Simmons College, Boston, MA, writing instructor in MFA program at Center for the Study of Children's Literature.

Member
Society of Children's Book Writers and Illustrators.

Jo Knowles (Photograph by Peter Carini. Reproduced by permission.)

Awards, Honors
Society of Children's Book Writers and Illustrators work-in-progress grant, 2002, for *Jumping off Swings*; PEN New England Children's Book Discovery Award, 2005, and New York Public Library Book for the Teen Age designation, and YALSA Quick Pick for Reluctant Readers designation, all for *Lessons from a Dead Girl*.

Writings

Huntington's Disease (nonfiction), Rosen Publishing (New York, NY), 2006.
Lessons from a Dead Girl, Candlewick Press (Cambridge, MA), 2007.
Junior Drug Awareness: Over-the-Counter Drugs (nonfiction), Chelsea House (New York, NY), 2008.
Jumping off Swings, Candlewick Press (Cambridge, MA), 2009.

Sidelights
Vermont-based writer Jo Knowles is the author of the young-adult novel *Lessons from a Dead Girl*. A sobering story about a teen who begins to reflect on her own life following the death of a childhood friend, the novel was inspired by an article about children who abuse children. "I began to wonder what makes childhood friendships so complex, so painful at times, and yet so binding," the author explained in discussing the origins of her highly praised first novel.

In *Lessons from a Dead Girl* Leah and Laine are long-time friends, but after Leah is killed in a car accident, Laine begins to reflect on their relationship, which be-

gan in elementary school. By fifth grade, pretty and popular Leah pronounces the two "Best Friends Forever," but for quiet Laine the friendship has more than its share of painful moments. By their teen years, Leah has shown herself to be domineering and insecure, and readers can see what Laine cannot: that Leah is demonstrating the behaviors of an abused girl. When Laine seeks out new friends, Leah reacts with anger and threats, using a secret from the girls' past to force Laine's continued loyalty. Writing that Knowles deals effectively with an unusual topic—sexual abuse among teenage peers—Meredith Robbins added in *School Library Journal* that "the concise, clear style of [*Lessons from a Dead Girl*] . . . belies the sophistication of its subject matter." According to a *Kirkus Reviews* writer, the author's "spare and evocative prose" brings to life a "rajor-sharp examination of friendship, abuse, and secrets," and in *Booklist* Cindy Dobrez dubbed the novel a "haunting story of a girl's journey to understanding."

"I love to write because I enjoy making something out of nothing," Knowles wrote on her home page. "I like to start a sentence at the top of the page and feel it turning into a story, into a living thing. Once those characters are on the page, they're alive. They're alive in my heart forever. And even though the characters usually have something that's causing them pain, that's OK. Because whatever that pain is, most likely it's a pain I've experienced, too. And this is my way of exploring it and working it out."

Biographical and Critical Sources

PERIODICALS

Booklist, December 1, 2007, Cindy Dobrez, review of *Lessons from a Dead Girl,* p. 34.

Bulletin of the Center for Children's Books, January, 2008, Karen Coats, review of *Lessons from a Dead Girl,* p. 215.

Kirkus Reviews, October 1, 2007, review of *Lessons from a Dead Girl.*

Kliatt, November, 2007, Janis Flint-Ferguson, review of *Lessons from a Dead Girl,* p. 11.

Publishers Weekly, December 3, 2007, review of *Lessons from a Dead Girl,* p. 72.

School Library Journal, December, 2007, Meredith Robbins, review of *Lessons from a Dead Girl,* p. 132.

Cover of Knowles' haunting young-adult novel **Lessons from a Dead Girl.** (Jacket photograph copyright © 2007 by Cheryl North Coughlan/Solus. Reproduced by permission of the publisher, Candlewick Press, Inc., Somerville, MA.)

Voice of Youth Advocates, Jamie S. Hansen, review of *Lessons from a Dead Girl,* p. 526.

ONLINE

Class of 2k7 Web site, http://classof2k7.com/ (January 15, 2009), "Jo Knowles."

Jo Knowles Home Page, http://www.joknowles.com (January 15, 2009).

*   *   *

KNOWLES, Johanna Beth See KNOWLES, Jo

L

LAFRANCE, Marie 1955-

Personal

Born 1955, in Quebec City, Quebec, Canada; married; husband a musician; children: Béatrice. *Education:* Attended Cégep du Vieux-Montréal and Studio Graff.

Addresses

Office—4398 boulevard St-Laurent, Studio 303, Montreal, Quebec H2W 1Z5, Canada. *E-mail*—marilaf@cam.org.

Career

Artist. Freelance illustrator; has also worked as a silk-screen printmaker.

Member

Association des Illustrateurs et Illustratrices du Québec (member of board).

Awards, Honors

Governor General's Award nomination, and Alcuin Society Design Award citation, both for *La Diablesse and the Baby* by Ricardo Keens-Douglas; Louis J. Battan Author's Award shortlist, and Information Book Award shortlist, both 2007, both for *Who Likes the Wind?* by Etta Kaner.

Illustrator

Madeleine Bouchet, *Le comment et le pourquoi,* Madibou (Notre-Dame-de-Ham, Quebec, Canada), 1982.

(With Philippe Germain) James Rousselle, Huguette Lachapelle, and Michel Monette, *À lire,* Centre Educatif et Culturel (Montreal, Quebec, Canada), 1988.

Mimi Legault, *Le club des moucs-moucs,* P. Tisseyre (Montreal, Quebec, Canada), 1988.

Joceline Sanschagrin, *Le prince Mathieu charmant,* Chouette (Montreal, Quebec, Canada), 1990, translation by Penelope Cowie published as *Matthew, Prince Charming,* 1990.

Nadia Ghalem, *La rose des sables,* Hurtubise HMH (La-Salle, Quebec, Canada), 1993.

Ricardo Keens-Douglas, *La Diablesse and the Baby: A Caribbean Folktale,* Annick Press (Toronto, Ontario, Canada), 1994.

Anne Louise MacDonald, *Nanny-Mac's Cat,* Ragweed Press (Charlottetown, Prince Edward Island, Canada), 1994.

Isabelle Clerc, *Mandarine,* Éditions Héritage (Saint-Lambert, Quebec, Canada), 1995.

Lynette Comissiong, *Mind Me Good Now!,* Annick Press (Toronto, Ontario, Canada), 1997.

Ricardo Keens-Douglas, *The Miss Meow Pageant,* Annick Press (Toronto, Ontario, Canada), 1998.

Gilles Tibo, *Le petit musicien,* Dominique et Cie. (Saint-Lambert, Quebec, Canada), 2001.

Gilles Tibo, *Le grand magicien,* Dominique et Cie. (Saint-Lambert, Quebec, Canada), 2002.

Angèle Delaunois, *Le grand voyage de monsieur Caca,* Les 400 Coups (Montreal, Quebec, Canada), 2003, bilingual English/Spanish edition translated by Daniel Zolinsky published as *The Long Journey of Mister Poop/El gran viaje del Señor Caca,* Cinco Puntos Press (El Paso, TX), 2007.

Gilles Tibo, *Émilie pleine de jouets,* Dominique et Cie. (Saint-Lambert, Quebec, Canada), 2003.

Paule Brière, *La poupée de Noël,* Les 400 Coups (Montreal, Quebec, Canada), 2003.

Marie-Danielle Croteau, *Réglisse solaire,* Dominique et Cie. (Saint-Lambert, Quebec, Canada), 2004.

(With Robert Dolbec and Céline Malépart) Nicole Durand-Lutzy, *Laisse-moi te raconter,* Fides-Médiaspaul (Montreal, Quebec, Canada), 2004.

Anique Poitras, *La fée des bonbons,* Dominique et Cie. (Saint-Lambert, Quebec, Canada), 2005.

Marie-Danielle Croteau, *Gouttes d'ocean,* Dominique et Cie. (Saint-Lambert, Quebec, Canada), 2005.

Lionel Daunais, *Le petit chien de laine,* Montagne secrète (Montreal, Quebec, Canada), 2005.

Marie-Danielle Croteau, *Le secret du carnet bleu,* Dominique et Cie. (Saint-Lambert, Quebec, Canada), 2006.

A.S. Gadot, *The First Gift,* Kar-Ben Publishing (Minneapolis, MN), 2006.

Etta Kaner, *Who Likes the Wind?* ("Exploring the Elements" series), Kids Can Press (Toronto, Ontario, Canada), 2006.

Etta Kaner, *Who Likes the Snow?* ("Exploring the Elements" series), Kids Can Press (Toronto, Ontario, Canada), 2006.

Etta Kaner, *Who Likes the Sun?* ("Exploring the Elements" series), Kids Can Press (Toronto, Ontario, Canada), 2007.

Etta Kaner, *Who Likes the Rain?* ("Exploring the Elements" series), Kids Can Press (Toronto, Ontario, Canada), 2007.

Carmen Campagne, *Dors mon petit, dors,* Dominique et Cie. (Saint-Lambert, Quebec, Canada), 2007.

Roger Poupart, *Edgar-la-bagarre,* Soulières (Saint-Lambert, Quebec, Canada), 2007.

Mireille Levert, *Le sorcier amoureux,* Dominique et Cie. (Saint-Lambert, Quebec, Canada), 2007, translation published as *A Wizard in Love,* Tundra Books (Toronto, Ontario, Canada), 2009.

Carmen Campagne, *Les douze jours de Noël,* Secret Mountain (Montreal, Quebec, Canada), 2007.

Carmen Campagne, *Nous sommes les musiciens!,* Secret Mountain (Montreal, Quebec, Canada), 2007.

Also illustrator of textbooks, magazines, book covers, and posters.

Sidelights

A former silk-screen printmaker, Marie Lafrance has illustrated numerous children's books that have been published in the United States and Canada. One of her illustration projects, *Mind Me Good Now!,* is a Caribbean version of "Hansel and Gretel" by Lynette Comissiong. The book centers on the misadventures of Dalby and Tina, two siblings who disobey their mother and cross a forbidden river, only to encounter Mama Zee, a seemingly gentle old woman who turns out to be an evil creature known as a cocoya. According to Janet McNaughton, writing in *Quill & Quire,* "Lafrance's illustrations are tropically lush and just surreal enough to suggest magic from the very first page." *The First Gift,* a work pairing Lafrance's art and a text by A.S. Gadot, examines naming customs around the world. A *Publishers Weekly* critic complimented the book's illustrations, stating that the "creamy acrylic paintings feature fluid, elongated characters and dreamlike background scenes with folk-art-style motifs." In *Booklist* Ilene Cooper similarly noted of *The First Gift* that Lafrance's "characters have the look of carved wooden figures."

Lafrance has collaborated with Etta Kaner on a series of early readers in the "Exploring the Elements" series; these works employ a lift-the-flap format to provide young readers with basic information about weather phenomena. *Quill & Quire* reviewer Philipp Sheppard praised Lafrance's artwork for series installment *Who Likes the Wind?,* stating that "the overall impression of each double-paged spread is dynamic," while Carolyn Phelan commented in *Booklist* that the "acrylic paintings offer attractive scenes of children at play as well as good visual explanations." Reviewing *Who Likes the Snow?* in the *Canadian Review of Materials,* Cheryl Archer observed that "the book flows smoothly in a visual sense," and a *Kirkus Reviews* writer stated of *Who Likes the Rain?* that Lafrance's "simply rendered groups of illustrations behind the gatefolds work to help children understand the scientific answers" presented in Kaner's text.

Marie Lafrance contributes colorful, stylized art to Etta Kanner's large-format picture book **Who Likes the Rain?** (Illustration copyright © 2007 by Marie Lafrance. All rights reserved. Used by permission of Kids Can Press Ltd., Toronto.)

Biographical and Critical Sources

PERIODICALS

Booklist, January 1, 1999, Hazel Rochman, review of *Mind Me Good Now!,* p. 818; April 1, 2006, Carolyn Phelan, review of *Who Likes the Wind?,* p. 67; October 1, 2006, Ilene Cooper, review of *The First Gift,* p. 64; March 1, 2007, Carolyn Phelan, review of *Who Likes the Sun?,* p. 86; January 1, 2008, Carolyn Phelan, review of *Who Likes the Rain?,* p. 66.

Canadian Review of Materials, December 8, 2006, Cheryl Archer, review of *Who Likes the Snow?*

Horn Book, July-August, 2006, Betty Carter, review of *Who Likes the Wind?,* p. 463.

Kirkus Reviews, August 15, 2007, review of *Who Likes the Rain?*

Publishers Weekly, July 31, 2006, review of *The First Gift,* p. 78.

Quill & Quire, September, 1997, Janet McNaughton, review of *Mind Me Good Now!;* March, 2006, Philipp Sheppard, review of *Who Likes the Wind?*

Resource Links, July-April, 2006, Suzanne Finkelstein, review of *Who Likes the Wind?,* p. 30; February, 2007, Tanya Boudreau, review of *Who Likes the Snow?,* p. 23; June, 2007, Tanya Boudreau, review of *Who Likes the Sun?,* p. 21.

School Library Journal, December, 2006, Mary Hazelton, review of *Who Likes the Snow?,* p. 124.

ONLINE

Annick Press Web site, http://www.annickpress.com/ (January 20, 2009), "Marie Lafrance."

Kids Can Press Web site, http://www.kidscanpress.com/ (January 20, 2009), "Marie Lafrance."*

* * *

LAWSON, Amy
See GORDON, Amy

* * *

LEFFLER, Silke

Personal

Born in Vorarlberg, Austria. *Education:* Studied design.

Addresses

Office—Silke Leffler Design & Illustration, Im Oberdorf 13, D 78661 Dietingen, Germany. *E-mail*—silke.leffler@leffler-design.de.

Career

Illustrator and graphic designer. Worked as a textile designer in England, early 1990s; children's book illustrator, beginning 1998.

Awards, Honors

Several design prizes; Nachwuchsförderpreis, Reinhold-Beitlich-Stiftung, 1998; Schönste Kinderbuch Österreichs, 2003, for *Das Fabelbuch;* Anerkennungspreis (Vienna, Austria), 2004, for *Freunde lässt man nicht im Stich;* Preis der Stadt Wien für das Kinderbuch, 2004, for *Der Blumenball;* Jugendbuchpreis, 2005, for *Der Tagesschlucker.*

Writings

SELF-ILLUSTRATED

Der Tatesschlucker, Annette Betz (Vienna, Austria), 2005.

ILLUSTRATOR

Weihnachten ganz wunderbar: Ein literarischer Adventskalender, Ueberreuter (Vienna, Austria), 2000, translated as *A Simply Wonderful Christmas: A Literary Advent Calendar,* 2000.

Schnip, Schnapp, Schnorum: Lieder und Reime für Große und Kleine, Annette Betz (Vienna, Austria), 2001.

Das Fabelbuch von Aesop bis heute, Annette Betz (Vienna, Austria), 2003.

Sigrid Laube, *Freunde lässt man nicht im Stich,* Annette Betz (Vienna, Austria), 2003.

Das Andersen Märchenbuch, Annette Betz (Vienna, Austria), 2004, translated by Friederun Reichenstetter as *Andersen's Fairy Tales,* North-South (New York, NY), 2007.

Aufgewacht der Frühling kommt, Annette Betz (Vienna, Austria), 2004.

Sigrid Laube, *Der Blumenball,* Annette Betz (Vienna, Austria), 2005, translated by Philip Boehm as *The Flower Ball,* Pumpkin House Ltd. (Columbus, OH), 2005.

Heinz Janisch, *Über die Liebe: Die schönsten Geschichten und Gedicht,* Annette Betz (Munich, Germany), 2006.

Heinz Janisch, *Über die Freundschaft: Die schönsten Geschichten und Gedicht,* Annette Betz (Munich, Germany), 2006.

Heinz Janisch, *"Ich hab ein kleines Problem," sagt der Bär,* Annette Betz (Munich, Germany), 2007, translated as *"I Have a Little Problem," Said Bear,* North-South (New York, NY), 2009.

Constanze Breckoff, *Geschenkbuch Liebe,* Annette Betz (Munich, Germany), 2009.

Constanze Breckoff, *Geschenkbuch Glück,* Annette Betz (Munich, Germany), 2009.

Constanze Breckoff, *Geschenkbuch Geburstag,* Annette Betz (Munich, Germany), 2009.

Constanze Breckoff, *Geschenkbuch Baby,* Annette Betz (Munich, Germany), 2009.

Biographical and Critical Sources

PERIODICALS

Booklist, October 15, 2007, Carolyn Phelan, review of *Andersen's Fairy Tales,* p. 48; December 15, 2008,

Carolyn Phelan, review of *"I Have a Little Problem,"* *Said Bear,* p. 52.

Kirkus Reviews, September 1, 2007, review of *Andersen's Fairy Tales.*

Publishers Weekly, April 24, 2006, review of *The Flower Ball,* p. 60.

School Library Journal, July, 2006, Donna Cardon, review of *The Flower Ball,* p. 82; October, 2006, Mara Alpert, review of *A Simply Wonderful Christmas: A Literary Advent Calendar,* p. 100; December, 2007, Susan Scheps, review of *Andersen's Fairy Tales,* p. 142.

ONLINE

Silke Leffler Home Page, http://www.leffler-design.de (January 15, 2009).*

*　　*　　*

LOCKE, Gary 1963-

Personal

Born 1963.

Addresses

Home—Rogersville, MO. *E-mail*—garyartgood@aol. com.

Career

Illustrator for books and advertising.

Illustrator

Larry Burkett with Kevin Miller, *All about Treasure: Discovering the History, Purpose, and Effect of Money,* FaithKids (Colorado Springs, CO), 2003.

Larry Burkett, with Kevin Miller, *All about Talent: Discovering Your Gifts and Personality,* FaithKids (Colorado Springs, CO), 2003.

Kevin Miller, *Larry Burkett's All about Time: Discovering How the Calendar Affects You,* FaithKids (Colorado Springs, CO), 2003.

Allison Bottke and Heather Gemmen, *Friend or Freak,* Faith Kidz (Colorado Springs, CO), 2004.

Allison Bottke and Heather Gemmen, *Pastrami Project,* Faith Kidz (Colorado Springs, CO), 2004.

Allison Bottke and Heather Gemmen, *Get Real!,* Faith Kidz (Colorado Springs, CO), 2004.

Ray Romano, with Richard and Robert Romano, *Raymie, Dickie, and the Bean: Why I Love and Hate My Brothers,* Simon & Schuster (New York, NY), 2005.

April Pulley Sayre, *Bird! Bird! Bird!,* NorthWord (Minnetonka, MN), 2007.

Biographical and Critical Sources

PERIODICALS

Kirkus Reviews, March 1, 2005, review of *Raymie, Dickie, and the Bean: Why I Love and Hate My Brothers,* p. 294; September 15, 2007, review of *Bird! Bird! Bird!: A Chirping Chant.*

Publishers Weekly, February 28, 2005, review of *Raymie, Dickie, and the Bean,* p. 65.

School Library Journal, June, 2005, Robin L. Gibson, review of *Raymie, Dickie, and the Bean,* p. 126; January, 2008, Martha Simpson, review of *Bird! Bird! Bird!,* p. 111.

ONLINE

Gary Locke Home Page, http://www.garyartgood.com (January 15, 2009).*

M

MacPHAIL, Catherine 1946-

Personal
Born January 25, 1946, in Scotland; daughter of James Moore (a shipyard worker) and Catherine (a cleaner) Green; married Archibald Gilchrist MacPhail (a computer worker), May 31, 1972; children: David Moore, Sarah Blue, Catherine Cleary Green. *Politics:* Socialist Labour. *Religion:* Roman Catholic.

Addresses
Home—Greenock, Inverclyde, Scotland.

Career
Writer. Formerly assembled computers for IBM. Speaker at schools and workshops; participant in author residencies.

Member
Scottish Children's Writers and Illustrators, Scottish Association of Writers (president), Society of Authors.

Awards, Honors
Kathleen Fidler Award, 1994, and Verghereto award (Italy), 1998, both for *Run, Zan, Run;* Scottish Children's Book Award, 1999, for *Fighting Back;* South Lanarkshire Book Award, 2000, for *Missing;* Stockport Book Award, 2003, for *Dark Waters;* Sheffield Book Award, 2002, for *Tribes;* Calderdale Book Award, 2005, for *Underworld* and *Catch Us If You Can;* Royal Mail Award for Scottish Children's Books, and North East Book Award, both 2006, and Grampian Book Award, 2007, all for *Roxy's Baby.*

Writings

YOUNG-ADULT NOVELS

Run, Zan, Run, Blackie Children's (London, England), 1994.
Fighting Back, Puffin (London, England), 1998.

Fugitive, Puffin (London, England), 1999.
Picking on Percy, illustrated by Karen Donnelly, Bloomsbury (London, England), 2000.
Missing, Puffin (London, England), 2000, Bloomsbury (New York, NY), 2002.
A Kind of Magic, Barrington Stoke (Edinburgh, Scotland), 2001.
Bad Company, Bloomsbury (London, England), 2001.
Tribes, Puffin (London, England), 2001.
Dark Waters, Bloomsbury (London, England), 2002, Bloomsbury (New York, NY), 2003.
Wheels, Puffin (London, England), 2003.
Get That Ghost to Go!, illustrated by Karen Donnelly, Barrington Stoke (Edinburgh, Scotland), 2003, Stone Arch Books (Mankato, MN), 2006.
Another Me, Bloomsbury (London, England), 2003.
Catch Us if You Can, Puffin (London, England), 2004.
Underworld, Bloomsbury (London, England), 2004, Bloomsbury (New York, NY), 2005.
Traitor's Gate, illustrated by Karen Donnelly, Barrington Stoke (Edinburgh, Scotland), 2005.
Sticks and Stones, Barrington Stoke (Edinburgh, Scotland), 2005.
Roxy's Baby, Bloomsbury (London, England), 2005.
Dead Man's Close, illustrated by Karen Donnelly, Barrington Stoke (Edinburgh, Scotland), 2006.
Get That Ghost to Go Too!, illustrated by Karen Donnelly, Barrington Stoke (Edinburgh, Scotland), 2006.
Under the Skin, illustrated by Tom Percival, Barrington Stoke (Edinburgh, Scotland), 2007.
Worse than Boys, Bloomsbury (London, England), 2007.

Author's works have been translated into several languages, including Italian and Welsh.

"GRANNY NOTHING" CHAPTER-BOOK SERIES

Granny Nothing, illustrated by Sarah Nayler, Scholastic (London, England), 2003.
Granny Nothing and the Shrunken Head, illustrated by Sarah Nayler, Scholastic (London, England), 2003.
Granny Nothing and the Secret Weapon, illustrated by Sarah Nayler, Scholastic (London, England), 2004.

Granny Nothing and the Rusty Key, illustrated by Sarah Nayler, Scholastic (London, England), 2004.

"NEMESIS" NOVEL SERIES

Into the Shadows, Bloomsbury (London, England), 2006.
The Beast Within, Bloomsbury (London, England), 2007.
Sinister Intent, Bloomsbury (London, England), 2007.
Ride of Death, Bloomsbury (London, England), 2008.

OTHER

Kintyre's Daughter (adult fiction), Love Images, 1989.
(With Jack Kirkland) *Blue Lights and Bandages* (nonfiction), Seanachaidh (Greenock, Scotland), 1990.
My Mammy and Me (radio plays), produced by British Broadcasting Corporation (London, England), 1994–98.
Takeaway (radio play), produced by British Broadcasting Corporation (London, England), 1999.

Contributor of fiction to periodicals, including *Tidbits, Woman's Weekly,* and London *Sunday Post.*

Sidelights

Scottish writer Catherine MacPhail made a name for herself writing humorous radio scripts for the British Broadcasting Corporation (BBC) before turning to juvenile literature. Like many writers of children's fiction, she has been inspired by events within her own family. Beginning with her award-winning first novel, *Run, Zan, Run,* MacPhail has become known for penning hard-hitting, realistic stories that confront issues faced by real teens and find something positive in even difficult situations. In addition, she has also produced the humorous "Granny Nothing" series of easy readers about a supersized and problem-solving grandma, and the "Nemesis" teen mystery series about a teen who wakes with amnesia and is forced to run when he learns he is suspected of murder.

"I can't remember wanting to be anything else but a writer," MacPhail once told *SATA,* "but with a widowed mother who was a school cleaner, and three sisters, it seemed like an impossible dream. Nothing interesting ever happened to me! So I grew up, left school, began working in our local mill and the dream seemed further away than ever. It was only after my youngest child was born, that I plucked up the courage to join our local writers' club. It was a major turning point, though I didn't know it at the time. There I was given all the encouragement I needed to start sending my stories away, and I wrote everything, ghost stories, horror stories, murder stories, romantic stories.

"I didn't know exactly what I wanted to write. However, I wrote so many romantic short stories I thought I was meant to be a romance novelist, but when I sent my romance novels off, they came back with letters

saying 'cut out the funny bits' and, know what? I realized then it was the funny bits I was good at. I love comedy. Even in the hard circumstances, my mother brought us up laughing. So, I started concentrating on comedy and ended up with two comedy series on BBC Radio, called *My Mammy and Me.* Other comedies followed, and *My Mammy and Me* has since been commissioned for television. I had found my niche at last.

"I never ever considered writing for young people, and then my wee daughter, Katie, was viciously assaulted by a gang in her school. The aftermath of that, the effect on Katie, was what fired me up to write my first children's book, *Run, Zan, Run.*"

Called a "powerful story" by a *Books for Keeps* reviewer, *Run, Zan, Run* follows Katie, the victim of school bullies, and her friendship with a homeless and streetwise girl named Zan, who helps Katie deal with the harassment. Predicting its appeal to teenage readers, *School Librarian* reviewer Cathy Sutton highly praised MacPhail's fiction debut for its "excellent" characterization, pace, and "breathtaking climax." *Run, Zan, Run* won several awards, convincing MacPhail that she had finally found her creative niche as a writer.

Continuing to focus on a young-adult readership, MacPhail's novel *Fugitive* recounts the story of Jack and his mother, Big Rose, who make the best of their hardscrabble life. Although Jack has been led to believe that his father is dead, after hearing news reports of an escaped criminal on the loose, he begins to think otherwise. As with *Run, Zan, Run,* many critics praised *Fugitive.* Writing in *Magpies,* Jo Goodman noted the book's "fully rounded" characters, "convincing" plot, suspenseful pacing, and "humorous touches," while a *Books for Keeps* contributor stressed the appeal of "Jack's engaging character and plenty of humour."

Fighting Back revolves around a mother and daughter who encounter prejudice when they move to a low-rent apartment complex. Although a *Books for Keeps* reviewer found the characters in the novel to be undeveloped, *School Librarian* critic Elspeth S. Scott judged the characters in *Fighting Back* to be "likeable" and the novel overall to be "tense and gripping" yet seasoned with humor.

In *Missing* thirteen-year-old Maxine Moody was devastated when her older brother Derek, ran away from home ten months ago in order to avoid a local bully named Sweeney. Now Derek has wound up dead, and his guilt-ridden parents, who identified the body, have held the funeral. Now she gets a phone call from someone who insists that he is her brother. When Maxine asks for help in dealing with the caller, her parents discount her claims, and other adults treat her as though she is speaking through her grief. Finally, classmate Cam comes to Maxine's rescue, and together the two teens track down the caller and learn the truth of Derek's situation. In *Kliatt* Claire Rosser recommended

Missing "as a mystery, a ghost story, as a good vs. evil battle" of appeal to teen readers, and a *Kirkus Reviews* writer concluded that MacPhail's novel—a "good old-fashioned ghost story"—"is so involving that when the ending arrives it is too soon."

In *Dark Waters* readers meet Col McCann, the younger brother of chronicle troublemaker Mungo McCann. The brothers' criminal father has been killed, and Mungo has become Col's hero. When the older teen is a suspect in a crime, Col knows that it is his place is to provide Mungo with an alibi. However, when he risks his life in an emergency, Col begins to reevaluate his family ethic. Then he meets Klaus, a frightened boy who can lead authorities to the truth regarding Mungo's crime. A difficult decision now faces the younger brother: should he remain loyal to Mungo or tell the truth about what he knows? Praising MacPhail's realistic characters, a *Kirkus Reviews* added of *Dark Waters* that the book's "fast-paced plot, with its element of the supernatural, explores moral and ethical issues, providing conflict and depth to the story's mystery and adventure." Noting that *Dark Waters* will appeal to teens who usually avoid reading, *Booklist* critic Debbie Carton ranked the novel "above most reluctant-reader fare," citing its "ample character development and thought-provoking issues."

"It . . . amazes me that I'm now known for writing 'gritty realism,'" MacPhail once told *SATA*. "My children always tell me I live in a Doris Day world. In a way, they're right. I think life is wonderful. I'm a very positive thinker, and when I go around to schools, I always tell children how, when I was wee, I thought wee girls like me couldn't become writers. Now I think you can do anything you put your mind to, no matter what your background. It's my advice to aspiring writers, too. If writing is really what you want to do, you'll do it. Just write every day, read, learn, and send those stories away. Sometimes you can learn as much from a rejection as you can from an acceptance."

Biographical and Critical Sources

BOOKS

Gormley, Julie, *Understanding the Author's Craft: A Kind of Magic,* Barrington Stoke (Edinburgh, Scotland), 2004.

PERIODICALS

Booklist, March 15, 2003, Debbie Carton, review of *Dark Waters,* p. 1317; July, 2005, Frances Bradburn, review of *Underworld,* p. 1917.
Books for Keeps, May, 1996, review of *Run, Zan, Run,* p. 16; January, 1999, review of *Fighting Back,* p. 25; November, 1999, review of *Fugitive,* p. 27.

Bulletin of the Center for Children's Books, March, 2003, review of *Dark Waters,* p. 280; September, 2005, Krista Hutley, review of *Underworld,* p. 26.
Journal of Adolescent and Adult Literacy, May, 2003, Pamela Osback, review of *Missing,* p. 702.
Kirkus Reviews, October 15, 2002, review of *Missing,* p. 1533; February 15, 2003, review of *Dark Waters,* p. 312; June 15, 2005, review of *Underworld,* p. 685.
Kliatt, November, 2002, Claire Rosser, review of *Missing,* p. 12.
Magpies, November, 1999, Jo Goodman, review of *Fugitive,* p. 35.
Publishers Weekly, October 28, 2002, review of *Missing,* p. 72; January 27, 2003, review of *Dark Waters,* p. 260.
School Library Journal, November, 2002, Angela M. Ottman, review of *Missing,* p. 173; June, 2003, Bruce Anne Shook, review of *Dark Waters,* p. 146; July, 2005, Jeffrey Hastings, review of *Underworld,* p. 106; July, 2006, Anne L. Tormohlen, review of *Get That Ghost to Go!,* p. 108.
School Librarian, May, 1995, Cathy Sutton, review of *Run, Zan, Run,* p. 78; summer, 1999, Elspeth S. Scott, review of *Fighting Back,* p. 90; winter, 2007, Elizabeth Finlayson, review of *The Beast Within,* p. 214.
Voice of Youth Advocates, June, 2003, review of *Dark Waters,* p. 139; August, 2005, Julie Watkins, review of *Underworld,* p. 235.

ONLINE

Catherine MacPhail Home Page, http://www.catherine macphail.co.uk (January 26, 2009).
Puffin Web site, http://www.puffin.co.uk/ (February 20, 2002), "Author Zone."
Scottish Book Trust Web site, http://www.scottishbooktrust. com/ (January 26, 2009), "Catherine MacPhail."*

*   *   *

MANDABACH, Brian 1962(?)-

Personal

Born c. 1962, in IL; married; children: one daughter, one son. *Education:* Colorado College, B.A. (English), M.A.T. *Hobbies and other interests:* Fishing.

Addresses

Home—Colorado Springs, CO. *E-mail*—mandabach@ gmail.com.

Career

Educator and writer. Teacher of English at Jenkins Middle School, Colorado Springs, CO; teacher at alternative high school. Producer of radio program *Lay of the Land.*

Writings

. . . *Or Not?*, Flux (Woodbury, MN), 2007.

Contributor to periodicals, including *Colorado Springs Independent*.

Sidelights

Brian Mandabach teaches English and literature in Colorado, where he has worked with students in middle school as well as in high school. His first young-adult novel, . . . *Or Not?*, came about after a teenaged girl living nearby Mandabach's home committed suicide, and he began to think about what would prompt someone so young to end their life before it actually began. In . . . *Or Not?* Cassie Sullivan is fourteen years old and starting the eighth grade when her world changes. The terrorist attacks of September 11, 2001, cause everyone to rethink their assumptions and to feel less secure in middle America. The idealistic and reflective Cassie is inspired to act out in accordance with the anti-establishment, vegan, hippie philosophy she has embraced. Her refusal to stand during the Pledge of Allegiance and her outspoken attitude against the U.S. military results in Cassie's ostracism by her fellow students. Ultimately, the teen seeks refuge in her writing and ultimately finds an accepting community in a writers group.

Calling Cassie "interesting and likable," *Booklist* critic Heather Booth predicted of . . . *Or Not?* that "introspective teens will . . . empathize with her struggles." In *Kliatt* Claire Rosser recommended Mandabach's novel for "precocious early teens" who are "facing similar alienation, depression, and bullying issues."

Biographical and Critical Sources

PERIODICALS

Booklist, September 15, 2007, Heather Booth, review of . . . *Or Not?*, p. 60.
Kirkus Reviews, September 15, 2007, review of . . . *Or Not?*
Kliatt, September, 2007, Claire Rosser, review of . . . *Or Not?*, p. 15.
School Library Journal, March, 2008, Jeffrey Hastings, review of . . . *Or Not?*, p. 206.
Voice of Youth Advocates, February, 2008, Amanda Mac-George, review of . . . *Or Not?*, p. 527.

ONLINE

Brian Mandabach Home Page, http://mandabach.com (January 15, 2009).
Colorado Springs Independent Online, http://www.csindy.com/ (May 29, 2008), Jill Thomas, "To Be, or Not" (profile).

MAROKVIA, Mireille 1908-2008
(Mireille Journet, Mireille Journet Marokvia)

OBITUARY NOTICE—

See index for *SATA* sketch: Born December 7, 1908, in France; died October 19, 2008, in Las Cruces, NM. Teacher, translator, children's writer, and memoirist. Marokvia worked as a teacher in Paris, France, and as a translator in Nazi Germany before she and her husband came to the United States in 1950. In the United States, except for a brief period as a dressmaker and costume design assistant, she worked as a writer. Marokvia wrote a few children's stories in the 1960s, usually illustrated by her artist husband, Artur Marokvia. For the next thirty years she contented herself with home duties, but the death of her husband prompted her to resume work on a memoir that she had begun many years before. *Immortelles: Memoir of a Will o' the Wisp* (1996) was well received as the enchanting story of a carefree childhood in the security of a French village before the horrors of World War II changed the author's life forever. *Sins of the Innocent: A Memoir* (2006) tells the story of those horrors as Marokvia experienced them. Trapped in Germany as the wife of a German national conscripted to serve (reluctantly) in the Wehrmacht (German Army), she was forced to fend for herself in a country where her motives were often regarded with suspicion. Marokvia kept a diary of those years, which she destroyed in 1944 out of fear of the Gestapo. She later told an interviewer that the second memoir was the harder one to write. There were memories, she commented, that her conscious mind simply did not want to revive. Marokvia persisted because she wanted readers to understand what life was like in those days, and her efforts were rewarded by the approval of critics who praised her perception and lack of bias. Marokvia was determined to write for the rest of her life, despite occasional difficulties, and that is reportedly what she did. Some short stories and autobiographical vignettes remained uncollected at the time of her death.

OBITUARIES AND OTHER SOURCES:

BOOKS

Marokvia, Mireille, *Immortelles: Memoir of a Will o' the Wisp,* MacMurray & Beck (Denver, CO), 1996.
Marokvia, Mireille, *Sins of the Innocent: A Memoir,* Unbridled Books (Denver, CO), 2006.

PERIODICALS

Los Angeles Times, November 4, 2008, p. B9.
New York Times, October 27, 2008, p. B9.

MAROKVIA, Mireille Journet
See MAROKVIA, Mireille

*   *   *

MAYR, Diane 1949-

Personal
Born 1949.

Addresses
Home—NH. *E-mail*—dianemayr@dianemayr.com.

Career
Writer and librarian. Nesmith Library, Windham, NH, children's librarian, then assistant director and adult-services librarian.

Member
New Hampshire Library Association (former president).

Writings

The Everything Kids' Money Book: From Saving to Spending to Investing, Adams Media (Holbrook, MA), 2000.
Littlebat's Halloween Story, illustrated by Gideon Kendall, Albert Whitman (Morton Grove, IL), 2001.
Out and About at the Apple Orchard, illustrated by Anne McMullen, Picture Window Books (Minneapolis, MN), 2003.
North Carolina, Gareth Stevens (Milwaukee, WI), 2006.
Run, Turkey, Run!, illustrated by Laura Rader, Walker & Company (New York, NY), 2007.
(With others) *Women of Granite: Twenty-five New Hampshire Women You Should Know,* Apprentice Shop Books (Bedford, NH), 2008.

Contributor or articles, stories, poems, and activities to periodicals, including *Writer, Boys' Quest, Ladybug,* and *Christian Science Monitor.*

Sidelights
A librarian and freelance writer, Diane Mayr is the author of such well-received picture books as *Littlebat's Halloween Story* and *Run, Turkey, Run!* In the former, a tiny creature enjoys story-time as much the children who visit the library he calls home. From his spot in the attic, Littlebat can hear the librarian read many wonderful tales, but he grows increasingly frustrated because he cannot see the illustrations. Although Littlebat's mother warns him to stay hidden, the tiny bat swoops down one day when he spies a moth on a book's pages, frightening the children nearby. Having learned his lesson, Littlebat waits patiently for the right time to rejoin the group, and when Halloween arrives, he seizes the opportunity. "Children who delight in sharing stories will find kindred spirits here," John Peters noted in *Booklist.*

Run, Turkey, Run!, another holiday tale, centers on an anxious bird who fears that he will be the main course at Thanksgiving dinner. Turkey tries rolling in the mud, hoping to convince the farmer that he is really a pig, and when that trick fails he begins swimming in order to persuade the farmer that he is actually a duck. Finally fleeing into the forest, Turkey learns that the farm family had other plans for their Thanksgiving feast all along. In *Booklist,* Julie Cummins remarked that although Mayr's "premise may put kids off eating turkey, they'll gobble up the humor" in her holiday-themed story.

Biographical and Critical Sources

PERIODICALS

Booklist, September 1, 2001, John Peters, review of *Littlebat's Halloween Story,* p. 121; September 15, 2007, Julie Cummins, review of *Run, Turkey, Run!,* p. 69.
Kirkus Reviews, September 1, 2007, review of *Run, Turkey, Run!*
Publishers Weekly, May 22, 2000, "Everything for Everybody," review of *The Everything Kids' Money Book: From Saving to Spending to Investing,* p. 95.
School Library Journal, September, 2001, Susan Marie Pitard, review of *Littlebat's Halloween Story,* p. 199.

ONLINE

Diane Mayr Home Page, http://www.dianemayr.com (January 20, 2009).*

*   *   *

McKEAN, Dave 1963-
(David Jeff McKean)

Personal
Born December 29, 1963, in Maidenhead, England; married; wife's name Claire; children: two. *Education:* Berkshire College of Art and Design, degree, 1986.

Addresses
Home—England.

Career
Illustrator, artist, and film director. Organizer, with others, of Unauthorised Sex Company, England, c. 1990; Feral Records (recording studio), cofounder with Iain

Ballamy. Time-Warner International, designer and animator. Wormwood Studios, director of short films, including *The Week Before,* 1998, and *N[eon],* 2002; director of full-length feature film *MirrorMask,* 2005. Designer and illustrator of book, album, and CD covers; conceptual artist for films *Harry Potter and the Prisoner of Azkaban* and *Harry Potter and the Goblet of Fire.* Jazz pianist. *Exhibitions:* Work included in shows at galleries.

Awards, Honors

World Fantasy Award for best artist, 1991; *Newsweek* Best Children's Books listee, 1997, for *The Day I Swapped My Dad for Two Goldfish* by Neil Gaiman; British Science-Fiction Association Award for Best Short Fiction, Elizabeth Burr/Worzalla Award, Bram Stoker Award, Hugo Award for Best Novella, and Prix Tam Tam Award, all 2003, all for *Coraline* by Gaiman.

Writings

SELF-ILLUSTRATED

A Small Book of Black and White Lies (photographs), 1995.
Dustcovers (collected "Sandman" covers), DC Comics/Vertigo (New York, NY), 1997.
Cages (graphic novel; published in ten comic-book issues, 1990-96), Kitchen Sink Press (Northampton, MA), 1998.

Author of short comic *Pictures That Tick,* 1995, and of photography collections *Option: Click,* 1998, and *The Particle Tarot.*

ILLUSTRATOR

Neil Gaiman, *Violent Cases* (graphic novel; originally published in comic-book form), Titan (London, England), 1987, Tundra (Northampton, MA), 1991, third edition, Kitchen Sink Press (Northampton, MA), 1997.
Neil Gaiman, *Black Orchid* (graphic novel; originally published in comic-book form), DC Comics (New York, NY), 1988.
Grant Morrison, *Arkham Asylum* (graphic novel; originally published in comic-book form), Titan (London, England), 1989, 15th anniversary edition published as *Arkham Asylum: A Serious House on Serious Earth,* afterword by Karen Berger, DC Comics (New York, NY), 2004.
Neil Gaiman, *Signal to Noise* (originally serialized in *The Face* magazine), Gollancz (London, England), 1992.
(With others) Neil Gaiman, *Death: The High Cost of Living* (graphic novel; "Sandman" series; originally published in comic-book form), DC Comics (New York, NY), 1994.
Neil Gaiman, *The Tragical Comedy, or Comical Tragedy, of Mr. Punch: A Romance,* DC Comics/Vertigo (New York, NY), 1994.

Neil Gaiman, *The Day I Swapped My Dad for Two Goldfish* (juvenile), Borealis (Clarkston, GA), 1997, revised edition, with a CD narrated by Gaiman, Harper-Collins (New York, NY), 2004.
Iain Sinclair, *Slow Chocolate Autopsy: Incidents from the Notorious Career of Norton, Prisoner of London,* Phoenix House (London, England), 1997.
John Cale and Victor Bockris, *What's Welsh for Zen?: The Autobiography of John Cale,* Bloomsbury (London, England), 1999.
Neil Gaiman, *Coraline* (juvenile), HarperCollins (New York, NY), 2002.
Neil Gaiman, *The Wolves in the Walls,* HarperCollins (New York, NY), 2003.
S.F. Said, *Varjak Paw,* David Fickling Books (New York, NY), 2003.
Neil Gaiman, *MirrorMask* (screenplay), William Morrow (New York, NY), 2005.
S.F. Said, *The Outlaw Varjak Paw,* David Fickling Books (New York, NY), 2006.
Neil Gaiman, *The Graveyard Book,* HarperCollins (New York, NY), 2008.
Neil Gaiman, *Crazy Hair,* HarperCollins (New York, NY), 2009.

Illustrator of comic-book series, including "Hellblazer" and "Sandman," and of hundreds of other comic books, including *Voodoo Lounge* (with the Rolling Stones). Contributor to periodicals, including the *New Yorker.*

Sidelights

British artist and filmmmaker Dave McKean is best known for the illustrations he has provided for book and CD covers as well as comics and graphic novels, especially those written by friend Neil Gaiman. McKean's talent is extensive, however, and his creativity extends to photography, painting, model-building, music performance, film direction, and digital and graphic design. As a visual artist he use a variety of mediums, including drawing, painting, photography, paper and found-object collage, and sculpture. Despite his wide-ranging credits, McKean is best known to younger fans as the illustrator of children's books by Gaiman, S.F. Said, and David Almond.

McKean and Gaiman first met in New York City in the mid-1980s, and they have since collaborated on many projects. In fact, McKean's artwork was first introduced to mass audiences in the pages of Gaiman's short graphic novel *Violent Cases.* Subsequent comic-book projects cemented the collaboration, among them *Black Orchid, Signal to Noise,* and Gaiman's groundbreaking "Sandman" comic-book series, all of which have subsequently been published in graphic-novel format.

From ongoing series work, Gaiman and McKean soon turned to stand-alone projects, such as the large-format graphic novel *The Tragical Comedy, or Comical Tragedy, of Mr. Punch: A Romance.* Featuring a haunting story by Gaiman, the book showcases McKean's multi-

Among his many illustration projects, Dave McKean creates evocative images for S.F. Said's unusual novel The Outlaw Varjak Paw. (Illustration copyright © 2006 by Dave McKean. All rights reserved. Used by permission of David Fickling Books, an imprint of Random House Children's Books, a division of Random House, Inc.)

media art, made eerie due to the darkly drawn and sometimes grotesque adult characters and surreal Punch-and-Judy images. Calling the work "stunning," Frank McConnell went on to assert in *Commonweal* that *The Tragical Comedy, or Comical Tragedy, of Mr. Punch* is "easily the most haunting, inescapable story I've read in years." Another creative collaboration, this time with writer Grant Morrison, resulted in the comic-book compilation *Arkham Asylum,* a "Batman" adventure. Roger Sabin, reviewing this work for *New Statesman & Society,* concluded that "McKean's artwork is often breathtaking—veering from gloomy photo-realism to brightly-coloured Steadmanesque abstraction."

Apart from their work in comics, McKean and Gaiman have also collaborated on several books for children, as well as on the McKean-directed film *MirrorMask,* based on a screenplay by Gaiman. In *The Day I Swapped My Dad for Two Goldfish,* an uninvolved father realizes that he is not important to his child when he is traded for a pair of desired pets. *Coraline* focuses on a little

girl who crosses over into a nightmarish dimension, while in *The Wolves in the Walls* an imaginative child named Lucy is the only one in her family who has seen the wolves living in the walls of her parents' house. Another imaginative child is the focus of Gaiman's rhyming story *Crazy Hair,* in which young Bonnie discovers strange animals and other unusual objects hiding in a man's unruly coiffure, while *The Graveyard Book* finds author and illustrator returning to their darker themes in a Newbery Award-winning book that *School Library Journal* contributor Megan Honig described as "a rich, surprising, and sometimes disturbing tale of dreams, ghouls, murderers, trickery, and family." Reviewing *Coraline* in *Kliatt,* Sherry Hoy concluded that McKean's surreal illustrations "create the true chills here," while *Booklist* critic Francisca Goldsmith credited the artist's "startling graphics" for making *The Wolves in the Walls* "visually and emotionally sophisticated, accessible, and inspired."

Other books featuring artwork by McKean include *The Savage,* by Almond, and Said's novels *Varjak Paw* and *The Outlaw Varjak Paw.* Gestured ink images bring to life Said's novels, which focus on a purebred cat with Mesopotamian antecedents and a talent for the martial arts that saves several threatened family members and lead them to a haven in a dark and dangerous world. In *Kirkus Reviews* a critic concluded of *Varjak Paw* that Said's "creepily off-kilter" fictional world is "effectively reinforced by [McKean's] vivid ink sketches," and a *Publishers Weekly* critic dubbed the book's illustrations "chilling" and "sinuous."

Biographical and Critical Sources

PERIODICALS

Booklist, September 15, 1998, Gordon Flagg, review of *Cages,* p. 185; August, 2003, Francisca Goldsmith, review of *The Wolves in the Walls,* p. 1989; April 1, 2006, Ed Sullivan, review of *The Outlaw Varjak Paw,* p. 41.
Bulletin of the Center for Children's Books, September, 2003, Janice Del Negro, review of *The Wolves in the Walls,* p. 14, and *Varjak Paw,* p. 32.
Commonweal, December 2, 1994, Frank McConnell, review of *The Tragical Comedy or Comical Tragedy of Mr. Punch: A Romance,* p. 27.
Horn Book, November-December, 2002, Anita L. Burkam, review of *Coraline,* p. 755; July-August, 2003, Anita L. Burkam, review of *Varjak Paw,* p. 467; September-October, 2008, Jonathan Hunt, review of *The Savage,* p. 575.
Kirkus Reviews, May 1, 2003, review of *Varjak Paw,* p. 683; July 1, 2003, review of *The Wolves in the Walls,* p. 910; December 15, 2005, review of *The Outlaw Varjak Paw,* p. 1327; August 15, 2008, review of *The Graveyard Book.*
Kliatt, July, 2004, Sherry Hoy, review of *Coraline,* p. 30.

Library Journal, November 15, 1998, Stephen Weiner, review of *Cages,* p. 64.

Magazine of Fantasy and Science Fiction, September, 1995, Charles de Lint, review of *The Vertigo Tarot,* p. 29; May, 1998, Charles de Lint, review of *Dustcovers,* p. 22.

New Statesman & Society, January 12, 1990, Roger Sabin, review of *Arkham Asylum,* p. 35.

Publishers Weekly, February 21, 1994, review of *Death: The High Cost of Living,* p. 248; July 22, 2002, review of *Cages,* p. 160; April 28, 2003, review of *Varjak Paw,* p. 70; June 30, 2003, review of *The Wolves in the Walls,* p. 77; September 29, 2008, review of *The Graveyard Book,* p. 82.

School Library Journal, September, 2003, Marian Creamer, review of *The Wolves in the Walls,* p. 178; February, 2006, Tasha Saecker, review of *The Outlaw Varjak Paw,* p. 136; October, 2008, Megan Honig, review of *The Graveyard Book,* p. 144; December, 2008, Johanna Lewis, review of *The Savage,* p. 118.

ONLINE

Dave McKean Home Page, http://www.davemckean.com (January 20, 2009).

Time Online, http://www.time.com/ (August 27, 2002), Andrew D. Arnold, review of *Cages.*

Underground Online, http://www.ugo.com/ (October 19, 2002), Dan Epstein, "The Art of Dave McKean" (interview).*

*   *   *

McKEAN, David Jeff
See McKEAN, Dave

*   *   *

MOHAMMED, Khadra

Personal

Born in Yemen; married; children: three children. *Education:* University of United Arab Emirates, B.S.

Addresses

Home—Pittsburgh, PA. *Office*—Pittsburgh Refugee Center, 1901-15 Centre Ave., Ste. 203, Pittsburgh, PA 15219. *E-mail*—Khadra@pittsburghrefugeecenter.org.

Career

Pittsburgh Refugee Center, Pittsburgh, PA, executive director. Has worked with refugee populations, both in United States and in refugee camps in Pakistan and Kenya, for more than twenty years.

Awards, Honors

Committed Collaborator Award, Education Law Center, 2005; named Woman of Distinction, Girl Scouts of America, 2005; 40 under 40 Award, *Pittsburgh* Magazine.

Writings

(With Karen Lynn Williams) *Four Feet, Two Sandals,* illustrated by Doug Chayka, Eerdmans Books (Grand Rapids, MI), 2007.

(With Karen Lynn Williams) *My Name Is Sangoel,* illustrated by Catherine Stock, Eerdmans Books (Grand Rapids, MI), 2009.

Sidelights

Khadra Mohammed, executive director of the Pittsburgh Refugee Center, is the coauthor of *Four Feet, Two Sandals,* a picture book based on her experiences working in the city of Peshawar, on the Afghanistan-Pakistan border. Mohammed, who was born in Yemen to Somali parents, has devoted her life to helping the disadvantaged. "Though I am not a refugee, I identify with their struggle to maintain their identity," the author remarked in an interview on the Eerdmans Books Web site. She added, "Writing *Four Feet, Two Sandals* has made me realize how much the publishing world lacks stories about the plight of refugees."

Four Feet, Two Sandals, cowritten with Karen Lynn Williams, centers on ten-year-old Lina, an Afghani girl who lives in a refugee camp. When relief workers distribute clothing to the camp, Lina takes possession of a single, bright yellow sandal, and she later spies another youngster, Feroza, wearing the one that matches. The girls agree to share the footwear, wearing the pair of sandals on alternate days, and they quickly become friends. When Lina receives word that her family will be relocating to the United States, the youngsters must decide who will keep the sandals. A *Publishers Weekly* reviewer called *Four Feet, Two Sandals* a "poignant story," and Hazel Rochman, writing in *Booklist,* praised the authenticity of the work, describing it as "the personal drama behind the daily news."

Biographical and Critical Sources

PERIODICALS

Booklist, September 15, 2007, review of *Four Feet, Two Sandals,* p. 72.

Pittsburgh Post-Gazette, September 5, 2001, Diana Nelson Jones, "A Rock for Refugees: She Helps Immigrants Navigate the Choppy Waters of U.S. Culture"; October 3, 2007, Cristina Rouvalis, "Book with Local Roots Speaks to Refugee Children."

Publishers Weekly, October 29, 2007, review of *Four Feet, Two Sandals,* p. 55.

ONLINE

Eerdmans Books Web site, http://www.eerdmans.com/ (September 1, 2007), interview with Karen Lynn Williams and Mohammed.

Pittsburgh Refugee Center Web site, http://www.pittsburgh refugeecenter.org/ (February 1, 2009), "Khadra Mohammed."

Publishers Weekly Web site, http://www.publishersweekly. com/ (February 21, 2008), Shannon Maughan, "From Pittsburgh to Pakistan and Back."

N

NELSON, R.A.

Personal

Born in AL; son of an aerospace engineer; married; children: four sons. *Hobbies and other interests:* Poetry, quantum physics, old movies, spelunking, history, traveling, astronomy, archeology, basketball, exploring, walking in the woods.

Addresses

Home—Madison, AL. *E-mail*—ranelson@ranelson1. com.

Career

Technical writer and novelist. Marshall Space Flight Center, Huntsville, AL, technical writer. Has also worked as a journalist and a linguist.

Member

Society of Children's Book Writers and Illustrators.

Awards, Honors

Silver Snoopy Award, National Aeronautics and Space Administration; Dona Vaughn work-in-progress grant, Society of Children's Book Writers and Illustrators, 2004, Books for the Teen Age listee, New York Public Library, 2006, and Best Books for Young Adults selection, American Library Association, all for *Teach Me*.

Writings

NOVELS

Teach Me, Razorbill (New York, NY), 2005.
Breathe My Name, Razorbill (New York, NY), 2005.
Days of Little Texas, Knopf (New York, NY), 2009.

Sidelights

R.A. Nelson, a technical writer for the National Aeronautics and Space Administration (NASA), is the author of the young-adult novels *Teach Me* and *Breathe My*

Cover of R.A. Nelson's young-adult novel Teach Me, *which focuses on a clandestine relationship between a high-school teacher and a bookish student.* (Razorbill, 2005. Cover photograph by Denis Scott/Getty Images. Reproduced by permission of Razorbill, a division of Penguin Putnam Books for Young Readers.)

Name, both of which feature young women facing difficult moral choices. "Somebody once said, 'Writers are failed actors,' and I tend to believe this," Nelson stated in a *Teenreads.com* interview with Alexis Burling. "When I'm writing, I completely inhabit the character and see the world through her eyes. I can't imagine writing any other way. I witness the story in front of me as I'm walking around inside of it, experiencing it as it unfolds, so that what I type almost seems like 'reporting' on something real that I'm observing."

Born and raised in north Alabama, Nelson began writing stories while in the second grade. He later developed an interest in science fiction and devoured works by Jules Verne, H.G. Wells, Ray Bradbury, Cyril Kornbluth, and Philip K. Dick, among other authors. Nelson also admired the novels of Charles Dickens and Mark Twain, especially Twain's *The Adventures of Huckleberry Finn,* "which is hilarious and a very brave book for its time," he remarked to Burling. Nelson's love of literature was further strengthened by an English teacher who introduced him to the works of William Shakespeare and the poetry of Robert Frost. "I will never forget her encouragement—like all good teachers, she made an imprint on my life that will last forever," he acknowledged.

Teach Me, Nelson's debut title, centers on Carolina "Nine" Livingston, a high-school senior who falls in love with her English teacher. Fiercely intelligent yet socially isolated, Nine longs for more than her small Alabama town can offer, and she finds herself drawn to the charismatic Mr. Mann. Though their relationship begins innocently enough, it soon develops into an intense affair that is consummated on Nine's eighteenth birthday. Just before graduation, however, Mr. Mann announces that he is engaged to another woman, and an angry and embittered Nine seeks her revenge.

Despite its controversial subject matter, *Teach Me* earned strong reviews. According to *Booklist* contributor Ilene Cooper, Nelson "eloquently captures . . . the yearning that comes with loving someone who doesn't seem attainable." Claire E. Gross, writing in *Kliatt,* noted that the sometimes-melodramatic narrative of *Teach Me* is "redeemed by the force of Nine's personality, which infuses the book with grit and humor." Discussing the novel's sensational plot with Burling, Nelson admitted: "I was aware that it would rile some critics who wouldn't be too happy with the subject matter, but I knew that if I did it with sensitivity and care, it could be an important book." According to the author, it was necessary to portray both Nine and Mr. Mann as three-dimensional characters. "I think it's harder to blame people and find fault when you like them, even if what they are doing is inappropriate and wrong," he explained. "By playing out the love story between these two, I think it gives readers a chance to get to know the characters well and get caught up in the romance rather than look to find fault. The more we examine them, the more human they become."

In *Breathe My Name,* Nelson's second work, a young woman deals with painful memories of her mother, who years earlier suffocated the teen's three younger siblings in the midst of a psychotic breakdown. Eighteen-year-old Frances Robinson is enjoying life with her adopted family in small-town Alabama when she receives a letter from Alton, her birth mother, who has been living in a psychiatric hospital. With her boyfriend, Nix, Frances embarks on a secret journey to visit Alton and confront her own horrific past. *Breathe My Name* "is a thoughtful, moody, and entirely thrilling book," Jennifer Barnes observed in *School Library Journal,* and a critic in *Kirkus Reviews* lauded Nelson's prose, stating that "its shimmering clarity transfixes the reader, candling both damaging and redemptive familial forces."

Biographical and Critical Sources

PERIODICALS

Booklist, November 15, 2005, Ilene Cooper, review of *Teach Me,* p. 55.

Cover of Nelson's teen novel **Breathe My Name,** *featuring photography by Tom Kates.* (Razorbill, 2007. Photograph by Tom Kates. Reproduced by permission of Razorbill, a division of Penguin Putnam Books for Young Readers.)

Horn Book, November-December, 2005, Claire E. Gross, review of *Teach Me,* p. 721.

Kirkus Reviews, August 1, 2005, review of *Teach Me,* p. 855; October 1, 2007, review of *Breathe My Name.*

Kliatt, November, 2007, Janis Flint-Ferguson, review of *Breathe My Name,* p. 13.

Publishers Weekly, August 29, 2005, review of *Teach Me,* p. 58; December 3, 2007, review of *Breathe My Name,* p. 72.

School Library Journal, October, 2005, Jane Cronkhite, review of *Teach Me,* p. 168; March, 2008, Jennifer Barnes, review of *Breathe My Name,* p. 207.

ONLINE

R.A. Nelson Home Page, http://www.ranelson1.com (January 20, 2009).

Teenreads.com, http://www.teenreads.com/ (October 18, 2005), Alexis Burling, interview with Nelson.*

*   *   *

G. Neri (Reproduced by permission of G. Neri.)

NERI, G.
(Greg Neri, Gregory Neri)

Personal

Married; wife's name Maggie (a professor of sociology); children: Zola.

Addresses

Home—Tampa, FL. *Agent*—Edward Necarsulmer, McIntosh & Otis, Inc., 353 Lexington Ave., New York, NY 10016. *E-mail*—greg@gregneri.com.

Career

Author, filmmaker, artist, and digital media producer. Head of production for two media companies, 1993-2003; AnimAction, Inc., Calabasas, CA, teacher of animation and storytelling and producer of films. Film work includes (co-director) *Fa'a Samoa* (documentary); (director and producer) *A Picasso on the Beach;* and (writer, producer, and director) *A Weekend with Barbara und Ingrid.*

Awards, Honors

Student Academy Award finalist, for *A Picasso on the Beach;* Notable Children's Book designation, American Library Association, Notable Children's Book designation, International Reading Association, Best Children's Book selection, Bank Street College of Education, and Best Book in the Language Arts designation, Society of School Librarians International, all 2008, all for *Chess Rumble.*

Writings

FOR YOUNG ADULTS

Chess Rumble, illustrated by Jesse Joshua Watson, Lee & Low (New York, NY), 2007.

Yummy: The Last Days of a Southside Shorty, illustrated by Randy DuBurke, Lee & Low (New York, NY), 2009.

Surf Mules, Putnam (New York, NY), 2009.

Caught, Putnam (New York, NY), 2010.

OTHER

(And producer and director; as Gregory Neri) *A Weekend with Barbara und Ingrid* (screenplay), Angelika Films, 1994.

(Illustrator; as Greg Neri) Gina Shaw, *Hooray for Teeth!,* Scholastic (New York, NY), 2001.

Sidelights

Storyteller, digital media producer, and film maker G. Neri is the author of *Chess Rumble,* an award-winning illustrated novella for young adults. "I came to writing late in my life, quite by accident," Neri remarked on his home page. "When I was a kid, I wanted to be a cartoonist. Most of my life I was a visual storyteller (film, artist, illustrator). The only connection now is that, as a language artist, I . . . paint with words."

Chess Rumble concerns Marcus, an angry youth from a tough neighborhood who learns to channel his frustrations with the help of a local chess master. "*Chess Rumble* was inspired by many of the black chess mentors out there running chess programs for inner city kids," Neri stated in an online interview with Heidi R. Kling. "The way some mentors applied chess strategy to real life was inspiring and something I personally believed in." Recalling his own work with youngsters in South Central Los Angeles, Neri added: "I dealt with a few kids who were the big and silent type. They kept everything bottled inside of them and it came out in

ugly ways sometimes. I thought a kid like this up against a tough love mentor in an urban setting would be rife with possibilities."

Told in free verse, *Chess Rumble* centers on the relationship between Marcus, a fatherless middle schooler who is still grieving over the recent death of his sister, and CM, a chess-club adviser who teaches the inner-city youngster to battle with wits instead of fists. According to *Booklist* critic Gillian Engberg, "Neri makes clear, without overstating, how Marcus' sense of being misunderstood amplifies his frustrations." Jill Heritage Maza, writing in *School Library Journal,* similarly noted that the author "expertly captures Marcus's voice and delicately teases out his alternating vulnerability and rage." "There's plenty of powerful emotion here," a contributor in *Kirkus Reviews* concluded of *Chess Rumble.*

Biographical and Critical Sources

PERIODICALS

Booklist, January 1, 2008, review of *Chess Rumble,* p. 74.
Kirkus Reviews, October 1, 2007, review of *Chess Rumble.*

Cover of Neri's highly praised young-adult novel Chess Rumble, *featuring artwork by Jesse Joshua Watson.* (Jacket art copyright © 2007 by Jesse Joshua Watson. Reproduced by permission of Lee & Low Books, Inc.)

School Library Journal, November, 2007, Jill Heritage Maza, review of *Chess Rumble,* p. 132.

ONLINE

G. Neri Home Page, http://www.gregneri.com (January 20, 2009).
G. Neri Web log, http://gneri.livejournal.com/ (January 20, 2009).
Heidi R. Kling Web log, http://seaheidi.livejournal.com/ (October 19, 2007), interview with Neri.

*   *   *

NERI, Greg
See NERI, G.

*   *   *

NERI, Gregory
See NERI, G.

*   *   *

NOBLE, Trinka Hakes 1944-

Personal

Born 1944, in MI. *Education:* Michigan State University, B.A., 1967; also attended Parsons School of Design, New School for Social Research (now New School University), Greenwich Village Workshop, and New York University.

Addresses

Home—Bernardsville, NJ. *E-mail*—trinka-studio@comcast.net.

Career

Children's author and illustrator. Has taught art in Michigan, Virginia, and Rhode Island. Member, Rutgers University Council on Children's Literature.

Awards, Honors

Notable Book designation, American Library Association (ALA), 1980, and Golden Sower Award Honor designation, Nebraska Library Association, and Children's Choice Book designation, International Reading Association (IRA)/Children's Book Council, both 1981, all for *The Day Jimmy's Boa Ate the Wash;* named Outstanding Woman in Arts and Letters in the state of New Jersey, 2002, for lifetime work in children's books; Teacher's Choice designation, IRA, 2005, for *The Scarlet Stockings Spy;* Independent Publisher Book Award, 2007, for *The Last Brother.*

Writings

SELF-ILLUSTRATED

The King's Tea, Dial (New York, NY), 1979.
Hansy's Mermaid, Dial (New York, NY), 1983.
Apple Tree Christmas, Dial (New York, NY), 1984, re-printed, Sleeping Bear Press (Chelsea, MI), 2005.

FOR CHILDREN

The Day Jimmy's Boa Ate the Wash, illustrated by Steven Kellogg, Dial (New York, NY), 1980.
Jimmy's Boa Bounces Back, illustrated by Steven Kellogg, Dial (New York, NY), 1984.
Meanwhile Back at the Ranch, illustrated by Tony Ross, Dial (New York, NY), 1987.
Jimmy's Boa and the Big Splash Birthday Bash, illustrated by Steven Kellogg, Dial (New York, NY), 1989.
Jimmy's Boa and the Bungee Jump Slam Dunk, illustrated by Steven Kellogg, Dial (New York, NY), 2003.
The Scarlet Stockings Spy, illustrated by Robert Papp, Sleeping Bear Press (Chelsea, MI), 2004.
One for All: A Pennsylvania Number Book, illustrated by Lisa Papp, Sleeping Bear Press (Chelsea, MI), 2005.
The Legend of Michigan, illustrated by Gijsbert van Fran-kenhuyzen, Sleeping Bear Press (Chelsea, MI), 2006.
The Last Brother: A Civil War Tale, illustrated by Robert Papp, Sleeping Bear Press (Chelsea, MI), 2006.
The Legend of the Cape May Diamond, illustrated by E.B. Lewis, Sleeping Bear Press (Chelsea, MI), 2007.
The Pennsylvania Reader, illustrated by K.L. Darnell, Sleeping Bear Press (Chelsea, MI), 2007.
The Orange Shoes, illustrated by Doris Ettlinger, Sleeping Bear Press (Chelsea, MI), 2007.

Several of Noble's books have been translated into Spanish.

ILLUSTRATOR

Mary Calhoun, *The Witch Who Lost Her Shadow,* Harper (New York, NY), 1979.
Susan Pearson, *Karin's Christmas Walk,* Dial (New York, NY), 1980.
Marilyn Singer, *Will You Take Me to Town on Strawberry Day?,* Harper (New York, NY), 1981.

Adaptations

Five of Noble's stories were recorded on audiocassette as *The Day Jimmy's Boa Ate the Wash and Other Stories,* read by Sandy Duncan, Caedmon, 1986.

Sidelights

The author of *The King's Tea, Jimmy's Boa and the Bungee Jump Slam Dunk,* and *The Orange Shoes,* among others, Trinka Hakes Noble has written and il-lustrated many books for children. In addition to writ-ing and illustrating her own work, Noble has contrib-uted her artistic talents to the works of other authors, including Marilyn Singer, Susan Pearson, and Mary Calhoun.

Raised on a farm in a rural area of Michigan, Noble was one of seven children. Her early schooling con-sisted of classes in a one-room schoolhouse that drew children of all ages together from miles around. In the fifth grade, her last year of attending school there, she was the only student working at her grade level. Art al-ways fascinated her; "The earliest memory I have of wanting to be an artist is the smell of crayons," Noble wrote on her home page. "Our crayons were kept in an old cigar box along with assorted Tinkertoys, odd checkers, and Monopoly pieces. They were broken, chewed, and well used. You couldn't even recognize the different colors, so you had to test each color first by drawing on the cigar box lid. That lid was a work of art in itself. But the smell when you opened the lid . . . ahhh . . . and a nice sheet of manila construction paper . . . and life's requirements were met!"

After graduating from high school, Noble worked for a year to save up enough money to attend art classes at Michigan State University. After graduating from col-lege, she put her art training to use by teaching at schools in Michigan, Virginia, and Rhode Island before settling down in the New York City area. In New York, Noble was fortunate to study illustration with artist Uri Shulevitz at his advanced workshop in Greenwich Vil-lage, and she supplemented that education with classes at the New School for Social Research.

Noble's first published book, the self-illustrated *The King's Tea,* was praised by a *Publishers Weekly* critic for its incorporation of "the snowballing effects that children love." In the book a cup of tea prepared for the king's breakfast is ruined when soured milk is added; this in turn ruins the king's mood, and the negative ef-fects spread throughout the kingdom as everyone from the tea steward to the milk cows in the field pass along the blame. Fortunately, by lunchtime the problem is solved—a rain shower has sweetened the buttercups eaten by the milk cows, who in turn provide sweeter milk for tea. Reviewers particularly praised Noble's earth-toned watercolor washes. *Horn Book* reviewer Kern M. Klockner noted that in her "gentle" artwork the author/illustrator "captures the rough features and peasant clothing of her characters, giving careful atten-tion to detail." Donnarae MacCann commented in *Wil-son Library Bulletin* that Noble's technique of "radi-cally [varying] the size of objects in her illustrations . . . adds a subtly comic aspect to many scenes, with-out the use of conventional cartoon devices."

Hansy's Mermaid takes place in Holland and is the story of a mermaid who is stranded in a pool left after a spring flood of the Zuider Zee river. Discovered by the Klumperty family, the mermaid, Seanora, is quickly dressed and taken under the wing of the Klumperty sis-

Trinka Hakes Noble treats readers to a simple story of appreciation in **The Orange Shoes,** *featuring detailed artwork by Doris Ettlinger.* (Illustration copyright © 2007 by Doris Ettlinger. All rights reserved. Reproduced by permission of the illustrator.)

ters, who decide that the best thing for their new friend would be to become as expert at sewing, butter churning, and cheese making as they are. Kept from her home in the sea, Seanora's unhappiness is detected by the family's young son, Hansy. While he brings her seaweed and helps her to participate in winter sports such as skating despite the fact that she has no legs, Hansy realizes that the landlocked mermaid will never be happy in the human world. Ultimately, he helps Seanora return to her home in the sea. Praising Noble's soft pencil drawings and the "fairy tale quality" of her text, Jonni Moore deemed *Hansy's Mermaid* a "thoroughly satisfying fantasy" in her *School Library Journal* assessment. *Horn Book* reviewer Ann A. Flowers also praised the book as "sensitive, imaginative, and thoughtful."

In *Apple Tree Christmas* the joys of a rural childhood are reflected by Noble in both prose and illustrations. Taking place in 1881, the story revolves around young Katrina's love for a local apple tree that succumbs to the extreme cold of a Michigan winter. After the tree falls, the girl realizes that her sadness is shared by every person in her family, each of whom loved the tree for a different reason. On Christmas Day, Father surprises each of the sisters with gifts he has crafted from the tree's wood, including a drawing table for budding artist Katrina. Praising the tale for its evocation of the

family-centered holiday spirit of years past, *School Library Journal* reviewer Elizabeth M. Simmons dubbed *Apple Tree Christmas* a "quiet, quaint story that will be enjoyed by children who love a touch of the old-fashioned," while a *Bulletin of the Center for Children's Books* writer praised Noble for her use of "period detail and some evocative watercolor paintings."

In *The Day Jimmy's Boa Ate the Wash* Noble introduces her popular young protagonist and his pet boa constrictor. In this story, a young girl named Meggie quietly relates what happens when Jimmy decided to bring his pet snake along on a class field trip to a local farm. In typical Noble fashion, confusion and fun are the result: pigs board the school bus and eat everyone's lunch, raw eggs become missiles in the hands of gleeful children, and the hungry snake makes away with the laundry, all of which is highlighted in colorful fashion through the illustrations of Steven Kellogg. Reviewing the work in the *Bulletin of the Center for Children's Books,* a critic described *The Day Jimmy's Boa Ate the Wash* as "total nonsense, [and] great fun," adding that Noble's "bland delivery is in effective contrast with the zany events, each strengthening the other." A *Booklist* contributor echoed this praise, calling the picture book "a top-notch choice that children will not want to put down."

Jimmy and his boa have appeared in several more collaborations between Noble and Kellogg, each told with what *School Library Journal* contributor Cynthia K. Leibold described as Noble's "now familiar droll . . . style." In *Jimmy's Boa Bounces Back* the pet snake makes a fussy garden-club party a memorable event through his entrance disguised as a flowery hat on the head of Meggie's mother. Not surprisingly, the genteel mood of the party quickly evaporates after the boa decides to uncurl and go in search of a light lunch. Meggie's mother is ultimately banished from the garden club, while the boa finds a new best friend in Miss Peachtree's pet poodle.

"The return of Jimmy and his boa is reason to cheer," proclaimed *School Library Journal* reviewer Trev Jones in announcing the publication of *Jimmy's Boa and the Big Splash Birthday Bash,* "for the action is as frenzied, frantic, and wacky as before." This time out, a birthday outing to SeaLand serves as the spark to a host of outrageous events, and by story's end everyone in the party has taken a plunge into the whale tank, frolicked with penguins, and dodged hungry sharks. Jones went on to praise Noble for her skill in "captur[ing] the logic of children and the way in which they tell a story" by leaving out the crucial bits until someone directly asks them "why?"

Jimmy and his reptilian pal create chaos for a group of dancers in *Jimmy's Boa and the Bungee Jump Slam Dunk,* "a highly entertaining treat to share with young (and old) children," remarked Mary Elam in *School Library Journal.* When Miss Peachtree commandeers the

gymnasium for her dance class, Jimmy insists on waltzing with his pet snake, which quickly winds up tangled with other unlikely participants, including the school basketball coach and a group of rabbits. A critic in *Kirkus Reviews* deemed the work "another slam-dunk for Jimmy fans."

Set in Philadelphia in 1777, *The Scarlet Stockings Spy* focuses on Maddy Rose, a young girl who devises a system to communicate with her brother, a soldier in General George Washington's colonial army. By hanging her petticoats and brightly colored stockings from a clothesline, Maddy is able to point out the location of suspicious vessels docked in the harbor. The system works well, until Maddy's brother fails to appear one night. Describing the tale as "well told in simple descriptive language," *School Library Journal* reviewer Susan Scheps added that young readers "with little knowledge of this period in American history will gain some background from Noble's story."

Based on her own family's history, Noble's *The Last Brother: A Civil War Tale* centers on eleven-year-old Gabriel, who joins the Union Army as a bugler so he can remain close to his last surviving brother, Davy. After marching to Gettysburg, Gabe meets a Confederate bugle boy named Orlee, and they strike up an unlikely friendship before the three-day battle commences. According to Christine Markley in *School Library Journal*, the story "resonates with courage and fear, love and loyalty."

In *The Orange Shoes,* a work with autobiographical overtones, young Delly Porter walks barefoot to her one-room schoolhouse each day. After her teacher announces a "Shoebox Social" to raise funds for art supplies, Delly receives a new pair of leather shoes from her father, despite the family's meager finances. The youngster is devastated when several of her classmates try to ruin the footwear, however, and she attempts to use her artistic skills to hide the damage. Noble's "warm, heartfelt story" drew praise from *School Library Journal* critic Andrea Tarr.

Discussing the importance of her work on the Powell's Books Web site, Noble stated: "We've all heard the expression that 'less is more,' or can be. But to truly understand this abstract concept requires life experience." "This is where children's literature comes in," Noble continued. "If a character in a story can believably illustrate the concept of less is more, then it becomes believable and understandable to the young reader, but only if they make an honest connection with the character. In other words, young readers can gain life experience through a character's story, even when they have not experienced something similar in real life."

Biographical and Critical Sources

PERIODICALS

Booklist, January 1, 1981, review of *The Day Jimmy's Boa Ate the Wash,* p. 625; April 1, 1987, Ilene Cooper, review of *Meanwhile, Back at the Ranch,* p. 1208; August, 2003, Michael Cart, review of *Jimmy's Boa and the Bungee Jump Slam Dunk,* p. 1990; February 1, 2005, Ilene Cooper, review of *The Scarlet Stockings Spy,* p. 959; September 1, 2006, GraceAnne A. DeCandido, review of *The Last Brother: A Civil War Tale,* p. 139.

Bulletin of the Center for Children's Books, April, 1981, review of *The Day Jimmy's Boa Ate the Wash,* p. 158; July, 1983, review of *Hansy's Mermaid,* p. 215; October, 1984, review of *Apple Tree Christmas,* p. 33.

Horn Book, December, 1979, Kern M. Klockner, review of *The King's Tea,* p. 656; February, 1981, Ann A. Flowers, review of *The Day Jimmy's Boa Ate the Wash,* p. 44; October, 1983, Ann A. Flowers, review of *Hansy's Mermaid,* p. 564; November, 1989, Ethel R. Twichell, review of *Jimmy's Boa and the Big Splash Birthday Bash,* p. 763.

Junior Bookshelf, August, 1987, review of *Meanwhile, Back at the Ranch,* pp. 165-166.

Kirkus Reviews, February 15, 1980, review of *The King's Tea,* p. 212; February 15, 1987, review of *Meanwhile, Back at the Ranch,* p. 303; August 15, 2003, review of *Jimmy's Boa and the Bungee Jump Slam Dunk,* p. 1077; August 1, 2007, review of *The Orange Shoes.*

New York Times Book Review, January 13, 1985, review of *The Day Jimmy's Boa Ate the Wash,* p. 26.

Publishers Weekly, June 11, 1982, review of *The King's Tea,* p. 63; May 25, 1984, review of *Jimmy's Boa Bounces Back,* p. 60; August 12, 1988, review of *Apple Tree Christmas,* p. 462.

School Library Journal, October, 1979, Carolyn K. Jenks, review of *The King's Tea,* pp. 143-144; January, 1981, p. 54; September, 1983, Jonni Moore, review of *Hansy's Mermaid,* p. 110; September, 1984, Cynthia K. Leibold, review of *Jimmy's Boa Bounces Back,* p. 108; October, 1984, Elizabeth M. Simmons, review of *Apple Tree Christmas,* p. 174; November, 1989, Trev Jones, review of *Jimmy's Boa and the Big Splash Birthday Bash,* p. 91; September, 2003, Mary Elam, review of *Jimmy's Boa and the Bungee Jump Slam Dunk,* p. 186; July, 2005, Susan Scheps, review of *The Scarlet Stockings Spy,* p. 79; December, 2006, Christine Markley, review of *The Last Brother,* p. 110; September, 2007, Andrea Tarr, review of *The Orange Shoes,* p. 173.

Times Literary Supplement, July 24, 1981, Kicki Moxon Browne, review of *The Day Jimmy's Boa Ate the Wash,* p. 840.

Wilson Library Bulletin, November, 1979, Donnarae MacCann, review of *The King's Tea,* pp. 183, 205.

ONLINE

Powell's Books Web site, http://www.powells.com/ (February 1, 2009), Trinka Hakes Noble, "Less Is More, Sometimes."

Trinka Hakes Noble Home Page, http://www.trinkahakesnoble.com (February 1, 2009).*

O

ÓLAFSDÓTTIR, Gudrún Elin
See GUNNELLA

*   *   *

OLIVER, Narelle 1960-

Personal

Born 1960, in Toowoomba, Queensland, Australia; mother an art teacher; married; husband's name Greg (an environmental scientist); children: Jessie, Liam. *Education:* B.Ed. (printmaking and design). *Hobbies and other interests:* Nature, conservation.

Addresses

Home—Brisbane, Queensland, Australia. *E-mail*—ne oliver@pacific.net.au.

Career

Author and illustrator. Queensland School for the Deaf, Queensland, Australia, former teacher; University of Southern Queensland, former tutor for faculty of education; University of Melbourne, May Gibbs Children's Literature Trust artist-in-residence, 2000. *Exhibitions:* Oliver's artwork has been exhibited in Australia at the Freemantle Children's Literature Center, Dromkeen Children's Literature Center, and State Library of Queensland.

Awards, Honors

Australian Picture Book of the Year Award, shortlist, 1994, for *The Best Beak in Boonaroo Bay,* winner, 1996, for *The Hunt;* Eve Pownall Award shortlist, and Wilderness Society Environmental Award for Children's Literature, both 2000, both for *Sand Swimmers;* Picture Book of the Year Award Honor Book designation, and Eve Pownall Award Honor Book designation, both 2002, both for *Baby Bilby, Where Do You Sleep?;* Chil-

Narelle Oliver (Photograph by Pete Campbell. Reproduced by permission.)

dren's Book Council of Australia (CBCA) Notable Book designation, 2002, for *Mermaids Most Amazing;* BILBY Award for Early Reader, 2003, and Young Australian Best Book Award shortlist for Picture Storybook, 2004, both for *The Very Blue Thingamajig;* Queensland Premier's Literary Award shortlist, 2006, and Wilderness Society Environmental Award for Children's Literature shortlist, Patricia Wrightson Prize, New South Wales Premier's Literary Awards, and CBCA Picture Book of the Year shortlist, all 2007, all for *Home.*

Writings

SELF-ILLUSTRATED

Leaf Tail, McCulloch Publishing (Carlton, Victoria, Australia), 1989.

High above the Sea, Jam Roll Press (Nundah, Queensland, Australia), 1991.

The Best Beak in Boonaroo Bay, Lothian (Port Melbourne, Victoria, Australia), 1993, Fulcrum Publishers (Golden, CO), 1995.

The Hunt, Lothian (Port Melbourne, Victoria, Australia), 1995.

Sand Swimmers: The Secret Life of Australia's Dead Heart, Lothian (Port Melbourne, Victoria, Australia), 1999.

Baby Bilby, Where Do You Sleep?, Lothian (Port Melbourne, Victoria, Australia), 2001.

Mermaids Most Amazing, Ommibus Scholastic (Gosford, New South Wales, Australia), 2001, G.P. Putnam's Sons (New York, NY), 2005.

The Very Blue Thingamajig, Omnibus Scholastic (Gosford, New South Wales, Australia), 2003.

Dancing the Boom Cha-Cha Boogie, Omnibus (Malvern, South Australia, Australia), 2005.

Home, Omnibus (Malvern, South Australia, Australia), 2006.

Twilight Hunt, Star Bright (New York, NY), 2007.

Fox and Fine Feathers, Omnibus (Malvern, South Australia, Australia), 2009.

Oliver's work has been published in Korean.

OTHER

Gary Crew, *The Well* ("After Dark" series), Lothian (Port Melbourne, Victoria, Australia), 1996, Franklin Watts (London, England), 1999.

(Illustrator) *What a Goat!,* illustrated by David Cox, Omnibus Scholastic (Gosford, New South Wales, Australia), 2003.

Adaptations

Several of Oliver's books have been published with CD audio.

Sidelights

Award-winning Australian-based author and illustrator Narelle Oliver feels extremely lucky to have a career that she enjoys so passionately. The creator of the picture books *The Best Beak in Boonaroo Bay* and *Sand Swimmers: The Secret Life of Australia's Dead Heart,* as well as a compilation of mermaid facts and lore titled *Mermaids Most Amazing,* Oliver first became interested in children's books while she was working as a teacher at the Queensland School for the Deaf. Utilizing picture books in the classroom, and often creating them with her students, Oliver thoroughly enjoyed the process so much that she decided to write and illustrate her own books. She also creates artwork for books by other Australian writers, among them Gary Crew. Reviewing *Mermaids Most Amazing* in *Booklist,* Connie Fletcher praised the "rich assemblage" of magical waterbeings profiled in Oliver's text and art, while Angela J. Reynolds noted that the "hand-colored, folksy linocuts . . . deftly illustrate the [book's] lively text."

Among Oliver's self-illustrated picture books is **The Hunt,** *which features her delicately tinted line art.* (Star Bright Books, 1998. Illustration copyright © 1998 bt Narelle Oliver. Reproduced by permission of the illustrator.)

Birds figure prominently in several of Oliver's books, such as *The Best Beak in Boonaroo Bay,* which finds a group of locals competing in a best-beak contest, as well as her award-winning picture books *The Hunt* and *Home.* In *Home,* Oliver's collage illustrations, which combine linocut rubbings and digitally enhanced photographs, bring to life her story about a pair of falcons that make their home on a skyscraper in a large city and manage to find food despite the seemingly inhospitable surroundings. The text, which includes descriptions of various features of a large city, is written through the eyes of the falcons themselves. Turning to the birds of North America, her self-illustrated *Twilight Hunt: A Seek-and-Find Book* finds a mother screech owl hunting in a forest as the sun sets. Readers can aid the sharp-eyed owl in her task and hunt through Oliver's intricate tinted linocut and collage images to discover the many small creatures hiding from sight. In *School Library Journal* Nancy Call dubbed *Twilight Hunt* a "stunning portrayal of predator and prey," and added that "Oliver's elegant text is highly descriptive and action packed." According to a *Kirkus Reviews* writer, *Twilight Hunt* will also serve teachers and parents alike as "a good prelude for a field trip of the outdoorsy sort."

In Oliver's humorous lift-the-flap book *The Very Blue Thingamajig,* a mysterious blue creature that is very unbirdlike hatches from an egg covered with spots. While other thingamajigs are interested at first, they soon wander off; then the newly hatched creature begins an amazing transformation. At the end of the week the thingamajig rushes to show the other thingamajigs its new appearance, with surprising results. Reviewing *The Very Blue Thingamajig* in *Aussiereviews.com,* Sally Murphy called the picture book a "fun" read highlighted by Oliver's block-printed illustrations featuring "rich pastel colours." While entertaining, Murphy added, the picture book also provides young children with opportunities to count, learn the days of the week, and gain "a gentle lesson on differences."

The vast desert that covers much of the center of the Australian continent is the focus of Oliver's self-illustrated picture book *Sand Swimmers,* which won the Queensland Premier's Literary Award in 2000. Other desert creatures are depicted in her interactive picture book *Baby Bilby, Where Do You Sleep?,* which features peepholes through which to discover burrowing rodents and other creatures. She engages in a bit of fantasy in *Dancing the Boom Cha-Cha Boogie,* telling a story about three fun-loving murmels, imaginary creatures that wash up on the shore of a place where everything around them is strange and rather scary. Teaming up with another illustrator, Oliver has also created a story geared for budding readers in *What a Goat!*

As Oliver noted in her profile posted on the *Scholastic Australia Web site,* her interest in the environment inspired her to begin her writing career. In the early 1980s, she traveled with her environmental scientist

Oliver's detailed woodcuts are a feature of her picture book **Mermaids Most Amazing,** *which collects stories and legends about the mysterious deep.* (Copyright © 2001 by Narelle Oliver. All rights reserved. Reproduced by permission of G.P. Putnam's Sons, a division of Penguin Putnam Books for Young Readers.)

husband. On these trips, she explained, "We explored many national parks on the east coast of Australia and I became convinced that there was a need for picture book stories about the many fascinating and less well-known Australian animals in their own unique habitats. I was especially interested in showing how these animals adapt to their surroundings, and using this idea as the basis of various story plots." "Most of the time I feel very lucky that something I enjoy doing so passionately is also my work," the author/illustrator added. "Coming up with a new picture book idea, and then creating it, is an irresistible challenge."

Biographical and Critical Sources

PERIODICALS

Booklist, February 1, 2005, Connie Fletcher, review of *Mermaids Most Amazing,* p. 956.
Bulletin of the Center for Children's Books, February, 2005, Timnah Card, review of *Mermaids Most Amazing,* p. 26.
Kirkus Reviews, December 15, 2004, review of *Mermaids Most Amazing,* p. 1206; August 1, 2007, review of *Twilight Hunt.*

Magpies, May, 2001, review of *Mermaids Most Amazing,* p. 9; March, 2003, review of *The Very Blue Thingamajig,* p. 27; July, 2003, review of *What a Goat!,* p. 30; September, 2005, Maurice Saxby, review of *Dancing the Boom-Cha-Cha Boogie,* p. 6.

School Library Journal, February, 2005, Angela J. Reynolds, review of *Mermaids Most Amazing,* p. 126; December, 2007, Nancy Call, review of *Twilight Hunt: A Seek-and-Find Adventure,* p. 98.

ONLINE

AussieReviews.com, http://www.aussiereviews.com/ (February 6, 2004), Sally Murphy, review of *The Very Blue Thingamajig.*

Scholastic Australia Web site, http://www.scholastic.com/au/ (January 23, 2009), "Narelle Oliver."

OTHER

Bellingham, Daryll, editor and producer, *Undercover Stories: Writing, Illustrating, Publishing, Printing: Book Creators Reveal Their Secrets* (videorecording), Book Links, 2007.

* * *

OLTEN, Manuela 1970-

Personal

Born 1970, in Germany; married; children: one son. *Education:* Studied at Kasseler Werkakademie and Hochschule für Gestaltung (Offenbach, Germany).

Addresses

Home—Offenbach am Main, Germany.

Career

Author and illustrator of children's books. Teacher of art.

Awards, Honors

Oldenburger Kinder-und Jugendbuchpreis, 2004, and Deutschen Jugendliteraturepreis nomination, 2005, both for *Echte Kerle.*

Writings

SELF-ILLUSTRATED

Echte Kerle, Bajazzo Verlag (Zurich, Switzerland), 2004, translated as *Boys Are Best!,* Sterling (New York, NY), 2007.

Muss mal Pipi, Carlsen Verlag (Hamburg, Germany), 2005.

Wahre Freunde, Bajazzo Verlag (Zurich, Switzerland), 2005.

Mama?, Calrsen Verlag (Hamburg, Germany), 2007.

Schnell ins Bett, Carlsen Verlag (Hamburg, Germany), 2008.

Author's books have been translated into Spanish.

ILLUSTRATOR

Brigitte Raab, *Wo Wächst der Pfeffer?,* Friedrich Oetinger Verlag (Hamburg, Germany), 2005, translated by J. Alison James as *Where Does Pepper Come From?, and Other Fun Facts,* North-South Books (New York, NY), 2006.

Brigitte Rabb, *Jetzt hol ich mir eine enue Mama,* Friedrich Oetinger Verlag (Hamburg, Germany), 2007.

Biographical and Critical Sources

PERIODICALS

Horn Book, July-August, 2006, Danielle J. Ford, review of *Where Does Pepper Come From?, and Other Fun Facts,* p. 467.

Kirkus Reviews, September 15, 2007, review of *Boys Are Best!*

School Library Journal, October, 2006, Lauralyn Person, review of *Where Does Pepper Come From?,* p. 142; November, 2007, Mary Jean Smith, review of *Boys Are Best!,* p. 98.*

* * *

ORBACK, Craig

Personal

Born in Los Osos, CA. *Education:* Cuesta Community College, A.A.; Cornish College of the Arts, B.F.A., 1998. *Hobbies and other interests:* Travel, hiking, movies, reading.

Addresses

Home—Seattle, WA. *Agent*—Liz Sanders Agency; lizlizsanders.com. *E-mail*—craig.orback@gmail.com; craig@craigorback.com.

Career

Illustrator, 1998—. Also teaches children's book illustration and oil painting.

Awards, Honors

Best Children's Books selection, Bank Street College of Education, 2007, for *The Flyer Flew!;* Best Children's Books selection, Bank Street College of Education, and

Editor's Choice for Picture Books, *Library Media Connection,* both 2008, both for *Nature's Paintbox;* Amelia Bloomer Project selection, American Library Association, 2008, for *Susan B. Anthony: Fighter for Freedom and Equality.*

Illustrator

Ginger Wadsworth, *Benjamin Banneker: Pioneering Scientist,* Carolrhoda Books (Minneapolis, MN), 2003.

Tami Lehman-Wilzig, *Keeping the Promise: A Torah's Journey,* Kar-Ben Publishing (Minneapolis, MN), 2004.

Laura Hamilton Waxman, *An Uncommon Revolutionary: A Story about Thomas Paine,* Carolrhoda Books (Minneapolis, MN), 2004.

Marlene Targ Brill, *Bronco Charlie and the Pony Express,* Carolrhoda Books (Minneapolis, MN), 2004.

Deborah Hopkinson, *John Adams Speaks for Freedom,* Aladdin (New York, NY), 2005.

Lee Sullivan Hill, *The Flyer Flew!: The Invention of the Airplane,* Millbrook Press (Minneapolis, MN), 2006.

Marty Rhodes Figley, *Washington Is Burning,* Millbrook Press (Minneapolis, MN), 2006.

Suzanne Slade, *Susan B. Anthony: Fighter for Freedom and Equality,* Picture Window Books (Minneapolis, MN), 2007.

Patricia Thomas, *Nature's Paintbox: A Seasonal Gallery of Art and Verse,* Millbrook Press (Minneapolis, MN), 2007.

Stephen Krensky, *Paul Bunyan,* Millbrook Press (Minneapolis, MN), 2007.

Marty Rhodes Figley, *Prisoner for Liberty,* Millbrook Press (Minneapolis, MN), 2008.

Ginger Wadsworth, *Survival in the Snow,* Millbrook Press (Minneapolis, MN), 2009.

Also contributor of illustrations to magazines and text books.

Craig Orback contributes detailed illustrations to Patricia Thomas's picture book **Nature's Paintbox.** (Illustration copyright © 2007 by Craig Orback. All rights reserved. Reprinted with the permission of Millbrook Press, Inc., a division of Lerner Publishing Group.)

Sidelights

A children's book illustrator based in the Pacific Northwest, Craig Orback has provided the artwork for such award-winning titles as *The Flyer Flew!: The Invention of the Airplane* by Lee Sullivan Hill and *Nature's Paintbox: A Seasonal Gallery of Art and Verse* by Patricia Thomas. Orback, who works primarily in oils, also paints portraits and landscapes and teaches art at colleges near his home in Seattle, Washington.

One of Orback's early efforts, the art in *Keeping the Promise: A Torah's Journey* by Tami Lehman-Wilzig, focuses on a story of survival. The work concerns a small Torah scroll that was given as a gift to a survivor of the Bergen-Belsen concentration camp; the scroll was later carried into space by an Israeli astronaut aboard the ill-fated space shuttle Columbia. "Orback's full-page oil paintings tell a story in themselves," Sandra Kitain noted in *School Library Journal.*

Thomas offers an ode to the four seasons in *Nature's Paintbox.* In his illustrations for this book, Orback depicts each season using a different medium: pen and ink for winter, pastel chalk for spring, water color for summer, and oils for fall. "It's a successful conceit," observed Susan Moorhead in *School Library Journal,* and *Booklist* contributor Carolyn Phelan credited the success of the work to "Orback's artistic ability and to the quality of the free verse." *Nature's Paintbox* exhibits "a strikingly rare synergy between the poetry and the illustrations," in the view of a *Kirkus Reviews* writer.

Orback has also served as the illustrator for a number of juvenile biographies. The accomplishments of Wilbur and Orville Wright are the focus of his collaboration with Hill for *The Flyer Flew!* According to *School Library Journal* reviewer Heather Ver Voort, the book's characters "are painted with clear expressions and details that add to the quality of the book." Suzanne Slade offers a portrait of a famed abolitionist and suffragist in *Susan B. Anthony: Fighter for Freedom and Equality.*

Ilene Cooper, writing in *Booklist,* complimented Orback's work for Slade's biography, in particular a "dramatic spread showing slaves and soldiers marching under a golden sky." *Prisoner for Liberty* tells the story of James Forten, an African-American teenager who enlisted as a sailor during the Revolutionary War. In *Booklist,* Hazel Rochman remarked that here Orback's "vivid paintings" added to the "inspiring" tale by Marty Rhodes Figley.

Biographical and Critical Sources

PERIODICALS

Booklist, June 1, 2006, Gillian Engberg, review of *The Flyer Flew!: The Invention of the Airplane,* p. 101; June 1, 2007, Ilene Cooper, review of *Susan B. Anthony: Fighter for Freedom and Equality,* p. 94; October 15, 2007, Carolyn Phelan, review of *Nature's Paintbox: A Seasonal Gallery of Art and Verse,* p. 50; January 1, 2008, Hazel Rochman, review of *Prisoner for Liberty,* p. 66.
Kirkus Reviews, October 1, 2007, review of *Nature's Paintbox.*
School Library Journal, December, 2002, Suzanne Crowder, review of *Nathan Hale: Patriot Spy,* p. 131; May, 2004, Rita Soltan, review of *Uncommon Revolutionary: A Story about Thomas Paine,* p. 138; August, 2004, Anne Knickerbocker, review of *Bronco Charlie and the Pony Express,* p. 106, and Sandra Kitain, review of *Keeping the Promise: A Torah's Journey,* p. 111; August, 2006, Heather Ver Voort, review of *The Flyer Flew!,* p. 105; November, 2007, Susan Moorhead, review of *Nature's Paintbox,* p. 113.

ONLINE

Craig Orback Home Page, http://www.craigorback.com (January 20, 2009).*

P

PARSONS, Garry

Personal
Born in England.

Addresses
Home—England. *Office*—07931 923934 Studio 002, 2 Limesford Rd., London SE15 3BX, England. *Agent*—Meiklejohn Illustration, 5 Risborough St., London SE1 0HF, England. *E-mail*—bachimitsu@btconnect.com.

Career
Illustrator and author of children's books.

Awards, Honors
Red House Children's Book Award, Stockport (England) Schools Book Award, and AOI Images 28 Children's Book Silver award, all 2004; Nottingham Children's Book Award, and Bronze Award, Society of Artists Agents Illustration Awards, both 2005; Perth & Kinross Word's Out! Picture Book award, 2006.

Writings

SELF-ILLUSTRATED

Krong!, Bodley Head (London, England), 2005, Tiger Tales (Wilton, CT), 2006.

ILLUSTRATOR

Valerie Bloom, compiler, *On a Camel to the Moon, and Other Poems about Journeys,* Belitha (London, England), 2001.

Judy Waite, *Digging for Dinosaurs,* Red Fox (London, England), 2001, Crabtree (New York, NY), 2004.

Jonathan Shipton, *Emily's Perfect Pet,* Gullane (London, England), 2002.

Kes Gray, *Billy's Bucket,* Candlewick Press (Cambridge, MA), 2003.

Sue Mayfield, *The Four Franks,* Egmont (London, England), 2003, Crabtree (New York, NY), 2006.

Sandra Glover, *Monkey-Man,* Orchard (London, England), 2003.

Louise Cooper, *Butch the Cat-Dog,* Pearson Longman (Harlow, England), 2003.

Kate Agnew, editor, *What's Cool about School?,* Egmont (London, England), 2003.

Kate Agnew, editor, *Would You Believe It?,* Egmont (London, England), 2003.

Kate Agnew, editor, *A Family like Mine,* Egmont (London, England), 2003.

Kate Agnew, editor, *Give Me Some Space!,* Egmont (London, England), 2003.

Julia Donaldson, *The Wrong Kind of Bark,* Egmont (London, England), 2004, Crabtree (New York, NY), 2005.

Jane Clarke, *Dino Dog,* Corgi Pups (London, England), 2004.

Karen Wallace, *Ooh La La, Lottie,* Kingfisher (Boston, MA), 2004.

Jane Clarke, *G.E.M,* Red Fox (London, England), 2006.

Brian Moses, *Trouble at the Dinosaur Café,* Walker & Co. (New York, NY), 2006.

Lucy and Stephen Hawking, with Christophe Gafard, *George's Secret Key to the Universe,* Simon & Schuster (New York, NY), 2007.

Jane Clarke, *Stuck in the Mud,* Puffin (London, England), 2007, Walker & Co. (New York, NY), 2008.

(With Nick Sharratt) Kes Gray, *Daisy and the Trouble with Life,* Red Fox (London, England), 2007.

Malachy Doyle, *The Football Ghosts,* Egmont (London, England), 2007.

Jeane Willis, *Ouch in My Pouch,* Puffin (London, England), 2008.

Lucy and Stephen Hawking, *George's Cosmic Treasure Hunt,* Simon & Schuster (New York, NY), 2009.

Contributor of illustrations to periodicals, including *Runner's World, Printweek,* and *MacUser.*

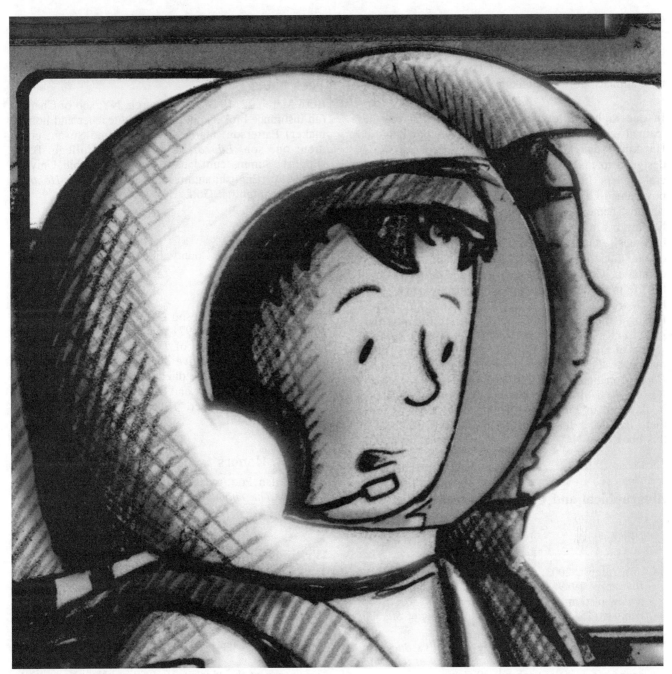

Garry Parsons' detailed cartoon drawings of a boy named George are the feature of a book series by Lucy and Stephen Hawking. (Courtesy of Garry Parsons.)

ILLUSTRATOR; "DREAM TEAM" SERIES

Ann Coburn *Showtime,* Walker (London, England), 2006.
Ann Coburn *Flying Solo,* Walker (London, England), 2006.
Ann Coburn *Speed Challenge,* Walker (London, England), 2007.
Ann Coburn *Daydream Shift,* Walker (London, England), 2007.

Sidelights

British illustrator Garry Parsons has combined his career creating editorial cartoons for magazines and newspapers with work creating art for children's books. In addition to his original self-illustrated picture book *Krong!,* about a boy whose life is disrupted when a spaceship lands in his backyard, Parsons has also contributed artwork to picture books and beginning readers by writers such as Malachy Doyle, Kes Gray, and Julia Donaldson. Collaborating with Ann Coburn, he has also illustrated several volumes in Coburn's "Dream Team" series of beginning readers. The acrylic paintings Parsons contributed to Gray's picture book *Billy's Bucket* were cited by *Booklist* critic Carolyn Phelan as "jaunty" additions to the text, "making this witty, offbeat picture

book an entertaining choice," Phelan wrote, while in *School Library Journal* Madeline Walton-Hadlock concluded of Jane Clarke's *Stuck in the Mud* that Parsons' "bright paintings . . . and simple, yet expressive cartoon animals are well suited to very young listeners."

In one high-profile illustration project, Parsons has teamed up with noted physicist Stephen Hawking and Hawking's daughter Lucy Hawking on several stories designed to make the complex understandable to general readers. In *George's Secret Key to the Universe,* a boy named George befriends his eccentric neighbors, a scientist named Eric and Eric's daughter, Annie. While helping his new friends with their experiments, George becomes fascinated with physics and is ultimately taken on an amazing adventure by the scientist's supercomputer, Cosmos. Continuing to pursue their search for life in the universe, Eric and Annie are again joined by George in *George's Cosmic Treasure Hunt.* Here Parsons' illustrations follow the two children as they join Annie's cousin Emmett and travel through space in search of alien life. Noting the wealth of factual information nested within the Hawkings' "fast-paced story," *Booklist* critic Debbie Carton dubbed *George's Secret Key to the Universe* "a charmingly illustrated chapter book," and in *Publishers Weekly* a reviewer asserted that "Parsons's cartoons enhance the broad appeal of this book."

Biographical and Critical Sources

PERIODICALS

Booklist, August, 2003, Carolyn Phelan, review of *Billy's Bucket,* p. 1989; December 1, 2007, Debbie Carton, review of *George's Secret Key to the Universe,* p. 40; February 15, 2008, Shauna Yusko, review of *Stuck in the Mud,* p. 86.

Kirkus Reviews, June 1, 2003, review of *Billy's Bucket,* p. 804; August 1, 2006, review of *Trouble at the Dinosaur Café,* p. 793; October 1, 2007, review of *George's Secret Key to the Universe.*

Publishers Weekly, May 12, 2003, review of *Billy's Bucket,* p. 65; March 10, 2008, review of *Stuck in the Mud,* p. 80; October 1, 2007, review of *George's Secret Key to the Universe,* p. 57.

School Library Journal, September, 2006, Andrea Tarr, review of *Trouble at the Dinosaur Café,* p. 180; December, 2007, Steven Engelfried, review of *George's Secret Key to the Universe,* p. 132; February, 2008, Madeline Walton-Hadlock, review of *Stuck in the Mud,* p. 84.

ONLINE

Gary Parsons Home Page, http://www.garryparsons.co.uk (January 15, 2009).

PATTERSON, James 1947-
(James B. Patterson)

Personal

Born March 22, 1947, in Newburgh, NY; son of Charles (an insurance broker) and Isabelle (a teacher and homemaker) Patterson; married; wife's name Susan; children: one son. *Education:* Manhattan College, B.A. (English; summa cum laude), 1969; Vanderbilt University, M.A. (English; summa cum laude), 1970. *Hobbies and other interests:* Golf.

Addresses

Home—Palm Beach County, FL.

Career

Writer. J. Walter Thompson Co., New York, NY, junior copywriter, beginning 1971, vice president and associate creative supervisor of JWT/U.S.A., 1976, senior vice president and creative director of JWT/New York, 1980, executive creative director and member of board of directors, 1984, chair and creative director, 1987, and chief executive officer, 1988, chair of JWT/North America, 1990-96.

Awards, Honors

Edgar Allan Poe Award, Mystery Writers of America, 1977, for *The Thomas Berryman Number.*

Writings

MYSTERY NOVELS; FOR ADULTS

The Thomas Berryman Number, Little, Brown (Boston, MA), 1976, reprinted, Compass Press (Boston, MA), 1997.

The Season of the Machete, Ballantine (New York, NY), 1977, reprinted, 1997.

The Jericho Commandment, Crown (New York, NY), 1979, published as *See How They Run,* Warner Books (New York, NY), 1997.

Virgin, McGraw Hill (New York, NY), 1980, revised as *Cradle and All,* Little, Brown (Boston, MA), 2000.

Black Market, Simon & Schuster (New York, NY), 1986, published as *Black Friday,* Warner Books (New York, NY), 2002.

The Midnight Club, Little, Brown (Boston, MA), 1989.

(With Peter de Jonge) *Miracle on the 17th Green,* Little, Brown (Boston, MA), 1996.

Hide and Seek, Little, Brown (Boston, MA), 1996.

When the Wind Blows, Little, Brown (Boston, MA), 1998.

(With Peter de Jonge) *The Beach House,* Little, Brown (Boston, MA), 2002.

The Lake House (sequel to *When the Wind Blows*), Little, Brown (Boston, MA), 2003.

(With Andrew Gross) *The Jester,* Little, Brown (Boston, MA), 2003.

(With Howard Roughan) *Honeymoon,* Little, Brown (New York, NY), 2005.

(With Andrew Gross) *Lifeguard,* Little, Brown (New York, NY), 2005.

(With Andrew Gross) *Judge and Jury,* Little, Brown (New York, NY), 2006.

(With Peter de Jonge) *Beach Road,* Little, Brown (New York, NY), 2006.

(With Michael Ledwidge) *Step on a Crack,* Little, Brown (New York, NY), 2007.

(With Michael Ledwidge) *The Quickie,* Little, Brown (New York, NY), 2007.

(With Howard Roughan) *You've Been Warned,* Little, Brown (New York, NY), 2007.

(With Howard Roughan) *Sail,* Little, Brown (New York, NY), 2008.

(With Gabrielle Charbonnet) *Sundays at Tiffany's,* Little, Brown (New York, NY), 2008.

(With Michael Ledwidge) *Run for Your Life,* Little, Brown (New York, NY), 2009.

"WOMEN'S MURDER CLUB" SERIES; FOR ADULTS

First to Die, Little, Brown (Boston, MA), 2001.

(With Andrew Gross) *Second Chance,* Little, Brown (Boston, MA), 2002.

(With Andrew Gross) *Third Degree,* Little, Brown (New York, NY), 2004.

(With Maxine Paetro) *Fourth of July,* Little, Brown (New York, NY), 2005.

(With Maxine Paetro) *The Fifth Horseman,* Little, Brown (New York, NY), 2006.

(With Maxine Paetro) *The Sixth Target,* Little, Brown (New York, NY), 2007.

(With Maxine Paetro) *Seventh Heaven,* Little, Brown (New York, NY), 2008.

"ALEX CROSS" MYSTERY SERIES; FOR ADULTS

Along Came a Spider, Little, Brown (Boston, MA), 1993.
Kiss the Girls, Little, Brown (Boston, MA), 1995.
Jack and Jill, Little, Brown (Boston, MA), 1996.
Cat and Mouse, Little, Brown (Boston, MA), 1997.
Pop Goes the Weasel, Little, Brown (Boston, MA), 1999.
Roses Are Red, Little, Brown (Boston, MA), 2000.
Violets Are Blue, Little, Brown (Boston, MA), 2001.
Four Blind Mice, Little, Brown (Boston, MA), 2002.
The Big Bad Wolf, Little, Brown (Boston, MA), 2003.
London Bridges, Little, Brown (New York, NY), 2004.
Mary, Mary, Little, Brown (New York, NY), 2005.
Cross, Little, Brown (New York, NY), 2007.
Double Cross, Little, Brown (New York, NY), 2007.
Cross Country, Little, Brown (New York, NY), 2008.

FOR YOUNGER READERS

SantaKid (picture book), illustrated by Michael Garland, Little, Brown (Boston, MA), 2004.

(With Michael Ledwidge) *The Dangerous Days of Daniel X* (also see below), Little, Brown (New York, NY), 2008.

(With Leopoldo Gout) *Daniel X: Alien Hunter* (graphic-novel adaptation of *The Dangerous Days of Daniel X*), Little, Brown (New York, NY), 2008.

"MAXIMUM RIDE" NOVEL SERIES; FOR YOUNG ADULTS

The Angel Experiment, Little Brown (New York, NY), 2005.

School's Out—Forever, Little, Brown (New York, NY), 2006.

Saving the World, and Other Extreme Sports, Little, Brown (New York, NY), 2007.

The Final Warning, Little, Brown (New York, NY), 2008.

OTHER

(With Peter Kim) *The Day America Told the Truth: What People Really Believe about Everything That Matters* (nonfiction), Prentice Hall (Englewood Cliffs, NJ), 1991.

(With Peter Kim) *The Second American Revolution* (nonfiction), Morrow (New York, NY), 1994.

Suzanne's Diary for Nicholas (adult fiction), Little, Brown (Boston, MA), 2001.

Sam's Letters to Jennifer (adult fiction), Little, Brown (New York, NY), 2004.

(Editor) *Thriller* (short stories), Mira (Toronto, Ontario, Canada), 2006.

Against Medical Advice: A True Story, Little, Brown (New York, NY), 2008.

Adaptations

Kiss the Girls was produced by Paramount in 1997. *Along Came a Spider* was produced by Paramount, 2001, starring Morgan Freeman and directed by Lee Tamahori. *Roses Are Red* was adapted for film by Ben Ramsey. *First to Die* was adapted for an NBC television mini-series. *Virgin* was adapted as a television film titled *Child of Darkness, Child of Light.* Film rights to *When the Wind Blows* and *Maximum Ride* were sold to Warner Bros. Film rights to *Santakid* and *Honeymoon* were sold to New Line Cinema. All Patterson's mystery novels have been adapted as audiobooks, as have his "Maximum Ride" books.

Sidelights

A best-selling novelist whose "Alex Cross" mystery thrillers have won him a loyal following, James Patterson moved to fiction writing after a stellar career in advertising where, as former chair of the J. Walter Thompson advertising agency, he created advertising campaigns for Kodak, Toys 'R' Us, Burger King, and other companies. His first novel to crack the bestseller list was *Along Came a Spider,* the story of a crazed math teacher who kidnaps two of his students. In addition to introducing Cross, a black police psychologist,

the novel marked the first of Patterson's books to be adapted as a feature film starring Morgan Freeman. Known for his addictive, fast-moving plots, Patterson dedicated his eighth "Alex Cross" mystery, *Pop Goes the Weasel,* to "the millions of Alex Cross readers who so frequently ask 'Can't you write faster?'"

In addition to his "Alex Cross" novels, Patterson has produced several other series novels, as well as mainstream novels, in his prolific career. *When the Wind Blows* and its sequel, *The Lake House,* proved to be a slight change of pace for the author because they combine a taut mystery with elements of science fiction. While written for an adult readership, *When the Wind Blows* focuses on a Colorado veterinarian who meets a strange preteen named Max who is trying to avoid the group of thugs attempting to return her to a secret genetic research laboratory located nearby. As the novel continues, five other children—Fang, Iggy, Nudge, the Gasman, and Angel—are introduced, all half-human, half clones with extraordinary abilities. *The Lake House* continues the story, as the members of the Flock confront a new threat in the form of a maniacal physician who wants to subject the young people to unpleasant forms of medical experimentation.

Learning that *When the Wind Blows* and *The Lake House* had gained him many teen readers, Patterson decided to rework Max's story in a book specifically geared for a young-adult audience. In *Maximum Ride: The Angel Experiment* Max is now fourteen, and her five friends are discovering how to use the retractable wings and other super-abilities resulting from the bird DNA that was grafted onto their human genes. Orphans, the children were held in cages at a place known only as the "School"; since their escape they have lived in hiding, migrating to New York City in search of answers and hoping to escape the half-wolf Erasers who are hunting them down.

Dubbing *Maximum Ride* "an action-packed cross between Gertrude Chandler Warner's "Boxcar Children" and Marvel Comics' X-Men," *Booklist* contributor Stephanie Zvirin predicted that the novel would attract both teen and adult readers. Noting that the novel's "fast-moving plot" is conveyed primarily through Max's first-person narration, Sharon Rawlins praised the novel as a "compelling read," while a *Kirkus Reviews* contributor noted that "nonstop action" propels Patterson's "page-turner breathlessly from start to finish." While several reviewers noted that *Maximum Ride* leaves several questions unanswered, the *Kirkus Reviews* contributor wrote that the novel closes, "leaving layers of mystery" for Patterson's planned sequel.

Patterson continues Max's adventures in three other "Maximum Ride" novels, as the young woman is guided toward her ultimate destiny: to save the world. In *School's Out—Forever* Max and her wingéd friends Fang, Iggy, Nudge, Gasman, and Angel are flying south when their location is made known to the FBI after

Fang becomes injured and must be taken to the hospital. Although FBI agent Anne Walker hides the six teens on her Virginia farm, their flirtation with real life proves to be short-lived. *Saving the World, and Other Extreme Sports* moves the action closer to the final countdown, as Max combats a group of scientists attempting to re-engineer humans into a superior master race. In *The Final Warning* the Flock travels to Antarctica, hoping to combat climate change, but their creator lies in wait, hoping to capture the teens and sell them to the highest bidder. "Patterson, an accomplished storyteller, . . . demonstrates his ability to write page-turning action scenes," concluded *Booklist* critic Diana Tixier Herald in her review of *School's Out—Forever,* the critic also citing the author's inclusion of "some surprising humor." In *Booklist* Jennifer Mattson predicted of *Saving the World, and Other Extreme Sports* that "affection for the dauntless characters and misadventures" in the series "will hold readers."

In more recent years, responding to the demands of his fans as well as those of his publisher, Patterson has begun collaborating with other writers, sketching the plot of many of his adult novels and then approving his collaborator's completed manuscript. The young-adult novel *The Dangerous Days of Daniel X* is also a collaboration. Devised by Patterson and written by Michael Ledwidge, the story finds fifteen-year-old Daniel working in the family trade: hunting alien life forms and exterminating the top twenty creatures on the official List of Alien Outlaws on Terra Firma. In addition to appearing in novel form, *The Dangerous Days of Daniel X* was also adapted as the graphic novel *Alien Hunter.*

In his books for both teens and adults, Patterson remains known for his high-speed plots and his tendency to avoid in-depth character development in favor of high-octane storytelling. As he explained to Steven Womak in a *Bookpage.com* interview, "I read *Ulysses* and figured I couldn't top that, so I never had any desire to write literary fiction." However, when he read William Peter Blatty's *The Exorcist* and Frederick Forsyth's *The Day of the Jackal,* he had a different reaction. "I went, 'Ooh! This is cool.' . . . And I set out to write that kind of book, the kind of book that would make an airplane ride disappear." In an interview posted on his home page, Patterson explained that writing for younger readers is an especially fulfilling experience: "I love the idea of getting people reading."

Biographical and Critical Sources

PERIODICALS

Booklist, May 15, 2001, Kristine Huntley, review of *Suzanne's Diary for Nicholas,* p. 1708; October 15, 2001, Kristine Huntley, review of *Violets Are Blue,* p. 356; January 1, 2002, Kristine Huntley, review of *Sec-*

ond Chance, p. 777; July, 2004, Kristine Huntley, review of *Sam's Letters to Jennifer,* p. 1799; February 1, 2005, Stephanie Zvirin, review of *Maximum Ride: The Angel Experiment,* p. 918; May 15, 2006, Diana Tixier Herald, review of *School's Out—Forever,* p. 54; August, 2007, Jennifer Mattson, review of *Saving the World, and Other Extreme Sports,* p. 62; October 1, 2008, Jesse Karp, review of *Daniel X: Alien Hunter,* p. 40.

Bulletin of the Center for Children's Books, April, 2005, Krista Hutley, review of *The Angel Experiment,* p. 353.

Kirkus Reviews, December 15, 2001, review of *Second Chance,* p. 1712; June 1, 2004, review of *Sam's Letters to Jennifer,* p. 513; April 1, 2005, review of *Maximum Ride,* p. 422; April 1, 2006, review of *School's Out—Forever,* p. 353; May 1, 2007, review of *Saving the World, and Other Extreme Sports;* November 1, 2008, review of *The Dangerous Days of Daniel X.*

Kliatt, March, 2005, Paula Rohrlick, review of *Maximum Ride,* p. 15; March, 2006, Paula Rohrlick, review of *School's Out—Forever,* p. 16; May, 2007, Paula Rohrlick, review of *Saving the World, and Other Extreme Sports,* p. 17.

Library Journal, October 1, 2000, Rebecca House Stankowski, review of *Roses Are Red,* p. 148; July 2001, Margaret Hanes, review of *Suzanne's Diary for Nicholas,* p. 126.

New York Times, July 24, 2001, Janet Maslin, "Love Story, or Is That Death Story?," p. 6; November 29, 2001, Janet Maslin, "Bodies Hang in California, and Bullets Fly in Florida," p. 7.

Publishers Weekly, August 2, 1999, review of *Pop Goes the Weasel,* p. 69; March 20, 2000, review of *Cradle and All,* p. 68; February 18, 2002, review of *Second Chance,* p. 75; March 18, 2002, Daisy Maryles and Dick Donahue, "Don't Get Mad, Get Even," p. 19; June 7, 2004, review of *Sam's Letters to Jennifer,* p. 33; July 12, 2004, Daisy Maryles, "A Passionate Patterson," p. 12; September 27, 2004, review of *SantaKid,* p. 60; March 21, 2005, review of *Maximum Ride,* p. 52.

School Library Journal, May, 2005, Sharon Rawlins, review of *Maximum Ride,* p. 135; August, 2006, Heather M. Campbell, review of *School's Out—Forever,* p. 127; July, 2007, Vicki Reutter, review of *Saving the World, and Other Extreme Sports,* p. 108.

Voice of Youth Advocates, April, 2005, Jenny Ingram, review of *Maximum Ride,* p. 60; February, 2007, review of *School's Out—Forever;* August, 2007, Jenny Ingram, review of *Saving the World, and Other Extreme Sports.*

ONLINE

Bookpage.com, http://www.bookpage.com/ (April 2, 2002), Steven Womak, "Stretching the Boundaries of the Thriller" (interview).

James Patterson Web site, http://www.jamespatterson.com (September 17, 2005).*

PATTERSON, James B.
See PATTERSON, James

*   *   *

PAZ, Natalia Toledo
See TOLEDO, Natalia

*   *   *

PEDLER, Caroline

Personal

Born in Cornwall, England. *Education:* Portsmouth University, B.F.A. (illustration), 1995.

Addresses

Home—Bristol, England. *Office*—Churchtown Arts, Churchtown, St. Agnes, Cornwall TR5 0QW, England.

Career

Illustrator and artist. Freelance illustrator, beginning 1997. *Exhibitions:* Work include in exhibitions at Roster Gallery, Bath, England, 2003.

Illustrator

The Twelve Days of Christmas, Marks & Spencer (London, England), 2001.

My Treasury of Christmas Stories, Marks & Spencer (London, England), 2001.

Gaby Goldsack, *A Letter to Santa,* Marks & Spencer (London, England), 2001.

Gaby Goldsack, reteller, *The Little Fir-Tree,* Marks & Spencer (London, England), 2001.

Gaby Goldsack, reteller, *A Christmas Carol,* Marks & Spencer (London, England), 2003.

Carrie Emma Weston, *Moonlight Lily,* Oxford University Press (Oxford, England), 2004.

Kenneth Steven, *Imagining Things, and Other Poems,* Lion Children's Books (London, England), 2005.

Vicki Howe, *Have You Seen Christmas?,* Bible Reading Fellowship, 2006.

M. Christina Butler, *A Star So Bright!: A Christmas Tale,* Little Tiger Press (London, England), 2006, Good Books (Intercourse, PA), 2007.

David Bedford, *Bedtime for Little Bears!,* Good Books (Intercourse, PA), 2006.

Christmas Animal Tales, Stripes (London, England), 2007.

M. Christina Butler, *Don't Be Afraid, Little Ones,* Little Tiger Press (London, England), 2007.

Claire Freedman, *A Kiss for Little Kitten,* Little Tiger Press (London, England), 2008.

Claire Freedman, *A Cuddle for Little Duck,* Little Tiger Press (London, England), 2008.

Elizabeth Baguley, *Little Pip and the Rainbow Wish,* Good Books (Intercourse, PA), 2008.

Julia Hubery, *A Friend like You,* Good Books (Intercourse, PA), 2009.

David Bedford, *Little Bear's Big Sweater,* Good Books (Intercourse, PA), 2009, published as *Little Bear's Big Jumper,* Little Tiger Press (London, England), 2009.

Also illustrator of board books, including *Kind Little Bear* and *Brave Little Deer.*

Books featuring Pedler's illustrations have been translated into several languages, including Spanish.

Biographical and Critical Sources

PERIODICALS

Bristol Evening Post (Bristol, England), April 24, 2003, "Budding Artist on Show."
Publishers Weekly, October 22, 2007, review of *A Star So Bright!: A Christmas Tale,* p. 54.

ONLINE

Caroline Pedler Home Page, http://www.carolinepedler. co.uk (January 20, 2009).*

*   *   *

PETERS, Julie Anne 1952-

Personal

Born January 16, 1952, in Jamestown, NY; partner of Sherri Leggett. *Education:* Colorado Women's College, B.A., 1974; Metropolitan State College of Denver, B.S. (summa cum laude), 1985; University of Colorado—Denver, M.B.A. (magna cum laude), 1989. *Hobbies and other interests:* Human rights, animal rights advocacy, reading, fostering kittens, sports, musical theater.

Addresses

Home—Lakewood, CO. *E-mail*—Julie@julieannepeters. com.

Career

Writer. Tracom Corporation, Denver, CO, secretary, research assistant, computer programmer, and systems analyst, 1975-84; Electronic Data Systems, Denver, computer systems engineer, 1985-88; Jefferson County School District, Lakewood, CO, special-needs educational assistant. Fifth grade teacher, 1975.

Member

Society of Children's Book Writers and Illustrators, Authors' Guild, Colorado Authors' League, Colorado Center for the Book, Denver Zoological Society, Cat Care Society, American Civil Liberties Union, GLBT Center of Colorado.

Julie Anne Peters (Reproduced by permission.)

Awards, Honors

KC3 Reading Award, Greater Kansas City Association of School Librarians, 1995, for *The Stinky Sneakers Contest;* Best Book in Language Arts: K-6 Novels, Society of School Librarians International, 1997, for *How Do You Spell GEEK?;* Top Hand Award for Young-Adult Fiction, Colorado Authors' League, 1998, for *Revenge of the Snob Squad;* Best Books for Young Adults selection, Popular Paperbacks for Young Adults selection, and Quick Pick for Reluctant Young Adult Readers selection, all American Library Association (ALA), all 2000, all for *Define "Normal";* Best Books for Young Adults selection, and Popular Paperbacks for Young Adults selection, both ALA, Books for the Teen Age selection, New York Public Library, and Lambda Literary Award finalist, all 2003, and Amelia Bloomer Project Recommended Feminist Books for Youth, and Stonewall Honor Book, both ALA, both 2004, all for *Keeping You a Secret;* Buxtehuder Bulle nomination, National Book Award in Young People's Literature finalist, 2004, and Best Books for Young Adults selection, ALA, Books for the Teen Age selection, New York Public Library, Stonewall Honor Book, and Lambda Literary Award finalist, all 2005, all for *Luna;* Rainbow Reads selection, ALA, 2005, and Best Books for Young Adults selection, and Quick Pick for Reluctant Young-Adult Readers selection, both ALA, and Books for the Teen Age selection, New York Public Library, all 2006,

all for *Far from Xanadu;* Lambda Literary Award, James Cook Teen Book Award, Ohio Library Council, Cybils Award finalist, and Rainbow Reads selection, all 2006, all for *Between Mom and Jo;* Golden Crown Literary Award finalist, and Rainbow Reads selection, both 2007, and Books for the Teen Age selection, New York Public Library, and Cooperative Children's Books Center Choice designation, both 2008, all for *grl2grl.*

Writings

The Stinky Sneakers Contest, illustrated by Cat Bowman Smith, Little, Brown (Boston, MA), 1992.
Risky Friends, Willowisp Press (St. Petersburg, FL), 1993.
B.J.'s Billion-Dollar Bet, illustrated by Cynthia Fisher, Little, Brown (Boston, MA), 1994.
How Do You Spell GEEK?, Little, Brown (Boston, MA), 1996.
Revenge of the Snob Squad, Little, Brown (Boston, MA), 1998.
Romance of the Snob Squad, Little, Brown (Boston, MA), 1999.
Love Me, Love My Broccoli, Avon/HarperCollins (New York, NY), 1999.
Define "Normal," Little, Brown (Boston, MA), 2000.
A Snitch in the Snob Squad, Little, Brown (Boston, MA), 2001.
Keeping You a Secret, Little, Brown (Boston, MA), 2003.
Luna, Little, Brown (Boston, MA), 2004.
Far from Xanadu, Little, Brown (Boston, MA), 2005.
Between Mom and Jo, Little, Brown (Boston, MA), 2006.
grl2grl: short fictions, Little, Brown (Boston, MA), 2007.
By the Time You Read This, I'll Be Dead, Disney/Hperion (New York, NY), 2008.
Rage: A Love Story, Knopf (New York, NY), 2009.

Also author of numerous articles for juvenile, young-adult, and adult periodicals, including *Wee Wisdom, Hopscotch, Career Woman, Purple Cow, Venture, My Friend, Free Spirit, Lollipops, Family Fun, On the Line, Touch, Guide, Children's Book Insider, Wilson Library Bulletin, Writer's Handbook, Writer, Accent on Living,* and *Good Housekeeping.* Contributing editor for *IEA News.*

Sidelights

Julie Anne Peters is the author of several award-winning titles for children and young adults, including *The Stinky Sneakers Contest, Define "Normal,"* and *Between Mom and Jo.* Peters has a special affinity for young-adult literature; "I've always loved reading it," she told interview Malinda Lo for *AfterEllen.com.* "I really just love the passion in it, and I love transporting back to that time in life, when you did live passionately, you lived with velocity. Every day was a lifetime, and the drama never ended."

After trying her hand at teaching and working as a systems engineer, Peters began her writing career in teh hopes that she could avoid the frustrations of corporate

life; "You can only waste so much of your life geeking out about 4GL and artificial intelligence," she remarked on her home page. She explored the possibility of writing fiction, leading to the sale of a number of short stories as well as nonfiction articles and educational activities to various children's periodicals. Soon thereafter, Peters was able to get her first two books published, formally launching her career as a young-adult and children's writer.

Peters' first book, *The Stinky Sneakers Contest,* is based on a real-life experience as well as a "grungy" shoe contest that Peters read about. "Reading about the contest reminded me of my own childhood humiliation of perpetually smelly feet," she once told *SATA.* The plot moves far beyond the title and presents a tale of a friendship in jeopardy because of cheating. The story depicts familiar themes of winning, losing, and honesty, as Earl and Damian compete in the Feetfirst shoe company's smelly sneakers contest. An *Instructor* reviewer commented that Peters' "pleasant, easy-to-read chapter book about two African-American boys will stimulate reflection on what it takes to be a winner." Lynnea McBurney, a reviewer for *School Library Journal,* also

Peters focuses on the disparate experiences of two teens in her young-adult novel Define "Normal." *(Little, Brown & Company, Ltd., 2000. Copyright © 2000 by Julie Anne Peters. Reproduced by permission.)*

Cover of Peters' middle-grade novel How Do You Spell GEEK?, *featuring artwork by Doran Ben-Ami.* (Little, Brown, 1996. Reproduced by permission.)

stated that, "on the whole, this is a nicely written, humorous story. It is short enough for those just getting into transitional readers, yet there is enough here for enjoyment and food for thought."

Peters' second book, *Risky Friends,* explores the issue of choosing friends while confronting the reality of single-parent households. Two best friends, Kacie and Vicky, are at risk of losing their friendship over Kacie's newfound companion, Skye, who wins Kacie's attention by buying her gifts. "As a kid, I always envied people with more money than me—thinking wealth solved the world's problems," Peters said. "That misperception, along with the inevitable growing pains accompanying young adulthood, are the themes explored in *Risky Friends.*" Sister Bernadette Marie Ondus stated in *Kliatt:* "The younger set, girls primarily, will enjoy this story since they will be able to identify closely with the characters."

Define "Normal" grew out of Peters' experiences working with special-needs children. According to her, "these kids weren't necessarily learning disabled, or intellectually challenged. They had so many family problems, so much responsibility, that school was the bottom rung on

their priority ladder." Peters noted that the children she worked with struggled daily to survive, and that theirs was a far-from-normal childhood. "I began to examine the concept of 'normal' and how we use it to label people—particularly teens. We react so negatively to kids who choose to express themselves a bit outrageously, who dress to shock, or ornament their bodies. But this is absolutely normal behavior. Young people are trying to figure out who they are, where they fit in. And conversely, how they'll set themselves apart." It was this exploration of "normal" says Peters that evolved into two of her novel's characters: Antonia and Jazz.

In *Define "Normal"* Antonia Dillon appears to be a perfectly normal teen: healthy, happy, and trouble free. She dresses conservatively, performs well in school, and never questions authority. Yet underneath her controlled exterior she is experiencing tremendous family turmoil. Peters explained to *SATA,* "Antonia has way too much responsibility for a fourteen-year-old girl. She has no time or energy to explore who she is as a person." On the other end of the spectrum is Jasmine Luther. "Jazz," noted Peters, "is all about self. She's this glorious expression of who she is. But Jazz is free to be herself because she has a solid family foundation. If she crashes and burns, she knows someone will be there to douse the flames. Antonia doesn't have this luxury." The conflict in the book occurs when Antonia is assigned to peer counsel Jazz in school, leading to a resounding clash of values. As both girls work through the counseling sessions, they each come to terms with their problems, eventually becoming friends. Writing in *School Library Journal,* Kimberly A. Ault lauded *Define "Normal"* as "believable" and "well written."

Peters is also the author of a series of books about a group of sixth-grade girls who call themselves the Snob Squad. Each book explores aspects in the lives of these girls as they bond in friendship to combat the loneliness of being outcasts and misfits. Along the way, they fall in love, uncover mysteries, and solve crimes. In *A Snitch in the Snob Squad,* Jenny, the main character, and her friends try to discover the truth about a theft at school and its related cover-up, while also grappling with issues of trust at home and with her friends. According to *Booklist* contributor Hazel Rochman, readers will "appreciate the honesty as Jenny wrestles with issues of friendship, guilt, and loyalty." *Romance of the Snob Squad* centers on a crush that one of the Snob Squad girls has on a classmate, while simultaneously addressing aspects of family love and loyalty to friends. Rochman noted that the narrator's "bossy, wry first-person narrative is candid . . . kind, and sad," predicting that many middle-graders will identify with the issues explored in this book.

At the suggestion of her editor, Peters, an openly gay woman, entered new literary territory with the novel *Keeping You a Secret.* A love story, the work centers on Holland Jaeger, a popular and intelligent high-school

senior who falls in love with Cecelia "Cece" Goddard, a strong-willed transfer student. After Holland's friends and family shun her, she must turn to members of the gay community for support. "Because Holland is such an analytical character, and one who begins the novel believing herself to be straight, the narrative of her self-discovery invites readers to appreciate the natural, gut-level way she falls for Cece," observed Nancy Boutilier in the *Lambda Book Report*. "The book is a window into one girl's efforts to fashion a lesbian sense of self amid high school pressures." Audience response to *Keeping You a Secret* was overwhelming, Peters remarked to Lo. "Once the book came out I just got thousands of letters, I could not believe it. It kind of gave my writing a higher purpose, I think. Kind of a greater calling. And I worked through all my fears about doing it, because it's just important. It's important to get that literature out there."

Peters' novel *Luna,* about a transgender teen, was nominated for a National Book Award. At night Regan watches as her older brother, Liam, slips into her room, puts on makeup, and transforms himself into Luna, his "female" self. When Liam begins dressing as a girl in

Cover of Peters' Between Mom and Jo, *which focuses on a teen dealing with a nontraditional family torn by divorce.* (Little, Brown & Company, 2006. Cover photo copyright © PhotoAlto/Veer. Reproduced by permission.)

public, Regan fears a backlash from their parents and classmates, and she also worries that constantly addressing her brother's needs prevents her from enjoying her own life. According to *Horn Book* reviewer Laurence Adams, Peters "succeeds in creating whole, complex characters confronting these issues." The author "does not shy away from the complexities of 'coming out' as a transgendered person, nor does she get on a soapbox about the myriad of issues surrounding transgenderism," reported Lynn Evarts in the *Lambda Book Report*. "She simply allows Regan to report and allows us to peek inside her life, as she desperately tries to hold herself and her brother together."

Far from Xanadu tells the story of Mike Szabo, a butch lesbian teenager living in rural Kansas. When beautiful, rebellious Xanadu moves into town to live with relatives, Mike falls head-over-heels in love. The new girl is straight, however, and although she has no intention of dating Mike, she enjoys the attention she receives from Mike and toys with her emotions. "Despite the multitude of difficulties the protagonist faces," noted Miranda Doyle in *School Library Journal,* "the story never slips into melodrama, and all of the issues are handled with sensitivity and compassion." Michael Cart, writing in *Booklist,* also praised *Far from Xanadu*, stating that "there's no arguing with the honest intensity of Mike's emotions."

In *Between Mom and Jo,* Peters "wanted to look at same-sex marriage and relationships from the child's point of view," she told Lo, adding: "I think a lot of times it's more of a burden on them than we think it is." The novel concerns Nick, a teenager who has been raised by Erin, his biological mother, and her partner, Jo. When their relationship ends, Nick is torn between his loyalty to Erin and his love for Jo, who has no legal rights to the boy. "This coming-of-age novel powerfully portrays the universal pain of a family breakup," observed *School Library Journal* contributor Beth Gallego, and Janis Flint-Ferguson remarked in *Kliatt* that Nick's "pain is palpable as Jo and Erin work through their differences to do what's right for their son."

In addition to her novels, Peters has also released *grl2grl: short fictions,* a collection of ten stories that focuses on lesbian and transgender teen issues. "To sustain a career in writing, a writer has to evolve," Peters told a *Mombian.com* interviewer. "I begin with the premise that each new work I undertake must be newer, fresher, bigger and better than the last. I'm always asking, What can I do that I've never done before? How can I stretch and risk and keep myself and my readers excited? Young adult literature is the ideal venue to experiment with style, form, voice and subject matter." *grl2grl* earned strong reviews. "Peters skillfully varies the subject matter and tone from piece to piece," *Horn Book* critic Anita L. Burkam wrote of the collection, and a *Publishers Weekly* reviewer complimented the authenticity of Peters' "voices."

Peters once told *SATA:* "The most gratifying aspect of writing for young people is discovering that your books transcend storytelling to making a difference in a person's life. I cry when I receive letters like this one from Joli in New York City. 'I read your book about three times,' she says. 'I'm not a person to sit down and read. But your book is wonderful.' Or this from Alexandra in Denver. 'You probably don't know that I don't like to read, but your books really get me going.'"

"Since I was a reluctant reader myself, I know how finding the one book that turns you onto reading is like being handed the keys to the kingdom," Peters added. "The kingdom is knowledge and adventure and self-discovery. Reading opens the realm of possibilities in life. It's life-changing, life-affirming. If my books can ignite one young person's love of reading, what greater reward could there be for a writer?"

Biographical and Critical Sources

PERIODICALS

Booklist, December 15, 1998, Ilene Cooper, review of *Revenge of the Snob Squad,* p. 751; April 1, 1999, Hazel Rochman, review of *Romance of the Snob Squad,* p. 1414; May 15, 2000, Jean Franklin, review of *Define "Normal,"* p. 1739; May 15, 2001, Hazel Rochman, review of *A Snitch in the Snob Squad,* p. 1753; July, 2004, Cindy Welch, review of *Luna,* p. 1834; September 1, 2005, Michael Cart, review of *Far from Xanadu,* p. 112; March 1, 2006, Krista Hutley, review of *Between Mom and Jo,* p. 83; August, 2007, Francisca Goldsmith, review of *grl2grl: short fictions,* p. 63.

Denver Post, June 24, 2003, Eric Hubler, "Editor Prods Peters to Reinvent Herself as 'Gay-lit' Author," p. F1.

Horn Book, July-August, 2004, Laurence Adams, review of *Luna,* p. 459; May-June, 2005, Lauren Adams review of *Far from Xanadu,* p. 332; September-October, 2007, Anita L. Burkam, review of *grl2grl,* p. 585.

Instructor, February, 1993, review of *The Stinky Sneakers Contest,* p. 5.

Kliatt, November, 1993, Sister Bernadette Marie Ondus, review of *Risky Friends,* p. 10; May, 2003, Claire Rosser, review of *Keeping You a Secret,* p. 12; May, 2006, Janis Flint-Ferguson, review of *Between Mom and Jo,* p. 13; July, 2007, Amanda MacGregor, review of *grl2grl,* p. 36.

Lambda Book Report, August-September, 2003, Nancy Boutilier, review of *Keeping You a Secret,* p. 32; October, 2004, Lynn Evarts, review of *Luna,* p. 13.

Publishers Weekly, August 19, 1996, review of *How Do You Spell GEEK?,* p. 67; March 13, 2000, review of *Define "Normal,"* p. 85; April 21, 2003, review of *Keeping You a Secret,* p. 63; May 17, 2004, review of *Luna,* p. 52; September 17, 2007, review of *grl2grl,* p. 56.

School Library Journal, March, 1993, Lynnea McBurney, review of *The Stinky Sneakers Contest,* p. 184; October, 1996, Harriett Fargnoli, review of *How Do You Spell GEEK?,* p. 124; July, 2000, Kimberly A. Ault, review of *Define "Normal,"* p. 108; April, 2001, Janet Hilburn, review of *A Snitch in the Snob Squad,* p. 148; June, 2005, Miranda Doyle, review of *Far from Xanadu,* p. 167; April, 2006, Beth Gallego, review of *Between Mom and Jo,* p. 146.

ONLINE

AfterEllen.com, http://www.afterellen.com/ (April 21, 2005), Malinda Lo, interview with Peters.

Julie Anne Peters Home Page, http://www.julieannepeters.com (February 1, 2009).

Mombian.com, http://www.mombian.com/ (March 28, 2007), interview with Peters.

*   *   *

PORFIRIO, Guy 1958-

Personal

Born 1958; married; children: two. *Education:* American Academy of Art, graduate; attended School of Visual Arts (New York, NY).

Addresses

Home—Tucson, AZ. *E-mail*—guyporfirio@msn.com.

Career

Artist and illustrator.

Illustrator

David F. Birchman, *The Raggly, Scraggly, No-Soap, No-Scrub Girl,* Lothrop, Lee & Shepard (New York, NY), 1995.

Marsha Wilson Chall, *Happy Birthday, America!,* Lothrop, Lee & Shepard (New York, NY), 2000.

Tony Johnston, *Clear Moon, Snow Soon,* Rising Moon (Flagstaff, AZ), 2001.

Kathleen Long Bostrom, *Papa's Gift: An Inspirational Story of Love and Loss,* Zonderkidz (Grand Rapids, MI), 2002.

Lynn Crosbie Loux, *The Day I Could Fly,* NorthWord Press (Chanhassen, MN), 2003.

Dianne M. MacMillan, *The Curse of Rafferty McGill,* Albert Whitman (Morton Grove, IL), 2003.

Charles Tazewell, *The Littlest Angel,* Ideals Children's Books (Nashville, TN), 2004.

Clement C. Moore, *The Night before Christmas,* Candy-Cane Press (Nashville, TN), 2004.

Myrna Strasser, *Silent Night, Holy Night,* Zonderkidz (Grand Rapids, MI), 2004.

Billy Crystal, *Grandpa's Little One,* HarperCollins (New York, NY), 2006.

Martin Luther, *From Heaven Above: A Christmas Carol,* Concordia Publishing House (St. Louis, MO), 2006.

Sonia Levitin, *Junk Man's Daughter,* Sleeping Bear Press (Chelsea, MI), 2007.

Dandi Daley Mackall, *The Legend of Saint Nicholas: A Story of Christmas Giving,* Zonderkidz (Grand Rapids, MI), 2007.

Sidelights

Illustrator Guy Porfirio has provided the artwork for a number of well-received children's books, including Sonia Levitin's *Junk Man's Daughter* and Tony Johnston's *Clear Moon, Snow Soon.* "I think of what I do as telling a story without using words," Porfirio remarked to *Foothills News* contributor Heather Stanton, adding: "I always say that as you read, before you realize it you are visualizing the story and pictures are forming in your mind."

One of Porfirio's early efforts, creating artwork for *Happy Birthday, America!* by Marsha Wilson Chall, focuses on a small-town family's Fourth of July celebration. "The clan's high spirits resonate in the intentionally grainy, sun-dappled watercolor and colored-pencil art," noted a contributor in *Publishers Weekly,* and JoAnn Jonas observed in *School Library Journal* that the characters' "facial expressions show the excitement and fun of the event." A young boy tries to catch a glimpse of Santa Claus in Johnston's *Clear Moon, Snow Soon,* a work told in verse. Here *Booklist* reviewer Ilene Cooper described Johnston's narrative as "warm and soothing," adding that "Porfirio's glowing oil paintings capture that same mood."

Junk Man's Daughter centers on the members of an immigrant family and their struggle to survive in the United States of America. According to *Booklist* contributor Hazel Rochman, Porfirio's illustrations for this book "include effective scenes of the family—hopeful, hard at work, angry, and blissful." A child's first birthday is the focus of *Grandpa's Little One,* a tale by actor and comedian Billy Crystal. Here Porfirio's pictures "convey the affection between grandfather and his cherubic granddaughter," remarked a critic in *Publishers Weekly.*

Biographical and Critical Sources

PERIODICALS

Booklist, September 1, 1995, Hazel Rochman, review of *The Raggly, Scraggly, No-Soap, No-Scrub Girl,* p. 82; May 1, 2000, John Peters, review of *Happy Birthday, America!,* p. 1676; November 1, 2001, Ilene Cooper, review of *Clear Moon, Snow Soon,* p. 482; December 1, 2007, Hazel Rochman, review of *Junk Man's Daughter,* p. 48.
Kirkus Reviews, September 15, 2007, review of *Junk Man's Daughter.*
Publishers Weekly, June 5, 2000, review of *Happy Birthday, America!,* p. 94; September 24, 2001, review of *Clear Moon, Snow Soon,* p. 52; March 6, 2006, review of *Grandpa's Little One,* p. 72.
School Library Journal, June, 2000, JoAnn Jonas, review of *Happy Birthday, America!,* p. 102; October, 2001, review of *Clear Moon, Snow Soon,* p. 66; October, 2003, Ann Joslin, review of *The Day I Could Fly,* p. 129; December, 2003, Donna Cardon, review of *The Curse of Rafferty McGill,* p. 120; April, 2008, Lucinda Snyder Whitehurst, review of *Junk Man's Daughter,* p. 115.

ONLINE

Foothills News Web site, http://www.thefoothillsnews.com/ (May 28, 2008), Heather Stanton, "Foothills Resident Makes Career out of Passion for Drawing."
Guy Porfirio Home Page, http://guyporfirio.com (January 20, 2009).*

R

RADER, Laura

Personal
Female. *Education:* Attended Pratt Institute.

Addresses
Home—Los Angeles, CA.

Career
Writer and illustrator.

Writings

A Child's Story of Thanksgiving, illustrated by Mary Ann Utt, Ideals Children's Books (Nashville, TN), 1998.

SELF-ILLUSTRATED

The Pudgy Where Is Your Nose? Book, Grosset & Dunlap (New York, NY), 1989.
The Best Smelling Mother Goose Book Ever!, Little Simon (New York, NY), 1996.
The Best Smelling Christmas Book Ever!, Little Simon (New York, NY), 1997.
(Reteller) *Chicken Little,* HarperCollins (New York, NY), 1998, published as *Chicken Licken,* illustrated by Thomas Sperling, Abrams (Waterbury, CT), 2005.
Santa's New Suit, HarperCollins (New York, NY), 2000.
These Little Piggies, Little Simon (New York, NY), 2001.
Tea for Me, Tea for You, HarperCollins(New York, NY), 2003.
Who'll Pull Santa's Sleigh Tonight?, HarperCollins (New York, NY), 2003.
Grow Little Turnip, Grow Big, Sterling (New York, NY), 2006.
When Santa Lost His Ho! Ho! Ho!, HarperCollins (New York, NY), 2007.

ILLUSTRATOR

Jane Yolen, *The Mermaid's Three Wisdoms,* Collins (New York, NY), 1978.
Edward Bartholic, *Cricket and Sparrow: Four Stories,* Collins (New York, NY), 1979.
Margo Mason, *Winter Coats,* Bantam (New York, NY), 1989.
Harriet Ziefert, *The Big Birthday Box,* Random House (New York, NY), 1989.
Harriet Ziefert, *In My Kitchen,* Random House (New York, NY), 1989.
Harriet Ziefert, *Penny Goes to the Movies,* Viking (New York, NY), 1990.
Harriet Ziefert, *Follow Me!,* Puffin (New York, NY), 1990.
Harriet Ziefert, *Getting Ready for New Baby,* Harper & Row (New York, NY), 1990.
Harriet Ziefert, *Bigger than a Baby,* HarperCollins (New York, NY), 1991.
Harriet Ziefert, *Dancing,* HarperCollins (New York, NY), 1991.
Harriet Ziefert, *Goody New Shoes,* Viking (New York, NY), 1991.
Harriet Ziefert, *I Hate Boots!,* HarperCollins (New York, NY), 1991.
Harriet Ziefert, *Move Over,* HarperCollins (New York, NY), 1991, republished, Sterling (New York, NY), 2005.
Harriet Ziefert, *My Apple Tree,* HarperCollins (New York, NY), 1991.
Mother Hubbard's Cupboard: A Mother Goose Surprise Book, Tambourine (New York, NY), 1993.
Beverly McLoughland, *A Hippo's Heap and Other Animal Poems,* Boyd Mills (New York, NY), 1993.
Harriet Ziefert, *My Camera,* Ziefert Inc., 1993.
Harriet Ziefert, *My Cassette Player,* Ziefert Inc., 1993.
Harriet Ziefert, *My Telephone,* Ziefert Inc., 1993.
Harriet Ziefert, *My Television,* Ziefert Inc., 1993.
My First Christmas Carols (song book), Troll (Mahwah, NJ), 1994.
Janet Palazzo-Craig, *A Letter to Santa,* Troll (Mahwah, NJ), 1994.

Harriet Ziefert, reteller, *Goldilocks and the Three Bears,* Tambourine (New York, NY), 1994.

Harriet Ziefert, *Pete's Chicken,* Tambourine (New York, NY), 1994.

Harriet Ziefert, reteller, *The Three Billy Goats Gruff,* Tambourine (New York, NY), 1994.

Paul Fehlner, *No Way!,* Scholastic (New York, NY), 1995.

Kirsten Hall, *A Bad, Bad Day,* Scholastic (New York, NY), 1995.

Kirsten Hall, *Duck, Duck, Goose!,* Childrens Press (Chicago, IL), 1995.

Harriet Ziefert, *The Best-smelling Alphabet Book Ever,* Little Simon (New York, NY), 1995.

Harriet Ziefert, reteller, *The Teeny-Tiny Woman,* Viking (New York, NY), 1995.

Harriet Ziefert, reteller, *The Three Little Pigs,* Viking (New York, NY), 1995.

Christmas Angel, Publications International (Lincolnwood, IL), 1996.

Christmas Snowman, Publications International (Lincolnwood, IL), 1996.

Kirsten Hall, *At the Carnival,* Scholastic (New York, NY), 1996.

Harriet Ziefert, reteller, *The Turnip,* Viking (New York, NY), 1996.

Christmas Snowman, Publications International (Lincolnwood, IL), 1997.

Harriet Ziefert, *Sleepy-O!,* Houghton-Mifflin (New York, NY), 1997.

Harriet Ziefert, *The Funny Red Christmas Stocking,* Little Simon (New York, NY), 1998.

Jeff Kindley, *Scamper's Year,* Gareth Stevens (Milwaukee, WI), 1999.

Mary Packard, *When I Am Big,* Reader's Digest Children's Books (Pleasantville, NY), 1999.

Dave Ross, *A Book of Friends,* HarperCollins (New York, NY), 1999.

Dave Ross, *A Book of Hugs,* HarperCollins (New York, NY), 1999.

Harriet Ziefert, *I Need an Easter Egg!: A Lift-the-Flap Story,* Little Simon (New York, NY), 1999.

H.M. Ehrlich, *Dr. Duck,* Orchard (New York, NY), 2000.

Heidi Murkoff, *What to Expect at Bedtime,* HarperFestival (New York, NY), 2000.

Heidi Murkoff, *What to Expect When Mommy's Having a Baby,* HarperFestival (New York, NY), 2000.

Heidi Murkoff, *What to Expect When the Babysitter Comes,* HarperFestival (New York, NY), 2000.

Heidi Murkoff, *What to Expect When You Go to the Doctor,* HarperFestival (New York, NY), 2000.

Heidi Murkoff, *What to Expect When You Go to the Potty,* HarperFestival (New York, NY), 2000.

Dave Ross, *A Book of Kisses,* HarperCollins (New York, NY), 2000.

Harriet Ziefert, *Presents for Santa,* Viking (New York, NY), 2000.

H.M. Ehrlich, *Dancing Class,* Orchard (New York, NY), 2001.

Heidi Murkoff, *What to Expect at a Play Date,* HarperFestival (New York, NY), 2001.

Heidi Murkoff, *What to Expect at Preschool,* HarperFestival (New York, NY), 2001.

Heidi Murkoff, *What to Expect When the New Baby Comes Home,* HarperFestival (New York, NY), 2001.

Heidi Murkoff, *What to Expect When You Go to Kindergarten,* HarperFestival (New York, NY), 2002.

Heidi Murkoff, *What to Expect When You Go to the Dentist,* HarperFestival (New York, NY), 2002.

Julie Markes, *I Can't Talk Yet, but When I Do—,* HarperCollins (New York, NY), 2003.

Where Is Humpty Dumpty?, Sterling (New York, NY), 2004.

Karma Wilson, *Dinos on the Go!,* Little, Brown (New York, NY), 2004.

Harriet Ziefert, *What Happened to Jack and Jill?,* Sterling (New York, NY), 2004.

H.M. Ehrlich, *Dr. Duck and the New Babies,* Blue Apple (Maplewood, NJ), 2005.

Karma Wilson, *Dinos in the Snow!,* Little, Brown (New York, NY), 2005.

Corrine Demas, *Yuck! Stuck in the Muck,* Scholastic (New York, NY), 2006.

Diane Mayr, *Run, Turkey Run!,* Walker & Co. (New York, NY), 2007.

Sidelights

Educated at the Pratt Institute in New York City and now based in Los Angeles, California, Laura Rader has been illustrating children's books since 1978. In addition to her own children's books, Rader has illustrated dozens of books by other authors, among them Harriet Ziefert, Karma Wilson, and Dave Ross.

Rader's self-illustrated works include both concept books and holiday stories. *Tea for Me, Tea for You,* a counting book about an overworked waiter and a tea party for ten pigs, features characters that were described as "sport[ing] a variety of spiffy outfits" and

Laura Rader's loosely drawn cartoon art pairs effectively with Dave Ross's **A Book of Hugs.** (Illustration copyright © 1998 by Laura Rader. Used by permission of HarperCollins Publishers.)

"drawn in bright crayon colors and strong black out-lines" by a *Kirkus Reviews* contributor. *Santa's New Suit*, a picture book detailing Santa's attempts at chang-ing his look, was described by a *Publishers Weekly* critic as "a snappily paced story" with "kicky watercol-ors brimming with comic detail." In the sequel *Who'll Pull Santa's Sleigh Tonight?*, all of Santa's reindeer are sick and can only be cured with a cup of hot chocolate, for which a recipe is provided. While a *Publishers Weekly* contributor commented that Rader's "follow-up isn't as kicky or clever as its predecessor," Carolyn Phelan noted in *Booklist* that in her artwork Rader "set the stage and warmed up her audience for laughs, not logic."

Rader's art is a potent part of the books she has illus-trated. In her *Booklist* review of Ross's *A Book of Hugs*, Ilene Cooper commented that the picture book "gets most of its humor from the engaging pictures." For the sequel, titled *A Book of Kisses, Booklist* reviewer Helen Rosenberg commented on Rader's "delightful water-color illustrations," and a *Publishers Weekly* critic noted that the "gently humorous, brightly colored cartoon drawings are guaranteed child-pleasers." For Rader's work on Wilson's *Dinos on the Go!*, Tana Elias pre-dicted in *School Library Journal* that "children will ap-preciate the action and energy in the acrylic-and-ink il-lustrations and fire rhyming text."

Rader worked with writer Heidi Murkoff on the "What to Expect Kids" series. Covering everything from potty training to babysitters, Rader's artwork helps to reas-sure and educate the series' fans. Discussing *What to Expect When the New Baby Comes Home, School Li-brary Journal* reviewer Martha Topol cited Rader's "full-colored cartoon drawings of family scenes," but cautioned that the book's "intended audience will be hard-pressed to sit still long enough to appreciate all of [Murkoff's] . . . lengthy yet well-intentioned advice."

Biographical and Critical Sources

PERIODICALS

Booklist, March 15, 1999, Ilene Cooper, review of *A Book of Hugs,* p. 1334; February 15, 2000, Helen Rosen-berg, review of *A Book of Kisses,* p. 1120; December 1, 2000, Carolyn Phelan, review of *Presents for Santa,* p. 727; July, 2001, Kathy Broderick, review of *What to Expect When the New Baby Comes Home,* p. 2020; November 15, 2001, Helen Rosenberg, review of *What to Expect at Preschool,* p. 578; June 1, 2002, Kathy Broderick, review of *What to Expect When You Go to the Dentist,* p. 1727; September 1, 2003, Carolyn Phelan, review of *Who'll Pull Santa's Sleigh Tonight?,* p. 135; September 15, 2007, Julie Cummins, review of *Run, Turkey, Run!,* p. 69.

Kirkus Reviews, April 1, 2003, review of *I Can't Talk Yet, but When I Do—,* p. 537; May 15, 2003, review of *Tea for Me, Tea for You,* p. 755; November 1, 2003, review of *Who'll Pull Santa's Sleigh Tonight?,* p. 1320; August 1, 2004, review of *Dinos on the Go!,* p. 751; October 1, 2005, review of *Dinos in the Snow!,* p. 1092; September 1, 2007, review of *Run, Turkey, Run!,* p. 125.

Publishers Weekly, June 27, 1994, review of *Pete's Chicken,* p. 78; January 3, 2000, review of *A Book of Kisses,* p. 75; February 28, 2000, review of *Dr. Duck,* p. 79; September 25, 2000, Elizabeth Devereaux, re-view of *Santa's New Suit,* p. 69; March 4, 2003, re-view of *I Can't Talk Yet, but When I Do—,* p. 75; May 26, 2003, review of *Tea for Me, Tea for You,* p. 69; September 22, 2003, review of *Who'll Pull Santa's Sleigh Tonight?,* p. 70; October 11, 2004, review of *Dinos on the Go!,* p. 78.

School Library Journal, May, 2000, Tana Elias, review of *Dr. Duck,* p. 140; October, 2000, review of *Santa's New Suit,* p. 62, and review of *Presents for Santa,* p. 64; June, 2001, Martha Topol, review of *What to Ex-pect When the New Baby Comes Home,* p. 140; De-cember, 2001, Karen J. Tannenbaum, review of *What to Expect at Preschool,* p. 126; May, 2003, Sandra Ki-tain, review of *I Can't Talk Yet, but When I Do—,* p. 125; November, 2003, Kristin de Lacoste, review of *Tea for Me, Tea for You,* p. 113; September, 2004, Tana Elias, review of *Dinos on the Go!,* p. 182; Au-gust, 2005, Kathleen Simonetta, review of *Dr. Duck and the New Babies,* p. 93; December, 2005, Lisa Gangemi Kropp, review of *Dinos in the Snow!,* p. 122.*

ONLINE

Scholastic Web site, http://www.scholastic.com/ (February 24, 2009), profile of Rader.*

*   *   *

REINHART, Matthew 1971-

Personal

Born September 21, 1971, in Cedar Rapids, IA; son of Garry (an oral surgeon) and Judith Reinhart; partner of Robert Sabuda (an illustrator). *Education:* Clemson University, B.S. (biology; cum laude); Pratt Institute, degree (industrial/toy design).

Addresses

Home—New York, NY.

Career

Model maker, paper engineer, educator, and illustrator. Pratt Institute, New York, NY, instructor in paper engi-neering; Eye Bank for Sight Restoration, New York, NY, technician; model maker for Nickelodon and *News-week.*

Writings

SELF-ILLUSTRATED

Animal Popposites: A Pop-up Book of Opposites, Little Si-mon (New York, NY), 2002.

Young Naturalist's Handbook: Insect-lo-pedia, Hyperion Books for Children (New York, NY), 2003.
Cinderella: A Pop-up Fairy Tale, Simon & Schuster (New York, NY), 2005.
The Ark, Simon & Schuster (New York, NY), 2005.
The Jungle Book: A Pop-up Adventure, Simon & Schuster (New York, NY), 2006.
Star Wars: A Pop-up Guide to the Galaxy, Orchard Books (New York, NY), 2007.

"ENCYCLOPEDIA PREHISTORICA" POP-UP SERIES

(With Robert Sabuda) *Dinosaurs,* Candlewick Press (Cambridge, MA), 2005.
(With Robert Sabuda) *Sharks and Other Sea Monsters,* Candlewick Press (Cambridge, MA), 2006.
(With Robert Sabuda) *Mega-Beasts,* Candlewick Press (Cambridge, MA), 2007.

ILLUSTRATOR/PAPER ENGINEER

(With Balvis Rubess) Gary Greenberg, *The Pop-up Book of Phobias,* Rob Weisbach Books (New York, NY), 1999.
(With Robert Sabuda) *The Movable Mother Goose,* Little Simon (New York, NY), 1999.
(With Balvis Rubess) Gary Greenberg, *The Pop-up Book of Nightmares,* St. Martin's Press (New York, NY), 2001.
(With Robert Sabuda) *Young Naturalist's Pop-up Handbook: Beetles,* Hyperion Books for Children (New York, NY), 2001.
(With Robert Sabuda) *Young Naturalist's Pop-up Handbook: Butterflies,* Hyperion Books for Children (New York, NY), 2003.
(With Robert Sabuda) *Castle: Medieval Days and Knights,* text by Kyle Olmon, illustrations by Tracy Sabin, Orchard Books (New York, NY), 2006.
Arthur Yorinks, *Mommy?,* illustrations by Maurice Sendak, Michael di Capua Books (New York, NY), 2006.
Margie Palatini, *No Biting, Louise,* Katherine Tegen Books (New York, NY), 2007.
(With Robert Sabuda) *Encyclopedia Mythologica: Fairies and Magical Creatures,* Candlewick Press (Cambridge, MA), 2008.
(With Robert Sabuda) Tomie de Paola, *Brava Strega Nona!: A Heartwarming Pop-up Book,* Putnam (New York, NY), 2008.

Books featuring Reinhart's paper engineering have been translated into numerous languages, including French, Arabic, German, Spanish, Italian, Greek, Portuguese, Korean, and Slovenian.

Sidelights

As the son of a doctor, Matthew Reinhart began his academic career preparing for a career in medicine, until a visit to New York City and an introduction to artist Robert Sabuda changed his life. In addition to building a lifelong personal partnership, the two men also began using their artistic talent in volunteer projects, and this work inspired Reinhart to enroll in a degree in industrial/toy design at the prestigious Pratt Institute. Reinhart has since achieved acclaim for his innovations in the art of paper engineering, and his pop-up illustrations have been featured in original projects such as *Animal Popposites: A Pop-up Book of Opposites, Star Wars: A Pop-up Guide to the Galaxy,* and *Cinderella: A Pop-up Fairy Tale,* in addition to numerous collaborations with Sabuda. According to *Booklist* critic Jennifer Mattson, "the exciting dimensional art and numerous bells and whistles . . ." in *Cinderella* "should dazzle both kids and collectors like."

Reinhart and Sabuda's multi-volume "Encyclopedia Prehistorica" includes the volumes *Dinosaurs, Sharks and Other Sea Monsters,* and *Mega-Beasts.* Praised by a *Publishers Weekly* contributor as "playful and edifying," *Dinosaurs* instructs readers in the structural differences between different prehistoric species and supplement their multi-colored interactive dino-constructs with information on extinction, advances in paleontology, and other facts. *Sharks and Other Sea Monsters* takes readers down to the briny deep, where they meet the megalodon as well as sharks and other ancient swimmers. *Mega-Beasts* focuses on other ancient creatures, such as woolly mammoths, saber-toothed tigers, and pterosaurs, and presents these creatures in what *Booklist* critic Carolyn Phelan described as "cleverly designed and beautifully crafted" paper sculptures of various sizes that "move . . . without a hitch."

In addition to his work with Sabuda, Reinhart has contributed interactive illustrations to Arthur Yorinks' *Mommy?,* a story that also includes artwork by noted artist Maurice Sendak. A *Publishers Weekly* critic described the book as a "light bite of spine-tingling fare," and listed among its strengths Reinhart's interactive "engineering feat": a miniature mummy-unwrapping mechanism hidden beneath one of the book's many flaps. The paper engineer and artist also creates two-dimensional illustrations for Margie Palatini's picture book *No Biting, Louise,* the story of a sharp-toothed young alligator with a penchant for nibbling where she should not. In augmenting Palatini's humorous verse, Reinhart "gleefully records the mayhem with nicely nutty watercolor-and-ink cartoons," wrote a *Publishers Weekly* contributor, while *School Library Journal* contributor Joy Fleishhacker dubbed *Mommy?* a "pop-up tour de force [that] abounds with humor, vibrant artwork, and visual fireworks."

Biographical and Critical Sources

BOOKS

Artist to Artist: 23 Major Illustrators Talk to Children about Their Art, Philomel (New York, NY), 2007.

PERIODICALS

Booklist, July, 2005, Jennifer Mattson, review of *Dinosaurs,* p. 1929; November 1, 2005, Jennifer Mattson, review of *Cinderella: A Pop-up Fairy Tale,* p. 50; June 1, 2006, Jennifer Mattson, review of *Sharks and Other Sea Monsters,* p. 65; August 1, 2006, Jennifer Matson, review of *Mommy?,* p. 90; November 1, 2006, Carolyn Phelan, review of *Castle: Medieval Days and Knights,* p. 46; August, 2007, Carolyn Phelan, review of *Mega-Beasts,* p. 80.

Bulletin of the Center for Children's Books, October, 2006, Deborah Stevenson, review of *Mommy?,* p. 102.

Horn Book, September-October, 2005, Danielle J. Ford, review of *Dinosaurs,* p. 607; July-August, 2006, Danielle J. Ford, review of *Sharks and Other Sea Monsters,* p. 468; November-December, 2006, Christine M. Heppermann, review of *Mommy?,* p. 703; July-August, 2007, Danielle J. Ford, review of *Mega-Beasts,* p. 414.

Kirkus Reviews, October 1, 2003, review of *Young Naturalists Pop-up Handbook: Insect-lo-Pedia,* p. 1229; October 15, 2005, review of *Cinderella: A Pop-up Fairy Tale,* p. 1145; August 15, 2006, review of *Mommy?,* p. 855; May 15, 2007, review of *Mega-Beasts;* August 1, 2007, review of *No Biting, Louise;* October 15, 2008, review of *Encyclopedia Mythologica: Fairies and Magical Beasts.*

New York Times Book Review, November 11, 2007, David Pogue, review of *Star Wars: A Pop-up Guide to the Galaxy,* p. 41.

Print, March, 2000, Caitlin Dover, review of *Pop Goes the Phobia,* p. 12.

Publishers Weekly, June 3, 2002, review of *Animal Popposites,* p. 89; October 13, 2003, review of *Young Naturalist's Pop-up Handbook: Insect-lo-Pedia,* p. 82; June 20, 2005, review of *Dinosaurs,* p. 77; July 17, 2006, review of *Mommy?,* p. 155; September 3, 2007, review of *No Biting, Louise,* p. 57; October 6, 2008, review of *Brava Strega Nona!: A Heartwarming Pop-up Book,* p. 53.

School Library Journal, December, 2003, Margaret Bush, review of *Young Naturalist's Pop-up Handbook: Insect-lo-pedia,* p. 138; February, 2005, Kathy Piehl, review of *The Ark,* p. 126; September, 2005, Joy Fleishhacker, review of *Dinosaurs,* p. 195; September, 2006, Joy Fleishhacker, review of *Mommy?,* p. 188; November, 2006, John Peters, review of *The Jungle Book,* p. 109; July, 2007, Joy Fleishhacker, review of *Mega-Beasts,* p. 95; September, 2007, Donna Atmur, review of *No Biting, Louise,* p. 173; December, 2008, Joy Fleishhacker, review of *Encyclopedia Mythologica,* p. 115.

Science News, March 6, 2004, review of *Young Naturalist's Pop-up Handbook: Insect-lo-pedia,* p. 159.

ONLINE

Hyperion Books for Children Web site, http://www.hyperionbooksforchildren.com/ (May 3, 2005), "Matthew Reinhart."

Matthew Reinhart Home Page, http://www.matthewreinhart.com (January 26, 2009).

Matthew Reinhart Web log, http://popupstudionyc.blogspot.com (January 26, 2009).

Robert Sabuda Web site, http://www.robersabuda.com/ (May 3, 2005), "Matthew Reinhart's 'The Ark.'"*

* * *

REYNOLDS, Aaron 1970-

Personal

Born June 4, 1970; married; wife's name Michelle; children: Reese, Ethan. *Education:* Illinois Wesleyan University, B.A.; attended Kendall Culinary School.

Addresses

Home and office—Fox River Grove, IL. *E-mail*—aaron reynolds@earthlink.net.

Career

Children's ministry consultant and writer. Former artistic director of Promiseland (children's ministry), Willow Creek Community Church, South Barrington, IL.

Member

Society of Children's Book Writers and Illustrators.

Writings

The Nineteenth of Maquerk, illustrated by Peter Whitehead, Zonderkidz (Grand Rapids, MI), 2005.

Breaking out of the Bungle Bird, illustrated by Peter Whitehead, Zonderkidz (Grand Rapids, MI), 2005.

Tale of the Poisonous Yuck Bugs, illustrated by Peter Whitehead, Zonderkidz (Grand Rapids, MI), 2005.

Chicks and Salsa, illustrated by Paulette Bogan, Bloomsbury (New York, NY), 2005.

Buffalo Wings, illustrated by Paulette Bogan, Bloomsbury (New York, NY), 2007.

The Fabulous Reinvention of Sunday School: Transformational Techniques for Reaching and Teaching Kids, Zondervan (Grand Rapids, MI), 2007.

Metal Man, illustrated by Paul Hoppe, Charlesbridge (Watertown, MA), 2008.

Back of the Bus, illustrated by Floyd Cooper, Philomel (New York, NY), 2009.

Superhero School, Bloomsbury (New York, NY), 2009.

Joey Fly, Private Eye in Creepy Crawly Crime, illustrated by Neil Numberman, Henry Holt (New York, NY), 2009.

"TIGER MOTH" SERIES; GRAPHIC NOVELS

Tiger Moth, Insect Ninja, illustrated by Erik Lervold, Stone Arch (Minneapolis, MN), 2007.

Aaron Reynolds (Photograph by Suzanne Plunkett. Reproduced by permission.)

Tiger Moth and the Dragon Kite Contest, illustrated by Erik Lervold, Stone Arch (Minneapolis, MN), 2007.

Tiger Moth: The Dung Beetle Bandits, illustrated by Erik Lervold, Stone Arch (Minneapolis, MN), 2007.

Tiger Moth: The Fortune Cookies of Weevil, illustrated by Erik Lervold, Stone Arch (Minneapolis, MN), 2007.

Tiger Moth: Kung Pow Chicken, illustrated by Erik Lervold, Stone Arch (Minneapolis, MN), 2008.

Tiger Moth: The Pest Show on Earth, illustrated by Erik Lervold, Stone Arch (Minneapolis, MN), 2008.

Adaptations

The "Tiger Moth" books have been adapted on CD-ROM.

Sidelights

Before he became a children's book writer, Aaron Reynolds worked with children. As the artistic director of Promiseland, a children's ministry at Willow Creek Community Church near Chicago, Illinois, Reynolds wrote scripts for children's programs and plays and produced classroom lessons and other materials to guide ministry programming. He draws on these experiences in his book for adults, *The Fabulous Reinvention of Sunday School: Transformational Techniques for Reaching and Teaching Kids* and credits this work with helping him develop a narrative voice that would appeal to children in picture books.

Reynolds' picture book *Chicks and Salsa* was featured on the Public Television program *Between the Lions* and earned many positive reviews. Here the author

"punctuates his wry, snappy text with the kind of knowing, running jokes that kids love," described a *Publishers Weekly* critic in a review of the picture book, which features artwork by Paulette Bogan. The story of a rooster foodie, *Chicks and Salsa* finds a group of farmyard animals tiring of the same feed they receive each and every day. Rooster soon spices up their diet, teaching the chickens how to mix tomatoes and onions to make salsa, and soon the whole farmyard is dining Southwestern style. *Chicks and Salsa* "is a fun read, with a refrain and a smooth pattern," wrote Susan E. Murray in her *School Library Journal* review of Reynolds' story. The farmyard characters return in *Buffalo Wings,* as Rooster attempts to create the titular dish for his farm friends. When the feathered chef discovers that buffalo wings are actually made from chicken, he has to hatch a new plan. "The resolution is silly but satisfying," wrote *School Library Journal* critic Lee Bock, while a *Kirkus Reviews* contributor concluded that Reynolds' "latest culinary misadventure will . . . provoke equal quantities of laughter and saliva."

In *Metal Man,* Reynolds tells a story about a real figure from his own life: Mitch Levin, a metal sculptor. When young Devon asks the sculptor what he is making, the artist replies with a question, asking the boy what he sees in the work of art in process. "The poetic text is visceral—readers experience the sounds, vibrations, textures, and heat of the metal shop," wrote Heidi Estrin in *School Library Journal.*

In addition to picture books, Reynolds has also written a series of graphic novels for young readers, beginning with *Tiger Moth, Insect Ninja.* Combining superhero and kung fu storylines with grade-school issues, the "Tiger Moth" books follow Tiger Moth and his sidekick, pill bug Kung Pow, as they heroically fight crime. Marilyn Hersh, reviewing the "Tiger Moth" books for *School Library Journal,* concluded that the graphic-novel format, with illustrations by Erik Lervold, will particularly appeal to young boys. Reynold's second graphic-novel series, "Joey Fly, Private Eye," debuted in 2009.

"I LOVE kids' books," Reynolds told *SATA,* "but never really read them growing up until the fifth grade. We didn't really have books in my house, so I wasn't much of a reader. Then, my fifth-grade teacher, Mr. Hunter, read a book aloud to us. It was the first time I remembered really having a book read aloud to me. The book was *Ramona the Pest* by Beverly Cleary. I loved it. I couldn't believe that THIS is what books were! I couldn't believe what I had been missing. I began devouring kids books—whatever I could get my hands on—and I haven't stopped yet.

"I love playing video games. I love watching TV and movies. But I LOVE reading. Books hold a power that none of these other things do . . . to utterly transport you."

Reynolds' humorous picture book Chicks and Salsa *is brought to life in colorful folkstyle art by Paulette Bogan.* (Illustration copyright © 2005 by Paulette Bogan. All rights reserved. Reprinted by permission of Bloomsbury USA.)

Biographical and Critical Sources

PERIODICALS

Kirkus Reviews, October 1, 2005, review of *Chicks and Salsa,* p. 1987; October 1, 2007, review of *Buffalo Wings*; June 15, 2008, review of *Metal Man.*

Publishers Weekly, November 14, 2005, review of *Chicks and Salsa,* p. 68.

School Library Journal, November, 2005, Susan E. Murray, review of *Chicks and Salsa,* p. 104; December, 2007, Lee Bock, review of *Buffalo Wings,* p. 98; April, 2008, Marilyn Hersh, review of *Tiger Moth, Insect Ninja,* p. 83; July, 2008, Heidi Estrin, review of *Metal Man,* p. 80.

ONLINE

Aaron Reynolds Home Page, http://www.aaron-reynolds.com (January 15, 2009).

Creative Kids Ministry Web site, http://www.creativekidsministry.com/ (January 15, 2009), profile of Reynolds.

Society of Children's Book Writers and Illustrators Illinois Web site, http://www.scbwi-illinois.org/ (January 15, 2009), profile of Reynolds.

Zondervan Web site, http://www.zondervan.com/ (January 15, 2009), profile of Reynolds.

ROBERTSON, Mark
See ROBERTSON, M.P.

* * *

ROBERTSON, M.P. 1965-
(Mark Robertson)

Personal

Born 1965, in London, England; partner of Sophy Williams (an illustrator); children: two sons. *Education:* Attended Hounslow Borough College; Kingston Polytechnic, degree.

Addresses

Home and office—Bradford on Avon, England.

Career

Writer and illustrator.

Writings

SELF-ILLUSTRATED

(With Meredith Hooper) *The Endurance: Shackleton's Perilous Expedition in Antarctica,* Abbeville (New York, NY), 2001.

The Egg, Phyllis Fogelman (New York, NY), 2001.

The Sandcastle, Rising Moon (Flagstaff, AZ), 2001.

The Great Dragon Rescue, Dial (New York, NY), 2004.

The Moon in Swampland, Frances Lincoln (London, Ontario, Canada), 2004.

The Dragon Snatcher, Dial (New York, NY), 2005.

Hieronymus Betts and His Unusual Pets, Frances Lincoln (London, Ontario, Canada), 2005.

Big Brave Brian, Frances Lincoln (London, Ontario, Canada), 2007.

Dragon and the Gruesome Twosome, Frances Lincoln (London, Ontario, Canada), 2008.

ILLUSTRATOR

Dragons: A Pop-up Book of Fantastic Adventures, Harry Abrams (New York, NY), 2006.

Adèle Geras, *Cleopatra,* Kingfisher (New York, NY), 2007.

Sidelights

M.P. Robertson was never particularly good at school. According to the *Love Reading 4 Kids* Web site, Robertson slept through most of school, only barely managing to get good enough grades to go on to study art at college. After leaving one college, he graduated from Kingston Polytechnic with a degree in illustration. He has been writing and illustrating children's books ever since.

M.P. Robertson's detailed artwork is a highlight of his picture book **The Sandcastle.** (Frances Lincoln Children's Books, 2001. Illustration copyright © 2001 by M.P. Robertson. All rights reserved. Reproduced by permission.)

Several of Robertson's titles feature tales about a boy named George and a dragon that hatches after being mothered by a hen. In *The Egg* George first sees a hen sitting atop a huge golden-brown egg, and he knows that this is no normal chicken egg. He brings the egg inside his home and hatches it himself, discovering the dragon inside. A *Publishers Weekly* critic commented on the author/illustrator's "delicate, detail-rich watercolors," and Lisa Gangemi Kropp noted in *School Library Journal* that *The Egg* is "a beautifully written fantasy with luminous, richly hued artwork that is as evocative as the text."

The adventures of George and the dragon continue in *The Great Dragon Rescue,* as the dragon is captured by a witch who lives in a dark, dark forest. In order to save his fire-breathing friend, George must beat the witch in a flying race around an enchanted castle. Although a *Kirkus Reviews* contributor found the book to be "lushly illustrated," the text was less successful. In *School Library Journal* Maryann H. Owen also found Robertson's story lacking, but approving of the "colorful, well-imagined artwork." While sharing a similar opinion of *The Great Dragon Rescue,* Gillian Engberg commented in *Booklist* that "Robertson's watercolor illustrations are a delight" that weighs out the book's negatives.

The Dragon Snatcher continues to chronicle George's adventures with "arresting, dramatically angled paint-

ings featuring big, leathery dragons," according to a *Kirkus Reviews* contributor. In this adventure, a wizard is keeping dragon eggs captive. George tries to save the final egg that has not been captured, only to have the dragon hatch during the battle. The young dragon makes such an impression on the wizard that the man's heart melts, allowing all of the other dragon eggs are freed to hatch. Robertson's "expansive illustrations . . . more than make up for any holes in the plot," wrote Kara Schaff Dean in *School Library Journal,* while in *Booklist* Jennifer Mattson noted that the series offers an "epic-fantasy experience in a form that is far more manageable" to reluctant readers than those in novels designed for older readers.

Like George, the main character in *Hieronymus Betts and His Unusual Pets* has a way with magical animals. From a slugapotamus to a porcupython, the mixed-up creatures that share Hieronymus's home are each worse than the last, until finally Hieronymus shows the weirdest creature of all: his younger brother. When the two conclude an adventure together, Hieronymus decides that his brother is actually more fun than any of his pets. "With its repetitive language and imaginative names, [*Hieronymus Betts and His Unusual Pets*] . . . is great for reading aloud," wrote Suzanne Myers Harold in *School Library Journal,* noting that Robertson's book would be especially well-liked by older sib-

In **Big Brave Brian** *Robertson introduces a brave young hero with a vivid imagination.* (Frances Lincoln Children's Books, 2007. Illustration copyright © 2007 by M.P. Robertson. All rights reserved. Reproduced by permission.)

lings. A *Publishers Weekly* critic noted that "the weird hybrids and monstrosities in Hieronymus's stable are hilariously imagined."

Biographical and Critical Sources

PERIODICALS

Booklist, December 1, 2004, Gillian Engberg, review of *The Great Dragon Rescue,* p. 662; December 1, 2005, Jennifer Mattson, review of *The Dragon Snatcher,* p. 57.
Kirkus Reviews, September 15, 2004, review of *The Great Dragon Rescue,* p. 919; October 15, 2004, review of *The Moon in Swampland,* p. 1013; October 1, 2005, review of *The Dragon Snatcher,* p. 1987; September 15, 2007, review of *Big Brave Brian*; October 1, 2007, review of *Cleopatra.*
Publishers Weekly, December 11, 2000, review of *The Egg,* p. 84; December 12, 2005, review of *Hieronymus Betts and His Unusual Pets,* p. 65.
School Library Journal, January, 2001, Lisa Gangemi Kropp, review of *The Egg,* p. 107; July, 2001, Lisa Gangemi, review of *The Sandcastle,* p. 87; January, 2005, Maryann H. Owen, review of *The Great Dragon Rescue,* p. 97; October, 2005, Kara Schaff Dean, review of *The Dragon Snatcher,* p. 126; February, 2006, Suzanne Myers Harold, review of *Hieronymus Betts and His Unusual Pets,* p. 109; June, 2009, Clare A. Dombrowski, review of *Cleopatra,* p. 123.

ONLINE

Love Reading 4 Kids Web site, http://www.lovereading 4kids.co.uk/ (February 25, 2009), "M.P. Robertson."*

* * *

ROBINSON, Sharon 1950-

Personal

Born January 13, 1950, in New York, NY; daughter of Jackie (a baseball player) and Rachel Robinson; married twice (both marriages ended); children: Jesse Simms. *Education:* Harvard University, B.S.; Columbia University, M.S.; University of Pennsylvania, certificate in teaching (nursing). *Hobbies and other interests:* Sports, reading.

Addresses

Home—New York, NY. *Agent*—Marie Brown, Marie Brown Associates, 625 Broadway, New York, NY 10012.

Career

Writer and director of educational programming. Worked as a nurse midwife, beginning 1975; Yale University, New Haven, CT, assistant professor of nursing; also taught at Columbia University, Howard University, and Georgetown University. Jackie Robinson Foundation, member of board of directors. Major League Baseball, director of educational programming, beginning 1997; manager of Breaking Barriers: In Sports, in Life (multi-curricular character-education program).

Member

American College of Nurse-Midwives (member, board of directors).

Awards, Honors

Medaille College, D.L.H. honoris causa, 1998.

Writings

Stealing Home: An Intimate Family Portrait by the Daughter of Jackie Robinson, HarperCollins (New York, NY), 1996.
Jackie's Nine: Jackie Robinson's Values to Live By, Scholastic Press (New York, NY), 2001.
Still the Storm, Genesis Press (Columbus, MS), 2002.
Promises to Keep: How Jackie Robinson Changed America, Scholastic Press (New York, NY), 2004.
Safe at Home, Scholastic Press (New York, NY), 2006.
Slam Dunk!, Scholastic Press (New York, NY), 2007.

Contributor to a women's health textbook; contributor of articles to *Essence* magazine and to professional journals.

Sidelights

Sharon Robinson was born in 1950 to a famous father: Jackie Robinson, the first African American to play major-league baseball. She recounts what it was like for her and her brothers to grow up in the public environment that came with their father's pioneering achievement in the world of sports in her 1996 book, *Stealing Home: An Intimate Family Portrait by the Daughter of Jackie Robinson.* Robinson also returns to her father's legacy in *Jackie's Nine: Jackie Robinson's Values to Live By* and *Promises to Keep: How Jackie Robinson Changed America.*

As Robinson reveals in *Stealing Home,* Jackie Robinson tried very hard to be a good family man and to give time and attention to his children despite his demanding career in professional baseball. Nevertheless, Sharon and her brothers, Jackie, Jr. and David, felt the strain of having to share their dad with his many admiring fans. As an adult, Sharon became a nurse midwife, and survived two failed marriages. In addition to the details of her life and her family's life in *Stealing Home,* she also includes a collection of family photographs that follow her father's career and his growing family. A *Publishers Weekly* critic responded favorably to the volume, predicting that Sharon Robinson's "loving biography" of her father "will add to his stature."

In *Jackie's Nine* Robinson presents a collection of essays on nine inspiring character traits that shaped her while growing up under her father's tutelage: courage, determination, teamwork, persistence, integrity, citizenship, justice, commitment, and excellence. As Robinson writes in the book, *Jackie's Nine* "presents values as principles by which to shape a life, rather than as mere buzz worlds." The text also describes the efforts the elder Robinson made to embody those traits, prompting readers "to nurture those same values within their own lives," according to Daniel R. Beach in *Book Report*.

Promises to Keep provides readers with insight into the active role the baseball legend played in fueling the civil rights movement. Here Robinson chronicles her father's legendary career and the trials he faced while growing up and encountered as he pursued his celebrated athletic career. "In captivating words and picture," the daughter includes telling glimpses into Robinson's life that reveal "information on the post-Civil War world, race relations, and the struggle for civil rights," commented Tracy Bell in *School Library Journal*. Gillian Engberg stated in *Booklist* that "there are numerous biographies about Robinson available for young people, but none have this book's advantage of family intimacy."

Cover of Sharon Robinson's middle-grade novel Safe at Home, *featuring artwork by Kadir Nelson.* (Cover illustration copyright © 2006 by Kadir Nelson. Reproduced by permission of Scholastic, Inc.)

Robinson turns to fiction in her middle-grade novels *Safe at Home* and *Slam Dunk!*, both of which feature sports themes. In *Safe at Home* ten-year-old Elijah Breeze moves with his recently widowed mom from their suburban home to Harlem, to live with his grandmother. Now the boy must deal with city culture in addition to his grief over his dad's death. A summer spent at neighborhood baseball camp crystallizes Elijah's feelings as well as his difficulty in finding his place in his new life. His ability to overcome the threats of a bullying campmate and develop the skills needed to make him a valuable team member ultimately symbolize the boy's emotional growth in a novel that a *Publishers Weekly* critic dubbed "a solid first novel about a likable 10-year-old who comes to terms with some big changes." In *School Library Journal* Jack Forman praised *Safe at Home* as a "quick-reading" story in which middle-grade readers will enjoy spending time with Robinson's "intriguing protagonists."

Elijah returns in *Slam Dunk!* A year older and now enrolled at Harlem's Langston Hughes Middle School, the boy is now nicknamed "Jumper" due to his skill on the basketball court. When the girl's basketball team beats the boys in a school exhibition game, Elijah's friend Nia—who organized the winning girls' team—decides to take her win on the court and use it to compete with Elijah in his bid for student-council representative. In *Booklist* Stephanie Zvirin praised *Slam Dunk!* as "an amiable story about friends who stay that way, a theme that translates well in any community." Robinson's well-paced novel is enriched by what a *Kirkus Reviews* writer described as "thoughtful moments where heartfelt revelations expertly transition to more complexities." As the critic concluded, *Slam Dunk!* "warrants a third installment" recounting Elijah's middle-school adventures.

Biographical and Critical Sources

BOOKS

Robinson, Sharon, *Jackie's Nine: Jackie Robinson's Values to Live By,* Scholastic (New York, NY), 2001.

PERIODICALS

Booklist, June 1, 1996, review of *Stealing Home: An Intimate Family Portrait by the Daughter of Jackie Robinson,* p. 1628; July, 2001, John Peters, review of *Jackie's Nine: Jackie Robinson's Values to Live By,* p. 2004; February 15, 2004, Gillian Engberg, review of *Promises to Keep: How Jackie Robinson Changed America,* p. 1077; September 1, 2007, Stephanie Zvirin, review of *Slam Dunk!,* p. 136.
Book Report, September-October, 2001, Daniel R. Beach, review of *Jackie's Nine,* p. 72.
Bulletin of the Center for Children's Books, January, 2007, Elizabeth Bush, review of *Safe at Home,* p. 74.

Emerge, October, 1996, review of *Stealing Home,* p. 73.
Kirkus Reviews, January 15, 2004, review of *Promises to Keep,* p. 88; August 1, 2007, review of *Slam Dunk!*
Kliatt, September, 2007, KaaVonia Hinton, review of *Slam Dunk!,* p. 17.
Library Journal, June 15, 1996, review of *Stealing Home,* p. 72.
New York Times Book Review, November 3, 1996, review of *Stealing Home,* p. 18.
Publishers Weekly, May 14, 2001, review of *Jackie's Nine,* p. 84; February 9, 2004, review of *Promises to Keep,* p. 82; August 21, 2006, review of *Safe at Home,* p. 69.
School Library Journal, June, 2001, review of *Jackie's Nine,* p. 180; March, 2004, Tracy Bell, review of *Promises to Keep,* p. 242; October, 2006, review of *Safe at Home,* p. 168; November, 2007, Debbie Whitbeck, review of *Slam Dunk!,* p. 136.

ONLINE

BookPage.com, http://www.bookpage.com/ (June 11, 2005), "Sharon Robinson."
Scholastic Web site, http://content.scholastic.com/ (January 26, 2009), "Sharon Robinson."
Sharon Robinson Home Page, http://www.sharonrobinsonink.com (January 26, 2009).*

*   *   *

RYAN, Pam Muñoz 1951-

Personal

Born 1951, in CA; married; children: four. *Education:* B.A. (child development); M.Ed. (post-secondary education).

Addresses

Home—San Diego County, CA.

Career

Teacher and writer.

Awards, Honors

Jane Addams Children's Book Award, 2001, Pura Belpré Award for Narrative, Association for Library Service to Children/National Association to Promote Library and Information Services to Latinos and the Spanish-speaking, 2002, Top Ten Best Books for Young Adults, American Library Association (ALA), and Américas Award Honor Book designation, all for *Esperanza Rising;* California Young Reader Medal, and Willa Cather Award, both 1997, both for *Riding Freedom;* Notable Book selection, ALA, 1999, for *Amelia and Eleanor Go for a Ride,* and 2001, for *Mice and Beans;* Robert Siebert Honor Book designation, ALA Notable Book designation, Parents Choice Gold Award,

Pam Muñoz Ryan (Cover illustration copyright © 2006 by Kadir Nelson. Reproduced by permission of Scholastic, Inc.)

and Orbis Pictus Award, all 2002, and Jefferson Cup Honor, Virginia Library Association, and National Council of Teachers of English (NCTE) Notable Children's Book in the Language Arts, both 2003, all for *When Marian Sang;* Pura Belpré Honor Book designation, Tomás Rivera Mexican-American Children's Book Award, International Reading Association Notable Book for a Global Society designation, ALA Notable Book designation and Schneider Award, NCTE Notable Children's Book in the Language Arts, and included in New York Public Library Top Ten Titles for Reading and Sharing, all 2006, all for *Becoming Naomi León.*

Writings

FOR CHILDREN

One Hundred Is a Family, illustrated by Benrei Huang, Hyperion (New York, NY), 1994.
The Flag We Love, illustrated by Ralph Masiello, Charlesbridge (Watertown, MA), 1996, tenth anniversary edition, 2006.
A Pinky Is a Baby Mouse; and Other Baby Animal Names, illustrated by Diane de Groat, Hyperion (New York, NY), 1997.

Armadillos Sleep in Dugouts; and Other Places Animals Live, illustrated by Diane de Groat, Hyperion (New York, NY), 1997.

California, Here We Come!, illustrated by Kay Salem, Charlesbridge (Watertown, MA), 1997.

Riding Freedom, illustrated by Brian Selznick, Scholastic (New York, NY), 1998.

Doug Counts Down, illustrated by Matthew C. Peters, Disney Press (New York, NY), 1998.

Disney's Doug's Treasure Hunt, created by Jim Jenkins, illustrated by Jumbo Pictures, Mouse Works (New York, NY), 1998.

Funnie Family Vacation, illustrated by William Presing and Tony Curanaj, Disney Press (New York, NY), 1999.

Amelia and Eleanor Go for a Ride, illustrated by Brian Selznick, Scholastic (New York, NY), 1999.

Hello, Ocean!, illustrated by Mark Astrella, Charlesbridge/Talewinds (Watertown, MA), 2001.

Mice and Beans, illustrated by Joe Cepeda, Scholastic (New York, NY), 2001.

When Marian Sang: The True Recital of Marian Anderson, illustrated by Brian Selznick, Scholastic (New York, NY), 2002.

Mud Is Cake, illustrated by David McPhail, Hyperion (New York, NY), 2002.

How Do You Raise a Raisin?, illustrated by Craig Brown, Charlesbridge (Watertown, MA), 2003.

A Box of Friends, illustrated by Mary Whyte, McGraw-Hill (New York, NY), 2003.

Nacho and Lolita, illustrated by Claudia Rueda, Scholastic (New York, NY), 2005.

There Was No Snow on Christmas Eve, illustrated by Dennis Nolan, Hyperion Books (New York, NY), 2005.

Our California, illustrated by Rafael López, Charlesbridge (Watertown, MA), 2008.

Also author of children's books *Netty, Netty Goes to School,* and *Netty Goes around the World,* published in Japan.

Authors works have been translated into Spanish.

YOUNG-ADULT NOVELS

Esperanza Rising, Scholastic (New York, NY), 2000.
Becoming Naomi León, Scholastic (New York, NY), 2004.
Paint the Wind, Scholastic (New York, NY), 2007.

Sidelights

Pam Muñoz Ryan is the author of several acclaimed books for young readers that draw upon her Hispanic heritage, among them the young-adult novel *Esperanza Rising* and the picture books *Our California, Nacho and Lolita,* and *How Do You Raise a Raisin?* A native of California's San Joaquin Valley, Ryan was an avid reader as a child and a frequent visitor to her local library during the hot summer weeks. In an interview for the Scholastic Web site, Ryan recalled that she did not harbor any early ambitions to become a writer. "I al-

ways loved books," she noted. "I didn't know when I was a young child that I could be an author, [however,] because when I went to school we didn't do the integrated writing activities kids do in school today." Praising *Nacho and Lolita,* Ryan's story about the romance between a colorful pitachoche bird and a brown barn swallow, *Booklist* contributor Jennifer Mattson called the work "a fanciful, broadly appealing affirmation of the transforming power of love," and *School Library Journal* critic Marian Drabkin dubbed *Our California* a "loving tribute to the state."

As a young adult, Ryan earned a college degree, married, and had four children. After working as a teacher she returned to school for a master's degree, and her papers were singled out by one professor. The professor asked if she had ever considered writing as a profession. "Until that time, it had never occurred to me. Within a few weeks, a colleague asked me if I'd consider helping her write a book. Then I knew that was something I wanted to try. First I wrote three books for grown-ups with my colleague. They were easy to get published. Then I started to write stories for children, but getting published in the children's market was a long struggle."

Ryan persevered, and her first book for a younger audience was published in 1994. *One Hundred Is a Family*

Cover of Ryan's award-winning young-adult novel **Esperanza Rising,** *featuring artwork by Joe Cepeda.* (Jacket illustration copyright © 2000 by Joe Cepeda. Reproduced by permission of Scholastic, Inc.)

Ryan's biography Amelia and Eleanor Go for a Ride! *teams a story featuring a noted aviatrix with art by Brian Selznick.* (Illustration copyright © 1999 by Brian Selznick. Reproduced by permission of Scholastic, Inc.)

is a counting book for children aged four to eight. It depicts groups of one through ten, and then continues on by stages of ten up to one hundred. Her aim was to show the human family in all its various permutations, and how people are related by kinship, community, and heritage. According to *Booklist* contributor Annie Ayres, Ryan's text is "comforting in that it presents and embraces a world in which every form of family is welcome."

After witnessing an American flag misused in a store one day, Ryan was inspired to write *The Flag We Love,* which has also been published in translation for young Spanish-speaking readers. The work traces the history of the American flag and touches upon related topics such as the national anthem written in homage to it and its use in various official ceremonies. The work "could help spark discussion on the basic elements of democracy," noted a *Publishers Weekly* contributor.

Based on the stories of her Mexican-American family, *Mice and Beans* focuses on a warm-hearted grandmother's excited preparations for the birthday feast of her little granddaughter, Catalina. Rosa Maria is obsessed with ridding her casita of mice and tries to keep the party food away from them. The woman is also a bit absentminded and she forgets to fill Catalina's birthday piñata, the showpiece of the celebration. The colorful tissue-paper sculpture proves to be laden with candy

and treats anyway, when it is broken on feast day, and Rosa Maria ultimately discovers that the mice she had tried to chase away were actually busy helping her. In *Booklist* reviewer Kelly Milner Halls wrote of *Mice and Beans* that "what makes it special is the quiet authenticity of the Hispanic characterizations."

Ryan embellished some details about an actual historical event in *Amelia and Eleanor Go for a Ride!,* a picture book featuring artwork by Brian Selznick. After a White House dinner in April of 1933, famed aviatrix Amelia Earhart took First Lady Eleanor Roosevelt, wife of newly elected President Franklin D. Roosevelt, up in her plane at a time when aircraft were a relatively scarce sight in the night sky. Roosevelt had actually taken some flying lessons but never earned a pilot's license, and Ryan's story concludes with the First Lady taking Earhart—who disappeared somewhere over the Pacific Ocean a few years later—for a reciprocal drive in her new automobile. Again, Ryan explains which parts of the story were fictionalized: for example, two male pilots actually flew the plane that night—but White House Secret Service agents were wary about the idea nonetheless. A reviewer for *Publishers Weekly* called Ryan's work "a brief but compelling slice from the lives of two determined, outspoken and passionate women." *School Library Journal* writer Steven Engelfried noted that "the fictionalized tale is lively and compelling, and the courage and sense of adventure that these individuals

shared will be evident" even to readers not familiar with these two women, who were quite famous in the 1930s. *Booklist* critic Ilene Cooper similarly stated that in the story "children will get a sense of the importance of Earhart and Roosevelt to America's history in general, and women's history in particular."

Ryan and Selznick team up again for *When Marian Sang: The True Recital of Marian Anderson.* Here author and illustrator profile one of the most dramatic incidents of the civil rights era: the day in 1939 that noted African-American vocalist Marian Anderson was turned away from performing at Washington, DC's Constitution Hall and instead gave a free concert on the steps of the Lincoln Memorial. Hazel Rochman described the picture book as "lush," adding in *Booklist* that Ryan's "passionate words and [Selznick's] beautifully detailed sepia-tone pictures . . . present a true story that seems like a theatrical Cinderella tale." While noting that author and illustrator "indulge in a . . . mythification" of their subject, *Horn Book* reviewer Roger Sutton concluded that *When Marian Sang* features "an intimacy of tone that gives life to the legend" upon which it is based.

Ryan's first lengthier work for children, *Riding Freedom,* is an historical novel about Charlotte Darkey Parkhurst, who came to be known as "One-Eyed Charley." Parkhurst is believed to be the first woman ever to cast a ballot in a federal election, although she did so by deception. Orphaned as a child in the mid-nineteenth century, Parkhurst endured some bleak years at a New Hampshire orphanage, where her only solace was helping out in the stables. She was forbidden to ride a horse, however, because she was a girl, and the orphanage authorities also prevented her from being adopted into a family, preferring to keep her on the grounds as a servant. In Ryan's story, Parkhurst listens to the stories another stable worker tells about his flight from slavery into freedom. Inspired, she escapes by donning boys' clothing—a ticket to independence during her era—and uses her skill with horses to find a well-paying job as a stagecoach driver. As Ryan notes, the real-life Parkhurst retained her disguise as a man, and was able to own property and even vote in an 1868 election in California. A *Publishers Weekly* critic praised *Riding Freedom* as "ebullient and tautly structured," adding that "with a pacing that moves along at a gallop, this is a skillful execution of a fascinating historical tale." In *School Library Journal* Carol A. Edwards described the book as "a compact and exciting story about real people who exemplify traits that readers admire."

Ryan's multi-award-winning young-adult novel *Esperanza Rising* is based on the life story of her own grandmother, who came to California from Mexico during the 1930s. The story's heroine is Esperanza Ortega, a thirteen year old who enjoys a privileged life in Aguascalientes, Mexico, where her beloved father, a landowner, instills in her a deep appreciation for the land as part of their family heritage. Tragedy strikes when Es-

peranza's father is slain by robbers, and the girl's stepuncles then try to force her mother into marrying one of them. After their home is destroyed by arson, mother and daughter flee north to California. Now refugees, with little of their possessions remaining, Esperanza and her mother must fend for themselves in a harsh and racist environment. Working as migrant laborers, they pick fruit for mere pennies and live in dire poverty in a camp with other workers. When some workers attempt to form a union, the increasing tensions lead to violence and foster worries that they will be deported to Mexico as troublemakers. When Esperanza's mother becomes ill, the girl supports the family and ultimately earns enough money to pay for the trip to bring her beloved Abuelita north.

Esperanza Rising won many accolades from reviewers. *Reading Today* contributor Lynne T. Burke, for example, termed it a "passionate novel" that is "written with an uncommon understanding of the plight of Mexican farm workers," while *School Library Journal* critic Francisca Goldsmith found it a "compelling story of immigration and assimilation, not only to a new country but also into a different social class." A reviewer for *Publishers Weekly* commented on Ryan's "lyrical, fairy tale-like style," and commended the author for interweaving into the story "subtle metaphors via Abuelita's pearls of wisdom, and not until story's end will readers recognize how carefully they have been strung." In *Booklist,* Gillian Engberg asserted that "Ryan's lyrical novel manages the contradictory: a story of migration and movement deeply rooted in the earth."

Another novel for older readers, *Becoming Naomi León* introduces another resilient young heroine in Naomi Soledad León Outlaw. Living in a trailer part in Lemon Tree, California, with her great-grandmother and her disabled younger brother Owen, eleven-year-old Naomi feels burdened by her name and her family's poverty. When her alcoholic mother, Skyla, resurfaces after seven years and wants to take her daughter to live with her and her boyfriend in Las Vegas, Naomi is confused. Ultimately, guardian Gran and the two children drive the trailer across the border into Mexico, hoping to find a way to stop Skyla's plan with the help of the children's father. "In true mythic tradition, Ryan . . . makes Naomi's search for her dad a search for identity, and both are exciting," wrote *Booklist* critic Hazel Rochman in a review of *Becoming Naomi León,* while a *Kirkus Reviews* writer praised the author's use of "potent, economic prose" in her "tender tale about family love and loyalty." In *Horn Book* Christine M. Heppermann noted that, "with its quirky characterizations and folksy atmosphere," *Becoming Naomi León* is an "engrossing family drama . . . [with an] uniquely affecting emotional core."

Narrated in alternating third-person accounts of eleven-year-old Maya and a wild mare named Artemesia, *Paint the Wind* focuses on how a girl's life changes when she must leave her pampered life for life on a working

ranch. Orphaned at age six, Maya has been catered to by her wealthy grandmother. When the woman has a stroke, the girl is sent to live with Great-Aunt Vi on Vi's Wyoming ranch. There, as Maya learns to know and love the herd of wild horses roaming hear her new home, she also reconnects with the mother she scarcely knew. "Details surrounding the care and riding of horses are both authentic and copious," asserted a *Publishers Weekly* reviewer, the critic adding that the combination of girls and horses is a perennial favorite among preteens. According to *Booklist* critic Francesca Goldsmith, *Paint the Wind* features "lots of adventure . . . (both human and equine), and the pace never lags for an instant."

As a writer, Ryan recognizes the value of family stories. "My advice for students would be to interview their grandparents and write down the stories that they have to tell," she noted in her Scholastic Web site interview. "I think when we're children, we tend to think it's sort of boring, but as we grow up we feel almost desperate for those stories, because they connect us with our history. The key is to write some of the stories down, and don't throw them away!" She often visits schools and offers budding writers this encouragement: "Like anything else in life, the harder you work the more lucky you get. The more you practice, the better you get. Writing is just the same."

Biographical and Critical Sources

PERIODICALS

Booklist, November 1, 1994, Annie Ayres, review of *One Hundred Is a Family,* p. 509; January 1, 1996, Caro-

Our California *teams Ryan with illustrator Rafael Lopez in a colorful ode to the popular westernmost U.S. state.* (Illustration copyright © 2008 by Rafael Lopez. All rights reserved. Used with permission by Charlesbridge Publishing, Inc.)

lyn Phelan, review of *The Flag We Love,* p. 841; January 1, 1998, Hazel Rochman, review of *Riding Freedom,* p. 814; October 15, 1999, Ilene Cooper, review of *Amelia and Eleanor Go for a Ride,* p. 447; December 1, 2000, Gillian Engberg, review of *Esperanza Rising,* p. 708; September 15, 2001, Kelly Milner Halls, review of *Mice and Beans,* p. 233; June 1, 2002, Lauren Peterson, review of *Mud Is Cake,* p. 1743; November 15, 2002, review of *When Marian Sang: The True Recital of Marian Anderson,* p. 799; July, 2003, GraceAnne A. DeCandido, review of *A Box of Friends,* p. 1898; August, 2003, Ellen Mandel, review of *How Do You Raise a Raisin?,* p. 1986; September 15, 2004, Hazel Rochman, review of *Becoming Naomi León,* p. 245; October 1, 2005, Jennifer Mattson, review of *Nacho and Lolita,* p. 66; October 15, 2005, Julie Cummins, review of *There Was No Snow on Christmas,* p. 60; November 15, 2007, Francisca Goldsmith, review of *Paint the Wind,* p. 44; December 15, 2007, Ilene Cooper, review of *Our California,* p. 48.

Horn Book, January, 2001, review of *Esperanza Rising,* p. 96; November-December, 2002, Roger Sutton, review of *When Marian Sang,* p. 780; September-October, 2004, Christine M. Heppermann, review of *Becoming Naomi León,* p. 598.

Instructor, October, 2001, Alice Quiocho, review of *Esperanza Rising,* p. 18.

Journal of Adolescent & Adult Literacy, December, 2001, Tasha Tropp, review of *Esperanza Rising,* p. 334.

Kirkus Reviews, December 1, 1997, review of *Riding Freedom,* pp. 1778-1779; August 1, 2001, review of *Mice and Beans,* p. 1131; September 1, 2002, review of *When Marian Sang,* p. 1319; September 1, 2004, review of *Becoming Naomi León,* p. 873; October 1, 2005, review of *Nacho and Lolita,* p. 1088; August 1, 2007, review of *Paint the Wind;* December 15, 2007, review of *Our California.*

Publishers Weekly, November 7, 1994, review of *One Hundred Is a Family,* p. 78; February 5, 1996, review of *The Flag We Love,* p. 88; February 2, 1998, review of *Riding Freedom,* p. 91; September 20, 1999, review of *Riding Freedom,* p. 90; September 27, 1999, review of *Amelia and Eleanor Go for a Ride!,* p. 105; October 9, 2000, review of *Esperanza Rising,* p. 88; January 8, 2001, review of *Hello, Ocean!,* p. 65; September 13, 2004, review of *Becoming Naomi León,* p. 79; August 22, 2005, review of *Nacho and Lolita,* p. 63; August 20, 2007, review of *Paint the Wind,* p. 68; December 17, 2007, review of *Our California,* p. 50.

Reading Today, October, 2000, Lynne T. Burke, review of *Esperanza Rising,* p. 32.

School Library Journal, October, 1994, Christine A. Moesch, review of *One Hundred Is a Family,* p. 97; May, 1996, Eunice Weech, review of *The Flag We Love,* p. 108; July, 1997, Lisa Wu Stowe, review of *A Pinky Is a Baby Mouse; and Other Baby Animal Names,* p. 87; December, 1997, Patricia Manning, review of *Armadillos Sleep in Dugouts; and Other Places Animals Live,* p. 114; March, 1998, Carol A. Edwards, review of *Riding Freedom,* p. 218; September, 1999, Steven Engelfried, review of *Amelia and Eleanor Go for a Ride!,* p. 202; October, 2000, Francisca Goldsmith, review of *Esperanza Rising,* p. 171; May, 2001, Sally R. Dow, review of *Hello, Ocean!,* p. 133; October, 2001, Mary Elam, review of *Mice and Beans,* p. 130; May, 2002, Sheilah Kosco, review of *Mud Is Cake,* p. 126; November, 2002, Wendy Lukehart, review of *When Marian Sang,* p. 147; August, 2003, Dona Ratterree, review of *How Do You Raise a Raisin?,* p. 151; September, 2003, Kathleen Kelly MacMillan, review of *A Box of Friends,* p. 189; September, 2004, Sharon Morrison, review of *Becoming Naomi León,* p. 216; October, 2005, Rosalyn Pierini, review of *Nacho and Lolita,* p. 144; November, 2007, Ann Robinson, review of *Paint the Wind,* p. 136; June, 2008, Marian Drabkin, review of *Our California,* p. 130.

ONLINE

Pam Muñoz Ryan Home Page, http://www.pammunozryan. com (January 15, 2009).

Scholastic Web site, http://www.scholastic.com/ (February 8, 2002), interview with Ryan.*

S

SAGE, Angie 1952-

Personal

Born 1952, in London, England; father a publisher; married; children: Laurie, Lois. *Education:* B.A. *Hobbies and other interests:* Sailing, the sea, boats, Cornwall, rock music.

Addresses

Home—Cornwall, England.

Career

Writer and illustrator.

Writings

(With Chris Sage) *The Trouble with Babies,* Viking Kestrel (London, England), 1989.
(With Chris Sage) *Happy Baby,* Dial Books for Young Readers (New York, NY), 1990.
(With Chris Sage) *Sleepy Baby,* Dial Books for Young Readers (New York, NY), 1990.
(With Chris Sage) *That's Mine, That's Yours,* Viking (New York, NY), 1991.
(And adaptor) *Give a Little Love: Stories of Love and Friendship,* illustrated by Valeria Petrone, Element Children's Books (Shaftesbury, England), 1999, Element Books (Scranton, PA), 2001.
The Lonely Puppy, illustrated by Edward Eaves, Puffin (London, England), 2003.

SELF-ILLUSTRATED

Monkeys in the Jungle, Methuen (London, England), 1989.
(With Laurie Sage) *The Little Blue Book of the Marie Celeste,* Puffin (London, England), 1993.
The Little Pink Book of the Woolly Mammoth, Puffin (London, England), 1994.

The Amazing Mushroom Mix-up, Young Lions (London, England), 1994.
Bats, Boilers, and Blackcurrant Jelly, Young Lions (London, England), 1994.
I Spy Baby!, Puffin (London, England), 1994.
Muriel and the Monster Maniac Spell, Hodder Children's (London, England), 1995.
Muriel and the Mystery Tour, Hodder Children's (London, England), 1995.
The Little Green Book of the Last Lost Dinosaur, Puffin (London, England), 1995.
Ellie's Slugbucket, Hodder Children's (London, England), 1996.
Ellie and the Wolves, Hodder Children's (London, England), 1996.
My Blue Book: A Play-doh Play Book (board book; packaged with Play-doh), Campbell (London, England), 1996.
Allie's Crocodile, Puffin (London, England), 1997.
Shark Island, Puffin (London, England), 1997.
In My Home, Dial Books for Young Readers (New York, NY), 1997.
On the Move, Dial Books for Young Readers (New York, NY), 1997.
Dear Alien, A. & C. Black (London, England), 1998.
Crocodile Canal, Puffin (London, England), 1998.
Stack-a-Car: Read the Books! Make the Toy!, David & Charles Children's Books (London, England), 1999.
Hello Ducks!, Hodder Children's (London, England), 2001.
Mouse, Puffin (London, England), 2001.
Molly and the Birthday Party, Peachtree (Atlanta, GA), 2001.
Molly at the Dentist Peachtree (Atlanta, GA), 2001.
No Banana!, Hodder Children's (London, England), 2001.

Work included in anthology *The Big Book of Pet Stories,* Viking (London, England), 2001.

"SEPTIMUS HEAP" FANTASY NOVEL SERIES

Magyk illustrated by Mark Zug, Katherine Tegen Books (New York, NY), 2005.

Flyte, illustrated by Mark Zug, Katherine Tegen Books (New York, NY), 2006.

Physik, illustrated by Mark Zug, Katherine Tegen Books (New York, NY), 2007.

Queste, illustrated by Mark Zug, Katherine Tegen Books (New York, NY), 2008.

The Magykal Papers, illustrated by Mark Zug, Katherine Tegen Books (New York, NY), 2009.

Syren, illustrated by Mark Zug, Katherine Tegen Books (New York, NY), 2009.

"ARAMINTA SPOOKIE" NOVEL SERIES

My Haunted House, illustrated by Jimmy Pickering, Katherine Tegen Books (New York, NY) 2006.

The Sword in the Grotto, illustrated by Jimmy Pickering, Katherine Tegen Books (New York, NY) 2006.

Frognapped, illustrated by Jimmy Pickering, Katherine Tegen Books (New York, NY) 2007.

Vampire Brat, illustrated by Jimmy Pickering, Katherine Tegen Books (New York, NY) 2007.

Ghostsitters, illustrated by Jimmy Pickering, Katherine Tegen Books (New York, NY) 2008.

ILLUSTRATOR

Fran Hunia, adaptor, *Ananse and the Sky God,* Ladybird Books (Loughborough, England), 1980.

Enid Blyton's Ruby Storybook, Knight (Sevenoaks, Kent, England), 1980.

The Nightmare Song (lyrics from Gilbert and Sullivan operetta *Iolanthe*), Angus & Robertson (London, England), 1981.

Enid Blyton's Turquoise Storybook, Hodder & Stoughton (Sevenoaks, Kent, England), 1983.

Enid Blyton's Coral Storybook, Hodder & Stoughton (Sevenoaks, Kent, England), 1983.

Saviour Pirotta, *Jasper Joe and the Best Trick in the World,* Blackie (London, England), 1988.

Jana Novotny Hunter, *Get up, Ben!,* Viking (London, England), 1991.

Christine Morton, *The Pig That Barked,* Hodder & Stoughton (London, England), 1992.

Susan Mayes, *The Usborne Book of Kites,* Usborne (London, England), 1992.

Peter Holland, *The Usborne Book of Paper Superplanes,* Usborne (London, England), 1992.

Linda Fisher, *Shape and Colour,* Headway (London, England), 1992.

Tony Mitton, *Nobody Laughed,* Collins Educational (London, England), 1994.

Sarah Bowen, *Laura's Granny: Explaining Death to Children,* Scripture Union (London, England), 1995.

Jill Atkins, *The Moonsnoop,* Heinemann Educational (Oxford, England), 1998.

Sidelights

Angie Sage ranges widely in her writing for children, from picture books for the youngest children to fantasy novels for middle-grade readers, such as her popular

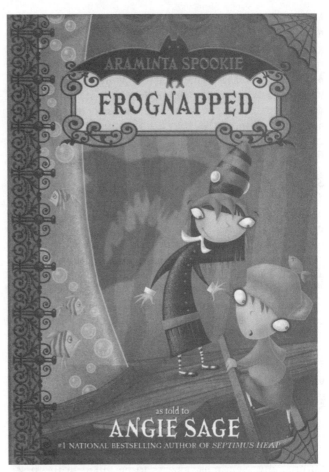

Cover of Angie Sage's middle-grade "Araminta Spookie" novel **Frognapped,** *featuring artwork by Jimmy Pickering.* (Cover art copyright © 2007 by Jimmy Pickering. Used by permission of HarperCollins Publishers.)

"Septimus Heap" and "Araminta Spookie" series. Although Sage trained as a radiographer and planned to attend medical school in her native England, she ultimately made the switch to art school. After creating dozens of original self-illustrated picture books and contributing artwork to texts by other several authors, Sage has more recently passed on the illustration duties; Mark Zug brings to life her "Septimus Heap" stories while Jimmy Pickering captures the weird whimsy in Sage's "Araminta Spookie" saga.

One of Sage's first books for children, *Happy Baby,* is a board book for toddlers that she created with Chris Sage. In the simple story, an appealingly drawn baby goes through the activities of his average day. Similarly, *Sleepy Baby* follows a drowsy tot as sleep approaches. In a playful twist, the baby's demeanor changes abruptly on the last page: sleepy baby is suddenly wide awake, and happy baby wails out a complaint against the world. The book's pleasing colors and first-person narration "are sure to draw children in," noted a contributor to *Publishers Weekly.*

In *Molly and the Birthday Party* Sage uses a lift-the-flap-format book to allow children to discover for themselves what Molly the Monster is doing next. When

Molly attends Olly's birthday party, she does not want to give up the present she has brought. She plays games and wins a prize, but only after she sees Olly's other friends give him presents is she ready to offer hers. In *Molly at the Dentist,* the reluctant Molly resists letting the dentist examine her teeth. When he takes out a small dental mirror, however, Molly agrees to have a look along with him. In *School Library Journal* Laura Scott called Molly's adventures "treats for storytime or laptime."

Sage tackles the sometimes tricky subject of sharing in *That's Mine, That's Yours.* Here an older sister butts heads with her baby sister when the younger of the pair becomes more interested in the older's belongings than her own. The older sister "displays admirable patience" as she tries to explain to her sibling that certain objects are "mine," and other objects are "yours," observed a *Publishers Weekly* reviewer. At first, the baby fails to grasp the concept, and tugging matches between the sisters ensue. Kindly big sister finally gives in, and in the end little sister shares too when the duo lie down for a nap in little sister's crib. The critic also called *That's Mine, That's Yours* a "good choice for toddlers as well as older siblings."

Sage turns to older readers in her "Septimus Heap" fantasy series for middle-school readers. In *Magyk,* she introduces the magically gifted Septimus, a boy born with powers only given to the seventh son of a seventh son. Surprisingly, Septimus appears to be killed in the first paragraph of the first book of his series. However, ten years later a powerful necromancer named DomDaniel arrives at the home of the large Heap family. Jenna Heap soon learns that she is not a member of the Heap family after all; she is actually a princess who was hidden among the raucous family of six boys a decade earlier. As Jenna and her protector, ExtraOrdinary Wizard Marcia Overstrand, flee from the menacing DomDaniel, other members of the Heap family join them, among them the unremarkable brother known as Boy 412. When Boy 412 demonstrates stunning powers and awesome magical potential, readers clue in that the infant Septimus was declared dead a little too early. In *Booklist,* Jennifer A. Mattson cited "Sage's fluent, charismatic storytelling" and character development, while a *Kirkus Reviews* contributor called *Magyk* "a quick-reading, stand-alone, deliciously spellbinding series opener."

Jenna and Septimus return in *Flyte,* as DomDaniel is reconstituted and continues to plan their demise. Now apprenticed to ExtraOrdinary wizard Marcia, Septimus works to help sister Jenna while his jealous brother Simon Heap teams up with DomDaniel to thwart both siblings' efforts. The villainy of DomDaniel is eclipsed by the ghost of an evil queen in *Physik,* as Septimus is pulled 500 years into the past. Ordered to apprentice himself to an ancient alchemist, Septimus is soon joined by several others from his own era, including Princess Jenna and several members of the Heap family. In *Queste* Nicko Heap and friend Snorri become trapped in the past, forcing Septimus and his sister Jenna to locate the place where all paths through Time meet in order to free his brother and his girlfriend. Although *School Library Journal* contributor Emily Rodriguez noted the sometimes-confusing cast of characters in *Flyte,* she added that fantasy buffs "will find themselves quickly immersed in [the author's] . . . imaginative world, moving from one well-crafted adventure to another at a suspenseful pace." Even Harry Potter fans, "won over by Sage's confiding, whimsical tone and tightly interlocking plot elements, [readers] will welcome Septimus Heap as their second-favorite wizard," predicted Mattson. Reviewing *Physik,* Mattson concluded that fans of the "Septimus Heap" novels will enjoy the author's "quirky storytelling, [which is] marked by a sprawling, omniscient purview and plenty of entertaining tangents."

Sage turns from frightening time-travel adventure to humorously creepy, spine-tickling tales in her "Araminta Spookie" series of middle-grade novels. In series opener *My Haunted House,* Araminta lives in a haunted house with her aunt Tabby and Uncle Drac. When Aunt Tabby attempts to put Spook House on the market because of the costs of maintaining it, Araminta gets help from several resident ghosts to keep interested real-estate agents fleeing from the house. When the fun-loving Wizzard family shows up, family members' love of ghostly haunts make them a perfect fit as roommates. Noting that Pickering's illustrations "add the perfect mood" for the story, *School Library Journal* critic Amelia Jenkins wrote that *My Haunted House* serves up "fun escapism for readers who like their spooky without the scary," while in *Publishers Weekly* the critic dubbed Sage's novel a "humorous, fast-paced . . . caper."

The "Araminta Spookie" series continues in *The Sword in the Grotto,* as Araminta and Wanda Wizzard join Edward the ghost and risk a trip into a hidden tunnel in Spook House. Their goal: to locate a long-missing sword that would make the perfect birthday gift for chief Spook House ghost Sir Horace. *Frognapped* finds the two girls on the hunt for Mr. Wizzard's five acrobatic frogs, even when the trail leads them to a bizarre marine park that has been constructed on the property of their crabby neighbor Old Morris. Uncle Drac's spoiled nephew is a guest at Spook House in *Vampire Brat,* while *Ghostsitters* finds the house thrown into chaos by a pair of poltergeists who moves in while Tabby and Drac are away on holiday. According to *School Library Journal* critic Walter Minkel, *Frognapped* will appeal to middle graders "who like the idea of spooky things such as secret passages and ghosts," but would like to avoid more gruesome fare.

Sage invests all of her characters with a sense of humor, an enjoyment in the company of others (whether ghost or human), and the ability to deal with oddities life as they happen. In an interview for *BookBrowse.*

com, she specifically reflected on the cast of her "Septimus Heap" novels. "I like their chaotic acceptance of life, and the fact that they don't do what they are told by authority if they think it is wrong," she explained. "Stuff happens to them that makes their life difficult at times but they don't moan about things, they just get on and sort it out as best they can. They are remarkably accepting of other people, I think because they are so strong as a unit." "They are also a family which becomes separated by circumstances," Sage added, "and I wanted to show that families can still be close to each other and care for each other even though they live apart."

Biographical and Critical Sources

PERIODICALS

Booklist, March 15, 2005, Jennifer Mattson, review of *Magyk,* p. 1295; May 15, 2006, Jennifer Mattson, review of *Flyte,* p. 59; April 1, 2007, Jennifer Mattson, review of *Physik,* p. 52; May 15, 2008, Jennifer Mattson, review of *Queste,* p. 56.

Christian Parenting Today, November-December, 2001, review of *Molly and the Birthday Party* and *Molly at the Dentist,* p. 60.

Kirkus Reviews, January 15, 2005, review of *Magyk,* p. 125; March 1, 2007, review of *Physik,* p. 231; April 15, 2008, review of *Queste.*

Publishers Weekly, June 29, 1990, review of *Happy Baby* and *Sleepy Baby,* p. 99; March 22, 1991, review of *That's Mine, That's Yours,* p. 79; August 9, 1999, review of *Stack-a-Car: Read the Books! Make the Toy!,* p. 355; January 31, 2000, review of *Give a Little Love: Stories of Love and Friendship,* p. 109; January 3, 2005, review of *Magyk,* p. 56l; August 14, 2006, review of *My Haunted House,* p. 205.

School Library Journal, August, 2000, Susan Helpler, review of *Give a Little Love,* p. 164; November, 2001, Laura Scott, review of *Molly and the Birthday Party,* p. 136; April, 2005, Steve Engelfried, review of *Magyk,* p. 140; June, 2006, Emily Rodriguez, review of *Flyte,* p. 165; February, 2007, Amelia Jenkins, review of *My Haunted House,* p. 96; June, 2007, Emily Rodriguez, review of *Physik,* p. 159; September, 2007, Walter Minkel, review of *Frognapped,* p. 175; June, 2008, Elizabeth Bird, review of *Queste,* p. 150.

Voice of Youth Advocates, April, 2005, review of *Magyk,* p. 13.

ONLINE

BookBrowse Web site, http://www.bookbrowse.com/ (January 28, 2009), interview with Sage.

Septimus Heap Web site, http://www.septimusheap.com/ (January 28, 2009), "Angie Sage."*

SANDIN, Joan 1942-

Personal

Surname pronounced "Sand-een"; born April 30, 1942, in Watertown, WI; daughter of Robert L. (a teacher) and Frances K. (an interviewer) Sandin; married Sigfrid Leijonhufvud (a journalist), April 30, 1971 (divorced, 1986); married; second husband's name Brian; children: Jonas, Jenny. *Education:* University of Arizona, B.F.A., 1964.

Addresses

Home—Tucson, AZ.

Career

Illustrator, author, and translator of children's books. *Exhibitions:* Work included in solo shows in Sweden and the United States.

Member

Authors Guild, FST, Swedish Society of Illustrators.

Awards, Honors

Best Children's Books citation, American Institute of Graphic Artists, 1970, for *Crocodile and Hen;* Forfattarfonden (Swedish Writers' Fund) travel and work grants; Bildkonstnarsfonden (Swedish Artists' Fund) exhibition grant; Notable Children's Trade Book in the Field of Social Studies citations, National Council for the Social Studies/Children's Book Council (CBC), 1971, for *Hill of Fire,* 1975, for *The Lemming Condition,* and 1981, for both *The Long Way to a New Land* and *Time for Uncle Joe;* Georgia Children's Award, 1973, for *"Hey, What's Wrong with This One?";* Outstanding Science Trade Book for Children citation, National Science Teachers Association/CBC, 1974, for *Woodchuck;* Edgar Allan Poe Award nominee, Mystery Writers of America, 1975, for *The Mysterious Red Tape Gang;* Notable Book citations, American Library Association, 1981, for *The Long Way to a New Land,* and 1988, for translation of Christina Bjork's *Linnea's Windowsill Garden.*

Writings

SELF-ILLUSTRATED

The Long Way to a New Land, Harper & Row (New York, NY), 1981.

The Long Way Westward, Harper & Row (New York, NY), 1989.

Pioneer Bear: Based on a True Story, Random House (New York, NY), 1995.

Coyote School News, Holt (New York, NY), 2003.

At Home in a New Land, HarperCollins (New York, NY), 2007.

ILLUSTRATOR

Carol Beach York, *The Blue Umbrella,* Franklin Watts (New York, NY), 1968.

Randolph Stow, *Midnite: The Story of a Wild Colonial Boy,* Prentice-Hall (Englewood Cliffs, NJ), 1968.

Harold Felton, *True Tall Tales of Stormalong: Sailor of the Seven Seas,* Prentice-Hall (Englewood Cliffs, NJ), 1968.

Edith Brecht, *The Little Fox,* Lippincott (Philadelphia, PA), 1968.

Eleanor Hull, *A Trainful of Strangers,* Atheneum (New York, NY), 1968.

Ellen Pugh, *Tales from the Welsh Hills,* Dodd (New York, NY), 1968.

Maia Wojciechowska, *"Hey, What's Wrong with This One?",* Harper (New York, NY), 1969.

Joan Lexau, *Crocodile and Hen,* Harper (New York, NY), 1969.

Jan M. Robinson, *The December Dog,* Lippincott (Philadelphia, PA), 1969.

Constantine Georgiou, *Rani, Queen of the Jungle,* Prentice-Hall (Englewood Cliffs, NJ), 1970.

Joan Lexau, *It All Began with a Drip, Drip, Drip,* McCall/Dutton (New York, NY), 1970.

Jean Little, *Look through My Window,* Harper (New York, NY), 1970.

Joanna Cole, *The Secret Box,* Morrow (New York, NY), 1971.

Thomas P. Lewis, *Hill of Fire,* Harper (New York, NY), 1971.

Barbara Brenner, *A Year in the Life of Rosie Bernard,* Harper (New York, NY), 1971.

Ellen Pugh, *More Tales from the Welsh Hills,* Dodd (New York, NY), 1971.

Jean Little, *From Anna,* Harper (New York, NY), 1972.

Nathaniel Benchley, *Small Wolf,* Harper (New York, NY), 1972.

Edna Mitchell Preston, *Ickle Bickle Robin,* Watts (New York, NY), 1973.

Alison Morgan, *A Boy Called Fish,* Harper (New York, NY), 1973.

Joan L. Nixon, *The Mysterious Red Tape Gang,* Putnam (New York, NY), 1974.

Hans Eric Hellberg, *Grandpa's Maria,* translated by Patricia Crampton, Morrow (New York, NY), 1974.

Faith McNulty, *Woodchuck,* Harper (New York, NY), 1974.

Kathryn Ewing, *A Private Matter,* Harcourt Brace Jovanovich (New York, NY), 1975.

Liesel Skorpen, *Michael,* Harper (New York, NY), 1975.

Liesel Skorpen, *Bird,* Harper (New York, NY), 1976.

Sandra Love, *But What about Me?,* Harcourt Brace Jovanovich (New York, NY), 1976.

Alan Arkin, *The Lemming Condition,* Harper (New York, NY), 1976.

Thomas P. Lewis, *Clipper Ship,* Harper & Row (New York, NY), 1978.

Clyde Robert Bulla, *Daniel's Duck,* Harper & Row (New York, NY), 1979.

Nancy Jewell, *Time for Uncle Joe,* Harper & Row (New York, NY), 1981.

Eleanor Coerr, *The Bell Ringer and the Pirates,* Harper & Row (New York, NY), 1983.

Doreen Rappaport, *Trouble at the Mines,* Crowell (New York, NY), 1987.

Aileen Fisher, *The House of a Mouse: Poems,* Harper & Row (New York, NY), 1988.

Aileen Fisher, *Always Wondering: Some Favorite Poems of Aileen Fisher,* HarperCollins (New York, NY), 1991.

Nancy Smiler Levinson, *Snowshoe Thompson,* HarperCollins (New York, NY), 1992.

Elaine Marie Alphin, *A Bear for Miguel,* HarperCollins (New York, NY), 1996.

Elizabeth Winthrop, *As the Crow Flies,* Clarion (New York, NY), 1998.

Illustrator of Betty Miles' "Army of Two," serialize in the *Boston Herald,* 2000.

Sandin's illustrations are represented in the Kerlan Collection.

TRANSLATOR

Gunilla Bergstrom, *Who's Scaring Alfie Atkins?,* Farrar, Straus & Giroux (New York, NY), 1987.

Christina Bjork and Lena Anderson, *Linnea's Windowsill Garden,* Farrar, Straus & Giroux (New York, NY), 1988.

Christina Bjork, *Elliot's Extraordinary Cookbook,* Farrar, Straus & Giroux (New York, NY), 1991.

Christina Bjork, *The Other Alice: The Story of Alice Liddell and Alice in Wonderland,* R & S Books (New York, NY), 1993.

Christina Bjork, *Big Bear's Book: By Himself,* Farrar, Straus & Giroux (New York, NY), 1994.

Olof and Lena Landström, *Boo and Baa in a Party Mood,* R & S Books (New York, NY), 1996.

Olof and Lena Landström, *Boo and Baa in Windy Weather,* R & S Books (New York, NY), 1996.

Olof and Lena Landström, *Boo and Baa at Sea,* R & S Books (New York, NY), 1997.

Olof and Lena Landström, *Boo and Baa on a Cleaning Spree,* R & S Books (New York, NY), 1997.

Lena Arro, *Good Night, Animals,* illustrated by Catarina Kruusval, R & S Books (New York, NY), 2002.

Lena Landström, *The Little Hippos' Adventure,* R & S Books (New York, NY), 2002.

Lena Landström, *The New Hippos,* R & S Books (New York, NY), 2003.

Peter Cohen, *Boris's Glasses,* illustrated by Olaf Landström, R & S Books (New York, NY), 2003.

Jeanette Milde, *Once upon a Wedding,* R & S Books (New York, NY), 2004.

Lena Landström, *Four Hens and a Rooster,* illustrated by Olof Landström, R & S Books (New York, NY), 2005.

Olof and Lena Landström, *Boo and Baa Have Company,* R & S Books (New York, NY), 2006.

Lena Anderson, *Hedgehog, Pig, and the Sweet Little Friend,* R & S Books (New York, NY), 2007.

Adam Dahlin, *Junk Collector School,* illustrated by Emma Akerman, R & S Books (New York, NY), 2007.

Catarina Kruusval, *Franny's Friends,* Farrar, Straus & Giroux (New York, NY), 2008.

Sidelights

A prolific illustrator, Joan Sandin is also a skilled translator and a storyteller in her own right. As Sandin once told *SATA:* "I most enjoy working with folktales and books demanding research and/or travel." Indeed, Sandin's self-illustrated works have all been well-researched historical tales, often based on her ancestors' experiences. Her extensive travels in Europe and Mexico as well as the United States have also inspired her work.

Among the many books Sandin has illustrated is *A Bear for Miguel,* written by Elaine Maria Alphin. It is an unusual story for early readers, according to reviewers, but one that is effectively done and sensitively rendered in pictures and words. When Maria brings her stuffed toy bear, Paco, along to the market with her father, she has no intention of trading him. Her feelings change, however, as she begins to understand how the war in her country of El Salvador has affected her father's ability to find work. Sensing that a little boy injured in the war would love to have Paco, Maria decides to trade the toy for food for her family. "Sandin's watercolors add to the emotional impact . . . and do an effective job of setting the scene," remarked Gale W. Sherman in *School Library Journal.*

Sandin lived in Sweden for more than a decade before returning to the United States in the mid-1980s. Since her return, she has translated several children's books from Swedish into English. Many of these translations have been of picture books by Olof and Lena Landström, including their series about Boo and Baa, two hapless little sheep who find themselves in humorous jams no matter what they try to do. In *Boo and Baa in a Party Mood,* the two prepare for a birthday party by practicing their dance steps, but things get sticky when they try to wrap the present. *Boo and Baa in Windy Weather* find the sheep at the grocery store during a snow storm, but dragging home a sled laden with their purchases presents a problem, and their attempts to rescue a cat in a tree provide the humor in *Boo and Ba Have Company.* Sandin also translated Lena Landström's self-illustrated books about a family of hippopotami, including *The Little Hippos' Adventure* and *The New Hippos.* In the first book, three baby hippos get bored with swimming in the safe river near their home. Instead, they want to go diving off of the forbidden Tall Cliff. When they are finally allowed to go swimming there, catastrophe nearly strikes. In the latter book, the hippos must get used to a new family who moves into their part of the jungle, discovering that the new family does not do everything the same way they do.

Big Bear's Book: By Himself, according to *School Library Journal* contributor Marilyn Taniguchi, is not a picture book but "a whimsical reminiscence of child-hood" best suited to sentimental adults. Written by Christina Bjork, *Big Bear's Book* tells the story of a toy bear's relationship to his owner, from childhood, through a sojourn in the attic, to a place in the child's adult life and a career in the movies. Sandin is also the translator of Bjork's tribute to the children's classic *Alice in Wonderland.* In *The Other Alice: The Story of Alice Liddell and Alice in Wonderland,* Bjork describes the model for Lewis Carroll's main character, Alice Liddell, and explains some of the games and other trivia associated with the book. The result is "a unique pleasure," Ann A. Flowers wrote in *Horn Book.*

Sandin's own background—her ancestors immigrated to the United States from Sweden in the nineteenth century—inspired the research that went into *The Long Way to a New Land, The Long Way Westward,* and *At Home in a New Land.* These self-illustrated early readers follow an immigrant family's journey from Sweden to the United States in the 1860s. Told from the perspective of Carl Erik, the family's elder son, *The Long Way to a New Land* describes the drought that forces Erik's family to sell their farm and try to make a fresh start in America. The story continues with an account of their trip by boat to the United States, where bad weather, bad smells, and crowding mean long days of discomfort before they reach their destination. Critics noted that Sandin uses her illustrations effectively to augment a necessarily spare text intended for beginning readers. "It isn't always easy to make history comprehensible to younger children," remarked Zena Sutherland of the *Bulletin of the Center for Children's Books,* but "Sandin does a nice job of it."

Praised as "an interesting, well-researched slice of history" by a critic for *Kirkus Reviews, The Long Way Westward* continues the story of the Erik family's journey as they travel from New York City by railroad to Minnesota to live among their relatives and make a claim on 160 acres of land through the Homestead Act. In *At Home in a New Land* Carl enjoys a traditional Swedish Christmas, but also takes on new responsibilities, such as learning English and hunting and trapping, when his father and uncle leave to work at a logging camp. In *Horn Book* Christine M. Heppermann praised *At Home in a New Land* as a "gentle yet balanced view of nineteenth-century homesteading life" that is "rendered affectionately in Sandin's ink-and-watercolor illustrations." Recommending the book for history buffs, a *Kirkus Reviews* writer also cited the author's artwork, writing that Sandin's "charming watercolor-washed black-line drawings show the worry and diligence of" young Carl as he shoulders his share of the tasks in his homesteading family.

Also set in the nineteenth century, *Pioneer Bear: Based on a True Story* introduces readers to John Lacy, a photographer who learns that young Andrew Irwin taught a bear to dance. Lacy travels thirty miles to the Irwin farm to photograph the bear; but when he arrives, Bearly the bear is nowhere to be found. Sandin provides a visual survey of pioneer life on a farm while the

Joan Sandin creates the detailed drawings in her history-themed picture book At Home in a New Land.

family goes from room to room, from barn to outhouse, in search of the cub. "Pioneer activities such as washing laundry in tubs . . . and smoking meats are realistically presented in warm watercolor illustrations," Mary Ann Bursk observed in *School Library Journal.* Reviewers also noted Sandin's sly infusion of humor into the story through her illustrations. "Primary schoolers will enjoy sighting Bearly . . . as he peeks from behind outbuildings and foliage," remarked Elizabeth Bush in the *Bulletin of the Center for Children's Books.*

Coyote School News was inspired by actual newspapers printed by five tiny rural schools in Depression-era Arizona. Sandin stumbled across the original newspapers, titled *The Little Cowpuncher,* while doing research for a book about her high school friend, who went to one of the schools located in the area covered by the paper. As well as writing *Coyote School News,* Sandin also got involved in a project to digitally archive the crumbling originals of *The Little Cowpuncher* so that the materials would be available to researchers in future generations.

A *Kirkus Reviews* contributor praised the "delightful authenticity" of *Coyote School News,* which follows student Monchi Ramirez and his five siblings through the 1938-39 school year. The story is partially told from Monchi's point of view and partially conveyed through nine included issues of *Coyote School News,* which are printed to look like they came from an old-fashioned, purple-inked mimeograph. "Sandin's love and knowledge of this land and its history are evident," the *Kirkus Reviews* critic concluded, as she sketches with pictures and words the lives of the twelve students of the Coyote School. Observing that the book offers young readers a look at "Mexican traditions [that] have been part of the American cultural landscape for generations," *School Library Journal* reviewer Eve Ortega found *Coyote School News* to capture and convey "an entertaining bit of historical fiction."

Biographical and Critical Sources

PERIODICALS

Arizona Daily Star (Tucson, AZ), September 17, 2002, Bonnie Henry, interview with Sandin, p. B1.

Booklist, December 1, 1993, Carolyn Phelan, review of *The Other Alice: The Story of Alice Liddell and Alice in Wonderland,* pp. 686-687; July, 1995, Stephanie Zvirin, review of *Pioneer Bear: Based on a True Story,* p. 1885; November 1, 1996, Carolyn Phelan, reviews of *Boo and Baa in Windy Weather* and *Boo and Baa in a Party Mood,* pp. 507-508; April, 1998, Hazel Rochman, review of *As the Crow Flies,* p. 1334.

Boston Herald, April 24, 2000, Kristen Bradley, review of *Army of Two,* p. 16.

Bulletin of the Center for Children's Books, March, 1982, Zena Sutherland, review of *The Long Way to a New Land,* p. 138; July, 1995, Elizabeth Bush, review of *Pioneer Bear,* p. 397.

Horn Book, February, 1982, Nancy Sheridan, review of *The Long Way to a New Land,* p. 39; March-April, 1987, Hanna B. Zeiger, review of *Trouble at the Mines,* p. 212; September-October, 1989, Mary M. Burns, review of *The Long Way Westward,* p. 618; January-February, 1992, Mary M. Burns, review of *Showshoe Thompson,* p. 66; March-April, 1994, Ann A. Flowers, review of *The Other Alice,* p. 215; May-June, 1996, Maeve Visser Knoth, review of *A Bear for Miguel,* pp. 331-332; September-October, 2006, Martha V. Parravano, review of *Boo and Baa Have Company,* p. 568; November-December, 2007, Christine M. Heppermann, review of *At Home in a New Land,* p. 686.

Kirkus Reviews, August 15, 1989, review of *The Long Way Westward,* p. 1250; August 1, 2002, review of *Good Night, Animals,* p. 1121; July 1, 2003, review of *Coyote School News,* p. 914; August 1, 2007, review of *At Home in a New Land.*

Publishers Weekly, April 10, 1987, review of *Trouble at the Mines,* p. 96; September 30, 1988, review of *Linnea's Windowsill Garden,* p. 64; August 25, 1989, review of *The Long Way Westward,* p. 63; January 19, 1990, review of *Linnea's Almanac,* p. 106; August 5, 1996, reviews of *Boo and Baa in Windy Weather* and *Boo and Baa in a Party Mood,* p. 440; April 8, 2002, review of *The Little Hippos' Adventure,* p. 225; July 28, 2003, review of *Coyote School News,* pp. 94-95.

Reading Teacher, October, 1989, Lee Galda, review of *The House of a Mouse,* pp. 66-71.

School Library Journal, December, 1981, review of *The Long Way to a New Land,* p. 75; April, 1987, Mary Beth Burgoyne, review of *Trouble at the Mines,* p. 102; February, 1988, Shirley Wilton, review of *Linnea in Monet's Garden,* p. 72; November, 1988, Frances E. Millhouser, review of *Linnea's Windowsill Garden,* p. 100; January, 1989, Kathleen Whalin, review of *The House of a Mouse,* p. 70; September, 1989, Sharron McElmeel, review of *The Long Way Westward,* p. 234; April, 1990, Amy Adler, review of *Linnea's Almanac,* p. 102; May, 1991, Carolyn Jenks, review of *Elliot's Extraordinary Cookbook,* p. 100; December, 1991, Barbara Chatton, review of *Always Wondering: Some Favorite Poems of Aileen Fisher,* pp. 109-110; January, 1992, Gale W. Sherman, review of *Snowshoe Thompson,* p. 104; December, 1993, Patricia A. Dollisch, review of *The Other Alice,* pp. 140-141; April, 1995, Marilyn Taniguchi, review of *Big Bear's Book: By Himself,* p. 130; October, 1995, Mary Ann Bursk, review of *Pioneer Bear,* p. 117; June, 1996, Gale W. Sherman, review of *A Bear for Miguel,* p. 92; July, 1997, Darla Remple, reviews of *Boo and Baa at Sea* and *Boo and Baa on a Cleaning Spree,* p. 70; June, 1998, Faith Brautigan, review of *As the Crow Flies,* pp. 124-125; April, 2002, Be Astengo, review of *The Little Hippos' Adventure,* p. 114; February, 2003, Kathy Piehl, review of *Good Night, Animals,* p. 102; April, 2003, Bina Williams, review of *The New Hippos,* pp. 130-131; September, 2003, Edith Ching, review of *Boris's Glasses,* p. 176; October, 2003, Eve Ortega, review of *Coyote School News,* p. 138; September, 2007, Mary Elam, review of *At Home in a New Land,* p. 175.

ONLINE

Joan Sandin Home Page, http://members.authorsguild.net/joansandin (January 25, 2009).*

*   *   *

SCHMATZ, Pat

Personal

Born in WI. *Education:* Michigan State University, B.S.; University of California at Berkeley, M.A.

Addresses

Home—WI. *Agent*—Andrea Cascardi, Transatlantic Literary Agency; andreatla1.com. *E-mail*—pschmatz@hotmail.com.

Pat Schmatz (Photograph by Edie Walker. Reproduced by permission.)

Career

Writer. Has worked variously as forklift operator, janitor, fitness consultant, stable hand, library assistant, legal secretary, and shipping clerk.

Awards, Honors

Minnesota State Arts Board fellowship grant, 2003; Outstanding Books for Children by a Wisconsin Author honor, Wisconsin Library Association, and Best Children's Books of the Year selection, Bank Street College of Education, both 2008, both for *Circle the Truth.*

Writings

NOVELS

Mrs. Estronsky and the U.F.O., Blue Works (Port Orchard, WA), 2001.
Circle the Truth, Carolrhoda Books (Minneapolis, MN), 2007.
Mousetraps, illustrated by Bill Hauser, Carolrhoda Books (Minneapolis, MN), 2008.

Sidelights

Born and raised in rural Wisconsin, young-adult novelist Pat Schmatz has set each of her books in the Midwest, "which certainly has a particular cultural flavor," the author remarked in an *Under the Covers* interview with Lisa Chellman. "I find the upper Midwest—both rural and urban—to have a particular kindness, something almost like innocence," Schmatz added. "That's not quite the right word, but it's a related concept . . ., and so characters with a gentle sort of progressive political sensibility . . . can be found everywhere."

Schmatz's debut title, *Mrs. Estronsky and the U.F.O.,* centers on the relationship between a girl and her piano teacher, who both spot an unidentified flying object. In her next work, *Circle the Truth,* she presents readers with a supernatural fantasy. The work concerns Orithian "Rith" Haley, an angry and resentful teen from a blended family whose father died when Rith was very young. When the boy begins having visions of an elderly man who quotes Biblical passages and is accompanied by a cat that guards him, Rith begins to question his spiritual beliefs. Schmatz's "rhapsody on faith, acceptance, patience and the relationship between 'truth' and 'reality' is an unusual and valuable addition" to young adult literature, asserted a critic in *Kirkus Reviews.*

Mousetraps, an illustrated novel, focuses on sixteen-year-old Maxie, a high-school junior who is reunited with Rick, her best pal from elementary school. Rick had disappeared years earlier, after he was attacked by gay-bashers. Although Maxie would like to rekindle the friendship, she has second thoughts after noticing some dangerous changes in her old friend. According to *School Library Journal* reviewer Natasha Forrester, "Maxie's voice captures the insecurity and wish to fit in that color the adolescent years." A *Kirkus Reviews* contributor described *Mousetraps* as "unexpectedly, richly dark, with no easy answers," resulting in a novel that is "both chilling and sweet."

Biographical and Critical Sources

PERIODICALS

Booklist, December 1, 2007, Ilene Cooper, review of *Circle the Truth,* p. 34.
Kirkus Reviews, October 1, 2007, review of *Circle the Truth;* September 15, 2008, review of *Mousetraps.*
School Library Journal, November, 2008, Natasha Forrester, review of *Mousetraps,* p. 136.

ONLINE

Pat Schmatz Home Page, http://www.patschmatz.com (January 20, 2009).
Pat Schmatz Web log, http://patschmatz.livejournal.com/ (January 20, 2009).
Transatlantic Literary Agency Web site, http://www.tla1.com/ (January 20, 2009), "Pat Schmatz."
Under the Covers Web site, http://lisachellman.com/ (October 30, 2008), Lisa Chellman, interview with Schmatz.

*   *   *

SCHY, Yael

Personal

Married David M. Schwartz (a children's book author). *Education:* University of California at Santa Cruz, bach-

Yael Schy (Photograph by Ed Aiona. Courtesy of Yael Schy.)

elor's degree (psychology and theatre arts); M.S.W. (community organization/social work); certifications in organizational psychology and human resource development).

Addresses

Home—Oakland, CA. *E-mail*—yael@dramaticstrides.com.

Career

Speaker, coach, and business consultant; also dance teacher and improvisational theatre/dance performer. Dramatic Strides Consulting, Oakland, CA, founder and principal. Formerly worked as a social worker and nonprofit manager. Member of faculty, American Management Association, and City College of San Francisco Contract education; CompassPoint Nonprofit Services, instructor.

Awards, Honors

American Association for the Advancement of Science/ Subaru Science Book and Films Prize for Excellence in Science Books, Animal Behavior Society Outstanding

Children's Book Award, and Outstanding Science Trade Book designation, National Science Teachers Association/Children's Book Council, all 2008, and Cybils Award finalist, all for *Where in the Wild?*

Writings

(With husband, David M. Schwartz) *Where in the Wild?: Camouflaged Animals Concealed—and Revealed: Ear-tickling Poems,* photography by Dwight Kuhn, Tricycle Press (Berkeley, CA), 2007.

(With Wendy C. Horikoshi) *Teamwork Tools: A Revolutionary Approach for Managers and Trainers,* Kagan Publishing 2008.

Sidelights

I have always loved writing poems and songs, ever since I was a child," Yael Schy told *SATA.* "Writing *Where in the Wild?: Camouflaged Animals Concealed—and Revealed: Ear-tickling Poems,* with my husband, children's author David M. Schwartz, gave me the opportunity to mix my love of poetry with his background in writing children's science and math books. We have just finished writing a sequel, called *Where Else in the Wild?: More Camouflaged Creatures Concealed . . . and Revealed,* which will be published by Tricycle Press in 2009. We will also be writing a third book in the series, called *What in the Wild?,* to be published in 2010.

"The other thing that I love most in life is dancing, which I use to teach teamwork."

Biographical and Critical Sources

PERIODICALS

Booklist, November 1, 2007, Carolyn Phelan, review of *Where in the Wild?: Camouflaged Animals Concealed—and Revealed: Ear-tickling Poems,* p. 50.

New York Times Book Review, April 13, 2008, review of *Where in the Wild?,* p. 19.

School Library Journal, August, 2007, Margaret Bush, review of *Where in the Wild?,* p. 105.

ONLINE

Dramatic Strides Web site, http://www.DramaticStrides.com/ (January 15, 2009).*

*   *   *

SEDGWICK, Marcus 1968-

Personal

Born 1968, in England; married; children: Alice.

Addresses

Home—Sussex, England.

Career

Writer, beginning 1994; Walker Books, London, England, sales manager. Formerly worked as a bookseller for Heffers (children's bookshop), Cambridge, England; as a sales manager for Ragged Bears (children's book publisher), Somerset, England; and as an editor for Templar Publishing, Dorking, England. Stone carver and wood engraver; performer with International Band of Mystery ("Austin Powers" tribute band and acting troupe), as drummer Basil Exposition.

Awards, Honors

Branford Boase Award, 2000, for *Floodland;* Edgar Allan Poe Award nomination, Mystery Writers of America, Independent Reading Association award nomination, and Portsmouth Book Award nomination, all 2001, all for *Witch Hill;* Carnegie Medal shortlist, London *Guardian* Children's Fiction Prize shortlist, and Blue Peter Book Award shortlist, all 2002, all for *The Dark Horse;* Sheffield Book Award shortlist, *Guardian* Book Award nomination, and Edgar Allan Poe shortlist, all for *The Book of Dead Days;* Booktrusted Teenage Prize shortlist, Salford Book Award shortlist, Angus Book Award shortlist, Best Book for Young Adults designation, American Library Association, Portsmouth Book Award, North East Teenage Book Award, and Notable Tradebooks for Young People selection, National Council for the Social Studies, all 2007, all for *The Foreshadowing;* Booktrusted Teenage Book Prize, 2007, for *My Swordhand Is Singing;* Costa Children's Book Award shortlist, 2007, for *Blood Red, Snow White.*

Writings

Floodland, Orion (London, England), 2000, Delacorte (New York, NY), 2001.

Witch Hill, Delacorte (New York, NY), 2001.

The Dark Horse, Orion (London, England), 2002, Wendy Lamb (New York, NY), 2003.

(Editor) Helen Ward, *The Dragon Machine,* illustrated by Wayne Anderson, Templar (Dorking, England), 2003.

Cowards, Orion (London, England), 2003.

The Book of Dead Days (also see below), Orion (London, England), 2003, Wendy Lamb (New York, NY), 2004.

A Winter's Tale (picture book), illustrated by Simon Bartram, Templar (London, England), 2003, published as *A Christmas Wish,* Dutton (New York, NY), 2003.

(Reteller) *The Emperor's New Clothes* (picture book), illustrated by Alison Jay, Chronicle Books (San Francisco, CA), 2004.

The Dark Flight Down (sequel to *The Book of Dead Days*), Orion (London, England), 2004, Wendy Lamb Books (New York, NY), 2005.

The Foreshadowing, Orion (London, England), 2005, Wendy Lamb Books (New York, NY), 2006.

My Swordhand Is Singing, Wendy Lamb Books (New York, NY), 2006.

Blood Red, Snow White, Orion (London, England), 2007.

The Kiss of Death, Orion (London, England), 2008.

Flood and Fang ("Raven Mysteries" series), Orion (London, England), 2008.

Contributor to *The Restless Dead: Ten Original Stories of the Supernatural,* edited by Deborah Noyes, Candlewick Press (Cambridge, MA), 2007. Contributor of book reviews to London *Guardian.*

ILLUSTRATOR

Nick Riddle, editor, *Outremer: Jaufre Rudel and the Countess of Tripoli: A Legend of the Crusades,* Fisher King, 1994.

June Counsel, *Once upon Our Time,* Glyndley Books, 2000.

Sidelights

British author Marcus Sedgwick is well known for the dark themes in his critically acclaimed fantasy novels for young adults, including *Witch Hill, The Book of Dead Days,* and *The Kiss of Death.* "I'm famous for

Cover of Marcus Sedgwick's fantasy novel The Dark Horse, *featuring artwork by Cliff Nielsen.* (Jacket illustration copyright © 2003 by Cliff Nielsen. All rights reserved. Used by permission of Random House Children's Books, a division of Random House, Inc.)

being a gloom merchant and for writing dark and serious books (not that I think that they are as dark or as serious as other people seem to . . .) but I do have a sense of humour," the author stated in a *Bookseller* interview with Caroline Horn. Sedgwick has written books about a world flooded by global warming, a magician who has made a pact with a demon for his soul, and a girl with magic powers living in an ancient Nordic tribe. He is also the author of several cheerful picture books and has illustrated a collection of myths and a book of folktales for adults.

After working as a bookseller and working inside children's publishing, Sedgwick began writing seriously in 1994. His first book, *Floodland,* was published in 2000 to praise from critics, and it received the Branford Boase Award for the best first children's novel of that year. *Floodland* tells the story of Zoe, who lives on her own on an island that used to be part of England before global warming caused the sea levels to rise. Trying to find her family, Zoe leaves her island and lands on the Island of Eels, where there is a power struggle over the limited food and supplies the island has to offer. "Most readers will enjoy this survival story for its heart-pounding plot and dystopic setting," commented Ellen Fader in *School Library Journal.*

Although a *Horn Book* reviewer commented that the story would have benefited from more-developed characters, Sedgwick's "first novel is sufficiently taut, accessible, and swift moving to make it an effective cautionary tale." Lynne T. Burke termed *Floodland* a "nailbiter" in her review for *Reading Today,* while Barry Schwartz praised the "gripping ending" in his *Book Report* review.

Sedgwick followed *Floodland* with *Witch Hill,* the tale of a boy named Jamie, whose house is destroyed by fire, and who believes that his baby sister was killed in the flames before he could rescue her. Unable to put his memories of the fire from his mind, Jamie begins dreaming of an evil old witch trying to harm him, and a girl who is the victim of a witch hunt. It seems that the dreams have more meaning than normal nightmares, and that Jamie's dreams are tied into both the history of the town and the series of strange and terrifying events now trouble the village. John Peters, writing in *Booklist,* warned: "Don't read this suspenseful tale at bedtime."

The Dark Horse borrows its tone from Norse myth. Sigurd's clan is threatened by a group of raiders known only as the Dark Horse. His adopted sister, Mouse, who was raised by animals when she was very young and can still communicate with them, seems to be connected to the Dark Horse in some strange way. Sigurd and Mouse must go together on a quest to retrieve a mysterious box that only one person can open, which they retrieve near a stranger, who at first seems helpful, but later seems to be more dangerous than either of them realize. As Coop Renner wrote in *School Library Journal,* "Making no concessions to moralizing or romanticizing, Sedgwick's tale is rich, involving, and vivifying."

Cover of Sedgwick's **The Book of Dead Days,** *featuring artwork by Geoff Taylor.* (Jacket illustration copyright © 2004 by Geoff Taylor. All rights reserved. Used by permission of Random House Children's Books, a division of Random House, Inc.)

ing." *Horn Book* reviewer Joanna Rudge Long wrote of *The Dark Horse* that "the bleak setting is fully realized . . . and the events are gripping."

In *The Book of Dead Days* Sedgwick returns to the themes of magic and its dangers. Here the magician Valerian and his servant, Boy, seek a way for Valerian to get out of a pact he made with a demon. In a city reminiscent of eighteenth-century Europe, Boy, along with an orphaned girl named Willow, follows Valerian, knowing only that if they do not help him, he will die. The three search for a mysterious book that may help Valerian find a way to avoid his fate. In *The Dark Flight Down* Boy and Willow are captured by Emperor Frederick, a terrifying man who employs necromancers. Reviewing *The Book of Dead Days* for *Horn Book,* Joanna Rudge Long commented that Sedgwick's "dark thriller reaches a satisfactory denouement" leaving readers waiting for answers in the sequel. "Readers who enjoy fast-paced melodrama with an overlay of the supernatural will devour this tale and wait eagerly for the next installment," predicted Bruce Anne Shook in a review for *School Library Journal.* A contributor to *Kirkus Reviews* named the first installment a "fascinatingly brooding tale," and Ilene Cooper noted in *Booklist,* that *The Book of Dead Days* "is a haunting novel, and the possibility of more is definitely enticing."

Sedgwick returns to a more modern setting with *Cowards,* a nonfiction work about two young men who refuse to fight during World War I, because they believe that killing is wrong. Labeled by many as cowards, the men are imprisoned, tortured, and eventually killed due to their beliefs. Staying away from the magical elements marking his earlier novels, in *Cowards* Sedgwick raises modern concerns about the morality of war. "Research is essential in historical writing because the details need to be accurate," the author stated in an online interview on the *Children's Literature Comprehensive Database,* adding that *Cowards* "took about nine months of research in the Imperial War Museum as well as background reading and online searching."

Like *Cowards, The Foreshadowing* is set during World War I. After her older brother is sent into combat, Alexandra "Sasha" Fox, a British teen, begins having frightening visions of her sibling's death. After training as a nurse, she journeys to France, where she hopes to warn her brother and prevent his untimely end. "Sedgwick keeps this story going relentlessly," noted Claire Rosser in *Kliatt,* citing the novel's "short chapters, haunting images, a courageous heroine, and questions about honor and patriotism that continue to resonate." The author's "fast-paced, minimalist style is well suited to the bleakness of war," observed *Horn Book* contributor Claire E. Gross, and Gillian Engberg, reviewing *The Foreshadowing* in *Booklist,* praised the "unusually powerful, visceral view of war's horrors . . . in which the real and the supernatural are inextricably linked."

A horror story set in seventeenth-century Europe, *My Swordhand Is Singing* concerns Peter, a woodcutter, and his violent, hard-drinking father, Tomas. The pair settles in a remote village where it is soon learned that the dead rise from their graves at night to hunt the living. When Peter meets Sofia, a gypsy girl, he learns of his father's mysterious past, and he must then convince Tomas to battle the zombie-like creatures with a powerful sword. *My Swordhand Is Singing* "is as dark and chilling as a foggy midnight," wrote Ian Chipman in *Booklist,* and a *Publishers Weekly* contributor remarked that Sedgwick "knows his way around a gothic setting, and readers will likely devour this bone-chiller." *My Swordhand Is Singing* received the prestigious Booktrusted Teenage Book Prize.

In *The Kiss of Death,* a sequel to *My Swordhand Is Singing,* young Marko travels to Venice to search for his missing father. He meets Sorrel, the daughter of a glassmaker who has gone mad, Sorrel's suspicious neighbor, Venetia, and Peter, now an old man who arrives in the city to vanquish the Shadow Queen. According to London *Guardian* reviewer Mary Hoffman, Sedgwick "is superb, as in the earlier book about the undead, at creating atmosphere. There it was all snow and ice and shambling zombies; here it is mist, corruption and masks, concealing whether figures in the night are friends or foes." Craig offered praise for the author's distinct narrative, stating that "each chapter is

only two or three pages long, and often interspersed with fairytales, letters, diary entries and so on. The effect is not unlike one of those collages, built up by glueing small pieces of torn-up colour magazines to form an image that is both disturbing and suggestive of a bigger picture."

Sedgwick examines the role one man played during the Russian Revolution of 1917 in *Blood Red, Snow White,* "a magical book that blends bloodthirsty folk tale, rip-roaring adventure, romance and the remarkable true story of one of our favourite children's authors: Arthur Ransome," noted Danuta Kean on the *Orion Books* Web site. Ransome, who created the popular "Swallows and Amazons" series, traveled to Russia in 1913. There he fell in love with Evgenia Petrovna Shelepina, the secretary of communist revolutionary Leon Trotsky, and also became involved in espionage activities against the Russian czar. "Sedgwick has a faultless ear for the narrative voice of his subject," observed London *Times* contributor Amanda Craig, "and the real-life story he reveals about spies, adultery, bloodshed and a fortune in gold that follows is irresistible."

Much lighter in tone than his novels, Sedgwick's picture books also involve magical occurrences. *A Winter's Tale,* published in the United States as *A Christmas Wish,* tells the story of a boy who lives in a fairly warm climate who wishes for snow for Christmas, so that his home will look like the world in his snow globe. In the night, his wish is granted, and snow surrounds his home, freezing the nearby lake to allow the boy to ice skate. Characters such as gingerbread men, polar bears, dancers, living snowmen, and a snow wizard—presumably the one responsible for the magic—appear to fill the snowy wonderland. "The reader must decide if [the story] is happening outdoors, in the snow globe, or in the boy's imagination," commented a contributor to *Kirkus Reviews.* Calling the plot fairly thin, Karin Snelson nevertheless admitted in *Booklist* that any reader who had ever been transfixed by the magic of a snow globe "may be transported by this visual winter fantasy."

In *The Emperor's New Clothes,* a retelling "true to the spirit of the original" according to Carolyn Phelan in *Booklist,* Sedgwick brings Hans Christian Andersen's story to readers in the form of rhymed couplets. The traditional tale relates how two swindling tailors, here depicted as weasels, convince an emperor that they have magical cloth which appears to be invisible to the unworthy. The emperor, drawn as a lion in Sedgwick's illustrated retelling, does not wish to seem unworthy, and commissions a robe made of the magical cloth. His advisors (a tortoise and a hare) take turns admiring the imaginary cloth, until a small frog child at the end of the book points out the obvious fact that the emperor is naked. Maria B. Salvadore called Sedgwick's version "a fresh look and sound for an old tale," and a reviewer for *Publishers Weekly* praised the book as a "buoyant collaboration" between Sedgwick and illustrator Allison Jay.

Cover of Sedgwick's novel The Dark Flight Down, *featuring artwork by Geoff Taylor.* (Cover illustration copyright © 2005 by Geoff Taylor. All rights reserved. Used by permission of Wendy Lamb Books, an imprint of Random House Children's Books, a division of Random House. Inc.)

Sedgwick lives in Sussex, England, with his daughter, Alice. When he is not writing, he performs as a drummer and actor with the International Band of Mystery, a group that pays tribute to the "Austin Powers" movies. Sedgwick also travels to schools and literary festivals to give workshops on writing. Describing his wishes for his readers, he stated on his home page: "I hope they finish one of my books having been entertained, and maybe moved. I hope that they might remember them for a while, and I hope that they might look at something a bit differently."

Biographical and Critical Sources

PERIODICALS

Booklist, October 1, 2001, John Peters, review of *Witch Hill,* p. 320; September 15, 2003, Karin Snelson, review of *A Christmas Wish,* p. 248; September 1, 2004, Ilene Cooper, review of *The Book of Dead Days,* p. 123; October 1, 2004, Carolyn Phelan, review of *The Book of Dead Days,* p. 338; June 1, 2005, Ilene Cooper, review of *The Dark Flight Down,* p. 1792; April 1, 2006, Gillian Engberg, review of *The Foreshadowing,* p. 43; November 15, 2007, Ian Chipman, review of *My Swordhand Is Singing,* p. 37.

Book Report, November-December, 2001, Barry Schwartz, review of *Floodland,* p. 66.

Bookseller, November 21, 2008, Caroline Horn, "A Raven with Something to Crow About," p. 26.

Guardian (London, England), October 11, 2008, Mary Hoffman, review of *The Kiss of Death,* p. 14.

Horn Book, March, 2001, Joanna Rudge Long, review of *Floodland,* p. 213; March-April, 2003, Joanna Rudge Long, review of *The Dark Horse,* p. 217; November-December, 2004, Joanna Rudge Long, review of *The Book of Dead Days,* p. 718; November-December, 2008, Joanna Rudge Long, review of *The Dark Flight Down,* p. 725; May-June, 2006, Claire E. Gross, review of *The Foreshadowing,* p. 330.

Kirkus Reviews, November 1, 2003, review of *A Christmas Wish,* p. 1320; September 1, 2004, review of *The Emperor's New Clothes,* p. 874; October 1, 2004, review of *The Book of Dead Days,* p. 968.

Kliatt, May, 2006, Claire Rosser, review of *The Foreshadowing,* p. 14; September, 2007, Paula Rohrlick, review of *My Swordhand Is Singing,* p. 18.

Publishers Weekly, January 29, 2001, review of *Floodland,* p. 90; September 22, 2003, review of *A Christmas Wish,* p. 71; September 6, 2004, review of *The Emperor's New Clothes,* p. 61; November 12, 2007, review of *My Swordhand Is Singing,* p. 57.

Reading Today, June, 2001, Lynne T. Burke, review of *Floodland,* p. 32.

School Library Journal, March, 2001, Ellen Fader, review of *Floodland,* p. 256; September, 2001, Janet Hilburn, review of *Witch Hill,* p. 232; November, 2001, Lori Craft, review of *Floodland,* p. 76; March, 2003, Coop Renner, review of *The Dark Horse,* p. 237; October, 2003, Susan Patron, review of *A Christmas Wish,* p. 67; October, 2004, Maria B. Salvadore, review of *The Emperor's New Clothes,* p. 129; November, 2004, Bruce Anne Shook, review of *The Book of Dead Days,* p. 154; February, 2006, Walter Minkel, review of *The Dark Flight Down,* p. 136.

Times (London, England), July 21, 2007, Nicolette Jones, review of *Blood Red, Snow White,* p. 49; August 23, 2008, Amanda Craig, review of *The Kiss of Death,* p. 15.

ONLINE

Children's Literature Comprehensive Database, http://www.childrenslit.com/ (February 1, 2009), "Q&A with Marcus Sedgwick."

Marcus Sedgwick Home Page, http://www.marcussedgwick.com (February 1, 2009).

Marcus Sedgwick Web log, http://marcussedgwick.blogspot.com/ (February 1, 2009).

Orion Books Web site, http://www.orionbooks.co.uk/ (February 1, 2009), Danuta Kean, interview with Sedgwick.

Random House Web site, http://www.randomhouse.com/ (February 1, 2009), "Marcus Sedgwick."*

*   *   *

SMALLMAN, Steve

Personal
Born in England.

Addresses
E-mail—sbsillustration@aol.com.

Career
Children's book author and illustrator.

Writings

Bumbletum, illustrated by Tim Warnes, Tiger Tales (Wilton, CT), 2006.
The Very Greedy Bee, illustrated by Jack Tickle, Tiger Tales (Wilton, CT), 2007.
The Lamb Who Came for Dinner, illustrated by Joelle Dreidemy, Tiger Tales (Wilton, CT), 2007.

ILLUSTRATOR

(Ellen Miles, reteller) Kenneth Grahame, *The Wind in the Willows,* Scholastic (New York, NY), 2002.
Gwen Ellis, reteller, *The Story of Easter,* Thomas Nelson (Nashville, TN), 2007.
Gwen Ellis, reteller, *Christmas Angels,* Thomas Nelson (Nashville, TN), 2007.
(With Jeffrey Ebbeler) Gwen Ellis, *Our Together-Time Bible,* Thomas Nelson (Nashville, TN), 2009.

Biographical and Critical Sources

PERIODICALS

Kirkus Reviews, August 1, 2007, review of *The Lamb Who Came for Dinner.*
School Librarian, summer, 2006, Joyce Banks, review of *Bumbletum,* p. 78; summer, 2007, Heidi Barton, review of *The Lamb Who Came for Dinner,* p. 53.
School Library Journal, May, 2007, DeAnn Okamura, review of *The Very Greedy Bee,* p. 108.

ONLINE

Steve Smallman Home Page, http://www.stevesmallman. info (January 15, 2009).*

*   *   *

SNEIDER, Marian 1932-2005

Personal
Born 1932; died in FL, 2005.

Career
Writer.

Writings

(With Ruth Vander Zee) *Eli Remembers,* illustrated by Bill Farnsworth, Eerdmans Books for Young Readers (Grand Rapids, MI), 2007.

Contributor to periodicals, including *Highlights for Children* and *Turtle.*

Sidelights
The late Marian Sneider was a family therapist and an author who wrote for *Highlights for Children, Turtle,* and two Miami area newspapers. At a writers' meeting, she presented a personal story, based on the experiences of her young grandson, Ely Sandler. Ely had just come back from a trip to Lithuania with his grandfather. He learned that between July, 1941 and August, 1944, between 70,000 and 80,000 Jews, including seven members of Sneider's family, as well as 20,000 Poles and 8,000 Russians, were killed and buried in mass graves near Ponary, Lithuania, in the Ponar Forest. Ruth Vander Zee heard this story, and having published a previous book about the Holocaust, she arranged with Sneider to coauthor *Eli Remembers.*

According to a contributor to *Publishers Weekly,* in *Eli Remembers* Sneider and Vander Zee "use simple, direct language to follow Eli's trajectory from puzzlement and ignorance to horrific realization and resolve." Hazel Rochman, writing in *Booklist,* respected the book as an experience in sharing family history in many Jewish survivor families, but added that, "unfortunately, the present-day scenario is sentimentalized; the characters are almost greeting-card icons of grief and love." In an interview with Sue Corbett for the *Miami Herald,* Vander Zee discussed how the book was written. "Having a Jew [Sneider] and a Christian write a book together is a unique experience because we look at life so differently," she explained. Vander Zee saw a story of forgiveness, while Sneider saw a story of remembrance. Sneider died in 2005, six months after *Eli Remembers* found a publisher.

Biographical and Critical Sources

PERIODICALS

Booklist, July 1, 2007, Hazel Rochman, review of *Eli Remembers,* p. 59.

Miami Herald, November 17, 2007, "Boy's Past Revives War Story."

Publishers Weekly, September 24, 2007, review of *Eli Remembers,* p. 71.

Social Education, May-June, 2008, review of *Eli Remembers,* p. S14.*

T

TALLEC, Olivier 1970-

Personal
Born 1970, in Morlaix, Brittany, France. *Education:* Attended École Duperré (Paris, France).

Addresses
Home—France. *E-mail*—otallec@gmail.com.

Career
Writer.

Writings

(Self-illustrated) *Noël dans le ciel,* Desclée de Brouwer (France), 2001.

ILLUSTRATOR

Emmanuel Viau, *Anton et la musique Cubaine,* Gallimard (Paris, France), 1998.

Jean-Marc Ligny, *Les dëmons de Mamyvone,* Nathan (Paris, France), 1999.

Mon imagier sonore, Gallimard (Paris, France), 2000.

Agnès Bertron, *La sieste des mamans,* Père Castor Flammarion (Paris, France), 2000.

Michel Butor, *Zoo,* Rue du Monde (Paris, France), 2001.

Anne Bustarret, *Mon imagier des amusettes,* Gallimard (Paris, France), 2001.

Sylvie Poillevé, *Le plus féroce des loups,* Père Castor Flammarion (Paris, France), 2001.

Alain Serres and Lily Franey, *L'Abëcëdire,* Rue du Monde (Paris, France), 2001.

Anne Tardy, *L'île aux Ëtoiles,* Desclée de Brouwer (France), 2001.

Evelyne Reberg, *Ito ou la vengeance du Samouraï,* Albin Michel (Paris, France), 2001.

Jean-François Chabas, *Aurélien Malte,* Hachette (Paris, France), 2001.

Alain Serres, *Salade de Comptines (+1 Dessert Offert),* Rue du Monde (Paris, France), 2002.

Françoise Kérisel, *Prëhistorique,* Desclée de Brouwer (France), 2002.

Mon imagier des animaux sauvages, Gallimard (Paris, France), 2002.

Alain Serres, *La devise de ma rëpublique,* Rue du Monde (Paris, France), 2002.

Sarah K., *J'suis pas à la mode,* Père Castor Flammarion (Paris, France), 2002.

Clotilde Bernos, *Oh là là Lola,* Rue du Monde (Paris, France), 2003.

Anne Bustarret, *Mon imagier des Rondes,* Gallimard (Paris, France), 2003.

René Gouichoux, *Manan ours est Partie,* Père Castor Flammarion (Paris, France), 2003.

Jarmila Kurucova, *La sorcière du bout de la rue,* Bibloquet (France), 2003.

Blandine Lathuillière, *Belle du nuit,* Casterman (Paris, France), 2003.

Claudine Aubrun, *Profession: Pirate!,* Desclée de Brouwer (France), 2004.

Thierry Lenain, *Il Faudra,* Sarbacane (Paris, France), 2004.

Claire Babin, *Gustave est un poisson,* La Baron Perché (France), 2004, translated by Claudia Zoe Bedrick as *Gus Is a Fish,* Enchanted Lion (New York, NY), 2008.

Claire Babin, *Gustave est un Arbre,* La Baron Perché (France), 2004, translated by Claudia Zoe Bedrick as *Gus Is a Tree,* Enchanted Lion (New York, NY), 2008.

Claire Babin, *Gustave est un oiseau,* La Baron Perché (France), 2004.

Daniel Picouly, reteller, *Poucette de Toulaba,* Rue du Monde (Paris, France), 2005, translated by Claudia Zoe Bedrick as *Thumbelina of Toulaba,* Enchanted Lion (New York, NY), 2007.

Barnard Davois and François Laurière, *Mon imagier de l'alphabet,* Gallimard (Paris, France), 2005.

Carl Norac, *Le carnaval des animaux,* Sarbacane (Paris, France), 2005.

Madame Leprince de Beaumont, *La belle et la Bête,* Père Castor Flammarion (Paris, France), 2005.

Nadine Brun-Cosme, *Grand loup et petit loup,* Père Castor Flammarion (Paris, France), 2005.

Jean-Pierre Siméon, *Ceci est un poème qui guërit les poissons,* Rue du Monde (Paris, France), 2005, translated by Claudia Zoe Bedrick as *This Is a Poem That Heals Fish,* Enchanted Lion (New York, NY), 2007.

Henri Troyat, *Babouchka,* Père Castor Flammarion (Paris, France), 2005.

Jean-Philipppe Arrou-Vignod, *Rita et Machin,* Gallimard (Paris, France), 2006, translated as *Rita and Whatsit,* Chronicle (San Francisco, CA), 2009.

Jean-Philipppe Arrou-Vignod, *Rita et Machin à l'école,* Gallimard (Paris, France), 2006.

Jean-Philipppe Arrou-Vignod, *Rita et Machin à la plage,* Gallimard (Paris, France), 2006.

Jean-Philipppe Arrou-Vignod, *Le noël de Rita et Machin,* Gallimard (Paris, France), 2006.

Jean-Philipppe Arrou-Vignod, *Le dimanche de Rita et Machin,* Gallimard (Paris, France), 2006.

Alain Serres, *Je vous aime tant,* Rue du Monde (Paris, France), 2006.

Sylvie Neeman, *Mercredi à la librairie,* Sarbacane (Paris, France), 2007.

Alain Serres, *Maintenant,* Rue du Monde (Paris, France), 2007.

Jean-Philipppe Arrou-Vignod, *L'invité de Rita et Machin,* Gallimard (Paris, France), 2007.

Jean-Philipppe Arrou-Vignod, *Les courses de Rita et Machin,* Gallimard (Paris, France), 2007.

Valentine Goby, *Le rève de Jacek de la pologne aux corons du nord,* Ricochet (Paris, France), 2007.

Nadine Brun-Cosme, *Le petite feuille qui ne tombait pas,* Père Castor Flammarion (Paris, France), 2007.

Roland Fuentès, *Charlepogne et Poilenfrac,* La Baron Perché (France), 2007.

Jean-Philipppe Arrou-Vignod, *Rita et Machin à la piscine,* Gallimard (Paris, France), 2008.

Jean-Philipppe Arrou-Vignod, *La cachette de Rita et Machin,* Gallimard (Paris, France), 2008.

Valentine Goby, *Adama ou la vie en 3D, du Mali a Saint-Denis,* Autrement (France), 2008.

Sidelights

French illustrator Olivier Tallec has been working on children's books since 1997, and has illustrated approximately thirty titles in France, several of which have also been released in the United States. Talec studied both visual and applied arts, attended the École Duperré in Paris, France, and has contributed art work to magazines, including *Libération* and *Elle.* He is also the author of the self-illustrated picture book *Noël dans le ciel.*

Tallec's illustrations have accompanied traditional tales and original stories. In a retelling of Hans Christian Andersen's *Thumbelina of Toulaba,* Tallec's "striking illustrations . . . inventively present the world through Thumbelina's perspective," wrote a contributor to *Kirkus Reviews.* Noting that the reteller gives the tale a Caribbean flare, Donna Cardon wrote in *School Library Journal* that "Tallec's bold, stylized illustrations reflect the exotic feel of the text."

Tallec has provided the illustrations for three titles by Claire Babin that focus on an imaginative boy named Gustave. Two of the tales (published in the United States as *Gus Is a Fish* and *Gus Is a Tree*) combine mixed-media and acrylic images with photography. For *This Is a Poem That Heals Fish,* by Jean-Pierre Siméon, Tallec contributes "stylized, simplified color paintings," according to a *Children's Bookwatch* critic. Tallec's "imaginative fauvist illustrations capture the fanciful, free mood" wrote a contributor to *Kirkus Reviews.* A *Publishers Weekly* critic described Tallec's contributions to Siméon's story as composed of "delicate pencil lines and wet strokes of vibrant color."

Biographical and Critical Sources

PERIODICALS

Children's Bookwatch, April, 2007, review of *This Is a Poem That Heals Fish;* September, 2007, review of *Thumbelina of Toulaba.*

Kirkus Reviews, March 1, 2007, review of *This Is a Poem That Heals Fish,* p. 232; September 15, 2007, review of *Thumbelina of Toulaba;* May, 2008, review of *Gus Is a Fish.*

Publishers Weekly, May 7, 2007, review of *This Is a Poem That Heals Fish,* p. 59.

School Library Journal, July, 2007, Kathleen Whalin, review of *This Is a Poem That Heals Fish,* p. 85; November, 2007, Donna Cardon, review of *Thumbelina of Toulaba,* p. 98.

ONLINE

Chez Antoine Agency Web site, http://www.chezantoine.com/ (February 24, 2009), "Olivier Tallec."

Olivier Tallec Home Page, http://www.oliviertallec.com (February 24, 2009).

Ricochet Jeunes Web site, http://www.ricochet-jeunes.org/ (February 24, 2009), "Olivier Tallec."*

*   *   *

THOMAS, Jan 1958-

Personal
Born 1958.

Addresses
Home—Sorroco, NM.

Career
Writer and illustrator.

Writings

SELF-ILLUSTRATED

What Will Fat Cat Sit On?, Harcourt (Orlando, FL), 2007.
A Birthday for Cow!, Harcourt (Orlando, FL), 2008.
In the Doghouse, Harcourt (Orlando, FL), 2008.
Rhyming Dust Bunnies, Atheneum (New York, NY), 2008.

Sidelights

Author and illustrator Jan Thomas is the creator of a series of picture-book tales about farmyard friends. In *What Will Fat Cat Sit On?,* the farmyard animals are less concerned about where Fat Cat will sit than who will wind up beneath him! A *Publishers Weekly* critic found the book to be "a rollicking and highly promising debut," while a contributor to *Kirkus Reviews* dubbed it

Cover of Jan Thomas's self-illustrated **The Doghouse,** ***which features large-format cartoon art.*** (Copyright © 2008 by Jan Thomas. All rights reserved. Reproduced by permission of Houghton Mifflin Harcourt Publishing Company. This material may not be reproduced in any form or by any means without the prior written permission of the publisher.)

a volume that "toddlers and new readers will reach for again and again." Blair Christolon commented in *School Library Journal* on the tale's "well-paced, laugh-out-loud humor."

Familiar characters return in *A Birthday for Cow!* and *In the Doghouse.* Pig and Mouse bake a cake for Cow in *A Birthday for Cow!,* while they try to keep Duck from adding an unwanted turnip to the recipe. Thomas's "riotous read-aloud is guaranteed to have them rolling in the aisles," wrote a contributor to *Kirkus Reviews.* G. Alyssa Parkinson noted in *School Library Journal* that Thomas's "whimsical story" is "told in simple language." Mouse, Duck, and Pig find themselves entering new territory when cow kicks a ball far afield in *In the Doghouse.* A *Kirkus Reviews* contributor noted of the same book that Thomas's "successful use of repetition [is] . . . realized through succinct sentences," making *In the Doghouse* approachable for new readers.

Biographical and Critical Sources

PERIODICALS

Kirkus Reviews, August 1, 2007, review of *What Will Fat Cat Sit On?*; March 1, 2008, review of *A Birthday for Cow!*; August 1, 2008, review of *In the Doghouse.*

Publishers Weekly, September 10, 2007, review of *What Will Fat Cat Sit On?,* p. 59.

School Library Journal, December, 2007, Blair Christolon, review of *What Will Fat Cat Sit On?,* p. 101; June, 2008, G. Alyssa Parkinson, review of *A Birthday for Cow!,* p. 114.

ONLINE

Jan Thomas Home Page, http://www.janthomasbooks.com (February 18, 2009).*

*   *   *

TOLEDO, Natalia 1967-
(Natalia Toledo Paz)

Personal

Born 1967, in Juchitán, Oaxaca, Mexico; daughter of Francisco Toledo (a painter).

Addresses

Home—Mexico.

Career

Poet and writer. President of Patronato de la Casa de la Cultura de Juchitán.

Awards, Honors

Scholarships in indigenous languages from Fondo Nacional para la Cultura y las Artes, 1994-95, 2001-02, and Fondo Estatal para la Cultura y las Artes de Oaxaca, 1995-96; Nezahualcyotl de Literatura, prize in contemporary indigenous literature, 2004, for *Guie' Yaasé'.*

Writings

(With Rocío González) *Paraíso de Fisuras,* Casa de la Cultura Oaxaqueña (Oaxaca de Juárez, Mexico), 1992.

(As Natalia Toledo Paz) *Ca Gunaa Gubidxa Ca Gunaa Guiiba Ìrisaca/Mujeres de sol, mujeres de oro,* Instituto Oaxaqueño, 2002.

Guie' Yaasé', 2003.

(With father, Francisco Toledo) *La muerte pies ligeros,* Instituto Estatal de Educación Pública de Oaxaca (Oaxaxa, México), 2006, bilingual edition published as *Light Foot/ Pies Ligeros,* Groundwood Books (Toronto, Ontario, Canada), 2007.

Author's works have been translated into several Mexican dialects.

Sidelights

Born in Juchitá, Oaxaca, Mexico in 1968, Natalia Toledo became involved with the indigenous language movement in Mexico while she studied at the Casa de la Cultura de Juchitán, her home city's "house of culture." While a student, she learned how to write in the Zapotec language, the tongue of the native culture of southern Oaxaca. Toledo herself grew up surrounded by two languages, speaking Zapotec at home and Spanish at school. Her poetry and stories draw heavily on the unique regional tales she has learned from people in her family and in the rural areas of Oaxaca near where she grew up.

A few of Toledo's books have been translated for an English-language audience and feature both Spanish and English texts. *Light Foot/ Pies Ligeros* is a picture book Toledo created to frame a series of paintings done by her father, well-known Mexican painter Francisco Toledo. With a bilingual English/Spanish text, the book retells a folk story in which Death challenges the animals to a jump rope contest in an effort to control the world's population. If Death wins, the animals will die; but fortunately Grasshopper is able to challenge Death before that happens. "The text includes little jump-rope rhymes that Death recites to his victims," wrote Tim Wadham in *School Library Journal,* the critic adding that the tale and the art might be too scary for a young audience. Although Michelle Gowans judged the themes in the book to be very subtle, she wrote in *Resource Links* that *Light Foot/ Pies Ligeros* "is a clever little folktale, with well-crafted rhymes peppered throughout the text."

Natalia Toledo teams up with artist father Francisco Toledo to create the bilingual, Mexican-themed picture book Light Foot/ Pies Ligeros. (Groundwood Books, 2006. Illustration copyright © 2006 by Francisco Toledo. All rights reserved. Reproduced by permission.)

Biographical and Critical Sources

PERIODICALS

Resource Links, December, 2007, Michelle Gowans, review of *Light Foot/ Pies Ligeros,* p. 13.
School Library Journal, March, 2008, Tim Wadham, review of *Light Foot/ Pies Ligeros,* p. 192.

ONLINE

Laventana Casa Web site, http://laventana.casa.cult.cu/ (January 23, 2006), Spanish-language interview with Toledo.
Letralia: Tierra de Letras Web site, http://www.letralia. com/ (November 22, 2004), Spanish-language article about Toledo.*

V-W

VERE, Ed

Personal
Born in England. *Education:* Attended Camberwell College of Arts.

Addresses
Home—London, England. *E-mail*—ed@edvere.com.

Career
Author and illustrator.

Awards, Honors
Kate Greenaway Medal shortlist, 2008, for *Banana!*

Writings

SELF-ILLUSTRATED

Everyone's Hungry, Orchard Books (New York, NY), 2000.
Everyone's Sleepy, Orchard Books (New York, NY), 2000.
Everyone's Little, Orchard Books (New York, NY), 2001.
Everyone's Noisy, Orchard Books (New York, NY), 2001.
It's Raining, Campbell Books (London, England), 2001.
It's Snowing, Campbell Books (London, England), 2001.
It's Sunny, Campbell Books (London, England), 2002.
It's Windy, Campbell Books (London, England), 2002.
The Getaway, Puffin (London, England), 2006, Margaret K. McElderry Books (New York, NY), 2007.
Banana!, Puffin (London, England), 2007.
Mr. Big, Puffin (London, England), 2007.

ILLUSTRATOR

Lisa Lawston, *Can You Hop?,* Orchard Books (New York, NY), 1999.

Lisa Lawston, *Can You Sing?,* Orchard Books (New York, NY), 1999.
Will Grace, *Red Train,* Scholastic (New York, NY), 2003.
Will Grace, *Five Little Dinosaurs,* Scholastic (New York, NY), 2004.

Sidelights
Ed Vere is a British artist and author known for his unconventional and slightly subversive children's books, including *The Getaway,* a self-illustrated title. "When I write I try to think about what would have entertained me when I was younger," Vere remarked in an interview for *Little Big* online. "I do sometimes think there's not much out there for small boys, so I try to appeal to that section of the market."

Vere, who grew up in the Peak District of central and northern England, developed an interest in art at a young age. He cites Maurice Sendak, Tomi Ungerer, and Richard Scarry as his first influences and describes E.H. Shepard, the original illustrator of Kenneth Grahame's *The Wind in the Willows,* as "one of my absolute heroes." Vere also developed a relationship with acclaimed author and illustrator Jan Pienkowski, a family friend and winner of the Kate Greenaway Medal. As Vere stated in his *Little Big* interview, "Visiting his [Pienkowki's] studio was always inspirational, to know someone whose job was to draw all day long—incredible!"

Vere studied fine art at the Camberwell College of Arts before launching his literary career; he now works from a studio in London, England. "My books, so far, are completely character driven," he noted. "I start the process of creating a book with a character rather than a plot. I need to find a compelling character who feels like they have a life of some kind, and then I'll try to find out what their story/motivation is."

The Getaway, a spoof of hard-boiled detective stories, centers on Fingers McGraw, a clever and notorious mouse with a penchant for pilfering cheese, and Jumbo

Wayne, Jr., the no-nonsense elephant detective assigned to bring Fingers to justice. As he speeds through the city aboard his yellow moped, Fingers appeals directly to the reader to help him avoid capture. The jumbo-sized lawman is not the only creature in hot pursuit, however; Fingers must also avoid some treacherous rats, an alert anteater, and a money-hungry rhino that plans to nab the cheese-pilfering rodent and claim the reward money. Vere uses mixed-media illustrations to depict the chase, with cartoon characters superimposed over photographs of urban areas. "Expository captions, printed in an uneven typewriter font, chart the crime Dragnet-style," noted a critic in *Publishers Weekly,* the reviewer comparing Vere's tale to the works of Mo Willems and Lauren Child.

Shelley B. Sutherland, reviewing *The Getaway* for *School Library Journal,* remarked that "the sheer energy and playfulness that are packed into every page will surely delight kids." In *Booklist* Randall Enos predicted that young readers "who like offbeat stories with quirky illustrations will enjoy this one." Other critics also praised the humorous deadpan dialogue in Vere's book, as well as his sly references to such classic noir films as *To Have and Have Not* starring Humphrey Bogart and Lauren Bacall. "There's terrific humour and surging energy in the wise-cracking text," observed Julia Eccleshare in the London *Guardian,* and London *Sunday Times* contributor Nicolette Jones wrote that, "verbally playful and visually stimulating, [*The Getaway*] . . . creates a complete world of its own."

Biographical and Critical Sources

PERIODICALS

Booklist, November 15, 2007, Randall Enos, review of *The Getaway,* p. 48.
Guardian (London, England), October 28, 2006, Julia Eccleshare, review of *The Getaway,* p. 20.
Kirkus Reviews, September 1, 2007, review of *The Getaway.*
Publishers Weekly, March 1, 1999, review of *Can You Hop?,* p. 71; September 4, 2000, review of *Everyone's Hungry,* p. 110; June 11, 2001, review of *Everyone's Noisy,* p. 87; September 17, 2007, review of *The Getaway,* p. 53.
School Library Journal, January, 2008, Shelley B. Sutherland, review of *The Getaway,* p. 100.
Sunday Times (London, England), October 22, 2006, Nicolette Jones, review of *The Getaway.*

ONLINE

Ed Vere Home Page, http://www.edvere.com (January 20, 2009).
Little Big Online, http://www.littlebigmagazine.com/ (October 1, 2008), "Bookish Type: Ed Vere."*

WALKER, David 1965-

Personal

Born 1965. *Education:* Graduated from University of Kansas.

Addresses

Office—David Walker Studios, 133 Graylyn Dr., Chapel Hill, NC 27516. *E-mail*—david@davidwalkerstudios.com.

Career

Artist and illustrator. Hallmark Cards, Kansas City, MO, former art director.

Illustrator

Ann Whitford Paul, *Little Monkey Says Good Night,* Farrar, Straus & Giroux (New York, NY), 2003.
Susan Meyers, *Puppies! Puppies! Puppies!,* Henry Abrams (New York, NY), 2005.
Susan Meyers, *Kittens! Kittens! Kittens!,* Henry Abrams (New York, NY), 2007.
Claire Masurel, *Domino,* Candlewick Press (Cambridge, MA), 2007.
Ann Whitford Paul, *If Animals Kissed Good Night,* Farrar, Straus & Giroux (New York, NY), 2008.
Maribeth Boelts, *Before You Were Mine,* Putnam (New York, NY), 2008.
Andy Hilford and Susan Hilford, *The Grandmother Book: A Book about You for Your Grandchild,* Andrews McMeel (Kansas City, MO), 2008.
Susan Middleton Elya, *No More, Por Favor,* Putnam (New York, NY), 2009.
Kim Norman, *Crocodaddy,* Sterling Publishing (New York, NY), 2009.
Phyllis Root, *Flip, Flap, Fly!: A Book for Babies Everywhere,* Random House (New York, NY), 2009.

Sidelights

Artist David Walker has contributed the illustrations to a number of picture books for young children. For one project, he teamed with author Ann Whitford Paul on *Little Monkey Says Good Night,* a humorous picture book about an energetic monkey's misadventures at the circus. When Little Monkey learns that he has to go to bed, he bounds into the Big Top to say good night to each of the performers, leaving chaos in his wake. Walker "presents the mischievous monkey's escapades via soft-edged, slapstick illustrations," noted a contributor in *Publishers Weekly,* and Marianne Saccardi wrote in *School Library Journal* that the illustrator's "whimsical cartoon paintings are essential to the enjoyment of the brief text." Walker and Paul also collaborate on *If Animals Kissed Good Night,* "a charming bedtime book," in the words of *School Library Journal* contributor Jane Marino. The story shows a host of animals—including pythons, sloths, and walruses—prepar-

ing for sleep. "Using soft color, Walker renders the nighttime rituals inventively," Abby Nolan wrote in her *Booklist* review of the work.

Walker also illustrated *Puppies! Puppies! Puppies!* and *Kittens! Kittens! Kittens!,* a pair of works by Susan Meyers that celebrates the enthusiasm of young animals. Reviewing the former in *School Library Journal,* Piper L. Nyman remarked that Walker's "delightful acrylic illustrations are warm and child friendly," and Ilene Cooper observed in *Booklist* that the pups have "a stuffed-animal look; kids will want to pick them up and give them a hug." In *Kittens! Kittens! Kittens!* Walker's soft-toned acrylic paintings give Meyers' text "a warm and fuzzy feeling," related Martha Simpson in *School Library Journal.*

A youngster adopts a shelter dog after his own pet dies in *Before You Were Mine,* a poignant story by Maribeth Boelts. Here Walker's "pastel illustrations use a variety of layouts to infuse the story with emotion," Kathleen Odean explained in *Booklist.* A *Kirkus Reviews* contributor also praised Boelts's narrative and Walker's illustrations, writing that they "combine to pack a small wallop directly to the hearts" of young readers.

Biographical and Critical Sources

PERIODICALS

Booklist, April 1, 2005, Ilene Cooper, review of *Puppies! Puppies! Puppies!,* p. 1359; January 1, 2007, Stephanie Zvirin, review of *Kittens! Kittens! Kittens!,* p. 115; December 1, 2007, Kathleen Odean, review of *Before You Were Mine,* p. 47; June 1, 2008, Abby Nolan, review of *If Animals Kissed Good Night,* p. 88.

Kirkus Reviews, March 15, 2007, review of *Kittens! Kittens! Kittens!;* September 1, 2007, review of *Before You Were Mine.*

Publishers Weekly, March 24, 2003, review of *Little Monkey Says Good Night,* p. 74; March 24, 2008, review of *If Animals Kissed Good Night,* p. 69.

School Library Journal, July, 2003, Marianne Saccardi, review of *Little Monkey Says Good Night,* p. 104; August, 2005, Piper L. Nyman, review of *Puppies! Puppies! Puppies!,* p. 103; March, 2007, Martha Simpson, review of *Kittens! Kittens! Kittens!,* p. 182; June, 2008, Jane Marino, review of *If Animals Kissed Good Night,* p. 113.

ONLINE

David Walker Home Page, http://www.davidwalkerstudios. com (January 20, 2009).*

*   *   *

WEAVER, Tess

Personal

Born in Coshocton, OH; married; children: two sons.

Addresses

Home—Iowa City, IA. *E-mail*—tessweaver@mcshi.com.

Career

Children's book author. Has also worked as a marketing manager, book reviewer, and copywriter.

Awards, Honors

Award for Excellence, Cat Writers' Association, New England Book Show Award, Oppenheim Toy Portfolio Best Book Platinum Award, and Oppenheim Toy Portfolio Best Book Gold Award, all 2003, all for *Opera Cat.*

Writings

Opera Cat, illustrated by Andréa Wesson, Clarion Books (New York, NY), 2002.

Cat Jumped In!, illustrated by Emily Arnold McCully, Clarion Books (New York, NY), 2007.

Frederick Finch, Loudmouth, illustrated by Debbie Tilley, Clarion Books (New York, NY), 2008.

Encore, Opera Cat, illustrated by Andréa Wesson, Clarion Books (New York, NY), 2009.

Sidelights

Tess Weaver is the author of such critically acclaimed picture books as *Opera Cat* and *Frederick Finch, Loudmouth.* Having worked as a marketing manager and book reviewer, Weaver began penning stories for young readers after her youngest child turned five years old. "Writing children's books is my over-the-moon dream job," she admitted on her home page.

Weaver's award-winning picture-book debut, *Opera Cat,* appeared in 2002. Illustrated by Andréa Wesson, the work concerns Alma, a music-loving feline, and her owner, Madame SoSo, an acclaimed opera singer. When the diva is felled by a case of laryngitis just before starring in a big performance, Alma unexpectedly comes to her companion's assistance. Having listened to every one of Madame SoSo's practice sessions, the cat knows all the tunes and astonishes her owner by singing them beautifully. The pair then devises a clever plan that allows both of them to take the stage together. A contributor in *Publishers Weekly* described *Opera Cat* as "a delightful star-is-born story," and a *Kirkus Reviews* critic remarked that Weaver's imaginative tale is "deftly drawn through detailed settings, sensory allusions, and just the right amount of melodrama and romance." According to Maryann H. Owen, writing in *School Library Journal,* "children will be charmed to see a cat earn her 15 minutes of fame." Weaver and Wesson have also collaborated on *Encore, Opera Cat,* a companion volume.

A curious feline is the focus of Weaver's *Cat Jumped In!,* a picture book illustrated by Emily Arnold McCully. When he spies an open window in the kitchen,

an energetic black-and-white cat leaps outdoors, in the process tipping over a trash can and creating a mess. Misadventure follows misadventure as the feline proceeds to invade a closet, where he brings down a shelf, as well as his owner's art studio, where he leaves a trail of paint. "Some 26 different verbs describe the cat's movements, infusing the story with plenty of action," Randall Enos stated in *Booklist.* Kate McClelland, reviewing the book for *School Library Journal,* predicted that *Cat Jumped In!* would make a good choice for read-alouds, noting that Weaver's "text is patterned and repetitive, containing many action and onomatopoeic words to delight teachers."

In Weaver's *Frederick Finch, Loudmouth,* illustrated by Debbie Tilley, a young boy gamely attempts to prove his worth. Even though the Finch family attends the State Fair each year, Frederick fails to win a single contest and comes home empty-handed while his siblings garner a host of prizes. Determined to get a ribbon of his own, the boy realizes that he must enter a competition that minimizes his greatest weakness: his incredibly loud voice. At the suggestion of his mother, the youngster creates a brightly colored shirt for the Boys' Fashion Fair that earns rave reviews, and he also finds a new event that is particularly well-suited to his tastes: a Mom-hollering Contest. A contributor in *Kirkus Reviews* described *Frederick Finch, Loudmouth* as "seriously zany," adding that "its goofiness is its saving grace." According to Lynne Mattern, writing in *School Library Journal,* "Frederick is a likable character who perseveres and continually tries to succeed."

Biographical and Critical Sources

PERIODICALS

Booklist, October 1, 2002, John Peters, review of *Opera Cat,* p. 339; December 15, 2007, Randall Enos, review of *Cat Jumped In!,* p. 49; June 1, 2008, Hazel Rochman, review of *Frederick Finch, Loudmouth,* p. 87.

Kirkus Reviews, October 1, 2002, review of *Opera Cat,* p. 1483; October 1, 2007, review of *Cat Jumped In!;* April 1, 2008, review of *Frederick Finch, Loudmouth.*

Publishers Weekly, September 16, 2002, review of *Opera Cat,* p. 68.

School Library Journal, December, 2002, Maryann H. Owen, review of *Opera Cat,* p. 112; December, 2007, Kate McClelland, review of *Cat Jumped In!,* p. 102; June, 2008, Lynne Mattern, review of *Frederick Finch, Loudmouth,* p. 116.

ONLINE

Tess Weaver Home Page, http://www.tessweaver.com (January 20, 2009).*

WILD, Margaret 1948-

Personal

Born 1948, in Eschew, South Africa; immigrated to Australia, 1972; children: two. *Education:* Attended Australian National University. *Hobbies and other interests:* Music, opera, frequenting cafés.

Addresses

Home—Sydney, New South Wales, Australia.

Career

Journalist, book editor, and children's author. ABC Books, Sydney, New South Wales, Australia, editor and publisher.

Awards, Honors

Book of the Year Award for Picture Book shortlist, Children's Book Council of Australia (CBCA). and Kate Greenaway Award shortlist, both 1984, both for *There's a Sea in My Bedroom;* Book of the Year Award for Picture Book, CBC, 1990, for *The Very Best of Friends;* Australian Books of the Year Awards shortlist, 1992, for *Let the Celebrations Begin!;* CBCA Book of the Year Award for Picture Book shortlist, 1997, for *The Midnight Gang;* Young Australian Best Book Award (YABBA) shortlist, 1999, for *Miss Lily's Fabulous Pink Feather Boa;* CBC Book of the Year for Early Childhood, 2002, and YABBA shortlist, and Bilby Award shortlist, both 2003, all for *The Pocket Dogs;* New South Wales State Literary Award shortlist, and CBC Book of the Year Award for Picture Book, both 2000, and YABBA shortlist, 2001, all for *Jenny Angel;* CBCA Book of the Year Award for Picture Book, and Queensland Premier's Literary Award for Children's Book, both 2001, both for *Fox;* May Gibbs Literature Trust fellowship, La Trobe University, 2001; CBCA Award shortlist for novel, 2002, for *Jinx;* Bilby Award for Early Reader, 2006, for *Baby Broomsticks;* CBCA Book of the Year Award for Picture Book shortlist, 2004, for *Seven More Sleeps,* 2007, for *Chatterbox;* Aurealis Award for Children's Book, 2006, and CBCA Book of the Year Award for Picture Book shortlist, 2007, both for *Woolvs in the Sitee.*

Writings

FOR CHILDREN

There's a Sea in My Bedroom, illustrated by Jane Tanner, Nelson (Melbourne, Victoria, Australia), 1984, reprinted, Puffin (Camberwell, Victoria, Australia), 2005.

Something Absolutely Enormous, illustrated by Jack Hannah, Ashton Scholastic (Sydney, New South Wales, Australia), 1984.

One Shoe On, illustrated by Hannah Koch, Hodder & Stoughton (Sydney, New South Wales, Australia), 1984.

Creatures in the Beard, illustrated by Margaret Power, Omnibus Books (Adelaide, South Australia, Australia), 1986.

Kathy's Umbrella, Hodder & Stoughton (Sydney, New South Wales, Australia), 1986.

The Diary of Megan Moon (Soon to Be Rich and Famous), illustrated by Shirley Peters, Collins Australia (Sydney, New South Wales, Australia), 1988.

Mr. Nick's Knitting, illustrated by Dee Huxley, Hodder & Stoughton (Sydney, New South Wales, Australia), 1988, Harcourt Brace (San Diego, CA), 1989.

The Very Best of Friends, illustrated by Julie Vivas, Margaret Hamilton (Sydney, New South Wales, Australia), 1989, Harcourt Brace (San Diego, CA), 1990.

Something Rich and Strange, illustrated by Janet Bridgland, Omnibus Books (Norwood, South Australia, Australia), 1990.

Harvey Jackson's Cubby, illustrated by Keith McEwan, Macmillan Australia (South Melbourne, Victoria, Australia), 1990.

Remember Me, Margaret Hamilton (Sydney, New South Wales, Australia), 1990, Albert Whitman (Morton Grove, IL), 1995.

A Bit of Company, illustrated by Wayne Harris, Ashton Scholastic (Sydney, New South Wales, Australia), 1991.

Let the Celebrations Begin!, illustrated by Julie Vivas, Orchard Books (New York, NY), 1991, published as *A Time for Toys,* Kids Can Press (Toronto, Ontario, Canada), 1992.

Thank You, Santa, illustrated by Kerry Argent, Omnibus Books (Norwood, South Australia, Australia), 1991, Scholastic (New York, NY), 1992.

Belinda's Blanket, illustrated by Alice Mak, Macmillan Australia (South Melbourne, Victoria, Australia), 1992.

Space Travellers, illustrated by Gregory Rogers, Scholastic (New York, NY), 1992.

The Queen's Holiday, illustrated by Sue O'Loughlin, Orchard Books (New York, NY), 1992.

First Best Friends, illustrated by Donna Rawlins, Roads and Traffic Authority of New South Wales (Sydney, New South Wales, Australia), 1992.

When Penny Was Mum, illustrated by Chantal Stewart, Roads and Traffic Authority of New South Wales (Sydney, New South Wales, Australia), 1992.

My Dearest Dinosaur, illustrated by Donna Rawlins, Orchard Books (New York, NY), 1992, reprinted, Scholastic Press (Gosford, New South Wales, Australia), 2005.

All the Better to See You With!, illustrated by Pat Reynolds, Allen & Unwin (St. Leonards, New South Wales, Australia), 1992, Albert Whitman (Morton Grove, IL), 1993.

The Slumber Party, illustrated by David Cox, Omnibus Books (Norwood, South Australia, Australia), 1992, Ticknor & Fields (New York, NY), 1993.

Beast, Omnibus Books (Norwood, South Australia, Australia), 1992, Scholastic (New York, NY), 1995.

(With Lorraine Hannay) *Sam's Sunday Dad,* Hodder & Stoughton (Sydney, New South Wales, Australia), 1992.

Going Home, illustrated by Wayne Harris, Ashton Scholastic (Sydney, New South Wales, Australia), 1993, Scholastic (New York, NY), 1994.

Our Granny, illustrated by Julie Vivas, Omnibus Books (Norwood, South Australia, Australia), 1993, Ticknor & Fields (New York, NY), 1994.

Toby, illustrated by Noela Young, Omnibus Books (Norwood, South Australia, Australia), 1993, Ticknor & Fields (New York, NY), 1994.

Light the Lamps, illustrated by Dee Huxley, Margaret Hamilton Books (Sydney, New South Wales, Australia), 1994, Scholastic (New York, NY), 1997.

But Granny Did!, illustrated by Ian Forss, SRA School Group (Santa Rosa, CA), 1994.

Morris the Reinbear, illustrated by David Francis, David Jones (Sydney, New South Wales, Australia), 1995.

Looking after Alice & Co., illustrated by David Cox, Margaret Hamilton (Sydney, New South Wales, Australia), 1995.

Old Pig, illustrated by Ron Brooks, Allen & Unwin (St. Leonards, New South Wales, Australia), 1995, Dial (New York, NY), 1996.

The Midnight Gang, illustrated by Ann James, Omnibus Books (Sydney, New South Wales, Australia), 1996.

Big Cat Dreaming, illustrated by Anne Spudvilas, Viking (Ringwood, Victoria, Australia), 1996.

Morris the Reinbear's Magic Books, illustrated by David Francis, David Jones (Sydney, New South Wales, Australia), 1997.

First Day, illustrated by Kim Gamble, Allen & Unwin (St. Leonards, New South Wales, Australia), 1998.

Rosie and Tortoise, illustrated by Ron Brooks, Allen & Unwin (St. Leonards, New South Wales, Australia), 1998, DK Publishing (New York, NY), 1999.

Bim, Bam, Boom!, illustrated by Wayne Harris, ABC Books (Sydney, New South Wales, Australia), 1998.

Miss Lily's Fabulous Pink Feather Boa, illustrated by Kerry Argent, Penguin (Ringwood, Victoria, Australia), 1998.

Jenny Angel, illustrated by Anne Spudvilas, Viking (New York, NY), 1999.

Midnight Babies, illustrated by Ann James, Clarion Books (New York, NY), 1999.

The Midnight Feast, illustrated by Ann James, ABC Books (Sydney, New South Wales, Australia), 1999.

Tom Goes to Kindergarten, illustrated by David Legge, ABC Books (Sydney, New South Wales, Australia), 1999, Albert Whitman (Morton Grove, IL), 2000.

(With Donna Rawlins) *Robber Girl,* Random House Australia (Milsons Point, New South Wales, Australia), 2000.

Fox, illustrated by Ron Brooks, Allen & Unwin (St. Leonards, New South Wales, Australia), 2000, Kane/Miller Book Publishers (La Jolla, CA), 2001.

Nighty Night!, illustrated by Kerry Argent, ABC Books (Sydney, New South Wales, Australia), 2000, Peachtree Publishers (Atlanta, GA), 2001.

The Pocket Dogs, illustrated by Stephen Michael King, Omnibus Books (Norwood, South Australia, Australia), 2000, Scholastic (New York, NY), 2001.

The House of Narcissus, illustrated by Wayne Harris, ABC Books (Sydney, New South Wales, Australia), 2001.

Jinx, Allen & Unwin (Crows Nest, New South Wales, Australia), 2001, Walker (New York, NY), 2002.

(With Jonathan Bentley) *Mr. Moo,* ABC Books (Sydney, New South Wales, Australia), 2002.

One Night, Allen & Unwin (Crows Nest, New South Wales, Australia), 2003, Knopf (New York, NY), 2004.

Babs the Baby and Fog the Dog, Working Title Press (Kingswood, South Australia, Australia), 2003.

Baby Boomsticks, illustrated by David Legge, ABC Books (Sydney, New South Wales, Australia), 2003.

Pat the Cat and Sailor Sam, illustrated by Tohby Riddle, Solo Books (Norwood, South Australia, Australia), 2003.

Too Many Monkeys, illustrated by Sally Rippin, Omnibus Books (Norwood, South Australia, Australia), 2004.

Fox, illustrated by Ron Brooks, Allen & Unwin (St. Leonards, New South Wales, Australia), 2004.

Kiss Kiss!, illustrated by Bridget Strevens-Marxo, Simon & Schuster (New York, NY), 2004.

Seven More Sleeps, illustrated by Donna Rawlins, Working Title Press (Kingswood, South Australia, Australia), 2004.

Farmer Fred's Cow, illustrated by David Waller, ABC Books (Sydney, New South Wales, Australia), 2004.

Piglet and Mama, illustrated by Stephen Michael King, Working Title Press (Kingswood, South Australia, Australia), 2004, Abrams Books for Young Readers (New York, NY), 2007.

Miss Lily's Fabulous Pink Feather Boa, illustrated by Kerry Argent, Puffin (Camberwell, Victoria, Australia), 2005.

The Little Crooked House, illustrated by Jonathan Bentley, ABC Books (Sydney, New South Wales, Australia), 2005.

The Bilbies of Bliss, illustrated by Noela Young ABC Books (Sydney, New South Wales, Australia), 2005.

Hop, Little Hare!, illustrated by Peter Shaw, Little Hare (Surry Hills, New South Wales, Australia), 2005.

Woolvs in the Sitee, illustrated by Anne Spudvilas, Penguin (Camberwell, Victoria, Australia), 2005, Front Street (Asheville, NC), 2007.

Bobbie Dazzler, illustrated by Janine Dawson, Working Title Press (Kingswood, South Australia, Australia), 2006.

Chatterbox, illustrated by Deborah Niland, Viking (Camberwell, Victoria, Australia), 2006.

Lucy Goosey, illustrated by Ann James, Little Hare (Surry Hills, New South Wales, Australia), 2007.

Ruby Roars, illustrated by Kerry Argent, Allen & Unwin (E. Melbourne, Victoria, Australia), 2007.

Little Dumpty, illustrated by Ann James, Little Hare (Surry Hills, New South Wales, Australia), 2007.

Piglet and Papa, illustrated by Stephen Michael King, Working Title Press (Kingswood, South Australia, Australia), 2007.

Puffing, illustrated by Julie Vivas, Omnibus (Malvern, South Australia, Australia), 2007, Feiwel & Friends (New York, NY), 2009.

The Pocket Dogs Go on Holiday, illustrated by Stephen Michael King, Omnibus Books (Norwood, South Australia, Australia), 2008.

Margaret Wild's warm-hearted picture book Old Pig *features illustrations by Ron Brooks.* (Illustration © 1995 by Ron Brooks. Reproduced by permission of Dial Books for Young Readers, a division of Penguin Books USA, Inc. In Australian/New Zealand by Allen & Unwin Pty Ltd., www.allenandunwin.com.)

Bit Red Hen and the Little Lost Egg, illustrated by Terry Denton, Penguin (Hawthorn, Victoria, Australia), 2008.

Baby Bird's Blankie, illustrated by Gwyn Perkins, Working Title Press (Kingswood, South Australia, Australia), 2008.

Piglet and Granny, illustrated by Stephen Michael King, Abrams Books for Young Readers (New York, NY), 2009.

Grandpa Baby, illustrated by Deborah Niland, Penguin (Camberwell, Victoria, Australia), 2009.

Harry and Hopper, illustrated by Freya Blackwood, Omnibus (Malvern, South Australia, Australia), 2009.

Going Home, illustrated by Wayne Harris, Walker Books (Newton, New South Wales, Australia), 2009.

A Bit of Company, illustrated by Wayne Harris, Walker Books (Newton, New South Wales, Australia), 2009.

Old Pig, illustrated by Ron Brooks, Allen & Unwin (Crows Nest, New South Wales, Australia), 2009.

Hush, Hush!, illustrated by Bridget Strevens-Marzo, Little Hare (Surry Hills, New South Wales, Australia), 2010.

Contributor to *Doctor Gemma* and *Out of Reach!,* education resource kits, New South Wales Department of Education and Training (Ryde, New South Wales, Australia), 2001.

Sidelights

Margaret Wild is a prolific author of children's books whose themes sometimes range to issues outside the genre's norm: death and dying, grief, divorce, aging, and fears of being lost, overwhelmed, or bullied. Her realistic portrayals of these difficult subjects have been widely praised by critics and reviewers alike. In contrast, Wild's picture books, such as *Our Granny, Little Humpty, Piglet and Papa,* and *Bobbie Dazzler,* are jubilant celebrations of grandmothers, babies, childhood, and friendship. Even her more sober works, such as her highly lauded picture book *Woolvs in the Sitee* and her verse novel *Jinx,* hold the message that children have the ability to understand and cope with a sad or scary situation.

Set in Wild's native Australia, *The Very Best of Friends* introduces a farm couple, James and Jessie, and their cat, William. James is especially fond of William, and Jessie tolerates the cat for her husband's sake. When James dies suddenly, Jessie shuts out everything, including William, and stops caring for the farm, the animals, and herself. The neglected cat becomes thin and vicious, in his own way shut out from the world. However, when William claws Jessie, she realizes how she has let herself and her world deteriorate, and the two develop a strong friendship. *The Very Best of Friends* is a "story about relationships, love and loss, survival and recovery," wrote Patricia Dooley in *School Library Journal.* "The poignant tale is superbly told by Wild . . . who achieves an enviable balance of detail and simplicity," added a reviewer in *Publishers Weekly.*

Let the Celebrations Begin!—also published as *A Time for Toys!*—has the unusual setting of the Bergen-Belsen concentration camp in Germany. Miriam, an older child prisoner, can remember what life was like before the camp, when she had parents and a home and toys. Because many of the younger children have known nothing but the camp, Miriam plans a very special party for the children, one that will happen when "the soldiers come to set us free" from their captivity. The women tear usable scraps of cloth from their already-threadbare clothing to make the toys, which are indeed given when the camp is liberated. Marjorie Gann, writing in *Canadian Children's Literature,* noted that *A Time for Toys* "tells an important story well." Susan Perren, reviewing the book in *Quill & Quire,* called Wild's story "a work of alchemy, creating something of beauty from the bleakest material."

The theme of death coupled with the hopeful message of moving on from grief while not forgetting a loved one informs two of Wild's more popular books. In *Old Pig* the title character and Granddaughter live happily together, and have for a very long time. Old Pig carefully teaches Granddaughter how to fend for herself; the two do their daily chores together, have their meals together, and sleep peacefully together. One day, after being unable to get up and go about her routine as usual, Old Pig realizes what is coming and begins tidying up—returning library books, closing bank accounts, paying bills, and feasting her eyes on nature for the very last time. The final picture in the book shows Granddaughter alone, feasting on nature the way Old Pig taught her to. "Beautiful in its simplicity, this captures the essence of a life; and children, even little ones, cannot help but feel the love that infuses it," wrote Ilene Cooper in *Booklist.*

In *Toby* the family dog is elderly and ailing, but twelve-year-old Sara is indifferent, sometimes even harsh to her lifelong pet. Her two younger brothers cannot understand Sara's anger toward the dog, so they decide to play with Toby and comfort him. When the vet announces that it would be kindest to put Toby to sleep, Sara reacts with hostility toward the ailing pup. Sara's mom realizes that the girl's reaction is a response to the sadness she feels at the prospect of losing Toby and the entirety of her childhood that he represents. Michael J. Rosen, writing in the *Washington Post Book World,* called *Toby* "a glorious book worth weeping over together," while *Booklist* critic Ellen Mandel deemed the work "a genuinely touching illumination of a family's loss of a beloved friend."

Wild also deals with the loss of a family member in *Jenny Angel.* Here young Davy is gravely ill and dying, but his older sister Jenny believes she can save his life by acting as his guardian angel and willing him to live. She perches protectively outside his window at night, and then spends time "flying" over the city in her imagination to bring back marvelous stories of her adventures. She even wears a heavy coat at school to hide her

***Illustrator Julie Vivas brings to life Wild's lighthearted story in* Let the Celebrations Begin!** (Illustration copyright © 1991 by Julie Vivas. All rights reserved. Reproduced by permission of Scholastic, Inc.)

"wings," enduring relentless teasing and questioning in order to maintain her illusion of being Davy's guardian angel. It is only after the boy's unavoidable death and his funeral that Jenny finally takes off her coat, visits the roof one last time, and accepts that Davy is gone. "Understated, honest, and ultimately hopefully, *Jenny Angel* does not simplify emotions nor does it give answers to impossible questions," remarked Nola Allen in a *Magpies* review. Rosemary Stores, writing in *Books for Keeps,* declared that "Wild's depiction of Jenny finding a way to accept her loss is . . . so sensitively

conveyed that young readers can only be enriched by it," and Margaret Dunkle remarked in the *Australian Book World* that *Jenny Angel* "is a tender, loving, beautiful story, splendidly reinforced by Anne Spudvilas's sensitive paintings."

Other children's books by Wild tackle complex subjects: divorce and visitation in *Sam's Sunday Dad,* coping with homelessness in *Space Travellers,* a child's need for glasses in *All the Better to See You With!,* the aging of a relative in *Remember Me* and *Big Cat Dream-*

ing, and the first day of school in both *First Day* and *Tom Goes to Kindergarten.* Joan Zahnleitner, writing in *Magpies,* observed that with *First Day,* Wild's approach "has been towards a more optimistic side of life even while acknowledging that what may seem small worries to adults can assume monumental proportions for young children."

In her verse novels *Jinx* and *One Night* Wild refocuses her writing for more sophisticated teen readers. Told in a series of interrelated poems, *Jinx* relates the story of Jen, a girl who considers herself a jinx and source of bad luck for those around her. Two consecutive boyfriends have died—the first by suicide, the second in an accident—and her parents have split up. Her sister is "born imperfect," and she has a stepmother she hates. In frustration, Jen blames another boy, Ben, for the accident that killed her second boyfriend, and she terrorizes him and his family relentlessly. Her circle of family and friends try to help her cope, but Jen adopts the "Jinx" nickname that she has been given at school. When she feels remorse for being so harsh to Ben and

begins to fall in love with the young man, she sheds her Jinx persona. "*Jinx* emerges as a subtly wrought, deeply affecting story dealing with friendship and familial and romantic love," commented a *Kirkus Reviews* critic. "The device of the poetry will attract many young readers; the skill with which it is told will keep them hooked."

Also told in short poems divided in three parts, *One Night* focuses on two teens, Gabe and Helen, who meet at a party, become intimate, and go their separate ways only to realize later that their lives have been altered forever by the events of that night. For Helen, a young woman with a disfigured face, her pregnancy changes her life course because of her decision to keep Gabe's baby. For Gabe the encounter initially has far less resonance; Helen is just one of many women he has had sex with. However, as time passes, Helen and Gabe reconnect and begin to deal more responsibly with the future. "It's quite amazing how a carefully crafted poem is able to reveal character so clearly on two levels of understanding: intellectual and emotional," noted Claire

Stephen Michael King creates the artwork for Wild's rural-themed picture book **Piglet and Papa.** (Harry N. Abrams, Inc., 2007. Illustration copyright © 2007 by Stephen Michael King. Reproduced by permission.)

Rosser in her *Kliatt* appraisal of Wild's verse novel. While maintaining an air of compassion, the author "doesn't pull back from the weaknesses and mistakes" exhibited by her protagonists, the critic added. Praising the "spare, lyrical poems" in *One Night, Booklist* critic Gillian Engberg also wrote that the novel contains "moments of exceptional beauty" and phrases that "shimmer with startling, intense feeling."

Featuring evocative illustrations by Spudvilas, Wild's award-winning large-format picture book *Woolvs in the Sitee* distills the horrors of being a survivor in a post-apocalyptic future into a minimal text. Living in the basement room in a stark, almost-empty apartment building, Ben is terrified of what he believes are wolves living in the shadows of his city neighborhood. For the teen, his only friend is Mrs. Radinski, an elderly woman who lives upstairs until she vanishes after rescuing Ben from the dangers in the outer world. Using a text designed to represent the words of a young man with limited education or understanding of the things around him, Wild creates what *Horn Book* contributor Claire E. Gross described as a "chilling" story "reinforcing the idea of a decayed society and adding a sense of otherness through accent and slang." "The jarring reading experience . . . heightens the impression of a brutal, off-kilter world," explained Kate McClelland in her *School Library Journal* review. Praising Spudvilas's haunting paintings, Gross noted that they combine with Wild's "deceptively simple poetic trajectory . . . to enhance the fear, ruin, longing, and hope of this eerie dystopian allegory."

In contrast to some of her books for older readers, optimism and exuberance take center stage in many of Wild's illustrated picture books. In *Our Granny,* for example, Wild offers a celebration of well-loved grandmothers in all colors, shapes, and sizes. "And they can take part in any activities they like," explained Russ Merrin in *Magpies.* "No white-haired buns pulled back from wrinkled brows here. These ladies are stirrers and doers and goers." In *The Queen's Holiday* Wild serves up a "royal romp" that will be "enjoyed by young and old," according to *School Library Journal* critic Nancy Seiner. Here Wild follows the queen's trip to the beach and the steadily increasing mayhem brought about by her attendants, until the regal woman decides to put things right in a suitably royal manner. In the picture book *Midnight Babies* a group of toddlers gathers at midnight to dance, feast, and cavort before returning to bed and "normal" life, while *Little Humpty* introduces readers to a young camel who lives with his mother in a hot, sandy desert. Ilene Cooper, writing in *Booklist,* called *Midnight Babies* a "fantastical ode to babydom" acted out with characters whose "actions are whimsical, bold, and delicious." Noting that the illustrations Ann James contributes to *Little Humpty* are "luminous and evincing an almost palpable fluidity," a *Publishers Weekly* critic added that Wild's "reassuring" story captures "the picture-perfect definition of the boundless love between parent and child."

Wild and artist Anne Spudvilas team up to create a disquieting futuristic story in their acclaimed Woolvs in the Sitee. (Illustration copyright © 2006 by Anne Spudvilas. All rights reserved. Reprinted with the permission of Boyds Mills Press, Inc.)

Biographical and Critical Sources

BOOKS

Children's Books and Their Creators, edited by Anita Silvey, Houghton Mifflin (New York, NY), 1995.
Wild, Margaret, *Let the Celebrations Begin!,* illustrated by Julie Vivas, Orchard Books (New York, NY), 1991.
Wild, Margaret, *The Queen's Holiday,* illustrated by Sue O'Loughlin, Orchard Books (New York, NY), 1992.
Wild, Margaret, *Jenny Angel,* illustrated by Anne Spudvilas, Viking (New York, NY), 1999.

PERIODICALS

Australian Book Review, June, 1992, Meg Sorensen, review of *Sam's Sunday Dad,* pp. 60-63; April, 1995, Linnet Hunter, review of *Light the Lamps,* pp. 61-62; December-January, 1996-97, Linnet Hunter, review of *The Midnight Gang,* pp. 91-92; October, 1999, Margaret Dunkle, review of *Jenny Angel,* pp. 43-44; February, 2001, review of *Robber Girl,* p. 52.
Booklist, November 1, 1992, Carolyn Phelan, review of *Thank You, Santa,* p. 88; July, 1993, Lisa Napoli, review of *All the Better to See You With!,* p. 1978; October 1, 1993, Stephanie Zvirin, review of *The Slumber Party,* p. 355; January 15, 1994, Hazel Rochman, review of *Our Granny,* p. 925; March 15, 1994, Ellen

Mandel, review of *Toby*, p. 1375; April 1, 1994, Hazel Rochman, review of *Going Home*, p. 463; February 1, 1996, Leone McDermott, review of *Remember Me*, p. 940; May 15, 1996, Ilene Cooper, review of *Old Pig*, p. 1578; February 1, 1998, Stephanie Zvirin, review of *Big Cat Dreaming*, p. 924; December 1, 1999, Michael Cart, review of *Rosie and Tortoise*, p. 715; May 1, 2000, Catherine Andronik, review of *Tom Goes to Kindergarten*, p. 1680; February 1, 2001, Carolyn Phelan, review of *The Pocket Dogs*, p. 1051; February 15, 2001, Ilene Cooper, review of *Midnight Babies*, p. 1135; September 1, 2001, Shelle Rosenfeld, review of *Nighty Night!*, p. 118; November 15, 2001, Gillian Engberg, review of *Fox*, p. 585; January 1, 2002, review of *Midnight Babies*, p. 769; September 15, 2002, Ilene Cooper, review of *Jinx*, p. 228; January 1, 2004, Hazel Rochman, review of *Kiss Kiss!*, p. 884; May 15, 2004, Gillian Engberg, review of *One Night*, p. 1615; March 1, 2005, Hazel Rochman, review of *Piglet and Mama*, p. 1207; May 1, 2007, Gillian Engberg, review of *Piglet and Papa*, p. 84; November 15, 2007, Jennifer Mattson, review of *Woolvs in the Sitee*, p. 40.

Book Report, September-October, 1995, Carol Burbridge, review of *Beast*, p. 42.

Books for Keeps, March, 2000, Rosemary Stores, review of *Jenny Angel*, p. 24.

Books in Canada, December, 1997, Gillian Chan, review of *Big Cat Dreaming*, p. 35.

Bulletin of the Center for Children's Books, September, 1991, review of *Let the Celebrations Begin!*, p. 25; November, 1992, review of *Thank You, Santa*, p. 94; May, 1993, review of *Space Travellers*, p. 298; June, 1994, review of *Toby*, p. 339; February, 1995, review of *Beast*, p. 218; March, 1996, review of *Old Pig*, p. 247; March, 2001, review of *The Pocket Dogs*, p. 283; September, 2001, review of *Nighty Night!*, p. 40; November, 2007, Deborah Stevenson, review of *Woolvs in the Sitee*, p. 155.

Canadian Children's Literature, 1993, Marjorie Gann, review of *A Time for Toys*, pp. 34-36.

Emergency Librarian, March-April, 1987, Anne Hazell, review of *Creatures in the Beard*, p. 23.

Family Matters, winter, 2000, Carole Jean, review of *Sam's Sunday Dad*, p. 70.

Horn Book, November-December, 1989, Hanna B. Zeiger, review of *Mr. Nick's Knitting*, p. 766; March-April, 1990, Karen Jameyson, review of *The Very Best of Friends*, p. 235; May-June, 1990, Margaret A. Bush, review of *The Very Best of Friends*, p. 331; September-October, 1992, Hanna B. Zeiger, review of *The Queen's Holiday*, pp. 580-581; March-April, 1993, Karen Jameyson, review of *My Dearest Dinosaur*, pp. 241-244; September-October, 1993, Maeve Visser Knoth, review of *The Slumber Party*, pp. 593-594; May-June, 1994, Hanna B. Zeiger, review of *Our Granny*, pp. 322-323; November-December, Lauren Adams, review of *Jinx*, p. 765; November-December, 2007, Claire E. Gross, review of *Woolvs in the Sitee*, p. 671.

Junior Bookshelf, December, 1984, *There's a Sea in My Bedroom*, pp. 244-245; August, 1991, review of *Let the Celebrations Begin!*, p. 149.

Kirkus Reviews, September 15, 1992, review of *Thank You, Santa*, p. 1195; May 1, 1994, review of *Going Home*, p. 638; November 15, 1997, review of *Big Cat Dreaming*, p. 1714; September 15, 2001, review of *Fox*, p. 1371; July 15, 2002, review of *Jinx*, p. 1048; April 15, 2004, review of *One Night*, p. 403; December 15, 2004, review of *Little Humpty*, p. 1211; April 15, 2005, review of *Piglet and Mama*, p. 428; May 1, 2007, review of *Piglet and Papa*; August 1, 2007, review of *Woolvs in the Sitee*; August 15, 2007, review of *Bobbie Dazzler.*

Kliatt, May, 2004, Claire Rosser, review of *One Night*, p. 15.

Los Angeles Times Book Review, December 17, 1989, Patricia MacLachlan, review of *Mr. Nick's Knitting*, p. 7; May 27, 1990, Patricia MacLachlan, review of *The Very Best of Friends*, p. 8; June 9, 1996, Michael Cart, review of *Old Pig*, p. 15.

Magpies, March, 1991, review of *Something Rich and Strange*, p. 28; July, 1991, Melanie Guile, review of *Remember Me*, p. 27; November, 1991, Margot Tyrrell, review of *Let the Celebrations Begin!*, p. 29; May, 1992, review of *A Bit of Company*, p. 27; November, 1992, Lynne Ferencz, review of *The Slumber Party*, p. 31; May, 1993, Stephanie Owen Reeder, review of *Sam's Sunday Dad*, p. 27, Mandy Cheetham, review of *All the Better to See You With!*, p. 26, and Robyn Shehan, review of *Beast*, p. 29; July, 1993, Stephanie Owen Reeder, review of *Space Travellers*, pp. 30-31, and Mandy Cheetham, review of *My Dearest Dinosaur*, p. 29; November, 1993, Renya Spratt, review of *Christmas Magic*, p. 27; July, 1994, Russ Merrin, review of *Our Granny*, p. 26; March, 1995, Melanie Guile, review of *Light the Lamps*, p. 24; July, 1996, Mandy Cheetham, review of *Big Cat Dreaming*, p. 25; March, 1996, Annette Dale-Meiklejohn, review of *Looking after Alice and Co.*, p. 34; May, 1998, Moira Robinson, review of *Rosie and Tortoise*, p. 27; September, 1998, Margaret Phillips, review of *Bim Bam Boom!*, p. 28, and Joan Zahnleitner, review of *First Day*, p. 24; November, 1998, Linnet Hunter, review of *Miss Lily's Fabulous Pink Feather Boa*, p. 24; November, 1999, Nola Allen, review of *Jenny Angel*, pp. 8-9, and Joan Zahnleitner, review of *The Midnight Feast*, p. 26; July, 2000, Anne Hanzl, review of *Robber Girl*, p. 46; November, 2001, Kevin Steinberger, review of *The House of Narcissus*, p. 17.

New York Times Book Review, February 18, 1990, review of *Mr. Nick's Knitting*, p. 25.

People, November 28, 1994, review of *Our Granny*, pp. 42-43.

Publishers Weekly, October 13, 1989, review of *Mr. Nick's Knitting*, p. 53; March 16, 1990, review of *The Very Best of Friends*, p. 69; July 25, 1991, review of *Let the Celebrations Begin!*, p. 52; August 24, 1992, review of *The Queen's Holiday*, p. 78; September 7, 1992, review of *Thank You, Santa*, p. 68; September 28, 1992, review of *My Dearest Dinosaur*, p. 78; April 12, 1993, review of *Space Travelers*, p. 63; July 19, 1993, review of *The Slumber Party*, p. 252; February 14, 1994, review of *Going Home*, pp. 88-89; September 20, 1999, review of *Rosie and Tortoise*, p. 87;

May 1, 2000, review of *Tom Goes to Kindergarten,* p. 70; February 5, 2001, review of *Midnight Babies,* p. 87; April, 2001, review of *The Pocket Dogs,* p. 63; July 9, 2001, review of *Nighty Night!,* p. 66; October 8, 2001, review of *Fox,* p. 65; August 5, 2002, review of *Jinx,* p. 74; January 19, 2004, review of *Kiss Kiss!,* p. 74; June 21, 2004, review of *One Night,* p. 64; January 17, 2005, review of *Little Humpty,* p. 54; August 27, 2007, review of *Woolvs in the Sitee,* p. 89.

Quill & Quire, May, 1991, Susan Perren, review of *A Time for Toys,* p. 24.

Reading Teacher, February, 1991, Barbara Kiefer, review of *The Very Best of Friends,* p. 410; October, 1992, Barbara Tolin, review of *The Very Best of Friends,* p. 146, and Barbara Tolin, review of *Let the Celebrations Begin,* p. 146.

School Librarian, summer, 2000, Trevor Dickinson, review of *Jenny Angel,* p. 91.

School Library Journal, October, 1989, Jeanne Marie Clancy, review of *Mr. Nick's Knitting,* pp. 98-99; June, 1990, Patricia Dooley, review of *The Very Best of Friends,* p. 106; July, 1991, Susan Scheps, review of *Let the Celebrations Begin!,* p. 75; October, 1992, review of *Thank You, Santa,* p. 45, and Nancy Seiner, review of *The Queen's Holiday,* pp. 99-100; January, 1993, Cathryn A. Camper, review of *My Dearest Dinosaur,* p. 88; April, 1993, Karen K. Radtke, review of *Space Travellers,* pp. 103-104; August, 1993, Anna DeWind, review of *All the Better to See You With,* p. 154; October, 1993, Karen James, review of *The Slumber Party,* p. 114; March, 1994, Patricia Pearl Dole, review of *Toby,* p. 212; April, 1994, Karen James, review of *Our Granny,* pp. 114-115, and Louise L. Sherman, review of *Going Home,* p. 114; February, 1995, Tim Rausch, review of *Beast,* pp. 100-101; January, 1996, Pamela K. Bomboy, review of *Remember Me,* p. 98; April, 1996, Christina Dorr, review of *Old Pig,* p. 121; February, 1998, Lauralyn Persson, review of *Big Cat Dreaming,* p. 92; September, 1999, Kathleen Staerkel, review of *Rosie and Tortoise,* p. 209; April,

2000, Ginny Gustin, review of *Tom Goes to Kindergarten,* p. 117; April, 2001, Joy Fleishhacker, review of *Midnight Babies,* p. 126; June, 2001, Lisa Gangemi Krapp, review of *The Pocket Dogs,* p. 132; September, 2001, Debbie Stewart, review of *Nighty Night!,* p. 208; December, 2001, Susan Scheps, review of *Fox,* pp. 114-115; November, 2002, Sharon Morrison, review of *Jinx,* p. 178; January, 2004, Faith Brautigam, review of *Kiss Kiss!,* p. 107; February, 2005, Suzanne Myers Harold, review of *Little Humpty,* p. 112; June, 2005, Shawn Brommer, review of *Piglet and Mama,* p. 131; July, 2007, Judith Constantinides, review of *Piglet and Papa,* p. 87; September, 2007, Kate McClelland, review of *Woolvs in the Sitee,* p. 210; September, 2007, Martha Simpson, review of *Bobbie Dazzler,* p. 178.

Spectator, December 5, 1992, Juliet Townsend, review of *The Queen's Holiday,* p. 49.

Times Educational Supplement, August, 1984, review of *There's a Sea in My Bedroom,* p. 21; May 31, 1991, Ann Thwaite, review of *Let the Celebrations Begin!,* p. 24; April 19, 1996, Robert Dunbar, review of *Old Pig,* p. B18.

Tribune Books (Chicago, IL), May 8, 1994, Mary Harris Veeder, review of *Our Granny,* p. 6.

Voice of Youth Advocates, April, 1995, Karen S.H. Roggenkamp, review of *Beast,* p. 29; December, 2002, review of *Jinx,* p. 392; August, 2004, review of *One Night,* p. 226.

Washington Post Book World, May 8, 1994, Michael J. Rosen, review of *Toby,* p. 18.

Wilson Library Bulletin, April, 1994, review of *The Slumber Party,* p. 119.

ONLINE

Allen & Unwin Web site, http://www.allen-unwin.com/ (December 12, 2002), "Margaret Wild."

Little Hare Books Web site, http://www.littleharebooks.com/ (January 27, 2009), "Margaret Wild."*

Illustrations Index

(In the following index, the number of the *volume* in which an illustrator's work appears is given *before* the colon, and the *page number* on which it appears is given *after* the colon. For example, a drawing by Adams, Adrienne appears in Volume 2 on page 6, another drawing by her appears in Volume 3 on page 80, another drawing in Volume 8 on page 1, and so on and so on. . . .)

YABC

Index references to *YABC* refer to listings appearing in the two-volume *Yesterday's Authors of Books for Children,* also published by Gale, Cengage Learning. *YABC* covers prominent authors and illustrators who died prior to 1960.

A

Aas, Ulf *5:* 174
Abbe, S. van
  See van Abbe, S.
Abel, Raymond *6:* 122; *7:* 195; *12:* 3; *21:* 86; *25:* 119
Abelliera, Aldo *71:* 120
Abolafia, Yossi *60:* 2; *93:* 163; *152:* 202
Abrahams, Hilary *26:* 205; *29:* 24, 25; *53:* 61
Abrams, Kathie *36:* 170
Abrams, Lester *49:* 26
Abulafia, Yossi *154:* 67; *177:* 3
Accardo, Anthony *191:* 3, 8
Accornero, Franco *184:* 8
Accorsi, William *11:* 198
Acs, Laszlo *14:* 156; *42:* 22
Adams, Adrienne *2:* 6; *3:* 80; *8:* 1; *15:* 107; *16:* 180; *20:* 65; *22:* 134, 135; *33:* 75; *36:* 103, 112; *39:* 74; *86:* 54; *90:* 2, 3
Adams, Connie J. *129:* 68
Adams, John Wolcott *17:* 162
Adams, Lynn *96:* 44
Adams, Norman *55:* 82
Adams, Pam *112:* 1, 2
Adams, Sarah *98:* 126; *164:* 180
Adamson, George *30:* 23, 24; *69:* 64
Addams, Charles *55:* 5
Addison, Kenneth *192:* 173
Addy, Sean *180:* 8
Ade, Rene *76:* 198; *195:* 162
Adinolfi, JoAnn *115:* 42; *176:* 2
Adkins, Alta *22:* 250
Adkins, Jan *8:* 3; *69:* 4; *144:* 2, 3, 4
Adler, Kelynn *195:* 47
Adler, Peggy *22:* 6; *29:* 31
Adler, Ruth *29:* 29
Adlerman, Daniel *163:* 2
Adragna, Robert *47:* 145
Agard, Nadema *18:* 1
Agee, Jon *116:* 8, 9, 10; *157:* 4; *196:* 3, 4, 5, 6, 7, 8
Agre, Patricia *47:* 195
Aguirre, Alfredo *152:* 218
Ahl, Anna Maria *32:* 24
Ahlberg, Allan *68:* 6, 7, 9; *165:* 5
Ahlberg, Janet *68:* 6, 7, 9
Aicher-Scholl, Inge *63:* 127
Aichinger, Helga *4:* 5, 45
Aitken, Amy *31:* 34

Akaba, Suekichi *46:* 23; *53:* 127
Akasaka, Miyoshi *YABC 2:* 261
Akib, Jamel *181:* 13; *182:* 99
Akino, Fuku *6:* 144
Alain *40:* 41
Alajalov *2:* 226
Alborough, Jez *86:* 1, 2, 3; *149:* 3
Albrecht, Jan *37:* 176
Albright, Donn *1:* 91
Alcala, Alfredo *91:* 128
Alcantará, Felipe Ugalde *171:* 186
Alcorn, John *3:* 159; *7:* 165; *31:* 22; *44:* 127; *46:* 23, 170
Alcorn, Stephen *110:* 4; *125:* 106; *128:* 172; *150:* 97; *160:* 188; *165:* 48
Alcott, May *100:* 3
Alda, Arlene *44:* 24; *158:* 2
Alden, Albert *11:* 103
Aldridge, Andy *27:* 131
Aldridge, George *105:* 125
Aldridge, Sheila *192:* 4
Alejandro, Cliff *176:* 75
Alex, Ben *45:* 25, 26
Alexander, Ellen *91:* 3
Alexander, Lloyd *49:* 34
Alexander, Martha *3:* 206; *11:* 103; *13:* 109; *25:* 100; *36:* 131; *70:* 6, 7; *136:* 3, 4, 5; *169:* 120
Alexander, Paul *85:* 57; *90:* 9
Alexeieff, Alexander *14:* 6; *26:* 199
Alfano, Wayne *80:* 69
Aliki
  See Brandenberg, Aliki
Allamand, Pascale *12:* 9
Allan, Judith *38:* 166
Alland, Alexandra *16:* 255
Allen, Gertrude *9:* 6
Allen, Graham *31:* 145
Allen, Jonathan *131:* 3, 4; *177:* 8, 9, 10
Allen, Joy *168:* 185
Allen, Pamela *50:* 25, 26, 27, 28; *81:* 9, 10; *123:* 4, 5
Allen, Rowena *47:* 75
Allen, Thomas B. *81:* 101; *82:* 248; *89:* 37; *104:* 9
Allen, Tom *85:* 176
Allender, David *73:* 223
Alley, R.W. *80:* 183; *95:* 187; *156:* 100, 153; *169:* 4, 5; *179:* 17
Allison, Linda *43:* 27
Allon, Jeffrey *119:* 174

Allport, Mike *71:* 55
Almquist, Don *11:* 8; *12:* 128; *17:* 46; *22:* 110
Aloise, Frank *5:* 38; *10:* 133; *30:* 92
Alsenas, Linas *186:* 2
Althea
  See Braithwaite, Althea
Altschuler, Franz *11:* 185; *23:* 141; *40:* 48; *45:* 29; *57:* 181
Alvin, John *117:* 5
Ambrus, Victor G. *1:* 6, 7, 194; *3:* 69; *5:* 15; *6:* 44; *7:* 36; *8:* 210; *12:* 227; *14:* 213; *15:* 213; *22:* 209; *24:* 36; *28:* 179; *30:* 178; *32:* 44, 46; *38:* 143; *41:* 25, 26, 27, 28, 29, 30, 31, 32; *42:* 87; *44:* 190; *55:* 172; *62:* 30, 144, 145, 148; *86:* 99, 100, 101; *87:* 66, 137; *89:* 162; *134:* 160
Ames, Lee J. *3:* 12; *9:* 130; *10:* 69; *17:* 214; *22:* 124; *151:* 13
Amon, Aline *9:* 9
Amoss, Berthe *5:* 5
Amstutz, Andre *152:* 102
Amundsen, Dick *7:* 77
Amundsen, Richard E. *5:* 10; *24:* 122
Ancona, George *12:* 11; *55:* 144; *145:* 7
Anderson, Alasdair *18:* 122
Andersen, Bethanne *116:* 167; *162:* 189; *175:* 17; *191:* 4, 5
Anderson, Bob *139:* 16
Anderson, Brad *33:* 28
Anderson, C.W. *11:* 10
Anderson, Carl *7:* 4
Anderson, Catherine Corley *72:* 2
Anderson, Cecil *127:* 152
Anderson, David Lee *118:* 176
Anderson, Derek *169:* 9; *174:* 180
Anderson, Doug *40:* 111
Anderson, Erica *23:* 65
Anderson, Laurie *12:* 153, 155
Anderson, Lena *99:* 26
Anderson, Peggy Perry *179:* 2
Anderson, Sara *173:* 3
Anderson, Scoular *138:* 13
Anderson, Susan *90:* 12
Anderson, Tara *188:* 132
Anderson, Wayne *23:* 119; *41:* 239; *56:* 7; *62:* 26; *147:* 6
Andreasen, Daniel *86:* 157; *87:* 104; *103:* 201, 202; *159:* 75; *167:* 106, 107; *168:* 184; *180:* 247; *186:* 9
Andrew, Ian *111:* 37; *116:* 12; *166:* 2
Andrew, John *22:* 4

Andrews, Benny *14:* 251; *31:* 24; *57:* 6, 7; *183:* 8
Andrews, Vaughn *166:* 28
Anelay, Henry *57:* 173
Angel, Marie *47:* 22
Angelo, Valenti *14:* 8; *18:* 100; *20:* 232; *32:* 70
Anglund, Joan Walsh *2:* 7, 250, 251; *37:* 198, 199, 200
Anholt, Catherine *74:* 8; *131:* 7; *141:* 5
Anholt, Laurence *141:* 4
Anno, Mitsumasa *5:* 7; *38:* 25, 26, 27, 28, 29, 30, 31, 32; *77:* 3, 4; *157:* 10, 11
Antal, Andrew *1:* 124; *30:* 145
Antram, David *152:* 133
Apostolou, Christy Hale
    See Hale, Christy
Apple, Margot *33:* 25; *35:* 206; *46:* 81; *53:* 8; *61:* 109; *64:* 21, 22, 24, 25, 27; *71:* 176; *77:* 53; *82:* 245; *92:* 39; *94:* 180; *96:* 107; *152:* 4, 5; *162:* 192, 194; *173:* 44
Appleyard, Dev *2:* 192
Aragones, Sergio *48:* 23, 24, 25, 26, 27
Araneus *40:* 29
Arbo, Cris *103:* 4
Archambault, Matt *85:* 173; *138:* 19, 20; *143:* 33; *145:* 144; *179:* 103; *187:* 7
Archer, Janet *16:* 69; *178:* 156
Ardizzone, Edward *1:* 11, 12; *2:* 105; *3:* 258; *4:* 78; *7:* 79; *10:* 100; *15:* 232; *20:* 69,178; *23:* 223; *24:* 125; *28:* 25, 26, 27, 28, 29, 30, 31,33, 34, 35, 36, 37; *31:* 192, 193; *34:* 215, 217; *60:* 173; *64:* 145; *87:* 176; *YABC 2:* 25
Arena, Jill *176:* 49
Arenella, Roy *14:* 9
Argemi, David *197:* 2
Argent, Kerry *103:* 56; *138:* 17; *158:* 134
Arisman, Marshall *162:* 50
Armer, Austin *13:* 3
Armer, Laura Adams *13:* 3
Armer, Sidney *13:* 3
Armitage, David *47:* 23; *99:* 5; *155:* 4
Armitage, Eileen *4:* 16
Armstrong, George *10:* 6; *21:* 72
Armstrong, Shelagh *102:* 114
Armstrong-Ellis, Carey *185:* 196
Arno, Enrico *1:* 217; *2:* 22, 210; *4:* 9; *5:* 43; *6:* 52; *29:* 217, 219; *33:* 152; *35:* 99; *43:* 31, 32, 33; *45:* 212, 213, 214; *72:* 72; *74:* 166; *100:* 169
Arnold, Alli *187:* 40, 41
Arnold, Caroline *174:* 5
Arnold, Emily *76:* 7, 9, 10
Arnold, Katya *115:* 11; *168:* 2, 3
Arnold, Tedd *116:* 14; *133:* 152; *160:* 5
Arnosky, Jim *22:* 20; *70:* 9, 10, 11; *118:* 3, 5; *160:* 8, 10; *189:* 5, 7, 8, 9, 10
Arnsteen, Katy Keck *105:* 97; *116:* 145
Arrowood, Clinton *12:* 193; *19:* 11; *65:* 210
Artell, Mike *89:* 8
Arting, Fred J. *41:* 63
Artzybasheff, Boris *13:* 143; *14:* 15; *40:* 152, 155
Aruego, Ariane *6:* 4
Aruego, José *4:* 140; *6:* 4; *7:* 64; *33:* 195; *35:* 208; *68:* 16, 17; *75:* 46; *93:* 91, 92; *94:* 197; *109:* 65, 67; *125:* 2, 3, 4, 5; *127:* 188; *143:* 25; *178:* 17, 19, 74; *188:* 166
Arzoumanian, Alik *177:* 12; *194:* 115
Asare, Meshack *86:* 9; *139:* 19
Ascensios, Natalie *105:* 139
Asch, Frank *5:* 9; *66:* 2, 4, 6, 7, 9, 10; *102:* 18, 19,21; *154:* 12
Ashby, Gail *11:* 135
Ashby, Gil *146:* 4
Ashby, Gwynneth *44:* 26
Ashley, C.W. *19:* 197
Ashmead, Hal *8:* 70
Aska, Warabe *56:* 10
Assel, Steven *44:* 153; *77:* 22, 97
Astrop, John *32:* 56

Atene, Ann *12:* 18
Atherton, Lisa *38:* 198
Atkinson, Allen *60:* 5
Atkinson, J. Priestman *17:* 275
Atkinson, Janet *86:* 147; *103:* 138
Atkinson, Mike *127:* 74
Atkinson, Wayne *40:* 46
Attard, Karl *196:* 22, 23
Attebery, Charles *38:* 170
Atwell, Debby *150:* 6
Atwood, Ann *7:* 9
Aubrey, Meg Kelleher *77:* 159
Auch, Herm *173:* 7, 8
Auch, Mary Jane *173:* 7
Augarde, Steve *25:* 22; *159:* 7
Austerman, Miriam *23:* 107
Austin, Margot *11:* 16
Austin, Robert *3:* 44
Austin, Virginia *81:* 205; *127:* 221
Auth, Tony *51:* 5; *192:* 18
Avendano, Dolores *158:* 74
Avedon, Richard *57:* 140
Averill, Esther *1:* 17; *28:* 39, 40, 41
Axeman, Lois *2:* 32; *11:* 84; *13:* 165; *22:* 8; *23:* 49; *61:* 116; *101:* 124
Axtel, David *155:* 110
Ayer, Jacqueline *13:* 7
Ayer, Margaret *15:* 12; *50:* 120
Ayers, Alan *91:* 58; *107:* 169
Ayliffe, Alex *95:* 164
Ayto, Russell *111:* 5; *112:* 54
Azarian, Mary *112:* 9, 10; *114:* 129; *117:* 171; *137:* 163; *171:* 4, 5; *181:* 161; *188:* 128

B

B.T.B.
    See Blackwell, Basil T.
Babbitt, Bradford *33:* 158
Babbitt, Natalie *6:* 6; *8:* 220; *68:* 20; *70:* 242, 243; *194:* 8, 9
Baca, Maria *104:* 5
Bacchus, Andy *94:* 87
Bacha, Andy *109:* 169
Bachelet, Gilles *196:* 18
Bachem, Paul *48:* 180; *67:* 65; *144:* 206
Back, Adam *63:* 125
Back, George *31:* 161
Backes, Nick *190:* 72
Backhouse, Colin *78:* 142
Bacon, Bruce *4:* 74
Bacon, Paul *7:* 155; *8:* 121; *31:* 55; *50:* 42; *56:* 175; *62:* 82, 84
Bacon, Peggy *2:* 11, 228; *46:* 44
Baek, Matthew J. *169:* 95
Baer, Julie *161:* 2
Baicker-McKee, Carol *177:* 15; *180:* 215
Bailey, Peter *58:* 174; *87:* 221; *194:* 12
Bailey, Sheila *155:* 11
Baker, Alan *22:* 22; *61:* 134; *93:* 11, 12; *146:* 6, 7, 10
Baker, Charlotte *2:* 12
Baker, Garin *89:* 65
Baker, Jeannie *23:* 4; *88:* 18, 19, 20
Baker, Jim *22:* 24
Baker, Joe *82:* 188; *111:* 55; *124:* 70; *197:* 73
Baker, Keith *179:* 6, 7
Baker, Leslie *112:* 214; *132:* 103, 246; *180:* 74, 246
Baldacci, Rudy *184:* 9
Baldridge, Cyrus LeRoy *19:* 69; *44:* 50
Baldus, Zachary *152:* 231; *187:* 60
Balet, Jan *11:* 22
Balian, Lorna *9:* 16; *91:* 16
Balit, Christina *102:* 24; *159:* 9; *162:* 118, 119
Ballantyne, R.M. *24:* 34
Ballis, George *14:* 199
Balouch, Kristen *176:* 11
Baltzer, Hans *40:* 30

Banbery, Fred *58:* 15
Banfill, A. Scott *98:* 7; *112:* 59
Bang, Molly Garrett *24:* 37, 38; *69:* 8, 9, 10; *111:* 7,9, 10, 11; *140:* 11; *158:* 37, 38, 39; *195:* 3
Banik, Yvette Santiago *21:* 136
Banner, Angela
    See Maddison, Angela Mary
Bannerman, Helen *19:* 13, 14
Bannon, Laura *6:* 10; *23:* 8
Bantock, Nick *74:* 229; *95:* 6
Banyai, Istvan *185:* 209; *193:* 14, 16
Baptist, Michael *37:* 208
Baracca, Sal *135:* 206
Baranaski, Marcin *182:* 113
Barasch, Lynne *126:* 16; *186:* 15
Barbarin, Lucien C., Jr. *89:* 88
Barbour, Karen *96:* 5; *74:* 209; *170:* 16
Bare, Arnold Edwin *16:* 31
Bare, Colleen Stanley *32:* 33
Barger, Jan *147:* 11
Bargery, Geoffrey *14:* 258
Barkat, Jonathan *149:* 177; *164:* 254; *181:* 106; *184:* 186; *196:* 11
Barker, Carol *31:* 27
Barker, Cicely Mary *49:* 50, 51
Barkley, James *4:* 13; *6:* 11; *13:* 112
Barks, Carl *37:* 27, 28, 29, 30, 31, 32, 33, 34
Barling, Joy *62:* 148
Barling, Tom *9:* 23
Barlow, Gillian *62:* 20
Barlow, Perry *35:* 28
Barlowe, Dot *30:* 223
Barlowe, Wayne *37:* 72; *84:* 43; *105:* 5
Barnard, Bryn *88:* 53; *13:* 55; *169:* 13; *193:* 194
Barner, Bob *29:* 37; *128:* 33; *136:* 19, 20; *177:* 27
Barnes, Hiram P. *20:* 28
Barnes, Tim *137:* 28
Barnes-Murphy, Rowan *88:* 22
Barnett, Charles II *175:* 150
Barnett, Ivan *70:* 14
Barnett, Moneta *16:* 89; *19:* 142; *31:* 102; *33:* 30, 31, 32; *41:* 153; *61:* 94, 97
Barney, Maginel Wright *39:* 32, 33, 34; *YABC 2:* 306
Barnum, Jay Hyde *11:* 224; *20:* 5; *37:* 189, 190
Baron, Alan *80:* 3; *89:* 123
Barr, George *60:* 74; *69:* 64
Barragan, Paula S. *134:* 116; *186:* 158
Barrall, Tim *115:* 152
Barraud, Martin *189:* 38
Barrauds *33:* 114
Barrer-Russell, Gertrude *9:* 65; *27:* 31
Barret, Robert *85:* 134
Barrett, Angela *40:* 136, 137; *62:* 74; *75:* 10; *76:* 142; *144:* 137; *145:* 14
Barrett, Jennifer *58:* 149
Barrett, John E. *43:* 119
Barrett, Moneta *74:* 10
Barrett, Peter *55:* 169; *86:* 111
Barrett, Robert *62:* 145; *77:* 146; *82:* 35
Barrett, Ron *14:* 24; *26:* 35
Barron, John N. *3:* 261; *5:* 101; *14:* 220
Barrow, Ann *136:* 27
Barrows, Walter *14:* 268
Barry, Ethelred B. *37:* 79; *YABC 1:* 229
Barry, James *14:* 25
Barry, Katharina *2:* 159; *4:* 22
Barry, Robert E. *6:* 12
Barry, Scott *32:* 35
Bartenbach, Jean *40:* 31
Barth, Ernest Kurt *2:* 172; *3:* 160; *8:* 26; *10:* 31
Bartlett, Alison *101:* 88; *165:* 93
Barton, Byron *8:* 207; *9:* 18; *23:* 66; *80:* 181; *90:* 18, 19, 20, 21; *126:* 29, 30
Barton, Harriett *30:* 71

Barton, Jill *129:* 108; *135:* 120; *145:* 185, 189; *184:* 177
Bartram, Robert *10:* 42
Bartsch, Jochen *8:* 105; *39:* 38
Bascove, Barbara *45:* 73
Base, Graeme *101:* 15, 16, 17, 18; *162:* 8, 10, 12
Baseman, Gary *174:* 12
Bash, Barbara *132:* 9
Baskin, Leonard *30:* 42, 43, 46, 47; *49:* 125, 126, 128, 129,133; *173:* 120
Bass, Saul *49:* 192
Bassett, Jeni *40:* 99; *64:* 30
Basso, Bill *99:* 139; *189:* 134
Batchelor, Joy *29:* 41, 47, 48
Bate, Norman *5:* 16
Bates, Amy June *188:* 170; *189:* 27, 28
Bates, Leo *24:* 35
Batet, Carmen *39:* 134
Batherman, Muriel *31:* 79; *45:* 185
Battaglia, Aurelius *50:* 44
Batten, John D. *25:* 161, 162
Batten, Mary *162:* 14, 15
Battles, Asa *32:* 94, 95
Bauer, Carla *193:* 6
Bauer, Jutta *150:* 32
Bauernschmidt, Marjorie *15:* 15
Baum, Allyn *20:* 10
Baum, Willi *4:* 24, 25; *7:* 173
Bauman, Leslie *61:* 121
Baumann, Jill *34:* 170
Baumhauer, Hans *11:* 218; *15:* 163, 165, 167
Baxter, Glen *57:* 100
Baxter, Leon *59:* 102
Baxter, Robert *87:* 129
Bayer, Herbert *181:* 16
Bayley, Dorothy *37:* 195
Bayley, Nicola *40:* 104; *41:* 34, 35; *69:* 15; *129:* 33, 34, 35
Baylin, Mark *158:* 233
Baynes, Pauline *2:* 244; *3:* 149; *13:* 133, 135,137, 141; *19:* 18, 19, 20; *32:* 208, 213, 214; *36:* 105, 108; *59:* 12, 13, 14, 16, 17, 18, 20; *100:* 158, 159, 243; *133:* 3, 4
Beach, Lou *150:* 150
Beame, Rona *12:* 40
Bean, Jonathan *196:* 102
Bear's Heart *73:* 215
Beard, Dan *22:* 31, 32
Beard, J.H. *YABC 1:* 158
Bearden, Romare *9:* 7; *22:* 35
Beardshaw, Rosalind *169:* 22; *190:* 22
Beardsley, Aubrey *17:* 14; *23:* 181; *59:* 130, 131
Bearman, Jane *29:* 38
Beaton, Cecil *24:* 208
Beaton, Clare *125:* 28
Beauce, J.A. *18:* 103
Beaujard, Sophie *81:* 54
Beccia, Carlyn *189:* 29
Beck, Charles *11:* 169; *51:* 173
Beck, Ian *138:* 27; *182:* 150; *190:* 25
Beck, Ruth *13:* 11
Becker, Harriet *12:* 211
Beckett, Sheilah *25:* 5; *33:* 37, 38
Beckhoff, Harry *1:* 78; *5:* 163
Beckhorn, Susan Williams *189:* 32
Beckman, Kaj *45:* 38, 39, 40, 41
Beckman, Per *45:* 42, 43
Beddows, Eric *72:* 70
Bedford, F.D. *20:* 118, 122; *33:* 170; *41:* 220, 221,230, 233
Bee, Joyce *19:* 62
Bee, William *188:* 6
Beeby, Betty *25:* 36
Beech, Carol *9:* 149
Beech, Mark *192:* 122
Beek *25:* 51, 55, 59
Beeke, Tiphanie *177:* 127
Beekman, Doug *125:* 146, 148
Beerbohm, Max *24:* 208

Beeson, Bob *108:* 57
Begin, Maryjane *82:* 13
Beha, Philippe *172:* 85
Behr, Joyce *15:* 15; *21:* 132; *23:* 161
Behrens, Hans *5:* 97
Beier, Ellen *135:* 170; *139:* 47; *183:* 164
Beinicke, Steve *69:* 18
Beisner, Monika *46:* 128, 131; *112:* 127
Belden, Charles J. *12:* 182
Belina, Renate *39:* 132
Bell, Corydon *3:* 20
Bell, Graham *54:* 48
Bell, Julia *151:* 214
Bell, Julie *159:* 172; *165:* 18
Bell, Thomas P. *76:* 182
Bellamy, Glen *127:* 15
Bemelmans, Ludwig *15:* 19, 21; *100:* 27
Ben-Ami, Doron *75:* 96; *84:* 107; *108:* 132; *110:* 63; *159:* 157; *197:* 142
Bendall-Brunello, John *150:* 4; *157:* 163; *185:* 3, 4
Benda, Wladyslaw T. *15:* 256; *30:* 76, 77; *44:* 182
Bender, Robert *77:* 162; *79:* 13; *160:* 23
Bendick, Jeanne *2:* 24; *68:* 27, 28
Benioff, Carol *121:* 42; *175:* 23
Benner, Cheryl *80:* 11
Bennett, Charles H. *64:* 6
Bennett, Erin Susanne *165:* 216
Bennett, F.I. *YABC 1:* 134
Bennett, James *146:* 240
Bennett, Jill *26:* 61; *41:* 38, 39; *45:* 54
Bennett, Rainey *15:* 26; *23:* 53
Bennett, Richard *15:* 45; *21:* 11, 12, 13; *25:* 175
Bennett, Susan *5:* 55
Benny, Mike *142:* 78
Benoit, Elise *77:* 74
Benson, Linda *60:* 130; *62:* 91; *75:* 101; *79:* 156; *134:* 129
Benson, Patrick *68:* 162; *147:* 17, 18, 19, 20
Bentley, Carolyn *46:* 153
Bentley, James *149:* 30
Bentley, Roy *30:* 162
Benton, Jim *172:* 22
Benton, Thomas Hart *2:* 99
Berelson, Howard *5:* 20; *16:* 58; *31:* 50
Berenstain, Jan *12:* 47; *64:* 33, 34, 36, 37, 38, 40, 42, 44; *135:* 25, 28, 31, 35
Berenstain, Stan *12:* 47; *64:* 33, 34, 36, 37, 38, 40, 42, 44; *135:* 25, 28, 31, 35
Berenzy, Alix *65:* 13; *73:* 6; *78:* 115
Berg, Joan *1:* 115; *3:* 156; *6:* 26, 58
Berg, Ron *36:* 48, 49; *48:* 37, 38; *67:* 72
Bergen, David *115:* 44
Berger, Barbara *77:* 14
Berger, Carin *185:* 6
Berger, William M. *14:* 143; *YABC 1:* 204
Bergherr, Mary *74:* 170; *151:* 123
Bergin, Mark *114:* 8, 9; *143:* 95; *160:* 26, 27
Bergstreser, Douglas *69:* 76
Bergum, Constance R. *121:* 14, 15
Bering, Claus *13:* 14
Berkeley, Jon *139:* 218
Berkowitz, Jeanette *3:* 249
Berman, Paul *66:* 14
Bernal, Richard *154:* 176
Bernadette
    See Watts, Bernadette
Bernardin, James *112:* 24; *167:* 94
Bernasconi, Pablo *183:* 10, 11
Bernath, Stefen *32:* 76
Bernhard, Durga *80:* 13
Bernstein, Michel J. *51:* 71
Bernstein, Ted *38:* 183; *50:* 131
Bernstein, Zena *23:* 46
Berridge, Celia *86:* 63
Berrill, Jacquelyn *12:* 50
Berry, Erick
    See Best, Allena

Berry, William D. *14:* 29; *19:* 48
Berry, William A. *6:* 219
Berson, Harold *2:* 17, 18; *4:* 28, 29, 220; *9:* 10; *12:* 19; *17:* 45; *18:* 193; *22:* 85; *34:* 172; *44:* 120; *46:* 42; *80:* 240
Bertholf, Bret *187:* 9; *189:* 32, 33
Berton, Patsy *99:* 16
Bertschmann, Harry *16:* 1
Besco, Don *70:* 99
Beskow, Elsa *20:* 13, 14, 15
Bess, Clayton *63:* 94
Best, Allena *2:* 26; *34:* 76
Betera, Carol *74:* 68
Bethell, Thomas N. *61:* 169
Bethers, Ray *6:* 22
Bettina
    See Ehrlich, Bettina
Betts, Ethel Franklin *17:* 161, 164, 165; *YABC 2:* 47
Betz, Rudolf *59:* 161
Bewick, Thomas *16:* 40, 41, 43, 44, 45, 47; *54:* 150; *YABC 1:* 107
Beyer, Paul J. III *74:* 24
Bezencon, Jacqueline *48:* 40
Biamonte, Daniel *40:* 90
Bianchi, John *91:* 19
Bianco, Pamela *15:* 31; *28:* 44, 45, 46
Bible, Charles *13:* 15
Bice, Clare *22:* 40
Biedrzycki, David *186:* 170
Bierman, Don *57:* 184
Biggers, John *2:* 123
Biggs, Brian *192:* 38; *196:* 15
Bileck, Marvin *3:* 102; *40:* 36, 37
Bilibin, Ivan *61:* 8, 9, 12, 13, 14, 15, 151, 152, 154, 162
Billington, Patrick *98:* 71
Billout, Guy *144:* 38, 39
Bimen, Levent *5:* 179
Binch, Caroline *81:* 18; *140:* 15, 16; *144:* 115
Binder, Hannes *169:* 163
Bing, Christopher *126:* 34
Binger, Bill *121:* 46
Binks, Robert *25:* 150
Binzen, Bill *24:* 47
Birch, Reginald *15:* 150; *19:* 33, 34, 35, 36; *37:* 196,197; *44:* 182; *46:* 176; *YABC 1:* 84; *2:* 34, 39
Birchall, Mark *123:* 188
Bird, Esther Brock *1:* 36; *25:* 66
Birdsong, Keith *167:* 85
Birkett, Rachel *78:* 206
Birling, Paul *109:* 30
Birmingham, Christian *132:* 243; *143:* 114
Birmingham, Lloyd P. *12:* 51; *83:* 13
Biro, Val *1:* 26; *41:* 42; *60:* 178; *67:* 23, 24; *84:* 242, 243
Bischoff, Ilse *44:* 51
Bishop, Gavin *97:* 17, 18; *144:* 42, 44
Bishop, Kathleen Wong *115:* 67
Bishop, Rich *56:* 43
Bite, I. *60:* 14
Bittinger, Ned *93:* 117
Bjorklund, Lorence *3:* 188, 252; *7:* 100; *9:* 113; *10:* 66; *19:* 178; *33:* 122, 123; *35:* 36, 37, 38, 39,41, 42, 43; *36:* 185; *38:* 93; *47:* 106; *66:* 194; *YABC 1:* 242
Bjorkman, Steve *91:* 199; *160:* 110
Black Sheep *164:* 100
Blackburn, Loren H. *63:* 10
Blackall, Sophie *194:* 140
Blackford, John *137:* 105; *180:* 36
Blackwell, Basil T. *YABC 1:* 68, 69
Blackwood, Gary L. *118:* 17
Blades, Ann *16:* 52; *37:* 213; *50:* 41; *69:* 21; *99:* 215
Blair, Jay *45:* 46; *46:* 155
Blaisdell, Elinore *1:* 121; *3:* 134; *35:* 63
Blake, Anne Catharine *189:* 71

Blake, Quentin *3:* 170; *10:* 48; *13:* 38; *21:* 180; *26:* 60; *28:* 228; *30:* 29, 31; *40:* 108; *45:* 219; *46:* 165, 168; *48:* 196; *52:* 10, 11, 12,13, 14, 15, 16, 17; *73:* 41, 43; *78:* 84, 86; *80:* 250, 251; *84:* 210, 211, 212; *87:* 177; *96:* 24, 26, 28; *124:* 79; *125:* 32, 34; *181:* 139
Blake, Robert J. *37:* 90; *53:* 67; *54:* 23; *160:* 28, 29
Blake, William *30:* 54, 56, 57, 58, 59, 60
Blanchard, N. Taylor *82:* 140
Blass, Jacqueline *8:* 215
Blazek, Scott R. *91:* 71
Bleck, Cathie *118:* 116
Blegvad, Erik *2:* 59; *3:* 98; *5:* 117; *7:* 131; *11:* 149; *14:* 34, 35; *18:* 237; *32:* 219; *60:* 106; *66:* 16, 17, 18, 19; *70:* 233; *76:* 18; *82:* 106; *87:* 45; *100:* 188; *129:* 125; *132:* 17, 18, 19, 20; *176:* 14; *YABC 1:* 201
Blessen, Karen *93:* 126
Bliss, Corinne Demas *37:* 38
Bliss, Harry *196:* 27, 28, 29
Blitt, Barry *179:* 199; *187:* 13
Bloch, Lucienne *10:* 12
Blondon, Herve *129:* 48; *183:* 22
Bloom, Lloyd *35:* 180; *36:* 149; *47:* 99; *62:* 117; *68:* 231; *72:* 136; *75:* 185; *83:* 99; *108:* 19
Bloom, Suzanne *172:* 23, 24
Blossom, Dave *34:* 29
Blumenschein, E.L. *YABC 1:* 113, 115
Blumer, Patt *29:* 214
Blundell, Kim *29:* 36
Bluthenthal, Diana Cain *93:* 32; *104:* 106; *177:* 26
Blythe, Benjamin *128:* 7
Blythe, Gary *112:* 52; *181:* 166; *182:* 64; *185:* 7; *186:* 116, 117
Boake, Kathy *176:* 185
Board, Perry *171:* 99
Boardman, Gwenn *12:* 60
Bober, Richard *125:* 145; *132:* 40
Bobri *30:* 138; *47:* 27
Bock, Vera *1:* 187; *21:* 41
Bock, William Sauts *8:* 7; *14:* 37; *16:* 120; *21:* 141; *36:* 177; *62:* 203
Bodecker, N(iels) M(ogens) *8:* 13; *14:* 2; *17:* 55, 56, 57; *73:* 22, 23, 24
Boehm, Linda *40:* 31
Bogacki, Tomek *138:* 31, 32; *144:* 123
Bogan, Paulette *197:* 152
Bogdan, Florentina *107:* 43
Bohdal, Susi *22:* 44; *101:* 20
Bohlen, Nina *58:* 13
Boies, Alex *96:* 53
Bolam, Emily *101:* 216; *159:* 12
Bolian, Polly *3:* 270; *4:* 30; *13:* 77; *29:* 197
Bolle, Frank *87:* 100
Bollen, Roger *79:* 186; *83:* 16
Bolling, Vickey *114:* 44
Bollinger, Peter *101:* 7; *128:* 198; *172:* 26
Bolognese, Don *2:* 147, 231; *4:* 176; *7:* 146; *17:* 43; *23:* 192; *24:* 50; *34:* 108; *36:* 133; *71:* 24, 25; *103:* 131; *129:* 39, 40
Bolster, Rob *186:* 169
Bolton, A.T. *57:* 158
Bond, Arnold *18:* 116
Bond, Barbara Higgins *21:* 102
Bond, Bruce *52:* 97
Bond, Felicia *38:* 197; *49:* 55, 56; *89:* 170; *90:* 171; *126:* 37
Bond, Higgins *177:* 22, 23
Bonn, Pat *43:* 40
Bonner, Hannah *197:* 13, 14
Bonners, Susan *41:* 40; *85:* 36; *94:* 99, 100; *151:* 105, 106
Bono, Mary *184:* 73
Bonsall, Crosby *23:* 6
Boon, Debbie *103:* 6; *144:* 188
Boon, Emilie *86:* 23, 24
Boone, Debbie *165:* 77

Boore, Sara *60:* 73
Bootman, Colin *155:* 13; *159:* 35; *174:* 192
Booth, Franklin *YABC 2:* 76
Booth, George *191:* 13
Booth, Graham *32:* 193; *37:* 41, 42
Borda, Juliette *102:* 188
Bordier, Georgette *16:* 54
Boren, Tinka *27:* 128
Borges, Jose Francisco *119:* 62
Borja, Robert *22:* 48
Born, Adolf *49:* 63
Bornstein, Ruth *14:* 44; *88:* 45, 46; *107:* 30
Borten, Helen *3:* 54; *5:* 24
Bosin, Blackbear *69:* 104
Bossom, Naomi *35:* 48
Bostock, Mike *83:* 221; *114:* 14; *188:* 205
Boston, Peter *19:* 42
Bosustow, Stephen *34:* 202
Boszko, Ron *75:* 47
Bottner, Barbara *14:* 46
Boucher, Joelle *41:* 138
Boulat, Pierre *44:* 40
Boulet, Susan Seddon *50:* 47
Bouma, Paddy *118:* 25; *128:* 16
Bour, Daniele *66:* 145
Bourke-White, Margaret *15:* 286, 287; *57:* 102
Boutet de Monvel, M. *30:* 61, 62, 63, 65
Bowen, Betsy *105:* 222
Bowen, Richard *42:* 134
Bowen, Ruth *31:* 188
Bower, Ron *29:* 33
Bowers, David *95:* 38; *115:* 20; *127:* 169, 170; *165:* 57
Bowers, Tim *185:* 35
Bowman, Claire *174:* 177
Bowman, Eric *151:* 23
Bowman, Leslie *85:* 203; *105:* 108; *116:* 76; *128:* 234; *182:* 24, 25
Bowman, Peter *146:* 214, 215; *150:* 115
Bowser, Carolyn Ewing *22:* 253
Boxall, Ed *178:* 28
Boyd, Aaron *158:* 242
Boyd, Patti *45:* 31
Boyle, Eleanor Vere *28:* 50, 51
Boynton, Sandra *57:* 13, 14, 15; *107:* 36, 37; *152:* 12, 13, 14
Bozzo, Frank *4:* 154
Brabbs, Derry *55:* 170
Brace, Eric *132:* 193, 194; *152:* 71; *184:* 195; *197:* 6
Brackers de Hugo, Pierre *115:* 21
Bradford, June *158:* 138
Bradford, Ron *7:* 157
Bradley, David P. *69:* 105
Bradley, Richard D. *26:* 182
Bradley, William *5:* 164
Brady, Irene *4:* 31; *42:* 37; *68:* 191
Bragg, Michael *32:* 78; *46:* 31
Bragg, Ruth Gembicki *77:* 18
Brainerd, John W. *65:* 19
Braithwaite, Althea *23:* 12, 13; *119:* 16
Brak, Syd *146:* 187
Bralds, Braldt *90:* 28; *91:* 151
Bram, Elizabeth *30:* 67
Bramley, Peter *4:* 3
Brandenberg, Aliki *2:* 36, 37; *24:* 222; *35:* 49, 50, 51,52, 53, 54, 56, 57; *75:* 15, 17; *92:* 205; *113:* 18, 19, 20; *157:* 28; *156:* 111
Brandenburg, Alexa *75:* 19
Brandenburg, Jim *47:* 58; *150:* 212
Brandi, Lillian *31:* 158
Brandon, Brumsic, Jr. *9:* 25
Bransom, Paul *17:* 121; *43:* 44
Braren, Loretta Trezzo *87:* 193
Brassard, France *186:* 22
Braun, Wendy *80:* 17, 18
Brautigam, Don *115:* 175, 176
Brazell, Derek *75:* 105; *79:* 9
Breathed, Berkeley *86:* 27, 28, 29; *161:* 13, 14
Breckenreid, Julia *192:* 209
Breen, Steve *186:* 23

Brennan, Steve *83:* 230; *101:* 184
Brenner, Fred *22:* 85; *36:* 34; *42:* 34
Brett, Bernard *22:* 54
Brett, Harold M. *26:* 98, 99, 100
Brett, Jan *30:* 135; *42:* 39; *71:* 31, 32; *130:* 23, 24, 25, 26, 27; *171:* 15, 16
Brewer, Paul *106:* 115; *145:* 202
Brewer, Sally King *33:* 44
Brewster, Patience *40:* 68; *45:* 22, 183; *51:* 20; *66:* 144; *89:* 4; *97:* 30, 31
Brick, John *10:* 15
Brickman, Robin D. *131:* 88; *142:* 150; *155:* 18; *178:* 109; *184:* 32
Bridge, David R. *45:* 28
Bridgman, L.J. *37:* 77
Bridwell, Norman *4:* 37; *138:* 36, 37, 40
Brierley, Louise *91:* 22; *96:* 165; *183:* 51
Briggs, Harry *172:* 187
Briggs, Raymond *10:* 168; *23:* 20, 21; *66:* 29, 31, 32; *131:* 28, 29; *184:* 15, 16
Brigham, Grace A. *37:* 148
Bright, Robert *24:* 55
Brighton, Catherine *107:* 39
Brinckloe, Julie *13:* 18; *24:* 79, 115; *29:* 35; *63:* 140; *81:* 131
Brion *47:* 116
Brisley, Joyce L. *22:* 57
Brisson, James F. *110:* 60
Brittingham, Geoffrey *88:* 37
Brix-Henker, Silke *81:* 194
Brock, Charles E. *15:* 97; *19:* 247, 249; *23:* 224, 225; *36:* 88; *42:* 41, 42, 43, 44, 45; *100:* 189; *YABC 1:* 194, 196, 203
Brock, Emma *7:* 21
Brock, Henry Matthew *15:* 81; *16:* 141; *19:* 71; *34:* 115; *40:* 164; *42:* 47, 48, 49; *49:* 66
Brocksopp, Arthur *57:* 157
Broda, Ron *136:* 180; *174:* 123
Brodkin, Gwen *34:* 135
Brodovitch, Alexi *52:* 22
Bromhall, Winifred *5:* 11; *26:* 38
Bromley, Lizzy *159:* 179
Bronson, Linda *150:* 210; *174:* 133
Brooke, L. Leslie *16:* 181, 182, 183, 186; *17:* 15, 16, 17; *18:* 194
Brooker, Christopher *15:* 251
Brooker, Krysten *111:* 94; *140:* 28; *162:* 111; *175:* 108; *186:* 42, 225
Brooks, Erik *166:* 52; *182:* 30
Brooks, Karen Stormer *186:* 110
Brooks, Maya Itzna *92:* 153
Brooks, Ron *94:* 15; *197:* 188
Brooks, S.G. *178:* 127
Broomfield, Maurice *40:* 141
Brotman, Adolph E. *5:* 21
Brown, Buck *45:* 48
Brown, Calef *179:* 18
Brown, Christopher *62:* 124, 125, 127, 128
Brown, Craig McFarland *73:* 28; *84:* 65
Brown, Dan *61:* 167; *115:* 183, 184; *116:* 28, 29; *193:* 190
Brown, David *7:* 47; *48:* 52
Brown, Denise *11:* 213
Brown, Don *172:* 29
Brown, Elbrite *195:* 39
Brown, Ford Madox *48:* 74
Brown, Hunter *191:* 111, 112
Brown, Judith Gwyn *1:* 45; *7:* 5; *8:* 167; *9:* 182, 190; *20:* 16, 17, 18; *23:* 142; *29:* 117; *33:* 97; *36:* 23, 26; *43:* 184; *48:* 201, 223; *49:* 69; *86:* 227; *110:* 188; *153:* 7
Brown, Kathryn *98:* 26
Brown, Lisa *187:* 175
Brown, Laurie Krasny *99:* 30
Brown, Marc (Tolon) *10:* 17, 197; *14:* 263; *51:* 18; *53:* 11, 12, 13, 15, 16, 17; *75:* 58; *80:* 24, 25, 26; *82:* 261; *99:* 29; *145:* 22, 23, 25, 27; *146:* 198
Brown, Marcia *7:* 30; *25:* 203; *47:* 31, 32, 33, 34, 35,36, 37, 38, 39, 40, 42, 43, 44; *YABC 1:* 27

Brown, Margery W. *5:* 32, 33; *10:* 3
Brown, Martin *101:* 43
Brown, Mary Barrett *97:* 74
Brown, Palmer *36:* 40
Brown, Paul *25:* 26; *26:* 107
Brown, Richard *61:* 18; *67:* 30
Brown, Rick *78:* 71; *150:* 154
Brown, Robert S. *85:* 33
Brown, Rod *157:* 142
Brown, Ruth *55:* 165; *86:* 112, 113; *105:* 16, 17, 18; *171:* 178
Brown, Trevor *99:* 160; *139:* 247; *189:* 206
Browne, Anthony *45:* 50, 51, 52; *61:* 21, 22, 23, 24, 25; *105:* 21, 22, 23, 25
Browne, Dik *8:* 212; *67:* 32, 33, 35, 37, 39
Browne, Gordon *16:* 97; *64:* 114, 116, 117, 119, 121
Browne, Hablot K. *15:* 65, 80; *21:* 14, 15, 16, 17, 18, 19,20; *24:* 25
Browne, Jane *165:* 222
Browning, Coleen *4:* 132
Browning, Mary Eleanor *24:* 84
Bruce, Robert *23:* 23
Brude, Dick *48:* 215
Bruel, Nick *166:* 41
Brule, Al *3:* 135
Brumbeau, Jeff *157:* 29
Bruna, Dick *43:* 48, 49, 50; *76:* 27, 28
Brundage, Frances *19:* 244
Brunhoff, Jean de *24:* 57, 58
Brunhoff, Laurent de *24:* 60; *71:* 35, 36, 37
Brunkus, Denise *84:* 50; *123:* 117; *178:* 209; *193:* 99
Brunson, Bob *43:* 135
Bryan, Ashley *31:* 44; *72:* 27, 28, 29; *107:* 92; *116:* 192; *132:* 24; *178:* 33, 34, 35
Bryant, Laura J. *176:* 36; *183:* 168
Bryant, Michael *93:* 74
Brychta, Alex *21:* 21
Bryer, Diana *107:* 121
Bryson, Bernarda *3:* 88, 146; *39:* 26; *44:* 185; *131:* 40
Buba, Joy *12:* 83; *30:* 226; *44:* 56
Buchanan, George *166:* 198
Buchanan, Lilian *13:* 16
Buchanan, Rachel *171:* 71
Bucholtz-Ross, Linda *44:* 137
Buchs, Thomas *40:* 38
Buck, Margaret Waring *3:* 30
Buckhardt, Marc *172:* 59
Buckley, Mike *166:* 180
Budwine, Greg *175:* 172
Buehner, Mark *104:* 12, 15; *105:* 160; *119:* 98; *157:* 188; *159:* 39, 40, 43; *192:* 111
Buehr, Walter *3:* 31
Buff, Conrad *19:* 52, 53, 54
Buff, Mary *19:* 52, 53
Bull, Charles Livingston *18:* 207; *88:* 175, 176
Bullen, Anne *3:* 166, 167
Bullock, Kathleen *77:* 24
Bumgarner-Kirby, Claudia *77:* 194
Burbank, Addison *37:* 43
Burchard, Peter Duncan *3:* 197; *5:* 35; *6:* 158, 218; *143:* 17
Burckhardt, Marc *94:* 48; *110:* 89; *196:* 41
Burger, Carl *3:* 33; *45:* 160, 162
Burgeson, Marjorie *19:* 31
Burgess, Anne *76:* 252
Burgess, Gelett *32:* 39, 42
Burgess, Mark *157:* 31
Burke, Jim *179:* 19; *185:* 63
Burke, Phillip *95:* 117
Burkert, Nancy Ekholm *18:* 186; *22:* 140; *24:* 62, 63,64, 65; *26:* 53; *29:* 60, 61; *46:* 171; *YABC 1:* 46
Burkhardt, Bruce *142:* 86
Burkhardt, Melissa A. *142:* 86
Burleson, Joe *104:* 35; *172:* 139
Burn, Doris *6:* 172
Burn, Jeffrey *89:* 125; *152:* 132

Burn, Ted
  See Burn, Thomas E.
Burn, Thomas E. *151:* 41
Burnard, Damon *115:* 23
Burnett, Virgil *44:* 42
Burningham, John *9:* 68; *16:* 60, 61; *59:* 28, 29, 30,31, 32, 33, 35; *111:* 18, 19, 21; *160:* 37
Burns, Howard M. *12:* 173
Burns, Jim *47:* 70; *86:* 32; *91:* 197; *123:* 16
Burns, M.F. *26:* 69
Burns, Raymond *9:* 29
Burns, Robert *24:* 106
Burr, Dan *65:* 28; *108:* 134; *164:* 203; *182:* 68
Burr, Dane *12:* 2
Burra, Edward *YABC 2:* 68
Burrell, Galen *56:* 76
Burri, Rene *41:* 143; *54:* 166
Burridge, Marge Opitz *14:* 42
Burris, Burmah *4:* 81
Burroughs, John Coleman *41:* 64
Burroughs, Studley O. *41:* 65
Burton, Marilee Robin *46:* 33
Burton, Virginia Lee *2:* 43; *44:* 49, 51; *100:* 46, 47; *YABC 1:* 24; *147:* 56
Busoni, Rafaello *1:* 186; *3:* 224; *6:* 126; *14:* 5; *16:* 62, 63
Butchkes, Sidney *50:* 58
Butler, Geoff *94:* 20
Butler, Ralph *116:* 212
Butterfield, Ned *1:* 153; *27:* 128; *79:* 63
Butterworth, Ian *184:* 48, 49
Butterworth, Nick *106:* 43, 44; *149:* 34
Buxton, John *123:* 12
Buzelli, Christopher *105:* 149
Buzonas, Gail *29:* 88
Buzzell, Russ W. *12:* 177
Byard, Carole *39:* 44; *57:* 18, 19, 20; *60:* 60; *61:* 93, 96; *69:* 210; *78:* 246; *79:* 227
Byars, Betsy *46:* 35
Byfield, Barbara Ninde *8:* 18
Byfield, Graham *32:* 29
Bynum, Janie *176:* 50
Byrd, Robert *13:* 218; *33:* 46; *158:* 70
Byrd, Samuel *123:* 104

C

Cabat, Erni *74:* 38
Cabban, Vanessa *138:* 73; *176:* 39; *185:* 65
Cabrera, Jane *103:* 24; *152:* 27; *182:* 33, 34
Caddy, Alice *6:* 41
Cady, Harrison *17:* 21, 23; *19:* 57, 58
Caffrey, Aileen *72:* 223; *141:* 154
Cairns, Julia *177:* 37
Caldecott, Randolph *16:* 98, 103; *17:* 32, 33, 36, 38, 39; *26:* 90; *100:* 49, 50; *YABC 2:* 172
Calder, Alexander *18:* 168
Calderón, Gloria *179:* 5
Calderon, W. Frank *25:* 160
Caldwell, Ben *105:* 75; *149:* 60; *195:* 61
Caldwell, Clyde *98:* 100; *116:* 39
Caldwell, Doreen *23:* 77; *71:* 41
Caldwell, John *46:* 225
Call, Greg *126:* 135; *165:* 49; *182:* 105, 163; *197:* 18, 19
Callahan, Kevin *22:* 42
Callahan, Philip S. *25:* 77
Callan, Jamie *59:* 37
Calvin, James *61:* 92
Camburn-Bracalente, Carol A. *118:* 22
Cameron, Chad *190:* 144
Cameron, Julia Margaret *19:* 203
Cameron, Scott *99:* 18
Camm, Martin *140:* 208, 209, 210
Campbell, Ann *11:* 43; *123:* 182; *183:* 68
Campbell, Bill *89:* 39
Campbell, Ken *126:* 143

Campbell, Robert *55:* 120
Campbell, Rod *51:* 27; *98:* 34
Campbell, Walter M. *YABC 2:* 158
Camps, Luis *28:* 120, 121; *66:* 35
Canga, C.B. *187:* 165
Cann, Helen *124:* 50; *141:* 78; *170:* 138; *179:* 22, 23
Cannell, Jon *196:* 43
Cannon, Janell *78:* 25; *128:* 40
Canright, David *36:* 162
Cantone, AnnaLaura *182:* 146; *196:* 80
Canty, Thomas *85:* 161; *92:* 47; *113:* 192; *134:* 60; *185:* 117
Canyon, Christopher *150:* 44; *151:* 112
Caporale, Wende *70:* 42
Capp, Al *61:* 28, 30, 31, 40, 41, 43, 44
Cappon, Manuela *154:* 64
Caras, Peter *36:* 64
Caraway, Caren *57:* 22
Caraway, James *3:* 200, 201
Carbe, Nino *29:* 183
Cares, Linda *67:* 176
Carigiet, Alois *24:* 67
Carle, Eric *4:* 42; *11:* 121; *12:* 29; *65:* 32,33, 34, 36; *73:* 63, 65; *163:* 55, 56
Carling, Amelia Lau *164:* 46
Carlino, Angela *168:* 43; *188:* 20
Carlson, Nancy L. *41:* 116; *56:* 25; *90:* 45; *144:* 48, 50
Carlluccio, Maria *175:* 129
Carmi, Giora *79:* 35; *149:* 40
Carpenter, Nancy *76:* 128; *86:* 173; *89:* 171; *131:* 186; *134:* 8; *138:* 215; *153:* 204; *159:* 93; *165:* 232
Carr, Archie *37:* 225
Carrick, Donald *5:* 194; *39:* 97; *49:* 70; *53:* 156; *63:* 15, 16, 17, 18, 19, 21; *80:* 131; *86:* 151; *118:* 24
Carrick, Malcolm *28:* 59, 60
Carrick, Paul *118:* 26; *194:* 28
Carrick, Valery *21:* 47
Carrier, Lark *71:* 43
Carroll, Jim *88:* 211; *140:* 177; *153:* 99; *195:* 75
Carroll, Lewis
  See Dodgson, Charles L.
Carroll, Michael *72:* 5
Carroll, Pamela *84:* 68; *128:* 214
Carroll, Ruth *7:* 41; *10:* 68
Carter, Abby *81:* 32; *97:* 121; *102:* 61; *163:* 139; *164:* 125; *184:* 22, 23; *191:* 85
Carter, Barbara *47:* 167, 169
Carter, David A. *114:* 24, 25; *170:* 42, 43
Carter, Don *124:* 54; *184:* 100; *192:* 43, 44, 45
Carter, Harry *22:* 179
Carter, Helene *15:* 38; *22:* 202, 203; *YABC 2:* 220, 221
Carter, Penny *173:* 91
Cartlidge, Michelle *49:* 65; *96:* 50, 51
Cartwright, Reg *63:* 61, 62; *78:* 26; *143:* 4
Cartwright, Shannon *176:* 81
Carty, Leo *4:* 196; *7:* 163; *58:* 131
Cary *4:* 133; *9:* 32; *20:* 2; *21:* 143
Cary, Page *12:* 41
Casale, Paul *71:* 63; *109:* 122; *136:* 28
Case, Sandra E. *16:* 2
Caseley, Judith *87:* 36; *159:* 47, 48, 49
Casilla, Robert *78:* 7; *167:* 124
Casino, Steve *85:* 193
Cassel, Lili
  See Wronker, Lili Cassel
Cassel-Wronker, Lili
  See Wronker, Lili Cassel
Cassels, Jean *8:* 50; *150:* 119; *173:* 37; *186:* 182
Cassen, Melody *140:* 51
Cassity, Don *104:* 24
Cassler, Carl *75:* 137, 138; *82:* 162
Casson, Hugh *65:* 38, 40, 42, 43
Castellon, Federico *48:* 45, 46, 47, 48
Castle, Jane *4:* 80

Castro, Antonio *84:* 71
Catalano, Dominic *94:* 79; *163:* 60, 61; *162:* 54
Catalanotto, Peter *63:* 170; *70:* 23; *71:* 182; *72:* 96; *74:* 114; *76:* 194, 195; *77:* 7; *79:* 157; *80:* 28, 67; *83:* 157; *85:* 27; *108:* 11; *113:* 30, 31, 33, 34, 36; *114:* 27, 28, 29; *117:* 53; *124:* 168; *159:* 54, 55; *195:* 19, 20, 21, 22, 24, 174
Catania, Tom *68:* 82
Cather, Carolyn *3:* 83; *15:* 203; *34:* 216
Catrow, David *117:* 179; *152:* 31, 33; *173:* 24
Cauley, Lorinda Bryan *44:* 135; *46:* 49
Cayard, Bruce *38:* 67
Cazet, Denys *52:* 27; *99:* 39, 40; *163:* 65, 66; *191:* 25, 27, 28
Ceccoli, Nicoletta *181:* 39; *188:* 99
Cecil, Randy *127:* 132, 133; *187:* 16, 17; *191:* 168
Cellini, Joseph *2:* 73; *3:* 35; *16:* 116; *47:* 103
Cepeda, Joe *90:* 62; *109:* 91; *134:* 172; *159:* 57, 58, 164; *197:* 157
Chabrian, Debbi *45:* 55
Chabrian, Deborah *51:* 182; *53:* 124; *63:* 107; *75:* 84; *79:* 85; *82:* 247; *89:* 93; *101:* 197
Chagnon, Mary *37:* 158
Chalmers, Mary *3:* 145; *13:* 148; *33:* 125; *66:* 214
Chamberlain, Christopher *45:* 57
Chamberlain, Margaret *46:* 51; *106:* 89; *188:* 193
Chamberlain, Nigel *78:* 140
Chambers, C.E. *17:* 230
Chambers, Dave *12:* 151
Chambers, Jill *134:* 110
Chambers, Mary *4:* 188
Chambliss, Maxie *42:* 186; *56:* 159; *93:* 163, 164; *103:* 178; *186:* 33, 34; *196:* 39
Champlin, Dale *136:* 124
Chan, Harvey *96:* 236; *99:* 153; *143:* 218; *179:* 144
Chandler, David P. *28:* 62
Chaney, Howard *139:* 27
Chang, Warren *101:* 209
Chapel, Jody *68:* 20
Chapman, C.H. *13:* 83, 85, 87
Chapman, Frederick T. *6:* 27; *44:* 28
Chapman, Gaynor *32:* 52, 53
Chapman, Jane *145:* 186; *150:* 56; *166:* 220; *174:* 202; *176:* 43, 44; *179:* 131
Chapman, Lynne *175:* 31; *197:* 25
Chappell, Warren *3:* 172; *21:* 56; *27:* 125
Charles, Donald *30:* 154, 155
Charlip, Remy *4:* 48; *34:* 138; *68:* 53, 54; *119:* 29, 30
Charlot, Jean *1:* 137, 138; *8:* 23; *14:* 31; *48:* 151; *56:* 21
Charlot, Martin *64:* 72
Charlton, Michael *34:* 50; *37:* 39
Charmatz, Bill *7:* 45
Chartier, Normand *9:* 36; *52:* 49; *66:* 40; *74:* 220; *145:* 169; *168:* 91; *177:* 108
Chase, Lynwood M. *14:* 4
Chast, Roz *97:* 39, 40
Chastain, Madye Lee *4:* 50
Chateron, Ann *152:* 19
Chatterton, Martin *68:* 102; *152:* 19
Chau, Tungwai *140:* 35
Chauncy, Francis *24:* 158
Chayka, Doug *145:* 97; *177:* 150; *196:* 46
Chee, Cheng-Khee *79:* 42; *81:* 224; *180:* 245
Chen, Chih-sien *90:* 226
Chen, Tony *6:* 45; *19:* 131; *29:* 126; *34:* 160
Chen, Yong *183:* 34
Cheney, T.A. *11:* 47
Cheng, Judith *36:* 45; *51:* 16
Chermayeff, Ivan *47:* 53
Cherry, David *93:* 40
Cherry, Lynne *34:* 52; *65:* 184; *87:* 111; *99:* 46, 47
Chesak, Lina *135:* 118

Chess, Victoria *12:* 6; *33:* 42, 48, 49; *40:* 194; *41:* 145; *69:* 80; *72:* 100; *92:* 33, 34; *104:* 167
Chessare, Michele *41:* 50; *56:* 48; *69:* 145
Chesterton, G.K. *27:* 43, 44, 45, 47
Chestnutt, David *47:* 217
Chesworth, Michael *75:* 24, 152; *88:* 136; *94:* 25; *98:* 155; *160:* 42
Chetham, Celia *134:* 34
Chetwin, Grace *86:* 40
Cheung, Irving *158:* 96
Chevalier, Christa *35:* 66
Chew, Ruth *7:* 46; *132:* 147
Chewning, Randy *92:* 206
Chichester Clark, Emma *72:* 121; *77:* 212; *78:* 209; *87:* 143; *117:* 37, 39, 40; *144:* 138; *156:* 24, 25
Chifflart *47:* 113, 127
Child, Lauren *119:* 32; *183:* 30, 31
Chin, Alex *28:* 54
Chitwood, Susan Tanner *163:* 16
Cho, Shinta *8:* 126
Chodos-Irvine, Margaret *52:* 102, 103, 107; *152:* 44
Choi, Yangsook *171:* 134; *173:* 135; *178:* 38, 39, 40
Chollat, Emilie *170:* 203
Chollick, Jay *25:* 175
Choma, Christina *99:* 169
Chomey, Steve *188:* 53
Chorao, Kay *7:* 200, 201; *8:* 25; *11:* 234; *33:* 187; *35:* 239; *69:* 35; *70:* 235; *123:* 174; *193:* 179
Chowdhury, Subrata *62:* 130; *162:* 22, 23
Christelow, Eileen *38:* 44; *83:* 198, 199; *90:* 57, 58; *184:* 26
Christensen, Bonnie *93:* 100; *153:* 67
Christensen, Gardell Dano *1:* 57
Christensen, James C. *140:* 226
Christiana, David *90:* 64; *135:* 13; *171:* 7; *195:* 26, 27
Christiansen, Per *40:* 24
Christie, R. Gregory *116:* 107; *127:* 20, 21; *162:* 179; *164:* 114; *165:* 137; *174:* 157; *179:* 172; *185:* 17, 18, 19
Christy, Howard Chandler *17:* 163, 164, 165, 168, 169; *19:* 186, 187; *21:* 22, 23, 24, 25
Christy, Jana *194:* 21
Chronister, Robert *23:* 138; *63:* 27; *69:* 167
Church, Caroline Jayne *179:* 27
Church, Frederick *YABC 1:* 155
Chute, Marchette *1:* 59
Chwast, Jacqueline *1:* 63; *2:* 275; *6:* 46, 47; *11:* 125; *12:* 202; *14:* 235
Chwast, Seymour *3:* 128, 129; *18:* 43; *27:* 152; *92:* 79; *96:* 56, 57, 58; *146:* 32, 33; *197:* 99
Cieslawksi, Steve *101:* 142; *127:* 116; *158:* 169, 171; *190:* 174
Cinelli, Lisa *146:* 253
Cirlin, Edgard *2:* 168
Clairin, Georges *53:* 109
Clapp, John *105:* 66; *109:* 58; *126:* 7; *129:* 148; *130:* 165; *195:* 48
Clark, Brenda *119:* 85; *153:* 55
Clark, David *77:* 164; *134:* 144, 145
Clark, Emma Chichester
See Chichester Clark, Emma
Clark, Victoria *35:* 159
Clarke, Greg *169:* 134
Clarke, Gus *72:* 226; *134:* 31
Clarke, Harry *23:* 172, 173
Clarke, Peter *75:* 102
Claverie, Jean *38:* 46; *88:* 29
Clavis, Philippe Goossens *182:* 167
Clayton, Elaine *159:* 60
Clayton, Robert *9:* 181
Cleary, Brian P. *186:* 37
Cleaver, Elizabeth *8:* 204; *23:* 36
Cleland, T.M. *26:* 92
Clemens, Peter *61:* 125

Clement, Charles *20:* 38
Clement, Gary *186:* 79; *191:* 32
Clement, Janet *182:* 50
Clement, Rod *97:* 42
Clement, Stephen *88:* 3
Clementson, John *84:* 213
Clemesha, David *192:* 49, 50
Clevin, Jorgen *7:* 50
Clifford, Judy *34:* 163; *45:* 198
Clokey, Art *59:* 44
Clouse, Dennis *187:* 158
Clouse, James *84:* 15
Clouse, Nancy L. *78:* 31; *114:* 90
Clover, Peter *152:* 45
Cneut, Carll *156:* 166; *165:* 67; *197:* 26
Coalson, Glo *9:* 72, 85; *25:* 155; *26:* 42; *35:* 212; *53:* 31; *56:* 154; *94:* 37, 38, 193
Cober, Alan E. *17:* 158; *32:* 77; *49:* 127
Cober-Gentry, Leslie *92:* 111
Cocca-Leffler, Maryann *80:* 46; *136:* 60; *139:* 193; *194:* 31, 33, 34
CoConis, Ted *4:* 41; *46:* 41; *51:* 104
Cocozza, Chris *87:* 18; *110:* 173; *111:* 149
Cockroft, Jason *152:* 20
Coerr, Eleanor *1:* 64; *67:* 52
Coes, Peter *35:* 172
Cogancherry, Helen *52:* 143; *69:* 131; *77:* 93; *78:* 220; *109:* 204; *110:* 129
Coggins, Jack *2:* 69
Cohen, Alix *7:* 53
Cohen, Miriam *155:* 23, 24
Cohen, Nancy R. *165:* 35
Cohen, Santiago *164:* 26
Cohen, Sheldon *105:* 33, 34; *166:* 46, 47
Cohen, Vincent O. *19:* 243
Cohen, Vivien *11:* 112
Coker, Paul *51:* 172
Colbert, Anthony *15:* 41; *20:* 193
Colby, C.B. *3:* 47
Cole, Babette *58:* 172; *96:* 63, 64; *155:* 29
Cole, Brock *68:* 223; *72:* 36, 37, 38, 192; *127:* 23; *136:* 64, 65; *197:*
Cole, Gwen *87:* 185
Cole, Henry *178:* 120; *181:* 42, 43; *189:* 60
Cole, Herbert *28:* 104
Cole, Michael *59:* 46
Cole, Olivia H.H. *1:* 134; *3:* 223; *9:* 111; *38:* 104
Colin, Paul *102:* 59; *123:* 118; *126:* 152; *192:* 129
Collicott, Sharleen *98:* 39; *143:* 29, 30
Collier, Bryan *126:* 54; *151:* 166; *174:* 16, 17, 18
Collier, David *13:* 127
Collier, John *27:* 179
Collier, Steven *50:* 52
Collier-Morales, Roberta *168:* 61
Collins, Heather *66:* 84; *67:* 68; *81:* 40; *98:* 192, 193; *129:* 95, 96, 98
Collins, Matt *167:* 90
Collins, Ross *140:* 23, 24
Colman, Audrey *146:* 161
Colón, Raul *108:* 112; *113:* 5; *117:* 167; *134:* 112; *146:* 23; *159:* 92; *166:* 73; *180:* 107; *186:* 156; *190:* 6; *193:* 24, 205
Colonna, Bernard *21:* 50; *28:* 103; *34:* 140; *43:* 180; *78:* 150
Comport, Sally Wern *117:* 169; *169:* 104; *190:* 42
Conde, J.M. *100:* 120
Condon, Grattan *54:* 85 *Condon, Ken 161:* 44; *195:* 28, 29
Cone, Ferne Geller *39:* 49
Cone, J. Morton *39:* 49
Conklin, Paul *43:* 62
Connolly, Howard *67:* 88
Connolly, Jerome P. *4:* 128; *28:* 52
Connolly, Peter *47:* 60
Conoly, Walle *110:* 224
Conover, Chris *31:* 52; *40:* 184; *41:* 51; *44:* 79

Contreras, Gerry 72: 9
Converse, James 38: 70
Conway 62: 62
Conway, Michael 69: 12; 81: 3; 92: 108
Cook, Ande 188: 135
Cook, G.R. 29: 165
Cook, Joel 108: 160
Cookburn, W.V. 29: 204
Cooke, Donald E. 2: 77
Cooke, Tom 52: 118
Coomaraswamy, A.K. 50: 100
Coombs, Charles 43: 65
Coombs, Deborah 139: 175
Coombs, Patricia 2: 82; 3: 52; 22: 119; 51: 32, 33, 34, 35, 36, 37, 38, 39, 40, 42, 43
Cooney, Barbara 6: 16, 17, 50; 12: 42; 13: 92; 15: 145; 16: 74, 111; 18: 189; 23: 38, 89, 93; 32: 138; 38: 105; 59: 48, 49, 51, 52, 53; 74: 222; 81: 100; 91: 25; 96: 71, 72, 74; 100: 149; YABC2: 10
Cooper, Elisha 157: 38, 39
Cooper, Floyd 79: 95; 81: 45; 84: 82; 85: 74; 91: 118; 96: 77, 78; 103: 149; 144: 54; 145: 151; 159: 198; 176: 133, 134; 187: 26, 27, 28, 29; 188: 22
Cooper, Heather 50: 39
Cooper, Helen 102: 42, 43, 44
Cooper, Mario 24: 107
Cooper, Marjorie 7: 112
Cope, Jane 61: 201; 108 52
Copeland, Mark 180: 12
Copelman, Evelyn 8: 61; 18: 25
Copley, Heather 30: 86; 45: 57
Corbett, Grahame 30: 114; 43: 67
Corbino, John 19: 248
Corcos, Lucille 2: 223; 10: 27; 34: 66
Cordell, Matthew 197: 93
Corey, Robert 9: 34
Corlass, Heather 10: 7
Cornell, James 27: 60
Cornell, Jeff 11: 58
Cornell, Laura 94: 179; 95: 25
Corrigan, Barbara 8: 37
Corrigan, Patrick 145: 149
Corwin, Judith Hoffman 10: 28
Corwin, Oliver 191: 119
Cory, Fanny Y. 20: 113; 48: 29
Cosentino, Ralph 169: 32
Cosgrove, Margaret 3: 100; 47: 63; 82: 133
Costabel, Eva Deutsch 45: 66, 67
Costanza, John 58: 7, 8, 9
Costello, Chris 86: 78
Costello, David F. 23: 55
Côté, Geneviéve 184: 37, 39
Cote, Nancy 126: 139; 156: 101; 174: 101; 182: 53, 54, 55
Cottenden, Jeff 190: 45
Couch, Greg 94: 124; 110: 13; 162: 31; 168: 149
Councell, Ruth Tietjen 79: 29
Courtney, Cathy 58: 69, 144; 59: 15; 61: 20, 87
Courtney, R. 35: 110
Counihan, Claire 133: 106
Cousineau, Normand 89: 180; 112: 76
Cousins, Lucy 172: 53, 54
Couture, Christin 41: 209
Covarrubias, Miguel 35: 118, 119, 123, 124, 125
Coville, Katherine 32: 57; 36: 167; 92: 38
Covington, Neverne 113: 87
Cowdrey, Richard 169: 170; 178: 205
Cowell, Cressida 140: 39
Cowell, Lucinda 77: 54
Cox 43: 93
Cox, Charles 8: 20
Cox, David 56: 37; 90: 63; 119: 38
Cox, Palmer 24: 76, 77
Cox, Steve 140: 96
Coxe, Molly 69: 44
Coxon, Michele 158: 80

Crabb, Gordon 70: 39
Crabtree, Judith 98: 42
Craft, Kinuko 22: 182; 36: 220; 53: 122, 123, 148,149; 74: 12; 81: 129; 86: 31; 89: 139; 127: 27, 28, 29; 132: 142; 139: 38
Craig, Daniel 177: 67; 180: 11; 185: 203
Craig, David 136: 198
Craig, Helen 49: 76; 62: 70, 71, 72; 69: 141; 94: 42, 43, 44; 112: 53; 135: 101, 102
Crane, Alan H. 1: 217
Crane, H.M. 13: 111
Crane, Jack 43: 183
Crane, Jordan 174: 21
Crane, Walter 18: 46, 47, 48, 49, 53, 54, 56, 57, 59, 60, 61; 22: 128; 24: 210, 217; 100: 70, 71
Cravath, Lynne W. 98: 45; 182: 58, 59
Crawford, Denise 137: 213
Crawford, Will 43: 77
Credle, Ellis 1: 69
Czernecki, Stefan 154: 104; 178: 68, 69
Crespi, Francesca 87: 90
Cressy, Michael 124: 55
Crews, Donald 32: 59, 60; 76: 42, 43, 44
Crews, Nina 97: 49
Crichlow, Ernest 74: 88; 83: 203
Croft, James 150: 57
Crofut, Bob 80: 87; 81: 47
Crofut, Susan 23: 61
Croll, Carolyn 80: 137; 102: 52
Cross, Peter 56: 78; 63: 60, 65
Crowe, Elizabeth 88: 144
Crowell, Pers 3: 125
Cruikshank, George 15: 76, 83; 22: 74, 75, 76, 77, 78, 79,80, 81, 82, 84, 137; 24: 22, 23
Crump, Fred H. 11: 62
Cruz, Ray 6: 55; 70: 234; 123: 173; 172: 192
Csatari, Joe 44: 82; 55: 152; 63: 25, 28; 102: 58
Cuetara, Mittie 158: 85
Cuffari, Richard 4: 75; 5: 98; 6: 56; 7: 13,84, 153; 8: 148, 155; 9: 89; 11: 19; 12: 55, 96,114; 15: 51, 202; 18: 5; 20: 139; 21: 197; 22: 14, 192; 23: 15, 106; 25: 97; 27: 133; 28: 196; 29: 54; 30: 85; 31: 35; 36: 101; 38: 171; 42: 97; 44: 92, 192; 45: 212, 213; 46: 36, 198; 50: 164; 54: 80, 136, 137, 145; 56: 17; 60: 63; 66: 49, 50; 70: 41; 71: 132; 77: 157; 78: 58, 149; 79: 120; 85: 2, 152
Cugat, Xavier 19: 120
Cumings, Art 35: 160
Cummings, Chris 29: 167
Cummings, Michael 159: 142
Cummings, Pat 42: 61; 61: 99; 69: 205; 71: 57,58; 78: 24, 25; 93: 75; 107: 49, 50; 164: 259
Cummings, Richard 24: 119
Cunette, Lou 20: 93; 22: 125
Cunningham, Aline 25: 180
Cunningham, David 11: 13
Cunningham, Imogene 16: 122, 127
Cunningham, Kelley 176: 159
Cupples, Pat 107: 12; 126: 109; 182: 13
Curlee, Lynn 98: 48; 141: 39; 190: 48
Currey, Anna 190: 145
Curry, John Steuart 2: 5; 19: 84; 34: 36; 144: 126
Curry, Tom 127: 131; 185: 25, 26
Curtis, Bruce 23: 96; 30: 88; 36: 22
Curtis, Neil 167: 30
Cusack, Margaret 58: 49, 50, 51
Cushman, Doug 65: 57; 101: 39, 40; 133: 179; 157: 45; 186: 157
Cutting, Ann 196: 194
Cyrus, Kurt 132: 39; 179: 36, 37
Czechowski, Alicia 95: 21; 171: 37
Czernecki, Stefan 117: 173

D

Dabcovich, Lydia 25: 105; 40: 114; 99: 75, 76
Dacey, Bob 82: 175; 152: 65
d'Achille, Gino 127: 175, 176
Dailey, Don 78: 197
Dain, Martin J. 35: 75
Dale, Penny 127: 224; 151: 57; 160: 89; 197: 75
Dale, Rae 72: 197
Daley, Joann 50: 22
Dalton, Anne 40: 62; 63: 119
Daly, Deborah M. 74: 213
Daly, Jim 103: 60; 150: 48
Daly, Jude 138: 118, 119
Daly, Nicholas 37: 53; 76: 48, 49
Daly, Niki 107: 15; 114: 38, 39, 40; 164: 86; 192: 53
Daly, Paul 97: 205
Dalziel, Brothers 33: 113
D'Amato, Alex 9: 48; 20: 25
D'Amato, Janet 9: 48; 20: 25; 26: 118
D'Amico, Steve 170: 52
Danalis, Johnny 167: 27
D'Andrea, Domenick 183: 108
Daniel, Alan 23: 59; 29: 110; 76: 50, 53, 55, 56; 153: 76 115: 74; 134: 70
Daniel, Lea 76: 53, 55; 153: 76
Daniel, Lewis C. 20: 216
Daniels, Beau 73: 4
Daniels, Steve 22: 16
Daniels, Stewart 56: 12
Dann, Bonnie 31: 83
Dann, Penny 82: 128
Danska, Herbert 24: 219
Danyell, Alice 20: 27
Darley, F.O.C. 16: 145; 19: 79, 86, 88, 185; 21: 28,36; 35: 76, 77, 78, 79, 80, 81; YABC 2: 175
Darling, Lois 3: 59; 23: 30, 31
Darling, Louis 1: 40, 41; 2: 63; 3: 59; 23: 30,31; 43: 54, 57, 59; 121: 53
Darrow, David R. 84: 101
Darrow, Whitney, Jr. 13: 25; 38: 220, 221
Darwin, Beatrice 43: 54
Darwin, Len 24: 82
Dastolfo, Frank 33: 179
Dauber, Liz 1: 22; 3: 266; 30: 49
Daugherty, James 3: 66; 8: 178; 13: 27, 28, 161; 18: 101; 19: 72; 29: 108; 32: 156; 42: 84; YABC 1: 256; 2: 174
d'Aulaire, Edgar Parin 5: 51; 66: 53
d'Aulaire, Ingri Parin 5: 51; 66: 53
Davalos, Felipe 99: 197; 159: 66; 174: 163
Davenier, Christine 125: 88; 127: 32; 128: 152; 179: 39, 40
Davick, Linda 151: 124
David, Jacques-Louis 193: 22
David, Jonathan 19: 37
Davidson, Kevin 28: 154
Davidson, Raymond 32: 61
Davie, Helen K. 77: 48, 49
Davis, Allen 20: 11; 22: 45; 27: 222; 29: 157; 41: 99; 47: 99; 50: 84; 52: 105
Davis, Bette J. 15: 53; 23: 95
Davis, Dimitris 45: 95
Davis, Hendon 151: 122
Davis, Jack E. 145: 139; 175: 84, 85
Davis, Jim 32: 63, 64
Davis, Katie 152: 52, 53, 54
Davis, Lambert 110: 23, 24; 176: 58
Davis, Marguerite 31: 38; 34: 69, 70; 100: 34; YABC 1: 126, 230
Davis, Nelle 69: 191
Davis, Paul 78: 214
Davis, Yvonne LeBrun 94: 144
Davisson, Virginia H. 44: 178
DaVolls, Andy 85: 53
Dawson, Diane 24: 127; 42: 126; 52: 130; 68: 104

Day, Alexandra *67:* 59; *97:* 54; *166:* 65; *169:* 40; *197:* 50, 51, 52, 54
Day, Larry *169:* 88; *185:* 59
Day, Rob *94:* 110; *127:* 24; *197:* 32
Dean, Bob *19:* 211
Dean, David *192:* 55
de Angeli, Marguerite *1:* 77; *27:* 62, 65, 66, 67, 69, 70, 72; *100:* 75, 76; *YABC 1:* 166
DeArmond, Dale *70:* 47
Deas, Michael *27:* 219, 221; *30:* 156; *67:* 134; *72:* 24; *75:* 155; *84:* 206; *88:* 124
Deas, Rich *191:* 87; *193:* 10
deBarros, Jim *196:* 60
Debon, Nicolas *151:* 60; *177:* 46
de Bosschere, Jean *19:* 252; *21:* 4; *186:* 44, 45
De Bruyn, M(onica) G. *13:* 30, 31
Decker, C.B. *172:* 120
De Cuir, John F. *1:* 28, 29
Deeter, Catherine *74:* 110; *103:* 150; *137:* 50
Degen, Bruce *40:* 227, 229; *57:* 28, 29; *56:* 156; *75:* 229; *76:* 19; *81:* 36, 37; *92:* 26; *93:* 199; *97:* 56, 58, 59; *124:* 40; *147:* 39, 40, 41; *168:* 23
De Grazia *14:* 59; *39:* 56, 57
DeGroat, George *88:* 40
deGroat, Diane *9:* 39; *18:* 7; *23:* 123; *28:* 200, 201; *31:* 58, 59; *34:* 151; *41:* 152; *43:* 88; *46:* 40, 200; *49:* 163; *50:* 89; *52:* 30, 34; *54:* 43; *63:* 5; *70:* 136; *71:* 99; *73:* 117,156; *77:* 34; *85:* 48; *86:* 201; *87:* 142; *90:* 72, 73, 143; *95:* 182; *111:* 123; *118:* 160; *126:* 8; *130:* 130; *138:* 93, 94; *169:* 46, 47
de Groot, Lee *6:* 21
Deines, Brian *110:* 139
DeJohn, Marie *89:* 78
Dekhteryov, B. *61:* 158
de Kiefte, Kees *94:* 107
Delacre, Lulu *36:* 66; *156:* 35
Delaney, A. *21:* 78
Delaney, Michael *180:* 16
Delaney, Molly *80:* 43
Delaney, Ned *28:* 68; *56:* 80; *102:* 11
DeLange, Alex Pardo *179:* 128
DeLapine, Jim *79:* 21
De La Roche Saint Andre, Anne *75:* 37
de Larrea, Victoria *6:* 119, 204; *29:* 103; *72:* 203; *87:* 199
Delessert, Étienne *7:* 140; *46:* 61, 62, 63, 65, 67, 68; *130:* 38, 39, 40, 41, 42; *179:* 46, 47, 48, 49; *YABC 2:* 209
Delezenne, Christine *186:* 126
Del Negro, Janice *196:* 161
DeLorenzo, Christopher *154:* 149
Delulio, John *15:* 54
DeLuna, Tony *88:* 95
Demarest, Chris L. *45:* 68, 69, 70; *73:* 172, 173, 176; *78:* 106; *82:* 48, 49; *89:* 212; *92:* 86; *128:* 57, 58; *175:* 46, 48
De Mejo, Oscar *40:* 67
Demi *11:* 135; *15:* 245; *66:* 129, 130; *89:* 216; *102:* 66, 67, 68
Denetsosie, Hoke *13:* 126; *82:* 34
Denise, Christopher *147:* 43, 44; *176:* 101; *193:* 35, 36, 37
Dennis, Morgan *18:* 68, 69; *64:* 89
Dennis, Wesley *2:* 87; *3:* 111; *11:* 132; *18:* 71, 72, 73, 74; *22:* 9; *24:* 196, 200; *46:* 178; *69:* 94, 96; *129:* 62
Denslow, W.W. *16:* 84, 85, 86, 87; *18:* 19, 20, 24; *29:* 211; *100:* 21
Denton, Kady MacDonald *110:* 82; *130:* 70; *181:* 54, 55, 56; *192:* 75
Denton, Terry *72:* 163; *174:* 26; *186:* 52; *196:* 83, 84
DePalma, Mary Newell *132:* 114; *139:* 75; *185:* 30, 31; *186:* 121
de Paola, Tomie *8:* 95; *9:* 93; *11:* 69; *25:* 103; *28:* 157; *29:* 80; *39:* 52, 53; *40:* 226; *46:* 187; *59:* 61, 62, 63, 64, 65, 66, 67, 68, 69, 71, 72, 74; *62:* 19; *108:* 63, 67, 68, 70; *155:* 62, 64, 66; *180:* 105

Deraney, Michael J. *77:* 35; *78:* 148
deRosa, Dee *70:* 48; *71:* 210; *91:* 78
Dervaux, Isabelle *111:* 117
DeSaix, Deborah Durland *180:* 15; *188:* 24
De Saulles, Tony *119:* 39
de Seve, Peter *146:* 261
Deshaprabhu, Meera Dayal *86:* 192
Desimini, Lisa *86:* 68; *94:* 47; *96:* 7; *104:* 107; *125:* 194; *131:* 180; *172:* 56
de St. Menin, Charles *70:* 17
Detmold, Edward J. *22:* 104, 105, 106, 107; *35:* 120; *64:* 5; *YABC 2:* 203
Detrich, Susan *20:* 133
Deutermann, Diana *77:* 175
DeVelasco, Joseph E. *21:* 51
de Veyrac, Robert *YABC 2:* 19
DeVille, Edward A. *4:* 235
de Visser, John *55:* 119
Devito, Bert *12:* 164
Devlin, Harry *11:* 74; *74:* 63, 65; *136:* 77, 78
Dewan, Ted *108:* 73; *157:* 55; *165:* 129
Dewar, Nick *133:* 122
Dewdney, Anna *184:* 43, 44
Dewey, Ariane *7:* 64; *33:* 195; *35:* 208; *68:* 16,17; *75:* 46; *93:* 91; *94:* 197; *109:* 65, 66, 67; *125:* 2, 3, 4, 5; *127:* 188; *143:* 25; *178:* 17, 19, 74; *188:* 166
Dewey, Jennifer (Owings) *58:* 54; *64:* 214; *65:* 207; *88:* 169; *103:* 45
Dewey, Kenneth *39:* 62; *51:* 23; *56:* 163
de Zanger, Arie *30:* 40
Diakité, Baba Wagué *174:* 28
Diamond, Donna *21:* 200; *23:* 63; *26:* 142; *35:* 83, 84, 85, 86, 87, 88, 89; *38:* 78; *40:* 147; *44:* 152; *50:* 144; *53:* 126; *69:* 46, 47, 48, 201; *71:* 133; *123:* 19
Dias, Ron *71:* 67
Diaz, David *80:* 213; *96:* 83, 84; *108:* 228; *110:* 29; *149:* 106; *150:* 63; *179:* 160; *184:* 95, 97; *189:* 51, 52, 53
Dibley, Glin *138:* 83; *141:* 128
DiCesare, Joe *70:* 38; *71:* 63, 106; *79:* 214; *93:* 147; *116:* 217; *143:* 111; *166:* 57
Dick, John Henry *8:* 181
Dickens, Frank *34:* 131
Dickey, Robert L. *15:* 279
Dickson, Mora *84:* 21
Didier, Sam *166:* 114
Dietz, James *128:* 223; *193:* 136
di Fate, Vincent *37:* 70; *90:* 11; *93:* 60; *109:* 219, 220
Di Fiori, Lawrence *10:* 51; *12:* 190; *27:* 97; *40:* 219; *93:* 57; *130:* 45
Digby, Desmond *97:* 180
Dignan, James *196:* 143
Di Grazia, Thomas *32:* 66; *35:* 241
Dillard, Annie *10:* 32
Dillard, Sarah *136:* 186
Dillon, Corinne B. *1:* 139
Dillon, Diane *4:* 104, 167; *6:* 23; *13:* 29; *15:* 99; *26:* 148; *27:* 136, 201; *51:* 29, 48, 51, 52, 53, 54,55, 56, 57, 58, 59, 60, 61, 62; *54:* 155; *56:* 69; *58:* 127,128; *61:* 95; *62:* 27; *64:* 46; *68:* 3; *69:* 209; *74:* 89; *79:* 92; *86:* 89; *92:* 28, 177; *93:* 7, 210; *94:* 239, 240; *97:* 167; *106:* 58, 59,61, 64; *107:* 3; *139:* 246; *167:* 77; *189:* 202; *191:* 191; *194:* 45, 46, 48, 49
Dillon, Leo *4:* 104, 167; *6:* 23; *13:* 29; *15:* 99; *26:* 148; *27:* 136, 201; *51:* 29, 48, 51, 52, 53, 54,55, 56, 57, 58, 59, 60, 61, 62; *54:* 155; *56:* 69; *58:* 127,128; *61:* 95; *62:* 27; *64:* 46; *68:* 3; *69:* 209; *74:* 89; *79:* 92; *86:* 89; *92:* 28, 177; *93:* 7, 210; *94:* 239, 240; *97:* 167; *106:* 58, 59,61, 64; *107:* 3; *139:* 246; *167:* 77; *189:* 202; *191:* 191; *194:* 45, 46, 48, 49
Dillon, Sharon Saseen *59:* 179, 188
DiMaccio, Gerald *121:* 80
DiMaggio, Joe *36:* 22
DiMassi, Gina *169:* 17

Dinan, Carol *25:* 169; *59:* 75
Dines, Glen *7:* 66, 67
Dinesen, Thomas *44:* 37
Dinh, Pham Viet *167:* 184
Dinnerstein, Harvey *42:* 63, 64, 65, 66, 67, 68; *50:* 146
Dinsdale, Mary *10:* 65; *11:* 171
Dinyer, Eric *86:* 148; *109:* 163; *110:* 239; *124:* 11; *150:* 69; *170:* 4; *171:* 30
Dion, Nathalie *170:* 124
DiRocco, Carl *181:* 23
DiSalvo-Ryan, DyAnne *59:* 77; *62:* 185; *117:* 46; *144:* 64; *150:* 153; *186:* 162
Disney, Walt *28:* 71, 72, 73, 76, 77, 78, 79, 80, 81, 87, 88, 89,90, 91, 94
DiTerlizzi, Tony *105:* 7; *147:* 22; *154:* 31, 32, 33
Divito, Anna *83:* 159
Dixon, Don *74:* 17; *109:* 196
Dixon, Larry *127:* 125
Dixon, Maynard *20:* 165
Doares, Robert G. *20:* 39
Dobias, Frank *22:* 162
Dobrin, Arnold *4:* 68
Dobson, Steven Gaston *102:* 103
Dockray, Tracy *139:* 77
Docktor, Irv *43:* 70
Dodd, Ed *4:* 69
Dodd, Julie *74:* 73
Dodd, Lynley *35:* 92; *86:* 71; *132:* 45, 46, 47
Dodge, Bill *96:* 36; *118:* 7, 8, 9; *133:* 135
Dodgson, Charles L. *20:* 148; *33:* 146; *YABC 2:* 98
Dodson, Bert *9:* 138; *14:* 195; *42:* 55; *54:* 8; *60:* 49; *101:* 125
Dodson, Liz Brenner *105:* 117; *111:* 15
Dohanos, Stevan *16:* 10
Dolce, J. Ellen *74:* 147; *75:* 41
Dolch, Marguerite P. *50:* 64
Dolesch, Susanne *34:* 49
Dollar, Diane *57:* 32
Dolobowsky, Mena *81:* 54
Dolson, Hildegarde *5:* 57
Domanska, Janina *6:* 66, 67; *YABC 1:* 166
Domi *134:* 113
Dominguez, El *53:* 94
Domjan, Joseph *25:* 93
Domm, Jeffrey C. *84:* 69; *135:* 70
Donahey, William *68:* 209
Donahue, Dorothy *76:* 170
Donahue, Vic *2:* 93; *3:* 190; *9:* 44
Donald, Elizabeth *4:* 18
Donalty, Alison *149:* 195, 196, 197
Donato *85:* 59; *149:* 204; *191:* 19
Doney, Todd L.W. *87:* 12; *93:* 112; *98:* 135; *101:* 57; *104:* 40; *118:* 163; *135:* 162, 163; *151:* 18
Donna, Natalie *9:* 52
Donohue, Dorothy *95:* 2; *132:* 30; *176:* 54, 55; *178:* 77, 78, 79
Dooling, Michael *82:* 19; *105:* 55; *106:* 224; *125:* 135; *171:* 46; *172:* 12; *176:* 120; *197:* 89
Doran, Ben-Ami *128:* 189
Dore, Gustave *18:* 169, 172, 175; *19:* 93, 94, 95, 96, 97, 98,99, 100, 101, 102, 103, 104, 105; *23:* 188; *25:* 197, 199
Doremus, Robert *6:* 62; *13:* 90; *30:* 95, 96, 97; *38:* 97
Dorfman, Ronald *11:* 128
Doriau *86:* 59; *91:* 152
Dorman, Brandon *197:* 35
Dorros, Arthur *78:* 42, 43; *91:* 28
Doruyter, Karel *165:* 105
dos Santos, Joyce Audy *57:* 187, 189
Doty, Roy *28:* 98; *31:* 32; *32:* 224; *46:* 157; *82:* 71; *142:* 7
Doucet, Bob *132:* 238; *169:* 159
Dougherty, Charles *16:* 204; *18:* 74
Doughty, Rebecca *177:* 174
Doughty, Thomas *118:* 31; *140:* 60

Douglas, Aaron *31:* 103
Douglas, Carole Nelson *73:* 48
Douglas, Goray *13:* 151
Dow, Brian *150:* 92
Dowd, Jason *132:* 51, 52; *164:* 244
Dowd, Vic *3:* 244; *10:* 97
Dowden, Anne Ophelia *7:* 70, 71; *13:* 120
Dowdy, Mrs. Regera *29:* 100
Downes, Belinda *180:* 29
Downing, Julie *60:* 140; *81:* 50; *86:* 200; *99:* 129
Doyle, Janet *56:* 31
Doyle, Richard *21:* 31, 32, 33; *23:* 231; *24:* 177; *31:* 87
Draper, Angie *43:* 84
Drath, Bill *26:* 34
Drawson, Blair *17:* 53; *126:* 65
Dray, Matt *177:* 47
Drescher, Henrik *105:* 60, 62, 63; *172:* 72
Drescher, Joan *30:* 100, 101; *35:* 245; *52:* 168; *137:* 52
Dressell, Peggy *186:* 41
Drew, Patricia *15:* 100
Drummond, V.H. *6:* 70
Drury, Christian Potter *105:* 97; *186:* 224
Dubanevich, Arlene *56:* 44
Dubois, Claude K. *196:* 2
Dubois, Gerard *182:* 9
DuBurke, Randy *187:* 89
Ducak, Danilo *99:* 130; *108:* 214
Duchesne, Janet *6:* 162; *79:* 8
Duda, Jana *102:* 155
Dudash, Michael *32:* 122; *77:* 134; *82:* 149
Duer, Douglas *34:* 177
Duewell, Kristina *195:* 76
Duffy, Daniel Mark *76:* 37; *101:* 196; *108:* 147, 148
Duffy, Joseph *38:* 203
Duffy, Pat *28:* 153
Dugan, Karen *181:* 26
Dugin, Andrej *77:* 60
Dugina, Olga *77:* 60
Duke, Chris *8:* 195; *139:* 164
Duke, Kate *87:* 186; *90:* 78, 79, 80, 81; *192:* 21, 59, 60, 61, 63
Duke, Marion *165:* 87
Dulac, Edmund *19:* 108, 109, 110, 111, 112, 113, 114, 115, 117; *23:* 187; *25:* 152; *YABC 1:* 37; *2:* 147
Dulac, Jean *13:* 64
Dumas, Philippe *52:* 36, 37, 38, 39, 40, 41, 42, 43, 45; *119:* 40, 41, 42
Dunaway, Nancy *108:* 161
Dunbar, James *76:* 63
Dunbar, Polly *181:* 60, 61
Duncan, Beverly *72:* 92
Duncan, John *116:* 94
Dunn, H.T. *62:* 196
Dunn, Harvey *34:* 78, 79, 80, 81
Dunn, Iris *5:* 175
Dunn, Phoebe *5:* 175
Dunne, Jeanette *72:* 57, 173, 222
Dunnick, Regan *176:* 51; *178:* 83, 84
Dunnington, Tom *3:* 36; *18:* 281; *25:* 61; *31:* 159; *35:* 168; *48:* 195; *79:* 144; *82:* 230
Dunn-Ramsey, Marcy *117:* 131
Dunrea, Olivier *59:* 81; *118:* 53, 54; *124:* 43
Duntze, Dorothee *88:* 28; *160:* 76
Dupasquier, Philippe *86:* 75; *104:* 76; *151:* 63
DuQuette, Keith *90:* 83; *155:* 73, 74
Durham, Sarah *192:* 248
Duroussy, Nathalie *146:* 150
Durrell, Julie *82:* 62; *94:* 62
Dutz *6:* 59
Duvoisin, Roger *2:* 95; *6:* 76, 77; *7:* 197; *28:* 125; *30:* 101, 102, 103, 104, 105, 107; *47:* 205; *84:* 254
Dyer, Dale *141:* 71
Dyer, Jane *75:* 219; *129:* 28; *147:* 49, 50, 51; *168:* 121; *190:* 4; *191:* 57, 59, 60
Dypold, Pat *15:* 37

E

E.V.B.
  See Boyle, Eleanor Vere (Gordon)
Eachus, Jennifer *29:* 74; *82:* 201; *164:* 153
Eadie, Bob *63:* 36
Eagle, Bruce *95:* 119
Eagle, Ellen *82:* 121; *89:* 3
Eagle, Jeremy *141:* 71
Eagle, Michael *11:* 86; *20:* 9; *23:* 18; *27:* 122; *28:* 57; *34:* 201; *44:* 189; *73:* 9; *78:* 235; *85:* 43
Earl-Bridges, Michele *159:* 128
Earle, Edwin *56:* 27
Earle, Olive L. *7:* 75
Earle, Vana *27:* 99
Earley, Lori *132:* 2; *186:* 4; *195:* 8
Early, Margaret *72:* 59
East, Stella *131:* 223
Eastman, P.D. *33:* 57
Easton, Reginald *29:* 181
Eaton, Tom *4:* 62; *6:* 64; *22:* 99; *24:* 124
Ebbeler, Jeffrey *193:* 62
Ebel, Alex *11:* 89
Eberbach, Andrea *192:* 115
Ebert, Len *9:* 191; *44:* 47
Echevarria, Abe *37:* 69
Echo Hawk, Bunky *187:* 192
Eckersley, Maureen *48:* 62
Eckert, Horst *72:* 62
Ede, Janina *33:* 59
Edens, Cooper *49:* 81, 82, 83, 84, 85; *112:* 58
Edens, John *109:* 115
Edgar, Sarah E. *41:* 97
Edgerton, Perky *195:* 144
Edliq, Emily S. *131:* 107
Edrien *11:* 53
Edwards, Freya *45:* 102
Edwards, George Wharton *31:* 155
Edwards, Gunvor *2:* 71; *25:* 47; *32:* 71; *54:* 106
Edwards, Jeanne *29:* 257
Edwards, Linda Strauss *21:* 134; *39:* 123; *49:* 88, 89
Edwards, Michelle *152:* 62, 63
Edwards, Wallace *170:* 55
Egan, Tim *155:* 76, 77, 78
Egge, David *102:* 71
Eggenhofer, Nicholas *2:* 81
Eggleton, Bob *74:* 40; *81:* 190, 191; *105:* 6; *121:* 183; *149:* 203; *166:* 215
Egielski, Richard *11:* 90; *16:* 208; *33:* 236; *38:* 35; *49:* 91, 92, 93, 95, 212, 213, 214, 216; *79:* 122; *106:* 67, 68, 69; *134:* 135; *144:* 244; *163:* 82, 84
Ehlert, Lois *35:* 97; *69:* 51; *112:* 7; *113:* 208; *128:* 63, 64, 65; *172:* 77, 79, 80
Ehrlich, Bettina *1:* 83
Eitan, Ora *160:* 165
Eichenberg, Fritz *1:* 79; *9:* 54; *19:* 248; *23:* 170; *24:* 200; *26:* 208; *50:* 67, 68, 69, 70, 71, 72, 73,74, 75, 76, 77, 78, 79, 80, 81; *60:* 165; *100:* 137; *YABC 1:* 104, 105; *2:* 213
Einsel, Naiad *10:* 35; *29:* 136
Einsel, Walter *10:* 37
Einzig, Susan *3:* 77; *43:* 78; *67:* 155; *129:* 154
Eisner, Will *165:* 82, 83
Eitzen, Allan *9:* 56; *12:* 212; *14:* 226; *21:* 194; *38:* 162; *76:* 218
Eldridge, H. *54:* 109
Eldridge, Harold *43:* 83
Elgaard, Greta *19:* 241
Elgin, Kathleen *9:* 188; *39:* 69
Ellacott, S.E. *19:* 118
Elliot, David *192:* 26
Elliott, Mark *93:* 69; *105:* 108; *107:* 123; *140:* 53; *165:* 189; *173:* 67; *195:* 95
Elliott, Sarah M. *14:* 58
Ellis, Dianne *130:* 208
Ellis, Jan Davey *88:* 50; *115:* 80

Ellis, Richard *130:* 47, 48
Ellison, Chris *196:* 66
Ellison, Pauline *55:* 21
Elmer, Richard *78:* 5
Elmore, Larry *90:* 8
Elschner, Géraldine *183:* 38
Elwell, Peter *195:* 150
Elwell, Tristan *110:* 39; *121:* 182; *127:* 46; *137:* 144; *141:* 173; *151:* 236; *158:* 264; *167:* 119, 120, 121; *169:* 20; *190:* 12
Elzbieta *88:* 80, 81
Emberley, Ed *8:* 53; *70:* 53, 54; *146:* 65, 69, 70
Emberley, Michael *34:* 83; *80:* 72; *119:* 47, 48; *147:* 100; *158:* 115; *189:* 62, 64
Emerling, Dorothy *104:* 27
Emery, Leslie *49:* 187
Emmett, Bruce *49:* 147; *80:* 175; *101:* 206
Emry-Perrott, Jennifer *61:* 57
Emshwiller, Ed *174:* 45
Endle, Kate *191:* 167
Engel, Diana *70:* 57
Engle, Mort *38:* 64
Englebert, Victor *8:* 54
English, Mark *101:* 207
Enik, Ted *142:* 39
Enos, Randall *20:* 183
Enright, Maginel Wright *19:* 240, 243; *39:* 31, 35, 36
Enrique, Romeo *34:* 135
Ensor, Barbara *180:* 30
Epstein, Stephen *50:* 142, 148
Erdogan, Buket *174:* 179
Erdrich, Louise *141:* 62
Erhard, Walter *1:* 152
Erickson, Jim *196:* 190
Erickson, Phoebe *11:* 83; *59:* 85
Erikson, Mel *31:* 69
Eriksson, Eva *63:* 88, 90, 92, 93
Ering, Timothy Basil *131:* 100; *176:* 63, 64
Erlbruch, Wolf *181:* 66
Ernst, Lisa Campbell *47:* 147; *95:* 47; *154:* 46, 47, 48; *164:* 88
Esco, Jo *61:* 103
Escourido, Joseph *4:* 81
Escrivá, Viví *119:* 51; *181:* 36
Este, Kirk *33:* 111
Estep, David *73:* 57
Estes, Eleanor *91:* 66
Estoril, Jean *32:* 27
Estrada, Pau *74:* 76
Estrada, Ric *5:* 52, 146; *13:* 174
Etchemendy, Teje *38:* 68
Etheredges, the *73:* 12
Etienne, Kirk-Albert *145:* 184
Ets, Marie Hall *2:* 102
Ettlinger, Doris *171:* 98; *186:* 106; *197:* 126
Eulalie *YABC 2:* 315
Evans, Greg *73:* 54, 55, 56; *143:* 40, 41
Evans, Katherine *5:* 64
Evans, Leslie *144:* 227
Evans, Shane W. *159:* 142; *160:* 190; *168:* 39; *188:* 88; *189:* 66, 67, 68
Everitt, Betsy *151:* 110
Ewart, Claire *76:* 69; *145:* 59, 60
Ewing, Carolyn *66:* 143; *79:* 52
Ewing, Juliana Horatia *16:* 92
Eyolfson, Norman *98:* 154

F

Fabian, Limbert *136:* 114
Facklam, Paul *132:* 62
Falconer, Ian *125:* 66; *179:* 59
Falconer, Pearl *34:* 23
Falkenstern, Lisa *70:* 34; *76:* 133; *78:* 171; *127:* 16; *191:* 151
Falls, C.B. *1:* 19; *38:* 71, 72, 73, 74
Falter, John *40:* 169, 170

Falwell, Cathryn *118:* 77; *137:* 185; *196:* 71, 72
Fancher, Lou *138:* 219; *141:* 64; *144:* 199; *177:* 51
Fanelli, Sara *89:* 63; *126:* 69
Faria, Rosana *150:* 143
Faricy, Patrick *185:* 182
Farmer, Andrew *49:* 102
Farmer, Peter *24:* 108; *38:* 75
Farnsworth, Bill *93:* 189; *116:* 147; *124:* 8; *135:* 52; *146:* 242, 243, 244; *182:* 176; *186:* 31, 83, 84, 85; *191:* 197
Farquharson, Alexander *46:* 75
Farrell, David *40:* 135
Farrell, Russell *196:* 38
Farris, David *74:* 42
Fasolino, Teresa *118:* 145
Fatigati, Evelyn *24:* 112
Fatus, Sophie *182:* 74; *190:* 218
Faul-Jansen, Regina *22:* 117
Faulkner, Jack *6:* 169
Faulkner, Matt *161:* 174; *167:* 75
Fava, Rita *2:* 29
Fax, Elton C. *1:* 101; *4:* 2; *12:* 77; *25:* 107
Fay *43:* 93
Fearnley, Jan *153:* 82, 83
Fearrington, Ann *146:* 80
Federspiel, Marian *33:* 51
Fedorov, Nickolai Ivanovich *110:* 102
Feelings, Tom *5:* 22; *8:* 56; *12:* 153; *16:* 105; *30:* 196; *49:* 37; *61:* 101; *69:* 56, 57; *93:* 74; *105:* 88
Fehr, Terrence *21:* 87
Feiffer, Jules *3:* 91; *8:* 58; *61:* 66, 67, 70, 74, 76,77, 78; *111:* 47, 48, 49, 50; *132:* 122; *157:* 62
Feigeles, Neil *41:* 242
Feldman, Elyse *86:* 7
Feller, Gene *33:* 130
Fellows, Muriel H. *10:* 42
Felstead, Cathie *116:* 85
Felts, Shirley *33:* 71; *48:* 59
Fennell, Tracy *171:* 69
Fennelli, Maureen *38:* 181
Fenton, Carroll Lane *5:* 66; *21:* 39
Fenton, Mildred Adams *5:* 66; *21:* 39
Ferguson, Peter *177:* 30, 31; *181:* 154; *197:* 4
Ferguson, Walter W. *34:* 86
Fernandes, Eugenie *77:* 67
Fernandes, Stanislaw *70:* 28
Fernandez, Fernando *77:* 57
Fernandez, Laura *77:* 153; *101:* 117; *131:* 222; *170:* 119; *175:* 182
Ferrari, Alex *188:* 121
Ferrington, Susan *172:* 22
Fetz, Ingrid *11:* 67; *12:* 52; *16:* 205; *17:* 59; *29:* 105; *30:* 108, 109; *32:* 149; *43:* 142; *56:* 29; *60:* 34; *85:* 48; *87:* 146
Fiammenghi, Gioia *9:* 66; *11:* 44; *12:* 206; *13:* 57, 59; *52:* 126, 129; *66:* 64; *85:* 83; *91:* 161; *166:* 169
Fiedler, Joseph Daniel *96:* 42; *113:* 173; *129:* 164; *146:* 17; *159:* 68; *162:* 104
Field, Rachel *15:* 113
Fielding, David *70:* 124
Fieser, Stephen *152:* 36
Fine, Howard *145:* 159; *159:* 64; *165:* 134; *174:* 129; *181:* 68
Fine, Peter K. *43:* 210
Finger, Helen *42:* 81
Fink, Sam *18:* 119
Finlay, Winifred *23:* 72
Finney, Pat *79:* 215
Fiore, Peter *99:* 196; *125:* 139; *144:* 225; *160:* 169; *180:* 72
Fiorentino, Al *3:* 240
Firehammer, Karla *174:* 202
Firmin, Charlotte *29:* 75; *48:* 70
Firmin, Peter *58:* 63, 64, 65, 67, 68, 70, 71
Firth, Barbara *81:* 208; *127:* 218; *179:* 62
Fischel, Lillian *40:* 204

Fischer, Hans *25:* 202
Fischer-Nagel, Andreas *56:* 50
Fischer-Nagel, Heiderose *56:* 50
Fisher, Carolyn *154:* 50
Fisher, Chris *79:* 62; *158:* 248; *188:* 195
Fisher, Cynthia *117:* 45; *137:* 118; *195:* 40
Fisher, Jeffrey *142:* 80
Fisher, Leonard Everett *3:* 6; *4:* 72, 86; *6:* 197; *9:* 59; *16:* 151, 153; *23:* 44; *27:* 134; *29:* 26; *34:* 87, 89, 90, 91, 93, 94, 95, 96; *40:* 206; *50:* 150; *60:* 158; *73:* 68, 70, 71, 72, 73; *176:* 71, 72, 73; *YABC 2:* 169
Fisher, Lois *20:* 62; *21:* 7
Fisher, Valorie *177:* 55
Fisk, Nicholas *25:* 112
Fitschen, Marilyn *2:* 20, 21; *20:* 48
Fitz-Maurice, Jeff *175:* 2
Fitzgerald, F.A. *15:* 116; *25:* 86, 87
Fitzhugh, Louise *1:* 94; *9:* 163; *45:* 75, 78
Fitzgerald, Joanne *157:* 153, 154
Fitzhugh, Susie *11:* 117
Fitzpatrick, Jim *109:* 130
Fitzpatrick, Marie-Louise *125:* 69, 70; *189:* 72, 73
Fitzsimmons, Arthur *14:* 128
Fix, Philippe *26:* 102
Flack, Marjorie *21:* 67; *100:* 93; *YABC 2:* 122
Flagg, James Montgomery *17:* 227
Flavin, Teresa *132:* 115; *186:* 119
Flax, Zeona *2:* 245
Fleetwood, Tony *171:* 51
Fleishman, Seymour *14:* 232; *24:* 87
Fleming, Denise *71:* 179; *81:* 58; *126:* 71, 72, 73; *173:* 52, 53
Fleming, Guy *18:* 41
Flesher, Vivienne *85:* 55
Fletcher, Claire *80:* 106; *157:* 159
Flint, Russ *74:* 80
Floate, Helen *111:* 163
Floca, Brian *155:* 88, 89; *190:* 10, 66, 67
Floethe, Richard *3:* 131; *4:* 90
Floherty, John J., Jr. *5:* 68
Flook, Helen *160:* 81
Flora, James *1:* 96; *30:* 111, 112
Florczak, Robert *166:* 51
Florian, Douglas *19:* 122; *83:* 64, 65; *125:* 71, 72, 74, 76; *128:* 130; *177:* 58, 60
Flory, Jane *22:* 111
Flower, Renee *125:* 109
Floyd, Gareth *1:* 74; *17:* 245; *48:* 63; *62:* 35,36, 37, 39, 40, 41; *74:* 245; *79:* 56
Fluchere, Henri A. *40:* 79
Flynn, Alice *183:* 2
Flynn, Barbara *7:* 31; *9:* 70
Fogarty, Thomas *15:* 89
Foley, Greg *190:* 69
Folger, Joseph *9:* 100
Folkard, Charles *22:* 132; *29:* 128, 257, 258
Foott, Jeff *42:* 202
Forberg, Ati *12:* 71, 205; *14:* 1; *22:* 113; *26:* 22; *48:* 64, 65
Ford, George *24:* 120; *31:* 70, 177; *58:* 126; *81:* 103; *107:* 91; *136:* 100; *194:* 47
Ford, H.J. *16:* 185, 186
Ford, Jason *174:* 119
Ford, Pamela Baldwin *27:* 104
Fordham, John *168:* 160, 161
Foreman, Michael *2:* 110, 111; *67:* 99; *73:* 78, 79, 80,81, 82; *93:* 146; *135:* 55, 56, 57; *184:* 58, 59
Forrester, Victoria *40:* 83
Forsey, Chris *140:* 210
Fortnum, Peggy *6:* 29; *20:* 179; *24:* 211; *26:* 76, 77, 78; *39:* 78; *58:* 19, 21, 23, 27; *YABC 1:* 148
Fortune, Eric *191:* 52
Foster, Brad W. *34:* 99
Foster, Genevieve *2:* 112
Foster, Gerald *7:* 78
Foster, Jon *146:* 18
Foster, Laura Louise *6:* 79

Foster, Marian Curtis *23:* 74; *40:* 42
Foster, Sally *58:* 73, 74
Foucher, Adele *47:* 118
Foust, Mitch *168:* 50
Fowler, Jim *184:* 190
Fowler, Mel *36:* 127
Fowler, Richard *87:* 219
Fowles, Selley *165:* 127
Fox, Charles Phillip *12:* 84
Fox, Christyan *188:* 36
Fox, Jim *6:* 187
Fox-Davies, Sarah *76:* 150; *182:* 63
Frace, Charles *15:* 118
Frailey, Joy *72:* 108
Frame, Paul *2:* 45, 145; *9:* 153; *10:* 124; *21:* 71; *23:* 62; *24:* 123; *27:* 106; *31:* 48; *32:* 159; *34:* 195; *38:* 136; *42:* 55; *44:* 139; *60:* 39, 40, 41, 42, 43, 44, 46; *73:* 183
Frampton, David *85:* 72; *102:* 33; *139:* 182; *152:* 37; *189:* 171
Francois, Andre *25:* 117
Francoise
    See Seignobosc, Francoise
Frank, Lola Edick *2:* 199
Frank, Mary *4:* 54; *34:* 100
Franke, Phil *45:* 91
Frankel, Alona *66:* 70
Frankel, Julie *40:* 84, 85, 202
Frankenberg, Robert *22:* 116; *30:* 50; *38:* 92, 94, 95; *68:* 111
Frankfeldt, Gwen *84:* 223; *110:* 92
Frankland, David *169:* 137; *182:* 164
Franklin, Ashton *165:* 144
Franklin, John *24:* 22
Franson, Leanne R. *111:* 57, 58; *151:* 7
Frascino, Edward *9:* 133; *29:* 229; *33:* 190; *48:* 80, 81, 82, 83, 84, 85, 86
Frasconi, Antonio *6:* 80; *27:* 208; *53:* 41, 43, 45, 47,48; *68:* 145; *73:* 226; *131:* 68
Fraser, Betty *2:* 212; *6:* 185; *8:* 103; *31:* 72,73; *43:* 136; *111:* 76
Fraser, Eric *38:* 78; *41:* 149, 151
Fraser, F.A. *22:* 234
Fraser, James *171:* 68
Fraser, Mary Ann *137:* 63
Frasier, Debra *69:* 60; *112:* 67; *182:* 81, 82, 83
Fraustino, Lisa Rowe *146:* 87
Frazee, Marla *72:* 98; *105:* 79, 80; *151:* 67, 68; *164:* 165; *171:* 190, 191; *187:* 53, 54,55, 56, 143
Frazetta, Frank *41:* 72; *58:* 77, 78, 79, 80, 81, 82, 83
Frazier, Craig *177:* 63
Freas, John *25:* 207
Fredrickson, Mark *103:* 33
Freeland, Michael J. *118:* 115
Freeman, Don *2:* 15; *13:* 249; *17:* 62, 63, 65, 67, 68; *18:* 243; *20:* 195; *23:* 213, 217; *32:* 155; *55:* 129
Freeman, Irving *67:* 150
Freeman, Laura *144:* 111
Freeman, Pietri *140:* 223
Freeman, Tom *167:* 118
Freeman, Tor *164:* 93
Fregosi, Claudia *24:* 117
Fremaux, Charlotte Murray *138:* 29; *141:* 95
French, Fiona *6:* 82, 83; *75:* 61; *109:* 170; *132:* 79, 80, 81, 82
French, Martin *163:* 4
Frendak, Rodney *126:* 97, 98
Freschet, Gina *175:* 73
Freynet, Gilbert *72:* 221
Friedman, Judith *43:* 197; *131:* 221
Friedman, Marvin *19:* 59; *42:* 86
Frinta, Dagmar *36:* 42
Frith, Michael K. *15:* 138; *18:* 120
Fritz, Ronald *46:* 73; *82:* 124
Fromm, Lilo *29:* 85; *40:* 197
Frost, A.B. *17:* 6, 7; *19:* 123, 124, 125, 126, 127, 128, 129,130; *100:* 119; *YABC 1:* 156, 157, 160; *2:* 107

Frost, Helen *183:* 51
Frost, Kristi *118:* 113
Frost, Michael *151:* 209
Froud, Brian *150:* 82, 83
Froud, Wendy *151:* 237
Fry, Guy *2:* 224
Fry, Rosalie *3:* 72; *YABC 2:* 180, 181
Fry, Rosalind *21:* 153, 168
Fryer, Elmer *34:* 115
Fuchs, Bernie *110:* 10; *162:* 46
Fuchs, Erich *6:* 84
Fuchshuber, Annegert *43:* 96
Fufuka, Mahiri *32:* 146
Fuge, Charles *144:* 91, 93
Fujikawa, Gyo *39:* 75, 76; *76:* 72, 73, 74
Fulford, Deborah *23:* 159
Fuller, Margaret *25:* 189
Fulweiler, John *93:* 99
Funai, Mamoru *38:* 105
Funfhausen, Christian *196:* 30
Funk, Tom *7:* 17, 99
Furchgott, Terry *29:* 86
Furness, William Henry, Jr. *94:* 18
Furukawa, Mel *25:* 42
Fusari, Erika *164:* 227

G

Gaadt, David *78:* 212; *121:* 166
Gaadt, George *71:* 9
Gaber, Susan *99:* 33; *115:* 57, 58; *164:* 195; *169:* 61, 62, 63; *185:* 50, 51; *188:* 124
Gaberell, J. *19:* 236
Gable, Brian *195:* 68, 69
Gabler, Mirko *99:* 71; *195:* 32
Gackenbach, Dick *19:* 168; *41:* 81; *48:* 89, 90, 91, 92, 93, 94; *54:* 105; *79:* 75, 76, 77
Gad, Victor *87:* 161
Gaetano, Nicholas *23:* 209
Gaffney-Kessell, Walter *94:* 219; *174:* 188
Gag, Flavia *17:* 49, 52
Gag, Wanda *100:* 101, 102; *YABC 1:* 135, 137, 138, 141, 143
Gagnon, Cecile *11:* 77; *58:* 87
Gal, Laszlo *14:* 127; *52:* 54, 55, 56; *65:* 142; *68:* 150; *81:* 185; *96:* 104, 105
Galazinski, Tom *55:* 13
Galdone, Paul *1:* 156, 181, 206; *2:* 40, 241; *3:* 42, 144; *4:* 141; *10:* 109, 158; *11:* 21; *12:* 118, 210; *14:* 12; *16:* 36, 37; *17:* 70, 71, 72, 73, 74; *18:* 111, 230; *19:* 183; *21:* 154; *22:* 150, 245; *33:* 126; *39:* 136, 137; *42:* 57; *51:* 169; *55:* 110; *66:* 80, 82, 139; *72:* 73; *100:* 84
Gale, Cathy *140:* 22; *143:* 52
Gall, Chris *176:* 79, 80
Gallagher, Jack *187:* 100
Gallagher, S. Saelig *105:* 154
Gallagher, Sears *20:* 112
Galloway, Ewing *51:* 154
Galouchka, Annouchka Gravel *95:* 55; *182:* 40
Galster, Robert *1:* 66
Galsworthy, Gay John *35:* 232
Galvez, Daniel *125:* 182
Gamble, Kim *112:* 64, 65; *124:* 77; *183:* 40, 42, 43, 56, 57; *187:* 170
Gammell, Stephen *7:* 48; *13:* 149; *29:* 82; *33:* 209; *41:* 88; *50:* 185, 186, 187; *53:* 51, 52, 53, 54, 55, 56, 57, 58; *54:* 24, 25; *56:* 147, 148, 150; *57:* 27, 66; *81:* 62, 63; *87:* 88; *89:* 10; *106:* 223; *126:* 2; *128:* 71, 73, 74, 77; *154:* 34
Gamper, Ruth *84:* 198
Gampert, John *58:* 94
Ganly, Helen *56:* 56
Gannett, Ruth Chrisman *3:* 74; *18:* 254; *33:* 77, 78
Gantschev, Ivan *45:* 32
Garafano, Marie *73:* 33

Garbot, Dave *131:* 106
Garbutt, Bernard *23:* 68
Garcia *37:* 71
Garcia, Manuel *74:* 145
Garcia-Franco, Rebecca *173:* 46
Gardiner, Lindsey *178:* 128; *186:* 137
Gardner, Earle *45:* 167
Gardner, Joan *40:* 87
Gardner, Joel *40:* 87, 92
Gardner, John *40:* 87
Gardner, Lucy *40:* 87
Gardner, Richard
    See Cummings, Richard
Gardner, Sally *171:* 177; *177:* 66, 68
Gargiulo, Frank *84:* 158
Garland, Michael *36:* 29; *38:* 83; *44:* 168; *48:* 78, 221, 222; *49:* 161; *60:* 139; *71:* 6, 11; *72:* 229; *74:* 142; *89:* 187; *93:* 183; *104:* 110; *131:* 55; *139:* 209; *168:* 56
Garland, Peggy *60:* 139
Garland, Sarah *62:* 45; *135:* 67, 68; *171:* 118
Garn, Aimee *75:* 47
Garner, Joan *128:* 170
Garneray, Ambroise Louis *59:* 140
Garnett, Eve *3:* 75
Garnett, Gary *39:* 184
Garns, Allen *80:* 125; *84:* 39; *165:* 231
Garófoli, Viviana *186:* 123
Garraty, Gail *4:* 142; *52:* 106
Garrett, Agnes *46:* 110; *47:* 157
Garrett, Edmund H. *20:* 29
Garrett, Tom *107:* 194
Garrick, Jacqueline *67:* 42, 43; *77:* 94
Garrison, Barbara *19:* 133; *104:* 146; *109:* 87
Garro, Mark *108:* 131; *128:* 210
Garvey, Robert *98:* 222
Garza, Carmen Lomas *80:* 211; *182:* 86
Garza, Xavier *184:* 64
Gates, Frieda *26:* 80
Gaughan, Jack *26:* 79; *43:* 185
Gaver, Becky *20:* 61
Gawing, Toby *72:* 52
Gay, Marie-Louise *68:* 76, 77, 78; *102:* 136; *126:* 76, 78, 81, 83; *127:* 55, 56; *179:* 70, 72, 73, 74
Gay, Zhenya *19:* 135, 136
Gaydos, Tim *62:* 201
Gazsi, Ed *80:* 48
Gazso, Gabriel *73:* 85
Geary, Clifford N. *1:* 122; *9:* 104; *51:* 74
Geary, Rick *142:* 44, 46
Gee, Frank *33:* 26
Geehan, Wayne *157:* 181
Geer, Charles *1:* 91; *3:* 179; *4:* 201; *6:* 168; *7:* 96; *9:* 58; *10:* 72; *12:* 127; *39:* 156, 157, 158, 159, 160; *42:* 88, 89, 90, 91; *55:* 111, 116
Geerinck, Manuel *173:* 128
Gehm, Charlie *36:* 65; *57:* 117; *62:* 60, 138
Geis, Alissa Imre *189:* 77
Geisel, Theodor Seuss *1:* 104, 105, 106; *28:* 108, 109, 110, 111, 112, 113; *75:* 67, 68, 69, 70, 71; *89:* 127, 128; *100:* 106, 107, 108
Geisert, Arthur *92:* 67, 68; *133:* 72, 73, 74; *165:* 97, 98; *171:* 64, 65
Geldart, William *15:* 121; *21:* 202
Genia *4:* 84
Gentry, Cyrille R. *12:* 66
Genzo, John Paul *136:* 74
George, Jean *2:* 113
George, Lindsay Barrett *95:* 57; *155:* 97, 98
Geraghty, Paul *130:* 60, 61
Gerard, Jean Ignace *45:* 80
Gerard, Rolf *27:* 147, 150
Gerber, Mark *61:* 105
Gerber, Mary Jane *112:* 124; *171:* 56
Gerber, Stephanie *71:* 195
Gerdstein, Mordecai *169:* 105
Gergely, Tibor *54:* 15, 16
Geritz, Franz *17:* 135
Gerlach, Geff *42:* 58
Gerrard, Roy *47:* 78; *90:* 96, 97, 98, 99

Gerritsen, Paula *177:* 69
Gershinowitz, George *36:* 27
Gerstein, Mordicai *31:* 117; *47:* 80, 81, 82, 83, 84, 85, 86; *51:* 173; *69:* 134; *107:* 122; *142:* 49, 52; *165:* 209; *176:* 119; *178:* 95, 97, 99
Gervase *12:* 27
Geter, Tyrone *146:* 249; *150:* 86
Getz, Arthur *32:* 148
Gévry, Claudine *188:* 47
Gewirtz, Bina *61:* 81
Giancola, Donato *95:* 146; *164:* 226
Gibbons, Gail *23:* 78; *72:* 77, 78, 79; *82:* 182; *104:* 65; *160:* 99, 100
Gibbs, Tony *40:* 95
Gibran, Kahlil *32:* 116
Gider, Iskender *81:* 193
Giebfried, Rosemary *170:* 135
Giesen, Rosemary *34:* 192, 193
Giffard, Hannah *83:* 70
Giguere, George *20:* 111
Gilbert, John *19:* 184; *54:* 115; *YABC 2:* 287
Gilbert, W.S. *36:* 83, 85, 96
Gilbert, Yvonne *116:* 70; *128:* 84; *149:* 119; *185:* 69; *192:* 25; *195:* 81
Gilchrist, Jan Spivey *72:* 82, 83, 84, 85, 87; *77:* 90; *105:* 89, 91; *130:* 63, 64; *155:* 105, 107; *182:* 67
Giles, Will *41:* 218
Gili, Phillida *70:* 73
Gill, Margery *4:* 57; *7:* 7; *22:* 122; *25:* 166; *26:* 146, 147
Gillen, Denver *28:* 216
Gillette, Henry J. *23:* 237
Gilliam, Stan *39:* 64, 81
Gillies, Chuck *62:* 31
Gilliland, Jillian *87:* 58
Gillman, Alec *98:* 105
Gilman, Esther *15:* 124
Gilman, Phoebe *104:* 70, 71
Ginsberg, Sari *111:* 184
Ginsburg, Max *62:* 59; *68:* 194 *Girard, Roge 161:* 30
Girouard, Patrick *155:* 100
Giovanopoulos, Paul *7:* 104; *60:* 36
Giovine, Sergio *79:* 12; *93:* 118; *139:* 118
Githens, Elizabeth M. *5:* 47
Gladden, Scott *99:* 108; *103:* 160; *193:* 46, 47
Gladstone, Gary *12:* 89; *13:* 190
Gladstone, Lise *15:* 273
Glanzman, Louis S. *2:* 177; *3:* 182; *36:* 97, 98; *38:* 120, 122; *52:* 141, 144; *71:* 191; *91:* 54, 56
Glaser, Byron *154:* 59, 60
Glaser, Milton *3:* 5; *5:* 156; *11:* 107; *30:* 26; *36:* 112; *54:* 141; *151:* 70
Glass, Andrew *36:* 38; *44:* 133; *48:* 205; *65:* 3; *68:* 43, 45; *90:* 104, 105; *150:* 89
Glass, Marvin *9:* 174
Glasser, Judy *41:* 156; *56:* 140; *69:* 79; *72:* 101
Glattauer, Ned *5:* 84; *13:* 224; *14:* 26
Glauber, Uta *17:* 76
Gleeson, J.M. *YABC 2:* 207
Glegg, Creina *36:* 100
Glienke, Amelie *63:* 150
Gliewe, Unada *3:* 78, 79; *21:* 73; *30:* 220
Gliori, Debi *72:* 91; *138:* 82; *162:* 37; *189:* 79, 81, 82
Glovach, Linda *7:* 105
Gobbato, Imero *3:* 180, 181; *6:* 213; *7:* 58; *9:* 150; *18:* 39; *21:* 167; *39:* 82, 83; *41:* 137, 251; *59:* 177
Goble, Paul *25:* 121; *26:* 86; *33:* 65; *69:* 68, 69; *131:* 79, 80
Goble, Warwick *46:* 78, 79; *194:* 143
Godal, Eric *36:* 93
Godkin, Celia *145:* 84, 86
Godfrey, Michael *17:* 279
Godon, Ingrid *166:* 163; *186:* 99
Goembel, Ponder *42:* 124

Goffe, Toni *61:* 83, 84, 85; *89:* 11; *90:* 124; *178:* 118
Goffstein, M.B. *8:* 71; *70:* 75, 76, 77
Golbin, Andre *15:* 125
Gold, Robert *166:* 151, 152
Goldfeder, Cheryl *11:* 191
Goldfinger, Jennifer P. *185:* 71
Goldsborough, June *5:* 154, 155; *8:* 92, *14:* 226; *19:* 139; *54:* 165
Goldsmith, Robert *110:* 77
Goldstein, Leslie *5:* 8; *6:* 60; *10:* 106
Goldstein, Nathan *1:* 175; *2:* 79; *11:* 41, 232; *16:* 55
Goldstrom, Robert *98:* 36; *145:* 51, 52
Golembe, Carla *79:* 80, 81; *136:* 91; *144:* 113; *193:* 53
Golin, Carlo *74:* 112
Gomez, Elena *188:* 122; *191:* 72
Gomez, Elizabeth *127:* 70; *133:* 76
Gomi, Taro *64:* 102; *103:* 74, 76
Gon, Adriano *101:* 112
Gonsalve, Ron *178:* 213
Gonzalez, Maya Christina *104:* 3; *136:* 92
Goodall, John S. *4:* 92, 93; *10:* 132; *66:* 92, 93; *YABC 1:* 198
Goode, Diane *15:* 126; *50:* 183; *52:* 114, 115; *76:* 195; *84:* 94; *99:* 141; *114:* 76, 77, 78; *170:* 99, 101
Goodelman, Aaron *40:* 203
Goodenow, Earle *40:* 97
Goodfellow, Peter *62:* 95; *94:* 202
Goodman, Joan Elizabeth *50:* 86
Goodman, Vivienne *82:* 251; *146:* 181, 182
Goodnow, Patti *117:* 33
Goodwin, Harold *13:* 74
Goodwin, Philip R. *18:* 206
Goor, Nancy *39:* 85, 86
Goor, Ron *39:* 85, 86
Goossens, Philippe *195:* 71
Gorbachev, Valeri *89:* 96; *112:* 97; *143:* 63, 64; *184:* 66, 67, 68, 101
Gordon, Gwen *12:* 151
Gordon, Margaret *4:* 147; *5:* 48, 49; *9:* 79
Gordon, Mike *101:* 62, 63, 64
Gordon, Russell *136:* 204; *137:* 214
Gordon, Walter *138:* 9
Gore, Leonid *89:* 51; *94:* 74; *136:* 8; *158:* 117; *166:* 136; *168:* 36; *170:* 107; *181:* 94; *185:* 73
Gorecka-Egan, Erica *18:* 35
Gorey, Edward *1:* 60, 61; *13:* 169; *18:* 192; *20:* 201; *29:* 90, 91, 92, 93, 94, 95, 96, 97, 98, 99, 100; *30:* 129; *32:* 90; *34:* 200, *65:* 48; *68:* 24, 25; *69:* 79; *70:* 80, 82, 83, 84; *85:* 136; *127:* 62
Gorsline, Douglas *1:* 98; *6:* 13; *11:* 113; *13:* 104; *15:* 14; *28:* 117; *YABC 1:* 15
Gorton, Julia *108:* 94; *178:* 81, 82
Gosfield, Josh *118:* 165, 166; *149:* 67
Gosner, Kenneth *5:* 135
Gosney, Joy *167:* 142
Gotlieb, Jules *6:* 127
Goto, Scott *115:* 86; *136:* 69
Gott, Barry *197:* 95
Gottlieb, Dale *67:* 162; *107:* 16; *149:* 6
Goudey, Ray *97:* 86
Gough, Alan *91:* 57
Gough, Philip *23:* 47; *45:* 90
Gould, Chester *49:* 112, 113, 114, 116, 117, 118
Gould, Jason *151:* 232
Gourbault, Martine *177:* 159
Govern, Elaine R. *26:* 94
Gower, Teri *102:* 184
Gowing, Toby *60:* 25; *63:* 33; *78:* 70, 252; *83:* 228; *86:* 187; *93:* 145; *108:* 133; *110:* 217; *184:* 125
Grabianski *20:* 144
Grabianski, Janusz *39:* 92, 93, 94, 95
Graboff, Abner *35:* 103, 104
Graef, Renee *61:* 188; *72:* 207

Grafe, Max *156:* 173; *178:* 237; *192:* 240
Graham, A.B. *11:* 61
Graham, Bob *101:* 66, 67, 68; *151:* 74, 75; *187:* 65, 67, 68, 70
Graham, Georgia *188:* 3; *190:* 75
Graham, L. *7:* 108
Graham, Margaret Bloy *11:* 120; *18:* 305, 307
Graham, Mark *88:* 208; *159:* 153; *182:* 3
Grahame-Johnstone, Janet *13:* 61
Grahame-Johnstone, Anne *13:* 61
Grainger, Sam *42:* 95
Gralley, Jean *166:* 86
Gramatky, Hardie *1:* 107; *30:* 116, 119, 120, 122, 123
Gran, Julie *168:* 118
Granahan, Julie *84:* 84
GrandPré, Mary *84:* 131; *109:* 199; *118:* 76; *180:* 65; *184:* 70, 71, 180; *192:* 87
Grandström, Brita *176:* 139
Grandville, J.J. *45:* 81, 82, 83, 84, 85, 86, 87, 88; *47:* 125; *64:* 10
Granger, Paul *39:* 153
Granström, Brita *162:* 35; *167:* 46
Grant, (Alice) Leigh *10:* 52; *15:* 131; *20:* 20; *26:* 119; *48:* 202
Grant, Gordon *17:* 230, 234; *25:* 123, 124, 125, 126; *52:* 69; *YABC 1:* 164
Grant, Melvyn *159:* 186, 187; *170:* 48, 49
Grant, Renee *77:* 40
Grant, Shirley *109:* 45
Graves, Elizabeth *45:* 101
Graves, Keith *167:* 89; *191:* 74
Gray, Harold *33:* 87, 88
Gray, Les *82:* 76; *83:* 232
Gray, Reginald *6:* 69
Greco, Tony *184:* 6
Greder, Armin *76:* 235
Green, Ann Canevari *62:* 48
Green, Eileen *6:* 97
Green, Elizabeth Shippen *139:* 109
Green, Jonathan *86:* 135; *105:* 109
Green, Ken *111:* 68
Green, Michael *32:* 216
Green, Robina *87:* 138
Green, Jonathan *157:* 105
Greene, Jeffrey *117:* 93
Greenaway, Kate *17:* 275; *24:* 180; *26:* 107; *41:* 222, 232; *100:* 115, 116; *YABC 1:* 88, 89; *2:* 131, 133, 136,138, 139, 141
Greenberg, Melanie Hope *72:* 93; *80:* 125; *101:* 174; *133:* 180; *186:* 189
Greenseid, Diane *178:* 106, 107
Greenstein, Elaine *150:* 100
Greenwald, Sheila *1:* 34; *3:* 99; *8:* 72
Greger, Carol *76:* 86
Gregorian, Joyce Ballou *30:* 125
Gregory, Emilian *177:* 146; *187:* 10
Gregory, Fran *130:* 4; *140:* 93
Gregory, Frank M. *29:* 107
Greiffenhagen, Maurice *16:* 137; *27:* 57; *YABC 2:* 288
Greiner, Robert *6:* 86
Gretter, J. Clemens *31:* 134
Gretz, Susanna *7:* 114
Gretzer, John *1:* 54; *3:* 26; *4:* 162; *7:* 125; *16:* 247; *18:* 117; *28:* 66; *30:* 85, 211; *33:* 235; *56:* 16
Grey, Mini *166:* 90; *192:* 71
Grey Owl *24:* 41
Gri *25:* 90
Grieder, Walter *9:* 84
Griesbach/Martucci *59:* 3
Grifalconi, Ann *2:* 126; *3:* 248; *11:* 18; *13:* 182; *46:* 38; *50:* 145; *66:* 99, 100, 101, 104, 106; *69:* 38; *70:* 64; *87:* 128; *90:* 53; *93:* 49; *128:* 48; *133:* 79, 81
Griffin, Gillett Good *26:* 96
Griffin, James *30:* 166
Griffin, John Howard *59:* 186
Griffin, Rachel *131:* 23
Griffith, Gershom *94:* 214

Griffiths, Dave *29:* 76
Griffiths, Dean *168:* 180; *169:* 182
Grimly, Gris *186:* 102; *192:* 112; *197:* 86
Grimsdell, Jeremy *83:* 75
Grimwood, Brian *82:* 89
Gringhuis, Dirk *6:* 98; *9:* 196
Gripe, Harald *2:* 127; *74:* 98
Grisha *3:* 71
Grohmann, Susan *84:* 97
Gropper, William *27:* 93; *37:* 193
Grose, Helen Mason *YABC 1:* 260; *2:* 150
Grossman, Nancy *24:* 130; *29:* 101
Grossman, Robert *11:* 124; *46:* 39
Groth, John *15:* 79; *21:* 53, 54; *83:* 230
Grover, Lorie Ann *168:* 59
Grubb, Lisa *160:* 116
Grue, Lisa *187:* 193
Gruelle, Johnny *35:* 107
Gschwind, William *11:* 72
Guay-Mitchell, Rebecca *110:* 95, 96; *135:* 240; *180:* 76; *181:* 71, 73
Guback, Georgia *88:* 102
Guerguerion, Claudine *105:* 73
Guevara, Susan *97:* 87; *167:* 49; *194:* 54
Guggenheim, Hans *2:* 10; *3:* 37; *8:* 136
Guhathaakurta, Ajanta *183:* 199
Guida, Lisa Chauncy *172:* 188
Guilbeau, Honore *22:* 69
Guillette, Joseph *137:* 37
Guisewite, Cathy *57:* 52, 53, 54, 56, 57
Gukova, Julia *95:* 104; *154:* 103; *168:* 195
Gundersheimer, Karen *35:* 240; *82:* 100
Gunderson, Nick *57:* 120
Gunnella *192:* 144
Gurney, James *76:* 97; *86:* 32
Gurney, John Steven *75:* 39, 82; *110:* 175; *143:* 67, 68; *169:* 172
Gusman, Annie *38:* 62
Gustafson, Scott *34:* 111; *43:* 40
Gustavson, Adam *104:* 10; *171:* 183; *176:* 87; *197:* 94
Guthridge, Bettina *108:* 79; *186:* 92
Guthrie, R. Dale *64:* 143
Guthrie, Robin *20:* 122
Gutierrez, Akemi *172:* 87
Gutierrez, Alan *136:* 31, 32
Gutierrez, Rudy *97:* 162
Gutmann, Bessie Pease *73:* 93, 94
Gwynne, Fred *41:* 94, 95
Gyberg, Bo-Erik *38:* 131

H

Haas, Irene *17:* 77; *87:* 46; *96:* 117
Hack, Konrad *51:* 127
Hader, Berta H. *16:* 126
Hader, Elmer S. *16:* 126
Haeffele, Deborah *76:* 99
Haemer, Alan *62:* 109
Hafner, Marylin *22:* 196, 216; *24:* 44; *30:* 51; *35:* 95; *51:* 25, 160, 164; *86:* 16; *105:* 196; *121:* 93, 94; *149:* 208, 209; *179:* 82, 83, 84, 115; *190:* 200
Hagerty, Sean *62:* 181
Hague, Michael *32:* 128; *48:* 98, 99, 100, 101, 103, 105,106, 107, 108, 109, 110; *49:* 121; *51:* 105; *64:* 14, 15; *79:* 134; *80:* 91, 92; *83:* 135; *100:* 241; *102:* 29; *129:* 101, 103, 104; *185:* 80, 81, 82
Hair, Jonathan *115:* 135
Halas, John *29:* 41, 47, 48
Haldane, Roger *13:* 76; *14:* 202
Hale, Christy *79:* 124; *84:* 200; *114:* 201; *128:* 2, 3; *146:* 203; *158:* 243; *167:* 99; *179:* 87
Hale, Irina *26:* 97
Hale, James Graham *88:* 207
Hale, Kathleen *17:* 79; *66:* 114, 116, 118

Haley, Gail E. *43:* 102, 103, 104, 105; *78:* 65, 67; *136:* 106, 107
Hall, Amanda *96:* 110
Hall, Chuck *30:* 189
Hall, Douglas *15:* 184; *43:* 106, 107; *86:* 100; *87:* 82; *129:* 72
Hall, H. Tom *1:* 227; *30:* 210
Hall, Melanie *116:* 48, 49; *169:* 77, 78
Hall, Sydney P. *31:* 89
Hall, Tim *164:* 196
Hall, Vicki *20:* 24
Hallinan, P.K. *39:* 98
Hallman, Tom *98:* 166
Hally, Greg *101:* 200; *151:* 224
Halperin, Wendy Anderson *96:* 151; *125:* 96, 97, 98, 99; *139:* 22; *140:* 84
Halpern, Joan *10:* 25
Halpern, Shari *174:* 172
Halsey, Megan *96:* 172; *114:* 185; *180:* 8; *185:* 85
Halstead, Virginia *125:* 105
Halverson, Janet *49:* 38, 42, 44
Hallensleben, Georg *134:* 5, 6; *172:* 17
Hamanaka, Sheila *71:* 100
Hamann, Brad *78:* 151
Hamann, Sigune *104:* 115
Hamberger, John *6:* 8; *8:* 32; *14:* 79; *34:* 136; *88:* 78
Hamil, Tom *14:* 80; *43:* 163
Hamilton, Bill and Associates *26:* 215
Hamilton, Helen S. *2:* 238
Hamilton, J. *19:* 83, 85, 87
Hamilton, Laurie *116:* 210
Hamilton, Todd Cameron *84:* 15
Hamlin, Janet *97:* 136; *124:* 90; *137:* 157; *182:* 117
Hamlin, Louise *71:* 135
Hammond, Chris *21:* 37
Hammond, Elizabeth *5:* 36, 203
Hampshire, Michael *5:* 187; *7:* 110, 111; *48:* 150; *51:* 129
Hampson, Denman *10:* 155; *15:* 130
Hampton, Blake *41:* 244
Handford, Martin *64:* 105, 106, 107, 109
Handforth, Thomas *42:* 100, 101, 102, 103, 104, 105, 107
Handville, Robert *1:* 89; *38:* 76; *45:* 108, 109
Hane, Roger *17:* 239; *44:* 54
Haney, Elizabeth Mathieu *34:* 84
Hanke, Ted *71:* 10
Hankinson, Phil *181:* 164
Hanley, Catherine *8:* 161
Hann, Jacquie *19:* 144
Hanna, Cheryl *91:* 133
Hanna, Wayne A. *67:* 145
Hannon, Mark *38:* 37
Hansen, Gaby *159:* 11; *186:* 25
Hansen, Mia *149:* 76
Hanson, Joan *8:* 76; *11:* 139
Hanson, Peter E. *52:* 47; *54:* 99, 100; *73:* 21; *84:* 79; *116:* 144
Hansson, Gunilla *64:* 111, 112
Hardcastle, Nick *121:* 82; *175:* 185
Hardy, David A. *9:* 96; *119:* 74
Hardy, Paul *YABC 2:* 245 Haring, Keith *145:* 65
Harlan, Jerry *3:* 96
Harlin, Greg *89:* 194; *103:* 82; *118:* 161; *121:* 167; *182:* 76
Harness, Cheryl *106:* 80; *131:* 87; *178:* 111
Harnischfeger *18:* 121
Harper, Arthur *YABC 2:* 121
Harper, Betty *126:* 90
Harper, Jamie *174:* 71
Harper, Piers *79:* 27; *105:* 102; *161:* 67
Harrington, Glenn *82:* 18; *94:* 66, 68; *185:* 118
Harrington, Jack *83:* 162
Harrington, Richard *5:* 81
Harris, Andrew N. *191:* 78
Harris, Jim *127:* 130; *183:* 4

Harris, John *83:* 25
Harris, Nick *86:* 177
Harris, Susan Yard *42:* 121
Harrison, Florence *20:* 150, 152
Harrison, Harry *4:* 103
Harrison, Jack *28:* 149
Harrison, Mark *105:* 157; *165:* 190
Harrison, Ted *56:* 73
Harsh, Fred *72:* 107
Harston, Jerry *105:* 143
Hart, Lewis *98:* 115
Hart, Thomas *181:* 165
Hart, William *13:* 72
Hartland, Jessie *171:* 80, 81; *186:* 165
Hartung, Susan Kathleen *150:* 107, 108; *173:* 106; *175:* 106; *192:* 78
Hartelius, Margaret *10:* 24
Hartshorn, Ruth *5:* 115; *11:* 129
Harvey, Amanda *145:* 44
Harvey, Bob *48:* 219
Harvey, Gerry *7:* 180
Harvey, Lisa *97:* 21
Harvey, Paul *88:* 74
Harvey, Roland *71:* 88; *123:* 63; *179:* 94
Haskamp, Steve *195:* 36
Hassall, Joan *43:* 108, 109
Hassell, Hilton *YABC 1:* 187
Hassett, John *162:* 59
Hasselriis, Else *18:* 87; *YABC 1:* 96
Hastings, Glenn *89:* 183
Hastings, Ian *62:* 67
Hauman, Doris *2:* 184; *29:* 58, 59; *32:* 85, 86, 87
Hauman, George *2:* 184; *29:* 58, 59; *32:* 85, 86, 87
Hausherr, Rosmarie *15:* 29
Hawkes, Kevin *78:* 72; *104:* 198; *105:* 197; *112:* 109; *126:* 87; *144:* 88; *149:* 210; *150:* 110, 135; *156:* 94; *164:* 35; *186:* 18; *190:* 197
Hawkins, Jacqui *112:* 86; *162:* 64
Hawkinson, John *4:* 109; *7:* 83; *21:* 64
Hawkinson, Lucy *21:* 64
Hawthorne, Mike *140:* 228
Haxton, Elaine *28:* 131
Haydock, Robert *4:* 95
Hayes, Geoffrey *26:* 111; *44:* 133; *91:* 85
Haynes, Max *72:* 107
Hays, Michael *73:* 207; *83:* 93; *139:* 197; *146:* 202, 250
Haywood, Carolyn *1:* 112; *29:* 104
Heale, Jonathan *104:* 117
Healy, Daty *12:* 143
Healy, Deborah *58:* 181, 182; *101:* 111
Heap, Sue *102:* 207; *150:* 113, 114; *187:* 84, 85, 87
Hearn, Diane Dawson *79:* 99; *113:* 13
Hearon, Dorothy *34:* 69
Heaslip, William *57:* 24, 25
Hechtkopf, H. *11:* 110
Heck, Ed *173:* 81
Hedderwick, Mairi *30:* 127; *32:* 47; *36:* 104; *77:* 86; *145:* 91, 93, 95
Heffernan, Phil *146:* 197; *195:* 172
Hefter, Richard *28:* 170; *31:* 81, 82; *33:* 183
Hehenberger, Shelly *126:* 91
Heigh, James *22:* 98
Heighway, Richard *25:* 160; *64:* 4
Heighway-Bury, Robin *159:* 89
Heine, Helme *67:* 86; *135:* 91, 92
Heinly, John *45:* 113
Hellard, Susan *81:* 21
Hellebrand, Nancy *26:* 57
Heller, Linda *46:* 86
Heller, Ruth M. *66:* 125; *77:* 30, 32
Hellmuth, Jim *38:* 164
Helms, Georgeann *33:* 62
Helquist, Brett *142:* 203; *146:* 133, 134; *156:* 10; *173:* 25; *180:* 106; *187:* 90, 91; *193:* 12
Helweg, Hans *41:* 118; *50:* 93; *58:* 22, 26
Hemphill, Helen *179:* 95

Henba, Bobbie *90:* 195
Henderson, Dave *73:* 76; *75:* 191, 192, 193, 194; *82:* 4
Henderson, Douglas *103:* 68
Henderson, Kathy *55:* 32; *155:* 118
Henderson, Keith *35:* 122
Henderson, Meryl *127:* 58, 60; *169:* 81
Hendrix, John *187:* 133
Hendry, Linda *80:* 104; *83:* 83; *164:* 216
Hengeveld, Dennis *142:* 86
Henkes, Kevin *43:* 111; *108:* 106, 107, 108
Henneberger, Robert *1:* 42; *2:* 237; *25:* 83
Henriquez, Celeste *103:* 137
Henriquez, Elsa *82:* 260
Henriquez, Emile F. *89:* 88
Henry, Everett *29:* 191
Henry, Matthew *117:* 58
Henry, Paul *93:* 121; *194:* 125
Henry, Thomas *5:* 102
Hensel *27:* 119
Henshaw, Jacqui *141:* 127
Henstra, Friso *8:* 80; *36:* 70; *40:* 222; *41:* 250; *73:* 100, 101
Henterly, Jamichael *93:* 4
Heo, Yumi *89:* 85, 86; *94:* 89, 90; *146:* 40, 137, 138; *163:* 227
Hepple, Norman *28:* 198
Herbert, Helen *57:* 70
Herbert, Jennifer *189:* 47
Herbert, Wally *23:* 101
Herbster, Mary Lee *9:* 33
Herder, Edwin *182:* 104
Herge
See Remi, Georges
Hermansen, Pal *133:* 113
Hermanson, Dennis *10:* 55
Hermes, Gertrude *54:* 161
Herr, Margo *57:* 191
Herr, Susan *83:* 163
Herriman, George *140:* 74, 75, 76, 77, 78
Herriman, Lisa *87:* 190
Herring, Michael *121:* 76; *182:* 103
Herrington, Roger *3:* 161
Herscovici, C. *165:* 240
Hescox, Richard *85:* 86; *90:* 30; *139:* 35
Heslop, Mike *38:* 60; *40:* 130
Hess, Lydia J. *85:* 17
Hess, Mark *111:* 146; *113:* 207
Hess, Paul *134:* 47; *166:* 133; *193:* 13
Hess, Richard *42:* 31
Hester, Ronnie *37:* 85
Heuser, Olga J. *121:* 116
Heusser, Sibylle *168:* 195
Heustis, Louise L. *20:* 28
Hewitson, Jennifer *74:* 119; *124:* 167
Hewitt, Kathryn *80:* 126; *149:* 105; *184:* 93; *196:* 36
Hewitt, Margaret *84:* 112
Heyduck-Huth, Hilde *8:* 82
Heyer, Carol *74:* 122; *130:* 72, 73; *192:* 35
Heyer, Hermann *20:* 114, 115
Heyer, Marilee *102:* 108
Heyman, Ken *8:* 33; *34:* 113
Heyne, Ulrike *146:* 151
Heywood, Karen *48:* 114
Hickling, P.B. *40:* 165
Hickman, Stephen *85:* 58; *136:* 33; *171:* 128
Hierstein, Judy *56:* 40; *162:* 168
Higashi, Sandra *154:* 59, 60
Higginbottom, J. Winslow *8:* 170; *29:* 105, 106
Higgins, Chester *101:* 79
Higham, David *50:* 104
Hilb, Nora *176:* 8
Hildebrandt, Greg *8:* 191; *55:* 35, 36, 38, 39, 40, 42, 46; *172:* 110
Hildebrandt, Tim *8:* 191; *55:* 44, 45, 46
Hilder, Rowland *19:* 207
Hill, Eric *66:* 127, 128; *133:* 91
Hill, Gregory *35:* 190

Hill, Pat *49:* 120
Hillenbrand, Will *84:* 115; *92:* 76, 80; *93:* 131; *104:* 168; *128:* 137; *145:* 187; *146:* 184; *147:* 105, 106, 107; *152:* 59; *184:* 179; *195:* 34, 180; *196:* 125
Hilliard, Richard *183:* 74
Hillier, Matthew *45:* 205
Hillman, Priscilla *48:* 115
Hills, Tad *113:* 4; *137:* 147; *173:* 83
Himler, Ronald *6:* 114; *7:* 162; *8:* 17, 84, 125; *14:* 76; *19:* 145; *26:* 160; *31:* 43; *38:* 116; *41:* 44, 79; *43:* 52; *45:* 120; *46:* 43; *54:* 44, 83; *58:* 180; *59:* 38; *68:* 146; *69:* 231; *70:* 98; *71:* 177, 178; *77:* 219; *79:* 212; *83:* 62; *89:* 5; *91:* 160; *92:* 91, 92, 93; *94:* 93; *95:* 69, 174, 194; *99:* 99, 112; *113:* 92; *118:* 114; *137:* 73, 74, 77, 167; *163:* 99; *165:* 138; *178:* 9, 220; *183:* 77, 79, 80, 81; *184:* 80, 83
Himmelman, John *47:* 109; *65:* 87; *94:* 96, 97; *159:* 85
Hinds, Bill *37:* 127, 130
Hines, Anna Grossnickle *51:* 90; *74:* 124; *95:* 78, 79, 80, 81
Hines, Bob *135:* 149, 150
Hiroko *99:* 61
Hiroshige *25:* 71
Hirsh, Marilyn *7:* 126
Hiscock, Bruce *137:* 80, 81
Hissey, Jane *103:* 90; *130:* 81
Hitch, Jeff *99:* 206; *128:* 86
Hitz, Demi *11:* 135; *15:* 245; *66:* 129, 130; *152:* 94, 95
Hnizdovsky, Jacques *32:* 96; *76:* 187
Ho, Kwoncjan *15:* 132
Hoban, Lillian *1:* 114; *22:* 157; *26:* 72; *29:* 53; *40:* 105, 107, 195; *47:* 80; *69:* 107, 108; *71:* 98; *77:* 168; *106:* 50; *113:* 86; *136:* 118
Hoban, Tana *22:* 159; *104:* 82, 83, 85
Hobbie, Jocelyn *190:* 78; *196:* 92
Hobbie, Nathaniel *196:* 92
Hobbs, Leigh *166:* 95
Hoberman, Norman *5:* 82
Hobson, Sally *77:* 185
Hockerman, Dennis *39:* 22; *56:* 23
Hodgell, P.C. *42:* 114
Hodges, C. Walter *2:* 139; *11:* 15; *12:* 25; *23:* 34; *25:* 96; *38:* 165; *44:* 197; *45:* 95; *100:* 57; *YABC 2:* 62, 63
Hodges, David *9:* 98
Hodgetts, Victoria *43:* 132
Hofbauer, Imre *2:* 162
Hoff, Syd *9:* 107; *10:* 128; *33:* 94; *72:* 115, 116, 117, 118; *138:* 114, 115
Hoffman, Rosekrans *15:* 133; *50:* 219; *63:* 97
Hoffman, Sanford *38:* 208; *76:* 174; *88:* 160, 161; *151:* 156
Hoffmann, Felix *9:* 109
Hoffnung, Gerard *66:* 76, 77
Hofsinde, Robert *21:* 70
Hogan, Inez *2:* 141
Hogan, Jamie *192:* 94
Hogarth, Burne *41:* 58; *63:* 46, 48, 49, 50, 52, 53, 54, 55, 56
Hogarth, Paul *41:* 102, 103, 104; *YABC 1:* 16
Hogarth, William *42:* 33
Hogenbyl, Jan *1:* 35
Hogner, Nils *4:* 122; *25:* 144
Hogrogian, Nonny *3:* 221; *4:* 106, 107; *5:* 166; *7:* 129; *15:* 2; *16:* 176; *20:* 154; *22:* 146; *25:* 217; *27:* 206; *74:* 127, 128, 129, 149, 152; *127:* 99; *YABC 2:* 84, 94
Hokanson, Lars *93:* 111; *172:* 137
Hokusai *25:* 71
Hol, Colby *126:* 96
Holberg, Richard *2:* 51
Holbrook, Kathy *107:* 114
Holdcroft, Tina *38:* 109
Holden, Caroline *55:* 159
Holder, Heidi *36:* 99; *64:* 9
Holder, Jimmy *151:* 224
Holiday, Henry *YABC 2:* 107

Holl, F. *36:* 91
Holland, Brad *45:* 59, 159
Holland, Gay W. *128:* 105
Holland, Janice *18:* 118
Holland, Marion *6:* 116
Holldobler, Turid *26:* 120
Holliday, Keaf *144:* 236
Holling, Holling C. *15:* 136, 137
Hollinger, Deanne *12:* 116
Holm, Sharon Lane *114:* 84; *115:* 52
Holmes, B. *3:* 82
Holmes, Bea *7:* 74; *24:* 156; *31:* 93
Holmes, Dave *54:* 22
Holmes, Lesley *135:* 96
Holmgren, George Ellen *45:* 112
Holmlund, Heather D. *150:* 140
Holt, Norma *44:* 106
Holt, Pater *151:* 188
Holtan, Gene *32:* 192
Holub, Joan *149:* 72
Holyfield, John *149:* 231
Holz, Loretta *17:* 81
Hom, Nancy *79:* 195
Homar, Lorenzo *6:* 2
Homer, Winslow *128:* 8; *YABC 2:* 87
Honey, Elizabeth *112:* 95, 96; *137:* 93, 94
Honeywood, Varnette P. *110:* 68, 70
Hong, Lily Toy *76:* 104
Honigman, Marian *3:* 2
Honore, Paul *42:* 77, 79, 81, 82
Hood, Alun *69:* 145, 218; *72:* 41; *80:* 226; *87:* 4; *95:* 139
Hood, Susan *12:* 43
Hook, Christian *104:* 103
Hook, Frances *26:* 188; *27:* 127
Hook, Jeff *14:* 137; *103:* 105
Hook, Richard *26:* 188
Hooks *63:* 30
Hooper, Hadley *177:* 145
Hoover, Carol A. *21:* 77
Hoover, Russell *12:* 95; *17:* 2; *34:* 156
Hope, James *141:* 116
Hopkins, Chris *99:* 127
Hopman, Philip *178:* 184
Hoppin, Augustus *34:* 66
Horacek, Petr *163:* 117
Horder, Margaret *2:* 108; *73:* 75
Horen, Michael *45:* 121
Horne, Daniel *73:* 106; *91:* 153; *109:* 127; *110:* 232; *164:* 176
Horne, Richard *111:* 80
Horse, Harry *128:* 195; *169:* 86
Horvat, Laurel *12:* 201
Horvath, David *192:* 95
Horvath, Ferdinand Kusati *24:* 176
Horvath, Maria *57:* 171
Horwitz, Richard *57:* 174
Hotchkiss, De Wolfe *20:* 49
Hough, Charlotte *9:* 112; *13:* 98; *17:* 83; *24:* 195
Houlihan, Ray *11:* 214
House, Caroline *183:* 121
Housman, Laurence *25:* 146, 147
Houston, James *13:* 107; *74:* 132, 134, 135
Hovland, Gary *88:* 172; *171:* 148
Hoyt, Eleanor *158:* 231
How, W.E. *20:* 47
Howard, Alan *16:* 80; *34:* 58; *45:* 114
Howard, Arthur *165:* 111, 112; *190:* 5
Howard, J.N. *15:* 234
Howard, John *33:* 179
Howard, Kim *116:* 71
Howard, Paul *142:* 126, 129; *144:* 187
Howard, Rob *40:* 161
Howarth, Daniel *170:* 34
Howe, John *115:* 47; *176:* 106
Howe, John F. *79:* 101; *80:* 150
Howe, Phillip *117:* 117; *175:* 115
Howe, Stephen *1:* 232
Howell, Karen *119:* 123
Howell, Pat *15:* 139

Howell, Troy *23:* 24; *31:* 61; *36:* 158; *37:* 184; *41:* 76, 235; *48:* 112; *56:* 13; *57:* 3; *59:* 174; *63:* 5; *74:* 46; *89:* 188; *90:* 231; *95:* 97; *98:* 130; *99:* 189; *153:* 156, 157, 158; *176:* 104
Howes, Charles *22:* 17
Hoyt, Ard *145:* 141; *190:* 82
Hranilovich, Barbara *127:* 51
Hu, Ying-Hwa *116:* 107; *152:* 236; *173:* 171
Huang, Benrei *137:* 55
Huang, Zhong-Yang *117:* 30, 32
Hubbard, Woodleigh Marx *98:* 67; *115:* 79; *160:* 138
Hubley, Faith *48:* 120, 121, 125, 130, 131, 132, 134
Hubley, John *48:* 125, 130, 131, 132, 134
Hudak, Michal *143:* 74
Hudnut, Robin *14:* 62
Huerta, Catherine *76:* 178; *77:* 44, 45; *90:* 182
Huffaker, Sandy *10:* 56
Huffman, Joan *13:* 33
Huffman, Tom *13:* 180; *17:* 212; *21:* 116; *24:* 132; *33:* 154; *38:* 59; *42:* 147
Hughes, Arthur *20:* 148, 149, 150; *33:* 114, 148, 149
Hughes, Darren *95:* 44
Hughes, David *36:* 197
Hughes, Shirley *1:* 20, 21; *7:* 3; *12:* 217; *16:* 163; *29:* 154; *63:* 118; *70:* 102, 103, 104; *73:* 169; *88:* 70; *110:* 118, 119; *159:* 103
Hugo, Victor *47:* 112
Hull, Cathy *78:* 29
Hull, Richard *95:* 120; *123:* 175; *172:* 195
Hulsmann, Eva *16:* 166
Hume, Lachie *189:* 93
Hummel, Berta *43:* 137, 138, 139
Hummel, Lisl *29:* 109; *YABC 2:* 333, 334
Humphrey, Henry *16:* 167
Humphreys, Graham *25:* 168
Humphries, Tudor *76:* 66; *80:* 4; *124:* 4, 5
Huneck, Stephen *183:* 88, 89
Hunt, James *2:* 143
Hunt, Jonathan *84:* 120
Hunt, Paul *119:* 104; *129:* 135; *139:* 160; *173:* 112
Hunt, Robert *110:* 206, 235; *147:* 136, 137; *170:* 3
Hunt, Scott *190:* 143
Hunter, Anne *133:* 190; *178:* 150
Huntington, Amy *180:* 99
Hurd, Clement *2:* 148, 149; *64:* 127, 128, 129, 131, 133, 134,135, 136; *100:* 37, 38
Hurd, Peter *24:* 30, 31,; *YABC 2:* 56
Hurd, Thacher *46:* 88, 89; *94:* 114, 115, 116; *123:* 81, 82, 84
Hurlimann, Ruth *32:* 99
Hurst, Carol Otis *185:* 92
Hurst, Philip *196:* 79
Hurst, Tracey *192:* 238
Hussar, Michael *114:* 113; *117:* 159
Hustler, Tom *6:* 105
Hutchins, Laurence *55:* 22
Hutchins, Pat *15:* 142; *70:* 106, 107, 108; *178:* 131, 132
Hutchinson, Sascha *95:* 211
Hutchinson, William M. *6:* 3, 138; *46:* 70
Hutchison, Paula *23:* 10
Hutton, Clarke *YABC 2:* 335
Hutton, Kathryn *35:* 155; *89:* 91
Hutton, Warwick *20:* 91
Huyette, Marcia *29:* 188
Hyatt, John *54:* 7
Hyatt, Mitch *178:* 162
Hyde, Maureen *82:* 17; *121:* 145, 146
Hyman, David *117:* 64
Hyman, Trina Schart *1:* 204; *2:* 194; *5:* 153; *6:* 106; *7:* 138, 145; *8:* 22; *10:* 196; *13:* 96; *14:* 114; *15:* 204; *16:* 234; *20:* 82; *22:* 133; *24:* 151; *25:* 79, 82; *26:* 82; *29:* 83; *31:* 37, 39; *34:* 104; *38:* 84, 100, 128; *41:* 49; *43:* 146; *46:* 91, 92, 93, 95, 96, 97, 98, 99, 100,

101, 102, 103, 104, 105,108, 109, 111, 197; *48:* 60, 61; *52:* 32; *60:* 168; *66:* 38; *67:* 214; *72:* 74; *75:* 92; *79:* 57; *82:* 95, 238; *89:* 46; *95:* 91, 92, 93; *100:* 33, 199; *132:* 12; *147:* 33, 35, 36; *167:* 58, 60; *177:* 189, 190

I

Ibarra, Rosa *147:* 91
Ibatoulline, Bagram *156:* 48; *174:* 33, 82
Ichikawa, Satomi *29:* 152; *41:* 52; *47:* 133, 134,135, 136; *78:* 93, 94; *80:* 81; *146:* 143, 145, 146
Ide, Jacqueline *YABC 1:* 39
Ilsley, Velma *3:* 1; *7:* 55; *12:* 109; *37:* 62; *38:* 184
Imai, Ayano *190:* 85, 86
in den Bosch, Nicole *150:* 204
Inga *1:* 142
Ingman, Bruce *134:* 50; *182:* 91, 92
Ingpen, Robert *109:* 103, 104; *132:* 138; *137:* 177; *166:* 103; *181:* 140
Ingraham, Erick *21:* 177; *84:* 256; *103:* 66
Inkpen, Mick *99:* 104, 105; *106:* 44
Innerst, Stacy *149:* 104
Innocenti, Roberto *21:* 123; *96:* 122; *159:* 111, 197
Inoue, Yosuke *24:* 118
Iofin, Michael *97:* 157
Iosa, Ann *63:* 189
Ipcar, Dahlov *1:* 124, 125; *49:* 137, 138, 139, 140, 141, 142,143, 144, 145; *147:* 122, 124, 126
Irvin, Fred *13:* 166; *15:* 143, 144; *27:* 175
Irving, Jay *45:* 72
Irving, Laurence *27:* 50
Isaac, Joanne *21:* 76
Isaacs, Gary *170:* 188
Isadora, Rachel *43:* 159, 160; *54:* 31; *79:* 106, 107,108; *121:* 100, 102; *165:* 116, 117
Ishmael, Woodi *24:* 111; *31:* 99
Ives, Ruth *15:* 257
Iwai, Melissa *149:* 233; *183:* 92

J

Jabar, Cynthia *101:* 201
Jackness, Andrew *94:* 237
Jackson, Julian *91:* 104, 106
Jackson, Michael *43:* 42
Jackson, Shelley *79:* 71; *99:* 109; *187:* 82
Jacob, Murv *89:* 30
Jacobi, Kathy *62:* 118
Jacobs, Barbara *9:* 136
Jacobs, Lou, Jr. *9:* 136; *15:* 128
Jacobsen, Laura *176:* 98; *177:* 85, 86
Jacobson, Rick *131:* 222; *170:* 119
Jacobus, Tim *79:* 140; *109:* 126; *129:* 180
Jacques, Robin *1:* 70; *2:* 1; *8:* 46; *9:* 20; *15:* 187; *19:* 253; *32:* 102, 103, 104; *43:* 184; *73:* 135; *YABC 1:* 42
Jaeggi, Yoshiko *186:* 184
Jaffee, Al *66:* 131, 132
Jagr, Miloslav *13:* 197
Jahn-Clough, Lisa *88:* 114; *152:* 104; *193:* 70, 71
Jahnke, Robert *84:* 24
Jainschigg, Nicholas *80:* 64; *91:* 138; *95:* 63; *99:* 25; *108:* 50; *171:* 41
Jakesavic, Nenad *85:* 102
Jakobsen, Kathy *116:* 83
Jakubowski, Charles *14:* 192
Jambor, Louis *YABC 1:* 11
James, Ann *73:* 50; *82:* 113; *158:* 61; *183:* 44
James, Brian *140:* 91
James, Curtis E. *182:* 93

James, Derek *35:* 187; *44:* 91; *61:* 133; *74:* 2; *80:* 57; *86:* 88; *130:* 30; *179:* 29
James, Gilbert *YABC 1:* 43
James, Gordon C. *195:* 89
James, Harold *2:* 151; *3:* 62; *8:* 79; *29:* 113; *51:* 195; *74:* 90
James, Kennon *126:* 211
James, Robin *50:* 106; *53:* 32, 34, 35
Janosch
　See Eckert, Horst
Janovitch, Marilyn *68:* 168
Janovitz, Marilyn *87:* 187; *130:* 198; *194:* 91
Jansons, Inese *48:* 117
Jansson, Tove *3:* 90; *41:* 106, 108, 109, 110, 111, 113, 114
Jaques, Faith *7:* 11, 132, 133; *21:* 83, 84; *69:* 114,116; *73:* 170
Jaques, Frances Lee *29:* 224
Jauss, Anne Marie *1:* 139; *3:* 34; *10:* 57, 119; *11:* 205; *23:* 194
Jay, Alison *158:* 97, 98; *183:* 126, 127; *196:* 95, 96, 97, 98
Jeffers, Oliver *175:* 111
Jeffers, Susan *17:* 86, 87; *25:* 164, 165; *26:* 112; *50:* 132, 134, 135; *70:* 111, 112, 113; *137:* 107, 108, 109, 110, 111
Jefferson, Louise E. *4:* 160
Jenkin-Pearce, Susie *78:* 16
Jenkins, Debra Reid *85:* 202; *114:* 89; *173:* 134
Jenkins, Jean *98:* 79, 102
Jenkins, Leonard *157:* 169; *167:* 128; *189:* 96, 97; *190:* 89
Jenkins, Patrick *72:* 126
Jenkins, Steve *124:* 177; *154:* 90, 91, 92, 93; *185:* 194; *188:* 81, 82, 83, 84, 85, 86
Jenks, Aleta *73:* 117; *124:* 225
Jenkyns, Chris *51:* 97
Jensen, Bruce *95:* 39
Jensinius, Kirsten *56:* 58
Jeram, Anita *89:* 135; *102:* 122, 123; *129:* 112; *154:* 96, 97, 98; *164:* 154
Jernigan, E. Wesley *85:* 92
Jerome, Karen A. *72:* 194
Jeruchim, Simon *6:* 173; *15:* 250
Jeschke, Susan *20:* 89; *39:* 161; *41:* 84; *42:* 120
Jessel, Camilla *29:* 115
Jessell, Tim *159:* 3; *177:* 87; *181:* 95
Jeyaveeran, Ruth *182:* 100
Jiang, Cheng An *109:* 108
Jiang, Wei *109:* 108
Jimenez, Maria *77:* 158; *93:* 127
Jobling, Curtis *138:* 74
Jocelyn, Marthe *118:* 83; *137:* 219; *163:* 119, 120
Joerns, Consuelo *38:* 36; *44:* 94
John, Diana *12:* 209
John, Helen *1:* 215; *28:* 204
Johns, Elizabeth *127:* 33
Johns, Jasper *61:* 172
Johns, Jeanne *24:* 114
Johnson, Adrian *143:* 50
Johnson, Bruce *9:* 47
Johnson, Cathy *92:* 136
Johnson, Crockett
　See Leisk, David
Johnson, D. William *23:* 104
Johnson, D.B. *183:* 98, 139
Johnson, David *175:* 18; *191:* 91
Johnson, Gillian *119:* 175; *164:* 217
Johnson, Harper *1:* 27; *2:* 33; *18:* 302; *19:* 61; *31:* 181; *44:* 46, 50, 95
Johnson, Ingrid *37:* 118
Johnson, James Ralph *1:* 23, 127
Johnson, James David *12:* 195
Johnson, Jane *48:* 136
Johnson, Joel Peter *98:* 18; *128:* 111
Johnson, John E. *34:* 133
Johnson, Kevin *72:* 44

Johnson, Kevin Eugene *109:* 215
Johnson, Larry *47:* 56; *123:* 107; *159:* 203
Johnson, Layne *187:* 94
Johnson, Margaret S. *35:* 131
Johnson, Meredith Merrell *71:* 181; *83:* 158; *89:* 103; *104:* 88
Johnson, Milton *1:* 67; *2:* 71; *26:* 45; *31:* 107; *60:* 112; *68:* 96
Johnson, Pamela *16:* 174; *52:* 145; *62:* 140; *73:* 116; *85:* 64
Johnson, Paul Brett *83:* 95; *132:* 119
Johnson, Stephen T. *80:* 15; *131:* 35; *141:* 96; *145:* 40; *164:* 187; *175:* 32; *189:* 99, 100
Johnson, Steve *138:* 219; *141:* 64; *144:* 199; *177:* 51
Johnson, William R. *38:* 91
Johnson-Petrov, Arden *115:* 206
Johnston, David McCall *50:* 131, 133
Johnston, Lynne *118:* 85, 87, 89
Johnstone, Anne *8:* 120; *36:* 89
Johnstone, Janet Grahame *8:* 120; *36:* 89
Jonas, Ann *50:* 107, 108, 109; *135:* 113
Jones, Bob *71:* 5; *77:* 199
Jones, Carol *5:* 131; *72:* 185, 186; *153:* 111, 112
Jones, Chuck *53:* 70, 71
Jones, Davy *89:* 176
Jones, Douglas B. *185:* 192
Jones, Elizabeth Orton *18:* 124, 126, 128, 129
Jones, Harold *14:* 88; *52:* 50
Jones, Holly *127:* 3
Jones, Jeff *41:* 64
Jones, Laurian *25:* 24, 27
Jones, Margaret *74:* 57
Jones, Noah Z. *182:* 37
Jones, Randy *131:* 104
Jones, Richard *127:* 222
Jones, Robert *25:* 67
Jones, Wilfred *35:* 115; *YABC 1:* 163
Jordan, Charles *89:* 58
Jordan, Jess *158:* 136
Jordan, Martin George *84:* 127
Jordan, Richard *84:* 36
Jorgenson, Andrea *91:* 111
Jorisch, Stéphane *153:* 56, 193; *177:* 29; *178:* 138, 139; *187:* 23
Joseph, James *53:* 88
Joudrey, Ken *64:* 145; *78:* 6
Joyce, William *72:* 131, 132, 133, 134; *73:* 227; *145:* 37
Joyner, Jerry *34:* 138
Juan, Ana *175:* 38; *179:* 111, 112
Jucker, Sita *5:* 93
Judge, Lita *192:* 99
Judkis, Jim *37:* 38
Juhasz, Victor *31:* 67
Jullian, Philippe *24:* 206; *25:* 203
Jung, Tom *91:* 217
Junge, Alexandra *183:* 37
Junge, Walter *67:* 150
Jupo, Frank *7:* 148, 149
Jurisch, Stephane *154:* 105
Justice, Martin *34:* 72

K

Kabatova-Taborska, Zdenka *107:* 153
Kachik, John *165:* 230
Kaczman, James *156:* 98
Kadair, Deborah Ousley *184:* 45, 89
Kahl, David *74:* 95; *97:* 35; *109:* 174; *110:* 213
Kahl, M.P. *37:* 83
Kahl, Virginia *48:* 138
Kahn, Katherine Janus *90:* 135
Kakimoo, Kozo *11:* 148
Kalett, Jim *48:* 159, 160, 161
Kalin, Victor *39:* 186
Kalman, Maira *96:* 131, 132; *137:* 115

Kalmenoff, Matthew 22: 191
Kalow, Gisela 32: 105
Kamen, Gloria 1: 41; 9: 119; 10: 178; 35: 157; 78: 236; 98: 82
Kaminsky, Jef 102: 153
Kandell, Alice 35: 133
Kane, Henry B. 14: 90; 18: 219, 220
Kane, Robert 18: 131
Kanfer, Larry 66: 141
Kappes, Alfred 28: 104
Karalus, Bob 41: 157
Karas, G. Brian 80: 60; 99: 179; 115: 41; 118: 50; 136: 168; 145: 166; 149: 245; 159: 65; 171: 192; 178: 142, 143
Karasz, Ilonka 128: 163
Karlin, Eugene 10: 63; 20: 131
Karlin, Nurit 63: 78; 103: 110
Karpinski, Tony 134: 160
Kasamatsu, Shiro 139: 155
Kasparavicius, Kestutis 139: 210
Kassian, Olena 64: 94
Kastner, Jill 79: 135; 117: 84, 85
Kasuya, Masahiro 41: 206, 207; 51: 100
Kasza, Keiko 191: 99, 100, 101, 102, 103
Katona, Robert 21: 85; 24: 126
Katz, Karen 158: 123
Kauffer, E. McKnight 33: 103; 35: 127; 63: 67
Kaufman, Angelika 15: 156
Kaufman, Joe 33: 119
Kaufman, John 13: 158
Kaufman, Stuart 62: 64; 68: 226; 137: 44
Kaufmann, John 1: 174; 4: 159; 8: 43, 1; 10: 102; 18: 133, 134; 22: 251
Kaye, Graham 1: 9; 67: 7, 8
Kaye, M.M. 62: 95
Kazalovski, Nata 40: 205
Keane, Bil 4: 135
Kearney, David 72: 47; 121: 83
Keating, Pamel T. 77: 37
Keats, Ezra Jack 3: 18, 105, 257; 14: 101, 102; 33: 129; 57: 79, 80, 82, 83, 84, 87
Keegan, Charles 166: 211
Keegan, Marcia 9: 122; 32: 93
Keeler, Patricia A. 81: 56; 183: 102, 103
Keely, Jack 119: 95
Keely, John 26: 104; 48: 214
Keen, Eliot 25: 213
Keep, Richard C. 170: 122
Keeping, Charles 9: 124, 185; 15: 28, 134; 18: 115; 44: 194, 196; 47: 25; 52: 3; 54: 156; 69: 123, 124; 74: 56; 155: 9
Keeter, Susan 168: 46; 183: 192
Keith, Eros 4: 98; 5: 138; 31: 29; 43: 220; 52: 91, 92, 93, 94; 56: 64, 66; 60: 37; 79: 93
Keleinikov, Andrei 65: 101, 102
Kelen, Emery 13: 115
Keller, A.J. 62: 198
Keller, Arthur I. 26: 106
Keller, Dick 36: 123, 125
Keller, Holly 45: 79; 76: 118, 119, 120, 121; 108: 137, 138, 140; 157: 117, 118, 119
Keller, Katie 79: 222; 93: 108
Keller, Laurie 196: 105, 106
Keller, Ronald 45: 208
Kelley, Gary 183: 105
Kelley, True 41: 114, 115; 42: 137; 75: 35; 92: 104, 105; 124: 62; 130: 100, 101; 179: 120, 121, 122; 192: 251
Kellogg, Steven 8: 96; 11: 207; 14: 130; 20: 58; 29: 140, 141; 30: 35; 41: 141; 57: 89, 90, 92, 93, 94, 96; 59: 182; 73: 141; 77: 129; 130: 105, 106; 177: 94, 95, 96, 97; YABC 1: 65, 73
Kelly, Billy 158: 143
Kelly, Geoff 97: 196; 112: 25
Kelly, Irene 147: 134
Kelly, John 194: 186
Kelly, Joseph 174: 94
Kelly, Kathleen M. 71: 109
Kelly, Laura 89: 217
Kelly, True 163: 87

Kelly, Walt 18: 136, 137, 138, 139, 140, 141, 144, 145, 146, 148, 149
Kemble, E.W. 34: 75; 44: 178; YABC 2: 54, 59
Kemp-Welsh, Lucy 24: 197; 100: 214
Kendall, Jane 150: 105; 186: 109
Kendall, Peter 152: 85
Kendrick, Dennis 79: 213
Kennaway, Adrienne 60: 55, 56; 171: 88, 89
Kennedy, Doug 189: 104
Kennedy, Paul Edward 6: 190; 8: 132; 33: 120
Kennedy, Richard 3: 93; 12: 179; 44: 193; 100: 15; YABC 1: 57
Kent, Jack 24: 136; 37: 37; 40: 81; 84: 89; 86: 150; 88: 77
Kent, Rockwell 5: 166; 6: 129; 20: 225, 226, 227,229; 59: 144
Kenyon, Tony 81: 201; 127: 74
Kepes, Juliet 13: 119
Kerins, Anthony 76: 84
Kerr, Judity 24: 137
Kerr, Phyllis Forbes 72: 141
Kessler, Leonard 1: 108; 7: 139; 14: 107, 227; 22: 101; 44: 96; 67: 79; 82: 123
Kest, Kristin 168: 99; 173: 23
Kesteven, Peter 35: 189
Ketcham, Hank 28: 140, 141, 142
Kettelkamp, Larry 2: 164
Key, Alexander 8: 99
Khalsa, Dayal Kaur 62: 99
Kiakshuk 8: 59
Kidd, Chip 94: 23
Kidd, Richard 152: 110
Kidd, Tom 64: 199; 81: 189; 185: 173
Kiddell-Monroe, Joan 19: 201; 55: 59, 60; 87: 174; 121: 112
Kidder, Harvey 9: 105; 80: 41
Kidwell, Carl 43: 145
Kieffer, Christa 41: 89
Kiesler, Kate 110: 105; 136: 142
Kiff, Ken 40: 45
Kilbride, Robert 37: 100
Kilby, Don 141: 144
Kim, Glenn 99: 82
Kimball, Anton 78: 114; 119: 105
Kimball, Yeffe 23: 116; 37: 88
Kimber, Murray 171: 91
Kimmel, Warren 176: 112
Kincade, Orin 34: 116
Kindersley, Barnabas 96: 110
Kindred, Wendy 7: 151
King, Colin 53: 3
King, Robin 10: 164, 165
King, Stephen Michael 141: 31; 197: 191
King, Tara Calahan 139: 172
King, Tony 39: 121
Kingman, Dong 16: 287; 44: 100, 102, 104
Kingsley, Charles YABC 2: 182
Kingston, Julie 147: 14
Kingston, Maxine Hong 53: 92
Kinney, Jeff 187: 97
Kipling, John Lockwood YABC 2: 198
Kipling, Rudyard YABC 2: 196
Kipniss, Robert 29: 59
Kirchherr, Astrid 55: 23
Kirchhoff, Art 28: 136
Kirk, Daniel 153: 115, 116, 117; 173: 101; 196: 113, 114, 115, 116
Kirk, David 117: 88, 89; 161: 97, 98
Kirk, Ruth 5: 96
Kirk, Steve 170: 37
Kirk, Tim 32: 209, 211; 72: 89; 83: 49
Kirmse, Marguerite 15: 283; 18: 153
Kirsch, Vincent X. 124: 207
Kirschner, Ruth 22: 154
Kish, Ely 73: 119; 79: 2
Kitamura, Satoshi 62: 102; 98: 91; 101: 147; 138: 2; 143: 83, 85, 86
Kiss, Andrew 168: 115
Kitchel, JoAnn E. 133: 32
Kitchen, Bert 70: 126; 193: 49

Kittelsen, Theodor 62: 14
Kiuchi, Tatsuro 114: 71
Kiwak, Barbara 172: 135
Klahr, Susan 176: 196
Klapholz, Mel 13: 35
Klein, Bill 89: 105
Klein, Robert 55: 77
Klein, Suzanna 63: 104
Kleinman, Zalman 28: 143
Kleven, Elisa 173: 96, 97
Kliban, B. 35: 137, 138
Kline, Michael 127: 66
Klise, M. Sarah 180: 117, 118; 181: 97
Knabel, Lonnie 73: 103; 75: 187, 228; 194: 216
Kneen, Maggie 140: 139
Knight, Ann 34: 143
Knight, Christopher 13: 125
Knight, Hilary 1: 233; 3: 21; 15: 92, 158, 159; 16: 258, 259, 260; 18: 235; 19: 169; 35: 242; 46: 167; 52: 116; 69: 126, 127; 132: 129; YABC 1: 168, 169, 172
Knorr, Peter 126: 92, 93
Knotts, Howard 20: 4; 25: 170; 36: 163
Knutson, Barbara 112: 134
Knutson, Kimberley 115: 90
Kobayashi, Ann 39: 58
Kochalka, James 196: 120, 121, 122
Kocsis, J.C.
   See Paul, James
Koehler, Hanne Lore 176: 203
Koehn, Ilse 34: 198; 79: 123
Koelsch, Michael 99: 182; 107: 164; 109: 239; 138: 142; 150: 94; 176: 105; 187: 63
Koering, Ursula 3: 28; 4: 14; 44: 5; 64: 140,141; 85: 46
Koerner, Henry
   See Koerner, W.H.D.
Koerner, W.H.D. 14: 216; 21: 88, 89, 90, 91; 23: 211
Koetsch, Mike 166: 68
Koffler, Camilla 36: 113
Kogan, Deborah Ray 161: 101, 102
Koide, Yasuko 50: 114
Kolado, Karen 102: 228
Komoda, Kiyo 9: 128; 13: 214
Kompaneyets, Marc 169: 92
Konashevich, Vladimir 61: 160
Konashevicha, V. YABC 1: 26
Konigsburg, E.L. 4: 138; 48: 141, 142, 144, 145; 94: 129, 130; 126: 129, 130, 131; 194: 95, 98
Kono, Erin Eitter 177: 99
Kooiker, Leonie 48: 148
Koonook, Simon 65: 157
Koontz, Robin Michal 136: 155
Koopmans, Loek 101: 121
Kopelke, Lisa 154: 107
Kopper, Lisa 72: 152, 153; 105: 135, 136
Korach, Mimi 1: 128, 129; 2: 52; 4: 39; 5: 159; 9: 129; 10: 21; 24: 69
Koren, Edward 5: 100; 65: 65, 67
Kosaka, Fumi 164: 130
Koscielniak, Bruce 99: 122; 153: 120, 121, 122
Koshkin, Alexander 92: 180
Kossin, Sandy 10: 71; 23: 105
Kostin, Andrej 26: 204
Kosturko, Bob 164: 56
Kotzky, Brian 68: 184
Kovacevic, Zivojin 13: 247
Kovalski, Maryann 58: 120; 84: 88; 97: 124, 125, 126; 158: 3; 186: 80
Krahn, Fernando 2: 257; 34: 206; 49: 152
Kramer, Anthony 33: 81
Kramer, David 96: 162; 109: 132; 150: 220
Kramer, Frank 6: 121
Krantz, Kathy 35: 83
Kratter, Paul 139: 65
Kraus, Robert 13: 217; 65: 113; 93: 93, 94
Krause, Jon 176: 62

Krauss, Trisha *174:* 10
Kredel, Fritz *6:* 35; *17:* 93, 94, 95, 96; *22:* 147; *24:* 175; *29:* 130; *35:* 77; *YABC 2:* 166, 300
Kreloff, Eliot *189:* 107, 108
Krementz, Jill *17:* 98; *49:* 41
Krenina, Katya *117:* 106; *125:* 133; *176:* 117
Kresin, Robert *23:* 19
Krieger, Salem *54:* 164
Kriegler, Lyn *73:* 29
Krinitz, Esther Nisenthal *193:* 196
Krommes, Beth *128:* 141; *149:* 136; *181:* 100, 101; *184:* 105; *188:* 125
Krone, Mike *101:* 71
Kronheimer, Ann *135:* 119
Krosoczka, Jarrett J. *155:* 142
Kruck, Gerald *88:* 181
Krupinski, Loretta *67:* 104; *102:* 131; *161:* 105, 106
Krupp, Robin Rector *53:* 96, 98
Krush, Beth *1:* 51, 85; *2:* 233; *4:* 115; *9:* 61; *10:* 191; *11:* 196; *18:* 164, 165; *32:* 72; *37:* 203; *43:* 57; *60:* 102, 103, 107, 108, 109
Krush, Joe *2:* 233; *4:* 115; *9:* 61; *10:* 191; *11:* 196; *18:* 164, 165; *32:* 72, 91; *37:* 203; *43:* 57; *60:* 102, 103, 107, 108, 109
Krych, Duane *91:* 43
Krykorka, Vladyana *96:* 147; *143:* 90, 91; *168:* 14
Kubick, Dana *165:* 91
Kubinyi, Laszlo *4:* 116; *6:* 113; *16:* 118; *17:* 100; *28:* 227; *30:* 172; *49:* 24, 28; *54:* 23; *167:* 149
Kubricht, Mary *73:* 118
Kucharik, Elena *139:* 31
Kuchera, Kathleen *84:* 5
Kuhn, Bob *17:* 91; *35:* 235
Kulikov, Boris *163:* 185; *185:* 23
Kulka, Joe *188:* 110
Kukalis, Romas *90:* 27; *139:* 37
Kuklin, Susan *63:* 82, 83, 84
Kunhardt, Dorothy *53:* 101
Kunhardt, Edith *67:* 105, 106
Kunstler, Mort *10:* 73; *32:* 143
Kurchevsky, V. *34:* 61
Kurczok, Belinda *121:* 118
Kurelek, William *8:* 107
Kuriloff, Ron *13:* 19
Kurisu, Jane *160:* 120
Kuskin, Karla *2:* 170; *68:* 115, 116; *111:* 116
Kutzer, Ernst *19:* 249
Kuzma, Steve *57:* 8; *62:* 93
Kuznetsova, Berta *74:* 45
Kvasnosky, Laura McGee *93:* 103; *142:* 83; *182:* 108
Kwas, Susan Estelle *179:* 116
Kyong, Yunmee *165:* 139

L

LaBlanc, Andre *24:* 146
Laboccetta, Mario *27:* 120
LaBrose, Darcie *157:* 134
Labrosse, Darcia *58:* 88; *108:* 77; *178:* 89
LaCava, Vince *95:* 118
Laceky, Adam *32:* 121
Lacis, Astra *85:* 117
Lacome, Julie *174:* 96, 97
La Croix *YABC 2:* 4
Ladwig, Tim *98:* 212; *117:* 76
La Farge, Margaret *47:* 141
LaFave, Kim *64:* 177; *72:* 39; *97:* 146; *99:* 172; *106:* 123; *149:* 126; *196:* 128, 129
Lafontaine, Roger *167:* 158
Lafrance, Marie *197:* 109
Lagarrigue, Jerome *136:* 102; *187:* 81
Laimgruber, Monika *11:* 153
Laite, Gordon *1:* 130, 131; *8:* 209; *31:* 113; *40:* 63; *46:* 117

Laliberté, Louise-Andrée *169:* 98
LaMarche, Jim *46:* 204; *61:* 56; *94:* 69; *114:* 22; *129:* 163; *162:* 78, 80
Lamb, Jim *10:* 117
Lambase, Barbara *101:* 185; *150:* 221; *166:* 234
Lambert, J.K. *38:* 129; *39:* 24
Lambert, Sally Anne *133:* 191
Lambert, Saul *23:* 112; *33:* 107; *54:* 136
Lambert, Stephen *109:* 33; *174:* 99
Lambo, Don *6:* 156; *35:* 115; *36:* 146
Lamontagne, Jacques *166:* 227
Lamut, Sonja *57:* 193
Lamut, Sonya *85:* 102
Landa, Peter *11:* 95; *13:* 177; *53:* 119
Landau, Jacob *38:* 111
Landis, Joan *104:* 23
Landon, Lucinda *79:* 31
Landshoff, Ursula *13:* 124
Landström, Lena *146:* 165, 166
Landström, Olof *146:* 166, 168; *170:* 22
Lane, Daniel *112:* 60
Lane, John R. *8:* 145
Lane, John *15:* 176, 177; *30:* 146
Lane, Nancy *74:* 74
Lang, G.D. *48:* 56
Lang, Gary *73:* 75
Lang, Jerry *18:* 295
Langdo, Bryan *186:* 187; *191:* 113, 114, 115
Lange, Dorothea *50:* 141
Langley, Jonathan *162:* 128
Langner, Nola *8:* 110; *42:* 36
Lanino, Deborah *105:* 148
Lantz, Paul *1:* 82, 102; *27:* 88; *34:* 102; *45:* 123
Larkin, Bob *84:* 225
Laroche, Giles *126:* 140; *146:* 81
LaRochelle, David *171:* 97
Larrecq, John *44:* 108; *68:* 56
Larsen, Suzanne *1:* 13
Larson, Gary *57:* 121, 122, 123, 124, 125, 126, 127
Larsson, Carl *35:* 144, 145, 146, 147, 148, 149, 150, 152, 153, 154
Larsson, Karl *35:* 144
Lartitegui, Ana G. *105:* 167
LaRue, Jenna *167:* 20
La Rue, Michael D. *13:* 215
Lasker, Joe *7:* 186, 187; *14:* 55; *38:* 115; *39:* 47; *83:* 113, 114, 115
Latham, Barbara *16:* 188, 189; *43:* 71
Lathrop, Dorothy *14:* 117, 118, 119; *15:* 109; *16:* 78, 79, 81; *32:* 201, 203; *33:* 112; *YABC 2:* 301
Lattimore, Eleanor Frances *7:* 156
Lauden, Claire *16:* 173
Lauden, George, Jr. *16:* 173
Laune, Paul *2:* 235; *34:* 31
Laure, Jason *49:* 53; *50:* 122
Lauter, Richard *63:* 29; *67:* 111; *77:* 198
Lavallee, Barbara *74:* 157; *92:* 154; *96:* 126; *145:* 193; *166:* 125, 126; *186:* 155; *192:* 172
Lave, Fitz Hugh *59:* 139
Lavis, Stephen *43:* 143; *87:* 137, 164, 165
Layton, Neal *152:* 120, 121; *182:* 65; *187:* 103, 105, 106
Lawrason, June *168:* 30
Lawrence, John *25:* 131; *30:* 141; *44:* 198, 200
Lawrence, Stephen *20:* 195
Lawson, Carol *6:* 38; *42:* 93, 131; *174:* 56; *189:* 89
Lawson, George *17:* 280
Lawson, Robert *5:* 26; *6:* 94; *13:* 39; *16:* 11; *20:* 100, 102, 103; *54:* 3; *66:* 12; *100:* 144, 145; *YABC 2:* 222, 224, 225, 227, 228, 229, 230, 231, 232, 233, 234, 235, 237, 238, 239, 240, 241
Layfield, Kathie *60:* 194
Lazare, Jerry *44:* 109; *74:* 28
Lazarevich, Mila *17:* 118

Lazarus, Claire *103:* 30
Lazarus, Keo Felker *21:* 94
Lazzaro, Victor *11:* 126
Lea, Bob *166:* 208
Lea, Tom *43:* 72, 74
Leacroft, Richard *6:* 140
Leaf, Munro *20:* 99
Leake, Donald *70:* 41
Leander, Patricia *23:* 27
Lear, Edward *18:* 183, 184, 185
Lear, Rebecca *149:* 46
Lebenson, Richard *6:* 209; *7:* 76; *23:* 145; *44:* 191; *87:* 153
Le Cain, Errol *6:* 141; *9:* 3; *22:* 142; *25:* 198; *28:* 173; *68:* 128, 129; *86:* 49
Lechon, Daniel *113:* 211
Leder, Dora *129:* 172
Ledger, Bill *181:* 58
Leduc, Bernard *102:* 36
Lee, Alan *62:* 25, 28
Lee, Bryce *99:* 60; *101:* 195; *196:* 53
Lee, Chinlun *181:* 138; *182:* 112
Lee, Declan *191:* 20
Lee, Dom *83:* 118, 120; *93:* 123; *121:* 121, 126; *146:* 174, 175, 206, 207; *174:* 204
Lee, Doris *13:* 246; *32:* 183; *44:* 111
Lee, Hector Viveros *115:* 96
Lee, Jeanne M. *158:* 56
Lee, Jared *93:* 200; *157:* 229
Lee, Jody *81:* 121; *82:* 225; *91:* 155; *100:* 182
Lee, Jody A. *127:* 124, 126, 127
    See also Lee, Jody
Lee, Manning de V. *2:* 200; *17:* 12; *27:* 87; *37:* 102, 103, 104; *YABC 2:* 304
Lee, Marie G. *138:* 157
Lee, Paul *97:* 100; *105:* 72, 209; *109:* 177; *128:* 113
Lee, Robert J. *3:* 97; *67:* 124
Lee, Victor *96:* 228; *105:* 182; *140:* 196
Leech, Dorothy *98:* 76
Leech, John *15:* 59
Leedy, Loreen *84:* 142; *128:* 144, 145, 146; *175:* 125, 126, 127
Leeman, Michael *44:* 157
Leeming, Catherine *87:* 39
Lees, Harry *6:* 112
LeFever, Bill *88:* 220, 221
Legenisel *47:* 111
Legrand, Edy *18:* 89, 93
Lehman, Barbara *73:* 123; *170:* 130
Lehrman, Rosalie *2:* 180
Leichman, Seymour *5:* 107
Leighton, Clare *25:* 130; *33:* 168; *37:* 105, 106, 108, 109
Leisk, David *1:* 140, 141; *11:* 54; *30:* 137, 142, 143,144
Leister, Brian *89:* 45; *106:* 37; *114:* 67; *149:* 236
Leloir, Maurice *18:* 77, 80, 83, 99
Lemaître, Pascal *144:* 175; *176:* 130; *189:* 135
Lemieux, Michele *100:* 148; *139:* 153
Lemke, Horst *14:* 98; *38:* 117, 118, 119
Lemke, R.W. *42:* 162
Lemon, David Gwynne *9:* 1
LeMoult, Adolph *82:* 116
Lenn, Michael *136:* 89
Lennon, John *114:* 100
Lennox, Elsie *95:* 163; *143:* 160
Lenski, Lois *1:* 144; *26:* 135, 137, 139, 141; *100:* 153, 154
Lent, Blair *1:* 116, 117; *2:* 174; *3:* 206, 207; *7:* 168, 169; *34:* 62; *68:* 217; *133:* 101; *183:* 60
Leonard, Richard *91:* 128
Leone, Leonard *49:* 190
Lerner, Carol *86:* 140, 141, 142
Lerner, Judith *11:* 138
Lerner, Sharon *11:* 157; *22:* 56
Leroux-Hugon, Helene *132:* 139
Leslie, Cecil *19:* 244
Lessac, Frane *80:* 182, 207; *96:* 182

Lessing, Erich *167:* 52; *173:* 60
Lester, Alison *50:* 124; *90:* 147, 148; *129:* 130
Lethcoe, Jason *191:* 116, 117
Le Tord, Bijou *49:* 156; *95:* 112
Leutz, Emanuel *165:* 27
Levai, Blaise *39:* 130
Levin, Ted *12:* 148
Levine, David *43:* 147, 149, 150, 151, 152; *64:* 11
Levine, Joe *71:* 88
Levine, Marge *81:* 127
Levinson, David *178:* 232
Levit, Herschel *24:* 223
Levstek, Ljuba *131:* 192; *134:* 216; *149:* 65; *168:* 180
Levy, Jessica Ann *19:* 225; *39:* 191
Levy, Lina *117:* 126
Lewin, Betsy *32:* 114; *48:* 177; *90:* 151; *91:* 125; *92:* 85; *115:* 105; *169:* 110, 111; *178:* 47; *186:* 188; *194:* 201
Lewin, Ted *4:* 77; *8:* 168; *20:* 110; *21:* 99,100; *27:* 110; *28:* 96, 97; *31:* 49; *45:* 55; *48:* 223; *60:* 20, 119, 120; *62:* 139; *66:* 108; *71:* 12; *72:* 21; *74:* 226; *76:* 139, 140; *77:* 82; *79:* 87; *85:* 49, 177; *86:* 55; *88:* 182; *93:* 28, 29; *94:* 34, 182, 194; *99:* 156; *104:* 8; *115:* 123; *118:* 74; *119:* 114, 116; *131:* 54; *145:* 99; *165:* 151; *177:* 75; *178:* 42; *190:* 30; *192:* 86; *195:* 101, 102
Lewis, Allen *15:* 112
Lewis, E.B. *88:* 143; *93:* 109; *119:* 79; *124:* 113; *128:* 49; *151:* 167; *168:* 110; *173:* 121; *174:* 66; *176:* 7; *184:* 150; *185:* 191
Lewis, H.B. *170:* 124
Lewis, J. Patrick *162:* 83
Lewis, Jan *81:* 22
Lewis, Kim *136:* 165
Lewis, Richard W. *52:* 25
Lewis, Robin Baird *98:* 193
Leydon, Rita Floden *21:* 101
Li, Xiojun *187:* 172
Lichtenheld, Tom *152:* 125, 126
Lieblich, Irene *22:* 173; *27:* 209, 214
Lieder, Rick *108:* 197
Lies, Brian *92:* 40; *141:* 101; *150:* 138; *190:* 97, 98, 99
Liese, Charles *4:* 222
Life, Kay *79:* 49
Lifton, Robert Jay *66:* 154
Lightburn, Ron *86:* 153; *91:* 122
Lightfoot, Norman R. *45:* 47
Lignell, Lois *37:* 114
Lill, Debra *121:* 70
Lilly, Charles *8:* 73; *20:* 127; *48:* 53; *72:* 9,16; *77:* 98; *102:* 94
Lilly, Ken *37:* 224
Lim, John *43:* 153
Limona, Mercedes *51:* 183
Lin, Grace *143:* 217; *162:* 86, 87; *174:* 185
Lincoln, Patricia Henderson *27:* 27; *78:* 127
Lindahn, Ron *84:* 17
Lindahn, Val *84:* 17
Lindberg, Howard *10:* 123; *16:* 190
Lindberg, Jeffrey *64:* 77; *77:* 71; *79:* 54; *80:* 149; *174:* 109; *179:* 52
Linden, Seymour *18:* 200, 201; *43:* 140
Lindenbaum, Pija *144:* 143; *183:* 113
Linder, Richard *27:* 119
Lindman, Maj *43:* 154
Lindsay, Norman *67:* 114
Lindsay, Vachel *40:* 118
Lindstrom, Jack *145:* 118
Line, Les *27:* 143
Linell
See Smith, Linell
Lionni, Leo *8:* 115; *72:* 159, 160, 161
Lipinsky, Lino *2:* 156; *22:* 175
Lippincott, Gary A. *70:* 35; *119:* 118
Lippman, Peter *8:* 31; *31:* 119, 120, 160
Lisi, Victoria *89:* 145
Lisker, Emily *169:* 114

Lisker, Sonia O. *16:* 274; *31:* 31; *44:* 113, 114
Lisowski, Gabriel *47:* 144; *49:* 157
Lissim, Simon *17:* 138
Little, Ed *89:* 145; *151:* 53
Little, Harold *16:* 72
Little, Mary E. *28:* 146
Littlewood, Karen *165:* 126
Litty, Julie *111:* 63
Litzinger, Rosanne *151:* 101; *176:* 118; *196:* 133, 134, 135
Liu, Lesley *143:* 72
Livesly, Lorna *19:* 216
Livingston, Susan *95:* 22
Liwska, Renata *164:* 113
Ljungkvist, Laura *180:* 120
Llerena, Carlos Antonio *19:* 181
Lloyd, Errol *11:* 39; *22:* 178
Lloyd, Megan *77:* 118; *80:* 113; *97:* 75; *117:* 94, 95; *189:* 121, 122
Lloyd, Sam *183:* 116, 117
Lo, Beth *165:* 154
Lo, Koon-chiu *7:* 134
Loates, Glen *63:* 76
Lobel, Anita *6:* 87; *9:* 141; *18:* 248; *55:* 85,86, 87, 88, 93, 104; *60:* 67; *78:* 263; *82:* 110; *96:* 157, 159; *101:* 84; *132:* 35; *162:* 93, 94
Lobel, Arnold *1:* 188, 189; *5:* 12; *6:* 147; *7:* 167, 209; *18:* 190, 191; *25:* 39, 43; *27:* 40; *29:* 174; *52:* 127; *55:* 89, 91, 94, 95, 97, 98, 99, 100, 101, 102,103, 105, 106; *60:* 18, 31; *66:* 181, 183; *75:* 57; *82:* 246; *136:* 146
Lobel, Gillian *190:* 21
Locker, Thomas *109:* 134
Lodge, Bernard *107:* 125, 126; *153:* 93
Loeb, Jeph *153:* 177
Lodge, Jo *112:* 119
Loefgren, Ulf *3:* 108
Loescher, Ann *20:* 108
Loescher, Gil *20:* 108
Loew, David *93:* 184; *171:* 120
Lofting, Hugh *15:* 182, 183; *100:* 161, 162
Lofts, Pamela *60:* 188
Loh, George *38:* 88
Lomberg, Jon *58:* 160
Lonette, Reisie *11:* 211; *12:* 168; *13:* 56; *36:* 122; *43:* 155
Long, Ethan *168:* 146; *178:* 12; *182:* 120, 121; *196:* 124
Long, Laurel *162:* 135; *190:* 11
Long, Loren *99:* 176; *172:* 65; *182:* 78; *188:* 114, 115
Long, Melinda *152:* 128
Long, Miles *115:* 174
Long, Sally *42:* 184
Long, Sylvia *74:* 168; *132:* 63; *179:* 134
Longoni, Eduardo *73:* 85
Longtemps, Ken *17:* 123; *29:* 221; *69:* 82
Looser, Heinz *YABC 2:* 208
Lopez, Loretta *190:* 100
Lopez, Rafael *197:* 160
Lopshire, Robert *6:* 149; *21:* 117; *34:* 166; *73:* 13
Lord, John Vernon *21:* 104; *23:* 25; *51:* 22
Lorenz, Albert *40:* 146; *115:* 127
Loretta, Sister Mary *33:* 73
Lorraine, Walter H. *3:* 110; *4:* 123; *16:* 192; *103:* 119
Los, Marek *146:* 22; *193:* 23
Loss, Joan *11:* 163
Louderback, Walt *YABC 1:* 164
Lousada, Sandra *40:* 138
Louth, Jack *149:* 252; *151:* 191, 192
Love, Judy *173:* 43; *196:* 40
Low, Joseph *14:* 124, 125; *18:* 68; *19:* 194; *31:* 166; *80:* 239
Low, William *62:* 175; *80:* 147; *112:* 194; *150:* 202; *169:* 175; *177:* 110; *192:* 27
Lowe, Vicky *177:* 130
Lowenheim, Alfred *13:* 65, 66
Lowenstein, Sallie *116:* 90, 91
Lowitz, Anson *17:* 124; *18:* 215

Lowrey, Jo *8:* 133
Lubach, Vanessa *142:* 152
Lubell, Winifred *1:* 207; *3:* 15; *6:* 151
Lubin, Leonard B. *19:* 224; *36:* 79, 80; *45:* 128, 129,131, 132, 133, 134, 135, 136, 137, 139, 140, 141; *70:* 95; *YABC2:* 96
Lucht, Irmgard *82:* 145
Ludwig, Helen *33:* 144, 145
Lufkin, Raymond *38:* 138; *44:* 48
Luhrs, Henry *7:* 123; *11:* 120
Lujan, Tonita *82:* 33
Lupo, Dom *4:* 204
Lustig, Loretta *30:* 186; *46:* 134, 135, 136, 137
Luthardt, Kevin *172:* 125, 126
Luxbacher, Irene *153:* 145
Luzak, Dennis *52:* 121; *99:* 142
Lydbury, Jane *82:* 98
Lydecker, Laura *21:* 113; *42:* 53
Lynch, Charles *16:* 33
Lynch, Marietta *29:* 137; *30:* 171
Lynch, P.J. *126:* 228; *129:* 110; *132:* 247; *183:* 64
Lyne, Alison Davis *188:* 118, 198
Lyon, Carol *102:* 26
Lyon, Elinor *6:* 154
Lyon, Fred *14:* 16
Lyon, Tammie *175:* 170
Lyons, Oren *8:* 193
Lyster, Michael *26:* 41

M

Maas, Dorothy *6:* 175
Maas, Julie *47:* 61
Macaulay, David *46:* 139, 140, 141, 142, 143, 144, 145, 147, 149, 150; *72:* 167, 168, 169; *137:* 129, 130, 131, 132
MacCarthy, Patricia *69:* 141
Macdonald, Alister *21:* 55
Macdonald, Roberta *19:* 237; *52:* 164
MacDonald, Norman *13:* 99
MacDonald, Suse *54:* 41; *109* 138; *130:* 156; *193:* 106, 107, 109, 110
Mace, Varian *49:* 159
Macguire, Robert Reid *18:* 67
Machetanz, Fredrick *34:* 147, 148
MacInnes, Ian *35:* 59
MacIntyre, Elisabeth *17:* 127, 128
Mack, Jeff *161:* 128; *194:* 119, 120
Mack, Stan *17:* 129; *96:* 33
Mackay, Donald *17:* 60
MacKaye, Arvia *32:* 119
Mackenzie, Stuart *73:* 213
MacKenzie, Garry *33:* 159
Mackie, Clare *87:* 134
Mackinlay, Miguel *27:* 22
MacKinstry, Elizabeth *15:* 110; *42:* 139, 140, 141, 142, 143,144, 145
MacLeod, Lee *91:* 167
Maclise, Daniel *YABC 2:* 257
Macnaughton, Tina *182:* 145
MacRae, Tom *181:* 112
Madden, Don *3:* 112, 113; *4:* 33, 108, 155; *7:* 193; *78:* 12; *YABC 2:* 211
Maddison, Angela Mary *10:* 83
Madsen, Jim *146:* 259; *152:* 237; *184:* 106; *197:* 21
Maestro, Giulio *8:* 124; *12:* 17; *13:* 108; *25:* 182; *54:* 147; *59:* 114, 115, 116, 117, 118, 121, 123, 124, 125,126, 127; *68:* 37, 38; *106:* 129, 130, 131, 136, 137, 138
Maffia, Daniel *60:* 200
Maggio, Viqui *58:* 136, 181; *74:* 150; *75:* 90; *85:* 159; *90:* 158; *109:* 184; *193:* 113
Magnus, Erica *77:* 123
Magnuson, Diana *28:* 102; *34:* 190; *41:* 175
Magoon, Scott *181:* 104
Magovern, Peg *103:* 123

Maguire, Sheila *41:* 100
Magurn, Susan *91:* 30
Mahony, Will *37:* 120
Mahony, Will *85:* 116
Mahood, Kenneth *24:* 141
Mahurin, Matt *164:* 225; *175:* 95; *189:* 37; *196:* 14
Maik, Henri *9:* 102
Maione, Heather *106:* 5; *178:* 8; *189:* 126, 127; *193:* 58
Maisto, Carol *29:* 87
Maitland, Antony *1:* 100, 176; *8:* 41; *17:* 246; *24:* 46; *25:* 177, 178; *32:* 74; *60:* 65, 195; *67:* 156; *87:* 131; *101:* 110
Majewski, Dawn W. *169:* 95
Mak, Kam *72:* 25; *75:* 43; *87:* 186; *97:* 24; *102:* 154; *149:* 195; *186:* 28
Makie, Pam *37:* 117
Maktima, Joe *116:* 191
Maland, Nick *99:* 77
Male, Alan *132:* 64
Malone, James Hiram *84:* 161
Malone, Nola Langner *82:* 239
Malone, Peter *191:* 121, 122, 123
Malsberg, Edward *51:* 175
Malvern, Corinne *2:* 13; *34:* 148, 149
Manchess, Gregory *165:* 241
Mancusi, Stephen *63:* 198, 199
Mandelbaum, Ira *31:* 115
Manders, John *138:* 152, 155; *188:* 171; *190:* 92
Manet, Edouard *23:* 170
Mangiat, Jeff *173:* 127
Mangurian, David *14:* 133
Manham, Allan *42:* 109; *77:* 180; *80:* 227
Manley, Matt *103:* 167; *117:* 98; *172:* 49
Manna, Giovanni *178:* 44
Manniche, Lise *31:* 121
Manning, Jane *96:* 203
Manning, Jo *63:* 154
Manning, Lawrence *191:* 153
Manning, Mick *176:* 139
Manning, Samuel F. *5:* 75
Mantel, Richard *57:* 73; *63:* 106; *82:* 255
Maraja *15:* 86; *YABC 1:* 28; *2:* 115
Marcellino, Fred *20:* 125; *34:* 222; *53:* 125; *58:* 205; *61:* 64, 121, 122; *68:* 154, 156, 157, 158, 159; *72:* 25; *86:* 184; *98:* 181; *118:* 129, 130, 131; *149:* 218; *194:* 7
Marchesi, Stephen *34:* 140; *46:* 72; *50:* 147; *66:* 239; *70:* 33; *73:* 18, 114, 163; *77:* 47, 76,147; *78:* 79; *80:* 30; *81:* 6; *89:* 66; *93:* 21,130; *94:* 94; *97:* 66; *98:* 96; *114:* 115, 116
Marchiori, Carlos *14:* 60
Marciano, John Bemelmans *118:* 133; *167:* 110, 111, 112
Marcus, Barry David *139:* 248; *145:* 18
Margules, Gabriele *21:* 120
Mariana
   See Foster, Marian Curtis
Mariano, Michael *52:* 108
Marino, Dorothy *6:* 37; *14:* 135
Mario, Heide Stetson *101:* 202
Maris, Ron *71:* 123
Maritz, Nicolaas *85:* 123
Mark, Mona *65:* 105; *68:* 205; *116:* 213
Markham, R.L. *17:* 240
Marks, Alan *104:* 104; *109:* 182; *164:* 92; *185:* 134; *187:* 120, 121, 122
Marks, Cara *54:* 9
Marokvia, Artur *31:* 122
Marquez, Susan *108:* 121
Marrella, Maria Pia *62:* 116
Marriott, Pat *30:* 30; *34:* 39; *35:* 164, 165, 166; *44:* 170; *48:* 186, 187, 188, 189, 191, 192, 193; *91:* 92
Mars, W.T. *1:* 161; *3:* 115; *4:* 208, 225; *5:* 92, 105, 186; *8:* 214; *9:* 12; *13:* 121; *27:* 151; *31:* 180; *38:* 102; *48:* 66; *62:* 164, 165; *64:* 62; *68:* 229; *79:* 55

Marschall, Ken *85:* 29
Marsh, Christine *3:* 164
Marsh, James *73:* 137
Marsh, Reginald *17:* 5; *19:* 89; *22:* 90, 96
Marshall, Anthony D. *18:* 216
Marshall, Felicia *170:* 190
Marshall, James *6:* 160; *40:* 221; *42:* 24, 25, 29; *51:* 111, 112, 113, 114, 115, 116, 117, 118, 119, 120, 121; *64:* 13; *75:* 126, 127, 128, 129; *102:* 10, 12
Marshall, Janet *97:* 154
Marstall, Bob *55:* 145; *84:* 153, 170; *104:* 145; *154:* 166, 167, 168
Martchenko, Michael *50:* 129, 153, 155, 156, 157; *83:* 144,145; *154:* 137, 138, 139
Marten, Ruth *129:* 52
Martin, Charles E. *70:* 144
Martin, David Stone *24:* 232; *62:* 4
Martin, Fletcher *18:* 213; *23:* 151
Martin, Rene *2:* 144; *42:* 148, 149, 150
Martin, Richard E. *51:* 157; *131:* 203
Martin, Ron *32:* 81
Martin, Stefan *8:* 68; *32:* 124, 126; *56:* 33
Martin, Whitney *166:* 137
Martinez, Ed *58:* 192; *72:* 231; *77:* 33; *80:* 214; *167:* 154
Martinez, John *6:* 113; *118:* 13; *139:* 143
Martinez, Sergio *158:* 190
Martini, Angela *183:* 161
Martiniere, Stephan *171:* 130
Marton, Jirina *95:* 127, 128; *144:* 145
Martorell, Antonio *84:* 6; *97:* 161
Martucci, Griesbach *52:* 106
Marvin, Frederic *83:* 86
Marx, Robert F. *24:* 143
Marzollo, Jean *190:* 127
Masefield, Judith *19:* 208, 209
Masheris, Robert *78:* 51
Masiello, Ralph *186:* 171
Mason, George F. *14:* 139
Mason, Robert *84:* 96
Massey, Barbara *68:* 142
Massie, Diane Redfield *16:* 194
Massie, Kim *31:* 43
Mataya, David *121:* 66
Mathers, Petra *119:* 125; *163:* 104; *176:* 143, 144; *187:* 142; *196:* 101
Mathewuse, James *51:* 143
Mathieu, Joseph *14:* 33; *39:* 206; *43:* 167; *56:* 180; *79:* 126; *94:* 147; *185:* 140
Matje, Martin *169:* 177, 178; *172:* 180
Matsubara, Naoko *12:* 121
Matsuda, Shizu *13:* 167
Matsuoka, Mei *192:* 135
Matte, L'Enc *22:* 183
Mattelson, Marvin *36:* 50, 51
Matheson, Jenny *180:* 132
Matthews, Elizabeth *194:* 128
Matthews, F. Leslie *4:* 216
Matthews, Tina *190:* 130
Mattingly, David *71:* 76, 77; *82:* 64; *91:* 216, 217; *109:* 25
Matulay, Laszlo *5:* 18; *43:* 168
Matus, Greta *12:* 142
Maughan, William *181:* 31
Mauldin, Bill *27:* 23
Mauterer, Erin Marie *119:* 5
Mawicke, Tran *9:* 137; *15:* 191; *47:* 100
Mawson, Matt *74:* 115
Max, Peter *45:* 146, 147, 148, 149, 150
Maxie, Betty *40:* 135
Maxwell, John Alan *1:* 148
Mayan, Earl *7:* 193
Mayer, Danuta *117:* 103
Mayer, Marianna *32:* 132
Mayer, Mercer *11:* 192; *16:* 195, 196; *20:* 55, 57; *32:* 129, 130, 132, 133, 134; *41:* 144, 248, 252; *58:* 186; *73:* 140, 142, 143; *137:* 137, 138
Mayforth, Hal *166:* 77
Mayhew, James *85:* 121; *138:* 187; *149:* 140

Mayhew, Richard *3:* 106
Mayo, Gretchen Will *38:* 81; *84:* 166
Mays, Victor *5:* 127; *8:* 45, 153; *14:* 245; *23:* 50; *34:* 155; *40:* 79; *45:* 158; *54:* 91; *66:* 240
Mazal, Chanan *49:* 104
Maze, Deborah *71:* 83
Mazellan, Ron *75:* 97, 98
Mazetti, Alan *112:* 72
Mazille, Capucine *96:* 168
Mazza, Adriana Saviozzi *19:* 215
Mazzella, Mary Jo *82:* 165
Mazzetti, Alan *45:* 210
McAfee, Steve *135:* 146; *167:* 176; *191:* 84
McAlinden, Paul *112:* 128
McBride, Angus *28:* 49; *103:* 40
McBride, Will *30:* 110
McCaffery, Janet *38:* 145
McCallum, Graham *78:* 78
McCallum, Stephen *141:* 143; *156:* 5; *166:* 228
McCann, Gerald *3:* 50; *4:* 94; *7:* 54; *41:* 121
McCarthy, Dan *174:* 74
McCarthy, Linda *177:* 128
McCarthy, Meghan *168:* 134
McCauley, Adam *157:* 36; *184:* 199; *193:* 100
McCay, Winsor *41:* 124, 126, 128, 129, 130, 131; *134:* 77, 79
McClary, Nelson *1:* 111
McClements, George *196:* 146
McClintock, Barbara *57:* 135; *95:* 130; *146:* 190
McClintock, Theodore *14:* 141
McCloskey, Robert *1:* 184, 185; *2:* 186, 187; *17:* 209; *39:* 139, 140, 141, 142, 143, 146, 147, 148; *85:* 150, 151; *100:* 172, 173, 174
McClung, Robert *2:* 189; *68:* 166, 167
McClure, Gillian *31:* 132; *150:* 53
McConnel, Jerry *31:* 75, 187
McConnell, Mary *102:* 49
McCord, Kathleen Garry *78:* 236
McCormack, John *66:* 193
McCormick, A.D. *35:* 119
McCormick, Dell J. *19:* 216
McCrady, Lady *16:* 198; *39:* 127
McCrea, James *3:* 122; *33:* 216
McCrea, Ruth *3:* 122; *27:* 102; *33:* 216
McCue, Lisa *65:* 148, 149; *77:* 54; *80:* 132; *175:* 33; *177:* 133, 135
McCully, Emily Arnold *2:* 89; *4:* 120, 121, 146, 197; *5:* 2, 129; *7:* 191; *11:* 122; *15:* 210; *33:* 23; *35:* 244; *37:* 122; *39:* 88; *40:* 103; *50:* 30,31, 32, 33, 34, 35, 36, 37; *52:* 89, 90; *57:* 6; *62:* 3; *70:* 195; *86:* 82; *96:* 192; *97:* 93; *110:* 143,144; *117:* 47; *167:* 96
McCurdy, Michael *13:* 153; *24:* 85; *81:* 160; *82:* 157, 158; *86:* 125; *97:* 92; *117:* 178; *132:* 6; *147:* 159, 160
McCusker, Paul *99:* 19
McDaniel, Jerry *132:* 135
McDaniel, Preston *160:* 206; *170:* 139
McDermott, Beverly Brodsky *11:* 180
McDermott, Gerald *16:* 201; *74:* 174, 175; *163:* 150, 151
McDermott, Mike *96:* 187
McDonald, Jill *13:* 155; *26:* 128
McDonald, Mercedes *169:* 118
McDonald, Ralph J. *5:* 123, 195
McDonnell, Flora *146:* 199, 200
McDonnell, Patrick *179:* 153, 154
McDonough, Don *10:* 163
McElligott, Matt *196:* 147
McElmurry, Jill *137:* 148; *163:* 141
McElrath-Eslick, Lori *129:* 145; *142:* 21; *173:* 123
McEntee, Dorothy *37:* 124
McEwan, Keith *88:* 116; *165:* 122, 123
McEwen, Katharine *169:* 34
McFall, Christie *12:* 144
McFeely, Daniel *160:* 213
McGaw, Laurie *109:* 243; *143:* 216

McGee, Barbara *6:* 165
McGee, Marni *163:* 153
McGillvray, Kim *158:* 171; *165:* 213; *186:* 183; *190:* 175
McGinley-Nally, Sharon *131:* 19
McGinnis, Robert *110:* 113; *177:* 80
McGovern, Tara *98:* 171
McGraw, Sheila *83:* 146
McGregor, Malcolm *23:* 27
McGrory, Anik *193:* 120
McGuirk, Leslie *152:* 159
McHale, John *138:* 190
McHenry, E.B. *193:* 122
McHugh, Tom *23:* 64
McIntosh, Jon *42:* 56
McKay, Donald *2:* 118; *32:* 157; *45:* 151, 152
McKean, Dave *150:* 71; *174:* 156; *197:* 83, 118
McKeating, Eileen *44:* 58
McKee, David *10:* 48; *21:* 9; *70:* 154, 155; *107:* 139, 140, 141; *134:* 218; *158:* 148, 149, 150, 151
McKee, Diana *109:* 185
McKelvey, Patrick *164:* 141
McKendry, Joe *170:* 136
McKeveny, Tom *164:* 60; *173:* 79
McKie, Roy *7:* 44
McKillip, Kathy *30:* 153
McKinney, Ena *26:* 39
McKinnon, James *136:* 75
McKowen, Scott *172:* 63
McLachlan, Edward *5:* 89
McLaren, Chesley *133:* 53
McLaren, Kirsty *123:* 99; *124:* 226
Mclean, Andrew *113:* 117, 118, 120, 121; *172:* 130, 131
Mclean, Janet *172:* 130
McLean, Meg *94:* 196
McLean, Sammis *32:* 197
McLean, Wilson *90:* 29; *113:* 195
McLoughlin, John C. *47:* 149
McLoughlin, Wayne *102:* 230; *134:* 178
McMahon, Robert *36:* 155; *69:* 169
McManus, Shawn *85:* 71
McMenemy, Sarah *156:* 139
McMillan, Bruce *22:* 184
McMullan, James *40:* 33; *67:* 172; *87:* 142; *99:* 63, 64; *189:* 133; *196:* 51
McMullen, Nigel *146:* 177
McNeely, Tom *162:* 55
McNaught, Harry *12:* 80; *32:* 136
McNaughton, Colin *39:* 149; *40:* 108; *92:* 144, 145, 146; *134:* 104, 106
McNicholas, Maureen *38:* 148
McNicholas, Shelagh *173:* 61; *191:* 125, 126
McPhail, David *14:* 105; *23:* 135; *37:* 217, 218, 220,221; *47:* 151, 152, 153, 154, 155, 156, 158, 159, 160, 162, 163, 164; *71:* 211; *81:* 139, 140, 142; *86:* 123; *132:* 150; *140:* 129, 131, 132; *183:* 134, 135, 137; *189:* 132
McPhee, Richard B. *41:* 133
McPheeters, Neal *78:* 132; *86:* 90; *99:* 162; *111:* 141; *142:* 162
McQuade, Jacqueline *124:* 223
McQueen, Lucinda *28:* 149; *41:* 249; *46:* 206; *53:* 103
McQuillan, Mary *153:* 97
McVay, Tracy *11:* 68
McVicker, Charles *39:* 150
Mead, Ben Carlton *43:* 75
Meade, Holly *90:* 102; *94:* 101; *149:* 8; *151:* 107
Mecray, John *33:* 62
Meddaugh, Susan *20:* 42; *29:* 143; *41:* 241; *77:* 50; *84:* 173, 174, 175, 176, 177, 178; *125:* 160, 161, 162; *176:* 148, 149, 150, 151
Meehan, Dennis B. *56:* 144
Meents, Len W. *73:* 147, 150
Meers, Tony *99:* 113
Meisel, Paul *98:* 137; *124:* 18; *162:* 180; *179:* 16; *181:* 62; *194:* 154

Melanson, Luc *149:* 229
Melendez, Francisco *72:* 180
Melnychuk, Monika *153:* 65
Melo, Esperança *196:* 90
Melo, John *16:* 285; *58:* 203
Meloni, Maria Teresa *98:* 62
Meltzer, Ericka
    See O'Rourke, Ericka
Menasco, Milton *43:* 85
Menchin, Scott *188:* 129
Mendelson, Steven T. *86:* 154
Mendelssohn, Felix *19:* 170
Mendola, Christopher *88:* 223
Meng, Heinz *13:* 158
Merian, Maria Sibylla *140:* 88
Mero, Lee *34:* 68
Merrill, Frank T. *16:* 147; *19:* 71; *YABC 1:* 226, 229,273
Merriman, Rachel *98:* 108; *114:* 122; *149:* 142
Meryman, Hope *27:* 41
Meryweather, Jack *10:* 179
Meseldzija, Petar *168:* 97
Meserve, Jess *184:* 137
Messick, Dale *64:* 150, 151, 152
Meth, Harold *24:* 203
Meyer, Herbert *19:* 189
Meyer, Renate *6:* 170
Meyers, Bob *11:* 136
Meyers, Nancy *172:* 124
Meynell, Louis *37:* 76
Micale, Albert *2:* 65; *22:* 185
Miccuci, Charles *82:* 163; *144:* 150
Micich, Paul *164:* 163
Middleton, Jeffrey *177:* 173
Middleton-Sandford, Betty *2:* 125
Mieke, Anne *45:* 74
Mighell, Patricia *43:* 134
Miglio, Paige *101:* 203; *151:* 223
Mikolaycak, Charles *9:* 144; *12:* 101; *13:* 212; *21:* 121; *22:* 168; *30:* 187; *34:* 103, 150; *37:* 183; *43:* 179; *44:* 90; *46:* 115, 118, 119; *49:* 25; *78:* 121, 122, 205, 207; *81:* 4
Milelli, Pascal *129:* 66; *135:* 153; *187:* 45
Miles, Elizabeth *117:* 77
Miles, Jennifer *17:* 278
Milgrim, David *158:* 157; *187:* 125, 126, 128
Milhous, Katherine *15:* 193; *17:* 51
Millais, John E. *22:* 230, 231
Millar, H.R. *YABC 1:* 194, 195, 203
Millard, C.E. *28:* 186
Millard, Kerry *105:* 124
Miller, Don *15:* 195; *16:* 71; *20:* 106; *31:* 178
Miller, Edna *29:* 148
Miller, Edward *115:* 64; *183:* 140, 141
Miller, Frank J. *25:* 94
Miller, Grambs *18:* 38; *23:* 16
Miller, Ian *99:* 128
Miller, Jane *15:* 196
Miller, Marcia *13:* 233
Miller, Marilyn *1:* 87; *31:* 69; *33:* 157
Miller, Mitchell *28:* 183; *34:* 207
Miller, Phil *175:* 150
Miller, Shane *5:* 140
Miller, Virginia *81:* 206
Millman, Isaac *172:* 18
Mills, Elaine *72:* 181
Mills, Judith Christine *130:* 168, 169
Mills, Lauren *92:* 170
Mills, Yaroslava Surmach *35:* 169, 170; *46:* 114
Millsap, Darrel *51:* 102
Milone, Karen *89:* 169
Milord, Susan *147:* 163, 164
Milton, Debbie *162:* 161
Mims, Ashley *170:* 51
Miner, Julia *98:* 69
Minor, Wendell *39:* 188; *52:* 87; *56:* 171; *58:* 116; *62:* 56; *109:* 74; *93; *78:* 129; *94:* 67; *117:* 12, 13; *124:* 84, 86; *136:* 121; *164:* 168, 169; *170:* 71
Minter, Daniel *176:* 154; *179:* 177

Mirocha, Paul *81:* 133; *192:* 148; *194:* 36
Misako Rocks! *192:* 149, 150
Mitchell, Judith *109:* 117
Mitchell, Mark *91:* 208
Mitchell, Tracy *190:* 15
Mitgutsch, Ali *76:* 161
Mitsuhashi, Yoko *45:* 153
Miyake, Yoshi *38:* 141
Mizumura, Kazue *10:* 143; *18:* 223; *36:* 159
Mochi, Ugo *8:* 122; *38:* 150
Mock, Paul *55:* 83; *123:* 32
Modarressi, Mitra *90:* 236; *126:* 168; *173:* 165, 166
Modell, Frank *39:* 152
Mogenson, Jan *74:* 183
Mohn, Susan *89:* 224
Mohr, Mark *133:* 201
Mohr, Nicholasa *8:* 139; *113:* 127
Molan, Christine *60:* 177; *84:* 183
Moldon, Peter L. *49:* 168
Molk, Laurel *92:* 150
Mollica, Gene *197:* 11
Momaday, N. Scott *48:* 159
Mombourquette, Paul *112:* 91; *126:* 142
Monk, Julie *165:* 231; *191:* 96
Monks, Lydia *189:* 136, 137
Montgomery, Lucy *150:* 126
Montgomery-Higham, Amanda *169:* 131
Montiel, David *69:* 106; *84:* 145
Montijo, Rhode *193:* 164
Montresor, Beni *2:* 91; *3:* 138; *38:* 152, 153, 154,155, 156, 157, 158, 159, 160; *68:* 63
Montserrat, Pep *128:* 135; *181:* 119; *184:* 53
Moon, Carl *25:* 183, 184, 185
Moon, Eliza *14:* 40
Moon, Ivan *22:* 39; *38:* 140
Moore, Adrienne *67:* 147
Moore, Agnes Kay Randall *43:* 187
Moore, Cyd *117:* 107, 108; *159:* 137, 138; *186:* 148, 149, 151
Moore, Gustav *127:* 181, 182; *170:* 162, 163
Moore, Jackie *128:* 79
Moore, Janet *63:* 153
Moore, Margie *176:* 156
Moore, Mary *29:* 160
Moore, Patrick *184:* 121
Moore, Yvette *101:* 11, 12; *154:* 141
Mora, Giovanni *179:* 127; *184:* 11
Mora, Raul Mina *20:* 41
Moraes, Odilon *102:* 144
Morales, Yuyi *154:* 144
Moran, Rosslyn *111:* 26
Moran, Tom *60:* 100
Mordan, C.B. *193:* 115
Mordvinoff, Nicolas *15:* 179
Moreno, René King *169:* 59; *190:* 133, 209
Morgan, Barbara *169:* 116
Morgan, Jacqui *58:* 57
Morgan, Mary *114:* 133, 134, 135; *123:* 11
Morgan, Tom *42:* 157
Morgan, Pierr *173:* 148
Morgenstern, Michael *158:* 7, 57; *171:* 103; *174:* 60
Morice, Dave *93:* 142
Moriuchi, Mique *177:* 203
Morozumi, Atsuko *110:* 155
Morrill, Leslie *18:* 218; *29:* 177; *33:* 84; *38:* 147; *42:* 127; *44:* 93; *48:* 164, 165, 167, 168, 169, 170,171; *49:* 162; *63:* 136, 180; *70:* 72; *71:* 70, 91,92; *72:* 228; *80:* 163, 164, 165; *90:* 121; *121:* 88; *178:* 117
Morrill, Rowena A. *84:* 16; *98:* 163
Morris *47:* 91
Morris, Frank *55:* 133; *60:* 28; *76:* 2
Morris, Harry O. *119:* 138
Morris, Jackie *128:* 194; *144:* 119; *151:* 146
Morris, Jennifer E. *179:* 157
Morris, Oradel Nolen *128:* 180
Morris, Tony *62:* 146; *70:* 97

Morrison, Bill *42:* 116; *66:* 170; *69:* 40
Morrison, Gordon *87:* 150; *113:* 93; *128:* 181, 182; *183:* 144, 145, 146
Morrison, Frank *169:* 162
Morrison, Taylor *159:* 144, 145; *187:* 131
Morrow, Gray *2:* 64; *5:* 200; *10:* 103, 114; *14:* 175
Morton, Lee Jack *32:* 140
Morton, Marian *3:* 185
Mosberg, Hilary *117:* 195; *118:* 164; *149:* 55
Moser, Barry *56:* 68, 117, 118, 119, 120, 121, 122, 123, 124; *59:* 141; *60:* 160; *79:* 91, 147, 149, 151, 152; *82:* 81; *90:* 118; *91:* 35; *95:* 210; *97:* 91, 93; *102:* 152; *126:* 4; *128:* 175; *133:* 141; *138:* 167, 171, 174; *153:* 205; *174:* 130; *185:* 152, 154; *195:* 163
Moser, Cara *90:* 118; *138:* 167
Moses, Grandma *18:* 228
Moses, Will *178:* 170, 171
Moskof, Martin Stephen *27:* 152
Mosley, Francis *57:* 144
Moss, Donald *11:* 184
Moss, Geoffrey *32:* 198
Moss, Marissa *71:* 130; *104:* 127; *163:* 156
Most, Bernard *48:* 173; *91:* 142, 143; *134:* 120
Mowll, Joshua *188:* 133
Mowry, Carmen *50:* 62
Moxley, Sheila *96:* 174; *169:* 26
Moyers, William *21:* 65
Moyler, Alan *36:* 142
Mozley, Charles *9:* 87; *20:* 176, 192, 193; *22:* 228; *25:* 205; *33:* 150; *43:* 170, 171, 172, 173, 174; *YABC2:* 89
Mueller, Hans Alexander *26:* 64; *27:* 52, 53
Mugnaini, Joseph *11:* 35; *27:* 52, 53; *35:* 62
Mujica, Rick *72:* 67; *88:* 95; *111:* 53; *180:* 185; *197:* 70
Mullen, Douglas *180:* 178
Muller, Robin *86:* 161
Muller, Steven *32:* 167
Muller, Jorg *35:* 215; *67:* 138, 139
Mulock, Julie *163:* 112
Mullins, Edward S. *10:* 101
Mullins, Patricia *51:* 68
Multer, Scott *80:* 108
Munari, Bruno *15:* 200
Munch, Edvard *140:* 143
Munowitz, Ken *14:* 148; *72:* 178, 179
Munro, Roxie *58:* 134; *136:* 177; *137:* 218; *184:* 133, 134
Munsinger, Lynn *33:* 161; *46:* 126; *71:* 92; *82:* 80; *89:* 218; *92:* 125; *94:* 157, 158, 159, 160; *98:* 196; *103:* 198; *142:* 143; *145:* 133, 134, 136; *153:* 203; *176:* 162; *177:* 140, 141, 142; *189:* 113, 114, 116, 117
Munson, Russell *13:* 9
Munster, Sebastian *166:* 107
Munoz, William *42:* 160
Munzar, Barbara *149:* 75
Murdocca, Salvatore *73:* 212; *98:* 132; *111:* 168; *157:* 228; *164:* 257
Murphy, Bill *5:* 138; *130:* 170
Murphy, Jill *37:* 142; *70:* 166; *142:* 132, 134
Murphy, Kelly *130:* 212; *143:* 119; *176:* 158; *190:* 135
Murphy, Mary *196:* 158
Murphy, Tom *192:* 40
Murr, Karl *20:* 62
Murray, Joe *175:* 37
Murray, Ossie *43:* 176
Mussino, Attilio *29:* 131; *100:* 164
Mutchler, Dwight *1:* 25
Myers, Bernice *9:* 147; *36:* 75; *81:* 146, 147, 148
Myers, Christopher *183:* 150; *193:* 139
Myers, Duane O. *99:* 145
Myers, Tim *147:* 168
Myers, V.G. *142:* 41
Myers, Lou *11:* 2

N

Nachreiner, Tom *29:* 182
Nacht, Merle *65:* 49
Nadler, Ellis *88:* 91
Nagle, Shane *180:* 223
Nagy, Ian *195:* 64
Najaka, Marlies *62:* 101
Nakai, Michael *30:* 217; *54:* 29
Nakata, Hiroe *157:* 156; *162:* 30
Nakatani, Chiyoko *12:* 124
Narahashi, Keiko *77:* 188; *82:* 213; *115:* 142, 143, 144
Nascimbene, Yan *133:* 128; *173:* 132, 133
Nash, Lesa *87:* 135
Nash, Linell *46:* 175
Nash, Scott *130:* 36; *188:* 196
Naso, John *33:* 183
Nason, Thomas W. *14:* 68
Nasser, Muriel *48:* 74
Nast, Thomas *21:* 29; *28:* 23; *51:* 132, 133, 134, 135,136, 137, 138, 139, 141
Nasta, Vincent *78:* 185
Natale, Vincent *76:* 3; *78:* 125; *112:* 47; *166:* 81; *174:* 189; *185:* 212; *197:* 59
Natchev, Alexi *96:* 177
Nathan, Charlott *125:* 151
Nathan, Cheryl *150:* 104; *186:* 112
Natti, Susanna *20:* 146; *32:* 141, 142; *35:* 178; *37:* 143; *71:* 49; *93:* 98; *125:* 166, 168; *126:* 228; *151:* 6; *178:* 8; *188:* 106
Navarra, Celeste Scala *8:* 142
Naylor, Penelope *10:* 104
Nazz, James *72:* 8
Nebel, M. *45:* 154
Neebe, William *7:* 93
Needham, Dave *196:* 85
Needler, Jerry *12:* 93
Neel, Alice *31:* 23
Neely, Beth *119:* 184
Neely, Keith R. *46:* 124
Neff, Leland *78:* 74
Negri, Rocco *3:* 213; *5:* 67; *6:* 91, 108; *12:* 159
Negrin, Fabian *174:* 125; *175:* 15
Neidigh, Sherry *128:* 53
Neilan, Eujin Kim *180:* 241
Neill, John R. *18:* 8, 10, 11, 21, 30; *100:* 22
Neilsen, Cliff *158:* 131; *177:* 112, 121
Neilsen, Terese *116:* 74
Nelson, Craig *62:* 151; *153:* *183:* 86
Nelson, Gail White *68:* 140
Nelson, Jennifer *129:* 152
Nelson, Kadir *151:* 185; *154:* 146, 147; *157:* 189, 222; *181:* 122, 124; *197:* 155
Nelson, S.D. *131:* 34; *181:* 126, 127
Ness, Evaline *1:* 164, 165; *2:* 39; *3:* 8; *10:* 147; *12:* 53; *26:* 150, 151, 152, 153; *49:* 30, 31, 32; *56:* 30; *60:* 113
Neubecker, Robert *170:* 143
Neville, Vera *2:* 182
Nevins, Daniel *191:* 173
Nevwirth, Allan *79:* 168
Newberry, Clare Turlay *1:* 170
Newbold, Greg *108:* 125; *145:* 199; *151:* 23; *193:* 178; *197:* 10
Newfeld, Frank *14:* 121; *26:* 154
Newman, Andy *149:* 61; *195:* 63
Newman, Ann *43:* 90
Newman, Barbara Johansen *191:* 137, 138
Newsham, Ian *143:* 162
Newsom, Carol *40:* 159; *44:* 60; *47:* 189; *65:* 29; *70:* 192; *80:* 36; *85:* 137, 138; *92:* 167; *191:* 82
Newsom, Tom *49:* 149; *71:* 13, 62; *75:* 156; *91:* 113
Newton, Jill *83:* 105
Ng, Michael *29:* 171
Ng, Simon *167:* 7
Nguyen, Vincent *189:* 49

Nicholson, William *15:* 33, 34; *16:* 48
Nickens, Bessie *104:* 153
Nicklaus, Carol *45:* 194; *62:* 132, 133
Nickle, John *181:* 128
Nickless, Will *16:* 139
Nicholas, Corasue *154:* 20
Nicolas *17:* 130, 132, 133; *YABC 2:* 215
Niebrugge, Jane *6:* 118
Nielsen, Jon *6:* 100; *24:* 202
Nielsen, Kay *15:* 7; *16:* 211, 212, 213, 215, 217; *22:* 143; *YABC 1:* 32, 33
Nielsen, Cliff *95:* 207, 208; *105:* 58; *114:* 112; *124:* 12; *125:* 91, 92; *132:* 224; *135:* 187; *136:* 40; *137:* 168; *145:* 54; *149:* 28; *158:* 129; *165:* 64, 158; *168:* 169; *170:* 6; *175:* 114, 116; *187:* 75, 76; *194:* 107; *197:* 172
Niemann, Christoph *191:* 141
Nikola-Lisa, W. *180:* 180
Niland, Deborah *25:* 191; *27:* 156; *135:* 50; *172:* 143
Niland, Kilmeny *25:* 191; *75:* 143
Nino, Alex *59:* 145
Ninon *1:* 5; *38:* 101, 103, 108
Nissen, Rie *44:* 35
Nithael, Mark *158:* 237
Nivola, Claire A. *78:* 126; *140:* 147
Nixon, K. *14:* 152
Nobati, Eugenia *194:* 118
Noble, Louise *61:* 170
Noble, Marty *97:* 168; *125:* 171
Noble, Trinka Hakes *39:* 162; *84:* 157
Noda, Takayo *168:* 143
Noguchi, Yoshie *30:* 99
Nolan, Dennis *42:* 163; *67:* 163; *78:* 189; *82:* 225; *83:* 26; *92:* 169, 170; *103:* 166; *111:* 35; *112:* 213; *127:* 171; *166:* 161; *194:* 218
Noll, Sally *82:* 171
Nolte, Larry *121:* 63, 65
Nones, Eric Jon *61:* 111; *76:* 38; *77:* 177
Noonan, Daniel *100:* 224
Noonan, Julia *4:* 163; *7:* 207; *25:* 151; *91:* 29; *95:* 149
Norcia, Ernie *108:* 155; *140:* 47
Nordenskjold, Birgitta *2:* 208
Noreika, Robert *173:* 20
Norling, Beth *149:* 153, 154
Norman, Elaine *77:* 72, 176; *94:* 35; *136:* 63; *178:* 42
Norman, Mary *36:* 138, 147
Norman, Michael *12:* 117; *27:* 168
Northway, Jennifer *85:* 96
Nostlinger, Christiana *162:* 131
Novak, Linda *166:* 205
Novak, Matt *104:* 132, 133; *165:* 173, 174
Novelli, Luca *61:* 137
Nugent, Cynthia *106:* 189
Numeroff, Laura Joffe *28:* 161; *30:* 177
Nurse, Chris *164:* 91
Nussbaumer, Paul *16:* 219; *39:* 117
Nutt, Ken *72:* 69; *97:* 170
Nyce, Helene *19:* 219
Nygren, Tord *30:* 148; *127:* 164

O

Oakley, Graham *8:* 112; *30:* 164, 165; *84:* 188,189, 190, 191, 192
Oakley, Thornton *YABC 2:* 189
Oberheide, Heide *118:* 37
Obligado, Lilian *2:* 28, 66, 67; *6:* 30; *14:* 179; *15:* 103; *25:* 84; *61:* 138, 139, 140, 141, 143
Oblinski, Rafael *190:* 139
Obrant, Susan *11:* 186
O'Brien, Anne Sibley *53:* 116, 117; *155:* 115
O'Brien, John *41:* 253; *72:* 12; *89:* 59, 60; *98:* 16; *161:* 185; *169:* 16; *180:* 196
O'Brien, Patrick *193:* 142, 143, 144
O'Brien, Teresa *87:* 89

O'Brien, Tim *93:* 25; *136:* 94; *164:* 57; *169:* 57; *173:* 55; *175:* 86; *184:* 192; *191:* 134; *193:* 137
O'Clair, Dennis *127:* 25
O'Connor, George *183:* 153
Odell, Carole *35:* 47
Odem, Mel *99:* 164; *167:* 84, 87
O'Donohue, Thomas *40:* 89
Oechsli, Kelly *5:* 144, 145; *7:* 115; *8:* 83, 183; *13:* 117; *20:* 94; *81:* 199
Offen, Hilda *42:* 207
Ogden, Bill *42:* 59; *47:* 55
Ogg, Oscar *33:* 34
Ogle, Nancy Gray *163:* 144
Ohi, Ruth *90:* 175, 177; *131:* 63; *135:* 106; *175:* 107; *179:* 55
Ohlsson, Ib *4:* 152; *7:* 57; *10:* 20; *11:* 90; *19:* 217; *41:* 246; *82:* 106; *92:* 213
Ohtomo, Yasuo *37:* 146; *39:* 212, 213
O'Keefe, Jennifer *136:* 184
O'Kelley, Mattie Lou *36:* 150
Olbinski, Rafal *149:* 27; *158:* 77
Oliver, Isaac *171:* 182
Oliver, Jenni *23:* 121; *35:* 112
Oliver, Narelle *152:* 192; *197:* 129, 130
Oller, Erika *128:* 186; *134:* 126
Olschewski, Alfred *7:* 172
Olsen, Ib Spang *6:* 178, 179; *81:* 164
Olson, Alan *77:* 229
Olson-Brown, Ellen *183:* 154
Olugebefola, Ademola *15:* 205
O'Malley, Kevin *94:* 180; *106:* 8; *113:* 108; *136:* 70; *157:* 193; *191:* 146
O'Neil, Dan IV *7:* 176
O'Neill, Catharine *72:* 113; *84:* 78; *134:* 153
O'Neill, Jean *22:* 146
O'Neill, Martin *187:* 39
O'Neill, Michael J. *54:* 172
O'Neill, Rose *48:* 30, 31
O'Neill, Steve *21:* 118
Ono, Chiyo *7:* 97
Orbaan, Albert *2:* 31; *5:* 65, 171; *9:* 8; *14:* 241; *20:* 109
Orbach, Ruth *21:* 112
Orback, Craig *197:* 132
Orfe, Joan *20:* 81
Org, Ed *119:* 93
Ormai, Stella *72:* 129
Ormerod, Jan *55:* 124; *70:* 170, 171; *90:* 39; *132:* 172, 173, 174; *147:* 98
Ormsby, Virginia H. *11:* 187
O'Rourke, Ericka *108:* 216; *117:* 194; *111:* 142; *119:* 194; *137:* 152; *150:* 134; *167:* 64; *172:* 164; *188:* 163; *191:* 172
O'Rourke, Ericka Meltzer
    See O'Rourke, Ericka
Orozco, Jose Clemente *9:* 177
Orr, Forrest W. *23:* 9
Orr, N. *19:* 70
Ortiz, Vilma *88:* 158
Osborn, Cathy *152:* 232
Osborn, Robert *65:* 49
Osborne, Billie Jean *35:* 209
Osmond, Edward *10:* 111
O'Sullivan, Tom *3:* 176; *4:* 55; *78:* 195
Otani, June *124:* 42; *156:* 53
Otis, Rebecca *185:* 92
Ottley, Matt *147:* 221; *171:* 133
Otto, Svend *22:* 130, 141; *67:* 188, 189
Oudry, J.B. *18:* 167
Oughton, Taylor *5:* 23; *104:* 136
Overeng, Johannes *44:* 36
Overlie, George *11:* 156
Owens, Carl *2:* 35; *23:* 521
Owens, Gail *10:* 170; *12:* 157; *19:* 16; *22:* 70; *25:* 81; *28:* 203, 205; *32:* 221, 222; *36:* 132; *46:* 40; *47:* 57; *54:* 66, 67, 68, 69, 70, 71, 72, 73; *71:* 100; *73:* 64; *77:* 157; *80:* 32; *82:* 3; *99:* 226
Owens, Mary Beth *113:* 202, 203; *191:* 148, 149

Owens, Nubia *84:* 74
Oxenbury, Helen *3:* 150, 151; *24:* 81; *68:* 174, 175,176; *81:* 209; *84:* 213, 245; *129:* 56; *149:* 159; *184:* 181
Oz, Robin *88:* 167; *185:* 181

P

Padgett, Jim *12:* 165
Page, Homer *14:* 145
Page, Mark *162:* 70
Paget, Sidney *24:* 90, 91, 93, 95, 97
Paget, Walter *64:* 122
Paillot, Jim *173:* 89
Pajouhesh, Noushin *160:* 121
Pak *12:* 76
Pak, Yu Cha *86:* 174
Paladino, Lance *134:* 30
Palazzo, Tony *3:* 152, 153
Palecek, Josef *56:* 136; *89:* 158
Palen, Debbie *135:* 88; *195:* 148, 149
Palencar, John Jude *84:* 12, 45; *85:* 87; *92:* 187; *99:* 128; *110:* 204; *150:* 122; *171:* 86
Palin, Nicki *81:* 201; *89:* 161
Palladini, David *4:* 113; *40:* 176, 177, 178, 179, 181,224, 225; *50:* 138; *78:* 186
Pallarito, Don *43:* 36
Palmer, Carol *158:* 230; *195:* 187
Palmer, Heidi *15:* 207; *29:* 102
Palmer, Jan *42:* 153; *82:* 161
Palmer, Judd *153:* 160, 161
Palmer, Juliette *6:* 89; *15:* 208
Palmer, Kate Salley *104:* 143; *154:* 169
Palmer, Lemuel *17:* 25, 29
Palmisciano, Diane *110:* 62; *162:* 26
Palmquist, Eric *38:* 133
Panesis, Nicholas *3:* 127
Panter, Gary *182:* 191
Panton, Doug *52:* 99
Paparone, Pamela *129:* 174
Papas, William *11:* 223; *50:* 160
Papin, Joseph *26:* 113
Papish, Robin Lloyd *10:* 80
Paradis, Susan *40:* 216
Paraquin, Charles H. *18:* 166
Paris, Peter *31:* 127
Parisi, Elizabeth B. *141:* 82; *164:* 57
Park, Nick *113:* 143
Park, Seho *39:* 110
Park, W.B. *22:* 189
Parker, Ant *82:* 87, 88; *104:* 121
Parker, Lewis *2:* 179
Parker, Nancy Winslow *10:* 113; *22:* 164; *28:* 47, 144; *52:* 7; *69:* 153; *91:* 171, 174; *132:* 175
Parker, Robert *4:* 161; *5:* 74; *9:* 136; *29:* 39
Parker, Robert Andrew *11:* 81; *29:* 186; *39:* 165; *40:* 25; *41:* 78; *42:* 123; *43:* 144; *48:* 182; *54:* 140; *74:* 141; *91:* 24; *111:* 115; *151:* 201; *154:* 156
Parker-Rees, Guy *149:* 145; *193:* 149, 150
Parkin, Trevor *140:* 151
Parkins, David *114:* 123; *146:* 176; *176:* 168; *192:* 107
Parkinson, Kathy *71:* 143; *144:* 234
Parkinson, Keith *70:* 66
Parks, Gordon, Jr. *33:* 228
Parnall, Peter *5:* 137; *16:* 221; *24:* 70; *40:* 78; *51:* 130; *69:* 17, 155; *136:* 22, 23, 24
Parnall, Virginia *40:* 78
Parow, Lorraine *158:* 127
Parr, Todd *134:* 139, 140; *179:* 163, 164, 165
Parrish, Anne *27:* 159, 160
Parrish, Dillwyn *27:* 159
Parrish, Maxfield *14:* 160, 161, 164, 165; *16:* 109; *18:* 12, 13; *YABC 1:* 149, 152, 267; *2:* 146, 149
Parry, David *26:* 156
Parry, Marian *13:* 176; *19:* 179

Parsons, Garry *197:* 135
Partch, Virgil *45:* 163, 165
Pascal, David *14:* 174
Paschkis, Julie *177:* 153, 154
Pasquier, J.A. *16:* 91
Pasternak, Robert *119:* 53
Paterson, Diane *13:* 116; *39:* 163; *59:* 164, 165, 166,167; *72:* 51, 53; *129:* 175; *177:* 156, 157
Paterson, Helen *16:* 93
Patkau, Karen *112:* 123
Paton, Jane *15:* 271; *35:* 176
Patrick, John *139:* 190
Patrick, Pamela *90:* 160; *93:* 211; *105:* 12
Patrick, Tom *190:* 103
Patterson, Geoffrey *54:* 75
Patterson, Robert *25:* 118
Patti, Joyce *187:* 145, 146
Patz, Nancy *111:* 40; *154:* 161
Paul, James *4:* 130; *23:* 161
Paul, Korky *102:* 85
Paull, Grace *24:* 157; *87:* 127
Paulsen, Ruth Wright *79:* 160, 164; *189:* 146
Pavlov, Elena *80:* 49
Payne, Adam S. *135:* 166
Payne, C.F. *145:* 138, 140; *179:* 168
Payne, Joan Balfour *1:* 118
Payne, Tom *170:* 27
Payson, Dale *7:* 34; *9:* 151; *20:* 140; *37:* 22
Payzant, Charles *21:* 147
Peacock, Ralph *64:* 118
Peake, Mervyn *22:* 136, 149; *23:* 162, 163, 164; *YABC2:* 307
Pearson, Larry *38:* 225
Pearson, Tracey Campbell *64:* 163, 164, 167, 168, 169; *118:* 51; *156:* 169, 171, 172; *163:* 140
Peat, Fern B. *16:* 115
Peck, Anne Merriman *18:* 241; *24:* 155
Peck, Beth *66:* 242; *79:* 166; *80:* 136; *91:* 34; *95:* 9; *101:* 77; *164:* 197; *190:* 170
Pedersen, Janet *193:* 152
Pedersen, Judy *66:* 217; *121:* 36; *172:* 67
Pedersen, Vilhelm *YABC 1:* 40
Pederson, Sharleen *12:* 92
Pedlar, Elaine *161:* 45
Peek, Merle *39:* 168
Peet, Bill *2:* 203; *41:* 159, 160, 161, 162, 163; *78:* 158, 159, 160, 161
Peguero, Adrian *116:* 133
Peguero, Gerard *116:* 133
Pels, Winslow Pinney *55:* 126
Peltier, Leslie C. *13:* 178
Penberthy, Mark *171:* 78
Pendle, Alexy *7:* 159; *13:* 34; *29:* 161; *33:* 215; *86:* 62
Pendola, Joanne *76:* 203; *81:* 125; *105:* 181; *178:* 152, 153
Pene du Bois, William *4:* 70; *10:* 122; *26:* 61; *27:* 145, 211; *35:* 243; *41:* 216; *68:* 180, 181; *73:* 45
Penfound, David *102:* 185
Pennington, Eunice *27:* 162
Peppe, Mark *28:* 142
Peppe, Rodney *4:* 164, 165; *74:* 187, 188, 189
Pepper, Hubert *64:* 143
Percy, Graham *63:* 2
Pericoli, Matteo *178:* 177
Perini, Ben *173:* 77
Perkins, David *60:* 68
Perkins, Lucy Fitch *72:* 199
Perkins, Lynne Rae *172:* 146
Perl, Susan *2:* 98; *4:* 231; *5:* 44, 45, 118; *6:* 199; *8:* 137; *12:* 88; *22:* 193; *34:* 54, 55; *52:* 128; *YABC 1:* 176
Perrone, Donna *78:* 166
Perry, Marie Fritz *165:* 180
Perry, Patricia *29:* 137; *30:* 171
Perry, Roger *27:* 163
Perske, Martha *46:* 83; *51:* 108, 147
Persson, Stina *175:* 166

Pesek, Ludek *15:* 237
Petach, Heidi *149:* 166
Peters, David *72:* 205; *182:* 116
Petersen, Jeff *181:* 95
Petersham, Maud *17:* 108, 147, 148, 149, 150, 151, 152, 153
Petersham, Miska *17:* 108, 147, 148, 149, 150, 151, 152, 153
Peterson, Eric *109:* 125
Peterson, Nisse *99:* 27
Peterson, R.F. *7:* 101
Peterson, Russell *7:* 130
Petie, Haris *2:* 3; *10:* 41, 118; *11:* 227; *12:* 70
Petricic, Dusan *153:* 75, 76, 77; *170:* 12; *172:* 13; *176:* 170; *179:* 56
Petrides, Heidrun *19:* 223
Petrone, Valeria *159:* 160; *171:* 92; *186:* 173
Petrosino, Tamara *177:* 40; *193:* 154, 155
Petruccio, Steven James *67:* 159; *127:* 5
Pettingill, Ondre *64:* 181; *70:* 64
Peyo *40:* 56, 57
Peyton, K.M. *15:* 212
Pfeifer, Herman *15:* 262
Pfister, Marcus *83:* 165, 166, 167; *146:* 152; *150:* 160
Pfloog, Jan *124:* 60
Pham, LeUyen *160:* 48; *175:* 154, 156; *179:* 149
Phelan, Matt *182:* 160; *184:* 222
Phillips, Craig *70:* 151
Phillips, Douglas *1:* 19
Phillips, F.D. *6:* 202
Phillips, Louise *133:* 67
Phillips, Matt *184:* 173
Phillips, Thomas *30:* 55
Philpot, Glyn *54:* 46
Phiz
    See Browne, Hablot K.
Piatti, Celestino *16:* 223
Pica, Steve *115:* 181
Picarella, Joseph *13:* 147
Picart, Gabriel *121:* 165
Pichon, Liz *174:* 139
Pickard, Charles *12:* 38; *18:* 203; *36:* 152
Picken, George A. *23:* 150
Pickens, David *22:* 156
Pickering, Jimmy *195:* 152; *197:* 163
Pienkowski, Jan *6:* 183; *30:* 32; *58:* 140, 141, 142,143, 146, 147; *73:* 3; *87:* 156, 157; *131:* 189
Pignataro, Anna *163:* 220 Pileggi, Steve *145:* 122
Pilkey, Dav *68:* 186; *115:* 164, 166; *166:* 173, 174, 175
Pimlott, John *10:* 205
Pincus, Harriet *4:* 186; *8:* 179; *22:* 148; *27:* 164, 165; *66:* 202
Pini, Wendy *89:* 166
Pinkett, Neil *60:* 8
Pinkney, Brian *81:* 184, 185; *94:* 107; *113:* 146, 147; *117:* 121, 166; *132:* 145; *158:* 108, 191; *160:* 189
Pinkney, Jerry *8:* 218; *10:* 40; *15:* 276; *20:* 66; *24:* 121; *33:* 109; *36:* 222; *38:* 200; *41:* 165, 166, 167, 168, 169, 170, 171, 173, 174; *44:* 198; *48:* 51; *53:* 20; *56:* 61, 68; *58:* 184; *60:* 59; *61:* 91; *71:* 146, 148, 149; *72:* 17; *73:* 149; *74:* 159,192; *75:* 45; *80:* 206; *81:* 44; *85:* 144; *95:* 50; *107:* 158, 159, 160; *108:* 164; *112:* 114, 115; *133:* 58; *195:* 140
Pinkwater, Daniel Manus *46:* 180, 181, 182, 185, 188, 189, 190; *151:* 161 *76:* 178, 179, 180
Pinkwater, Manus *8:* 156; *46:* 180
    See also Pinkwater, Daniel Manus
Pinkwater, Jill *114:* 160, 161; *158:* 179; *188:* 143, 145, 146
Pinto, Ralph *10:* 131; *45:* 93
Pinon, Mark *74:* 22
Piven, Hanoch *173:* 142
Pistolesi *73:* 211

Pitcairn, Ansel *188:* 10
Pittman, Helena Clare *71:* 151
Pitz, Henry C. *4:* 168; *19:* 165; *35:* 128; *42:* 80; *YABC 2:* 95, 176
Pitzenberger, Lawrence J. *26:* 94
Pitzer, Susanna *181:* 131
Player, Stephen *82:* 190
Plecas, Jennifer *84:* 201; *106:* 124; *149:* 168
Ploog, Mike *180:* 19
Plowden, David *52:* 135, 136
Plume, Ilse *170:* 149
Plummer, William *32:* 31
Podevin, Jean François *184:* 185
Podwal, Mark *56:* 170, 173; *101:* 154, 155, 157; *149:* 176; *160:* 194
Pogany, Willy *15:* 46, 49; *19:* 222, 256; *25:* 214; *44:* 142, 143, 144, 145, 146, 147, 148
Pohrt, Tom *67:* 116; *104:* 80; *152:* 199; *195:* 154
Poirson, V.A. *26:* 89
Polacco, Patricia *74:* 195, 196, 197, 198; *123:* 121, 122, 123; *180:* 189, 190, 191, 193, 194
Polgreen, John *21:* 44
Politi, Leo *1:* 178; *4:* 53; *21:* 48; *47:* 173,174, 176, 178, 179, 180, 181
Pollema-Cahill, Phyllis *123:* 126
Pollen, Samson *64:* 80
Polonsky, Arthur *34:* 168
Polseno, Jo *1:* 53; *3:* 117; *5:* 114; *17:* 154; *20:* 87; *32:* 49; *41:* 245
Pomaska, Anna *117:* 148
Pons, Bernadette *184:* 100
Ponter, James *5:* 204
Poole, Colin *111:* 27
Poortvliet, Rien *6:* 212; *65:* 165, 166, 167
Pope, Kevin *183:* 158
Popp, Wendy *72:* 122; *158:* 68
Poppel, Hans *71:* 154, 155
Porfirio, Guy *76:* 134
Portal, Colette *6:* 186; *11:* 203
Porter, George *7:* 181
Porter, Janice Lee *136:* 175; *164:* 37
Porter, John *113:* 47
Porter, Pat Grant *84:* 112; *125:* 101
Porter, Sue *146:* 246, 247
Porter, Walter *124:* 175
Posada, Mia *187:* 151
Posen, Michael *175:* 82
Posthuma, Sieb *150:* 163
Postma, Lidia *79:* 17
Potter, Beatrix *100:* 194, 195; *132:* 179, 180, 181, 182; *YABC 1:* 208, 209, 210, 212, 213
Potter, Giselle *117:* 123; *143:* 44; *144:* 170, 197; *149:* 7; *150:* 165; *187:* 152, 153; *190:* 198; *196:* 152
Potter, Katherine *104:* 147; *171:* 135; *173:* 136
Potter, Miriam Clark *3:* 162
Poulin, Stephane *98:* 140, 141
Poullis, Nick *146:* 210
Powell, Constance Buffington *174:* 141
Powell, Gary *151:* 208
Powell, Ivan *67:* 219
Power, Margaret *105:* 122
Powers, Daniel *161:* 173
Powers, Richard M. *1:* 230; *3:* 218; *7:* 194; *26:* 186
Powledge, Fred *37:* 154
Powzyk, Joyce *74:* 214
Poydar, Nancy *96:* 149; *190:* 180, 181, 182
Pracher, Richard *91:* 166
Prachaticka, Marketa *126:* 126
Prange, Beckie *181:* 169
Prap, Lila *177:* 165
Prater, John *103:* 142, 143, 144; *149:* 172
Pratt, Charles *23:* 29
Pratt, George *116:* 208
Pratt, Pierre *150:* 73; *166:* 183; *168:* 172
Prebenna, David *73:* 174
Preiss-Glasser, Robin *123:* 176; *152* 40; *172:* 194
Press, Jenny *116:* 95

Preston, Mark *152:* 162
Pretro, Korinna *91:* 126
Price, Christine *2:* 247; *3:* 163, 253; *8:* 166
Price, Cynthia *118:* 156
Price, Edward *33:* 34
Price, Garrett *1:* 76; *2:* 42
Price, Hattie Longstreet *17:* 13
Price, Norman *YABC 1:* 129
Price, Willard *48:* 184
Priceman, Marjorie *81:* 171; *136:* 169; *156:* 200; *168:* 153, 154; *188:* 45
Priestley, Alice *168:* 33
Primavera, Elise *26:* 95; *58:* 151; *73:* 37; *80:* 79; *86:* 156; *105:* 161
Primrose, Jean *36:* 109
Prince, Alison *86:* 188, 189
Prince, Leonora E. *7:* 170
Pritchett, Shelley *116:* 148
Prittie, Edwin J. *YABC 1:* 120
Proimos, James *176:* 4
Proimos, John *173:* 144
Prosmitsky, Jenya *132:* 33
Provensen, Alice *37:* 204, 215, 222; *70:* 176, 177, 178, 180, *71:* 213; *147:* 184; *191:* 190
Provensen, Martin *37:* 204, 215, 222; *70:* 176, 177, 178, 180; *71:* 213; *191:* 190
Pucci, Albert John *44:* 154
Pudlo *8:* 59
Puggaard, Ulla *196:* 25
Pulver, Harry, Jr. *129:* 159
Pulver, Robin *160:* 4
Punchatz, Don *99:* 57
Purdy, Susan *8:* 162
Pursell, Weimer *55:* 18
Purtscher, Alfons *97:* 6
Puskas, James *5:* 141
Pyk, Jan *7:* 26; *38:* 123
Pyle, Chuck *99:* 149; *191:* 83
Pyle, Howard *16:* 225, 226, 227, 228, 230, 231, 232, 235; *24:* 27; *34:* 124, 125, 127, 128; *59:* 132; *100:* 198

Q

Quackenbush, Robert *4:* 190; *6:* 166; *7:* 175, 178; *9:* 86; *11:* 65, 221; *41:* 154; *43:* 157; *70:* 185, 186; *71:* 137; *85:* 47; *92:* 148; *133:* 154, 164, 169
Qualls, Sean *177:* 167, 168; *193:* 43
Quennell, Marjorie (Courtney) *29:* 163, 164
Quidor, John *19:* 82
Quirk, John *62:* 170
Quirk, Thomas *12:* 81

R

Rackham, Arthur *15:* 32, 78, 214-227; *17:* 105, 115; *18:* 233; *19:* 254; *20:* 151; *22:* 129, 131, 132, 133; *23:* 175; *24:* 161, 181; *26:* 91; *32:* 118; *64:* 18; *100:* 9, 16, 203, 204; *YABC 1:* 25, 45, 55, 147; *2:* 103, 142, 173, 210
Racz, Michael *56:* 134
Raczka, Bob *191:* 155, 156
Radcliffe, Andrew *82:* 215
Rader, Laura *101:* 219; *197:* 147
Radunsky, Vladimir *177:* 170; *192:* 30
Rafilson, Sidney *11:* 172
Raglin, Tim *125:* 24
Raible, Alton *1:* 202, 203; *28:* 193; *35:* 181; *110:* 207
Raine, Patricia *82:* 74; *88:* 154
Ramá, Sue *173:* 45; *185:* 186; *190:* 184
Ramhorst, John *117:* 11
Ramirez, Gladys *177:* 19
Ramsey, James *16:* 41

Ramsey, Marcy Dunn 82: 11; 180: 186
Ramus, Michael 51: 171
Rand, Paul 6: 188
Rand, Ted 67: 9, 10, 121, 123; 74: 190; 84: 170; 103: 170; 112: 6; 114: 73; 139: 168; 143: 194; 156: 154; 161: 9, 10
Randazzo, Tony 81: 98
Randell, William 55: 54
Rane, Walter 93: 144; 143: 109; 184: 126
Rankin, Joan 163: 40
Rankin, Laura 176: 173, 174; 179: 150
Ransome, Arthur 22: 201
Ransome, James E. 74: 137; 75: 80; 84: 181; 94: 108; 117: 115; 123: 128, 129, 130; 158: 101, 102; 159: 205; 178: 188, 189, 190
Rantz, Don 119: 184
Rao, Anthony 28: 126
Raphael, Elaine 23: 192; 71: 24, 25
Rappaport, Eva 6: 190
Raschka, Chris 80: 187, 189, 190; 97: 211; 115: 210; 117: 151, 152, 153, 154; 143: 195; 145: 153; 166: 190, 191; 170: 114
Rash, Andy 158: 178; 162: 172
Raskin, Ellen 2: 208, 209; 4: 142; 13: 183; 22: 68; 29: 139; 36: 134; 38: 173, 174, 175, 176, 177, 178,179, 180, 181; 60: 163; 86: 81
Rathmann, Peggy 93: 32; 94: 168; 157: 212, 214
Ratkus, Tony 77: 133
Ratzkin, Lawrence 40: 143
Rau, Margaret 9: 157
Ravid, Joyce 61: 73
Ravielli, Anthony 1: 198; 3: 168; 11: 143
Ravilious, Robin 77: 169
Rawlins, Donna 72: 198; 73: 15, 129
Rawlins, Janet 76: 79
Rawlings, Steve 143: 139; 151: 54
Rawlinson, Debbie 75: 132
Ray, Deborah Kogan 8: 164; 29: 238; 50: 112, 113; 62: 119; 78: 191
Ray, Jane 96: 166; 97: 104; 152: 208; 190: 221; 196: 165
Ray, Ralph 2: 239; 5: 73
Rayann, Omar 162: 205; 186: 29, 30
Rayevsky, Robert 64: 17; 70: 173; 80: 204; 117: 79; 190: 187, 188
Raymond, Larry 31: 108; 97: 109
Rayner, Hugh 151: 170
Rayner, Mary 22: 207; 47: 140; 72: 191; 87: 171, 172; 192: 104
Rayner, Shoo
    See Rayner, Hugh
Raynes, John 71: 19
Raynor, Dorka 28: 168
Raynor, Paul 24: 73
Rayyan, Omar 110: 222; 112: 17; 125: 131
Razzi, James 10: 127
Read, Alexander D. 20: 45
Reader, Dennis 71: 157
Reasoner, Charles 53: 33, 36, 37
Reczuch, Karen 115: 132; 145: 131
Redlich, Ben 163: 221
Reed, Joseph 116: 139
Reed, Lynn Rowe 115: 173; 171: 146
Reed, Tom 34: 171
Reeder, Colin 74: 202; 77: 113
Rees, Mary 134: 219
Reese, Bob 60: 135
Reeve, Philip 171: 50
Reeves, Eira B. 130: 173, 174; 141: 151
Reeves, Rick 181: 179
Regan, Dana 117: 116
Regan, Laura 103: 198; 153: 206
Reichert, Renée 169: 127
Reid, Barbara 82: 178; 92: 17; 93: 169, 170
Reid, Stephen 19: 213; 22: 89
Reim, Melanie 104: 151; 150: 98
Reinert, Kirk 89: 138; 195: 129
Reinertson, Barbara 44: 150; 62: 103
Reiniger, Lotte 40: 185

Reisberg, Mira 119: 2
Reisch, Jesse 158: 130
Reiser, Lynn 81: 175; 138: 184; 180: 200
Reiss, John J. 23: 193
Relf, Douglas 3: 63
Relyea, C.M. 16: 29; 31: 153
Remi, Georges 13: 184
Remington, Frederic 19: 188; 41: 178, 179, 180, 181, 183,184, 185, 186, 187, 188; 62: 197
Remkiewicz, Frank 67: 102; 77: 171; 80: 130; 113: 107; 152: 116; 152: 211, 212; 157: 148
Rendon, Maria 116: 141; 192: 134: 152
Renfro, Ed 79: 176
Renlie, Frank 11: 200
Reschofsky, Jean 7: 118
Rethi 60: 181
Rethi, Lili 2: 153; 36: 156
Reusswig, William 3: 267
Revell, Cindy 195: 93
Rex, Adam 156: 172; 169: 91; 186: 178, 179
Rex, Michael 157: 147; 191: 159, 160
Rey, H.A. 1: 182; 26: 163, 164, 166, 167, 169; 69: 172, 173, 174, 175; 86: 195, 196, 197; 100: 211; YABC 2: 17
Reynolds, Adrian 192: 159, 160
Reynolds, Doris 5: 71; 31: 77
Reynolds, Peter H. 142: 12; 179: 175, 176
Rhead, Louis 31: 91; 100: 228
Rhodes, Andrew 38: 204; 50: 163; 54: 76; 61: 123, 124; 87: 200
Ribbons, Ian 3: 10; 37: 161; 40: 76
Ricci, Regolo 93: 22; 164: 148
Rice, Elizabeth 2: 53, 214
Rice, Eve 34: 174, 175; 91: 172
Rice, James 22: 210; 93: 173
Rich, Martha 195: 16
Richards, Chuck 170: 154
Richards, George 40: 116, 119, 121; 44: 179
Richards, Henry YABC 1: 228, 231
Richardson, Ernest 2: 144
Richardson, Frederick 18: 27, 31
Richardson, John 110: 88
Richman, Hilda 26: 132
Richmond, George 24: 179
Riddell, Chris 114: 170, 195; 166: 179
Riddle, Tohby 74: 204; 151: 179
Riding, Peter 63: 195
Rieniets, Judy King 14: 28
Riger, Bob 2: 166
Riggio, Anita 73: 191; 85: 63; 137: 184; 172: 165
Riley, Jon 74: 70
Riley, Kenneth 22: 230
Riley-Webb, Charlotte 153: 143
Rinaldi, Angelo 165: 60, 69
Ringgold, Faith 71: 162; 114: 173, 174, 176; 187: 160, 161, 163
Ringi, Kjell 12: 171
Rios, Tere
    See Versace, Marie
Ripper, Charles L. 3: 175
Ripplinger, Henry 117: 31
Ritchie, William 74: 183
Ritter, John 175: 14
Ritz, Karen 41: 117; 72: 239; 87: 125; 102: 7; 106: 6
Rivers, Ruth 178: 193
Rivkin, Jay 15: 230
Rivoche, Paul 45: 125
Roach, Marilynne 9: 158
Robbin, Jodi 44: 156, 159
Robbins, Frank 42: 167
Robbins, Ken 147: 191, 192
Robbins, Ruth 52: 102
Roberts, Cliff 4: 126
Roberts, David 154: 4, 6; 191: 162; 196: 184; 197: 105
Roberts, Doreen 4: 230; 28: 105
Roberts, Jim 22: 166; 23: 69; 31: 110
Roberts, Tony 109: 195, 214

Roberts, W. 22: 2, 3
Robertson, M.P. 197: 153
Robins, Arthur 137: 172; 151: 225
Robinson, Aminah Brenda Lynn 86: 205; 103: 55; 159: 159
Robinson, Charles [1870-1937] 17: 157, 171, 172, 173, 175, 176; 24: 207; 25: 204; YABC 2: 308, 309, 310, 331
Robinson, Charles 3: 53; 5: 14; 6: 193; 7: 150; 7: 183; 8: 38; 9: 81; 13: 188; 14: 248, 249; 23: 149; 26: 115; 27: 48; 28: 191; 32: 28; 35: 210; 36: 37; 48: 96; 52: 33; 53: 157; 56: 15; 62: 142; 77: 41; 111: 148
Robinson, Jerry 3: 262
Robinson, Joan G. 7: 184
Robinson, Lolly 90: 227
Robinson, T.H. 17: 179, 181, 182, 183; 29: 254
Robinson, W. Heath 17: 185, 187, 189, 191, 193, 195, 197, 199, 202; 23: 167; 25: 194; 29: 150; YABC 1: 44; 2: 183
Rocco, John 187: 4; 188: 151
Roche, Christine 41: 98
Roche, Denis 99: 184; 180: 32; 196: 168
Roche, P.K. 57: 151, 152
Rocker, Fermin 7: 34; 13: 21; 31: 40; 40: 190,191
Rocklen, Margot 101: 181
Rockwell, Anne 5: 147; 33: 171, 173; 71: 166, 167,168; 114: 183, 184; 194: 152, 155
Rockwell, Gail 7: 186
Rockwell, Harlow 33: 171, 173, 175
Rockwell, Lizzy 114: 182; 162: 182; 185: 189
Rockwell, Norman 23: 39, 196, 197, 199, 200, 203, 204, 207; 41: 140, 143; 123: 47; YABC 2: 60
Rockwood, Richard 119: 75
Rodanas, Kristina 156: 183, 184
Rodegast, Roland 43: 100
Rodgers, Frank 69: 177
Rodriguez, Albert G. 182: 50
Rodriguez, Christina 184: 12
Rodriguez, Joel 16: 65
Rodriguez, Robert 145: 145
Rodriguez-Howard, Pauline 177: 18
Roeckelein, Katrina 134: 223
Roennfeldt, Robert 66: 243
Roever, J.M. 4: 119; 26: 170
Roffey, Maureen 33: 142, 176, 177
Rogasky, Barbara 46: 90
Rogé 173: 160
Rogers, Carol 2: 262; 6: 164; 26: 129
Rogers, Chris M. 150: 59; 196: 61
Rogers, Forest 87: 160; 101: 76
Rogers, Frances 10: 130
Rogers, Gregory 104: 76; 126: 57; 171: 26
Rogers, Jacqueline 78: 249; 80: 34; 86: 54 103: 70; 115: 72; 129: 173; 131: 57, 225; 143: 211; 153: 100; 193: 186
Rogers, Sherry 191: 66
Rogers, Walter S. 31: 135, 138; 67: 65, 168; 100: 81
Rogers, William A. 15: 151, 153, 154; 33: 35
Rogoff, Barbara 95: 20
Rohmann, Eric 103: 152
Rojankovsky, Feodor 6: 134, 136; 10: 183; 21: 128,129, 130; 25: 110; 28: 42; 68: 120
Rolfsen, Alf 62: 15
Romain, Trevor 134: 157
Roman, Barbara J. 103: 171
Romas 114: 111; 165: 63
Romano, Robert 64: 68
Romero, Alejandro 187: 185
Roos, Maryn 168: 198
Root, Barry 80: 212; 90: 196; 146: 78; 156: 165; 159: 161; 182: 18, 172
Root, Kimberly Bulcken 86: 72; 98: 21; 108: 111; 127: 114; 159: 162; 176: 134; 192: 163
Roper, Bob 65: 153
Roraback, Robin 111: 156
Rorer, Abigail 43: 222; 85: 155

Rosales, Melodye *80:* 35
Rosamilia, Patricia *36:* 120
Rose, Carl *5:* 62
Rose, David S. *29:* 109; *70:* 120
Rose, Gerald *68:* 200, 201; *86:* 48
Rose, Ted *93:* 178
Rosenbaum, Jonathan *50:* 46
Rosenberg, Amye *74:* 207, 208
Rosenberry, Vera *87:* 22, 26; *144:* 212, 213; *158:* 120
Rosenblum, Richard *11:* 202; *18:* 18
Rosier, Lydia *16:* 236; *20:* 104; *21:* 109; *22:* 125; *30:* 151, 158; *42:* 128; *45:* 214; *77:* 227, 228
Rosing, Jens *85:* 142
Ross
 See Thomson, Ross
Ross, Christine *83:* 172, 173
Ross, Clare Romano *3:* 123; *21:* 45; *48:* 199
Ross, Dave *32:* 152; *57:* 108
Ross, Herbert *37:* 78
Ross, John *3:* 123; *21:* 45
Ross, Johnny *32:* 190
Ross, Larry *47:* 168; *60:* 62
Ross, Ruth *109:* 233
Ross, Tony *17:* 204; *56:* 132; *65:* 176, 177, 179; *90:* 123; *123:* 186, 187, 190; *130:* 188, 190, 191, 192; *132:* 242; *174:* 159; *176:* 181, 182, 183
Rossetti, Dante Gabriel *20:* 151, 153
Rostant, Larry *180:* 221; *194:* 108; *195:* 96; *197:* 12
Roth, Arnold *4:* 238; *21:* 133
Roth, Julie Jersild *180:* 206
Roth, Marci *135:* 223
Roth, R.G. *184:* 50
Roth, Rob *105:* 98; *146:* 41
Roth, Robert *176:* 159
Roth, Roger *61:* 128; *190:* 192
Roth, Stephanie *136:* 171, 172
Roth, Susan L. *80:* 38; *93:* 78; *134:* 165, 166; *181:* 145, 146
Rothenberg, Joani Keller *162:* 190, 191
Rothman, Michael *139:* 62; *184:* 34 Rotman, Jeffrey L. *145:* 30
Rotondo, Pat *32:* 158
Roughsey, Dick *35:* 186
Rouille, M. *11:* 96
Rounds, Glen *8:* 173; *9:* 171; *12:* 56; *32:* 194; *40:* 230; *51:* 161, 162, 166; *56:* 149; *70:* 198, 199; *YABC 1:* 1, 2, 3; *112:* 163
Roundtree, Katherine *114:* 88; *168:* 102
Rowan, Evadne *52:* 51
Rowe, Eric *111:* 161
Rowe, Gavin *27:* 144; *72:* 47; *88:* 201
Rowe, John *132:* 70, 71; *180:* 126
Rowell, Kenneth *40:* 72
Rowen, Amy *52:* 143
Rowena *116:* 101
Rowland, Andrew *164:* 136
Rowland, Jada *83:* 73
Rowles, Daphne *58:* 24
Roy, Jeroo *27:* 229; *36:* 110
Royo *118:* 32; *144:* 105, 106, 108; *165:* 19; *166:* 166
Rubel, Nicole *18:* 255; *20:* 59; *81:* 66, 67; *95:* 169, 170; *119:* 60; *135:* 177, 179, 180; *169:* 68; *181:* 150
Rubel, Reina *33:* 217
Rud, Borghild *6:* 15
Ruddell, Gary *110:* 238; *116:* 207
Rudolph, Norman Guthrie *17:* 13
Rue, Leonard Lee III *37:* 164
Rueda, Claudia *183:* 170, 171
Ruelle, Karen Gray *126:* 193
Ruff, Donna *50:* 173; *72:* 203; *78:* 49; *80:* 120,121; *93:* 162; *164:* 121
Ruffins, Reynold *10:* 134, 135; *41:* 191, 192, 193, 194, 195, 196; *125:* 187, 188, 189; *162:* 197
Ruhlin, Roger *34:* 44

Ruiz, Art *95:* 154; *110:* 91
Rumford, James *193:* 167
Runnerstroem, Bengt Arne *75:* 161
Ruse, Margaret *24:* 155
Rush, Ken *98:* 74
Rush, Peter *42:* 75
Russell, Charles M. *167:* 171
Russell, E.B. *18:* 177, 182
Russell, Jim *53:* 134
Russell, P. Craig *80:* 196; *146:* 102; *162:* 186
Russo, Marisabina *84:* 51; *106:* 164; *151:* 183; *188:* 153, 154, 155, 156
Russo, Susan *30:* 182; *36:* 144
Russon, Mary *87:* 145
Ruth, Greg *183:* 125
Ruth, Rod *9:* 161
Rutherford, Alexa *110:* 108
Rutherford, Jenny *78:* 5
Rutherford, Meg *25:* 174; *34:* 178, 179; *69:* 73; *72:* 31
Rutland, Jonathan *31:* 126
Ruurs, Margriet *147:* 195
Ruzzier, Sergio *159:* 176, 177; *163:* 184
Ryan, Amy *188:* 50
Ryan, Will *86:* 134
Ryden, Hope *8:* 176
Rylant, Cynthia *112:* 170, 172
Rymer, Alta M. *34:* 181
Ryniak, Christopher *178:* 11
Rystedt, Rex *49:* 80

S

Saaf, Chuck *49:* 179
Saaf, Donald *101:* 220; *124:* 180
Sabaka, Donna R. *21:* 172
Sabin, Robert *45:* 35; *60:* 30; *99:* 161
Sabuda, Robert *170:* 166, 167, 168
Sacker, Amy *16:* 100
Saelig, S.M. *129:* 73; *173:* 59
Saffioti, Lino *36:* 176; *48:* 60
Saflund, Birgitta *94:* 2
Sagsoorian, Paul *12:* 183; *22:* 154; *33:* 106; *87:* 152
Sahara, Tony *168:* 106; *177:* 181; *178:* 228; *186:* 132
Sahlberg, Myron *57:* 165
Saidens, Amy *145:* 162; *191:* 131
Saint Exupery, Antoine de *20:* 157
Saint James, Synthia *152:* 220; *188:* 90
Saldutti, Denise *39:* 186; *57:* 178
Sale, Morton *YABC 2:* 31
Sale, Tim *153:* 177
Salerno, Steven *150:* 79; *176:* 188
Salter, George *72:* 128, 130
Saltzberg, Barney *135:* 184, 185; *194:* 160
Saltzman, David *86:* 209
Salwowski, Mark *71:* 54
Salzman, Yuri *86:* 12
Sambourne, Linley *YABC 2:* 181
Sampson, Katherine *9:* 197
Samson, Anne S. *2:* 216
San Souci, Daniel *40:* 200; *96:* 199, 200; *113:* 171; *157:* 149; *170:* 69; *192:* 167, 168
Sancha, Sheila *38:* 185
Sanchez, Enrique O. *155:* 84
Sand, George X. *45:* 182
Sandberg, Lasse *15:* 239, 241
Sanders, Beryl *39:* 173
Sanderson, Ruth *21:* 126; *24:* 53; *28:* 63; *33:* 67; *41:* 48, 198, 199, 200, 201, 202, 203; *43:* 79; *46:* 36,44; *47:* 102; *49:* 58; *62:* 121, 122; *85:* 3; *109:* 207, 208, 209, 210; *172:* 157, 158
Sandia *119:* 74

Sandin, Joan *4:* 36; *6:* 194; *7:* 177; *12:* 145,185; *20:* 43; *21:* 74; *26:* 144; *27:* 142; *28:* 224, 225; *38:* 86; *41:* 46; *42:* 35; *59:* 6; *80:* 136; *94:* 188; *140:* 116; *153:* 179, 180; *197:* 168
Sandland, Reg *39:* 215
Sandoz, Edouard *26:* 45, 47
Sanford, John *66:* 96, 97
Sankey, Tom *72:* 103
Sano, Kazuhiko *153:* 208; *195:* 171
Santat, Dan *188:* 160
Santore, Charles *54:* 139
Santoro, Christopher *74:* 215
Santos, Jesse J. *99:* 24
Sapieha, Christine *1:* 180
Saport, Linda *123:* 137, 138
Sara
 See De La Roche Saint Andre, Anne
Sardinha, Rick *175:* 151
Sarg, Tony *YABC 2:* 236
Sargent, Claudia *64:* 181
Sargent, Robert *2:* 217
Saris *1:* 33
Sarony *YABC 2:* 170
Sasaki, Goro *170:* 46
Sasek, Miroslav *16:* 239, 240, 241, 242
Sassman, David *9:* 79
Satty *29:* 203, 205
Sauber, Robert *40:* 183; *76:* 256; *78:* 154; *87:* 92
Saunders, Dave *85:* 163, 164, 165
Savadier, Elivia *84:* 50; *145:* 45; *164:* 206
Savage, Naomi *56:* 172
Savage, Steele *10:* 203; *20:* 77; *35:* 28
Savage, Stephen *174:* 182
Savio *76:* 4
Savitt, Sam *8:* 66, 182; *15:* 278; *20:* 96; *24:* 192; *28:* 98
Sawyer, Kem Knapp *84:* 228, 229
Say, Allen *28:* 178; *69:* 182, 183, 232; *110:* 194, 195,196; *161:* 154, 155
Sayles, Elizabeth *82:* 93; *105:* 155; *109:* 116; *180:* 64
Scabrini, Janet *13:* 191; *44:* 128
Scanlan, Peter *83:* 27; *153:* 165; *187:* 149
Scanlon, Paul *83:* 87
Scannell, Reece *105:* 105
Scarry, Huck *35:* 204, 205
Scarry, Richard *2:* 220, 221; *18:* 20; *35:* 193, 194, 195,196, 197, 198, 199, 200, 201, 202; *75:* 165, 167, 168
Schachner, Judith Byron *88:* 180; *92:* 163; *93:* 102; *142:* 82; *178:* 199, 200; *190:* 140
Schaeffer, Mead *18:* 81, 94; *21:* 137, 138, 139; *47:* 128
Schaffer, Amanda *90:* 206
Schanzer, Rosalyn *138:* 192, 193
Scharl, Josef *20:* 132; *22:* 128
Scheel, Lita *11:* 230
Scheffler, Axel *180:* 23, 24
Scheib, Ida *29:* 28
Schermer, Judith *30:* 184
Schick, Eleanor *82:* 210, 211; *144:* 222
Schick, Joel *16:* 160; *17:* 167; *22:* 12; *27:* 176; *31:* 147, 148; *36:* 23; *38:* 64; *45:* 116, 117; *52:* 5, 85; *104:* 159
Schields, Gretchen *75:* 171, 203
Schindelman, Joseph *1:* 74; *4:* 101; *12:* 49; *26:* 51; *40:* 146; *56:* 158; *73:* 40
Schindler, Edith *7:* 22
Schindler, S.D. *38:* 107; *46:* 196; *74:* 162; *75:* 172, 173; *99:* 133; *112:* 177; *118:* 185, 186; *121:* 71; *136:* 159; *143:* 45; *149:* 120; *156:* 30; *169:* 135; *171:* 161, 162, 163; *172:* 9; *186:* 163; *194:* 109; *195:* 35
Schlesinger, Bret *7:* 77
Schmid, Eleanore *12:* 188; *126:* 196, 197
Schmiderer, Dorothy *19:* 224
Schmidt, Bill *73:* 34; *76:* 220, 222, 224
Schmidt, Elizabeth *15:* 242
Schmidt, George Paul *132:* 122

Schmidt, Karen Lee *54:* 12; *71:* 174; *92:* 56; *94:* 190, 191; *127:* 103
Schmidt, Lynette *76:* 205
Schneider, Christine M. *171:* 165
Schneider, Howie *181:* 159
Schneider, Rex *29:* 64; *44:* 171
Schnurr, Edward *170:* 62
Schoberle, Cecile *80:* 200; *92:* 134
Schoenherr, Ian *32:* 83; *173:* 41
Schoenherr, John *1:* 146, 147, 173; *3:* 39, 139; *17:* 75; *29:* 72; *32:* 83; *37:* 168, 169, 170; *43:* 164, 165; *45:* 160, 162; *51:* 127; 66; 196, 197, 198; *68:* 83; *72:* 240; *75:* 225; *88:* 176
Scholder, Fritz *69:* 103
Schomburg, Alex *13:* 23
Schongut, Emanuel *4:* 102; *15:* 186; *47:* 218, 219; *52:* 147, 148, 149, 150; *185:* 27
Schoonover, Frank *17:* 107; *19:* 81, 190, 233; *22:* 88,129; *24:* 189; *31:* 88; *41:* 69; *YABC 2:* 282, 316
Schories, Pat *164:* 210
Schottland, Miriam *22:* 172
Schramm, Ulrik *2:* 16; *14:* 112
Schreiber, Elizabeth Anne *13:* 193
Schreiber, Ralph W. *13:* 193
Schreiter, Rick *14:* 97; *23:* 171; *41:* 247; *49:* 131
Schroeder, Binette *56:* 128, 129
Schroeder, E. Peter *12:* 112
Schroeder, Ted *11:* 160; *15:* 189; *30:* 91; *34:* 43
Schrotter, Gustav *22:* 212; *30:* 225
Schubert, Dieter *101:* 167, 168
Schubert-Gabrys, Ingrid *101:* 167, 168
Schucker, James *31:* 163
Schuett, Stacey *72:* 137
Schulder, Lili *146:* 29
Schulke, Debra *57:* 167
Schulke, Flip *57:* 167
Schulz, Barbara *167:* 24
Schulz, Charles M. *10:* 137, 138, 139, 140, 141, 142; *118:* 192, 193, 194, 196, 199
Schutzer, Dena *109:* 32
Schwark, Mary Beth *51:* 155; *72:* 175
Schwartz, Amy *47:* 191; *82:* 100; *83:* 178, 179, 180,181; *129:* 107; *131:* 197, 198; *189:* 166, 168
Schwartz, Carol *124:* 41; *130:* 199
Schwartz, Charles *8:* 184
Schwartz, Daniel *46:* 37
Schwartz, Joanie *124:* 170
Schwartzberg, Joan *3:* 208
Schweitzer, Iris *2:* 137; *6:* 207
Schweninger, Ann *29:* 172; *82:* 246; *159:* 202; *168:* 166
Schwinger, Laurence *84:* 44; *91:* 61
Scofield, Penrod *61:* 107; *62:* 160
Scott, Anita Walker *7:* 38
Scott, Art *39:* 41
Scott, Frances Gruse *38:* 43
Scott, Julian *34:* 126
Scott, Roszel *33:* 238
Scott, Sally *87:* 27
Scott, Steve *166:* 230, 231; *171:* 93
Scott, Trudy *27:* 172
Scrace, Carolyn *143:* 95, 96
Scribner, Joanne *14:* 236; *29:* 78; *33:* 185; *34:* 208; *78:* 75; *164:* 237
Scrofani, Joseph *31:* 65; *74:* 225
Scroggs, Kirk *187:* 169
Seaman, Mary Lott *34:* 64
Searle, Ronald *24:* 98; *42:* 172, 173, 174, 176, 177, 179; *66:* 73, 74; *70:* 205, 206, 207
Searle, Townley *36:* 85
Sebree, Charles *18:* 65
Sedacca, Joseph M. *11:* 25; *22:* 36
Seder, Jason *108:* 102
Seeger, Laura Vaccaro *172:* 162
Seegmiller, Don *174:* 57
Seely, David *164:* 173

Seeley, Laura L. *97:* 105
Segal, John *178:* 202
Segar, E.C. *61:* 179, 181
Segur, Adrienne *27:* 121
Seibold, J. Otto *83:* 188, 190, 191; *149:* 212, 214, 215, 216; *196:* 177, 179
Seignobosc, Francoise *21:* 145, 146
Sejima, Yoshimasa *8:* 187
Selig, Sylvie *13:* 199
Seltzer, Isadore *6:* 18; *133:* 59
Seltzer, Meyer *17:* 214
Selven, Maniam *144:* 133
Selway, Martina *169:* 157
Selznick, Brian *79:* 192; *104:* 25; *117:* 175; *126:* 156; *134:* 171; *158:* 76, 78; *169:* 70; *171:* 172, 173; *191:* 106; *192:* 130; *197:* 158
Sempe, Jean-Jacques *47:* 92; *YABC 2:* 109
Sendak, Maurice *1:* 135, 190; *3:* 204; *7:* 142; *15:* 199; *17:* 210; *27:* 181, 182, 183, 185, 186, 187, 189,190, 191, 192, 193, 194, 195, 197, 198, 199, 203; *28:* 181, 182; *32:* 108; *33:* 148, 149; *35:* 238; *44:* 180, 181; *45:* 97, 99; *46:* 174; *73:* 225; *91:* 10, 11 *YABC1:* 167; *113:* 163, 165, 167, 168; *118:* 153; *127:* 161
Senders, Marci *180:* 79
Sengler, Johanna *18:* 256
Senn, Steve *60:* 145
Seredy, Kate *1:* 192; *14:* 20, 21; *17:* 210
Sergeant, John *6:* 74
Servello, Joe *10:* 144; *24:* 139; *40:* 91; *70:* 130, 131; *146:* 159
Seton, Ernest Thompson *18:* 260-269, 271
Seuss, Dr.
  See Geisel, Theodor
Severin, John Powers *7:* 62
Sewall, Marcia *15:* 8; *22:* 170; *37:* 171, 172, 173; *39:* 73; *45:* 209; *62:* 117; *69:* 185, 186; *71:* 212; *90:* 232; *96:* 127; *102:* 101; *107:* 129; *119:* 176, 177, 178, 180
Seward, James *70:* 35
Seward, Prudence *16:* 243
Sewell, Helen *3:* 186; *15:* 308; *33:* 102; *38:* 189, 190, 191, 192
Seymour, Stephen *54:* 21
Sfar, Joann *182:* 183
Shachat, Andrew *82:* 179
Shahn, Ben *39:* 178; *46:* 193
Shalansky, Len *38:* 167
Shanks, Anne Zane *10:* 149
Shannon, David *57:* 137; *107:* 184; *112:* 216; *135:* 12; *152:* 223, 224, 225; *158:* 192
Sharp, Paul *52:* 60
Sharp, William *6:* 131; *19:* 241; *20:* 112; *25:* 141
Sharratt, Nick *102:* 207, 208; *104:* 163; *153:* 198; *175:* 176; *192:* 208
Shaw, Barclay *74:* 14, 16; *118:* 138
Shaw, Charles *21:* 135; *38:* 187; *47:* 124; *126:* 219
Shaw, Charles G. *13:* 200
Shaw-Smith, Emma *144:* 117
Shea, Edmund *56:* 19
Shearer, Ted *43:* 193, 194, 195, 196
Sheban, Chris *182:* 185; *190:* 102, 104
Shecter, Ben *16:* 244; *25:* 109; *33:* 188, 191; *41:* 77
Shed, Greg *74:* 94; *84:* 204; *129:* 149, 167: 91; *179:* 192
Sheeban, Chris *144:* 190; *158:* 163
Shefcik, James *48:* 221, 222; *60:* 141
Shefelman, Karl *58:* 168
Shefts, Joelle *48:* 210
Shein, Bob *139:* 189
Shekerjian, Haig *16:* 245
Shekerjian, Regina *16:* 245; *25:* 73
Sheldon, David *184:* 174; *185:* 204
Shelley, John *186:* 223
Shemie, Bonnie *96:* 207
Shenton, Edward *45:* 187, 188, 189; *YABC 1:* 218, 219, 221

Shepard, Ernest H. *3:* 193; *4:* 74; *16:* 101; *17:* 109; *25:* 148; *33:* 152, 199, 200, 201, 202, 203, 204, 205, 206,207; *46:* 194; *98:* 114; *100:* 111, 178, 179, 217, 219, 220,221; *YABC 1:* 148, 153, 174, 176, 180, 181
Shepard, Mary *4:* 210; *22:* 205; *30:* 132, 133; *54:* 150, 152, 153, 157, 158; *59:* 108, 109, 111; *100:* 246
Shepherd, Irana *171:* 112
Sheppard, Kate *195:* 176
Shepperson, Rob *96:* 153; *177:* 163; *178:* 204; *197:* 34
Sheridan, Brian *196:* 193
Sherman, Theresa *27:* 167
Sherwan, Earl *3:* 196
Shields, Charles *10:* 150; *36:* 63
Shields, Leonard *13:* 83, 85, 87
Shiffman, Lena *139:* 167; *168:* 136
Shigley, Neil K. *66:* 219
Shillabeer, Mary *35:* 74
Shilston, Arthur *49:* 61; *62:* 58
Shimin, Symeon *1:* 93; *2:* 128, 129; *3:* 202; *7:* 85; *11:* 177; *12:* 139; *13:* 202, 203; *27:* 138; *28:* 65; *35:* 129; *36:* 130; *48:* 151; *49:* 59; *56:* 63, 65, 153
Shine, Andrea *104:* 165; *128:* 34
Shinn, Everett *16:* 148; *18:* 229; *21:* 149, 150, 151; *24:* 218
Shinn, Florence Scovel *63:* 133, 135
Shore, Robert *27:* 54; *39:* 192, 193; *YABC 2:* 200
Shortall, Leonard *4:* 144; *8:* 196; *10:* 166; *19:* 227, 228, 229, 230; *25:* 78; *28:* 66, 167; *33:* 127; *52:* 125; *73:* 12, 212
Shortt, T.M. *27:* 36
Shpitalnik, Vladimir *83:* 194
Shropshire, Sandy *170:* 191
Shtainments, Leon *32:* 161
Shulevitz, Uri *3:* 198, 199; *17:* 85; *22:* 204; *27:* 212; *28:* 184; *50:* 190, 191, 192, 193, 194, 195, 196,197, 198, 199, 201; *106:* 181, 182, 183; *165:* 203, 205; *166:* 138
Shulman, Dee *180:* 140
Shupe, Bobbi *139:* 80, 81
Shute, A.B. *67:* 196
Shute, Linda *46:* 59; *74:* 118
Siberell, Anne *29:* 193
Sibley, Don *1:* 39; *12:* 196; *31:* 47
Sibthorp, Fletcher *94:* 111, 112
Sidjakov, Nicolas *18:* 274
Siebel, Fritz *3:* 120; *17:* 145
Siebold, J. Otto *158:* 227
Siegel, Hal *74:* 246
Sieger, Ted *189:* 172
Siegl, Helen *12:* 166; *23:* 216; *34:* 185, 186
Silin-Palmer, Pamela *184:* 102
Sill, John *140:* 194; *141:* 157
Sills, Joyce *5:* 199
Silva, Simon *108:* 122
Silver, Maggie *85:* 210
Silveria, Gordon *96:* 44
Silverstein, Alvin *8:* 189
Silverstein, Shel *33:* 211; *92:* 209, 210
Silverstein, Virginia *8:* 189
Silvey, Joe *135:* 203
Simard, Remy *95:* 156
Simmons, Elly *110:* 2; *127:* 69; *134:* 181
Simon, Eric M. *7:* 82
Simon, Hilda *28:* 189
Simon, Howard *2:* 175; *5:* 132; *19:* 199; *32:* 163, 164, 165
Simont, Marc *2:* 119; *4:* 213; *9:* 168; *13:* 238,240; *14:* 262; *16:* 179; *18:* 221; *26:* 210; *33:* 189, 190; *44:* 132; *58:* 122; *68:* 117; *73:* 204, 205, 206; *74:* 221; *126:* 199, 200; *133:* 195; *164:* 128
Sims, Agnes *54:* 152
Sims, Blanche *44:* 116; *57:* 129; *75:* 179, 180; *77:* 92; *104:* 192; *152:* 117; *156:* 160; *160:* 70; *168:* 174, 175
Singer, Edith G. *2:* 30

Singer, Gloria *34:* 56; *36:* 43
Singer, Julia *28:* 190
Singh, Jen *178:* 146
Siomades, Lorianne *134:* 45
Simont, Marc *163:* 40
Siracusa, Catherine *68:* 135; *82:* 218
Sís, Peter *67:* 179, 181, 183, 184, 185; *96:* 96, 98; *106:* 193, 194, 195; *149:* 224, 226; *180:* 177; *192:* 180, 182
Sivard, Robert *26:* 124
Sivertson, Liz *116:* 84
Skardinski, Stanley *23:* 144; *32:* 84; *66:* 122; *84:* 108
Slack, Michael *185:* 108; *189:* 173, 174
Slackman, Charles B. *12:* 201
Slade, Christian *193:* 187
Slade, Paul *61:* 170
Slark, Albert *99:* 212
Slater, Rod *25:* 167
Slavin, Bill *182:* 14, 15; *196:* 90
Sloan, Joseph *16:* 68
Sloane, Eric *21:* 3; *52:* 153, 154, 155, 156, 157, 158, 160
Sloat, Teri *164:* 231
Slobodkin, Louis *1:* 200; *3:* 232; *5:* 168; *13:* 251; *15:* 13, 88; *26:* 173, 174, 175, 176, 178, 179; *60:* 180
Slobodkina, Esphyr *1:* 201
Slonim, David *166:* 167, 168
Small, David *50:* 204, 205; *79:* 44; *95:* 189, 190, 191; *126:* 203, 204; *136:* 119; *143:* 201, 202, 203; *144:* 246; *150:* 5; *161:* 176; *183:* 181, 182, 183, 184
Small, W. *33:* 113
Smalley, Janet *1:* 154
Smedley, William T. *34:* 129
Smee, David *14:* 78; *62:* 30
Smee, Nicola *167:* 156
Smith, A.G., Jr. *35:* 182
Smith, Alvin *1:* 31, 229; *13:* 187; *27:* 216; *28:* 226; *48:* 149; *49:* 60
Smith, Andy *188:* 20
Smith, Anne *194:* 147
Smith, Anne Warren *41:* 212
Smith, Barry *75:* 183
Smith, Carl *36:* 41
Smith, Cat Bowman *146:* 39; *164:* 219
Smith, Craig *97:* 197; *172:* 175
Smith, Donald A. *178:* 7
Smith, Doris Susan *41:* 139
Smith, Douglas *189:* 159
Smith, Duane *171:* 152
Smith, E. Boyd *19:* 70; *22:* 89; *26:* 63; *YABC 1:* 4, 5, 240, 248, 249
Smith, Edward J. *4:* 224
Smith, Elwood H. *157:* 231; *181:* 79
Smith, Eunice Young *5:* 170
Smith, Gary *113:* 216
Smith, George *102:* 169
Smith, Howard *19:* 196
Smith, J. Gerard *95:* 42
Smith, Jacqueline Bardner *27:* 108; *39:* 197
Smith, Jay J. *61:* 119
Smith, Jeff *93:* 191
Smith, Jessie Willcox *15:* 91; *16:* 95; *18:* 231; *19:* 57, 242; *21:* 29, 156, 157, 158, 159, 160, 161; *34:* 65; *100:* 223; *YABC 1:* 6; *2:* 180, 185, 191, 311, 325
Smith, Jos. A. *52:* 131; *72:* 120; *74:* 151; *84:* 147, 148; *85:* 146; *87:* 96; *94:* 219; *96:* 97; *104:* 33; *108:* 126, 127, 128; *111:* 140; *136:* 145; *181:* 173
Smith, Kenneth R. *47:* 182
Smith, Kevin Warren *89:* 112
Smith, L.H. *35:* 174
Smith, Lane *76:* 211, 213; *88:* 115; *105:* 202, 203, 204, 205; *131:* 207; *160:* 217, 221; *179:* 183, 184, 185, 186
Smith, Lee *29:* 32
Smith, Linell Nash *2:* 195

Smith, Maggie Kaufman *13:* 205; *35:* 191; *110:* 158; *178:* 226; *190:* 204
Smith, Mavis *101:* 219
Smith, Moishe *33:* 155
Smith, Philip *44:* 134; *46:* 203
Smith, Ralph Crosby *2:* 267; *49:* 203
Smith, Robert D. *5:* 63
Smith, Sally J. *84:* 55
Smith, Susan Carlton *12:* 208
Smith, Terry *12:* 106; *33:* 158
Smith, Virginia *3:* 157; *33:* 72
Smith, William A. *1:* 36; *10:* 154; *25:* 65
Smith-Moore, J.J. *98:* 147
Smolinski, Dick *84:* 217
Smoljan, Joe *112:* 201
Smollin, Mike *39:* 203
Smyth, Iain *105:* 207
Smyth, M. Jane *12:* 15
Smythe, Fiona *151:* 213
Smythe, Theresa *141:* 37
Snair, Andy *176:* 4
Sneed, Brad *125:* 25; *191:* 175, 176
Snyder, Andrew A. *30:* 212
Snyder, Jerome *13:* 207; *30:* 173
Snyder, Joel *28:* 163
So, Meilo *162:* 201
Soentpiet, Chris K. *97:* 208; *110:* 33; *159:* 184; *161:* 10; *163:* 130
Sofia *1:* 62; *5:* 90; *32:* 166; *86:* 43
Sofilas, Mark *93:* 157
Sohn, Jiho *182:* 78
Sokol, Bill *37:* 178; *49:* 23
Sokolov, Kirill *34:* 188
Solbert, Ronni *1:* 159; *2:* 232; *5:* 121; *6:* 34; *17:* 249
Solomon, Michael *174:* 115
Solonevich, George *15:* 246; *17:* 47
Soma, Liana *81:* 118
Soman, David *90:* 122; *102:* 126; *140:* 120; *93:* 188; *188:* 43, 89
Sommer, Robert *12:* 211
Sorel, Edward *4:* 61; *36:* 82; *65:* 191, 193; *126:* 214
Sorensen, Henri *196:* 58
Sorensen, Henrik *62:* 16
Sorensen, Svend Otto *22:* 130, 141; *67:* 188, 189
Sorra, Kristin *155:* 80
Sostre, Maria *187:* 36
Sotomayor, Antonio *11:* 215
Souhami, Jessica *112:* 128; *176:* 193
Souza, Diana *71:* 139
Sovak, Jan *115:* 190
Soyer, Moses *20:* 177
Spaenkuch, August *16:* 28
Spafford, Suzy *160:* 228
Spain, Valerie *105:* 76
Spain, Sunday Sahara *133:* 204
Spalenka, Greg *149:* 69; *151:* 228; *184:* 195; *191:* 21; *196:* 12
Spanfeller, James *1:* 72, 149; *2:* 183; *19:* 230, 231,232; *22:* 66; *36:* 160, 161; *40:* 75; *52:* 166; *76:* 37
Sparks, Mary Walker *15:* 247
Spears, Rick *182:* 187
Speidel, Sandra *78:* 233; *94:* 178; *134:* 180
Speirs, John *67:* 178
Spence, Geraldine *21:* 163; *47:* 196
Spence, Jim *38:* 89; *50:* 102
Spencer, Laurie *113:* 12
Spencer, Mark *57:* 170
Spengler, Kenneth J. *146:* 256
Sperling, Andrea *133:* 182
Spiegel, Beth *184:* 203
Spiegel, Doris *29:* 111
Spiegelman, Art *109:* 227
Spier, Jo *10:* 30
Spier, Peter *3:* 155; *4:* 200; *7:* 61; *11:* 78; *38:* 106; *54:* 120, 121, 122, 123, 124, 125, 126, 127, 128, 129, 130,131, 132, 133, 134
Spilka, Arnold *5:* 120; *6:* 204; *8:* 131

Spirin, Gennady *95:* 196, 197; *113:* 172; *128:* 9; *129:* 49; *134:* 210; *153:* 9
Spivak, I. Howard *8:* 10; *13:* 172
Spohn, David *72:* 233
Spohn, Kate *87:* 195; *147:* 201, 202
Spollen, Christopher J. *12:* 214
Spooner, Malcolm *40:* 142
Spowart, Robin *82:* 228; *92:* 149; *133:* 131; *176:* 163; *177:* 183, 184
Sprague, Kevin *150:* 60; *196:* 62
Sprattler, Rob *12:* 176
Spring, Bob *5:* 60
Spring, Ira *5:* 60
Springer, Harriet *31:* 92
Spudvilas, Anne *110:* 74; *197:* 192
Spurll, Barbara *78:* 199; *88:* 141, 142; *99:* 215
Spurrier, Steven *28:* 198
Spuvilas, Anne *85:* 114
Spy
    See Ward, Leslie
Squires, Stuart *127:* 74
St. Aubin, Bruno *179:* 54
St. John, J. Allen *41:* 62
Stabin, Victor *101:* 131; *164:* 158
Stadler, John *62:* 33
Staffan, Alvin E. *11:* 56; *12:* 187
Stahl, Ben *5:* 181; *12:* 91; *49:* 122; *71:* 128; *87:* 206; *112:* 107
Stair, Gobin *35:* 214
Stallwood, Karen *73:* 126
Stamaty, Mark Alan *12:* 215
Stammen, JoEllen McAllister *113:* 14
Stampnick, Ken *51:* 142
Stanbridge, Joanne *150:* 91
Stanley, Diane *3:* 45; *37:* 180; *80:* 217, 219
Stanley, Sanna *145:* 228
Starcke, Helmut *86:* 217
Stark, Ken *197:* 102
Starr, Branka *73:* 25
Stasiak, Krystyna *49:* 181; *64:* 194
Staub, Leslie *103:* 54
Staunton, Ted *112:* 192
Stawicki, Matt *164:* 250
Stead, L. *55:* 51, 56
Steadman, Broeck *97:* 185, 186; *99:* 56; *121:* 48
Steadman, Ralph *32:* 180; *123:* 143, 145
Stearn, Nick *183:* 26
Steckler, June *90:* 178
Steele, Robert Gantt *169:* 174
Steichen, Edward *30:* 79
Steig, William *18:* 275, 276; *70:* 215, 216, 217, 218; *111:* 173, 174, 175, 176, 177
Stein, Harve *1:* 109
Steinberg, Saul *47:* 193
Steinel, William *23:* 146
Steiner, Charlotte *45:* 196
Steiner, Joan *110:* 219
Steirnagel, Michael *80:* 56
Stemp, Eric *60:* 184
Stephens, Alice Barber *66:* 208, 209
Stephens, Charles H. *YABC 2:* 279
Stephens, Pat *126:* 110; *128:* 101
Stephens, William M. *21:* 165
Steptoe, Javaka *151:* 203, 204; *190:* 169
Steptoe, John *8:* 197; *57:* 9; *63:* 158, 159, 160, 161,163, 164, 165, 166, 167; *96:* 4; *105:* 87
Stern, Simon *15:* 249, 250; *17:* 58; *34:* 192, 193
Sterret, Jane *53:* 27
Stetsios, Debbie *165:* 108, 109
Steven, Kat *158:* 237
Stevens, David *62:* 44
Stevens, Helen *189:* 31
Stevens, Janet *40:* 126; *57:* 10, 11; *80:* 112; *90:* 221, 222; *109:* 156; *130:* 34; *166:* 202; *176:* 53, 116; *193:* 199, 200, 202
Stevens, Mary *11:* 193; *13:* 129; *43:* 95
Stevenson, Harvey *66:* 143; *80:* 201, 221; *153:* 60; *191:* 166

Stevenson, James *42:* 182, 183; *51:* 163; *66:* 184; *71:* 185, 187, 188; *78:* 262; *87:* 97; *113:* 182, 183,184, 185; *161:* 182, 183
Stevenson, Sucie *92:* 27; *104:* 194, 195; *112:* 168; *160:* 202; *194:* 172, 173; *195:* 166
Stewart, April Blair *75:* 210
Stewart, Arvis *33:* 98; *36:* 69; *60:* 118; *75:* 91; *127:* 4
Stewart, Charles *2:* 205
Stewart, Joel *151:* 205
Stieg, William *172:* 58
Stiles, Fran *26:* 85; *78:* 56; *82:* 150
Stillman, Susan *44:* 130; *76:* 83
Stimpson, Tom *49:* 171
Stinemetz, Morgan *40:* 151
Stinson, Paul *110:* 86
Stirnweis, Shannon *10:* 164
Stites, Joe *86:* 96
Stobbs, William *1:* 48, 49; *3:* 68; *6:* 20; *17:* 117, 217; *24:* 150; *29:* 250; *60:* 179; *87:* 204, 205,206
Stock, Catherine *37:* 55; *65:* 198; *72:* 7; *99:* 225; *114:* 197, 198, 199; *126:* 3; *145:* 161; *161:* 82; *173:* 149
Stockman, Jack *113:* 24
Stoeke, Janet Morgan *90:* 225; *136:* 196
Stoerrle, Tom *55:* 147
Stolp, Jaap *49:* 98
Stolp, Todd *89:* 195
Stone, David L. *87:* 154
Stone, David *9:* 173
Stone, David K. *4:* 38; *6:* 124; *9:* 180; *43:* 182; *60:* 70
Stone, Helen V. *6:* 209
Stone, Helen *44:* 121, 122, 126
Stone, Kazuko G. *134:* 43
Stone, Phoebe *86:* 212; *134:* 213; *162:* 188
Stone, Steve *166:* 213
Stone, Tony *150:* 34, 35
Storrings, Michael *191:* 108
Stoud, Virginia A. *89:* 31
Stover, Jill *82:* 234
Stratton, Helen *33:* 151
Stratton-Porter, Gene *15:* 254, 259, 263, 264, 268, 269
Straub, Matt *192:* 176
Straub, Phillip *197:* 22
Streano, Vince *20:* 173
Street, Janet Travell *84:* 235
Streeter, Clive *121:* 2
Stringer, Lauren *129:* 187; *154:* 172, 173; *161:* 127; *183:* 187, 188
Strodl, Daniel *47:* 95
Strogart, Alexander *63:* 139
Stromoski, Rick *111:* 179; *124:* 161, 190
Strong, Joseph D., Jr. *YABC 2:* 330
Stroyer, Poul *13:* 221
Strugnell, Ann *27:* 38
Struzan, Drew *117:* 6
Stubbs, William *73:* 196
Stubis, Talivaldis *5:* 182, 183; *10:* 45; *11:* 9; *18:* 304; *20:* 127
Stubley, Trevor *14:* 43; *22:* 219; *23:* 37; *28:* 61; *87:* 26
Stuck, Marion *104:* 44
Stuecklen, Karl W. *8:* 34, 65; *23:* 103
Stull, Betty *11:* 46
Stutzman, Mark *119:* 99
Stutzmann, Laura *73:* 185
Suarez, Maribel *162:* 208
Suba, Susanne *4:* 202, 203; *14:* 261; *23:* 134; *29:* 222; *32:* 30
Sueling, Barbara *98:* 185
Sueling, Gwenn *98:* 186
Sugarman, Tracy *3:* 76; *8:* 199; *37:* 181, 182
Sugimoto, Yugo *170:* 144
Sugita, Yutaka *36:* 180, 181
Suh, John *80:* 157
Sullivan, Dorothy *89:* 113
Sullivan, Edmund J. *31:* 86
Sullivan, James F. *19:* 280; *20:* 192

Sully, Tom *104:* 199, 200; *182:* 77
Sumichrast, Jozef *14:* 253; *29:* 168, 213
Sumiko *46:* 57
Summers, Leo *1:* 177; *2:* 273; *13:* 22
Summers, Mark *118:* 144
Summers, Mike *190:* 176
Sutton, Judith *94:* 164
Svarez, Juan *56:* 113
Svendsen, Mark *181:* 176
Svolinsky, Karel *17:* 104
Swain, Carol *172:* 182
Swain, Su Zan Noguchi *21:* 170
Swan, Susan *22:* 220, 221; *37:* 66; *60:* 146; *145:* 205; *181:* 168
Swann, Susan *86:* 55
Swanson, Karl *79:* 65; *89:* 186
Swayne, Sam *53:* 143, 145
Swayne, Zoa *53:* 143, 145
Swearingen, Greg *152:* 56; *165:* 135; *173:* 2
Sweat, Lynn *25:* 206; *57:* 176; *73:* 184; *168:* 178
Sweet, Darrell K. *60:* 9; *69:* 86; *74:* 15; *75:* 215; *76:* 130, 131; *81:* 96, 122; *82:* 253; *83:* 11; *84:* 14; *85:* 37; *89:* 140; *90:* 6; *91:* 137,139; *95:* 160, 161; *126:* 25; *185:* 175; *195:* 132
Sweet, Darrell K. *1:* 163; *4:* 136; *164:* 175
Sweet, Melissa *71:* 94; *72:* 172; *111:* 82; *139:* 53, 58; *141:* 88; *142:* 231; *155:* 121; *159:* 121, 122; *172:* 185; *188:* 127
Sweet, Ozzie *31:* 149, 151, 152
Sweetland, Robert *12:* 194
Swiatkowska, Gabi *132:* 43; *175:* 139; *180:* 218; *183:* 176
Swope, Martha *43:* 160; *56:* 86, 87, 89
Sylvada, Peter *154:* 174
Sylvester, Natalie G. *22:* 222
Szafran, Gene *24:* 144
Szasz, Susanne *13:* 55, 226; *14:* 48
Szekeres, Cyndy *2:* 218; *5:* 185; *8:* 85; *11:* 166; *14:* 19; *16:* 57, 159; *26:* 49, 214; *34:* 205; *60:* 150, 151, 152, 153, 154; *73:* 224; *74:* 218; *131:* 213, 215
Szpura, Beata *81:* 68; *119:* 65; *168:* 201

T

Taback, Simms *40:* 207; *52:* 120; *57:* 34; *80:* 241; *104:* 202, 203; *170:* 176, 177
Taber, Patricia *75:* 124
Tabor, Nancy Maria Grande *89:* 210; *161:* 188
Taddei, Richard *112:* 13, 14
Tadgell, Nicole *150:* 77; *161:* 20; *177:* 186
Tadiello, Ed *133:* 200
Tafuri, Nancy *39:* 210; *75:* 199, 200; *92:* 75; *130:* 215, 216, 217
Tailfeathers, Gerald *86:* 85
Tait, Douglas *12:* 220; *74:* 105, 106
Takabayashi, Mari *113:* 112; *130:* 22; *156:* 169
Takahashi, Hideko *136:* 160; *187:* 6
Takakjian, Portia *15:* 274
Takashima, Shizuye *13:* 228
Talarczyk, June *4:* 173
Talbott, Hudson *84:* 240; *163:* 100
Tallarico, Tony *116:* 197
Tallon, Robert *2:* 228; *43:* 200, 201, 202, 203, 204, 205,206, 207, 209
Tamas, Szecsko *29:* 135
Tamburine, Jean *12:* 222
Tandy, H.R. *13:* 69
Tandy, Russell H. *65:* 9; *100:* 30, 131
Tang, Charles *81:* 202; *90:* 192
Tang, Susan *80:* 174; *108:* 158
Tang, You-shan *63:* 100
Tankersley, Paul *69:* 206; *133:* 219
Tannenbaum, Robert *48:* 181
Tanner, Jane *87:* 13; *97:* 37
Tanner, Tim *72:* 192; *84:* 35
Tanobe, Miyuki *23:* 221

Tarabay, Sharif *110:* 149; *113:* 123; *169:* 83
Tarkington, Booth *17:* 224, 225
Tarlow, Phyllis *61:* 198
Tate, Don *159:* 141, 191; *183:* 69; *186:* 120
Tauss, Herbert *95:* 179
Tauss, Marc *117:* 160; *126:* 155; *178:* 221; *197:* 7
Tavares, Matt *159:* 192, 193
Taylor, Ann *41:* 226
Taylor, Dahl *129:* 157
Taylor, Geoff *93:* 156; *197:* 173, 175
Taylor, Isaac *41:* 228
Taylor, Mike *143:* 99, 100
Teague, Mark *83:* 6; *139:* 241; *170:* 180, 181
Teale, Edwin Way *7:* 196
Teason, James *1:* 14
Teeple, Lyn *33:* 147
Tee-Van, Helen Damrosch *10:* 176; *11:* 182
Teicher, Dick *50:* 211
Teichman, Mary *77:* 220; *124:* 208; *127:* 22; *197:* 33
Temertey, Ludmilla *96:* 232; *104:* 43, 45; *109:* 244
Tempest, Margaret *3:* 237, 238; *88:* 200
Temple, Frances *85:* 185, 186, 187
Temple, Herbert *45:* 201
Templeton, Owen *11:* 77
ten Cate, Marijke *183:* 193
Tenggren, Gustaf *18:* 277, 278, 279; *19:* 15; *28:* 86; *YABC2:* 145
Tennent, Julie *81:* 105
Tenneson, Joyce *153:* 166
Tenney, Gordon *24:* 204
Tenniel, John *74:* 234, 235; *100:* 89; *YABC 2:* 99; *153:* 63
Tepper, Matt *116:* 80
Terkel, Ari *103:* 162
Terry, Michael *180:* 209
Terry, Will *131:* 73
Teskey, Donald *71:* 51
Thacher, Mary M. *30:* 72
Thackeray, William Makepeace *23:* 224, 228
Thamer, Katie *42:* 187
Tharlet, Eve *146:* 149
Thelwell, Norman *14:* 201
Theobalds, Prue *40:* 23
Theurer, Marilyn Churchill *39:* 195
Thiesing, Lisa *89:* 134; *95:* 202; *156:* 190; *159:* 195
Thiewes, Sam *133:* 114
Thistlethwaite, Miles *12:* 224
Thollander, Earl *11:* 47; *18:* 112; *22:* 224
Thomas, Allan *22:* 13
Thomas, Art *48:* 217
Thomas, Eric *28:* 49
Thomas, Harold *20:* 98
Thomas, Jacqui *125:* 95
Thomas, Jan *197:* 180
Thomas, Mark *42:* 136
Thomas, Martin *14:* 255
Thomas, Middy *177:* 114
Thompson, Arthur *34:* 107
Thompson, Carol *85:* 189; *95:* 75; *102:* 86; *147:* 166; *189:* 179, 180, 181; *190:* 84
Thompson, Colin *95:* 204
Thompson, Ellen *51:* 88, 151; *60:* 33; *67:* 42; *77:* 148; *78:* 75, 219; *79:* 122, 170; *84:* 219; *85:* 97; *87:* 37; *88:* 192, 194; *89:* 80; *93:* 37; *98:* 59; *132:* 14
Thompson, George W. *22:* 18; *28:* 150; *33:* 135
Thompson, John *58:* 201; *102:* 226; *124:* 154; *128:* 228; *129:* 157; *150:* 49; *185:* 160; *191:* 192
Thompson, Julie *44:* 158
Thompson, Katherine *132:* 146
Thompson, K. Dyble *84:* 6
Thompson, Miles *152:* 77
Thompson, Sharon *74:* 113; *158:* 60; *165:* 87
Thomson, Arline K. *3:* 264
Thomson, Bill *186:* 160

Illustrations Index

Thomson, Hugh 26: 88
Thomson, Ross 36: 179
Thorkelson, Gregg 95: 183, 184; 98: 58; 165: 30, 31
Thorn, Lori 189: 119
Thornberg, Dan 104: 125
Thornburgh, Rebecca McKillip 143: 37
Thorne, Diana 25: 212
Thornhill, Jan 77: 213
Thorpe, Peter 58: 109
Thorvall, Kerstin 13: 235
Threadgall, Colin 77: 215
Thurber, James 13: 239, 242, 243, 245, 248, 249
Thurman, Mark 63: 173; 168: 116
Tibbles, Jean-Paul 115: 200
Tibbles, Paul 45: 23
Tibo, Gilles 67: 207; 107: 199, 201
Tichenor, Tom 14: 207
Tichnor, Richard 90: 218
Tiegreen, Alan 36: 143; 43: 55, 56, 58; 77: 200; 94: 216, 217; 121: 54, 59
Tierney, Tom 113: 198, 200, 201
Tilley, Debbie 102: 134; 133: 226; 137: 101; 159: 96; 190: 211, 212
Tilney, F.C. 22: 231
Timbs, Gloria 36: 90
Timmins, Harry 2: 171
Timmons, Bonnie 194: 189
Tinkelman, Murray 12: 225; 35: 44
Titherington, Jeanne 39: 90; 58: 138; 75: 79; 135: 161
Tobin, Nancy 145: 197
Toddy, Irving 172: 144
Tokunbo, Dimitrea 181: 183; 187: 182, 183
Tolbert, Jeff 128: 69
Toledo, Francisco 197: 182
Toledo, Natalia 197: 182
Tolford, Joshua 1: 221
Tolkien, J.R.R. 2: 243; 32: 215
Tolman, Marije 195: 43
Tolmie, Ken 15: 292
Tomei, Lorna 47: 168, 171
Tomes, Jacqueline 2: 117; 12: 139
Tomes, Margot 1: 224; 2: 120, 121; 16: 207; 18: 250; 20: 7; 25: 62; 27: 78, 79; 29: 81, 199; 33: 82; 36: 186, 187, 188, 189, 190; 46: 129; 56: 71; 58: 183; 70: 228; 75: 73, 75; 80: 80; 83: 97; 90: 205
Toner, Raymond John 10: 179
Tong, Gary 66: 215
Tongier, Stephen 82: 32
Tooke, Susan 173: 162
Toothill, Harry 6: 54; 7: 49; 25: 219; 42: 192
Toothill, Ilse 6: 54
Topolski, Feliks 44: 48
Torbert, Floyd James 22: 226
Torgersen, Don 55: 157
Torline, Kevin 169: 171
Tormey, Bertram M. 75: 3, 4
Torrecilla, Pablo 176: 207
Torres, Leyla 156: 199, 201
Torrey, Helen 87: 41
Torrey, Marjorie 34: 105
Torrey, Richard 189: 182
Toschik, Larry 6: 102
Totten, Bob 13: 93
Toy, Julie 128: 112
Trachok, Cathy 131: 16
Tracy, Libba 82: 24
Trago, Keith 158: 253
Trail, Lee 55: 157
Trang, To Ngoc 167: 180
Trang, Winson 89: 151
Trapani, Iza 116: 202
Travers, Bob 49: 100; 63: 145
Treatner, Meryl 95: 180
Tremain, Ruthven 17: 238
Tresilian, Stuart 25: 53; 40: 212
Trez, Alain 17: 236
Trezzo, Loretta 86: 45

Trier, Walter 14: 96
Trimby, Elisa 47: 199
Trinkle, Sally 53: 27
Triplett, Gina 182: 193; 188: 100
Tripp, F.J. 24: 167
Tripp, Wallace 2: 48; 7: 28; 8: 94; 10: 54,76; 11: 92; 31: 170, 171; 34: 203; 42: 57; 60: 157; 73: 182
Trivas, Irene 53: 4; 54: 168; 82: 46, 101
Trnka, Jiri 22: 151; 43: 212, 213, 214, 215; YABC 1: 30, 31
Trondheim, Lewis 182: 183
Troughton, Joanna 37: 186; 48: 72
Troyer, Johannes 3: 16; 7: 18
Trudeau, G.B. 35: 220, 221, 222; 48: 119, 123, 126, 127,128, 129, 133; 168: 189
Trueman, Matthew 165: 208; 183: 191
Truesdell, Sue 55: 142; 108: 219, 220
Tryon, Leslie 84: 7; 139: 214; 143: 10; 181: 10
Tseng, Jean 72: 195; 94: 102; 119: 126; 151: 106; 173: 138, 139
Tseng, Mou-sien 72: 195; 94: 102; 119: 126; 151: 106; 173: 138, 139
Tsinajinie, Andy 2: 62
Tsinganos, Jim 180: 142
Tsugami, Kyuzo 18: 198, 199
Tucker, Ezra 156: 31
Tuckwell, Jennifer 17: 205
Tudor, Bethany 7: 103
Tudor, Tasha 18: 227; 20: 185, 186, 187; 36: 111; 69: 196, 198; 100: 44; YABC 2: 46, 314; 160: 234
Tuerk, Hanne 71: 201
Tulloch, Maurice 24: 79
Tunis, Edwin 1: 218, 219; 28: 209, 210, 211, 212
Tunnicliffe, C.F. 62: 176; 177; 178, 179; 181
Turkle, Brinton 1: 211, 213; 2: 249; 3: 226; 11: 3; 16: 209; 20: 22; 50: 23; 67: 50; 68: 65; 79: 205, 206, 207; 128: 47; YABC 1: 79
Turnbull, Christopher J. 143: 99, 100
Turner, Gwenda 59: 195
Turska, Krystyna 12: 103; 31: 173, 174, 175; 56: 32,34; 100: 66
Tusa, Tricia 72: 242; 111: 180, 181; 157: 165; 164: 186; 189: 40
Tusan, Stan 6: 58; 22: 236, 237
Tworkov, Jack 47: 207
Tyers, Jenny 89: 220
Tylden-Wright, Jenny 114: 119
Tyrol, Adelaide Murphy 103: 27
Tyrrell, Frances 107: 204
Tzimoulis, Paul 12: 104

U

Uchida, Yoshiko 1: 220
Uderzo 47: 88
Udovic, David 189: 185; 195: 201
Ueno, Noriko 59: 155
Ugliano, Natascia 196: 186
Ulm, Robert 17: 238
Ulrich, George 73: 15; 75: 136, 139; 99: 150
Ulriksen, Mark 101: 58; 182: 43
Unada 84: 67
    See Gliewe, Unada
Underhill, Liz 53: 159
Underwood, Beck 192: 36
Underwood, Clarence 40: 166
Unger, Jim 67: 208
Ungerer, Tomi 5: 188; 9: 40; 18: 188; 29: 175; 33: 221, 222, 223, 225; 71: 48; 106: 209, 210, 211, 212
Unwin, Nora S. 3: 65, 234, 235; 4: 237; 44: 173, 174; YABC 1: 59; 2: 301
Upitis, Alvis 145: 179
Urban, Helle 149: 243
Urbanovic, Jackie 86: 86; 189: 186, 187

Uris, Jill 49: 188, 197
Ursell, Martin 50: 51
Utpatel, Frank 18: 114
Utz, Lois 5: 190

V

Vagin, Vladimir 66: 10; 142: 215
Vaillancourt, Francois 107: 199
Vainio, Pirkko 123: 157, 158
Valério, Geraldo 180: 225; 194: 116
Vallejo, Boris 62: 130; 72: 212; 91: 38; 93: 61
Van Abbe, S. 16: 142; 18: 282; 31: 90; YABC 2: 157, 161
Van Allsburg, Chris 37: 205, 206; 53: 161, 162, 163, 165,166, 167, 168, 169, 170, 171; 105: 215, 216, 217, 218; 156: 176, 177, 178
Vance, James 65: 28
Van Der Linde, Henry 99: 17
van der Meer, Ron 98: 204, 205
van der Meer, Atie 98: 204, 205
Vandivert, William 21: 175
Van Dongen, H.R. 81: 97
Van Dusen, Chris W. 173: 169
Van Everen, Jay 13: 160; YABC 1: 121
Van Fleet, John 165: 12, 13
Van Frankenhuyzen, Gijsbert 145: 230; 149: 164; 184: 151
van Genechten, Guido 165: 226
van Haeringen, Annemarie 193: 206
Van Horn, William 43: 218
van Hout, Mies 195: 191
van Kampen, Vlasta 194: 217
van Lawick, Hugo 62: 76, 79
Van Loon, Hendrik Willem 18: 285, 289, 291
Van Munching, Paul 83: 85
van Ommen, Sylvia 186: 192
Van Patter, Bruce 183: 195
Van Rynbach, Iris 102: 192
Van Sciver, Ruth 37: 162
VanSeveren, Joe 63: 182
Van Stockum, Hilda 5: 193
Van Wely, Babs 16: 50; 79: 16
Van Wright, Cornelius 72: 18; 102: 208; 116: 107; 152: 236; 173: 170, 171
Van Zyle, Jon 103: 125; 160: 181, 182; 176: 199, 200
Vardzigulyants, Ruben 90: 54
Varga, Judy 29: 196
Vargo, Kurt 79: 224
Varley, Susan 61: 199; 63: 176, 177; 101: 148; 134: 220
Varon, Sara 195: 208
Vasconcellos, Daniel 80: 42
Vasiliu, Mircea 2: 166, 253; 9: 166; 13: 58; 68: 42
Vaughn, Frank 34: 157
Vavra, Robert 8: 206
Vawter, Will 17: 163
Vayas, Diana 71: 61
Vazquez, Carlos 125: 184
Veeder, Larry 18: 4
Velasquez, Eric 45: 217; 61: 45; 63: 110, 111; 88: 162; 90: 34, 144; 94: 213; 107: 147; 132: 192; 138: 213; 159: 126; 181: 184; 184: 96; 191: 16; 192: 234
Velasquez, Jose A. 63: 73
Velez, Walter 71: 75; 91: 154; 121: 181; 168: 49
Velthuijs, Max 110: 228, 229
Vendrell, Carme Sole 42: 205
Venezia, Mike 54: 17
Venti, Anthony Bacon 124: 103; 126: 26
Venturo, Piero 61: 194, 195
Ver Beck, Frank 18: 16, 17
Verkaaik, Ben 110: 209
Verling, John 71: 27
Verney, John 14: 225; 75: 8
Verrier, Suzanne 5: 20; 23: 212

Versace, Marie *2:* 255
Verstraete, Randy *108:* 193
Vestal, H.B. *9:* 134; *11:* 101; *27:* 25; *34:* 158
Vestergaard, Hope *190:* 203
Vicatan *59:* 146
Vickrey, Robert *45:* 59, 64
Victor, Joan Berg *30:* 193
Viereck, Ellen *3:* 242; *14:* 229
Vigna, Judith *15:* 293; *102:* 194, 195, 196, 197
Vilato, Gaspar E. *5:* 41
Villiard, Paul *51:* 178
Vimnera, A. *23:* 154
Vincent, Eric *34:* 98
Vincent, Felix *41:* 237
Vincent, Gabrielle *121:* 175
Vip *45:* 164
Viskupic, Gary *83:* 48
Vitale, Stefano *109:* 71, 107; *114:* 219, 220; *123:* 106; *138:* 232; *180:* 228, 229
Vivas, Julie *51:* 67, 69; *96:* 225; *197:* 190
Voake, Charlotte *114:* 221, 222; *180:* 232
Vo-Dinh, Mai *16:* 272; *60:* 191
Vogel, Ilse-Margret *14:* 230
Voigt, Erna *35:* 228
Vojnar, Kamil *95:* 31; *114:* 4; *115:* 62; *121:* 90; *124:* 72; *130:* 31; *141:* 81; *146:* 196; *150:* 123; *158:* 5, 6; *158:* 154; *171:* 119, 188; *179:* 15; *180:* 112
Vojtech, Anna *42:* 190; *108:* 222, 223; *150:* 203; *174:* 173
von Buhler, Cynthia *149:* 237; *162:* 177; *177:* 205; *180:* 77; *185:* 214, 215, 216
von Roehl, Angela *126:* 191
von Schmidt, Eric *8:* 62; *50:* 209, 210
von Schmidt, Harold *30:* 80
Vosburgh, Leonard *1:* 161; *7:* 32; *15:* 295, 296; *23:* 110; *30:* 214; *43:* 181
Voss, Tom *127:* 104
Voter, Thomas W. *19:* 3, 9
Vroman, Tom *10:* 29
Vulliamy, Clara *72:* 65

W

Waber, Bernard *47:* 209, 210, 211, 212, 213, 214; *95:* 215, 216, 217; *156:* 203, 205, 206, 207
Wachenje, Benjamin *194:* 170
Wack, Jeff *95:* 140; *110:* 90
Wagner, John *8:* 200; *52:* 104
Wagner, Ken *2:* 59
Waide, Jan *29:* 225; *36:* 139
Wainwright, Jerry *14:* 85
Waites, Joan C. *171:* 2
Wakeen, Sandra *47:* 97
Wakiyama, Hanako *171:* 96; *192:* 236
Waldherr, Kris *81:* 186
Waldman, Bruce *15:* 297; *43:* 178
Waldman, Neil *35:* 141; *50:* 163; *51:* 180; *54:* 78; *77:* 112; *79:* 162; *82:* 174; *84:* 5, 56, 106; *94:* 232, 233, 234; *96:* 41; *111:* 139; *113:* 9; *118:* 30; *142:* 220, 223
Waldrep, Richard *111:* 147
Walker, Brian *144:* 128
Walker, Charles *1:* 46; *4:* 59; *5:* 177; *11:* 115; *19:* 45; *34:* 74; *62:* 168; *72:* 218
Walker, Dugald Stewart *15:* 47; *32:* 202; *33:* 112
Walker, Gil *8:* 49; *23:* 132; *34:* 42
Walker, Jeff *55:* 154; *123:* 116
Walker, Jim *10:* 94
Walker, Mort *8:* 213
Walker, Norman *41:* 37; *45:* 58
Walker, Stephen *12:* 229; *21:* 174
Wallace, Beverly Dobrin *19:* 259
Wallace, Cly *87:* 93
Wallace, Ian *53:* 176, 177; *56:* 165, 166; *58:* 4; *98:* 4; *101:* 191; *112:* 124; *141:* 197, 198, 199, 200; *151:* 212

Wallace, John *105:* 228
Wallace, Nancy Elizabeth *141:* 204; *186:* 195, 197, 199
Wallenta, Adam *123:* 180
Waller, S.E. *24:* 36
Wallner, Alexandra *15:* 120; *156:* 183
Wallner, John C. *9:* 77; *10:* 188; *11:* 28; *14:* 209; *31:* 56, 118; *37:* 64; *51:* 186, 187, 188, 189, 190, 191,192, 193, 194, 195; *52:* 96; *53:* 23, 26; *71:* 99; *73:* 158; *89:* 215; *141:* 9
Wallner, John *162:* 17
Wallower, Lucille *11:* 226
Walotsky, Ron *93:* 87
Walsh, Ellen Stoll *99:* 209; *147:* 219; *194:* 194, 195, 196
Walsh, Rebecca *158:* 193
Walsh, Vivian *149:* 215; *158:* 227
Walters, Audrey *18:* 294
Walther, Tom *31:* 179
Walton, Garry *69:* 149
Walton, Tony *11:* 164; *24:* 209; *153:* 8; *177:* 73
Waltrip, Lela *9:* 195
Waltrip, Mildred *3:* 209; *37:* 211
Waltrip, Rufus *9:* 195
Wan *12:* 76
Wang, Suling *191:* 183
Warburton, Sarah *154:* 187
Wappers, G. *121:* 40
Ward, Fred *52:* 19
Ward, Helen *72:* 244; *144:* 240, 242
Ward, John *42:* 191; *96:* 54; *97:* 110; *123:* 105; *124:* 71; *173:* 66
Ward, Keith *2:* 107; *132:* 69
Ward, Leslie *34:* 126; *36:* 87
Ward, Lynd *1:* 99, 132, 133, 150; *2:* 108, 158, 196, 259; *18:* 86; *27:* 56; *29:* 79, 187, 253, 255; *36:* 199,200, 201, 202, 203, 204, 205, 206, 207, 209; *43:* 34; *56:* 28; *60:* 116; *100:* 65
Ward, Peter *37:* 116
Waring, Geoff *172:* 84
Warhola, James *92:* 5; *115:* 85, 87; *118:* 174, 175, 177; *176:* 84; *187:* 189, 190
Warner, Ben *159:* 171
Warner, Peter *14:* 87
Warnes, Tim *175:* 159
Warnick, Elsa *113:* 223
Warren, Betsy *2:* 101
Warren, Jim *85:* 81
Warren, Marion Cray *14:* 215
Warshaw, Jerry *30:* 197, 198; *42:* 165
Wasden, Kevin *102:* 162
Washington, Nevin *20:* 123
Washington, Phyllis *20:* 123
Wasserman, Amy L. *92:* 110
Waterman, Stan *11:* 76
Watkins-Pitchford, D.J. *6:* 215, 217
Watling, James *67:* 210; *78:* 112; *101:* 81; *117:* 189, 190; *127:* 119, 120
Watson, Aldren A. *2:* 267; *5:* 94; *13:* 71; *19:* 253; *32:* 220; *42:* 193, 194, 195, 196, 197, 198, 199, 200, 201; *YABC 2:* 202
Watson, G. *83:* 162
Watson, Gary *19:* 147; *36:* 68; *41:* 122; *47:* 139
Watson, J.D. *22:* 86
Watson, Jesse Joshua *197:* 124
Watson, Karen *11:* 26
Watson, Mary *117:* 193
Watson, Richard Jesse *62:* 188, 189
Watson, Wendy *5:* 197; *13:* 101; *33:* 116; *46:* 163; *64:* 12; *74:* 242, 243; *91:* 21; *142:* 228
Watt, Mélanie *136:* 206; *193:* 211
Wattenberg, Jane *174:* 200; *185:* 46; *187:* 108
Watterson, Bill *66:* 223, 225, 226
Watts, Bernadette *4:* 227; *103:* 182, 183
Watts, James *59:* 197; *74:* 145; *86:* 124
Watts, John *37:* 149
Watts, Leslie Elizabeth *150:* 207; *165:* 106
Watts, Stan *116:* 205

Weatherby, Mark Alan *77:* 141
Webb, Jennifer *110:* 79
Webb, Lanny *142:* 175
Webb, Sophie *135:* 214
Webber, Helen *3:* 141
Webber, Irma E. *14:* 238
Weber, Erik *56:* 19, 20
Weber, Florence *40:* 153
Weber, Jill *127:* 227, 228; *189:* 163
Weber, Roland *61:* 204
Weber, Sam *190:* 227
Weber, William J. *14:* 239
Webster, Jean *17:* 241
Weeks, Sarah *162:* 39
Wegman, William *78:* 243
Wegner, Fritz *14:* 250; *20:* 189; *44:* 165; *86:* 62
Weidenear, Reynold H. *21:* 122
Weigel, Jeff *170:* 193
Weihs, Erika *4:* 21; *15:* 299; *72:* 201; *107:* 207, 208
Weil, Lisl *7:* 203; *10:* 58; *21:* 95; *22:* 188,217; *33:* 193
Weiman, Jon *50:* 162, 165; *52:* 103; *54:* 78, 79, 81; *78:* 80; *82:* 107; *93:* 82; *97:* 69; *105:* 179; *193:* 65
Weiner, Sandra *14:* 240
Weiner, Scott *55:* 27
Weinhaus, Karen Ann *53:* 90; *71:* 50; *86:* 124
Weinman, Brad *197:* 20
Weisgard, Leonard *1:* 65; *2:* 191, 197, 204, 264, 265; *5:* 108; *21:* 42; *30:* 200, 201, 203, 204; *41:* 47; *44:* 125; *53:* 25; *85:* 196, 198, 200, 201; *100:* 139,207; *YABC 2:* 13
Weisman, David *173:* 47
Weiss, Ellen *44:* 202
Weiss, Emil *1:* 168; *7:* 60
Weiss, Harvey *1:* 145, 223; *27:* 224, 227; *68:* 214; *76:* 245, 246, 247
Weiss, Nicki *33:* 229
Weissman, Bari *49:* 72; *90:* 125; *139:* 142
Weitzman, David L. *172:* 199
Welch, Sheila Kelly *130:* 221
Welkes, Allen *68:* 218
Wellington, Monica *99:* 223; *157:* 259, 260, 261
Welliver, Norma *76:* 94
Wellner, Fred *127:* 53
Wells, Frances *1:* 183
Wells, H.G. *20:* 194, 200
Wells, Haru *53:* 120, 121
Wells, Robert E. *184:* 208
Wells, Rosemary *6:* 49; *18:* 297; *60:* 32; *66:* 203; *69:* 215, 216; *114:* 227; *118:* 149, 150; *156:* 188, 189, 190, 191
Wells, Rufus III *56:* 111, 113
Wells, Susan *22:* 43
Wendelin, Rudolph *23:* 234
Wengenroth, Stow *37:* 47
Weninger, Brigitte *189:* 192, 194
Werenskiold, Erik *15:* 6; *62:* 17
Werner, Honi *24:* 110; *33:* 41; *88:* 122
Werth, Kurt *7:* 122; *14:* 157; *20:* 214; *39:* 128
West, Harry A. *124:* 38
Westcott, Nadine Bernard *68:* 46; *84:* 49; *86:* 133; *106:* 199; *111:* 78; *113:* 111; *130:* 224; *139:* 54; *158:* 256; *194:* 199
Westerberg, Christine *29:* 226
Westerduin, Anne *105:* 229
Westerman, Johanna *162:* 206
Weston, Martha *29:* 116; *30:* 213; *33:* 85, 100; *53:* 181, 182, 183, 184; *77:* 95; *80:* 152; *119:* 196,197, 198, 199; *127:* 189; *133:* 196
Wetherbee, Margaret *5:* 3
Wexler, Jerome *49:* 73; *150:* 129
Whalley, Peter *50:* 49
Whatley, Bruce *186:* 93, 95
Wheatley, Arabelle *11:* 231; *16:* 276
Wheeler, Cindy *49:* 205
Wheeler, Dora *44:* 179
Wheelright, Rowland *15:* 81; *YABC 2:* 286

Whelan, Michael *56:* 108; *70:* 27, 29, 67, 68, 148; *74:* 18; *84:* 14; *91:* 195, 196; *95:* 147; *98:* 150, 151; *106:* 157; *113:* 218, 220; *116:* 99, 100
Whelan, Patrick *135:* 145
Whistler, Rex *16:* 75; *30:* 207, 208
White, Craig *110:* 130; *119:* 193; *130:* 33; *179:* 31
White, David Omar *5:* 56; *18:* 6
White, Joan *83:* 225
White, Martin *51:* 197; *85:* 127
Whitear *32:* 26
Whitehead, Beck *86:* 171
Whitehead, S.B. *154:* 132
Whithorne, H.S. *7:* 49
Whitney, George Gillett *3:* 24
Whitney, Jean *99:* 53
Whitson, Paul *102:* 161
Whittam, Geoffrey *30:* 191
Whyte, Mary *96:* 127
Wiberg, Harald *38:* 127; *93:* 215
Wick, Walter *77:* 128
Wickstrom, Sylvie *106:* 87; *169:* 180
Widener, Terry *105:* 230; *106:* 7; *163:* 23
Wiese, Kurt *3:* 255; *4:* 206; *14:* 17; *17:* 18, 19; *19:* 47; *24:* 152; *25:* 212; *32:* 184; *36:* 211,213, 214, 215, 216, 217, 218; *45:* 161; *100:* 92
Wiesner, David *33:* 47; *51:* 106; *57:* 67; *58:* 55; *64:* 78, 79, 81; *69:* 233; *72:* 247, 248, 249, 251,252, 253, 254; *83:* 134; *104:* 31; *117:* 197, 199, 200, 202; *139:* 223, 224; *151:* 51; *181:* 189, 190
Wiesner, William *4:* 100; *5:* 200, 201; *14:* 262
Wiggins, George *6:* 133
Wijngaard, Juan *111:* 36; *114:* 124
Wikkelsoe, Otto *45:* 25, 26
Wikland, Ilon *5:* 113; *8:* 150; *38:* 124, 125, 130; *127:* 162
Wikler, Madeline *114:* 233
Wilbur, C. Keith, M.D. *27:* 228
Wilburn, Kathy *53:* 102; *68:* 234
Wilcox, Cathy *105:* 123
Wilcox, J.A.J. *34:* 122
Wilcox, R. Turner *36:* 219
Wild, Jocelyn *46:* 220, 221, 222; *80:* 117
Wilde, George *7:* 139
Wildsmith, Brian *16:* 281, 282; *18:* 170, 171; *66:* 25; *69:* 224, 225, 227; *77:* 103; *83:* 218; *124:* 214,217, 219
Wildsmith, Mike *140:* 229
Wilhelm, Hans *58:* 189, 191; *73:* 157; *77:* 127; *135:* 229, 230, 233, 234; *196:* 209
Wilkin, Eloise *36:* 173; *49:* 208, 209, 210
Wilkinson, Barry *50:* 213
Wilkinson, Gerald *3:* 40
Wilkon, Jozef *31:* 183, 184; *71:* 206, 207, 209; *133:* 222
Wilks, Mike *34:* 24; *44:* 203
Willems, Mo *154:* 245, 246, 247; *180:* 236, 237, 239
Willey, Bee *103:* 129; *139:* 159; *173:* 115
Willhoite, Michael A. *71:* 214
William, Maria *168:* 51
Williams, Berkeley, Jr. *64:* 75
Williams, Ferelith Eccles *22:* 238
Williams, Garth *1:* 197; *2:* 49, 270; *4:* 205; *15:* 198, 302, 304, 307; *16:* 34; *18:* 283, 298, 299, 300, 301; *29:* 177, 178, 179, 232, 233, 241, 242, 243, 244, 245, 248; *40:* 106; *66:* 229, 230, 231, 233, 234; *71:* 192; *73:* 218, 219, 220; *78:* 261; *100:* 251, 252, 255; *136:* 117; *YABC 2:* 15, 16, 19
Williams, J. Scott *48:* 28
Williams, Jennifer *102:* 201
Williams, Jenny *60:* 202; *81:* 21; *88:* 71
Williams, Kent *180:* 18
Williams, Kit *44:* 206, 207, 208, 209, 211, 212
Williams, Marcia *97:* 214; *159:* 208, 209
Williams, Maureen *12:* 238
Williams, Patrick *14:* 218

Williams, Richard *44:* 93; *72:* 229; *74:* 133; *78:* 155, 237; *91:* 178; *110:* 212; *136:* 201, 202, 203; *152:* 115
Williams, Sam *124:* 222; *153:* 11; *177:* 201, 202; *180:* 34
Williams, Sophy *135:* 236
Williams, Vera B. *53:* 186, 187, 188, 189; *102:* 201, 202, 203
Williamson, Alex *177:* 180
Williamson, Mel *60:* 9
Willingham, Fred *104:* 206; *154:* 157
Willis, Adam *181:* 75
Willmore, J.T. *54:* 113, 114
Wilsdorf, Anne *180:* 122; *189:* 124; *191:* 195
Wilson, Anne *160:* 114
Wilson, Charles Banks *17:* 92; *43:* 73
Wilson, Connie *113:* 179
Wilson, Dagmar *10:* 47
Wilson, Dawn *67:* 161; *81:* 120; *113:* 158
Wilson, Edward A. *6:* 24; *16:* 149; *20:* 220, 221; *22:* 87; *26:* 67; *38:* 212, 214, 215, 216, 217
Wilson, Forrest *27:* 231
Wilson, Gahan *35:* 234; *41:* 136
Wilson, George *76:* 87
Wilson, Helen Miranda *140:* 61
Wilson, Jack *17:* 139
Wilson, Janet *77:* 154; *96:* 114; *99:* 219, 220; *153:* 64 *106:* 122; *130:* 210; *145:* 178; *173:* 64
Wilson, John *22:* 240
Wilson, Maurice *46:* 224
Wilson, Patten *35:* 61
Wilson, Peggy *15:* 4; *84:* 20
Wilson, Phil *181:* 29
Wilson, Rowland B. *30:* 170
Wilson, Sarah *50:* 215
Wilson, Tom *33:* 232
Wilson, W.N. *22:* 26
Wilson-Max, Ken *170:* 196; *180:* 181
Wilton, Nicholas *103:* 52; *183:* 111
Wilwerding, Walter J. *9:* 202
Wimmer, Mike *63:* 6; *70:* 121; *75:* 186; *76:* 21,22, 23; *91:* 114; *97:* 45, 68; *98:* 28; *107:* 130; *146:* 21; *149:* 47; *173:* 126; *193:* 21, 25; *194:* 204, 205
Winborn, Marsha *78:* 34; *99:* 70; *192:* 20
Winch, John *165:* 233
Winchester, Linda *13:* 231
Wind, Betty *28:* 158
Windham, Kathryn Tucker *14:* 260
Windham, Sophie *184:* 212
Winfield, Alison *115:* 78
Winfield, Wayne *72:* 23
Wing, Gary *64:* 147
Wing, Ron *50:* 85
Wingerter, Linda S. *132:* 199; *174:* 181
Winick, Judd *124:* 227, 228, 229
Winslow, Will *21:* 124
Winstead, Rosie *180:* 243
Winsten, Melanie Willa *41:* 41
Winter, Jeanette *151:* 240, 241, 242; *184:* 215, 217, 218, 219
Winter, Milo *15:* 97; *19:* 221; *21:* 181, 203, 204, 205; *64:* 19; *YABC 2:* 144
Winter, Paula *48:* 227
Winter, Susan *163:* 177; *182:* 201
Winters, Greg *70:* 117
Winters, Nina *62:* 194
Wise, Louis *13:* 68
Wiseman, Ann *31:* 187
Wiseman, B. *4:* 233
Wishnefsky, Phillip *3:* 14
Wiskur, Darrell *5:* 72; *10:* 50; *18:* 246
Wisniewski, David *95:* 220, 221
Wisniewski, Robert *95:* 10; *119:* 192
Witschonke, Alan *153:* 149, 150
Witt, Dick *80:* 244
Wittmann, Patrick *162:* 204
Wittman, Sally *30:* 219
Wittner, Dale *99:* 43

Wittwer, Hala *158:* 267; *195:* 80
Woehr, Lois *12:* 5
Wohlberg, Meg *12:* 100; *14:* 197; *41:* 255
Wohnoutka, Mike *137:* 68; *190:* 199; *195:* 218
Wojtowycz, David *167:* 168
Woldin, Beth Weiner *34:* 211
Wolf, Elizabeth *133:* 151
Wolf, J. *16:* 91
Wolf, Janet *78:* 254
Wolf, Linda *33:* 163
Wolfe, Corey *72:* 213
Wolff, Ashley *50:* 217; *81:* 216; *156:* 216, 217; *170:* 57; *174:* 174; *184:* 72
Wolff, Glenn *178:* 230
Wolfsgruber, Linda *166:* 61
Wondriska, William *6:* 220
Wong, Janet S. *98:* 225; *152:* 43
Wong, Nicole *174:* 13
Wonsetler, John C. *5:* 168
Wood, Audrey *50:* 221, 222, 223; *81:* 219, 221
Wood, Don *50:* 220, 225, 226, 228, 229; *81:* 218, 220; *139:* 239, 240
Wood, Grant *19:* 198
Wood, Heather *133:* 108
Wood, Ivor *58:* 17
Wood, Muriel *36:* 119; *77:* 167; *171:* 55; *187:* 46
Wood, Myron *6:* 220
Wood, Owen *18:* 187; *64:* 202, 204, 205, 206, 208, 210
Wood, Rob *193:* 48
Wood, Ruth *8:* 11
Woodbridge, Curtis *133:* 138
Wooding, Sharon L. *66:* 237
Woodruff, Liza *132:* 239; *182:* 46, 204
Woodruff, Thomas *171:* 73
Woods, John, Jr. *109:* 142
Woodson, Jack *10:* 201
Woodson, Jacqueline *94:* 242
Woodward, Alice *26:* 89; *36:* 81
Wool, David *26:* 27
Woolley, Janet *112:* 75
Woolman, Steven *106:* 47; *163:* 73
Wooten, Vernon *23:* 70; *51:* 170
Worboys, Evelyn *1:* 166, 167
Word, Reagan *103:* 204
Wormell, Christopher *154:* 251
Worth, Jo *34:* 143
Worth, Wendy *4:* 133
Wosmek, Frances *29:* 251
Wrenn, Charles L. *38:* 96; *YABC 1:* 20, 21
Wright, Barbara Mullarney *98:* 161
Wright, Cliff *168:* 203
Wright, Dare *21:* 206
Wright-Frierson, Virginia *58:* 194; *110:* 246
Wright, George *YABC 1:* 268
Wright, Joseph *30:* 160
Wronker, Lili Cassel *3:* 247; *10:* 204; *21:* 10
Wummer, Amy *154:* 181; *168:* 150; *176:* 85
Wyant, Alexander Helwig *110:* 19
Wyatt, David *97:* 9; *101:* 44; *114:* 194; *140:* 20; *167:* 13; *188:* 48
Wyatt, Stanley *46:* 210
Wyeth, Andrew *13:* 40; *YABC 1:* 133, 134
Wyeth, Jamie *41:* 257
Wyeth, N.C. *13:* 41; *17:* 252, 253, 254, 255, 256, 257, 258, 259, 264, 265, 266, 267, 268; *18:* 181; *19:* 80, 191, 200; *21:* 57, 183; *22:* 91; *23:* 152; *24:* 28, 99; *35:* 61; *41:* 65; *100:* 206; *YABC1:* 133, 223; *2:* 53, 75, 171, 187, 317
Wyman, Cherie R. *91:* 42

X

Xuan, YongSheng *119:* 202, 207, 208; *140:* 36; *187:* 21

Y

Yaccarino, Dan *141:* 208, 209; *147:* 171; *192:* 244, 245
Yakovetic, Joe *59:* 202; *75:* 85
Yalowitz, Paul *93:* 33
Yamaguchi, Marianne *85:* 118
Yamasaki, James *167:* 93
Yang, Belle *170:* 198
Yang, Jay *1:* 8; *12:* 239
Yap, Weda *6:* 176
Yaroslava
    See Mills, Yaroslava Surmach
Yashima, Taro *14:* 84
Yates, John *74:* 249, 250
Yayo *178:* 88
Yee, Cora *166:* 233
Yee, Wong Herbert *115:* 216, 217; *172:* 204, 205; *194:* 59
Yeo, Brad *135:* 121; *192:* 106
Yerxa, Leo *181:* 195
Yezerski, Thomas F. *162:* 29
Ylla
    See Koffler, Camilla
Yohn, F.C. *23:* 128; *YABC 1:* 269
Yoo, Taeeun *191:* 198
Yorinks, Adrienne *144:* 248
Yorke, David *80:* 178
Yoshida, Toshi *77:* 231
Yoshikawa, Sachiko *168:* 104; *177:* 28; *181:* 196, 197
Youll, Paul *91:* 218
Youll, Stephen *92:* 227; *118:* 136, 137; *164:* 248
Young, Amy L. *185:* 218; *190:* 46
Young, Cybéle *167:* 9
Young, Ed *7:* 205; *10:* 206; *40:* 124; *63:* 142; *74:* 250, 251, 252, 253; *75:* 227; *81:* 159; *83:* 98; *94:* 154; *115:* 160; *137:* 162; *YABC 2:* 242; *173:* 174, 175, 176

Young, Mary O'Keefe *77:* 95; *80:* 247; *134:* 214; *140:* 213
Young, Noela *8:* 221; *89:* 231; *97:* 195
Young, Paul *190:* 222
Young, Selina *153:* 12
Yun, Cheng Mung *60:* 143

Z

Zacharow, Christopher *88:* 98
Zacks, Lewis *10:* 161
Zadig *50:* 58
Zaffo, George *42:* 208
Zagwyn, Deborah Turney *138:* 227
Zahares, Wade *193:* 219
Zaid, Barry *50:* 127; *51:* 201
Zaidenberg, Arthur *34:* 218, 219, 220
Zalben, Jane Breskin *7:* 211; *79:* 230, 231, 233; *170:* 202
Zallinger, Jean *4:* 192; *8:* 8, 129; *14:* 273; *68:* 36; *80:* 254; *115:* 219, 220, 222
Zallinger, Rudolph F. *3:* 245
Zakrajsek, Molly *177:* 146
Zappa, Ahmet *180:* 250
Zebot, George *83:* 214
Zeck, Gerry *40:* 232
Zeff, Joe *181:* 98
Zeifert, Harriet *154:* 265, 267
Zeiring, Bob *42:* 130
Zeldich, Arieh *49:* 124; *62:* 120
Zeldis, Malcah *86:* 239; *94:* 198; *146:* 265, 266
Zelinsky, Paul O. *14:* 269; *43:* 56; *49:* 218-223; *53:* 111; *68:* 195; *102:* 219, 222, 221, 222; *154:* 255, 256, 257; *171:* 141; *185:* 96
Zelvin, Diana *72:* 190; *76:* 101; *93:* 207
Zemach, Kaethe *149:* 250

Zemach, Margot *3:* 270; *8:* 201; *21:* 210, 211; *27:* 204, 205, 210; *28:* 185; *49:* 22, 183, 224; *53:* 151; *56:* 146; *70:* 245, 246, *92:* 74
Zeman, Ludmila *153* 212
Zemsky, Jessica *10:* 62
Zepelinsky, Paul *35:* 93
Zerbetz, Evon *127:* 34; *158:* 109
Zezejl, Daniel *197:* 74
Zhang, Ange *101:* 190; *172:* 41
Zhang, Son Nang *163:* 113; *170:* 206
Ziegler, Jack *84:* 134
Zimdars, Berta *129:* 155
Zimet, Jay *147:* 94; *152:* 74; *196:* 75
Zimic, Tricia *72:* 95
Zimmer, Dirk *38:* 195; *49:* 71; *56:* 151; *65:* 214; *84:* 159; *89:* 26; *147:* 224
Zimmer, Tracie Vaughn *169:* 183
Zimmerman, Andrea *192:* 49, 50
Zimmermann, H. Werner *101:* 223; *112:* 197
Zimnik, Reiner *36:* 224
Zingone, Robin *180:* 134
Zinkeisen, Anna *13:* 106
Zinn, David *97:* 97
Zoellick, Scott *33:* 231
Zollars, Jaime *190:* 190
Zonia, Dhimitri *20:* 234, 235
Zorn, Peter A., Jr. *142:* 157
Zudeck, Darryl *58:* 129; *63:* 98; *80:* 52
Zug, Mark *88:* 131
Zulewski, Tim *164:* 95
Zuma *99:* 36
Zvorykin, Boris *61:* 155
Zweifel, Francis *14:* 274; *28:* 187
Zwerger, Lisbeth *54:* 176, 178; *66:* 246, 247, 248; *130:* 230, 231, 232, 233; *181:* 92; *194:* 224, 225, 226
Zwinger, Herman H. *46:* 227
Zwolak, Paul *67:* 69, 71, 73, 74

Author Index

The following index gives the number of the volume in which an author's biographical sketch, Autobiography Feature, Brief Entry, or Obituary appears.

This index includes references to all entries in the following series, which are also published by The Gale Group.

YABC—*Yesterday's Authors of Books for Children: Facts and Pictures about Authors and Illustrators of Books for Young People from Early Times to 1960*
CLR—*Children's Literature Review: Excerpts from Reviews, Criticism, and Commentary on Books for Children*
SAAS—*Something about the Author Autobiography Series*

A

Aardema, Verna 1911-2000 107
  Obituary 119
  Earlier sketches in SATA :4, 68
  See also CLR 17
  See also SAAS 8
Aaron, Chester 1923- 74
  Earlier sketch in SATA 9
  See also SAAS 12
Aaseng, Nate
  See Aaseng, Nathan
Aaseng, Nathan 1953- 172
  Brief entry 38
  Earlier sketches in SATA 51, 88
  See also CLR 54
  See also SAAS 12
Abadzis, Nick 1965- 193
Ábalos, Rafael 1956- 197
Abbas, Jailan 1952- 91
Abbey, Lynn
  See Abbey, Marilyn Lorraine
Abbey, Marilyn Lorraine 1948- 156
Abbott, Alice
  See Borland, Kathryn Kilby
  and Speicher, Helen Ross S(mith)
Abbott, Jacob 1803-1879 22
Abbott, Manager Henry
  See Stratemeyer, Edward L.
Abbott, R(obert) Tucker 1919-1995 61
  Obituary 87
Abbott, Sarah
  See Zolotow, Charlotte
Abbott, Tony 1952- 159
Abdelsayed, Cindy 1962- 123
Abdul, Raoul 1929- 12
Abeele, Veronique van den 196
Abel, Raymond 1911- 12
Abell, Kathleen 1938- 9
Abelove, Joan 110
Abels, Harriette S(heffer) 1926- 50
Abercrombie, Barbara 1939- 182
  Earlier sketch in SATA 16
Abercrombie, Barbara Mattes
  See Abercrombie, Barbara
Abercrombie, Lynn
  See Sorrells, Walter
Abernethy, Robert G(ordon) 1927- 5
Abisch, Roslyn Kroop 1927- 9

Abisch, Roz
  See Abisch, Roslyn Kroop
Ablow, Gail 1962- 198
Abodaher, David J. (Naiph) 1919- 17
Abolafia, Yossi 1944-
  See Abulafia, Yossi
Abouzeid, Chris 175
Abrahall, Clare Hoskyns
  See Hoskyns-Abrahall, Clare (Constance Drury)
Abrahams, Hilary (Ruth) 1938- 29
Abrahams, Peter 1947- 194
Abrahams, Robert David 1905-1998 4
Abramovitz, Anita (Zeltner Brooks) 1914- 5
Abrams, Joy 1941- 16
Abrams, Lawrence F. 58
  Brief entry 47
Abrashkin, Raymond 1911-1960 50
Abulafia, Yossi 1944- 177
  Brief entry 46
  Earlier sketch in SATA 60
Acampora, Paul 175
Accardo, Anthony 191
Achebe, Albert Chinualumogu
  See Achebe, Chinua
Achebe, Chinua 1930- 40
  Brief entry 38
  Earlier sketch in SATA 38
  See also CLR 20
Ackerman, Diane 1948- 102
Ackerman, Eugene (Francis) 1888-1974 10
Ackerman, Karen 1951- 126
Ackerman, Susan Yoder 1945- 92
Ackison, Wendy Wassink 1956- 103
Ackley, Peggy Jo 1955- 58
Ackroyd, Peter 1949- 153
Acorn, John (Harrison) 1958- 79
Acredolo, Linda (Potter) 1947- 159
Acs, Laszlo (Bela) 1931- 42
  Brief entry 32
Acuff, Selma Boyd 1924- 45
Ada, Alma Flor 1938- 181
  Earlier sketches in SATA 43, 84, 143
  See also CLR 62
Adair, Gilbert 1944- 98
Adair, Ian 1942- 53
Adair, Margaret Weeks (?)-1971 10
Adam, Cornel
  See Lengyel, Cornel Adam

Adam, Mark
  See Alexander, Marc
Adam, Robert 1948- 93
Adams, Adrienne 1906- 90
  Earlier sketch in SATA 8
  See also CLR 73
Adams, Andy 1859-1935
  See YABC 1
Adams, Barbara Johnston 1943- 60
Adams, Bruin
  See Ellis, Edward S(ylvester)
Adams, Captain Bruin
  See Ellis, Edward S(ylvester)
Adams, Captain J. F. C.
  See Ellis, Edward S(ylvester)
Adams, Dale
  See Quinn, Elisabeth
Adams, Daniel
  See Nicole, Christopher (Robin)
Adams, Debra
  See Speregen, Devra Newberger
Adams, Douglas 1952-2001 116
  Obituary 128
Adams, Douglas Noel
  See Adams, Douglas
Adams, Edith
  See Shine, Deborah
Adams, Florence 1932- 61
Adams, Harriet S(tratemeyer) 1892(?)-1982 .. 1
  Obituary 29
Adams, Harrison
  See Rathborne, St. George (Henry)
  and Stratemeyer, Edward L.
Adams, Hazard 1926- 6
Adams, Hazard Simeon
  See Adams, Hazard
Adams, John Anthony 1944- 67
Adams, Laurie 1941- 33
Adams, Lowell
  See Joseph, James (Herz)
Adams, Nicholas
  See Pine, Nicholas
Adams, Nicholas
  See Smith, Sherwood
Adams, Nicholas
  See Doyle, Debra
  and Macdonald, James D.
Adams, Pam 1919- 112

Adams, Pamela
See Adams, Pam
Adams, Richard (George) 1920- 69
Earlier sketch in SATA 7
See also CLR 121
Adams, Ruth Joyce 14
Adams, Tricia
See Kite, Pat
Adams, William Taylor 1822-1897 28
Adam Smith, Janet (Buchanan) 1905-1999 .. 63
Adamson, Gareth 1925-1982(?) 46
Obituary 30
Adamson, George 1906-1989
Obituary 63
Adamson, George (Worsley) 1913-2005 30
Adamson, Graham
See Groom, Arthur William
Adamson, Joy(-Friederike Victoria)
1910-1980 11
Obituary 22
Adamson, Wendy Writson 1942- 22
Addison, Kenneth 1949(?)-2005 187
Addison, Kenneth L.
See Addison, Kenneth
Addona, Angelo F. 1925- 14
Addy, Sharon Hart 1943- 192
Earlier sketch in SATA 108
Addy, Ted
See Winterbotham, R(ussell) R(obert)
Adelberg, Doris
See Orgel, Doris
Adelson, Leone 1908- 11
Adinolfi, JoAnn 176
Adkins, Jan 1944- 144
Earlier sketches in SATA 8, 69
See also CLR 77
See also SAAS 19
Adler, C(arole) S(chwerdtfeger) 1932- 126
Earlier sketches in SATA 26, 63, 102
See also CLR 78
See also SAAS 15
Adler, David A. 1947- 178
Earlier sketches in SATA 14, 70, 106, 151
See also CLR 108
Adler, Irene
See Penzler, Otto
and Storr, Catherine (Cole)
Adler, Irving 1913- 29
Autobiography Feature 164
Earlier sketch in SATA 1
See also CLR 27
See also SAAS 15
Adler, Larry 1939- 36
Adler, Peggy 22
Adler, Ruth 1915-1968 1
Adlerman, Daniel (Ezra) 1963- 163
Earlier sketch in SATA 96
Adlerman, Kim
See Adlerman, Kimberly M(arie)
Adlerman, Kimberly M(arie) 1964- 163
Earlier sketch in SATA 96
Adoff, Arnold 1935- 96
Earlier sketches in SATA 5, 57
See also CLR 7
See also SAAS 15
Adoff, Jaime (Levi) 163
Adorjan, Carol (Madden) 1934- 71
Earlier sketch in SATA 10
Adrian, Frances
See Polland, Madeleine A(ngela Cahill)
Adrian, Mary
See Jorgensen, Mary Venn
Adshead, Gladys L(ucy) 1896-1985 3
Aesop 620(?)B.C.-560(?)B.C. 64
See also CLR 14
Aesop, Abraham
See Newbery, John
Affabee, Eric
See Stine, R.L.
Agapida, Fray Antonio
See Irving, Washington

Agard, John 1949- 138
Agard, Nadema 1948- 18
Agarwal, Deepa 1947- 141
Agee, Jon 1960- 196
Earlier sketches in SATA 116, 157
Agell, Charlotte 1959- 150
Earlier sketch in SATA 99
Agent Orange
See Moseley, James W(illett)
Aghill, Gordon
See Garrett, (Gordon) Randall (Phillip)
and Silverberg, Robert
Agle, Nan Hayden 1905- 3
See also SAAS 10
Agnew, Edith J(osephine) 1897-1988 11
Agonito, Joseph 177
Agonito, Rosemary 1937- 177
Ahern, Margaret McCrohan 1921- 10
Ahl, Anna Maria 1926- 32
Ahlberg, Allan 1938- 165
Brief entry 35
Earlier sketches in SATA 68, 120
See also CLR 18
Ahlberg, Janet 1944-1994 120
Brief entry 32
Obituary 83
Earlier sketch in SATA 68
See also CLR 18
Aichinger, Helga 1937- 4
Aiken, Clarissa (M.) Lorenz 1899-1992 12
Obituary 109
Aiken, Conrad (Potter) 1889-1973 30
Earlier sketch in SATA 3
Aiken, Joan (Delano) 1924-2004 73
Autobiography Feature 109
Obituary 152
Earlier sketches in SATA 2, 30
See also CLR 90
See also SAAS 1
Aillaud, Cindy Lou 1955- 184
Ainsley, Alix
See Steiner, Barbara A(nnette)
Ainsworth, Catherine Harris 1910- 56
Ainsworth, Norma 1911-1987 9
Ainsworth, Ruth (Gallard) 1908- 73
Earlier sketch in SATA 7
Ainsworth, William Harrison 1805-1882 24
Aistrop, Jack 1916- 14
Aitken, Amy 1952- 54
Brief entry 40
Aitken, Dorothy 1916- 10
Aitmatov, Chingiz 1928-2008 56
Aitmatov, Chingiz Torekulovich
See Aitmatov, Chingiz
Akaba, Suekichi 1910- 46
Akers, Floyd
See Baum, L(yman) Frank
Akib, Jamel 181
Aks, Patricia 1926-1994 68
Alagoa, Ebiegberi Joe 1933- 108
Alain
See Brustlein, Daniel
Alajalov, Constantin 1900-1987
Obituary 53
Alan, David
See Horsfield, Alan
Alan, Robert
See Silverstein, Robert Alan
Alarcon, Francisco X(avier) 1954- 104
Albert, Burton 1936- 22
Albert, Louise 1928- 157
Albert, Richard E. 1909-1999 82
Albert, Susan Wittig 1940- 107
Alberts, Frances Jacobs 1907-1989 14
Albertson, Susan
See Wojciechowski, Susan
Albion, Lee Smith 29
Alborough, Jez 1959- 149
Earlier sketch in SATA 86
Albrecht, Lillie (Vanderveer H.)
1894-1985 12

Albyn, Carole Lisa 1955- 83
Alchemy, Jack
See Gershator, David
Alcock, Gudrun 1908- 56
Brief entry 33
Alcock, Vivien (Dolores) 1924-2003 76
Brief entry 38
Obituary 148
Earlier sketch in SATA 45
See also CLR 26
Alcorn, John 1935- 31
Brief entry 30
Alcorn, Stephen 1958- 110
Alcott, Louisa May 1832-1888 100
See also YABC 1
See also CLR 109
Alda, Arlene 1933- 158
Brief entry 36
Earlier sketches in SATA 44, 106
See also CLR 93
Alden, Isabella (Macdonald) 1841-1930 115
See also YABC 2
Alden, Sue
See Francis, Dorothy
Alderman, Clifford Lindsey 1902-1988 3
Alderson, Sue Ann 1940- 59
Brief entry 48
Alding, Peter
See Jeffries, Roderic
Aldis, Dorothy (Keeley) 1896-1966 2
Aldiss, Brian W. 1925- 34
Aldiss, Brian Wilson
See Aldiss, Brian W.
Aldon, Adair
See Meigs, Cornelia Lynde
Aldous, Allan (Charles) 1911- 27
Aldrich, Ann
See Meaker, Marijane
Aldrich, Bess Streeter 1881-1954
See CLR 70
Aldrich, Thomas (Bailey) 1836-1907 114
Earlier sketch in SATA 17
Aldridge, (Harold Edward) James 1918- 87
Aldridge, Josephine Haskell 14
Aldridge, Sheila 1974- 192
Aleas, Richard
See Appelt, Kathi
Alegria, Malin 1974(?)- 190
Alegria, Ricardo E(nrique) 1921- 6
Aleksin, Anatolii Georgievich 1924- 36
Alenov, Lydia 1948- 61
Alex, Ben (a pseudonym) 1946- 45
Alex, Marlee (a pseudonym) 1948- 45
Alexander, Anna B(arbara Cooke) 1913- 1
Alexander, Anne
See Alexander, Anna B(arbara Cooke)
Alexander, Ellen 1938- 91
Alexander, Frances (Laura) 1888-1979 4
Alexander, Janet 1907-1994 97
Earlier sketch in SATA 1
Alexander, Jocelyn Anne Arundel 1930- 22
Alexander, Linda 1935- 2
Alexander, Lloyd 1924-2007 135
Obituary 182
Earlier sketches in SATA 3, 49, 81, 129
See also CLR 48
See also SAAS 19
Alexander, Lloyd Chudley
See Alexander, Lloyd
Alexander, Marc 1929- 117
Alexander, Martha 1920- 136
Earlier sketches in SATA 11, 70
Alexander, Rae Pace
See Alexander, Raymond Pace
Alexander, Raymond Pace 1898-1974 22
Alexander, Rod
See Pellowski, Michael (Joseph)
Alexander, Sally Hobart 1943- 84

Alexander, Sue 1933-2008 .... *136*
 Obituary *195*
 Earlier sketches in SATA *12, 89*
 See also SAAS *15*
Alexander, Vincent Arthur 1925-1980
 Obituary *23*
Alexeieff, Alexandre A. 1901-1979 .... *14*
Alger, Horatio, Jr.
 See Stratemeyer, Edward L.
Alger, Horatio, Jr. 1832-1899 .... *16*
 See also CLR *87*
Alger, Leclaire (Gowans) 1898-1969 .... *15*
Aliki
 See Brandenberg, Aliki (Liacouras)
Alkema, Chester Jay 1932- *12*
Al-Khalili, Jim 1962- *124*
Alkiviades, Alkis 1953- *105*
Alkouatli, Claire *186*
Allaby, John Michael
 See Allaby, Michael
Allaby, Michael 1933- *167*
Allamand, Pascale 1942- *12*
Allan, Mabel Esther 1915-1998 .... *75*
 Earlier sketches in SATA *5, 32*
 See also CLR *43*
 See also SAAS *11*
Allan, Nicholas 1956- *123*
 Earlier sketch in SATA *79*
Allan-Meyer, Kathleen 1918- *51*
 Brief entry *46*
Allard, Harry
 See Allard, Harry G(rover), Jr.
Allard, Harry G(rover), Jr. 1928- *102*
 Earlier sketch in SATA *42*
 See also CLR *85*
Allee, Marjorie Hill 1890-1945 .... *17*
Allen, Adam
 See Epstein, Beryl (M. Williams)
 and Epstein, Samuel
Allen, Alex B.
 See Heide, Florence Parry
Allen, Allyn
 See Eberle, Irmengarde
Allen, Betsy
 See Harrison, Elizabeth (Allen) Cavanna
Allen, Bob 1961- *76*
Allen, Gertrude E(lizabeth) 1888-1984 .... *9*
Allen, Grace
 See Hogarth, Grace (Weston Allen)
Allen, Jeffrey (Yale) 1948- *42*
Allen, John
 See Perry, Ritchie (John Allen)
Allen, Jonathan 1957- *177*
 Earlier sketch in SATA *131*
Allen, Jonathan Dean
 See Allen, Jonathan
Allen, Judy (Christina) 1941- *124*
 Earlier sketch in SATA *80*
Allen, Kenneth S. 1913-1981 .... *56*
Allen, Leroy 1912- *11*
Allen, Linda 1925- *33*
Allen, Marjorie 1931- *22*
Allen, Maury 1932- *26*
Allen, Merritt Parmelee 1892-1954 .... *22*
Allen, Nancy Kelly 1949- *171*
 Earlier sketch in SATA *127*
Allen, Nina (Stroemgren) 1935- *22*
Allen, Pamela (Kay) 1934- *123*
 Earlier sketches in SATA *50, 81*
 See also CLR *44*
Allen, Rodney F. 1938-1999 .... *27*
Allen, Roger MacBride 1957- *105*
Allen, Ruth
 See Peterson, Esther (Allen)
Allen, Samuel W(ashington) 1917- *9*
Allen, T. D.
 See Allen, Terril Diener
Allen, Terril Diener 1908- *35*
Allen, Terry D.
 See Allen, Terril Diener

Allen, Thomas B. 1929- *193*
 Earlier sketches in SATA *45, 140*
Allen, Thomas B. 1929- *193*
Allen, Thomas Benton
 See Allen, Thomas B.
Allen, Tom
 See Allen, Thomas B.
Allende, Isabel 1942- *163*
 See also CLR *99*
Allerton, Mary
 See Govan, (Mary) Christine Noble
Alley, Robert W.
 See Alley, R.W.
Alley, R.W. *169*
Alleyn, Ellen
 See Rossetti, Christina
Allington, Richard L(loyd) 1947- *39*
 Brief entry *35*
Allison, Amy 1956- *138*
Allison, Bob *14*
Allison, Diane Worfolk *78*
Allison, Jennifer *173*
Allison, Linda 1948- *43*
Allison, Margaret
 See Klam, Cheryl
Allman, Barbara 1950- *137*
Allmendinger, David F(rederick), Jr. 1938- . *35*
Allred, Alexandra Powe 1965- *144*
Allred, Gordon T(hatcher) 1930- *10*
Allsop, Kenneth 1920-1973 .... *17*
Allsopp, Sophie *188*
Almedingen, E. M.
 See Almedingen, Martha Edith von
Almedingen, Martha Edith von 1898-1971 .... *3*
Almon, Russell
 See Clevenger, William R.
 and Downing, David A(lmon)
Almond, David 1951- *158*
 Earlier sketch in SATA *114*
 See also CLR *85*
Almond, Linda Stevens 1881(?)-1987
 Obituary *50*
Almquist, Don 1929- *11*
Alonzo, Sandra *199*
Alphin, Elaine Marie 1955- *139*
 Autobiography Feature *139*
 Earlier sketches in SATA *80, 130*
Alsenas, Linas 1979- *186*
Alsop, Mary O'Hara 1885-1980 .... *34*
 Obituary *24*
 Earlier sketch in SATA *2*
Alter, Anna 1974- *135*
Alter, Judith (MacBain) 1938- *101*
 Earlier sketch in SATA *52*
Alter, Judy
 See Alter, Judith (MacBain)
Alter, Robert Edmond 1925-1965 .... *9*
Alter, Stephen 1956- *187*
Althea
 See Braithwaite, Althea
Altman, Linda Jacobs 1943- *21*
Altman, Suzanne
 See Orgel, Doris
 and Schecter, Ellen
Alton, Steve *169*
Altschuler, Franz 1923- *45*
Altsheler, Joseph A(lexander) 1862-1919
 See YABC *1*
Alvarez, John
 See del Rey, Lester
Alvarez, Joseph A. 1930- *18*
Alvarez, Julia 1950- *129*
al-Windawi, Thura
 See Windawi, Thura al-
Alyer, Philip A.
 See Stratemeyer, Edward L.
Amado, Elisa *193*
Amann, Janet 1951- *79*
Amato, Carol A. 1942- *92*
Amato, Mary 1961- *178*
 Earlier sketch in SATA *140*

Ambrose, Stephen E. 1936-2002 .... *138*
 Earlier sketch in SATA *40*
Ambrose, Stephen Edward
 See Ambrose, Stephen E.
Ambrus, Gyozo Laszlo 1935- *1*
 See also SAAS *4*
Ambrus, Victor G.
 See Ambrus, Gyozo Laszlo
Amend, Bill 1962- *147*
Amerman, Lockhart 1911-1969 .... *3*
Ames, Evelyn 1908-1990 .... *13*
 Obituary *64*
Ames, Gerald 1906-1993 .... *11*
 Obituary *74*
Ames, Lee J(udah) 1921- *151*
 Earlier sketch in SATA *3*
Ames, Mildred 1919-1994 .... *85*
 Earlier sketches in SATA *22, 81*
Amico, Tom 1960(?)- *176*
Ammon, Richard 1942- *124*
Amon, Aline 1928- *9*
Amoss, Berthe 1925- *112*
 Earlier sketch in SATA *5*
Anastasio, Dina 1941- *94*
 Brief entry *30*
 Earlier sketch in SATA *37*
Anaya, Rudolfo A. 1937-
 See CLR *129*
Anaya, Rudolpho Alfonso
 See Anaya, Rudolfo A.
Anckarsvard, Karin Inez Maria 1915-1969 .... *6*
Ancona, George 1929- *192*
 Earlier sketches in SATA *12, 85, 145*
 See also SAAS *18*
Anders, C. J.
 See Bennett, Cherie
Anders, Isabel 1946- *101*
Anders, Lou *176*
Andersdatter, Karla M(argaret) 1938- *34*
Andersen, Bethanne 1954- *191*
Andersen, Hans Christian 1805-1875 .... *100*
 See also YABC *1*
 See also CLR *113*
Andersen, Ted
 See Boyd, Waldo T.
Andersen, Yvonne 1932- *27*
Anderson, Bernice G(oudy) 1894-1997 .... *33*
Anderson, Bob 1944- *139*
 Earlier sketch in SATA *136*
Anderson, Brad(ley Jay) 1924- *33*
 Brief entry *31*
Anderson, C. C.
 See Anderson, Catherine Corley
Anderson, C(larence) W(illiam) 1891-1971 . *11*
Anderson, Catherine C.
 See Anderson, Catherine Corley
Anderson, Catherine Corley 1909-2001 .... *72*
Anderson, Clifford
 See Gardner, Richard (M.)
Anderson, Daryl Shon 1963- *93*
Anderson, Dave
 See Anderson, David (Poole)
Anderson, David (Poole) 1929- *60*
Anderson, Derek 1969- *169*
Anderson, Eloise Adell 1927- *9*
Anderson, George
 See Groom, Arthur William
Anderson, Grace Fox 1932- *43*
Anderson, J(ohn) R(ichard) L(ane)
 1911-1981 .... *15*
 Obituary *27*
Anderson, Jodi Lynn *182*
Anderson, John David 1975- *197*
Anderson, John L(onzo) 1905- *2*
Anderson, Joy 1928- *1*
Anderson, Kevin J. 1962- *117*
 Earlier sketch in SATA *74*
Anderson, Kevin James
 See Anderson, Kevin J.
Anderson, Kirsty 1978- *108*

Anderson, K.J.
    See Moesta, Rebecca
Anderson, Laurie Halse 1961- *186*
    Earlier sketches in SATA *95, 132*
    See also CLR *138*
Anderson, LaVere Francis Shoenfelt
    1907-1998 .... *27*
Anderson, Leone Castell 1923- *53*
    Brief entry *49*
Anderson, Lisa G. 1963- *108*
Anderson, Lonzo
    See Anderson, John L(onzo)
Anderson, Lucia (Lewis) 1922- *10*
Anderson, Madelyn Klein 1926-2005 .... *28*
Anderson, Margaret J(ean) 1931- *27*
    See also SAAS *8*
Anderson, Marilyn D. 1943- *144*
Anderson, Mary 1939- *82*
    Earlier sketch in SATA *7*
    See also SAAS *23*
Anderson, Matthew Tobin
    See Anderson, M.T.
Anderson, Mona 1910-2004 .... *40*
Anderson, Mrs. Melvin
    See Anderson, Catherine Corley
Anderson, M.T. 1968- *182*
    Earlier sketches in SATA *97, 146*
Anderson, Norman Dean 1928- *22*
Anderson, Peggy Perry 1953- *179*
    Earlier sketch in SATA *84*
Anderson, Poul 1926-2001 .... *90*
    Autobiography Feature *106*
    Brief entry *39*
    See also CLR *58*
Anderson, Poul William
    See Anderson, Poul
Anderson, Rachel 1943- *86*
    Earlier sketch in SATA *34*
    See also SAAS *18*
Anderson, Rebecca M.
    See Moesta, Rebecca
Anderson, Rebecca Moesta
    See Moesta, Rebecca
Anderson, Richard
    See Anderson, J(ohn) R(ichard) L(ane)
Anderson, Sara *173*
Anderson, (Tom) Scoular *138*
Anderson, Susan 1952- *90*
Anderson, W. B.
    See Schultz, James Willard
Anderson, Wayne 1946- *147*
    Earlier sketch in SATA *56*
Andre, Evelyn M(arie) 1924- *27*
Andreasen, Dan *186*
Andreassen, Karl
    See Boyd, Waldo T.
Andreassi, K. Robert
    See DeCandido, Keith R.A.
Andree, Louise
    See Coury, Louise Andree
Andrew, Ian 1962- *166*
    Earlier sketch in SATA *116*
Andrew, Ian Peter
    See Andrew, Ian
Andrew, Prudence (Hastings) 1924- *87*
Andrews, Benny 1930-2006 .... *31*
    Obituary *178*
Andrews, Eleanor Lattimore
    See Lattimore, Eleanor Frances
Andrews, Elton V.
    See Pohl, Frederik
Andrews, F(rank) Emerson 1902-1978 .... *22*
Andrews, J(ames) S(ydney) 1934- *4*
Andrews, Jan 1942- *167*
    Brief entry *49*
    Earlier sketches in SATA *58, 98*
Andrews, Julie 1935- *153*
    Earlier sketch in SATA *7*
    See also CLR *85*
Andrews, Laura
    See Coury, Louise Andree

Andrews, Roy Chapman 1884-1960 .... *19*
Andrews, Tamra 1959- *129*
Andrews, V(irginia) C(leo) 1924(?)-1986
    Obituary *50*
Andrews, Wendy
    See Sharmat, Marjorie Weinman
Andrews, William G(eorge) 1930- *74*
Andrezel, Pierre
    See Blixen, Karen (Christentze Dinesen)
Andriani, Renee
    See Williams-Andriani, Renee
Andriola, Alfred J. 1912-1983
    Obituary *34*
Andrist, Ralph K. 1914-2004 .... *45*
Andronik, Catherine M. *189*
Andryszewski, Tricia 1956- *148*
    Earlier sketch in SATA *88*
Angel, Ann 1952- *192*
Angel, Carl *178*
Angel, Marie 1923- *47*
Angeles, Peter A. 1931- *40*
Angeletti, Roberta 1964- *124*
Angeli, Marguerite (Lofft) de
    See de Angeli, Marguerite (Lofft)
Angell, Judie 1937- *78*
    Earlier sketch in SATA *22*
    See also CLR *33*
Angell, Madeline 1919- *18*
Angelo, Valenti 1897- *14*
Angelou, Maya 1928- *136*
    Earlier sketch in SATA *49*
    See also CLR *53*
Angier, Bradford -1997 .... *12*
Angle, Paul M(cClelland) 1900-1975
    Obituary *20*
Anglund, Joan Walsh 1926- *2*
    See also CLR *94*
Ango, Fan D.
    See Longyear, Barry B(rookes)
Angrist, Stanley W(olff) 1933- *4*
Anholt, Catherine 1958- *131*
    Earlier sketch in SATA *74*
Anholt, Laurence 1959- *141*
    Earlier sketch in SATA *74*
Anita
    See Daniel, Anita
Anmar, Frank
    See Nolan, William F(rancis)
Annett, Cora
    See Scott, Cora Annett (Pipitone)
Annie-Jo
    See Blanchard, Patricia
    and Suhr, Joanne
Annixter, Jane
    See Sturtzel, Jane Levington
Annixter, Paul
    See Sturtzel, Howard A(llison)
Anno, Mitsumasa 1926- *157*
    Earlier sketches in SATA *5, 38, 77*
    See also CLR *122*
Anrooy, Francine Van
    See Van Anrooy, Francine
Ansary, Mir Tamim 1948- *140*
Anstey, Caroline 1958- *81*
Antell, Will D. 1935- *31*
Anthony, Barbara
    See Barber, Antonia
Anthony, C. L.
    See Smith, Dorothy Gladys
Anthony, Edward 1895-1971 .... *21*
Anthony, John
    See Beckett, Ronald Brymer
    and Ciardi, John (Anthony)
    and Sabini, John Anthony
Anthony, Joseph Patrick 1964- *103*
Anthony, Patricia 1947- *109*
Anthony, Piers 1934- *129*
    Autobiography Feature *129*
    Earlier sketch in SATA *84*
    See also CLR *118*
    See also SAAS *22*

Anthony, Susan C(arol) 1953- *87*
Anticaglia, Elizabeth 1939- *12*
Antilles, Kem
    See Moesta, Rebecca
Antle, Nancy 1955- *102*
Antolini, Margaret Fishback 1904-1985
    Obituary *45*
Anton, Michael J(ames) 1940- *12*
Antonacci, Robert J(oseph) 1916- *45*
    Brief entry *37*
Anvil, Christopher
    See Crosby, Harry C., Jr.
Anzaldua, Gloria (Evanjelina) 1942-2004
    Obituary *154*
Aoki, Hisako 1942- *45*
Apfel, Necia H(alpern) 1930- *51*
    Brief entry *41*
Aphrodite, J.
    See Livingston, Carole
Apikuni
    See Schultz, James Willard
Apostolina, M. *184*
Apostolina, Michael
    See Apostolina, M.
Apostolou, Christine Hale 1955- *179*
    Earlier sketches in SATA *82, 128*
Appel, Allen (R.) 1945- *115*
Appel, Benjamin 1907-1977 .... *39*
    Obituary *21*
Appel, Martin 1948- *45*
Appel, Martin Eliot
    See Appel, Martin
Appel, Marty
    See Appel, Martin
Appelbaum, Diana Muir Karter 1953- *132*
Appelt, Kathi 1954- *190*
    Earlier sketches in SATA *83, 129*
Apperley, Dawn 1969- *135*
Appiah, Peggy 1921-2006 .... *84*
    Earlier sketch in SATA *15*
    See also SAAS *19*
Apple, Margot *152*
    Brief entry *42*
    Earlier sketch in SATA *64*
Applebaum, Stan 1922- *45*
Applegate, K.A.
    See Applegate, Katherine
Applegate, Katherine 1956- *196*
    Earlier sketches in SATA *109, 162*
    See also CLR *90*
Applegate, Katherine Alice
    See Applegate, Katherine
Appleton, Victor
    See Barrett, Neal, Jr.
    and Doyle, Debra
    and Macdonald, James D.
    and Stratemeyer, Edward L.
    and Vardeman, Robert E(dward)
Appleton, Victor II
    See Goulart, Ron(ald Joseph)
Apsler, Alfred 1907-1982 .... *10*
Aragones, Sergio 1937- *48*
    Brief entry *39*
Araujo, Frank P. 1937- *86*
Arbo, Cris 1950- *103*
Arbuckle, Dorothy Fry 1910-1982
    Obituary *33*
Arbuthnot, May Hill 1884-1969 .... *2*
Archambault, John *163*
    Earlier sketches in SATA *67, 112*
Archbold, Rick 1950- *97*
Archer, Colleen Rutherford 1949- *164*
Archer, Frank
    See O'Connor, Richard
Archer, Jules 1915- *85*
    Earlier sketch in SATA *4*
    See also SAAS *5*
Archer, Lily 1981- *193*
Archer, Marion Fuller 1917- *11*
Archer, Nathan
    See Watt-Evans, Lawrence

Archer, Peggy 1947- *199*
Archibald, Joe
    See Archibald, Joseph S(topford)
Archibald, Joseph S(topford) 1898-1986 ...... *3*
    Obituary *47*
Ard, William
    See Jakes, John
Ardagh, Philip 1961- *154*
Ardai, Charles 1969- *85*
Arden, Barbi
    See Stoutenburg, Adrien (Pearl)
Arden, William
    See Lynds, Dennis
Ardizzone, Edward (Jeffrey Irving)
    1900-1979 .... *28*
    Obituary *21*
    Earlier sketch in SATA *1*
    See also CLR *3*
Ardley, Neil (Richard) 1937- *121*
    Earlier sketch in SATA *43*
Arehart-Treichel, Joan 1942- *22*
Arena, Felice 1968- *151*
Arenella, Roy 1939- *14*
Argent, Kerry 1960- *138*
Argueta, Jorge *179*
Arkin, Alan 1934- *59*
    Brief entry *32*
Arkin, Alan Wolf
    See Arkin, Alan
Arksey, Neil *158*
Arlen, Leslie
    See Nicole, Christopher (Robin)
Arley, Robert
    See Jackson, Mike
Armer, Alberta (Roller) 1904-1986 .... *9*
Armer, Laura Adams 1874-1963 .... *13*
Armistead, John 1941- *130*
Armitage, David 1943- *155*
    Brief entry *38*
    Earlier sketch in SATA *99*
Armitage, Frank
    See Carpenter, John (Howard)
Armitage, Ronda (Jacqueline) 1943- *155*
    Brief entry *38*
    Earlier sketches in SATA *47, 99*
Armour, Richard (Willard) 1906-1989 .... *14*
    Obituary *61*
Armstrong, Alan 1939- *172*
Armstrong, Alan W.
    See Armstrong, Alan
Armstrong, George D. 1927- *10*
Armstrong, Gerry (Breen) 1929- *10*
Armstrong, Jeannette (C.) 1948- *102*
Armstrong, Jennifer 1961- *165*
    Autobiography Feature *120*
    Earlier sketches in SATA *77, 111*
    See also CLR *66*
    See also SAAS *24*
Armstrong, Louise *43*
    Brief entry *33*
Armstrong, Martin Donisthorpe
    1882-1974 .... *115*
Armstrong, Matthew 1975- *188*
Armstrong, Matthew S.
    See Armstrong, Matthew
Armstrong, Ralph Richard
    See Armstrong, Richard
Armstrong, Richard 1903-1986 .... *11*
Armstrong, William H(oward) 1914-1999 ..... *4*
    Obituary *111*
    See also CLR *117*
    See also SAAS *7*
Armstrong-Ellis, Carey (Fraser) 1956- *145*
Arndt, Ursula (Martha H.) *56*
    Brief entry *39*
Arneson, D(on) J(on) 1935- *37*
Arnett, Caroline
    See Cole, Lois Dwight
Arnett, Jack
    See Goulart, Ron(ald Joseph)

Arnette, Robert
    See Silverberg, Robert
Arno, Enrico 1913-1981 .... *43*
    Obituary *28*
Arnold, Caroline 1944- *174*
    Brief entry *34*
    Earlier sketches in SATA *36, 85, 131*
    See also CLR *61*
    See also SAAS *23*
Arnold, Elizabeth 1944- *164*
Arnold, Elliott 1912-1980 .... *5*
    Obituary *22*
Arnold, Emily 1939- *134*
    Autobiography Feature *134*
    Earlier sketches in SATA *5, 50, 76, 110*
    See also CLR *46*
    See also SAAS *7*
Arnold, Katya 1947- *168*
    Earlier sketches in SATA *82, 115*
Arnold, Louise *175*
Arnold, Marsha Diane 1948- *147*
    Earlier sketch in SATA *93*
Arnold, Nick 1961- *113*
Arnold, Oren 1900-1980 .... *4*
Arnold, Susan (Riser) 1951- *58*
Arnold, Tedd 1949- *160*
    Earlier sketches in SATA *69, 116*
Arnoldy, Julie
    See Bischoff, Julia Bristol
Arnosky, James Edward 1946- *189*
    Earlier sketches in SATA *70, 118*
    See also CLR *93*
Arnosky, Jim
    See Arnosky, James Edward
Arnott, Kathleen 1914- *20*
Arnov, Boris, Jr. 1926- *12*
Arnow, Harriette (Louisa) Simpson
    1908-1986 .... *42*
    Obituary *47*
Arnsteen, Katy Keck 1934- *68*
Arnstein, Helene S(olomon) 1915- *12*
Arntson, Herbert E(dward) 1911-1982 .... *12*
Aroner, Miriam *82*
Aronin, Ben 1904-1980
    Obituary *25*
Aronson, Marc 1950- *189*
    Autobiography Feature *189*
    Earlier sketches in SATA *126, 175*
Aronson, Marc Henry
    See Aronson, Marc
Aronson, Sarah *196*
Aronson, Virginia 1954- *122*
Arora, Shirley (Lease) 1930- *2*
Arrasmith, Patrick *176*
Arrick, Fran
    See Angell, Judie
Arrigan, Mary 1943- *142*
Arrington, Aileen *183*
Arrington, Stephen L. 1948- *97*
Arrington, Stephen Lee
    See Arrington, Stephen L.
Arrley, Richmond
    See Delany, Samuel R., Jr.
Arrowood, (McKendrick Lee) Clinton
    1939- *19*
Arrowsmith, Pat 1930- *59*
Artell, Mike 1948- *183*
    Earlier sketches in SATA *89, 134*
Arthur, Robert (Andrew) 1909-1969
    See Arthur, Robert, (Jr.)
Arthur, Robert, (Jr.) 1909-1969 .... *118*
Arthur, Ruth M(abel) 1905-1979 .... *26*
    Earlier sketch in SATA *7*
Artis, Vicki Kimmel 1945- *12*
Artzybasheff, Boris (Miklailovich)
    1899-1965 .... *14*
Aruego, Ariane
    See Dewey, Ariane
Aruego, Jose 1932- *178*
    Earlier sketches in SATA *6, 68, 125*
    See also CLR *5*

Aruego, Jose Espiritu
    See Aruego, Jose
Arundel, Honor (Morfydd) 1919-1973 .... *4*
    Obituary *24*
    See also CLR *35*
Arundel, Jocelyn
    See Alexander, Jocelyn Anne Arundel
Arvey, Michael 1948- *79*
Arzoumanian, Alik *177*
Asare, Meshack (Yaw) 1945- *139*
    Earlier sketch in SATA *86*
Asaro, Catherine 1955- *165*
    Earlier sketch in SATA *101*
    See Asaro, Catherine Ann
Asaro, Catherine Ann 1955-
    See Asaro, Catherine
Asay, Donna Day 1945- *127*
Asbjørnsen, Peter Christen 1812-1885 .... *15*
    See also CLR *104*
Asch, Frank 1946- *154*
    Earlier sketches in SATA *5, 66, 102*
Ash, Jutta 1942- *38*
Ashabranner, Brent 1921- *166*
    Earlier sketches in SATA *1, 67, 130*
    See also CLR *28*
    See also SAAS *14*
Ashabranner, Brent Kenneth
    See Ashabranner, Brent
Ashbless, William
    See Blaylock, James P.
    and Powers, Tim
Ashby, Gil 1958- *146*
Ashby, Gwynneth 1922- *44*
Ashby, Ruth *170*
Ashby, Yvonne 1955- *121*
Ashe, Arthur (Robert, Jr.) 1943-1993 .... *65*
    Obituary *87*
Ashe, Geoffrey (Thomas) 1923- *17*
    Autobiography Feature *125*
Ashe, Mary Ann
    See Lewis, Mary (Christianna)
Asher, Sandra Fenichel
    See Asher, Sandy
Asher, Sandy 1942- *71*
    Autobiography Feature *158*
    Brief entry *34*
    Earlier sketch in SATA *36*
    See also SAAS *13*
Asheron, Sara
    See Moore, Lilian
Ashey, Bella
    See Breinburg, Petronella
Ashford, Daisy
    See Ashford, Margaret Mary
Ashford, Jeffrey
    See Jeffries, Roderic
Ashford, Margaret Mary 1881-1972 .... *10*
Ashley, Bernard (John) 1935- *155*
    Brief entry *39*
    Earlier sketches in SATA *47, 79*
    See also CLR *4*
Ashley, Elizabeth
    See Salmon, Annie Elizabeth
Ashley, Ray
    See Abrashkin, Raymond
Ashman, Linda 1960- *150*
Ashton, Lorayne
    See Gottfried, Theodore Mark
Ashton, Warren T.
    See Adams, William Taylor
Asimov, Isaac 1920-1992 .... *74*
    Earlier sketches in SATA *1, 26*
    See also CLR *79*
Asinof, Eliot 1919-2008 .... *6*
Asinof, Eliot Tager
    See Asinof, Eliot
Aska, Warabe
    See Masuda, Takeshi
Asprin, Robert L. 1946-2008 .... *92*
Asprin, Robert Lynn
    See Asprin, Robert L.

Asquith, Cynthia Mary Evelyn (Charteris)
1887-1960 107
Asquith, Ros 153
Astley, Juliet
See Lofts, Norah (Robinson)
Aston, Dianna Hutts 1964- 176
Aston, James
See White, T(erence) H(anbury)
Ata, Te 1895-1995 119
Atene, Ann
See Atene, (Rita) Anna
Atene, (Rita) Anna 1922- 12
Atheling, William, Jr.
See Blish, James (Benjamin)
Atkins, Catherine 160
Atkins, Jeannine 1953- 172
Earlier sketch in SATA 113
Atkinson, Allen G. 1953(?)-1987 60
Brief entry 46
Obituary 55
Atkinson, M. E.
See Frankau, Mary Evelyn Atkinson
Atkinson, Margaret Fleming 14
Atteberry, Kevan J. 186
Attema, Martha 1949- 156
Earlier sketch in SATA 94
Atticus
See Davies, Hunter
and Fleming, Ian
and Pawle, Gerald Strachan
and Wilson, (Thomas) Woodrow
Atwater, Florence (Hasseltine Carroll)
1896-1979 66
Earlier sketch in SATA 16
See also CLR 19
Atwater, Montgomery Meigs 1904-1976 15
Atwater, Richard (Tupper) 1892-1948 66
Brief entry 27
Earlier sketch in SATA 54
See also CLR 19
Atwater-Rhodes, Amelia 1984- 170
Earlier sketch in SATA 124
Atwell, Debby 1953- 150
Earlier sketch in SATA 87
Atwood, Ann (Margaret) 1913-1992 7
Atwood, Margaret 1939- 170
Earlier sketch in SATA 50
Atwood, Margaret Eleanor
See Atwood, Margaret
Aubrey, Meg Kelleher 1963- 83
Aubry, Claude B. 1914-1984 29
Obituary 40
Auch, Herm 173
Auch, Mary Jane 173
Earlier sketch in SATA 138
Auch, M.J.
See Auch, Mary Jane
Auclair, Joan 1960- 68
Auel, Jean M(arie) 1936- 91
Auer, Martin 1951- 77
Augarde, Steve 1950- 159
Earlier sketch in SATA 25
Augelli, John P(at) 1921- 46
Augustine, Mildred
See Benson, Mildred (Augustine Wirt)
Ault, Phil
See Ault, Phillip H(alliday)
Ault, Phillip H(alliday) 1914- 23
Ault, Rosalie Sain 1942- 38
Ault, Roz
See Ault, Rosalie Sain
Aung, (Maung) Htin 1909- 21
Auntie Deb
See Coury, Louise Andree
Auntie Louise
See Coury, Louise Andree
Aunt Weedy
See Alcott, Louisa May
Auseon, Andrew 1976- 166
Austen, Carrie
See Bennett, Cherie

Austin, Carrie
See Seuling, Barbara
Austin, Elizabeth S. 1907-1977 5
Austin, Harry
See McInerny, Ralph
Austin, Margot 1909(?)-1990 11
Obituary 66
Austin, Michael 178
Austin, Oliver L(uther), Jr. 1903-1988 7
Obituary 59
Austin, Patricia 1950- 137
Austin, R. G.
See Gelman, Rita Golden
and Lamb, Nancy
Austin, Virginia 1951- 152
Earlier sketch in SATA 80
Auteur, Hillary
See Gottfried, Theodore Mark
Auth, Tony
See Auth, William Anthony, Jr.
Auth, William Anthony, Jr. 1942- 192
Autry, Gloria Diener
See Allen, Terril Diener
Auvil, Peggy A 1954- 122
Auvil, Peggy Appleby
See Auvil, Peggy A
Aveni, Anthony F. 1938- 181
Aveni, Anthony Francis
See Aveni, Anthony F.
Averill, Esther (Holden) 1902-1992 28
Obituary 72
Earlier sketch in SATA 1
Avery, A. A.
See Montgomery, Rutherford George
Avery, Al
See Montgomery, Rutherford George
Avery, Gillian (Elise) 1926- 137
Autobiography Feature 137
Earlier sketches in SATA 7, 75
See also SAAS 6
Avery, Kay 1908- 5
Avery, Lorraine
See Older, Effin
and Older, Jules
Avery, Lynn
See Cole, Lois Dwight
Avi 1937- 190
Earlier sketches in SATA 14, 71, 108, 156
See also CLR 68
Avishai, Susan 1949- 82
Avril, Francois 1961- 191
Avril, Lynne
See Cravath, Lynne W.
Awdry, Christopher Vere 1940- 67
Awdry, Wilbert Vere 1911-1997 94
See also CLR 23
Axelrod, Amy 131
Axelsen, Stephen 1953- 165
Axton, David
See Koontz, Dean R.
Ayars, James S(terling) 1898-1986 4
Aye, A. K.
See Edwards, Hazel (Eileen)
Ayer, Eleanor H. 1947-1998 121
Earlier sketch in SATA 78
Ayer, Jacqueline 1930- 13
Ayer, Margaret (?)-1981 15
Aylesworth, Jim 1943- 139
Earlier sketches in SATA 38, 89
See also CLR 89
Aylesworth, Thomas G(ibbons) 1927-1995 .. 88
Earlier sketch in SATA 4
See also CLR 6
See also SAAS 17
Ayliffe, Alex 190
Aylward, Marcus
See Alexander, Marc
Aymar, Brandt 1911- 22
Ayme, Marcel (Andre) 1902-1967 91
See also CLR 25

Ayres, Becky
See Hickox, Rebecca (Ayres)
Ayres, Katherine 1947- 187
Ayres, Pam 1947- 90
Ayres, Patricia Miller 1923-1985
Obituary 46
Aytmatov, Chingiz
See Aitmatov, Chingiz
Ayto, Russell 1960- 166
Earlier sketch in SATA 111
Azaid
See Zaidenberg, Arthur
Azar, Penny 1952- 121
Azarian, Mary 1940- 171
Earlier sketch in SATA 112
Azore, Barbara 1934- 188

B

Baastad, Babbis Friis
See Friis-Baastad, Babbis Ellinor
Bab
See Gilbert, W(illiam) S(chwenck)
Babbis, Eleanor
See Friis-Baastad, Babbis Ellinor
Babbitt, Lucy Cullyford 1960- 85
Babbitt, Natalie 1932- 194
Earlier sketches in SATA 6, 68, 106
See also CLR 53
See also SAAS 5
Babbitt, Natalie Zane Moore
See Babbitt, Natalie
Babcock, Chris 1963- 83
Babcock, Dennis 1948- 22
Babcock, Dennis Arthur
See Babcock, Dennis
Baber, Carolyn Stonnell 1936- 96
Baboni, Elena 198
Baca, Ana 1967- 191
Baca, Maria 1951- 104
Bach, Alice (Hendricks) 1942- 93
Brief entry 27
Earlier sketch in SATA 30
Bach, Bellamy
See Windling, Terri
Bach, Mary 1960- 125
Bach, Richard 1936- 13
Bach, Richard David
See Bach, Richard
Bache, Ellyn 1942- 124
Bachel, Beverly K. 1957- 142
Bachelet, Gilles 1952- 196
Bachman, Fred 1949- 12
Bachman, Richard
See King, Stephen
Bachrach, Deborah 80
Backus, James Gilmore 1913-1989
Obituary 63
Backus, Jim
See Backus, James Gilmore
Bacmeister, Rhoda W(arner) 1893-1991 11
Bacon, Betty
See Bacon, Elizabeth
Bacon, Elizabeth 1914-2001 3
Obituary 131
Bacon, Joan Chase
See Bowden, Joan Chase
Bacon, Josephine Dodge (Daskam)
1876-1961 48
Bacon, Margaret Frances
See Bacon, Peggy
Bacon, Margaret Hope 1921- 6
Bacon, Martha Sherman 1917-1981 18
Obituary 27
See also CLR 3
Bacon, Melvin 1950- 93
Bacon, Melvin L.
See Bacon, Melvin
Bacon, Peggy 1895-1987 50

Bacon, R(onald) L(eonard) 1924- 84
 Earlier sketch in SATA 26
Baden, Robert 1936- 70
Baden-Powell, Robert (Stephenson Smyth)
 1857-1941 16
Badt, Karin L(uisa) 1963- 91
Bae, Hyun-Joo 186
Baehr, Kingsley M. 1937- 89
Baehr, Patricia 1952- 65
Baehr, Patricia Goehner
 See Baehr, Patricia
Baer, Jill
 See Gilbert, (Agnes) Joan (Sewell)
Baer, Judy 1951- 71
Baer, Julie 1960- 161
Baer-Block, Roxanna 172
Baerg, Harry J(ohn) 1909-1996 12
Baeten, Lieve 1954- 83
Bagert, Brod 1947- 191
 Earlier sketch in SATA 80
Baggette, Susan K. 1942- 126
Baggott, Julianna 1969- 197
Bagnold, Enid 1889-1981 25
 Earlier sketch in SATA 1
Baguley, Elizabeth 1959- 199
Bahlke, Valerie Worth -1994
 See Worth, Valerie
Bahous, Sally 1939- 86
Bahr, Mary (Madelyn) 1946- 95
Bahr, Robert 1940- 38
Bahti, Tom 1926-1972 57
 Brief entry 31
Baicker-McKee, Carol 1958- 177
Bailey, Alice Cooper 1890-1978 12
Bailey, Anne 1958- 71
Bailey, Bernadine (Freeman) 1901-1995 14
Bailey, Carolyn Sherwin 1875-1961 14
Bailey, Debbie 1954- 123
Bailey, Donna (Veronica Anne) 1938- 68
Bailey, Jane H(orton) 1916- 12
Bailey, John (Robert) 1940- 52
Bailey, Len 193
Bailey, Linda 1948- 182
 Earlier sketch in SATA 107
Bailey, Maralyn Collins (Harrison) 1941- 12
Bailey, Matilda
 See Radford, Ruby L(orraine)
Bailey, Maurice Charles 1932- 12
Bailey, Pearl (Mae) 1918-1990 81
Bailey, Peter 1946- 194
Bailey, Ralph Edgar 1893-1982 11
Bailey, Sheila (Lucas) 1960- 155
Baillie, Allan 1943- 151
 Earlier sketch in SATA 87
 See also CLR 49
 See also SAAS 21
Baillie, Allan Stuart
 See Baillie, Allan
Baines, John (David) 1943- 71
Bains, Larry
 See Sabin, Louis
Baird, Alison 1963- 138
Baird, Bil 1904-1987 30
 Obituary 52
Baird, Thomas (P.) 1923-1990 45
 Brief entry 39
 Obituary 64
Baird, William Britton
 See Baird, Bil
Baity, Elizabeth Chesley 1907-1989 1
Baiul, Oksana 1977- 108
Bajoria, Paul 1964- 187
Bakeless, John (Edwin) 1894-1978 9
Bakeless, Katherine Little 1895-1992 9
Baker, Alan 1951- 146
 Earlier sketches in SATA 22, 93
Baker, Augusta 1911-1998 3
Baker, Barbara 1947- 192
Baker, Betty Lou 1928-1987 73
 Obituary 54
 Earlier sketch in SATA 5

Baker, Carin Greenberg 1959- 79
Baker, Charlotte 1910- 2
Baker, Christina
 See Kline, Christina Baker
Baker, Christopher W. 1952- 144
Baker, Deirdre 1955- 195
Baker, E.D. 190
Baker, (Mary) Elizabeth (Gillette) 1923- 7
Baker, Gayle Cunningham 1950- 39
Baker, James W. 1924- 65
 Earlier sketch in SATA 22
Baker, James W. 1926- 122
Baker, Janice E(dla) 1941- 22
Baker, Jeanette 178
Baker, Jeannie 1950- 156
 Earlier sketches in SATA 23, 88
 See also CLR 28
Baker, Jeffrey J(ohn) W(heeler) 1931- 5
Baker, Jim
 See Baker, James W.
Baker, Keith 1953- 179
Baker, Ken 1962- 133
Baker, Laura Nelson 1911- 3
Baker, Margaret 1890-1965 4
Baker, Margaret J(oyce) 1918- 12
 See also SAAS 8
Baker, Mary Gladys Steel 1892-1974 12
Baker, (Robert) Michael (Graham) 1938- 4
Baker, Nina (Brown) 1888-1957 15
Baker, Pamela J. 1947- 66
Baker, Rachel 1904-1978 2
 Obituary 26
Baker, Rosalie F. 1945- 166
Baker, Samm Sinclair 1909-1997 12
 Obituary 96
Baker, Susan (Catherine) 1942-1991 29
Balaam
 See Lamb, G(eoffrey) F(rederick)
Balan, Bruce 1959- 113
Balcavage, Dynise 1965- 137
Balch, Glenn 1902-1989 3
 Obituary 83
 See also SAAS 11
Baldacci, David 1960- 184
Baldacci, David G.
 See Baldacci, David
 and Baldacci, David
Balderose, Nancy Ward 1952- 93
Balderson, Margaret 1935- 151
Baldry, Cherith 1947- 167
 Earlier sketch in SATA 72
Balducci, Carolyn 1946- 5
Balducci, Carolyn Feleppa
 See Balducci, Carolyn
Baldwin, Alex
 See Griffin, W.E.B
Baldwin, Anne Norris 1938- 5
Baldwin, Clara 11
Baldwin, Gordo
 See Baldwin, Gordon C(ortis)
Baldwin, Gordon C(ortis) 1908-1983 12
Baldwin, James 1841-1925 24
Baldwin, James 1924-1987 9
 Obituary 54
Baldwin, Louis 1919- 110
Baldwin, Margaret
 See Weis, Margaret
Baldwin, Stan(ley C.) 1929- 62
 Brief entry 28
Bales, Carol Ann 1940- 57
 Brief entry 29
Balet, Jan (Bernard) 1913- 11
Balgassi, Haemi 1971- 131
Balian, Lorna 1929- 91
 Earlier sketch in SATA 9
Balit, Christina 1961- 159
 Earlier sketch in SATA 102
Ball, Duncan 1941- 73
Ball, Zachary
 See Janas, Frankie-Lee
 and Masters, Kelly R(ay)

Ballantine, Lesley Frost
 See Frost, Lesley
Ballantyne, R(obert) M(ichael) 1825-1894 ... 24
 See also CLR 137
Ballard, James Graham
 See Ballard, J.G.
Ballard, Jane
 See Gorman, Carol
Ballard, J.G. 1930- 93
Ballard, John 1945- 110
Ballard, Lowell C(lyne) 1904-1986 12
 Obituary 49
Ballard, (Charles) Martin 1929- 1
Ballard, Mignon F. 1934- 64
 Brief entry 49
Ballard, Mignon Franklin
 See Ballard, Mignon F.
Ballard, Robert D(uane) 1942- 85
 See also CLR 60
Ballard, Robin 1965- 126
Balliett, Blue 1955- 156
Ballinger, Bryan 1968- 161
Ballouhey, Pierre 1944- 90
Balogh, Penelope 1916-1975 1
 Obituary 34
Balouch, Kristen 176
Balow, Tom 1931- 12
Baltazzi, Evan S(erge) 1921- 90
Balterman, Marcia Ridlon 1942- 22
Baltimore, J.
 See Catherall, Arthur
Baltzer, Hans (Adolf) 1900- 40
Balzano, Jeanne (Koppel) 1912- 7
Bambara, Toni Cade 1939-1995 112
Bamfylde, Walter
 See Bevan, Tom
Bamman, Henry A. 1918- 12
Banat, D. R.
 See Bradbury, Ray
Bancroft, Griffing 1907-1999 6
Bancroft, Laura
 See Baum, L(yman) Frank
Bandel, Betty 1912- 47
Baner, Skulda Vanadis 1897-1964 10
Banerjee, Anjali 174
Banfill, A. Scott 1956- 98
Bang, Betsy 1912- 48
 Brief entry 37
Bang, Garrett
 See Bang, Molly
Bang, Molly 1943- 158
 Earlier sketches in SATA 24, 69, 111
 See also CLR 8
Bang, Molly Garrett
 See Bang, Molly
Bang-Campbell, Monika 1975(?)- 195
 Earlier sketch in SATA 140
Banjo, The
 See Paterson, A(ndrew) B(arton)
Banke, Cecile de
 See de Banke, Cecile
Banks, Kate 1960- 172
 Earlier sketch in SATA 134
Banks, Laura Stockton Voorhees 1908(?)-1980
 Obituary 23
Banks, Lynne Reid
 See Reid Banks, Lynne
Banks, Merry 197
Banks, Michael A. 1951- 101
Banks, Paul 1952- 174
Banks, Sara (Jeanne Gordon Harrell) 26
 See Harrell, Sara (Jeanne) Gordon
Bannatyne-Cugnet, Elizabeth Jo-Anne
 See Bannatyne-Cugnet, Jo
Bannatyne-Cugnet, Jo 1951- 101
Banner, Angela
 See Maddison, Angela Mary
Bannerman, Helen (Brodie Cowan Watson)
 1862(?)-1946 19
 See also CLR 21
Banning, Evelyn I. 1903-1993 36

Bannon, Laura (?)-1963 6
Bannor, Brett 1959- 143
Banta, Susan 181
Bantock, Nick 1950(?)- 95
Banyai, Istvan 193
Barakat, Ibtisam 1963- 186
Barasch, Lynne 1939- 186
  Earlier sketches in SATA *74, 126*
Barbalet, Margaret 1949- 77
Barbary, James
  See Beeching, Jack
Barbash, Shepard 1957- 84
Barbe, Walter Burke 1926- 45
Barber, Antonia 1932- 163
  Earlier sketch in SATA *29*
Barber, Atiim Kiambu
  See Barber, Tiki
Barber, Lynda
  See Graham-Barber, Lynda
Barber, Lynda Graham
  See Graham-Barber, Lynda
Barber, Richard (William) 1941- 35
Barber, Ronde 1975- 182
Barber, Tiki 1975- 182
Barbera, Joe 1911-2006 51
  Obituary 179
Barbera, Joseph
  See Barbera, Joe
Barbera, Joseph Roland
  See Barbera, Joe
Barberis, Juan C(arlos) 1920- 61
Barbour, Karen 1956- 170
  Earlier sketches in SATA *63, 121*
Barbour, Ralph Henry 1870-1944 16
Barclay, Bill
  See Moorcock, Michael
Barclay, Isabel
  See Dobell, I(sabel) M(arian) B(arclay)
Barclay, William Ewert
  See Moorcock, Michael
Bardhan-Quallen, Sudipta 168
Bardoe, Cheryl 181
Bare, Arnold Edwin 1920- 16
Bare, Colleen Stanley 32
Bar-el, Dan 199
Barenholtz, Bernard 1914-1989
  Obituary 64
Bargar, Gary W. 1947-1985 63
Barger, Jan 1948- 147
Barish, Matthew 1907-2000 12
Barkan, Joanne 127
  Earlier sketch in SATA *77*
Barker, Albert W. 1900- 8
Barker, Carol (Minturn) 1938- 31
Barker, Cicely Mary 1895-1973 49
  Brief entry 39
  See also CLR *88*
Barker, Melvern 1907-1989 11
Barker, S(quire) Omar 1894-1985 10
Barker, Will 1913-1983 8
Barkin, Carol 1944- 52
  Earlier sketch in SATA *42*
Barklem, Jill 1951- 96
  See also CLR *31*
Barkley, Brad 178
Barkley, James Edward 1941- 6
Barks, Carl 1901-2000 37
Barley, Janet Crane 1934- 95
Barnaby, Ralph S(tanton) 1893-1986 9
Barnard, A. M.
  See Alcott, Louisa May
Barnard, Bryn 1956- 169
  Earlier sketch in SATA *115*
Barne, Kitty
  See Barne, Marion Catherine
Barne, Marion Catherine 1883-1957 97
Barner, Bob 1947- 136
  Earlier sketch in SATA *29*
Barnes, Dawn 1957- 175
Barnes, Derrick 191

Barnes, Derrick D.
  See Barnes, Derrick
Barnes, (Frank) Eric Wollencott 1907-1962 . 22
Barnes, Joyce Annette 1958- 85
Barnes, Laura T. 1958- 119
Barnes, Loutricia
  See Barnes-Svarney, Patricia L(ou)
Barnes, Malcolm 1909(?)-1984
  Obituary 41
Barnes, Michael 1934- 55
Barnes-Murphy, Frances 1951- 88
Barnes-Murphy, Rowan 1952- 88
Barnes-Svarney, Patricia L(ou) 1953- 67
Barnet, Nancy 1954- 84
Barnett, Ivan 1947- 70
Barnett, Lincoln (Kinnear) 1909-1979 36
Barnett, Moneta 1922-1976 33
Barnett, Naomi 1927- 40
Barney, Maginel Wright 1881(?)-1966 39
  Brief entry 32
Barnhart, Clarence L(ewis) 1900-1993 48
  Obituary 78
Barnouw, Adriaan Jacob 1877-1968
  Obituary 27
Barnouw, Victor 1915-1989 43
  Brief entry 28
Barnstone, Willis 1927- 20
Barnum, Jay Hyde 1888(?)-1962 20
Barnum, P. T., Jr.
  See Stratemeyer, Edward L.
Barnum, Richard 67
  Earlier sketch in SATA *1*
Barnum, Theodore
  See Stratemeyer, Edward L.
Baron, Kathy 1954- 90
Baron, Virginia Olsen 1931- 46
  Brief entry 28
Barr, Donald 1921-2004 20
  Obituary 152
Barr, George 1907-1992 2
Barr, Jene 1922-1985 16
  Obituary 42
Barr, Nevada 1952- 126
  Earlier sketch in SATA *115*
Barrer, Gertrude
  See Barrer-Russell, Gertrude
Barrer-Russell, Gertrude 1921- 27
Barrett, Angela (Jane) 1955- 145
  Earlier sketch in SATA *75*
Barrett, Ethel 87
  Brief entry 44
Barrett, Joyce Durham 1943- 138
Barrett, Judi
  See Barrett, Judith
Barrett, Judith 1941- 26
  See also CLR *98*
Barrett, Robert T(heodore) 1949- 92
Barrett, Ron 1937- 14
Barrett, Susan (Mary) 1938- 113
Barrett, Tracy 1955- 156
  Earlier sketches in SATA *84, 115*
Barrett, William E(dmund) 1900-1986
  Obituary 49
Barretta, Gene 176
Barretton, Grandall
  See Garrett, (Gordon) Randall (Phillip)
Barrie, J(ames) M(atthew) 1860-1937 100
  See also YABC *1*
  See also CLR *124*
Barringer, William 1940-1996 153
Barrington, Michael
  See Moorcock, Michael
Barris, George 1925- 47
Barrol, Grady
  See Bograd, Larry
Barron, Rex 1951- 84
Barron, T.A. 1952- 192
  Earlier sketches in SATA *83, 126*
  See also CLR *86*
Barron, Thomas Archibald
  See Barron, T.A.

Barron, Tom
  See Barron, T.A.
Barrow, Lloyd H. 1942- 73
Barrows, Annie 1962- 180
Barry, Dan 1958- 177
Barry, Dana (Marie Malloy) 1949- 139
Barry, James P(otvin) 1918- 14
Barry, Katharina Watjen 1936- 4
Barry, Robert (Everett) 1931- 6
Barry, Scott 1952- 32
Barry, Sheila Anne -2003 91
Bartell, Susan S. 175
Bartenbach, Jean 1918- 40
Barth, Edna 1914-1980 7
  Obituary 24
Barth, Kelly L. 1964- 152
Barthelme, Donald 1931-1989 7
  Obituary 62
Barth-Grozinger, Inge 1950- 185
Bartholomew, Barbara 1941- 86
  Brief entry 42
Bartholomew, Jean
  See Beatty, Patricia (Robbins)
Bartlett, Alison 153
Bartlett, Philip A. 1
Bartlett, Robert Merrill 1899-1995 12
Bartoletti, Susan Campbell 1958- 173
  Earlier sketches in SATA *88, 129, 135*
Barton, Byron 1930- 126
  Earlier sketches in SATA *9, 90*
Barton, Jill(ian) 1940- 75
Barton, May Hollis 67
  Earlier sketch in SATA *1*
Barton, Pat
  See Arrowsmith, Pat
Bartos-Hoeppner, Barbara 1923- 5
Bartram, Simon 156
Bartsch, Jochen 1906- 39
Baruch, Dorothy W(alter) 1899-1962 21
Barunga, Albert 1912(?)-1977 120
Baryshnikov, Mikhail 1948- 192
Bas, Rutger
  See Rutgers van der Loeff-Basenau, An(na)
  Maria Margaretha
Base, Graeme (Rowland) 1958- 162
  Earlier sketches in SATA *67, 101*
  See also CLR *22*
Baseman, Gary 1960- 174
Bash, Barbara 1948- 132
Bashevis, Isaac
  See Singer, Isaac Bashevis
Bashevis, Yitskhok
  See Singer, Isaac Bashevis
Basile, Gloria Vitanza 1929- 180
Baskin, Leonard 1922-2000 120
  Brief entry 27
  Earlier sketch in SATA *30*
Baskin, Nora Raleigh 1961- 189
  Earlier sketch in SATA *129*
Bason, Lillian 1913- 20
Bass, L. G.
  See Geringer, Laura
Bassett, Jeni 1959- 64
  Brief entry 43
Bassett, John Keith
  See Keating, Lawrence A.
Bassett, Lisa 1958- 61
Bassil, Andrea
  See Nilsen, Anna
Bastyra, Judy 108
Bat-Ami, Miriam 1950- 150
  Autobiography Feature 150
  Earlier sketches in SATA *82, 122*
Bate, Lucy 1939-1993 18
Bate, Norman (Arthur) 1916- 5
Bateman, Colin 1962- 172
Bateman, Donna M. 190
Bateman, Teresa 1957- 168
  Earlier sketch in SATA *112*
Bates, Amy June 189
Bates, Barbara S(nedeker) 1919- 12

Bates, Betty
   See Bates, Elizabeth
Bates, Dianne 1948- *147*
Bates, Elizabeth 1921- *19*
Bates, Ivan *175*
Bates, Katharine Lee 1859-1929 .... *113*
Bates, Martine
   See Leavitt, Martine
Bateson, Catherine 1960- *197*
   Earlier sketch in SATA *157*
Batey, Tom 1946- *52*
   Brief entry *41*
Bath, Kevin P.
   See Bath, K.P.
Bath, K.P. 1959- *171*
Batherman, Muriel
   See Sheldon, Muriel
Batson, Larry 1930- *35*
Batt, Tanya Robyn 1970- *131*
Battaglia, Aurelius 1910- *50*
   Brief entry *33*
Batten, H(arry) Mortimer 1888-1958 .... *25*
Batten, Mary 1937- *162*
   Earlier sketches in SATA *5, 102*
Batterberry, Ariane Ruskin 1935- *13*
Batterberry, Michael Carver 1932- *32*
Battle-Lavert, Gwendolyn 1951- *155*
   Earlier sketches in SATA *85, 131*
Battles, (Roxy) Edith 1921- *7*
Baudouy, Michel-Aime 1909- *7*
Bauer, Caroline Feller 1935- *98*
   Brief entry *46*
   Earlier sketch in SATA *52*
   See also SAAS *24*
Bauer, Fred 1934- *36*
Bauer, Helen 1900-1988 .... *2*
Bauer, Joan 1951- *160*
   Earlier sketch in SATA *117*
Bauer, Jutta 1955- *150*
Bauer, Marion Dane 1938- *192*
   Autobiography Feature *144*
   Earlier sketches in SATA *20, 69, 113, 144*
   See also SAAS *9*
Bauer, Michael Gerard 1955(?)- *167*
Bauer, Steven 1948- *125*
Bauerschmidt, Marjorie 1926- *15*
Baughman, Dorothy 1940- *61*
Baum, Allyn Z(elton) 1924-1997 .... *98*
   Earlier sketch in SATA *20*
Baum, L. Frank
   See Thompson, Ruth Plumly
Baum, L(yman) Frank 1856-1919 .... *100*
   Earlier sketch in SATA *18*
   See also CLR *107*
Baum, Louis 1948- *182*
   Brief entry *52*
   Earlier sketch in SATA *64*
Baum, Louis F.
   See Baum, L(yman) Frank
Baum, Maxie *188*
Baum, Willi 1931- *4*
Baumann, Amy (Brown) Beeching 1922- *10*
Baumann, Hans 1914- *2*
   See also CLR *35*
Baumann, Kurt 1935- *21*
Baumgartner, Barbara 1939- *86*
Baurys, Flo(rence) 1938- *122*
Bausum, Ann *173*
Bawden, Nina 1925- *132*
   Earlier sketches in SATA *4, 72*
   See also CLR *51*
   See also SAAS *16*
Bawden, Nina Mary Mabey
   See Bawden, Nina
Baxter, Valerie
   See Meynell, Laurence Walter
Bay, Jeanette Graham 1928- *88*
Bayer, Harold
   See Gregg, Andrew K.
Bayer, Jane E. (?)-1985
   Obituary *44*

Bayley, Nicola 1949- *129*
   Earlier sketches in SATA *41, 69*
Baylor, Byrd 1924- *136*
   Earlier sketches in SATA *16, 69*
   See also CLR *3*
Baynes, Pauline 1922-2008 .... *133*
   Obituary *196*
   Earlier sketches in SATA *19, 59*
Baynes, Pauline Diana
   See Baynes, Pauline
Bayoc, Cbabi *186*
BB
   See Watkins-Pitchford, Denys James
Beach, Charles
   See Reid, (Thomas) Mayne
Beach, Charles Amory *1*
Beach, Edward L. 1918-2002 .... *12*
   Obituary *140*
Beach, Edward Latimer
   See Beach, Edward L.
Beach, Lisa 1957- *111*
Beach, Lynn
   See Lance, Kathryn
Beach, Stewart T(aft) 1899-1979 .... *23*
Beachcroft, Nina 1931- *18*
Beagle, Peter S. 1939- *130*
   Earlier sketch in SATA *60*
Beagle, Peter Soyer
   See Beagle, Peter S.
Beaglehole, Helen 1946- *117*
Beale, Fleur *107*
Bealer, Alex W(inkler III) 1921-1980 .... *8*
   Obituary *22*
Beales, Valerie 1915- *74*
Beals, Carleton 1893-1979 .... *12*
Beals, Frank Lee 1881-1972
   Obituary *26*
Beam, Matt 1970- *187*
Beame, Rona 1934- *12*
Beamer, (George) Charles (Jr.) 1942- *43*
Bean, Jonathan 1979- *194*
Bean, Normal
   See Burroughs, Edgar Rice
Beaney, Jan
   See Udall, Jan Beaney
Beaney, Jane
   See Udall, Jan Beaney
Bear, Carolyn
   See Rayban, Chloe
Bear, Greg(ory Dale) 1951- *105*
   Earlier sketch in SATA *65*
Bearanger, Marie
   See Messier, Claire
Beard, Charles A(ustin) 1874-1948 .... *18*
Beard, Dan(iel Carter) 1850-1941 .... *22*
Beard, Darleen Bailey 1961- *96*
Bearden, Romare (Howard) 1914(?)-1988 ... *22*
   Obituary *56*
Beardmore, Cedric
   See Beardmore, George
Beardmore, George 1908-1979 .... *20*
Beardshaw, Rosalind 1969- *190*
Beardsley, Martyn R. 1957- *150*
Bearman, Jane (Ruth) 1917- *29*
Beaton, Clare 1947- *125*
Beatty, Elizabeth
   See Holloway, Teresa (Bragunier)
Beatty, Hetty Burlingame 1907-1971 .... *5*
Beatty, Jerome, Jr. 1918- *5*
Beatty, John (Louis) 1922-1975 .... *6*
   Obituary *25*
Beatty, Patricia (Robbins) 1922-1991 .... *73*
   Obituary *68*
   Earlier sketches in SATA *1, 30*
   See also SAAS *4*
Beaty, Andrea *186*
Beaty, Mary (T.) 1947- *146*
Beccia, Carlyn *189*
Bechard, Margaret 1953- *164*
   Earlier sketch in SATA *85*

Bechtel, Louise Seaman 1894-1985 .... *4*
   Obituary *43*
Beck, Barbara L. 1927- *12*
Beck, Ian 1947- *190*
   Earlier sketch in SATA *138*
   See Beck, Ian Archibald
Beck, Peggy 1949- *171*
Beck, Scott *197*
Becker, Beril 1901-1999 .... *11*
Becker, Bonny *184*
Becker, Deborah Zimmett 1955- *138*
Becker, Helaine 1961- *142*
Becker, John (Leonard) 1901- *12*
Becker, John E(mil) 1942- *148*
Becker, Joyce 1936- *39*
Becker, May Lamberton 1873-1958 .... *33*
Becker, Neesa 1951- *123*
Becker, Shari *174*
Beckerman, Chad W. *198*
Beckett, Sheilah 1913- *33*
Beckhorn, Susan Williams 1953- *189*
Beckles Willson, Robina (Elizabeth) 1930- . *27*
Beckman, Delores 1914-1994 .... *51*
Beckman, Gunnel 1910- *6*
   See also CLR *25*
   See also SAAS *9*
Beckman, Kaj
   See Beckman, Karin
Beckman, Karin 1913- *45*
Beckman, Per (Frithiof) 1913- *45*
Bedard, Michael 1949- *154*
   Earlier sketch in SATA *93*
   See also CLR *35*
Beddor, Frank *194*
Beddows, Eric
   See Nutt, Ken
Bedford, A. N.
   See Watson, Jane Werner
Bedford, Annie North
   See Watson, Jane Werner
Bedford, David *159*
Bedoukian, Kerop 1907-1981 .... *53*
Bee, Jay
   See Brainerd, John W(hiting)
Bee, William *188*
Beebe, B(urdetta) F(aye)
   See Johnson, B(urdetta) F(aye)
Beebe, (Charles) William 1877-1962 .... *19*
Beeby, Betty 1923- *25*
Beech, Mark 1971- *191*
Beech, Webb
   See Griffin, W.E.B
Beecham, Jahnna *161*
Beechcroft, William
   See Hallstead, William F(inn III)
Beeching, Jack 1922- *14*
Beeke, Tiphanie *163*
Beeler, Janet
   See Shaw, Janet
Beeler, Nelson F(rederick) 1910-1978 .... *13*
Beere, Peter 1951- *97*
Beers, Dorothy Sands 1917- *9*
Beers, Lorna 1897-1989 .... *14*
Beers, V(ictor) Gilbert 1928- *130*
   Earlier sketch in SATA *9*
Beeton, Max
   See Redding, Robert Hull
Begay, Shonto 1954- *137*
Begaye, Lisa Shook
   See Beach, Lisa
Begin, Maryjane 1963- *82*
Begin-Callanan, Maryjane
   See Begin, Maryjane
Begley, Kathleen A. 1948- *21*
Begley, Kathleen Anne
   See Begley, Kathleen A.
Behan, Leslie
   See Gottfried, Theodore Mark
Behler, Deborah A. 1947- *145*
Behler, John L. 1943-2006 .... *145*
   Obituary *173*

Behler, John Luther
  See Behler, John L.
Behn, Harry 1898-1973 2
  Obituary 34
Behnke, Frances L. 8
Behr, Joyce 1929- 15
Behrens, June York 1925- 19
Behrman, Carol H(elen) 1925- 144
  Earlier sketch in SATA 14
Beifuss, John, (Jr.) 1959- 92
Beil, Karen Magnuson 1950- 124
Beiler, Edna 1923- 61
Beinicke, Steve 1956- 69
Beirne, Barbara 1933- 71
Beiser, Arthur 1931- 22
Beiser, Germaine 1931- 11
Belair, Richard L. 1934- 45
Belaney, Archibald Stansfeld 1888-1938 24
  See also CLR 32
Belbin, David 1958- 164
  Earlier sketch in SATA 106
Belden, Wilanne Schneider 1925- 56
Belfrage, Sally 1936-1994 65
  Obituary 79
Belknap, B. H.
  See Ellis, Edward S(ylvester)
Belknap, Boynton
  See Ellis, Edward S(ylvester)
Belknap, Boynton M.D.
  See Ellis, Edward S(ylvester)
Bell, Anthea 1936- 148
  Earlier sketch in SATA 88
Bell, Clare (Louise) 1952- 99
Bell, Corydon Whitten 1894-1980 3
Bell, David Owen 1949- 99
Bell, Emerson
  See Stratemeyer, Edward L.
Bell, Emily Mary
  See Cason, Mabel Earp
Bell, Frank
  See Benson, Mildred (Augustine Wirt)
Bell, Gertrude (Wood) 1911-1987 12
Bell, Gina
  See Balzano, Jeanne (Koppel)
Bell, Hilari 1958- 197
  Earlier sketch in SATA 151
Bell, Jadrien
  See Golden, Christie
Bell, Janet
  See Clymer, Eleanor
Bell, Janet Cheatham 1937- 127
Bell, Krista 1950- 126
Bell, Krista Anne Blakeney
  See Bell, Krista
Bell, Margaret E(lizabeth) 1898-1990 2
Bell, Mary Reeves 1946- 88
Bell, Norman (Edward) 1899- 11
Bell, Raymond Martin 1907-1999 13
Bell, Siobhan 177
Bell, Thelma Harrington 1896-1985 3
Bell, William 1945- 90
  See also CLR 91
Bellairs, John (Anthony) 1938-1991 160
  Obituary 66
  Earlier sketches in SATA 2, 68
  See also CLR 37
Beller, Susan Provost 1949- 128
  Earlier sketch in SATA 84
  See also CLR 106
Bellingham, Brenda 1931- 99
  Brief entry 51
Bello, Rosario de
  See De Bello, Rosario
Belloc, (Joseph) Hilaire (Pierre Sebastien Rene
  Swanton) 1870-1953 112
  See also YABC 1
  See also CLR 102
Belloc, Joseph Peter Rene Hilaire
  See Belloc, (Joseph) Hilaire (Pierre Sebastien
  Rene Swanton)

Belloc, Joseph Pierre Hilaire
  See Belloc, (Joseph) Hilaire (Pierre Sebastien
  Rene Swanton)
Belloli, Andrea P. A. 1947- 86
Bell-Rehwoldt, Sheri 1962- 199
Bellville, Cheryl Walsh 1944- 54
  Brief entry 49
Bell-Zano, Gina
  See Balzano, Jeanne (Koppel)
Belpre, Pura 1899-1982 16
  Obituary 30
Belting, Natalia Maree 1915-1997 6
Belton, John Raynor 1931- 22
Belton, Sandra 1939- 186
  Earlier sketches in SATA 85, 134
Belton, Sandra Yvonne
  See Belton, Sandra
Belton, Sandra Yvonne
  See Belton, Sandra
Beltran, Alberto 1923- 43
Beltran-Hernandez, Irene 1945- 74
Belvedere, Lee
  See Grayland, Valerie (Merle Spanner)
Bemelmans, Ludwig 1898-1962 100
  Earlier sketch in SATA 15
  See also CLR 93
Benander, Carl D. 1941- 74
Benary, Margot
  See Benary-Isbert, Margot
Benary-Isbert, Margot 1889-1979 2
  Obituary 21
  See also CLR 12
Benasutti, Marion 1908-1992 6
Benatar, Raquel 1955- 167
Benchley, Nathaniel (Goddard) 1915-1981 .. 25
  Obituary 28
  Earlier sketch in SATA 3
Benchley, Peter 1940-2006 164
  Earlier sketches in SATA 3, 89
Benchley, Peter Bradford
  See Benchley, Peter
Bendall-Brunello, John 185
Bender, Edna 1941- 92
Bender, Esther 1942- 88
Bender, Lucy Ellen 1942- 22
Bender, Robert 1962- 160
  Earlier sketch in SATA 79
Bendick, Jeanne 1919- 135
  Earlier sketches in SATA 2, 68
  See also CLR 5
  See also SAAS 4
Bendick, Robert L(ouis) 1917- 11
Benedetto, William R. 1928- 180
Benedetto, William Ralph
  See Benedetto, William R.
Benedict, Andrew
  See Arthur, Robert, (Jr.)
Benedict, Dorothy Potter 1889-1979 11
  Obituary 23
Benedict, Lois Trimble 1902-1967 12
Benedict, Rex 1920-1995 8
Benedict, Stewart H(urd) 1924- 26
Beneduce, Ann Keay 128
Benet, Laura 1884-1979 3
  Obituary 23
Benet, Stephen Vincent 1898-1943
  See YABC 1
Benet, Sula 1906-1982 21
  Obituary 33
Ben-Ezer, Ehud 1936- 122
Benezra, Barbara (Beardsley) 1921- 10
Benham, Leslie 1922- 48
Benham, Lois (Dakin) 1924- 48
Benham, Mary Lile 1914-1991 55
Benjamin, E. M. J.
  See Bache, Ellyn
Benjamin, Nora
  See Kubie, Nora Gottheil Benjamin
Benjamin, Saragail Katzman 1953- 86
Benner, Cheryl 1962- 80
Benner, Judith Ann 1942- 94

Bennett, Alice
  See Ziner, Florence
Bennett, Cherie 1960- 158
  Earlier sketch in SATA 97
Bennett, Dorothea
  See Young, Dorothea Bennett
Bennett, Holly 1957- 181
Bennett, Holly 1957- 181
Bennett, James (W.) 1942- 153
  Autobiography Feature 153
  Earlier sketches in SATA 93, 148
Bennett, Jay 1912- 87
  Brief entry 27
  Earlier sketch in SATA 41
  See also SAAS 4
Bennett, Jill (Crawford) 1934- 41
Bennett, John 1865-1956
  See YABC 1
Bennett, Penelope (Agnes) 1938- 94
Bennett, Rachel
  See Hill, Margaret (Ohler)
Bennett, Rainey 1907-1998 15
  Obituary 111
Bennett, Richard 1899- 21
Bennett, Russell H(oradley) 1896- 25
Bennett, Veronica 1953- 178
Bennett, William (John) 1943- 102
Benning, Elizabeth
  See Rice, Bebe Faas
Benson, Elizabeth P(olk) 1924- 65
Benson, Kathleen 1947- 183
  Earlier sketches in SATA 62, 111
Benson, Linda M(aria) 1959- 84
Benson, Mildred (Augustine Wirt)
  1905-2002 100
  Obituary 135
  Earlier sketches in SATA 1, 65, 67
Benson, Mildred Wirt
  See Benson, Mildred (Augustine Wirt)
Benson, Millie
  See Benson, Mildred (Augustine Wirt)
Benson, Patrick 1956- 147
Benson, Sally 1900-1972 35
  Obituary 27
  Earlier sketch in SATA 1
Bentley, Judith (McBride) 1945- 89
  Earlier sketch in SATA 40
Bentley, Karen
  See Taschek, Karen
Bentley, Nancy (L.) 1946- 78
Bentley, Nicolas Clerihew 1907-1978
  Obituary 24
Bentley, Phyllis Eleanor 1894-1977 6
  Obituary 25
Bentley, Roy 1947- 46
Bentley, William (George) 1916- 84
Benton, Jim 1963- 172
ben Uzair, Salem
  See Horne, Richard Henry Hengist
Bercaw, Edna Coe 1961- 124
Berck, Judith 1960- 75
Berelson, Howard 1940- 5
Berends, Polly Berrien 1939- 50
  Brief entry 38
Berenstain, Jan 1923- 135
  Earlier sketches in SATA 12, 64, 129
  See also CLR 19
  See also SAAS 20
Berenstain, Janice
  See Berenstain, Jan
Berenstain, Michael 1951- 45
Berenstain, Mike
  See Berenstain, Michael
Berenstain, Stan 1923-2005 135
  Obituary 169
  Earlier sketches in SATA 12, 64, 129
  See also CLR 19
  See also SAAS 20
Berenstain, Stanley
  See Berenstain, Stan

Berenzy, Alix 1957- 168
Earlier sketch in SATA 65
Beresford, Elisabeth 1928- 141
Earlier sketches in SATA 25, 86
See also SAAS 20
Berg, Adriane G(ilda) 1948- 152
Berg, Dave
See Berg, David
Berg, David 1920-2002 27
Obituary 137
Berg, Elizabeth 1948- 104
Berg, Jean Horton 1913-1995 6
Berg, Joan
See Victor, Joan Berg
Berg, Ron 1952- 48
Bergaust, Erik 1925-1978 20
Bergel, Colin J. 1963- 137
Bergen, Joyce 1949- 95
Berger, Barbara (Helen) 1945- 77
Berger, Carin 185
Berger, Gilda 1935- 88
Brief entry 42
Berger, Josef 1903-1971 36
Berger, Melvin H. 1927- 158
Autobiography Feature 124
Earlier sketches in SATA 5, 88
See also CLR 32
See also SAAS 2
Berger, Phil 1942-2001 62
Berger, Samantha (Allison) 1969- 140
Berger, Terry 1933- 8
Bergey, Alyce (Mae) 1934- 45
Bergin, Mark 1961- 160
Earlier sketch in SATA 114
Berglin, Ruth Marie 1970- 181
Bergman, Donna 1934- 73
Bergman, Mara 1956- 196
Bergman, Tamar 1939- 95
Bergsma, Jody Lynn 163
Bergum, Constance R. 1952- 121
Berkebile, Fred D(onovan) 1900-1978
Obituary 26
Berkes, Marianne 173
Berkey, Barry Robert 1935- 24
Berkowitz, Freda Pastor 1908-1994 12
Berkus, Clara Widess 1909- 78
Berlan, Kathryn Hook 1946- 78
Berlfein, Judy Reiss 1958- 79
Berlin, Eric 195
Berliner, Don 1930- 33
Berliner, Franz 1930- 13
Berlitz, Charles (L. Frambach) 1914-2003 ... 32
Obituary 151
Berman, Linda 1948- 38
Berman, Paul (Lawrence) 1949- 66
Berna, Paul 1910-1994 15
Obituary 78
See also CLR 19
Bernadette
See Watts, (Anna) Bernadette
Bernard, Bruce 1928-2000 78
Obituary 124
Bernard, George I. 1949- 39
Bernard, Jacqueline (de Sieyes) 1921-1983 ... 8
Obituary 45
Bernard, Patricia 1942- 181
Earlier sketch in SATA 106
Bernard, Trish
See Bernard, Patricia
Bernardin, James (B.) 1966- 112
Bernardo, Anilu 184
Bernards, Neal 1963- 71
Bernasconi, Pablo 1973- 183
Bernays, Anne 1930- 32
Bernhard, Durga T. 1961- 80
Bernhard, Emery 1950- 80
Bernstein, Daryl (Evan) 1976- 81
Bernstein, Joanne E(ckstein) 1943- 15
Bernstein, Margery 1933- 114
Bernstein, Nina 1949- 180

Bernstein, Theodore M(enline) 1904-1979 ... 12
Obituary 27
Berrien, Edith Heal
See Heal, Edith
Berrill, Jacquelyn (Batsel) 1905- 12
Berrington, John
See Brownjohn, Alan
Berry, B. J.
See Berry, Barbara J.
Berry, Barbara J. 1937- 7
Berry, Erick
See Best, (Evangel) Allena Champlin
Berry, James 1925- 110
Earlier sketch in SATA 67
See also CLR 22
Berry, Jane Cobb 1915(?)-1979
Obituary 22
Berry, Joy
See Berry, Joy Wilt
Berry, Joy Wilt 1944- 58
Brief entry 46
Berry, Lynne 190
Berry, William D(avid) 1926- 14
Bersani, Shennen 1961- 164
Berson, Harold 1926- 4
Bertagna, Julie 1962- 151
Bertholf, Bret 189
Bertin, Charles-Francois
See Berlitz, Charles (L. Frambach)
Bertolet, Paul
See McLaughlin, Frank
Berton, Pierre (Francis de Marigny)
1920-2004 99
Obituary 158
Bertrand, Cecile 1953- 76
Bertrand, Diane Gonzales 1956- 177
Earlier sketch in SATA 106
Bertrand, Lynne 1963- 164
Earlier sketch in SATA 81
Beskow, Elsa (Maartman) 1874-1953 20
See also CLR 17
Bess, Clayton
See Locke, Robert
Besson, Luc 1959- 199
Best, (Evangel) Allena Champlin 1892-1974 . 2
Obituary 25
Best, Cari 1951- 149
Earlier sketch in SATA 107
Best, (Oswald) Herbert 1894-1980 2
Bestall, A(lfred) E(dmeades) 1892-1986 97
Obituary 48
Betancourt, Jeanne 1941- 148
Brief entry 43
Earlier sketches in SATA 55, 96
Beth, Mary
See Miller, Mary Beth
Bethancourt, T. Ernesto
See Paisley, Tom
Bethel, Dell 1929- 52
Bethell, Jean (Frankenberry) 1922- 8
Bethers, Ray 1902-1973 6
Bethke, Bruce Raymond 1955- 114
Bethlen, T.D.
See Silverberg, Robert
Bethune, J. G.
See Ellis, Edward S(ylvester)
Bethune, J. H.
See Ellis, Edward S(ylvester)
Betteridge, Anne
See Potter, Margaret (Newman)
Bettina
See Ehrlich, Bettina Bauer
Bettmann, Otto Ludwig 1903-1998 46
Bettoli, Delana 187
Betts, James
See Haynes, Betsy
Betz, Eva Kelly 1897-1968 10
Bevan, Tom 1868-1930(?)
See YABC 2
Bewick, Thomas 1753-1828 16
Beyer, Audrey White 1916- 9

Beyer, Paul J. III 1950- 74
Beynon, John
See Harris, John (Wyndham Parkes Lucas)
Beynon
Bezencon, Jacqueline (Buxcel) 1924- 48
Bhatia, Jamunadevi 1919- 48
Bhatia, June
See Bhatia, Jamunadevi
Bial, Morrison David 1917- 62
Bial, Raymond 1948- 165
Earlier sketches in SATA 76, 116
Biala
See Brustlein, Janice Tworkov
Biale, Rachel 1952- 99
Bialk, Elisa
See Krautter, Elisa (Bialk)
Bianchi, John 1947- 91
Bianchi, Robert S(teven) 1943- 92
Bianco, Margery
See Bianco, Margery Williams
Bianco, Margery Williams 1881-1944 15
See also CLR 19
Bianco, Pamela 1906- 28
Bibby, Violet 1908-1996 24
Bible, Charles 1937- 13
Bibo, Bobette
See Gugliotta, Bobette
Bice, Clare 1909-1976 22
Bickerstaff, Isaac
See Swift, Jonathan
Bidner, Jenni 1963- 193
Biegel, Paul 1925- 79
Earlier sketch in SATA 16
See also CLR 27
See also SAAS 18
Biemiller, Carl L(udwig), Jr.) 1912-1979 40
Obituary 21
Bienenfeld, Florence L(ucille) 1929- 39
Bierhorst, John (William) 1936- 149
Autobiography Feature 149
Earlier sketches in SATA 6, 91
See also SAAS 10
Biggar, Joan R(awlins) 1936- 120
Biggle, Lloyd, Jr. 1923-2002 65
Biggs, Brian 1968- 192
Bilal, Abdel W(ahab) 1970- 92
Bilbrough, Norman 1941- 111
Bildner, Phil 173
Bileck, Marvin 1920- 40
Bilibin, Ivan (Iakolevich) 1876-1942 61
Bill, Alfred Hoyt 1879-1964 44
Billam, Rosemary 1952- 61
Billings, Charlene W(interer) 1941- 41
Billingsley, Franny 1954- 132
Billington, Elizabeth T(hain) 50
Brief entry 43
Billout, Guy (Rene) 1941- 144
Earlier sketch in SATA 10
See also CLR 33
Bilson, Geoffrey 1938-1987 99
Binch, Caroline (Lesley) 1947- 140
Earlier sketch in SATA 81
Bing, Christopher (H.) 126
Bingham, Caroline 1962- 158
Bingham, Jane M. 1941- 163
Bingham, Jane Marie
See Bingham, Jane M.
Bingham, Sam(uel A.) 1944- 96
Bingley, Margaret (Jane Kirby) 1947- 72
Binkley, Anne
See Rand, Ann (Binkley)
Binzen, Bill
See Binzen, William
Binzen, William 24
Birch, David (W.) 1913-1996 89
Birch, Reginald B(athurst) 1856-1943 19
Birchman, David 1949- 72
Birchmore, Daniel A. 1951- 92
Bird, Carmel 1940- 124
Bird, E(lzy) J(ay) 1911- 58
Birdsall, Jeanne 1952(?)- 170

Birdseye, Tom 1951- *148*
  Earlier sketches in SATA *66, 98*
Birenbaum, Barbara 1941- *65*
Birmingham, Lloyd P(aul) 1924- *83*
  Earlier sketch in SATA *12*
Birmingham, Ruth
  See Sorrells, Walter
Birney, Betty G. 1947- *169*
  Earlier sketch in SATA *98*
Biro, B.
  See Biro, B(alint) S(tephen)
Biro, B(alint) S(tephen) 1921- *1*
  See also CLR *28*
  See also SAAS *13*
Biro, Val
  See Biro, B(alint) S(tephen)
Bischoff, Julia Bristol 1899-1970 .... *12*
Bishop, Bonnie 1943- *37*
Bishop, Claire Huchet 1899(?)-1993 .... *14*
  Obituary *74*
  See also CLR *80*
Bishop, Courtney
  See Ruemmler, John D(avid)
Bishop, Curtis (Kent) 1912-1967 .... *6*
Bishop, Elizabeth 1911-1979
  Obituary *24*
Bishop, Gavin 1946- *144*
  Earlier sketch in SATA *97*
Bishop, Kathleen Wong 1954- *120*
Bishop, Kathy
  See Bishop, Kathleen Wong
Bishop, Nic 1955- *161*
  Earlier sketch in SATA *107*
Bisset, Donald 1910-1995 .... *86*
  Earlier sketch in SATA *7*
Bisson, Terry 1942- *99*
Bisson, Terry Ballantine
  See Bisson, Terry
Bitter, Gary G(len) 1940- *22*
Bixby, William (Courtney) 1920-1986 .... *6*
  Obituary *47*
Bjoerk, Christina 1938- *99*
  Earlier sketch in SATA *67*
  See also CLR *22*
Bjork, Christina
  See Bjoerk, Christina
Bjorklund, Lorence F. 1913-1978 .... *35*
  Brief entry *32*
Bjorkman, Steve *163*
Black, Algernon David 1900-1993 .... *12*
  Obituary *76*
Black, Holly 1971- *147*
Black, Irma Simonton 1906-1972 .... *2*
  Obituary *25*
Black, Mansell
  See Trevor, Elleston
Black, MaryAnn
  See Easley, MaryAnn
Black, Susan Adams 1953- *40*
Blackall, Bernie 1956- *126*
Blackall, Sophie *182*
Blackburn, Claire
  See Altman, Linda Jacobs
Blackburn, John(ny) Brewton 1952- *15*
Blackburn, Joyce Knight 1920- *29*
Blacker, Terence 1948- *194*
Blacker, Tina
  See Louise, Tina
Blackett, Veronica Heath 1927- *12*
Blackie, Jean Cutler 1943- *79*
Blacklin, Malcolm
  See Chambers, Aidan
Blacklock, Dyan 1951- *112*
Blackman, Malorie 1962- *196*
  Earlier sketches in SATA *83, 128*
Blackton, Peter
  See Wilson, Lionel
Blackwood, Alan 1932- *70*
Blackwood, Freya *199*
Blackwood, Gary L. 1945- *169*
  Earlier sketches in SATA *72, 118*

Blade, Alexander
  See Garrett, (Gordon) Randall (Phillip)
  and Hamilton, Edmond
  and Silverberg, Robert
Blades, Ann (Sager) 1947- *69*
  Earlier sketch in SATA *16*
  See also CLR *15*
Bladow, Suzanne Wilson 1937- *14*
Blaine, Chris
  See Gardner, Craig Shaw
Blaine, John
  See Goodwin, Harold L(eland)
Blaine, Marge
  See Blaine, Margery Kay
Blaine, Margery Kay 1937- *11*
Blair, Alison
  See Lerangis, Peter
Blair, Anne Denton 1914-1993 .... *46*
Blair, David Nelson 1954- *80*
Blair, Eric (Arthur) 1903-1950 .... *29*
  See also CLR *68*
Blair, Jay 1953- *45*
Blair, Lucile
  See Yeakley, Marjory Hall
Blair, Margaret Whitman 1951- *124*
Blair, Mary 1911-1978 .... *195*
Blair, Pauline Hunter
  See Clarke, Pauline
Blair, Ruth Van Ness 1912-1999 .... *12*
Blair, Shannon
  See Kaye, Marilyn
Blair, Walter 1900-1992 .... *12*
  Obituary *72*
Blaisdell, Bob
  See Blaisdell, Robert
Blaisdell, Robert 1959- *105*
Blake, Bronwyn 1940- *149*
Blake, Francis *198*
Blake, Jon 1954- *171*
  Earlier sketch in SATA *78*
Blake, Olive
  See Supraner, Robyn
Blake, Quentin (Saxby) 1932- *125*
  Earlier sketches in SATA *9, 52, 96*
  See also CLR *31*
Blake, Robert 1949- *42*
Blake, Robert J. *160*
Blake, Walker E.
  See Griffin, W.E.B
Blake, William 1757-1827 .... *30*
  See also CLR *52*
Blakely, Gloria 1950- *139*
Blakely, Roger K. 1922- *82*
Blakeney, Jay D.
  See Chester, Deborah
Blakey, Nancy 1955- *94*
Blanc, Esther S. 1913-1997 .... *66*
Blanc, Mel 1908-1989
  Obituary *64*
Blanchard, Patricia *125*
Blanchet, M(uriel) Wylie 1891-1961 .... *106*
Blanco, Richard L(idio) 1926- *63*
Bland, E.
  See Nesbit, E.
Bland, Edith Nesbit
  See Nesbit, E.
Bland, Fabian
  See Nesbit, E.
Blane, Gertrude
  See Blumenthal, Gertrude
Blank, Clarissa Mabel 1915-1965 .... *62*
Blankenship, LeeAnn 1944- *181*
Blassingame, Wyatt Rainey 1909-1985 .... *34*
  Obituary *41*
  Earlier sketch in SATA *1*
Blatchford, Claire H. 1944- *94*
Blauer, Ettagale 1940- *49*
Bledsoe, Glen L. 1951- *108*
Bledsoe, Glen Leonard
  See Bledsoe, Glen L.

Bledsoe, Karen E. 1962- *167*
  Earlier sketch in SATA *108*
Bledsoe, Karen Elizabeth
  See Bledsoe, Karen E.
Bledsoe, Lucy Jane 1957- *162*
  Earlier sketch in SATA *97*
Bleeker, Sonia
  See Zim, Sonia Bleeker
Blegen, Daniel M. 1950- *92*
Blegvad, Erik 1923- *132*
  Earlier sketches in SATA *14, 66*
Blegvad, Lenore 1926- *176*
  Earlier sketches in SATA *14, 66*
Bley, Anette 1967- *188*
Blish, James (Benjamin) 1921-1975 .... *66*
Blishen, Edward (William) 1920-1996 .... *66*
  Obituary *93*
  Earlier sketch in SATA *8*
Bliss, Corinne Demas 1947- *131*
  Earlier sketch in SATA *37*
Bliss, Frederick
  See Card, Orson Scott
Bliss, Gillian
  See Paton Walsh, Jill
Bliss, Harry 1964- *196*
  Earlier sketch in SATA *156*
Bliss, Reginald
  See Wells, H(erbert) G(eorge)
Bliss, Ronald G(ene) 1942- *12*
Blitt, Barry *187*
Bliven, Bruce, Jr. 1916-2002 .... *2*
Blixen, Karen (Christentze Dinesen)
  1885-1962 .... *44*
Blizzard, Gladys S. (?)-1992 .... *79*
Blobaum, Cindy 1966- *123*
Bloch, Lucienne 1909-1999 .... *10*
Bloch, Marie Halun 1910-1998 .... *6*
  See also SAAS *9*
Bloch, Robert (Albert) 1917-1994 .... *12*
  Obituary *82*
Blochman, Lawrence G(oldtree)
  1900-1975 .... *22*
Block, Francesca Lia 1962- *158*
  Earlier sketches in SATA *80, 116*
  See also CLR *116*
  See also SAAS *21*
Block, Irvin 1917- *12*
Blomgren, Jennifer (Alice) 1954- *136*
Blood, Charles Lewis 1929- *28*
Bloom, Barbara Lee 1943- *146*
Bloom, Freddy 1914-2000 .... *37*
  Obituary *121*
Bloom, Lloyd 1947- *108*
  Brief entry *43*
Bloom, Suzanne 1950- *172*
Bloomfield, Michaela 1966- *70*
Bloor, Edward 1950- *155*
  Earlier sketch in SATA *98*
Bloor, Edward William
  See Bloor, Edward
Blos, Joan W. 1928- *153*
  Autobiography Feature *153*
  Brief entry *27*
  Earlier sketches in SATA *33, 69, 109*
  See also CLR *18*
  See also SAAS *11*
Blos, Joan Winsor
  See Blos, Joan W.
Blough, Glenn O(rlando) 1907-1995 .... *1*
Blue, Rose 1931- *166*
  Autobiography Feature *117*
  Earlier sketches in SATA *5, 91, 93*
  See also SAAS *24*
Blue, Zachary
  See Stine, R.L.
Bluggage, Oranthy
  See Alcott, Louisa May
Blumberg, Leda 1956- *59*
Blumberg, Rhoda 1917- *123*
  Earlier sketches in SATA *35, 70*
  See also CLR *21*

Blume, Judy 1938- 195
  Earlier sketches in SATA 2, 31, 79, 142
  See also CLR 69
Blume, Judy Sussman
  See Blume, Judy
Blume, Lesley M.M. 1975- 180
Blumenthal, Deborah 161
Blumenthal, Gertrude 1907-1971
  Obituary 27
Blumenthal, Shirley 1943- 46
Blutig, Eduard
  See Gorey, Edward (St. John)
Bly, Janet (Chester) 1945- 43
Bly, Stephen A(rthur) 1944- 116
  Earlier sketch in SATA 43
Blyler, Allison Lee 1966- 74
Blythe, Gary 1959- 185
Blyton, Carey 1932-2002 9
  Obituary 138
Blyton, Enid 1897-1968 25
  See also CLR 31
Blyton, Enid Mary
  See Blyton, Enid
Bo, Ben
  See Richardson, V.A.
Boardman, Fon Wyman, Jr. 1911-2000 6
Boardman, Gwenn R.
  See Petersen, Gwenn Boardman
Boase, Wendy 1944-1999 28
  Obituary 110
Boatner, Mark Mayo III 1921- 29
Bobbe, Dorothie de Bear 1905-1975 1
  Obituary 25
Bober, Natalie S. 1930- 134
  Earlier sketch in SATA 87
  See also SAAS 23
Bobette, Bibo
  See Gugliotta, Bobette
Bobri, Vladimir V. 1898-1986 47
  Brief entry 32
Bobritsky, Vladimir
  See Bobri, Vladimir V.
Bochak, Grayce 1956- 76
Bock, Hal
  See Bock, Harold I.
Bock, Harold I. 1939- 10
Bock, William Sauts Netamux'we 1939- 14
Bodanis, David 179
Bode, Janet 1943-1999 96
  Obituary 118
  Earlier sketch in SATA 60
Bode, N.E.
  See Baggott, Julianna
Bodecker, N(iels) M(ogens) 1922-1988 73
  Obituary 54
  Earlier sketch in SATA 8
Boden, Hilda
  See Bodenham, Hilda Morris
Bodenham, Hilda Morris 1901- 13
Bodett, Thomas Edward 1955- 70
Bodett, Tom
  See Bodett, Thomas Edward
Bodie, Idella F(allaw) 1925- 89
  Earlier sketch in SATA 12
Bodker, Cecil 1927- 133
  Earlier sketch in SATA 14
  See also CLR 23
Bodker, Cecil 1927-
  See Bodker, Cecil
Bodsworth, (Charles) Fred(erick) 1918- 27
Boeckman, Charles 1920- 12
Boegehold, Betty (Doyle) 1913-1985
  Obituary 42
Boelts, Maribeth 1964- 163
  Earlier sketch in SATA 78
Boerst, William J. 1939- 170
  Earlier sketch in SATA 121
Boesch, Mark J(oseph) 1917- 12
Boesen, Victor 1908- 16
Bogacki, Tomek 1950- 138
Bogaerts, Gert 1965- 80

Bogan, Paulette 1960- 129
Bogart, Jo Ellen 1945- 92
  See also CLR 59
Boggs, Ralph Steele 1901-1994 7
Bograd, Larry 1953- 89
  Earlier sketch in SATA 33
  See also SAAS 21
Bogue, Gary 1938- 195
Bogue, Gary L.
  See Bogue, Gary
Bohdal, Susi 1951- 101
  Earlier sketch in SATA 22
Bohlen, Nina 1931- 58
Bohlmeijer, Arno 1956- 94
Bohner, Charles (Henry) 1927- 62
Bohnhoff, Maya Kaathryn 1954- 88
Boiger, Alexandra 178
Boissard, Janine 1932- 59
Bojunga, Lygia
  See Nunes, Lygia Bojunga
Bojunga-Nunes, Lygia
  See Nunes, Lygia Bojunga
Boland, Janice 98
Bolden, Tonya 1959- 188
  Earlier sketches in SATA 79, 138
Bolden, Tonya Wilyce
  See Bolden, Tonya
Boles, Paul Darcy 1916-1984 9
  Obituary 38
Bolian, Polly 1925- 4
Bollen, Roger 1941(?)- 83
  Brief entry 29
Bolliger, Max 1929- 7
Bollinger, Max 1929- 167
Bollinger, Peter 172
Bolognese, Don(ald Alan) 1934- 129
  Earlier sketches in SATA 24, 71
Bolognese, Elaine (Raphael Chionchio)
  1933- 23
Bolotin, Norman (Phillip) 1951- 93
Bolton, Carole 1926- 6
Bolton, Elizabeth
  See St. John, Nicole
Bolton, Evelyn
  See Bunting, Eve
Bonar, Veronica
  See Bailey, Donna (Veronica Anne)
Bond, B. J.
  See Heneghan, James
Bond, Bruce 1939- 61
Bond, Felicia 1954- 126
  Earlier sketch in SATA 49
Bond, Gladys Baker 1912- 14
Bond, Higgins 1951- 177
  Earlier sketch in SATA 83
Bond, J. Harvey
  See Winterbotham, R(ussell) R(obert)
Bond, (Thomas) Michael 1926- 157
  Earlier sketches in SATA 6, 58
  See also CLR 95
  See also SAAS 3
Bond, Nancy 1945- 159
  Autobiography Feature 159
  Earlier sketches in SATA 22, 82
  See also CLR 11
  See also SAAS 13
Bond, Nancy Barbara
  See Bond, Nancy
Bond, Rebecca 1972- 130
Bond, Ruskin 1934- 87
  Earlier sketch in SATA 14
Bondie, J. D.
  See Cunningham, Chet
Bondoux, Anne-Laure 1971- 175
Bone, Ian 1956- 158
  Earlier sketch in SATA 117
Bonehill, Captain Ralph
  See Stratemeyer, Edward L.
Bonestell, Chesley 1888-1986
  Obituary 48
Bonham, Barbara Thomas 1926- 7

Bonham, Frank 1914-1989 49
  Obituary 62
  Earlier sketch in SATA 1
  See also SAAS 3
Boniface, William 1963- 182
  Earlier sketch in SATA 102
Bonino, Louise
  See Williams, Louise Bonino
Bonk, John J. 189
Bonn, Pat
  See Bonn, Patricia Carolyn
Bonn, Patricia Carolyn 1948- 43
Bonner, Hannah 197
Bonner, Mary Graham 1890-1974 19
Bonner, Mike 1951- 121
Bonners, Susan 1947- 85
  Brief entry 48
Bonnett-Rampersaud, Louise 173
Bonning, Tony 1948- 169
Bonsall, Crosby Barbara (Newell)
  1921-1995 23
  Obituary 84
Bonsall, Joseph S. 1948- 119
Bonsignore, Joan 1959- 140
Bontemps, Arna(ud Wendell) 1902-1973 44
  Obituary 24
  Earlier sketch in SATA 2
  See also CLR 6
Bonzon, Paul-Jacques 1908-1978 22
Boock, Paula 1964- 134
Booher, Dianna Daniels 1948- 33
Book, Rick 1949- 119
Book, Rita
  See Holub, Joan
Bookman, Charlotte
  See Zolotow, Charlotte
Boon, Debbie 1960- 103
Boon, Emilie (Laetitia) 1958- 86
Boone, Charles Eugene
  See Boone, Pat
Boone, Pat 1934- 7
Boorman, Linda (Kay) 1940- 46
Boorstin, Daniel J(oseph) 1914-2004 52
Booth, Coe 187
Booth, Ernest Sheldon 1915-1984 43
Booth, George 1926- 191
Booth, Graham (Charles) 1935- 37
Bootman, Colin 159
Borden, Louise 1949- 190
  Autobiography Feature 141
  Earlier sketches in SATA 68, 104, 141
Bordier, Georgette 1924- 16
Borgman, James
  See Borgman, Jim
Borgman, James Mark
  See Borgman, Jim
Borgman, Jim 1954- 122
Borgo, Lacy Finn 1972- 194
Boring, Mel 1939- 168
  Earlier sketch in SATA 35
Borja, Corinne 1929- 22
Borja, Robert 1923- 22
Borland, Hal
  See Borland, Harold Glen
Borland, Harold Glen 1900-1978 5
  Obituary 24
Borland, Kathryn Kilby 1916- 16
Borlenghi, Patricia 1951- 79
Born, Adolf 1930- 49
Bornstein, Ruth Lercher
  See Bornstein-Lercher, Ruth
Bornstein-Lercher, Ruth 1927- 88
  Autobiography Feature 107
  Earlier sketch in SATA 14
Borski, Lucia Merecka 18
Borten, Helen Jacobson 1930- 5
Bortolotti, Dan 1969- 157
Borton, Elizabeth
  See Trevino, Elizabeth B(orton) de
Borton, Lady 1942- 98

Borton de Trevino, Elizabeth
  See Trevino, Elizabeth B(orton) de
Bortstein, Larry 1942- 16
Bortz, Alfred B(enjamin) 1944- 139
  Earlier sketch in SATA 74
Bortz, Fred
  See Bortz, Alfred B(enjamin)
Bosch, Pseudonymous 199
Bosco, Jack
  See Holliday, Joseph
Boshell, Gordon 1908-1991 15
Boshinski, Blanche 1922- 10
Bosman, Paul 1929- 107
Bosse, Malcolm (Joseph, Jr.) 1926-2002 136
  Earlier sketch in SATA 35
Bosserman, (Charles) Phillip 1931- 84
Bossom, Naomi 1933- 35
Bostock, Mike 1962- 114
Boston, L(ucy) M(aria Wood) 1892-1990 19
  Obituary 64
  See also CLR 3
Bostrom, Kathleen (Susan) Long 1954- 139
Bostrom, Kathy
  See Bostrom, Kathleen (Susan) Long
Bosworth, J. Allan 1925- 19
Bothwell, Jean (?)-1977 2
Botkin, B(enjamin) A(lbert) 1901-1975 40
Botsford, Ward 1927-2004 66
Botting, Douglas (Scott) 1934- 43
Bottner, Barbara 1943- 170
  Autobiography Feature 121
  Earlier sketches in SATA 14, 93
  See also SAAS 26
Bottone, Frank G., Jr. 1969- 141
Bouchard, David 1952- 117
Boucher, (Clarence) Carter 1954- 129
Boudelang, Bob
  See Pell, Ed(ward)
Boughton, Richard 1954- 75
Boulet, Susan Seddon 1941- 50
Boulle, Pierre (Francois Marie-Louis)
  1912-1994 22
  Obituary 78
Boulton, Jane 1921- 91
Bouma, Paddy 1947- 128
Bour, Daniele 1939- 62
Bourbonniere, Sylvie 1966- 182
Bourdon, David 1934-1998 46
Bourgeois, Paulette 1951- 153
Bourne, Lesley
  See Marshall, Evelyn
Bourne, Miriam Anne 1931-1989 16
  Obituary 63
Boutet de Monvel, (Louis) M(aurice)
  1850(?)-1913 30
  See also CLR 32
Bova, Ben 1932- 133
  Earlier sketches in SATA 6, 68
  See also CLR 96
Bova, Benjamin William
  See Bova, Ben
Bovaird, Anne E(lizabeth) 1960- 90
Bow, Patricia 1946- 168
Bowden, Joan Chase 1925- 51
  Brief entry 38
Bowe, Julie 1962- 194
Bowen, Alexandria Russell 97
Bowen, Andy Russell
  See Bowen, Alexandria Russell
Bowen, Anne 1952- 170
Bowen, Betty Morgan
  See West, Betty
Bowen, Catherine (Shober) Drinker
  1897-1973 7
Bowen, David
  See Bowen, Joshua David
Bowen, Fred 1953- 136
Bowen, Joshua David 1930- 22
Bowen, Rhys
  See Quin-Harkin, Janet

Bowen, Robert Sydney 1900-1977 52
  Obituary 21
Bowermaster, Jon 1954- 135
  Earlier sketch in SATA 77
Bowers, Terrell L. 1945- 101
Bowers, Terry
  See Bowers, Terrell L.
Bowers, Tim 185
Bowie, C. W.
  See Old, Wendie C(orbin)
  and Wirths, Claudine (Turner) G(ibson)
Bowie, Jim
  See Norwood, Victor G(eorge) C(harles)
  and Stratemeyer, Edward L.
Bowkett, Stephen 1953- 67
Bowler, Jan Brett
  See Brett, Jan
Bowler, Tim 1953- 149
Bowman, Crystal 1951- 105
Bowman, James Cloyd 1880-1961 23
Bowman, John S(tewart) 1931- 16
Bowman, Kathleen (Gill) 1942- 52
  Brief entry 40
Bowman, Leslie
  See Bowman, Leslie W.
Bowman, Leslie W. 182
Bowsher, Melodie 195
Boxall, Ed 178
Boyce, Frank Cottrell 182
Boyce, George A(rthur) 1898- 19
Boyd, Candy Dawson 1946- 72
  See also CLR 50
Boyd, Pauline
  See Schock, Pauline
Boyd, Selma
  See Acuff, Selma Boyd
Boyd, Waldo T. 1918- 18
Boyden, Linda 1948- 143
Boyer, Allen B. 1963- 153
Boyer, Robert E(rnst) 1929- 22
Boyes, Vivien 1952- 106
Boyes, Vivien Elizabeth
  See Boyes, Vivien
Boyle, Ann (Peters) 1916- 10
Boyle, Eleanor Vere (Gordon) 1825-1916 28
Boyle, Robert H. 1928- 65
Boylston, Helen Dore 1895-1984 23
  Obituary 39
Boyne, John 1971- 181
Boynton, Sandra (Keith) 1953- 152
  Brief entry 38
  Earlier sketches in SATA 57, 107
  See also CLR 105
Boz
  See Dickens, Charles (John Huffam)
Bracken, Charles
  See Pellowski, Michael (Joseph)
Brackers de Hugo, Pierre 1960- 115
Brackett, Dolli Tingle 1911-1993 137
Brackett, Virginia 1950- 166
  Earlier sketch in SATA 121
Brackett, Virginia Roberts Meredith
  See Brackett, Virginia
Bradbury, Bianca (Ryley) 1908-1982 56
  Earlier sketch in SATA 3
Bradbury, Edward P.
  See Moorcock, Michael
Bradbury, Ray 1920- 123
  Earlier sketches in SATA 11, 64
Bradbury, Ray Douglas
  See Bradbury, Ray
Bradby, Marie 161
Bradfield, Carl 1942- 91
Bradford, Ann (Liddell) 1917- 56
  Brief entry 38
Bradford, Barbara Taylor 1933- 66
Bradford, Karleen 1936- 96
  Earlier sketch in SATA 48
Bradford, Lois J(ean) 1936- 36
Bradford, Richard (Roark) 1932-2002 59
  Obituary 135

Bradley, Duane
  See Sanborn, Duane
Bradley, Kimberly Brubaker 1967- 179
Bradley, Marion Zimmer 1930-1999 139
  Obituary 116
  Earlier sketch in SATA 90
Bradley, Timothy J. 193
Bradley, Virginia 1912- 23
Bradley, Will
  See Strickland, (William) Brad(ley)
Bradman, Tony 1954- 152
  Earlier sketch in SATA 81
Bradshaw, Gillian (Joan) 1949- 118
Bradshaw, Gillian 1956- 127
Bradshaw, Gillian Marucha
  See Bradshaw, Gillian
Bradstreet, T. J.
  See Thesman, Jean
Brady, Esther Wood 1905-1987 31
  Obituary 53
Brady, Irene 1943- 4
Brady, Kimberley S. 1953- 101
Brady, Kimberley Smith
  See Brady, Kimberley S.
Brady, Lillian 1902- 28
Bragdon, Elspeth MacDuffie 1897-1980 6
Bragdon, Lillian Jacot 24
Brager, Bruce L. 1949- 146
Bragg, Mabel Caroline 1870-1945 24
Bragg, Michael 1948- 46
Bragg, Ruth Gembicki 1943- 77
Brahm, Sumishta 1954- 58
Brailsford, Frances
  See Wosmek, Frances
Brainerd, John W(hiting) 1918- 65
Braithwaite, Althea 1940- 23
  Autobiography Feature 119
  See also SAAS 24
Bram, Elizabeth 1948- 30
Brancato, Robin F(idler) 1936- 97
  See also CLR 32
  See also SAAS 9
Branch, Muriel Miller 1943- 152
  Earlier sketch in SATA 94
Brand, Christianna
  See Lewis, Mary (Christianna)
Brand, Rebecca
  See Charnas, Suzy McKee
Brande, Robin 194
Brandel, Marc 1919- 71
Brandenberg, Alexa (Demetria) 1966- 97
Brandenberg, Aliki (Liacouras) 1929- 157
  Earlier sketches in SATA 2, 35, 75, 113
  See also CLR 71
Brandenberg, Franz 1932- 75
  Earlier sketches in SATA 8, 35
Brandenburg, Jim 1945- 87
Brandhorst, Carl T(heodore) 1898-1988 23
Brandis, Marianne 1938- 149
  Earlier sketches in SATA 59, 96
Brandon, Brumsic, Jr. 1927- 9
Brandon, Curt
  See Bishop, Curtis (Kent)
Brandreth, Gyles 1948- 28
Brandreth, Gyles Daubeney
  See Brandreth, Gyles
Brandt, Catharine 1905-1997 40
Brandt, Keith
  See Sabin, Louis
Brandt, Sue R(eading) 1916- 59
Branfield, John (Charles) 1931- 11
Branford, Henrietta 1946-1999 106
Branley, Franklyn M(ansfield) 1915-2002 .. 136
  Earlier sketches in SATA 4, 68
  See also CLR 13
  See also SAAS 16
Branscum, Robbie (Tilley) 1937-1997 72
  Obituary 96
  Earlier sketch in SATA 23
  See also SAAS 17
Bransom, (John) Paul 1885-1979 43

Brashares, Ann 1967- *188*
  Earlier sketch in SATA *145*
  See also CLR *113*
Brassard, France 1963- *186*
Braswell, E.J.
  See Lynn, Tracy
Braswell, Elizabeth J.
  See Lynn, Tracy
Braswell, Liz
  See Lynn, Tracy
Bratton, Helen 1899-1986 .... *4*
Bratun, Katy 1950- *160*
  Earlier sketch in SATA *83*
Braude, Michael 1936- *23*
Braun, Lilian Jackson 1916(?)- *109*
Brautigan, Richard (Gary) 1935-1984 .... *56*
Bray, Libba *159*
Bray, Martha E.
  See Bray, Libba
Braymer, Marjorie Elizabeth 1911-1988 .... *6*
Breathed, Berke 1957- *161*
  Earlier sketch in SATA *86*
Breathed, Guy Berkeley
  See Breathed, Berke
Brecht, Edith 1895-1975 .... *6*
  Obituary *25*
Breck, Vivian
  See Breckenfeld, Vivian Gurney
Breckenfeld, Vivian Gurney 1895-1992 .... *1*
Breda, Tjalmar
  See DeJong, David C(ornel)
Bredeson, Carmen 1944- *163*
  Earlier sketch in SATA *98*
Breen, Steve 1970- *186*
Breinburg, Petronella 1927- *11*
  See also CLR *31*
Breisky, William J(ohn) 1928- *22*
Brenaman, Miriam *172*
Brennan, Caitlin
  See Tarr, Judith
Brennan, Gale (Patrick) 1927- *64*
  Brief entry *53*
Brennan, Herbie 1940- *183*
  Earlier sketch in SATA *140*
Brennan, James Herbert
  See Brennan, Herbie
Brennan, Jan
  See Brennan, Herbie
Brennan, J.H.
  See Brennan, Herbie
Brennan, Joseph Lomas 1903-2000 .... *6*
Brennan, Linda Crotta 1952- *130*
Brennan, Tim
  See Conroy, John Wesley
Brenner, Anita 1905-1974 .... *56*
Brenner, Barbara (Johnes) 1925- *124*
  Earlier sketches in SATA *4, 42, 76*
  See also SAAS *14*
Brenner, Fred 1920- *36*
  Brief entry *34*
Brent, Hope 1935(?)-1984
  Obituary *39*
Brent, Stuart *14*
Breskin, Jane
  See Zalben, Jane Breskin
Breslin, Theresa *128*
  Autobiography Feature *128*
  Earlier sketch in SATA *70*
Breslow, Maurice 1935- *72*
Breslow, Maurice A
  See Breslow, Maurice
Breslow, Susan 1951- *69*
Brett, Bernard 1925- *22*
Brett, Grace N(eff) 1900-1975 .... *23*
Brett, Jan 1949- *171*
  Earlier sketches in SATA *42, 71, 130*
  See also CLR *27*
Brett, Jan Churchill
  See Brett, Jan
Brett Bowler, Jan
  See Brett, Jan

Brewer, Heather 1973- *196*
Brewer, James D. 1951- *108*
Brewer, Sally King 1947- *33*
Brewer, Benjamin
  See Folsom, Franklin (Brewster)
Brewster, Hugh 1950- *191*
  Earlier sketch in SATA *95*
Brewster, Patience 1952- *97*
Brewton, John E(dmund) 1898-1982 .... *5*
Brian, Janeen (Paulette) 1948- *141*
Briant, Ed *180*
Brick, John 1922-1973 .... *10*
Brickman, Robin D. 1954- *155*
Bride, Nadja
  See Nobisso, Josephine
Bridgers, Sue Ellen 1942- *90*
  Autobiography Feature *109*
  Earlier sketch in SATA *22*
  See also CLR *18*
  See also SAAS *1*
Bridges, Laurie
  See Bruck, Lorraine
Bridges, Ruby (Nell) 1954- *131*
Bridges, William (Andrew) 1901-1984 .... *5*
Bridwell, Norman (Ray) 1928- *138*
  Earlier sketches in SATA *4, 68*
  See also CLR *96*
Brier, Howard M(axwell) 1903-1969 .... *8*
Brierley, (Louise) 1958- *59*
Briggs, Katharine Mary 1898-1980 .... *101*
  Obituary *25*
Briggs, Peter 1921-1975 .... *39*
  Obituary *31*
Briggs, Raymond 1934- *184*
  Earlier sketches in SATA *23, 66, 131*
  See also CLR *10*
Briggs, Raymond Redvers
  See Briggs, Raymond
Bright, Paul 1949- *182*
Bright, Robert (Douglas Sr.) 1902-1988 .... *63*
  Obituary *60*
  Earlier sketch in SATA *24*
Bright, Sarah
  See Shine, Deborah
Brightfield, Richard 1927- *65*
  Brief entry *53*
Brightfield, Rick
  See Brightfield, Richard
Brighton, Catherine 1943- *107*
  Earlier sketch in SATA *65*
Brill, Marlene Targ 1945- *124*
  Earlier sketch in SATA *77*
Brimberg, Stanlee 1947- *9*
Brimner, Larry Dane 1949- *170*
  Autobiography Feature *112*
  Earlier sketch in SATA *79*
Brin, David 1950- *65*
Brin, Ruth Firestone 1921- *22*
Brinckloe, Julie 1950- *13*
Brinckloe, Julie Lorraine
  See Brinckloe, Julie
Brindel, June (Rachuy) 1919- *7*
Brindle, Max
  See Fleischman, Sid
Brindze, Ruth 1903-1984 .... *23*
Brink, Carol Ryrie 1895-1981 .... *100*
  Obituary *27*
  Earlier sketches in SATA *1, 31*
  See also CLR *30*
Brinsmead, H. F(ay)
  See Brinsmead, H(esba) F(ay)
Brinsmead, H. F.
  See Brinsmead, H(esba) F(ay)
Brinsmead, H(esba) F(ay) 1922- *78*
  Earlier sketch in SATA *18*
  See also CLR *47*
  See also SAAS *5*
Briquebec, John
  See Rowland-Entwistle, (Arthur) Theodore
  (Henry)

Brisbane, Henry R.
  See Ellis, Edward S(ylvester)
Brisco, P. A.
  See Matthews, Patricia
Brisco, Patty
  See Matthews, Patricia
  and Matthews, Clayton (Hartley)
Briscoe, Jill (Pauline) 1935- *56*
  Brief entry *47*
Brisley, Joyce Lankester 1896-1978 .... *22*
  Obituary *84*
Brissenden, Connie
  See Brissenden, Constance
Brissenden, Constance 1947- *150*
Brisson, Pat 1951- *177*
  Autobiography Feature *133*
  Earlier sketches in SATA *67, 128, 133*
Britt, Albert 1874-1969
  Obituary *28*
Britt, Dell 1934- *1*
Brittain, Bill
  See Brittain, William (E.)
Brittain, C. Dale 1948- *82*
Brittain, William (E.) 1930- *76*
  Earlier sketch in SATA *36*
  See also SAAS *7*
Brittingham, Geoffrey (Hugh) 1959- *76*
Britton, Kate
  See Stegeman, Janet Allais
Britton, Louisa
  See McGuire, Leslie (Sarah)
Britton, Rick 1952- *82*
Bro, Marguerite (Harmon) 1894-1977 .... *19*
  Obituary *27*
Broach, Elise 1963- *173*
Broadhead, Helen Cross 1913- *25*
Brochmann, Elizabeth 1938- *41*
Brock, Betty (Carter) 1923-2003 .... *4*
  Obituary *150*
Brock, C(harles) E(dmund) 1870-1938 .... *42*
  Brief entry *32*
Brock, Delia
  See Ephron, Delia
Brock, Emma L(illian) 1886-1974 .... *8*
Brock, H(enry) M(atthew) 1875-1960 .... *42*
Brockett, Eleanor Hall 1913-1967 .... *10*
Brockman, C(hristian) Frank 1902-1985 .... *26*
Brockmeier, Kevin 1972- *176*
Broderick, Dorothy M. 1929- *5*
Brodeur, Ruth Wallace
  See Wallace-Brodeur, Ruth
Brodie, Sally
  See Cavin, Ruth (Brodie)
Brodsky, Beverly
  See McDermott, Beverly Brodsky
Brody, Wendy
  See Staub, Wendy Corsi
Broeger, Achim 1944- *31*
Broekel, Rainer Lothar 1923- *38*
Broekel, Ray
  See Broekel, Rainer Lothar
Broekstra, Lorette 1964- *189*
  Earlier sketch in SATA *124*
Brogden, Sherryl
  See Jordan, Sherryl
Broger, Achim
  See Broeger, Achim
Broida, Marian *154*
Brokamp, Marilyn 1920- *10*
Broman, Fred
  See Moseley, James W(illett)
Bromhall, Winifred *26*
Brommer, Gerald F(rederick) 1927- *28*
Brondfield, Jerome 1913-1998 .... *22*
Brondfield, Jerry
  See Brondfield, Jerome
Bronner, Stephen Eric 1949- *101*
Bronowski, Jacob 1908-1974 .... *55*
Bronson, Alice
  See Watkins, Dawn L.

Bronson, Lynn
  See Lampman, Evelyn Sibley
Bronson, Wilfrid Swancourt 1894-1985
  Obituary *43*
Brook, Judith (Penelope) 1926- *59*
  Brief entry *51*
Brook, Judy
  See Brook, Judith (Penelope)
Brooke, L(eonard) Leslie 1862-1940 .... *17*
  See also CLR *20*
Brooke, William J. 1946- *139*
Brooke-Haven, P.
  See Wodehouse, P(elham) G(renville)
Brooker, Kyrsten *199*
Brookins, Dana 1931- *28*
Brooks, Anita
  See Abramovitz, Anita (Zeltner Brooks)
Brooks, Bill 1939- *59*
Brooks, Bruce 1950- *112*
  Brief entry *53*
  Earlier sketch in SATA *72*
  See also CLR *25*
Brooks, Caryl 1924- *84*
Brooks, Charlotte K(endrick) 1918-1998 ..... *24*
  Obituary *112*
Brooks, Erik 1972- *182*
  Earlier sketch in SATA *152*
Brooks, George
  See Baum, L(yman) Frank
Brooks, Gwendolyn 1917-2000 .... *6*
  Obituary *123*
  See also CLR *27*
Brooks, Gwendolyn Elizabeth
  See Brooks, Gwendolyn
Brooks, Jerome 1931- *23*
Brooks, Kevin 1959- *197*
  Earlier sketch in SATA *150*
Brooks, Kevin M.
  See Brooks, Kevin
Brooks, Lester 1924- *7*
Brooks, Martha 1944- *134*
  Autobiography Feature *134*
  Earlier sketches in SATA *68, 121*
Brooks, Maurice (Graham) 1900- *45*
Brooks, Polly Schoyer 1912- *12*
Brooks, Ron 1948- *94*
  Brief entry *33*
Brooks, Ronald George
  See Brooks, Ron
Brooks, Terry 1944- *60*
Brooks, Walter R(ollin) 1886-1958 .... *17*
Brooks-Hill, Helen (Mason) 1908-1994 .... *59*
Broome, Errol 1937- *158*
  Earlier sketch in SATA *105*
Brophy, Nannette 1963- *73*
Brosnan, James Patrick 1929- *14*
Brosnan, Jim
  See Brosnan, James Patrick
Brostoff, Anita 1931- *132*
Brothers Grimm
  See Grimm, Jacob Ludwig Karl
  and Grimm, Wilhelm Karl
Brothers Hildebrandt, The
  See Hildebrandt, Greg
  and Hildebrandt, Tim
Broun, Emily
  See Sterne, Emma Gelders
Brouwer, S. W.
  See Brouwer, Sigmund (W.)
Brouwer, Sigmund (W.) 1959- *109*
Brow, Thea 1934- *60*
Brower, Millicent *8*
Brower, Pauline 1929- *22*
Browin, Frances Williams 1898-1986 .... *5*
Brown, Alexis
  See Baumann, Amy (Brown) Beeching
Brown, Anne Ensign 1937- *61*
Brown, Beverly Swerdlow *97*
Brown, Bill
  See Brown, William L(ouis)

Brown, Billye Walker
  See Cutchen, Billye Walker
Brown, Bob
  See Brown, Robert Joseph
Brown, Buck 1936- *45*
Brown, Calef *179*
Brown, Cassie 1919-1986 .... *55*
Brown, Charlotte Lewis *181*
Brown, Conrad 1922- *31*
Brown, Craig McFarland 1947- *73*
Brown, David
  See Brown, David A(lan)
  and Myller, Rolf
Brown, Dee 1908-2002 .... *110*
  Obituary *141*
  Earlier sketch in SATA *5*
Brown, Dee Alexander
  See Brown, Dee
Brown, Don 1949- *172*
Brown, Drew T. III 1955- *83*
Brown, Drollene P. 1939- *53*
Brown, Elbrite *198*
Brown, Eleanor Frances 1908-1987 .... *3*
Brown, Elizabeth Ferguson 1937- *153*
Brown, Elizabeth M(yers) 1915- *43*
Brown, Fern G. 1918- *34*
Brown, (Robert) Fletch 1923- *42*
Brown, Fornan 1901-1996 .... *71*
  Obituary *88*
Brown, George Earl 1883-1964 .... *11*
Brown, George Mackay 1921-1996 .... *35*
Brown, Irene Bennett 1932- *3*
Brown, Irving
  See Adams, William Taylor
Brown, Ivor (John Carnegie) 1891-1974 .... *5*
  Obituary *26*
Brown, Jane Clark 1930- *81*
Brown, Janet Mitsui *87*
Brown, Jo 1964- *170*
Brown, Joanne 1933- *147*
Brown, Joe David 1915-1976 .... *44*
Brown, Joseph E(dward) 1929- *59*
  Brief entry *51*
Brown, Judith Gwyn 1933- *20*
Brown, Kathryn 1955- *168*
  Earlier sketch in SATA *98*
Brown, Kathy
  See Brown, Kathryn
Brown, Ken (James) *129*
Brown, Kevin 1960- *101*
Brown, Laurene Krasny 1945- *99*
  Earlier sketch in SATA *54*
Brown, Laurie Krasny
  See Brown, Laurene Krasny
Brown, Lloyd Arnold 1907-1966 .... *36*
Brown, Mahlon A.
  See Ellis, Edward S(ylvester)
Brown, Marc (Tolon) 1946- *145*
  Earlier sketches in SATA *10, 53, 80*
  See also CLR *29*
Brown, Marcia (Joan) 1918- *47*
  Earlier sketch in SATA *7*
  See also CLR *12*
Brown, Margaret Wise 1910-1952 .... *100*
  See also YABC *2*
  See also CLR *107*
Brown, Margery (Wheeler) *78*
  Earlier sketch in SATA *5*
Brown, Marion Marsh 1908-2001 .... *6*
Brown, Myra Berry 1918- *6*
Brown, Palmer 1919- *36*
Brown, Pamela (Beatrice) 1924-1989 .... *5*
  Obituary *61*
Brown, Peter 1979- *178*
Brown, Reeve Lindbergh
  See Lindbergh, Reeve
Brown, Richard E. 1946- *61*
Brown, Robert Joseph 1907-1989 .... *14*
Brown, Roderick (Langmere) Haig-
  See Haig-Brown, Roderick (Langmere)

Brown, Rosalie
  See Moore, Rosalie (Gertrude)
Brown, Roswell
  See Webb, Jean Francis (III)
Brown, Roy (Frederick) 1921-1982 .... *51*
  Obituary *39*
Brown, Ruth 1941- *170*
  Earlier sketch in SATA *105*
Brown, Scott 1971- *134*
Brown, Sue Ellen 1954- *81*
Brown, Tricia 1954- *114*
Brown, Vinson 1912-1991 .... *19*
Brown, Walter R(eed) 1929- *19*
Brown, Will
  See Ainsworth, William Harrison
Brown, William L(ouis) 1910-1964 .... *5*
Browne, Anthony 1946- *163*
  Brief entry *44*
  Earlier sketches in SATA *45, 61, 105*
  See also CLR *19*
Browne, Anthony Edward Tudor
  See Browne, Anthony
Browne, Dik
  See Browne, Richard Arthur Allen
Browne, Hablot Knight 1815-1882 .... *21*
Browne, Matthew
  See Rands, William Brighty
Browne, Nicki M.
  See Browne, N.M.
Browne, Nicky Matthews
  See Browne, N.M.
Browne, N.M. 1960- *167*
Browne, Richard Arthur Allen 1917-1989 ... *67*
  Brief entry *38*
Browne, Vee F(rances) 1956- *90*
Browning, Robert 1812-1889
  See YABC *1*
  See also CLR *97*
Brownjohn, Alan 1931- *6*
Brownlee, Walter 1930- *62*
Brownlie, Betty 1946- *159*
Brownlow, Kevin 1938- *65*
Brownlow, Mike *183*
Brownridge, William R(oy) 1932- *94*
Bruce, Dorita Fairlie 1885-1970
  Obituary *27*
Bruce, (William) Harry 1934- *77*
Bruce, Mary 1927- *1*
Bruchac, Joseph III
  See Bruchac, Joseph
Bruchac, Joseph 1942- *176*
  Autobiography Feature *176*
  Earlier sketches in SATA *42, 89, 131*
  See also CLR *46*
Bruchac, Margaret M.
  See Bruchac, Marge
Bruchac, Marge *181*
Bruck, Lorraine 1921- *55*
  Brief entry *46*
Bruel, Nick *166*
Bruel, Robert O. 1929-2002 .... *189*
Bruemmer, Fred 1929- *47*
Brugman, Alyssa (F.) 1974- *152*
Brumbeau, Jeff 1955- *157*
Bruna, Dick 1927- *76*
  Brief entry *30*
  Earlier sketch in SATA *43*
  See also CLR *7*
Brunhoff, Jean de 1899-1937 .... *24*
  See also CLR *116*
Brunhoff, Laurent de 1925- *150*
  Earlier sketches in SATA *24, 71*
  See also CLR *116*
Brunskill, Elizabeth Ann Flatt
  See Flatt, Lizann
Brush, Karen A(lexandra) 1960- *85*
Brussel-Smith, Bernard 1914- *58*
Brust, Steven 1955- *121*
  Earlier sketch in SATA *86*
Brust, Steven K. Zoltan
  See Brust, Steven

Brustlein, Daniel 1904- *40*
Brustlein, Janice Tworkov -2000 .... *40*
  Obituary *126*
Brutschy, Jennifer 1960- *84*
Bryan, Ashley 1923- *178*
  Earlier sketches in SATA *31, 72, 132*
  See also CLR *66*
Bryan, Ashley F.
  See Bryan, Ashley
Bryan, Dorothy M. 1896(?)-1984
  Obituary *39*
Bryan, Jennifer *190*
Bryan, Sean *192*
Bryant, Bernice (Morgan) 1908-1976 .... *11*
Bryant, Jen 1960- *175*
  Earlier sketch in SATA *94*
Bryant, Jennifer Fisher
  See Bryant, Jen
Bryant, Laura J. *176*
Brychta, Alex 1956- *21*
Brynie, Faith H. 1946- *113*
Brynie, Faith Hickman
  See Brynie, Faith H.
Bryson, Bernarda 1903-2004 .... *9*
Buba, Joy Flinsch 1904- *44*
Buchan, Bryan 1945- *36*
Buchan, John 1875-1940
  See YABC *2*
Buchan, Stuart 1942-1987
  Obituary *54*
Buchanan, Debby 1952- *82*
Buchanan, Deborah Leevonne
  See Buchanan, Debby
Buchanan, Jane 1956- *160*
Buchanan, Paul 1959- *116*
Buchanan, Sue 1939- *139*
Buchheimer, Naomi Barnett
  See Barnett, Naomi
Buchignani, Walter 1965- *84*
Buchmann, Stephen L. *194*
Buchwald, Art 1925-2007 .... *10*
Buchwald, Arthur
  See Buchwald, Art
Buchwald, Emilie 1935- *7*
Buck, Gisela 1941- *101*
Buck, Lewis 1925- *18*
Buck, Margaret Waring 1905-1997 .... *3*
Buck, Nola
  See Godwin, Laura
Buck, Pearl S(ydenstricker) 1892-1973 .... *25*
  Earlier sketch in SATA *1*
Buck, Siegfried 1941- *101*
Buckeridge, Anthony (Malcolm)
  1912-2004 .... *85*
  Earlier sketch in SATA *6*
Buckholtz, Eileen (Garber) 1949- *54*
  Brief entry *47*
Buckler, Ernest 1908-1984 .... *47*
Buckless, Andrea K. 1968- *117*
Buckley, Helen E(lizabeth) 1918- *90*
  Earlier sketch in SATA *2*
Buckley, James, Jr. 1963- *166*
  Earlier sketch in SATA *114*
Buckley, Michael *177*
Buckley, Susan *184*
Buckley, Susan Washburn
  See Buckley, Susan
Buckley-Archer, Linda *185*
Buckmaster, Henrietta
  See Stephens, Henrietta Henkle
Bucks, Brad
  See Holub, Joan
Budd, E. S.
  See Sirimarco, Elizabeth
Budd, Lillian (Peterson) 1897-1989 .... *7*
Budhos, Marina *173*
Buehler, Stephanie Jona 1956- *83*
Buehner, Caralyn (M.) 1963- *159*
  Earlier sketch in SATA *104*
Buehner, Mark 1959- *159*
  Earlier sketch in SATA *104*

Buehr, Walter Franklin 1897-1971 .... *3*
Buell, Ellen Lewis
  See Cash, Ellen Lewis Buell
Buell, Janet 1952- *185*
  Earlier sketch in SATA *106*
Buergel, Paul-Hermann H. 1949- *83*
Buettner, Dan 1960- *95*
Buff, Conrad 1886-1975 .... *19*
Buff, Mary (E. Marsh) 1890-1970 .... *19*
Buffett, Jimmy 1946- *110*
  Earlier sketch in SATA *76*
Buffie, Margaret 1945- *161*
  Earlier sketches in SATA *71, 107*
  See also CLR *39*
Bugbee, Emma 1888(?)-1981
  Obituary *29*
Bugni, Alice 1951- *122*
Buhhos, Marina Tamar
  See Budhos, Marina
Bujold, Lois McMaster 1949- *136*
Bulfinch, Thomas 1796-1867 .... *35*
Bulion, Leslie 1958- *161*
Bull, Angela (Mary) 1936- *45*
Bull, Emma 1954- *190*
  Autobiography Feature *103*
  Earlier sketch in SATA *99*
Bull, Norman John 1916- *41*
Bull, Peter (Cecil) 1912-1984
  Obituary *39*
Bull, Schuyler M. 1974- *138*
Bulla, Clyde R. 1914-2007 .... *139*
  Obituary *182*
  Earlier sketches in SATA *2, 41, 91*
  See also SAAS *6*
Bullard, Lisa 1961- *142*
Bullock, Kathleen (Mary) 1946- *77*
Bullock, Robert (D.) 1947- *92*
Bulpin, (Barbara) Vicki *92*
Bumstead, Kathleen Mary 1918-1987 .... *53*
Bundles, A'Lelia Perry 1952- *76*
Bunin, Catherine 1967- *30*
Bunin, Sherry 1925- *30*
Bunkers, Suzanne L. 1950- *136*
Bunting, A.E.
  See Bunting, Eve
Bunting, Anne Evelyn
  See Bunting, Eve
Bunting, Eve 1928- *196*
  Earlier sketches in SATA *18, 64, 110, 158*
  See also CLR *82*
Bunting, Glenn (Davison) 1957- *22*
Bunyan, John 1628-1688
  See CLR *124*
Bupp, Walter
  See Garrett, (Gordon) Randall (Phillip)
Burack, Sylvia K. 1916-2003 .... *35*
  Obituary *143*
Burbank, Addison (Buswell) 1895-1961 .... *37*
Burch, Joann J(ohansen) *75*
Burch, Robert J(oseph) 1925- *74*
  Earlier sketch in SATA *1*
  See also CLR *63*
Burchard, Peter Duncan 1921- *143*
  Earlier sketches in SATA *5, 74*
  See also SAAS *13*
Burchard, S. H.
  See Burchard, Sue
Burchard, Sue 1937- *22*
Burchardt, Nellie 1921- *7*
Burckhardt, Marc 1962- *196*
Burdett, Lois *117*
Burdick, Eugene (Leonard) 1918-1965 .... *22*
Burford, Eleanor
  See Hibbert, Eleanor Alice Burford
Burgan, Michael 1960- *167*
  Earlier sketch in SATA *118*
Burger, Carl 1888-1967 .... *9*
Burgess, Ann Marie
  See Gerson, Noel Bertram
Burgess, Barbara Hood 1926- *69*

Burgess, Em
  See Burgess, Mary Wyche
Burgess, (Frank) Gelett 1866-1951 .... *32*
  Brief entry *30*
Burgess, Mark *157*
Burgess, Mary Wyche 1916- *18*
Burgess, Melvin 1954- *198*
  Earlier sketches in SATA *96, 146*
Burgess, Michael
  See Gerson, Noel Bertram
Burgess, Robert F(orrest) 1927- *4*
Burgess, Starling
  See Tudor, Tasha
Burgess, Thornton Waldo 1874-1965 .... *17*
Burgess, Trevor
  See Trevor, Elleston
Burgwyn, Mebane Holoman 1914-1992 .... *7*
Burke, David 1927- *46*
Burke, Diana G.
  See Gallagher, Diana G.
Burke, Diana Gallagher
  See Gallagher, Diana G.
Burke, Dianne O'Quinn 1940- *89*
Burke, Janine 1952- *139*
Burke, Jim 1973- *179*
Burke, John
  See O'Connor, Richard
Burke, Katie 1953- *168*
Burke, Patrick 1958- *114*
Burke, Ralph
  See Garrett, (Gordon) Randall (Phillip)
  and Silverberg, Robert
Burkert, Nancy Ekholm 1933- *24*
  See also SAAS *14*
Burkett, D. Brent *194*
Burke-Weiner, Kimberly 1962- *95*
Burks, Brian 1955- *95*
Burland, Brian (Berkeley) 1931- *34*
Burland, C. A.
  See Burland, Cottie (Arthur)
Burland, Cottie (Arthur) 1905-1983 .... *5*
Burleigh, Robert 1936- *193*
  Earlier sketches in SATA *55, 98, 146*
Burlingame, (William) Roger 1889-1967 .... *2*
Burman, Alice Caddy 1896(?)-1977
  Obituary *24*
Burman, Ben Lucien 1896-1984 .... *6*
  Obituary *40*
Burn, Doris 1923- *1*
Burn, Ted
  See Burn, Thomas E.
Burn, Thomas E. 1940- *150*
Burnard, Damon 1963- *115*
Burnett, Constance Buel 1893-1975 .... *36*
Burnett, Frances (Eliza) Hodgson
  1849-1924 .... *100*
  See also YABC *2*
  See also CLR *122*
Burnett Bossi, Lisa *193*
Burney, Anton
  See Hopkins, (Hector) Kenneth
Burnford, Sheila (Philip Cochrane Every)
  1918-1984 .... *3*
  Obituary *38*
  See also CLR *2*
Burnham, Gretchen
  See Sprague, Gretchen
Burnham, Nicole 1970- *161*
Burnham, Niki
  See Burnham, Nicole
Burnham, Sophy 1936- *65*
Burningham, John 1936- *160*
  Earlier sketches in SATA *16, 59, 111*
  See also CLR *9*
Burns, Diane L. 1950- *81*
  See also SAAS *24*
Burns, Eloise Wilkin
  See Wilkin, Eloise
Burns, Florence M. 1905-1988 .... *61*
Burns, Khephra 1950- *92*
Burns, Loree Griffin *193*

Burns, Marilyn 1941- *96*
   Brief entry *33*
Burns, Olive Ann 1924-1990 .... *65*
Burns, Paul C. *5*
Burns, Ray
   See Burns, Raymond (Howard)
Burns, Raymond (Howard) 1924- *9*
Burns, Theresa 1961- *84*
Burns, William A. 1909-1999 .... *5*
Burr, Dan 1951- *65*
Burr, Lonnie 1943- *47*
Burrell, Roy E(ric) C(harles) 1923- *72*
Burroughs, Edgar Rice 1875-1950 .... *41*
Burroughs, Jean Mitchell 1908- *28*
Burroughs, Polly 1925- *2*
Burroway, Janet (Gay) 1936- *23*
Burstein, Chaya M(alamud) 1923- *64*
Burstein, Fred 1950- *83*
Burstein, John 1949- *54*
   Brief entry *40*
Burstein, Stanley M.
   See Burstein, Stanley Mayer
Burstein, Stanley Mayer 1941- *175*
Bursztynski, Sue 1953- *114*
Burt, Jesse Clifton 1921-1976 .... *46*
   Obituary *20*
Burt, Olive Woolley 1894-1981 .... *4*
Burtinshaw, Julie *185*
Burton, Gennett 1945- *95*
Burton, Hester (Wood-Hill) 1913-2000 .... *74*
   Earlier sketch in SATA *7*
   See also CLR *1*
   See also SAAS *8*
Burton, Leslie
   See McGuire, Leslie (Sarah)
Burton, Marilee Robin 1950- *82*
   Earlier sketch in SATA *46*
Burton, Maurice 1898-1992 .... *23*
Burton, Rebecca 1970- *183*
Burton, Robert (Wellesley) 1941- *22*
Burton, Virginia Lee 1909-1968 .... *100*
   Earlier sketch in SATA *2*
   See also CLR *11*
Burton, William H(enry) 1890-1964 .... *11*
Busby, Ailie *192*
Busby, Cylin 1970- *118*
Busby, Edith (A. Lake) (?)-1964
   Obituary *29*
Buscaglia, (Felice) Leo(nardo) 1924-1998 ... *65*
Buscaglia, Leo F.
   See Buscaglia, (Felice) Leo(nardo)
Busch, Phyllis S. 1909- *30*
Bush, Anne Kelleher
   See Kelleher, Anne
Bush, Catherine 1961- *128*
Bushmiller, Ernest Paul 1905-1982 .... *31*
Bushmiller, Ernie
   See Bushmiller, Ernest Paul
Bushnell, Jack 1952- *86*
Busoni, Rafaello 1900-1962 .... *16*
Buss, Helen M.
   See Clarke, Margaret
Busse, Sarah Martin *194*
Busselle, Rebecca 1941- *80*
Bustard, Anne 1951- *173*
Butcher, Kristin 1951- *140*
Butenko, Bohdan 1931- *90*
Butler, Beverly Kathleen 1932- *7*
Butler, Bill
   See Butler, William (Arthur) Vivian
   and Butler, Ernest Alton
   and Butler, William Huxford
Butler, Charles 1963- *175*
   Earlier sketch in SATA *121*
Butler, Charles Cadman
   See Butler, Charles
Butler, Dori Hillestad 1965- *164*
Butler, Dorothy 1925- *73*
Butler, Geoff 1945- *94*
Butler, M. Christina 1934- *170*
   Earlier sketch in SATA *72*

Butler, Octavia E. 1947-2006 .... *84*
   See also CLR *65*
Butler, Octavia Estelle
   See Butler, Octavia E.
Butler, Vivian
   See Butler, William (Arthur) Vivian
Butler, William
   See Butler, William (Arthur) Vivian
Butler, William (Arthur) Vivian 1927-1987 . *79*
Butters, Dorothy Gilman
   See Gilman, Dorothy
Butterworth, Emma Macalik 1928- *43*
Butterworth, Nick 1946- *149*
   Earlier sketch in SATA *106*
Butterworth, Oliver 1915-1990 .... *1*
   Obituary *66*
Butterworth, W.E.
   See Griffin, W.E.B
Butterworth, William E.
   See Griffin, W.E.B
Butterworth, William Edmund III
   See Griffin, W.E.B
Butts, Ed 1951- *177*
Butts, Edward P.
   See Butts, Ed
Butts, Ellen R(ubinstein) 1942- *93*
Buxton, Ralph
   See Silverstein, Alvin
   and Silverstein, Virginia B(arbara Opshelor)
Buzzeo, Toni 1951- *135*
Byalick, Marcia 1947- *141*
   Earlier sketch in SATA *97*
Byard, Carole (Marie) 1941- *57*
Byars, Betsy 1928- *163*
   Autobiography Feature *108*
   Earlier sketches in SATA *4, 46, 80*
   See also CLR *72*
   See also SAAS *1*
Byars, Betsy Cromer
   See Byars, Betsy
Byfield, Barbara Ninde 1930- *8*
Byman, Jeremy 1944- *129*
Bynum, Janie *133*
Byrd, Elizabeth 1912-1989 .... *34*
Byrd, Nicole
   See Zach, Cheryl (Byrd)
Byrd, Robert (John) 1942- *158*
   Earlier sketches in SATA *33, 112*
Byrne, Mary Gregg 1951- *162*

C

C. 3. 3.
   See Wilde, Oscar
C. E. M.
   See Mastrangelo, Charles E(lmer)
Cabaniss, J(ames) Allen 1911-1997 .... *5*
Cabat, Erni 1914- *74*
Cabban, Vanessa 1971- *176*
Cable, Mary 1920- *9*
Cabot, Meg 1967- *175*
   Earlier sketch in SATA *127*
   See also CLR *85*
Cabot, Meggin
   See Cabot, Meg
Cabot, Meggin Patricia
   See Cabot, Meg
Cabot, Patricia
   See Cabot, Meg
Cabral, O. M.
   See Cabral, Olga
Cabral, Olga 1909- *46*
Cabrera, Cozbi A. 1963- *177*
Cabrera, Jane 1968- *182*
   Earlier sketches in SATA *103, 152*
Cabrera, Marcela 1966- *90*
Caddy, Alice
   See Burman, Alice Caddy

Cade, Toni
   See Bambara, Toni Cade
Cadmus and Harmonia
   See Buchan, John
Cadnum, Michael 1949- *165*
   Earlier sketches in SATA *87, 121*
   See also CLR *78*
Caduto, Michael J. 1955- *103*
Cadwallader, Sharon 1936- *7*
Cady, (Walter) Harrison 1877(?)-1970 .... *19*
Caffey, Donna (J.) 1954- *110*
Cagle, Malcolm W(infield) 1918- *32*
Cahn, Rhoda 1922- *37*
Cahn, William 1912-1976 .... *37*
Cain, Arthur H(omer) 1913-1981 .... *3*
Cain, Christopher
   See Fleming, Thomas
Cain, Sheridan 1952- *186*
Caine, Geoffrey
   See Walker, Robert W(ayne)
Caines, Jeannette (Franklin) 1938- *78*
   Brief entry *43*
   See also CLR *24*
Cairns, Trevor 1922- *14*
Calabro, Marian 1954- *79*
Caldecott, Moyra 1927- *22*
Caldecott, Randolph (J.) 1846-1886 .... *100*
   Earlier sketch in SATA *17*
   See also CLR *110*
Calder, Charlotte 1952- *125*
Calder, David 1932-1997 .... *105*
Calder, Lyn
   See Calmenson, Stephanie
Calder, Marie D(onais) 1948- *96*
Calderone-Stewart, Lisa
   See Calderone-Stewart, Lisa-Marie
Calderone-Stewart, Lisa-Marie 1958- *123*
Caldwell, Doreen (Mary) 1942- *71*
Caldwell, John C(ope) 1913-1984 .... *7*
Caletti, Deb 1963- *171*
Calhoun, B. B. 1961- *98*
Calhoun, Chad
   See Barrett, Neal, Jr.
   and Cunningham, Chet
   and Goulart, Ron(ald Joseph)
Calhoun, Dia 1959- *183*
   Earlier sketch in SATA *129*
Calhoun, Mary
   See Wilkins, Mary Huiskamp
Calhoun, T.B.
   See Bisson, Terry
Cali, Davide 1972- *190*
Calif, Ruth 1922- *67*
Calkins, Franklin
   See Stratemeyer, Edward L.
Call, Greg *197*
Call, Hughie Florence 1890-1969 .... *1*
Callahan, Dorothy M(onahan) 1934- *39*
   Brief entry *35*
Callahan, Philip Serna 1923- *25*
Callan, Jamie 1954- *59*
Callan, Jim 1951- *181*
Callaway, Bernice (Anne) 1923- *48*
Callaway, Kathy 1943- *36*
Callen, Larry
   See Callen, Lawrence Willard, Jr.
Callen, Lawrence Willard, Jr. 1927- *19*
Calley, Karin 1965- *92*
Calmenson, Stephanie 1952- *139*
   Brief entry *37*
   Earlier sketches in SATA *51, 84*
Calvert, Elinor H.
   See Lasell, Elinor H.
Calvert, John
   See Leaf, (Wilbur) Munro
Calvert, Patricia 1931- *132*
   Earlier sketches in SATA *45, 69*
   See also SAAS *17*
Camburn, Carol A.
   See Camburn-Bracalente, Carol A.
Camburn-Bracalente, Carol A. 1962- *118*

Cameron, Ann 1943- *129*
　Earlier sketches in SATA *27, 89*
　See also SAAS *20*
Cameron, Edna M. 1905-1999 .... *3*
Cameron, Eleanor (Frances) 1912-1996 .... *25*
　Obituary *93*
　Earlier sketch in SATA *1*
　See also CLR *72*
　See also SAAS *10*
Cameron, Elizabeth
　See Nowell, Elizabeth Cameron
Cameron, Elizabeth Jane 1910-1976 .... *32*
　Obituary *30*
Cameron, Ian
　See Payne, Donald Gordon
Cameron, M(alcolm) G(ordon) Graham
　See Graham-Cameron, M(alcolm) G(ordon)
Cameron, M. Graham
　See Graham-Cameron, M(alcolm) G(ordon)
Cameron, Mike Graham
　See Graham-Cameron, M(alcolm) G(ordon)
Cameron, Polly 1928- *2*
Cameron, Scott 1962- *84*
Camp, Charles L. 1893-1975
　Obituary *31*
Camp, Lindsay 1957- *133*
Camp, Madeleine L'Engle
　See L'Engle, Madeleine
Camp, Walter (Chauncey) 1859-1925
　See YABC *1*
Campbell, (Elizabeth) Andrea 1963- *50*
Campbell, Ann R. 1925- *11*
Campbell, Bill 1960- *89*
Campbell, Bruce
　See Epstein, Samuel
Campbell, Camilla 1905-1992 .... *26*
Campbell, Carole R. 1939- *125*
Campbell, Hope 1925- *20*
Campbell, Hugh 1930- *90*
Campbell, Jane
　See Edwards, Jane Campbell
Campbell, Julie
　See Tatham, Julie Campbell
Campbell, Patricia J(ean) 1930- *45*
Campbell, Patty
　See Campbell, Patricia J(ean)
Campbell, Peter A. 1948- *99*
Campbell, R. W.
　See Campbell, Rosemae Wells
Campbell, Robin
　See Strachan, Ian
Campbell, Rod 1945- *98*
　Brief entry *44*
　Earlier sketch in SATA *51*
Campbell, Rosemae Wells 1909- *1*
Camper, Cathy 1956- *170*
Campion, Nardi Reeder 1917-2007 .... *22*
Campling, Elizabeth 1948- *53*
Campoy, F. Isabel 1946- *181*
　Earlier sketch in SATA *143*
Camps, Luis 1928- *66*
Canales, Viola 1957- *141*
Candell, Victor 1903-1977
　Obituary *24*
Canfield, Dorothea F.
　See Fisher, Dorothy (Frances) Canfield
Canfield, Dorothea Frances
　See Fisher, Dorothy (Frances) Canfield
Canfield, Dorothy
　See Fisher, Dorothy (Frances) Canfield
Canfield, Jack 1944- *164*
Canfield, Jane White 1897-1984 .... *32*
　Obituary *38*
Canfield, Muriel 1935- *94*
Caniff, Milton 1907-1988
　Obituary *58*
Caniff, Milton Arthur Paul
　See Caniff, Milton
Cann, Helen 1969- *179*
　Earlier sketch in SATA *124*

Cann, Kate 1954- *152*
　Earlier sketch in SATA *103*
Cannan, Joanna
　See Pullein-Thompson, Joanna Maxwell
Cannell, Jon *196*
Cannell, Jonathan C.
　See Cannell, Jon
Cannon, A(nn) E(dwards) *163*
　Earlier sketch in SATA *93*
Cannon, Bettie (Waddell) 1922- *59*
Cannon, Curt
　See Hunter, Evan
Cannon, Eileen E(mily) 1948- *119*
Cannon, Frank
　See Mayhar, Ardath
Cannon, Janell 1957- *128*
　Earlier sketch in SATA *78*
　See also CLR *120*
Cannon, Marian G. 1923- *85*
Cannon, Taffy
　See Cannon, Eileen E(mily)
Cantone, AnnaLaura *182*
Canusi, Jose
　See Barker, S(quire) Omar
Canyon, Christopher 1966- *150*
　Earlier sketch in SATA *104*
Capek, Michael 1947- *142*
　Earlier sketch in SATA *96*
Capes, Bernard (Edward Joseph)
　1854-1918 .... *116*
Caple, Kathy *193*
Caplin, Alfred Gerald 1909-1979 .... *61*
　Obituary *21*
Caponigro, John Paul 1965- *84*
Capote, Truman 1924-1984 .... *91*
Capp, Al
　See Caplin, Alfred Gerald
Cappel, Constance 1936- *22*
Cappetta, Cynthia 1949- *125*
Cappo, Nan Willard 1955- *143*
Capps, Benjamin (Franklin) 1922- *9*
Cappy Dick
　See Cleveland, George
Captain Kangaroo
　See Keeshan, Robert J.
Captain Wheeler
　See Ellis, Edward S(ylvester)
Captain Young of Yale
　See Stratemeyer, Edward L.
Capucilli, Alyssa Satin 1957- *163*
　Earlier sketch in SATA *115*
Capucine
　See Mazille, Capucine
Caraher, Kim(berley Elizabeth) 1961- *105*
Caraker, Mary 1929- *74*
Caras, Roger A(ndrew) 1928-2001 .... *12*
　Obituary *127*
Caravantes, Peggy 1935- *140*
Caraway, Caren 1939- *57*
Carbone, Elisa 1954- *173*
　Earlier sketches in SATA *81, 137*
Carbone, Elisa Lynn
　See Carbone, Elisa
Carbonnier, Jeanne 1894-1974 .... *3*
　Obituary *34*
Card, Orson Scott 1951- *127*
　Earlier sketch in SATA *83*
　See also CLR *116*
Care, Felicity
　See Coury, Louise Andree
Carew, Jan 1925- *51*
　Brief entry *40*
Carew, Jan Rynveld
　See Carew, Jan
Carey, Bonnie
　See Marshall, Bonnie C.
Carey, Charles W., Jr. 1951- *170*
Carey, Ernestine Gilbreth 1908-2006 .... *2*
　Obituary *177*
Carey, Janet Lee 1959(?)- *185*
Carey, Lisa *110*

Carey, M. V.
　See Carey, Mary V(irginia)
Carey, Mary V(irginia) 1925-1994 .... *44*
　Brief entry *39*
Carey, Peter 1943- *94*
Carey, Peter Philip
　See Carey, Peter
Carey, Valerie Scho 1949- *60*
Carheden, Goorel Kristina
　See Naaslund, Goorel Kristina
Carigiet, Alois 1902-1985 .... *24*
　Obituary *47*
　See also CLR *38*
Carini, Edward 1923- *9*
Carkeet, David 1946- *75*
Carle, Eric 1929- *163*
　Earlier sketches in SATA *4, 65, 120*
　See also CLR *72*
　See also SAAS *6*
Carleton, Captain L. C.
　See Ellis, Edward S(ylvester)
Carleton, Captain Latham C.
　See Ellis, Edward S(ylvester)
Carleton, Latham C.
　See Ellis, Edward S(ylvester)
Carley, V(an Ness) Royal 1906-1976
　Obituary *20*
Carling, Amelia Lau 1949- *164*
　Earlier sketch in SATA *119*
Carlisle, Carolyn
　See Hawes, Louise
Carlisle, Clark
　See Holding, James (Clark Carlisle, Jr.)
Carlisle, Olga Andreyev 1930- *35*
Carlock, Miriam
　See Eyerly, Jeannette
Carls, Claudia 1978- *198*
Carlsen, G(eorge) Robert 1917- *30*
Carlsen, Ruth C(hristoffer) 1918- *2*
Carlson, Bernice Wells 1910- *8*
Carlson, Dale (Bick) 1935- *1*
Carlson, Daniel (Bick) 1960- *27*
Carlson, Kirsten 1968- *192*
Carlson, Kirsten M.
　See Carlson, Kirsten
Carlson, Laurie 1952- *173*
　Earlier sketch in SATA *101*
Carlson, Laurie Winn
　See Carlson, Laurie
Carlson, Melody 1956- *171*
　Earlier sketch in SATA *113*
Carlson, Nancy L.
　See Carlson, Nancy L(ee)
Carlson, Nancy L(ee) 1953- *144*
　Brief entry *45*
　Earlier sketches in SATA *56, 90*
Carlson, Natalie Savage 1906-1997 .... *68*
　Earlier sketch in SATA *2*
　See also SAAS *4*
Carlson, Susan Johnston 1953- *88*
Carlson, Vada F. 1897- *16*
Carlstrom, Nancy White 1948- *156*
　Brief entry *48*
　Earlier sketches in SATA *53, 92*
Carlton, Keith
　See Robertson, Keith (Carlton)
Carlton, Susan 1960- *195*
Carlyon, Richard *55*
Carman, Patrick *197*
　Earlier sketch in SATA *161*
Carmer, Carl (Lamson) 1893-1976 .... *37*
　Obituary *30*
Carmer, Elizabeth Black 1904- *24*
Carmi, Giora 1944- *149*
　Earlier sketch in SATA *79*
Carmichael, Carrie
　See Carmichael, Harriet
Carmichael, Harriet *40*
Carmody, Isobelle 1958- *191*
　Earlier sketch in SATA *161*

Carmody, Isobelle Jane
  See Carmody, Isobelle
Carney, Elizabeth 1981- 199
Carney, Jeff 1962- 196
Carney, Mary Lou 1949- 170
Carol, Bill J.
  See Knott, William C(ecil, Jr.)
Caron, Romi
  See Caron-Kyselkova', Romana
Caron-Kyselkova', Romana 1967- 94
Caroselli, Remus F(rancis) 1916- 36
Carpelan, Bo 1926- 8
Carpelan, Bo Gustaf Bertelsson
  See Carpelan, Bo
Carpenter, (John) Allan 1917- 81
  Earlier sketch in SATA *3*
Carpenter, Angelica Shirley 1945- 153
  Earlier sketch in SATA *71*
Carpenter, Frances 1890-1972 3
  Obituary 27
Carpenter, John (Howard) 1948- 58
Carpenter, Johnny
  See Carpenter, John (Howard)
Carpenter, Patricia (Healy Evans) 1920- 11
Carr, Glyn
  See Styles, (Frank) Showell
Carr, Harriett H(elen) 1899-1977 3
Carr, Jan 1953- 132
  Earlier sketch in SATA *89*
Carr, M. J.
  See Carr, Jan
Carr, Mary Jane 1899-1988 2
  Obituary 55
Carr, Philippa
  See Hibbert, Eleanor Alice Burford
Carr, Roger Vaughan 1937- 95
Carrel, Annette Felder 1929- 90
Carrick, Carol (Hatfield) 1935- 118
  Earlier sketches in SATA *7, 63*
  See also SAAS *18*
Carrick, Donald (F.) 1929-1989 63
  Earlier sketch in SATA *7*
Carrick, Malcolm 1945- 28
Carrick, Paul 1972- 194
Carrier, Lark 1947- 71
  Brief entry 50
Carrier, Roch 1937- 166
  Earlier sketch in SATA *105*
Carrighar, Sally 1898-1985 24
Carrington, G. A.
  See Cunningham, Chet
Carrington, Marsha Gray 1954- 168
  Earlier sketch in SATA *111*
Carris, Joan 1938- 182
  Brief entry 42
  Earlier sketch in SATA *44*
Carris, Joan Davenport
  See Carris, Joan
Carroll, Curt
  See Bishop, Curtis (Kent)
Carroll, Elizabeth
  See Barkin, Carol
  and James, Elizabeth
Carroll, Jenny
  See Cabot, Meg
Carroll, (Archer) Latrobe 1894-1996 7
Carroll, Laura
  See Parr, Lucy
Carroll, Lewis
  See Dodgson, Charles L(utwidge)
Carroll, Raymond 1924- 86
  Brief entry 47
Carruth, Hayden 1921-2008 47
  Obituary 197
Carryl, Charles E. 1841-1920 114
Carryl, Charles Edward
  See Carryl, Charles E.
Carse, Robert 1902-1971 5
Carson, J(ohn) Franklin 1920-1981 1
  Obituary 107
Carson, Mary Kay 1964- 150

Carson, Rachel
  See Carson, Rachel Louise
Carson, Rachel Louise 1907-1964 23
Carson, Rosalind
  See Chittenden, Margaret
Carson, S. M.
  See Gorsline, (Sally) Marie
Carson, William C. 1928- 154
Carter, Abby 184
Carter, Alden R 1947- 137
  Earlier sketch in SATA *67*
  See also CLR *22*
  See also SAAS *18*
Carter, Alden Richardson
  See Carter, Alden R
Carter, Andy 1948- 134
Carter, Angela 1940-1992 66
  Obituary 70
Carter, Angela Olive
  See Carter, Angela
Carter, Anne Laurel 1953- 135
Carter, Asa Earl
  See Carter, Forrest
Carter, Avis Murton
  See Allen, Kenneth S.
Carter, Bruce
  See Hough, Richard (Alexander)
Carter, Carol S(hadis) 1948- 124
Carter, David A. 1957- 170
  Earlier sketch in SATA *114*
Carter, Don 1958- 192
  Earlier sketch in SATA *124*
Carter, Dorothy Sharp 1921- 8
Carter, Forrest 1927(?)-1979 32
Carter, Helene 1887-1960 15
Carter, (William) Hodding, Jr. 1907-1972 2
  Obituary 27
Carter, James Earl, Jr.
  See Carter, Jimmy
Carter, Jimmy 1924- 79
Carter, Katharine J(ones) 1905-1984 2
Carter, Lin(wood Vrooman) 1930-1988 91
Carter, Mike 1936- 138
Carter, Nick
  See Avallone, Michael (Angelo, Jr.)
  and Ballard, (Willis) Todhunter
  and Crider, Bill
  and Cassiday, Bruce (Bingham)
  and Chastain, Thomas
  and Dey, Frederic (Merrill) Van Rensselaer
  and Garside, (Clifford) Jack
  and Hayes, Ralph E(ugene)
  and Henderson, M(arilyn) R(uth)
  and Lynds, Dennis
  and Lynds, Gayle (Hallenbeck)
  and Randisi, Robert J.
  and Rasof, Henry
  and Stratemeyer, Edward L.
  and Smith, Martin Cruz
  and Swain, Dwight V(reeland)
  and Vardeman, Robert E(dward)
  and Wallmann, Jeffrey M(iner)
  and White, Lionel
Carter, Peter 1929- 57
Carter, Phyllis Ann
  See Eberle, Irmengarde
Carter, Samuel (Thomson) III 1904-1988 37
  Obituary 60
Carter, William E. 1926-1983 1
  Obituary 35
Cartlidge, Michelle 1950- 96
  Brief entry 37
  Earlier sketch in SATA *49*
Cartner, William Carruthers 1910- 11
Cartwright, Ann 1940- 78
Cartwright, Reg(inald Ainsley) 1938- 64
Cartwright, Sally 1923- 9
Carusone, Al 1949- 89
Carvell, Marlene 172
Carver, John
  See Gardner, Richard (M.)

Carwell, L'Ann
  See McKissack, Patricia C.
Cary
  See Cary, Louis F(avreau)
Cary, Barbara Knapp 1912(?)-1975
  Obituary 31
Cary, Kate 1967(?)- 174
Cary, Louis F(avreau) 1915- 9
Caryl, Jean
  See Kaplan, Jean Caryl Korn
Casanova, Mary 1957- 186
  Earlier sketches in SATA *94, 136*
Cascone, A.G. 103
  See Cascone, Annette
  and Cascone, Gina
Cascone, Annette 1960- 103
  See Cascone, A.G.
Case, Marshal T(aylor) 1941- 9
Case, Michael
  See Howard, Robert West
Caseley, Judith 1951- 159
  Brief entry 53
  Earlier sketch in SATA *87*
Casewit, Curtis W(erner) 1922-2002 4
Casey, Barbara (Louise) 1944- 147
  Earlier sketch in SATA *79*
Casey, Brigid 1950- 9
Casey, Tina 1959- 141
Cash, Ellen Lewis Buell 1905-1989
  Obituary 64
Cash, Megan Montague 160
Casilla, Robert 1959- 146
  Earlier sketch in SATA *75*
Cason, Mabel Earp 1892-1965 10
Cass, Joan E(velyn) 1
Cass-Beggs, Barbara 1904- 62
Cassedy, Patrice (Rinaldo) 1953- 149
Cassedy, Sylvia 1930-1989 77
  Obituary 61
  Earlier sketch in SATA *27*
  See also CLR *26*
Cassel, Lili
  See Wronker, Lili Cassel
Cassels, Jean 173
Cassidy, Anne 1952- 166
Cassidy, Cathy 1962- 183
Casson, Hugh Maxwell 1910-1999 65
  Obituary 115
Cassutt, Michael 1954- 78
Cassutt, Michael Joseph
  See Cassutt, Michael
Castaldi, Elicia 194
Castaldo, Nancy Fusco 1962- 151
  Earlier sketch in SATA *93*
Castaneda, Omar S. 1954- 71
Castell, Megan
  See Williams, Jeanne
Castellanos, Jane Mollie Robinson
  1913-2001 9
Castellon, Federico 1914-1971 48
Castellucci, Cecil 1969- 176
Castillo, Edmund L. 1924-2005 1
  Obituary 167
Castillo, Lauren 195
Castle, Lee
  See Ogan, George F.
  and Ogan, Margaret E. (Nettles)
Castle, Paul
  See Howard, Vernon (Linwood)
Castle, Robert
  See Hamilton, Edmond
Castrovilla, Selene 1966- 186
Caswell, Brian 1954- 171
  Earlier sketch in SATA *97*
Caswell, Helen (Rayburn) 1923- 12
Catalano, Dominic 1956- 163
  Earlier sketch in SATA *76*
Catalano, Grace (A.) 1961- 99

Catalanotto, Peter 1959- *195*
  Autobiography Feature *113*
  Earlier sketches in SATA *70, 114, 159*
  See also CLR *68*
  See also SAAS *25*
Catanese, P.W. 1961- *179*
Cate, Annette LeBlanc *196*
Cate, Dick
  See Cate, Richard Edward Nelson
Cate, Richard Edward Nelson 1932- *28*
Cather, Willa (Sibert) 1873-1947 .... *30*
  See also CLR *98*
Catherall, Arthur 1906-1980 .... *74*
  Earlier sketches in SATA *3, 4*
Cathon, Laura E(lizabeth) 1908-1991 .... *27*
Catlett, Elizabeth 1919(?)- *82*
Catlin, Wynelle 1930- *13*
Catlow, Nikalas
  See Catlow, Niki
Catlow, Niki 1975- *193*
Cato, Heather *105*
Cato, Sheila *114*
Catran, Ken 1944- *190*
Catrow, David
  See Catrow, David J. III
Catrow, David J. III *152*
Catt, Louis
  See French, Vivian
Cattell, James 1954- *123*
Catton, (Charles) Bruce 1899-1978 .... *2*
  Obituary *24*
Catz, Max
  See Glaser, Milton
Caudell, Marian 1930- *52*
Caudill, Rebecca 1899-1985 .... *1*
  Obituary *44*
Cauley, Lorinda Bryan 1951- *46*
  Brief entry *43*
Caulfield, Peggy F. 1926-1987
  Obituary *53*
Cauman, Samuel 1910-1971 .... *48*
Causley, Charles (Stanley) 1917-2003 .... *66*
  Obituary *149*
  Earlier sketch in SATA *3*
  See also CLR *30*
Cavallaro, Ann (Abelson) 1918- *62*
Cavallo, Diana 1931- *7*
Cavanagh, Helen (Carol) 1939- *98*
  Brief entry *37*
  Earlier sketch in SATA *48*
Cavanah, Frances 1899-1982 .... *31*
  Earlier sketch in SATA *1*
Cavanna, Betty
  See Harrison, Elizabeth (Allen) Cavanna
Cavanna, Elizabeth
  See Harrison, Elizabeth (Allen) Cavanna
Cave, Kathryn 1948- *123*
  Earlier sketch in SATA *76*
Cavendish, Peter
  See Horler, Sydney
Cavin, Ruth (Brodie) 1918- *38*
Cavoukian, Raffi 1948- *68*
Cawley, Winifred 1915- *13*
Caxton, Pisistratus
  See Lytton, Edward G(eorge) E(arle) L(ytton)
  Bulwer-Lytton Baron
Cazeau, Charles J(ay) 1931- *65*
Cazet, Denys 1938- *191*
  Brief entry *41*
  Earlier sketches in SATA *52, 99, 163*
Cazzola, Gus 1934- *73*
Cebulash, Mel 1937- *91*
  Earlier sketch in SATA *10*
Ceccoli, Nicoletta *181*
Cecil, Randy 1968- *187*
Cecka, Melanie *199*
Ceder, Georgiana Dorcas -1985 .... *10*
Celenza, Anna Harwell *133*
Celestino, Martha Laing
  See Laing, Martha
Cepeda, Joe *159*

Cerf, Bennett (Alfred) 1898-1971 .... *7*
Cerf, Christopher (Bennett) 1941- *2*
Cermak, Martin
  See Duchacek, Ivo D(uka)
Cerullo, Mary M. 1949- *145*
  Earlier sketch in SATA *86*
Cervon, Jacqueline
  See Moussard, Jacqueline
Cetin, Frank Stanley 1921- *2*
Chabon, Michael 1963- *145*
Chaconas, D.J.
  See Chaconas, Dori
Chaconas, Dori 1938- *175*
  Earlier sketch in SATA *145*
Chaconas, Doris J.
  See Chaconas, Dori
Chadwick, Lester *67*
  Earlier sketch in SATA *1*
Chaffee, Allen *3*
Chaffin, Lillie D(orton) 1925- *4*
Chaikin, Miriam 1924- *152*
  Earlier sketches in SATA *24, 102*
Chall, Marsha Wilson *150*
Challand, Helen J(ean) 1921- *64*
Challans, Mary 1905-1983 .... *23*
  Obituary *36*
Chalmers, Mary (Eileen) 1927- *6*
  See also SAAS *14*
Chamberlain, Barbara A.
  See Azore, Barbara
Chamberlain, Margaret 1954- *46*
Chamberlin, Kate 1945- *105*
Chamberlin, Mary 1960- *177*
Chamberlin, Rich *177*
Chamberlin, Richard
  See Chamberlin, Rich
Chambers, Aidan 1934- *171*
  Earlier sketches in SATA *1, 69, 108*
  See also SAAS *12*
Chambers, Bradford 1922-1984
  Obituary *39*
Chambers, Catherine E.
  See St. John, Nicole
Chambers, John W. 1933- *57*
  Brief entry *46*
Chambers, Kate
  See St. John, Nicole
Chambers, Margaret Ada Eastwood 1911- *2*
Chambers, Peggy
  See Chambers, Margaret Ada Eastwood
Chambers, Robert W(illiam) 1865-1933 .... *107*
Chambliss, Maxie *186*
Chan, Gillian 1954- *147*
  Earlier sketch in SATA *102*
Chance, James T.
  See Carpenter, John (Howard)
Chance, John T.
  See Carpenter, John (Howard)
Chance, Stephen
  See Turner, Philip (William)
Chandler, Caroline A(ugusta) 1906-1979 ..... *22*
  Obituary *24*
Chandler, David P(orter) 1933- *28*
Chandler, Edna Walker 1908-1982 .... *11*
  Obituary *31*
Chandler, Jennifer
  See Westwood, Jennifer
Chandler, Karen 1959- *122*
Chandler, Linda S(mith) 1929- *39*
Chandler, Pauline *175*
Chandler, Robert 1953- *40*
Chandler, Ruth Forbes 1894-1978 .... *2*
  Obituary *26*
Chandonnet, Ann F. 1943- *92*
Chaney, Jill 1932- *87*
Chang, Chih-Wei 1966- *111*
Chang, Cindy 1968- *90*
Chang, Margaret 1941- *71*
Chang, Margaret Scrogin
  See Chang, Margaret

Chang, Raymond 1939- *142*
  Earlier sketches in SATA *71, 142 PEN*
Chanin, Michael 1952- *84*
Channel, A. R.
  See Catherall, Arthur
Chapian, Marie 1938- *29*
Chapin, Alene Olsen Dalton 1915(?)-1986
  Obituary *47*
Chapin, Tom 1945- *83*
Chapman, Allen *67*
  Earlier sketch in SATA *1*
Chapman, Cheryl O(rth) 1948- *80*
Chapman, (Constance) Elizabeth (Mann)
  1919- *10*
Chapman, Gaynor 1935- *32*
Chapman, Gillian 1955- *120*
Chapman, Jane 1970- *176*
  Earlier sketch in SATA *122*
Chapman, Jean *104*
  Earlier sketch in SATA *34*
  See also CLR *65*
Chapman, John Stanton Higham 1891-1972
  Obituary *27*
Chapman, Lee
  See Bradley, Marion Zimmer
Chapman, Lynne 1960- *197*
Chapman, Lynne F(erguson) 1963- *150*
  Earlier sketch in SATA *94*
Chapman, Maristan
  See Chapman, John Stanton Higham
Chapman, Vera (Ivy May) 1898-1996 .... *33*
Chapman, Walker
  See Silverberg, Robert
Chappell, Audrey 1954- *72*
Chappell, Crissa-Jean *198*
Chappell, Warren 1904-1991 .... *68*
  Obituary *67*
  Earlier sketch in SATA *6*
  See also SAAS *10*
Chapra, Mimi *182*
Charbonneau, Eileen 1951- *118*
  Earlier sketch in SATA *84*
Charbonnet, Gabrielle 1961- *81*
Chardiet, Bernice (Kroll) 1927(?)- *27*
Charest, Emily MacLachlan *198*
Charles, Donald
  See Meighan, Donald Charles
Charles, Louis
  See Stratemeyer, Edward L.
Charles, Nicholas J.
  See Kuskin, Karla
Charles, Norma *153*
Charles, Veronika Martenova *182*
Charlip, Remy 1929- *119*
  Earlier sketches in SATA *4, 68*
  See also CLR *8*
Charlot, Jean 1898-1979 .... *8*
  Obituary *31*
Charlot, Martin (Day) 1944- *64*
Charlton, Michael (Alan) 1923- *34*
Charlton-Trujillo, e.E. *189*
Charmatz, Bill 1925-2005 .... *7*
Charnas, Suzy McKee 1939- *110*
  Earlier sketch in SATA *61*
Charosh, Mannis 1906- *5*
Chartier, Normand L. 1945- *66*
Chase, Alice
  See McHargue, Georgess
Chase, Alyssa 1965- *92*
Chase, Andra 1942- *91*
Chase, Emily
  See Aks, Patricia
  and Garwood, Julie
  and Sachs, Judith
  and White, Carol
Chase, Mary (Coyle) 1907-1981 .... *17*
  Obituary *29*
Chase, Mary Ellen 1887-1973 .... *10*
Chase, Richard 1904-1988 .... *64*
  Obituary *56*

Chase, Samantha
  See Glick, Ruth (Burtnick)
Chast, Roz 1954- 97
Chastain, Madye Lee 1908-1989 4
Chataway, Carol 1955- 140
Chatterjee, Debjani 1952- 83
Chauncy, Nan(cen Beryl Masterman)
  1900-1970 6
  See also CLR 6
Chaundler, Christine 1887-1972 1
  Obituary 25
Chayka, Doug 196
Chbosky, Stephen 1972- 164
Cheaney, Janie B.
  See Cheaney, J.B.
Cheaney, J.B. 1950- 188
Chee, Cheng-Khee 1934- 79
Cheese, Chloe 1952- 118
Chekhonte, Antosha
  See Chekhov, Anton (Pavlovich)
Chekhov, Anton (Pavlovich) 1860-1904 90
Chelushkin, Kirill 1968- 186
Chen, Anthony 1929- 6
Chen, Chih-Yuan 1975- 155
Chen, Ju-Hong 1941- 78
Chen, Sara
  See Odgers, Sally Farrell
Chen, Tony
  See Chen, Anthony
Chen, Yong 1963- 183
Chen, Yuan-tsung 1932- 65
Chenault, Nell
  See Smith, Linell Nash
Chenery, Janet (Dai) 1923- 25
Cheney, Cora 1916-1999 3
  Obituary 110
Cheney, Glenn (Alan) 1951- 99
Cheney, Lynne V. 1941- 152
Cheney, Ted
  See Cheney, Theodore Albert
Cheney, Theodore A. Rees
  See Cheney, Theodore Albert
Cheney, Theodore Albert 1928- 11
Cheng, Andrea 1957- 172
  Earlier sketch in SATA 128
Cheng, Christopher 1959- 173
  Earlier sketch in SATA 106
Cheng, Judith 1955- 36
Cheng, Shan
  See Jiang, Cheng An
Cheripko, Jan 1951- 155
  Earlier sketch in SATA 83
Chermayeff, Ivan 1932- 47
Chernenko, Dan
  See Chernenko, Dan
Chernoff, Dorothy A.
  See Ernst, (Lyman) John
Chernoff, Goldie Taub 1909- 10
Cherry, Carolyn Janice
  See Cherryh, C.J.
Cherry, Lynne 1952- 99
  Earlier sketch in SATA 34
Cherryh, C.J. 1942- 172
  Earlier sketch in SATA 93
Cherryholmes, Anne
  See Price, Olive
Cheshire, Simon 172
Chesler, Bernice 1932-2002 59
Chess, Victoria (Dickerson) 1939- 92
  Earlier sketch in SATA 33
Chessa, Francesca 191
Chester, Deborah 1957- 85
Chester, Kate
  See Guccione, Leslie Davis
Chesterton, G(ilbert) K(eith) 1874-1936 27
Chesworth, Michael 160
Chetin, Helen 1922- 6
Chetwin, Grace 86
  Brief entry 50
Chevalier, Christa 1937- 35
Chevalier, Tracy 1962- 128

Chew, Ruth 1920- 7
Chichester Clark, Emma 1955- 69
  Earlier sketches in SATA 117, 156
Chidsey, Donald Barr 1902-1981 3
  Obituary 27
Chiefari, Janet D. 1942- 58
Chien, Catia 193
Chien-min, Lin
  See Rumford, James
Child, L. Maria
  See Child, Lydia Maria
Child, Lauren 1965- 183
  Earlier sketches in SATA 119, 160
Child, Lincoln 1957- 113
Child, Lincoln B.
  See Child, Lincoln
Child, Lydia Maria 1802-1880 67
Child, Mrs.
  See Child, Lydia Maria
Child, Philip 1898-1978 47
Children's Shepherd, The
  See Westphal, Arnold Carl
Childress, Alice 1920-1994 81
  Earlier sketches in SATA 7, 48
  See also CLR 14
Childs, H(alla) Fay (Cochrane) 1890-1971 1
  Obituary 25
Chilton, Charles (Frederick William)
  1917- 102
Chima, Cinda Williams 192
Chimaera
  See Farjeon, Eleanor
Chin, Richard (M.) 1946- 52
Chinery, Michael 1938- 26
Chin-Lee, Cynthia 1958- 102
Chin-Lee D., Cynthia
  See Chin-Lee, Cynthia
Chippendale, Lisa A. 158
Chipperfield, Joseph Eugene 1912-1980(?) .. 87
  Earlier sketch in SATA 2
Chisholm, P. F.
  See Finney, Patricia
Chislett, Gail (Elaine) 1948- 58
Chittenden, Elizabeth F. 1903-1999 9
Chittenden, Margaret 1935- 28
Chittum, Ida 1918- 7
Chitwood, Suzanne Tanner 1958- 160
Chmielarz, Sharon Lee 1940- 72
Choate, Judith (Newkirk) 1940- 30
Chocolate, Debbi 1954- 96
Chocolate, Deborah M. Newton
  See Chocolate, Debbi
Chodos-Irvine, Margaret 152
Choi, Sook Nyul 1937- 73
  Autobiography Feature 126
  See also CLR 53
Choi, Yangsook 178
Choldenko, Gennifer 1957- 182
  Earlier sketch in SATA 135
Chorao, (Ann Mc)Kay (Sproat) 1936- 162
  Earlier sketches in SATA 8, 69
Choron, Sandra (Zena Samelson) 1950- 146
Choung, Eun-hee 199
Chown, Marcus 1959- 137
Choyce, Lesley 1951- 165
  Earlier sketch in SATA 94
Chrisman, Arthur Bowie 1889-1953 124
  See also YABC 1
Christelow, Eileen 1943- 184
  Autobiography Feature 120
  Brief entry 35
  Earlier sketches in SATA 38, 90
Christensen, Bonnie 1951- 157
  Earlier sketch in SATA 110
Christensen, Gardell Dano 1907-1991 1
Christensen, Laurie
  See Steding, Laurie
Christesen, Barbara 1940- 40
Christgau, Alice Erickson 1902-1977 13
Christian, Mary Blount 1933- 9
Christiana, David 195

Christie, Agatha (Mary Clarissa)
  1890-1976 36
Christie, Ann Philippa
  See Pearce, Philippa
Christie, Gregory
  See Christie, R. Gregory
Christie, Philippa
  See Pearce, Philippa
Christie, R. Gregory 1971- 185
  Earlier sketch in SATA 127
Christopher, John
  See Youd, (Christopher) Samuel
Christopher, Louise
  See Hale, Arlene
Christopher, Matt(hew Frederick)
  1917-1997 80
  Obituary 99
  Earlier sketches in SATA 2, 47
  See also CLR 119
  See also SAAS 9
Christopher, Milbourne 1914(?)-1984 46
Christy, Howard Chandler 1873-1952 21
Chrustowski, Rick 176
Chrystie, Frances N(icholson) 1904-1986 60
Chu, Daniel 1933- 11
Chukovsky, Kornei (Ivanovich) 1882-1969 . 34
  Earlier sketch in SATA 5
Church, Caroline Jayne 179
Church, Richard 1893-1972 3
Churchill, E(lmer) Richard 1937- 11
Churchill, Elizabeth
  See Hough, Richard (Alexander)
Chute, B(eatrice) J(oy) 1913-1987 2
  Obituary 53
Chute, Marchette (Gaylord) 1909-1994 1
Chwast, Jacqueline 1932- 6
Chwast, Seymour 1931- 146
  Earlier sketches in SATA 18, 96
Ciardi, John (Anthony) 1916-1986 65
  Obituary 46
  Earlier sketch in SATA 1
  See also CLR 19
  See also SAAS 26
Ciccone, Madonna Louise Veronica
  See Madonna
Ciment, James D. 1958- 140
Cirrone, Dorian 182
Cisneros, Sandra 1954-
  See CLR 123
Citra, Becky 1954- 137
Citrin, Michael 1965(?)- 183
Clair, Andree 19
Clampett, Bob 1914(?)-1985 44
  Obituary 38
Clampett, Robert
  See Clampett, Bob
Clapp, John 1968- 109
Clapp, Patricia 1912- 74
  Earlier sketch in SATA 4
  See also SAAS 4
Clare, Ellen
  See Sinclair, Olga
Clare, Helen
  See Clarke, Pauline
Claremont, Chris 1950- 87
Claremont, Christopher Simon
  See Claremont, Chris
Clark, Ann Nolan 1896-1995 82
  Obituary 87
  Earlier sketch in SATA 4
  See also CLR 16
  See also SAAS 16
Clark, Champ 1923-2002 47
Clark, Christopher (Anthony) Stuart
  See Stuart-Clark, Christopher (Anthony)
Clark, Clara Gillow 1951- 154
  Earlier sketch in SATA 84
Clark, David
  See Hardcastle, Michael
Clark, David Allen
  See Ernst, (Lyman) John

Clark, Emma Chichester
    See Chichester Clark, Emma
Clark, Frank J(ames) 1922- 18
Clark, Garel
    See Garelick, May
Clark, Halsey
    See Deming, Richard
Clark, Joan
    See Benson, Mildred (Augustine Wirt)
Clark, Joan 1934- 182
    Earlier sketches in SATA 59, 96
Clark, Leonard 1905-1981 30
    Obituary 29
Clark, M. R.
    See Clark, Mavis Thorpe
Clark, Margaret (D.) 1943- 126
Clark, Margaret Goff 1913- 82
    Earlier sketch in SATA 8
Clark, Mary Higgins 1929- 46
Clark, Mavis Thorpe 1909-1999 74
    Earlier sketch in SATA 8
    See also CLR 30
    See also SAAS 5
Clark, Merle
    See Gessner, Lynne
Clark, Patricia Denise 1921- 117
Clark, Patricia Finrow 1929- 11
Clark, Ronald Harry 1904-1999 193
Clark, Ronald William 1916-1987 2
    Obituary 52
Clark, Sherryl 1956- 149
Clark, Van D(eusen) 1909-1974 2
Clark, Virginia
    See Gray, Patricia (Clark)
Clark, Walter Van Tilburg 1909-1971 8
Clarke, Arthur
    See Clarke, Arthur C.
Clarke, Arthur C. 1917-2008 115
    Obituary 191
    Earlier sketches in SATA 13, 70
    See also CLR 119
Clarke, Arthur Charles
    See Clarke, Arthur C.
Clarke, Clorinda 1917- 7
Clarke, Gus 1948- 134
Clarke, J.
    See Clarke, Judith
Clarke, James Hall
    See Rowland-Entwistle, (Arthur) Theodore
    (Henry)
Clarke, Joan B. 1921- 42
    Brief entry 27
Clarke, John
    See Laklan, Carli
    and Sontup, Dan(iel)
Clarke, Judith 1943- 164
    Earlier sketches in SATA 75, 110
    See also CLR 61
Clarke, Julia 1950- 138
Clarke, Kenneth 1957- 107
Clarke, Lea
    See Rowland-Entwistle, (Arthur) Theodore
    (Henry)
Clarke, Margaret 1941-
    See CLR 99
Clarke, Mary Stetson 1911-1994 5
Clarke, Michael
    See Newlon, (Frank) Clarke
Clarke, Pauline 1921- 131
    See also CLR 28
    See Hunter Blair, Pauline
Clarke-Rich, Elizabeth L. 1934- 103
Clarkson, E(dith) Margaret 1915- 37
Clarkson, Ewan 1929- 9
Claudia, Susan
    See Goulart, Ron(ald Joseph)
    and Johnston, William
Claverie, Jean 1946- 38
Clay, Patrice 1947- 47
Clayman, Deborah Paula
    See Da Costa, Deborah

Claypool, Jane
    See Miner, Jane Claypool
Clayton, Elaine 1961- 159
    Earlier sketch in SATA 94
Clayton, Lawrence (Otto, Jr.) 1945- 75
Clayton, Sandra 1951- 110
Cleary, Beverly 1916- 121
    Earlier sketches in SATA 2, 43, 79
    See also CLR 72
    See also SAAS 20
Cleary, Beverly Atlee Bunn
    See Cleary, Beverly
Cleary, Brian P. 1959- 186
    Earlier sketches in SATA 93, 132
Cleaver, Bill
    See Cleaver, William J(oseph)
Cleaver, Carole 1934- 6
Cleaver, Elizabeth (Ann Mrazik)
    1939-1985 23
    Obituary 43
    See also CLR 13
Cleaver, Hylton Reginald 1891-1961 49
Cleaver, Vera (Allen) 1919-1993 76
    Earlier sketch in SATA 22
    See also CLR 6
Cleaver, William J(oseph) 1920-1981 22
    Obituary 27
    See also CLR 6
Cleishbotham, Jebediah
    See Scott, Sir Walter
Cleland, Mabel
    See Widdemer, Mabel Cleland
Clem, Margaret H(ollingsworth) 1923- 90
Clemens, Samuel Langhorne
    See Twain, Mark
Clemens, Virginia Phelps 1941- 35
Clement, Gary 191
Clement, Janet 182
Clement, Priscilla Ferguson 1942- 171
Clement, Rod 97
Clement-Moore, Rosemary 188
Clements, Andrew 1949- 158
    Earlier sketch in SATA 104
Clements, Bruce 1931- 178
    Earlier sketches in SATA 27, 94
Clemesha, David 192
Clemons, Elizabeth
    See Nowell, Elizabeth Cameron
Clerk, N. W.
    See Lewis, C.S.
Cleveland, Bob
    See Cleveland, George
Cleveland, George 1903(?)-1985
    Obituary 43
Cleveland-Peck, Patricia 80
Cleven, Cathrine
    See Cleven, Kathryn Seward
Cleven, Kathryn Seward 2
Clevenger, William R. 1954- 84
Clevenger, William Russell
    See Clevenger, William R.
Clevin, Joergen 1920- 7
Clevin, Jorgen
    See Clevin, Joergen
Clewes, Dorothy (Mary) 1907-2003 86
    Obituary 138
    Earlier sketch in SATA 1
Clifford, David
    See Rosenberg, Eth(el) Clifford
Clifford, Eth
    See Rosenberg, Eth(el) Clifford
Clifford, Harold B(urton) 1893-1988 10
Clifford, Margaret Cort 1929- 1
Clifford, Martin
    See Hamilton, Charles (Harold St. John)
Clifford, Mary Louise Beneway 1926- 23
Clifford, Peggy
    See Clifford, Margaret Cort
Clifford, Rachel Mark
    See Lewis, Brenda Ralph

Clifton, Lucille 1936- 128
    Earlier sketches in SATA 20, 69
    See also CLR 5
Clifton, Thelma Lucille
    See Clifton, Lucille
Climo, Shirley 1928- 166
    Autobiography Feature 110
    Brief entry 35
    Earlier sketches in SATA 39, 77
    See also CLR 69
Clinton, Cathryn 1957- 136
Clinton, Dirk
    See Silverberg, Robert
Clinton, Jon
    See Prince, J(ack) H(arvey)
Clippinger, Carol 193
Clish, (Lee) Marian 1946- 43
Clive, Clifford
    See Hamilton, Charles (Harold St. John)
Clokey, Art 1921- 59
Cloudsley-Thompson, J(ohn) L(eonard)
    1921- 19
Clouse, Nancy L. 1938- 78
Clover, Peter 1952- 152
Clutha, Janet Paterson Frame
    See Frame, Janet
Clymer, Eleanor 1906-2001 85
    Obituary 126
    Earlier sketch in SATA 9
    See also SAAS 17
Clyne, Patricia (Edwards) 31
Cneut, Carll 1969- 197
Coalson, Glo 1946- 94
    Earlier sketch in SATA 26
Coates, Anna 1958- 73
Coates, Belle 1896-1986 2
Coates, Ruth Allison 1915- 11
Coats, Alice M(argaret) 1905-1976 11
Coatsworth, Elizabeth (Jane) 1893-1986 100
    Obituary 49
    Earlier sketches in SATA 2, 56
    See also CLR 2
Cobalt, Martin
    See Mayne, William (James Carter)
Cobb, Jane
    See Berry, Jane Cobb
Cobb, Mary 1931- 88
Cobb, Vicki 1938- 136
    Autobiography Feature 136
    Earlier sketches in SATA 8, 69, 131
    See also CLR 2
    See also SAAS 6
Cobbett, Richard
    See Pluckrose, Henry (Arthur)
Cober, Alan E(dwin) 1935-1998 7
    Obituary 101
Cobham, Sir Alan
    See Hamilton, Charles (Harold St. John)
Coburn, Jake 1978- 155
Cocagnac, Augustin Maurice(-Jean) 1924- 7
Cocca-Leffler, Maryann 1958- 194
    Earlier sketches in SATA 80, 136
Cochran, Bill 187
Cochran, Bobbye A. 1949- 11
Cochran, Thomas 1955- 198
Cockett, Mary 3
Coddell, Esme Raji
    See Codell, Esme Raji
Codell, Esme Raji 1968- 160
Cody, C. S.
    See Waller, Leslie
Cody, Jess
    See Cunningham, Chet
Coe, Anne (E.) 1949- 95
Coe, Douglas
    See Epstein, Beryl (M. Williams)
    and Epstein, Samuel
Coe, Lloyd 1899(?)-1976
    Obituary 30
Coen, Rena Neumann 1925- 20

Coerr, Eleanor (Beatrice) 1922- 67
  Earlier sketch in SATA *1*
Cofer, Judith Ortiz 1952- 164
  Earlier sketch in SATA *110*
Coffelt, Nancy 1961- 189
Coffey, Brian
  See Koontz, Dean R.
Coffin, Geoffrey
  See Mason, F(rancis) van Wyck
Coffin, M. T.
  See Stanley, George Edward
Coffman, Ramon Peyton 1896-1989 4
Cogan, Karen 1954- 125
Coggins, Jack (Banham) 1911-2006 2
Cohen, Barbara 1932-1992 77
  Obituary 74
  Earlier sketch in SATA *10*
  See also SAAS *7*
Cohen, Daniel (E.) 1936- 70
  Earlier sketch in SATA *8*
  See also CLR *43*
  See also SAAS *4*
Cohen, Deborah Bodin 1968- 180
Cohen, Jan Barger
  See Barger, Jan
Cohen, Jene Barr
  See Barr, Jene
Cohen, Joan Lebold 1932- 4
Cohen, Judith Love 1933- 78
Cohen, Miriam 1926-1955 155
  Earlier sketches in SATA *29, 106*
  See also SAAS *11*
Cohen, Nora 75
Cohen, Paul S. 1945- 58
Cohen, Peter Zachary 1931- 150
  Earlier sketch in SATA *4*
Cohen, Robert Carl 1930- 8
Cohen, Sholom 1951- 94
Cohn, Angelo 1914-1997 19
Cohn, Diana 194
Cohn, Rachel 1968- 161
Coit, Margaret Louise 1922-2003 2
  Obituary 142
Colato Lainez, Rene 1970- 176
Colbert, Anthony 1934-2007 15
Colbert, Nancy A. 1936- 139
Colby, C(arroll) B(urleigh) 1904-1977 35
  Earlier sketch in SATA *3*
Colby, Jean Poindexter 1909-1993 23
Cole, Annette
  See Steiner, Barbara A(nnette)
Cole, Babette 1949- 155
  Earlier sketches in SATA *61, 96*
Cole, Betsy 1940- 83
Cole, Brock 1938- 136
  Earlier sketch in SATA *72*
  See also CLR *18*
Cole, Davis
  See Elting, Mary
Cole, Hannah 1954- 74
Cole, Henry 1955- 181
Cole, Jack -1974
  See Stewart, John (William)
Cole, Jackson
  See Curry, Thomas Albert
  and Germano, Peter B.
  and Heckelmann, Charles N(ewman)
  and Newton, D(wight) B(ennett)
  and Schisgall, Oscar
Cole, Jennifer
  See Zach, Cheryl (Byrd)
Cole, Joanna 1944- 168
  Brief entry 37
  Earlier sketches in SATA *49, 81, 120*
  See also CLR *40*
Cole, Lois Dwight 1903-1979 10
  Obituary 26
Cole, Michael 1947- 59
Cole, Sheila R. 1939- 171
  Earlier sketches in SATA *24, 95*

Cole, Sheila Rotenberg
  See Cole, Sheila R.
Cole, Stephen 1971- 161
Cole, William (Rossa) 1919-2000 71
  Earlier sketch in SATA *9*
  See also SAAS *9*
Coleman, Andrew
  See Pine, Nicholas
Coleman, Clare
  See Bell, Clare (Louise)
  and Easton, M(alcolm) Coleman
Coleman, Janet Wyman 184
Coleman, Loren 1947- 164
Coleman, Loren Elwood, Jr.
  See Coleman, Loren
Coleman, Mary Ann 1928- 83
Coleman, Michael 199
  See Jones, Frewin
Coleman, Michael (Lee) 1946- 133
  Autobiography Feature 133
  Earlier sketch in SATA *108*
Coleman, Rowan 187
Coleman, William L(eRoy) 1938- 49
  Brief entry 34
Coles, Robert (Martin) 1929- 23
Colfer, Eoin 1965- 197
  Earlier sketch in SATA *148*
  See also CLR *112*
Colin, Ann
  See Ure, Jean
Collard, Sneed B. III 1959- 184
  Earlier sketches in SATA *84, 139*
Colledge, Anne 1939- 142
Collicott, Sharleen 1937- 143
  Earlier sketch in SATA *98*
Collier, Bryan 174
  Earlier sketch in SATA *126*
Collier, Christopher 1930- 70
  Earlier sketch in SATA *16*
  See also CLR *126*
Collier, Ethel 1903-1999 22
Collier, James Lincoln 1928- 166
  Earlier sketches in SATA *8, 70*
  See also CLR *126*
  See also SAAS *21*
Collier, Jane
  See Collier, Zena
Collier, Kristi 182
Collier, Steven 1942- 61
Collier, Zena 1926- 23
Collings, Gillian 1939- 102
Collington, Peter 1948- 99
  Earlier sketch in SATA *59*
Collins, Ace 1953- 82
Collins, Andrew J.
  See Collins, Ace
Collins, David R(aymond) 1940-2001 121
  Earlier sketch in SATA *7*
Collins, Heather 1946- 81
Collins, Hunt
  See Hunter, Evan
Collins, Michael
  See Lynds, Dennis
Collins, Michael 1930- 58
Collins, Pat(ricia) Lowery 1932- 151
  Earlier sketch in SATA *31*
Collins, Paul 1954- 126
Collins, Ruth Philpott 1890-1975
  Obituary 30
Collins, Suzanne 180
Collins, Yvonne 194
Collinson, A. S.
  See Collinson, Alan S.
Collinson, Alan S. 1934- 80
Collinson, Roger (Alfred) 1936- 133
Collison, Linda 1953- 185
Collodi, Carlo
  See Lorenzini, Carlo
Colloms, Brenda 1919- 40

Colman, Hila 53
  Earlier sketch in SATA *1*
  See also SAAS *14*
Colman, Morris 1899(?)-1981
  Obituary 25
Colman, Penny (Morgan) 1944- 160
  Autobiography Feature 160
  Earlier sketches in SATA *77, 114*
Colman, Warren (David) 1944- 67
Colombo, John Robert 1936- 50
Colon, Raul 156
Colonius, Lillian 1911-1992 3
Colorado, Antonio J.
  See Colorado (Capella), Antonio J(ulio)
Colorado (Capella), Antonio J(ulio)
  1903-1994 23
  Obituary 79
Colquhoun, Glenn 1964- 165
Colston, Fifi E. 1960- 150
Colt, Martin
  See Epstein, Beryl (M. Williams)
  and Epstein, Samuel
Colum, Padraic 1881-1972 15
  See also CLR *36*
Columbus, Chris 1959- 97
Columbus, Christopher
  See Columbus, Chris
Columella
  See Moore, Clement Clarke
Colver, Anne 1908- 7
Colvin, James
  See Moorcock, Michael
Colwell, Eileen (Hilda) 1904-2002 2
Colwyn, Stewart
  See Pepper, Frank S.
Coman, Carolyn 1951- 197
  Earlier sketch in SATA *127*
Combs, Lisa M.
  See McCourt, Lisa
Combs, Robert
  See Murray, John
Comfort, Jane Levington
  See Sturtzel, Jane Levington
Comfort, Mildred Houghton 1886-1976 3
Comins, Ethel M(ae) 11
Comins, Jeremy 1933- 28
Commager, Henry Steele 1902-1998 23
  Obituary 102
Comora, Madeleine 190
Compere, Mickie
  See Davidson, Margaret
Compestine, Ying Chang 1963- 187
  Earlier sketch in SATA *140*
Comport, Sally Wern 190
Compton, Patricia A. 1936- 75
Comte, The Great
  See Hawkesworth, Eric
Comus
  See Ballantyne, R(obert) M(ichael)
Comyns, Nance
  See Comyns-Toohey, Nantz
Comyns-Toohey, Nantz 1956- 86
Conan Doyle, Arthur
  See Doyle, Sir Arthur Conan
Condit, Martha Olson 1913- 28
Condon, Bill 1949- 142
Condon, Judith 83
Condon, Ken 195
Condy, Roy 1942- 96
Cone, Ferne Geller 1921- 39
Cone, Molly (Lamken) 1918- 151
  Autobiography Feature 151
  Earlier sketches in SATA *1, 28, 115*
  See also SAAS *11*
Cone, Patrick 1954- 89
Coney, Michael G. 1932-2005 61
  Obituary 170
Coney, Michael Greatrex
  See Coney, Michael G.
Coney, Mike
  See Coney, Michael G.

Conford, Ellen 1942- 162
Earlier sketches in SATA *6, 68, 110*
See also CLR *71*
Conger, Lesley
See Suttles, Shirley (Smith)
Conklin, Gladys Plemon 1903- 2
Conklin, Paul S. 1929(?)-2003 43
Brief entry 33
Obituary 147
Conkling, Hilda 1910-1986 23
Conlan, Kathleen Elizabeth 1950- 145
Conlan, Kathy
See Conlan, Kathleen Elizabeth
Conley-Weaver, Robyn 1963- 125
Conlon-McKenna, Marita 1956- 71
Conly, Jane Leslie 1948- 164
Earlier sketches in SATA *80, 112*
Conly, Robert Leslie 1918(?)-1973 23
See also CLR *2*
Connell, Kirk
See Chapman, John Stanton Higham
Connelly, Marc(us Cook) 1890-1980
Obituary 25
Connolly, Jerome P(atrick) 1931- 8
Connolly, Pat 1943- 74
Connolly, Peter 1935- 105
Earlier sketch in SATA *47*
Conover, Chris 1950- 31
Conquest, Owen
See Hamilton, Charles (Harold St. John)
Conrad, Joseph 1857-1924 27
Conrad, Pam 1947-1996 133
Brief entry 49
Obituary 90
Earlier sketches in SATA *52, 80*
See also CLR *18*
See also SAAS *19*
Conroy, Jack
See Conroy, John Wesley
Conroy, John Wesley 1899-1990 19
Obituary 65
Conroy, Robert
See Goldston, Robert (Conroy)
Constable, Kate 1966- 172
Constant, Alberta Wilson 1908-1981 22
Obituary 28
Constantin, Pascale 185
Conway, Diana C(ohen) 1943- 91
Conway, Gordon
See Hamilton, Charles (Harold St. John)
Cook, Ande 192
Cook, Bernadine 1924- 11
Cook, Fred J(ames) 1911-2003 2
Obituary 145
Cook, Glen 1944- 171
Earlier sketch in SATA *108*
Cook, Glen Charles
See Cook, Glen
Cook, Hugh 1956- 85
Cook, Hugh, Walter Gilbert
See Cook, Hugh
Cook, Jean Thor 1930- 94
Cook, Joel 1934- 79
Cook, Joseph Jay 1924- 8
Cook, Lisa Broadie 157
Cook, Lyn
See Waddell, Evelyn Margaret
Cook, Roy
See Silverberg, Robert
Cook, Trish 175
Cooke, Ann
See Cole, Joanna
Cooke, Arthur
See Lowndes, Robert A(ugustine) W(ard)
Cooke, Barbara
See Alexander, Anna B(arbara Cooke)
Cooke, David Coxe 1917- 2
Cooke, Donald Ewin 1916-1985 2
Obituary 45
Cooke, Frank E. 1920- 87
Cooke, Jean (Isobel Esther) 1929- 74

Cooke, John Estes
See Baum, L(yman) Frank
Cooke, Trish 1962- 129
Cookson, Catherine (McMullen) 1906-1998 .. 9
Obituary 116
Cooley, Regina Francoise 1940- 177
Coolidge, Olivia E(nsor) 1908- 26
Earlier sketch in SATA *1*
Cooling, Wendy 169
Earlier sketch in SATA *111*
Coombs, Charles I(ra) 1914-1994 43
Earlier sketch in SATA *3*
See also SAAS *15*
Coombs, Chick
See Coombs, Charles I(ra)
Coombs, Kate 190
Coombs, Patricia 1926- 51
Earlier sketch in SATA *3*
See also SAAS *22*
Cooney, Barbara 1917-2000 96
Obituary 123
Earlier sketches in SATA *6, 59*
See also CLR *23*
Cooney, Caroline B. 1947- 179
Brief entry 41
Earlier sketches in SATA *48, 80, 113, 130*
Cooney, Doug 181
Cooney, Nancy Evans 1932- 42
Coontz, Otto 1946- 33
Cooper, Ann (Catharine) 1939- 104
Cooper, Dutch
See Kuyper, Sjoerd
Cooper, Elisha 1971- 157
Earlier sketch in SATA *99*
Cooper, Elizabeth Keyser -1992 47
Cooper, Floyd 187
Earlier sketches in SATA *96, 144*
See also CLR *60*
Cooper, Gordon 1932- 23
Cooper, Helen 1963- 169
Earlier sketch in SATA *102*
Cooper, Henry S(potswood) F(enimore), Jr.
1933- 65
Cooper, Ilene 1948- 145
Earlier sketches in SATA *66, 97*
Cooper, James Fenimore 1789-1851 19
See also CLR *105*
Cooper, John R. 1
Cooper, Kay 1941- 11
Cooper, Lee Pelham 1926- 5
Cooper, Lester (Irving) 1919-1985 32
Obituary 43
Cooper, Lettice (Ulpha) 1897-1994 35
Obituary 82
Cooper, Louise 1952- 152
Cooper, M.E.
See Lerangis, Peter
Cooper, M.E.
See Davis, Maggie S.
Cooper, Melrose
See Kroll, Virginia L.
Cooper, Michael L. 1950- 181
Earlier sketches in SATA *79, 117*
Cooper, Patrick 1949- 134
Cooper, Susan 1935- 151
Earlier sketches in SATA *4, 64, 104*
See also CLR *67*
See also SAAS *6*
Cooper, Susan Mary
See Cooper, Susan
Cope, Jane U(rsula) 1949- 108
Copeland, Helen 1920- 4
Copeland, Mark 1956- 180
Copeland, Paul W. 23
Coplans, Peta 1951- 84
Copley (Diana) Heather Pickering 1918- 45
Coppard, A(lfred) E(dgar) 1878-1957
See YABC *1*
Copper, Melinda 1952- 172
Copper, Melinda McConnaughey
See Copper, Melinda

Coralie
See Anderson, Catherine Corley
Corbett, Grahame 43
Brief entry 36
Corbett, Scott 1913- 42
Earlier sketch in SATA *2*
See also CLR *1*
See also SAAS *2*
Corbett, Sue 174
Corbett, W(illiam) J(esse) 1938- 102
Brief entry 44
Earlier sketch in SATA *50*
See also CLR *19*
Corbin, Sabra Lee
See Malvern, Gladys
Corbin, William
See McGraw, William Corbin
Corbman, Marjorie 1987- 179
Corby, Dan
See Catherall, Arthur
Corcoran, Barbara (Asenath) 1911- 77
Autobiography Feature 125
Earlier sketch in SATA *3*
See also CLR *50*
See also SAAS *20*
Corcos, Lucille 1908-1973 10
Cordell, Alexander
See Graber, Alexander
Cordell, Alexander
See Graber, (George) Alexander
Cordell, Matthew 1975- 199
Corder, Zizou
See Young, Louisa
Corella, Joseph
See Odgers, Sally Farrell
Coren, Alan 1938-2007 32
Obituary 187
Corey, Dorothy 23
Corey, Shana 1974- 133
Corfe, Thomas Howell 1928- 27
Corfe, Tom
See Corfe, Thomas Howell
Corfield, Robin Bell 1952- 74
Corlett, William 1938-2005 46
Brief entry 39
Cormack, M(argaret) Grant 1913- 11
Cormack, Maribelle B. 1902-1984 39
Cormier, Robert 1925-2000 83
Obituary 122
Earlier sketches in SATA *10, 45*
See also CLR *55*
Cormier, Robert Edmund
See Cormier, Robert
Cornelius, Carol 1942- 40
Cornelius, Kay 1933- 157
Cornell, J.
See Cornell, Jeffrey
Cornell, James (Clayton, Jr.) 1938- 27
Cornell, Jean Gay 1920- 23
Cornell, Jeffrey 1945- 11
Cornell, Laura 189
Cornish, D.M. 1972- 185
Cornish, Sam(uel James) 1935- 23
Cornwall, Nellie
See Sloggett, Nellie
Cornwell, Autumn 195
Corr, Christopher 1955- 189
Correy, Lee
See Stine, G(eorge) Harry
Corrick, James A. 1945- 76
Corrigan, (Helen) Adeline 1909- 23
Corrigan, Barbara 1922- 8
Corrigan, Eireann 1977- 163
Corrin, Sara 1918- 86
Brief entry 48
Corrin, Stephen 86
Brief entry 48
Corsi, Wendy
See Staub, Wendy Corsi
Cort, M. C.
See Clifford, Margaret Cort

Cort, Margaret
See Clifford, Margaret Cort
Corwin, Judith H(offman) 1946- 10
Cory, Rowena
See Lindquist, Rowena Cory
Cosby, Bill
See Cosby, William Henry, Jr.
Cosby, William Henry, Jr. 1937- 110
Earlier sketch in SATA 66
Cosentino, Ralph 169
Cosgrave, John O'Hara II 1908-1968
Obituary 21
Cosgrove, Margaret (Leota) 1926- 47
Cosgrove, Stephen E(dward) 1945- 53
Brief entry 40
Coskey, Evelyn 1932- 7
Cosner, Shaaron 1940- 43
Cossi, Olga 1921- 102
Earlier sketch in SATA 67
Costabel, Eva Deutsch 1924- 45
Costabel-Deutsch, Eva
See Costabel, Eva Deutsch
Coste, Marion 1938- 183
Costello, David 174
Costello, David F(rancis) 1904-1990 23
Cte, Genevieve 1964- 184
Cote, Nancy 182
Cott, Jonathan 1942- 23
Cottam, Clarence 1899-1974 25
Cotten, Cynthia 188
Cottle, Joan 1960- 135
Cottler, Joseph 1899-1996 22
Cottonwood, Joe 1947- 92
Cottrell, Leonard 1913-1974 24
Cottringer, Anne 1952- 150
Earlier sketch in SATA 97
Couch, Greg 199
Coulman, Valerie 1969- 161
Couloumbis, Audrey 173
Counsel, June 1926- 70
Countryman, The
See Whitlock, Ralph
Courlander, Harold 1908-1996 6
Obituary 88
Coursen, Valerie 1965(?)- 102
Courtis, Stuart Appleton 1874-1969
Obituary 29
Courtland, Tyler
See Stevens, Serita
Courtney, Dayle
See Goldsmith, Howard
Coury, Louise Andree 1895(?)-1983
Obituary 34
Cousins, Linda 1946- 90
Cousins, Lucy 1964- 172
Cousins, Margaret 1905-1996 2
Obituary 92
Cousteau, Jacques-Yves 1910-1997 98
Earlier sketch in SATA 38
Couture, Christin 1951- 73
Couvillon, Jacques 195
Covert, Ralph 1968- 197
Coville, Bruce 1950- 155
Autobiography Feature 155
Earlier sketches in SATA 32, 77, 118
Covington, Dennis 109
Covington, Linda
See Windsor, Linda
Cowan, Catherine 121
Cowan, Rebecca M.
See Moesta, Rebecca
Cowan, Rebecca Moesta
See Moesta, Rebecca
Coward, Fiona 1963- 178
Cowell, Cressida 1966- 140
Cowen, Eve
See Werner, Herma
Cowen, Ida 1898-1993 64
Cowie, Leonard W(allace) 1919- 4
Cowles, Kathleen
See Krull, Kathleen

Cowley, Cassia Joy
See Cowley, Joy
Cowley, Joy 1936- 164
Cowley, (Cassia) Joy 1936- 90
Autobiography Feature 118
Earlier sketch in SATA 4
See also CLR 55
See also SAAS 26
Cowley, Marjorie 1925- 111
Cox, (Christopher) Barry 1931- 62
Cox, Clinton 1934- 108
Earlier sketch in SATA 74
Cox, David (Dundas) 1933- 56
Cox, Donald William 1921- 23
Cox, Jack
See Cox, John Roberts
Cox, John Roberts 1915-1981 191
Earlier sketch in SATA 9
Cox, Judy 1954- 198
Earlier sketches in SATA 117, 160
Cox, Marion Monroe 1898-1983
Obituary 34
Cox, Palmer 1840-1924 24
See also CLR 24
Cox, Vic 1942- 88
Cox, Vicki 1945- 158
Cox, Victoria
See Garretson, Victoria Diane
Cox, Wallace (Maynard) 1924-1973 25
Cox, Wally
See Cox, Wallace (Maynard)
Cox, William R(obert) 1901-1988 46
Brief entry 31
Obituary 57
Coxe, Molly 1959- 101
Earlier sketch in SATA 69
Coxon, Michele 1950- 158
Earlier sketch in SATA 76
Coy, Harold 1902-1986 3
Coy, John 1958- 171
Earlier sketch in SATA 120
Craats, Rennay 1973- 131
Crabtree, Judith 1928- 98
Earlier sketch in SATA 63
Cracker, Edward E.B.
See Odgers, Sally Farrell
Craft, K. Y.
See Craft, Kinuko Y(amabe)
Craft, Kinuko
See Craft, Kinuko Y(amabe)
Craft, Kinuko Y(amabe) 1940- 127
Earlier sketch in SATA 65
Craft, Ruth 1935- 87
Brief entry 31
Craig, A. A.
See Anderson, Poul
Craig, Alisa
See MacLeod, Charlotte (Matilda)
Craig, Helen 1934- 94
Earlier sketches in SATA 46, 49
Craig, Joe 1979- 198
Craig, Joe Alexander
See Craig, Joe
Craig, John Eland
See Chipperfield, Joseph Eugene
Craig, John Ernest 1921- 23
Craig, Kit
See Reed, Kit
Craig, M. F.
See Craig, Mary (Francis) Shura
Craig, M. Jean 17
Craig, M. S.
See Craig, Mary (Francis) Shura
Craig, Margaret (Maze) 1911-1964 9
Craig, Mary
See Craig, Mary (Francis) Shura
Craig, Mary Shura
See Craig, Mary (Francis) Shura

Craig, Mary (Francis) Shura 1923-1991 86
Obituary 65
Earlier sketch in SATA 6
See also SAAS 7
Craig, Ruth 1922- 95
Craik, Mrs.
See Craik, Dinah Maria (Mulock)
Craik, Dinah Maria (Mulock) 1826-1887 34
Crandall, Court 1965- 175
Crandell, Rachel 1943- 152
Crane, Barbara (Joyce) 1934- 31
Crane, Caroline 1930- 11
Crane, Jordan 1973- 174
Crane, M. A.
See Wartski, Maureen (Ann Crane)
Crane, Royston Campbell 1901-1977
Obituary 22
Crane, Stephen (Townley) 1871-1900
See YABC 2
See also CLR 132
Crane, Walter 1845-1915 100
Earlier sketch in SATA 18
See also CLR 56
Crane, William D(wight) 1892-1976 1
Cranfield, Ingrid 1945- 74
Cranshaw, Stanley
See Fisher, Dorothy (Frances) Canfield
Crary, Elizabeth (Ann) 1942- 99
Brief entry 43
Crary, Margaret (Coleman) 1906-1986 9
Cravath, Lynne Avril
See Cravath, Lynne W.
Cravath, Lynne W. 1951- 182
Earlier sketches in SATA 98, 148
Craven, Thomas 1889-1969 22
Crawford, Charles P. 1945- 28
Crawford, Deborah 1922- 6
Crawford, John E(dmund) 1904-1971 3
Crawford, K(aren) Michael 1959- 155
Crawford, Mel 1925- 44
Brief entry 33
Crawford, Phyllis 1899- 3
Crawley, Dave 177
Cray, Roberta
See Emerson, Ru
Crayder, Dorothy 7
Crayder, Teresa
See Colman, Hila
Crayon, Geoffrey
See Irving, Washington
Craz, Albert G. 1926- 24
Crebbin, June 1938- 169
Earlier sketch in SATA 80
Crecy, Jeanne
See Williams, Jeanne
Credle, Ellis 1902-1998 1
Creech, Sharon 1945- 172
Earlier sketches in SATA 94, 139
See also CLR 89
Creeden, Sharon 1938- 91
Creel, Ann Howard 1953- 187
Creighton, (Mary) Helen 1899-1989
Obituary 64
Creighton, Jill 1949- 96
Crenson, Victoria 1952- 159
Earlier sketch in SATA 88
Cresp, Gael 1954- 119
Crespo, George 1962- 82
Cresswell, Helen 1934-2005 79
Obituary 168
Earlier sketches in SATA 1, 48
See also CLR 18
See also SAAS 20
Cressy, Michael 1955- 124
Cressy, Mike
See Cressy, Michael
Cretan, Gladys (Yessayan) 1921- 2
Cretzmeyer, Stacy (Megan) 1959- 124
Crew, Gary 1947- 163
Earlier sketches in SATA 75, 110
See also CLR 42

Crew, Helen (Cecilia) Coale 1866-1941
    See YABC 2
Crew, Linda (Jean) 1951- 137
    Earlier sketch in SATA 71
Crews, Donald 1938- 76
    Brief entry 30
    Earlier sketch in SATA 32
    See also CLR 7
Crews, Nina 1963- 158
    Earlier sketch in SATA 97
Crichton, John Michael
    See Crichton, Michael
Crichton, Michael 1942-2008 88
    Obituary 199
    Earlier sketch in SATA 9
Crider, Allen Billy
    See Crider, Bill
Crider, Bill 1941- 99
Crilley, Mark 1966- 148
    Autobiography Feature 148
    Earlier sketch in SATA 120
Crimi, Carolyn 1959- 176
Cripps, Enid Margaret
    See Appiah, Peggy
Crisler, Curtis L. 188
Crisman, Ruth 1914- 73
Crisp, Marta Marie 1947- 128
Crisp, Marty
    See Crisp, Marta Marie
Crispin, A(nn) C(arol) 1950- 86
Crist, James J. 1961- 168
Cristall, Barbara 79
Crist-Evans, Craig 1954- 153
Crocker, Carter 193
Crocker, Nancy 1956- 185
Crofford, Emily (Ardell) 1927- 61
Crofut, William E. III 1934- 23
Croggon, Alison 1962- 194
Croll, Carolyn 1945- 102
    Brief entry 52
    Earlier sketch in SATA 56
Croman, Dorothy Young
    See Rosenberg, Dorothy
Cromie, Alice Hamilton 1914-2000 24
Cromie, William J(oseph) 1930- 4
Crompton, Anne Eliot 1930- 73
    Earlier sketch in SATA 23
Crompton, Richmal
    See Lamburn, Richmal Crompton
Cronbach, Abraham 1882-1965 11
Crone, Ruth 1919-2003 4
Cronin, A(rchibald) J(oseph) 1896-1981 47
    Obituary 25
Cronin, Doreen (A.) 125
Cronin, Doreen 1966(?)- 178
    See also CLR 136
Cronin, Doreen A.
    See Cronin, Doreen
Crook, Beverly Courtney 38
    Brief entry 35
Crook, Connie Brummel 1930- 168
    Earlier sketch in SATA 98
Crook, Constance
    See Crook, Connie Brummel
Crosby, Alexander L. 1906-1980 2
    Obituary 23
Crosby, Harry C., Jr. 102
Crosby, Margaret
    See Rathmann, Peggy
Crosher, G. R. 14
Cross, Gilbert B. 1939- 60
    Brief entry 51
Cross, Gillian 1945- 178
    Autobiography Feature 178
    Earlier sketches in SATA 38, 71, 110, 165
    See also CLR 28
Cross, Gillian Clare
    See Cross, Gillian
Cross, Helen Reeder
    See Broadhead, Helen Cross
Cross, Peter 1951- 95

Cross, Shauna 1976(?)- 196
Cross, Tom 1954- 146
Cross, Verda 1914- 75
Cross, Wilbur Lucius III 1918- 2
Crossland, Caroline 1964- 83
Crossley-Holland, Kevin 1941- 165
    Earlier sketches in SATA 5, 74, 120
    See also CLR 84
    See also SAAS 20
Crossley-Holland, Kevin John William
    See Crossley-Holland, Kevin
Crouch, Marcus 1913-1996 4
Crout, George C(lement) 1917- 11
Crow, Donna Fletcher 1941- 40
Crow, Francis Luther
    See Luther, Frank
Crowe, Andrew 111
Crowe, John
    See Lynds, Dennis
Crowe, (Bettina) Peter Lum 1911- 6
Crowell, Grace Noll 1877-1969 34
Crowell, Pers 1910-1990 2
Crowell, Robert Leland 1909-2001 63
Crowfield, Christopher
    See Stowe, Harriet (Elizabeth) Beecher
Crowley, Arthur McBlair 1945- 38
Crowley, John 1942- 140
    Earlier sketch in SATA 65
Crowley, Suzanne 1963- 196
Crowley, Suzanne Carlisle
    See Crowley, Suzanne
Crownfield, Gertrude 1867-1945
    See YABC 1
Crowther, James Gerald 1899-1983 14
Crowther, Robert 1948- 163
Cruikshank, George 1792-1878 22
    See also CLR 63
Cruise, Robin 1951- 179
Crum, Shutta 192
    Earlier sketch in SATA 134
Crummel, Susan Stevens 1949- 176
    Earlier sketch in SATA 130
Crump, Fred H., Jr. 1931- 76
    Earlier sketch in SATA 11
Crump, J(ames) Irving 1887-1979 57
    Obituary 21
Crump, William D(rake) 1949- 138
Crunden, Reginald
    See Cleaver, Hylton Reginald
Crunk, T.
    See Crunk, Tony
Crunk, Tony 1956- 130
Crutcher, Chris 1946- 196
    Earlier sketches in SATA 52, 99, 153
    See also CLR 28
Crutcher, Christopher C.
    See Crutcher, Chris
Cruz, Ray(mond) 1933- 6
Cruz Martinez, Alejandro (?)-1987 74
Crystal, Billy 1947- 154
Ctvrtek, Vaclav 1911-1976
    Obituary 27
Cuetara, Mittie 1957- 158
    Earlier sketch in SATA 106
Cuffari, Richard 1925-1978 66
    Obituary 25
    Earlier sketch in SATA 6
Cuffe-Perez, Mary 1946- 199
Cullen, Countee 1903-1946 18
Cullen, Lynn 190
Culliford, Pierre 1928-1992 40
    Obituary 74
Cullinan, Bernice E(llinger) 1926- 135
Culp, Louanna McNary 1901-1965 2
Culper, Felix
    See McCaughrean, Geraldine
Cumbaa, Stephen 1947- 72
Cumming, Peter 1951- 168
Cumming, Primrose Amy 1915- 24
Cumming, Robert 1945- 65

Cummings, Betty Sue 1918- 15
    See also SAAS 9
Cummings, Mary 1951- 185
Cummings, Parke 1902-1987 2
    Obituary 53
Cummings, Pat (Marie) 1950- 107
    Earlier sketches in SATA 42, 71
    See also CLR 48
    See also SAAS 13
Cummings, Phil 1957- 123
    Earlier sketch in SATA 74
Cummings, Priscilla 1951- 170
    Earlier sketch in SATA 129
Cummings, Richard
    See Gardner, Richard (M.)
Cummins, Maria Susanna 1827-1866
    See YABC 1
Cuneo, Mary Louise -2001 85
Cunliffe, John Arthur 1933- 86
    Earlier sketch in SATA 11
Cunliffe, Marcus (Falkner) 1922-1990 37
    Obituary 66
Cunnane, Kelly 175
Cunningham, Bob
    See May, Julian
Cunningham, Captain Frank
    See Glick, Carl (Cannon)
Cunningham, Cathy
    See Cunningham, Chet
Cunningham, Chet 1928- 23
Cunningham, Dale S(peers) 1932- 11
Cunningham, Dru 91
Cunningham, E. V.
    See Fast, Howard
Cunningham, Julia (Woolfolk) 1916- 132
    Earlier sketches in SATA 1, 26
    See also SAAS 2
Cunningham, Lawrence J. 1943- 125
Cunningham, Virginia
    See Holmgren, Virginia C(unningham)
Curiae, Amicus
    See Fuller, Edmund (Maybank)
Curie, Eve 1904-2007 1
    Obituary 188
Curlee, Lynn 1947- 190
    Earlier sketches in SATA 98, 141
Curley, Daniel 1918-1988 23
    Obituary 61
Curley, Marianne 1959- 175
    Earlier sketch in SATA 131
Currey, Anna 194
Currie, Robin 1948- 120
Currie, Stephen 1960- 132
    Earlier sketch in SATA 82
Curry, Ann (Gabrielle) 1934- 72
Curry, Jane L(ouise) 1932- 138
    Autobiography Feature 138
    Earlier sketches in SATA 1, 52, 90
    See also CLR 31
    See also SAAS 6
Curry, Peggy Simson 1911-1987 8
    Obituary 50
Curry, Tom 185
Curtis, Bruce (Richard) 1944- 30
Curtis, Chara M(ahar) 1950- 78
Curtis, Christopher Paul 1954(?)- 187
    Earlier sketches in SATA 93, 140
    See also CLR 68
Curtis, Gavin 1965- 107
Curtis, Jamie Lee 1958- 144
    Earlier sketch in SATA 95
    See also CLR 88
Curtis, Jennifer Keats 185
Curtis, Marci 160
Curtis, Patricia 1921- 101
    Earlier sketch in SATA 23
Curtis, Peter
    See Lofts, Norah (Robinson)
Curtis, Philip (Delacourt) 1920- 62
Curtis, Richard (Alan) 1937- 29

Curtis, Richard Hale
  See Deming, Richard
  and Levinson, Leonard
  and Rothweiler, Paul Roger
Curtis, Wade
  See Pournelle, Jerry (Eugene)
Curtiss, A(rlene) B. 1934- 90
Cusack, Margaret 1945- 58
Cushman, Doug 1953- 157
  Earlier sketches in SATA *65, 101*
Cushman, Jerome 2
Cushman, Karen 1941- 147
  Earlier sketch in SATA *89*
  See also CLR *55*
Cusick, Richie Tankersley 1952- 140
  Earlier sketch in SATA *67*
Cutchen, Billye Walker 1930- 15
Cutchins, Judy 1947- 59
Cutler, Daniel S(olomon) 1951- 78
Cutler, Ebbitt 1923- 9
Cutler, Ivor 1923-2006 24
  Obituary 174
Cutler, Jane 1936- 162
  Earlier sketches in SATA *75, 118*
Cutler, May Ebbitt
  See Cutler, Ebbitt
Cutler, Samuel
  See Folsom, Franklin (Brewster)
Cutlip, Kimbra L(eigh-Ann) 1964- 128
Cutrate, Joe
  See Spiegelman, Art
Cutt, W(illiam) Towrie 1898-1981 16
  Obituary 85
Cuyler, Margery 1948- 195
  Earlier sketches in SATA *39, 99, 156*
Cuyler, Margery Stuyvesant
  See Cuyler, Margery
Cuyler, Stephen
  See Bates, Barbara S(nedeker)
Cyrus, Kurt 1954- 179
  Earlier sketch in SATA *132*
Czernecki, Stefan 1946- 178

D

Dabba Smith, Frank 174
Dabcovich, Lydia 99
  Brief entry 47
  Earlier sketch in SATA *58*
Dace, Dolores B(oelens) 1929- 89
Da Costa, Deborah 193
Daddo, Andrew 1967- 198
Dadey, Debbie 1959- 136
  Earlier sketch in SATA *73*
Dahl, Borghild (Margarethe) 1890-1984 7
  Obituary 37
Dahl, Roald 1916-1990 73
  Obituary 65
  Earlier sketches in SATA *1, 26*
  See also CLR *111*
Dahlberg, Maurine F. 1951- 171
Dahlstedt, Marden (Stewart) 1921-1983 8
  Obituary 110
Dain, Martin J. 1924-2000 35
Dakos, Kalli 1950- 115
  Earlier sketch in SATA *80*
Dale, Anna 1971- 170
Dale, Gary
  See Reece, Colleen L.
Dale, George E.
  See Asimov, Isaac
Dale, Jack
  See Holliday, Joseph
Dale, Kim 1957- 123
Dale, Margaret J(essy) Miller 1911- 39
Dale, Mitzi
  See Hemstock, Gillian
Dale, Norman
  See Denny, Norman (George)

Dale, Penny 1954- 151
  Earlier sketch in SATA *70*
Daley, Michael J. 170
Dalgliesh, Alice 1893-1979 17
  Obituary 21
  See also CLR *62*
Dalkey, Kara 1953- 132
Dalkey, Kara Mia
  See Dalkey, Kara
Dallas, Ruth 1919- 86
Dalmas, John
  See Jones, John R(obert)
Dalton, Alene
  See Chapin, Alene Olsen Dalton
Dalton, Annie 1948- 140
  Earlier sketch in SATA *40*
Dalton, Kit
  See Cunningham, Chet
Dalton, Pamela
  See Johnson, Pamela
Dalton, Sean
  See Chester, Deborah
Dalton, Sheila 1949- 108
Daly, Jim
  See Stratemeyer, Edward L.
Daly, Jude 1951- 177
Daly, Kathleen N(orah) 124
  Brief entry 37
Daly, Maureen 1921-2006 129
  Obituary 176
  Earlier sketch in SATA *2*
  See also CLR *96*
  See also SAAS *1*
Daly, Nicholas 1946- 164
  Earlier sketches in SATA *37, 76, 114*
  See also CLR *41*
  See also SAAS *21*
  See Daly, Niki
Daly, Niki 198
  See Daly, Nicholas
D'Amato, Alex 1919- 20
D'Amato, Janet (Potter) 1925- 9
Damerow, Gail 1944- 83
Damerow, Gail Jane
  See Damerow, Gail
D'Amico, Carmela 170
D'Amico, Steve 170
Damrell, Liz 1956- 77
Damrosch, Helen
  See Tee-Van, Helen Damrosch
Dana, Barbara 1940- 22
Dana, Richard Henry, Jr. 1815-1882 26
Danachair, Caoimhin O
  See Danaher, Kevin
Danaher, Kevin 1913-2002 22
Danakas, John 1963- 94
Dandi
  See Mackall, Dandi Daley
D'Andrea, Kate
  See Steiner, Barbara A(nnette)
Dangerfield, Balfour
  See McCloskey, (John) Robert
Daniel, Alan 1939- 76
  Brief entry 53
Daniel, Anita 1893(?)-1978 23
  Obituary 24
Daniel, Anne
  See Steiner, Barbara A(nnette)
Daniel, Becky 1947- 56
Daniel, Claire 1949- 164
Daniel, Colin
  See Windsor, Patricia
Daniel, Hawthorne 1890- 8
Daniel, (Donna) Lee 1944- 76
Daniel, Rebecca
  See Daniel, Becky
Daniels, Guy 1919-1989 11
  Obituary 62
Daniels, Lucy
  See Oldfield, Jenny

Daniels, Max
  See Gellis, Roberta
Daniels, Olga
  See Sinclair, Olga
Daniels, Patricia 1955- 93
Daniels, Zoe
  See Laux, Constance
Dank, Gloria Rand 1955- 56
  Brief entry 46
Dank, Leonard D(ewey) 1929- 44
Dank, Milton 1920- 31
Dann, Max 1955- 62
Danneberg, Julie 1958- 173
Dantz, William R.
  See Philbrick, Rodman
Danziger, Paula 1944-2004 149
  Brief entry 30
  Obituary 155
  Earlier sketches in SATA *36, 63, 102*
  See also CLR *20*
Darby, Gene Kegley
  See Darby, Jean (Kegley)
Darby, J. N.
  See Govan, (Mary) Christine Noble
Darby, Jean (Kegley) 1921- 68
Darby, Patricia (Paulsen) 14
Darby, Ray(mond) 1912-1982 7
d'Arcy, Willard
  See Cox, William R(obert)
Dare, Geena
  See McNicoll, Sylvia (Marilyn)
Darian, Shea 1959- 97
Daringer, Helen Fern 1892-1986 1
Darke, Marjorie 1929- 87
  Earlier sketch in SATA *16*
Darley, F(elix) O(ctavius) C(arr)
  1822-1888 35
Darling, David J. 1953- 60
  Brief entry 44
Darling, Kathy
  See Darling, Mary Kathleen
Darling, Lois (MacIntyre) 1917-1989 3
  Obituary 64
Darling, Louis, (Jr.) 1916-1970 3
  Obituary 23
Darling, Mary Kathleen 1943- 124
  Earlier sketches in SATA *9, 79*
Darling, Sandra Louise Woodward
  See Day, Alexandra
Darnell, K(athryn) L(ynne) 1955- 150
Darroll, Sally
  See Odgers, Sally Farrell
Darrow, Sharon 181
Darrow, Whitney, (Jr.) 1909-1999 13
  Obituary 115
Darwin, Len
  See Darwin, Leonard
Darwin, Leonard 1916- 24
Dasent, Sir George Webbe 1817-1896 62
  Brief entry 29
Dash, Joan 1925- 142
Daskam, Josephine Dodge
  See Bacon, Josephine Dodge (Daskam)
D'ath, Justin 1953- 174
  Earlier sketch in SATA *106*
Dauer, Rosamond 1934- 23
Daugherty, Charles Michael 1914- 16
Daugherty, James (Henry) 1889-1974 13
  See also CLR *78*
Daugherty, Richard D(eo) 1922- 35
Daugherty, Sonia Medwedeff (?)-1971
  Obituary 27
d'Aulaire, Edgar Parin 1898-1986 66
  Obituary 47
  Earlier sketch in SATA *5*
  See also CLR *21*
d'Aulaire, Ingri (Mortenson Parin)
  1904-1980 66
  Obituary 24
  Earlier sketch in SATA *5*
  See also CLR *21*

Dave, Dave
　See Berg, David
Daveluy, Paule Cloutier 1919- *11*
Davenier, Christine 1961- *179*
　Earlier sketch in SATA *127*
Davenport, John 1960- *156*
Daves, Michael 1938- *40*
David, A. R.
　See David, A(nn) Rosalie
David, A(nn) Rosalie 1946- *103*
David, Jonathan
　See Ames, Lee J(udah)
David, Lawrence 1963- *165*
　Earlier sketch in SATA *111*
David, Peter 1956- *72*
David, Peter Allen
　See David, Peter
David, Rosalie
　See David, A(nn) Rosalie
Davidson, Alice Joyce 1932- *54*
　Brief entry *45*
Davidson, Basil 1914- *13*
Davidson, (Marie) Diane 1924- *91*
Davidson, Hugh
　See Hamilton, Edmond
Davidson, Jessica 1915-1986 .... *5*
Davidson, Judith 1953- *40*
Davidson, Lionel 1922- *87*
Davidson, Margaret 1936- *5*
Davidson, Marion
　See Garis, Howard R(oger)
Davidson, Mary R. 1885-1973 .... *9*
Davidson, Mary S. 1940- *61*
Davidson, Mickie
　See Davidson, Margaret
Davidson, Nicole
　See Jensen, Kathryn
Davidson, R.
　See Davidson, Raymond
Davidson, Raymond 1926- *32*
Davidson, Rosalie 1921- *23*
Davie, Helen K(ay) 1952- *148*
　Earlier sketch in SATA *77*
Davies, Andrew (Wynford) 1936- *27*
Davies, Bettilu D(onna) 1942- *33*
Davies, Hunter 1936- *55*
　Brief entry *45*
Davies, Jacqueline 1962- *186*
　Earlier sketch in SATA *155*
Davies, Joan 1934- *50*
　Brief entry *47*
Davies, Nicola 1958- *182*
　Earlier sketches in SATA *99, 150*
Davies, Peter J(oseph) 1937- *52*
Davies, Sumiko 1942- *46*
Davis, (A.) Aubrey 1949- *153*
Davis, Barbara Steincrohn
　See Davis, Maggie S.
Davis, Bette J. 1923- *15*
Davis, Burke 1913- *4*
Davis, Christopher 1928- *6*
Davis, D(elbert) Dwight 1908-1965 .... *33*
Davis, Daniel S(heldon) 1936- *12*
Davis, David R. 1948- *106*
Davis, Donald 1944- *169*
　Earlier sketch in SATA *93*
Davis, Donald D.
　See Davis, Donald
Davis, Emma
　See Davis, Maggie S.
Davis, Gibbs 1953- *102*
　Brief entry *41*
　Earlier sketch in SATA *46*
Davis, Grania 1943- *88*
　Brief entry *50*
Davis, H(arold) L(enoir) 1896-1960 .... *114*
Davis, Hubert J(ackson) 1904-1997 .... *31*
Davis, James Robert 1945- *32*
Davis, Jenny 1953- *74*
Davis, Jim
　See Davis, James Robert

Davis, Julia 1900(?)-1993 .... *6*
　Obituary *75*
Davis, Karen (Elizabeth) 1944- *109*
Davis, Katie 1959(?)- *152*
Davis, Lambert *176*
Davis, Leslie
　See Guccione, Leslie Davis
Davis, Louise Littleton 1921- *25*
Davis, Maggie S. 1943- *57*
Davis, Marguerite 1889- *34*
Davis, Mary L(ee) 1935- *9*
Davis, Mary Octavia 1901-1976 .... *6*
Davis, Nelle 1958- *73*
Davis, Ossie 1917-2005 .... *81*
　See also CLR *56*
Davis, Paxton 1925-1994 .... *16*
Davis, Robert 1881-1949
　See YABC *1*
Davis, Robin W(orks) 1962- *87*
Davis, Russell Gerard 1922- *3*
Davis, Tim(othy N.) 1957- *94*
Davis, Verne Theodore 1889-1973 .... *6*
Davis, Yvonne 1927- *115*
Davol, Marguerite W. 1928- *146*
　Earlier sketch in SATA *82*
DaVolls, Andy (P.) 1967- *85*
DaVolls, Linda 1966- *85*
Davys, Sarah
　See Manning, Rosemary (Joy)
Dawes, Claiborne 1935- *111*
Dawson, Elmer A. *67*
　Earlier sketch in SATA *1*
Dawson, Imogen (Zoe) 1948- *126*
　Earlier sketch in SATA *90*
Dawson, Janine 1957- *196*
Dawson, Mary 1919- *11*
Day, A(rthur) Grove 1904-1994 .... *59*
Day, Alexandra 1941- *197*
　Autobiography Feature *197*
　Earlier sketches in SATA *67, 97, 169*
　See also CLR *22*
　See also SAAS *19*
Day, Beth (Feagles) 1924- *33*
Day, Donna
　See Asay, Donna Day
Day, Edward C. 1932- *72*
Day, Jon 1936(?)- *79*
Day, Karen *187*
Day, Larry 1956- *181*
Day, Nancy 1953- *140*
Day, Nancy Raines 1951- *148*
　Earlier sketch in SATA *93*
Day, Shirley 1962- *94*
Day, Thomas 1748-1789
　See YABC *1*
Day, Trevor 1955- *124*
Dazey, Agnes J(ohnston) *2*
Dazey, Frank M. *2*
Deacon, Alexis 1978- *139*
Deacon, Eileen
　See Geipel, Eileen
Deacon, Richard
　See McCormick, (George) Donald (King)
Deadman, Ronald 1919-1988(?)
　Obituary *56*
Deak, Erzsi 1959- *152*
Dean, Anabel 1915- *12*
Dean, Carolee 1962- *148*
Dean, David 1976- *192*
Dean, Karen Strickler 1923- *49*
Dean, Ruth (Brigham) 1947- *145*
Dean, Zoey
　See Bennett, Cherie
de Angeli, Marguerite (Lofft) 1889-1987 ... *100*
　Obituary *51*
　Earlier sketches in SATA *1, 27*
　See also CLR *1*
Deans, Karen *195*
Deans, Sis Boulos 1955- *136*
　Earlier sketch in SATA *78*

DeArmand, Frances Ullmann 1904(?)-1984 . *10*
　Obituary *38*
DeArmond, Dale 1914- *70*
DeArmond, Dale Burlison
　See DeArmond, Dale
Deary, Terry 1946- *171*
　Brief entry *41*
　Earlier sketches in SATA *51, 101*
Deaver, Julie Reece 1953- *68*
de Banke, Cecile 1889-1965 .... *11*
De Bello, Rosario 1923- *89*
Debon, Nicolas *186*
　Earlier sketch in SATA *151*
de Bono, Edward 1933- *66*
de Brissac, Malcolm
　See Dickinson, Peter (Malcolm de Brissac)
de Brunhoff, Jean
　See Brunhoff, Jean de
De Brunhoff, Laurent
　See Brunhoff, Laurent de
De Bruyn, Monica G. 1952- *13*
De Bruyn, Monica Jean Grembowicz
　See De Bruyn, Monica G.
DeBry, Roger K. 1942- *91*
de Camp, Catherine Crook 1907-2000 .... *83*
　Earlier sketch in SATA *12*
de Camp, L(yon) Sprague 1907-2000 .... *83*
　Earlier sketch in SATA *9*
DeCandido, Keith R.A. *112*
Dechausay, Sonia E. *94*
Decker, C.B. *172*
Decker, Cynthia B.
　See Decker, C.B.
Decker, Duane 1910-1964 .... *5*
Decker, Timothy 1974- *197*
DeClements, Barthe (Faith) 1920- *131*
　Earlier sketches in SATA *35, 71*
　See also CLR *23*
de Clercq Zubli, Rita la Fontaine 1929- *199*
de Conte, Sieur Louis
　See Twain, Mark
Dedman, Stephen *108*
Dee, Catherine 1964- *138*
Dee, Ruby
　See Wallace, Ruby Ann
Deedy, Carmen Agra 1960- *196*
Deedy, John 1923- *24*
Deegan, Paul Joseph 1937- *48*
　Brief entry *38*
Deem, James M. 1950- *191*
　Autobiography Feature *191*
　Earlier sketches in SATA *75, 134*
Deem, James Morgan
　See Deem, James M.
Deeter, Catherine 1947- *137*
DeFelice, Cynthia 1951- *165*
　Earlier sketches in SATA *79, 121*
DeFelice, Cynthia C.
　See DeFelice, Cynthia
Defoe, Daniel 1660(?)-1731 .... *22*
　See also CLR *61*
DeFord, Deborah H. *123*
deFrance, Anthony
　See DiFranco, Anthony (Mario)
Degen, Bruce 1945- *147*
　Brief entry *47*
　Earlier sketches in SATA *57, 97*
DeGering, Etta (Belle) Fowler 1898-1996 ..... *7*
De Goldi, Kate
　See De Goldi, Kathleen Domenica
De Goldi, Kathleen Domenica 1959- *123*
de Goursac, Olivier 1959- *184*
De Grazia, Ettore 1909-1982 .... *39*
De Grazia, Ted
　See De Grazia, Ettore
deGroat, Diane 1947- *169*
　Earlier sketches in SATA *31, 90*
deGros, J. H.
　See Villiard, Paul
de Grummond, Lena Young *62*
　Earlier sketch in SATA *6*

de Hamel, Joan Littledale 1924- 86
De Haven, Tom 1949- 72
de Hugo, Pierre
    See Brackers de Hugo, Pierre
Deiss, Joseph Jay 1915- 12
de Jenkins, Lyll Becerra 1925-1997 102
DeJong, David C(ornel) 1905-1967 10
de Jong, Dola 1911-2003
    See de Jong, Dorothea Rosalie
de Jong, Dorothea Rosalie 1911-2003 7
    Obituary 149
DeJong, Meindert 1906-1991 2
    Obituary 68
    See also CLR 73
DeJonge, Joanne E. 1943- 56
Deka, Connie
    See Laux, Constance
de Kay, Ormonde (Jr.) 1923-1998 7
    Obituary 106
de Kiriline, Louise
    See Lawrence, Louise de Kiriline
Dekker, Carl
    See Laffin, John (Alfred Charles)
    and Lynds, Dennis
deKruif, Paul (Henry) 1890-1971 50
    Earlier sketch in SATA 5
Delacre, Lulu 1957- 156
    Earlier sketch in SATA 36
DeLaCroix, Alice 1940- 195
    Earlier sketch in SATA 75
de la Cruz, Melissa 1971- 179
De la Garza, Phyllis 1942- 169
De Lage, Ida 1918- 11
de la Mare, Walter (John) 1873-1956 16
    See also CLR 23
Delaney, Harry 1932- 3
Delaney, Joseph 1945- 172
Delaney, M.C.
    See Delaney, Michael
Delaney, Michael 1955- 180
    Earlier sketch in SATA 96
Delaney, Michael Clark
    See Delaney, Michael
Delaney, Ned
    See Delaney, Thomas Nicholas III
Delaney, Thomas Nicholas III 1951- 28
Delano, Hugh 1933- 20
Delany, Samuel R., Jr. 1942- 92
Delany, Samuel Ray
    See Delany, Samuel R., Jr.
De La Ramee, Marie Louise 1839-1908 20
de la Roche, Mazo 1879-1961 64
De La Roche Saint Andre, Anne 1950- 75
Delaune, (Jewel) Lynn (de Grummond) 7
DeLaurentis, Louise Budde 1920- 12
del Barco, Lucy Salamanca 1900(?)-1989
    Obituary 64
Delderfield, Eric R(aymond) 1909-1995 14
Delderfield, Ronald Frederick 1912-1972 20
DeLeeuw, Adele (Louise) 1899-1988 30
    Obituary 56
    Earlier sketch in SATA 1
De Leon, Nephtali 1945- 97
Delessert, Etienne 1941- 179
    Brief entry 27
    Earlier sketches in SATA 46, 130
    See also CLR 81
Delgado, James P. 1958- 122
de Lint, Charles 1951- 157
    Earlier sketch in SATA 115
de Lint, Charles Henri Diederick Hofsmit
    See de Lint, Charles
Delmar, Roy
    See Wexler, Jerome (LeRoy)
Del Negro, Janice M. 197
Deloria, Vine, Jr. 1933-2005 21
    Obituary 171
Deloria, Vine Victor, Jr.
    See Deloria, Vine, Jr.
del Rey, Lester 1915-1993 22
    Obituary 76

Delrio, Martin
    See Doyle, Debra
    and Macdonald, James D.
Delton, Judy 1931-2001 77
    Obituary 130
    Earlier sketch in SATA 14
    See also SAAS 9
Delulio, John 1938- 15
Delving, Michael
    See Williams, Jay
de Marcken, Gail 186
Demarest, Chris L. 1951- 175
    Brief entry 44
    Earlier sketches in SATA 45, 82, 128
Demarest, Christopher Lynn
    See Demarest, Chris L.
Demarest, Doug
    See Barker, Will
De Mari, Silvana 1953- 193
Demas, Corinne
    See Bliss, Corinne Demas
Demas, Vida 1927- 9
DeMatteis, J.M. 1953- 180
DeMatteis, John Marc
    See DeMatteis, J.M.
De Mejo, Oscar 1911-1992 40
Demers, Dominique 1956- 177
de Messieres, Nicole 1930- 39
Demi
    See Hitz, Demi
Demijohn, Thom
    See Disch, Thomas M.
    and Sladek, John
Deming, Richard 1915-1983 24
Deming, Sarah 191
de Monfreid, Dorothee 1973- 189
Demuth, Patricia Brennan 1948- 84
    Brief entry 51
Dendinger, Roger E. 1952- 158
Denenberg, Barry 175
Dengler, Marianna (Herron) 1935- 103
Dengler, Sandy 1939- 54
    Brief entry 40
Denim, Sue
    See Pilkey, Dav
Denise, Christopher 1968- 193
    Earlier sketch in SATA 147
Denman, K.L. 1957- 186
Denmark, Harrison
    See Zelazny, Roger
Dennard, Deborah 1953- 136
    Earlier sketch in SATA 78
Denney, Diana 1910-2000 25
    Obituary 120
Dennis, Morgan 1891(?)-1960 18
Dennis, Wesley 1903-1966 18
Denniston, Elinore 1900-1978
    Obituary 24
Denny, Norman (George) 1901-1982 43
Denslow, Sharon Phillips 1947- 142
    Earlier sketch in SATA 68
Denslow, W(illiam) W(allace) 1856-1915 16
    See also CLR 15
Dent, Grace 1973- 187
Denton, Kady MacDonald 181
    Earlier sketches in SATA 66, 110
    See also CLR 71
Denton, Terry 1950- 186
Denver, Walt
    See Redding, Robert Hull
    and Sherman, Jory (Tecumseh)
Denzel, Justin F(rancis) 1917-1999 46
    Brief entry 38
Denzer, Ann Wiseman
    See Wiseman, Ann (Sayre)
DePalma, Mary Newell 1961- 185
    Earlier sketch in SATA 139
De Palma, Toni 199

dePaola, Thomas Anthony 1934- 155
    Earlier sketches in SATA 11, 59, 108
    See also CLR 81
    See also SAAS 15
dePaola, Tomie
    See dePaola, Thomas Anthony
deParrie, Paul 1949- 74
DePauw, Linda Grant 1940- 24
DeRan, David 1946- 76
Derby, Ken 1956- 181
Derby, Kenneth R.
    See Derby, Ken
Derby, Pat 1942- 172
Derby, Sally 1934- 189
    Earlier sketches in SATA 89, 132
de Regniers, Beatrice Schenk (Freedman)
    1914-2000 68
    Obituary 123
    Earlier sketch in SATA 2
    See also SAAS 6
Dereske, Jo 1947- 72
Derleth, August (William) 1909-1971 5
Derman, Martha (Winn) 74
Derman, Sarah Audrey 1915- 11
DeRoberts, Lyndon
    See Silverstein, Robert Alan
de Roo, Anne Louise 1931-1997 84
    Earlier sketch in SATA 25
    See also CLR 63
deRosa, Dee 70
Derrick, Lionel
    See Cunningham, Chet
Derrickson, Jim 1959- 141
Derry Down Derry
    See Lear, Edward
Dervaux, Isabelle 1961- 106
Derwent, Lavinia 14
Desai, Anita 1937- 126
    Earlier sketch in SATA 63
DeSaix, Deborah Durland 188
De Saulles, Tony 1958- 119
Desbarats, Peter 1933- 39
de Selincourt, Aubrey 1894-1962 14
de Seve, Randall 198
Deshpande, Chris 1950- 69
Desimini, Lisa 1964- 148
    Earlier sketch in SATA 86
Desjarlais, John 1953- 71
Desjarlais, John J.
    See Desjarlais, John
Desmoinaux, Christel 1967- 149
    Earlier sketch in SATA 103
Desmond, Adrian J(ohn) 1947- 51
Desmond, Alice Curtis 1897-1990 8
Desnoettes, Caroline 183
DeSpain, Pleasant 1943- 87
Desputeaux, Helene 1959- 95
Dessen, Sarah 1970- 172
    Earlier sketch in SATA 120
Detine, Padre
    See Olsen, Ib Spang
de Trevino, Elizabeth B.
    See Trevino, Elizabeth B(orton) de
de Trevino, Elizabeth Borton
    See Trevino, Elizabeth B(orton) de
Detwiler, Susan Dill 1956- 58
Deuker, Carl 1950- 196
    Earlier sketches in SATA 82, 150
Deutsch, Babette 1895-1982 1
    Obituary 33
Deutsch, Eva Costabel
    See Costabel, Eva Deutsch
Deutsch, Helen 1906-1992 76
Deutsch, Kurt
    See Singer, Kurt D.
De Valera, Sinead 1879(?)-1975
    Obituary 30
Devaney, John 1926-1994 12
de Varennes, Monique 1947- 168
de Varona, Frank J. 1943- 83

Devereux, Frederick L(eonard), Jr.
1914-1993 9
Devi, Nila
See Woody, Regina Jones
deVinck, Christopher 1951- 85
DeVita, James 195
DeVito, Cara 1956- 80
Devlin, Dorothy Wende
See Devlin, Wende
Devlin, Harry 1918-2001 136
Earlier sketches in SATA 11, 74
Devlin, Wende 1918-2002 74
Earlier sketch in SATA 11
Devon, Paddie 1953- 92
Devons, Sonia 1974- 72
Devorah-Leah 111
de Vos, Gail 1949- 122
DeVries, Douglas 1933- 122
De Waard, E(lliott) John 1935- 7
Dewan, Ted 1961- 157
Earlier sketch in SATA 108
Dewdney, Anna 184
Dewdney, Selwyn (Hanington) 1909-1979 ... 64
DeWeese, Gene
See DeWeese, Thomas Eugene
DeWeese, Jean
See DeWeese, Thomas Eugene
DeWeese, Thomas Eugene 1934- 46
Brief entry 45
Dewey, Ariane 1937- 178
Earlier sketches in SATA 7, 109
Dewey, Jennifer (Owings) 1941- 103
Brief entry 48
Earlier sketch in SATA 58
Dewey, Kenneth Francis 1940- 39
De Wire, Elinor 1953- 180
deWit, Dorothy (May Knowles) 1916-1980 . 39
Obituary 28
Dexter, Alison 1966- 125
Dexter, John
See Bradley, Marion Zimmer
Deyneka, Anita 1943- 24
Deyrup, Astrith Johnson 1923- 24
Dhami, Narinder 1958- 152
Dhondy, Farrukh 1944- 152
Earlier sketch in SATA 65
See also CLR 41
Diakite, Baba Wague 1961- 174
Diakite, Penda 1993(?)- 174
Diamond, Arthur 1957- 76
Diamond, Donna 1950- 69
Brief entry 30
Earlier sketch in SATA 35
Diamond, Petra
See Sachs, Judith
Diamond, Rebecca
See Sachs, Judith
Dias, Earl Joseph 1916- 41
Dias, Ron 1937- 71
Diaz, David 1959(?)- 189
Earlier sketches in SATA 96, 150
See also CLR 65
Dibley, Glin 188
DiCamillo, Kate 1964- 163
Earlier sketch in SATA 121
See also CLR 117
Di Certo, J(oseph) J(ohn) 1933- 60
DiCianni, Ron 1952- 107
Dick, Trella Lamson 1889-1974 9
Dickens, Charles (John Huffam)
1812-1870 15
See also CLR 95
Dickens, Frank
See Huline-Dickens, Frank William
Dickens, Monica (Enid) 1915-1992 4
Obituary 74
Dickerson, Roy Ernest 1886-1965
Obituary 26
Dickinson, Emily (Elizabeth) 1830-1886 29
Dickinson, Mary 1949- 48
Brief entry 41

Dickinson, Mary-Anne
See Rodda, Emily
Dickinson, Peter (Malcolm de Brissac)
1927- 150
Earlier sketches in SATA 5, 62, 95
See also CLR 125
Dickinson, Susan 1931- 8
Dickinson, Terence 1943- 102
Dickinson, W(illiam) Croft 1897-1963 13
Dickson, Gordon R. 1923-2001 77
Dickson, Gordon Rupert
See Dickson, Gordon R.
Dickson, Helen
See Reynolds, Helen Mary Greenwood Camp-
bell
Dickson, Naida 1916- 8
Diehn, Gwen 1943- 80
Dierssen, Andreas 1962- 190
Dieterich, Michele M. 1962- 78
Dietz, David H(enry) 1897-1984 10
Obituary 41
Dietz, Lew 1907-1997 11
Obituary 95
Diffily, Deborah 159
Di Fiori, Larry
See Di Fiori, Lawrence
Di Fiori, Lawrence 1934- 130
DiFranco, Anthony (Mario) 1945- 42
Digby, Anne 1935- 72
Digges, Jeremiah
See Berger, Josef
Digman, Kristina 1959- 176
D'Ignazio, Fred(erick) 1949- 39
Brief entry 35
Di Grazia, Thomas (?)-1983 32
Dijkstra, Lida 1961- 195
Dikty, Julian May
See May, Julian
Dillard, Annie 1945- 140
Earlier sketch in SATA 10
Dillard, Kristine 1964- 113
Dillard, Polly Hargis 1916- 24
Diller, Harriett 1953- 78
Dillon, Barbara 1927- 44
Brief entry 39
Dillon, Diane 1933- 194
Earlier sketches in SATA 15, 51, 106
See also CLR 44
Dillon, Diane Claire
See Dillon, Diane
Dillon, Eilis 1920-1994 74
Autobiography Feature 105
Obituary 83
Earlier sketch in SATA 2
See also CLR 26
Dillon, Jana (a pseudonym) 1952- 117
Dillon, Leo 1933- 194
Earlier sketches in SATA 15, 51, 106
See also CLR 44
Dillon, Sharon Saseen
See Saseen, Sharon (Dillon)
Dils, Tracey E. 1958- 83
Dilson, Jesse 1914-1988 24
Dinan, Carolyn 59
Brief entry 47
Dines, Carol 1956- 175
Dines, (Harry) Glen 1925-1996 7
Dinesen, Isak
See Blixen, Karen (Christentze Dinesen)
Dinessi, Alex
See Schembri, Jim
Dinneen, Betty 1929- 61
Dinnerstein, Harvey 1928- 42
Dinsdale, Tim(othy Kay) 1924-1987 11
Diop, Birago (Ismael) 1906-1989
Obituary 64
Diouf, Sylviane A. 168
Diouf, Sylviane Anna
See Diouf, Sylviane A.
DiPucchio, Kelly 159

Dirk
See Gringhuis, Richard H.
Dirks, Wilhelmina 1916- 59
Dirks, Willy
See Dirks, Wilhelmina
Dirtmeister
See Tomecek, Steve
DiSalvo, DyAnne 1960- 144
Earlier sketch in SATA 59
DiSalvo-Ryan, DyAnne
See DiSalvo, DyAnne
Disch, Thomas M. 1940-2008 92
Obituary 195
See also CLR 18
See also SAAS 15
Disch, Thomas Michael
See Disch, Thomas M.
Disch, Tom
See Disch, Thomas M.
Disher, Garry 1949- 125
Earlier sketch in SATA 81
Disney, Walt(er Elias) 1901-1966 28
Brief entry 27
Ditchfield, Christin 1973- 189
DiTerlizzi, Tony 1969- 154
Divakaruni, Chitra Banerjee 1956- 160
Di Valentin, Maria (Amelia) Messuri
1911-1985 7
Divine, Arthur Durham 1904-1987
Obituary 52
Divine, David
See Divine, Arthur Durham
Dixon, Ann R. 1954- 127
Earlier sketch in SATA 77
Dixon, Ann Renee
See Dixon, Ann R.
Dixon, Dougal 1947- 190
Earlier sketches in SATA 45, 127
Dixon, Franklin W.
See Barrett, Neal, Jr.
and Goulart, Ron(ald Joseph)
and Lantz, Francess L(in)
and Lerangis, Peter
and McFarlane, Leslie (Charles)
and Stanley, George Edward
and Stratemeyer, Edward L.
Dixon, Jeanne 1936- 31
Dixon, Paige
See Corcoran, Barbara (Asenath)
Dixon, Peter L(ee) 1931- 6
Dixon, Rachel 1952- 74
Djoleto, (Solomon Alexander) Amu 1929- ... 80
d'lacey, Chris 1949- 165
Doak, Annie
See Dillard, Annie
Doane, Pelagie 1906-1966 7
Dobell, I(sabel) M(arian) B(arclay)
1909-1998 11
Dobie, J(ames) Frank 1888-1964 43
Dobkin, Alexander 1908-1975
Obituary 30
Dobler, Lavinia G. 1910- 6
Dobrin, Arnold 1928- 4
Dobson, Jill 1969- 140
Dobson, Julia 1941- 48
Dobson, Mary 1954- 117
Dockery, Wallene T. 1941- 27
Dockray, Tracy 1962- 139
Dockrey, Karen 1955- 103
Doctor, Bernard
See Doctor, Bernard Aquina
Doctor, Bernard Aquina 1950- 81
Doctor X
See Nourse, Alan E(dward)
Dodd, Ed(ward Benton) 1902-1991 4
Obituary 68
Dodd, Lynley (Stuart) 1941- 132
Earlier sketches in SATA 35, 86
See also CLR 62
Dodd, Marty 1921- 142
Dodd, Quentin 1972- 137

Dodds, Bill 1952- *78*
Dodds, Dayle Ann 1952- *150*
  Earlier sketch in SATA 75
Doder, Josh 1968- *187*
Dodge, Bertha S(anford) 1902-1995 .... *8*
Dodge, Fremont
  See Grimes, Lee
Dodge, Gil
  See Hano, Arnold
Dodge, Mary (Elizabeth) Mapes
  1831(?)-1905 .... *100*
  Earlier sketch in SATA 21
  See also CLR 62
Dodgson, Charles L(utwidge) 1832-1898 ... *100*
  See also YABC 2
  See also CLR 108
Dodson, Kenneth MacKenzie 1907-1999 ..... *11*
Dodson, Susan 1941- *50*
  Brief entry *40*
Dogyear, Drew
  See Gorey, Edward (St. John)
Doherty, Berlie 1943- *111*
  Earlier sketch in SATA 72
  See also CLR 21
  See also SAAS 16
Doherty, Charles Hugh 1913- *6*
Doherty, Craig A. 1951- *169*
  Earlier sketch in SATA 83
Doherty, Katherine M(ann) 1951- *83*
Doherty, Kieran 1945- *164*
Dokey, Cameron 1956- *97*
Dolan, Edward F(rancis), Jr. 1924- *94*
  Brief entry *31*
  Earlier sketch in SATA 45
Dolan, Ellen M(eara) 1929-1998 .... *88*
Dolan, Sean J. 1958- *74*
Dolce, J. Ellen 1948- *75*
Dolch, Edward William 1889-1961 .... *50*
Dolch, Marguerite Pierce 1891-1978 .... *50*
Dollar, Diane (Hills) 1933- *57*
Dolson, Hildegarde
  See Lockridge, Hildegarde (Dolson)
Domanska, Janina 1913(?)-1995 .... *68*
  Obituary *84*
  Earlier sketch in SATA 6
  See also CLR 40
  See also SAAS 18
Dominguez, Angel 1953- *76*
Domino, John
  See Averill, Esther (Holden)
Domjan, Joseph (Spiri) 1907-1992 .... *25*
Domm, Jeffrey C. 1958- *84*
Donahue, Dorothy *178*
Donald, Rhonda Lucas 1962- *147*
Donalds, Gordon
  See Shirreffs, Gordon D(onald)
Donaldson, Bryna
  See Stevens, Bryna
Donaldson, Gordon 1913-1993 .... *64*
  Obituary *76*
Donaldson, Joan 1953- *78*
Donaldson, Julia 1948- *180*
  Earlier sketches in SATA 82, 132
Donaldson, Stephen R. 1947- *121*
Donaldson, Stephen Reeder
  See Donaldson, Stephen R.
Doner, Kim 1955- *91*
Doney, Todd L. W. 1959- *104*
Dong-Sung, Kim 1970- *195*
Dong-Sung Kim
  See Dong-Sung, Kim
Donkin, Nance (Clare) 1915- *95*
Donna, Natalie 1934-1979 .... *9*
Donnelly, Elfie 1950-
  See CLR 104
Donnelly, Jennifer 1963- *154*
Donnelly, Matt 1972- *148*
Donnio, Sylviane *188*
Donoghue, Emma 1969- *101*
Donoughue, Carol 1935- *139*

Donovan, Frank (Robert) 1906-1975
  Obituary *30*
Donovan, John 1928-1992 .... *72*
  Brief entry *29*
  See also CLR 3
Donovan, Mary Lee 1961- *86*
Donovan, William
  See Berkebile, Fred D(onovan)
Donze, Mary Terese 1911- *89*
Doob, Leonard W(illiam) 1909-2000 .... *8*
Dooley, Norah 1953- *74*
Dooling, Michael 1958- *105*
Dor, Ana
  See Ceder, Georgiana Dorcas
Dore, (Louis Christophe Paul) Gustave
  1832-1883 .... *19*
Doremus, Robert 1913- *30*
Doren, Marion (Walker) 1928- *57*
Dorenkamp, Michelle 1957- *89*
Dorflinger, Carolyn 1953- *91*
Dorfman, Joaquin 1979- *180*
Dorfman, Joaquin Emiliano
  See Dorfman, Joaquin
Dorian, Edith M(cEwen) 1900-1983 .... *5*
Dorian, Harry
  See Hamilton, Charles (Harold St. John)
Dorian, Marguerite *7*
Dorin, Patrick C(arberry) 1939- *59*
  Brief entry *52*
Dorman, Brandon *194*
Dorman, Michael 1932- *7*
Dorman, N. B. 1927- *39*
Dorris, Michael 1945-1997 .... *75*
  Obituary *94*
  See also CLR 58
Dorris, Michael A.
  See Dorris, Michael
Dorris, Michael Anthony
  See Dorris, Michael
Dorritt, Susan
  See Schlein, Miriam
Dorros, Alex 1991- *194*
Dorros, Arthur 1950- *168*
  Earlier sketches in SATA 78, 122
  See also CLR 42
  See also SAAS 20
Dorros, Arthur M.
  See Dorros, Arthur
Dorson, Richard M(ercer) 1916-1981 .... *30*
Doss, Helen (Grigsby) 1918- *20*
Doss, Margot Patterson *6*
dos Santos, Joyce Audy 1949- *57*
  Brief entry *42*
Dothers, Anne
  See Chess, Victoria (Dickerson)
Dotlich, Rebecca Kai 1951- *182*
Dottig
  See Grider, Dorothy
Dotts, Maryann J. 1933- *35*
Doty, Jean Slaughter 1929- *28*
Doty, Roy 1922- *28*
Doubtfire, Dianne (Abrams) 1918- *29*
Doucet, Sharon Arms 1951- *144*
  Autobiography Feature *144*
  Earlier sketch in SATA 125
Dougherty, Charles 1922- *18*
Dougherty, Terri (L.) 1964- *146*
Doughty, Rebecca 1955- *174*
Douglas, Blaise 1960- *101*
Douglas, Carole Nelson 1944- *73*
Douglas, Garry
  See Kilworth, Garry
Douglas, James McM.
  See Griffin, W.E.B
Douglas, Kathryn
  See Ewing, Kathryn
Douglas, Leonard
  See Bradbury, Ray
Douglas, Lola
  See Zeises, Lara M.
Douglas, Marjory Stoneman 1890-1998 .... *10*

Douglas, Michael
  See Bright, Robert (Douglas Sr.)
Douglas, Michael
  See Crichton, Michael
Douglas, Shirley Stewart
  See Tepper, Sheri S.
Douglass, Barbara 1930- *40*
Douglass, Frederick 1817(?)-1895 .... *29*
Douglass, Keith
  See Cunningham, Chet
Douty, Esther M(orris) 1909-1978 .... *8*
  Obituary *23*
Dow, Emily R. 1904-1987 .... *10*
Dow, Vicki
  See McVey, Vicki
Dowd, John David 1945- *78*
Dowdell, Dorothy (Florence) Karns 1910- ... *12*
Dowden, Anne Ophelia Todd 1907-2007 .... *7*
  Obituary *180*
  See also SAAS 10
Dowdey, Landon Gerald 1923- *11*
Dowdy, Mrs. Regera
  See Gorey, Edward (St. John)
Dowell, Frances O'Roark *157*
Dower, Laura *185*
Dowling, Terry 1947- *101*
Downer, Ann 1960- *155*
Downer, Marion 1892(?)-1971 .... *25*
Downes, Belinda 1962- *180*
Downey, Fairfax D(avis) 1893-1990 .... *3*
  Obituary *66*
Downey, Lynn 1961- *185*
Downham, Jenny 1964- *192*
Downie, John 1931- *87*
Downie, Mary Alice 1934- *171*
  Earlier sketches in SATA 13, 87
Downie, Mary Alice Dawe
  See Downie, Mary Alice
Downing, David A(lmon) 1958- *84*
Downing, Johnette *184*
Downing, Julie 1956- *148*
  Earlier sketch in SATA 81
Downing, Paula E. 1951- *80*
Downing, Warwick 1931- *138*
Downing, Wick
  See Downing, Warwick
Dowswell, Paul 1957- *184*
Doyle, A. Conan
  See Doyle, Sir Arthur Conan
Doyle, Sir Arthur Conan 1859-1930 .... *24*
  See also CLR 106
Doyle, Brian 1935- *156*
  Earlier sketches in SATA 67, 104
  See also CLR 22
  See also SAAS 16
Doyle, Charlotte 1937- *178*
  Earlier sketch in SATA 94
Doyle, Charlotte Lackner
  See Doyle, Charlotte
Doyle, Conan
  See Doyle, Sir Arthur Conan
Doyle, Debra 1952- *165*
  Earlier sketch in SATA 105
Doyle, Donovan
  See Boegehold, Betty (Doyle)
Doyle, John
  See Graves, Robert
Doyle, Malachy 1954- *165*
  Earlier sketch in SATA 120
  See also CLR 83
Doyle, Richard 1824-1883 .... *21*
Doyle, Sir A. Conan
  See Doyle, Sir Arthur Conan
Dr. A
  See Asimov, Isaac
  and Silverstein, Alvin
  and Silverstein, Virginia B(arbara Opshelor)
Dr. Alphabet
  See Morice, Dave
Dr. Fred
  See Bortz, Alfred B(enjamin)

Dr. Laura
See Schlessinger, Laura (Catherine)
Dr. Seuss
See Geisel, Theodor Seuss
and LeSieg, Theo.
and Seuss, Dr.
and Stone, Rosetta
Dr. Zed
See Penrose, Gordon
Drabble, Margaret 1939- 48
Drackett, Phil(ip Arthur) 1922- 53
Draco, F.
See Davis, Julia
Dracup, Angela 1943- 74
Dragisic, Patricia 116
Dragonwagon, Crescent 1952- 186
Autobiography Feature 186
Earlier sketches in SATA 11, 41, 75, 133
See also SAAS 14
Drake, David 1945- 85
Drake, David Allen
See Drake, David
Drake, Frank
See Hamilton, Charles (Harold St. John)
Drake, Jane 1954- 82
Drakeford, Dale B 1952- 113
Drakeford, Dale Benjamin
See Drakeford, Dale B
Draper, Hastings
See Jeffries, Roderic
Draper, Sharon
See Draper, Sharon M.
Draper, Sharon M. 1948- 195
Autobiography Feature 146
Earlier sketches in SATA 98, 146
See also CLR 57
Draper, Sharon Mills
See Draper, Sharon M.
Drapier, M. B.
See Swift, Jonathan
Drawson, Blair 1943- 126
Earlier sketch in SATA 17
Dray, Matt 1967- 177
Dray, Matthew Frederick
See Dray, Matt
Dresang, Eliza (Carolyn Timberlake) 1941- . 19
Drescher, Henrik 1955- 172
Earlier sketches in SATA 67, 105
See also CLR 20
Drescher, Joan E(lizabeth) 1939- 137
Earlier sketch in SATA 30
Dressen-McQueen, Stacey 191
Dreves, Veronica R. 1927-1986
Obituary 50
Drew, Patricia (Mary) 1938- 15
Drewery, Mary 1918- 6
Drewery, Melanie 1970- 165
Drewry, Henry N(athaniel) 1924- 138
Dreyer, Ellen 177
Drial, J. E.
See Laird, Jean E(louise)
Drimmer, Frederick 1916-2000 60
Obituary 124
Driskill, J. Lawrence 1920- 90
Driskill, Larry
See Driskill, J. Lawrence
Driving Hawk, Virginia
See Sneve, Virginia Driving Hawk
Dron, Laura
See Matthews, L.S.
Dronzek, Laura 199
Drucker, Malka 1945- 111
Brief entry 29
Earlier sketch in SATA 39
Drucker, Olga Levy 1927- 79
Druitt, Tobias
See Purkiss, Diane
Drummond, V(iolet) H(ilda) 1911-2000 6
Drummond, Walter
See Silverberg, Robert

Drury, Clare Marie
See Hoskyns-Abrahall, Clare (Constance Drury)
Drury, Roger W(olcott) 1914-1996 15
Druse, Eleanor
See King, Stephen
Dryden, Pamela
See St. John, Nicole
D.T., Hughes
See Hughes, Dean
Duane, Diane (Elizabeth) 1952- 145
Brief entry 46
Earlier sketches in SATA 58, 95
Dubanevich, Arlene 1950- 56
Dubelaar, Thea 1947- 60
du Blane, Daphne
See Groom, Arthur William
Duble, Kathleen Benner 1958- 164
Dubois, Claude K. 1960- 196
DuBois, Rochelle (Lynn) Holt 1946- 41
Du Bois, Shirley Graham 1907(?)-1977 24
See Graham, Shirley
Du Bois, W(illiam) E(dward) B(urghardt)
1868-1963 42
Obituary
du Bois, William Pene
See Pene du Bois, William (Sherman)
Duboise, Novella 1911-1999 88
Dubosarsky, Ursula 1961- 193
Earlier sketches in SATA 107, 147
DuBose, LaRocque (Russ) 1926- 2
Dubrovin, Vivian 1931- 139
Earlier sketch in SATA 65
DuBurke, Randy 172
Ducey, Jean Sparks 1915- 93
Duchacek, Ivo D(uka) 1913-1988
Obituary 55
Du Chaillu, Paul (Belloni) 1835(?)-1903 26
Ducharme, Dede Fox
See Ducharme, Lilian Fox
Ducharme, Lilian Fox 1950- 122
Ducornet, Erica 1943- 7
Ducornet, Rikki
See Ducornet, Erica
Duden, Jane 1947- 136
Duder, Tessa 1940- 117
Earlier sketch in SATA 80
See also CLR 43
See also SAAS 23
Dudley, Helen
See Hope Simpson, Jacynth
Dudley, Martha Ward 1909(?)-1985
Obituary 45
Dudley, Nancy
See Cole, Lois Dwight
Dudley, Robert
See Baldwin, James
Dudley, Ruth H(ubbell) 1905-2001 11
Dudley-Smith, T.
See Trevor, Elleston
Due, Linnea A. 1948- 64
Dueck, Adele 1955- 97
Dueland, Joy V(ivian) 27
Duerr, Gisela 1968- 89
Duey, Kathleen 1950- 199
Earlier sketch in SATA 132
Dufault, Joseph Ernest Nephtali
See James, Will(iam Roderick)
Duff, Annis (James) 1904(?)-1986
Obituary 49
Duff, Maggie
See Duff, Margaret K(app)
Duff, Margaret K(app) 1916-2003 37
Obituary 144
Duffey, Betsy (Byars) 1953- 131
Earlier sketch in SATA 80
Duffie, Charles 1960- 144
Duffield, Katy S. 1961- 147
Duffy, Carol Ann 1955- 165
Earlier sketch in SATA 95
Dugan, Jack
See Griffin, W.E.B

Dugan, John Kevin
See Griffin, W.E.B
Dugan, Michael (Gray) 1947- 15
Duggan, Alfred Leo 1903-1964 25
Duggan, Maurice (Noel) 1922-1974 40
Obituary 30
Duggleby, John 1952- 94
Dugin, Andrej 1955- 77
Dugina, Olga 1964- 77
du Jardin, Rosamond Neal 1902-1963 2
Duka, Ivo
See Duchacek, Ivo D(uka)
Duke, Kate 1956- 192
Earlier sketches in SATA 90, 148
See also CLR 51
Duke, Will
See Gault, William Campbell
Dulac, Edmund 1882-1953 19
Dumas, Alexandre (pere) 1802-1870 18
See also CLR 134
Dumas, Jacqueline 1946- 55
Dumas, Philippe 1940- 119
Earlier sketch in SATA 52
du Maurier, Daphne 1907-1989 27
Obituary 60
Dumbleton, Mike 1948- 124
Earlier sketch in SATA 73
Dunbar, Fiona 1961- 167
Dunbar, Joyce 1944- 162
Earlier sketches in SATA 76, 112
Dunbar, Paul Laurence 1872-1906 34
Dunbar, Polly 1980(?)- 181
Dunbar, Robert E(verett) 1926- 32
Duncan, Alexandra
See Moore, Ishbel (Lindsay)
Duncan, Alice Faye 1967- 168
Earlier sketch in SATA 95
Duncan, Gregory
See McClintock, Marshall
Duncan, Jane
See Cameron, Elizabeth Jane
Duncan, Julia K.
See Benson, Mildred (Augustine Wirt)
Duncan, Lois 1934- 141
Autobiography Feature 141
Earlier sketches in SATA 1, 36, 75, 133
See also CLR 129
See also SAAS 2
Duncan, Norman 1871-1916
See YABC 1
Duncan, Terence
See Nolan, William F(rancis)
Duncombe, Frances (Riker) 1900-1994 25
Obituary 82
Dunham, Montrew 1919- 162
Dunham, Montrew Goetz
See Dunham, Montrew
Dunkle, Clare B. 1964- 155
Dunlap, Julie 1958- 84
Dunleavy, Deborah 1951- 133
Dunlop, Agnes M. R. (?)-1982 87
Dunlop, Eileen (Rhona) 1938- 76
Earlier sketch in SATA 24
See also SAAS 12
Dunn, Anne M. 1940- 107
Dunn, Harvey T(homas) 1884-1952 34
Dunn, Herb
See Gutman, Dan
Dunn, John M. (III) 1949- 93
Dunn, Judy
See Spangenberg, Judith Dunn
Dunn, Mary Lois 1930- 6
Dunnahoo, Terry Janson 1927- 7
Dunne, Jeanette 1952- 72
Dunne, Kathleen 1933- 126
Dunne, Marie
See Clark, Ann Nolan
Dunne, Mary Collins 1914- 11
Dunne, Mary Jo
See Dunne, Mary Collins

Dunnett, Kaitlyn
    See Emerson, Kathy Lynn
Dunnett, Margaret (Rosalind) 1909-1977 ..... *42*
Dunnick, Regan *178*
Dunrea, Olivier 1953- *160*
    Brief entry *46*
    Earlier sketches in SATA *59, 118*
Dunrea, Olivier Jean-Paul Dominique
    See Dunrea, Olivier
Dunton, Dorothy 1912- *92*
Dupasquier, Philippe 1955- *151*
    Earlier sketch in SATA *86*
DuPrau, Jeanne 1944- *144*
Dupuy, T(revor) N(evitt) 1916-1995 .... *4*
    Obituary *86*
DuQuette, Keith 1960- *155*
    Earlier sketch in SATA *90*
Duran, Gloria 1924- *171*
Duran, Gloria Bradley
    See Duran, Gloria
Duranceau, Suzanne 1952- *162*
Durango, Julia 1967- *173*
Durant, Alan 1958- *165*
    Earlier sketch in SATA *121*
Durant, John 1902- *27*
Durbin, William 1951- *174*
    Earlier sketch in SATA *143*
Durell, Ann 1930- *66*
Durkee, Sarah *173*
Durrant, Lynda 1954- *148*
    Earlier sketch in SATA *96*
Durrell, Gerald (Malcolm) 1925-1995 .... *8*
    Obituary *84*
Durrell, Julie 1955- *94*
Durrett, Deanne 1940- *144*
    Earlier sketch in SATA *92*
Du Soe, Robert C. 1892-1958
    See YABC *2*
Dussling, Jennifer 1970- *143*
    Earlier sketch in SATA *96*
DuTemple, Lesley A. 1952- *113*
Dutton, Sandra *191*
Dutz
    See Davis, Mary Octavia
Duval, Katherine
    See James, Elizabeth
Duval, Kathy 1946- *181*
Duvall, Aimee
    See Thurlo, Aimee
    and Thurlo, David
Duvall, Evelyn Millis 1906- *9*
Duvall, Jill D(onovan) 1932- *102*
Duvoisin, Roger (Antoine) 1904-1980 .... *30*
    Obituary *23*
    Earlier sketch in SATA *2*
    See also CLR *23*
Dwiggins, Don(ald J.) 1913-1988 .... *4*
    Obituary *60*
Dwight, Allan
    See Cole, Lois Dwight
Dwyer, Deanna
    See Koontz, Dean R.
Dwyer, K.R.
    See Koontz, Dean R.
Dyck, Peter J. 1914- *75*
Dyer, James (Frederick) 1934- *37*
Dyer, Jane *191*
    Earlier sketch in SATA *147*
Dyess, John (Foster) 1939- *76*
Dygard, Thomas J. 1931-1996 .... *97*
    Obituary *92*
    Earlier sketch in SATA *24*
    See also SAAS *15*
Dyke, John 1935- *35*

E

E. V. L.
    See Lucas, E(dward) V(errall)

Eagar, Frances (Elisabeth Stuart)
    1940-1978 .... *11*
    Obituary *55*
Eager, Edward (McMaken) 1911-1964 .... *17*
    See also CLR *43*
Eager, George 1921- *56*
    See Eager, George B.
Eager, George B.
    See Eager, George
Eagle, Ellen 1953- *61*
Eagle, Kin
    See Adlerman, Daniel (Ezra)
    and Adlerman, Kimberly M(arie)
Eagle, Mike 1942- *11*
Earle, Olive L(ydia) 1888-1982 .... *7*
Earle, William
    See Johns, W(illiam) E(arle)
Earls, Nick 1963- *156*
    Earlier sketch in SATA *95*
Early, Jack
    See Scoppettone, Sandra
Early, Jon
    See Johns, W(illiam) E(arle)
Early, Margaret 1951- *72*
Earnshaw, Brian 1929- *17*
Earnshaw, Micky
    See Earnshaw, Spencer Wright
Earnshaw, Spencer Wright 1939- *88*
Easley, MaryAnn *94*
Eason, Alethea 1957- *197*
Eastman, Charles A(lexander) 1858-1939
    See YABC *1*
Eastman, P(hilip) D(ey) 1909-1986 .... *33*
    Obituary *46*
Easton, Kelly 1960- *192*
    Earlier sketch in SATA *141*
Eastwick, Ivy (Ethel) O(live) *3*
Eaton, Anne T(haxter) 1881-1971 .... *32*
Eaton, Anthony 1971- *167*
Eaton, George L.
    See Verral, Charles Spain
Eaton, Janet
    See Givens, Janet E(aton)
Eaton, Jeanette 1886-1968 .... *24*
Eaton, Maxwell III 1981- *199*
Eaton, Tom 1940- *22*
Ebel, Alex 1927- *11*
Eber, Dorothy (Margaret) Harley 1930- *27*
Eberhart, Sheri S.
    See Tepper, Sheri S.
Eberle, Irmengarde 1898-1979 .... *2*
    Obituary *23*
Eble, Diane 1956- *74*
Eboch, Chris *113*
Eccles Williams, Ferelith 1920- *22*
Echlin, Kim 1955- *166*
Eckblad, Edith Berven 1923- *23*
Ecke, Wolfgang 1927-1983
    Obituary *37*
Eckert, Allan W. 1931- *91*
    Brief entry *27*
    Earlier sketch in SATA *29*
    See also SAAS *21*
Eckert, Horst 1931- *72*
    Earlier sketch in SATA *8*
    See also CLR *26*
Ecklar, Julia (Marie) 1964- *112*
Eddings, David 1931- *91*
Eddings, David Carroll
    See Eddings, David
Ede, Janina 1937- *33*
Edell, Celeste *12*
Edelman, Lily (Judith) 1915-1981 .... *22*
Edelson, Edward 1932- *51*
Edens, Cooper 1945- *166*
    Earlier sketches in SATA *49, 112*
Edens, (Bishop) David 1926- *39*
Edey, Maitland A(rmstrong) 1910-1992 .... *25*
    Obituary *71*
Edgerton, Perky *196*
Edgeworth, Maria 1768-1849 .... *21*

Edgy, Wardore
    See Gorey, Edward (St. John)
Edison, Theodore
    See Stratemeyer, Edward L.
Edler, Tim(othy) 1948- *56*
Edmiston, Jim 1948- *80*
Edmonds, I(vy) G(ordon) 1917- *8*
Edmonds, Walter D(umaux) 1903-1998 .... *27*
    Obituary *99*
    Earlier sketch in SATA *1*
    See also SAAS *4*
Edmund, Sean
    See Pringle, Laurence
Edsall, Marian (Stickney) 1920- *8*
Edwards, Al
    See Nourse, Alan E(dward)
Edwards, Anne 1927- *35*
Edwards, Audrey 1947- *52*
    Brief entry *31*
Edwards, Becky (Jane) 1966- *125*
Edwards, Bertram
    See Edwards, Herbert Charles
Edwards, Bronwen Elizabeth
    See Rose, Wendy
Edwards, Cecile Pepin 1916- *25*
Edwards, David 1962- *198*
Edwards, Dorothy 1914-1982 .... *88*
    Obituary *31*
    Earlier sketch in SATA *4*
Edwards, F. E.
    See Nolan, William F(rancis)
Edwards, Frank B. 1952- *93*
Edwards, Gunvor *32*
Edwards, Harvey 1929- *5*
Edwards, Hazel (Eileen) 1945- *135*
Edwards, Herbert Charles 1912- *12*
Edwards, Jane Campbell 1932- *10*
Edwards, Julia
    See Stratemeyer, Edward L.
Edwards, Julie
    See Andrews, Julie
Edwards, Julie Andrews
    See Andrews, Julie
Edwards, June
    See Bhatia, Jamunadevi
Edwards, Linda Strauss 1948- *49*
    Brief entry *42*
Edwards, Margaret (Alexander) 1902-1988
    Obituary *56*
Edwards, Michelle 1955- *152*
    Earlier sketch in SATA *70*
Edwards, Monica le Doux Newton
    1912-1998 .... *12*
Edwards, Olwen
    See Gater, Dilys
Edwards, Page (Lawrence, Jr.) 1941-1999 ... *59*
Edwards, Pamela Duncan *189*
Edwards, R. T.
    See Goulart, Ron(ald Joseph)
Edwards, Sally (Cary) 1929- *7*
Edwards, Samuel
    See Gerson, Noel Bertram
Edwards, Wallace 1957(?)- *170*
Egan, E(dward) W(elstead) 1922- *35*
Egan, Kerry *175*
Egan, Lorraine Hopping 1960- *134*
    Earlier sketch in SATA *91*
Egan, Tim 1957- *191*
    Earlier sketches in SATA *89, 155*
Egermeier, Elsie E(milie) 1890-1986 .... *65*
Eggenberger, David 1918- *6*
Eggleston, Edward 1837-1902 .... *27*
Egielski, Richard 1952- *163*
    Earlier sketches in SATA *11, 49, 106*
Egypt, Ophelia Settle 1903-1984 .... *16*
    Obituary *38*
Ehlert, Lois 1934- *172*
    Earlier sketches in SATA *35, 69, 128*
    See also CLR *28*
Ehlert, Lois Jane
    See Ehlert, Lois

Ehling, Katalin Olah 1941- 93
Ehrenfreund, Norbert 1921- 86
Ehrenhaft, Daniel 1970- 185
Ehrhardt, Karen 1963- 184
Ehrlich, Amy 1942- 132
    Earlier sketches in SATA 25, 65, 96
Ehrlich, Bettina Bauer 1903-1985 1
Ehrlich, H. M.
    See Ziefert, Harriet
Eichenberg, Fritz 1901-1990 50
    Earlier sketch in SATA 9
Eichler, Margrit 1942- 35
Eichner, James A. 1927- 4
Eidson, Thomas 1944- 112
Eifert, Virginia (Louise) S(nider) 1911-1966 . 2
Eige, (Elizabeth) Lillian 1915- 65
Eiken, J. Melia 1967- 125
Einsel, Naiad 10
Einsel, Walter 1926- 10
Einzig, Susan 1922- 43
Eiseman, Alberta 1925- 15
Eisenberg, Azriel (Louis) 1903-1985 12
Eisenberg, Lisa 1949- 155
    Brief entry 50
    Earlier sketch in SATA 57
Eisenberg, Phyllis Rose 1924- 41
Eisner, Vivienne
    See Margolis, Vivienne
Eisner, Will 1917-2005 165
    Earlier sketch in SATA 31
Eisner, William Erwin
    See Eisner, Will
Eitzen, Allan 1928- 9
Eitzen, Ruth (Carper) 1924- 9
Ekwensi, C. O. D.
    See Ekwensi, Cyprian
Ekwensi, Cyprian 1921-2007 66
Ekwensi, Cyprian Odiatu Duaka
    See Ekwensi, Cyprian
Elam, Richard M(ace, Jr.) 1920- 9
Elborn, Andrew
    See Clements, Andrew
    and Clements, Andrew
Elboz, Stephen 1956- 152
Eldin, Peter 1939- 154
Eldon, Kathy 1946- 107
Eldridge, Marion 199
Elfman, Blossom 1925- 8
Elgin, Kathleen 1923- 39
Elia
    See Lamb, Charles
Eliot, A. D.
    See Jewett, (Theodora) Sarah Orne
Eliot, Alice
    See Jewett, (Theodora) Sarah Orne
Eliot, Anne
    See Cole, Lois Dwight
Eliot, Dan
    See Silverberg, Robert
Elish, Dan 1960- 129
    Earlier sketch in SATA 68
Elisha, Ron 1951- 104
Elisofon, Eliot 1911-1973
    Obituary 21
Elkeles, Simone 187
Elkin, Benjamin 1911-1995 3
Elkins, Dov Peretz 1937- 5
Ellacott, S(amuel) E(rnest) 1911- 19
Elleman, Barbara 1934- 147
Ellen, Jaye
    See Nixon, Joan Lowery
Eller, Scott
    See Holinger, William (Jacques)
    and Shepard, Jim
Ellestad, Myrvin
    See Ellestad, Myrvin H.
Ellestad, Myrvin H. 1921- 120
Elliot, David 1952- 122
Elliott, Bruce
    See Field, Edward
Elliott, David 1947- 163

Elliott, Don
    See Silverberg, Robert
Elliott, Elizabeth Shippen Green
    See Green, Elizabeth Shippen
Elliott, Janice 1931-1995 119
Elliott, Joey
    See Houk, Randy
Elliott, Laura Malone 1957- 197
Elliott, Louise 111
Elliott, Odette 1939- 75
Elliott, Patricia 1946- 176
Elliott, Sarah M(cCarn) 1930- 14
Elliott, (Robert) Scott 1970- 153
Elliott, William
    See Bradbury, Ray
Ellis, (Mary) Amabel (Nassau Strachey)
Williams
    See Williams-Ellis, (Mary) Amabel (Nassau
    Strachey)
Ellis, Anyon
    See Rowland-Entwistle, (Arthur) Theodore
    (Henry)
Ellis, Carson 1975- 190
Ellis, Carson Friedman
    See Ellis, Carson
Ellis, Deborah 1960- 187
    Earlier sketch in SATA 129
Ellis, E. S.
    See Ellis, Edward S(ylvester)
Ellis, Edward S(ylvester) 1840-1916
    See YABC 1
Ellis, Ella Thorp 1928- 127
    Earlier sketch in SATA 7
    See also SAAS 9
Ellis, Harry Bearse 1921-2004 9
Ellis, Herbert
    See Wilson, Lionel
Ellis, Mel(vin Richard) 1912-1984 7
    Obituary 39
Ellis, Richard 1938- 130
Ellis, Sarah 1952- 179
    Earlier sketches in SATA 68, 131
    See also CLR 42
Ellison, Chris 196
Ellison, Emily 114
Ellison, Lucile Watkins 1907(?)-1979 50
    Obituary 22
Ellison, Virginia H(owell) 1910- 4
Ellsberg, Edward 1891-1983 7
Ellsworth, Loretta 1954- 199
Ellsworth, Mary Ellen (Tressel) 1940- 146
Elmer, Robert 1958- 154
    Earlier sketch in SATA 99
Elmore, (Carolyn) Patricia 1933- 38
    Brief entry 35
El-Moslimany, Ann P(axton) 1937- 90
Elschner, Geraldine 1954- 183
Elspeth
    See Bragdon, Elspeth MacDuffie
Elster, Jean Alicia 1953- 150
Elting, Mary 1906- 88
    Earlier sketch in SATA 2
    See also SAAS 20
Elvgren, Jennifer Riesmeyer 179
Elwart, Joan Potter 1927- 2
Elwood, Ann 1931- 55
    Brief entry 52
Elwood, Roger 1943-2007 58
Elya, Susan M(iddleton) 1955- 159
    Earlier sketch in SATA 106
Elzbieta 88
Ember, Kathi 190
Emberley, Barbara A(nne) 1932- 146
    Earlier sketches in SATA 8, 70
    See also CLR 5
Emberley, Ed(ward Randolph) 1931- 146
    Earlier sketches in SATA 8, 70
    See also CLR 81
Emberley, Michael 1960- 189
    Earlier sketches in SATA 34, 80, 119
Embry, Margaret Jacob 1919-1975 5

Emecheta, Buchi 1944- 66
Emecheta, Florence Onye Buchi
    See Emecheta, Buchi
Emerson, Alice B.
    See Benson, Mildred (Augustine Wirt)
Emerson, Kathy Lynn 1947- 63
Emerson, Ru 1944- 107
    Earlier sketch in SATA 70
Emerson, Sally 1952- 111
Emerson, William K(eith) 1925- 25
Emert, Phyllis R(aybin) 1947- 93
Emery, Anne (McGuigan) 1907- 33
    Earlier sketch in SATA 1
Emmens, Carol Ann 1944- 39
Emmett, Jonathan 1965- 188
    Earlier sketch in SATA 138
Emmons, Della (Florence) Gould 1890-1983
    Obituary 39
Emory, Jerry 1957- 96
Emrich, Duncan (Black Macdonald)
    1908-1970(?) 11
Emshwiller, Carol 1921- 174
    Autobiography Feature 174
Emshwiller, Carol Fries
    See Emshwiller, Carol
Emslie, M. L.
    See Simpson, Myrtle L(illias)
Ende, Michael (Andreas Helmuth)
    1929-1995 130
    Brief entry 42
    Obituary 86
    Earlier sketch in SATA 61
    See also CLR 138
Enderle, Dotti 1954- 145
Enderle, Judith (Ann) Ross 1941- 89
    Autobiography Feature 114
    Earlier sketch in SATA 38
    See also SAAS 26
Enell, Trinka (Gochenour) 1951- 79
Enfield, Carrie
    See Smith, Susan Vernon
Engdahl, Sylvia Louise 1933- 4
    Autobiography Feature 122
    See also CLR 2
    See also SAAS 5
Engel, Diana 1947- 70
Engelbreit, Mary 1952- 169
Engelhart, Margaret S. 1924- 59
Engelmann, Kim (V.) 1959- 87
England, George Allan 1877-1936 102
Englart, Mindi Rose 1965- 146
Engle, Eloise
    See Paananen, Eloise (Katherine)
Engle, Margarita 1951- 193
Englebert, Victor 1933- 8
English, James W(ilson) 1915- 37
Engstrom, Elizabeth 1951- 110
Enright, D(ennis) J(oseph) 1920-2002 25
    Obituary 140
Enright, Dominique 194
Enright, Elizabeth (Wright) 1909-1968 9
    See also CLR 4
Ensor, Barbara 180
Ensor, Robert (T.) 1922- 93
Enthoven, Sam 1974- 187
Entwistle, (Arthur) Theodore (Henry) Rowland
    See Rowland-Entwistle, (Arthur) Theodore
    (Henry)
Enys, Sarah L.
    See Sloggett, Nellie
Epanya, Christian A(rthur Kingue) 1956- 91
Ephraim, Shelly S(chonebaum) 1952- 97
Ephron, Delia 1944- 197
    Brief entry 50
    Earlier sketch in SATA 65
Epler, Doris M. 1928- 73
Epp, Margaret A(gnes) 1913- 20
Eppenstein, Louise (Kohn) 1892-1987
    Obituary 54
Epple, Anne Orth 1927- 20
Epstein, Anne Merrick 1931- 20

Epstein, Beryl (M. Williams) 1910- *31*
  Earlier sketch in SATA *1*
  See also CLR 26
  See also SAAS 17
Epstein, Perle S(herry) 1938- *27*
Epstein, Rachel S. 1941- *102*
Epstein, Samuel 1909-2000 .... *31*
  Earlier sketch in SATA *1*
  See also CLR 26
  See also SAAS 17
Erdman, Loula Grace 1905(?)-1976 .... *1*
Erdoes, Richard 1912- *33*
  Brief entry *28*
Erdogan, Buket *187*
Erdrich, Karen Louise
  See Erdrich, Louise
Erdrich, Louise 1954- *141*
  Earlier sketch in SATA *94*
Erickson, Betty J. 1923- *97*
Erickson, Betty Jean
  See Erickson, Betty J.
Erickson, John R. 1943- *136*
  Earlier sketch in SATA *70*
Erickson, Jon 1948- *141*
Erickson, Phoebe *59*
Erickson, Russell E(verett) 1932- *27*
Erickson, Sabra Rollins 1912-1995 .... *35*
Erickson, Walter
  See Fast, Howard
Ericson, Walter
  See Fast, Howard
Ericsson, Jennifer A. *170*
Erikson, Mel 1937- *31*
Ering, Timothy Basil *176*
Erlanger, Baba
  See Trahey, Jane
Erlbach, Arlene 1948- *160*
  Earlier sketches in SATA *78, 115*
Erlbruch, Wolf 1948- *181*
Erlich, Lillian (Feldman) 1910-1983 .... *10*
Erlings, Fridrik 1962- *196*
Erlingsson, Frierik
  See Erlings, Fridrik
Ermatinger, James W. 1959- *170*
Ernest, William
  See Berkebile, Fred D(onovan)
Ernst, (Lyman) John 1940- *39*
Ernst, Kathleen
  See Ernst, Kathleen A.
Ernst, Kathleen A. 1959- *162*
Ernst, Kathryn (Fitzgerald) 1942- *25*
Ernst, Lisa Campbell 1957- *154*
  Brief entry *44*
  Earlier sketches in SATA *55, 95*
Erskine, Kathryn *193*
Ervin, Janet Halliday 1923- *4*
Erwin, Will
  See Eisner, Will
Esbaum, Jill *174*
Esbensen, Barbara J(uster) 1925-1996 .... *97*
  Brief entry *53*
  Earlier sketch in SATA *62*
Eschbacher, Roger *160*
Eschmeyer, R(einhart) E(rnst) 1898-1989 .... *29*
Escriva, Vivi *182*
Eseki, Bruno
  See Mphahlele, Es'kia
Esekie, Bruno
  See Mphahlele, Es'kia
Eshmeyer, R. E.
  See Eschmeyer, R(einhart) E(rnst)
Eskridge, Ann E. 1949- *84*
Espeland, Pamela (Lee) 1951- *128*
  Brief entry *38*
  Earlier sketch in SATA *52*
Espriella, Don Manuel Alvarez
  See Southey, Robert
Espy, Willard R(ichardson) 1910-1999 .... *38*
  Obituary *113*
Essrig, Harry 1912- *66*
Estep, Irene Compton *5*

Esterl, Arnica 1933- *77*
Estes, Eleanor (Ruth) 1906-1988 .... *91*
  Obituary *56*
  Earlier sketch in SATA *7*
  See also CLR 70
Estoril, Jean
  See Allan, Mabel Esther
Estrada, Pau 1961- *74*
Etchemendy, Nancy 1952- *166*
  Earlier sketch in SATA *38*
Etchemendy, Nancy Elise Howell
  See Etchemendy, Nancy
Etchison, Birdie L(ee) 1937- *38*
Etchison, Craig 1945- *133*
Etherington, Frank 1945- *58*
Eton, Robert
  See Meynell, Laurence Walter
Ets, Marie Hall 1893-1984 .... *2*
  See also CLR 33
Ettlinger, Doris 1950- *173*
Eunson, (John) Dale 1904-2002 .... *5*
  Obituary *132*
Evan, Frances Y. 1951- *167*
Evanoff, Vlad 1916- *59*
Evans, Cambria 1981- *178*
Evans, Douglas 1953- *144*
  Earlier sketch in SATA *93*
Evans, Eva (Knox) 1905-1998 .... *27*
Evans, Freddi Williams 1957- *134*
Evans, Greg 1947- *143*
  Earlier sketch in SATA *73*
Evans, Hubert Reginald 1892-1986 .... *118*
  Obituary *48*
Evans, Katherine (Floyd) 1901-1964 .... *5*
Evans, Larry
  See Evans, Laurence Chubb
Evans, Laurence Chubb 1939- *88*
Evans, Lawrence Watt
  See Watt-Evans, Lawrence
Evans, Lezlie *180*
Evans, Mari 1923- *10*
Evans, Mark *19*
Evans, Nancy 1950- *65*
Evans, Patricia Healy
  See Carpenter, Patricia (Healy Evans)
Evans, (Alice) Pearl 1927- *83*
Evans, Shane W. *189*
Evans, Shirlee 1931- *58*
Evans, Tabor
  See Cameron, Lou
  and Knott, William C(ecil, Jr.)
  and Wallmann, Jeffrey M(iner)
  and Whittington, Harry (Benjamin)
Evarts, Esther
  See Benson, Sally
Evarts, Hal G., (Jr.) 1915-1989 .... *6*
Everett, Gail
  See Hale, Arlene
Evernden, Margery 1916- *5*
Eversole, Robyn 1971- *74*
Eversole, Robyn H.
  See Eversole, Robyn
Eversole, Robyn Harbert
  See Eversole, Robyn
Evslin, Bernard 1922-1993 .... *83*
  Brief entry *28*
  Obituary *77*
  Earlier sketch in SATA *45*
Ewart, Claire 1958- *145*
  Earlier sketch in SATA *76*
Ewen, David 1907-1985 .... *4*
  Obituary *47*
Ewing, Juliana (Horatia Gatty) 1841-1885 ... *16*
  See also CLR 78
Ewing, Kathryn 1921- *20*
Eyerly, Jeannette 1908-2008 .... *86*
  Obituary *196*
  Earlier sketch in SATA *4*
  See also SAAS 10
Eyerly, Jeannette Hyde
  See Eyerly, Jeannette

Eyre, Dorothy
  See McGuire, Leslie (Sarah)
Eyre, Frank 1910-1988
  Obituary *62*
Eyre, Katherine Wigmore 1901-1970 .... *26*
Ezzell, Marilyn 1937- *42*
  Brief entry *38*

F

Fabe, Maxene 1943- *15*
Faber, Doris (Greenberg) 1924- *78*
  Earlier sketch in SATA *3*
Faber, Harold 1919- *5*
Fabre, Jean Henri (Casimir) 1823-1915 .... *22*
Facklam, Margery (Metz) 1927- *132*
  Earlier sketches in SATA *20, 85*
Fadden, David Kanietakeron *196*
Fadiman, Clifton (Paul) 1904-1999 .... *11*
  Obituary *115*
Fagan, Cary 1957- *186*
Fahs, Sophia Blanche Lyon 1876-1978 ...... *102*
Failing, Barbara Larmon *182*
Fair, David 1952- *96*
Fair, Sylvia 1933- *13*
Fairfax-Lucy, Brian (Fulke Cameron-Ramsay)
  1898-1974 .... *6*
  Obituary *26*
Fairfield, Flora
  See Alcott, Louisa May
Fairlie, Gerard 1899-1983
  Obituary *34*
Fairman, Joan A(lexandra) 1935- *10*
Faithfull, Gail 1936- *8*
Falcone, L(ucy) M. 1951- *155*
Falconer, Ian 1959- *179*
  Earlier sketch in SATA *125*
  See also CLR 90
Falconer, James
  See Kirkup, James
Falconer, Lee N.
  See May, Julian
Falkner, Leonard 1900-1977 .... *12*
Fall, Andrew
  See Arthur, Robert, (Jr.)
Fall, Thomas
  See Snow, Donald Clifford
Faller, Regis 1968- *187*
Falls, C(harles) B(uckles) 1874-1960 .... *38*
  Brief entry *27*
Falstein, Louis 1909-1995 .... *37*
Falwell, Cathryn 1952- *196*
Fancher, Lou 1960- *177*
Fanelli, Sara 1969- *126*
  Earlier sketch in SATA *89*
Fanning, Leonard M(ulliken) 1888-1967 .... *5*
Faralla, Dana 1909- *9*
Faralla, Dorothy W.
  See Faralla, Dana
Farb, Peter 1929-1980 .... *12*
  Obituary *22*
Farber, Norma 1909-1984 .... *75*
  Obituary *38*
  Earlier sketch in SATA *25*
Fardell, John 1967- *195*
Farish, Terry 1947- *146*
  Earlier sketch in SATA *82*
Farjeon, (Eve) Annabel 1919-2004 .... *11*
  Obituary *153*
Farjeon, Eleanor 1881-1965 .... *2*
  See also CLR 34
Farley, Carol (J.) 1936- *137*
  Earlier sketch in SATA *4*
Farley, Terri *165*
Farley, Walter (Lorimer) 1915-1989 .... *132*
  Earlier sketches in SATA *2, 43*
Farlow, James O(rville, Jr.) 1951- *75*
Farmer, Nancy 1941- *161*
  Earlier sketches in SATA *79, 117*

Farmer, Patti 1948- 79
Farmer, Penelope (Jane) 1939- *105*
  Brief entry *39*
  Earlier sketch in SATA *40*
  See also CLR 8
  See also SAAS 22
Farmer, Peter 1950- *38*
Farmer, Philip Jose 1918-2009 .... *93*
Farnham, Burt
  See Clifford, Harold B(urton)
Farnsworth, Bill 1958- *186*
  Earlier sketches in SATA *84, 135*
Farquhar, Margaret C(utting) 1905-1988 ...... *13*
Farquharson, Alexander 1944- *46*
Farquharson, Martha
  See Finley, Martha
Farr, Diana (Pullein-Thompson) *82*
  Earlier sketch in SATA *3*
Farr, Finis (King) 1904-1982 .... *10*
Farrar, Jill
  See Morris, Jill
Farrar, Susan Clement 1917- *33*
Farrell, Ben
  See Cebulash, Mel
Farrell, Patrick
  See Odgers, Sally Farrell
Farrell, Sally
  See Odgers, Sally Farrell
Farrer, Vashti *167*
Farrington, Benjamin 1891-1974
  Obituary *20*
Farrington, S(elwyn) Kip, Jr. 1904-1983 ...... *20*
Farshtey, Greg(ory T.) 1965- *148*
Farthing, Alison 1936- *45*
  Brief entry *36*
Farthing-Knight, Catherine 1933- *92*
Fassler, Joan (Grace) 1931- *11*
Fast, Howard 1914-2003 .... *7*
  Autobiography Feature *107*
Fast, Howard Melvin
  See Fast, Howard
Fasulo, Michael 1963- *83*
Fatchen, Max 1920- *84*
  Earlier sketch in SATA *20*
  See also SAAS 20
Fate, Marilyn
  See Collins, Paul
Father Goose
  See Ghigna, Charles
Fatigati, (Frances) Evelyn 1948- *24*
Fatio, Louise 1904-1993 .... *6*
Fatus, Sophie 1957- *182*
Faulhaber, Martha 1926- *7*
Faulkner, Anne Irvin 1906- *23*
Faulkner, Frank
  See Ellis, Edward S(ylvester)
Faulkner, Nancy
  See Faulkner, Anne Irvin
Faulknor, Cliff(ord Vernon) 1913- *86*
Favole, Robert J(ames) 1950- *125*
Fax, Elton Clay 1909-1993 .... *25*
Faxon, Lavinia
  See Russ, Lavinia (Faxon)
Feagles, Anita M(acRae) 1927- *9*
Feagles, Elizabeth
  See Day, Beth (Feagles)
Feague, Mildred H. 1915- *14*
Fearnley, Jan 1965- *153*
Fearrington, Ann (Peyton) 1945- *146*
Fecher, Constance
  See Heaven, Constance (Christina)
Feder, Chris Welles 1938- *81*
Feder, Harriet K. 1928- *73*
Feder, Paula (Kurzband) 1935- *26*
Federici, Debbie 1965- *175*
Federici, Debbie Tanner
  See Federici, Debbie
Feelings, Muriel (Lavita Grey) 1938- *16*
  See also CLR 5
  See also SAAS 8

Feelings, Thomas 1933-2003 .... *69*
  Obituary *148*
  Earlier sketch in SATA *8*
  See also CLR 58
  See also SAAS 19
Feelings, Tom
  See Feelings, Thomas
Fehler, Gene 1940- *74*
Fehrenbach, T(heodore) R(eed, Jr.) 1925- *33*
Feiffer, Jules 1929- *157*
  Earlier sketches in SATA *8, 61, 111*
Feiffer, Jules Ralph
  See Feiffer, Jules
Feiffer, Kate 1964- *170*
Feig, Barbara Krane 1937- *34*
Feikema, Feike
  See Manfred, Frederick (Feikema)
Feil, Hila 1942- *12*
Feilen, John
  See May, Julian
Feinberg, Barbara Jane 1938- *123*
  Earlier sketch in SATA *58*
Feinberg, Barbara Silberdick
  See Feinberg, Barbara Jane
Feinstein, John 1956- *195*
  Earlier sketch in SATA *163*
Feldman, Anne (Rodgers) 1939- *19*
Feldman, Elane *79*
Felin, M. Sindy *194*
Felix
  See Vincent, Felix
Fell, Derek 1939- *167*
Fell, Derek John
  See Fell, Derek
Fellowes, Julian 1950- *198*
Fellows, Muriel H. *10*
Fellows, Stan 1957- *177*
Fellows, Stanley
  See Fellows, Stan
Felsen, Henry Gregor 1916-1995 .... *1*
  See also SAAS 2
Felstead, Cathie 1954- *192*
Feltenstein, Arlene (H.) 1934- *119*
Felton, Harold William 1902-1991 .... *1*
Felton, Ronald Oliver 1909- *3*
Felts, Shirley 1934- *33*
Fenderson, Lewis H., Jr. 1907-1983 .... *47*
  Obituary *37*
Fenner, Carol (Elizabeth) 1929-2002 .... *89*
  Obituary *132*
  Earlier sketch in SATA *7*
  See also SAAS 24
Fenner, Phyllis R(eid) 1899-1982 .... *1*
  Obituary *29*
Fensham, Elizabeth *169*
Fenten, Barbara D(oris) 1935- *26*
Fenten, D(onald) X. 1932- *4*
Fenton, Carroll Lane 1900-1969 .... *5*
Fenton, Edward 1917-1995 .... *7*
  Obituary *89*
Fenton, Mildred Adams 1899-1995 .... *21*
Fenwick, Patti
  See Grider, Dorothy
Feravolo, Rocco Vincent 1922- *10*
Ferber, Brenda A. 1967- *184*
Ferber, Edna 1887-1968 .... *7*
Fergus, Charles *114*
Ferguson, Alane 1957- *182*
  Earlier sketch in SATA *85*
Ferguson, Bob
  See Ferguson, Robert Bruce
Ferguson, Cecil 1931- *45*
Ferguson, Peter 1968- *199*
Ferguson, Robert Bruce 1927-2001 .... *13*
Ferguson, Sarah 1959- *180*
  Earlier sketches in SATA *66, 110*
Ferguson, Sarah Margaret
  See Ferguson, Sarah
Ferguson, Walter (W.) 1930- *34*
Fergusson, Erna 1888-1964 .... *5*

Fermi, Laura 1907-1977 .... *6*
  Obituary *28*
Fern, Eugene A. 1919-1987 .... *10*
  Obituary *54*
Fernandes, Eugenie 1943- *139*
  Earlier sketch in SATA *77*
Fernandez, Laura 1960- *171*
Ferrari, Maria *123*
Ferreiro, Carmen 1958- *158*
Ferrell, Nancy Warren 1932- *70*
Ferri, Giuliano 1965- *197*
Ferrier, Lucy
  See Penzler, Otto
Ferris, Helen Josephine 1890-1969 .... *21*
Ferris, James Cody
  See McFarlane, Leslie (Charles)
Ferris, Jean 1939- *149*
  Brief entry *50*
  Earlier sketches in SATA *56, 105*
Ferris, Jeri Chase 1937- *84*
Ferry, Charles 1927- *92*
  Earlier sketch in SATA *43*
  See also CLR 34
  See also SAAS 20
Fetz, Ingrid 1915- *30*
Feydy, Anne Lindbergh
  See Sapieyevski, Anne Lindbergh
Fiammenghi, Gioia 1929- *66*
  Earlier sketch in SATA *9*
Fiarotta, Noel
  See Ficarotta, Noel
Fiarotta, Phyllis
  See Ficarotta, Phyllis
Ficarotta, Noel 1944- *15*
Ficarotta, Phyllis 1942- *15*
Fichter, George S. 1922-1993 .... *7*
Ficocelli, Elizabeth *189*
Fidler, Kathleen (Annie) 1899-1980 .... *87*
  Obituary *45*
  Earlier sketch in SATA *3*
Fiedler, Jean(nette Feldman) *4*
Fiedler, Joseph Daniel *159*
Fiedler, Lisa *185*
Field, Dorothy 1944- *97*
Field, Edward 1924- *109*
  Earlier sketch in SATA *8*
Field, Elinor Whitney 1889-1980
  Obituary *28*
Field, Eugene 1850-1895 .... *16*
Field, Gans T.
  See Wellman, Manly Wade
Field, James 1959- *113*
Field, Peter
  See Drago, Harry Sinclair
  and Dresser, Davis
  and Mann, E(dward) B(everly)
Field, Rachel (Lyman) 1894-1942 .... *15*
  See also CLR 21
Fielding, Kate
  See Oldfield, Jenny
Fields, Bryan W. 1958(?)- *188*
Fields, Terri 1948- *191*
Fields, T.S.
  See Fields, Terri
Fienberg, Anna 1956- *183*
  Earlier sketch in SATA *112*
Fife, Dale (Odile Hollerbach) 1901- *18*
Fighter Pilot, A
  See Johnston, H(ugh) A(nthony) S(tephen)
Figler, Jeanie 1949- *123*
Figley, Marty Rhodes 1948- *158*
  Earlier sketch in SATA *88*
Figueredo, D(anilo) H. 1951- *155*
Figueroa, Pablo 1938- *9*
Fijan, Carol 1918- *12*
Filderman, Diane E(lizabeth) 1959- *87*
Files, Meg 1946- *107*
Fillmore, Parker H(oysted) 1878-1944
  See YABC 1
Filstrup, Chris
  See Filstrup, E(dward) Christian

Filstrup, E(dward) Christian 1942- *43*
Filstrup, Janie
  See Merrill, Jane
Finchler, Judy 1943- *93*
Finder, Martin
  See Salzmann, Siegmund
Findlay, Jamieson 1958- *169*
Findon, Joanne 1957- *161*
Fine, Anne 1947- *197*
  Earlier sketches in SATA *29, 72, 111, 160*
  See also CLR *25*
  See also SAAS *15*
Fine, Edith Hope *169*
Fine, Howard 1961- *181*
Fine, Jane
  See Ziefert, Harriet
Finger, Charles J(oseph) 1869(?)-1941 .... *42*
Fink, William B(ertrand) 1916- *22*
Finke, Blythe Foote 1922- *26*
Finkel, George (Irvine) 1909-1975 .... *8*
Finkelstein, Norman H. 1941- *137*
  Earlier sketch in SATA *73*
Finkelstein, Norman Henry
  See Finkelstein, Norman H.
Finlay, Alice Sullivan 1946- *82*
Finlay, Winifred Lindsay Crawford
  (McKissack) 1910-1989 .... *23*
Finlayson, Ann 1925- *8*
Finley, Martha 1828-1909 .... *43*
Finley, Mary Peace 1942- *83*
Finney, Jack
  See Finney, Walter Braden
Finney, Patricia 1958- *163*
Finney, Shan 1944- *65*
Finney, Walter Braden 1911-1995 .... *109*
Firer, Ben Zion
  See Firer, Benzion
Firer, Benzion 1914- *64*
Fireside, Bryna J. 1932- *73*
Firmin, Charlotte 1954- *29*
Firmin, Peter 1928- *58*
  Earlier sketch in SATA *15*
Firth, Barbara *179*
Fischbach, Julius 1894-1988 .... *10*
Fischer, John
  See Fluke, Joanne
Fischer, R.J.
  See Fluke, Joanne
Fischer, Scott M. 1971- *195*
Fischer-Nagel, Andreas 1951- *56*
Fischer-Nagel, Heiderose 1956- *56*
Fischler, Shirley (Walton) *66*
Fischler, Stan(ley I.) *66*
  Brief entry *36*
Fischtrom, Harvey 1933-1974 .... *3*
Fishback, Margaret
  See Antolini, Margaret Fishback
Fishbone, Greg R. *195*
Fisher, Aileen (Lucia) 1906-2002 .... *73*
  Obituary *143*
  Earlier sketches in SATA *1, 25*
  See also CLR *49*
Fisher, Barbara 1940- *44*
  Brief entry *34*
Fisher, Carolyn 1968- *154*
Fisher, Catherine 1957- *155*
Fisher, Chris 1958- *80*
Fisher, Clavin C(argill) 1912- *24*
Fisher, Cynthia *195*
Fisher, Dorothy (Frances) Canfield 1879-1958
  See YABC *1*
  See also CLR *71*
Fisher, Gary L. 1949- *86*
Fisher, John 1909-1996 .... *15*
Fisher, John Oswald Hamilton
  See Fisher, John
Fisher, Laura Harrison 1934- *5*

Fisher, Leonard Everett 1924- *176*
  Autobiography Feature *122*
  Earlier sketches in SATA *4, 34, 73, 120*
  See also CLR *18*
  See also SAAS *1*
Fisher, Lois I. 1948- *38*
  Brief entry *35*
Fisher, Margery (Turner) 1913-1992 .... *20*
  Obituary *74*
Fisher, Marshall Jon 1963- *113*
Fisher, Nikki
  See Strachan, Ian
Fisher, Robert (Tempest) 1943- *47*
Fisher, Suzanne
  See Staples, Suzanne Fisher
Fisher, Valorie *177*
Fishman, Cathy Goldberg 1951- *106*
Fisk, Nicholas
  See Higginbottom, David
Fisk, Pauline 1948- *160*
  Earlier sketch in SATA *66*
Fiske, Tarleton
  See Bloch, Robert (Albert)
Fisscher, Catharina G. M. 1958- *142*
Fisscher, Tiny
  See Fisscher, Catharina G. M.
Fitch, Clarke
  See Sinclair, Upton
Fitch, John IV
  See Cormier, Robert
Fitch, Sheree 1956- *178*
  Earlier sketch in SATA *108*
Fitschen, Dale 1937- *20*
Fitzalan, Roger
  See Trevor, Elleston
Fitzgerald, Captain Hugh
  See Baum, L(yman) Frank
FitzGerald, Cathleen 1932-1987
  Obituary *50*
Fitzgerald, Dawn *175*
Fitzgerald, Edward Earl 1919-2001 .... *20*
Fitzgerald, F(rancis) A(nthony) 1940- *15*
Fitzgerald, Joanne 1956- *198*
Fitzgerald, John D(ennis) 1907(?)-1988 .... *20*
  Obituary *56*
  See also CLR *1*
Fitzgerald, Merni Ingrassia 1955- *53*
Fitzgibbon, Terry 1948- *121*
Fitzhardinge, Joan Margaret 1912- *73*
  Earlier sketch in SATA *2*
  See also CLR *5*
  See also SAAS *3*
Fitzhugh, Louise (Perkins) 1928-1974 .... *45*
  Obituary *24*
  Earlier sketch in SATA *1*
  See also CLR *72*
Fitzhugh, Percy Keese 1876-1950 .... *65*
Fitzpatrick, Marie-Louise 1962- *189*
  Earlier sketch in SATA *125*
FitzRalph, Matthew
  See McInerny, Ralph
Fitz-Randolph, Jane (Currens) 1915- *51*
Fitzsimons, Cecilia 1952- *97*
Fitzsimons, Cecilia A.L.
  See Fitzsimons, Cecilia
Flack, Marjorie 1897-1958 .... *100*
  See also YABC *2*
  See also CLR *28*
Flack, Naomi John White -1999 .... *40*
  Brief entry *35*
Flake, Sharon G. *166*
Flanagan, John 1944- *180*
Flanagan, John Anthony
  See Flanagan, John
Flannery, Kate
  See De Goldi, Kathleen Domenica
Flatt, Lizann 1966- *88*
Fleagle, Gail S(hatto) 1940- *117*
Fleetwood, Jenni 1947- *80*
Fleischer, Jane
  See Oppenheim, Joanne

Fleischhauer-Hardt, Helga 1936- *30*
Fleischman, Albert Sidney
  See Fleischman, Sid
Fleischman, John 1948- *145*
Fleischman, Paul 1952- *156*
  Brief entry *32*
  Earlier sketches in SATA *39, 72, 110*
  See also CLR *66*
  See also SAAS *20*
Fleischman, Sid 1920- *185*
  Earlier sketches in SATA *8, 59, 96, 148*
  See also CLR *15*
Fleischner, Jennifer 1956- *188*
  Earlier sketch in SATA *93*
Fleisher, Paul 1948- *132*
  Earlier sketch in SATA *81*
Fleisher, Robbin 1951-1977 .... *52*
  Brief entry *49*
Fleishman, Seymour 1918- *66*
  Brief entry *32*
Fleming, A. A.
  See Arthur, Robert, (Jr.)
Fleming, Alice Mulcahey 1928- *9*
Fleming, Candace 1962- *190*
  Earlier sketches in SATA *94, 143*
Fleming, Denise 1950- *173*
  Earlier sketches in SATA *81, 126*
Fleming, Elizabeth P. 1888-1985
  Obituary *48*
Fleming, Ian 1908-1964 .... *9*
Fleming, Ian Lancaster
  See Fleming, Ian
Fleming, Ronald Lee 1941- *56*
Fleming, Sally
  See Walker, Sally M(acArt)
Fleming, Stuart
  See Knight, Damon (Francis)
Fleming, Susan 1932- *32*
Fleming, Thomas 1927- *8*
Fleming, Thomas James
  See Fleming, Thomas
Fleming, Virginia (Edwards) 1923- *84*
Flesch, Y.
  See Flesch, Yolande (Catarina)
Flesch, Yolande (Catarina) 1950- *55*
Fletcher, Charlie May Hogue 1897-1977 .... *3*
Fletcher, Colin 1922-2007 .... *28*
Fletcher, Dirk
  See Cunningham, Chet
Fletcher, George U.
  See Pratt, (Murray) Fletcher
Fletcher, Helen Jill 1910- *13*
Fletcher, Ralph 1953- *195*
  Earlier sketches in SATA *105, 149*
  See also CLR *104*
Fletcher, Ralph J.
  See Fletcher, Ralph
Fletcher, Richard E. 1917(?)-1983
  Obituary *34*
Fletcher, Rick
  See Fletcher, Richard E.
Fletcher, Susan 1951- *181*
  Earlier sketches in SATA *70, 110*
Fletcher, Susan Clemens
  See Fletcher, Susan
Fleur, Paul
  See Pohl, Frederik
Flexner, James Thomas 1908-2003 .... *9*
Flinn, Alex 1966- *198*
  Earlier sketch in SATA *159*
Flint, Helen 1952- *102*
Flint, Russ 1944- *74*
Flitner, David P(erkins), Jr. 1949- *7*
Floca, Brian *190*
  Earlier sketch in SATA *155*
Floethe, Louise Lee 1913-1988 .... *4*
Floethe, Richard 1901-1998 .... *4*
Floherty, John Joseph 1882-1964 .... *25*
Flood, Bo
  See Flood, Nancy Bo
Flood, Nancy Bo 1945- *130*

Flood, Pansie Hart 1964- *140*
Flood, William 1942- *129*
Flooglebuckle, Al
  See Spiegelman, Art
Flora, James (Royer) 1914-1998 .... *30*
  Obituary *103*
  Earlier sketch in SATA *1*
  See also SAAS *6*
Flores-Galbis, Enrique 1952- *186*
Florian, Douglas 1950- *177*
  Earlier sketches in SATA *19, 83, 125*
Flory, Jane Trescott 1917- *22*
Flournoy, Valerie 1952- *95*
Flournoy, Valerie Rose
  See Flournoy, Valerie
Flowerdew, Phyllis -1994 .... *33*
Flowers, Pam 1946- *136*
Flowers, Sarah 1952- *98*
Floyd, Gareth 1940- *62*
  Brief entry *31*
Fluchere, Henri 1914-1991 .... *40*
Fluke, Joanne 1943- *88*
Flutsztejn-Gruda, Ilona 1930- *170*
Flynn, Barbara 1928- *9*
Flynn, Jackson
  See Bensen, Donald R.
  and Shirreffs, Gordon D(onald)
Flynn, Nicholas
  See Odgers, Sally Farrell
Flynn, Rachel 1953- *171*
  Earlier sketch in SATA *109*
Flynn, Warren (G.) 1950- *154*
Fodor, R(onald) V(ictor) 1944- *25*
Fogelin, Adrian 1951- *175*
  Earlier sketch in SATA *129*
Foley, (Anna) Bernice Williams 1902-1987 . *28*
Foley, Greg E. 1969- *190*
Foley, June 1944- *44*
Foley, (Mary) Louise Munro 1933- *106*
  Brief entry *40*
  Earlier sketch in SATA *54*
Foley, Rae
  See Denniston, Elinore
Folke, Will
  See Bloch, Robert (Albert)
Follett, Helen Thomas 1884(?)-1970
  Obituary *27*
Folsom, Franklin (Brewster) 1907-1995 .... *5*
  Obituary *88*
Folsom, Michael (Brewster) 1938-1990 .... *40*
  Obituary *88*
Fontenot, Mary Alice 1910- *91*
  Earlier sketch in SATA *34*
Fontes, Justine *172*
Fontes, Ron 1952- *183*
Foon, Dennis 1951- *119*
Fooner, Michael *22*
Foote, Timothy (Gilson) 1926- *52*
Forberg, Ati
  See Forberg, Beate Gropius
Forberg, Beate Gropius 1925- *22*
Forbes, Anna 1954- *101*
Forbes, Bryan 1926- *37*
Forbes, Cabot L.
  See Hoyt, Edwin P(almer), Jr.
Forbes, Esther 1891-1967 .... *100*
  Earlier sketch in SATA *2*
  See also CLR *27*
Forbes, Graham B. *1*
Forbes, Kathryn
  See McLean, Kathryn (Anderson)
Forbes, Robert
  See Arthur, Robert, (Jr.)
Ford, Albert Lee
  See Stratemeyer, Edward L.
Ford, Barbara *56*
  Brief entry *34*
Ford, Brian J(ohn) 1939- *49*
Ford, Carolyn (Mott) 1938- *98*
Ford, Christine 1953- *176*

Ford, David
  See Baldacci, David
  and Baldacci, David
Ford, David B.
  See Baldacci, David
Ford, David Baldacci
  See Baldacci, David
Ford, Elbur
  See Hibbert, Eleanor Alice Burford
Ford, Ellen 1949- *89*
Ford, George (Jr.) *31*
Ford, Hilary
  See Youd, (Christopher) Samuel
Ford, Hildegarde
  See Morrison, Velma Ford
Ford, Jerome W. 1949- *78*
Ford, Jerry
  See Ford, Jerome W.
Ford, Juwanda G(ertrude) 1967- *102*
Ford, Marcia
  See Radford, Ruby L(orraine)
Ford, Nancy K(effer) 1906-1961
  Obituary *29*
Ford, Peter 1936- *59*
Ford, S. M.
  See Uhlig, Susan
Forde, Catherine 1961- *170*
Foreman, Mark *199*
Foreman, Michael 1938- *184*
  Earlier sketches in SATA *2, 73, 129, 135*
  See also CLR *32*
  See also SAAS *21*
Foreman, Wilmoth 1939- *153*
Forest, Dial
  See Gault, William Campbell
Forest, Heather 1948- *185*
  Earlier sketch in SATA *120*
Forester, C(ecil) S(cott) 1899-1966 .... *13*
Forman, Brenda 1936- *4*
Forman, James
  See Forman, James D.
Forman, James D. 1932- *70*
  Earlier sketch in SATA *8*
Forman, James Douglas
  See Forman, James D.
Forman, Ruth 1970- *186*
Forrest, Elizabeth
  See Salsitz, Rhondi Vilott
Forrest, Mary
  See Pausacker, Jenny
Forrest, Sybil
  See Markun, Patricia Maloney
Forrestal, Elaine 1941- *165*
  Earlier sketch in SATA *117*
Forrester, Frank H. 1919(?)-1986
  Obituary *52*
Forrester, Helen
  See Bhatia, Jamunadevi
Forrester, Jade
  See Pausacker, Jenny
Forrester, Marian
  See Schachtel, Roger
Forrester, Sandra 1949- *166*
  Earlier sketch in SATA *90*
Forrester, Victoria 1940- *40*
  Brief entry *35*
Forsee, (Frances) Aylesa -1986 .... *1*
Forsey, Chris 1950- *59*
Forshay-Lunsford, Cin 1965- *60*
Forster, E(dward) M(organ) 1879-1970 .... *57*
Forsyth, Kate 1966- *154*
Fort, Paul
  See Stockton, Francis Richard
Forte, Maurizio 1961- *110*
Fortey, Richard 1946- *109*
Fortey, Richard A.
  See Fortey, Richard
Fortey, Richard Alan
  See Fortey, Richard
Forth, Melissa D(eal) *96*

Fortnum, Peggy
  See Nuttall-Smith, Margaret Emily Noel
Fortune, Eric *182*
Forward, Robert L(ull) 1932-2002 .... *82*
Foster, Alan Dean 1946- *70*
Foster, Brad W. 1955- *34*
Foster, Doris Van Liew 1899-1993 .... *10*
Foster, E(lizabeth) C(onnell) 1902- *9*
Foster, Elizabeth 1902- *12*
Foster, Elizabeth 1905-1963 .... *10*
Foster, F. Blanche 1919- *11*
Foster, G(eorge) Allen 1907-1969 .... *26*
Foster, Genevieve (Stump) 1893-1979 .... *2*
  Obituary *23*
  See also CLR *7*
Foster, Gerald L. *198*
Foster, Hal
  See Foster, Harold (Rudolf)
Foster, Harold (Rudolf) 1892-1982 .... *31*
Foster, Jeanne
  See Williams, Jeanne
Foster, John
  See Foster, John L(ouis)
  and Furcolo, Foster
Foster, John (Thomas) 1925- *8*
Foster, John L(ouis) 1941- *102*
Foster, Juliana *196*
Foster, Laura Louise (James) 1918- *6*
Foster, Leila Merrell 1929- *73*
Foster, Lynne 1937- *74*
Foster, Margaret Lesser 1899(?)-1979
  Obituary *21*
Foster, Marian Curtis 1909-1978 .... *23*
Foster, Mark 1961- *197*
Foster, Sally *58*
Foulds, E. V.
  See Foulds, Elfrida Vipont
Foulds, Elfrida Vipont 1902-1992 .... *52*
Fountas, Angela Jane *180*
Fourie, Corlia 1944- *91*
Fourth Brother, The
  See Aung, (Maung) Htin
Fowke, Edith (Margaret) 1913-1996 .... *14*
Fowles, John 1926-2005 .... *22*
  Obituary *171*
Fowles, John Robert
  See Fowles, John
Fox, Aileen 1907-2005 .... *58*
  Obituary *170*
Fox, Aileen Mary
  See Fox, Aileen
Fox, Annie 1950- *175*
Fox, Charles Philip 1913-2003 .... *12*
  Obituary *150*
Fox, Christyan *188*
Fox, Diane *188*
Fox, Eleanor
  See St. John, Wylly Folk
Fox, Fontaine Talbot, Jr. 1884-1964
  Obituary *23*
Fox, Fred 1903(?)-1981
  Obituary *27*
Fox, Freeman
  See Hamilton, Charles (Harold St. John)
Fox, Geoffrey 1941- *73*
Fox, Grace
  See Anderson, Grace Fox
Fox, Helen 1962- *181*
Fox, Larry *30*
Fox, Lorraine 1922-1976 .... *27*
  Earlier sketch in SATA *11*
Fox, Louisa
  See Kroll, Virginia L.
Fox, Mary Virginia 1919- *152*
  Brief entry *39*
  Earlier sketches in SATA *44, 88*
Fox, Mem
  See Fox, Merrion Frances
Fox, Merrion Frances 1946- *155*
  Earlier sketches in SATA *51, 103*
  See also CLR *80*

Fox, Michael W(ilson) 1937- *15*
Fox, Paula 1923- *167*
  Earlier sketches in SATA *17, 60, 120*
  See also CLR *96*
Fox, Robert J. 1927- *33*
Fox-Davies, Sarah 1956- *199*
Foyt, Victoria .... *187.*
Fradin, Dennis
  See Fradin, Dennis Brindell
Fradin, Dennis Brindell 1945- *185*
  Earlier sketches in SATA *29, 90, 135*
Fradin, Judith Bloom 1945- *185*
  Earlier sketches in SATA *90, 152*
Frailey, Paige (Menefee) 1965- *82*
Frame, Janet 1924-2004 .... *119*
Frame, Paul 1913-1994 .... *60*
  Brief entry *33*
  Obituary *83*
Frances, Miss
  See Horwich, Frances R(appaport)
Franchere, Ruth *18*
Francis, Charles
  See Holme, Bryan
Francis, Dee
  See Haas, Dorothy F.
Francis, Dorothy 1926- *127*
  Earlier sketch in SATA *10*
Francis, Dorothy B.
  See Francis, Dorothy
Francis, Dorothy Brenner
  See Francis, Dorothy
Francis, Jaye
  See Pausacker, Jenny
Francis, Pamela (Mary) 1926- *11*
Franck, Eddie
  See Cooke, Frank E.
Franco, Betsy *188*
  Earlier sketch in SATA *150*
Franco, Eloise (Bauder) 1910- *62*
Franco, Johan (Henri Gustave) 1908-1988 ... *62*
Franco, Marjorie *38*
Francois, Andre 1915-2005 .... *25*
Francoise
  See Seignobosc, Francoise
Frank, Anne(lies Marie) 1929-1945 .... *87*
  Brief entry *42*
  See also CLR *101*
Frank, Daniel B. 1956- *55*
Frank, Emily R.
  See Frank, E.R.
Frank, E.R. 1967- *157*
Frank, Helene
  See Vautier, Ghislaine
Frank, Hillary 1976- *148*
Frank, John *199*
Frank, Josette 1893-1989 .... *10*
  Obituary *63*
Frank, Lucy 1947- *166*
  Earlier sketch in SATA *94*
Frank, Mary 1933- *34*
Frank, R., Jr.
  See Ross, Frank (Xavier), Jr.
Frankau, Mary Evelyn Atkinson 1899-1974 .. *4*
Frankel, Alona 1937- *66*
Frankel, Bernice *9*
Frankel, Edward 1910- *44*
Frankel, Ellen 1951- *78*
Frankel, Julie 1947- *40*
  Brief entry *34*
Frankenberg, Robert 1911- *22*
Franklin, Cheryl J. 1955- *70*
Franklin, Harold 1926- *13*
Franklin, Kristine L. 1958- *124*
  Earlier sketch in SATA *80*
Franklin, Lance
  See Lantz, Francess L(in)
Franklin, Madeleine
  See L'Engle, Madeleine
Franklin, Madeleine L'Engle
  See L'Engle, Madeleine

Franklin, Madeleine L'Engle Camp
  See L'Engle, Madeleine
Franklin, Max
  See Deming, Richard
Franklin, Steve
  See Stevens, Franklin
Franson, Leanne R. 1963- *111*
Franson, Scott E. 1966- *192*
Franzen, Nils-Olof 1916- *10*
Frascino, Edward *48*
  Brief entry *33*
  See also SAAS *9*
Frasconi, Antonio 1919- *131*
  Earlier sketches in SATA *6, 53*
  See also SAAS *11*
Fraser, Betty
  See Fraser, Elizabeth Marr
Fraser, Elizabeth Marr 1928- *31*
Fraser, Eric (George) 1902-1983 .... *38*
Fraser, Mary Ann 1959- *137*
  Earlier sketch in SATA *76*
  See also SAAS *23*
Fraser, Wynnette (McFaddin) 1925- *90*
Frasier, Debra 1953- *182*
  Earlier sketches in SATA *69, 112*
Fraustino, Lisa Rowe 1961- *146*
  Autobiography Feature *146*
  Earlier sketch in SATA *84*
Frazee, Marla 1958- *187*
  Earlier sketches in SATA *105, 151*
Frazetta, Frank 1928- *58*
Frazier, Craig 1955- *177*
Frazier, Neta (Osborn) Lohnes 1890-1990 ..... *7*
Frazier, Sundee T.
  See Frazier, Sundee Tucker
Frazier, Sundee Tucker 1968- *198*
Frederic, Mike
  See Cox, William R(obert)
Fredericks, Anthony D. 1947- *113*
Freed, Alvyn M. 1913-1993 .... *22*
Freedman, Benedict 1919- *27*
Freedman, Claire *185*
Freedman, Deborah 1960- *191*
Freedman, Jeff 1953- *90*
Freedman, Nancy 1920- *27*
Freedman, Russell 1929- *175*
  Earlier sketches in SATA *16, 71, 123*
  See also CLR *71*
Freedman, Russell Bruce
  See Freedman, Russell
Freeman, Barbara C. 1906-1999 .... *28*
Freeman, Barbara Constance
  See Freeman, Barbara C.
Freeman, Bill
  See Freeman, William Bradford
Freeman, Don 1908-1978 .... *17*
  See also CLR *90*
Freeman, Ira Maximilian 1905-1987 .... *21*
Freeman, Lucy (Greenbaum) 1916-2004 ...... *24*
Freeman, Mae 1907-1985 .... *25*
Freeman, Mae Blacker
  See Freeman, Mae
Freeman, Marcia S. 1937- *102*
Freeman, Martha 1956- *152*
  Earlier sketch in SATA *101*
Freeman, Nancy 1932- *61*
Freeman, Peter J.
  See Calvert, Patricia
Freeman, Sarah (Caroline) 1940- *66*
Freeman, Tor 1977- *164*
Freeman, VicToria
  See Freeman, Tor
Freeman, William Bradford 1938- *58*
  Brief entry *48*
Fregosi, Claudia (Anne Marie) 1946- *24*
French, Allen 1870-1946
  See YABC *1*
French, Dorothy Kayser 1926- *5*

French, Fiona 1944- *132*
  Earlier sketches in SATA *6, 75*
  See also CLR *37*
  See also SAAS *21*
French, Jackie *186*
  Autobiography Feature *139*
  Earlier sketches in SATA *108, 139*
  See French, Jackie Anne
  and French, Jacqueline Anne
French, Kathryn
  See Mosesson, Gloria R(ubin)
French, Martin *176*
French, Michael 1944- *49*
  Brief entry *38*
French, Paul
  See Asimov, Isaac
French, Simon 1957- *147*
  Earlier sketch in SATA *86*
French, Vivian *165*
Frenette, Liza *126*
Freschet, Gina 1960- *175*
  Earlier sketch in SATA *139*
Frewer, Glyn (M.) 1931- *11*
Frey, Darcy *98*
Freymann, Saxton 1958(?)- *178*
Freymann-Weyr, (Rhoda) Garret (Michaela)
  1965- *145*
Frick, C. H.
  See Irwin, Constance (H.) Frick
Frick, Constance
  See Irwin, Constance (H.) Frick
Fricke, Aaron 1962- *89*
Fridell, Ron 1943- *124*
Fried, Janice *197*
Friedlander, Joanne K(ohn) 1930- *9*
Friedman, Aimee 1979- *189*
Friedman, D. Dina 1957- *180*
Friedman, Debra 1955- *150*
Friedman, Estelle (Ehrenwald) 1920- *7*
Friedman, Frieda 1905- *43*
Friedman, Ina R(osen) 1926- *136*
  Brief entry *41*
  Earlier sketch in SATA *49*
Friedman, Jerrold David
  See Gerrold, David
Friedman, Judi 1935- *59*
Friedman, Laurie 1964- *179*
  Earlier sketch in SATA *138*
Friedman, Marvin 1930- *42*
  Brief entry *33*
Friedman, Robin 1968- *162*
Friedmann, Stan 1953- *80*
Friedrich, Otto (Alva) 1929-1995 .... *33*
Friedrich, Priscilla 1927- *39*
Friend, Catherine 1957(?)- *194*
Friend, David Michael 1975- *195*
Friend, Natasha 1972- *184*
Friendlich, Dick
  See Friendlich, Richard J.
Friendlich, Richard J. 1909- *11*
Friermood, Elisabeth Hamilton 1903-1992 .... *5*
Friesen, Bernice (Sarah Anne) 1966- *105*
Friesen, Gayle 1960- *109*
Friesner, Esther M. 1951- *168*
  Earlier sketch in SATA *71*
Friis-Baastad, Babbis Ellinor 1921-1970 .... *7*
Frimmer, Steven 1928- *31*
Frischmuth, Barbara 1941- *114*
Friskey, Margaret (Richards) 1901-1995 .... *5*
Fritts, Mary Bahr
  See Bahr, Mary (Madelyn)
Fritz, Jean (Guttery) 1915- *163*
  Autobiography Feature *122*
  Earlier sketches in SATA *1, 29, 72, 119*
  See also CLR *96*
  See also SAAS *2*
Froehlich, Margaret W(alden) 1930- *56*
Frois, Jeanne 1953- *73*
Froissart, Jean 1338(?)-1410(?) *28*
Froman, Elizabeth Hull 1920-1975 .... *10*
Froman, Robert (Winslow) 1917- *8*

Fromm, Lilo 1928- *29*
Frommer, Harvey 1937- *41*
Frost, A(rthur) B(urdett) 1851-1928 .... *19*
Frost, Elizabeth
　　See Frost-Knappman, Elizabeth
Frost, Erica
　　See Supraner, Robyn
Frost, Helen 1949- *194*
　　Autobiography Feature *194*
　　Earlier sketches in SATA *157, 183*
Frost, Helen Marie
　　See Frost, Helen
Frost, Lesley 1899-1983 .... *14*
　　Obituary *34*
Frost, Robert 1874-1963 .... *14*
　　See also CLR *67*
Frost, Robert Lee
　　See Frost, Robert
Frost, Shelley 1960- *138*
Frost-Knappman, Elizabeth 1943- *179*
Froud, Brian 1947- *150*
Fry, Annette R(iley) *89*
Fry, Christopher 1907-2005 .... *66*
Fry, Edward Bernard 1925- *35*
Fry, Rosalie Kingsmill 1911-1992 .... *3*
　　See also SAAS *11*
Fry, Virginia Lynn 1952- *95*
Frye, Sally
　　See Moore, Elaine
Fuchs, Bernie 1932- *162*
　　Earlier sketch in SATA *95*
Fuchs, Erich 1916- *6*
Fuchshuber, Annegert 1940- *43*
Fuerst, Jeffrey B. 1956- *143*
Fuertes, Gloria 1918-1998 .... *115*
Fuge, Charles 1966- *144*
　　Earlier sketch in SATA *74*
Fujikawa, Gyo 1908-1998 .... *76*
　　Brief entry *30*
　　Obituary *110*
　　Earlier sketch in SATA *39*
　　See also CLR *25*
　　See also SAAS *16*
Fujita, Tamao 1905-1999 .... *7*
Fujiwara, Kim 1957- *81*
Fujiwara, Michiko 1946- *15*
Fuka, Vladimir 1926-1977
　　Obituary *27*
Fulcher, Jennifer
　　See Westwood, Jennifer
Fuller, Catherine Leuthold 1916- *9*
Fuller, Edmund (Maybank) 1914- *21*
Fuller, Iola
　　See McCoy, Iola Fuller
Fuller, John G(rant, Jr.) 1913-1990 .... *65*
Fuller, Kathleen
　　See Gottfried, Theodore Mark
Fuller, Lois Hamilton 1915- *11*
Fuller, Margaret
　　See Ossoli, Sarah Margaret (Fuller)
Fuller, Maud
　　See Petersham, Maud (Sylvia Fuller)
Fuller, Roy (Broadbent) 1912-1991 .... *87*
Fuller, Sarah Margaret
　　See Ossoli, Sarah Margaret (Fuller)
Fuller, Sarah Margaret
　　See Ossoli, Sarah Margaret (Fuller)
Fults, John Lee 1932- *33*
Funk, Thompson 1911- *7*
Funk, Tom
　　See Funk, Thompson
Funke, Cornelia 1958- *174*
　　Earlier sketch in SATA *154*
Funke, Cornelia Caroline
　　See Funke, Cornelia
Funke, Lewis 1912-1992 .... *11*
Fuqua, Jonathon Scott 1966- *141*
Furbee, Mary R.
　　See Furbee, Mary Rodd
Furbee, Mary Rodd 1954- *138*
Furchgott, Terry 1948- *29*

Furlong, Monica (Mavis) 1930-2003 .... *86*
　　Obituary *142*
Furman, Gertrude Lerner Kerman 1909- *21*
Furniss, Tim 1948- *49*
Furrow, Robert 1985- *172*
Furukawa, Toshi 1924- *24*
Fusillo, Archimede 1962- *137*
Futcher, Jane P. 1947- *76*
Futehali, Zahida
　　See Whitaker, Zai
Fyleman, Rose (Amy) 1877-1957 .... *21*
Fyson, Jenny Grace
　　See Fyson, J.G.
Fyson, J.G. 1904-1998 .... *42*

G

Gaan, Margaret 1914- *65*
Gaber, Susan 1956- *169*
　　Earlier sketch in SATA *115*
Gaberman, Judie Angell
　　See Angell, Judie
Gabhart, Ann
　　See Gabhart, Ann H.
Gabhart, Ann H. 1947- *75*
Gable, Brian 1949- *195*
Gabler, Mirko 1951- *77*
Gabriel, Adriana
　　See Rojany, Lisa
Gabrys, Ingrid Schubert
　　See Schubert-Gabrys, Ingrid
Gackenbach, Dick 1927- *79*
　　Brief entry *30*
　　Earlier sketch in SATA *48*
Gadd, Jeremy 1949- *116*
Gaddis, Vincent H. 1913-1997 .... *35*
Gadler, Steve J. 1905-1985 .... *36*
Gaeddert, Lou Ann (Bigge) 1931- *103*
　　Earlier sketch in SATA *20*
Gaeddert, Louann
　　See Gaeddert, Lou Ann (Bigge)
Gaer, Joseph 1897-1969 .... *118*
Gaer, Yossef
　　See Gaer, Joseph
Gaetz, Dayle Campbell 1947- : *138*
Gaffney, Timothy R. 1951- *170*
　　Earlier sketch in SATA *69*
Gaffron, Norma (Bondeson) 1931- *97*
Gag, Flavia 1907-1979
　　Obituary *24*
Gag, Wanda (Hazel) 1893-1946 .... *100*
　　See also YABC *1*
　　See also CLR *4*
Gage, Brian *162*
Gage, Wilson
　　See Steele, Mary Q(uintard Govan)
Gagliano, Eugene M. 1946- *150*
Gagliardo, Ruth Garver 1895(?)-1980
　　Obituary *22*
Gagnon, Cecile 1936- *58*
Gaiman, Neil 1960- *197*
　　Earlier sketches in SATA *85, 146*
　　See also CLR *109*
Gaiman, Neil Richard
　　See Gaiman, Neil
Gainer, Cindy 1962- *74*
Gaines, Ernest J. 1933- *86*
　　See also CLR *62*
Gaines, Ernest James
　　See Gaines, Ernest J.
Gaither, Gloria 1942- *127*
Gal, Laszlo 1933- *96*
　　Brief entry *32*
　　Earlier sketch in SATA *52*
　　See also CLR *61*
Galbraith, Kathryn O(sebold) 1945- *85*

Galdone, Paul 1907(?)-1986 .... *66*
　　Obituary *49*
　　Earlier sketch in SATA *17*
　　See also CLR *16*
Galinsky, Ellen 1942- *23*
Gall, Chris 1961- *176*
Gallagher, Diana G. 1946- *153*
Gallagher, Lurlene Nora
　　See McDaniel, Lurlene
Gallant, Roy A(rthur) 1924- *110*
　　Earlier sketches in SATA *4, 68*
　　See also CLR *30*
Gallardo, Evelyn 1948- *78*
Gallaz, Christophe 1948- *162*
　　See also CLR *126*
Gallego Garcia, Laura 1977- *173*
Gallico, Paul (William) 1897-1976 .... *13*
Gallo, Donald R. 1938- *112*
　　Autobiography Feature *104*
Gallo, Donald Robert
　　See Gallo, Donald R.
Galloway, Owateka (S.) 1981- *121*
Galloway, Priscilla 1930- *112*
　　Earlier sketch in SATA *66*
Gallup, Joan 1957- *128*
Galouchko, Annouchka Gravel 1960- *95*
Galt, Thomas Franklin, Jr. 1908-1989 .... *5*
Galt, Tom
　　See Galt, Thomas Franklin, Jr.
Galvin, Matthew R. 1950- *93*
Galvin, Matthew Reppert
　　See Galvin, Matthew R.
Gamble, Kim 1952- *183*
　　Earlier sketches in SATA *81, 124*
Gambrell, Jamey *82*
Gamerman, Martha 1941- *15*
Gammell, Stephen 1943- *128*
　　Earlier sketches in SATA *53, 81*
　　See also CLR *83*
Ganly, Helen (Mary) 1940- *56*
Gannett, Ruth Chrisman (Arens)
　　1896-1979 .... *33*
Gannett, Ruth Stiles 1923- *3*
Gannon, Robert Haines 1931- *8*
Gano, Lila 1949- *76*
Gans, Roma 1894-1996 .... *45*
　　Obituary *93*
Gant, Matthew
　　See Hano, Arnold
Gantner, Susan (Verble) 1939- *63*
Gantos, Jack 1951- *169*
　　Earlier sketches in SATA *20, 81, 119*
　　See also CLR *85*
Gantos, John Bryan, Jr.
　　See Gantos, Jack
Ganz, Yaffa 1938- *61*
　　Brief entry *52*
Garafano, Marie 1942- *84*
Garant, Andre J. 1968- *123*
Garbe, Ruth Moore
　　See Moore, Ruth (Ellen)
Garber, Esther
　　See Lee, Tanith
Garcia, Emma 1969- *198*
Garcia, Yolanda P. 1952- *113*
Garcia, Yolanda Pacheco
　　See Garcia, Yolanda P.
Gard, Janice
　　See Latham, Jean Lee
Gard, Joyce
　　See Reeves, Joyce
Gard, Robert Edward 1910-1992 .... *18*
　　Obituary *74*
Gard, (Sanford) Wayne 1899-1986
　　Obituary *49*
Gardam, Jane 1928- *130*
　　Brief entry *28*
　　Earlier sketches in SATA *39, 76*
　　See also CLR *12*
　　See also SAAS *9*

Gardam, Jane Mary
  See Gardam, Jane
Gardella, Tricia 1944- 96
Garden, Nancy 1938- 147
  Autobiography Feature 147
  Earlier sketches in SATA *12, 77, 114*
  See also CLR *51*
  See also SAAS *8*
Gardiner, John Reynolds 1944-2006 64
  Obituary 174
Gardiner, Lindsey 1971- 144
Gardner, Craig Shaw 1949- 99
Gardner, Dic
  See Gardner, Richard (M.)
Gardner, Graham 159
Gardner, Hugh 1910-1986
  Obituary 49
Gardner, Jane Mylum 1946- 83
Gardner, Jeanne LeMonnier 1925- 5
Gardner, John, Jr. 1933-1982 40
  Obituary 31
Gardner, John Champlin, Jr.
  See Gardner, John, Jr.
Gardner, John E(dward) 1917- 192
Gardner, Lyn 192
Gardner, Martin 1914- 142
  Earlier sketch in SATA *16*
Gardner, Miriam
  See Bradley, Marion Zimmer
Gardner, Richard (M.) 1931- 24
Gardner, Richard A(lan) 1931-2003 13
  Obituary 144
Gardner, Sally 177
Gardner, Sandra 1940- 70
Gardner, Scot 1968- 143
Gardner, Sheldon 1934- 33
Gardner, Ted
  See Gardner, Theodore Roosevelt II
Gardner, Theodore Roosevelt
  See Gardner, Theodore Roosevelt II
Gardner, Theodore Roosevelt II 1934- 84
Garelick, May 1910-1989 19
Garfield, James B. 1881-1984 6
  Obituary 38
Garfield, Leon 1921-1996 76
  Obituary 90
  Earlier sketches in SATA *1, 32*
  See also CLR *21*
Garfinkle, Debra L.
  See Garfinkle, D.L.
Garfinkle, D.L. 187
Garis, Howard R(oger) 1873-1962 13
Garland, Mark 1953- 79
Garland, Mark A.
  See Garland, Mark
Garland, Michael 1952- 168
Garland, Sarah 1944- 135
  Earlier sketch in SATA *62*
Garland, Sherry 1948- 145
  Autobiography Feature 145
  Earlier sketches in SATA *73, 114*
Garner, Alan 1934- 69
  Autobiography Feature 108
  Earlier sketch in SATA *18*
  See also CLR *130*
Garner, David 1958- 78
Garner, Eleanor Ramrath 1930- 122
Garner, James Finn 1960(?)- 92
Garnet, A. H.
  See Slote, Alfred
Garnett, Eve C. R. 1900-1991 3
  Obituary 70
Garofoli, Viviana 1970- 186
Garou, Louis P.
  See Bowkett, Stephen
Garraty, John A. 1920-2007 23
  Obituary 189
Garraty, John Arthur
  See Garraty, John A.
Garren, Devorah-Leah
  See Devorah-Leah

Garret, Maxwell R. 1917- 39
Garretson, Victoria Diane 1945- 44
Garrett, Helen 1895- 21
Garrett, (Gordon) Randall (Phillip)
  1927-1987 180
Garrett, Richard 1920- 82
Garrigue, Sheila 1931- 21
Garrison, Barbara 1931- 163
  Earlier sketch in SATA *19*
Garrison, Frederick
  See Sinclair, Upton
Garrison, Mary 1952- 146
Garrison, Peter
  See Gardner, Craig Shaw
Garrison, Webb B(lack) 1919-2000 25
Garrity, Jennifer Johnson 1961- 124
Garrity, Linda K. 1947- 128
Garsee, Jeannine 199
Garst, Doris Shannon 1894-1981 1
Garst, Shannon
  See Garst, Doris Shannon
Garth, Will
  See Hamilton, Edmond
  and Kuttner, Henry
Garthwaite, Marion H(ook) 1893-1981 7
Garton, Malinda D(ean) (?)-1976
  Obituary 26
Garvie, Maureen 1944- 175
Garvie, Maureen McCallum
  See Garvie, Maureen
Garza, Carmen Lomas 1948- 182
Garza, Xavier 184
Gascoigne, Bamber 1935- 62
Gaskins, Pearl Fuyo 1957- 134
Gasperini, Jim 1952- 54
  Brief entry 49
Gater, Dilys 1944- 41
Gates, Doris 1901-1987 34
  Obituary 54
  Earlier sketch in SATA *1*
  See also SAAS *1*
Gates, Frieda 1933- 26
Gates, Susan 1950- 153
Gates, Viola R. 1931- 101
Gathorne-Hardy, Jonathan G. 1933- 124
  Earlier sketch in SATA *26*
Gatti, Anne 1952- 103
Gatty, Juliana Horatia
  See Ewing, Juliana (Horatia Gatty)
Gauch, Patricia Lee 1934- 80
  Earlier sketch in SATA *26*
  See also CLR *56*
  See also SAAS *21*
Gaudasinska, Elzbieta 1943- 190
Gaul, Randy 1959- 63
Gault, Clare 1925- 36
Gault, Frank 1926-1982 36
  Brief entry 30
Gault, William Campbell 1910-1995 8
Gauthier, Gail 1953- 160
  Earlier sketch in SATA *118*
Gaver, Becky
  See Gaver, Rebecca
Gaver, Rebecca 1952- 20
Gavin, Jamila 1941- 125
  Earlier sketch in SATA *96*
Gay, Amelia
  See Hogarth, Grace (Weston Allen)
Gay, Francis
  See Gee, H(erbert) L(eslie)
Gay, Kathlyn 1930- 144
  Earlier sketch in SATA *9*
Gay, Marie-Louise 1952- 179
  Earlier sketches in SATA *68, 126*
  See also CLR *27*
  See also SAAS *21*
Gay, Michel 1947- 162
Gay, Zhenya 1906-1978 19
Gaze, Gillian
  See Barklem, Jill

Gear, Kathleen M. O'Neal
  See Gear, Kathleen O'Neal
Gear, Kathleen O'Neal 1954- 166
  Earlier sketch in SATA *71*
Gear, W. Michael 1955- 166
  Earlier sketch in SATA *71*
Geary, Rick 1946- 142
Geason, Susan 1946- 122
Gedalof, Robin
  See McGrath, Robin
Gedge, Pauline (Alice) 1945- 101
Gee, H(erbert) L(eslie) 1901-1977
  Obituary 26
Gee, Maurice 1931- 101
  Earlier sketch in SATA *46*
  See also CLR *56*
Gee, Maurice Gough
  See Gee, Maurice
Geehan, Wayne (E.) 1947- 107
Geer, Charles 1922- 42
  Brief entry 32
Geeslin, Campbell 1925- 163
  Earlier sketch in SATA *107*
Gehman, Mary W. 1923- 86
Gehr, Mary 1910(?)-1997 32
  Obituary 99
Geipel, Eileen 1932- 30
Geis, Alissa Imre 1976- 189
Geis, Darlene Stern 1918(?)-1999 7
  Obituary 111
Geisel, Helen 1898-1967 26
Geisel, Theodor Seuss 1904-1991 100
  Obituary 67
  Earlier sketches in SATA *1, 28, 75*
  See also CLR *100*
Geisert, Arthur 1941- 171
  Brief entry 52
  Earlier sketches in SATA *56, 92, 133*
  See also CLR *87*
  See also SAAS *23*
Geisert, Arthur Frederick
  See Geisert, Arthur
Geisert, Bonnie 1942- 165
  Earlier sketch in SATA *92*
Geist, Ken 191
Geldart, William 1936- 15
Gelinas, Paul J. 1904-1996 10
Gellis, Roberta 1927- 128
Gellis, Roberta Leah Jacobs
  See Gellis, Roberta
Gellman, Marc 112
Gelman, Amy 1961- 72
Gelman, Jan 1963- 58
Gelman, Rita Golden 1937- 131
  Brief entry 51
  Earlier sketch in SATA *84*
Gelman, Steve 1934- 3
Gemming, Elizabeth 1932- 11
Gendel, Evelyn W. 1916(?)-1977
  Obituary 27
Gennaro, Joseph F(rancis), Jr. 1924- 53
Gentile, Petrina 1969- 91
Gentle, Mary 1956- 48
Gentleman, David (William) 1930- 7
Geoghegan, Adrienne 1962- 143
George, Barbara
  See Katz, Bobbi
George, Emily
  See Katz, Bobbi
George, Gail
  See Katz, Bobbi
George, Jean
  See George, Jean Craighead
George, Jean Craighead 1919- 170
  Earlier sketches in SATA *2, 68, 124*
  See also CLR *136*
George, John L(othar) 1916- 2
George, Kristine O'Connell 1954- 156
  Earlier sketch in SATA *110*
George, Lindsay Barrett 1952- 155
  Earlier sketch in SATA *95*

George, S(idney) C(harles) 1898- *11*
George, Sally
  See Orr, Wendy
George, Twig C. 1950- *114*
George, W(illiam) Lloyd 1900(?)-1975
  Obituary *30*
Georgiou, Constantine 1927- *7*
Georgiou, Theo
  See Odgers, Sally Farrell
Geraghty, Paul 1959- *130*
Gerard, Jean Ignace Isidore 1803-1847 .... *45*
Geras, Adele 1944- *180*
  Autobiography Feature *180*
  Earlier sketches in SATA *23, 87, 129, 173*
  See also SAAS *21*
Geras, Adele Daphne Weston
  See Geras, Adele
Gerber, Merrill Joan 1938- *170*
  Autobiography Feature *170*
  Earlier sketches in SATA *64, 127*
Gerber, Perren 1933- *104*
Gerberg, Mort 1931- *64*
Gergely, Tibor 1900-1978 .... *54*
  Obituary *20*
Geringer, Laura 1948- *164*
  Earlier sketches in SATA *29, 94*
Gerler, William R(obert) 1917-1996 .... *47*
Gerrard, Jean 1933- *51*
Gerrard, Roy 1935-1997 .... *90*
  Brief entry *45*
  Obituary *99*
  Earlier sketch in SATA *47*
  See also CLR *23*
Gerritsen, Paula 1956- *177*
Gerrold, David 1944- *144*
  Earlier sketch in SATA *66*
Gershator, David 1937- *180*
Gershator, Phillis 1942- *188*
  Earlier sketches in SATA *90, 158*
Gershon, Dann 1955- *187*
Gershon, Gina 1962- *187*
Gerson, Corinne 1927- *37*
Gerson, Mary-Joan *136*
  Earlier sketch in SATA *79*
Gerson, Noel Bertram 1914-1988 .... *22*
  Obituary *60*
Gerstein, Mordicai 1935- *178*
  Brief entry *36*
  Earlier sketches in SATA *47, 81, 142*
  See also CLR *102*
Gertridge, Allison 1967- *132*
Gervais, Bernadette 1959- *80*
Gervay, Susanne *183*
Gesner, Clark 1938-2002 .... *40*
  Obituary *143*
Gessner, Lynne 1919- *16*
Geter, Tyrone *150*
Getz, David 1957- *91*
Getzinger, Donna 1968- *128*
Gevirtz, Eliezer 1950- *49*
Gevry, Claudine *188*
Gewe, Raddory
  See Gorey, Edward (St. John)
Ghan, Linda (R.) 1947- *77*
Ghent, Natale 1962- *148*
Gherman, Beverly 1934- *123*
  Earlier sketch in SATA *68*
Ghigna, Charles 1946- *153*
  Earlier sketch in SATA *108*
Giacobbe, Beppe 1953- *174*
Giambastiani, Kurt R. A. 1958- *141*
Giannini, Enzo 1946- *68*
Gibbons, Alan 1953- *198*
  Earlier sketch in SATA *124*
Gibbons, Faye 1938- *103*
  Earlier sketch in SATA *65*
Gibbons, Gail 1944- *160*
  Earlier sketches in SATA *23, 72, 104*
  See also CLR *8*
  See also SAAS *12*

Gibbons, Gail Gretchen
  See Gibbons, Gail
Gibbons, Kaye 1960- *117*
Gibbs, Adrea 1960- *126*
Gibbs, Alonzo (Lawrence) 1915-1992 .... *5*
Gibbs, (Cecilia) May 1877-1969
  Obituary *27*
Gibbs, Tony
  See Gibbs, Wolcott, Jr.
Gibbs, Wolcott, Jr. 1935- *40*
Giblin, James Cross 1933- *197*
  Earlier sketches in SATA *33, 75, 122*
  See also CLR *29*
  See also SAAS *12*
Gibson, Andrew (William) 1949- *72*
Gibson, Betty 1911- *75*
Gibson, Jo
  See Fluke, Joanne
Gibson, Josephine
  See Hine, Sesyle Joslin
  and Hine, Al(fred Blakelee)
Gibson, William 1914-2008 .... *66*
  Obituary *199*
Gibson, William Ford
  See Gibson, William
Gidal, Nachum
  See Gidal, Tim Nachum
Gidal, Sonia (Epstein) 1922- *2*
Gidal, Tim Nachum 1909-1996 .... *2*
Gidalewitsch, Nachum
  See Gidal, Tim Nachum
Gideon, Melanie 1963- *175*
Giegling, John A(llan) 1935- *17*
Gifaldi, David 1950- *76*
Giff, Patricia Reilly 1935- *160*
  Earlier sketches in SATA *33, 70, 121*
Giffard, Hannah 1962- *83*
Gifford, Clive 1966- *198*
Gifford, Griselda 1931- *171*
  Earlier sketch in SATA *42*
Gifford, Kerri 1961- *91*
Gifford, Peggy 1952- *191*
Gilbert, Ann
  See Taylor, Ann
Gilbert, Anne Yvonne 1951- *185*
Gilbert, Barbara Snow 1954- *97*
Gilbert, Catherine
  See Murdock, Catherine Gilbert
Gilbert, Frances
  See Collings, Gillian
Gilbert, Harriett 1948- *30*
Gilbert, (Agnes) Joan (Sewell) 1931- *10*
Gilbert, John (Raphael) 1926- *36*
Gilbert, Nan
  See Gilbertson, Mildred Geiger
Gilbert, Roby Goodale 1966- *90*
Gilbert, Ruth Gallard Ainsworth
  See Ainsworth, Ruth (Gallard)
Gilbert, Sara (Dulaney) 1943- *82*
  Earlier sketch in SATA *11*
Gilbert, Sheri L. *157*
Gilbert, Suzie 1956- *97*
Gilbert, W(illiam) S(chwenck) 1836-1911 ... *36*
Gilbert, Yvonne
  See Gilbert, Anne Yvonne
Gilbertson, Mildred Geiger 1908-1988 .... *2*
Gilbreath, Alice 1921- *12*
Gilbreth, Frank B(unker), Jr. 1911-2001 .... *2*
Gilchrist, Jan Spivey 1949- *130*
  Earlier sketch in SATA *72*
Gilden, Mel 1947- *97*
Giles, Gail *196*
  Earlier sketch in SATA *152*
Gilfond, Henry *2*
Gilge, Jeanette 1924- *22*
Gili, Phillida 1944- *70*
Gill, Derek (Lewis Theodore) 1919-1997 ...... *9*
Gill, Margery Jean 1925- *22*
Gill, Shelley *176*
Gill, Stephen 1932- *63*
Gillespie, Carol Ann 1951- *158*

Gillett, Mary (Bledsoe) *7*
Gillette, Henry Sampson 1915- *14*
Gillette, J(an) Lynett 1946- *103*
Gilley, Jeremy 1969- *174*
Gillham, Bill
  See Gillham, W(illiam) E(dwin) C(harles)
Gillham, W(illiam) E(dwin) C(harles)
  1936- *42*
Gilliam, Stan 1946- *39*
  Brief entry *35*
Gilliland, Alexis A(rnaldus) 1931- *72*
Gilliland, (Cleburne) Hap 1918- *92*
Gilliland, Judith Heide *180*
Gillmor, Don 1954- *127*
Gilman, Dorothy 1923- *5*
Gilman, Esther 1925- *15*
Gilman, Laura Anne *178*
Gilman, Phoebe 1940-2002 .... *104*
  Obituary *141*
  Earlier sketch in SATA *58*
Gilmore, Iris 1900-1982 .... *22*
Gilmore, Kate 1931- *87*
Gilmore, Mary (Jean Cameron) 1865-1962 . *49*
Gilmore, Susan 1954- *59*
Gilpin, Stephen *177*
Gilroy, Beryl (Agatha) 1924- *80*
Gilson, Barbara
  See Gilson, Charles James Louis
Gilson, Charles James Louis 1878-1943
  See YABC *2*
Gilson, Jamie 1933- *176*
  Brief entry *34*
  Earlier sketches in SATA *37, 91*
Ginsburg, Mirra 1909-2000 .... *92*
  Earlier sketch in SATA *6*
  See also CLR *45*
Giovanni, Nikki 1943- *107*
  Earlier sketch in SATA *24*
  See also CLR *73*
Giovanni, Yolanda Cornelia
  See Giovanni, Nikki
Giovanni, Yolande Cornelia
  See Giovanni, Nikki
Giovanni, Yolande Cornelia, Jr.
  See Giovanni, Nikki
Giovanopoulos, Paul (Arthur) 1939- *7*
Gipson, Fred(erick Benjamin) 1908-1973 ...... *2*
  Obituary *24*
Girard, Linda (Walvoord) 1942- *41*
Girion, Barbara 1937- *78*
  Earlier sketch in SATA *26*
  See also SAAS *14*
Girouard, Patrick 1957- *155*
Girzone, Joseph F. 1930- *76*
Girzone, Joseph Francis
  See Girzone, Joseph F.
Gise, Joanne
  See Mattern, Joanne
Gittings, Jo (Grenville) Manton 1919- *3*
Gittings, Robert (William Victor) 1911-1992 . *6*
  Obituary *70*
Givens, Janet E(aton) 1932- *60*
Givner, Joan 1936- *171*
Givner, Joan Mary
  See Givner, Joan
Gladstone, Eve
  See Werner, Herma
Gladstone, Gary 1935- *12*
Gladstone, M(yron) J. 1923- *37*
Glanville, Brian (Lester) 1931- *42*
Glanzman, Louis S. 1922- *36*
Glaser, Byron 1954- *154*
Glaser, Dianne E(lizabeth) 1937- *50*
  Brief entry *31*
Glaser, Isabel Joshlin 1929- *94*
Glaser, Milton 1929- *151*
  Earlier sketch in SATA *11*
Glaser, Shirley *151*
Glaspell, Susan 1882(?)-1948
  See YABC *2*

Glass, Andrew 1949- *150*
  Brief entry *46*
  Earlier sketch in SATA *90*
Glass, Linzi *175*
Glass, Linzi Alex
  See Glass, Linzi
Glasscock, Amnesia
  See Steinbeck, John (Ernst)
Glassman, Bruce 1961- *76*
Glauber, Uta (Heil) 1936- *17*
Glazer, Thomas (Zachariah) 1914-2003 .... *9*
Glazer, Tom
  See Glazer, Thomas (Zachariah)
Gleasner, Diana (Cottle) 1936- *29*
Gleason, Judith 1929- *24*
Gleason, Katherine (A.) 1960- *104*
Gleeson, Libby 1950- *142*
  Autobiography Feature *142*
  Earlier sketches in SATA *82, 118*
Gleiter, Jan 1947- *111*
Gleitzman, Morris 1953- *156*
  Earlier sketch in SATA *88*
  See also CLR *88*
Glen, Maggie 1944- *88*
Glendinning, Richard 1917-1988 .... *24*
Glendinning, Sally
  See Glendinning, Sara W(ilson)
Glendinning, Sara W(ilson) 1913-1993 .... *24*
Glenn, John W. *195*
Glenn, Mel 1943- *93*
  Brief entry *45*
  Earlier sketch in SATA *51*
  See also CLR *51*
Glenn, Patricia Brown 1953- *86*
Glenn, Sharlee *159*
Glenn, Sharlee Mullins
  See Glenn, Sharlee
Glennon, Karen M. 1946- *85*
Gles, Margaret Breitmaier 1940- *22*
Glick, Carl (Cannon) 1890-1971 .... *14*
Glick, Ruth (Burtnick) 1942- *125*
Glick, Virginia Kirkus 1893-1980
  Obituary *23*
Gliewe, Unada (Grace) 1927- *3*
Glimmerveen, Ulco 1958- *85*
Glines, Carroll V(ane), Jr. 1920- *19*
Gliori, Debi 1959- *189*
  Earlier sketches in SATA *72, 138*
Globe, Leah Ain 1900- *41*
Glori Ann
  See Blakely, Gloria
Glovach, Linda 1947- *105*
  Earlier sketch in SATA *7*
Glover, Denis (James Matthews) 1912-1980 . *7*
Glubok, Shirley (Astor) *146*
  Autobiography Feature *146*
  Earlier sketches in SATA *6, 68*
  See also CLR *1*
  See also SAAS *7*
Gluck, Felix 1923-1981
  Obituary *25*
Glyman, Caroline A. 1967- *103*
Glynne-Jones, William 1907-1977 .... *11*
Gobbato, Imero 1923- *39*
Gobbletree, Richard
  See Quackenbush, Robert M(ead)
Goble, Dorothy *26*
Goble, Paul 1933- *131*
  Earlier sketches in SATA *25, 69*
  See also CLR *21*
Goble, Warwick (?)-1943 .... *46*
Godden, (Margaret) Rumer 1907-1998 .... *36*
  Obituary *109*
  Earlier sketch in SATA *3*
  See also CLR *20*
  See also SAAS *12*
Gode, Alexander
  See Gode von Aesch, Alexander (Gottfried Friedrich)
Gode von Aesch, Alexander (Gottfried Friedrich) 1906-1970 .... *14*

Godfrey, Jane
  See Bowden, Joan Chase
Godfrey, Martyn
  See Godfrey, Martyn N.
  and Godfrey, Martyn N.
Godfrey, Martyn N. 1949-2000 .... *95*
  See also CLR *57*
Godfrey, William
  See Youd, (Christopher) Samuel
Godin, Celia (Marilyn) 1948- *145*
  Earlier sketch in SATA *66*
Godon, Ingrid 1958- *186*
Godwin, Laura 1956- *179*
Godwin, Sam
  See Pirotta, Saviour
Goedecke, Christopher (John) 1951- *81*
Goekler, Susan
  See Wooley, Susan Frelick
Goertzen, Glenda *172*
Goettel, Elinor 1930- *12*
Goetz, Delia 1898-1996 .... *22*
  Obituary *91*
Goffe, Toni 1936- *61*
Goffstein, Brooke
  See Goffstein, M(arilyn) B(rooke)
Goffstein, M(arilyn) B(rooke) 1940- *70*
  Earlier sketch in SATA *8*
  See also CLR *3*
Goforth, Ellen
  See Francis, Dorothy
Gogol, Sara 1948-2004 .... *80*
Goh, Chan Hon 1969- *145*
Going, Kelly L.
  See Going, K.L.
Going, Kelly Louise
  See Going, K.L.
Going, K.L. *199*
  Earlier sketch in SATA *156*
Golann, Cecil Paige 1921-1995 .... *11*
Golbin, Andree 1923- *15*
Gold, Alison Leslie 1945- *104*
Gold, Bernice *150*
Gold, Phyllis
  See Goldberg, Phyllis
Gold, Robert S(tanley) 1924- *63*
Gold, Sharlya *9*
Gold, Susan
  See Gold, Susan Dudley
Gold, Susan Dudley 1949- *147*
Goldberg, Grace 1956- *78*
Goldberg, Herbert S. 1926- *25*
Goldberg, Jacob 1943- *94*
Goldberg, Jake
  See Goldberg, Jacob
Goldberg, Phyllis 1941- *21*
Goldberg, Stan J. 1939- *26*
Goldberg, Susan 1948- *71*
Goldberg, Whoopi 1955- *119*
Goldberger, Judith M. 1948- *80*
Goldblatt, Stacey 1969(?)- *191*
Golden, Christie 1963- *167*
  Earlier sketch in SATA *116*
Goldentyer, Debra 1960- *84*
Goldfeder, Cheryl
  See Pahz, Cheryl Suzanne
Goldfeder, James
  See Pahz, James Alon
Goldfeder, Jim
  See Pahz, James Alon
Goldfinger, Jennifer P. 1963- *185*
Goldfrank, Helen Colodny 1912- *6*
Goldin, Augusta 1906-1999 .... *13*
Goldin, Barbara Diamond 1946- *129*
  Autobiography Feature *129*
  Earlier sketch in SATA *92*
  See also SAAS *26*
Goldin, David 1963- *101*
Golding, Julia 1969- *188*
Golding, Theresa Martin 1960- *150*
Golding, William 1911-1993
  See CLR *130*

Golding, William Gerald
  See Golding, William
Goldman, Alex J. 1917- *65*
Goldman, E(leanor) M(aureen) 1943- *103*
Goldman, Elizabeth 1949- *90*
Goldring, Ann 1937- *149*
Goldsborough, June 1923- *19*
Goldsmith, Connie 1945- *147*
Goldsmith, Howard 1943- *108*
  Earlier sketch in SATA *24*
Goldsmith, John Herman Thorburn 1903-1987
  Obituary *52*
Goldsmith, Oliver 1730(?)-1774 .... *26*
Goldsmith, Ruth M. 1919- *62*
Goldstein, Nathan 1927- *47*
Goldstein, Philip 1910-1997 .... *23*
Goldston, Robert (Conroy) 1927- *6*
Goldstone, Bruce *183*
Goldstone, Lawrence A.
  See Treat, Lawrence
Goldszmit, Henryk 1878-1942 .... *65*
Golembe, Carla 1951- *79*
Golenbock, Peter 1946- *99*
Goll, Reinhold W(eimar) 1897-1993 .... *26*
Gollub, Matthew 1960- *134*
  Earlier sketch in SATA *83*
Gomes, Filomena 1965- *183*
Gomez, Elena *191*
Gomez, Elizabeth *133*
Gomez-Freer, Elizabeth
  See Gomez, Elizabeth
Gomi, Taro 1945- *103*
  Earlier sketch in SATA *64*
  See also CLR *57*
Gondosch, Linda 1944- *58*
Gonyea, Mark *194*
Gonzalez, Catherine Troxell 1917-2000 .... *87*
Gonzalez, Christina
  See Gonzalez, Maya Christina
Gonzalez, Gloria 1940- *23*
Gonzalez, Julie 1958- *174*
Gonzalez, Maya
  See Gonzalez, Maya Christina
Gonzalez, Maya Christina 1964- *175*
  Earlier sketch in SATA *115*
Gonzalez, Rigoberto 1970- *147*
Goobie, Beth 1959- *128*
Good, Alice 1950- *73*
Good, Clare
  See Romano, Clare
Goodall, Daphne Machin
  See Machin Goodall, Daphne (Edith)
Goodall, Jane 1934- *111*
Goodall, John S(trickland) 1908-1996 .... *66*
  Obituary *91*
  Earlier sketch in SATA *4*
  See also CLR *25*
Goodbody, Slim
  See Burstein, John
Goode, Diane 1949- *170*
  Earlier sketches in SATA *15, 84, 114*
Goode, Diane Capuozzo
  See Goode, Diane
Goode, Stephen Ray 1943- *55*
  Brief entry *40*
Goodenow, Earle 1913- *40*
Goodhart, Pippa 1958- *196*
  Earlier sketch in SATA *153*
Goodhue, Thomas W. 1949- *143*
Goodin, Sallie (Brown) 1953- *74*
Goodman, Alison 1966- *111*
Goodman, Deborah Lerme 1956- *50*
  Brief entry *49*
Goodman, Elaine 1930- *9*
Goodman, Joan Elizabeth 1950- *162*
  Earlier sketches in SATA *50, 94*
Goodman, Susan E. 1952- *181*
Goodman, Walter 1927-2002 .... *9*
Goodrich, Samuel Griswold 1793-1860 .... *23*
Goodsell, Jane Neuberger 1921(?)-1988
  Obituary *56*

GoodWeather, Hartley
  See King, Thomas
Goodweather, Hartley
  See King, Thomas
Goodwin, Hal
  See Goodwin, Harold L(eland)
Goodwin, Harold L(eland) 1914-1990 51
  Obituary 65
  Earlier sketch in SATA 13
Goodwin, William 1943- 117
Goor, Nancy (Ruth Miller) 1944- 39
  Brief entry 34
Goor, Ron(ald Stephen) 1940- 39
  Brief entry 34
Goossen, Agnes
  See Epp, Margaret A(gnes)
Goossens, Philippe 1963- 195
Gootman, Marilyn E. 1944- 179
Gopnik, Adam 1956- 171
Gorbachev, Valeri 1944- 184
  Autobiography Feature 143
  Earlier sketches in SATA 98, 143
Gordion, Mark
  See Turtledove, Harry
Gordon, Ad
  See Hano, Arnold
Gordon, Amy 1949- 197
  Earlier sketches in SATA 115, 156
Gordon, Bernard Ludwig 1931- 27
Gordon, Colonel H. R.
  See Ellis, Edward S(ylvester)
Gordon, David
  See Garrett, (Gordon) Randall (Phillip)
Gordon, Donald
  See Payne, Donald Gordon
Gordon, Dorothy 1893-1970 20
Gordon, Esther S(aranga) 1935- 10
Gordon, Frederick 1
Gordon, Gaelyn 1939-1997
  See CLR 75
Gordon, Garrett
  See Garrett, (Gordon) Randall (Phillip)
Gordon, Gary
  See Edmonds, I(vy) G(ordon)
Gordon, Hal
  See Goodwin, Harold L(eland)
Gordon, Jeffie Ross
  See Enderle, Judith (Ann) Ross
  and Gordon, Stephanie Jacob
Gordon, John
  See Gesner, Clark
Gordon, John (William) 1925- 84
Gordon, Lew
  See Baldwin, Gordon C(ortis)
Gordon, Margaret (Anna) 1939- 9
Gordon, Mike 1948- 101
Gordon, Mildred 1912-1979
  Obituary 24
Gordon, Selma
  See Lanes, Selma Gordon
Gordon, Sheila 1927- 88
  See also CLR 27
Gordon, Shirley 1921- 48
  Brief entry 41
Gordon, Sol 1923- 11
Gordon, Stephanie Jacob 1940- 89
  Autobiography Feature 114
  Earlier sketch in SATA 64
  See also SAAS 26
Gordon, Stewart
  See Shirreffs, Gordon D(onald)
Gordons, The
  See Gordon, Mildred
  and Gordon, Gordon
Gore, Leonid 185
Gorelick, Molly C(hernow) 1920-2003 9
  Obituary 153

Gorey, Edward (St. John) 1925-2000 70
  Brief entry 27
  Obituary 118
  Earlier sketch in SATA 29
  See also CLR 36
Gorham, Charles Orson 1868-1936 36
Gorham, Michael
  See Folsom, Franklin (Brewster)
Gorman, Carol 187
  Earlier sketch in SATA 150
Gorman, Jacqueline Laks 1955- 148
Gormley, Beatrice 1942- 127
  Brief entry 35
  Earlier sketch in SATA 39
Gorog, Judith (Katharine Allen) 1938- 75
  Earlier sketch in SATA 39
Gorrell, Gena K. 1946- 170
Gorsline, Douglas (Warner) 1913-1985 11
  Obituary 43
Gorsline, (Sally) Marie 1928- 28
Gorsline, S. M.
  See Gorsline, (Sally) Marie
Gorton, Kaitlyn
  See Emerson, Kathy Lynn
Gorton, Kathy Lynn
  See Emerson, Kathy Lynn
Goryan, Sirak
  See Saroyan, William
Goscinny, Rene 1926-1977 47
  Brief entry 39
  See also CLR 37
Goss, Clay(ton E.) 1946- 82
Goss, Gary 1947- 124
Goss, Mini 1963- 186
Gott, Barry 197
Gottesman, S. D.
  See Kornbluth, C(yril) M.
  and Lowndes, Robert A(ugustine) W(ard)
  and Pohl, Frederik
Gottfried, Ted
  See Gottfried, Theodore Mark
Gottfried, Theodore Mark 1928- 150
  Earlier sketch in SATA 85
Gottlieb, Gerald 1923- 7
Gottlieb, William P. 1917-2006 24
Gottlieb, William Paul
  See Gottlieb, William P.
Goudey, Alice E(dwards) 1898-1993 20
Goudge, Eileen 1950- 88
Goudge, Elizabeth (de Beauchamp)
  1900-1984 2
  Obituary 38
  See also CLR 94
Gough, Catherine
  See Mulgan, Catherine
Gough, Philip 1908-1986 45
Gough, Sue 1940- 106
Goulart, Ron(ald Joseph) 1933- 67
  Earlier sketch in SATA 1
Gould, Alberta 1945- 96
Gould, Chester 1900-1985 49
  Obituary 43
Gould, Jean R(osalind) 1909-1993 11
  Obituary 77
Gould, Lilian 6
Gould, Marilyn 1928- 76
  Earlier sketch in SATA 15
Gould, Robert 154
Gould, Steven 1955- 95
Gould, Steven Charles
  See Gould, Steven
Gourley, Catherine 1950- 190
  Earlier sketch in SATA 95
Gourse, Leslie 1939-2004 89
Govan, (Mary) Christine Noble 1898-1985 ... 9
Gove, Doris 1944- 72
Govenar, Alan 1952- 189
Govenar, Alan Bruce
  See Govenar, Alan
Govern, Elaine 1939- 26
Gowen, L. Kris 1968- 156

Graaf, Peter
  See Youd, (Christopher) Samuel
Graber, Alexander 1914-1997 98
  Earlier sketch in SATA 7
Graber, (George) Alexander 1914-1997 98
Graber, Janet 1942- 170
Graber, Richard (Fredrick) 1927- 26
Grabianski, Janusz 1928-1976 39
  Obituary 30
Graboff, Abner 1919-1986 35
Grace, Fran(ces Jane) 45
Grace, N.B.
  See Harper, Suzanne
Grace, Theresa
  See Mattern, Joanne
Gracza, Margaret Young 1928- 56
Graduate of Oxford, A
  See Ruskin, John
Grady, Denise 1952- 189
Graeber, Charlotte Towner 106
  Brief entry 44
  Earlier sketch in SATA 56
Graeme, Roderic
  See Jeffries, Roderic
Graf, Michael
  See Graf, Mike
Graf, Mike 1960- 164
Grafe, Max 198
Graff, Lisa 1981- 188
Graff, Polly Anne Colver
  See Colver, Anne
Graff, (S.) Stewart 1908- 9
Graham, Ada 1931- 11
Graham, Alastair 1945- 74
Graham, Arthur Kennon
  See Harrison, David L.
Graham, Bob 1942- 187
  Earlier sketches in SATA 63, 101, 151
  See also CLR 31
Graham, Brenda Knight 1942- 32
Graham, Charlotte
  See Bowden, Joan Chase
Graham, Eleanor 1896-1984 18
  Obituary 38
Graham, Ennis
  See Molesworth, Mary Louisa
Graham, Frank, Jr. 1925- 11
Graham, Georgia 1959- 190
Graham, Ian 1953- 112
Graham, John 1926-2007 11
Graham, Kennon
  See Harrison, David L.
Graham, Larry
  See Graham, Lawrence
Graham, Lawrence 1962- 63
Graham, Lawrence Otis
  See Graham, Lawrence
Graham, Linda
  See Graham-Barber, Lynda
Graham, Lorenz (Bell) 1902-1989 74
  Obituary 63
  Earlier sketch in SATA 2
  See also CLR 10
  See also SAAS 5
Graham, Margaret Bloy 1920- 11
Graham, Robin Lee 1949- 7
Graham, Shirley 1896(?)-1977
  See Du Bois, Shirley Graham
Graham-Barber, Lynda 1944- 159
  Earlier sketch in SATA 42
Graham-Cameron, M.
  See Graham-Cameron, M(alcolm) G(ordon)
Graham-Cameron, M(alcolm) G(ordon)
  1931- 53
  Brief entry 45
Graham-Cameron, Mike
  See Graham-Cameron, M(alcolm) G(ordon)
Grahame, Kenneth 1859-1932 100
  See also YABC 1
  See also CLR 135
Gralley, Jean 166

Gramatky, Hardie 1907-1979 30
  Obituary 23
  Earlier sketch in SATA 1
  See also CLR 22
Grambling, Lois G. 1927- 148
  Earlier sketch in SATA 71
Grambo, Rebecca L(ynn) 1963- 109
Grammer, June Amos 1927- 58
Grand, Samuel 1912-1988 42
Grandits, John 1949- 192
GrandPre, Mary 1954- 184
Grandville, J. J.
  See Gerard, Jean Ignace Isidore
Grandville, Jean Ignace Isidore Gerard
  See Gerard, Jean Ignace Isidore
Granfield, Linda 1950- 160
  Earlier sketch in SATA 96
Grange, Peter
  See Nicole, Christopher (Robin)
Granger, Margaret Jane 1925(?)-1977
  Obituary 27
Granger, Michele 1949- 88
Granger, Peggy
  See Granger, Margaret Jane
Granowsky, Alvin 1936- 101
Granstaff, Bill 1925- 10
Granstrom, Brita 1969- 167
  Earlier sketch in SATA 111
Grant, Bruce 1893-1977 5
  Obituary 25
Grant, Cynthia D. 1950- 147
  Earlier sketches in SATA 33, 77
Grant, Eva 1907-1996 7
Grant, Evva H. 1913-1977
  Obituary 27
Grant, Gordon 1875-1962 25
Grant, Gwen(doline Ellen) 1940- 47
Grant, Katie M.
  See Grant, K.M.
Grant, K.M. 175
Grant, (Alice) Leigh 1947- 10
Grant, Matthew G.
  See May, Julian
Grant, Maxwell
  See Gibson, Walter B(rown)
  and Lynds, Dennis
Grant, Melvyn 183
Grant, Myrna (Lois) 1934- 21
Grant, Neil 1938- 154
  Earlier sketch in SATA 14
Grant, Nicholas
  See Nicole, Christopher (Robin)
Grant, Richard 1948- 80
Grant, Skeeter
  See Spiegelman, Art
Grater, Michael 1923- 57
Gravel, Fern
  See Hall, James Norman
Gravelle, Karen 1942- 166
  Earlier sketch in SATA 78
Graves, Charles Parlin 1911-1972 4
Graves, Keith 191
  Earlier sketch in SATA 156
Graves, Robert 1895-1985 45
Graves, Robert von Ranke
  See Graves, Robert
Graves, Valerie
  See Bradley, Marion Zimmer
Gravett, Emily 1972(?)- 189
Gray, Betsy
  See Poole, Gray Johnson
Gray, Caroline
  See Nicole, Christopher (Robin)
Gray, Dianne E. 183
Gray, Elizabeth Janet
  See Vining, Elizabeth Gray
Gray, Genevieve S(tuck) 1920-1995 4
Gray, Harold (Lincoln) 1894-1968 33
  Brief entry 32
Gray, Jenny
  See Gray, Genevieve S(tuck)

Gray, John Lee
  See Jakes, John
Gray, Judith A. 1949- 93
Gray, Judith Anne
  See Gray, Judith A.
Gray, Keith 151
Gray, Kes 1960- 153
Gray, Les 1929- 82
Gray, Libba Moore 1937- 83
Gray, Luli 1945- 149
  Earlier sketch in SATA 90
Gray, Marian
  See Pierce, Edith Gray
Gray, Nicholas Stuart 1922-1981 4
  Obituary 27
Gray, Nigel 1941- 104
  Earlier sketch in SATA 33
Gray, (Lucy) Noel (Clervaux) 1898-1983 47
Gray, Patricia (Clark) 7
Gray, Patsey
  See Gray, Patricia (Clark)
Gray, Rita 184
Graydon, Shari 1958- 158
Grayland, V. Merle
  See Grayland, Valerie (Merle Spanner)
Grayland, Valerie (Merle Spanner) 7
Grayson, Devin (Kalile) 1970- 119
Grayson, Kristine
  See Rusch, Kristine Kathryn
Grayson, Paul 1946- 79
Graystone, Lynn
  See Brennan, Joseph Lomas
Great Comte, The
  See Hawkesworth, Eric
Greaves, Margaret 1914-1995 87
  Earlier sketch in SATA 7
Greaves, Nick 1955- 77
Gree, Alain 1936- 28
Green, Adam
  See Weisgard, Leonard (Joseph)
Green, Anne Canevari 1943- 62
Green, Brian
  See Card, Orson Scott
Green, Cliff(ord) 1934- 126
Green, Connie Jordan 1938- 80
Green, D.
  See Casewit, Curtis W(erner)
Green, Elizabeth Shippen 1871-1954 139
Green, Hannah
  See Greenberg, Joanne (Goldenberg)
Green, Jane 1937- 9
Green, John 1977(?)- 170
Green, Mary Moore 1906- 11
Green, Morton 1937- 8
Green, Norma B(erger) 1925- 11
Green, Phyllis 1932- 20
Green, Roger (Gilbert) Lancelyn 1918-1987 . 2
  Obituary 53
Green, (James Le)Roy 1948- 89
Green, Sheila Ellen 1934- 148
  Earlier sketches in SATA 8, 87
Green, Timothy 1953- 91
Greenaway, Kate 1846-1901 100
  See also YABC 2
  See also CLR 111
Greenbank, Anthony Hunt 1933- 39
Greenberg, David 1954- 171
Greenberg, David T.
  See Greenberg, David
Greenberg, Harvey R. 1935- 5
Greenberg, Jan 1942- 125
  Earlier sketch in SATA 61
Greenberg, Joanne (Goldenberg) 1932- 25
Greenberg, Melanie Hope 1954- 72
Greenberg, Polly 1932- 52
  Brief entry 43
Greenblat, Rodney Alan 1960- 106
Greenburg, Dan 1936- 175
  Earlier sketch in SATA 102

Greene, Bette 1934- 161
  Earlier sketches in SATA 8, 102
  See also CLR 140
  See also SAAS 16
Greene, Carla 1916- 67
  Earlier sketch in SATA 1
Greene, Carol 102
  Brief entry 44
  Earlier sketch in SATA 66
Greene, Constance C(larke) 1924- 72
  Earlier sketch in SATA 11
  See also CLR 62
  See also SAAS 11
Greene, Edgar
  See Papademetriou, Lisa
Greene, Ellin 1927- 23
Greene, Graham 1904-1991 20
Greene, Graham Henry
  See Greene, Graham
Greene, Jacqueline Dembar 1946- 131
  Earlier sketch in SATA 76
Greene, Laura Offenhartz 1935- 38
Greene, Meg
  See Malvasi, Meg Greene
Greene, Michele 1962- 178
Greene, Michele Dominguez
  See Greene, Michele
Greene, Rhonda Gowler 1955- 160
  Earlier sketch in SATA 101
Greene, Stephanie 1953- 173
  Earlier sketch in SATA 127
Greene, Wade 1933- 11
Greene, Yvonne
  See Flesch, Yolande (Catarina)
Greenfeld, Howard (Scheinman) 1928- 140
  Earlier sketch in SATA 19
Greenfeld, Josh(ua Joseph) 1928- 62
Greenfield, Eloise 1929- 155
  Earlier sketches in SATA 19, 61, 105
  See also CLR 38
  See also SAAS 16
Greenhaus, Thelma Nurenberg 1903-1984
  Obituary 45
Greenhut, Josh
  See Mercer, Sienna
Greenhut, Josh
  See Mercer, Sienna
Greening, Hamilton
  See Hamilton, Charles (Harold St. John)
Greenlaw, M. Jean 1941- 107
Greenleaf, Barbara Kaye 1942- 6
Greenleaf, Peter 1910-1997 33
Greenlee, Sharon 1935- 77
Greeno, Gayle 1949- 81
Greenseid, Diane 1948- 178
  Earlier sketch in SATA 93
Greenspun, Adele Aron 1938- 142
  Earlier sketch in SATA 76
Greenstein, Elaine 1959- 150
  Earlier sketch in SATA 82
Greenwald, Sheila
  See Green, Sheila Ellen
Greenwood, Barbara 1940- 129
  Earlier sketch in SATA 90
Greenwood, Pamela D. 1944- 115
Greer, Richard
  See Garrett, (Gordon) Randall (Phillip)
  and Silverberg, Robert
Gregg, Andrew K. 1929- 81
Gregg, Charles T(hornton) 1927- 65
Gregg, Walter H(arold) 1919- 20
Gregor, Arthur 1923- 36
Gregor, Lee
  See Pohl, Frederik
Gregori, Leon 1919- 15
Gregorian, Joyce Ballou 1946-1991 30
  Obituary 83
Gregorich, Barbara 1943- 184
  Earlier sketch in SATA 66
Gregorowski, Christopher 1940- 30

Gregory, Diana (Jean) 1933- *49*
  Brief entry *42*
Gregory, Harry
  See Gottfried, Theodore Mark
Gregory, Jean
  See Ure, Jean
Gregory, Kristiana 1951- *136*
  Earlier sketch in SATA *74*
Gregory, Nan 1944- *192*
  Earlier sketch in SATA *148*
Gregory, Philippa 1954- *122*
Gregory, Stephen
  See Penzler, Otto
Gregory, Valiska 1940- *82*
Greif, Jean-Jacques 1944- *195*
Greisman, Joan Ruth 1937- *31*
Grendon, Stephen
  See Derleth, August (William)
Grenville, Pelham
  See Wodehouse, P(elham) G(renville)
Gretz, Susanna 1937- *7*
Gretzer, John *18*
Grewdead, Roy
  See Gorey, Edward (St. John)
Grey, Carol
  See Lowndes, Robert A(ugustine) W(ard)
Grey, Christopher *191*
Grey, Christopher Peter
  See Grey, Christopher
Grey, Jerry 1926- *11*
Grey, Mini *166*
Greybeard the Pirate
  See Macintosh, Brownie
Grey Owl
  See Belaney, Archibald Stansfeld
Gri
  See Denney, Diana
Gribbin, John 1946- *159*
Gribbin, John R.
  See Gribbin, John
Grice, Frederick 1910-1983 .... *6*
Grider, Dorothy 1915- *31*
Gridley, Marion E(leanor) 1906-1974 ...... *35*
  Obituary *26*
Grieco-Tiso, Pina 1954- *108*
Grieder, Walter 1924- *9*
Griego, Tony A. 1955- *77*
Griese, Arnold A(lfred) 1921- *9*
Griessman, Annette 1962- *170*
  Earlier sketch in SATA *116*
Grieve, James 1934- *146*
Grifalconi, Ann 1929- *133*
  Earlier sketches in SATA *2, 66*
  See also CLR *35*
  See also SAAS *16*
Griffin, Adele 1970- *195*
  Earlier sketches in SATA *105, 153*
Griffin, Elizabeth May 1985- *89*
Griffin, Gillett Good 1928- *26*
Griffin, Judith Berry *34*
Griffin, Kitty 1951- *137*
Griffin, Peni R. 1961- *193*
  Earlier sketches in SATA *67, 99*
Griffin, Steven A. 1953- *89*
Griffin, Steven Arthur
  See Griffin, Steven A.
Griffin, W.E.B 1929- *5*
Griffith, Connie 1946- *89*
Griffith, Gershom 1960- *85*
Griffith, Helen V(irginia) 1934- *87*
  Autobiography Feature *107*
  Earlier sketch in SATA *39*
Griffith, Jeannette
  See Eyerly, Jeannette
Griffiths, Andy 1961- *196*
  Earlier sketch in SATA *152*
Griffiths, G(ordon) D(ouglas) 1910-1973
  Obituary *20*

Griffiths, Helen 1939- *86*
  Earlier sketch in SATA *5*
  See also CLR *75*
  See also SAAS *5*
Grigson, Jane (McIntire) 1928-1990 .... *63*
Grimes, Lee 1920- *68*
Grimes, Nikki 1950- *174*
  Earlier sketches in SATA *93, 136*
  See also CLR *42*
Grimly, Gris *186*
Grimm, Jacob Ludwig Karl 1785-1863 .... *22*
  See also CLR *112*
Grimm, Wilhelm Karl 1786-1859 .... *22*
  See also CLR *112*
Grimm, William C(arey) 1907-1992 .... *14*
Grimm and Grim
  See Grimm, Jacob Ludwig Karl
  and Grimm, Wilhelm Karl
Grimm Brothers
  See Grimm, Jacob Ludwig Karl
  and Grimm, Wilhelm Karl
Grimsdell, Jeremy 1942- *83*
Grimshaw, Nigel (Gilroy) 1925- *23*
Grimsley, Gordon
  See Groom, Arthur William
Grindley, Jane Sally
  See Grindley, Sally
Grindley, Sally 1953- *148*
Gringhuis, Dirk
  See Gringhuis, Richard H.
Gringhuis, Richard H. 1918-1974 .... *6*
  Obituary *25*
Grinnell, David
  See Wollheim, Donald A(llen)
Grinnell, George Bird 1849-1938 .... *16*
Grinspoon, David
  See Grinspoon, David H.
Grinspoon, David H. 1959- *156*
Grinspoon, David Harry
  See Grinspoon, David H.
Gripe, Maria 1923- *74*
  Earlier sketch in SATA *2*
  See also CLR *5*
Gripe, Maria Kristina
  See Gripe, Maria
Groch, Judith (Goldstein) 1929- *25*
Grode, Redway
  See Gorey, Edward (St. John)
Groener, Carl
  See Lowndes, Robert A(ugustine) W(ard)
Groening, Matt 1954- *116*
  Earlier sketch in SATA *81*
Grohmann, Susan 1948- *84*
Grohskopf, Bernice *7*
Grol, Lini R(icharda) 1913- *9*
Grollman, Earl A. 1925- *22*
Groom, Arthur William 1898-1964 .... *10*
Grooms, Duffy 1964- *169*
Gross, Alan 1947- *54*
  Brief entry *43*
Gross, Ernie 1913- *67*
Gross, Philip 1952- *164*
  Earlier sketch in SATA *84*
Gross, Philip John
  See Gross, Philip
Gross, Ruth Belov 1929- *33*
Gross, Sarah Chokla 1906-1976 .... *9*
  Obituary *26*
Grosser, Morton 1931- *74*
Grosser, Vicky 1958- *83*
Grossman, Bill 1948- *126*
  Earlier sketch in SATA *72*
Grossman, Nancy 1940- *29*
Grossman, Patricia 1951- *73*
Grossman, Robert 1940- *11*
Grote, JoAnn A. 1951- *113*
Groten, Dallas 1951- *64*
Groth, John (August) 1908-1988 .... *21*
  Obituary *56*
Groth-Fleming, Candace
  See Fleming, Candace

Grove, Vicki 1948- *151*
  Autobiography Feature *151*
  Earlier sketch in SATA *122*
Grover, Lorie Ann 1964- *168*
Grover, Wayne 1934- *69*
Groves, Georgina
  See Symons, (Dorothy) Geraldine
Groves, Maketa 1950- *107*
Groves, Seli *77*
Grubb, Lisa *160*
Gruber, Michael 1940- *173*
Gruber, Terry (deRoy) 1953- *66*
Gruelle, John (Barton) 1880-1938 .... *35*
  Brief entry *32*
  See also CLR *34*
Gruelle, Johnny
  See Gruelle, John (Barton)
Gruenberg, Sidonie Matsner 1881-1974 ...... *2*
  Obituary *27*
Gruhzit-Hoyt, Olga (Margaret) 1922- *127*
  Earlier sketch in SATA *16*
Grummer, Arnold E(dward) 1923- *49*
Grunewalt, Pine
  See Kunhardt, Edith
Grunwell, Jeanne Marie 1971- *147*
Grupper, Jonathan *137*
Gryski, Camilla 1948- *72*
Guarino, Dagmar
  See Guarino, Deborah
Guarino, Deborah 1954- *68*
Guay, Georgette (Marie Jeanne) 1952- *54*
Guback, Georgia *88*
Guccione, Leslie Davis 1946- *111*
  Earlier sketch in SATA *72*
Guck, Dorothy 1913-2002 .... *27*
Guerny, Gene
  See Gurney, Gene
Guest, Elissa Haden 1953- *125*
Guest, Jacqueline 1952- *135*
Guevara, Susan *167*
  Earlier sketch in SATA *97*
Gugler, Laurel Dee *95*
Gugliotta, Bobette 1918-1994 .... *7*
Guianan, Eve 1965- *102*
Guiberson, Brenda Z. 1946- *124*
  Earlier sketch in SATA *71*
Guibert, Emmanuel 1964- *181*
Guile, Melanie 1949- *152*
  Earlier sketch in SATA *104*
Guillaume, Jeanette G. Flierl 1899-1990 ... *8*
Guillot, Rene 1900-1969 .... *7*
  See also CLR *22*
Guisewite, Cathy (Lee) 1950- *57*
Gulbis, Stephen 1959- *142*
Gulley, Judie 1942- *58*
Gump, P. Q.
  See Card, Orson Scott
Gump, P.Q.
  See Card, Orson Scott
Gundrey, Elizabeth 1924- *23*
Gunn, James E. 1923- *35*
Gunn, James Edwin
  See Gunn, James E.
Gunn, Robin Jones 1955- *84*
Gunnella 1956- *197*
Gunning, Monica Olwen 1930- *161*
Gunston, Bill
  See Gunston, William Tudor
Gunston, William Tudor 1927- *9*
Gunterman, Bertha Lisette 1886(?)-1975
  Obituary *27*
Gunther, John 1901-1970
Guravich, Dan 1918- *74*
Gurko, Leo 1914- *9*
Gurko, Miriam 1910(?)-1988 .... *9*
  Obituary *58*
Gurney, Gene 1924- *65*
Gurney, James 1958- *120*
  Earlier sketch in SATA *76*
Gurney, John Steven 1962- *143*
  Earlier sketch in SATA *75*

Gustafson, Sarah R.
    See Riedman, Sarah R(egal)
Gustafson, Scott 1956- 34
Gustavson, Adam 176
Guthrie, A(lfred) B(ertram), Jr. 1901-1991 .. 62
    Obituary 67
Guthrie, Anne 1890-1979 28
Guthrie, Donna W. 1946- 105
    Earlier sketch in SATA 63
Gutierrez, Akemi 172
Gutman, Bill 128
    Brief entry 43
    Earlier sketch in SATA 67
Gutman, Dan 1955- 188
    Earlier sketches in SATA 77, 139
Gutman, Naham 1899(?)-1981
    Obituary 25
Gutmann, Bessie Pease 1876-1960 73
Guy, Geoffrey 1942- 153
Guy, Ginger Foglesong 1954- 171
Guy, Rosa (Cuthbert) 1925- 122
    Earlier sketches in SATA 14, 62
    See also CLR 137
Guy, Susan 1948- 149
Guymer, (Wilhelmina) Mary 1909- 50
Guzman, Lila 1952- 168
Guzman, Rick 1957- 168
Gwaltney, Doris 1932- 181
Gwynne, Fred(erick Hubbard) 1926-1993 41
    Brief entry 27
    Obituary 75
Gwynne, Oscar A.
    See Ellis, Edward S(ylvester)
Gwynne, Oswald A.
    See Ellis, Edward S(ylvester)

H

Haab, Sherri 1964- 169
    Earlier sketch in SATA 91
Haar, Jaap ter
    See ter Haar, Jaap
Haarsma, P.J. 183
Haas, Carolyn Buhai 1926- 43
Haas, Dan 1957- 105
Haas, Dorothy F. 46
    Brief entry 43
    See also SAAS 17
Haas, Irene 1929- 96
    Earlier sketch in SATA 17
Haas, James E(dward) 1943- 40
Haas, (Katherine) Jessie 1959- 135
    Autobiography Feature 135
    Earlier sketch in SATA 98
Haas, Merle S. 1896(?)-1985
    Obituary 41
Habenstreit, Barbara 1937- 5
Haber, Karen 1955- 78
Haber, Louis 1910-1988 12
Hacker, Randi 1951- 185
Hacker, Randi Dawn
    See Hacker, Randi
Hackett, John Winthrop 1910-1997 65
Hacks, Peter 1928-2003
    Obituary 151
Haddix, Margaret Peterson 1964- 187
    Earlier sketches in SATA 94, 125
Haddon, Mark 1962- 155
Hader, Berta (Hoerner) 1891(?)-1976 16
Hader, Elmer (Stanley) 1889-1973 16
Hadithi, Mwenye
    See Hobson, Bruce
Hadley, Franklin
    See Winterbotham, R(ussell) R(obert)

Hadley, Lee 1934-1995 89
    Brief entry 38
    Obituary 86
    Earlier sketch in SATA 47
    See also CLR 40
    See also SAAS 14
Haeffele, Deborah 1954- 76
Haenel, Wolfram 1956- 89
    See also CLR 64
Hafner, Marylin 1925- 179
    Earlier sketches in SATA 7, 121
Haft, Erin
    See Ehrenhaft, Daniel
Hager, Alan 1940- 176
Hager, Alice Rogers 1894-1969
    Obituary 26
Hager, Betty 1923- 89
Hager, Sarah 171
Hager, Thomas 1953- 119
Hager, Tom
    See Hager, Thomas
Hagerup, Klaus 1946- 186
Haggard, H(enry) Rider 1856-1925 16
Haggerty, James J(oseph) 1920- 5
Hagon, Priscilla
    See Allan, Mabel Esther
Hague, (Susan) Kathleen 1949- 49
    Brief entry 45
Hague, Michael 1948- 185
    Brief entry 32
    Earlier sketches in SATA 48, 80, 129
Hague, Michael R.
    See Hague, Michael
Hahn, Emily 1905-1997 3
    Obituary 96
Hahn, Hannelore 8
Hahn, James (Sage) 1947- 9
Hahn, (Mona) Lynn 1949- 9
Hahn, Mary Downing 1937- 157
    Autobiography Feature 157
    Brief entry 44
    Earlier sketches in SATA 50, 81, 138
    See also SAAS 12
Hahn, Michael T. 1953- 92
Haig-Brown, Roderick (Langmere)
    1908-1976 12
    See also CLR 31
Haight, Anne Lyon 1895-1977
    Obituary 30
Haight, Rip
    See Carpenter, John (Howard)
Haight, Sandy 1949- 79
Haij, Vera
    See Jansson, Tove (Marika)
Haines, Gail Kay 1943- 11
Haines, Margaret Ann Beck
    See Beck, Peggy
Haining, Peter 1940-2007 14
    Obituary 188
Haining, Peter Alexander
    See Haining, Peter
Hains, Harriet
    See Watson, Carol
Hajdusiewicz, Babs Bell 163
Hakim, Joy 1931- 173
    Earlier sketch in SATA 83
Halacy, D(aniel) S(tephen), Jr. 1919-2002 ... 36
    See also SAAS 8
Halacy, Dan
    See Halacy, D(aniel) S(tephen), Jr.
Halam, Ann
    See Jones, Gwyneth A(nn)
Haldane, Roger John 1945- 13
Hale, Arlene 1924-1982 49
Hale, Bruce 1957- 123
Hale, Christy
    See Apostolou, Christine Hale
Hale, Edward Everett 1822-1909 16
Hale, Glenn
    See Walker, Robert W(ayne)

Hale, Helen
    See Mulcahy, Lucille Burnett
Hale, Irina 1932- 26
Hale, Kathleen 1898-2000 66
    Obituary 121
    Earlier sketch in SATA 17
Hale, Linda (Howe) 1929- 6
Hale, Lucretia P.
    See Hale, Lucretia Peabody
Hale, Lucretia Peabody 1820-1900 26
    See also CLR 105
Hale, Marian 194
Hale, Nancy 1908-1988 31
    Obituary 57
Hale, Shannon 158
Haley, Gail E(inhart) 1939- 161
    Autobiography Feature 161
    Brief entry 28
    Earlier sketches in SATA 43, 78, 136
    See also CLR 21
    See also SAAS 13
Haley, Neale 52
Hall, Adam
    See Trevor, Elleston
Hall, Adele 1910- 7
Hall, Anna Gertrude 1882-1967 8
Hall, Barbara 1960- 68
Hall, Becky 1950- 186
Hall, Beverly B. 1918- 95
Hall, Borden
    See Yates, Raymond F(rancis)
Hall, Brian P(atrick) 1935- 31
Hall, Cameron
    See del Rey, Lester
Hall, Caryl
    See Hansen, Caryl (Hall)
Hall, Donald 1928- 97
    Earlier sketch in SATA 23
Hall, Donald Andrew, Jr.
    See Hall, Donald
Hall, Douglas 1931- 43
Hall, Elizabeth 1929- 77
Hall, Elvajean 1910-1984 6
Hall, Francie 1940- 166
Hall, James Norman 1887-1951 21
Hall, Jesse
    See Boesen, Victor
Hall, Katy
    See McMullan, Kate
Hall, Kirsten Marie 1974- 67
Hall, Lynn 1937- 79
    Earlier sketches in SATA 2, 47
    See also SAAS 4
Hall, Malcolm 1945- 7
Hall, Marjory
    See Yeakley, Marjory Hall
Hall, Melanie W. 1949- 169
    Earlier sketches in SATA 78, 116
Hall, Patricia 1940- 136
Hall, Rosalys Haskell 1914- 7
Hall, Willis 1929-2005 66
Hallard, Peter
    See Catherall, Arthur
Hallas, Richard
    See Knight, Eric
Hall-Clarke, James
    See Rowland-Entwistle, (Arthur) Theodore
    (Henry)
Hallensleben, Georg 1958- 173
Haller, Dorcas Woodbury 1946- 46
Hallett, Mark 1947- 83
Halliburton, Richard 1900-1939(?) 81
Halliburton, Warren J. 1924- 19
Halliday, Brett
    See Dresser, Davis
    and Johnson, (Walter) Ryerson
    and Terrall, Robert
Halliday, William R(oss) 1926- 52
Hallin, Emily Watson 1916-1995 6
Hallinan, P(atrick) K(enneth) 1944- 39
    Brief entry 37

Hallman, Ruth 1929- *43*
  Brief entry *28*
Hallowell, Tommy
  See Hill, Thomas
Hall-Quest, (Edna) Olga W(ilbourne)
  1899-1986 .... *11*
  Obituary *47*
Halls, Kelly Milner 1957- *131*
Hallstead, William F(inn III) 1924- *11*
Hallward, Michael 1889-1982 .... *12*
Halperin, Michael *156*
Halperin, Wendy Anderson 1952- *125*
  Earlier sketch in SATA *80*
Halpern, Julie 1975- *198*
Halpin, Brendan 1968- *193*
Halpin, Marlene 1927- *88*
Halsell, Grace (Eleanor) 1923-2000 .... *13*
Halsey, Megan *185*
Halsted, Anna Roosevelt 1906-1975
  Obituary *30*
Halter, Jon C(harles) 1941- *22*
Halvorson, Marilyn 1948- *123*
Hamalian, Leo 1920- *41*
Hamberger, John 1934- *14*
Hamblin, Dora Jane 1920- *36*
Hambly, Barbara 1951- *108*
Hambly, Barbara Joan
  See Hambly, Barbara
Hamer, Martyn
  See Eldin, Peter
Hamerstrom, Frances 1907-1998 .... *24*
Hamil, Thomas Arthur 1928- *14*
Hamill, Ethel
  See Webb, Jean Francis (III)
Hamilton, (John) Alan 1943- *66*
Hamilton, Alice
  See Cromie, Alice Hamilton
Hamilton, Anita 1919- *92*
Hamilton, Buzz
  See Hemming, Roy G.
Hamilton, Carol (Jean Barber) 1935- *94*
Hamilton, Charles (Harold St. John)
  1876-1961 .... *13*
Hamilton, Charles 1913-1996 .... *65*
  Obituary *93*
Hamilton, Clive
  See Lewis, C.S.
Hamilton, Dorothy (Drumm) 1906-1983 ...... *12*
  Obituary *35*
Hamilton, Edith 1867-1963 .... *20*
Hamilton, Edmond 1904-1977 .... *118*
Hamilton, (Muriel) Elizabeth (Mollie)
  1906- *23*
Hamilton, Emma Walton 1962- *177*
Hamilton, Franklin
  See Silverberg, Robert
Hamilton, Gail
  See Corcoran, Barbara (Asenath)
  and Dodge, Mary Abigail
Hamilton, Kersten 1958- *134*
Hamilton, Martha 1953- *183*
  Earlier sketch in SATA *123*
Hamilton, Mary (E.) 1927- *55*
Hamilton, Mollie
  See Kaye, M.M.
Hamilton, Morse 1943-1998 .... *101*
  Earlier sketch in SATA *35*
Hamilton, Peter F. 1960- *109*
Hamilton, Priscilla
  See Gellis, Roberta
Hamilton, Ralph
  See Stratemeyer, Edward L.
Hamilton, Virginia 1936-2002 .... *123*
  Obituary *132*
  Earlier sketches in SATA *4, 56, 79*
  See also CLR *127*
Hamilton, Virginia Esther
  See Hamilton, Virginia
Hamilton-Paterson, James 1941- *82*
Hamlet, Ova
  See Lupoff, Richard A(llen)

Hamley, Dennis 1935- *69*
  Earlier sketch in SATA *39*
  See also CLR *47*
  See also SAAS *22*
Hamlin, Peter J. 1970- *84*
Hamm, Diane Johnston 1949- *78*
Hammer, Charles 1934- *58*
Hammer, Richard 1928- *6*
Hammerman, Gay M(orenus) 1926- *9*
Hammond, Andrew 1970- *181*
Hammond, Ralph
  See Hammond Innes, Ralph
Hammond, Winifred G(raham) 1899-1992 ... *29*
  Obituary *107*
Hammond Innes, Ralph 1913-1998 .... *116*
Hammontree, Marie (Gertrude) 1913- *13*
Hample, Zack 1977- *161*
Hampshire, Joyce Gregorian
  See Gregorian, Joyce Ballou
Hampshire, Susan 1942- *98*
Hampson, (Richard) Denman 1929- *15*
Hampson, Frank 1918(?)-1985
  Obituary *46*
Hampton, Wilborn 1940- *196*
  Earlier sketch in SATA *156*
Hamre, Leif 1914- *5*
Hamsa, Bobbie 1944- *52*
  Brief entry *38*
Han, Jenny 1981- *175*
Han, Lu
  See Stickler, Soma Han
Han, Soma
  See Stickler, Soma Han
Han, Suzanne Crowder 1953- *89*
Hancock, Mary A. 1923- *31*
Hancock, Sibyl 1940- *9*
Hand, Elizabeth 1957- *167*
  Earlier sketch in SATA *118*
Handford, Martin (John) 1956- *64*
  See also CLR *22*
Handforth, Thomas (Schofield) 1897-1948 .. *42*
Handler, Daniel
  See Snicket, Lemony
Handville, Robert (Tompkins) 1924- *45*
Hane, Roger 1940-1974
  Obituary *20*
Hanel, Wolfram
  See Haenel, Wolfram
Haney, Lynn 1941- *23*
Hanff, Helene 1916-1997 .... *97*
  Earlier sketch in SATA *11*
Hanft, Josh 1956- *197*
Hanft, Joshua E.
  See Hanft, Josh
Hanley, Boniface Francis 1924- *65*
Hanlon, Emily 1945- *15*
Hann, Jacquie 1951- *19*
Hann, Judith 1942- *77*
Hanna, Bill
  See Hanna, William (Denby)
Hanna, Cheryl 1951- *84*
Hanna, Jack (Bushnell) 1947- *74*
Hanna, Nell(ie L.) 1908- *55*
Hanna, Paul R(obert) 1902-1988 .... *9*
Hanna, William (Denby) 1910-2001 .... *51*
  Obituary *126*
Hannam, Charles 1925- *50*
Hannan, Peter 1954- *187*
Hannigan, Katherine *170*
Hannon, Ezra
  See Hunter, Evan
Hann-Syme, Marguerite *127*
Hano, Arnold 1922- *12*
Hano, Renee Roth
  See Roth-Hano, Renee
Hanover, Terri
  See Huff, Tanya
Hansen, Ann Larkin 1958- *96*
Hansen, Brooks 1965- *104*
Hansen, Caryl (Hall) 1929- *39*
Hansen, Ian V. 1929- *113*

Hansen, Jennifer 1972- *156*
Hansen, Joyce 1942- *172*
  Autobiography Feature *172*
  Brief entry *39*
  Earlier sketches in SATA *46, 101*
  See also CLR *21*
  See also SAAS *15*
Hansen, Joyce Viola
  See Hansen, Joyce
Hansen, Mark Victor *112*
Hansen, Ron(ald Thomas) 1947- *56*
Hanser, Richard (Frederick) 1909-1981 .... *13*
Hanson, Joan 1938- *8*
Hanson, Joseph E. 1894(?)-1971
  Obituary *27*
Hanson, Mary Elizabeth *188*
Hanson, Warren 1949- *155*
Hansson, Gunilla 1939- *64*
Harald, Eric
  See Boesen, Victor
Harcourt, Ellen Knowles 1890(?)-1984
  Obituary *36*
Hard, Charlotte (Ann) 1969- *98*
Hardcastle, Michael 1933- *47*
  Brief entry *38*
Harding, Lee 1937- *32*
  Brief entry *31*
Hardt, Helga Fleischhauer
  See Fleischhauer-Hardt, Helga
Hardwick, Richard Holmes, Jr. 1923- *12*
Hardy, Alice Dale *67*
  Earlier sketch in SATA *1*
Hardy, David A(ndrews) 1936- *9*
Hardy, Jon 1958- *53*
Hardy, LeAnne 1951- *154*
Hardy, Stuart
  See Schisgall, Oscar
Hare, Norma Q(uarles) 1924- *46*
  Brief entry *41*
Harel, Nira 1936- *154*
Harford, Henry
  See Hudson, W(illiam) H(enry)
Hargrave, Leonie
  See Disch, Thomas M.
Hargreaves, (Charles) Roger 1935-1988
  Obituary *56*
Hargrove, James 1947- *57*
  Brief entry *50*
Hargrove, Jim
  See Hargrove, James
Hariton, Anca I. 1955- *79*
Hark, Mildred
  See McQueen, Mildred Hark
Harkaway, Hal
  See Stratemeyer, Edward L.
Harkins, Philip 1912-1997 .... *6*
  Obituary *129*
Harlan, Elizabeth 1945- *41*
  Brief entry *35*
Harlan, Glen
  See Cebulash, Mel
Harlan, Judith 1949- *135*
  Earlier sketch in SATA *74*
  See also CLR *81*
Harland, Richard 1947- *152*
Harlee, J. V.
  See Leese, Jennifer L.B.
Harler, Ann
  See Van Steenwyk, Elizabeth (Ann)
Harley, Avis *183*
Harley, Bill 1954- *87*
Harlow, Joan Hiatt 1932- *157*
Harman, Fred 1902(?)-1982
  Obituary *30*
Harman, Hugh 1903-1982
  Obituary *33*
Harmelink, Barbara (Mary) *9*
Harmer, Mabel 1894-1992 .... *45*
Harmon, Dan
  See Harmon, Daniel E(lton)
Harmon, Daniel E(lton) 1949- *157*

Harmon, Margaret 1906- *20*
Harmon, Michael 1969- *189*
Harmon, William (Ruth) 1938- *65*
Harnan, Terry 1920- *12*
Harness, Cheryl 1951- *178*
  Earlier sketch in SATA *131*
Harnett, Cynthia (Mary) 1893-1981 .... *5*
  Obituary *32*
Harper, Anita 1943- *41*
Harper, Betty 1946- *126*
Harper, Charise
  See Harper, Charise Mericle
Harper, Charise Mericle *179*
Harper, Elaine
  See Hallin, Emily Watson
Harper, Ellen
  See Noble, Marty
Harper, Jamie *174*
Harper, Jessica (R.) 1949- *148*
Harper, Jo 1932- *169*
  Earlier sketch in SATA *97*
Harper, Mary Wood
  See Dixon, Jeanne
Harper, Piers 1966- *161*
  Earlier sketch in SATA *105*
Harper, Suzanne *194*
Harper, Wilhelmina 1884-1973 .... *4*
  Obituary *26*
Harrah, Madge 1931- *154*
Harrah, Michael 1940- *41*
Harrah, Monique
  See Harrah, Madge
Harrar, George E. 1949- *124*
Harrell, Beatrice Orcutt 1943- *93*
Harrell, Janice 1945- *70*
Harries, Joan 1922- *39*
Harrill, Ronald 1950- *90*
Harrington, Denis J(ames) 1932- *88*
Harrington, Evelyn Davis 1911- *5*
Harrington, Janice N. 1956- *187*
Harrington, Lyn
  See Harrington, Evelyn Davis
Harris, Alan 1944- *71*
Harris, Aurand 1915-1996 .... *37*
  Obituary *91*
Harris, Bob
  See Harris, Robert J.
Harris, Carol Flynn 1933- *135*
Harris, Catherine
  See Ainsworth, Catherine Harris
Harris, Christie
  See Harris, Christie (Lucy) Irwin
Harris, Christie (Lucy) Irwin 1907-2002 ...... *74*
  Autobiography Feature *116*
  Earlier sketch in SATA *6*
  See also CLR *47*
  See also SAAS *10*
Harris, Christine 1955- *105*
Harris, Colver
  See Colver, Anne
Harris, David 1942- *118*
Harris, David William
  See Harris, David
Harris, Dorothy Joan 1931- *153*
  Earlier sketch in SATA *13*
Harris, Geraldine (Rachel) 1951- *54*
Harris, Jacqueline L. 1929- *62*
Harris, Janet 1932-1979 .... *4*
  Obituary *23*
Harris, Jesse
  See Standiford, Natalie
Harris, Joan 1946- *146*
Harris, Joel Chandler 1848-1908 .... *100*
  See also YABC *1*
  See also CLR *128*
Harris, John (Wyndham Parkes Lucas) Beynon
  1903-1969 .... *118*
Harris, Johnson
  See Harris, John (Wyndham Parkes Lucas)
  Beynon
Harris, Jonathan 1921-1997 .... *52*

Harris, Larry Vincent 1939- *59*
Harris, Lavinia
  See St. John, Nicole
Harris, Leon A., Jr. 1926-2000 .... *4*
Harris, Lois V. *199*
Harris, Lorle K(empe) 1912-2001 .... *22*
Harris, Marilyn
  See Springer, Marilyn Harris
Harris, Mark Jonathan 1941- *84*
  Earlier sketch in SATA *32*
Harris, Mary K(athleen) 1905-1966 .... *119*
Harris, Robert J. 1955- *195*
Harris, Robie H. 1940- *147*
  Brief entry *53*
  Earlier sketch in SATA *90*
Harris, Robin
  See Shine, Deborah
Harris, Rosemary (Jeanne) *82*
  Earlier sketch in SATA *4*
  See also CLR *30*
  See also SAAS *7*
Harris, Ruth Elwin 1935- *164*
Harris, Sherwood 1932- *25*
Harris, Steven Michael 1957- *55*
Harris, Trudy 1949- *191*
  Earlier sketch in SATA *128*
Harris-Filderman, Diane
  See Filderman, Diane E(lizabeth)
Harrison, C(hester) William 1913-1994 .... *35*
Harrison, Carol
  See Harrison, Carol Thompson
Harrison, Carol Thompson *113*
Harrison, David L. 1937- *186*
  Earlier sketches in SATA *26, 92, 150*
Harrison, Deloris 1938- *9*
Harrison, Edward Hardy 1926- *56*
Harrison, Elizabeth (Allen) Cavanna
  1909-2001 .... *30*
  Earlier sketch in SATA *1*
  See also SAAS *4*
Harrison, Harry 1925- *4*
Harrison, Harry Max
  See Harrison, Harry
Harrison, Mette Ivie 1970- *149*
Harrison, Michael 1939- *106*
Harrison, Molly (Hodgett) 1909-2002 .... *41*
Harrison, Sarah 1946- *63*
Harrison, Ted
  See Harrison, Edward Hardy
Harsh, Fred (T.) 1925- *72*
Harshaw, Ruth H(etzel) 1890-1968 .... *27*
Harshman, Marc 1950- *109*
  Earlier sketch in SATA *71*
Hart, Alexandra 1939- *14*
Hart, Alison
  See Leonhardt, Alice
Hart, Bruce 1938-2006 .... *57*
  Brief entry *39*
Hart, Carole 1943- *57*
  Brief entry *39*
Hart, Carolyn 1936- *74*
Hart, Carolyn G.
  See Hart, Carolyn
Hart, Carolyn Gimpel
  See Hart, Carolyn
Hart, Jan Siegel 1940- *79*
Hart, Joyce 1954- *148*
Hart, Karen *185*
Hart, Lenore *171*
Hart, Philip S. 1944- *180*
Hart, Virginia 1949- *83*
Harte, (Francis) Bret(t) 1836(?)-1902 .... *26*
Harter, Debbie 1963- *107*
Hartfield, Claire 1957- *147*
Hartinger, Brent 1964- *174*
  Earlier sketch in SATA *145*
Hartland, Jessie *171*
Hartley, Ellen (Raphael) 1915-1980 .... *23*
Hartley, Fred Allan III 1953- *41*
Hartley, William B(rown) 1913-1980 .... *23*

Hartling, Peter
  See Hartling, Peter
Hartling, Peter 1933- *66*
  See also CLR *29*
Hartman, Evert 1937- *38*
  Brief entry *35*
Hartman, Jane E(vangeline) 1928- *47*
Hartman, Louis F(rancis) 1901-1970 .... *22*
Hartman, Rachel *174*
Hartman, Victoria 1942- *91*
Hartnett, Sonya 1968- *176*
  Earlier sketches in SATA *93, 130*
Hartshorn, Ruth M. 1928- *11*
Hartung, Susan Kathleen *192*
  Earlier sketch in SATA *150*
Hartwig, Manfred 1950- *81*
Harvey, Brett 1936- *61*
Harvey, Edith 1908(?)-1972
  Obituary *27*
Harvey, Gill *189*
Harvey, Karen D. 1935- *88*
Harvey, Roland 1945- *179*
  Earlier sketches in SATA *71, 123*
Harvey-Fitzhenry, Alyxandra 1974- *189*
Harwick, B. L.
  See Keller, Beverly L(ou)
Harwin, Brian
  See Henderson, LeGrand
Harwood, Pearl Augusta (Bragdon)
  1903-1998 .... *9*
Haseley, Dennis 1950- *157*
  Brief entry *44*
  Earlier sketches in SATA *57, 105*
Hashmi, Kerri 1955- *108*
Haskell, Arnold L(ionel) 1903-1981(?) *6*
Haskins, James
  See Haskins, James S.
Haskins, James S. 1941-2005 .... *132*
  Autobiography Feature *132*
  Earlier sketches in SATA *9, 69, 105*
  See also CLR *39*
  See also SAAS *4*
Haskins, Jim
  See Haskins, James S.
Hasler, Eveline 1933- *181*
Hasler, Joan 1931- *28*
Hass, Robert 1941- *94*
Hassall, Joan 1906-1988 .... *43*
  Obituary *56*
Hassett, Ann 1958- *162*
Hassett, John *162*
Hassler, Jon 1933-2008 .... *19*
  Obituary *191*
Hassler, Jon Francis
  See Hassler, Jon
Hastings, Beverly
  See Barkin, Carol
  and James, Elizabeth
Hastings, Graham
  See Jeffries, Roderic
Hastings, Ian 1912- *62*
Hastings, Victor
  See Disch, Thomas M.
Haszard, Patricia Moyes 1923-2000 .... *63*
Hatch, Lynda S. 1950- *90*
Hathaway, Barbara *164*
Hathorn, Elizabeth
  See Hathorn, Elizabeth Helen
Hathorn, Elizabeth Helen 1943- *156*
  Autobiography Feature *156*
  Earlier sketches in SATA *74, 120*
Hathorn, Libby 1943-
  See Hathorn, Elizabeth Helen
Hatkoff, Craig 1954- *192*
Hatlo, Jimmy 1898-1963
  Obituary *23*
Haugaard, Erik Christian 1923- *68*
  Earlier sketch in SATA *4*
  See also CLR *11*
  See also SAAS *12*
Haugaard, Kay *117*

Haugen, Hayley Mitchell 1968- *172*
Haugen, Tormod 1945- *66*
Hauman, Doris 1898-1984 .... *32*
Hauman, George 1890-1961 .... *32*
Hauptly, Denis J(ames) 1945- *57*
Hauser, Jill Frankel 1950- *127*
Hauser, Margaret L(ouise) 1909- *10*
Hausherr, Rosmarie 1943- *86*
Hausman, Gerald 1945- *180*
    Earlier sketches in SATA *13, 90, 132*
    See also CLR *89*
Hausman, Gerry
    See Hausman, Gerald
Hauth, Katherine B. 1940- *99*
Hautman, Pete 1952- *173*
    Earlier sketches in SATA *82, 128*
Hautman, Peter Murray
    See Hautman, Pete
Hautzig, Deborah 1956- *106*
    Earlier sketch in SATA *31*
Hautzig, Esther Rudomin 1930- *148*
    Earlier sketches in SATA *4, 68*
    See also CLR *22*
    See also SAAS *15*
Havel, Geoff 1955- *152*
Havel, Jennifer
    See Havill, Juanita
Havelin, Kate 1961- *143*
Havighurst, Walter (Edwin) 1901-1994 .... *1*
    Obituary *79*
Haviland, Virginia 1911-1988 .... *6*
    Obituary *54*
Havill, Juanita 1949- *155*
    Earlier sketch in SATA *74*
Hawes, Judy 1913- *4*
Hawes, Louise 1943- *180*
    Earlier sketch in SATA *60*
Hawke, Rosanne 1953- *165*
    Earlier sketch in SATA *124*
Hawke, Rosanne Joy
    See Hawke, Rosanne
Hawkes, Kevin (Cliff) 1959- *150*
    Earlier sketch in SATA *78*
Hawkes, Nigel 1943- *119*
Hawkesworth, Eric 1921- *13*
Hawking, Lucy 1969- *197*
Hawkins, Arthur 1903-1985 .... *19*
Hawkins, Colin 1945- *162*
    Earlier sketch in SATA *112*
Hawkins, Jacqui *162*
    Earlier sketch in SATA *112*
Hawkins, Jimmy 1941- *188*
Hawkins, Laura 1951- *74*
Hawkins, (Helena Ann) Quail 1905-2002 .... *6*
    Obituary *141*
Hawkinson, John (Samuel) 1912-1994 .... *4*
Hawkinson, Lucy (Ozone) 1924-1971 .... *21*
Hawks, Robert 1961- *85*
Hawley, Mabel C. *67*
    Earlier sketch in SATA *1*
Hawthorne, Captain R. M.
    See Ellis, Edward S(ylvester)
Hawthorne, Nathaniel 1804-1864
    See YABC *2*
    See also CLR *103*
Hay, Jeff T. *154*
Hay, John 1915- *13*
Hay, Timothy
    See Brown, Margaret Wise
Hayashi, Leslie Ann 1954- *115*
Hayashi, Nancy 1939- *186*
    Earlier sketch in SATA *80*
Haycak, Cara 1961- *180*
Haycock, Kate 1962- *77*
Haycraft, Howard 1905-1991 .... *6*
    Obituary *70*
Haycraft, Molly Costain 1911- *6*
Hayden, Gwendolen Lampshire 1904- *35*
Hayden, Robert C(arter), Jr. 1937- *47*
    Brief entry *28*

Hayden, Robert E(arl) 1913-1980 .... *19*
    Obituary *26*
Hayden, Torey L. 1951- *163*
    Earlier sketch in SATA *65*
Hayden, Torey Lynn
    See Hayden, Torey L.
Hayes, Carlton J(oseph) H(untley)
    1882-1964 .... *11*
Hayes, Daniel 1952- *109*
    Earlier sketch in SATA *73*
Hayes, Geoffrey 1947- *91*
    Earlier sketch in SATA *26*
Hayes, Joe 1945- *131*
    Earlier sketch in SATA *88*
Hayes, John F. 1904-1980 .... *11*
Hayes, Rosemary *158*
Hayes, Sheila 1937- *51*
    Brief entry *50*
Hayes, Will *7*
Hayes, William D(imitt) 1913-1976 .... *8*
Haynes, Betsy 1937- *94*
    Brief entry *37*
    Earlier sketch in SATA *48*
    See also CLR *90*
Haynes, David 1955- *97*
Haynes, Linda
    See Swinford, Betty (June Wells)
Haynes, Mary 1938- *65*
Haynes, Max 1956- *72*
Hays, H(offmann) R(eynolds) 1904-1980 .... *26*
Hays, Thomas Anthony 1957- *84*
Hays, Tony
    See Hays, Thomas Anthony
Hays, Wilma Pitchford 1909- *28*
    Earlier sketch in SATA *1*
    See also CLR *59*
    See also SAAS *3*
Hayward, Linda 1943- *185*
    Brief entry *39*
    Earlier sketch in SATA *101*
Haywood, Carolyn 1898-1990 .... *75*
    Obituary *64*
    Earlier sketches in SATA *1, 29*
    See also CLR *22*
Hazell, Rebecca (Eileen) 1947- *141*
Hazen, Barbara Shook 1930- *178*
    Earlier sketches in SATA *27, 90*
Head, Gay
    See Hauser, Margaret L(ouise)
Head, Tom 1978- *167*
Headley, Elizabeth
    See Harrison, Elizabeth (Allen) Cavanna
Headley, Justina Chen 1968- *176*
Headstrom, (Birger) Richard 1902-1985 .... *8*
Heady, Eleanor B(utler) 1917-1979 .... *8*
Heagy, William D. 1964- *76*
Heal, Edith 1903-1995 .... *7*
Heal, Gillian 1934- *89*
Heale, Jay (Jeremy Peter Wingfield) 1937- .. *84*
Healey, Brooks
    See Albert, Burton
Healey, Larry 1927- *44*
    Brief entry *42*
Heap, Sue 1954- *187*
    Earlier sketch in SATA *150*
Heaps, Willard A(llison) 1908-1987 .... *26*
Hearn, Diane Dawson 1952- *79*
Hearn, Emily
    See Valleau, Emily
Hearn, Julie 1958- *152*
Hearn, Lian
    See Rubinstein, Gillian
Hearn, Sneed
    See Gregg, Andrew K.
Hearne, Betsy 1942- *146*
    Earlier sketches in SATA *38, 95*
Heath, Charles D(ickinson) 1941- *46*
Heath, Veronica
    See Blackett, Veronica Heath
Heaven, Constance (Christina) 1911- *7*
Hebert-Collins, Sheila 1948- *111*

Hecht, George J(oseph) 1895-1980
    Obituary *22*
Hecht, Henri Joseph 1922- *9*
Hechtkopf, Henryk 1910- *17*
Heck, Bessie (Mildred) Holland 1911-1995 . *26*
Heck, Ed 1963- *173*
Heckert, Connie K(aye Delp) 1948- *82*
Hedderwick, Mairi 1939- *145*
    Earlier sketches in SATA *30, 77*
Hedges, Sid(ney) G(eorge) 1897-1974 .... *28*
Hedrick, Irene Hope 1920- *175*
Heelan, Jamee Riggio 1965- *146*
Heerboth, Sharon
    See Leon, Sharon
Heffernan, John 1949- *168*
    Earlier sketch in SATA *121*
Heffron, Dorris 1944- *68*
Hefter, Richard 1942- *31*
Hegarty, Reginald Beaton 1906-1973 .... *10*
Hehenberger, Shelly 1968- *126*
Heidbreder, Robert 1947- *196*
    Earlier sketch in SATA *130*
Heidbreder, Robert K.
    See Heidbreder, Robert
Heide, Florence Parry 1919- *192*
    Earlier sketches in SATA *32, 69, 118*
    See also CLR *60*
    See also SAAS *6*
Heiderstadt, Dorothy 1907-2001 .... *6*
Heidi Louise
    See Erdrich, Louise
Heidler, David S(tephen) 1955- *132*
Heidler, Jeanne T. 1956- *132*
Heilbroner, Joan Knapp 1922- *63*
Heilbrun, Lois Hussey 1922(?)-1987
    Obituary *54*
Heiligman, Deborah 1958- *193*
    Earlier sketches in SATA *90, 144*
Heilman, Joan Rattner *50*
Heimann, Rolf 1940- *164*
    Earlier sketch in SATA *120*
Hein, Lucille Eleanor 1915-1994 .... *20*
Heine, Helme 1941- *135*
    Earlier sketch in SATA *67*
    See also CLR *18*
Heinlein, Robert A. 1907-1988 .... *69*
    Obituary *56*
    Earlier sketch in SATA *9*
    See also CLR *75*
Heinlein, Robert Anson
    See Heinlein, Robert A.
Heins, Ethel L(eah) 1918-1997 .... *101*
Heins, Paul 1909- *13*
Heintze, Carl 1922- *26*
Heinz, Bill
    See Heinz, W.C.
Heinz, Brian J. 1946- *181*
    Earlier sketch in SATA *95*
Heinz, Brian James
    See Heinz, Brian J.
Heinz, W.C. 1915-2008 .... *26*
Heinz, Wilfred Charles
    See Heinz, W.C.
Heinzen, Mildred
    See Masters, Mildred
Heisel, Sharon E(laine) 1941- *125*
    Earlier sketch in SATA *84*
Heitzmann, William Ray 1948- *73*
Heitzmann, Wm. Ray
    See Heitzmann, William Ray
Helakoski, Leslie *178*
Helberg, Shirley Adelaide Holden 1919- ... *138*
Helfer, Andrew *187*
Helfer, Ralph 1937- *177*
Helfman, Elizabeth S(eaver) 1911-2001 .... *3*
Helfman, Harry Carmozin 1910-1995 .... *3*
Helgerson, Joseph 1950- *181*
Hellard, Susan *182*
Hellberg, Hans-Eric 1927- *38*
Heller, Linda 1944- *46*
    Brief entry *40*

Heller, Mike
  See Hano, Arnold
Heller, Ruth M. 1924- 112
  Earlier sketch in SATA 66
Hellman, Hal
  See Hellman, Harold
Hellman, Harold 1927- 4
Helman, Andrea (Jean) 1946- 160
  Earlier sketch in SATA 107
Helmer, Diana Star 1962- 86
Helmer, Marilyn 160
  Earlier sketch in SATA 112
Helps, Racey 1913-1971 2
  Obituary 25
Helquist, Brett 187
  Earlier sketch in SATA 146
Helweg, Hans H. 1917- 50
  Brief entry 33
Helyar, Jane Penelope Josephine 1933- 5
  Autobiography Feature 138
  See also SAAS 2
Hemmant, Lynette 1938- 69
Hemming, Roy G. 1928-1995 11
  Obituary 86
Hemphill, Helen 1955- 179
Hemphill, Kris (Harrison) 1963- 118
Hemphill, Martha Locke 1904-1973 37
Hemphill, Stephanie 190
Hemstock, Gillian 1956- 173
Henba, Bobbie 1926- 87
Henbest, Nigel 1951- 55
  Brief entry 52
Henderley, Brooks 1
Henderson, Aileen Kilgore 1921- 178
Henderson, Aileen Mary
  See Fox, Aileen
Henderson, Gordon 1950- 53
Henderson, Kathy 1949- 155
  Brief entry 53
  Earlier sketches in SATA 55, 95
Henderson, LeGrand 1901-1965 9
Henderson, Nancy Wallace 1916- 22
Henderson, Zenna (Chlarson) 1917-1983 5
Hendrickson, Walter Brookfield, Jr. 1936- 9
Hendry, Diana 1941- 106
  Earlier sketch in SATA 68
Hendry, Frances Mary 1941- 171
  Earlier sketch in SATA 110
Hendry, Linda (Gail) 1961- 83
Heneghan, James 1930- 160
  Earlier sketches in SATA 53, 97
Henkes, Kevin 1960- 154
  Earlier sketches in SATA 43, 76, 108
  See also CLR 108
Hennessy, Barbara G.
  See Hennessy, B.G.
Hennessy, Barbara Gulbrandsen
  See Hennessy, B.G.
Hennessy, B.G. 1951- 175
Henney, Carolee Wells 1928- 102
Henriod, Lorraine 1925- 26
Henriquez, Emile F. 1937- 170
  Earlier sketch in SATA 89
Henry, April 1959- 174
Henry, Ernest 1948- 107
Henry, Joanne Landers 1927- 6
Henry, Maeve 1960- 75
Henry, Marguerite 1902-1997 100
  Obituary 99
  See also CLR 4
  See also SAAS 7
Henry, Marie H. 1935- 65
Henry, Marilyn 1939- 117
Henry, Marion
  See del Rey, Lester
Henry, O. 1862-1910
  See YABC 2
Henry, Oliver
  See Henry, O.

Henry, T. E.
  See Rowland-Entwistle, (Arthur) Theodore
  (Henry)
Henschel, Elizabeth Georgie 56
Henson, James Maury
  See Henson, Jim
Henson, Jim 1936-1990 43
  Obituary 65
Henstra, Friso 1928- 73
  Earlier sketch in SATA 8
  See also SAAS 14
Hentoff, Nat(han Irving) 1925- 133
  Brief entry 27
  Earlier sketches in SATA 42, 69
  See also CLR 52
Henty, G(eorge) A(lfred) 1832-1902 64
  See also CLR 76
Heo, Yumi 1964- 146
  Earlier sketch in SATA 94
Hepler, Heather 177
Herald, Kathleen
  See Peyton, Kathleen Wendy (Herald)
Herb, Angela M. 1970- 92
Herbert, Cecil
  See Hamilton, Charles (Harold St. John)
Herbert, Don 1917-2007 2
  Obituary 184
Herbert, Donald Jeffrey
  See Herbert, Don
Herbert, Frank 1920-1986 37
  Obituary 47
  Earlier sketch in SATA 9
Herbert, Frank Patrick
  See Herbert, Frank
Herbert, Helen (Jean) 1947- 57
Herbert, Janis 1956- 139
Herbert, Wally 1934-2007 23
Herbert, Walter William
  See Herbert, Wally
Herbst, Judith 1947- 74
Herda, D.J. 1948- 80
Herge
  See Remi, Georges
Heritage, Martin
  See Horler, Sydney
Herkimer, L(awrence) R(ussell) 1925(?)- 42
Herlihy, Dirlie Anne 1935- 73
Herman, Charlotte 1937- 99
  Earlier sketch in SATA 20
Hermanson, Dennis (Everett) 1947- 10
Hermes, Jules 1962- 92
Hermes, Patricia 1936- 191
  Earlier sketches in SATA 31, 78, 141
Hermes, Patricia Mary
  See Hermes, Patricia
Hernandez, Natalie Nelson 1929- 123
Herndon, Ernest 91
Herold, Ann Bixby 1937- 72
Herrera, Juan Felipe 1948- 127
Herrick, Steven 1958- 156
  Earlier sketch in SATA 103
Herriman, George (Joseph) 1880-1944 140
Herriot, James 1916-1995
  See Wight, James Alfred
Herrmanns, Ralph 1933- 11
Herrold, Tracey
  See Dils, Tracey E.
Herron, Edward A(lbert) 1912- 4
Herschler, Mildred Barger 130
Hersey, John 1914-1993 25
  Obituary 76
Hersey, John Richard
  See Hersey, John
  and Hersey, John
Hershberger, Priscilla (Gorman) 1951- 81
Hershenhorn, Esther 1945- 151
Hershey, Kathleen M. 1934- 80
Hershey, Mary 173
Hersom, Kathleen 1911- 73
Hertz, Grete Janus 1915- 23
Herzig, Alison Cragin 1935- 87

Herzog, Brad 1968- 131
Heslewood, Juliet 1951- 82
Hess, Lilo 1916- 4
Hess, Paul 1961- 134
Hesse, Hermann 1877-1962 50
Hesse, Karen 1952- 158
  Autobiography Feature 113
  Earlier sketches in SATA 74, 103
  See also CLR 54
  See also SAAS 25
Hest, Amy 1950- 193
  Earlier sketches in SATA 55, 82, 129
Heuer, Kenneth John 1927- 44
Heuman, William 1912-1971 21
Heuston, Kimberley 1960- 167
Heuston, Kimberley Burton
  See Heuston, Kimberley
Hewes, Agnes Danforth 1874-1963 35
Hewett, Anita 1918-1989 13
Hewett, Joan 1930- 140
  Earlier sketch in SATA 81
Hewett, Richard 1929- 81
Hewitson, Jennifer 1961- 97
Hewitt, Margaret 1961- 84
Hewitt, Sally 1949- 127
Hext, Harrington
  See Phillpotts, Eden
Hey, Nigel S(tewart) 1936- 20
Heyduck-Huth, Hilde 1929- 8
Heyer, Carol 1950- 130
  Earlier sketch in SATA 74
Heyer, Marilee 1942- 102
  Earlier sketch in SATA 64
Heyerdahl, Thor 1914-2002 52
  Earlier sketch in SATA 2
Heyes, (Nancy) Eileen 1956- 150
  Earlier sketch in SATA 80
Heyliger, William 1884-1955
  See YABC 1
Heyman, Ken(neth Louis) 1930- 114
  Earlier sketch in SATA 34
Heyward, (Edwin) DuBose 1885-1940 21
Heywood, Karen 1946- 48
Hezlep, William (Earl) 1936- 88
Hibbert, Arthur Raymond
  See Hibbert, Christopher
Hibbert, Christopher 1924-2008 4
Hibbert, Eleanor Alice Burford 1906-1993 2
  Obituary 74
Hickman, Estella (Lee) 1942- 111
Hickman, Janet 1940- 127
  Earlier sketch in SATA 12
Hickman, Martha Whitmore 1925- 26
Hickman, Pamela 1958- 186
  Earlier sketch in SATA 128
Hickock, Will
  See Harrison, C(hester) William
Hickok, Lorena A. 1893-1968 20
Hickox, Rebecca (Ayres) 116
Hicks, Barbara Jean 1953- 165
Hicks, Betty 191
Hicks, Clifford B. 1920- 50
Hicks, Eleanor B.
  See Coerr, Eleanor (Beatrice)
Hicks, Harvey
  See Stratemeyer, Edward L.
Hicks, Peter 1952- 111
Hicyilmaz, Gaye 1947- 157
  Earlier sketch in SATA 77
Hieatt, Constance B(artlett) 1928- 4
Hiebert, Ray Eldon 1932- 13
Higdon, Hal 1931- 4
Higginbottom, David 1923- 87
  Earlier sketch in SATA 25
Higginbottom, J(effrey) Winslow 1945- 29
Higgins, Joanna 1945- 125
Higgins, Simon (Richard) 1958- 105
Higginsen, Vy 79
High, Linda Oatman 1958- 188
  Autobiography Feature 188
  Earlier sketches in SATA 94, 145

High, Philip E. 1914- 119
High, Philip Empson
  See High, Philip E.
Higham, David (Michael) 1949- 50
Higham, Jon Atlas
  See Higham, Jonathan Huw
Higham, Jonathan Huw 1960- 59
Highet, Helen
  See MacInnes, Helen (Clark)
Hightman, Jason 1971(?)- 189
Hightman, J.P.
  See Hightman, Jason
Hightower, Florence Cole 1916-1981 4
  Obituary 27
Highwater, Jamake (Mamake)
  1942(?)-2001 69
  Brief entry 30
  Earlier sketch in SATA *32*
  See also CLR *17*
Hilb, Nora 1953- 178
Hildebrandt, Greg 1939- 172
  Brief entry 33
  Earlier sketch in SATA *55*
Hildebrandt, Tim 1939-2006 55
  Brief entry 33
Hildebrandt, Timothy
  See Hildebrandt, Tim
Hildebrandts, The
  See Hildebrandt, Greg
  and Hildebrandt, Tim
Hilder, Rowland 1905-1993 36
  Obituary 77
Hildick, E. W.
  See Hildick, (Edmund) Wallace
Hildick, (Edmund) Wallace 1925-2001 68
  Earlier sketch in SATA *2*
  See also SAAS *6*
Hilgartner, Beth 1957- 58
Hill, Alexis
  See Craig, Mary (Francis) Shura
  and Glick, Ruth (Burtnick)
Hill, Anthony R. 1942- 164
  Earlier sketch in SATA *91*
Hill, Anthony Robert
  See Hill, Anthony R.
Hill, David 1942- 152
  Earlier sketch in SATA *103*
Hill, Donna (Marie) 1921- 124
  Earlier sketch in SATA *24*
Hill, Douglas 1935-2007 78
  Earlier sketch in SATA *39*
Hill, Douglas Arthur
  See Hill, Douglas
Hill, Elizabeth Starr 1925- 143
  Earlier sketch in SATA *24*
Hill, Eric 1927- 133
  Brief entry 53
  Earlier sketch in SATA *66*
  See also CLR *13*
Hill, Gordon
  See Eldin, Peter
Hill, Grace Brooks 67
  Earlier sketch in SATA *1*
Hill, Grace Livingston 1865-1947
  See YABC *2*
Hill, Helen M(orey) 1915- 27
Hill, John
  See Koontz, Dean R.
Hill, Johnson
  See Kunhardt, Edith
Hill, Judy I. R.
  See Roberts, Judy I.
Hill, Kathleen Louise 1917- 4
Hill, Kay
  See Hill, Kathleen Louise
Hill, Kirkpatrick 1938- 188
  Earlier sketches in SATA *72, 126*
Hill, Laban Carrick 170
Hill, Lee Sullivan 1958- 96
Hill, Lorna 1902-1991 12
Hill, Margaret (Ohler) 1915- 36

Hill, Meg
  See Hill, Margaret (Ohler)
Hill, Meredith
  See Craig, Mary (Francis) Shura
Hill, Monica
  See Watson, Jane Werner
Hill, Pamela Smith 1954- 112
Hill, Ralph Nading 1917-1987 65
Hill, Robert W(hite) 1919-1982 12
  Obituary 31
Hill, Ruth A.
  See Viguers, Ruth Hill
Hill, Ruth Livingston
  See Munce, Ruth Hill
Hill, Stuart 1958- 186
Hill, Susan 1942- 183
Hill, Susan Elizabeth
  See Hill, Susan
Hill, Susanna Leonard 1965- 193
Hill, Thomas 1960- 82
Hillcourt, William 1900-1992 27
Hillenbrand, Will 1960- 147
  Earlier sketch in SATA *84*
Hiller, Ilo (Ann) 1938- 59
Hillerman, Anthony Grove
  See Hillerman, Tony
Hillerman, Tony 1925-2008 6
  Obituary 198
Hillert, Margaret 1920- 91
  Earlier sketch in SATA *8*
Hilliard, Richard 183
Hillman, Elizabeth 1942- 75
Hillman, John 1952- 120
Hillman, Martin
  See Hill, Douglas
Hillman, Priscilla 1940- 48
  Brief entry 39
Hills, C.A.R. 1955- 39
Hills, Charles Albert Reis
  See Hills, C.A.R.
Hills, Tad 173
Hilton, Irene Pothus -1979 7
Hilton, James 1900-1954 34
Hilton, Margaret Lynette 1946- 105
  Earlier sketch in SATA *68*
  See also CLR *25*
  See also SAAS *21*
Hilton, Nette
  See Hilton, Margaret Lynette
Hilton, Ralph 1907-1982 8
Hilton, Suzanne 1922- 4
Hilton-Bruce, Anne
  See Hilton, Margaret Lynette
Him, George 1937-1982
  Obituary 30
Himelblau, Linda -2005 179
Himelstein, Shmuel 1940- 83
Himler, Ann 1946- 8
Himler, Ronald 1937- 183
  Earlier sketches in SATA *6, 92, 137*
Himler, Ronald Norbert
  See Himler, Ronald
Himmelman, John C(arl) 1959- 159
  Earlier sketches in SATA *47, 94*
Hinckley, Helen
  See Jones, Helen Hinckley
Hind, Dolores (Ellen) 1931- 53
  Brief entry 49
Hindin, Nathan
  See Bloch, Robert (Albert)
Hindley, Judy 1940- 179
  Earlier sketch in SATA *120*
Hinds, P(atricia) Mignon 98
Hine, Sesyle Joslin 1929- 2
Hines, Anna Grossnickle 1946- 141
  Brief entry 45
  Earlier sketches in SATA *51, 95*
  See also SAAS *16*
Hines, Gary (Roger) 1944- 136
  Earlier sketch in SATA *74*
Hinojosa, Maria (de Lourdes) 1961- 88

Hinton, Nigel 1941- 166
Hinton, Sam 1917- 43
Hinton, S.E. 1950- 160
  Earlier sketches in SATA *19, 58, 115*
  See also CLR *23*
Hinton, Susan Eloise
  See Hinton, S.E.
Hintz, Martin 1945- 128
  Brief entry 39
  Earlier sketch in SATA *47*
Hintz, Stephen V. 1975- 129
Hippopotamus, Eugene H.
  See Kraus, (Herman) Robert
Hirano, Cathy 1957- 68
Hirsch, Karen 1941- 61
Hirsch, Odo 157
  Earlier sketch in SATA *111*
Hirsch, Phil 1926- 35
Hirsch, S. Carl 1913-1990 2
  See also SAAS *7*
Hirschfelder, Arlene B. 1943- 138
  Earlier sketch in SATA *80*
Hirschi, Ron 1948- 192
  Earlier sketches in SATA *56, 95*
Hirschmann, Linda (Ann) 1941- 40
Hirsh, Marilyn 1944-1988 7
  Obituary 58
Hirshberg, Al(bert Simon) 1909-1973 38
Hiscock, Bruce 1940- 137
  Earlier sketch in SATA *57*
Hiser, Constance 1950- 71
Hiser, Iona Seibert -1998 4
Hislop, Julia Rose Catherine 1962- 74
Hissey, Jane 1952- 130
  Autobiography Feature 130
  Earlier sketches in SATA *58, 103*
Hissey, Jane Elizabeth
  See Hissey, Jane
Hitchcock, Alfred (Joseph) 1899-1980 27
  Obituary 24
Hite, Sid 1954- 175
  Earlier sketches in SATA *75, 136*
Hitte, Kathryn 1919- 16
Hitz, Demi 1942- 152
  Earlier sketches in SATA *11, 66, 102*
  See also CLR *58*
Hitzeroth, Deborah L. 1961- 78
Hnizdovsky, Jacques 1915- 32
Ho, Louise 185
Ho, Minfong 1951- 151
  Earlier sketches in SATA *15, 94*
  See also CLR *28*
Hoagland, Edward (Morley) 1932- 51
Hoare, Robert J(ohn) 1921-1975 38
Hoban, Lillian 1925-1998 69
  Obituary 104
  Earlier sketch in SATA *22*
  See also CLR *67*
Hoban, Russell 1925- 136
  Earlier sketches in SATA *1, 40, 78*
  See also CLR *139*
Hoban, Russell Conwell
  See Hoban, Russell
Hoban, Tana 1917(?)-2006 104
  Obituary 173
  Earlier sketches in SATA *22, 70*
  See also CLR *76*
  See also SAAS *12*
Hobart, Lois (Elaine) 7
Hobbie, Holly 1944- 178
  See also CLR *88*
Hobbie, Jocelyn 190
Hobbie, Nathaniel 196
Hobbs, Leigh 1953- 166
Hobbs, Valerie 1941- 193
  Autobiography Feature 145
  Earlier sketches in SATA *93, 145*
Hobbs, Will 1947- 177
  Autobiography Feature 127
  Earlier sketches in SATA *72, 110*
  See also CLR *59*

Hobbs, William Carl
See Hobbs, Will
Hoberman, Mary Ann 1930- 158
Earlier sketches in SATA *5, 72, 111*
See also CLR *22*
See also SAAS *18*
Hobson, Bruce 1950- 62
Hobson, Burton (Harold) 1933- 28
Hobson, Laura Z(ametkin) 1900-1986 52
Hobson, Sally 1967- 172
Earlier sketch in SATA *84*
Hoce, Charley E. 174
Hochschild, Arlie Russell 1940- 11
Hockaby, Stephen
See Mitchell, Gladys (Maude Winifred)
Hockenberry, Hope
See Newell, Hope Hockenberry
Hodge, Deborah 1954- 163
Earlier sketch in SATA *122*
Hodge, P. W.
See Hodge, Paul W(illiam)
Hodge, Paul W(illiam) 1934- 12
Hodgell, P(atricia) C(hristine) 1951- 42
Hodges, C. Walter 1909-2004 2
Obituary 158
Hodges, Carl G. 1902-1964 10
Hodges, Cyril Walter
See Hodges, C. Walter
Hodges, Elizabeth Jamison 1
Hodges, Margaret 1911-2005 167
Obituary 172
Earlier sketches in SATA *1, 33, 75, 117*
See also SAAS *9*
Hodges, Margaret Moore
See Hodges, Margaret
Hodgetts, Blake Christopher 1967- 43
Hodgkins, Fran 1964- 199
Hodgman, Ann 1956- 198
Hodgson, Harriet (W.) 1935- 84
Hoehne, Marcia 1951- 89
Hoellwarth, Cathryn Clinton
See Clinton, Cathryn
Hoestlandt, Jo 1948- 94
Hoestlandt, Jocelyne
See Hoestlandt, Jo
Hoexter, Corinne K. 1927- 6
Hoeye, Michael 1947- 136
Hoff, Carol 1900-1979 11
Hoff, Mary (King) 1956- 157
Earlier sketch in SATA *74*
Hoff, Syd(ney) 1912-2004 138
Obituary 154
Earlier sketches in SATA *9, 72*
See also CLR *83*
See also SAAS *4*
Hoffman, Edwin D. 49
Hoffman, Elizabeth P(arkinson) 1921-2003
Obituary 153
Hoffman, Mary (Margaret) 1945- 144
Earlier sketches in SATA *59, 97*
See also SAAS *24*
Hoffman, Mat 1972- 150
Hoffman, Nina Kiriki 1955- 160
Hoffman, Phyllis M(iriam) 1944- 4
Hoffman, Rosekrans 1926- 15
Hoffmann, E(rnst) T(heodor) A(madeus)
1776-1822 27
See also CLR *133*
Hoffmann, Felix 1911-1975 9
Hoffmann, Heinrich 1809-1894
See CLR *122*
Hoffmann, Margaret Jones 1910- 48
Hoffmann, Peggy
See Hoffmann, Margaret Jones
Hofher, Catherine Baxley 1954- 130
Hofher, Cathy
See Hofher, Catherine Baxley
Hofmeyr, Dianne (Louise) 138
Hofsepian, Sylvia A. 1932- 74
Hofsinde, Robert 1902-1973 21
Hogan, Bernice Harris 1929- 12

Hogan, Inez 1895-1973 2
Hogan, James P(atrick) 1941- 81
Hogan, Jamie 1947- 192
Hogan, Linda 1947- 132
Hogarth, Burne 1911-1996 89
Earlier sketch in SATA *63*
Hogarth, Grace (Weston Allen) 1905-1995 .. 91
Hogarth, Jr.
See Kent, Rockwell
Hogarth, (Arthur) Paul 1917-2001 41
Hogg, Garry 1902-1976 2
Hogg, Gary 1957- 172
Earlier sketch in SATA *105*
Hogner, Dorothy Childs 4
Hogner, Nils 1893-1970 25
Hogrogian, Nonny 1932- 74
Autobiography Feature 127
Earlier sketch in SATA *7*
See also CLR *95*
See also SAAS *1*
Hoh, Diane 1937- 102
Brief entry 48
Earlier sketch in SATA *52*
Hoke, Helen
See Watts, Helen L. Hoke
Hoke, Helen L.
See Watts, Helen L. Hoke
Hoke, John (Lindsay) 1925- 7
Hokenson, Terry 1948- 193
Hol, Coby 1943- 126
Holabird, Katharine 1948- 135
Earlier sketch in SATA *62*
Holaday, Bobbie 1922- 153
Holbeach, Henry
See Rands, William Brighty
Holberg, Ruth L(angland) 1889-1984 1
Holbrook, Kathy 1963- 107
Holbrook, Peter
See Glick, Carl (Cannon)
Holbrook, Sabra
See Erickson, Sabra Rollins
Holbrook, Sara 131
Holbrook, Stewart Hall 1893-1964 2
Holcomb, Jerry (Leona) Kimble 1927- 113
Holcomb, Nan
See McPhee, Norma H.
Holden, Elizabeth Rhoda
See Lawrence, Louise
Holding, James (Clark Carlisle, Jr.)
1907-1997 3
Holeman, Linda 1949- 136
Autobiography Feature 136
Earlier sketch in SATA *102*
Holinger, William (Jacques) 1944- 90
Holisher, Desider 1901-1972 6
Holl, Adelaide Hinkle 1910- 8
Holl, Kristi D(iane) 1951- 51
Holland, Gay W. 1941- 128
Holland, Isabelle (Christian) 1920-2002 70
Autobiography Feature 103
Obituary 132
Earlier sketch in SATA *8*
See also CLR *57*
Holland, Janice 1913-1962 18
Holland, John L(ewis) 1919- 20
Holland, Joyce
See Morice, Dave
Holland, Julia 1954- 106
Holland, Lynda (H.) 1959- 77
Holland, Lys
See Gater, Dilys
Holland, Marion 1908-1989 6
Obituary 61
Hollander, John 1929- 13
Hollander, Nicole 1940(?)- 101
Hollander, Paul
See Silverberg, Robert
Hollander, Phyllis 1928- 39
Hollander, Zander 1923- 63
Holldobler, Turid 1939- 26

Holliday, Joe
See Holliday, Joseph
Holliday, Joseph 1910- 11
Holling, Holling C(lancy) 1900-1973 15
Obituary 26
See also CLR *50*
Hollingsworth, Alvin C(arl) 1930- 39
Hollingsworth, Mary 1947- 166
Earlier sketch in SATA *91*
Holloway, Teresa (Bragunier) 1906- 26
Holm, (Else) Anne (Lise) 1922-1998 1
See also CLR *75*
See also SAAS *7*
Holm, Jennifer L. 1968(?)- 183
Earlier sketches in SATA *120, 163*
Holm, Matthew 1974- 174
Holm, Sharon Lane 1955- 114
Earlier sketch in SATA *78*
Holman, Felice 1919- 82
Earlier sketch in SATA *7*
See also SAAS *17*
Holm and Hamel
See Holm, Jennifer L.
Holme, Bryan 1913-1990 26
Obituary 66
Holmes, Barbara Ware 1945- 127
Earlier sketch in SATA *65*
Holmes, Elizabeth 1957- 191
Holmes, Elizabeth Ann
See Holmes, Elizabeth
Holmes, John
See Souster, (Holmes) Raymond
Holmes, Marjorie (Rose) 1910-2002 43
Holmes, Martha 1961- 72
Holmes, Mary Tavener 1954- 199
Holmes, Mary Z(astrow) 1943- 80
Holmes, Oliver Wendell 1809-1894 34
Holmes, Peggy 1898- 60
Holmes, Raymond
See Souster, (Holmes) Raymond
Holmes, Rick
See Hardwick, Richard Holmes, Jr.
Holmes, Sara Lewis 186
Holmgren, Helen Jean 1930- 45
Holmgren, Sister George Ellen
See Holmgren, Helen Jean
Holmgren, Virginia C(unningham) 1909- 26
Holmquist, Eve 1921- 11
Holt, Kimberly Willis 1960- 179
Earlier sketch in SATA *122*
Holt, Margaret 1937- 4
Holt, Margaret Van Vechten (Saunders)
1899-1963 32
Holt, Michael (Paul) 1929- 13
Holt, Rackham
See Holt, Margaret Van Vechten (Saunders)
Holt, Rochelle L.
See DuBois, Rochelle (Lynn) Holt
Holt, Stephen
See Thompson, Harlan (Howard)
Holt, Victoria
See Hibbert, Eleanor Alice Burford
Holton, Leonard
See Wibberley, Leonard (Patrick O'Connor)
Holtze, Sally Holmes 1952- 64
Holtzman, Jerome 1926-2008 57
Obituary 194
Holub, Joan 1956- 149
Earlier sketch in SATA *99*
Holub, Josef 1926- 175
Holubitsky, Katherine 1955- 165
Earlier sketch in SATA *121*
Holyer, Erna Maria 1925- 22
Holyer, Ernie
See Holyer, Erna Maria
Holz, Loretta (Marie) 1943- 17
Homel, David 1952- 97
Homze, Alma C. 1932- 17
Honey, Elizabeth 1947- 137
Autobiography Feature 137
Earlier sketch in SATA *112*

Honeycutt, Natalie 1945- 97
Hong, Lily Toy 1958- 76
Hong, Maxine Ting Ting
  See Kingston, Maxine Hong
Honig, Donald 1931- 18
Honness, Elizabeth H. 1904- 2
Hoobler, Dorothy 1941- 161
  Earlier sketches in SATA *28, 109*
Hoobler, Thomas 161
  Earlier sketches in SATA *28, 109*
Hood, Joseph F. 1925- 4
Hood, Robert E. 1926- 21
Hood, Sarah
  See Killough, (Karen) Lee
Hook, Brendan 1963- 105
Hook, Frances 1912-1983 27
Hook, Geoffrey R(aynor) 1928- 103
Hook, Jeff
  See Hook, Geoffrey R(aynor)
Hook, Martha 1936- 27
Hooker, Richard
  See Heinz, W.C.
Hooker, Ruth 1920-1998 21
hooks, bell 1952(?)- 170
  Earlier sketch in SATA *115*
Hooks, William H(arris) 1921- 94
  Earlier sketch in SATA *16*
Hoon, Patricia Easterly 1954- 90
Hooper, Byrd
  See St. Clair, Byrd Hooper
Hooper, Mary 1948- 160
Hooper, Maureen Brett 1927- 76
Hooper, Meredith 1939- 159
  Earlier sketches in SATA *28, 101*
Hooper, Meredith Jean
  See Hooper, Meredith
Hooper, Patricia 1941- 95
Hoopes, Lyn Littlefield 1953- 49
  Brief entry 44
Hoopes, Ned E(dward) 1932- 21
Hoopes, Roy 1922- 11
Hoose, Phillip M. 1947- 137
Hoover, H(elen) M(ary) 1935- 132
  Brief entry 33
  Earlier sketches in SATA *44, 83*
  See also SAAS *8*
Hoover, Helen (Drusilla Blackburn)
  1910-1984 12
  Obituary 39
Hope, Christopher 1944- 62
Hope, Christopher David Tully
  See Hope, Christopher
Hope, Laura Lee
  See Goulart, Ron(ald Joseph)
  and Stanley, George Edward
Hope Simpson, Jacynth 1930- 12
Hopf, Alice (Martha) L(ightner) 1904-1988 ... 5
  Obituary 55
Hopkins, A. T.
  See Turngren, Annette
Hopkins, C. M.
  See Hopkins, Cathy
Hopkins, Cathy 1953- 165
Hopkins, Cathy M.
  See Hopkins, Cathy
Hopkins, Clark 1895-1976
  Obituary 34
Hopkins, Ellen L. 1955- 128
Hopkins, Jackie
  See Hopkins, Jackie Mims
Hopkins, Jackie Mims 1952- 178
  Earlier sketch in SATA *92*
Hopkins, Joseph G(erard) E(dward) 1909- ... 11
Hopkins, (Hector) Kenneth 1914-1988
  Obituary 58
Hopkins, Lee Bennett 1938- 168
  Earlier sketches in SATA *3, 68, 125*
  See also CLR *44*
  See also SAAS *4*
Hopkins, Lyman
  See Folsom, Franklin (Brewster)

Hopkins, Marjorie 1911-1999 9
Hopkins, Mary R(ice) 1956- 97
Hopkinson, Amanda 1948- 84
Hopkinson, Deborah 1952- 180
  Autobiography Feature 180
  Earlier sketches in SATA *76, 108, 159*
  See also CLR *118*
Hopman, Philip 1961- 177
Hoppe, Joanne 1932- 42
Hoppe, Matthias 1952- 76
Hopper, Nancy J. 1937- 38
  Brief entry 35
Hopping, Lorraine Jean
  See Egan, Lorraine Hopping
Horacek, Petr 163
Horenstein, Henry 1947- 108
Horgan, Paul (George Vincent O'Shaughnessy)
  1903-1995 13
  Obituary 84
Horlak, E.E.
  See Tepper, Sheri S.
Horler, Sydney 1888-1954 102
Horn, Sandra Ann 1944- 154
Hornblow, Arthur, Jr. 1893-1976 15
Hornblow, Leonora 1920-2005 18
  Obituary 171
Hornblow, Leonora Schinasi
  See Hornblow, Leonora
Horne, Constance 1927- 149
Horne, Richard 1960-2007 169
  Obituary 180
  Earlier sketch in SATA *111*
Horne, Richard Henry Hengist
  1802(?)-1884 29
Horner, Althea (Jane) 1926- 36
Horner, Dave 1934- 12
Horner, Jack
  See Horner, John R(obert)
Horner, John R(obert) 1946- 106
Hornik, Laurie Miller 159
Horniman, Joanne 1951- 167
  Earlier sketch in SATA *98*
Hornos, Axel 1907-1994 20
Hornstein, Reuben Aaron 1912- 64
Horowitz, Anthony 1955- 195
  Earlier sketch in SATA *137*
Horowitz, Dave 1973(?)- 172
Horowitz, Ruth 1957- 136
Horrocks, Anita 1958- 169
Horse, Harry
  See Horne, Richard
Horsfield, Alan 1939- 153
Hort, Lenny 179
Horton, James O. 1943- 173
Horton, James Oliver
  See Horton, James O.
Horton, Madelyn (Stacey) 1962- 77
Horvath, Betty 1927- 4
Horvath, David 1972(?)- 192
Horvath, Polly 1957- 194
  Earlier sketches in SATA *85, 140*
  See also CLR *90*
Horwich, Frances R(appaport) 1908-2001 11
  Obituary 130
Horwitz, Elinor Lander 45
  Brief entry 33
Horwood, William 1944- 85
Hosford, Dorothy (Grant) 1900-1952 22
Hosford, Jessie 1892-1990 5
Hoshi, Shin'ichi 1926- 101
Hoshino, Felicia 1968- 189
Hoskyns-Abrahall, Clare (Constance
  Drury) 13
Hosler, Danamarie 1978- 184
Hossack, Sylvia 1939- 83
Hossack, Sylvie Adams
  See Hossack, Sylvia
Hosseini, Khaled 1965- 156
Hossell, Karen Price
  See Price, Karen
Hosta, Dar 192

Hostetler, Marian 1932- 91
Houck, Carter 1924- 22
Hough, Charlotte 1924-2008 9
Hough, Helen Charlotte
  See Hough, Charlotte
Hough, Judy Taylor 1932- 63
  Brief entry 51
  Earlier sketch in SATA *56*
Hough, Richard (Alexander) 1922-1999 17
Houghton, Eric 1930- 7
Houk, Randy 1944- 97
Houlehen, Robert J. 1918- 18
Houlton, Peggy Mann 1925(?)-1990 6
Household, Geoffrey (Edward West)
  1900-1988 14
  Obituary 59
Housman, Laurence 1865-1959 25
Houston, Dick 1943- 74
Houston, Gloria 138
  Autobiography Feature 138
  Earlier sketch in SATA *81*
Houston, James A(rchibald) 1921-2005 74
  Obituary 163
  Earlier sketch in SATA *13*
  See also CLR *3*
  See also SAAS *17*
Houston, James D. 1933- 78
Houston, Jeanne Toyo Wakatsuki
  See Houston, Jeanne Wakatsuki
Houston, Jeanne Wakatsuki 1934- 168
  Autobiography Feature 168
  Earlier sketch in SATA *78*
Houston, Juanita C. 1921- 129
Houton, Kathleen
  See Kilgore, Kathleen
Houts, Amy F. 164
Hovey, Kate 158
Howard, Alan 1922- 45
Howard, Alyssa
  See Buckholtz, Eileen (Garber)
  and Glick, Ruth (Burtnick)
  and Titchener, Louise
Howard, Arthur 1948- 165
Howard, Arthur Charles
  See Howard, Arthur
Howard, Elizabeth Fitzgerald 1927- 119
  Earlier sketch in SATA *74*
Howard, Ellen 1943- 184
  Earlier sketches in SATA *67, 99*
Howard, Jane R(uble) 1924- 87
Howard, Norman Barry 1949- 90
Howard, P. M.
  See Howard, Pauline Rodriguez
Howard, Paul 1967- 190
  Earlier sketch in SATA *118*
Howard, Pauline Rodriguez 1951- 124
Howard, Prosper
  See Hamilton, Charles (Harold St. John)
Howard, Robert West 1908-1988 5
Howard, Todd 1964- 135
Howard, Tristan
  See Currie, Stephen
Howard, Vernon (Linwood) 1918-1992 40
  Obituary 73
Howard, Warren F.
  See Pohl, Frederik
Howarth, Daniel 188
Howarth, David (Armine) 1912-1991 6
  Obituary 68
Howarth, Lesley 1952- 94
Howe, Deborah 1946-1978 29
Howe, James 1946- 161
  Earlier sketches in SATA *29, 71, 111*
  See also CLR *9*
Howe, John F. 1957- 79
Howe, Norma 1930- 126
Howell, Pat 1947- 15
Howell, S.
  See Styles, (Frank) Showell
Howell, Virginia
  See Ellison, Virginia H(owell)

Howes, Barbara 1914-1996 .... *5*
Howie, Diana 1945- *122*
Howie, Diana Melson
  See Howie, Diana
Howker, Janni 1957- *72*
  Brief entry *46*
  See also CLR *14*
  See also SAAS *13*
Howland, Ethan 1963- *131*
Hoy, Linda 1946- *65*
Hoy, Nina
  See Roth, Arthur J(oseph)
Hoyle, Geoffrey 1942- *18*
Hoyt, Ard *190*
Hoyt, Edwin P(almer), Jr. 1923- *28*
Hoyt, Erich 1950- *140*
  Earlier sketch in SATA *65*
Hoyt, Olga
  See Gruhzit-Hoyt, Olga (Margaret)
Hrdlitschka, Shelley 1956- *167*
  Earlier sketch in SATA *111*
Hrdlitschka, Shelley Joanne
  See Hrdlitschka, Shelley
Htin Aung, U.
  See Aung, (Maung) Htin
Hu, Ying-Hwa *173*
Huang, Benrei 1959- *86*
Hubalek, Linda K. 1954- *111*
Hubbard, Margaret Ann
  See Priley, Margaret (Ann) Hubbard
Hubbard, Michelle Calabro 1953- *122*
Hubbard, Patricia 1945- *124*
Hubbard, Woodleigh Marx *160*
  Earlier sketch in SATA *98*
Hubbell, Patricia 1928- *186*
  Earlier sketches in SATA *8, 132*
Hubery, Julia *195*
Hubley, Faith Elliot 1924-2001 .... *48*
  Obituary *133*
Hubley, John 1914-1977 .... *48*
  Obituary *24*
Huck, Charlotte S. 1922- *136*
  Earlier sketch in SATA *82*
Hudak, Michal 1956- *143*
Hudson, Cheryl Willis 1948- *160*
  Earlier sketch in SATA *81*
Hudson, Jan 1954-1990 .... *77*
  See also CLR *40*
Hudson, Jeffery
  See Crichton, Michael
Hudson, Jeffrey
  See Crichton, Michael
Hudson, (Margaret) Kirsty 1947- *32*
Hudson, Margaret
  See Shuter, Jane (Margaret)
Hudson, W(illiam) H(enry) 1841-1922 .... *35*
Hudson, Wade 1946- *162*
  Earlier sketch in SATA *74*
Huelsmann, Eva 1928- *16*
Huerlimann, Bettina 1909-1983 .... *39*
  Obituary *34*
Huerlimann, Ruth 1939- *32*
  Brief entry *31*
Huff, Barbara A. 1929- *67*
Huff, Tanya 1957- *171*
  Earlier sketch in SATA *85*
Huff, Tanya Sue
  See Huff, Tanya
Huff, T.S.
  See Huff, Tanya
Huff, Vivian 1948- *59*
Huffaker, Sandy 1943- *10*
Huffman, Tom *24*
Huggins, Nathan Irvin 1927-1989 .... *63*
Huggins, Peter *178*
Hughes, Carol 1955- *108*
Hughes, Dean 1943- *139*
  Earlier sketches in SATA *33, 77*
  See also CLR *76*
Hughes, Eden
  See Griffin, W.E.B

Hughes, Edward James
  See Hughes, Ted
Hughes, (James Mercer) Langston
  1902-1967 .... *33*
  Earlier sketch in SATA *4*
  See also CLR *17*
Hughes, Libby *71*
Hughes, Matilda
  See MacLeod, Charlotte (Matilda)
Hughes, Monica 1925-2003 .... *162*
  Earlier sketches in SATA *15, 70, 119*
  See also CLR *60*
  See also SAAS *11*
Hughes, Monica Ince
  See Hughes, Monica
Hughes, Pat *197*
Hughes, Richard (Arthur Warren)
  1900-1976 .... *8*
  Obituary *25*
Hughes, Sara
  See Saunders, Susan
Hughes, Shirley 1927- *159*
  Earlier sketches in SATA *16, 70, 110*
  See also CLR *15*
Hughes, Ted 1930-1998 .... *49*
  Brief entry *27*
  Obituary *107*
  See also CLR *131*
Hughes, Thomas 1822-1896 .... *31*
Hughes, Virginia
  See Campbell, Hope
Hughes, Walter (Llewellyn) 1910-1993 .... *26*
Hughey, Roberta 1942- *61*
Hugo, Pierre Brackers de
  See Brackers de Hugo, Pierre
Hugo, Victor (Marie) 1802-1885 .... *47*
Huline-Dickens, Frank William 1931- *34*
Huling, Jan *172*
Huliska-Beith, Laura *175*
Hull, Eleanor (Means) 1913- *21*
Hull, Eric Traviss
  See Harnan, Terry
Hull, H. Braxton
  See Jacobs, Helen Hull
Hull, Jesse Redding
  See Hull, Jessie Redding
Hull, Jessie Redding 1932- *51*
Hull, Katharine 1921-1977 .... *23*
Hull, Lise (E.) 1954- *148*
Hull, Maureen 1949- *142*
Hulme, Joy N. 1922- *161*
  Earlier sketches in SATA *74, 112*
Hults, Dorothy Niebrugge 1898-2000 .... *6*
Humble, Richard 1945- *60*
Hume, Lachie *189*
Hume, Lotta Carswell *7*
Hume, Ruth Fox 1922-1980 .... *26*
  Obituary *22*
Hume, Stephen Eaton 1947- *136*
Hummel, Berta 1909-1946 .... *43*
Hummel, Sister Maria Innocentia
  See Hummel, Berta
Humphrey, Carol Sue 1956- *167*
Humphrey, Henry (III) 1930- *16*
Humphrey, Kate
  See Forsyth, Kate
Humphrey, Sandra McLeod 1936- *95*
Humphreys, Martha 1943- *71*
Humphreys, Susan L.
  See Lowell, Susan
Hundal, Nancy 1957- *128*
Huneck, Stephen 1949- *183*
  Earlier sketch in SATA *129*
Hungerford, Hesba Fay
  See Brinsmead, H(esba) F(ay)
Hungerford, Pixie
  See Brinsmead, H(esba) F(ay)
Hunkin, Timothy Mark Trelawney 1950- *53*
Hunt, Angela Elwell 1957- *159*
  Earlier sketch in SATA *75*
Hunt, Bernice (Kohn) 1920- *4*

Hunt, Francesca
  See Holland, Isabelle (Christian)
Hunt, Irene 1907-2001 .... *91*
  Earlier sketch in SATA *2*
  See also CLR *1*
Hunt, Janie Louise 1963- *102*
Hunt, Jonathan 1966- *84*
Hunt, Joyce 1927- *31*
Hunt, Linda 1940- *39*
Hunt, Lisa B(ehnke) 1967- *84*
Hunt, Mabel Leigh 1892-1971 .... *1*
  Obituary *26*
Hunt, Morton M(agill) 1920- *22*
Hunt, Nigel
  See Greenbank, Anthony Hunt
Hunt, Peter (Leonard) 1945- *76*
Hunter, Anne B. 1966- *118*
Hunter, Bernice Thurman 1922-2002 .... *85*
  Brief entry *45*
Hunter, Bobbi Dooley 1945- *89*
Hunter, Captain Marcy
  See Ellis, Edward S(ylvester)
Hunter, Chris
  See Fluke, Joanne
Hunter, Clingham M.D.
  See Adams, William Taylor
Hunter, Edith Fisher 1919- *31*
Hunter, Erin
  See Cary, Kate
Hunter, Evan 1926-2005 .... *25*
  Obituary *167*
Hunter, George E.
  See Ellis, Edward S(ylvester)
Hunter, Hilda 1921- *7*
Hunter, Jana
  See Hunter, Jana Novotny
Hunter, Jana Novotny *190*
Hunter, Jim 1939- *65*
Hunter, Kristin
  See Lattany, Kristin (Elaine Eggleston) Hunter
Hunter, Leigh
  See Etchison, Birdie L(ee)
Hunter, Lieutenant Ned
  See Ellis, Edward S(ylvester)
Hunter, Mel 1927-2004 .... *39*
Hunter, Mollie 1922- *139*
  Autobiography Feature *139*
  Earlier sketches in SATA *2, 54, 106*
  See also CLR *25*
  See also SAAS *7*
Hunter, Ned
  See Ellis, Edward S(ylvester)
Hunter, Norman (George Lorimer)
  1899-1995 .... *84*
  Earlier sketch in SATA *26*
Hunter, Ryan Ann
  See Greenwood, Pamela D.
  and Macalaster, Elizabeth G.
Hunter, Sara Hoagland 1954- *98*
Hunter Blair, Pauline *3*
  See Clarke, Pauline
Huntington, Amy 1956- *180*
  Earlier sketch in SATA *138*
Huntington, Geoffrey *145*
Huntington, Harriet E(lizabeth) 1909- *1*
Huntsberry, William E(mery) 1916- *5*
Hurd, Clement (G.) 1908-1988 .... *64*
  Obituary *54*
  Earlier sketch in SATA *2*
  See also CLR *49*
Hurd, Edith Thacher 1910-1997 .... *64*
  Obituary *95*
  Earlier sketch in SATA *2*
  See also CLR *49*
  See also SAAS *13*
Hurd, (John) Thacher 1949- *94*
  Autobiography Feature *123*
  Brief entry *45*
  Earlier sketch in SATA *46*
Hurley, Jo
  See Dower, Laura

Hurlimann, Bettina
  See Huerlimann, Bettina
Hurlimann, Ruth
  See Huerlimann, Ruth
Hurmence, Belinda 1921- 77
  See also CLR 25
  See also SAAS 20
Hurst, Carol Otis 1933-2007 185
  Earlier sketch in SATA 130
Hurt-Newton, Tania 1968- 84
Hurwin, Davida Wills 1950- 180
Hurwitz, Johanna 1937- 175
  Earlier sketches in SATA 20, 71, 113
  See also SAAS 18
Hurwood, Bernhardt J. 1926-1987 12
  Obituary 50
Husain, Shahrukh 1950- 108
Huser, Glen 1943- 151
Hutchens, Paul 1902-1977 31
Hutchins, Carleen Maley 1911- 9
Hutchins, Hazel J. 1952- 175
  Brief entry 51
  Earlier sketches in SATA 81, 135
  See also SAAS 24
Hutchins, Pat 1942- 178
  Earlier sketches in SATA 15, 70, 111
  See also CLR 20
  See also SAAS 16
Hutchins, Ross Elliott 1906- 4
Hutchison, Linda 1942- 152
Huthmacher, J. Joseph 1929- 5
Hutto, Nelson (Allen) 1904-1985 20
Hutton, Kathryn 1915- 89
Hutton, Warwick 1939-1994 20
  Obituary 83
  See also SAAS 17
Huxley, Aldous (Leonard) 1894-1963 63
Huxley, Elspeth (Josceline Grant)
  1907-1997 62
  Obituary 95
Hyde, Catherine R.
  See Hyde, Catherine Ryan
Hyde, Catherine Ryan 1955- 141
Hyde, Dayton O(gden) 9
Hyde, Hawk
  See Hyde, Dayton O(gden)
Hyde, Jeannette
  See Eyerly, Jeannette
Hyde, Margaret O. 1917- 139
  Earlier sketches in SATA 1, 42, 76
  See also CLR 23
  See also SAAS 8
Hyde, Margaret Oldroyd
  See Hyde, Margaret O.
Hyde, Shelley
  See Reed, Kit
Hyde, Wayne Frederick 1922- 7
Hylander, Clarence J(ohn) 1897-1964 7
Hyman, Robin P(hilip) 1931- 12
Hyman, Trina Schart 1939-2004 95
  Obituary 158
  Earlier sketches in SATA 7, 46
  See also CLR 50
Hymes, Lucia M(anley) 1907-1998 7
Hyndman, Jane Andrews Lee 1912-1978 46
  Obituary 23
  Earlier sketch in SATA 1
Hyndman, Robert Utley 1906-1973 18
Hynes, Pat 98

                        I

Iannone, Jeanne
  See Balzano, Jeanne (Koppel)
Ibatoulline, Bagram 1965(?)- 174
Ibbitson, John Perrie 1955- 102
Ibbotson, Eva 1925- 156
  Earlier sketches in SATA 13, 103
Ibbotson, M. C(hristine) 1930- 5

Icenoggle, Jodi 1967- 168
Icenoggle, Jodi O.
  See Icenoggle, Jodi
Ichikawa, Satomi 1949- 146
  Brief entry 36
  Earlier sketches in SATA 47, 78
  See also CLR 62
Iggulden, Hal 1972- 196
Ignoffo, Matthew 1945- 92
Igus, Toyomi 1953- 112
  Earlier sketch in SATA 76
Ihimaera, Witi (Tame) 1944- 148
Ikeda, Daisaku 1928- 77
Ilowite, Sheldon A. 1931- 27
Ilsey, Dent
  See Chapman, John Stanton Higham
Ilsley, Dent
  See Chapman, John Stanton Higham
Ilsley, Velma (Elizabeth) 1918- 12
Imai, Ayano 1980- 190
Imai, Miko 1963- 90
Imershein, Betsy 1953- 62
Immel, Mary Blair 1930- 28
Immell, Myra H. 1941- 92
Impey, Rose 1947- 152
  Earlier sketch in SATA 69
Ingelow, Jean 1820-1897 33
Ingermanson, Randall 1958- 134
Ingermanson, Randy
  See Ingermanson, Randall
Ingersoll, Norman 1928- 79
Ingham, Colonel Frederic
  See Hale, Edward Everett
Ingman, Bruce 1963- 182
  Earlier sketch in SATA 134
Ingman, Nicholas 1948- 52
Ingold, Jeanette 128
Ingpen, Robert 1936- 166
  Earlier sketch in SATA 109
Ingpen, Robert Roger
  See Ingpen, Robert
Ingraham, Erick 1950- 145
Ingraham, Leonard W(illiam) 1913-2003 4
Ingram, Scott 1948- 167
  Earlier sketch in SATA 92
Ingram, W. Scott
  See Ingram, Scott
Ingrams, Doreen 1906-1997 97
  Earlier sketch in SATA 20
Ingrid, Charles
  See Salsitz, Rhondi Vilott
Ingves, Gunilla (Anna Maria Folkesdotter)
  1939- 101
Inkpen, Mick 1952- 154
  Earlier sketch in SATA 99
Innes, (Ralph) Hammond
  See Hammond Innes, Ralph
Innes, Ralph Hammond
  See Hammond Innes, Ralph
Innocenti, Roberto 1940- 159
  Earlier sketch in SATA 96
  See also CLR 126
Innocenti and Gallaz
  See Gallaz, Christophe
  and Innocenti, Roberto
Inyart, Gene
  See Namovicz, Gene Inyart
Ionesco, Eugene 1912-1994 7
  Obituary 79
Ipcar, Dahlov (Zorach) 1917- 147
  Autobiography Feature 147
  Earlier sketches in SATA 1, 49
  See also SAAS 8
Ireland, Karin 151
  Earlier sketch in SATA 101
Ironside, Jetske 1940- 60
Irvin, Fred 1914- 15
Irvine, Georgeanne 1955- 72
Irvine, Joan 1951- 80
Irving, Alexander
  See Hume, Ruth Fox

Irving, Robert
  See Adler, Irving
Irving, Washington 1783-1859
  See YABC 2
  See also CLR 97
Irwin, Ann(abelle Bowen) 1915-1998 89
  Brief entry 38
  Obituary 106
  Earlier sketch in SATA 44
  See also CLR 40
  See also SAAS 14
Irwin, Constance (H.) Frick 1913-1995 6
Irwin, Hadley
  See Hadley, Lee
  and Irwin, Ann(abelle Bowen)
Irwin, Keith Gordon 1885-1964 11
Isaac, Joanne 1934- 21
Isaacs, Anne 1949- 185
  Earlier sketch in SATA 90
Isaacs, Jacob
  See Kranzler, George G(ershon)
Isaacson, Philip M(arshal) 1924- 87
Isadora, Rachel 1953(?)- 165
  Brief entry 32
  Earlier sketches in SATA 54, 79, 121
  See also CLR 7
Isbell, Rebecca T(emple) 1942- 125
Isham, Charlotte H(ickock) 1912- 21
Ishida, Jui 176
Ish-Kishor, Judith 1892-1972 11
Ish-Kishor, Sulamith 1896-1977 17
Ishmael, Woodi 1914-1995 31
  Obituary 109
Isle, Sue 1963- 105
Israel, Elaine 1945- 12
Israel, Marion Louise 1882-1973
  Obituary 26
Iterson, S(iny) R(ose) Van
  See Van Iterson, S(iny) R(ose)
Ivanko, John D. 1966- 111
Ivanko, John Duane
  See Ivanko, John D.
Iversen, Jeremy 1980(?)- 174
Iversen, Jeremy Watt
  See Iversen, Jeremy
Iverson, Carol (L.) 1941- 145
Iverson, Diane 1950- 122
Iverson, Eric G.
  See Turtledove, Harry
Ivery, Martha M. 1948- 124
Ives, David 1951- 173
Ives, Morgan
  See Bradley, Marion Zimmer
Iwai, Melissa 183
Iwamatsu, Jun Atsushi 1908-1994 81
  Earlier sketch in SATA 14
  See also CLR 4
Iwasaki (Matsumoto), Chihiro 1918-1974
  See CLR 18

                        J

Jablonski, Carla 184
Jac, Lee
  See Morton, Lee Jack, Jr.
Jacka, Martin 1943- 72
Jackson, Alison 1953- 160
  Earlier sketches in SATA 73, 108
Jackson, Anne 1896(?)-1984
  Obituary 37
Jackson, C(aary) Paul 1902-1991 6
Jackson, Caary
  See Jackson, C(aary) Paul
Jackson, Charlotte E. (Cobden) 1903(?)-1989
  Obituary 62
Jackson, Dave
  See Jackson, J. David
Jackson, Ellen B. 1943- 167
  Earlier sketches in SATA 75, 115

Jackson, Garnet Nelson 1944- 87
Jackson, Geoffrey (Holt Seymour) 1915-1987
  Obituary 53
Jackson, Gina
  See Fluke, Joanne
Jackson, Guida M. 1930- 71
Jackson, J. David 1944- 91
Jackson, Jacqueline 1928- 65
Jackson, Jacqueline Dougan
  See Jackson, Jacqueline
Jackson, Jesse 1908-1983 29
  Obituary 48
  Earlier sketch in SATA *2*
  See also CLR *28*
Jackson, Marjorie 1928- 127
Jackson, Melanie 1956- 141
Jackson, Mike 1946- 91
Jackson, Neta J. 1944- 91
Jackson, O. B.
  See Jackson, C(aary) Paul
Jackson, Rob 1961- 176
Jackson, Robert B(lake) 1926- 8
Jackson, Robert Bradley
  See Jackson, Rob
Jackson, Sally
  See Kellogg, Jean (Defrees)
Jackson, Shirley 1919-1965 2
Jackson, Woody 1948- 92
Jacob, Helen Pierce 1927- 21
Jacobin
  See Bisson, Terry
Jacobs, Deborah Lynn 187
Jacobs, Flora Gill 1918-2006 5
  Obituary 178
Jacobs, Francine 1935- 150
  Brief entry 42
  Earlier sketch in SATA *43*
Jacobs, Frank 1929- 30
Jacobs, Helen Hull 1908-1997 12
Jacobs, Joseph 1854-1916 25
Jacobs, Judy 1952- 69
Jacobs, Laurie A. 1956- 89
Jacobs, Leah
  See Gellis, Roberta
Jacobs, Leland Blair 1907-1992 20
  Obituary 71
Jacobs, Linda
  See Altman, Linda Jacobs
Jacobs, Lou(is), Jr. 1921- 2
Jacobs, Shannon K. 1947- 77
Jacobs, Susan
  See Quinn, Susan
Jacobs, William Jay 1933- 89
  Earlier sketch in SATA *28*
Jacobsen, Laura 177
Jacobson, Daniel 1923- 12
Jacobson, Jennifer
  See Jacobson, Jennifer Richard
Jacobson, Jennifer Richard 1958- 170
Jacobson, Morris K(arl) 1906- 21
Jacobson, Rick 170
Jacopetti, Alexandra
  See Hart, Alexandra
Jacques, Brian 1939- 176
  Earlier sketches in SATA *62, 95, 138*
  See also CLR *21*
Jacques, Robin 1920-1995 32
  Brief entry 30
  Obituary 86
  See also SAAS *5*
Jaekel, Susan M. 1948- 89
Jaffe, Michele 179
Jaffe, Michele Sharon
  See Jaffe, Michele
Jaffee, Al(lan) 1921- 66
  Earlier sketch in SATA *37*
Jagendorf, Moritz (Adolf) 1888-1981 2
  Obituary 24
Jahn, Michael
  See Jahn, (Joseph) Michael
Jahn, (Joseph) Michael 1943- 28

Jahn, Mike
  See Jahn, (Joseph) Michael
Jahn-Clough, Lisa 1967- 193
  Earlier sketches in SATA *88, 152*
Jahsmann, Allan Hart 1916- 28
Jakes, John 1932- 62
Jakes, John William
  See Jakes, John
James, Andrew
  See Kirkup, James
James, Ann 1952- 168
  Earlier sketches in SATA *82, 117*
James, Betsy 183
James, Brian 1976- 140
James, Bronte
  See Nash, Renea Denise
James, Captain Lew
  See Stratemeyer, Edward L.
James, Charlie 1961- 185
James, Curtis E. 182
James, Dynely
  See Mayne, William (James Carter)
James, Edwin
  See Gunn, James E.
James, Elizabeth 1942- 97
  Earlier sketches in SATA *39, 45, 52*
James, Emily
  See Standiford, Natalie
James, Gordon C. 1973- 195
James, Harry Clebourne 1896-1978 11
James, J. Alison 1962- 146
  Earlier sketch in SATA *83*
James, Josephine
  See Sterne, Emma Gelders
James, Mary
  See Meaker, Marijane
James, Philip
  See del Rey, Lester
  and Moorcock, Michael
James, Robin 1953- 50
James, Robin Irene
  See James, Robin
James, Tegan
  See Odgers, Sally Farrell
James, T.F.
  See Fleming, Thomas
James, Will(iam Roderick) 1892-1942 19
Jameson, W. C. 1942- 93
Jamieson, Ian R.
  See Goulart, Ron(ald Joseph)
Jamiolkowski, Raymond M. 1953- 81
Jane, Mary Childs 1909- 6
Jane, Pamela 158
Janeczko, Paul B(ryan) 1945- 155
  Earlier sketches in SATA *53, 98*
  See also CLR *47*
  See also SAAS *18*
Janes, Edward C. 1908-1984 25
Janes, J(oseph) Robert 1935- 148
  Brief entry 50
  Earlier sketch in SATA *101*
Janeway, Elizabeth (Hall) 1913-2005 19
Janger, Kathleen N. 1940- 66
Janice
  See Brustlein, Janice Tworkov
Janisch, Heinz 1960- 181
Janosch
  See Eckert, Horst
Janover, Caroline (Davis) 1943- 141
  Earlier sketch in SATA *89*
Janovitz, Marilyn 194
Jansen, Jared
  See Cebulash, Mel
Janson, Dora Jane (Heineberg) 1916- 31
Janson, H(orst) W(oldemar) 1913-1982 9
Jansson, Tove (Marika) 1914-2001 41
  Earlier sketch in SATA *3*
  See also CLR *125*
Janus, Grete
  See Hertz, Grete Janus

Jaques, Faith 1923-1997 97
  Earlier sketches in SATA *21, 69*
Jaquith, Priscilla 1908- 51
Jaramillo, Mari-Luci 1928- 139
Jarman, Julia 1946- 198
  Earlier sketch in SATA *133*
Jarman, Rosemary Hawley 1935- 7
Jarrell, Mary Von Schrader 1914- 35
Jarrell, Randall 1914-1965 7
  See also CLR *111*
Jarrett, Roxanne
  See Werner, Herma
Jarrow, Gail 1952- 185
  Earlier sketch in SATA *84*
Jarvis, E.K.
  See Ellison, Harlan
  and Silverberg, Robert
Jarvis, Robin 1963- 181
Jaskol, Julie 1958- 127
Jasner, W. K.
  See Watson, Jane Werner
Jassem, Kate
  See Oppenheim, Joanne
Jauss, Anne Marie 1902(?)-1991 10
  Obituary 69
Javernick, Ellen 1938- 89
Jay, Alison 196
Jayne, Lieutenant R. H.
  See Ellis, Edward S(ylvester)
Jaynes, Clare
  See Mayer, Jane Rothschild
Jeake, Samuel, Jr.
  See Aiken, Conrad (Potter)
Jean-Bart, Leslie 1954- 121
Jeapes, Ben 1965- 174
Jefferds, Vincent H(arris) 1916- 59
  Brief entry 49
Jefferies, (John) Richard 1848-1887 16
Jeffers, Dawn 189
Jeffers, Oliver 1977- 175
Jeffers, Susan 1942- 137
  Earlier sketches in SATA *17, 70, 129*
  See also CLR *30*
Jefferson, Sarah
  See Farjeon, (Eve) Annabel
Jeffries, Roderic 1926- 4
Jeffries, Roderic Graeme
  See Jeffries, Roderic
Jenkin-Pearce, Susie 1943- 80
Jenkins, A.M. 174
Jenkins, Amanda McRaney
  See Jenkins, A.M.
Jenkins, Debra Reid
  See Reid Jenkins, Debra
Jenkins, Emily 1967- 174
  Earlier sketch in SATA *144*
Jenkins, Jean 98
Jenkins, Jerry B. 1949- 149
Jenkins, Jerry Bruce
  See Jenkins, Jerry B.
Jenkins, Leonard 189
Jenkins, Marie M(agdalen) 1909- 7
Jenkins, Patrick 1955- 72
Jenkins, Steve 1952- 188
  Earlier sketch in SATA *154*
Jenkins, William A(twell) 1922-1998 9
Jenkyns, Chris 1924- 51
Jennings, Coleman A(lonzo) 1933- 64
Jennings, Dana Andrew 1957- 93
Jennings, Elizabeth (Joan) 1926-2001 66
Jennings, Gary 1928-1999 9
  Obituary 117
Jennings, Gary Gayne
  See Jennings, Gary
Jennings, Patrick 1962- 160
  Earlier sketch in SATA *96*
Jennings, Paul 1943- 165
  Earlier sketch in SATA *88*
  See also CLR *40*
Jennings, Richard W. 1945- 185
  Earlier sketch in SATA *136*

Jennings, Robert
　See Hamilton, Charles (Harold St. John)
Jennings, S. M.
　See Meyer, Jerome Sydney
Jennings, Sharon 1954- 95
Jennings, Sharon Elizabeth
　See Jennings, Sharon
Jennison, C. S.
　See Starbird, Kaye
Jennison, Keith Warren 1911-1995 14
Jensen, Kathryn 1949- 81
Jensen, Kristine Mary 1961- 78
Jensen, Niels 1927- 25
Jensen, Vickie (Dee) 1946- 81
Jensen, Virginia Allen 1927- 8
Jenson-Elliott, Cynthia L(ouise) 1962- 143
Jeram, Anita 1965- 154
　Earlier sketches in SATA *71, 102*
Jerman, Jerry 1949- 89
Jernigan, E. Wesley 1940- 85
Jernigan, Gisela (Evelyn) 1948- 85
Jeschke, Susan 1942- 42
　Brief entry 27
Jessel, Camilla (Ruth) 1937- 143
　Earlier sketch in SATA *29*
Jessell, Tim 177
Jessey, Cornelia
　See Sussman, Cornelia Silver
Jewel
　See Kilcher, Jewel
Jewell, Nancy 1940- 109
　Brief entry 41
Jewett, Eleanore Myers 1890-1967 5
Jewett, (Theodora) Sarah Orne 1849-1909 ... 15
Jezard, Alison 1919- 57
　Brief entry 34
Jiang, Cheng An 1943- 109
Jiang, Ji-li 1954- 101
Jiang, Zheng An
　See Jiang, Cheng An
Jiler, John 1946- 42
　Brief entry 35
Jimenez, Francisco 1943- 108
Jinks, Catherine 1963- 155
　Earlier sketch in SATA *94*
Jobb, Jamie 1945- 29
Jobling, Curtis 131
Jocelyn, Ann Henning 1948- 92
Jocelyn, Marthe 1956- 198
　Earlier sketches in SATA *118, 163*
Joerns, Consuelo 44
　Brief entry 33
Joey D
　See Macaulay, Teresa (E.)
Johansen, Krista V.
　See Johansen, K.V.
Johansen, K.V 1968- 186
Johansen, K.V. 1968- 186
　Earlier sketch in SATA *129*
Johansson, Philip 163
John, Joyce 59
Johns, Avery
　See Cousins, Margaret
Johns, Elizabeth 1943- 88
Johns, Janetta
　See Quin-Harkin, Janet
Johns, Linda 1945- 173
Johns, W(illiam) E(arle) 1893-1968 55
Johns, Captain W. E.
　See Johns, W(illiam) E(arle)
Johnson, A.
　See Johnson, Annabell (Jones)
Johnson, A. E.
　See Johnson, Annabell (Jones)
　and Johnson, Edgar (Raymond)
Johnson, Angela 1961- 188
　Earlier sketches in SATA *69, 102, 150*
　See also CLR *33*
Johnson, Annabel
　See Johnson, Annabell (Jones)

Johnson, Annabell (Jones) 1921- 72
　Earlier sketch in SATA *2*
Johnson, Art 1946- 123
Johnson, B(urdetta) F(aye) 1920- 1
Johnson, Benjamin F., of Boone
　See Riley, James Whitcomb
Johnson, Bettye 1858-1919
　See Rogers, Bettye
Johnson, Caryn
　See Goldberg, Whoopi
Johnson, Caryn E.
　See Goldberg, Whoopi
Johnson, Caryn Elaine
　See Goldberg, Whoopi
Johnson, Charles R. 1925- 11
Johnson, Charlotte Buel
　See von Wodtke, Charlotte Buel Johnson
Johnson, Chuck
　See Johnson, Charles R.
Johnson, Crockett
　See Leisk, David (Johnson)
Johnson, D(ana) William 1945- 23
Johnson, Daniel Shahid 1954- 73
Johnson, David
　See Johnson, David A.
Johnson, David A. 1951- 191
Johnson, D.B. 1944- 183
　Earlier sketch in SATA *146*
Johnson, Dianne 1960- 130
Johnson, Dinah
　See Johnson, Dianne
Johnson, Dolores 1949- 69
Johnson, Donald B.
　See Johnson, D.B.
Johnson, Dorothy M(arie) 1905-1984 6
　Obituary 40
Johnson, E(ugene) Harper 44
Johnson, Edgar (Raymond) 1912-1990 72
　Earlier sketch in SATA *2*
Johnson, Eleanor Murdock 1892-1987
　Obituary 54
Johnson, Elizabeth 1911-1984 7
　Obituary 39
Johnson, Eric W(arner) 1918-1994 ....
　Obituary 82
　Earlier sketch in SATA *8*
Johnson, Evelyne 1922- 20
Johnson, Fred 19(?)-1982 63
Johnson, Gaylord 1884-1972 7
Johnson, Gerald White 1890-1980 19
　Obituary 28
Johnson, Harper
　See Johnson, E(ugene) Harper
Johnson, Harriett 1908-1987
　Obituary 53
Johnson, James Ralph 1922- 1
Johnson, James Weldon 1871-1938 31
　See also CLR *32*
Johnson, Jane 1951- 48
Johnson, Joan J. 1942- 59
Johnson, John E(mil) 1929- 34
Johnson, Johnny 1901-1995
　See Johnson, (Walter) Ryerson
Johnson, Kathleen Jeffrie 1950- 186
Johnson, La Verne B(ravo) 1925- 13
Johnson, Layne 187
Johnson, Lee Kaiser 1962- 78
Johnson, Lissa H(alls) 1955- 65
Johnson, Lois Smith 1894-1993 6
Johnson, Lois Walfrid 1936- 130
　Earlier sketches in SATA *22, 91*
Johnson, Margaret S(weet) 1893-1964 35
Johnson, Marguerite Annie
　See Angelou, Maya
Johnson, Mary Frances K. 1929(?)-1979
　Obituary 27
Johnson, Maud Battle 1918(?)-1985
　Obituary 46
Johnson, Meredith Merrell 1952- 104
Johnson, Milton 1932- 31

Johnson, Neil 1954- 135
　Earlier sketch in SATA *73*
Johnson, Pamela 1949- 71
Johnson, Patricia Polin 1956- 84
Johnson, Paul Brett 1947- 132
　Earlier sketch in SATA *83*
Johnson, Rebecca L. 1956- 147
　Earlier sketch in SATA *67*
Johnson, Rick L. 1954- 79
Johnson, (Walter) Ryerson 1901-1995 10
　Obituary 106
Johnson, Scott 1952- 119
　Earlier sketch in SATA *76*
Johnson, Sherrie 1948- 87
Johnson, Shirley K(ing) 1927- 10
Johnson, Siddie Joe 1905-1977
　Obituary 20
Johnson, Spencer 1938- 145
　Brief entry 38
Johnson, Stacie
　See Myers, Walter Dean
Johnson, Stephen T. 1964- 189
　Earlier sketches in SATA *84, 141*
Johnson, Steve 1960- 177
Johnson, Sue Kaiser 1963- 78
Johnson, Sylvia A. 166
　Brief entry 52
　Earlier sketch in SATA *104*
Johnson, William R. 38
Johnson, William Weber 1909-1992 7
Johnson-Feelings, Dianne
　See Johnson, Dianne
Johnston, Agnes Christine
　See Dazey, Agnes J(ohnston)
Johnston, Annie Fellows 1863-1931 37
Johnston, Dorothy Grunbock 1915-1979 54
Johnston, Ginny 1946- 60
Johnston, H(ugh) A(nthony) S(tephen)
　1913-1967 14
Johnston, Janet 1944- 71
Johnston, Jeffry W. 188
Johnston, Johanna 1914(?)-1982 12
　Obituary 33
Johnston, Julie 1941- 110
　Autobiography Feature 128
　Earlier sketch in SATA *78*
　See also CLR *41*
　See also SAAS *24*
Johnston, Lynn 1947- 118
Johnston, Lynn Beverley
　See Johnston, Lynn
Johnston, Mark 194
Johnston, Norma
　See St. John, Nicole
Johnston, Portia
　See Takakjian, Portia
Johnston, Susan Taylor 1942- 180
　Earlier sketches in SATA *8, 83, 128*
Johnston, Tim(othy Patrick) 1962- 146
Johnston, Tony
　See Johnston, Susan Taylor
Joinson, Carla 160
Jolin, Paula 186
Jonas, Ann 1932- 135
　Brief entry 42
　Earlier sketch in SATA *50*
　See also CLR *74*
Jonell, Lynne 1956- 196
　Earlier sketch in SATA *109*
Jones, Adrienne 1915-2000 82
　Earlier sketch in SATA *7*
　See also SAAS *10*
Jones, Annabel
　See Lewis, Mary (Christianna)
Jones, Betty Millsaps 1940- 54
Jones, Carol 1942- 153
　Earlier sketch in SATA *79*
Jones, Carrie 1971- 191
Jones, Charles M(artin) 1912-2002 53
　Obituary 133

Jones, Charlotte Foltz 1945- 122
  Earlier sketch in SATA 77
Jones, Chuck
  See Jones, Charles M(artin)
Jones, Constance 112
Jones, Constance A.
  See Jones, Constance
Jones, Diana Wynne 1934- 160
  Earlier sketches in SATA 9, 70, 108
  See also CLR 120
  See also SAAS 7
Jones, Douglas C(lyde) 1924-1998 52
Jones, Elizabeth McDavid 155
Jones, Elizabeth Orton 1910-2005 18
  Obituary 164
Jones, Evan 1915-1996 3
Jones, Geraldine
  See McCaughrean, Geraldine
Jones, Gillingham
  See Hamilton, Charles (Harold St. John)
Jones, Gwyneth A(nn) 1952- 159
Jones, Harold 1904-1992 14
  Obituary 72
Jones, Helen Hinckley 1903-1991 26
Jones, Helen L(ouise) 1903-1973
  Obituary 22
Jones, Hettie 1934- 42
  Brief entry 27
Jones, Hortense P. 1918- 9
Jones, J. Sydney 1948- 101
Jones, Jasmine
  See Papademetriou, Lisa
Jones, Jennifer (Berry) 1947- 90
Jones, Jessie Mae Orton 1887(?)-1983
  Obituary 37
Jones, John R(obert) 1926- 76
Jones, Jon Sydney
  See Jones, J. Sydney
Jones, Kimberly K. 1957- 187
Jones, Marcia Thornton 1958- 115
  Earlier sketch in SATA 73
Jones, Martha T(annery) 1931- 130
Jones, Mary Alice 1898(?)-1980 6
Jones, McClure 34
Jones, Noah Z. 182
Jones, Patrick 1961- 136
Jones, Penelope 1938- 31
Jones, Rebecca C(astaldi) 1947- 99
  Earlier sketch in SATA 33
Jones, Robin D(orothy) 1959- 80
Jones, Sanford W.
  See Thorn, John
Jones, Sylvie 185
Jones, Sylvie Michelle
  See Jones, Sylvie
Jones, Terence Graham Parry 1942- 127
  Brief entry 51
  Earlier sketch in SATA 67
Jones, Terry
  See Jones, Terence Graham Parry
Jones, Tim Wynne
  See Wynne-Jones, Tim
Jones, Traci L. 186
Jones, V(ictoria) M(ary) 1958- 147
Jones, Veda Boyd 1948- 119
Jones, Volcano
  See Mitchell, Adrian
Jones, Weyman (B.) 1928- 4
  See also SAAS 11
Jones, William Glynne
  See Glynne-Jones, William
Jonk, Clarence 1906-1987 10
Jonsberg, Barry 1951- 168
Joos, Francoise 1956- 78
Joos, Frederic 1953- 78
Joosse, Barbara M. 1949- 164
  Earlier sketches in SATA 52, 96
Joosse, Barbara Monnot
  See Joosse, Barbara M.

Jordan, Alexis Hill
  See Glick, Ruth (Burtnick)
  and Titchener, Louise
Jordan, Anne Devereaux 1943- 80
Jordan, Chris
  See Philbrick, Rodman
Jordan, Deloris 191
Jordan, Don
  See Howard, Vernon (Linwood)
Jordan, Hope Dahle 1905-1995 15
Jordan, Jael (Michal) 1949- 30
Jordan, June 1936-2002 136
  Earlier sketch in SATA 4
  See also CLR 10
Jordan, June Meyer
  See Jordan, June
Jordan, Lee
  See Scholefield, Alan
Jordan, Martin George 1944- 84
Jordan, Robert 1948-2007 95
Jordan, Robert K.
  See Jordan, Robert
Jordan, Rosa 1939- 191
Jordan, Roslyn M. 189
Jordan, Sherryl 1949- 122
  Earlier sketch in SATA 71
  See also SAAS 23
Jordan, Shirley 1930- 154
Jordan, Tanis 1946- 84
Jorgensen, Ivar
  See Ellison, Harlan
  and Garrett, (Gordon) Randall (Phillip)
Jorgensen, Mary Venn -1995 36
Jorgensen, Norman 1954- 157
Jorgenson, Ivar
  See Silverberg, Robert
Jorisch, Stephane 178
Joseph, Anne
  See Coates, Anna
Joseph, James (Herz) 1924- 53
Joseph, Joan 1939- 34
Joseph, Joseph M(aron) 1903-1979 22
Joseph, Patrick
  See O'Malley, Kevin
Josephs, Rebecca
  See Talbot, Toby
Josephson, Judith Pinkerton 1943- 198
Josh
  See Twain, Mark
Joshua, Peter
  See Stone, Peter
Joslin, Mary 1953- 176
Joslin, Sesyle
  See Hine, Sesyle Joslin
Journet, Mireille
  See Marokvia, Mireille
Joyce, Bill
  See Joyce, William
Joyce, J(ames) Avery 1902-1987 11
  Obituary 50
Joyce, Peter 1937- 127
Joyce, William 1957- 118
  Brief entry 46
  Earlier sketch in SATA 72
  See also CLR 26
Joyner, Jerry 1938- 34
Juan, Ana 1961- 179
Jubert, Herve 185
Juby, Susan 1969- 156
Jucker, Sita 1921- 5
Judah, Aaron 1923- 118
Judd, Cyril
  See Kornbluth, C(yril) M.
  and Merril, Judith
  and Pohl, Frederik
Judd, Denis (O'Nan) 1938- 33
Judd, Frances K.
  See Benson, Mildred (Augustine Wirt)
Jude, Conny 81
Judge, Lita 192

Judson, Clara Ingram 1879-1960 38
  Brief entry 27
Judy, Stephen
  See Tchudi, Stephen N.
Judy, Stephen N.
  See Tchudi, Stephen N.
Juhasz, Victor 1954- 177
Jukes, Mavis 1947- 111
  Brief entry 43
  Earlier sketch in SATA 72
  See also SAAS 12
Jules, Jacqueline 1956- 183
  Earlier sketch in SATA 148
Julesberg, Elizabeth Rider Montgomery
  1902-1985 34
  Obituary 41
  Earlier sketch in SATA 3
Julian, Jane
  See Wiseman, David
Jumpp, Hugo
  See MacPeek, Walter G.
Jungman, Ann 165
Jupo, Frank J. 1904-1981 7
Jurmain, Suzanne 1945- 169
  Earlier sketch in SATA 72
Jurmain, Suzanne Tripp
  See Jurmain, Suzanne
Juster, Norton 1929- 132
  Earlier sketch in SATA 3
  See also CLR 112
Justus, May 1898-1989 1
  Obituary 106
Juvenilia
  See Taylor, Ann

                        K

Kaaberbol, Lene
  See Kaaberbol, Lene
Kaaberbol, Lene 1960- 159
Kabdebo, Tamas
  See Kabdebo, Thomas
Kabdebo, Thomas 1934- 10
Kabibble, Osh
  See Jobb, Jamie
Kacer, Kathy 1954- 184
  Earlier sketch in SATA 142
Kaczman, James 156
Kadair, Deborah Ousley 184
Kadesch, Robert R(udstone) 1922- 31
Kadohata, Cynthia 1956(?)- 180
  Earlier sketch in SATA 155
  See also CLR 121
Kaempfert, Wade
  See del Rey, Lester
Kaestner, Erich 1899-1974 14
  See also CLR 4
Kahl, Jonathan (D.) 1959- 77
Kahl, M(arvin) P(hilip) 1934- 37
Kahl, Virginia (Caroline) 1919-2004 48
  Brief entry 38
  Obituary 158
Kahn, Joan 1914-1994 48
  Obituary 82
Kahn, Katherine Janus 1942- 167
  Earlier sketch in SATA 90
Kahn, Peggy
  See Katz, Bobbi
Kahn, Roger 1927- 37
Kahukiwa, Robyn 1940- 134
Kains, Josephine
  See Goulart, Ron(ald Joseph)
Kaizuki, Kiyonori 1950- 72
Kakimoto, Kozo 1915- 11
Kalashnikoff, Nicholas 1888-1961 16
Kalb, Jonah 1926- 23
Kalbacken, Joan 1925- 96
Kalechofsky, Roberta 1931- 92
Kaler, James Otis 1848-1912 15

Kalish, Claire M. 1947- 92
Kallen, Stuart A(rnold) 1955- 126
  Earlier sketch in SATA 86
Kallevig, Christine Petrell 1955- 164
Kalman, Bobbie 1947- 63
Kalman, Maira 1949- 137
  Earlier sketch in SATA 96
  See also CLR 32
Kalnay, Francis 1899-1992 7
Kaloustian, Rosanne 1955- 93
Kalow, Gisela 1946- 32
Kalstein, Dave 175
Kamen, Gloria 1923- 98
  Earlier sketch in SATA 9
Kamerman, Sylvia E.
  See Burack, Sylvia K.
Kamm, Josephine (Hart) 1905-1989 24
Kammerman, Sylvia K.
  See Burack, Sylvia K.
Kandel, Michael 1941- 93
Kandell, Alice S. 1938- 35
Kane, Bob 1916-1998 120
Kane, Henry Bugbee 1902-1971 14
Kane, L. A.
  See Mannetti, Lisa
Kane, Robert W. 1910- 18
Kane, Wilson
  See Bloch, Robert (Albert)
Kanefield, Teri 1960- 135
Kaner, Etta 1947- 198
  Earlier sketch in SATA 126
Kanetzke, Howard W(illiam) 1932- 38
Kann, Elizabeth 180
Kann, Victoria 180
Kanninen, Barbara 196
Kanninen, Barbara J.
  See Kanninen, Barbara
Kanoza, Muriel Canfield
  See Canfield, Muriel
Kantner, Seth 1965- 179
Kanzawa, Toshiko
  See Furukawa, Toshi
Kanzler, John 1963- 188
Kaplan, Andrew 1960- 78
Kaplan, Anne Bernays
  See Bernays, Anne
Kaplan, Bess 1927- 22
Kaplan, Boche 1926- 24
Kaplan, Elizabeth 1956- 83
Kaplan, Elizabeth A.
  See Kaplan, Elizabeth
Kaplan, Irma 1900- 10
Kaplan, Jean Caryl Korn 1926- 10
Kaplow, Robert 1954- 70
Karageorge, Michael
  See Anderson, Poul
Karas, G. Brian 1957- 178
Karas, George Brian
  See Karas, G. Brian
Karasz, Ilonka 1896-1981
  Obituary 29
Karen, Ruth 1922-1987 9
  Obituary 54
Kark, Nina Mary
  See Bawden, Nina
Karl, Herb 1938- 73
Karl, Jean E(dna) 1927-2000 122
  Earlier sketch in SATA 34
  See also SAAS 10
Karlin, Bernie 1927- 68
Karlin, Eugene 1918- 10
Karlin, Nurit 103
  Earlier sketch in SATA 63
Karnes, Frances A. 1937- 110
Karp, Naomi J. 1926- 16
Karpinski, J. Rick
  See Karpinski, John Eric
Karpinski, John Eric 1952- 81
Karpinski, Rick
  See Karpinski, John Eric

Karr, Kathleen 1946- 127
  Earlier sketch in SATA 82
Karr, Phyllis Ann 1944- 119
Karwoski, Gail 1949- 127
Karwoski, Gail Langer
  See Karwoski, Gail
Kashiwagi, Isami 1925- 10
Kaslik, Ibi 185
  See Kaslik, Ibolya Emma
Kassem, Lou 1931- 62
  Brief entry 51
Kastel, Warren
  See Silverberg, Robert
Kastner, Erich
  See Kaestner, Erich
Kastner, Jill (Marie) 1964- 117
  Earlier sketch in SATA 70
Kasuya, Masahiro 1937- 51
Kasza, Keiko 1951- 191
  Earlier sketch in SATA 124
Kataphusin
  See Ruskin, John
Katchen, Carole 1944- 9
Kathryn
  See Searle, Kathryn Adrienne
Katona, Robert 1949- 21
Katsarakis, Joan Harries
  See Harries, Joan
Katz, Alan 185
Katz, Avi 1949- 199
Katz, Avner 1939- 103
Katz, Bobbi 1933- 179
  Earlier sketch in SATA 12
Katz, Fred(eric Phillip) 1938- 6
Katz, Jane B(resler) 1934- 33
Katz, Karen 1947- 195
  Earlier sketch in SATA 158
Katz, Marjorie P.
  See Weiser, Marjorie P(hillis) K(atz)
Katz, Susan 1945- 156
Katz, Welwyn Wilton 1948- 96
  Autobiography Feature 118
  Earlier sketch in SATA 62
  See also CLR 45
Katz, William 1940- 98
Katz, William Loren 1927- 13
Kaufman, Bel 57
Kaufman, Jeff 1955- 84
Kaufman, Joe 1911-2001 33
Kaufman, Joseph
  See Kaufman, Joe
Kaufman, Mervyn D. 1932- 4
Kaufmann, Angelika 1935- 15
Kaufmann, John 1931- 18
Kaula, Edna Mason 1906-1987 13
Kaur Khalsa, Dayal
  See Khalsa, Dayal Kaur
Kavaler, Lucy 1930- 23
Kavanagh, Jack 1920- 85
Kavanagh, P(atrick) J(oseph Gregory)
  1931- 122
Kavanaugh, Ian
  See Webb, Jean Francis (III)
Kay, Alan N. 1965- 144
Kay, Elizabeth 1949- 165
Kay, Guy Gavriel 1954- 167
  Earlier sketch in SATA 121
Kay, Helen
  See Goldfrank, Helen Colodny
Kay, Jackie 1961- 165
  Earlier sketch in SATA 97
Kay, Jacqueline Margaret
  See Kay, Jackie
Kay, Mara 13
Kay, Verla 1946- 120
Kaye, Danny 1913-1987
  Obituary 50
Kaye, Geraldine (Hughesdon) 1925- 85
  Earlier sketch in SATA 10
Kaye, Judy
  See Baer, Judy

Kaye, Marilyn 1949- 110
  Earlier sketch in SATA 56
Kaye, Mary Margaret
  See Kaye, M.M.
Kaye, M.M. 1908-2004 62
  Obituary 152
Kaye, Mollie
  See Kaye, M.M.
Kaye, Peggy 1948- 143
Keach, James P. 1950- 125
Keams, Geri 1951- 117
Keane, Bil 1922- 4
Keaney, Brian 1954- 188
  Earlier sketch in SATA 106
Kearney, Meg 1964- 178
Kearny, Jillian
  See Goulart, Ron(ald Joseph)
Keating, Bern
  See Keating, Leo Bernard
Keating, Frank 1944- 143
Keating, Lawrence A. 1903-1966 23
Keating, Leo Bernard 1915- 10
Keats, Emma 1899(?)-1979(?) 68
Keats, Ezra Jack 1916-1983 57
  Obituary 34
  Earlier sketch in SATA 14
  See also CLR 35
Keefer, Catherine
  See Ogan, George F.
  and Ogan, Margaret E. (Nettles)
Keefer, Janice Kulyk
  See Kulyk Keefer, Janice
Keegan, Marcia 1943- 104
  Earlier sketch in SATA 9
Keehn, Sally M. 1947- 165
  Earlier sketch in SATA 87
Keel, Frank
  See Keeler, Ronald F(ranklin)
Keeler, Patricia 183
Keeler, Patricia A.
  See Keeler, Patricia
Keeler, Ronald F(ranklin) 1913-1983 47
Keely, Jack 1951- 119
Keen, Martin L. 1913-1992 4
Keenan, Sheila 1953- 95
Keene, Ann T(odd) 1940- 86
Keene, Carolyn
  See Benson, Mildred (Augustine Wirt)
  and Goulart, Ron(ald Joseph)
  and Lerangis, Peter
  and McFarlane, Leslie (Charles)
  and Stanley, George Edward
  and Stratemeyer, Edward L.
Keens-Douglas, Richardo 1953- 154
  Earlier sketch in SATA 95
Keep, Linda Lowery
  See Lowery, Linda
Keep, Richard 1949- 170
Keep, Richard Cleminson
  See Keep, Richard
Keeping, Charles (William James)
  1924-1988 69
  Obituary 56
  Earlier sketch in SATA 9
  See also CLR 34
Keeshan, Robert J. 1927-2004 32
  Obituary 151
Kehlenbeck, Angela 1959- 186
Kehret, Peg 1936- 149
  Autobiography Feature 149
  Earlier sketches in SATA 73, 108
Keillor, Garrison 1942- 58
Keillor, Gary Edward
  See Keillor, Garrison
Keir, Christine
  See Pullein-Thompson, Christine
Keister, Douglas 1948- 88
Keith, Doug 1952- 81
Keith, Eros 1942- 52
Keith, Hal 1934- 36

Keith, Harold (Verne) 1903-1998 .... *74*
  Earlier sketch in SATA *2*
Keith, Robert
  See Applebaum, Stan
Keleinikov, Andrei 1924- *65*
Kelemen, Julie 1959- *78*
Kelen, Emery 1896-1978 .... *13*
  Obituary *26*
Kelleam, Joseph E(veridge) 1913-1975 .... *31*
Kelleher, Anne 1959- *97*
Kelleher, Annette 1950- *122*
Kelleher, Daria Valerian 1955- *79*
Kelleher, Victor (Michael Kitchener)
  1939- *129*
  Brief entry *52*
  Earlier sketch in SATA *75*
  See also CLR *36*
Keller, Beverly L(ou) *91*
  Earlier sketch in SATA *13*
Keller, Charles 1942- *82*
  Earlier sketch in SATA *8*
Keller, Debra 1958- *94*
Keller, Dick 1923- *36*
Keller, Emily *96*
Keller, Gail Faithfull
  See Faithfull, Gail
Keller, Holly 1942- *157*
  Brief entry *42*
  Earlier sketches in SATA *76, 108*
  See also CLR *45*
Keller, Irene (Barron) 1927-2002 .... *36*
  Obituary *139*
Keller, Laurie 1961(?)- *196*
Kelley, Ellen A. *185*
Kelley, Ellen Chavez
  See Kelley, Ellen A.
Kelley, Gary 1945- *183*
Kelley, Leo P(atrick) 1928- *32*
  Brief entry *31*
Kelley, Patrick (G.) 1963- *129*
Kelley, Patte 1947- *93*
Kelley, True 1946- *179*
Kelley, True (Adelaide) 1946- *130*
  Brief entry *39*
  Earlier sketches in SATA *41, 92*
Kelley, True Adelaide
  See Kelley, True
Kellin, Sally Moffet 1932- *9*
Kelling, Furn L. 1914-2000 .... *37*
Kellogg, Gene
  See Kellogg, Jean (Defrees)
Kellogg, Jean (Defrees) 1916-1978 .... *10*
Kellogg, Steven 1941- *177*
  Earlier sketches in SATA *8, 57, 130*
  See also CLR *6*
Kellogg, Steven Castle
  See Kellogg, Steven
Kellow, Kathleen
  See Hibbert, Eleanor Alice Burford
Kelly, C. M. O.
  See Gibbs, (Cecilia) May
Kelly, Clint 1950- *140*
Kelly, Eric P(hilbrook) 1884-1960
  See YABC *1*
Kelly, Fiona
  See Coleman, Michael (Lee)
  and Hendry, Frances Mary
  and Oldfield, Jenny
  and Welford, Sue
Kelly, Irene 1957- *147*
Kelly, Jeff
  See Kelly, Jeffrey
Kelly, Jeffrey 1946- *65*
Kelly, Joanne (W.) 1934- *87*
Kelly, Kate 1958- *91*
Kelly, Kathleen M. 1964- *71*
Kelly, Katy 1955- *169*
Kelly, Lauren
  See Oates, Joyce Carol
Kelly, Laurene 1954- *123*
Kelly, Martha Rose 1914-1983 .... *37*

Kelly, Marty
  See Kelly, Martha Rose
Kelly, Mij *166*
Kelly, Ralph
  See Geis, Darlene Stern
Kelly, Regina Z(immerman) 1898-1986 .... *5*
Kelly, Rosalie (Ruth) *43*
Kelly, Tom 1961- *191*
Kelly, Walt(er Crawford) 1913-1973 .... *18*
Kelsey, Alice Geer 1896-1982 .... *1*
Kelsey, Elin *159*
Kemly, Kathleen 1958- *197*
Kemnitz, Thomas Milton, Jr. 1984- *152*
Kemnitz, Tom, Jr.
  See Kemnitz, Thomas Milton, Jr.
Kemp, Gene 1926- *75*
  Earlier sketch in SATA *25*
  See also CLR *29*
Kempner, Mary Jean 1913-1969 .... *10*
Kempter, Christa 1945- *187*
Kempton, Jean Welch 1914- *10*
Kenah, Katharine 1949- *182*
Kenda, Margaret 1942- *71*
Kendall, Carol (Seeger) 1917- *74*
  Earlier sketch in SATA *11*
  See also SAAS *7*
Kendall, Katherine
  See Applegate, Katherine
Kendall, Lace
  See Stoutenburg, Adrien (Pearl)
Kendall, Martha E. *87*
Kendall, Russ 1957- *83*
Kenealy, James P. 1927- *52*
  Brief entry *29*
Kenealy, Jim
  See Kenealy, James P.
Kennaway, Adrienne 1945- *171*
  Earlier sketch in SATA *60*
Kennedy, Anne 1955- *198*
Kennedy, Anne Vittur
  See Kennedy, Anne
Kennedy, Brendan 1970- *57*
Kennedy, Dana Forrest 1917- *74*
Kennedy, Dorothy M(intzlaff) 1931- *53*
Kennedy, Doug 1963- *189*
  Earlier sketch in SATA *122*
Kennedy, Frances 1937- *192*
Kennedy, John Fitzgerald 1917-1963 .... *11*
Kennedy, Joseph Charles 1929- *130*
  Autobiography Feature *130*
  Earlier sketches in SATA *14, 86*
  See also CLR *27*
  See also SAAS *22*
  See Kennedy, X. J.
Kennedy, Kim *189*
Kennedy, Pamela (J.) 1946- *87*
Kennedy, Paul E(dward) 1929- *113*
  Earlier sketch in SATA *33*
Kennedy, Richard (Pitt) 1910-1989
  Obituary *60*
Kennedy, (Jerome) Richard 1932- *22*
Kennedy, Robert 1938- *63*
Kennedy, T.A. 1953- *42*
  Brief entry *35*
Kennedy, Teresa
  See Kennedy, T.A.
Kennedy, Teresa A.
  See Kennedy, T.A.
Kennedy, William 1928- *57*
Kennedy, William Joseph
  See Kennedy, William
Kennedy, X. J.
  See CLR *27*
  See also SAAS *22*
  See Kennedy, Joseph Charles
Kennell, Ruth Epperson 1893-1977 .... *6*
  Obituary *25*
Kennemore, Tim 1957- *133*
Kennen, Ally *190*
Kennett, David 1959- *121*

Kenny, Ellsworth Newcomb 1909-1971
  Obituary *26*
Kenny, Herbert Andrew 1912-2002 .... *13*
Kenny, Jude
  See Daly, Jude
Kenny, Kathryn
  See Bowden, Joan Chase
  and Krull, Kathleen
  and Sanderlin, Owenita (Harrah)
  and Stack, Nicolete Meredith
Kenny, Kevin
  See Krull, Kathleen
Kensinger, George
  See Fichter, George S.
Kensington, Kathryn Wesley
  See Rusch, Kristine Kathryn
Kent, Alexander
  See Reeman, Douglas Edward
Kent, David
  See Lambert, David (Compton)
Kent, Deborah Ann 1948- *155*
  Brief entry *41*
  Earlier sketches in SATA *47, 104*
Kent, Jack
  See Kent, John Wellington
Kent, John Wellington 1920-1985 .... *24*
  Obituary *45*
Kent, Lisa 1942- *90*
Kent, Mallory
  See Lowndes, Robert A(ugustine) W(ard)
Kent, Margaret 1894- *2*
Kent, Rockwell 1882-1971 .... *6*
Kent, Rose *188*
Kent, Sherman 1903-1986 .... *20*
  Obituary *47*
Kenward, Jean 1920- *42*
Kenworthy, Leonard S. 1912-1991 .... *6*
Kenyon, Karen (Smith) 1938- *145*
Kenyon, Kate
  See Adorjan, Carol (Madden)
  and Ransom, Candice F.
Kenyon, Ley 1913-1990 .... *6*
Keown, Elizabeth *78*
Kepes, Juliet A(ppleby) 1919-1999 .... *13*
Kephart, Beth 1960- *196*
Kerby, Mona 1951- *75*
Kerigan, Florence 1896-1984 .... *12*
Kerley, Barbara 1960- *191*
  Earlier sketch in SATA *138*
Kerman, Gertrude
  See Furman, Gertrude Lerner Kerman
Kerns, Thelma 1929- *116*
Kerr, Anne Louise
  See Mackey, Weezie Kerr
Kerr, Bob 1951- *120*
Kerr, Jessica 1901-1991 .... *13*
Kerr, (Anne-)Judith 1923-1970 .... *24*
Kerr, M. E.
  See Meaker, Marijane
Kerr, P.B.
  See Kerr, Philip
Kerr, Philip 1956- *168*
Kerr, Phyllis Forbes 1942- *72*
Kerr, Tom 1950- *77*
Kerrin, Jessica Scott *174*
Kerry, Frances
  See Kerigan, Florence
Kerry, Lois
  See Duncan, Lois
Kershen, (L.) Michael 1982- *82*
Kerven, Rosalind 1954- *83*
Ker Wilson, Barbara 1929- *121*
  Earlier sketches in SATA *20, 70*
  See also SAAS *18*
Keselman, Gabriela 1953- *128*
Kesey, Ken 1935-2001 .... *66*
  Obituary *131*
Kesey, Ken Elton
  See Kesey, Ken
Kesler, Jay 1935- *65*
Kessel, Joyce Karen 1937- *41*

Kessler, Cristina *190*
Kessler, Ethel 1922- *44*
  Brief entry *37*
Kessler, Leonard P. 1921- *14*
Kest, Kristin 1967- *168*
  Earlier sketch in SATA *118*
Kesteven, G. R.
  See Crosher, G. R.
Ketcham, Hank
  See Ketcham, Henry King
Ketcham, Henry King 1920-2001 .... *28*
  Brief entry *27*
  Obituary *128*
Ketcham, Sallie 1963- *124*
Ketchum, Liza 1946-
  See Murrow, Liza Ketchum
Ketner, Mary Grace 1946- *75*
Kettelkamp, Larry (Dale) 1933- *2*
  See also SAAS *3*
Ketteman, Helen 1945- *167*
  Earlier sketches in SATA *73, 115*
Kettle, Peter
  See Glover, Denis (James Matthews)
Kevles, Bettyann Holtzmann 1938- *23*
Key, Alexander (Hill) 1904-1979 .... *8*
  Obituary *23*
Key, Samuel M.
  See de Lint, Charles
Key, Watt 1970- *189*
Keyes, Daniel 1927- *37*
Keyes, Fenton 1915-1999 .... *34*
Keyes, Greg 1963- *116*
Keyes, J. Gregory
  See Keyes, Greg
Keyser, Marcia 1933- *42*
Keyser, Sarah
  See McGuire, Leslie (Sarah)
Khalid, Mohamed Nor
  See Lat
Khalsa, Dayal Kaur 1943-1989 .... *62*
  See also CLR *30*
Khan, Rukhsana 1962- *165*
  Earlier sketch in SATA *118*
Khanshendel, Chiron
  See Rose, Wendy
Kheirabadi, Masoud 1951- *158*
Khemir, Sabiha *87*
Kherdian, David 1931- *74*
  Autobiography Feature *125*
  Earlier sketch in SATA *16*
  See also CLR *24*
Khing, T.T. 1933- *192*
Kibbe, Pat (Hosley) *60*
Kidd, Diana 1933-2000 .... *150*
Kidd, Richard 1952-2008 .... *152*
  Obituary *194*
Kidd, Ronald 1948- *173*
  Earlier sketches in SATA *42, 92*
Kiddell, John 1922- *3*
Kiddell-Monroe, Joan 1908-1972 .... *55*
Kidwell, Carl 1910- *43*
Kiefer, Irene 1926- *21*
Kiefer, Kathleen Balmes 1957- *142*
Kiepper, Shirley Morgan 1933- *10*
Kierstead, Vera M.
  See Kierstead-Farber, Vera M.
Kierstead-Farber, Vera M. 1913- *121*
Kierstead-Farber, Vera May
  See Kierstead-Farber, Vera M.
Kiesel, Stanley 1925- *35*
Kiesler, Kate (A.) 1971- *152*
  Earlier sketch in SATA *90*
Kihn, Greg 1952- *110*
Kikukawa, Cecily H(arder) 1919- *44*
  Brief entry *35*
Kilcher, Jewel 1974- *109*
Kile, Joan 1940- *78*
Kilgore, Kathleen 1946- *42*
Kilian, Crawford 1941- *35*
Killdeer, John
  See Mayhar, Ardath

Killien, Christi 1956- *73*
Killilea, Marie (Lyons) 1913-1991 .... *2*
Killingback, Julia 1944- *63*
Killough, (Karen) Lee 1942- *64*
Kilreon, Beth
  See Walker, Barbara (Jeanne) K(erlin)
Kilworth, Garry 1941- *94*
Kilworth, Garry D.
  See Kilworth, Garry
Kilworth, Garry Douglas
  See Kilworth, Garry
Kim, Helen 1899-1970 .... *98*
Kimball, Gayle 1943- *90*
Kimball, Violet T(ew) 1932- *126*
Kimball, Yeffe 1914-1978 .... *37*
Kimber, Murray 1964- *171*
Kimble, Warren *176*
Kimbrough, Emily 1899-1989 .... *2*
  Obituary *59*
Kimeldorf, Martin 1948- *121*
Kimeldorf, Martin R.
  See Kimeldorf, Martin
Kimenye, Barbara 1940(?)- *121*
Kimmel, Elizabeth Cody *170*
Kimmel, Eric A. 1946- *176*
  Earlier sketches in SATA *13, 80, 125*
Kimmel, Margaret Mary 1938- *43*
  Brief entry *33*
Kimmelman, Burt 1947- *180*
Kimmelman, Leslie (Grodinsky) 1958- *156*
  Earlier sketch in SATA *85*
Kincaid, Jamaica 1949-
  See CLR *63*
Kincher, Jonni 1949- *79*
Kindl, Patrice 1951- *128*
  Earlier sketch in SATA *82*
  See also CLR *132*
Kindred, Wendy (Good) 1937- *7*
Kinerk, Robert *199*
Kines, Pat Decker 1937- *12*
King, Adam
  See Hoare, Robert J(ohn)
King, Alison
  See Martini, Teri
King, (Maria) Anna 1964- *72*
King, Billie Jean 1943- *12*
King, Christopher (L.) 1945- *84*
King, (David) Clive 1924- *144*
  Earlier sketch in SATA *28*
King, Colin 1943- *76*
King, Cynthia 1925- *7*
King, Daniel (John) 1963- *130*
King, Dave 1972- *197*
King, Elizabeth 1953- *83*
King, Frank O. 1883-1969
  Obituary *22*
King, Frank R. 1904-1999 .... *127*
King, Jane
  See Currie, Stephen
King, Jeanette (Margaret) 1959- *105*
King, Larry L. 1929- *66*
King, Laurie R. 1952- *88*
King, Marian 1900(?)-1986 .... *23*
  Obituary *47*
King, Martin Luther, Jr. 1929-1968 .... *14*
King, Mary Ellen 1958- *93*
King, Paul
  See Drackett, Phil(ip Arthur)
King, Paula
  See Downing, Paula E.
King, Stephen 1947- *161*
  Earlier sketches in SATA *9, 55*
  See also CLR *124*
King, Stephen Edwin
  See King, Stephen
King, Stephen Michael *157*
King, Steve
  See King, Stephen
King, Thomas 1943- *96*
King, Thomas Hunt
  See King, Thomas

King, Tony 1947- *39*
Kingman, Dong (Moy Shu) 1911-2000 .... *44*
Kingman, Lee
  See Natti, (Mary) Lee
Kingsland, Leslie William 1912- *13*
Kingsley, Charles 1819-1875
  See YABC *2*
  See also CLR *77*
Kingsley, Emily Perl 1940- *33*
Kingsley, Kaza *193*
King-Smith, Dick 1922- *192*
  Brief entry *38*
  Earlier sketches in SATA *47, 80, 135*
  See also CLR *40*
Kingston, Maxine Hong 1940- *53*
Kingston, Maxine Ting Ting Hong
  See Kingston, Maxine Hong
Kinney, C. Cle(land) 1915- *6*
Kinney, Harrison 1921- *13*
Kinney, Jean Stout 1912- *12*
Kinney, Jeff 1971- *187*
Kinsey, Elizabeth
  See Clymer, Eleanor
Kinsey, Helen 1948- *82*
Kinsey-Warnock, Natalie 1956- *167*
  Earlier sketches in SATA *71, 116*
Kinzel, Dorothy 1950- *57*
Kinzel, Dottie
  See Kinzel, Dorothy
Kipling, (Joseph) Rudyard 1865-1936 .... *100*
  See also YABC *2*
  See also CLR *65*
Kippax, Frank
  See Needle, Jan
Kirby, David K. 1944- *78*
Kirby, David Kirk
  See Kirby, David K.
Kirby, Margaret
  See Bingley, Margaret (Jane Kirby)
Kirby, Susan E. 1949- *62*
Kirk, Connie Ann 1957- *167*
Kirk, Daniel 1952- *196*
  Earlier sketches in SATA *107, 153*
Kirk, David 1955- *161*
  Earlier sketch in SATA *117*
Kirk, Heather 1949- *166*
Kirk, Ruth (Kratz) 1925- *5*
Kirkham, Dinah
  See Card, Orson Scott
Kirkland, Will
  See Hale, Arlene
Kirkpatrick, Katherine (Anne) 1964- *113*
Kirkup, James 1918- *12*
Kirkus, Virginia
  See Glick, Virginia Kirkus
Kirkwood, Kathryn
  See Fluke, Joanne
Kirshenbaum, Binnie *79*
Kirshner, David S. 1958- *123*
Kirtland, G. B.
  See Hine, Sesyle Joslin
  and Hine, Al(fred Blakelee)
Kirwan, Wednesday *198*
Kish, Eleanor M(ary) 1924- *73*
Kish, Ely
  See Kish, Eleanor M(ary)
Kishida, Eriko 1929- *12*
Kisinger, Grace Gelvin (Maze) 1913-1965 .. *10*
Kissin, Eva H. 1923- *10*
Kissinger, Rosemary K.
  See Updyke, Rosemary K.
Kistler, John M. 1967- *160*
Kitamura, Satoshi 1956- *143*
  Earlier sketches in SATA *62, 98*
  See also CLR *60*
Kitchen, Bert
  See Kitchen, Herbert Thomas
Kitchen, Herbert Thomas 1940- *70*
Kite, L. Patricia
  See Kite, Pat
Kite, Pat 1940- *78*

Kitt, Tamara
    See de Regniers, Beatrice Schenk (Freedman)
Kittinger, Jo S(usenbach) 1955- 148
    Earlier sketch in SATA 96
Kituomba
    See Odaga, Asenath (Bole)
Kitzinger, Sheila 1929- 57
Kiwak, Barbara 1966- 103
Kjelgaard, James Arthur 1910-1959 17
    See also CLR 81
    See Kjelgaard, Jim
Kjelgaard, Jim
    See Kjelgaard, James Arthur
Kjelle, Marylou Morano 1954- 146
Klages, Ellen 1954- 196
Klagsbrun, Francine (Lifton) 36
Klaits, Barrie 1944- 52
Klam, Cheryl 191
Klaperman, Gilbert 1921- 33
Klaperman, Libby Mindlin 1921-1982 33
    Obituary 31
Klass, David 1960- 142
    Earlier sketch in SATA 88
Klass, Morton 1927-2001 11
Klass, Sheila Solomon 1927- 99
    Autobiography Feature 126
    Earlier sketch in SATA 45
    See also SAAS 26
Klause, Annette Curtis 1953- 175
    Earlier sketch in SATA 79
    See also CLR 104
Klaveness, Jan O'Donnell 1939- 86
Kleberger, Ilse 1921- 5
Kleeberg, Irene (Flitner) Cumming 1932- 65
Klein, Aaron E. 1930-1998 45
    Brief entry 28
Klein, Bill 1945- 89
Klein, David 1919-2001 59
Klein, Frederick C. 1938- 154
Klein, Gerda Weissmann 1924- 44
Klein, H(erbert) Arthur 8
Klein, James 1932- 115
Klein, Leonore (Glotzer) 1916- 6
Klein, Mina C(ooper) 1906-1979 8
Klein, Norma 1938-1989 57
    Earlier sketch in SATA 7
    See also CLR 19
    See also SAAS 1
Klein, Rachel S. 1953- 105
Klein, Robin 1936- 164
    Brief entry 45
    Earlier sketches in SATA 55, 80
    See also CLR 21
Klemin, Diana 65
Klemm, Barry 1945- 104
Klemm, Edward G., Jr. 1910-2001 30
Klemm, Roberta K(ohnhorst) 1884-1975 30
Kleven, Elisa 1958- 173
    Earlier sketch in SATA 76
    See also CLR 85
Klevin, Jill Ross 1935- 39
    Brief entry 38
Kliban, B(ernard) 1935-1990 35
    Obituary 66
Klimowicz, Barbara 1927- 10
Kline, Christina Baker 1964- 101
Kline, James
    See Klein, James
Kline, Jim
    See Kline, Jim
Kline, Lisa Williams 1954- 143
Kline, Suzy 1943- 193
    Autobiography Feature 193
    Brief entry 48
    Earlier sketches in SATA 67, 99, 152
Kliros, Thea 1935- 106
Klise, Kate 181
Klise, M. Sarah 1961- 180
    Earlier sketch in SATA 128
Klots, Alexander Barrett 1903-1989
    Obituary 62

Klug, Ron(ald) 1939- 31
Knaak, Richard A. 1961- 166
    Earlier sketch in SATA 86
Knaak, Richard Allen
    See Knaak, Richard A.
Knapp, Edward
    See Kunhardt, Edith
Knapp, Ron 1952- 34
Knebel, Fletcher 1911-1993 36
    Obituary 75
Kneeland, Linda Clarke 1947- 94
Knickerbocker, Diedrich
    See Irving, Washington
Knifesmith
    See Cutler, Ivor
Knigge, Robert (R.) 1921(?)-1987 50
Knight, Anne (Katherine) 1946- 34
Knight, Brenda 112
Knight, Christopher G. 1943- 96
Knight, Damon (Francis) 1922-2002 9
    Obituary 139
Knight, David C(arpenter) 1925-1984 14
    See also CLR 38
Knight, Eric 1897-1943 18
Knight, Eric Mowbray
    See Knight, Eric
Knight, Francis Edgar 1905- 14
Knight, Frank
    See Knight, Francis Edgar
Knight, Hilary 1926- 132
    Earlier sketches in SATA 15, 69
Knight, Joan (MacPhail) 159
    Earlier sketch in SATA 82
Knight, Joan
    See Knight, Joan (MacPhail)
Knight, Kathryn Lasky
    See Lasky, Kathryn
Knight, Mallory T.
    See Hurwood, Bernhardt J.
Knight, Ruth Adams 1898-1974
    Obituary 20
Knight, Theodore O. 1946- 77
Knobloch, Dorothea 1951- 88
Knoepfle, John (Ignatius) 1923- 66
Knott, Bill
    See Knott, William C(ecil, Jr.)
Knott, William C(ecil, Jr.) 1927- 3
Knotts, Howard (Clayton, Jr.) 1922- 25
Knowles, Anne 1933- 37
Knowles, Jo 1970- 197
Knowles, Johanna Beth
    See Knowles, Jo
Knowles, John 1926-2001 89
    Obituary 134
    Earlier sketch in SATA 8
    See also CLR 98
Knox, Calvin M.
    See Silverberg, Robert
Knox, (Mary) Eleanor Jessie 1909-2000 59
    Earlier sketch in SATA 30
Knox, Elizabeth 1959- 176
Knox, Elizabeth Fiona
    See Knox, Elizabeth
Knox, James
    See Brittain, William (E.)
Knox, Jolyne 1937- 76
Knudsen, James 1950- 42
Knudsen, Michelle 171
Knudson, R. R.
    See Knudson, Rozanne
Knudson, Richard L(ewis) 1930- 34
Knudson, Rozanne 1932-2008 79
    Earlier sketch in SATA 7
    See also SAAS 18
Knutson, Barbara 1959-2005 166
Knutson, Kimberley 115
Knye, Cassandra
    See Disch, Thomas M.
Kobayashi, Masako Matsuno 1935- 6
Koch, Dorothy Clarke 1924- 6
Koch, Kenneth 1925-2002 65

Koch, Kenneth Jay
    See Koch, Kenneth
Koch, Phyllis (Mae) McCallum 1911- 10
Kochalka, James 1967- 196
Kocsis, J. C.
    See Paul, James
Koda-Callan, Elizabeth 1944- 140
    Earlier sketch in SATA 67
Koehler, Phoebe 1955- 85
Koehler-Pentacoff, Elizabeth 1957- 160
    Earlier sketch in SATA 96
Koehn, Ilse
    See Van Zwienen, Ilse Charlotte Koehn
Koeller, Carol 192
Koenig, Viviane 1950- 80
Koering, Ursula 1921-1976 64
Koerner, W(illiam) H(enry) D(avid)
    1878-1938 21
Koertge, Ronald 1940- 131
    Earlier sketches in SATA 53, 92
Koestler-Grack, Rachel A. 1973- 156
Koff, Richard Myram 1926- 62
Koffinke, Carol 1949- 82
Kogan, Deborah
    See Kogan Ray, Deborah
Kogan Ray, Deborah 1940- 161
    Earlier sketches in SATA 8, 50
Kogawa, Joy Nozomi 1935- 99
Kogler, Jennifer Anne 1982(?)- 174
Kohl, Herbert 1937- 47
Kohl, Herbert R.
    See Kohl, Herbert
Kohl, MaryAnn F(aubion) 1947- 144
    Earlier sketch in SATA 74
Kohler, Julilly H(ouse) 1908-1976
    Obituary 20
Kohn, Bernice
    See Hunt, Bernice (Kohn)
Kohn, Rita (T.) 1933- 89
Kohner, Frederick 1905-1986 10
    Obituary 48
Koide, Tan 1938-1986 50
Koike, Kay 1940- 72
Koja, Kathe 1960- 199
    Earlier sketch in SATA 155
Koja, Stephan 198
Kolb, Larry J. 1953- 175
Kolba, St. Tamara 22
Kolibalova, Marketa
    See Kolibalova, Marketa
Kolibalova, Marketa 1953- 126
Koller, Jackie French 1948- 157
    Earlier sketches in SATA 72, 109
    See also CLR 68
Kolodny, Nancy J. 1946- 76
Kolosov, Jacqueline 1967- 199
Komaiko, Leah 1954- 164
    Earlier sketch in SATA 97
Komisar, Lucy 1942- 9
Komoda, Beverly 1939- 25
Komoda, Kiyo 1937- 9
Kompaneyets, Marc 1974- 169
Komroff, Manuel 1890-1974 2
    Obituary 20
Konigsburg, E.L. 1930- 194
    Earlier sketches in SATA 4, 48, 94, 126
    See also CLR 81
Konigsburg, Elaine Lobl
    See Konigsburg, E.L.
Koning, Hans 1921-2007 5
    Obituary 182
Koningsberger, Hans
    See Koning, Hans
Konkle, Janet Everest 1917- 12
Kono, Erin Eitter 1973- 177
Konzak, Burt 1946- 151
Koob, Theodora (J. Foth) 1918- 23
Kooiker, Leonie
    See Kooyker-Romijn, Johanna Maria
Koons, James
    See Pernu, Dennis

Author Index

Koontz, Dean
See Koontz, Dean R.
Koontz, Dean R. 1945- 165
Earlier sketch in SATA 92
Koontz, Dean Ray
See Koontz, Dean R.
Koontz, Robin Michal 1954- 136
Earlier sketch in SATA 70
Kooyker, Leonie
See Kooyker-Romijn, Johanna Maria
Kooyker-Romijn, Johanna Maria 1927- 48
Kooyker-Romyn, Johanna Maria
See Kooyker-Romijn, Johanna Maria
Kopelke, Lisa 1963- 154
Kopper, Lisa (Esther) 1950- 105
Brief entry 51
Koppes, Steven N. 1957- 169
Koppes, Steven Nelson
See Koppes, Steven N.
Korach, Mimi 1922- 9
Koralek, Jenny 1934- 140
Earlier sketch in SATA 71
Korczak, Janusz
See Goldszmit, Henryk
Koren, Edward (Benjamin) 1935- 148
Earlier sketch in SATA 5
Korinets, Iurii Iosifovich
See Korinetz, Yuri (Iosifovich)
Korinetz, Yuri (Iosifovich) 1923- 9
See also CLR 4
Korman, Bernice 1937- 78
Korman, Gordon 1963- 167
Brief entry 41
Earlier sketches in SATA 49, 81, 119
See also CLR 25
Korman, Gordon Richard
See Korman, Gordon
Korman, Justine 1958- 70
Kornblatt, Marc 1954- 147
Earlier sketch in SATA 84
Kornprobst, Jacques 1937- 177
Korte, Gene J. 1950- 74
Korty, Carol 1937- 15
Koscielniak, Bruce 1947- 153
Earlier sketches in SATA 67, 99
Koshin, Alexander (A.) 1952- 86
Kositsky, Lynne 1947- 158
Koskenmaki, Rosalie
See Maggio, Rosalie
Koss, Amy Goldman 1954- 158
Earlier sketch in SATA 115
Kossin, Sandy (Sanford) 1926- 10
Kossman, Nina 1959- 84
Kostick, Conor 1964- 186
Kotzwinkle, William 1938- 146
Earlier sketches in SATA 24, 70
See also CLR 6
Kouhi, Elizabeth 1917- 54
Brief entry 49
Kouts, Anne 1945- 8
Koutsky, Jan Dale 1955- 146
Kovacs, Deborah 1954- 132
Earlier sketch in SATA 79
Kovalski, Maryann 1951- 175
Earlier sketches in SATA 58, 97
See also CLR 34
See also SAAS 21
Kowalski, Kathian M. 1955- 151
Earlier sketch in SATA 96
Kraft, Betsy Harvey 1937- 157
Kraft, Erik P. 193
Krahn, Fernando 1935- 49
Brief entry 31
See also CLR 3
Krakauer, Hoong Yee Lee 1955- 86
Krakauer, Jon 1954- 108
Kramer, George
See Heuman, William
Kramer, Nora 1896(?)-1984 26
Obituary 39
Kramer, Remi (Thomas) 1935- 90

Krantz, Hazel (Newman) 12
Kranzler, George G(ershon) 1916- 28
Kranzler, Gershon
See Kranzler, George G(ershon)
Krasilovsky, Phyllis 1926- 38
Earlier sketch in SATA 1
See also CLR 83
See also SAAS 5
Krasne, Betty
See Levine, Betty K(rasne)
Krasner, Steven 1953- 154
Krasno, Rena 1923- 104
Kratman, Tom 175
Kraus, Joanna Halpert 1937- 87
Kraus, (Herman) Robert 1925-2001 93
Obituary 130
Earlier sketches in SATA 4, 65
See also SAAS 11
Krauss, Ruth (Ida) 1911-1993 30
Obituary 75
Earlier sketch in SATA 1
See also CLR 42
Krautter, Elisa (Bialk) 1912(?)-1990 1
Obituary 65
Krautwurst, Terry 1946- 79
Kray, Robert Clement 1930- 82
Krech, Bob 1956- 185
Krech, Robert
See Krech, Bob
Kredel, Fritz 1900-1973 17
Kreikemeier, Gregory Scott 1965- 85
Kreloff, Elliot 189
Krementz, Jill 1940- 134
Earlier sketches in SATA 17, 71
See also CLR 5
See also SAAS 8
Kremer, Marcie
See Sorenson, Margo
Krenina, Katya 1968- 101
Krensky, Stephen 1953- 188
Brief entry 41
Earlier sketches in SATA 47, 93, 136
Krensky, Stephen Alan
See Krensky, Stephen
Kresh, Paul 1919-1997 61
Obituary 94
Kress, Nancy 1948- 147
Autobiography Feature 147
Earlier sketch in SATA 85
Kricher, John C. 1944- 113
Krieger, Melanie 96
Krinitz, Esther Nisenthal 1927-2001 194
Kripke, Dorothy Karp 30
Krisher, Trudy 1946- 160
Earlier sketch in SATA 86
Krisher, Trudy B.
See Krisher, Trudy
Krishnaswami, Uma 1956- 182
Earlier sketch in SATA 144
Kristof, Jane 1932- 8
Kroeber, Theodora (Kracaw) 1897-1979 1
Kroeger, Mary Kay 1950- 92
Krohn, Katherine E(lizabeth) 1961- 125
Earlier sketch in SATA 84
Kroll, Francis Lynde 1904-1973 10
Kroll, Steven 1941- 135
Autobiography Feature 135
Earlier sketches in SATA 19, 66, 125
See also SAAS 7
Kroll, Virginia L. 1948- 168
Earlier sketches in SATA 76, 114
Kroll, Virginia Louisa
See Kroll, Virginia L.
Kromhout, Rindert 1958- 189
Krommes, Beth 1956- 181
Earlier sketch in SATA 128
Kronenwetter, Michael 1943- 62
Kroniuk, Lisa
See Berton, Pierre (Francis de Marigny)

Kropp, Paul 1948- 38
Brief entry 34
See also CLR 96
Kropp, Paul Stephan
See Kropp, Paul
Krosoczka, Jarrett J. 1977- 155
Krovatin, Christopher 1985- 171
Kruess, James
See Kruss, James
Kruglik, Gerald 187
Krull, Kathleen 1952- 184
Autobiography Feature 106
Brief entry 39
Earlier sketches in SATA 52, 80, 149
See also CLR 44
Krumgold, Joseph (Quincy) 1908-1980 48
Obituary 23
Earlier sketch in SATA 1
Krupinski, Loretta 1940- 161
Earlier sketches in SATA 67, 102
Krupnick, Karen 1947- 89
Krupp, E(dwin) C(harles) 1944- 123
Earlier sketch in SATA 53
Krupp, Robin Rector 1946- 53
Krush, Beth 1918- 18
Krush, Joe 1918-
See Krush, Joseph P.
Krush, Joseph P. 1918- 18
Kruss, James 1926-1997 8
See also CLR 9
Krykorka, Vladyana 1945- 96
Krystoforski, Andrej 1943- 196
Kubie, Eleanor Gottheil
See Kubie, Nora Gottheil Benjamin
Kubie, Nora Benjamin
See Kubie, Nora Gottheil Benjamin
Kubie, Nora Gottheil Benjamin 1899-1988 . 39
Obituary 59
Kubinyi, Laszlo 1937- 94
Earlier sketch in SATA 17
Kudlinski, Kathleen V. 1950- 150
Kuenstler, Morton 1927- 10
Kuh, Charlotte 1892(?)-1985
Obituary 43
Kuharski, Janice 1947- 128
Kuhn, Dwight 199
Kuijer, Guus 1942- 179
Kujoth, Jean Spealman 1935-1975
Obituary 30
Kuklin, Susan 1941- 163
Earlier sketches in SATA 63, 95
See also CLR 51
Kulikov, Boris 1966- 170
Kulka, Joe 188
Kulling, Monica 1952- 89
Kullman, Harry 1919-1982 35
Kulyk Keefer, Janice 1952- 132
Kumin, Maxine 1925- 12
Kumin, Maxine Winokur
See Kumin, Maxine
Kunhardt, Dorothy (Meserve) 1901-1979 53
Obituary 22
Kunhardt, Edith 1937- 67
Kunjufu, Jawanza 1953- 73
Kunstler, Morton
See Kuenstler, Morton
Kuntz, J(ohn) L. 1947- 91
Kuntz, Jerry 1956- 133
Kupferberg, Herbert 1918-2001 19
Kuratomi, Chizuko 1939- 12
See also CLR 32
Kurczok, Belinda 1978- 121
Kurelek, William 1927-1977 8
Obituary 27
See also CLR 2
Kurian, George 1928- 65
Kurjian, Judi(th M.) 1944- 127
Kurland, Gerald 1942- 13
Kurland, Michael 1938- 118
Earlier sketch in SATA 48

Kurland, Michael Joseph
See Kurland, Michael
Kuroi, Ken 1947- 120
Kurokawa, Mitsuhiro 1954- 88
Kurten, Bjorn (Olof) 1924-1988 64
Kurtz, Jane 1952- 139
Earlier sketch in SATA 91
See also CLR 123
Kurtz, Katherine 1944- 182
Earlier sketches in SATA 76, 126
Kurtz, Katherine Irene
See Kurtz, Katherine
Kurz, Rudolf 1952- 95
Kushner, Donn (J.) 1927- 52
See also CLR 55
Kushner, Ellen 1955- 98
Kushner, Ellen Ruth
See Kushner, Ellen
Kushner, Jill Menkes 1951- 62
Kushner, Lawrence 1943- 169
Earlier sketch in SATA 83
Kushner, Tony 1956- 160
Kuskin, Karla 1932- 164
Earlier sketches in SATA 2, 68, 111
See also CLR 4
See also SAAS 3
Kuskin, Karla Seidman
See Kuskin, Karla
Kusugak, Michael 1948- 143
Kusugak, Michael Arvaarluk
See Kusugak, Michael
Kutner, Merrily 1948- 196
Kuttner, Paul 1922- 18
Kuyper, Sjoerd 1952- 177
Kuzma, Kay 1941- 39
Kvale, Velma R(uth) 1898-1979 8
Kvasnosky, Laura McGee 1951- 182
Earlier sketches in SATA 93, 142
Kwasney, Michelle D. 1960- 162
Kyle, Benjamin
See Gottfried, Theodore Mark
Kyle, Elisabeth
See Dunlop, Agnes M. R.
Kyte, Kathy S. 1946- 50
Brief entry 44

L

L., Barry
See Longyear, Barry B(rookes)
L., Tommy
See Lorkowski, Thomas V(incent)
Labouisse, Eve Curie
See Curie, Eve
Labouisse, Eve Denise
See Curie, Eve
Lace, William W. 1942- 126
Lacey, Joshua
See Doder, Josh
Lachner, Dorothea
See Knobloch, Dorothea
Lachtman, Ofelia Dumas 1919- 179
Lackey, Mercedes R. 1950- 127
Earlier sketch in SATA 81
Lackey, Mercedes Ritchie
See Lackey, Mercedes R.
Lacoe, Addie 78
Lacombe, Benjamin 1982- 198
Lacome, Julie 1961- 174
Earlier sketch in SATA 80
Lacy, Leslie Alexander 1937- 6
Ladd, Cheryl (Jean) 1951- 113
Ladd, Louise 1943- 97
Ladd, Veronica
See Miner, Jane Claypool
Laden, Nina 1962- 148
Earlier sketch in SATA 85
Lader, Lawrence 1919-2006 6
Obituary 178

LaDoux, Rita C. 1951- 74
Lady, A
See Taylor, Ann
Lady Mears
See Tempest, Margaret Mary
Lady of Quality, A
See Bagnold, Enid
La Farge, Oliver 1901-1963 19
La Farge, Oliver Hazard Perry
See La Farge, Oliver
La Farge, Phyllis 14
LaFave, Kim 196
LaFaye, A. 1970- 156
Earlier sketch in SATA 105
LaFaye, Alexandria R.T.
See LaFaye, A.
LaFevers, R.L. 191
LaFevers, Robin L.
See LaFevers, R.L.
Laffin, John (Alfred Charles) 1922- 31
LaFontaine, Bruce 1948- 176
Earlier sketch in SATA 114
La Fontaine, Jean de 1621-1695 18
Lafrance, Marie 1955- 197
Lager, Claude
See Lapp, Christiane (Germain)
Lager, Marilyn 1939- 52
Lagercrantz, Rose (Elsa) 1947- 39
Lagerloef, Selma (Ottiliana Lovisa)
See Lagerlof, Selma (Ottiliana Lovisa)
Lagerlof, Selma (Ottiliana Lovisa)
1858-1940 15
See also CLR 7
Laguna, Sofie 1968- 158
LaHaye, Tim F. 1926- 149
LaHaye, Timothy F.
See LaHaye, Tim F.
Laiken, Deirdre S(usan) 1948- 48
Brief entry 40
Laimgruber, Monika 1946- 11
Lain, Anna
See Lamb, Nancy
Laing, Alexander (Kinnan) 1903-1976 117
Laing, Martha 1951- 39
Laird, Christa 1944- 108
Autobiography Feature 120
See also SAAS 26
Laird, Elizabeth (Mary Risk) 1943- 159
Earlier sketches in SATA 77, 114
See also CLR 65
Laird, Jean E(louise) 1930- 38
Laite, Gordon 1925- 31
Lake, Harriet
See Taylor, Paula (Wright)
Lakin, Patricia 1944- 190
Laklan, Carli 1907-1988 5
Laliberte, Louise-Andree 1958- 169
Lalicki, Barbara 61
Lalicki, Tom 1949- 186
Lally, Soinbhe 1945- 119
LaMarche, Jim 162
Lamb, Albert 187
Lamb, Beatrice Pitney 1904-1997 21
Lamb, Charles 1775-1834 17
Lamb, Elizabeth Searle 1917- 31
Lamb, G(eoffrey) F(rederick) 10
Lamb, Harold (Albert) 1892-1962 53
Lamb, Lynton (Harold) 1907-1977 10
Lamb, Mary Ann 1764-1847 17
Lamb, Nancy 1939- 80
Lamb, Robert (Boyden) 1941- 13
Lamba, Marie 195
Lambert, David (Compton) 1932- 84
Brief entry 49
Lambert, Janet 1895(?)-1973 25
Lambert, Martha L. 113
Lambert, Saul 1928- 23
Lambert, Stephen 174
Lamburn, Richmal Crompton 1890-1969 5
Lamensdorf, Len 1930- 120

Lamensdorf, Leonard
See Lamensdorf, Len
Laminack, Lester L. 1956- 163
Earlier sketch in SATA 120
Lamorisse, Albert (Emmanuel) 1922-1970 ... 23
Lampert, Emily 1951- 52
Brief entry 49
Lamplugh, Lois 1921- 17
Lampman, Evelyn Sibley 1907-1980 87
Obituary 23
Earlier sketch in SATA 4
Lamprey, Louise 1869-1951
See YABC 2
Lampton, Chris
See Lampton, Christopher F.
Lampton, Christopher
See Lampton, Christopher F.
Lampton, Christopher F. 67
Brief entry 47
Lamstein, Sarah 1943- 174
Earlier sketch in SATA 126
Lamstein, Sarah Marwil
See Lamstein, Sarah
Lanagan, Margo 1960- 163
Lancaster, Bruce 1896-1963 9
Lancaster, Matthew 1973(?)-1983
Obituary 45
Lance, Kathryn 1943- 76
Land, Barbara (Neblett) 1923- 16
Land, Jane
See Borland, Kathryn Kilby
and Speicher, Helen Ross S(mith)
Land, Myrick (Ebben) 1922-1998 15
Land, Ross
See Borland, Kathryn Kilby
and Speicher, Helen Ross S(mith)
Landau, Elaine 1948- 141
Earlier sketches in SATA 10, 94
Landau, Jacob 1917- 38
Landeck, Beatrice 1904-1978 15
Landin, Les 1923- 2
Landis, J(ames) D(avid) 1942- 60
Brief entry 52
Landis, James D.
See Landis, J(ames) D(avid)
Landis, Jill Marie 1948- 101
Landmann, Bimba 1968- 176
Landon, Dena 1978(?)- 168
Landon, Lucinda 1950- 56
Brief entry 51
Landon, Margaret (Dorothea Mortenson)
1903-1993 50
Landshoff, Ursula 1908-1989 13
Landstrom, Lena 1943- 146
Landstrom, Olof 1943- 146
Lane, Carolyn 1926-1993 10
Lane, Connie
See Laux, Constance
Lane, Dakota 1959- 166
Earlier sketch in SATA 105
Lane, Jerry
See Martin, Patricia Miles
Lane, John (Richard) 1932- 15
Lane, Leena 199
Lane, Margaret 1907-1994 65
Brief entry 38
Obituary 79
Lane, Rose Wilder 1887-1968 29
Brief entry 28
Lanes, Selma Gordon 1929- 3
Lanfredi, Judy 1964- 83
Lang, Andrew 1844-1912 16
See also CLR 101
Lang, Aubrey 169
Lang, Paul 1948- 83
Lang, Susan S. 1950- 68
Lang, T.T.
See Taylor, Theodore
Langart, Darrell T.
See Garrett, (Gordon) Randall (Phillip)

Langdo, Bryan 1973- *191*
    Earlier sketch in SATA *138*
Lange, John
    See Crichton, Michael
Lange, Karen E. *190*
Lange, Suzanne 1945- *5*
Langley, Andrew 1949- *166*
    Earlier sketch in SATA *104*
Langley, Charles P(itman) III 1949- *103*
Langley, Jonathan 1952- *122*
Langley, Noel 1911-1980
    Obituary *25*
Langley, Wanda *173*
Langner, Nola
    See Malone, Nola Langner
Langone, John (Michael) 1929- *46*
    Brief entry *38*
Langreuter, Jutta 1944- *122*
Langrish, Katherine *177*
Langsen, Richard C. 1953- *95*
Langstaff, John 1920-2005 .... *68*
    Obituary *172*
    Earlier sketch in SATA *6*
    See also CLR *3*
Langstaff, John Meredith
    See Langstaff, John
Langstaff, Launcelot
    See Irving, Washington
Langston, Laura 1958- *186*
Langton, Jane (Gillson) 1922- *140*
    Autobiography Feature *140*
    Earlier sketches in SATA *3, 68, 129*
    See also CLR *33*
    See also SAAS *5*
Lanier, Sidney 1842-1881 .... *18*
Lanier, Sterling E. 1927-2007 .... *109*
Lanier, Sterling Edmund
    See Lanier, Sterling E.
Lanino, Deborah 1964- *123*
Lankford, Mary D. 1932- *112*
    Earlier sketch in SATA *77*
Lannin, Joanne 1951- *121*
Lannin, Joanne A.
    See Lannin, Joanne
Lansdale, Joe R. 1951- *116*
Lansdale, Joe Richard
    See Lansdale, Joe R.
Lansing, Alfred 1921-1975 .... *35*
Lansing, Karen E. 1954- *71*
Lansky, Vicki 1942- *177*
Lantier-Sampon, Patricia 1952- *92*
Lantz, Fran
    See Lantz, Francess L(in)
Lantz, Francess L(in) 1952-2004 .... *153*
    Autobiography Feature *153*
    Obituary *159*
    Earlier sketches in SATA *63, 109*
Lantz, Paul 1908- *45*
Lantz, Walter 1900-1994 .... *37*
    Obituary *79*
Lanza, Barbara 1945- *101*
Lapp, Christiane (Germain) 1948- *74*
Lappin, Peter 1911-1999 .... *32*
Larbalestier, Justine *178*
Lardy, Philippe 1963- *168*
LaReau, Jenna *181*
LaReau, Kara *181*
Larios, Julie 1949- *178*
Larios, Julie Hofstrand
    See Larios, Julie
Larkin, Amy
    See Burns, Olive Ann
Larkin, Maia
    See Wojciechowska, Maia (Teresa)
Laroche, Giles 1956- *126*
    Earlier sketch in SATA *71*
LaRochelle, David 1960- *171*
    Earlier sketch in SATA *115*
Larom, Henry V. 1903(?)-1975
    Obituary *30*
LaRose, Linda *125*

Larrabee, Lisa 1947- *84*
Larrecq, John M(aurice) 1926-1980 .... *44*
    Obituary *25*
Larrick (Crosby), Nancy 1910-2004 .... *4*
Larsen, Anita 1942- *78*
Larsen, Egon 1904- *14*
Larsen, Rebecca 1944- *54*
Larson, Eve
    See St. John, Wylly Folk
Larson, Gary 1950- *57*
Larson, Ingrid D(ana) 1965- *92*
Larson, Jean Russell 1930- *121*
Larson, Kirby 1954- *181*
    Earlier sketch in SATA *96*
Larson, Norita D(ittberner) 1944- *29*
Larson, William H. 1938- *10*
Larsson, Carl (Olof) 1853-1919 .... *35*
LaSalle, Charles A.
    See Ellis, Edward S(ylvester)
LaSalle, Charles E.
    See Ellis, Edward S(ylvester)
Lasell, Elinor H. 1929- *19*
Lasell, Fen H.
    See Lasell, Elinor H.
Lasenby, Jack 1931- *172*
    Earlier sketches in SATA *65, 103*
Laser, Michael 1954- *117*
Lash, Joseph P. 1909-1987 .... *43*
Lasher, Faith B. 1921- *12*
Lasker, David 1950- *38*
Lasker, Joe
    See Lasker, Joseph Leon
Lasker, Joseph Leon 1919- *83*
    Earlier sketch in SATA *9*
    See also SAAS *17*
Laski, Marghanita 1915-1988 .... *55*
Laskin, Pamela L. 1954- *75*
Lasky, Kathryn 1944- *157*
    Earlier sketches in SATA *13, 69, 112*
    See also CLR *140*
Lasky Knight, Kathryn
    See Lasky, Kathryn
Lass, Bonnie *131*
Lassalle, C. E.
    See Ellis, Edward S(ylvester)
Lassiter, Mary
    See Hoffman, Mary (Margaret)
Lassiter, Rhiannon 1977- *157*
Lat 1951- *196*
Latham, Barbara 1896- *16*
Latham, Frank B(rown) 1910-2000 .... *6*
Latham, Jean Lee 1902-1995 .... *68*
    Earlier sketch in SATA *2*
    See also CLR *50*
Latham, Mavis
    See Clark, Mavis Thorpe
Latham, Philip
    See Richardson, Robert S(hirley)
Lathrop, Dorothy P(ulis) 1891-1980 .... *14*
    Obituary *24*
Lathrop, Francis
    See Leiber, Fritz (Reuter, Jr.)
Latimer, Jim 1943- *80*
Latta, Rich
    See Latta, Richard
Latta, Richard 1946- *113*
Latta, Sara L. 1960- *174*
Lattany, Kristin
    See Lattany, Kristin (Elaine Eggleston) Hunter
Lattany, Kristin (Eggleston) Hunter 1931- . *154*
    Autobiography Feature *154*
    Earlier sketch in SATA *132*
Lattany, Kristin (Elaine Eggleston) Hunter
    1931- *132*
    Earlier sketch in SATA *12*
    See also CLR *3*
    See also SAAS *10*
Lattimore, Eleanor Frances 1904-1986 .... *7*
    Obituary *48*
Lattin, Ann
    See Cole, Lois Dwight

Lauber, Patricia (Grace) 1924- *138*
    Earlier sketches in SATA *1, 33, 75*
    See also CLR *16*
Laugesen, Mary E(akin) 1906-1995 .... *5*
Laughbaum, Steve 1945- *12*
Laughlin, Florence Young 1910-2001 .... *3*
Laughlin, Rosemary 1941- *123*
Laure, Ettagale
    See Blauer, Ettagale
Laure, Jason 1940- *50*
    Brief entry *44*
Laurence, Ester Hauser 1935- *7*
Laurence, Jean Margaret Wemyss
    See Laurence, Margaret
Laurence, Margaret 1926-1987
    Obituary *50*
Laurie, Rona 1916- *55*
Laurin, Anne
    See McLaurin, Anne
Lauritzen, Jonreed 1902-1979 .... *13*
Lauscher, Hermann
    See Hesse, Hermann
Lauture, Denize 1946- *86*
Laux, Connie
    See Laux, Constance
Laux, Constance 1952- *97*
Laux, Dorothy 1920- *49*
Lavallee, Barbara 1941- *166*
    Earlier sketch in SATA *74*
Lavender, David (Sievert) 1910-2003 .... *97*
    Obituary *145*
    Earlier sketch in SATA *64*
Lavender, William D. 1921- *143*
Laverne, Christine *175*
Lavert, Gwendolyn Battle 1951-
    See Battle-Lavert, Gwendolyn
Laverty, Donald
    See Blish, James (Benjamin)
    and Knight, Damon (Francis)
Lavigne, Louis-Dominique *107*
Lavine, David 1928- *31*
Lavine, Sigmund Arnold 1908-1986 .... *82*
    Earlier sketch in SATA *3*
    See also CLR *35*
Lavond, Paul Dennis
    See Kornbluth, C(yril) M.
    and Lowndes, Robert A(ugustine) W(ard)
    and Pohl, Frederik
Lawford, Paula Jane 1960- *57*
    Brief entry *53*
Lawhead, Stephen R. 1950- *109*
Lawhead, Steve
    See Lawhead, Stephen R.
Lawlor, Laurie 1953- *137*
    Earlier sketch in SATA *80*
Lawlor, William
    See Lawlor, William T.
Lawlor, William T. 1951- *183*
Lawrence, Ann (Margaret) 1942-1987 .... *41*
    Obituary *54*
Lawrence, Iain 1955- *183*
    Earlier sketch in SATA *135*
Lawrence, J. T.
    See Rowland-Entwistle, (Arthur) Theodore
    (Henry)
Lawrence, Jerome 1915-2004 .... *65*
Lawrence, John 1933- *30*
Lawrence, Josephine 1890(?)-1978
    Obituary *24*
Lawrence, Louise 1943- *119*
    Earlier sketches in SATA *38, 78*
Lawrence, Louise de Kiriline 1894-1992 ..... *13*
Lawrence, Lynn
    See Garland, Sherry
Lawrence, Margery H. 1889-1969 .... *120*
Lawrence, Michael 1943- *132*
Lawrence, Mildred Elwood 1907-1997 .... *3*
Lawrence, R(onald) D(ouglas) 1921- *55*
Lawrinson, Julia 1969- *141*
Lawson, Amy
    See Gordon, Amy

Lawson, Carol (Antell) 1946- 42
Lawson, Don(ald Elmer) 1917-1990 9
Lawson, Joan 1906- 55
Lawson, Julie 1947- 126
 Earlier sketch in SATA 79
 See also CLR 89
Lawson, Marion Tubbs 1896-1994 22
Lawson, Robert 1892-1957 100
 See also YABC 2
 See also CLR 73
Lawton, Clive A. 1951- 145
Laxdal, Vivienne 1962- 112
Laybourn, Emma 193
Laycock, George (Edwin) 1921- 5
Layne, Laura
 See Knott, William C(ecil, Jr.)
Layne, Steven L. 171
Layton, Neal 1971- 187
 Earlier sketch in SATA 152
Layton, Neal Andrew
 See Layton, Neal
Lazare, Gerald John 1927- 44
Lazare, Jerry
 See Lazare, Gerald John
Lazarevich, Mila 1942- 17
Lazarus, Keo Felker 1913-1993 21
 Obituary 129
Lea, Alec 1907- 19
Lea, Joan
 See Neufeld, John (Arthur)
Leach, Maria 1892-1977 39
 Brief entry 28
Leacock, Elspeth 1946- 131
Leacroft, Helen (Mabel Beal) 1919- 6
Leacroft, Richard (Vallance Becher) 1914- 6
Leaf, Margaret P. 1909(?)-1988
 Obituary 55
Leaf, (Wilbur) Munro 1905-1976 20
 See also CLR 25
Leaf, VaDonna Jean 1929- 26
Leah, Devorah
 See Devorah-Leah
Leakey, Richard E(rskine Frere) 1944- 42
Leander, Ed
 See Richelson, Geraldine
Lear, Edward 1812-1888 100
 Earlier sketch in SATA 18
 See also CLR 75
Lears, Laurie 1955- 127
Leasor, James 1923-2007 54
Leasor, Thomas James
 See Leasor, James
Leavitt, Jerome E(dward) 1916- 23
Leavitt, Martine 1953- 170
LeBar, Mary E(velyn) 1910-1982 35
LeBlanc, Annette M. 1965- 68
LeBlanc, L(ee) 1913- 54
LeBox, Annette 1943- 145
Lebrun, Claude 1929- 66
Le Cain, Errol (John) 1941-1989 68
 Obituary 60
 Earlier sketch in SATA 6
Lecourt, Nancy (Hoyt) 1951- 73
Ledbetter, Suzann 1953- 119
Leder, Jane Mersky 1945- 61
 Brief entry 51
Lederer, Muriel 1929- 48
Lederer, William J(ulius) 1912- 62
Lee, Amanda
 See Baggett, Nancy
 and Buckholtz, Eileen (Garber)
 and Glick, Ruth (Burtnick)
Lee, Benjamin 1921- 27
Lee, Betsy 1949- 37
Lee, Carol
 See Fletcher, Helen Jill
Lee, Carol Ann 1969- 185
Lee, Chinlun 182
Lee, Cora
 See Anderson, Catherine Corley

Lee, Dennis (Beynon) 1939- 102
 Earlier sketch in SATA 14
 See also CLR 3
Lee, Dom 1959- 146
 Autobiography Feature 121
 Earlier sketch in SATA 83
 See also SAAS 26
Lee, Doris Emrick 1905-1983 44
 Obituary 35
Lee, Edward
 See Lee, J. Edward
Lee, Elizabeth Rogers 1940- 90
Lee, Harper 1926- 11
Lee, Hector Viveros 1962- 115
Lee, Howard N.
 See Goulart, Ron(ald Joseph)
Lee, Huy Voun 1969- 129
Lee, J. Edward 1953- 130
Lee, Jeanne M. 1943- 138
Lee, John R(obert) 1923-1976 27
Lee, Jordan
 See Scholefield, Alan
Lee, Joseph Edward
 See Lee, J. Edward
Lee, Julian
 See Latham, Jean Lee
Lee, Linda
 See Eyerly, Jeannette
Lee, Liz
 See Lee, Elizabeth Rogers
Lee, Lucy
 See Talbot, Charlene Joy
Lee, Lyn 1953- 128
Lee, Manning de Villeneuve 1894-1980 37
 Obituary 22
Lee, Marian
 See Clish, (Lee) Marian
Lee, Marie G. 1964- 178
 Earlier sketches in SATA 81, 130
Lee, Marie Myung-Ok
 See Lee, Marie G.
Lee, Mary Price 1934- 82
 Earlier sketch in SATA 8
Lee, Mildred
 See Scudder, Mildred Lee
Lee, Nelle Harper
 See Lee, Harper
Lee, Richard S. 1927- 82
Lee, Robert C. 1931- 20
Lee, Robert E(dwin) 1918-1994 65
 Obituary 82
Lee, Robert J. 1921- 10
Lee, Roy
 See Hopkins, Clark
Lee, Sally 1943- 67
Lee, Suzy 193
Lee, Tammie
 See Townsend, Thomas L.
Lee, Tanith 1947- 185
 Earlier sketches in SATA 8, 88, 134
Leech, Ben
 See Bowkett, Stephen
Leeds, Contance 188
Leedy, Loreen 1959- 175
 Brief entry 50
 Earlier sketches in SATA 54, 84, 128
Leedy, Loreen Janelle
 See Leedy, Loreen
Lee-Hostetler, Jeri 1940- 63
Leekley, Thomas B(riggs) 1910-2001 23
Leeming, Jo Ann
 See Leeming, Joseph
Leeming, Joseph 1897-1968 26
Leemis, Ralph B. 1954- 72
Leese, Jennifer L.B. 1970- 163
Leeson, Muriel 1920- 54
Leeson, R. A.
 See Leeson, Robert (Arthur)
Leeson, Robert (Arthur) 1928- 76
 Earlier sketch in SATA 42
Lee Tae-Jun 1904-1956(?) 194

Lee-Tai, Amy 1964- 189
Leffland, Ella 1931- 65
Leffler, Silke 197
Lefler, Irene (Whitney) 1917- 12
LeFrak, Karen 182
Le Gallienne, Eva 1899-1991 9
 Obituary 68
Legg, Gerald 1947- 143
Legg, Sarah Martha Ross Bruggeman (?)-1982
 Obituary 40
LeGrand
 See Henderson, LeGrand
Le Guin, Ursula K. 1929- 194
 Earlier sketches in SATA 4, 52, 99, 149
 See also CLR 91
Le Guin, Ursula Kroeber
 See Le Guin, Ursula K.
Legum, Colin 1919-2003 10
Lehman, Barbara 1963- 170
 Earlier sketch in SATA 115
Lehman, Bob 91
Lehman, Elaine 91
Lehmann, Debra Lynn
 See Vanasse, Deb
Lehn, Cornelia 1920- 46
Lehne, Judith Logan 1947- 93
Lehr, Delores 1920- 10
Lehr, Norma 1930- 71
Leiber, Fritz (Reuter, Jr.) 1910-1992 45
 Obituary 73
Leibold, Jay 1957- 57
 Brief entry 52
Leichman, Seymour 1933- 5
Leigh, Nila K. 1981- 81
Leigh, Tom 1947- 46
Leigh-Pemberton, John 1911-1997 35
Leighton, Clare (Veronica Hope)
 1899-1989 37
Leighton, Margaret (Carver) 1896-1987 1
 Obituary 52
Leiner, Al(an) 1938- 83
Leiner, Katherine 1949- 93
Leipold, L. Edmond 1902-1983 16
Leisk, David (Johnson) 1906-1975 30
 Obituary 26
 Earlier sketch in SATA 1
 See also CLR 98
Leister, Mary 1917- 29
Leitch, Patricia 1933- 98
 Earlier sketch in SATA 11
Leitner, Isabella 1924- 86
Leland, Bob 1956- 92
Leland, Robert E.
 See Leland, Bob
Lemaitre, Pascal 1967- 176
Lember, Barbara Hirsch 1941- 92
LeMieux, A.C. 1954- 125
 Earlier sketch in SATA 90
LeMieux, Anne
 See LeMieux, A.C.
LeMieux, Anne Connelly
 See LeMieux, A.C.
Lemieux, Michele 1955- 139
Lemke, Horst 1922- 38
Lenanton, Carola Mary Anima Oman
 See Oman, Carola (Mary Anima)
Lenard, Alexander 1910-1972
 Obituary 21
L'Engle, Madeleine 1918-2007 128
 Obituary 186
 Earlier sketches in SATA 1, 27, 75
 See also CLR 57
 See also SAAS 15
L'Engle, Madeleine Camp Franklin
 See L'Engle, Madeleine
Lengyel, Cornel Adam 1915- 27
Lengyel, Emil 1895-1985 3
 Obituary 42
Lennon, John (Ono) 1940-1980 114
Leno, Jay 1950- 154
LeNoir, Janice 1941- 89

Lens, Sidney 1912-1986 .... *13*
  Obituary *48*
Lenski, Lois 1893-1974 .... *100*
  Earlier sketches in SATA *1, 26*
  See also CLR 26
Lent, Blair 1930-2009 .... *133*
  Earlier sketch in SATA *2*
Lent, Henry Bolles 1901-1973 .... *17*
Lent, John 1948- *108*
Leodhas, Sorche Nic
  See Alger, Leclaire (Gowans)
Leokum, Arkady 1916(?)- *45*
Leon, Sharon 1959- *79*
Leonard, Alison 1944- *70*
Leonard, Constance (Brink) 1923- *42*
  Brief entry *40*
Leonard, Dutch
  See Leonard, Elmore
Leonard, Elmore 1925- *163*
Leonard, Elmore John, Jr.
  See Leonard, Elmore
Leonard, Jonathan N(orton) 1903-1975 .... *36*
Leonard, Laura 1923- *75*
Leong, Gor Yun
  See Ellison, Virginia H(owell)
Leonhardt, Alice 1950- *152*
Lerangis, Peter 1955- *171*
  Earlier sketch in SATA *72*
Lerner, Aaron 1920-2007 .... *35*
  Obituary *179*
Lerner, Aaron Bunsen
  See Lerner, Aaron
Lerner, Carol 1927- *86*
  Earlier sketch in SATA *33*
  See also CLR 34
  See also SAAS 12
Lerner, Gerda 1920- *65*
Lerner, Harriet 1944- *101*
Lerner, Marguerite Rush 1924-1987 .... *11*
  Obituary *51*
Lerner, Sharon (Ruth) 1938-1982 .... *11*
  Obituary *29*
Leroe, Ellen W(hitney) 1949- *99*
  Brief entry *51*
  Earlier sketch in SATA *61*
Leroux, Gaston 1868-1927 .... *65*
Leroux-Hugon, Helene 1955- *132*
LeRoy, Gen *52*
  Brief entry *36*
Lerrigo, Marion Olive 1898-1968
  Obituary *29*
LeShan, Eda J(oan) 1922-2002 .... *21*
  See also CLR 6
LeSieg, Theo.
  See Dr. Seuss
  and Geisel, Theodor Seuss
  and Seuss, Dr.
  and Stone, Rosetta
Lesinski, Jeanne M. 1960- *120*
Leslie, Robert Franklin 1911-1990 .... *7*
Leslie, Roger 1961- *168*
Leslie, Roger James
  See Leslie, Roger
Leslie, Sarah
  See McGuire, Leslie (Sarah)
LeSourd, Catherine
  See Marshall, (Sarah) Catherine (Wood)
Lessac, Frane
  See Lessac, Frane
Lessac, Frane 1954- *148*
  Earlier sketch in SATA *61*
Lessem, Dino Don
  See Lessem, Don
Lessem, Don 1951- *182*
  Earlier sketches in SATA *97, 155*
Lesser, Margaret 1899(?)-1979
  Obituary *22*
Lesser, Rika 1953- *53*
Lester, Alison 1952- *129*
  Earlier sketches in SATA *50, 90*

Lester, Helen 1936- *189*
  Earlier sketches in SATA *46, 92, 145*
Lester, Julius 1939- *157*
  Earlier sketches in SATA *12, 74, 112*
  See also CLR 41
Lester, Julius Bernard
  See Lester, Julius
Lester, Mike 1955- *131*
Le Sueur, Meridel 1900-1996 .... *6*
Lethcoe, Jason *191*
Le Tord, Bijou 1945- *95*
  Earlier sketch in SATA *49*
Letts, Billie 1938- *121*
Leuck, Laura 1962- *192*
  Earlier sketches in SATA *85, 146*
Leutscher, Alfred (George) 1913- *23*
Levai, Blaise 1919- *39*
Levenkron, Steven 1941- *86*
Leverich, Kathleen 1948- *103*
LeVert, (William) John 1946- *55*
Levete, Sarah 1961- *153*
Levin, Betty 1927- *137*
  Earlier sketches in SATA *19, 84*
  See also SAAS 11
Levin, Ira 1929-2007 .... *66*
  Obituary *187*
Levin, Ira Marvin
  See Levin, Ira
Levin, Ira Marvin
  See Levin, Ira
Levin, Marcia Obrasky 1918- *13*
Levin, Meyer 1905-1981 .... *21*
  Obituary *27*
Levin, Miriam (Ramsfelder) 1962- *97*
Levine, Abby 1943- *54*
  Brief entry *52*
Levine, Betty K(rasne) 1933- *66*
Levine, David 1926- *43*
  Brief entry *35*
Levine, Edna S(imon) *35*
Levine, Ellen 1939- *190*
Levine, Evan 1962- *77*
  Earlier sketch in SATA *74*
Levine, Gail Carson 1947- *195*
  Earlier sketches in SATA *98, 161*
  See also CLR 85
Levine, I(srael) E. 1923-2003 .... *12*
  Obituary *146*
Levine, Joan Goldman *11*
Levine, Joseph 1910- *33*
Levine, Marge 1934- *81*
Levine, Rhoda *14*
Levine, Sarah 1970- *57*
Levine, Shar 1953- *131*
Levine-Freidus, Gail
  See Provost, Gail Levine
Levinson, Nancy Smiler 1938- *140*
  Earlier sketches in SATA *33, 80*
Levinson, Riki *99*
  Brief entry *49*
  Earlier sketch in SATA *52*
Levithan, David 1972- *166*
Levitin, Sonia 1934- *192*
  Autobiography Feature *131*
  Earlier sketches in SATA *4, 68, 119, 131*
  See also CLR 53
  See also SAAS 2
Levitt, Sidney (Mark) 1947- *68*
Levon, O. U.
  See Kesey, Ken
Levoy, Myron *49*
  Brief entry *37*
Levy, Barrie *112*
Levy, Constance 1931- *140*
  Earlier sketch in SATA *73*
  See also SAAS 22
Levy, Elizabeth 1942- *169*
  Earlier sketches in SATA *31, 69, 107*
  See also SAAS 18
Levy, Janice *172*
Levy, Marilyn 1937- *67*

Levy, Nathan 1945- *63*
Levy, Robert 1945- *82*
Lewees, John
  See Stockton, Francis Richard
Lewin, Betsy 1937- *169*
  Autobiography Feature *115*
  Earlier sketches in SATA *32, 90*
Lewin, Hugh 1939- *72*
  Brief entry *40*
  See also CLR 9
Lewin, Ted 1935- *195*
  Autobiography Feature *115*
  Earlier sketches in SATA *21, 76, 119, 165*
Lewis, Alice C. 1936- *46*
Lewis, Alice Hudson 1895(?)-1971
  Obituary *29*
Lewis, Amanda 1955- *80*
Lewis, Anthony 1927- *27*
Lewis, Anthony 1966- *120*
Lewis, Barbara A. 1943- *73*
Lewis, Beverly 1949- *80*
Lewis, Brenda Ralph 1932- *72*
Lewis, Brian 1963- *128*
Lewis, Claudia (Louise) 1907-2001 .... *5*
Lewis, Clive Staples
  See Lewis, C.S.
Lewis, C.S. 1898-1963 .... *100*
  Earlier sketch in SATA *13*
  See also CLR 109
Lewis, Cynthia Copeland 1960- *111*
Lewis, E. M. *123*
  Earlier sketch in SATA *20*
Lewis, Earl Bradley
  See Lewis, E.B.
Lewis, E.B. 1956- *168*
  Earlier sketches in SATA *93, 124*
Lewis, Elizabeth Foreman 1892-1958 .... *121*
  See also YABC 2
Lewis, Francine
  See Wells, Helen
Lewis, Hilda (Winifred) 1896-1974
  Obituary *20*
Lewis, J. Patrick 1942- *162*
  Earlier sketches in SATA *69, 104*
Lewis, Jack P(earl) 1919- *65*
Lewis, Jean 1924- *61*
Lewis, Joseph Anthony
  See Lewis, Anthony
Lewis, Julinda
  See Lewis-Ferguson, Julinda
Lewis, Kevin *173*
Lewis, Kim 1951- *136*
  Earlier sketch in SATA *84*
Lewis, Linda (Joy) 1946- *67*
Lewis, Lucia Z.
  See Anderson, Lucia (Lewis)
Lewis, Marjorie 1929- *40*
  Brief entry *35*
Lewis, Mary (Christianna) 1907(?)-1988 ..... *64*
  Obituary *56*
Lewis, Mervyn
  See Frewer, Glyn (M.)
Lewis, Michael
  See Untermeyer, Louis
Lewis, Naomi *144*
  Earlier sketch in SATA *76*
Lewis, Paeony 1960- *173*
Lewis, Paul
  See Gerson, Noel Bertram
Lewis, Richard 1935- *3*
Lewis, Rob 1962- *72*
Lewis, Roger
  See Zarchy, Harry
Lewis, Shannon
  See Llywelyn, Morgan
Lewis, Shari 1934-1998 .... *35*
  Brief entry *30*
  Obituary *104*
Lewis, Sylvan R.
  See Aronson, Virginia
Lewis, Thomas P(arker) 1936- *27*

Lewis, Wendy A. 1966- 150
Lewis-Ferguson, Julinda 1955- 85
Lewison, Wendy Cheyette 177
Lewiton, Mina 1904-1970 2
Lew-Vriethoff, Joanne 186
Lexau, Joan M. 130
   Earlier sketches in SATA *1, 36*
Ley, Willy 1906-1969 2
Leydon, Rita (Floden) 1949- 21
Leyland, Eric (Arthur) 1911- 37
L'Hommedieu, Dorothy Keasley 1885-1961
   Obituary 29
Li, Xiao Jun 1952- 86
Liatsos, Sandra Olson 1942- 103
Libby, Alisa M. 189
Libby, Barbara M. 153
Libby, Bill
   See Libby, William M.
Libby, William M. 1927-1984 5
   Obituary 39
Liberty, Gene 1924- 3
Lichtenheld, Tom 152
Lichtman, Wendy 1946- 193
Liddell, Kenneth 1912-1975 63
Lidz, Jane 120
Lieberman, E(dwin) James 1934- 62
Liebers, Arthur 1913-1984 12
Lieblich, Irene 1923- 22
Liers, Emil E(rnest) 1890-1975 37
Lies, Brian 1963- 190
   Earlier sketch in SATA *131*
Liestman, Vicki 1961- 72
Lietz, Gerald S. 1918- 11
Life, Kay (Guinn) 1930- 83
Lifton, Betty Jean 118
   Earlier sketch in SATA *6*
Lifton, Robert Jay 1926- 66
Lightburn, Ron 1954- 91
Lightburn, Sandra 1955- 91
Lightner, A. M.
   See Hopf, Alice (Martha) L(ightner)
Lightner, Alice
   See Hopf, Alice (Martha) L(ightner)
Lignell, Lois 1911- 37
Liles, Maurine Walpole 1935- 81
Lillegard, Dee 184
Lilley, Stephen R. 1950- 97
Lilley, Stephen Ray
   See Lilley, Stephen R.
Lillington, Kenneth (James) 1916-1998 39
Lilly, Nate 182
Lilly, Ray
   See Curtis, Richard (Alan)
Lim, John 1932- 43
Liman, Ellen (Fogelson) 1936- 22
Limb, Sue 1946- 158
Limburg, Peter R(ichard) 1929- 13
Lin, Grace 1974- 198
   Earlier sketches in SATA *111, 162*
Lincoln, C(harles) Eric 1924-2000 5
Lincoln, Hazel 187
Lincoln, James
   See Bates, Katharine Lee
Lindbergh, Anne
   See Sapieyevski, Anne Lindbergh
Lindbergh, Anne Morrow 1906-2001 33
   Obituary 125
Lindbergh, Anne Spencer Morrow
   See Lindbergh, Anne Morrow
Lindbergh, Charles A(ugustus, Jr.)
   1902-1974 33
Lindbergh, Reeve 1945- 163
   Earlier sketch in SATA *116*
Lindblom, Steven (Winther) 1946- 94
   Brief entry 39
   Earlier sketch in SATA *42*
Linde, Gunnel 1924- 5
Lindenbaum, Pija 1955- 183
   Earlier sketches in SATA *77, 144*

Lindgren, Astrid (Anna Emilia Ericsson)
   1907-2002 38
   Obituary 128
   Earlier sketch in SATA *2*
   See also CLR *119*
Lindgren, Barbro 1937- 120
   Brief entry 46
   Earlier sketch in SATA *63*
   See also CLR *86*
Lindman, Maj (Jan) 1886-1972 43
Lindop, Edmund 1925- 5
Lindquist, Jennie Dorothea 1899-1977 13
Lindquist, Rowena Cory 1958- 98
Lindquist, Willis 1908-1988 20
Lindsay, Norman Alfred William
   1879-1969 67
   See also CLR *8*
Lindsay, (Nicholas) Vachel 1879-1931 40
Lindsey, Kathleen D(orothy) 1949- 153
Line, David
   See Davidson, Lionel
Line, Les 1935- 27
Lines, Kathleen Mary 1902-1988
   Obituary 61
Linfield, Esther 40
Lingard, Joan (Amelia) 1932- 130
   Autobiography Feature 130
   Earlier sketches in SATA *8, 74, 114*
   See also CLR *89*
   See also SAAS *5*
Link, Martin 1934- 28
Linn, Margot
   See Ziefert, Harriet
Linnea, Sharon 1956- 82
Lion, Melissa 1976- 176
Lionni, Leo(nard) 1910-1999 72
   Obituary 118
   Earlier sketch in SATA *8*
   See also CLR *71*
Lipinsky de Orlov, Lino S. 1908- 22
Lipkind, William 1904-1974 15
Lipman, David 1931-2008 21
Lipman, Matthew 1923- 14
Lippincott, Bertram 1898(?)-1985
   Obituary 42
Lippincott, Gary A. 1953- 119
   Earlier sketch in SATA *73*
Lippincott, Joseph W(harton) 1887-1976 17
Lippincott, Sarah Lee 1920- 22
Lippman, Peter J. 1936- 31
Lipsyte, Robert 1938- 198
   Earlier sketches in SATA *5, 68, 113, 161*
   See also CLR *76*
Lipsyte, Robert Michael
   See Lipsyte, Robert
Lisandrelli, Elaine Slivinski 1951- 94
Lisker, Sonia O. 1933- 44
Lisle, Holly 1960- 98
Lisle, Janet Taylor 1947- 150
   Brief entry 47
   Earlier sketches in SATA *59, 96*
   See also SAAS *14*
Lisle, Rebecca 162
Lisle, Seward D.
   See Ellis, Edward S(ylvester)
Lisowski, Gabriel 1946- 47
   Brief entry 31
Liss, Howard 1922-1995 4
   Obituary 84
Lissiat, Amy
   See Thompson, Colin
Lisson, Deborah 1941- 110
   Earlier sketch in SATA *71*
List, Ilka Katherine 1935- 6
Liston, Robert A. 1927- 5
Litchfield, Ada B(assett) 1916-1999 5
Litchfield, Jo 1973- 116
Lithgow, John (Arthur) 1945- 145
Litowinsky, Olga (Jean) 1936- 26
Littke, Lael J. 1929- 140
   Earlier sketches in SATA *51, 83*

Little, A. Edward
   See Klein, Aaron E.
Little, Douglas 1942- 96
Little, (Flora) Jean 1932- 149
   Earlier sketches in SATA *2, 68, 106*
   See also CLR *4*
   See also SAAS *17*
Little, Lessie Jones 1906-1986 60
   Obituary 50
Little, Mary E. 1912-1999 28
Littlechild, George 1958- 85
Littledale, Freya (Lota) 1929-1992 74
   Earlier sketch in SATA *2*
Littlefield, Bill 1948- 83
Littlefield, Holly 1963- 97
Littlesugar, Amy 1953- 176
   Earlier sketch in SATA *122*
Littleton, Mark R. 1950- 142
   Earlier sketch in SATA *89*
Littman, Sarah Darer 175
Litty, Julie 1971- 181
Litzinger, Rosanne 1948- 196
Lively, Penelope 1933- 164
   Earlier sketches in SATA *7, 60, 101*
   See also CLR *7*
Lively, Penelope Margaret
   See Lively, Penelope
Liverakos, L.A.
   See Gilman, Laura Anne
Liversidge, (Henry) Douglas 1913- 8
Livesey, Claire (Warner) 1927- 127
Livingston, Carole 1941- 42
Livingston, (M.) Irene 1932- 150
Livingston, Myra Cohn 1926-1996 68
   Obituary 92
   Earlier sketch in SATA *5*
   See also CLR *7*
   See also SAAS *1*
Livingston, Richard R(oland) 1922- 8
Livo, Norma J. 1929- 76
Liwska, Renata 199
Ljungkvist, Laura 180
Llerena Aguirre, Carlos 1952- 19
Llerena Aguirre, Carlos Antonio
   See Llerena Aguirre, Carlos
Llewellyn, Claire 1954- 196
   Earlier sketches in SATA *77, 143*
Llewellyn, Grace 1964- 110
Llewellyn, Richard
   See Llewellyn Lloyd, Richard Dafydd Vivian
Llewellyn, Sam 1948- 185
   Earlier sketch in SATA *95*
Llewellyn Lloyd, Richard Dafydd Vivian
   1906-1983 11
   Obituary 37
Llewelyn, T. Harcourt
   See Hamilton, Charles (Harold St. John)
Lloyd, Alan
   See Lloyd, A.R.
Lloyd, Alan Richard
   See Lloyd, A.R.
Lloyd, A.R. 1927- 168
   Earlier sketch in SATA *97*
Lloyd, David
   See Lloyd, David T.
Lloyd, David T. 1954- 167
Lloyd, E. James
   See James, Elizabeth
Lloyd, Errol 1943- 22
Lloyd, Hugh
   See Fitzhugh, Percy Keese
Lloyd, James
   See James, Elizabeth
Lloyd, Megan 1958- 189
   Earlier sketches in SATA *77, 117*
Lloyd, Norman 1909-1980
   Obituary 23
Lloyd, (Mary) Norris 1908-1993 10
   Obituary 75
Lloyd, Sam 183
Lloyd-Jones, Sally 1960- 179

Lloyd Webber, Andrew 1948- 56
Llywelyn, Morgan 1937- 109
Lo, Ginnie 165
Lo, Virginia M.
   See Lo, Ginnie
Lobato, Jose Bento Monteiro 1882-1948 ... 114
Lobel, Anita (Kempler) 1934- 162
   Earlier sketches in SATA *6, 55, 96*
Lobel, Arnold (Stark) 1933-1987 55
   Obituary 54
   Earlier sketch in SATA *6*
   See also CLR *5*
Lobel, Gillian 181
Lobsenz, Amelia 12
Lobsenz, Norman M(itchell) 1919- 6
Lochak, Michele 1936- 39
Lochlons, Colin
   See Jackson, C(aary) Paul
Locke, Clinton W. 1
Locke, Elsie (Violet) 1912-2001 87
Locke, Gary 1963- 197
Locke, Lucie 1904-1989 10
Locke, Robert 1944- 63
   See also CLR *39*
Locker, Thomas 1937- 109
   Earlier sketch in SATA *59*
   See also CLR *14*
Lockhart, E.
   See Jenkins, Emily
Lockridge, Hildegarde (Dolson)
   1908-1981 121
   Earlier sketch in SATA *5*
Lockwood, Mary
   See Spelman, Mary
Lodge, Bernard 1933- 107
   Earlier sketch in SATA *33*
Lodge, Jo 1966- 173
   Earlier sketch in SATA *112*
Loeb, Jeffrey 1946- 57
Loeb, Robert H., Jr. 1917- 21
Loefgren, Ulf 1931- 3
Loehfelm, Bill 1969- 153
Loehr, Mallory 184
Loehr, Patrick 1968(?)- 194
Loeper, John J(oseph) 1929- 118
   Earlier sketch in SATA *10*
Loescher, Ann Dull 1942- 20
Loescher, Gil(burt Damian) 1945- 20
Loewer, Jean Jenkins
   See Jenkins, Jean
Loewer, (Henry) Peter 1934- 98
LoFaro, Jerry 1959- 77
Lofo
   See Heimann, Rolf
Lofthouse, Liz 199
Lofting, Hugh (John) 1886-1947 100
   Earlier sketch in SATA *15*
   See also CLR *19*
Lofts, Norah (Robinson) 1904-1983 8
   Obituary 36
Logan, Jake
   See Knott, William C(ecil, Jr.)
   and Krepps, Robert W(ilson)
   and Pearl, Jacques Bain
   and Riefe, Alan
   and Rifkin, Shepard
   and Smith, Martin Cruz
Logan, Mark
   See Nicole, Christopher (Robin)
Logan, Rochelle 1954- 169
Logston, Anne 1962- 112
Logue, Christopher 1926- 23
Logue, Mary 1952- 161
   Earlier sketch in SATA *112*
Logue, Mary Louise
   See Logue, Mary
Loh, Morag 1935- 73
Lohans, Alison 1949- 101
Loizeaux, William 185
Loken, Newton Clayton 1919- 26

Lomas, Steve
   See Brennan, Joseph Lomas
Lomask, Milton (Nachman) 1909-1991 20
Lombard, Jenny 178
Lombino, Salvatore
   See Hunter, Evan
LoMonaco, Palmyra 1932- 102
London, Jack 1876-1916
   See London, John Griffith
London, Jane
   See Geis, Darlene Stern
London, John Griffith 1876-1916 18
   See also CLR *108*
London, Jonathan (Paul) 1947- 157
   Earlier sketches in SATA *74, 113*
Lonergan, (Pauline) Joy (MacLean) 1909- ... 10
Lonette, Reisie (Dominee) 1924- 43
Long, Cathryn J. 1946- 89
Long, Earlene (Roberta) 1938- 50
Long, Emmett
   See Leonard, Elmore
Long, Ethan 1968(?)- 182
Long, Helen Beecher 1
Long, Judith Elaine 1953- 20
Long, Judy
   See Long, Judith Elaine
Long, Kim 1949- 69
Long, Laura Mooney 1892-1967
   Obituary 29
Long, Loren 1966(?)- 188
   Earlier sketch in SATA *151*
Long, Melinda 1960- 152
Long, Sylvia 1948- 179
   Earlier sketch in SATA *120*
Longbeard, Frederick
   See Longyear, Barry B(rookes)
Longfellow, Henry Wadsworth 1807-1882 ... 19
   See also CLR *99*
Longfellow, Layne (A.) 1937- 102
Longman, Harold S. 1919- 5
Longsworth, Polly 1933- 28
Longtemps, Kenneth 1933- 17
Longway, A. Hugh
   See Lang, Andrew
Longyear, Barry B(rookes) 1942- 117
Look, Lenore 180
Loomans, Diane 1955- 90
Loomis, Christine 160
   Earlier sketch in SATA *113*
Loomis, Jennifer A. 1942- 101
Loomis, Robert D. 5
Lopez, Angelo (Cayas) 1967- 83
Lopez, Barry (Holstun) 1945- 67
Lopez, Jack 1950- 178
Lopez, Loretta 1963- 190
Lopez, Lorraine M. 1956- 181
Lopez, Rafael 1961(?)- 198
Lopshire, Robert M(artin) 1927- 6
Loraine, Connie
   See Reece, Colleen L.
Lorbiecki, Marybeth 1959- 172
   Earlier sketch in SATA *121*
Lord, Athena V. 1932- 39
Lord, Beman 1924-1991 5
   Obituary 69
Lord, Bette Bao 1938- 58
Lord, Cynthia 182
Lord, Doreen Mildred Douglas
   See Lord, Douglas
Lord, Douglas 1904-1992 12
Lord, John Vernon 1939- 21
Lord, Nancy
   See Titus, Eve
Lord, Patricia C. 1927-1988
   Obituary 58
Lord, Walter 1917-2002 3
Lorde, Diana
   See Reno, Dawn E(laine)
Lorenz, Albert 1941- 115

Lorenzini, Carlo 1826-1890 100
   Earlier sketch in SATA *29*
   See also CLR *120*
Lorey, Dean 1967- 193
Lorimer, Janet 1941- 60
Loring, Emilie (Baker) 1864(?)-1951 51
Lorkowski, Thomas V(incent) 1950- 92
Lorkowski, Tom
   See Lorkowski, Thomas V(incent)
Lorraine, Walter (Henry) 1929- 16
Lorrimer, Claire
   See Clark, Patricia Denise
Loss, Joan 1933- 11
Lothrop, Harriet Mulford Stone 1844-1924 . 20
Lottridge, Celia Barker 1936- 157
   Earlier sketch in SATA *112*
LoTurco, Laura 1963- 84
Lotz, Wolfgang 1912-1981 65
Louie, Ai-Ling 1949- 40
   Brief entry 34
Louis, Catherine 1963- 186
Louis, Pat
   See Francis, Dorothy
Louisburgh, Sheila Burnford
   See Burnford, Sheila (Philip Cochrane Every)
Louise, Anita
   See Riggio, Anita
Louise, Tina 1934- 191
Lourie, Helen
   See Storr, Catherine (Cole)
Lourie, Peter 1952- 183
   Earlier sketches in SATA *82, 142*
Lourie, Peter King
   See Lourie, Peter
Love, Ann 1947- 168
   Earlier sketch in SATA *79*
Love, D. Anne 1949- 180
   Earlier sketches in SATA *96, 145*
Love, Douglas 1967- 92
Love, Judith Dufour
   See Love, Judy
Love, Judy 188
Love, Katherine (Isabel) 1907- 3
Love, Kathleen Ann
   See Love, Ann
Love, Sandra (Weller) 1940- 26
Lovejoy, Jack 1937- 116
Lovelace, Delos Wheeler 1894-1967 7
Lovelace, Maud Hart 1892-1980 2
   Obituary 23
Lovell, Ingraham
   See Bacon, Josephine Dodge (Daskam)
Loverseed, Amanda (Jane) 1965- 75
Lovett, Margaret (Rose) 1915- 22
Low, Alice 1926- 156
   Earlier sketches in SATA *11, 76*
Low, Elizabeth Hammond 1898-1991 5
Low, Joseph 1911-2007 14
Low, Penelope Margaret
   See Lively, Penelope
Low, William 177
Lowe, Jay, Jr.
   See Loeper, John J(oseph)
Lowell, Pamela 187
Lowell, Susan 1950- 127
   Earlier sketch in SATA *81*
Lowenstein, Dyno 1914-1996 6
Lowenstein, Sallie 1949- 116
Lowery, Linda 1949- 151
   Earlier sketch in SATA *74*
Lowitz, Anson C. 1901(?)-1978 18
Lowitz, Sadyebeth Heath 1901-1969 17
Lowndes, Robert A(ugustine) W(ard)
   1916-1998 117
Lowrey, Janette Sebring 1892-1986 43
Lowry, Lois 1937- 177
   Autobiography Feature 127
   Earlier sketches in SATA *23, 70, 111*
   See also CLR *72*
   See also SAAS *3*

Lowry, Lois Hammersberg
   See Lowry, Lois
Lowry, Peter 1953- 7
Lowther, George F. 1913-1975
   Obituary 30
Loyie, Larry 1933- 150
Lozansky, Edward D. 1941- 62
Lozier, Herbert 1915- 26
Lubar, David 1954- 190
   Earlier sketch in SATA *133*
Lubell, Cecil 1912-2000 6
Lubell, Winifred (A. Milius) 1914- 6
Lubin, Leonard
   See Lubin, Leonard B.
Lubin, Leonard B. 1943-1994 45
   Brief entry 37
Lubka, S. Ruth 1948- 154
Lubner, Susan 185
Luby, Thia 1954- 124
Lucado, Max (Lee) 1955- 104
Lucas, Cedric 1962- 101
Lucas, E(dward) V(errall) 1868-1938 20
Lucas, Eileen 1956- 113
   Earlier sketch in SATA *76*
Lucas, George 1944- 56
Lucas, Jerry 1940- 33
Lucas, Margeaux 186
Lucas, Victoria
   See Plath, Sylvia
Lucashenko, Melissa 1967- 104
Luccarelli, Vincent 1923- 90
Luce, Celia (Geneva Larsen) 1914- 38
Luce, Willard (Ray) 1914-1990 38
Lucht, Irmgard 1937- 82
Luckett, Dave 1951- 167
   Earlier sketch in SATA *106*
Luckhardt, Mildred Corell 1898-1990 5
Ludden, Allen (Ellsworth) 1918(?)-1981
   Obituary 27
Ludel, Jacqueline 1945- 64
Ludlow, Geoffrey
   See Meynell, Laurence Walter
Ludlum, Mabel Cleland
   See Widdemer, Mabel Cleland
Ludwig, Helen 33
Ludwig, Lyndell 1923- 63
Ludwig, Trudy 1959- 166
Lueders, Edward (George) 1923- 14
Luenn, Nancy 1954- 79
   Earlier sketch in SATA *51*
Lufkin, Raymond H. 1897- 38
Lugard, Flora Louisa Shaw 1852-1929 21
Luger, Harriett Mandelay 1914- 23
Luhrmann, Winifred B(ruce) 1934- 11
Luis, Earlene W. 1929- 11
Luke, Pauline 178
Luke, Pauline R.
   See Luke, Pauline
Lum, Peter
   See Crowe, (Bettina) Peter Lum
Lumry, Amanda (R.) 159
Lund, Deb 157
Lund, Doris Herold 1919- 12
Lung, Chang
   See Jordan, Robert
Lunge-Larsen, Lise 1955- 184
   Earlier sketch in SATA *138*
Lunn, Carolyn (Kowalczyk) 1960- 67
Lunn, Janet (Louise Swoboda) 1928- 110
   Earlier sketches in SATA *4, 68*
   See also CLR *18*
   See also SAAS *12*
Lunsford, Cin Forshay
   See Forshay-Lunsford, Cin
Lupica, Michael 1952- 177
Lupica, Michael Thomas
   See Lupica, Michael
Lupica, Mike
   See Lupica, Michael
Lupoff, Dick
   See Lupoff, Richard A(llen)

Lupoff, Richard A(llen) 1935- 60
Lurie, Alison 1926- 112
   Earlier sketch in SATA *46*
Lurie, Morris 1938- 72
Lussert, Anneliese 1929- 101
Lusted, Marcia Amidon 1962- 143
Lustig, Arnost 1926- 56
Lustig, Loretta 1944- 46
Luthardt, Kevin 1973- 172
Luther, Frank 1905-1980
   Obituary 25
Luther, Rebekah (Lyn) S(tiles) 1960- 90
Luttmann, Gail
   See Damerow, Gail
Luttrell, Guy L. 1938- 22
Luttrell, Ida (Alleene) 1934- 91
   Brief entry 35
   Earlier sketch in SATA *40*
Luttrell, William (J. III) 1954- 149
Lutz, John 1939- 180
Lutz, John Thomas
   See Lutz, John
Lutz, Norma Jean 1943- 122
Lutzeier, Elizabeth 1952- 72
Lutzker, Edythe 1904-1991 5
Luxbacher, Irene M. 1970- 153
Luzadder, Patrick 1954- 89
Luzzati, Emanuele 1921-2007 7
Luzzatto, Paola Caboara 1938- 38
Lybbert, Tyler 1970- 88
Lydon, Michael 1942- 11
Lyfick, Warren
   See Reeves, Lawrence F.
Lyle, Katie Letcher 1938- 8
Lynch, Chris 1962- 171
   Earlier sketches in SATA *95, 131*
   See also CLR *58*
Lynch, Lorenzo 1932- 7
Lynch, Marietta 1947- 29
Lynch, P(atrick) J(ames) 1962- 122
   Earlier sketch in SATA *79*
Lynch, Patricia (Nora) 1898-1972 9
Lynds, Dennis 1924-2005 47
   Brief entry 37
Lyne, Alison Davis 188
Lyngseth, Joan
   See Davies, Joan
Lynn, Elizabeth A(nne) 1946- 99
Lynn, Mary
   See Brokamp, Marilyn
Lynn, Patricia
   See Watts, Mabel Pizzey
Lynn, Tracy 175
Lyon, Elinor 1921-2008 6
   Obituary 192
Lyon, Elinor Bruce
   See Lyon, Elinor
Lyon, George Ella 1949- 148
   Autobiography Feature 148
   Earlier sketches in SATA *68, 119*
Lyon, Lyman R.
   See de Camp, L(yon) Sprague
Lyons, Dorothy M(arawee) 1907-1997 3
Lyons, Grant 1941- 30
Lyons, Marcus
   See Blish, James (Benjamin)
Lyons, Mary E. 1947- 195
   Autobiography Feature 195
   Earlier sketches in SATA *93, 142*
Lyons, Mary Evelyn
   See Lyons, Mary E.
Lystad, Mary (Hanemann) 1928- 11
Lytle, Elizabeth Stewart 1949- 79
Lytle, Robert A. 1944- 119
Lyttle, Richard B(ard) 1927- 23
Lytton, Edward G(eorge) E(arle) L(ytton)
   Bulwer-Lytton Baron 1803-1873 23

M

Ma, Wenhai 1954- 84
Maar, Leonard (Frank, Jr.) 1927- 30
Maartens, Maretha 1945- 73
Maas, Selve -1997 14
Maass, Robert 195
Mabie, Grace
   See Mattern, Joanne
Mac
   See MacManus, Seumas
   and Maccari, Ruggero
Macalaster, Elizabeth G. 1951- 115
MacAlister, Katie 159
MacAllan, Andrew
   See Leasor, James
MacAodhagain, Eamon
   See Egan, E(dward) W(elstead)
MacArthur-Onslow, Annette Rosemary
   1933- 26
Macaulay, David (Alexander) 1946- 137
   Brief entry 27
   Earlier sketches in SATA *46, 72*
   See also CLR *14*
Macaulay, Teresa (E.) 1947- 95
Macavinta, Courtney 176
MacBeth, George (Mann) 1932-1992 4
   Obituary 70
MacBride, Roger Lea 1929-1995 85
MacCarter, Don 1944- 91
MacClintock, Dorcas 1932- 8
MacCready, Robin Merrow 1959(?)- 190
MacCullough, Carolyn 174
MacDonald, Alan 1958- 192
MacDonald, Amy 1951- 156
   Autobiography Feature 156
   Earlier sketches in SATA *76, 136*
MacDonald, Anne Elizabeth Campbell Bard
   -1958
   See MacDonald, Betty
MacDonald, Anson
   See Heinlein, Robert A.
MacDonald, Betty 1908-1958
   See YABC *1*
Macdonald, Blackie
   See Emrich, Duncan (Black Macdonald)
Macdonald, Caroline 1948- 86
   Obituary 111
   See also CLR *60*
Macdonald, Dwight 1906-1982 29
   Obituary 33
MacDonald, George 1824-1905 100
   Earlier sketch in SATA *33*
   See also CLR *67*
MacDonald, Golden
   See Brown, Margaret Wise
Macdonald, Guy 195
Macdonald, James D. 1954- 67
   Earlier sketches in SATA *81, 114, 165, 1*
Macdonald, Marcia
   See Hill, Grace Livingston
MacDonald, Margaret Read 1940- 194
   Earlier sketches in SATA *94, 164*
Macdonald, Marianne 1934- 113
Macdonald, Mary
   See Gifford, Griselda
Macdonald, Maryann 1947- 189
   Earlier sketch in SATA *72*
Macdonald, Shelagh 1937- 25
MacDonald, Suse 1940- 193
   Brief entry 52
   Earlier sketches in SATA *54, 109*
Macdonald, Zillah K(atherine) 1885-1979 ... 11
MacDonnell, Megan
   See Stevens, Serita
MacDougal, John
   See Blish, James (Benjamin)
Mace, Elisabeth 1933- 27
Mace, Varian 1938- 49

MacEwen, Gwendolyn (Margaret)
  1941-1987 50
  Obituary 55
Macfarlan, Allan A. 1892-1982 35
MacFarlane, Iris 1922- 11
MacGill-Callahan, Sheila 1926-2000 78
MacGregor, Carol Lynn 153
MacGregor, Ellen 1906-1954 39
  Brief entry 27
MacGregor-Hastie, Roy (Alasdhair Niall)
  1929- 3
MacGrory, Yvonne 1948- 142
Machado, Ana Maria 1941- 150
MacHale, D.J. 1956- 175
MacHale, Donald James
  See MacHale, D.J.
Machetanz, Frederick 1908- 34
Machin Goodall, Daphne (Edith) 37
Macht, Norm
  See Macht, Norman L.
Macht, Norman L. 1929- 122
Macht, Norman Lee
  See Macht, Norman L.
MacInnes, Helen (Clark) 1907-1985 22
  Obituary 44
Macintosh, Brownie 1950- 98
MacIntyre, Elisabeth 1916- 17
MacIntyre, Wendy 1947- 196
Mack, Jeff 194
Mack, L.V.
  See Kimmelman, Burt
Mack, Stan(ley) 17
Mack, Todd 168
Mack, Tracy 1968- 183
  Earlier sketch in SATA *128*
Mackall, Dandi D.
  See Mackall, Dandi Daley
Mackall, Dandi Daley 1949- 182
  Earlier sketches in SATA *118, 177*
Mackay, Claire 1930- 97
  Autobiography Feature 124
  Earlier sketch in SATA *40*
  See also CLR *43*
Mackay, Constance D'Arcy (?)-1966 125
Mackay, Donald 1914-2005 81
  Obituary 173
Mackay, Donald Alexander
  See Mackay, Donald
MacKaye, Percy (Wallace) 1875-1956 32
Mackel, Kathryn 1950- 162
Mackel, Kathy
  See Mackel, Kathryn
MacKellar, William 1914- 4
Macken, Walter 1915-1967 36
MacKenzie, Jill (Kelly) 1947- 75
Mackey, Ernan
  See McInerny, Ralph
Mackey, Weezie Kerr 188
Mackie, Maron
  See McNeely, Jeannette
Mackin, Edward
  See McInerny, Ralph
MacKinnon, Bernie 1957- 69
MacKinnon Groomer, Vera 1915- 57
MacKinstry, Elizabeth 1879-1956 42
Mackler, Carolyn 1973- 156
MacLachlan, Emily
  See Charest, Emily MacLachlan
MacLachlan, Patricia 1938- 168
  Brief entry 42
  Earlier sketches in SATA *62, 107*
  See also CLR *14*
MacLane, Jack
  See Crider, Bill
MacLean, Alistair (Stuart) 1922(?)-1987 23
  Obituary 50
Maclean, Art
  See Shirreffs, Gordon D(onald)
MacLean, Christine Kole 177
MacLean, Glynne 1964- 150

MacLeod, Beatrice 1910- 162
  Earlier sketch in SATA *10*
MacLeod, Beatrice Beach
  See MacLeod, Beatrice
MacLeod, Charlotte (Matilda) 1922-2005 28
  Obituary 160
MacLeod, Doug 1959- 60
MacLeod, Elizabeth 184
  Earlier sketch in SATA *158*
MacLeod, Ellen Jane (Anderson) 1916- 14
MacManus, James
  See MacManus, Seumas
MacManus, Seumas 1869-1960 25
MacMaster, Eve (Ruth) B(owers) 1942- 46
MacMillan, Annabelle
  See Quick, Annabelle
MacMillan, Dianne M(arie) 1943- 125
  Earlier sketch in SATA *84*
Macnaughton, Tina 182
Macneill, Janet
  See McNeely, Jeannette
MacPeek, Walter G. 1902-1973 4
  Obituary 25
MacPhail, Catherine 1946- 197
  Earlier sketch in SATA *130*
MacPherson, Margaret 1908-2001 9
  See also SAAS *4*
MacPherson, Thomas George 1915-1976
  Obituary 30
MacPherson, Winnie 1930- 107
MacRae, Tom 1980- 181
Macrae, Travis
  See Feagles, Anita M(acRae)
MacRaois, Cormac 1944- 72
Macumber, Mari
  See Sandoz, Mari(e Susette)
Macy, Sue 1954- 134
  Earlier sketch in SATA *88*
Madaras, Lynda 1947- 151
Madden, Don 1927- 3
Madden, Kerry 1961- 168
Madden-Lunsford, Kerry
  See Madden, Kerry
Maddern, Eric 1950- 166
Maddigan, Beth 1967- 174
Maddison, Angela Mary 1923- 10
  See also CLR *24*
Maddock, Reginald (Bertram) 1912-1994 15
Madenski, Melissa (Ann) 1949- 77
Madian, Jon 1941- 9
Madison, Alan 182
Madison, Arnold 1937- 6
Madison, Winifred 5
Madonna 1958- 149
Madsen, Gunnar 171
Madsen, Ross Martin 1946- 82
Madsen, Susan A. 1954- 90
Madsen, Susan Arrington
  See Madsen, Susan A.
Maehlqvist, (Karl) Stefan 1943- 30
Maestro, Betsy (Crippen) 1944- 106
  Brief entry 30
  Earlier sketch in SATA *59*
  See also CLR *45*
Maestro, Giulio 1942- 106
  Earlier sketches in SATA *8, 59*
  See also CLR *45*
Maeterlinck, Maurice 1862-1949 66
Magee, Doug 1947- 78
Magee, Wes 1939- 64
Maggio, Rosalie 1943- 69
Magid, Ken(neth Marshall) 65
Magnus, Erica 1946- 77
Magoon, Scott 182
Magorian, James 1942- 92
  Earlier sketch in SATA *32*
Magorian, Michelle 1947- 128
  Earlier sketch in SATA *67*
Magorian, Michelle Jane
  See Magorian, Michelle
Magovern, Peg 103

Maguire, Anne
  See Nearing, Penny
Maguire, Gregory 1954- 129
  Earlier sketches in SATA *28, 84*
  See also SAAS *22*
Maguire, Gregory Peter
  See Maguire, Gregory
Maguire, Jack 1920-2000 74
Maguire, Jesse
  See Smith, Sherwood
Maguire, Jessie
  See Smith, Sherwood
Maher, Ramona 1934- 13
Mahlqvist, (Karl) Stefan
  See Maehlqvist, (Karl) Stefan
Mahon, Julia C(unha) 1916- 11
Mahony, Elizabeth Winthrop 1948- 164
  Autobiography Feature 116
  Earlier sketches in SATA *8, 76*
  See also CLR *89*
Mahood, Kenneth 1930- 24
Mahy, Margaret 1936- 171
  Earlier sketches in SATA *14, 69, 119*
  See also CLR *78*
Mahy, Margaret May
  See Mahy, Margaret
Maiden, Cecil (Edward) 1902-1981 52
Maidoff, Ilka
  See List, Ilka Katherine
Maifair, Linda Lee 1947- 83
Maik, Henri
  See Hecht, Henri Joseph
Maillu, David G(ian) 1939- 111
Maine, Trevor
  See Catherall, Arthur
Mains, Randolph P. 1946- 80
Maione, Heather 189
Maiorano, Robert 1946- 43
Maisner, Heather 1947- 89
Maison, Della
  See Katz, Bobbi
Maitland, Antony Jasper 1935- 25
Maitland, Barbara 102
Mai-Wyss, Tatjana 1972- 187
Major, Kevin (Gerald) 1949- 134
  Earlier sketches in SATA *32, 82*
  See also CLR *11*
Majure, Janet 1954- 96
Makhijani, Pooja 188
Makie, Pam 1943- 37
Makowski, Silk
  See Makowski, Silvia Ann
Makowski, Silvia Ann 1940- 101
Malam, John 1957- 152
  Earlier sketch in SATA *89*
Maland, Nick 195
Malcolm, Dan
  See Silverberg, Robert
Malcolm, Jahnna N.
  See Beecham, Jahnna
Malcolmson, Anne
  See von Storch, Anne B.
Malcolmson, David 1899-1978 6
Maletta, Dr. Arlene
  See Feltenstein, Arlene (H.)
Mali, Jane Lawrence 1937-1995 51
  Brief entry 44
  Obituary 86
Malkin, Nina 1959(?)- 179
Mallett, Jerry J. 1939- 76
Malley, Gemma 198
Malley, G.R.
  See Malley, Gemma
Mallory, Kenneth 1945- 185
  Earlier sketch in SATA *128*
Mallowan, Agatha Christie
  See Christie, Agatha (Mary Clarissa)
Malmberg, Carl 1904-1979 9
Malmgren, Dallin 1949- 65
Malo, John W. 1911-2000 4
Malone, James Hiram 1930- 84

Malone, Nola Langner 1930-2003 8
  Obituary 151
Malone, Patricia 1932- 155
Malone, Peter 1953- 191
Maloney, Pat
  See Markun, Patricia Maloney
Malory, Sir Thomas 1410(?)-1471(?) 59
  Brief entry 33
Maltese, Michael 1909(?)-1981
  Obituary 24
Malvasi, Meg Greene 143
Malvern, Corinne 1905-1956 34
Malvern, Gladys (?)-1962 23
Mama G.
  See Davis, Grania
Mammano, Julie (Lynn) 1962- 107
Mamonova, Tatyana 1943- 93
Manchel, Frank 1935- 10
Manchester, William (Raymond)
  1922-2004 65
Mandabach, Brian 1962(?)- 197
Mandel, Brett H. 1969- 108
Mandel, Peter 1957- 87
Mandel, Sally (Elizabeth) 1944- 64
Mandell, Muriel (Hortense Levin) 1921- 63
Manders, John 1957- 175
Manes, Stephen 1949- 99
  Brief entry 40
  Earlier sketch in SATA 42
Manfred, Frederick (Feikema) 1912-1994 30
Mangin, Marie France 1940- 59
Mangione, Gerlando 1909-1998 6
  Obituary 104
Mangione, Jerre
  See Mangione, Gerlando
Mango, Karin N. 1936- 52
Mangurian, David 1938- 14
Mania, Cathy 1950- 102
Mania, Robert 1952- 102
Mania, Robert C., Jr.
  See Mania, Robert
Maniatty, Taramesha 1978- 92
Maniscalco, Joseph 1926- 10
Manley, Deborah 1932- 28
Manley, Seon 1921- 15
  See also CLR 3
  See also SAAS 2
Mann, Elizabeth 1948- 153
Mann, Josephine
  See Pullein-Thompson, Josephine (Mary
  Wedderburn)
Mann, Kenny 1946- 91
Mann, Pamela 1946- 91
Mann, Patrick
  See Waller, Leslie
Mann, Peggy
  See Houlton, Peggy Mann
Mannetti, Lisa 1953- 57
  Brief entry 51
Mannheim, Grete (Salomon) 1909-1986 10
Manniche, Lise 1943- 31
Manning, Jane K. 185
Manning, Mick 1959- 176
Manning, Rosemary (Joy) 1911-1988 10
Manning, Sarra 162
Manning-Sanders, Ruth (Vernon)
  1895(?)-1988 73
  Obituary 57
  Earlier sketch in SATA 15
Mannion, Diane
  See Paterson, Diane
Mannis, Celeste Davidson 173
Mannon, Warwick
  See Hopkins, (Hector) Kenneth
Manos, Helen 199
Mansir, A. Richard 1932- 170
Manson, Ainslie Kertland 1938- 115
Manson, Beverlie 1945- 57
  Brief entry 44
Manthorpe, Helen 1958- 122
Mantinband, Gerda (B.) 1917- 74

Manton, Jo
  See Gittings, Jo (Grenville) Manton
Manuel, Lynn 1948- 179
  Earlier sketch in SATA 99
Manushkin, Fran 1942- 166
  Earlier sketches in SATA 7, 54, 93
Manushkin, Frances
  See Manushkin, Fran
Man Without a Spleen, A
  See Chekhov, Anton (Pavlovich)
Manzano, Sonia 1950- 167
Mapes, Mary A.
  See Ellison, Virginia H(owell)
Maple, Marilyn 1931- 80
Mappin, Strephyn 1956- 109
Mara, Barney
  See Roth, Arthur J(oseph)
Mara, Jeanette
  See Cebulash, Mel
Marais, Josef 1905-1978
  Obituary 24
Marasmus, Seymour
  See Rivoli, Mario
Marbach, Ethel
  See Pochocki, Ethel (Frances)
Marcal, Annette B.
  See Callaway, Bernice (Anne)
Marcelino
  See Agnew, Edith J(osephine)
Marcellino, Fred 1939-2001 118
  Obituary 127
  Earlier sketch in SATA 68
March, Carl
  See Fleischman, Sid
Marchant, Bessie 1862-1941
  See YABC 2
Marchant, Catherine
  See Cookson, Catherine (McMullen)
Marcher, Marion Walden 1890-1987 10
Marchesi, Stephen 1951- 114
Marchesi, Steve
  See Marchesi, Stephen
  and Older, Effin
  and Older, Jules
Marchetta, Melina 1965- 170
Marciano, John Bemelmans 1970- 167
  Earlier sketch in SATA 118
  See also CLR 93
Marco, Lou
  See Gottfried, Theodore Mark
Marcus, Leonard S. 1950- 187
  Earlier sketch in SATA 133
Marcus, Paul 1953- 82
Marcus, Rebecca B(rian) 1907- 9
Marcuse, Aida E. 1934- 89
Marek, Margot L. 1934(?)-1987
  Obituary 54
Maren, Julie 1970- 199
Margaret, Karla
  See Andersdatter, Karla M(argaret)
Margolin, Harriet
  See Ziefert, Harriet
Margolis, Jeffrey A. 1948- 108
Margolis, Leslie 187
Margolis, Richard J(ules) 1929-1991 86
  Obituary 67
  Earlier sketch in SATA 4
Margolis, Vivienne 1922- 46
Mariana
  See Foster, Marian Curtis
Marie, Geraldine 1949- 61
Mariner, Scott
  See Pohl, Frederik
Marino, Dorothy Bronson 1912- 14
Marino, Jan 1936- 114
Marino, Nick
  See Deming, Richard
Marino, Peter 1960- 179
Mario, Anna
  See Odgers, Sally Farrell

Marion, Henry
  See del Rey, Lester
Maris, Ron 71
  Brief entry 45
Mark, Jan 1943-2006 164
  Obituary 173
  Earlier sketches in SATA 22, 69, 114
  See also CLR 11
Mark, Janet Marjorie
  See Mark, Jan
Mark, Joan T. 1937- 122
Mark, Pauline (Dahlin) 1913-1997 14
Mark, Polly
  See Mark, Pauline (Dahlin)
Mark, Ted
  See Gottfried, Theodore Mark
Markel, Michelle 169
Marker, Sherry 1941- 76
Markert, Jennifer 1965- 83
Markert, Jenny
  See Markert, Jennifer
Markham, Lynne 1947- 102
Markham, Marion M. 1929- 60
Markham, Wendy
  See Staub, Wendy Corsi
Markins, W. S.
  See Jenkins, Marie M(agdalen)
Markle, Sandra L. 1946- 185
  Brief entry 41
  Earlier sketches in SATA 57, 92, 148
Markle, Sandra Lee
  See Markle, Sandra L.
Marko, Katherine D(olores) 28
Markoosie
  See Patsauq, Markoosie
Marks, Alan 1957- 187
  Earlier sketches in SATA 77, 151
Marks, Burton 1930- 47
  Brief entry 43
Marks, Graham 158
Marks, Hannah K.
  See Trivelpiece, Laurel
Marks, J.
  See Highwater, Jamake (Mamake)
Marks, J(ames) M(acdonald) 1921- 13
Marks, Laurie J. 1957- 68
Marks, Margaret L. 1911(?)-1980
  Obituary 23
Marks, Mickey Klar -1986 12
Marks, Peter
  See Smith, Robert Kimmel
Marks, Rita 1938- 47
Marks, Stan(ley) 1929- 14
Marks-Highwater, J.
  See Highwater, Jamake (Mamake)
Markun, Patricia Maloney 1924- 15
Markusen, Bruce (Stanley Rodriguez)
  1965- 141
Marley, Louise 1952- 173
  Earlier sketch in SATA 120
Marlin, Hilda
  See Van Stockum, Hilda
Marlow, Max
  See Nicole, Christopher (Robin)
Marlow, Susan K. 1953- 178
Marlowe, Amy Bell 67
  Earlier sketch in SATA 1
Marlowe, Jack
  See Deary, Terry
Marney, Dean 1952- 90
Marokvia, Artur 1909- 31
Marokvia, Mireille 1908-2008 5
  Obituary 197
Marokvia, Mireille Journet
  See Marokvia, Mireille
Marol, Jean-Claude 1946- 125
Marr, John S(tuart) 1940- 48
Marr, Melissa 1972- 189
Marric, J. J.
  See Butler, William (Arthur) Vivian
  and Creasey, John

Marrin, Albert 1936- 193
  Brief entry 43
  Earlier sketches in SATA 53, 90, 126
  See also CLR 53
Marriott, Alice Lee 1910-1992 31
  Obituary 71
Marriott, Janice 1946- 134
Marriott, Pat(ricia) 1920- 35
Marroquin, Patricio
  See Markun, Patricia Maloney
Mars, W. T.
  See Mars, Witold Tadeusz J.
Mars, Witold Tadeusz J. 1912-1985 3
Marsden, Carolyn 1950- 175
  Earlier sketch in SATA 140
Marsden, John 1950- 146
  Earlier sketches in SATA 66, 97
  See also CLR 34
  See also SAAS 22
Marsh, Carole 1946- 127
Marsh, Dave 1950- 66
Marsh, J. E.
  See Marshall, Evelyn
Marsh, James 1946- 73
Marsh, Jean
  See Marshall, Evelyn
Marsh, Joan F. 1923- 83
Marsh, Paul
  See Hopkins, (Hector) Kenneth
Marsh, Valerie 1954- 89
Marshall, Anthony D(ryden) 1924- 18
Marshall, Bonnie C. 1941- 141
  Earlier sketch in SATA 18
Marshall, Bridget M(ary) 1974- 103
Marshall, (Sarah) Catherine (Wood)
  1914-1983 2
  Obituary 34
Marshall, Douglas
  See McClintock, Marshall
Marshall, Edmund
  See Hopkins, (Hector) Kenneth
Marshall, Edward
  See Marshall, James
Marshall, Evelyn 1897-1991 11
Marshall, Felicity 1950- 116
Marshall, Garry 1934- 60
Marshall, H. H.
  See Jahn, (Joseph) Michael
Marshall, James 1942-1992 75
  Earlier sketches in SATA 6, 51
  See also CLR 21
Marshall, James Edward
  See Marshall, James
Marshall, James Vance
  See Payne, Donald Gordon
Marshall, Janet (Perry) 1938- 97
Marshall, Jeff
  See Laycock, George (Edwin)
Marshall, Kim
  See Marshall, Michael (Kimbrough)
Marshall, Michael (Kimbrough) 1948- 37
Marshall, Percy
  See Young, Percy M(arshall)
Marshall, S(amuel) L(yman) A(twood)
  1900-1977 21
Marsoli, Lisa Ann 1958- 101
  Brief entry 53
Marsten, Richard
  See Hunter, Evan
Marston, Elsa 1933- 156
Marston, Hope Irvin 1935- 127
  Earlier sketch in SATA 31
Marszalek, John F. 1939- 167
Marszalek, John Francis, Jr.
  See Marszalek, John F.
Marszalek, John Francis 1939-
  See Marszalek, John F.
Martchenko, Michael 1942- 154
  Earlier sketches in SATA 50, 95

Martel, Aimee
  See Thurlo, Aimee
  and Thurlo, David
Martel, Suzanne 1924- 99
Martignoni, Margaret E. 1908(?)-1974
  Obituary 27
Martin, Ann M. 1955- 192
  Brief entry 41
  Earlier sketches in SATA 44, 70, 126
  See also CLR 32
Martin, Bill, Jr.
  See Martin, William Ivan, Jr.
Martin, Charles E(lmer)
  See Mastrangelo, Charles E(lmer)
Martin, Christopher
  See Hoyt, Edwin P(almer), Jr.
Martin, Claire 1933- 76
Martin, David Stone 1913-1992 39
Martin, Del 1921-2008 47
Martin, Donald
  See Honig, Donald
Martin, Dorothy
  See Martin, Del
Martin, Dorothy L.
  See Martin, Del
Martin, Eugene 1
Martin, Eva M. 1939- 65
Martin, Frances M(cEntee) 1906-1998 36
Martin, Francesca 1947- 101
Martin, Fred 1948- 119
Martin, Fredric
  See Christopher, Matt(hew Frederick)
Martin, George Raymond Richard
  See Martin, George R.R.
Martin, George R.R. 1948- 118
Martin, J(ohn) P(ercival) 1880(?)-1966 15
Martin, Jacqueline Briggs 1945- 188
  Earlier sketches in SATA 98, 149
Martin, Jane Read 1957- 84
Martin, Jeremy
  See Levin, Marcia Obrasky
Martin, Les
  See Schulman, L(ester) M(artin)
Martin, Linda 1961- 82
Martin, Lynne 1923- 21
Martin, Marcia
  See Levin, Marcia Obrasky
Martin, Marvin 1926- 126
Martin, Melanie
  See Pellowski, Michael (Joseph)
Martin, Nancy
  See Salmon, Annie Elizabeth
Martin, Patricia Miles 1899-1986 43
  Obituary 48
  Earlier sketch in SATA 1
Martin, Peter
  See Chaundler, Christine
Martin, Rafe 1946- 175
Martin, Rene 1891-1977 42
  Obituary 20
Martin, Rupert (Claude) 1905- 31
Martin, S. R.
  See Mappin, Strephyn
Martin, Stefan 1936- 32
Martin, Vicky
  See Storey, Victoria Carolyn
Martin, Webber
  See Silverberg, Robert
Martin, Wendy
  See Martini, Teri
Martin, William Ivan, Jr. 1916-2004 145
  Brief entry 40
  Earlier sketches in SATA 40, 67
  See also CLR 97
Martineau, Diane 1940- 178
Martineau, Harriet 1802-1876
  See YABC 2
Martinet, Jeanne 1958- 80
Martinez, Agnes 167
Martinez, Arturo O. 1933- 192
Martinez, Ed(ward) 1954- 98

Martinez, Elizabeth Coonrod 1954- 85
Martinez, Victor 1954- 95
Martini, Teri 1930- 3
Martini, Therese
  See Martini, Teri
Martino, Alfred C. 1964- 174
Martinson, Janis
  See Herbert, Janis
Marton, Jirina 1946- 144
  Earlier sketch in SATA 95
Marton, Pierre
  See Stone, Peter
Martson, Del
  See Lupoff, Richard A(llen)
Martyr, Paula (Jane)
  See Lawford, Paula Jane
Maruki, Toshi 1912-2000 112
  See also CLR 19
Marvin, Isabel R(idout) 1924- 84
Marx, Patricia Windschill 1948- 160
  Earlier sketch in SATA 112
Marx, Robert F(rank) 1936- 24
Marx, Trish
  See Marx, Patricia Windschill
Marzani, Carl (Aldo) 1912-1994 12
Marzollo, Jean 1942- 190
  Autobiography Feature 190
  Earlier sketches in SATA 29, 77, 130
  See also SAAS 15
Masefield, John (Edward) 1878-1967 19
Masoff, Joy 1951- 118
Mason, Adrienne 1962- 163
Mason, Cherie 170
Mason, Edwin A. 1905-1979
  Obituary 32
Mason, Ernst
  See Pohl, Frederik
Mason, F(rancis) van Wyck 1901-1978 3
  Obituary 26
Mason, Frank W.
  See Mason, F(rancis) van Wyck
Mason, George Frederick 1904-2000 14
Mason, Miriam E(vangeline) 1900-1973 2
  Obituary 26
Mason, Prue 195
Mason, Simon 1962- 178
Mason, Tally
  See Derleth, August (William)
Mason, Van Wyck
  See Mason, F(rancis) van Wyck
Mass, Wendy 1967- 196
  Earlier sketch in SATA 158
Mass, William
  See Gibson, William
Masselman, George 1897-1971 19
Massie, Dianne Redfield 1938- 125
  Earlier sketch in SATA 16
Massie, Elizabeth 108
Masson, Sophie 1959- 179
  Earlier sketch in SATA 133
Masters, Anthony (Richard) 1940-2003 112
  Obituary 145
Masters, Kelly R(ay) 1897-1987 3
Masters, Mildred 1932- 42
Masters, William
  See Cousins, Margaret
Masters, Zeke
  See Bensen, Donald R.
  and Goulart, Ron(ald Joseph)
Mastrangelo, Charles E(lmer) 1910-1995 70
  Earlier sketch in SATA 69
Masuda, Takeshi 1944- 56
Matas, Carol 1949- 194
  Autobiography Feature 112
  Earlier sketch in SATA 93
  See also CLR 52
Matchette, Katharine E. 1941- 38
Math, Irwin 1940- 42
Mathabane, Mark 1960- 123
Mather, Kirtley F(letcher) 1888-1978 65

Mathers, Petra 1945- 176
  Earlier sketch in SATA 119
  See also CLR 76
Matheson, Richard (Christian) 1953- 119
Matheson, Shirlee Smith 1942- 155
Mathews, Eleanor
  See Mathews, Ellie
Mathews, Ellie 1946(?)- 193
Mathews, Janet 1914-1992 41
Mathews, Judith
  See Goldberger, Judith M.
Mathews, Louise
  See Tooke, Louise Mathews
Mathiesen, Egon 1907-1976
  Obituary 28
Mathieu, Joe 1949- 185
  Brief entry 36
  Earlier sketches in SATA 43, 94
Mathieu, Joseph P.
  See Mathieu, Joe
Mathis, Sharon Bell 1937- 58
  Earlier sketch in SATA 7
  See also CLR 3
  See also SAAS 3
Matlin, Marlee 1965- 181
Matlin, Marlee Beth
  See Matlin, Marlee
Matloff, Gregory 1945- 73
Matott, Justin 1961- 109
Matranga, Frances Carfi 1922- 78
Matray, James I. 1948- 161
Matray, James Irving
  See Matray, James I.
Matson, Emerson N(els) 1926- 12
Matsui, Tadashi 1926- 8
Matsuno, Masako
  See Kobayashi, Masako Matsuno
Matsuoka, Mei 1981- 192
Matte, (Encarnacion) L'Enc 1936- 22
Mattern, Joanne 1963- 122
Mattheson, Jenny 180
Matthews, Aline
  See De Wire, Elinor
Matthews, Andrew 1948- 138
Matthews, Caitlin 1952- 122
Matthews, Downs 1925- 71
Matthews, Elizabeth 1978- 194
Matthews, Ellen
  See Bache, Ellyn
Matthews, Ellen 1950- 28
Matthews, Harold Downs
  See Matthews, Downs
Matthews, Jacklyn Meek
  See Meek, Jacklyn O'Hanlon
Matthews, John (Kentigern) 1948- 116
Matthews, Laura S.
  See Matthews, L.S.
Matthews, Liz
  See Pellowski, Michael (Joseph)
Matthews, L.S. 183
Matthews, Morgan
  See Pellowski, Michael (Joseph)
Matthews, Nicola
  See Browne, N.M.
Matthews, Patricia 1927-2006 28
Matthews, Patricia Anne
  See Matthews, Patricia
Matthews, Tina 1961- 190
Matthews, Tom L.
  See Lalicki, Tom
Matthews, William Henry III 1919- 45
  Brief entry 28
Matthiessen, Peter 1927- 27
Mattingley, Christobel (Rosemary) 1931- 85
  Earlier sketch in SATA 37
  See also CLR 24
  See also SAAS 18
Matulay, Laszlo 1912- 43
Matus, Greta 1938- 12
Maugham, W. S.
  See Maugham, W(illiam) Somerset

Maugham, W(illiam) Somerset 1874-1965 .. 54
Maugham, William Somerset
  See Maugham, W(illiam) Somerset
Maurer, Diane Philippoff
  See Maurer-Mathison, Diane V(ogel)
Maurer, Diane Vogel
  See Maurer-Mathison, Diane V(ogel)
Maurer-Mathison, Diane V(ogel) 1944- 89
Mauser, Pat Rhoads
  See McCord, Patricia
Mauser, Patricia Rhoads
  See McCord, Patricia
Maves, Mary Carolyn 1916- 10
Maves, Paul B(enjamin) 1913-1994 10
Mavor, Salley 1955- 125
Mawicke, Tran 1911- 15
Max 1906-1989
  See Diop, Birago (Ismael)
Max, Peter 1939- 45
Maxon, Anne
  See Best, (Evangel) Allena Champlin
Maxwell, Arthur S. 1896-1970 11
Maxwell, Edith 1923- 7
Maxwell, Gavin 1914-1969 65
Maxwell, Katie
  See MacAlister, Katie
Maxwell, William (Keepers, Jr.) 1908-2000
  Obituary 128
Maxwell-Hyslop, Miranda 1968- 154
May, Charles Paul 1920- 4
May, Elaine Tyler 1947- 120
May, J. C.
  See May, Julian
May, Julian 1931- 11
May, Robert Lewis 1905-1976
  Obituary 27
May, Robert Stephen 1929-1996 46
May, Robin
  See May, Robert Stephen
Mayall, Beth 171
Mayberry, Florence V(irginia) Wilson 10
Maybury, Richard J. 1946- 72
Maybury, Rick
  See Maybury, Richard J.
Mayer, Agatha
  See Maher, Ramona
Mayer, Albert Ignatius, Jr. 1906-1994
  Obituary 29
Mayer, Ann M(argaret) 1938- 14
Mayer, Danuta 1958- 117
Mayer, Hannelore Valencak 1929- 42
Mayer, Jane Rothschild 1903-2001 38
Mayer, Marianna 1945- 132
  Earlier sketches in SATA 32, 83
Mayer, Mercer 1943- 137
  Earlier sketches in SATA 16, 32, 73, 129
  See also CLR 11
Mayerson, Charlotte Leon 36
Mayerson, Evelyn Wilde 1935- 55
Mayfield, Katherine 1958- 118
Mayfield, Sue 1963- 146
  Earlier sketch in SATA 72
Mayhar, Ardath 1930- 38
Mayhew, James (John) 1964- 149
  Earlier sketch in SATA 85
Maynard, Olga 1920- 40
Mayne, William (James Carter) 1928- 122
  Earlier sketches in SATA 6, 68
  See also CLR 123
  See also SAAS 11
Maynes, J. O. Rocky, Jr.
  See Maynes, J. Oscar, Jr.
Maynes, J. Oscar, Jr. 1929- 38
Mayo, Gretchen Will 1936- 163
  Earlier sketch in SATA 84
Mayo, Margaret 1935- 165
  Earlier sketches in SATA 38, 96
Mayo, Margaret Mary
  See Mayo, Margaret
Mayr, Diane 1949- 197
Mays, Lucinda L(a Bella) 1924- 49

Mays, (Lewis) Victor (Jr.) 1927- 5
Mazer, Anne 1953- 192
  Earlier sketches in SATA 67, 105
Mazer, Harry 1925- 167
  Earlier sketches in SATA 31, 67, 105
  See also CLR 16
  See also SAAS 11
Mazer, Norma Fox 1931- 198
  Earlier sketches in SATA 24, 67, 105, 168
  See also CLR 23
  See also SAAS 1
Mazille, Capucine 1953- 96
Mazza, Adriana 1928- 19
Mazzio, Joann 1926- 74
Mbugua, Kioi Wa 1962- 83
McAfee, Carol 1955- 81
McAllister, Amanda
  See Dowdell, Dorothy (Florence) Karns
  and Hager, Jean
  and Meaker, Eloise
McAllister, Angela 182
McAllister, Margaret I. 1956- 169
  Earlier sketch in SATA 117
McAllister, M.I.
  See McAllister, Margaret I.
McArdle, Paula 1971- 198
McArthur, Nancy 96
McAvoy, Jim 1972- 142
McBain, Ed
  See Hunter, Evan
McBain, Georgina 189
McBratney, Sam 1943- 164
  Earlier sketch in SATA 89
  See also CLR 44
McBrier, Michael
  See Older, Effin
  and Older, Jules
McCafferty, Jim 1954- 84
McCaffery, Janet 1936- 38
McCaffrey, Anne 1926- 152
  Autobiography Feature 152
  Earlier sketches in SATA 8, 70, 116
  See also CLR 130
  See also SAAS 11
McCaffrey, Anne Inez
  See McCaffrey, Anne
McCaffrey, Mary
  See Szudek, Agnes S(usan) P(hilomena)
McCain, Becky Ray 1954- 138
McCain, Murray (David, Jr.) 1926-1981 7
  Obituary 29
McCall, Edith (Sansom) 1911- 6
McCall, Virginia Nielsen 1909-2000 13
McCall, Wendell
  See Pearson, Ridley
McCallum, Phyllis
  See Koch, Phyllis (Mae) McCallum
McCallum, Stephen 1960- 91
McCampbell, Darlene Z. 1942- 83
McCann, Edson
  See del Rey, Lester
  and Pohl, Frederik
McCann, Gerald 1916- 41
McCann, Helen 1948- 75
McCannon, Dindga 41
McCants, William D. 1961- 82
McCarter, Neely Dixon 1929- 47
McCarthy, Agnes 1933- 4
McCarthy, Colin (John) 1951- 77
McCarthy, Meghan 199
  Earlier sketch in SATA 168
McCarthy, Ralph F. 1950- 139
McCarthy-Tucker, Sherri N. 1958- 83
McCarty, Peter 1966- 182
McCarty, Rega Kramer 1904-1986 10
McCaslin, Nellie 1914-2005 12
McCaughrean, Geraldine 1951- 173
  Earlier sketches in SATA 87, 139
  See also CLR 38
McCaughren, Tom 1936- 75
McCauley, Adam 1965- 128

McCay, (Zenas) Winsor 1869-1934 .... *134*
  Earlier sketch in SATA *41*
McClafferty, Carla Killough 1958- *137*
McClary, Jane Stevenson 1919-1990
  Obituary *64*
McCleery, Patsy R. 1925- *133*
  Earlier sketch in SATA *88*
McClements, George *196*
McClintock, Barbara 1955- *146*
  Earlier sketches in SATA *57, 95*
McClintock, Marshall 1906-1967 .... *3*
McClintock, May Garelick
  See Garelick, May
McClintock, Mike
  See McClintock, Marshall
McClintock, Norah *178*
McClintock, Theodore 1902-1971 .... *14*
McClinton, Leon 1933- *11*
McCloskey, Kevin 1951- *79*
McCloskey, (John) Robert 1914-2003 .... *100*
  Obituary *146*
  Earlier sketches in SATA *2, 39*
  See also CLR *7*
McCloy, James F(loyd) 1941- *59*
McClung, Robert M(arshall) 1916- *135*
  Earlier sketch in SATA *2, 68*
  See also CLR *11*
  See also SAAS *15*
McClure, Gillian Mary 1948- *31*
McColley, Kevin 1961- *80*
  See also SAAS *23*
McConduit, Denise Walter 1950- *89*
McConnell, James Douglas Rutherford
  1915-1988 .... *40*
  Obituary *56*
McCord, Anne 1942- *41*
McCord, David (Thompson Watson)
  1897-1997 .... *18*
  Obituary *96*
  See also CLR *9*
McCord, Jean 1924- *34*
McCord, Pat Mauser
  See McCord, Patricia
McCord, Patricia 1943- *159*
  Earlier sketch in SATA *37*
McCord, Patricia Sue Rhoads Mauser
  See McCord, Patricia
McCormick, Brooks
  See Adams, William Taylor
McCormick, Dell J. 1892-1949 .... *19*
McCormick, (George) Donald (King)
  1911-1998 .... *14*
McCormick, Edith (Joan) 1934- *30*
McCormick, Kimberly A. 1960- *153*
McCormick, Patricia 1956- *181*
  Earlier sketch in SATA *128*
McCourt, Edward (Alexander) 1907-1972
  Obituary *28*
McCourt, Lisa 1964- *159*
  Earlier sketch in SATA *117*
McCourt, Malachy 1931- *126*
McCoy, Iola Fuller *3*
McCoy, J(oseph) J(erome) 1917- *8*
McCoy, Karen Kawamoto 1953- *82*
McCoy, Lois (Rich) 1941- *38*
McCrady, Lady 1951- *16*
McCrea, James (Craig, Jr.) 1920- *3*
McCrea, Ruth (Pirman) 1921- *3*
McCreigh, James
  See Pohl, Frederik
McCrumb, Sharyn 1948- *109*
McCue, Lisa 1959- *177*
  Earlier sketch in SATA *65*
McCue, Lisa Emiline
  See McCue, Lisa
McCullen, Andrew
  See Arthur, Robert, (Jr.)
McCullers, (Lula) Carson (Smith)
  1917-1967 .... *27*
McCulloch, Derek (Ivor Breashur) 1897-1967
  Obituary *29*

McCulloch, John Tyler
  See Burroughs, Edgar Rice
McCulloch, Sarah
  See Ure, Jean
McCullough, David 1933- *62*
McCullough, David Gaub
  See McCullough, David
McCullough, Frances Monson 1938- *8*
McCullough, Sharon Pierce 1943- *131*
McCully, Emily Arnold
  See Arnold, Emily
McCune, Dan
  See Haas, Dorothy F.
McCunn, Ruthanne Lum 1946- *63*
McCurdy, Michael (Charles) 1942- *147*
  Earlier sketches in SATA *13, 82*
McCutcheon, Elsie (Mary Jackson) 1937- ... *60*
McCutcheon, John 1952- *97*
McDaniel, Becky Bring 1953- *61*
McDaniel, Lurlene 1944- *146*
  Earlier sketch in SATA *71*
McDaniels, Pellom III 1968- *121*
McDaniels, Preston 1952- *192*
McDearmon, Kay *20*
McDermott, Beverly Brodsky 1941- *11*
McDermott, Eleni *156*
McDermott, Gerald (Edward) 1941- *163*
  Earlier sketches in SATA *16, 74*
  See also CLR *9*
McDermott, Michael 1962- *76*
McDevitt, Jack 1935- *155*
  Earlier sketch in SATA *94*
McDevitt, John Charles
  See McDevitt, Jack
McDole, Carol
  See Farley, Carol (J.)
McDonald, Collin 1943- *79*
McDonald, Gerald D(oan) 1905-1970 .... *3*
McDonald, Jamie
  See Heide, Florence Parry
McDonald, Janet 1953-2007 .... *148*
McDonald, Jill (Masefield) 1927-1982 .... *13*
  Obituary *29*
McDonald, Joyce 1946- *164*
  Earlier sketch in SATA *101*
McDonald, Lucile Saunders 1898-1992 .... *10*
McDonald, Mary Ann 1956- *84*
McDonald, Megan 1959- *151*
  Autobiography Feature *151*
  Earlier sketches in SATA *67, 99, 148*
  See also CLR *94*
McDonald, Meme 1954- *112*
McDonald, Mercedes 1956- *169*
  Earlier sketch in SATA *97*
McDonell, Chris 1960- *138*
McDonnell, Christine 1949- *115*
  Earlier sketch in SATA *34*
McDonnell, Flora (Mary) 1963- *146*
  Earlier sketch in SATA *90*
McDonnell, Kathleen 1947- *186*
McDonnell, Lois Eddy 1914-2001 .... *10*
McDonnell, Patrick 1956- *179*
McDonough, Yona Zeldis 1957- *73*
McElligott, Matt 1968- *196*
  Earlier sketch in SATA *135*
McElligott, Matthew
  See McElligott, Matt
McElmeel, Sharron L. 1942- *128*
McElmurry, Jill *198*
  Earlier sketch in SATA *159*
McElrath, William N. 1932- *65*
McElrath-Eslick, Lori 1960- *96*
McEntee, Dorothy (Layng) 1902- *37*
McEwen, Katharine *183*
McEwen, Robert (Lindley) 1926-1980
  Obituary *23*
McFadden, Kevin Christopher
  See Pike, Christopher
McFall, Christie 1918- *12*
McFall, Gardner 1952- *183*
McFarlan, Donald M(aitland) 1915- *59*

McFarland, Henry "Hammer"
  See McFarland, Henry O.
McFarland, Henry O. 1934- *143*
McFarland, Kenton D(ean) 1920- *11*
McFarland, Martha
  See Smith-Ankrom, M. E.
McFarlane, Leslie (Charles) 1902-1977 ..... *100*
  Earlier sketches in SATA *31, 1, 65, 67*
  See also CLR *118*
McFarlane, Peter (William) 1940- *95*
McFarlane, Sheryl P. 1954- *86*
McFarlane, Todd 1961- *117*
McGaw, Jessie Brewer 1913-1997 .... *10*
McGee, Barbara 1943- *6*
McGee, Marni *163*
McGhee, Alison 1960- *196*
McGiffin, (Lewis) Lee (Shaffer) 1908-1978 ... *1*
McGill, Alice *159*
McGill, Ormond 1913- *92*
McGinley, Jerry 1948- *116*
McGinley, Phyllis 1905-1978 .... *44*
  Obituary *24*
  Earlier sketch in SATA *2*
McGinnis, Lila S(prague) 1924- *44*
McGinty, Alice B. 1963- *134*
McGivern, Justin 1985- *129*
McGivern, Maureen Daly
  See Daly, Maureen
McGivern, Maureen Patricia Daly
  See Daly, Maureen
McGough, Elizabeth (Hemmes) 1934- *33*
McGovern, Ann 1930- *132*
  Earlier sketches in SATA *8, 69, 70*
  See also CLR *50*
  See also SAAS *17*
McGowen, Thomas E. 1927- *109*
  Earlier sketch in SATA *2*
McGowen, Tom
  See McGowen, Thomas E.
McGrady, Mike 1933- *6*
McGrath, Barbara Barbieri 1953- *169*
  Earlier sketch in SATA *108*
McGrath, Robin 1949- *121*
McGrath, Thomas (Matthew) 1916-1990 ..... *41*
  Obituary *66*
McGraw, Eloise Jarvis 1915-2000 .... *67*
  Obituary *123*
  Earlier sketch in SATA *1*
  See also SAAS *6*
McGraw, William Corbin 1916-1999 .... *3*
McGreal, Elizabeth
  See Yates, Elizabeth
McGregor, Barbara 1959- *82*
McGregor, Craig 1933- *8*
McGregor, Iona 1929- *25*
McGrory, Anik *193*
McGuffey, Alexander Hamilton 1816-1896 . *60*
McGuigan, Mary Ann 1949- *106*
McGuire, Edna 1899- *13*
McGuire, Leslie (Sarah) 1945- *94*
  Brief entry *45*
  Earlier sketch in SATA *52*
McGuire, Robert *187*
McGuirk, Leslie (A.) 1960- *152*
McGurk, Slater
  See Roth, Arthur J(oseph)
McHargue, Georgess 1941- *77*
  Earlier sketch in SATA *4*
  See also CLR *2*
  See also SAAS *5*
McHenry, E.B. 1963(?)- *193*
McHugh, (Berit) Elisabet 1941- *55*
  Brief entry *44*
McIlvaine, Jane
  See McClary, Jane Stevenson
McIlwraith, Maureen Mollie Hunter
  See Hunter, Mollie
McInerney, Judith W(hitelock) 1945- *49*
  Brief entry *46*
McInerny, Ralph 1929- *93*

McInerny, Ralph Matthew
  See McInerny, Ralph
McKaughan, Larry (Scott) 1941- *75*
McKay, Donald 1895- *45*
McKay, Hilary (Jane) 1959- *145*
  Earlier sketch in SATA *92*
  See also SAAS *23*
McKay, Lawrence, Jr. 1948- *114*
McKay, Robert W. 1921- *15*
McKay, Sharon E. 1954- *165*
McKay, Simon
  See Nicole, Christopher (Robin)
McKean, Dave 1963- *197*
McKean, David Jeff
  See McKean, Dave
McKeating, Eileen 1957- *81*
McKee, David (John) 1935- *158*
  Earlier sketches in SATA *70, 107*
  See also CLR *38*
McKee, Tim 1970- *111*
McKeever, Marcia
  See Laird, Jean E(louise)
McKelvey, Carole A. 1942- *78*
McKelvy, Charles 1950- *124*
McKendrick, Melveena (Christine) 1941- *55*
McKendry, Joe 1972- *170*
McKenna, Colleen O'Shaughnessy 1948- .. *136*
  Earlier sketch in SATA *76*
McKenzie, Dorothy Clayton 1910-1981
  Obituary *28*
McKenzie, Ellen Kindt 1928- *80*
McKernan, Victoria 1957- *171*
McKie, Robin *112*
McKillip, Patricia A. 1948- *174*
  Earlier sketches in SATA *30, 80, 126*
McKillip, Patricia Anne
  See McKillip, Patricia A.
McKim, Audrey Margaret 1909-1999 .... *47*
McKimmie, Chris *194*
McKinley, Jennifer Carolyn Robin
  See McKinley, Robin
McKinley, Robin 1952- *195*
  Brief entry *32*
  Earlier sketches in SATA *50, 89, 130*
  See also CLR *127*
McKinney, Barbara Shaw 1951- *116*
McKinney, Nadine 1938- *91*
McKinty, Adrian *186*
McKissack, Fredrick L. 1939- *162*
  Brief entry *53*
  Earlier sketches in SATA *73, 117*
  See also CLR *55*
McKissack, Fredrick Lemuel
  See McKissack, Fredrick L.
McKissack, Patricia C. 1944- *195*
  Earlier sketches in SATA *51, 73, 117, 162*
  See also CLR *129*
McKissack, Patricia L'Ann Carwell
  See McKissack, Patricia C.
McKissack and McKissack
  See McKissack, Fredrick L.
  and McKissack, Patricia C.
McKown, Robin (?)-1976 .... *6*
McKy, Katie 1956- *184*
McLaren, Clemence 1938- *158*
  Earlier sketch in SATA *105*
McLaughlin, Frank 1934- *73*
McLaurin, Anne 1953- *27*
McLean, Andrew 1946- *172*
  Earlier sketch in SATA *113*
McLean, J. Sloan
  See Gillette, Virginia M(ary)
  and Wunsch, Josephine (McLean)
McLean, Janet 1946- *113*
McLean, Kathryn (Anderson) 1909-1966 .... *9*
McLean, Virginia Overton 1946- *90*
McLean-Carr, Carol 1948- *122*
McLeish, Kenneth 1940-1997 .... *35*
McLenighan, Valjean 1947- *46*
  Brief entry *40*
McLennan, Connie *171*

McLennan, Will
  See Wisler, G(ary) Clifton
McLeod, Bob 1951- *173*
McLeod, Chum 1955- *95*
McLeod, Emilie Warren 1926-1982 .... *23*
  Obituary *31*
McLeod, Kirsty
  See Hudson, (Margaret) Kirsty
McLeod, Margaret Vail
  See Holloway, Teresa (Bragunier)
McLerran, Alice 1933- *137*
  Earlier sketch in SATA *68*
McLimans, David 1949- *182*
McLoughlin, John C. 1949- *47*
McManus, Patrick F. 1933- *46*
McManus, Patrick Francis
  See McManus, Patrick F.
McMeekin, Clark
  See McMeekin, Isabel McLennan
McMeekin, Isabel McLennan 1895-1973 .... *3*
McMenemy, Sarah 1965- *156*
McMillan, Bruce 1947- *192*
  Earlier sketches in SATA *22, 70, 129*
  See also CLR *47*
McMillan, Naomi
  See Grimes, Nikki
McMorey, James L.
  See Moyer, Terry J.
McMorrow, Annalisa 1969- *104*
McMullan, Jim 1934- *150*
  Earlier sketch in SATA *87*
McMullan, K. H.
  See McMullan, Kate
McMullan, Kate 1947- *189*
  Brief entry *48*
  Earlier sketches in SATA *52, 87, 132*
McMullan, Kate Hall
  See McMullan, Kate
McMurtrey, Martin A(loysias) 1921- *21*
McNabb, Linda 1963- *147*
McNair, Kate *3*
McNair, Sylvia 1924-2002 .... *74*
McNamara, Margaret C(raig) 1915-1981
  Obituary *24*
McNaught, Harry *32*
McNaughton, Colin 1951- *134*
  Earlier sketches in SATA *39, 92*
  See also CLR *54*
McNaughton, Janet 1953- *162*
  Earlier sketch in SATA *110*
McNeal, Laura *194*
McNeal, Tom *194*
McNeely, Jeannette 1918- *25*
McNeer, May (Yonge) 1902-1994 .... *81*
  Earlier sketch in SATA *1*
McNeese, Tim 1953- *139*
McNeill, Janet
  See Alexander, Janet
McNicholas, Shelagh *191*
McNickle, (William) D'Arcy 1904-1977
  Obituary *22*
McNicoll, Sylvia (Marilyn) 1954- *113*
  See also CLR *99*
McNulty, Faith 1918-2005 .... *168*
  Earlier sketches in SATA *12, 84, 139*
McPhail, David 1940- *183*
  Brief entry *32*
  Earlier sketches in SATA *47, 81, 140*
McPhail, David M.
  See McPhail, David
McPhail, David Michael
  See McPhail, David
McPhee, Norma H. 1928- *95*
McPhee, Richard B(yron) 1934- *41*
McPherson, James M. 1936- *141*
  Earlier sketch in SATA *16*
McPherson, James Munro
  See McPherson, James M.
McQueen, Lucinda 1950- *58*
  Brief entry *48*
McQueen, Mildred Hark 1908-1978 .... *12*

McRae, Russell (William) 1934- *63*
McShean, Gordon 1936- *41*
Mc Swigan, Marie 1907-1962 .... *24*
McTavish, Sandy
  See Eyerly, Jeannette
McVeity, Jen *148*
McVey, Vicki 1946- *80*
McVicker, Charles (Taggart) 1930- *39*
McVicker, Chuck
  See McVicker, Charles (Taggart)
McWhirter, A(lan) Ross 1925-1975 .... *37*
  Obituary *31*
McWhirter, Norris (Dewar) 1925-2004 .... *37*
McWilliams, Karen 1943- *65*
Mdurvwa, Hajara E. 1962- *92*
Meacham, Margaret 1952- *95*
Meachum, Virginia 1918- *133*
  Earlier sketch in SATA *87*
Mead, Alice 1952- *146*
  Earlier sketch in SATA *94*
Mead, Margaret 1901-1978
  Obituary *20*
Mead, Russell (M., Jr.) 1935- *10*
Mead, Stella (?)-1981
  Obituary *27*
Meade, Ellen
  See Roddick, Ellen
Meade, Marion 1934- *127*
  Earlier sketch in SATA *23*
Meader, Stephen W(arren) 1892-1977 .... *1*
Meadmore, Susan
  See Sallis, Susan (Diana)
Meadow, Charles T(roub) 1929- *23*
Meadowcroft, Enid LaMonte
  See Wright, Enid Meadowcroft (LaMonte)
Meadows, Graham (W.) 1934- *161*
Meaker, M. J.
  See Meaker, Marijane
Meaker, Marijane 1927- *160*
  Autobiography Feature *111*
  Earlier sketches in SATA *20, 61, 99*
  See also CLR *29*
  See also SAAS *1*
Meaker, Marijane Agnes
  See Meaker, Marijane
Means, Florence Crannell 1891-1980 .... *1*
  Obituary *25*
  See also CLR *56*
Mearian, Judy Frank 1936- *49*
Mecca, Judy Truesdell 1955- *127*
Mechling, Lauren 1978(?)- *194*
Medary, Marjorie 1890-1980 .... *14*
Meddaugh, Susan 1944- *176*
  Earlier sketches in SATA *29, 84, 125*
Medearis, Angela Shelf 1956- *123*
  Earlier sketch in SATA *72*
Medearis, Mary 1915- *5*
Medina, Jane 1953- *167*
  Earlier sketch in SATA *122*
Medina, Nico 1982- *193*
Medlicott, Mary 1946- *88*
Mee, Charles L., Jr. 1938- *72*
  Earlier sketch in SATA *8*
Meek, Jacklyn O'Hanlon 1933- *51*
  Brief entry *34*
Meek, S(terner St.) P(aul) 1894-1972
  Obituary *28*
Meeker, Clare Hodgson 1952- *96*
Meeker, Oden 1919(?)-1976 .... *14*
Meeker, Richard
  See Brown, Fornan
Meeks, Esther MacBain *1*
Meggs, Libby Phillips 1943- *130*
Mehdevi, Alexander (Sinclair) 1947- *7*
Mehdevi, Anne (Marie) Sinclair 1947- *8*
Meidell, Sherry 1951- *73*
Meier, Minta 1906- *55*
Meighan, Donald Charles 1929- *30*
Meigs, Cornelia Lynde 1884-1973 .... *6*
  See also CLR *55*
Meilach, Dona Z(weigoron) 1926- *34*

Meilman, Philip W(arren) 1951- 79
Meinstereifel, Ronald L. 1960- 134
Meisel, Paul 184
Melanson, Luc 198
Melcher, Daniel 1912-1985
  Obituary 43
Melcher, Frederic Gershom 1879-1963
  Obituary 22
Melcher, Marguerite Fellows 1879-1969 10
Melendez, Francisco 1964- 72
Melhuish, Eva 199
Melin, Grace Hathaway 1892-1973 10
Mellersh, H(arold) E(dward) L(eslie)
  1897- 10
Melling, David 186
Melmoth, Sebastian
  See Wilde, Oscar
Melnikoff, Pamela (Rita) 97
Meltzer, Milton 1915- 128
  Autobiography Feature 124
  Earlier sketches in SATA *1, 50, 80*
  See also CLR *13*
  See also SAAS *1*
Melville, Anne
  See Potter, Margaret (Newman)
Melville, Herman 1819-1891 59
Melwood, Mary
  See Lewis, E. M.
Melzack, Ronald 1929- 5
Memling, Carl 1918-1969 6
Menchin, Scott 188
Mendel, Jo
  See Bond, Gladys Baker
  and Gilbertson, Mildred Geiger
Mendelson, Steven T. 1958-1995 86
Mendelson-Stevens, Serita Deborah
  See Stevens, Serita
Mendes, Valerie 1939- 157
Mendez, Raymond A. 1947- 66
Mendonca, Susan
  See Smith, Susan Vernon
Mendoza, George 1934- 41
  Brief entry 39
  See also SAAS *7*
Menendez, Shirley (C.) 1937- 146
Meng, Cece 194
Meng, Heinz (Karl) 1924- 13
Mennen, Ingrid 1954- 85
Menotti, Gian Carlo 1911-2007 29
  Obituary 180
Menuhin, Sir Yehudi 1916-1999 40
  Obituary 113
Menville, Douglas 1935- 64
Menzel, Barbara Jean 1946- 63
Mercati, Cynthia 164
Mercati, Cynthia J.
  See Mercati, Cynthia
Mercer, Charles (Edward) 1917-1988 16
  Obituary 61
Mercer, Jessie 21
Mercer, Sienna 192
Meredith, Arnold
  See Hopkins, (Hector) Kenneth
Meredith, David William
  See Miers, Earl Schenck
Meringoff, Laurene Krasny
  See Brown, Laurene Krasny
Meriwether, Louise 1923- 52
  Brief entry 31
Merlin, Arthur
  See Blish, James (Benjamin)
Merlin, Christina
  See Heaven, Constance (Christina)
Merriam, Eve 1916-1992 73
  Earlier sketches in SATA *3, 40*
  See also CLR *14*
Merrill, Jane 1946- 42
Merrill, Jane Merrill
  See Merrill, Jane

Merrill, Jean (Fairbanks) 1923- 82
  Earlier sketch in SATA *1*
  See also CLR *52*
Merrill, Phil
  See Merrill, Jane
Merriman, Alex
  See Silverberg, Robert
Merriman, Rachel 1971- 149
  Earlier sketch in SATA *98*
Merrit, Elizabeth
  See Goudge, Eileen
Merski, Patricia K.
  See Merski, P.K.
Merski, P.K. 172
Mertz, Barbara
  See Peters, Elizabeth
Mertz, Barbara Gross
  See Peters, Elizabeth
Merz, Jennifer J. 196
Meschel, Susan V. 1936- 83
Messenger, Charles (Rynd Milles) 1942- 59
Messick, Dale 1906-2005 64
  Brief entry 48
Messier, Claire 1956- 103
Messieres, Nicole de
  See de Messieres, Nicole
Messinger, Carla 198
Messmer, Otto 1892(?)-1983 37
Mesta, Gabriel
  See Moesta, Rebecca
Metcalf, Doris H(unter) 91
Metcalf, Suzanne
  See Baum, L(yman) Frank
Metos, Thomas H(arry) 1932- 37
Metter, Bert(ram Milton) 1927- 56
Metzenthen, David 1958- 167
  Earlier sketch in SATA *106*
Meunier, Brian 1954- 195
Meyer, Barbara 1939- 77
Meyer, Carolyn 1935- 142
  Autobiography Feature 142
  Earlier sketches in SATA *9, 70, 118*
  See also SAAS *9*
Meyer, Carolyn Mae
  See Meyer, Carolyn
Meyer, Edith Patterson 1895-1993 5
Meyer, F(ranklyn) E(dward) 1932- 9
Meyer, Jean Shepherd 11
Meyer, Jerome Sydney 1895-1975 3
  Obituary 25
Meyer, June
  See Jordan, June
Meyer, Kerstin 1966- 190
Meyer, L. A.
  See Meyer, Louis A(lbert), Jr.
Meyer, Louis A(lbert), Jr. 1942- 144
  Earlier sketch in SATA *12*
Meyer, Renate 1930- 6
Meyer, Stephenie 1973- 193
Meyer, Susan E. 1940- 64
Meyers, Susan 1942- 164
  Earlier sketches in SATA *19, 108*
Meynell, Laurence Walter 1899-1989
  Obituary 61
Meynier, Yvonne (Pollet) 1908- 14
Mezey, Robert 1935- 33
Micale, Albert 1913- 22
Michael, James
  See Scagnetti, Jack
Michael, Livi 1960- 172
Michael, Manfred
  See Winterfeld, Henry
Michael, Olivia
  See Michael, Livi
Michaels, Barbara
  See Peters, Elizabeth
Michaels, Jamie 195
Michaels, Joanne Louise
  See Teitelbaum, Michael
Michaels, Kristin
  See Williams, Jeanne

Michaels, Molly
  See Untermeyer, Louis
Michaels, Neal
  See Teitelbaum, Michael
Michaels, Rune 194
Michaels, Ski
  See Pellowski, Michael (Joseph)
Michaels, Steve 1955- 71
Michaels, William M. 1917- 77
Michel, Anna 1943- 49
  Brief entry 40
Michel, Francois 1948- 82
Michelin, Linda 183
Michelson, Richard 198
  Earlier sketch in SATA *173*
Micich, Paul 74
Micklish, Rita 1931- 12
Micklos, John, Jr. 1956- 173
  Earlier sketch in SATA *129*
Micklos J., John, Jr. 1956-
  See Micklos, John, Jr.
Micucci, Charles (Patrick, Jr.) 1959- 144
  Earlier sketch in SATA *82*
Middleton, Haydn 1955- 152
  Earlier sketch in SATA *85*
Miers, Earl Schenck 1910-1972 1
  Obituary 26
Migdale, Lawrence 1951- 89
Mikaelsen, Ben 1952- 173
  Earlier sketches in SATA *73, 107*
Mikaelsen, Benjamin John
  See Mikaelsen, Ben
Miklowitz, Gloria D. 1927- 129
  Earlier sketches in SATA *4, 68*
  See also SAAS *17*
Mikolaycak, Charles 1937-1993 78
  Obituary 75
  Earlier sketch in SATA *9*
  See also SAAS *4*
Mild, Warren (Paul) 1922- 41
Milelli, Pascal 1965- 135
Miles, Betty 1928- 78
  Earlier sketch in SATA *8*
  See also SAAS *9*
Miles, Miska
  See Martin, Patricia Miles
Miles, (Mary) Patricia 1930- 29
Miles, Patricia A.
  See Martin, Patricia Miles
Miles, Victoria 1966- 188
Milgrim, David 187
  Earlier sketch in SATA *158*
Milgrom, Harry 1912-1978 25
Milhous, Katherine 1894-1977 15
Milich, Zoran 174
Milios, Rita 1949- 79
Militant
  See Sandburg, Carl (August)
Millais, Raoul 1901- 77
Millar, Barbara F. 1924- 12
Millar, Margaret (Ellis Sturm) 1915-1994 61
  Obituary 79
Millbank, Captain H. R.
  See Ellis, Edward S(ylvester)
Millen, C(ynthia) M. 1955- 114
Miller, Albert G(riffith) 1905-1982 12
  Obituary 31
Miller, Alice Ann 1958- 150
Miller, Alice P(atricia McCarthy) 22
Miller, Debbie 1951- 160
  Earlier sketch in SATA *103*
Miller, Debbie S.
  See Miller, Debbie
Miller, Deborah Uchill 1944- 61
Miller, Don 1923- 15
Miller, Doris R.
  See Mosesson, Gloria R(ubin)
Miller, Eddie
  See Miller, Edward
Miller, Edna Anita 1920- 29
Miller, Edward 1905-1974 8

Miller, Edward 1964- 183
Miller, Elizabeth 1933- 41
Miller, Ellanita 1957- 87
Miller, Eugene 1925- 33
Miller, Frances A. 1937- 52
  Brief entry 46
Miller, Helen M(arkley) -1984 5
Miller, Helen Topping 1884-1960
  Obituary 29
Miller, Jane (Judith) 1925-1989 15
Miller, Jewel 1956- 73
Miller, John
  See Samachson, Joseph
Miller, Judi 117
Miller, Kate 1948- 193
Miller, Kirsten 1973- 185
Miller, Louise (Rolfe) 1940- 76
Miller, M. L. 85
Miller, Madge 1918- 63
Miller, Margaret J.
  See Dale, Margaret J(essy) Miller
Miller, Marilyn (Jean) 1925- 33
Miller, Marvin 65
Miller, Mary
  See Northcott, (William) Cecil
Miller, Mary Beth 1942- 9
Miller, Mary Beth 1964- 185
Miller, Maryann 1943- 73
Miller, Natalie 1917-1976 35
Miller, Robert H. 1944- 91
Miller, Ron 1947- 185
Miller, Ruth White
  See White, Ruth C.
Miller, Sandra
  See Miller, Sandy
Miller, Sandra Peden
  See Miller, Sandy
Miller, Sandy 1948- 41
  Brief entry 35
Miller, Sarah 1969- 175
Miller, Virginia
  See Austin, Virginia
Miller, William R. 1959- 116
Milligan, Bryce 1953- 170
Milligan, Spike
  See Milligan, Terence Alan
Milligan, Terence Alan 1918-2002 29
  Obituary 134
  See also CLR 92
Millington, Ada
  See Deyneka, Anita
Millman, Isaac 1933- 140
Mills, Adam
  See Stanley, George Edward
Mills, Claudia 1954- 191
  Brief entry 41
  Earlier sketches in SATA 44, 89, 145
Mills, Elaine (Rosemary) 1941- 72
Mills, G. Riley 196
Mills, Joyce C. 1944- 102
Mills, Judith Christine 1956- 130
Mills, Yaroslava Surmach 1925- 35
Millspaugh, Ben P. 1936- 77
Millstead, Thomas E. 30
Milne, A. A. 1882-1956 100
  See also YABC 1
  See also CLR 108
Milne, Alan Alexander
  See Milne, A. A.
Milne, Lorus J. 5
  See also CLR 22
  See also SAAS 18
Milne, Margery 5
  See also CLR 22
  See also SAAS 18
Milne, Terry
  See Milne, Theresa Ann
Milne, Theresa Ann 1964- 84
Milnes, Irma McDonough 1924- 101
Milonas, Rolf
  See Myller, Rolf

Milord, Susan 1954- 147
  Earlier sketch in SATA 74
Milotte, Alfred G(eorge) 1904-1989 11
  Obituary 62
Milstein, Linda 1954- 80
Milton, Ann 134
Milton, Hilary (Herbert) 1920- 23
Milton, John R(onald) 1924- 24
Milton, Joyce 1946- 101
  Brief entry 41
  Earlier sketch in SATA 52
Milverton, Charles A.
  See Penzler, Otto
Minahan, John A. 1956- 92
Minar, Barbra (Goodyear) 1940- 79
Minard, Rosemary 1939- 63
Minarik, Else Holmelund 1920- 127
  Earlier sketch in SATA 15
  See also CLR 33
Miner, Jane Claypool 1933- 103
  Brief entry 37
  Earlier sketch in SATA 38
Miner, Lewis S. 1909-1971 11
Mines, Jeanette 1948- 61
Mines, Jeanette Marie
  See Mines, Jeanette
Minier, Nelson
  See Stoutenburg, Adrien (Pearl)
Minnitt, Ronda Jacqueline
  See Armitage, David
Minor, Wendell 1944- 199
  Earlier sketches in SATA 78, 109, 164
Minter, Daniel 1961- 176
Mintonye, Grace 4
Miranda, Anne 1954- 109
  Earlier sketch in SATA 71
Mirocha, Paul 192
Mirsky, Jeannette 1903-1987 8
  Obituary 51
Mirsky, Reba Paeff 1902-1966 1
Misako Rocks! 192
Mishica, Clare 1960- 91
Miskovits, Christine 1939- 10
Miss Frances
  See Horwich, Frances R(appaport)
Miss Read
  See Saint, Dora Jessie
Mister Rogers
  See Rogers, Fred McFeely
Mitchard, Jacquelyn 1956- 168
  Earlier sketch in SATA 98
Mitchell, Adrian 1932-2008 166
  Earlier sketch in SATA 104
Mitchell, Allison
  See Griffin, W.E.B
Mitchell, Betty Jo
  See Mitchell, B.J.
Mitchell, B.J. 1931- 120
Mitchell, Clyde
  See Ellison, Harlan
  and Silverberg, Robert
Mitchell, Cynthia 1922- 29
Mitchell, (Sibyl) Elyne (Keith) 1913- 10
Mitchell, Gladys (Maude Winifred)
  1901-1983 46
  Obituary 35
Mitchell, Jay
  See Roberson, Jennifer
Mitchell, Joyce Slayton 1933- 142
  Brief entry 43
  Earlier sketch in SATA 46
Mitchell, K. L.
  See Lamb, Elizabeth Searle
Mitchell, Kathy 1948- 59
Mitchell, Lori 1961- 128
Mitchell, Margaree King 1953- 84
Mitchell, Marianne 1947- 145
Mitchell, Rhonda 89
Mitchell, Stephen 1943- 199
Mitchell, Todd 1974- 191

Mitchell, Yvonne 1925-1979
  Obituary 24
Mitchelson, Mitch
  See Mitchelson, Peter Richard
Mitchelson, Peter Richard 1950- 104
Mitchison, Naomi (Margaret Haldane)
  1897-1999 24
  Obituary 112
Mitchnik, Helen 1901-1982 41
  Brief entry 35
Mitchum, Hank
  See Knott, William C(ecil, Jr.)
  and Murray, Stuart A. P.
  and Newton, D(wight) B(ennett)
  and Sherman, Jory (Tecumseh)
Mitgutsch, Ali 1935- 76
Mitsuhashi, Yoko 45
  Brief entry 33
Mitton, Jacqueline 1948- 162
  Earlier sketches in SATA 66, 115
Mitton, Simon 1946- 66
Mitton, Tony 1951- 149
  Earlier sketch in SATA 104
Miura, Taro 1968- 181
Mizner, Elizabeth Howard 1907- 27
Mizumura, Kazue 18
Mlynowski, Sarah 1977(?)- 180
Mobin-Uddin, Asma 172
Mobley, Joe A. 1945- 91
Moche, Dinah (Rachel) L(evine) 1936- 44
  Brief entry 40
Mochi, Ugo (A.) 1889-1977 38
Mochizuki, Ken 1954- 146
  Earlier sketch in SATA 81
  See also SAAS 22
Modarressi, Mitra 1967- 126
Modell, Frank B. 1917- 39
  Brief entry 36
Modesitt, Jeanne 1953- 143
  Earlier sketch in SATA 92
Modesitt, L.E., Jr. 1943- 164
  Earlier sketch in SATA 91
Modesitt, Leland Exton, Jr.
  See Modesitt, L.E., Jr.
Modrell, Dolores 1933- 72
Moe, Barbara 1937- 20
Moe, Jorgen (Ingebretsen) 1813-1882
  See CLR 104
Moed-Kass, Pnina 169
Moerbeek, Kees 1955- 98
Moeri, Louise 1924- 93
  Earlier sketch in SATA 24
  See also SAAS 10
Moesta, Rebecca 1956- 182
Moffett, Jami 1952- 84
Moffett, Martha (Leatherwood) 1934- 8
Mogensen, Suzanne A(ncher) 1946- 129
Mohammed, Khadra 197
Mohn, Peter B(urnet) 1934- 28
Mohn, Viola Kohl 1914- 8
Mohr, Nicholasa 1938- 97
  Autobiography Feature 113
  Earlier sketch in SATA 8
  See also CLR 22
  See also SAAS 8
Mok, Esther 1953- 93
Molan, Christine 1943- 84
Molarsky, Osmond 1909- 16
Moldon, Peter L(eonard) 1937- 49
Mole, John 1941- 103
  Earlier sketch in SATA 36
  See also CLR 61
Molesworth, Mary Louisa 1839-1921 98
Molin, Charles
  See Mayne, William (James Carter)
Molina, Silvia 1946- 97
Molk, Laurel 1957- 162
  Earlier sketch in SATA 92
Mollel, Tololwa M. 1952- 88
Molloy, Anne Baker 1907-1999 32
Molloy, Michael (John) 1940- 162

Molloy, Paul (George) 1924- *5*
Moloney, James 1954- *144*
  Autobiography Feature *144*
  Earlier sketch in SATA *94*
Momaday, N. Scott 1934- *48*
  Brief entry *30*
Momaday, Navarre Scott
  See Momaday, N. Scott
Monaco, Octavia 1963- *169*
Monagle, Bernie 1957- *121*
Moncure, Jane Belk 1926- *23*
Monjo, F(erdinand) N(icholas III)
  1924-1978 .... *16*
  See also CLR *2*
Monk, Isabell 1952- *136*
Monks, Lydia *189*
Monroe, Lyle
  See Heinlein, Robert A.
Monroe, Marion
  See Cox, Marion Monroe
Monroy, Manuel 1970- *196*
Monsell, Helen Albee 1895-1971 .... *24*
Monson-Burton, Marianne 1975- *139*
Montana, Bob 1920-1975
  Obituary *21*
Montecalvo, Janet *177*
Montenegro, Laura Nyman 1953- *95*
Montero, Gloria 1933- *109*
Montes, Marisa 1951- *144*
Montgomerie, Norah (Mary) 1913- *26*
Montgomery, Constance
  See Cappel, Constance
Montgomery, Elizabeth
  See Julesberg, Elizabeth Rider Montgomery
Montgomery, Elizabeth Rider
  See Julesberg, Elizabeth Rider Montgomery
Montgomery, Hugh (Edward) 1962- *146*
Montgomery, L(ucy) M(aud) 1874-1942 .... *100*
  See also YABC *1*
  See also CLR *91*
Montgomery, Raymond A. (Jr.) 1936- *39*
Montgomery, Rutherford George 1894-1985 . *3*
Montgomery, Sy 1958- *184*
  Autobiography Feature *132*
  Earlier sketches in SATA *114, 132*
Montgomery, Vivian *36*
Monthei, Betty *179*
Montijo, Rhode *179*
Montileaux, Donald F. 1948- *183*
Montpetit, Charles 1958- *101*
Montresor, Beni 1926-2001 .... *38*
  Earlier sketch in SATA *3*
  See also SAAS *4*
Montserrat, Pep *181*
Monty Python
  See Chapman, Graham
  and Cleese, John (Marwood)
  and Gilliam, Terry
  and Idle, Eric
  and Jones, Terence Graham Parry
  and Palin, Michael
Moodie, Craig 1956- *172*
Moodie, Fiona 1952- *133*
Moody, Minerva
  See Alcott, Louisa May
Moody, Ralph Owen 1898-1982 .... *1*
Moon, Carl 1879(?)-1948 .... *25*
Moon, Grace (Purdie) 1877(?)-1947 .... *25*
Moon, Lily
  See Warnes, Tim
Moon, Nicola 1952- *147*
  Earlier sketch in SATA *96*
Moon, Pat 1946- *113*
Moon, Sheila 1910-1991 .... *5*
  Obituary *114*
Moon, Sheila Elizabeth
  See Moon, Sheila
Mooney, Bel 1946- *95*
Mooney, Bill 1936- *122*
Mooney, Elizabeth C(omstock) 1918-1986
  Obituary *48*

Mooney, William
  See Mooney, Bill
Moor, Emily
  See Deming, Richard
Moorcock, Michael 1939- *166*
  Earlier sketch in SATA *93*
Moorcock, Michael John
  See Moorcock, Michael
Moore, Anne Carroll 1871-1961 .... *13*
Moore, Cheri
  See Ladd, Cheryl (Jean)
Moore, Clement Clarke 1779-1863 .... *18*
Moore, Cyd 1957- *186*
  Earlier sketch in SATA *83, 133*
Moore, Don W. 1905(?)-1986
  Obituary *48*
Moore, Elaine 1944- *86*
Moore, Eva 1942- *103*
  Earlier sketch in SATA *20*
Moore, Ishbel (Lindsay) 1954- *140*
Moore, Jack (William) 1941- *46*
  Brief entry *32*
Moore, Janet Gaylord 1905-1992 .... *18*
Moore, Jim 1946- *42*
Moore, John Travers 1908- *12*
Moore, Lilian 1909-2004 .... *137*
  Obituary *155*
  Earlier sketch in SATA *52*
  See also CLR *15*
Moore, Liz
  See Moore, M. Elizabeth
Moore, M. Elizabeth 1959- *156*
Moore, Margaret R(umberger) 1903- *12*
Moore, Margie *176*
Moore, Marianne (Craig) 1887-1972 .... *20*
Moore, Patrick (Alfred Caldwell) 1923- *49*
  Brief entry *39*
  See also SAAS *8*
Moore, Patrick 1959- *184*
Moore, Perry *193*
Moore, Peter 1963- *175*
Moore, Peter G.
  See Moore, Peter
Moore, Ray (S.) 1905(?)-1984
  Obituary *37*
Moore, Regina
  See Dunne, Mary Collins
Moore, Rosalie (Gertrude) 1910-2001 .... *9*
Moore, Ruth (Ellen) 1908-1989 .... *23*
Moore, Ruth Nulton 1923- *38*
Moore, S(arah) E. *23*
Moore, Sarah Margaret
  See Hodges, Margaret
Moore, Tara 1950- *61*
Moore, Yvette 1958- *154*
  Earlier sketches in SATA *69, 70*
Moores, Dick
  See Moores, Richard (Arnold)
Moores, Richard (Arnold) 1909-1986
  Obituary *48*
Mooser, Stephen 1941- *75*
  Earlier sketch in SATA *28*
Mora, Francisco X(avier) 1952- *90*
Mora, Pat 1942- *186*
  Earlier sketches in SATA *92, 134*
  See also CLR *58*
Mora, Patricia
  See Mora, Pat
Morales, Yuyi *180*
  Earlier sketch in SATA *154*
Moran, Tom 1943- *60*
Moranville, Sharelle Byars *196*
  Earlier sketch in SATA *152*
Moray Williams, Ursula 1911-2006 .... *3*
  Obituary *177*
  See also SAAS *9*
Mordvinoff, Nicolas 1911-1973 .... *17*
More, Caroline
  See Cone, Molly (Lamken)
  and Strachan, Margaret Pitcairn
Moreno, Rene King *190*

Moreton, Andrew Esq.
  See Defoe, Daniel
Morey, Charles
  See Fletcher, Helen Jill
Morey, Walt(er Nelson) 1907-1992 .... *51*
  Obituary *70*
  Earlier sketch in SATA *3*
  See also SAAS *9*
Morgan, Alfred P(owell) 1889-1972 .... *33*
Morgan, Alison (Mary) 1930- *85*
  Earlier sketch in SATA *30*
Morgan, Anne 1954- *121*
Morgan, Christopher 1956- *199*
Morgan, Clay 1950- *198*
Morgan, Douglas
  See Macdonald, James D.
Morgan, Ellen
  See Bumstead, Kathleen Mary
Morgan, Geoffrey 1916- *46*
Morgan, Helen (Gertrude Louise)
  1921-1990 .... *29*
Morgan, Jane
  See Cooper, James Fenimore
  and Franklin, Jane (Morgan)
  and Moren, Sally M(oore)
Morgan, Lenore H. 1908-1976 .... *8*
Morgan, Mary 1957- *114*
  Earlier sketch in SATA *81*
Morgan, McKayla
  See Basile, Gloria Vitanza
Morgan, Michaela
  See Basile, Gloria Vitanza
Morgan, Nicola 1961- *161*
Morgan, Nina 1953- *110*
Morgan, Pierr 1952- *122*
  Earlier sketch in SATA *77*
Morgan, Robin (Evonne) 1941- *80*
Morgan, Roxanne
  See Gentle, Mary
Morgan, Sarah (Nicola) 1959- *68*
Morgan, Shirley
  See Kiepper, Shirley Morgan
Morgan, Stacy T(owle) 1959- *104*
Morgan, Stevie
  See Davies, Nicola
Morgan, Tom 1942- *42*
Morgan, Wendy
  See Staub, Wendy Corsi
Morgan-Vanroyen, Mary
  See Morgan, Mary
Morgenstern, Susie Hoch 1945- *133*
Mori, Hana 1909-1990(?) *88*
Mori, Kyoko 1957- *122*
  Autobiography Feature *126*
  See also CLR *64*
  See also SAAS *26*
Moriarty, Jaclyn *162*
Moriarty, William J. 1930- *127*
Morice, Dave 1946- *93*
Morin, Isobel V. 1928- *110*
Morine, Hoder
  See Conroy, John Wesley
Morley, Taia *199*
Morley, Wilfred Owen
  See Lowndes, Robert A(ugustine) W(ard)
Morningstar, Mildred (Whaley) 1912-1997 .. *61*
  Obituary *114*
Morozumi, Atsuko *110*
Morpurgo, Michael 1943- *184*
  Earlier sketches in SATA *93, 143*
  See also CLR *51*
Morrah, Dave
  See Morrah, David Wardlaw, Jr.
Morrah, David Wardlaw, Jr. 1914-1991 .... *10*
Morreale-de la Garza, Phyllis
  See De la Garza, Phyllis
Morressy, John 1930-2006 .... *23*
Morrill, Leslie H(olt) 1934-2003 .... *48*
  Brief entry *33*
  Obituary *148*
  See also SAAS *22*

Morris, Chris(topher Crosby) 1946- *66*
Morris, Deborah 1956- *91*
Morris, Desmond 1928- *14*
Morris, Desmond John
  See Morris, Desmond
Morris, Don 1954- *83*
Morris, Gerald 1963- *150*
  Earlier sketch in SATA *107*
Morris, Gerald Paul
  See Morris, Gerald
Morris, Gilbert (Leslie) 1929- *104*
Morris, Jackie *151*
Morris, Janet (Ellen) 1946- *66*
Morris, Jay
  See Tatham, Julie Campbell
Morris, (Margaret) Jean 1924- *98*
Morris, Jeffrey B(randon) 1941- *92*
Morris, Jennifer E. 1969- *179*
Morris, Jill 1936- *165*
  Earlier sketch in SATA *119*
Morris, Juddi *85*
Morris, Judy K. 1936- *61*
Morris, Oradel Nolen *128*
Morris, Robert A(da) 1933- *7*
Morris, William 1913-1994 .... *29*
Morrison, Bill 1935- *66*
  Brief entry *37*
Morrison, Chloe Anthony Wofford
  See Morrison, Toni
Morrison, Dorothy Nafus *29*
Morrison, Frank 1971- *185*
Morrison, Gordon 1944- *183*
  Earlier sketches in SATA *87, 128*
Morrison, Joan 1922- *65*
Morrison, Lillian 1917- *108*
  Earlier sketch in SATA *3*
Morrison, Lucile Phillips 1896- *17*
Morrison, Martha A. 1948- *77*
Morrison, Meighan 1966- *90*
Morrison, P.R. *196*
Morrison, Richard
  See Lowndes, Robert A(ugustine) W(ard)
Morrison, Robert
  See Lowndes, Robert A(ugustine) W(ard)
Morrison, Roberta
  See Webb, Jean Francis (III)
Morrison, Susan Dudley
  See Gold, Susan Dudley
Morrison, Taylor 1971- *187*
  Earlier sketches in SATA *95, 159*
Morrison, Toni 1931- *144*
  Earlier sketch in SATA *57*
  See also CLR *99*
Morrison, Velma Ford 1909- *21*
Morrison, Wilbur Howard 1915- *64*
Morrison, William
  See Samachson, Joseph
Morriss, James E(dward) 1932- *8*
Morrissey, Dean *183*
Morrow, Barbara Olenyik 1952- *167*
Morrow, Betty
  See Bacon, Elizabeth
Morse, Carol
  See Yeakley, Marjory Hall
Morse, Dorothy B(ayley) 1906-1979
  Obituary *24*
Morse, Flo 1921- *30*
Morse, Tony 1953- *129*
Mort, Vivian
  See Cromie, Alice Hamilton
Mortensen, Denise Dowling *179*
Mortimer, Anne 1958- *116*
Mortimer, Mary H.
  See Coury, Louise Andree
Morton, Alexandra (Hubbard) 1957- *144*
Morton, Anthony
  See Arthur, Robert, (Jr.)
Morton, Jane 1931- *50*
Morton, Joseph C. 1932- *156*
Morton, Lee Jack, Jr. 1928- *32*

Morton, Miriam 1918(?)-1985 .... *9*
  Obituary *46*
Mosatche, Harriet
  See Mosatche, Harriet
Mosatche, Harriet 1949- *122*
Moscow, Alvin 1925- *3*
Mosel, Arlene (Tichy) 1921-1996 .... *7*
Moseley, James W(illett) 1931- *139*
Moseng, Elisabeth 1967- *90*
Moser, Barry 1940- *185*
  Earlier sketches in SATA *56, 79, 138*
  See also CLR *49*
  See also SAAS *15*
Moser, Don(ald Bruce) 1932- *31*
Moser, Laura *194*
Moser, Lisa *192*
Moses, Sheila P. 1961- *168*
Moses, Will 1956- *178*
  Earlier sketch in SATA *120*
Mosesson, Gloria R(ubin) *24*
Mosher, Richard 1949- *120*
Moskin, Marietta D(unston) 1928- *23*
Moskof, Martin Stephen 1930- *27*
Mosley, Francis 1957- *57*
Moss, Don(ald) 1920- *11*
Moss, Elaine (Dora) 1924- *57*
  Brief entry *31*
Moss, Jeff(rey) 1942-1998 .... *73*
  Obituary *106*
Moss, Marissa 1959- *163*
  Earlier sketches in SATA *71, 104*
  See also CLR *134*
Moss, Miriam 1955- *140*
  Earlier sketch in SATA *76*
Moss, Thylias 1954- *108*
Moss, Thylias Rebecca Brasier
  See Moss, Thylias
Most, Bernard 1937- *134*
  Brief entry *40*
  Earlier sketches in SATA *48, 91*
Mosz, Gosia 1972- *194*
Mott, Evelyn Clarke 1962- *133*
  Earlier sketch in SATA *75*
Motz, Lloyd 1909-2004 .... *20*
Mould, Edwin
  See Whitlock, Ralph
Mouly, Francoise *155*
Mountain, Robert
  See Montgomery, Raymond A. (Jr.)
Mountfield, David
  See Grant, Neil
Mourlevat, Jean-Claude 1952- *187*
Moussard, Jacqueline 1924- *24*
Mowat, Claire 1933- *123*
Mowat, Claire Angel Wheeler
  See Mowat, Claire
Mowat, Farley 1921- *55*
  Earlier sketch in SATA *3*
  See also CLR *20*
Mowat, Farley McGill
  See Mowat, Farley
Mowll, Joshua 1970(?)- *188*
Mowry, Jess 1960- *131*
  Autobiography Feature *131*
  Earlier sketch in SATA *109*
  See also CLR *65*
Moxley, Sheila 1966- *96*
Moyer, Terry J. 1937- *94*
Moyes, Patricia
  See Haszard, Patricia Moyes
Moyler, Alan (Frank Powell) 1926- *36*
Mozelle, Shirley *179*
Mozley, Charles 1915- *43*
  Brief entry *32*
Mphahlele, Es'kia 1919-2008 .... *119*
  Obituary *198*
Mphahlele, Ezekiel
  See Mphahlele, Es'kia
Mphahlele, Zeke
  See Mphahlele, Es'kia

Mr. McGillicuddy
  See Abisch, Roslyn Kroop
Mr. Sniff
  See Abisch, Roslyn Kroop
Mr. Tivil
  See Lorkowski, Thomas V(incent)
Mr. Wizard
  See Herbert, Don
Mrs. Fairstar
  See Horne, Richard Henry Hengist
Muchamore, Robert 1972- *175*
Muchmore, Jo Ann 1937- *103*
Mude, O.
  See Gorey, Edward (St. John)
Mudgeon, Apeman
  See Mitchell, Adrian
Mueller, Jorg 1942- *67*
  See also CLR *43*
Mueller, Virginia 1924- *28*
Muggs
  See Watkins, Lois
Muir, Diana
  See Appelbaum, Diana Muir Karter
Muir, Frank (Herbert) 1920-1998 .... *30*
Muir, Helen 1937- *65*
Mukerji, Dhan Gopal 1890-1936 .... *40*
  See also CLR *10*
Mulcahy, Lucille Burnett *12*
Mulford, Philippa G. 1948- *112*
  Earlier sketch in SATA *43*
Mulford, Philippa Greene
  See Mulford, Philippa G.
Mulgan, Catherine 1931- *24*
Mulila, Vigad G.
  See Maillu, David G(ian)
Mull, Brandon 1974- *190*
Mullen, Michael 1937- *122*
Muller, Billex
  See Ellis, Edward S(ylvester)
Muller, Jorg
  See Mueller, Jorg
Muller, (Lester) Robin 1953- *86*
Mullin, Caryl Cude 1969- *130*
Mullins, Edward S(wift) 1922- *10*
Mullins, Hilary 1962- *84*
Mulock, Dinah Maria
  See Craik, Dinah Maria (Mulock)
Mulvihill, William Patrick 1923- *8*
Mumford, Ruth
  See Dallas, Ruth
Mumy, Bill 1954- *112*
Mun
  See Leaf, (Wilbur) Munro
Munari, Bruno 1907-1998 .... *15*
  See also CLR *9*
Munce, Ruth Hill 1898- *12*
Mundy, Simon 1954- *64*
Mundy, Simon Andrew James Hainault
  See Mundy, Simon
Munger, Nancy *170*
Munowitz, Ken 1935-1977 .... *14*
Munoz, William 1949- *92*
  Earlier sketch in SATA *42*
Munro, Alice 1931- *29*
Munro, Alice Anne
  See Munro, Alice
Munro, Eleanor 1928- *37*
Munro, Roxie 1945- *184*
  Earlier sketches in SATA *58, 136*
Munsch, Bob
  See Munsch, Robert (Norman)
Munsch, Robert (Norman) 1945- *120*
  Brief entry *48*
  Earlier sketches in SATA *50, 83*
  See also CLR *19*
Munsinger, Lynn 1951- *177*
  Earlier sketches in SATA *33, 94*
Munson, Derek 1970- *139*
Munson, R. W.
  See Karl, Jean E(dna)
Munson-Benson, Tunie 1946- *15*

Munsterberg, Peggy 1921- *102*
Muntean, Michaela *182*
Munthe, Nelly 1947- *53*
Munves, James (Albert) 1922- *30*
Munzer, Martha E. 1899-1999 .... *4*
Murawski, Darlyne A. *193*
Murch, Mel
  See Manes, Stephen
Murdoch, David H(amilton) 1937- *96*
Murdoch, Patricia 1957- *192*
Murdock, Catherine Gilbert *185*
Murhall, J(acqueline) J(ane) 1964- *143*
Murphy, Barbara Beasley 1933- *130*
  Earlier sketch in SATA *5*
Murphy, Claire Rudolf 1951- *137*
  Earlier sketch in SATA *76*
Murphy, E(mmett) Jefferson 1926- *4*
Murphy, Jill (Frances) 1949- *142*
  Earlier sketches in SATA *37, 70*
  See also CLR *39*
Murphy, Jim 1947- *185*
  Brief entry *32*
  Earlier sketches in SATA *37, 77, 124*
  See also CLR *53*
Murphy, Joseph E., Jr. 1930- *65*
Murphy, Kelly 1977- *190*
  Earlier sketch in SATA *143*
Murphy, Louise 1943- *155*
Murphy, Mary 1961- *196*
Murphy, Pat
  See Murphy, E(mmett) Jefferson
Murphy, Patricia J. 1963- *132*
Murphy, Rita *180*
Murphy, Robert (William) 1902-1971 .... *10*
Murphy, Shirley Rousseau 1928- *126*
  Earlier sketches in SATA *36, 71*
  See also SAAS *18*
Murphy, Stuart J. 1942- *157*
  Earlier sketch in SATA *115*
Murphy, Thomas Basil, Jr. 1935- *191*
Murphy, Tim
  See Murphy, Jim
Murphy, Tom
  See Murphy, Thomas Basil, Jr.
Murray, John 1923- *39*
Murray, Kirsty 1960- *165*
  Earlier sketch in SATA *108*
Murray, Marguerite 1917- *63*
Murray, Marian *5*
Murray, Martine 1965- *125*
Murray, (Judith) Michele (Freedman)
  1933-1974 .... *7*
Murray, Ossie 1938- *43*
Murray, Peter
  See Hautman, Pete
Murrow, Liza Ketchum 1946- *132*
  Earlier sketch in SATA *78*
Musgrave, Florence 1902-1999 .... *3*
Musgrove, Margaret W(ynkoop) 1943- *124*
  Earlier sketch in SATA *26*
Mussey, Virginia Howell
  See Ellison, Virginia H(owell)
Mussey, Virginia T.H.
  See Ellison, Virginia H(owell)
Mutel, Cornelia F. 1947- *74*
Muth, Jon J. *165*
Mutz
  See Kuenstler, Morton
Mwangi, Meja 1948- *174*
My Brother's Brother
  See Chekhov, Anton (Pavlovich)
Myers, Anna *160*
Myers, Arthur 1917- *91*
  Earlier sketch in SATA *35*
Myers, Bernice *81*
  Earlier sketch in SATA *9*
Myers, Caroline Elizabeth Clark
  1887-1980 .... *28*
Myers, Christopher 1975- *183*
  See also CLR *97*

Myers, Edward 1950- *172*
  Earlier sketch in SATA *96*
Myers, Elisabeth P(erkins) 1918- *36*
Myers, (Mary) Hortense (Powner)
  1913-1987 .... *10*
Myers, Jack 1913-2006 .... *83*
  Obituary *178*
Myers, Jack Edgar
  See Myers, Jack
Myers, Lou 1915-2005 .... *81*
  Obituary *171*
Myers, Louis
  See Myers, Lou
Myers, R.E. 1924- *119*
Myers, Robert Eugene
  See Myers, R.E.
Myers, Tim 1953- *176*
  Earlier sketch in SATA *147*
Myers, Timothy Joseph
  See Myers, Tim
Myers, Walter Dean 1937- *193*
  Brief entry *27*
  Earlier sketches in SATA *41, 71, 109, 157*
  See also CLR *110*
  See also SAAS *2*
Myers, Walter M.
  See Myers, Walter Dean
Myller, Rolf 1926-2006 .... *27*
  Obituary *175*
Myra, Harold L(awrence) 1939- *46*
  Brief entry *42*
Myracle, Lauren 1969- *162*
Myrus, Donald (Richard) 1927- *23*
Mysterious Traveler, The
  See Arthur, Robert, (Jr.)

N

Na, An *149*
Naaslund, Goorel Kristina 1940- *170*
Nadel, Laurie 1948- *74*
Naden, Corinne J. 1930- *166*
  Earlier sketch in SATA *79*
Nadimi, Suzan *188*
Nagda, Ann Whitehead *199*
Nagel, Andreas Fischer
  See Fischer-Nagel, Andreas
Nagel, Heiderose Fischer
  See Fischer-Nagel, Heiderose
Nagle, Shane *176*
Naidoo, Beverley 1943- *180*
  Earlier sketches in SATA *63, 135*
  See also CLR *29*
Nakae, Noriko 1940- *59*
Nakatani, Chiyoko 1930-1981 .... *55*
  Brief entry *40*
  See also CLR *30*
Nally, Susan W. 1947- *90*
Namioka, Lensey 1929- *157*
  Autobiography Feature *116*
  Earlier sketches in SATA *27, 89*
  See also CLR *48*
  See also SAAS *24*
Namovicz, Gene Inyart 1927- *6*
Nanji, Shenaaz 1954- *131*
Nanogak Agnes 1925- *61*
Napier, Mark
  See Laffin, John (Alfred Charles)
Napoli, Donna Jo 1948- *190*
  Earlier sketches in SATA *92, 137*
  See also CLR *51*
  See also SAAS *23*
Narahashi, Keiko 1959- *115*
  Earlier sketch in SATA *79*
Narayan, Rasipuram Krishnaswami
  See Narayan, R.K.
Narayan, R.K. 1906-2001 .... *62*
Nascimbene, Yan 1949- *173*
  Earlier sketch in SATA *133*

Nash, Bruce M(itchell) 1947- *34*
Nash, Fredric Ogden
  See Nash, Ogden
Nash, Linell
  See Smith, Linell Nash
Nash, Mary (Hughes) 1925- *41*
Nash, Ogden 1902-1971 .... *46*
  Earlier sketch in SATA *2*
Nash, Renea Denise 1963- *81*
Nast, Elsa Ruth
  See Watson, Jane Werner
Nast, Thomas 1840-1902 .... *51*
  Brief entry *33*
Nastick, Sharon 1954- *41*
Natale, Vince *196*
Natarajan, Srividya *187*
Nathan, Adele (Gutman) 1900(?)-1986
  Obituary *48*
Nathan, Amy *155*
  Earlier sketch in SATA *104*
Nathan, Dorothy (Goldeen) (?)-1966 .... *15*
Nathan, Robert (Gruntal) 1894-1985 .... *6*
  Obituary *43*
Nathanson, Laura Walther 1941- *57*
Natti, (Mary) Lee 1919- *67*
  Earlier sketch in SATA *1*
  See also SAAS *3*
Natti, Susanna 1948- *125*
  Earlier sketch in SATA *32*
Nau, Thomas *186*
Naughtie, Eleanor
  See Updale, Eleanor
Naughton, Bill
  See Naughton, William John (Francis)
Naughton, James Franklin 1957- *85*
Naughton, Jim
  See Naughton, James Franklin
Naughton, William John (Francis)
  1910-1992 .... *86*
Navarra, John Gabriel 1927- *8*
Naylor, Penelope 1941- *10*
Naylor, Phyllis 1933- *152*
  Autobiography Feature *152*
  Earlier sketches in SATA *12, 66, 102*
  See also CLR *135*
  See also SAAS *10*
Naylor, Phyllis Reynolds 1933-
  See Naylor, Phyllis
Nazarian, Nikki
  See Nichols, Cecilia Fawn
Nazaroff, Alexander I(vanovich) 1898-1981 .. *4*
Nazoa, Aquiles 1920-1976 .... *198*
Neal, Harry Edward 1906-1993 .... *5*
  Obituary *76*
Neal, Michael
  See Teitelbaum, Michael
Nearing, Penny 1916- *47*
  Brief entry *42*
Nebel, Gustave E. *45*
  Brief entry *33*
Nebel, Mimouca
  See Nebel, Gustave E.
Nee, Kay Bonner *10*
Needham, Kate 1962- *95*
Needle, Jan 1943- *98*
  Earlier sketch in SATA *30*
  See also CLR *43*
  See also SAAS *23*
Needleman, Jacob 1934- *6*
Neel, David 1960- *82*
Neel, Preston 1959- *93*
Negri, Rocco 1932- *12*
Negrin, Fabian 1963- *189*
Neier, Aryeh 1937- *59*
Neigoff, Anne *13*
Neigoff, Mike 1920- *13*
Neilson, Frances Fullerton (Jones)
  1910-2001 .... *14*
Neimark, Anne E. 1935- *145*
  Earlier sketch in SATA *4*

Neimark, Paul G. 1934- *80*
  Brief entry *37*
Neitzel, Shirley 1941- *134*
  Earlier sketch in SATA 77
Nell
  See Hanna, Nell(ie L.)
Nelscott, Kris
  See Rusch, Kristine Kathryn
Nelson, Blake 1960- *177*
Nelson, Catherine Chadwick 1926- *87*
Nelson, Cordner (Bruce) 1918- *54*
  Brief entry *29*
Nelson, Drew 1952- *77*
Nelson, Esther L. 1928- *13*
Nelson, Jim A.
  See Stotter, Mike
Nelson, Julie L. 1970- *117*
Nelson, Kadir *181*
  Earlier sketch in SATA 154
Nelson, Kris
  See Rusch, Kristine Kathryn
Nelson, Lawrence E(rnest) 1928-1977
  Obituary *28*
Nelson, Marilyn 1946- *60*
  Autobiography Feature *180*
Nelson, Mary Carroll 1929- *23*
Nelson, O. Terry 1941- *62*
Nelson, Peter N. 1953- *73*
Nelson, R.A. *197*
Nelson, Richard K(ing) 1941- *65*
Nelson, Robin Laura 1971- *141*
Nelson, Roy Paul 1923- *59*
Nelson, S.D. *181*
Nelson, Sharlene (P.) 1933- *96*
Nelson, Suzanne 1976- *184*
Nelson, Ted (W.) 1931- *96*
Nelson, Theresa 1948- *143*
  Autobiography Feature *143*
  Earlier sketch in SATA 79
Nemeth, Sally *187*
Neri, G. *197*
Neri, Greg
  See Neri, G.
Neri, Gregory
  See Neri, G.
Nerlove, Miriam 1959- *53*
  Brief entry *49*
Nesbit, E. 1858-1924 .... *100*
  See also YABC 1
  See also CLR 70
Nesbit, Edith
  See Nesbit, E.
Nesbit, Troy
  See Folsom, Franklin (Brewster)
Nespojohn, Katherine V(eronica) 1912-1975 . *7*
Ness, Evaline (Michelow) 1911-1986 .... *26*
  Obituary *49*
  Earlier sketch in SATA 1
  See also CLR 6
  See also SAAS 1
Nestor, Larry 1940- *149*
Nestor, William P(rodromos) 1947- *49*
Nethery, Mary *93*
Neubecker, Robert *170*
Neuberger, Julia (Babette Sarah) 1950- *142*
  Earlier sketch in SATA 78
Neufeld, John (Arthur) 1938- *131*
  Autobiography Feature *131*
  Earlier sketches in SATA 6, 81
  See also CLR 52
  See also SAAS 3
Neuhaus, David 1958- *83*
Neumeyer, Peter F(lorian) 1929- *13*
Neurath, Marie (Reidemeister) 1898-1986 ..... *1*
Neuschwander, Cindy 1953- *157*
  Earlier sketch in SATA 107
Neusner, Jacob 1932- *38*
Neville, Charles
  See Bodsworth, (Charles) Fred(erick)
Neville, Emily Cheney 1919- *1*
  See also SAAS 2

Neville, Mary
  See Woodrich, Mary Neville
Nevins, Albert (Francis) J(erome)
  1915-1997 .... *20*
Nevius, Carol 1955- *186*
Newberger, Devra
  See Speregen, Devra Newberger
Newberry, Clare Turlay 1903-1970 .... *1*
  Obituary *26*
Newbery, John 1713-1767 .... *20*
Newbery, Linda 1952- *184*
  Earlier sketch in SATA 142
Newbigging, Martha *198*
Newbold, Greg *199*
Newcomb, Ellsworth
  See Kenny, Ellsworth Newcomb
Newcombe, Eugene A. 1923-1990 .... *45*
  Brief entry *33*
Newcombe, Jack
  See Newcombe, Eugene A.
Newcome, Robert 1955- *91*
Newcome, Zita 1959- *88*
Newell, Crosby
  See Bonsall, Crosby Barbara (Newell)
Newell, Edythe W(eatherford) 1910-1989 .... *11*
Newell, Hope Hockenberry 1896-1965 .... *24*
Newfeld, Frank 1928- *26*
Newgarden, Mark 1959- *194*
Newlon, (Frank) Clarke 1905(?)-1982 .... *6*
  Obituary *33*
Newman, Barbara Johansen *191*
Newman, Daisy 1904-1994 .... *27*
  Obituary *78*
Newman, Gerald 1939- *46*
  Brief entry *42*
Newman, Jerry 1935- *82*
Newman, Leslea 1955- *134*
  Earlier sketches in SATA 71, 128
Newman, Margaret
  See Potter, Margaret (Newman)
Newman, Marjorie *146*
Newman, Matthew (Harrison) 1955- *56*
Newman, Nanette 1934- *162*
Newman, Robert (Howard) 1909-1988 .... *87*
  Obituary *60*
  Earlier sketch in SATA 4
Newman, Shirlee P(etkin) *144*
  Earlier sketches in SATA 10, 90
Newsom, Carol 1948- *92*
  Earlier sketch in SATA 40
Newsom, Tom 1944- *80*
Newth, Mette 1942- *140*
Newton, David E(dward) 1933- *67*
Newton, James R(obert) 1935- *23*
Newton, Robert 1965- *191*
Newton, Suzanne 1936- *77*
  Earlier sketch in SATA 5
Ney, John 1923- *43*
  Brief entry *33*
Nez, John *155*
Ng, Franklin *82*
Nguyen, Vincent *187*
Nichol, B(arrie) P(hillip) 1944-1988 .... *66*
Nicholas, Louise D.
  See Watkins, Dawn L.
Nicholls, Judith (Ann) 1941- *61*
Nichols, Cecilia Fawn 1906-1987 .... *12*
Nichols, Grace 1950- *164*
  Earlier sketch in SATA 98
Nichols, Janet (Louise) 1952- *67*
Nichols, Judy 1947- *124*
Nichols, Leigh
  See Koontz, Dean R.
Nichols, Paul
  See Hawks, Robert
Nichols, Peter
  See Youd, (Christopher) Samuel
Nichols, (Joanna) Ruth 1948- *15*
Nicholson, C. R.
  See Nicole, Christopher (Robin)

Nicholson, Christina
  See Nicole, Christopher (Robin)
Nicholson, Joyce Thorpe 1919- *35*
Nicholson, Lois P. 1949- *88*
Nicholson, Robin
  See Nicole, Christopher (Robin)
Nicholson, William *180*
Nicholson, William 1872-1949
  See CLR 76
Nickel, Barbara 1966- *188*
Nickell, Joe 1944- *167*
  Earlier sketch in SATA 73
Nickelsburg, Janet 1893-1983 .... *11*
Nickerson, Betty 1922- *14*
Nickerson, Elizabeth
  See Nickerson, Betty
Nickl, Barbara (Elisabeth) 1939- *56*
Nicklaus, Carol *62*
  Brief entry *33*
Nickle, John *181*
Nickless, Will 1902-1979(?) *66*
Nic Leodhas, Sorche
  See Alger, Leclaire (Gowans)
Nicol, Ann
  See Turnbull, Ann
Nicolas
  See Mordvinoff, Nicolas
Nicolay, Helen 1866-1954
  See YABC 1
Nicole, Christopher (Robin) 1930- *5*
Nicoll, Helen 1937- *87*
Nicolson, Cynthia Pratt 1949- *141*
Ni Dhuibhne, Eilis 1954- *91*
Niehaus, Paddy Bouma
  See Bouma, Paddy
Nields, Nerissa 1967- *166*
Nielsen, Kay (Rasmus) 1886-1957 .... *16*
  See also CLR 16
Nielsen, Laura F(arnsworth) 1960- *93*
Nielsen, Nancy J. 1951- *77*
Nielsen, Susin 1964- *195*
Nielsen, Virginia
  See McCall, Virginia Nielsen
Nielsen-Fernlund, Susin
  See Nielsen, Susin
Niemann, Christoph 1970- *191*
Nieuwsma, Milton J(ohn) 1941- *142*
Nightingale, Sandy 1953- *76*
Nikolajeva, Maria 1952- *127*
Nikola-Lisa, W. 1951- *180*
  Earlier sketch in SATA 71
Niland, Deborah 1951- *172*
  Earlier sketch in SATA 27
Niland, Kilmeny *75*
Nilsen, Anna 1948- *174*
  Earlier sketch in SATA 96
Nilsson, Eleanor 1939- *117*
  Earlier sketch in SATA 81
  See also SAAS 23
Nilsson, Per 1954- *159*
Nimmo, Jenny 1944- *144*
  Earlier sketch in SATA 87
  See also CLR 44
Nishimura, Kae *196*
Niven, Larry 1938- *171*
  Earlier sketch in SATA 95
Niven, Laurence VanCott
  See Niven, Larry
Nivola, Claire A. 1947- *140*
  Earlier sketch in SATA 84
Nix, Garth 1963- *143*
  Earlier sketch in SATA 97
  See also CLR 68
Nixon, Hershell Howard 1923- *42*
Nixon, Joan Lowery 1927-2003 .... *115*
  Obituary *146*
  Earlier sketches in SATA 8, 44, 78
  See also CLR 24
  See also SAAS 9
Nixon, K.
  See Nixon, Kathleen Irene (Blundell)

Nixon, Kathleen Irene (Blundell)
  1894-1988(?) *14*
  Obituary *59*
Nobisso, Josephine 1953- *121*
  Earlier sketch in SATA *78*
Noble, Iris (Davis) 1922-1986 .... *5*
  Obituary *49*
Noble, Marty 1947- *125*
  Earlier sketch in SATA *97*
Noble, Trinka Hakes 1944- *197*
  Brief entry *37*
  Earlier sketch in SATA *123*
Noda, Takayo 1961- *168*
Nodelman, Perry 1942- *101*
Nodset, Joan L.
  See Lexau, Joan M.
Noel Hume, Ivor 1927- *65*
Noestlinger, Christine
  See Nostlinger, Christine
Noguere, Suzanne 1947- *34*
Nolan, Dennis 1945- *166*
  Brief entry *34*
  Earlier sketches in SATA *42, 92*
Nolan, Han 1956- *157*
  Earlier sketch in SATA *109*
Nolan, Janet 1956- *191*
  Earlier sketch in SATA *145*
Nolan, Jeannette Covert 1897-1974 .... *2*
  Obituary *27*
Nolan, Paul T(homas) 1919- *48*
Nolan, William F(rancis) 1928- *88*
  Brief entry *28*
Nolen, Jerdine 1953- *157*
  Earlier sketch in SATA *105*
Noll, Sally 1946- *82*
Noonan, Brandon 1979- *184*
Noonan, Diana 1960- *146*
Noonan, Julia 1946- *148*
  Earlier sketches in SATA *4, 95*
Norac, Carl 1960- *166*
Norcross, John
  See Conroy, John Wesley
Nordan, Robert W(arren) 1934-2004 ...... *133*
Nordhoff, Charles Bernard 1887-1947 ...... *23*
Nordlicht, Lillian *29*
Nordstrom, Ursula 1910-1988 .... *3*
  Obituary *57*
Nordtvedt, Matilda 1926- *67*
Norling, Beth 1969- *149*
Norman, Charles 1904-1996 .... *38*
  Obituary *92*
Norman, Howard
  See Norman, Howard A.
Norman, Howard A. 1949- *81*
Norman, James
  See Schmidt, James Norman
Norman, Jay
  See Arthur, Robert, (Jr.)
Norman, Lilith 1927- *120*
  Earlier sketch in SATA *86*
Norman, Mary 1931- *36*
Norman, Steve
  See Pashko, Stanley
Norment, Lisa 1966- *91*
Norris, Gunilla Brodde 1939- *20*
North, Andrew
  See Norton, Andre
North, Anthony
  See Koontz, Dean R.
North, Captain George
  See Stevenson, Robert Louis (Balfour)
North, Captain George
  See Stevenson, Robert Louis (Balfour)
North, Howard
  See Trevor, Elleston
North, Joan 1920- *16*
North, Milou
  See Erdrich, Louise
North, Robert
  See Withers, Carl A.

North, Sara
  See Bonham, Barbara Thomas
  and Hager, Jean
North, Sterling 1906-1974 .... *45*
  Obituary *26*
  Earlier sketch in SATA *1*
Northcott, (William) Cecil 1902-1987
  Obituary *55*
Northeast, Brenda V(ictoria) 1948- *106*
Northmore, Elizabeth Florence 1906-1974 . *122*
Norton, Alice Mary
  See Norton, Andre
Norton, Andre 1912-2005 .... *91*
  Earlier sketches in SATA *1, 43*
  See also CLR *50*
Norton, Browning
  See Norton, Frank R. B(rowning)
Norton, Frank R. B(rowning) 1909-1989 ..... *10*
Norton, Mary 1903-1992 .... *60*
  Obituary *72*
  Earlier sketch in SATA *18*
  See also CLR *140*
Nosredna, Trebor
  See Anderson, Bob
Nostlinger, Christine 1936- *162*
  Brief entry *37*
  Earlier sketch in SATA *64*
  See also CLR *12*
Nourse, Alan E(dward) 1928-1992 .... *48*
  See also CLR *33*
Novak, Matt 1962- *165*
  Brief entry *52*
  Earlier sketches in SATA *60, 104*
Novelli, Luca 1947- *61*
Nowell, Elizabeth Cameron *12*
Noyes, Deborah 1965- *194*
  Earlier sketch in SATA *145*
Nugent, Nicholas 1949- *73*
Numeroff, Laura Joffe 1953- *142*
  Earlier sketches in SATA *28, 90*
  See also CLR *85*
Nunes, Lygia Bojunga 1932- *154*
  Earlier sketch in SATA *75*
  See Bojunga, Lygia
Nunn, Laura (Donna) Silverstein 1968- *124*
Nurenberg, Thelma
  See Greenhaus, Thelma Nurenberg
Nurnberg, Maxwell 1897-1984 .... *27*
  Obituary *41*
Nussbaumer, Paul (Edmund) 1934- *16*
Nutt, Ken 1951- *163*
  Earlier sketch in SATA *97*
Nuttall-Smith, Margaret Emily Noel 1919- .. *26*
Nuygen, Mathieu 1967- *80*
Nuzum, K.A. *195*
Nyberg, (Everett Wayne) Morgan 1944- *87*
Nyce, (Nellie) Helene von Strecker
  1885-1969 .... *19*
Nyce, Vera 1862-1925 .... *19*
Nye, Naomi Shihab 1952- *198*
  Earlier sketches in SATA *86, 147*
  See also CLR *59*
Nye, Robert 1939- *6*
Nyikos, Stacy A. 1969- *164*
Nystrom, Carolyn 1940- *130*
  Earlier sketch in SATA *67*

O

Oakes, Elizabeth H. 1964- *132*
Oakes, Vanya 1909-1983 .... *6*
  Obituary *37*
Oakley, Don(ald G.) 1927- *8*
Oakley, Graham 1929- *84*
  Earlier sketch in SATA *30*
  See also CLR *7*
Oakley, Helen (McKelvey) 1906- *10*
Oana, Katherine 1929- *53*
  Brief entry *37*

Oates, Eddie H. 1943- *88*
Oates, Joyce Carol 1938- *159*
Oates, Stephen B(aery) 1936- *59*
Obed, Ellen Bryan 1944- *74*
Oberle, Joseph 1958- *69*
Oberman, Sheldon 1949-2004 .... *85*
  Autobiography Feature *114*
  Obituary *153*
  See also CLR *54*
  See also SAAS *26*
Obligado, Lilian (Isabel) 1931- *61*
  Brief entry *45*
Obrant, Susan 1946- *11*
O'Brian, E.G.
  See Clarke, Arthur C.
O'Brien, Anne Sibley 1952- *80*
  Brief entry *48*
  Earlier sketch in SATA *53*
O'Brien, E.G.
  See Clarke, Arthur C.
O'Brien, Esse Forrester 1895(?)-1975
  Obituary *30*
O'Brien, Patrick 1960- *193*
O'Brien, Robert C.
  See Conly, Robert Leslie
O'Brien, Thomas C(lement) 1938- *29*
O'Callaghan, Julie 1954- *113*
O'Callahan, Jay 1938- *88*
O'Carroll, Ryan
  See Markun, Patricia Maloney
Ochiltree, Dianne 1953- *117*
Ockham, Joan Price
  See Price, Joan
O'Connell, Margaret F(orster) 1935-1977 .... *30*
  Obituary *30*
O'Connell, Peg
  See Ahern, Margaret McCrohan
O'Connell, Rebecca 1968- *130*
O'Connor, Barbara 1950- *193*
  Earlier sketch in SATA *154*
O'Connor, Francine M(arie) 1930- *90*
O'Connor, Genevieve A. 1914- *75*
O'Connor, George *183*
O'Connor, Ian 1965- *188*
O'Connor, Jane 1947- *186*
  Brief entry *47*
  Earlier sketches in SATA *59, 103, 150*
O'Connor, Karen 1938- *89*
  Earlier sketch in SATA *34*
O'Connor, Patrick
  See Wibberley, Leonard (Patrick O'Connor)
O'Connor, Richard 1915-1975
  Obituary *21*
O'Conor, Jane 1958- *78*
Odaga, Asenath (Bole) 1937- *130*
  Earlier sketch in SATA *67*
  See also SAAS *19*
O Danachair, Caoimhin
  See Danaher, Kevin
Odanaka, Barbara *159*
O'Daniel, Janet 1921- *24*
O'Day, Cathy
  See Crane, Barbara (Joyce)
O'Dell, Scott 1898-1989 .... *134*
  Earlier sketches in SATA *12, 60*
  See also CLR *126*
Odenwald, Robert P(aul) 1899-1965 .... *11*
Odgers, Sally
  See Odgers, Sally Farrell
Odgers, Sally Farrell 1957- *139*
  Earlier sketch in SATA *72*
O'Donnell, Dick
  See Lupoff, Richard A(llen)
  and Thompson, Don(ald Arthur)
Odriozola, Elena *186*
Oechsli, Kelly 1918-1999 .... *5*
Oesterle, Virginia Rorby
  See Rorby, Ginny
Ofek, Uriel 1926- *36*
  See also CLR *28*
Offenbacher, Ami 1958- *91*

Offit, Sidney 1928- *10*
Ofosu-Appiah, L(awrence) H(enry) 1920- ... *13*
Ogan, George F. 1912-1983 .... *13*
Ogan, M. G.
    See Ogan, George F.
    and Ogan, Margaret E. (Nettles)
Ogan, Margaret E. (Nettles) 1923-1979 .... *13*
Ogburn, Charlton (Jr.) 1911-1998 .... *3*
    Obituary *109*
Ogburn, Jacqueline K. *162*
Ogilvie, Elisabeth May 1917-2006 .... *40*
    Brief entry *29*
    Obituary *176*
Ogilvy, Gavin
    See Barrie, J(ames) M(atthew)
Ogilvy, Ian 1943- *177*
Ogilvy, Ian Raymond
    See Ogilvy, Ian
Ogle, Lucille Edith 1904-1988
    Obituary *59*
Ogletree, Charles J. 1952- *175*
O'Green, Jennifer
    See Roberson, Jennifer
O'Green, Jennifer Roberson
    See Roberson, Jennifer
O'Hagan, Caroline 1946- *38*
O'Hanlon, Jacklyn
    See Meek, Jacklyn O'Hanlon
O'Hara, Elizabeth
    See Ni Dhuibhne, Eilis
O'Hara, Kenneth
    See Morris, (Margaret) Jean
O'Hara, Mary
    See Alsop, Mary O'Hara
O'Hara (Alsop), Mary
    See Alsop, Mary O'Hara
O'Hare, Jeff(rey A.) 1958- *105*
Ohi, Ruth 1964- *95*
Ohiyesa
    See Eastman, Charles A(lexander)
Ohlsson, Ib 1935- *7*
Ohmi, Ayano 1959- *115*
Ohtomo, Yasuo 1946- *37*
o huigin, sean 1942- *138*
    See also CLR 75
Oiseau
    See Moseley, James W(illett)
Oke, Janette 1935- *97*
O'Keefe, Susan Heyboer *176*
    Earlier sketch in SATA *133*
O'Keeffe, Frank 1938- *99*
O'Kelley, Mattie Lou 1908-1997 .... *97*
    Earlier sketch in SATA *36*
Okimoto, Jean Davies 1942- *103*
    Earlier sketch in SATA *34*
Okomfo, Amasewa
    See Cousins, Linda
olafsdottir, Gudrun Elin
    See Gunnella
Olaleye, Isaac O. 1941- *96*
    See also SAAS 23
Olcott, Frances Jenkins 1872(?)-1963 .... *19*
Old, Wendie C(orbin) 1943- *154*
Old Boy
    See Hughes, Thomas
Oldenburg, E(gbert) William 1936-1974 ...... *35*
Older, Effin 1942- *114*
Older, Jules 1940- *156*
    Earlier sketch in SATA *114*
Oldfield, Jenny 1949- *140*
Oldfield, Margaret J(ean) 1932- *56*
Oldfield, Pamela 1931- *86*
Oldham, June *70*
Oldham, Mary 1944- *65*
Olds, Elizabeth 1896-1991 .... *3*
    Obituary *66*
Olds, Helen Diehl 1895-1981 .... *9*
    Obituary *25*
Oldstyle, Jonathan
    See Irving, Washington
O'Leary, Brian (Todd) 1940- *6*

O'Leary, Patsy B(aker) 1937- *97*
Oliphant, B.J.
    See Tepper, Sheri S.
Oliver, Burton
    See Burt, Olive Woolley
Oliver, Chad
    See Oliver, Symmes C(hadwick)
Oliver, John Edward 1933- *21*
Oliver, Marilyn Tower 1935- *89*
Oliver, Narelle 1960- *197*
    Earlier sketch in SATA *152*
Oliver, Shirley (Louise Dawkins) 1958- *74*
Oliver, Symmes C(hadwick) 1928-1993 .... *101*
Oliviero, Jamie 1950- *84*
Olmsted, Lorena Ann 1890-1989 .... *13*
Olney, Ross R. 1929- *13*
Olschewski, Alfred (Erich) 1920- *7*
Olsen, Barbara *148*
Olsen, Carol 1945- *89*
Olsen, Ib Spang 1921- *81*
    Earlier sketch in SATA *6*
Olsen, Violet (Mae) 1922-1991 .... *58*
Olson, Arielle North 1932- *67*
Olson, David J. 1974- *198*
Olson, Gene 1922- *32*
Olson, Gretchen *187*
Olson, Helen Kronberg *48*
Olson, Kay Melchisedech 1948- *175*
Olson, Marianne
    See Mitchell, Marianne
Olson-Brown, Ellen 1967- *183*
Olten, Manuela 1970- *197*
Olugebefola, Ademole 1941- *15*
Oluonye, Mary N(kechi) 1955- *111*
Om
    See Gorey, Edward (St. John)
O'Malley, Kevin 1961- *191*
    Earlier sketch in SATA *157*
Oman, Carola (Mary Anima) 1897-1978 ..... *35*
O'Mara, Carmel 1965- *166*
O'Mara-Horwitz, Carmel
    See O'Mara, Carmel
O'Meara, Walter (Andrew) 1897-1989 .... *65*
Ommanney, F(rancis) D(ownes) 1903-1980 . *23*
O Mude
    See Gorey, Edward (St. John)
Oneal, Elizabeth 1934- *82*
    Earlier sketch in SATA *30*
    See also CLR 13
O'Neal, Reagan
    See Jordan, Robert
O'Neal, Regan
    See Jordan, Robert
Oneal, Zibby
    See Oneal, Elizabeth
O'Neill, Amanda 1951- *111*
O'Neill, Gerard K(itchen) 1927-1992 .... *65*
O'Neill, Judith (Beatrice) 1930- *34*
O'Neill, Mary L(e Duc) 1908(?)-1990 .... *2*
    Obituary *64*
O'Neill, Reagan
    See Jordan, Robert
Onslow, Annette Rosemary MacArthur
    See MacArthur-Onslow, Annette Rosemary
Onslow, John 1906-1985
    Obituary *47*
Onyefulu, Ifeoma 1959- *157*
    Earlier sketches in SATA *81, 115*
Opie, Iona (Margaret Balfour) 1923- *118*
    Earlier sketches in SATA *3, 63*
    See also SAAS 6
Opie, Peter (Mason) 1918-1982 .... *118*
    Obituary *28*
    Earlier sketches in SATA *3, 63*
Oppel, Kenneth 1967- *199*
    Earlier sketches in SATA *99, 153*
Oppel, Kenneth Kerry
    See Oppel, Kenneth
Oppenheim, Joanne 1934- *174*
    Earlier sketches in SATA *5, 82, 136*
Oppenheim, Shulamith Levey 1928- *177*

Oppenheimer, Joan L(etson) 1925- *28*
Oppong, Joseph Ransford 1953- *160*
Optic, Oliver
    See Adams, William Taylor
    and Stratemeyer, Edward L.
Oram, Hiawyn 1946- *101*
    Earlier sketch in SATA *56*
Orbach, Ruth Gary 1941- *21*
Orback, Craig *197*
Orczy, Emma
    See Orczy, Baroness Emmuska
Orczy, Emma Magdalena Rosalia Maria Josefa
    See Orczy, Baroness Emmuska
Orczy, Emmuska
    See Orczy, Baroness Emmuska
Orczy, Baroness Emmuska 1865-1947 .... *40*
Orde, A.J.
    See Tepper, Sheri S.
O'Reilly, Jackson
    See Jordan, Robert
Orenstein, Denise Gosliner 1950- *157*
Orgad, Dorit 1936- *199*
Orgel, Doris 1929- *148*
    Earlier sketches in SATA *7, 85*
    See also CLR 48
    See also SAAS 19
Orgill, Roxane *198*
Oriolo, Joe
    See Oriolo, Joseph D.
Oriolo, Joseph D. 1913-1985
    Obituary *46*
Orleans, Ilo 1897-1962 .... *10*
Orlev, Uri 1931- *135*
    Earlier sketch in SATA *58*
    See also CLR 30
    See also SAAS 19
Ormai, Stella *57*
    Brief entry *48*
Ormerod, Jan 1946- *132*
    Brief entry *44*
    Earlier sketches in SATA *55, 70*
    See also CLR 20
Ormes, Jackie
    See Ormes, Zelda J.
Ormes, Zelda J. 1914-1986
    Obituary *47*
Ormondroyd, Edward 1925- *14*
Ormsby, Virginia H(aire) 1906-1990 .... *11*
Orona-Ramirez, Kristy 1964- *189*
Orozco, Jose-Luis 1948- *179*
Orr, Katherine S(helley) 1950- *72*
Orr, Wendy 1953- *141*
    Earlier sketch in SATA *90*
Orris
    See Ingelow, Jean
Orth, Richard
    See Gardner, Richard (M.)
Ortiz Cofer, Judith
    See Cofer, Judith Ortiz
Orwell, George
    See Blair, Eric (Arthur)
Orwin, Joanna 1944- *141*
Osborn, Elinor 1939- *145*
Osborn, Kathy 1955(?)- *199*
Osborn, Lois D(orothy) 1915- *61*
Osborne, Charles 1927- *59*
Osborne, Chester G(orham) 1915-1987 .... *11*
Osborne, David
    See Silverberg, Robert
Osborne, George
    See Silverberg, Robert
Osborne, Leone Neal 1914-1996 .... *2*
Osborne, Mary Pope 1949- *144*
    Earlier sketches in SATA *41, 55, 98*
    See also CLR 88
Osceola
    See Blixen, Karen (Christentze Dinesen)
Osgood, William E(dward) 1926- *37*
O'Shaughnessy, Darren
    See Shan, Darren
O'Shaughnessy, Ellen Cassels 1937- *78*

O'Shea, Catherine Patricia Shiels
  See O'Shea, Pat
O'Shea, Pat 1931-2007 87
  See also CLR 18
Osmond, Edward 1900- 10
Ossoli, Sarah Margaret (Fuller) 1810-1850 .. 25
Ostendorf, (Arthur) Lloyd, (Jr.) 1921-2000 .. 65
  Obituary 125
Ostow, Micol 1976- 170
Otfinoski, Steven 1949- 116
  Earlier sketch in SATA 56
Otis, James
  See Kaler, James Otis
O'Toole, Thomas 1941- 71
O'Trigger, Sir Lucius
  See Horne, Richard Henry Hengist
Otten, Charlotte
  See Otten, Charlotte F.
Otten, Charlotte F. 1926- 98
Otten, Charlotte Fennema
  See Otten, Charlotte F.
Ottley, Matt 1962- 171
  Earlier sketch in SATA 102
Ottley, Reginald Leslie 1909-1985 26
  See also CLR 16
Otto, Margaret Glover 1909-1976
  Obituary 30
Otto, Svend
  See Soerensen, Svend Otto
Oughton, Jerrie (Preston) 1937- 131
  Earlier sketch in SATA 76
Oughton, (William) Taylor 1925- 104
Ouida
  See De La Ramee, Marie Louise
Ousley, Odille 1896-1976 10
Outcalt, Todd 1960- 123
Overmyer, James E. 1946- 88
Overton, Jenny (Margaret Mary) 1942- 52
  Brief entry 36
Owen, Ann
  See Qualey, Marsha
Owen, Annie 1949- 75
Owen, Caroline Dale
  See Snedeker, Caroline Dale (Parke)
Owen, Clifford
  See Hamilton, Charles (Harold St. John)
Owen, Dilys
  See Gater, Dilys
Owen, (Benjamin) Evan 1918-1984 38
Owen, (John) Gareth 1936-2002 162
  Earlier sketch in SATA 83
  See also CLR 31
  See also SAAS 14
Owen, James A. 185
Owens, Bryant 1968- 116
Owens, Dana Elaine
  See Queen Latifah
Owens, Gail 1939- 54
Owens, Mary Beth 191
Owens, Thomas S(heldon) 1960- 86
Owens, Tom
  See Owens, Thomas S(heldon)
Oxenbury, Helen 1938- 149
  Earlier sketches in SATA 3, 68
  See also CLR 70
Oxendine, Bess Holland 1933- 90
Oz, Frank (Richard) 1944- 60
Ozer, Jerome S. 1927- 59

                          P

Paananen, Eloise (Katherine) 1923-1993 9
Pace, Lorenzo 1943- 131
Pace, Mildred Mastin 1907- 46
  Brief entry 29
Pachter, Hedwig (?)-1988 63
Pack, Janet 1952- 77
Pack, Robert 1929- 118

Packard, Edward 1931- 148
  Earlier sketches in SATA 47, 90
Packer, Kenneth L. 1946- 116
Packer, Vin
  See Meaker, Marijane
Pad, Peter
  See Stratemeyer, Edward L.
Page, Eileen
  See Heal, Edith
Page, Eleanor
  See Coerr, Eleanor (Beatrice)
Page, Jake 1936- 81
Page, James Keena, Jr.
  See Page, Jake
Page, Lou Williams 1912-1997 38
Page, Mary
  See Heal, Edith
Page, Robin 1943- 154
Pagnucci, Susan 1944- 90
Pahlen, Kurt 1907-2003
  Obituary 147
Pahz, Cheryl
  See Pahz, Cheryl Suzanne
Pahz, Cheryl Suzanne 1949- 11
Pahz, James Alon 1943- 11
Paice, Margaret 1920- 10
Paige, Harry W(orthington) 1922- 41
  Brief entry 35
Paige, Richard
  See Koontz, Dean R.
Paige, Robin
  See Albert, Susan Wittig
Paine, Penelope Colville 1946- 87
Paine, Roberta M. 1925- 13
Paisley, Tom 1932- 11
  See also CLR 3
Palatini, Margie 174
  Earlier sketch in SATA 134
Palazzo, Anthony D.
  See Palazzo, Tony
Palazzo, Tony 1905-1970 3
Palder, Edward L. 1922- 5
Palecek, Josef 1932- 56
Palecek, Libuse 1937- 89
Palen, Debbie 195
Palin, Michael 1943- 67
Palin, Michael Edward
  See Palin, Michael
Palladini, David (Mario) 1946- 40
  Brief entry 32
Pallas, Norvin 1918-1983 23
Pallister, John C(lare) 1891-1980
  Obituary 26
Pallotta, Gerard Larry
  See Pallotta, Jerry
Pallotta, Jerry 1953- 186
Pallotta-Chiarolli, Maria 1960- 117
Palmer, Bernard (Alvin) 1914-1998 26
Palmer, C. Everard 1930- 14
Palmer, (Ruth) Candida 1926- 11
Palmer, Cyril Everard
  See Palmer, C. Everard
Palmer, Don
  See Benson, Mildred (Augustine Wirt)
Palmer, Hap 1942- 68
Palmer, Heidi 1948- 15
Palmer, Helen Marion
  See Geisel, Helen
Palmer, Jessica 1953- 120
Palmer, Judd 1972- 153
Palmer, Juliette 1930- 15
Palmer, Kate Salley 1946- 97
Palmer, Maria
  See Strachan, Ian
Palmer, Maria
  See Brennan, Herbie
Palmer, Robin 1909-2000 43
Palmero Caceres, Ana 198
Paltrowitz, Donna 1950- 61
  Brief entry 50

Paltrowitz, Donna Milman
  See Paltrowitz, Donna
Paltrowitz, Stuart 1946- 61
  Brief entry 50
Pamintuan, Macky 178
Panagopoulos, Janie Lynn 149
Panati, Charles 1943- 65
Panchyk, Richard 1970- 138
Panetta, George 1915-1969 15
Panetta, Joseph N. 1953- 96
Panik, Sharon 1952- 82
Panowski, Eileen Thompson 1920- 49
Pansy
  See Alden, Isabella (Macdonald)
Pantell, Dora (Fuchs) 39
Panter, Carol 1936- 9
Paolini, Christopher 1983- 157
  See also CLR 102
Papademetriou, Lisa 175
Paparone, Pam 185
Paparone, Pamela
  See Paparone, Pam
Papas, Bill
  See Papas, William
Papas, William 1927-2000 50
Papashvily, George 1898-1978 17
Papashvily, Helen (Waite) 1906-1996 17
Pape, D. L.
  See Pape, Donna (Lugg)
Pape, Donna (Lugg) 1930- 82
  Earlier sketch in SATA 2
Paperny, Myra (Green) 1932- 51
  Brief entry 33
Paradis, Adrian A(lexis) 1912- 67
  Earlier sketch in SATA 1
  See also SAAS 8
Paradis, Marjorie Bartholomew
  1886(?)-1970 17
Paradiz, Valerie 1963- 176
Parenteau, Shirley 1935- 199
  Brief entry 40
  Earlier sketch in SATA 47
Parish, Margaret (Cecile) 1927-1988 73
  Obituary 59
  Earlier sketch in SATA 17
  See also CLR 22
Parish, Margaret Holt
  See Holt, Margaret
Parish, Peggy
  See Parish, Margaret (Cecile)
Park, Barbara 1947- 123
  Brief entry 35
  Earlier sketches in SATA 40, 78
  See also CLR 34
Park, Bill
  See Park, W(illiam) B(ryan)
Park, Frances 1955- 171
Park, Ginger 173
Park, Janie Jaehyun 150
Park, Jordan
  See Kornbluth, C(yril) M.
  and Pohl, Frederik
Park, Linda Sue 1960- 173
  Earlier sketch in SATA 127
  See also CLR 84
Park, Nick 1958- 113
Park, (Rosina) Ruth (Lucia) 1923(?)- 93
  Earlier sketch in SATA 25
  See also CLR 51
Park, W(illiam) B(ryan) 1936- 22
Parke, Marilyn 1928- 82
Parker, Barbara Keevil 1938- 157
Parker, Daniel
  See Ehrenhaft, Daniel
Parker, Elinor Milnor 1906- 3
Parker, Julie F. 1961- 92
Parker, Kim 1963- 174
Parker, Kristy 1957- 59
Parker, Lois M(ay) 1912-1996 30
Parker, Margot M. 1937- 52
Parker, Marjorie Blain 1960- 145

Parker, Mary Jessie 1948- 71
Parker, Nancy Winslow 1930- 132
   Earlier sketches in SATA 10, 69
   See also SAAS 20
Parker, Richard 1915-1990 14
Parker, Robert
   See Boyd, Waldo T.
Parker, Toni Trent 1947-2005 142
   Obituary 169
Parker-Rees, Guy 193
Parkes, Lucas
   See Harris, John (Wyndham Parkes Lucas)
   Beynon
Parkhill, John
   See Cox, William R(obert)
Parkins, David 1955- 176
Parkinson, Ethelyn M(inerva) 1906-1999 11
Parkinson, Kathryn N. 1954- 71
Parkinson, Kathy
   See Parkinson, Kathryn N.
Parkinson, Siobhan
   See Parkinson, Siobhan
Parkinson, Siobhan 1954- 178
Parks, Deborah A. 1948- 133
   Earlier sketch in SATA 91
Parks, Edd Winfield 1906-1968 10
Parks, Gordon 1912-2006 108
   Obituary 175
   Earlier sketch in SATA 8
Parks, Gordon Roger Alexander
   See Parks, Gordon
Parks, Peggy J. 1951- 143
Parks, PJ
   See Parks, Peggy J.
Parks, Rosa 1913-2005 83
   Obituary 169
Parks, Rosa Louise Lee
   See Parks, Rosa
Parks, Van Dyke 1943- 62
Parley, Peter
   See Goodrich, Samuel Griswold
Parlin, John
   See Graves, Charles Parlin
Parme, Fabrice 1966- 191
Parnall, Peter 1936- 69
   Earlier sketch in SATA 16
   See also SAAS 11
Parotti, Phillip (Elliott) 1941- 109
Parr, Ann 1943- 144
Parr, Danny
   See Parr, Ann
Parr, Letitia (Evelyn) 1906-1985(?) 37
Parr, Lucy 1924- 10
Parr, Todd 179
   Earlier sketch in SATA 134
Parrish, Anne 1888-1957 27
Parrish, Mary
   See Cousins, Margaret
Parrish, Maxfield
   See Parrish, (Frederick) Maxfield
Parrish, (Frederick) Maxfield 1870-1966 14
Parry, Marian 1924- 13
Parson Lot
   See Kingsley, Charles
Parsons, Alexandra 1947- 92
Parsons, Ellen
   See Dragonwagon, Crescent
Parsons, Garry 197
Parsons, Martin 1951- 116
Parsons, Martin Leslie
   See Parsons, Martin
Parsons, Tom
   See MacPherson, Thomas George
Parsons-Yazzi, Evangeline 172
Partch, Virgil Franklin II 1916-1984 39
   Obituary 39
Parton, Dolly 1946- 94
Parton, Dolly Rebecca
   See Parton, Dolly
Partridge, Benjamin W., Jr. 1915-2005 28
   Obituary 163

Partridge, Benjamin Waring, Jr.
   See Partridge, Benjamin W., Jr.
Partridge, Cora Cheney
   See Cheney, Cora
Partridge, Elizabeth 134
Partridge, Jenny (Lilian) 1947- 52
   Brief entry 37
Pasachoff, Naomi 1947- 147
Pascal, David 1918- 14
Pascal, Francine 1938- 143
   Brief entry 37
   Earlier sketches in SATA 51, 80
   See also CLR 25
Paschal, Nancy
   See Trotter, Grace V(iolet)
Paschkis, Julie 1957- 177
Pascudniak, Pascal
   See Lupoff, Richard A(llen)
Pashko, Stanley 1913-1982 29
Passailaigue, Thomas E.
   See Paisley, Tom
Pateman, Robert 1954- 84
Patent, Dorothy Hinshaw 1940- 162
   Autobiography Feature 162
   Earlier sketches in SATA 22, 69, 120
   See also CLR 19
   See also SAAS 13
Paterson, A(ndrew) B(arton) 1864-1941 97
Paterson, Banjo
   See Paterson, A(ndrew) B(arton)
Paterson, Diane 1946- 177
   Brief entry 33
   Earlier sketch in SATA 59
Paterson, John (Barstow) 1932- 114
Paterson, Katherine 1932- 133
   Earlier sketches in SATA 13, 53, 92
   See also CLR 127
Paterson, Katherine Womeldorf
   See Paterson, Katherine
Patience, John 1949- 90
Patneaude, David 1944- 159
   Earlier sketch in SATA 85
Paton, Alan 1903-1988 11
   Obituary 56
Paton, Alan Stewart
   See Paton, Alan
Paton, Jane (Elizabeth) 1934- 35
Paton, Priscilla 1952- 98
Paton Walsh, Gillian
   See Paton Walsh, Jill
Paton Walsh, Jill 1937- 190
   Autobiography Feature 190
   Earlier sketches in SATA 4, 72, 109
   See also CLR 128
   See also SAAS 3
Patrick, Susan
   See Clark, Patricia Denise
Patron, Susan 1948- 182
   Earlier sketch in SATA 76
Patsauq, Markoosie 1942-
   See CLR 23
Patschke, Steve 1955- 125
Patten, Brian 1946- 152
   Earlier sketch in SATA 29
Patterson, Charles 1935- 59
Patterson, Geoffrey 1943- 54
   Brief entry 44
Patterson, James 1947- 197
   Earlier sketch in SATA 164
Patterson, James B.
   See Patterson, James
Patterson, Lillie G. -1999 88
   Earlier sketch in SATA 14
Patterson, Nancy Ruth 1944- 148
   Earlier sketch in SATA 72
Pattison, Darcy (S.) 1954- 126
   Earlier sketch in SATA 72
Pattou, Edith 164
Patz (Blaustein), Nancy 154
Paul, Aileen 1917- 12
Paul, Alison 196

Paul, Ann Whitford 1941- 168
   Earlier sketches in SATA 76, 110
Paul, David (Tyler) 1934-1988
   Obituary 56
Paul, Dominique 1973- 184
Paul, Elizabeth
   See Crow, Donna Fletcher
Paul, Hamish Vigne Christie 1951- 151
   See also CLR 87
Paul, James 1936- 23
Paul, Korky
   See Paul, Hamish Vigne Christie
Paul, Robert
   See Roberts, John G(aither)
Paul, Tessa 1944- 103
Pauli, Hertha (Ernestine) 1909-1973 3
   Obituary 26
Paull, Grace A. 1898- 24
Paulsen, Gary 1939- 189
   Earlier sketches in SATA 22, 50, 54, 79, 111, 158
   See also CLR 82
Paulson, Jack
   See Jackson, C(aary) Paul
Pauquet, Gina Ruck
   See Ruck-Pauquet, Gina
Pausacker, Jenny 1948- 72
   See also SAAS 23
Pausewang, Gudrun 1928- 165
   Earlier sketch in SATA 104
Pavel, Frances 1907- 10
Paver, Michelle 170
Paxton, Thomas R. 1937- 70
Paxton, Tom
   See Paxton, Thomas R.
Paye, Won-Ldy 185
Payne, Alan
   See Jakes, John
Payne, Bernal C., Jr. 1941- 60
Payne, C. Douglas
   See Payne, C.D.
Payne, C.D. 1949- 133
Payne, C.F. 1956- 179
Payne, Chris Fox
   See Payne, C.F.
Payne, Donald Gordon 1924- 37
Payne, Emmy
   See West, Emily Govan
Payne, Nina 135
Payne, Rachel Ann
   See Jakes, John
Payson, Dale 1943- 9
Payzant, Charles 18
Paz, A.
   See Pahz, James Alon
Paz, Natalia Toledo
   See Toledo, Natalia
Paz, Zan
   See Pahz, Cheryl Suzanne
Peace, Mary
   See Finley, Mary Peace
Peacock, Shane 1957- 192
Peake, Mervyn 1911-1968 23
Peale, Norman Vincent 1898-1993 20
   Obituary 78
Pearce, Ann Philippa
   See Pearce, Philippa
Pearce, Emily Smith 1975- 199
Pearce, Jacqueline 1962- 146
Pearce, Margaret 104
Pearce, Philippa 1920-2006 129
   Obituary 179
   Earlier sketches in SATA 1, 67
   See also CLR 9
Peare, Catherine Owens 1911- 9
Pearsall, Shelley 1966- 190
Pearson, Gayle 1947- 119
   Earlier sketch in SATA 53
Pearson, Jean Mary
   See Gardam, Jane

Pearson, Kit 1947- 77
    Autobiography Feature 117
    See also CLR 26
Pearson, Mary E. 1955- 134
Pearson, Ridley 1953- 182
Pearson, Susan 1946- 166
    Brief entry 27
    Earlier sketches in SATA 39, 91
Pearson, Tracey Campbell 1956- 155
    Earlier sketch in SATA 64
Pease, (Clarence) Howard 1894-1974 2
    Obituary 25
Peavy, Linda 1943- 54
Peck, Anne Merriman 1884-1976 18
Peck, Beth 1957- 190
    Earlier sketch in SATA 79
Peck, Jan 159
Peck, Jeanie J. 1967- 147
Peck, Marshall III 1951- 92
Peck, Richard 1934- 190
    Autobiography Feature 110
    Earlier sketches in SATA 18, 55, 97, 110, 158
    See also CLR 15
    See also SAAS 2
Peck, Richard Wayne
    See Peck, Richard
Peck, Robert Newton 1928- 156
    Autobiography Feature 108
    Earlier sketches in SATA 21, 62, 111
    See also CLR 45
    See also SAAS 1
Peck, Sylvia 1953- 133
Peck-Whiting, Jeanie J.
    See Peck, Jeanie J.
Peddicord, Jane Ann 199
Pedersen, Janet 193
Pederson, Sharleen
    See Collicott, Sharleen
Pedler, Caroline 197
Peebles, Anne
    See Galloway, Priscilla
Peek, Merle 1938- 39
Peel, John 1954- 79
Peel, Norman Lemon
    See Hirsch, Phil
Peeples, Edwin A(ugustus, Jr.) 1915-1994 6
Peers, Judi 1956- 119
Peers, Judith May West
    See Peers, Judi
Peet, Bill
    See Peet, William Bartlett
Peet, Creighton B. 1899-1977 30
Peet, Mal 171
Peet, Malcolm
    See Peet, Mal
Peet, William Bartlett 1915-2002 78
    Obituary 137
    Earlier sketches in SATA 2, 41
    See also CLR 12
Peguero, Leone 116
Pelaez, Jill 1924- 12
Pelham, David 1938- 70
Pell, Ed(ward) 1950- 157
Pelletier, Andrew T. 195
Pelletier, Andrew Thomas
    See Pelletier, Andrew T.
Pellowski, Anne 1933- 20
Pellowski, Michael (Joseph) 1949- 151
    Brief entry 48
    Earlier sketch in SATA 88
Pellowski, Michael Morgan
    See Pellowski, Michael (Joseph)
Pelta, Kathy 1928- 18
Peltier, Leslie C(opus) 1900-1980 13
Pemberton, Bonnie 191
Pemberton, John Leigh
    See Leigh-Pemberton, John
Pembury, Bill
    See Groom, Arthur William
Pemsteen, Hans
    See Manes, Stephen

Pendennis, Arthur Esquir
    See Thackeray, William Makepeace
Pender, Lydia Podger 1907- 61
Pendery, Rosemary (Schmitz) 7
Pendle, Alexy 1943- 29
Pendle, George 1906-1977
    Obituary 28
Pendleton, Don
    See Cunningham, Chet
    and Garside, (Clifford) Jack
    and Jagninski, Tom
    and Krauzer, Steven M(ark)
    and Obstfeld, Raymond
Pendziwol, Jean E. 1965- 177
Pene du Bois, William (Sherman)
    1916-1993 68
    Obituary 74
    Earlier sketch in SATA 4
    See also CLR 1
Penn, Audrey 1950- 22
Penn, Ruth Bonn
    See Rosenberg, Eth(el) Clifford
Pennac, Daniel 1944- 155
Pennage, E. M.
    See Finkel, George (Irvine)
Penner, Fred 1946- 169
    Earlier sketch in SATA 67
Penner, Frederick Ralph Cornelius
    See Penner, Fred
Penney, Grace Jackson 1904-2000 35
Penney, Ian 1960- 76
Penney, Sue 1957- 152
    Earlier sketch in SATA 102
Pennington, Eunice 1923- 27
Pennington, Lillian Boyer 1904-2003 45
Pennypacker, Sara 1951- 187
Penrose, Gordon 1925- 66
Penson, Mary E. 1917- 78
Penzler, Otto 1942- 38
Pepe, Phil 1935- 20
Pepe, Philip
    See Pepe, Phil
Peppe, Rodney (Darrell) 1934- 74
    Earlier sketch in SATA 4
    See also SAAS 10
Pepper, Frank S. 1910-1988
    Obituary 61
Percy, Charles Henry
    See Smith, Dorothy Gladys
Percy, Rachel 1930- 63
Perdrizet, Marie-Pierre 1952- 79
Perenyi, Constance 1954- 93
Perenyi, Constance Marie
    See Perenyi, Constance
Perera, Hilda 1926- 105
Perera, Thomas Biddle 1938- 13
Peretti, Frank E. 1951- 141
    Earlier sketch in SATA 80
Perez, L. King 1940- 199
Perez, Lana
    See Perez, Marlene
Perez, Lucia Angela 1973- 182
Perez, Marlene 170
Pericoli, Matteo 1968- 178
Perkins, Al(bert Rogers) 1904-1975 30
Perkins, Lucy Fitch 1865-1937 72
Perkins, Lynne Rae 172
    Earlier sketch in SATA 131
Perkins, (Richard) Marlin 1905-1986 21
    Obituary 48
Perkins, Mitali 1963- 188
    Earlier sketch in SATA 88
Perks, Anne-Marie 1955- 122
Perl, Erica S. 188
Perl, Lila 72
    Earlier sketch in SATA 6
Perl, Susan 1922-1983 22
    Obituary 34
Perlman, Rhea 1948- 183
Perlmutter, O(scar) William 1920-1975 8
Pernu, Dennis 1970- 87

Perrault, Charles 1628-1703 25
    See also CLR 134
Perret, Delphine 1980- 190
Perret, Gene (Richard) 1937- 76
Perrine, Mary 1913-1976 2
Perrins, Lesley 1953- 56
Perrow, Angeli 1954- 121
Perry, Andrea 1956- 190
    Earlier sketch in SATA 148
Perry, Barbara Fisher
    See Fisher, Barbara
Perry, Elizabeth 1959- 174
Perry, Elizabeth Goodwin
    See Perry, Elizabeth
Perry, Marie Fritz 165
Perry, Patricia 1949- 30
Perry, Phyllis J(ean) 1933- 152
    Earlier sketches in SATA 60, 101
Perry, Ritchie (John Allen) 1942- 105
Perry, Roger 1933- 27
Perry, Steve(n Carl) 1947- 76
Pershall, Mary K. 1951- 172
    Earlier sketch in SATA 70
Pershing, Marie
    See Schultz, Pearle Henriksen
Perske, Robert 1927- 57
Persun, Morgan Reed
    See Watkins, Dawn L.
Petach, Heidi 149
Peter
    See Stratemeyer, Edward L.
Peters, Alexander
    See Hollander, Zander
Peters, Andrew Fusek 1965- 169
    Earlier sketch in SATA 107
Peters, Caroline
    See Betz, Eva Kelly
Peters, David
    See David, Peter
Peters, Elizabeth 1927- 49
Peters, Emma
    See Price, Karen
Peters, Gabriel
    See Matott, Justin
Peters, Julie Anne 1952- 197
    Earlier sketches in SATA 82, 128
Peters, Linda
    See Catherall, Arthur
Peters, Lisa Westberg 1951- 161
    Earlier sketches in SATA 74, 115
Peters, Patricia 1953- 84
Peters, Russell M. 1929- 78
Peters, S. H.
    See Henry, O.
    and Proffitt, Nicholas
Petersen, David 1946- 109
    Earlier sketch in SATA 62
Petersen, Gwenn Boardman 1924- 12
Petersen, P(eter) J(ames) 1941- 118
    Brief entry 43
    Earlier sketches in SATA 48, 83
Petersen, Palle 1943- 85
Petersham, Maud (Sylvia Fuller)
    1890-1971 17
    See also CLR 24
Petersham, Miska 1888-1960 17
    See also CLR 24
Peterson, Cris 1952- 174
    Earlier sketches in SATA 84, 145
Peterson, Dawn 1934- 86
Peterson, Esther (Allen) 1934- 35
Peterson, Hans 1922- 8
Peterson, Harold L(eslie) 1922-1978 8
Peterson, Helen Stone 1910- 8
Peterson, Jean Sunde 1941- 108
Peterson, Jeanne Whitehouse 1939- 159
    Earlier sketch in SATA 29
Peterson, Kathleen B. 1951- 119
Peterson, Lorraine 1940- 56
    Brief entry 44
Peterson, Shelley 1952- 146

Petie, Haris
See Petty, Roberta
Petricic, Dusan 1946- 176
Petrides, Heidrun 1944- 19
Petrie, Catherine 1947- 52
Brief entry 41
Petrone, Valeria 186
Petrosino, Tamara 193
Petroski, Catherine (Ann Groom) 1939- 48
Petrovich, Michael B(oro) 1922- 40
Petrovskaya, Kyra
See Wayne, Kyra Petrovskaya
Petruccio, Steven James 1961- 67
Petry, Ann (Lane) 1908-1997 5
Obituary 94
See also CLR 12
Pettit, Jayne 1932- 108
Petty, J.T. 1977- 189
Petty, Roberta 1915- 10
Pevsner, Stella 131
Earlier sketches in SATA 8, 77
See also SAAS 14
Peyo
See Culliford, Pierre
Peyton, K. M.
See Peyton, Kathleen Wendy (Herald)
Peyton, Kathleen Wendy (Herald) 1929- 157
Earlier sketches in SATA 15, 62
See also CLR 3
See also SAAS 17
Pfanner, (Anne) Louise 1955- 68
Pfeffer, Susan Beth 1948- 180
Earlier sketches in SATA 4, 83
See also CLR 11
See also SAAS 17
Pfeffer, Wendy 1929- 142
Earlier sketch in SATA 78
Pfeiffer, Janet (B.) 1949- 96
Pfister, Marcus 150
Earlier sketch in SATA 83
See also CLR 42
Pfitsch, Patricia Curtis 1948- 148
Pflieger, Pat 1955- 84
Pham, LeUyen 1973- 175
Phelan, Mary Kay 1914- 3
Phelan, Matt 1970- 172
Phelan, Terry Wolfe 1941- 56
Phelps, Ethel Johnston 1914-1984 35
Philbrick, Rodman 1951- 163
Philbrick, W. R.
See Philbrick, Rodman
Philbrick, W. Rodman
See Philbrick, Rodman
Philbrook, Clem(ent E.) 1917- 24
Phillips, Aileen Paul
See Paul, Aileen
Phillips, Betty Lou
See Phillips, Elizabeth Louise
Phillips, Bob 1940- 95
Phillips, Douglas A. 1949- 161
Phillips, Elizabeth Louise 58
Brief entry 48
Phillips, Irv(ing W.) 1905-2000 11
Obituary 125
Phillips, Jack
See Sandburg, Carl (August)
Phillips, Leon
See Gerson, Noel Bertram
Phillips, Loretta (Hosey) 1893-1987 10
Phillips, Louis 1942- 102
Earlier sketch in SATA 8
Phillips, Mark
See Garrett, (Gordon) Randall (Phillip)
and Janifer, Laurence M(ark)
Phillips, Mary Geisler 1881-1964 10
Phillips, Michael
See Nolan, William F(rancis)
Phillips, (Woodward) Prentice 1894-1981 10
Phillpotts, Eden 1862-1960 24
Phin
See Thayer, Ernest Lawrence

Phipson, Joan
See Fitzhardinge, Joan Margaret
Phiz
See Browne, Hablot Knight
Phleger, Fred B. 1909-1993 34
Phleger, Marjorie Temple 1908(?)-1986 1
Obituary 47
Piaget, Jean 1896-1980
Obituary 23
Piatti, Celestino 1922- 16
Picard, Barbara Leonie 1917- 89
Earlier sketch in SATA 2
See also SAAS 10
Pichon, Liz 174
Pickard, Charles 1932- 36
Pickering, James Sayre 1897-1969 36
Obituary 28
Pickering, Jimmy 195
Pickering, Robert B. 1950- 93
Pielichaty, Helena 1955- 142
Pienkowski, Jan (Michal) 1936- 131
Earlier sketches in SATA 6, 58
See also CLR 6
Pierce, Edith Gray 1893-1977 45
Pierce, Katherine
See St. John, Wylly Folk
Pierce, Meredith Ann 1958- 127
Brief entry 48
Earlier sketch in SATA 67
See also CLR 20
Pierce, Ruth (Ireland) 1936- 5
Pierce, Sharon
See McCullough, Sharon Pierce
Pierce, Tamora 1954- 187
Brief entry 49
Earlier sketches in SATA 51, 96, 153
Pierce, Terry 178
Pierik, Robert 1921- 13
Piernas-Davenport, Gail 199
Piers, Robert
See Anthony, Piers
Pig, Edward
See Gorey, Edward (St. John)
Pike, Bob
See Pike, Robert W(ilson)
Pike, Christopher 1954(?)- 156
Earlier sketch in SATA 68
See also CLR 29
Pike, Deborah 1951- 89
Pike, E(dgar) Royston 1896-1980 22
Obituary 56
Pike, R. William 1956- 92
Pike, Robert W(ilson) 1931- 102
Pilarski, Laura 1926- 13
Pilgrim, Anne
See Allan, Mabel Esther
Pilkey, Dav 1966- 166
Earlier sketches in SATA 68, 115
See also CLR 48
Pilkey, David Murray, Jr.
See Pilkey, Dav
Pilkington, Francis Meredyth 1907-1993 4
Pilkington, Roger (Windle) 1915-2003 10
Obituary 144
Pin, Isabel 1975- 183
Pinchot, David 1914(?)-1983
Obituary 34
Pincus, Harriet 1938- 27
Pinczes, Elinor J(ane) 1940- 81
Pine, Nicholas 1951- 91
Pine, Tillie S(chloss) 1896-1999 13
Pini, Richard (Alan) 1950- 89
Pini, Wendy 1951- 89
Pinkerton, Kathrene Sutherland (Gedney)
1887-1967
Obituary 26
Pinkett, Jada
See Smith, Jada Pinkett
Pinkney, Andrea Davis 1963- 160
Earlier sketch in SATA 113

Pinkney, (Jerry) Brian 1961- 148
Earlier sketch in SATA 74
See also CLR 54
Pinkney, Gloria Jean 1941- 85
Pinkney, J. Brian
See Pinkney, (Jerry) Brian
Pinkney, Jerry 1939- 198
Autobiography Feature 198
Brief entry 32
Earlier sketches in SATA 41, 71, 107, 151
See also CLR 43
See also SAAS 12
Pinkney, John 97
Pinkney, Sandra L. 193
Earlier sketch in SATA 128
Pinkwater, D. Manus
See Pinkwater, Daniel Manus
Pinkwater, Daniel
See Pinkwater, Daniel Manus
Pinkwater, Daniel M.
See Pinkwater, Daniel Manus
Pinkwater, Daniel Manus 1941- 158
Earlier sketches in SATA 8, 46, 76, 114
See also CLR 4
See also SAAS 3
Pinkwater, Jill 188
Pinkwater, Manus
See Pinkwater, Daniel Manus
Pinner, Joma
See Werner, Herma
Pioneer
See Yates, Raymond F(rancis)
Piowaty, Kim Kennelly 1957- 49
Piper, Roger
See Fisher, John
Pirner, Connie White 1955- 72
Piro, Richard 1934- 7
Pirot, Alison Lohans
See Lohans, Alison
Pirotta, Saviour 184
Pirsig, Robert M(aynard) 1928- 39
Pita
See Rendon, Maria
Pitcher, C.
See Pitcher, Caroline
Pitcher, Caroline 1948- 128
Pitcher, Caroline Nell
See Pitcher, Caroline
Pitman, (Isaac) James 1901-1985
Obituary 46
Pitre, Felix 1949- 84
Pitrone, Jean Maddern 1920- 4
Pittman, Helena Clare 1945- 71
Pitz, Henry C(larence) 1895-1976 4
Obituary 24
Pitzer, Susanna 1958- 181
Piven, Hanoch 1963- 173
Pixley, Marcella 194
Pizer, Vernon 1918- 21
Place, Marian T(empleton) 1910- 3
Place, Robin (Mary) 1926- 71
Plaidy, Jean
See Hibbert, Eleanor Alice Burford
Plain, Belva 1919- 62
Plaine, Alfred R. 1898(?)-1981
Obituary 29
Plath, Sylvia 1932-1963 96
Platt, Chris 1959- 185
Platt, Kin 1911- 86
Earlier sketch in SATA 21
See also SAAS 17
Platt, Randall 1948- 95
Platt, Randall Beth
See Platt, Randall
Platt, Richard 1953- 166
Earlier sketch in SATA 120
Playfellow, Robin
See Ellis, Edward S(ylvester)
Playsted, James
See Wood, James Playsted

Plecas, Jennifer 1966- *149*
    Earlier sketch in SATA *84*
Plimpton, George 1927-2003 .... *10*
    Obituary *150*
Plimpton, George Ames
    See Plimpton, George
Plomer, William Charles Franklin
    1903-1973 .... *24*
Plotz, Helen Ratnoff 1913-2000 .... *38*
Plourde, Lynn 1955- *168*
    Earlier sketch in SATA *122*
Plowden, David 1932- *52*
Plowden, Martha Ward 1948- *98*
Plowhead, Ruth Gipson 1877-1967 .... *43*
Plowman, Stephanie 1922- *6*
Pluckrose, Henry (Arthur) 1931- *141*
    Earlier sketch in SATA *13*
Plum, J.
    See Wodehouse, P(elham) G(renville)
Plum, Jennifer
    See Kurland, Michael
Plumb, Charles P. 1900(?)-1982
    Obituary *29*
Plume, Ilse *170*
    Brief entry *43*
Plumme, Don E.
    See Katz, Bobbi
Plummer, Margaret 1911- *2*
Plum-Ucci, Carol *184*
Pochocki, Ethel (Frances) 1925- *76*
Podendorf, Illa (E.) 1903(?)-1983 .... *18*
    Obituary *35*
Podwal, Mark 1945- *160*
    Earlier sketch in SATA *101*
Podwal, Mark H.
    See Podwal, Mark
Poe, Edgar Allan 1809-1849 .... *23*
Poe, Ty (Christopher) 1975- *94*
Pogany, William Andrew 1882-1955 .... *44*
    Brief entry *30*
Pogany, Willy
    See Pogany, William Andrew
Pohl, Frederik 1919- *24*
Pohlmann, Lillian (Grenfell) 1902-1997 ...... *11*
Pohrt, Tom 1953- *195*
    Earlier sketches in SATA *67, 152*
Pointon, Robert
    See Rooke, Daphne
Points, Larry G. 1945- *177*
    Earlier sketch in SATA *133*
Points, Larry Gene
    See Points, Larry G.
Pokeberry, P.J.
    See Mitchell, B.J.
POLA
    See Watson, Pauline
Polacco, Patricia 1944- *180*
    Earlier sketches in SATA *74, 123*
    See also CLR *40*
Polacco, Patricia Ann
    See Polacco, Patricia
Polak, Monique 1960- *178*
Polatnick, Florence T. 1923- *5*
Polder, Markus
    See Kruss, James
Polese, Carolyn 1947- *58*
Polese, James 1914- *87*
Polette, Nancy (Jane) 1930- *42*
Polhamus, Jean Burt 1928- *21*
Policoff, Stephen Phillip 1948- *77*
Polikoff, Barbara G. 1929- *162*
    Earlier sketch in SATA *77*
Polikoff, Barbara Garland
    See Polikoff, Barbara G.
Polisar, Barry Louis 1954- *134*
    Earlier sketch in SATA *77*
Politi, Leo 1908-1996 .... *47*
    Obituary *88*
    Earlier sketch in SATA *1*
    See also CLR *29*
Polking, Kirk 1925- *5*

Pollack, Jill S. 1963- *88*
Pollack, Merrill S. 1924-1988
    Obituary *55*
Polland, Barbara K(ay) 1939- *44*
Polland, Madeleine A(ngela Cahill) 1918- ... *68*
    Earlier sketch in SATA *6*
    See also SAAS *8*
Pollema-Cahill, Phyllis 1958- *123*
Pollock, Bruce 1945- *46*
Pollock, Mary
    See Blyton, Enid
Pollock, Penny 1935- *137*
    Brief entry *42*
    Earlier sketch in SATA *44*
Pollowitz, Melinda Kilborn 1944- *26*
Polner, Murray 1928- *64*
Polonsky, Arthur 1925- *34*
Polseno, Jo *17*
Pomaska, Anna 1946- *117*
Pomerantz, Charlotte 1930- *177*
    Earlier sketches in SATA *20, 80*
Pomeroy, Pete
    See Roth, Arthur J(oseph)
Pond, Alonzo W(illiam) 1894-1986 .... *5*
Pontiflet, Ted 1932- *32*
Poole, Gray Johnson 1906- *1*
Poole, Josephine
    See Helyar, Jane Penelope Josephine
Poole, (Jane Penelope) Josephine
    See Helyar, Jane Penelope Josephine
Poole, Lynn 1910-1969 .... *1*
Poole, Peggy 1925- *39*
Poortvliet, Rien 1932- *65*
    Brief entry *37*
Pope, Elizabeth Marie 1917-1992 .... *38*
    Brief entry *36*
Pope, Kevin 1958- *183*
Popescu, Christine
    See Pullein-Thompson, Christine
Poploff, Michelle 1956- *67*
Popp, K. Wendy *91*
Poppel, Hans 1942- *71*
Porfirio, Guy 1958- *197*
Portal, Colette 1936- *6*
Porte, Barbara Ann 1943- *152*
    Brief entry *45*
    Earlier sketches in SATA *57, 93*
Porter, A(nthony) P(eyton) 1945- *68*
Porter, Connie (Rose) 1959(?)- *129*
    Earlier sketch in SATA *81*
Porter, Donald Clayton
    See Gerson, Noel Bertram
Porter, Eleanor H(odgman) 1868-1920
    See CLR *110*
Porter, Gene(va Grace) Stratton
    See Stratton-Porter, Gene(va Grace)
Porter, Janice Lee 1953- *108*
    Earlier sketch in SATA *68*
Porter, Katherine Anne 1890-1980 .... *39*
    Obituary *23*
Porter, Kathryn
    See Swinford, Betty (June Wells)
Porter, Pamela 1956- *193*
Porter, Sheena 1935- *24*
    See also SAAS *10*
Porter, Sue
    See Limb, Sue
Porter, Sue 1951- *76*
Porter, Tracey *191*
Porter, William Sydney
    See Henry, O.
Portis, Antoinette *189*
Porto, Tony 1960- *153*
Portteus, Eleanora Marie Manthei (?)-1983
    Obituary *36*
Posada, Mia *187*
Posell, Elsa Z(eigerman) -1995 .... *3*
Posten, Margaret L(ois) 1915- *10*
Posthuma, Sieb 1960- *150*

Potok, Chaim 1929-2002 .... *106*
    Obituary *134*
    Earlier sketch in SATA *33*
    See also CLR *92*
Potok, Herbert Harold -2002
    See Potok, Chaim
Potok, Herman Harold
    See Potok, Chaim
Potter, Beatrix 1866-1943 .... *132*
    Earlier sketch in SATA *100*
    See also YABC *1*
    See also CLR *73*
Potter, Giselle *187*
    Earlier sketch in SATA *150*
Potter, Helen Beatrix
    See Potter, Beatrix
Potter, Margaret (Newman) 1926-1998 .... *21*
    Obituary *104*
Potter, Marian 1915- *9*
Potter, Miriam Clark 1886-1965 .... *3*
Poulin, Stephane 1961- *98*
    See also CLR *28*
Poulton, Kimberly 1957(?)- *136*
Pournelle, Jerry (Eugene) 1933- *161*
    Earlier sketches in SATA *26, 91*
Povelite, Kay 1955- *102*
Pow, Tom 1950- *163*
Powe-Allred, Alexandra
    See Allred, Alexandra Powe
Powell, A. M.
    See Morgan, Alfred P(owell)
Powell, Consie *174*
Powell, E. Sandy 1947- *72*
Powell, E.S.
    See Powell, E. Sandy
Powell, Pamela 1960- *78*
Powell, Patricia Hruby 1951- *136*
Powell, Randy 1956- *118*
Powell, Richard Stillman
    See Barbour, Ralph Henry
Powell, Robert (Stephenson Smyth) Baden
    See Baden-Powell, Robert (Stephenson
    Smyth)
Powell, Stephanie 1953- *93*
Power, Margaret (M.) 1945- *125*
    Earlier sketch in SATA *75*
Powers, Anne
    See Schwartz, Anne Powers
Powers, Bill 1931- *52*
    Brief entry *31*
Powers, Daniel 1959- *164*
Powers, Jessica Lynn
    See Powers, J.L.
Powers, J.L. 1974- *195*
Powers, Margaret
    See Heal, Edith
Powers, Tim 1952- *107*
Powers, Timothy Thomas
    See Powers, Tim
Powledge, Fred 1935- *37*
Poydar, Nancy *190*
Poynter, Margaret 1927- *27*
Prachaticka, Marketa
    See Kolibalova, Marketa
Prachatika, Marketa
    See Kolibalova, Marketa
Prager, Arthur *44*
Prager, Ellen J. 1962- *136*
Prange, Beckie *172*
Prap, Lila 1955- *177*
Praprotnik-Zupancic, Lilijana
    See Prap, Lila
Pratchett, Terence David John
    See Pratchett, Terry
Pratchett, Terry 1948- *185*
    Earlier sketches in SATA *82, 139*
    See also CLR *64*
Prater, John 1947- *149*
    Earlier sketches in SATA *72, 103*
Prato, Rodica *184*
Pratt, (Murray) Fletcher 1897-1956 .... *102*

Pratt, Kristin Joy 1976- 87
Pratt, Pierre 1962- 166
  Earlier sketch in SATA 95
Preiss, Byron 1953-2005 166
  Brief entry 42
  Earlier sketch in SATA 47
Preiss, Byron Cary
  See Preiss, Byron
Preller, James 1961- 88
Prelutsky, Jack 1940- 171
  Earlier sketches in SATA 22, 66, 118
  See also CLR 115
Prentice, Amy
  See Kaler, James Otis
Prescott, Casey
  See Morris, Chris(topher Crosby)
Presnall, Judith (Ann) Janda 1943- 96
Pressler, Mirjam 1940- 155
Preston, Douglas 1956- 113
Preston, Edna Mitchell 40
Preston, Lillian Elvira 1918- 47
Preussler, Otfried 1923- 24
Prevert, Jacques (Henri Marie) 1900-1977
  Obituary 30
Prevost, Guillaume 1964- 192
Price, Beverley Joan 1931- 98
Price, Charlie 187
Price, Christine (Hilda) 1928-1980 3
  Obituary 23
Price, Garrett 1896-1979
  Obituary 22
Price, Jennifer
  See Hoover, Helen (Drusilla Blackburn)
Price, Joan 1931- 124
Price, Jonathan (Reeve) 1941- 46
Price, Karen 1957- 125
Price, Kathy Z. 1957- 172
Price, Lucie Locke
  See Locke, Lucie
Price, Olive 1903-1991 8
Price, Susan 1955- 128
  Earlier sketches in SATA 25, 85
Price, Willard 1887-1983 48
  Brief entry 38
Price-Groff, Claire 127
Priceman, Marjorie 1958- 168
  Earlier sketches in SATA 81, 120
Prichard, Katharine Susannah 1883-1969 66
Prideaux, Tom 1908-1993 37
  Obituary 76
Priestley, Alice 1962- 95
Priestley, Chris 1958- 198
Priestley, Lee (Shore) 1904-1999 27
Priestly, Doug 1954- 122
Priestly, Douglas Michael
  See Priestly, Doug
Prieto, Mariana Beeching 1912-1999 8
Priley, Margaret (Ann) Hubbard 1909-1992
  Obituary 130
Primavera, Elise 1954- 185
  Brief entry 48
  Earlier sketches in SATA 58, 109
Prime, Derek (James) 1931- 34
Prince, Alison (Mary) 1931- 86
  Earlier sketch in SATA 28
Prince, April Jones 1975- 180
Prince, J(ack) H(arvey) 1908- 17
Prince, Joshua 188
Prince, Maggie 102
Pringle, Eric 138
Pringle, Laurence 1935- 154
  Earlier sketches in SATA 4, 68, 104
  See also CLR 57
  See also SAAS 6
Pringle, Laurence Patrick
  See Pringle, Laurence
Prinz, Yvonne 1960- 175
Prior, Natalie Jane 1963- 106
Pritchett, Elaine H(illyer) 1920- 36
Pritchett, Laura 1971- 178

Pritchett, Laura Rose
  See Pritchett, Laura
Pritts, Kim Derek 1953- 83
Prochazkova, Iva 1953- 68
Proctor, Everitt
  See Montgomery, Rutherford George
Proeysen, Alf 1914-1970 67
  See also CLR 24
Professor Scribbler
  See Hollingsworth, Mary
Proimos, James 1955- 173
Prose, Francine 1947- 198
  Earlier sketches in SATA 101, 149
Protopopescu, Orel 186
Protopopescu, Orel Odinov
  See Protopopescu, Orel
Provensen, Alice 1918- 147
  Earlier sketches in SATA 9, 70
  See also CLR 11
Provensen, Martin (Elias) 1916-1987 70
  Obituary 51
  Earlier sketch in SATA 9
  See also CLR 11
Provenzo, Eugene (F., Jr.) 1949- 142
  Earlier sketch in SATA 78
Provist, d'Alain 1906-1989
  See Diop, Birago (Ismael)
Provost, Gail Levine 1944- 65
Provost, Gary (Richard) 1944-1995 66
Proysen, Alf
  See Proeysen, Alf
Pruett, Candace (J.) 1968- 157
Pryor, Bonnie H. 1942- 69
Pryor, Boori (Monty) 1950- 112
Pryor, Helen Brenton 1897-1972 4
Pryor, Michael 1957- 153
Pucci, Albert John 1920- 44
Pudney, John (Sleigh) 1909-1977 24
Pugh, Ellen (Tiffany) 1920- 7
Pullein-Thompson, Christine 1925-2005 82
  Obituary 172
  Earlier sketch in SATA 3
Pullein-Thompson, Diana
  See Farr, Diana (Pullein-Thompson)
Pullein-Thompson, Joanna Maxwell
  1898-1961 82
Pullein-Thompson, Josephine (Mary
  Wedderburn) 82
  Earlier sketch in SATA 3
Pullen, Zachary 189
Pullman, Philip 1946- 198
  Earlier sketches in SATA 65, 103, 150
  See also CLR 84
  See also SAAS 17
Pullman, Philip Nicholas
  See Pullman, Philip
Pulver, Harry, Jr. 1960- 129
Pulver, Robin 1945- 133
  Earlier sketch in SATA 76
Puner, Helen W(alker) 1915-1989 37
  Obituary 63
Purdy, Carol 1943- 120
  Earlier sketch in SATA 66
Purdy, Susan G(old) 1939- 8
Purkiss, Diane 1961- 194
Purmell, Ann 1953- 147
Purnell, Idella 1901-1982 120
Purscell, Phyllis 1934- 7
Purtill, Richard L. 1931- 53
Pushker, Gloria 1927- 162
  Earlier sketch in SATA 75
Pushker, Gloria Teles
  See Pushker, Gloria
Pushkin, Aleksandr Sergeevich
  See Pushkin, Alexander (Sergeyevich)
Pushkin, Alexander (Sergeyevich)
  1799-1837 61
Putnam, Alice 1916- 61
Putnam, Arthur Lee
  See Alger, Horatio, Jr.

Putnam, Peter B(rock) 1920-1998 30
  Obituary 106
Puttapipat, Niroot 199
Puttock, Simon 178
Puybaret, Eric 1976- 195
Pyle, Howard 1853-1911 100
  Earlier sketch in SATA 16
  See also CLR 117
Pyle, Katharine 1863-1938 66
Pyne, Mable Mandeville 1903-1969 9
Pyrnelle, Louise-Clarke 1850-1907 114

Q

Quackenbush, Robert M(ead) 1929- 133
  Autobiography Feature 133
  Earlier sketches in SATA 7, 70
  See also CLR 122
  See also SAAS 7
Qualey, Marsha 1953- 124
  Earlier sketch in SATA 79
Qualls, Sean 177
Quammen, David 1948- 7
Quark, Jason
  See Eldin, Peter
Quarles, Benjamin (Arthur) 1904-1996 12
Quatermass, Martin
  See Carpenter, John (Howard)
Quattlebaum, Mary 1958- 185
  Earlier sketches in SATA 88, 134
Quay, Emma 173
  Earlier sketch in SATA 119
Queen, Ellery
  See Deming, Richard
  and Dannay, Frederic
  and Davidson, Avram (James)
  and Fairman, Paul W.
  and Flora, Fletcher
  and Holding, James (Clark Carlisle, Jr.)
  and Hoch, Edward D.
  and Kane, Henry
  and Lee, Manfred B.
  and Marlowe, Stephen
  and Powell, (Oval) Talmage
  and Sheldon, Walter J(ames)
  and Sturgeon, Theodore (Hamilton)
  and Tracy, Don(ald Fiske)
  and Vance, Jack
Queen Latifah 1970- 185
Quennell, Marjorie Courtney 1884-1972 29
Quentin
  See Sheldon, David
Quentin, Brad
  See Bisson, Terry
Quest, (Edna) Olga W(ilbourne) Hall
  See Hall-Quest, (Edna) Olga W(ilbourne)
Quick, Annabelle 1922-1986 2
Quigg, Jane (Hulda) (?)-1986
  Obituary 49
Quill, Monica
  See McInerny, Ralph
Quin-Harkin, Janet 1941- 165
  Earlier sketches in SATA 18, 90, 119
Quin-Harkin, Janet Elizabeth
  See Quin-Harkin, Janet
Quinlan, Susan E. 1954- 88
Quinlan, Susan Elizabeth
  See Quinlan, Susan E.
Quinn, Elisabeth 1881-1962 22
Quinn, Pat 1947- 130
Quinn, Patrick 1950- 73
Quinn, Rob 1972- 138
Quinn, Susan 1940- 30
Quinn, Theodora K.
  See Kroeber, Theodora (Kracaw)
Quinn, Vernon
  See Quinn, Elisabeth
Quintano, D.M.
  See Sheldon, Dyan

Quirk, Anne (E.) 1956- 99
Quixley, Jim 1931- 56
Quyth, Gabriel
    See Jennings, Gary

R

Ra, Carol F. 1939- 76
Raab, Evelyn 1951- 129
Rabb, Margo 1972- 188
Rabb, M.E.
    See Rabb, Margo
Rabe, Berniece (Louise) 1928- 148
    Autobiography Feature 148
    Earlier sketches in SATA 7, 77
    See also SAAS 10
Rabe, Olive H(anson) (?)-1968 13
Rabin, Staton 1958- 162
    Earlier sketch in SATA 84
Rabinowich, Ellen 1946- 29
Rabinowitz, Sandy 1954- 52
    Brief entry 39
Rachlin, Carol K(ing) 1919- 64
Rachlin, Harvey 1951- 47
Rachlin, Harvey Brant
    See Rachlin, Harvey
Rachlin, Nahid 64
Rachlis, Eugene (Jacob) 1920-1986
    Obituary 50
Rackham, Arthur 1867-1939 100
    Earlier sketch in SATA 15
    See also CLR 57
Raczka, Bob 1963- 191
    Earlier sketch in SATA 163
Radencich, Marguerite C. 1952-1998 79
Rader, Laura 197
Radford, Ruby L(orraine) 1891-1971 6
Radin, Ruth Yaffe 1938- 107
    Brief entry 52
    Earlier sketch in SATA 56
Radlauer, David 1952- 28
Radlauer, Edward 1921- 15
Radlauer, Ruth Shaw 1926- 98
    Earlier sketch in SATA 15
Radley, Gail 1951- 112
    Earlier sketch in SATA 25
Radunsky, Vladimir 177
Rae, Gwynedd 1892-1977 37
Raebeck, Lois 1921- 5
Rael, Elsa Okon 1927-
    See CLR 84
Raffi
    See Cavoukian, Raffi
Raftery, Gerald (Bransfield) 1905-1986 11
Ragan-Reid, Gale 1956- 90
Rahaman, Vashanti 1953- 98
Rahn, Joan Elma 1929- 27
Rai, Bali 1971- 152
Raible, Alton (Robert) 1918- 35
Raiff, Stan 1930- 11
Raines, Shirley C(arol) 1945- 128
Rainey, W. B.
    See Blassingame, Wyatt Rainey
Rake, Jody 1961- 157
Rallison, Janette 1966- 183
Ralston, Jan
    See Dunlop, Agnes M. R.
Rama, Sue 190
Ramal, Walter
    See de la Mare, Walter (John)
Ramanujan, A(ttipat) K(rishnaswami)
    1929-1993 86
Rame, David
    See Divine, Arthur Durham
Ramirez, Jose 1967- 198
Ramirez, Orlando L. 1972- 194
Ramstad, Ralph L. 1919- 115
Rana, Indi
    See Rana, Indira Higham

Rana, Indira Higham 1944- 82
Rana, J.
    See Bhatia, Jamunadevi
Ranadive, Gail 1944- 10
Rand, Ann (Binkley) 30
Rand, Gloria 1925- 156
    Earlier sketch in SATA 101
Rand, Paul 1914-1996 6
Randall, Carrie
    See Ransom, Candice F.
Randall, David 1972- 167
Randall, Florence Engel 1917-1997 5
Randall, Janet
    See Young, Janet Randall
    and Young, Robert W(illiam)
Randall, Robert
    See Garrett, (Gordon) Randall (Phillip)
    and Silverberg, Robert
Randall, Ruth (Elaine) Painter 1892-1971 3
Randell, Beverley
    See Price, Beverley Joan
Randle, Kristen D. 1952- 92
    Autobiography Feature 119
    See also SAAS 24
Randle, Kristen Downey
    See Randle, Kristen D.
Randolph, Boynton M.D.
    See Ellis, Edward S(ylvester)
Randolph, Ellen
    See Rawn, Melanie
Randolph, Geoffrey
    See Ellis, Edward S(ylvester)
Randolph, J. H.
    See Ellis, Edward S(ylvester)
Randolph, Lieutenant J. H.
    See Ellis, Edward S(ylvester)
Rands, William Brighty 1823-1882 17
Raney, Ken 1953- 74
Rankin, Joan 1940- 148
    Earlier sketch in SATA 88
Rankin, Laura 1953(?)- 176
Ranney, Agnes V. 1916-1985 6
Ransom, Candice F. 1952- 183
    Brief entry 49
    Earlier sketches in SATA 52, 89, 135
Ransom, Jeanie Franz 1957- 187
Ransome, Arthur (Michell) 1884-1967 22
    See also CLR 8
Ransome, James E. 1961- 178
    Earlier sketches in SATA 76, 123
    See also CLR 86
Rant, Tol E.
    See Longyear, Barry B(rookes)
Raphael, Elaine
    See Bolognese, Elaine (Raphael Chionchio)
Raposo, Joseph Guilherme 1938-1989
    Obituary 61
Rapp, Adam 1968(?)- 148
Rappaport, Doreen 151
Rappaport, Eva 1924- 6
Rappoport, Ken 1935- 167
    Earlier sketch in SATA 89
Rarick, Carrie 1911-2002 41
Raschka, Chris 1959- 166
    Earlier sketches in SATA 80, 117
Raschka, Christopher
    See Raschka, Chris
Rascol, Sabina I. 159
Rash, Andy 162
Raskin, Edith Lefkowitz 1908-1987 9
Raskin, Ellen 1928-1984 139
    Earlier sketches in SATA 2, 38
    See also CLR 12
Raskin, Joseph 1897-1982 12
    Obituary 29
Rathjen, Carl Henry 1909-1984 11
Rathmann, Peggy 1953- 157
    Earlier sketch in SATA 94
    See also CLR 77
Ratliff, Thomas M. 1948- 118

Ratner, Sue Lynn
    See Alexander, Sue
Rattigan, Jama Kim 1951- 99
Ratto, Linda Lee 1952- 79
Rattray, Simon
    See Trevor, Elleston
Ratz de Tagyos, Paul 1958- 198
    Earlier sketch in SATA 76
Rau, Dana Meachen 1971- 167
    Earlier sketch in SATA 94
Rau, Margaret 1913- 168
    Earlier sketch in SATA 9
    See also CLR 8
Rauch, Mabel Thompson 1888-1972
    Obituary 26
Raucher, Herman 1928- 8
Raude, Karina 199
Raum, Elizabeth 1949- 155
Raven, Margot Theis 184
RavenWolf, Silver 1956- 155
Ravielli, Anthony 1916-1997 3
    Obituary 95
Ravilious, Robin 1944- 77
Rawding, F(rederick) W(illiam) 1930- 55
Rawlings, Marjorie Kinnan 1896-1953 100
    See also YABC 1
    See also CLR 63
Rawlinson, Julia 175
Rawls, (Woodrow) Wilson 1913-1984 22
    See also CLR 81
Rawlyk, George Alexander 1935- 64
Rawn, Melanie 1954- 98
Rawn, Melanie Robin
    See Rawn, Melanie
Rawson, Katherine 1955- 190
Ray, Carl 1943-1978 63
Ray, Deborah
    See Kogan Ray, Deborah
Ray, Delia 1963- 179
    Earlier sketch in SATA 70
Ray, Irene
    See Sutton, Margaret Beebe
Ray, Jane 1960- 196
    Earlier sketches in SATA 72, 152
Ray, JoAnne 1935- 9
Ray, Mary (Eva Pedder) 1932- 127
    Earlier sketch in SATA 2
Ray, Mary Lyn 1946- 154
    Earlier sketch in SATA 90
Rayban, Chloe 1944- 167
Rayevsky, Robert 1955- 190
    Earlier sketch in SATA 81
Raymond, James Crossley 1917-1981
    Obituary 29
Raymond, Robert
    See Alter, Robert Edmond
Rayner, Hugh 151
Rayner, Mary 1933- 87
    Earlier sketch in SATA 22
    See also CLR 41
Rayner, Shoo
    See Rayner, Hugh
Rayner, William 1929- 55
    Brief entry 36
Raynor, Dorka 28
Rayson, Steven 1932- 30
Razzell, Arthur (George) 1925- 11
Razzell, Mary (Catherine) 1930- 102
Razzi, James 1931- 10
Read, Elfreida 1920- 2
Read, Nicholas 1956- 146
Read, Piers Paul 1941- 21
Reade, Deborah 1949- 69
Reader, Dennis 1929- 71
Reading, Richard P(atrick) 1962- 161
Readman, Jo 1958- 89
Ready, Kirk L(ewis) 1943- 39
Reaney, James 1926-2008 43
Reaney, James Crerar
    See Reaney, James

Reardon, Joyce
  See Pearson, Ridley
Reaver, Chap 1935-1993 69
  Obituary 77
Reaver, Herbert R.
  See Reaver, Chap
Reaves, J. Michael
  See Reaves, (James) Michael
Reaves, (James) Michael 1950- 99
Reber, Deborah 189
Recorvits, Helen 191
Redding, Robert Hull 1919- 2
Redekopp, Elsa 61
Redlich, Ben 1977- 181
Redsand, Anna 1948- 184
Redway, Ralph
  See Hamilton, Charles (Harold St. John)
Redway, Ridley
  See Hamilton, Charles (Harold St. John)
Reece, Colleen L. 1935- 116
Reece, Gabrielle 1970- 108
Reed, Betty Jane 1921- 4
Reed, E.
  See Evans, Mari
Reed, Gwendolyn E(lizabeth) 1932- 21
Reed, Kit 1932- 184
  Autobiography Feature 184
  Earlier sketches in SATA *34, 116*
Reed, Lynn Rowe 171
Reed, Neil 1961- 99
Reed, Talbot Baines 1852-1893
  See CLR *76*
Reed, Thomas (James) 1947- 34
Reed, William Maxwell 1871-1962 15
Reeder, Carolyn 1937- 97
  Earlier sketch in SATA *66*
  See also CLR *69*
Reeder, Colin (Dawson) 1938- 74
Reeder, Colonel Red
  See Reeder, Russell P(otter), Jr.
Reeder, Russell P(otter), Jr. 1902-1998 4
  Obituary 101
Reeder, Stephanie Owen 1951- 102
Reed-Jones, Carol 1955- 112
Reef, Catherine 1951- 189
  Earlier sketches in SATA *73, 128*
Reekie, Jocelyn (Margaret) 1947- 145
Reeman, Douglas Edward 1924- 63
  Brief entry 28
Rees, Celia 1949- 124
Rees, David (Bartlett) 1936-1993 69
  Obituary 76
  Earlier sketch in SATA *36*
  See also SAAS *5*
Rees, Douglas 1947- 169
Rees, Ennis (Samuel, Jr.) 1925- 3
Rees, (George) Leslie (Clarence)
  1905-2000 105
  Obituary 135
Reese, Bob
  See Reese, Robert A.
Reese, Carolyn Johnson 1938- 64
Reese, Della 1931(?)- 114
Reese, Lyn
  See Reese, Carolyn Johnson
Reese, Robert A. 1938- 60
  Brief entry 53
Reese, (John) Terence 1913-1996 59
Reeve, Joel
  See Cox, William R(obert)
Reeve, Kirk 1934- 117
Reeve, Philip 170
Reeve, Rosie 186
Reeve, Rosie 188
Reeves, Faye Couch 1953- 76
Reeves, James
  See Reeves, John Morris
Reeves, Jeni 1947- 111
Reeves, John Morris 1909-1978 87
  Earlier sketch in SATA *15*
Reeves, Joyce 1911- 17

Reeves, Lawrence F. 1926- 29
Reeves, Ruth Ellen
  See Ranney, Agnes V.
Regan, Dian Curtis 1950- 149
  Autobiography Feature 149
  Earlier sketches in SATA *75, 133*
Regehr, Lydia 1903-1991 37
Reger, James P. 1952- 106
Reggiani, Renee 1925- 18
Rehm, Karl M. 1935- 72
Reich, Ali
  See Katz, Bobbi
Reich, Susanna 1954- 113
Reiche, Dietlof 1941- 159
Reichert, Edwin C(lark) 1909-1988
  Obituary 57
Reichert, Mickey Zucker
  See Reichert, Miriam Zucker
Reichert, Miriam Zucker 1962- 85
Reichert, Renee 172
Reichhold, Jane(t E.) 1937- 147
Reid, Alastair 1926- 46
Reid, Barbara 1922- 21
Reid, Barbara (Jane) 1957- 93
  See also CLR *64*
Reid, Desmond
  See Moorcock, Michael
  and McNeilly, Wilfred (Glassford)
Reid, Eugenie Chazal 1924- 12
Reid, John Calvin 21
Reid, (Thomas) Mayne 1818-1883 24
Reid, Meta Mayne 1905-1991 58
  Brief entry 36
Reid, Robin (Nicole) 1969- 145
Reid Banks, Lynne 1929- 165
  Earlier sketches in SATA *22, 75, 111*
  See also CLR *86*
Reider, Katja 1960- 126
Reid Jenkins, Debra 1955- 87
Reiff, Stephanie Ann 1948- 47
  Brief entry 28
Reig, June 1933- 30
Reigot, Betty Polisar 1924- 55
  Brief entry 41
Reilly, Joan 195
Reim, Melanie (K.) 1956- 104
Reinach, Jacquelyn (Krasne) 1930-2000 28
Reiner, Carl 1922- 151
Reiner, William B(uck) 1910-1976 46
  Obituary 30
Reinfeld, Fred 1910-1964 3
Reinhardt, Dana 1971- 175
Reinhart, Matthew 1971- 197
  Earlier sketch in SATA *161*
Reiniger, Lotte 1899-1981 40
  Obituary 33
Reinsma, Carol 1949- 91
Reinstedt, Randall A. 1935- 101
Reinstedt, Randy
  See Reinstedt, Randall A.
Reisberg, Mira 1955- 82
Reisberg, Veg
  See Reisberg, Mira
Reiser, Lynn 1944- 180
  Earlier sketches in SATA *81, 138*
Reiser, Lynn Whisnant
  See Reiser, Lynn
Reisgies, Teresa (Maria) 1966- 74
Reiss, Johanna (de Leeuw) 1929(?)- 18
  See also CLR *19*
Reiss, John J. 23
Reiss, Kathryn 1957- 144
  Earlier sketch in SATA *76*
Reit, Seymour Victory 1918-2001 21
  Obituary 133
Reit, Sy
  See Reit, Seymour Victory
Relf, Patricia 1954- 134
  Earlier sketch in SATA *71*

Remi, Georges 1907-1983 13
  Obituary 32
  See also CLR *114*
Remington, Frederic S(ackrider)
  1861-1909 41
Remkiewicz, Frank 1939- 152
  Earlier sketch in SATA *77*
Rempt, Fiona 1973- 198
Remy, Georges
  See Remi, Georges
Renaud, Bernadette 1945- 66
Renault, Mary
  See Challans, Mary
Rendell, Joan 28
Rendina, Laura (Jones) Cooper 1902- 10
Rendon, Marcie R. 1952- 97
Rendon, Maria 1965- 116
Renee, Janina 1956- 140
Renfro, Ed 1924- 79
Renick, Marion (Lewis) 1905-1983 1
Renken, Aleda 1907- 27
Renlie, Frank H. 1936- 11
Rennert, Richard Scott 1956- 67
Rennison, Louise 1951- 149
Reno, Dawn E(laine) 1953- 130
Rensie, Willis
  See Eisner, Will
Renton, Cam
  See Armstrong, Richard
Renvoize, Jean 5
Resau, Laura 1973- 190
Resciniti, Angelo G. 1952- 75
Resnick, Michael David
  See Resnick, Mike
Resnick, Mike 1942- 159
  Earlier sketches in SATA *38, 106*
Resnick, Seymour 1920- 23
Retla, Robert
  See Alter, Robert Edmond
Rettig, Liz 199
Reuter, Bjarne (B.) 1950- 142
  Earlier sketch in SATA *68*
Reuter, Carol (Joan) 1931- 2
Revena
  See Wright, Betty Ren
Revsbech, Vicki
  See Liestman, Vicki
Rex, Adam 186
Rex, Michael 191
Rey, H(ans) A(ugusto) 1898-1977 100
  Earlier sketches in SATA *1, 26, 69*
  See also CLR *93*
Rey, Margret (Elisabeth) 1906-1996 86
  Obituary 93
  Earlier sketch in SATA *26*
  See also CLR *93*
Reyher, Becky
  See Reyher, Rebecca Hourwich
Reyher, Rebecca Hourwich 1897-1987 18
  Obituary 50
Reynold, Ann
  See Bernardo, Anilu
Reynolds, Aaron 1970- 197
Reynolds, Adrian 1963- 192
Reynolds, C. Buck 1957- 107
Reynolds, Dickson
  See Reynolds, Helen Mary Greenwood Campbell
Reynolds, Helen Mary Greenwood Campbell
  1884-1969
  Obituary 26
Reynolds, Jan 1956- 180
Reynolds, John
  See Whitlock, Ralph
Reynolds, Madge
  See Whitlock, Ralph
Reynolds, Malvina 1900-1978 44
  Obituary 24
Reynolds, Marilyn 1935- 121
  See also SAAS *23*

Reynolds, Marilyn M.
    See Reynolds, Marilyn
Reynolds, Marilynn 1940- 141
    Earlier sketch in SATA 80
Reynolds, Pamela 1923- 34
Reynolds, Peter H. 1961- 128
Reynolds, Peter J. 1961- 179
Reynolds, Susan 179
Rhine, Richard
    See Silverstein, Alvin
    and Silverstein, Virginia B(arbara Opshelor)
Rhoades, Diane 1952- 90
Rhodes, Bennie (Loran) 1927- 35
Rhodes, Donna McKee 1962- 87
Rhodes, Frank Harold Trevor 1926- 37
Rhue, Morton
    See Strasser, Todd
Rhyne, Nancy 1926- 66
Rhynes, Martha E. 1939- 141
Ribbons, Ian 1924- 37
    Brief entry 30
    See also SAAS 3
Ricciuti, Edward R(aphael) 1938- 10
Rice, Alice (Caldwell) Hegan 1870-1942 63
Rice, Bebe Faas 1932- 89
Rice, Charles D(uane) 1910-1971
    Obituary 27
Rice, Dale R. 1948- 42
Rice, Dale Richard
    See Rice, Dale R.
Rice, Dick
    See Rice, R. Hugh
Rice, Earle (Wilmont), Jr. 1928- 151
    Earlier sketch in SATA 92
Rice, Edward 1918-2001 47
    Brief entry 42
Rice, Elizabeth 1913-1976 2
Rice, Eve 1951- 91
    Earlier sketch in SATA 34
Rice, Eve Hart
    See Rice, Eve
Rice, Inez 1907- 13
Rice, James 1934- 93
    Earlier sketch in SATA 22
Rice, John F. 1958- 82
Rice, R. Hugh 1929- 115
Rice, Richard H.
    See Rice, R. Hugh
Rich, Barbara
    See Graves, Robert
Rich, Elaine Sommers 1926- 6
Rich, Josephine Bouchard 1912- 10
Rich, Louise Dickinson 1903-1991 54
    Obituary 67
Richard, Adrienne 1921- 5
    See also SAAS 9
Richard, James Robert
    See Bowen, Robert Sydney
Richards, Chuck 1957- 170
Richards, Frank
    See Hamilton, Charles (Harold St. John)
Richards, Hilda
    See Hamilton, Charles (Harold St. John)
Richards, Jackie 1925- 102
Richards, Jean 1940- 135
Richards, Justin 169
Richards, Kay
    See Baker, Susan (Catherine)
Richards, Laura E(lizabeth Howe) 1850-1943
    See YABC 1
    See also CLR 54
Richards, Leigh
    See King, Laurie R.
Richards, Marlee
    See Brill, Marlene Targ
Richards, Norman 1932- 48
Richards, R(onald) C(harles) W(illiam)
    1923- 59
    Brief entry 43
Richards, Walter Alden (Jr.) 1907-1988
    Obituary 56

Richardson, Andrew (William) 1986- 120
Richardson, Carol 1932- 58
Richardson, Frank Howard 1882-1970
    Obituary 27
Richardson, Grace Lee
    See Dickson, Naida
Richardson, Jean (Mary) 59
Richardson, Judith Benet 1941- 77
Richardson, Nigel 1957- 187
Richardson, Robert S(hirley) 1902-1981 8
Richardson, Sandy 1949- 116
Richardson, V.A. 189
Richardson, Willis 1889-1977 60
Richelson, Geraldine 1922- 29
Richemont, Enid 1940- 82
Richler, Mordecai 1931-2001 98
    Brief entry 27
    Earlier sketch in SATA 44
    See also CLR 17
Richman, Sophia 1941- 142
Rich-McCoy, Lois
    See McCoy, Lois (Rich)
Richmond, Robin 1951- 75
Richoux, Pat(ricia) 1927- 7
Richter, Alice 1941- 30
Richter, Conrad (Michael) 1890-1968 3
Richter, Hans Peter 1925-1993 6
    See also CLR 21
    See also SAAS 11
Richter, Jutta 1955- 184
Rickard, Graham 1949- 71
Rico, Don(ato) 1917-1985
    Obituary 43
Riddell, Chris 1962- 166
    Earlier sketch in SATA 114
Riddell, Christopher Barry
    See Riddell, Chris
Riddell, Edwina 1955- 82
Ridden, Brian (John) 1934- 123
Riddle, Tohby 1965- 151
    Earlier sketch in SATA 74
Riddles, Libby 1956- 140
Rideout, Sandy 194
Ridge, Antonia (Florence) (?)-1981 7
    Obituary 27
Ridge, Martin 1923-2003 43
Ridley, Philip 171
    Earlier sketch in SATA 88
Ridlon, Marci
    See Balterman, Marcia Ridlon
Riedman, Sarah R(egal) 1902-1995 1
Riehecky, Janet 1953- 164
Ries, Lori 185
Riesenberg, Felix, Jr. 1913-1962 23
Rieu, E(mile) V(ictor) 1887-1972 46
    Obituary 26
Riffenburgh, Beau 1955- 175
Rigg, Sharon
    See Creech, Sharon
Riggio, Anita 1952- 148
    Earlier sketch in SATA 73
Riggs, Shannon 190
Riggs, Sidney Noyes 1892-1975
    Obituary 28
Riggs, Stephanie 1964- 138
Riglietti, Serena 1969- 189
Rigney, James Oliver, Jr.
    See Jordan, Robert
Rikhoff, Jean 1928- 9
Rikki
    See Ducornet, Erica
Riley, James A. 1939- 97
Riley, James Whitcomb 1849-1916 17
Riley, Jocelyn 1949- 60
    Brief entry 50
Riley, Jocelyn Carol
    See Riley, Jocelyn
Riley, Linda Capus 1950- 85
Riley, Martin 1948- 81
Rimbauer, Steven
    See Pearson, Ridley

Rimes, (Margaret) LeAnn 1982- 154
Rinaldi, Ann 1934- 161
    Brief entry 50
    Earlier sketches in SATA 51, 78, 117
    See also CLR 46
Rinard, Judith E(llen) 1947- 140
    Earlier sketch in SATA 44
Rinder, Lenore 1949- 92
Ring, Elizabeth 1920- 79
Ringdahl, Mark
    See Longyear, Barry B(rookes)
Ringgold, Faith 1930- 187
    Earlier sketches in SATA 71, 114
    See also CLR 30
Ringi, Kjell (Arne Soerensen) 1939- 12
Rinkoff, Barbara Jean (Rich) 1923-1975 4
    Obituary 27
Rinn, Miriam 1946- 127
Riordan, James 1936- 95
Riordan, Rick 174
Rios, Tere
    See Versace, Marie Teresa Rios
Ripken, Cal, Jr. 1960- 114
Ripken, Calvin Edward, Jr.
    See Ripken, Cal, Jr.
Ripley, Catherine 1957- 82
Ripley, Elizabeth Blake 1906-1969 5
Ripper, Charles L(ewis) 1929- 3
Ripper, Chuck
    See Ripper, Charles L(ewis)
Riq
    See Atwater, Richard (Tupper)
Rish, David 1955- 110
Riskind, Mary 1944- 60
Rissinger, Matt 1956- 93
Rissman, Art
    See Sussman, Susan
Rissman, Susan
    See Sussman, Susan
Ritchie, Barbara Gibbons 14
Ritter, Felix
    See Kruss, James
Ritter, John H. 1951- 137
    Earlier sketch in SATA 129
Ritter, Lawrence S(tanley) 1922-2004 58
    Obituary 152
Ritthaler, Shelly 1955- 91
Ritts, Paul 1920(?)-1980
    Obituary 25
Ritz, Karen 1957- 80
Rivera, Geraldo (Miguel) 1943- 54
    Brief entry 28
Rivers, Elfrida
    See Bradley, Marion Zimmer
Rivers, Karen 1970- 131
Riverside, John
    See Heinlein, Robert A.
Rivkin, Ann 1920- 41
Rivoli, Mario 1943- 10
Roach, Marilynne K. 1946- 9
Roach, Marilynne Kathleen
    See Roach, Marilynne K.
Roach, Portia
    See Takakjian, Portia
Robb, Don 1937- 194
Robb, Laura 1937- 95
Robberecht, Thierry 1960- 182
Robbins, Frank 1917-1994(?) 42
    Brief entry 32
Robbins, Ken 1945- 147
    Brief entry 53
    Earlier sketch in SATA 94
Robbins, Raleigh
    See Hamilton, Charles (Harold St. John)
Robbins, Ruth 1917(?)- 14
Robbins, Tony
    See Pashko, Stanley
Robbins, Wayne
    See Cox, William R(obert)
Robel, S. L.
    See Fraustino, Lisa Rowe

Roberson, Jennifer 1953- 72
Roberson, John R(oyster) 1930- 53
Robert, Adrian
   See St. John, Nicole
Roberts, Bethany 133
Roberts, Bruce (Stuart) 1930- 47
   Brief entry 39
Roberts, Charles G(eorge) D(ouglas)
   1860-1943 88
   Brief entry 29
   See also CLR 33
Roberts, David
   See Cox, John Roberts
Roberts, Diane 1937- 184
Roberts, Elizabeth 1944- 80
Roberts, Elizabeth Madox 1886-1941 33
   Brief entry 27
   See also CLR 100
Roberts, Jim
   See Bates, Barbara S(nedeker)
Roberts, John G(aither) 1913-1993 27
Roberts, Judy I. 1957- 93
Roberts, Katherine 1962- 152
Roberts, M. L.
   See Mattern, Joanne
Roberts, Nancy Correll 1924- 52
   Brief entry 28
Roberts, Priscilla 1955- 184
Roberts, Terence
   See Sanderson, Ivan T(erence)
Roberts, Willo Davis 1928-2004 150
   Autobiography Feature 150
   Obituary 160
   Earlier sketches in SATA 21, 70, 133
   See also CLR 95
   See also SAAS 8
Robertson, Barbara (Anne) 1931- 12
Robertson, Don 1929-1999 8
   Obituary 113
Robertson, Dorothy Lewis 1912- 12
Robertson, Ellis
   See Ellison, Harlan
   and Silverberg, Robert
Robertson, James I., Jr. 1930- 182
Robertson, James Irvin
   See Robertson, James I., Jr.
Robertson, Janet (E.) 1935- 68
Robertson, Jennifer Sinclair 1942-1998 12
Robertson, Jenny
   See Robertson, Jennifer Sinclair
Robertson, Keith (Carlton) 1914-1991 85
   Obituary 69
   Earlier sketch in SATA 1
   See also SAAS 15
Robertson, Mark
   See Robertson, M.P.
Robertson, M.P. 1965- 197
Robertson, Stephen
   See Walker, Robert W(ayne)
Robertus, Polly M. 1948- 73
Robeson, Kenneth
   See Dent, Lester
   and Goulart, Ron(ald Joseph)
Robeson, Kenneth
   See Johnson, (Walter) Ryerson
Robinet, Harriette Gillem 1931- 104
   Earlier sketch in SATA 27
   See also CLR 64
Robins, Deri 1958- 166
   Earlier sketch in SATA 117
Robins, Patricia
   See Clark, Patricia Denise
Robins, Rollo, Jr.
   See Ellis, Edward S(ylvester)
Robins, Seelin
   See Ellis, Edward S(ylvester)
Robinson, Adjai 1932- 8
Robinson, Aminah Brenda Lynn 1940- 159
   Earlier sketch in SATA 77
Robinson, Barbara (Webb) 1927- 84
   Earlier sketch in SATA 8

Robinson, C(harles) A(lexander), Jr.
   1900-1965 36
Robinson, Charles 1870-1937 17
Robinson, Charles 1931- 6
Robinson, Dorothy W. 1929- 54
Robinson, Eve
   See Tanselle, Eve
Robinson, Glen 1953- 92
Robinson, Glendal P.
   See Robinson, Glen
Robinson, Jan M. 1933- 6
Robinson, Jean O. 1934- 7
Robinson, Joan (Mary) G(ale Thomas)
   1910-1988 7
Robinson, Kim Stanley 1952- 109
Robinson, Lee 1948- 110
Robinson, Lloyd
   See Silverberg, Robert
Robinson, Lynda S(uzanne) 1951- 107
Robinson, Marileta 1942- 32
Robinson, Maudie Millian Oller 1914- 11
Robinson, Maurice R(ichard) 1895-1982
   Obituary 29
Robinson, Nancy K(onheim) 1942-1994 91
   Brief entry 31
   Obituary 79
   Earlier sketch in SATA 32
Robinson, Ray 1920- 23
Robinson, Raymond Kenneth
   See Robinson, Ray
Robinson, Shari
   See McGuire, Leslie (Sarah)
Robinson, Sharon 1950- 197
   Earlier sketch in SATA 162
Robinson, Spider 1948- 118
Robinson, Sue
   See Robinson, Susan Maria
Robinson, Susan Maria 1955- 105
Robinson, Suzanne
   See Robinson, Lynda S(uzanne)
Robinson, T(homas) H(eath) 1869-1950 17
Robinson, (Wanda) Veronica 1926- 30
Robinson, W(illiam) Heath 1872-1944 17
Robison, Bonnie 1924- 12
Robison, Nancy L(ouise) 1934- 32
Robles, Harold E. 1948- 87
Robottom, John 1934- 7
Robson, Eric 1939- 82
Rocco, John 1967- 188
Roche, A. K.
   See Abisch, Roslyn Kroop
   and Kaplan, Boche
Roche, Denis 1967- 196
   Earlier sketch in SATA 99
Roche, Denis Mary
   See Roche, Denis
Roche, Luane 1937- 170
Roche, P(atricia) K. 1935- 57
   Brief entry 34
Roche, Terry
   See Poole, Peggy
Rochman, Hazel 1938- 105
Rock, Lois
   See Joslin, Mary
Rock, Maxine 1940- 108
Rocker, Fermin 1907- 40
Rocklin, Joanne 1946- 134
   Earlier sketch in SATA 86
Rockwell, Anne F. 1934- 194
   Earlier sketches in SATA 33, 71, 114, 162
   See also SAAS 19
Rockwell, Anne Foote
   See Rockwell, Anne F.
Rockwell, Bart
   See Pellowski, Michael (Joseph)
Rockwell, Harlow 1910-1988 33
   Obituary 56
Rockwell, Lizzy 1961- 185
Rockwell, Norman (Percevel) 1894-1978 23

Rockwell, Thomas 1933- 70
   Earlier sketch in SATA 7
   See also CLR 6
Rockwood, Joyce 1947- 39
Rockwood, Roy
   See McFarlane, Leslie (Charles)
   and Stratemeyer, Edward L.
Rodanas, Kristina 1952- 155
Rodari, Gianni 1920-1980
   See CLR 24
Rodd, Kathleen Tennant
   See Rodd, Kylie Tennant
Rodd, Kylie Tennant 1912-1988 57
   Obituary 55
   Earlier sketch in SATA 6
Rodda, Emily 1948- 146
   Earlier sketch in SATA 97
   See also CLR 32
Roddenberry, Eugene Wesley 1921-1991 45
   Obituary 69
Roddenberry, Gene
   See Roddenberry, Eugene Wesley
Roddick, Ellen 1936- 5
Roddie, Shen 153
Roddy, Lee 1921- 57
Rodenas, Paula 73
Rodgers, Frank 1944- 69
Rodgers, Mary 1931- 130
   Earlier sketch in SATA 8
   See also CLR 20
Rodman, Emerson
   See Ellis, Edward S(ylvester)
Rodman, Eric
   See Silverberg, Robert
Rodman, Maia
   See Wojciechowska, Maia (Teresa)
Rodman, Mary Ann 185
Rodman, (Cary) Selden 1909-2002 9
Rodowsky, Colby 1932- 164
   Earlier sketches in SATA 21, 77, 120
   See also SAAS 22
Rodowsky, Colby F.
   See Rodowsky, Colby
Rodriguez, Alejo 1941- 83
Rodriguez, Alex 1975- 189
Rodriguez, Christina 1981- 177
Rodriguez, Edel 1971- 196
Rodriguez, Luis J. 1954- 125
Rodriguez, Rachel 180
Rodriguez, Rachel Victoria
   See Rodriguez, Rachel
Roeder, Virginia Marsh 1926- 98
Roehrig, Catharine H. 1949- 67
Roennfeldt, Robert 1953- 78
Roessel-Waugh, C. C.
   See Waugh, Carol-Lynn Rossel
   and Waugh, Charles G(ordon)
Roets, Lois F. 1937- 91
Roever, J(oan) M(arilyn) 1935- 26
Rofes, Eric 1954-2006 52
Rofes, Eric Edward 1954-2006
   See Rofes, Eric
Roffey, Maureen 1936- 33
Rogak, Lisa 1962- 80
Rogak, Lisa Angowski
   See Rogak, Lisa
Rogan, S. Jones 199
Rogan, Sally Jones
   See Rogan, S. Jones
Rogasky, Barbara 1933- 144
   Earlier sketch in SATA 86
Rogers, (Thomas) Alan (Stinchcombe)
   1937- 81
   Earlier sketch in SATA 2
Rogers, Bettye 1858-1919 103
Rogers, Cindy 1950- 89
Rogers, Emma 1951- 74
Rogers, Frances 1888-1974 10
Rogers, Fred McFeely 1928-2003 33
   Obituary 138

Rogers, Hal
  See Sirimarco, Elizabeth
Rogers, Jean 1919- 55
  Brief entry 47
Rogers, Matilda 1894-1976 5
  Obituary 34
Rogers, Pamela 1927- 9
Rogers, Paul 1950- 98
  Earlier sketch in SATA 54
Rogers, Robert
  See Hamilton, Charles (Harold St. John)
Rogers, Sherry 193
Rogers, W(illiam) G(arland) 1896-1978 23
Rohan, M. S.
  See Rohan, Michael Scott
Rohan, Michael Scott 1951- 98
Rohan, Mike Scott
  See Rohan, Michael Scott
Rohmann, Eric 1957- 171
  See also CLR 100
Rohmer, Harriet 1938- 56
Rohrer, Doug 1962- 89
Rojan
  See Rojankovsky, Feodor (Stepanovich)
Rojankovsky, Feodor (Stepanovich)
  1891-1970 21
Rojany, Lisa 94
Rokeby-Thomas, Anna E(lma) 1911- 15
Roland, Albert 1925-2002 11
Roland, Mary
  See Lewis, Mary (Christianna)
Roleff, Tamara L. 1959- 143
Rolerson, Darrell A(llen) 1946- 8
Roll, Winifred 1909-1998 6
Rollins, Charlemae Hill 1897-1979 3
  Obituary 26
Rollock, Barbara T(herese) 1924- 64
Romack, Janice Reed
  See LeNoir, Janice
Romain, Trevor 134
Romanenko, Vitaliy 1962- 101
Romano, Clare 1922- 111
  Earlier sketch in SATA 48
Romano, Louis G. 1921- 35
Romano, Melora A. 1966- 118
Romano, Ray 1957- 170
Romano, Raymond
  See Romano, Ray
Romijn, Johanna Maria Kooyker
  See Kooyker-Romijn, Johanna Maria
Romyn, Johanna Maria Kooyker
  See Kooyker-Romijn, Johanna Maria
Rong, Yu 1970- 174
Rongen, Bjoern 1906- 10
Rongen, Bjorn
  See Rongen, Bjoern
Ronson, Mark
  See Alexander, Marc
Rood, Ronald (N.) 1920- 12
Rook, Sebastian
  See Jeapes, Ben
Rooke, Daphne 1914-2009 12
Rooke, Daphne Marie
  See Rooke, Daphne
Roop, Connie 1951- 167
  Brief entry 49
  Earlier sketches in SATA 54, 116
Roop, Constance Betzer
  See Roop, Connie
Roop, Peter 1951- 167
  Brief entry 49
  Earlier sketches in SATA 54, 116
Roop, Peter G.
  See Roop, Peter
Roop, Peter Geiger
  See Roop, Peter
Roos, Stephen 1945- 128
  Brief entry 41
  Earlier sketches in SATA 47, 77
Roose-Evans, James 1927- 65
Roosevelt, (Anna) Eleanor 1884-1962 50

Root, Barry 182
Root, Betty 84
Root, Kimberly Bulcken 192
Root, Phyllis 1949- 184
  Brief entry 48
  Earlier sketches in SATA 55, 94, 145
Root, Shelton L., Jr. 1923-1986
  Obituary 51
Roper, Laura (Newbold) Wood 1911-2003 .. 34
  Obituary 150
Roper, Robert 1946- 142
  Earlier sketch in SATA 78
Roraback, Robin (Ellan) 1964- 111
Rorby, Ginny 1944- 94
Rorer, Abigail 1949- 85
Rosamel, Godeleine de 1968- 151
Roscoe, D(onald) T(homas) 1934- 42
Rose, Anne 8
Rose, Deborah Lee 1955- 185
  Earlier sketches in SATA 71, 124
Rose, Elizabeth (Jane Pretty) 1933- 68
  Brief entry 28
Rose, Florella
  See Carlson, Vada F.
Rose, Gerald (Hembdon Seymour) 1935- 68
  Brief entry 30
Rose, Malcolm 1953- 168
  Earlier sketch in SATA 107
Rose, Nancy A.
  See Sweetland, Nancy A(nn)
Rose, Ted 1940- 93
Rose, Wendy 1948- 12
Rosen, Lillian (Diamond) 1928- 63
Rosen, Marvin 1933- 161
Rosen, Michael 1946- 181
  Brief entry 40
  Earlier sketches in SATA 48, 84, 137
  See also CLR 45
Rosen, Michael J. 1954- 199
  Earlier sketch in SATA 86
Rosen, Michael Wayne
  See Rosen, Michael
Rosen, Sidney 1916- 1
Rosen, Winifred 1943- 8
Rosenbaum, Maurice 1907-1987 6
Rosenberg, Amye 1950- 74
Rosenberg, Dorothy 1906- 40
Rosenberg, Eth(el) Clifford 1915- 92
  See also SAAS 22
Rosenberg, Jane 1949- 58
Rosenberg, Liz 1958- 129
  Earlier sketch in SATA 75
Rosenberg, Maxine B(erta) 1939- 93
  Brief entry 47
  Earlier sketch in SATA 55
Rosenberg, Nancy (Sherman) 1931- 4
Rosenberg, Sharon 1942- 8
Rosenberry, Vera 1948- 144
  Earlier sketch in SATA 83
Rosenblatt, Arthur
  See Rosenblatt, Arthur S.
Rosenblatt, Arthur S. 1938- 68
  Brief entry 45
Rosenblatt, Lily 1956- 90
Rosenbloom, Joseph 1928- 21
Rosenblum, Richard 1928- 11
Rosenburg, John M. 1918- 6
Rosenfeld, Dina 1962- 99
Rosenthal, Amy Krouse 1965- 177
Rosenthal, Betsy R. 1957- 178
Rosenthal, Harold 1914-1999 35
Rosenthal, M(acha) L(ouis) 1917-1996 59
Rosenthal, Marc 1949- 193
Rosenthal, Mark A(lan) 1946- 64
Rosing, Norbert 1953- 196
Rosman, Steven M 1956- 81
Rosman, Steven Michael
  See Rosman, Steven M
Rosoff, Meg 1956- 160
Ross, Alan
  See Warwick, Alan R(oss)

Ross, Christine 1950- 172
  Earlier sketch in SATA 83
Ross, Clare
  See Romano, Clare
Ross, Dana Fuller
  See Cockrell, Amanda
  and Gerson, Noel Bertram
Ross, Dave
  See Ross, David
Ross, David 1896-1975 49
  Obituary 20
Ross, David 1949- 133
  Earlier sketch in SATA 32
Ross, Deborah J.
  See Wheeler, Deborah
Ross, Diana
  See Denney, Diana
Ross, Edward S(hearman) 1915- 85
Ross, Eileen 1950- 115
Ross, Frank (Xavier), Jr. 1914- 28
Ross, Jane 1961- 79
Ross, John 1921- 45
Ross, Judy 1942- 54
Ross, Katharine Reynolds
  See Ross, Kathy
Ross, Kathy 1948- 169
  Earlier sketch in SATA 89
Ross, Kent 1956- 91
Ross, Lillian Hammer 1925- 72
Ross, Michael Elsohn 1952- 170
  Earlier sketches in SATA 80, 127
Ross, Pat(ricia Kienzle) 1943- 53
  Brief entry 48
Ross, Ramon R(oyal) 1930- 62
Ross, Stewart 1947- 134
  Earlier sketch in SATA 92
  See also SAAS 23
Ross, Tom 1958- 84
Ross, Tony 1938- 176
  Earlier sketches in SATA 17, 65, 130
Ross, Wilda 1915- 51
  Brief entry 39
Rossel, Seymour 1945- 28
Rossell, Judith 1953- 187
Rossel-Waugh, C. C.
  See Waugh, Carol-Lynn Rossel
Rossetti, Christina 1830-1894 20
  See also CLR 115
Rossetti, Christina Georgina
  See Rossetti, Christina
Rossi, Joyce 1943- 116
Rossotti, Hazel Swaine 1930- 95
Rostkowski, Margaret I. 1945- 59
Roth, Arnold 1929- 21
Roth, Arthur J(oseph) 1925-1993 43
  Brief entry 28
  Obituary 75
  See also SAAS 11
Roth, David 1940- 36
Roth, Julie Jersild 180
Roth, Matthue 1978(?)- 174
Roth, Roger 190
Roth, Susan L. 181
  Earlier sketch in SATA 134
Rothberg, Abraham 1922- 59
Roth-Hano, Renee 1931- 85
Rothkopf, Carol Z. 1929- 4
Rothman, Joel 1938- 7
Rotner, Shelley 1951- 169
  Earlier sketch in SATA 76
Rottman, S(usan) L(ynn) 1970- 157
  Earlier sketch in SATA 106
Roueche, Berton 1911-1994 28
Roughsey, Dick 1921(?)-1985 35
  See also CLR 41
Roughsey, Goobalathaldin
  See Roughsey, Dick
Rounds, Glen (Harold) 1906-2002 112
  Obituary 141
  Earlier sketches in SATA 8, 70

Rourke, Constance Mayfield 1885-1941
  See YABC *1*
Rowan, Deirdre
  See Williams, Jeanne
Rowe, Jennifer
  See Rodda, Emily
Rowe, John A. 1949- 198
  Earlier sketch in SATA *146*
Rowe, Viola Carson 1903-1969
  Obituary 26
Rowh, Mark 1952- 90
Rowland, Florence Wightman 1900-1997 8
  Obituary 108
Rowland-Entwistle, (Arthur) Theodore (Henry)
  1925- 94
  Earlier sketch in SATA *31*
Rowling, J.K. 1965- 174
  Earlier sketch in SATA *109*
  See also CLR *112*
Rowling, Joanne Kathleen
  See Rowling, J.K.
Rowsome, Frank (Howard), Jr. 1914-1983 .. 36
Roy, Gabrielle 1909-1983 104
Roy, Jacqueline 1954- 74
Roy, Jennifer
  See Roy, Jennifer Rozines
Roy, Jennifer Rozines 1967- 178
Roy, Jessie Hailstalk 1895-1986
  Obituary 51
Roy, Liam
  See Scarry, Patricia (Murphy)
Roy, Ron(ald) 1940- 110
  Brief entry 35
  Earlier sketch in SATA *40*
Roybal, Laura 1956- 85
Roybal, Laura Husby
  See Roybal, Laura
Royds, Caroline 1953- 55
Royston, Angela 1945- 169
  Earlier sketch in SATA *120*
Rozakis, Laurie E. 1952- 84
Rubel, Nicole 1953- 181
  Earlier sketches in SATA *18, 95, 135*
Rubin, Eva Johanna 1925- 38
Rubin, Susan Goldman 1939- 182
  Earlier sketches in SATA *84, 132*
Rubin, Vicky 1964- 193
Rubinetti, Donald 1947- 92
Rubinstein, Gillian 1942- 158
  Autobiography Feature 116
  Earlier sketches in SATA *68, 105*
  See also CLR *35*
  See also SAAS *25*
Rubinstein, Gillian Margaret
  See Rubinstein, Gillian
Rubinstein, Patricia (Giulia Caulfield Kate)
  -2003 29
  Obituary 149
  See Forest, Antonia
Rubinstein, Robert E(dward) 1943- 49
Rublowsky, John M(artin) 1928- 62
Rubright, Lynn 1936- 171
Ruby, Laura 181
  Earlier sketch in SATA *155*
Ruby, Lois 1942- 184
  Autobiography Feature 105
  Brief entry 34
  Earlier sketches in SATA *35, 95*
Ruby, Lois F.
  See Ruby, Lois
Ruchlis, Hy(man) 1913-1992 3
  Obituary 72
Rucker, Mike 1940- 91
Ruckman, Ivy 1931- 93
  Earlier sketch in SATA *37*
Ruck-Pauquet, Gina 1931- 40
  Brief entry 37
Ruditis, Paul 190
Rudley, Stephen 1946- 30
Rudolph, Marguerita 1908- 21

Rudomin, Esther
  See Hautzig, Esther Rudomin
Rue, Leonard Lee III 1926- 142
  Earlier sketch in SATA *37*
Rueda, Claudia 183
Ruedi, Norma Paul
  See Ainsworth, Norma
Ruelle, Karen Gray 1957- 126
  Earlier sketch in SATA *84*
Ruemmler, John D(avid) 1948- 78
Ruepp, Krista 1947- 143
Ruffell, Ann 1941- 30
Ruffins, Reynold 1930- 125
  Earlier sketch in SATA *41*
Rugoff, Milton 1913- 30
Ruhen, Olaf 1911-1989 17
Rukeyser, Muriel 1913-1980
  Obituary 22
Rumbaut, Hendle 1949- 84
Rumford, James 1948- 193
  Earlier sketch in SATA *116*
Rumsey, Marian (Barritt) 1928- 16
Rumstuckle, Cornelius
  See Brennan, Herbie
Runnerstroem, Bengt Arne 1944- 75
Runyan, John
  See Palmer, Bernard (Alvin)
Runyon, Catherine 1947- 62
Ruoff, A. LaVonne Brown 1930- 76
Rupp, Rebecca 185
Rusch, Elizabeth 1966- 198
Rusch, Kris
  See Rusch, Kristine Kathryn
Rusch, Kristine Kathryn 1960- 113
Rush, Alison 1951- 41
Rush, Peter 1937- 32
Rushdie, Ahmed Salman
  See Rushdie, Salman
Rushdie, Salman 1947-
  See CLR *125*
Rushford, Patricia H(elen) 1943- 134
Rushmore, Helen 1898-1994 3
Rushmore, Robert (William) 1926-1986 8
  Obituary 49
Ruskin, Ariane
  See Batterberry, Ariane Ruskin
Ruskin, John 1819-1900 24
Russ, Lavinia (Faxon) 1904-1992 74
Russell, Charlotte
  See Rathjen, Carl Henry
Russell, Ching Yeung 1946- 107
Russell, Don(ald Bert) 1899-1986
  Obituary 47
Russell, Franklin (Alexander) 1926- 11
Russell, Gertrude Barrer
  See Barrer-Russell, Gertrude
Russell, Helen Ross 1915- 8
Russell, James 1933- 53
Russell, Jim
  See Russell, James
Russell, Joan Plummer 1930- 139
Russell, P(hilip) Craig 1951- 162
  Earlier sketch in SATA *80*
Russell, Patrick
  See Sammis, John
Russell, Paul (Gary) 1942- 57
Russell, Sarah
  See Laski, Marghanita
Russell, Sharman Apt 1954- 123
Russell, Solveig Paulson 1904-1985 3
Russo, Marisabina 1950- 188
  Earlier sketches in SATA *106, 151*
Russo, Monica J. 1950- 83
Russo, Susan 1947- 30
Russon, Penni 1974- 179
Rutgers van der Loeff, An
  See Rutgers van der Loeff-Basenau, An(na)
  Maria Margaretha
Rutgers van der Loeff-Basenau, An(na) Maria
  Margaretha 1910- 22
Ruth, Rod 1912-1987 9

Rutherford, Douglas
  See McConnell, James Douglas Rutherford
Rutherford, Meg 1932- 34
Ruthin, Margaret
  See Catherall, Arthur
Rutledge, Jill Zimmerman 1951- 155
Rutz, Viola Larkin 1932- 12
Ruurs, Margriet 1952- 147
  Earlier sketch in SATA *97*
Ruzicka, Rudolph 1883-1978
  Obituary 24
Ruzzier, Sergio 1966- 159
Ryan, Betsy
  See Ryan, Elizabeth (Anne)
Ryan, Cheli Duran 20
Ryan, Darlene 1958- 176
Ryan, Elizabeth (Anne) 1943- 30
Ryan, Jeanette
  See Mines, Jeanette
Ryan, John (Gerald Christopher) 1921- 22
Ryan, Margaret 1950- 166
  Earlier sketch in SATA *78*
Ryan, Mary E. 1953- 61
Ryan, Mary Elizabeth
  See Ryan, Mary E.
Ryan, Pam Munoz 1951- 197
  Earlier sketch in SATA *134*
Ryan, Patrick 1957- 138
Ryan, Peter (Charles) 1939- 15
Ryan-Lush, Geraldine 1949- 89
Rybakov, Anatoli (Naumovich) 1911-1998 .. 79
  Obituary 108
  See Rybakov, Anatolii (Naumovich)
Rybakov, Anatolii (Naumovich)
  See Rybakov, Anatoli (Naumovich)
Rybolt, Thomas R. 1954- 62
Rybolt, Thomas Roy
  See Rybolt, Thomas R.
Rybolt, Tom
  See Rybolt, Thomas R.
Rydberg, Ernest E(mil) 1901-1993 21
Rydberg, Lou(isa Hampton) 1908- 27
Rydell, Katy 1942- 91
Rydell, Wendell
  See Rydell, Wendy
Rydell, Wendy 4
Ryden, Hope 91
  Earlier sketch in SATA *8*
Ryder, Joanne (Rose) 1946- 163
  Brief entry 34
  Earlier sketches in SATA *65, 122*
  See also CLR *37*
Ryder, Pamela
  See Lamb, Nancy
Rye, Anthony
  See Youd, (Christopher) Samuel
Rylant, Cynthia 1954- 195
  Brief entry 44
  Earlier sketches in SATA *50, 76, 112, 160*
  See also CLR *86*
  See also SAAS *13*
Rymer, Alta May 1925- 34
Rymond, Lynda Gene 199

S

S. L. C.
  See Twain, Mark
S., Svend Otto
  See Soerensen, Svend Otto
Saaf, Donald W(illiam) 1961- 124
Saal, Jocelyn
  See Sachs, Judith
Sabbeth, Carol (Landstrom) 1957- 125
Saberhagen, Fred 1930-2007 89
  Obituary 184
  Earlier sketch in SATA *37*
Saberhagen, Fred T.
  See Saberhagen, Fred

Saberhagen, Fred Thomas
　See Saberhagen, Fred
Saberhagen, Frederick Thomas
　See Saberhagen, Fred
Sabin, Edwin L(egrand) 1870-1952
　See YABC 2
Sabin, Francene 27
Sabin, Lou
　See Sabin, Louis
Sabin, Louis 1930- 27
Sabre, Dirk
　See Laffin, John (Alfred Charles)
Sabuda, Robert (James) 1965- 120
　Earlier sketch in SATA 81
Sabuda, Robert 1965- 170
Sabuda, Robert James
　See Sabuda, Robert
Sachar, Louis 1954- 154
　Brief entry 50
　Earlier sketches in SATA 63, 104
　See also CLR 79
Sachs, Elizabeth-Ann 1946- 48
Sachs, Judith 1947- 52
　Brief entry 51
Sachs, Marilyn 1927- 164
　Autobiography Feature 110
　Earlier sketches in SATA 3, 68
　See also CLR 2
　See also SAAS 2
Sachs, Marilyn Stickle
　See Sachs, Marilyn
Sackett, S(amuel) J(ohn) 1928- 12
Sackson, Sid 1920- 16
Sacre, Antonio 1968- 152
Saddler, Allen
　See Richards, R(onald) C(harles) W(illiam)
Saddler, K. Allen
　See Richards, R(onald) C(harles) W(illiam)
Sadie, Stanley 1930-2005 14
Sadie, Stanley John
　See Sadie, Stanley
Sadiq, Nazneen 1944- 101
Sadler, Catherine Edwards 1952- 60
　Brief entry 45
Sadler, Marilyn (June) 1950- 79
Sadler, Mark
　See Lynds, Dennis
Saffer, Barbara 144
Sagan, Carl 1934-1996 58
　Obituary 94
Sagan, Carl Edward
　See Sagan, Carl
Sage, Angie 197
Sage, Juniper
　See Brown, Margaret Wise
　and Hurd, Edith Thacher
Sagsoorian, Paul 1923- 12
Said, S.F. 1967- 174
Saidman, Anne 1952- 75
Saint, Dora Jessie 1913- 10
St. Anthony, Jane 175
St. Antoine, Sara L. 1966- 84
St. Clair, Byrd Hooper 1905-1976
　Obituary 28
Saint-Exupery, Antoine de 1900-1944 20
　See also CLR 10
Saint-Exupery, Antoine Jean Baptiste Marie
　Roger de
　See Saint-Exupery, Antoine de
St. George, Judith 1931- 161
　Earlier sketches in SATA 13, 99
　See also CLR 57
　See also SAAS 12
St. James, Blakely
　See Gottfried, Theodore Mark
　and Platt, Charles
St. James, Blakely
　See Griffin, W.E.B
St. James, Sierra
　See Rallison, Janette

Saint James, Synthia 1949- 152
　Earlier sketch in SATA 84
St. John, Nicole 143
　Autobiography Feature 143
　Earlier sketches in SATA 29, 89
　See also CLR 46
　See also SAAS 7
St. John, Patricia Mary 1919-1993
　Obituary 79
St. John, Philip
　See del Rey, Lester
St. John, Wylly Folk 1908-1985 10
　Obituary 45
St. Max, E. S.
　See Ellis, Edward S(ylvester)
St. Meyer, Ned
　See Stratemeyer, Edward L.
St. Mox, E. A.
　See Ellis, Edward S(ylvester)
St. Myer, Ned
　See Stratemeyer, Edward L.
St. Tamara
　See Kolba, St. Tamara
Saito, Michiko
　See Fujiwara, Michiko
Sakaki, Ichiro 1969- 192
Sakamoto, Miki 198
Sakers, Don 1958- 72
Sakharnov, S.
　See Sakharnov, Svyatoslav
Sakharnov, Svyatoslav 1923- 65
Sakharnov, Svyatoslav Vladimirovich
　See Sakharnov, Svyatoslav
Saksena, Kate 148
Sakurai, Gail 1952- 153
　Earlier sketch in SATA 87
Salamanca, Lucy
　See del Barco, Lucy Salamanca
Salassi, Otto R(ussell) 1939-1993 38
　Obituary 77
Salat, Cristina 82
Saldana, Rene, Jr. 186
Saldutti, Denise 1953- 39
Sale, Tim 1956- 153
Salem, Kay 1952- 92
Salerno, Steven 176
Salinger, J.D. 1919- 67
　See also CLR 18
Salinger, Jerome David
　See Salinger, J.D.
Salisbury, Graham 1944- 195
　Earlier sketches in SATA 76, 108, 161
Salisbury, Joyce E(llen) 1944- 138
Salkey, (Felix) Andrew (Alexander)
　1928-1995 118
　Earlier sketch in SATA 35
Salley, Coleen 166
Sallis, Susan (Diana) 1929- 55
Salmon, Annie Elizabeth 1899- 13
Salonen, Roxane Beauclair 1968- 184
Salsi, Lynn 1947- 130
Salsitz, R. A. V.
　See Salsitz, Rhondi Vilott
Salsitz, Rhondi Vilott 115
Salten, Felix
　See Salzmann, Siegmund
Salter, Cedric
　See Knight, Francis Edgar
Saltman, Judith 1947- 64
Saltzberg, Barney 1955- 194
　Earlier sketch in SATA 135
Saltzman, David (Charles Laertes)
　1967-1990 86
Salvadori, Mario (George) 1907-1997 97
　Earlier sketch in SATA 40
Salwood, F.K.
　See Kilworth, Garry
Salzer, L. E.
　See Wilson, Lionel
Salzman, Marian 1959- 77
Salzmann, Siegmund 1869-1945 25

Samachson, Dorothy (Mirkin) 1914-1997 3
Samachson, Joseph 1906-1980 3
　Obituary 52
Sammis, John 1942- 4
Sampson, Emma (Keats) Speed 1868-1947 . 68
Sampson, Fay (Elizabeth) 1935- 151
　Brief entry 40
　Earlier sketch in SATA 42
Sampson, Michael 1952- 143
　Earlier sketch in SATA 95
Samson, Anne S(tringer) 1933- 2
Samson, Joan 1937-1976 13
Samson, Suzanne M. 1959- 91
Samuels, Barbara 199
Samuels, Charles 1902-1982 12
Samuels, Cynthia K(alish) 1946- 79
Samuels, Gertrude 1910(?)-2003 17
　Obituary 147
Sanborn, Duane 1914-1996 38
Sancha, Sheila 1924- 38
Sanchez, Alex 1957- 151
Sanchez, Sonia 1934- 136
　Earlier sketch in SATA 22
　See also CLR 18
Sanchez-Silva, Jose Maria 1911- 132
　Earlier sketch in SATA 16
　See also CLR 12
Sand, George X. 45
Sandak, Cass R(obert) 1950-2001 51
　Brief entry 37
Sandberg, (Karin) Inger 1930- 15
Sandberg, Karl C. 1931- 35
Sandberg, Lasse (E. M.) 1924- 15
Sandburg, Carl (August) 1878-1967 8
　See also CLR 67
Sandburg, Charles
　See Sandburg, Carl (August)
Sandburg, Charles A.
　See Sandburg, Carl (August)
Sandburg, Helga 1918- 3
　See also SAAS 10
Sandell, Lisa Ann 1977- 175
Sander, Heather L. 1947- 157
Sanderlin, George 1915- 4
Sanderlin, Owenita (Harrah) 1916- 11
Sanders, Betty Jane
　See Monthei, Betty
Sanders, Nancy I. 1960- 141
　Earlier sketch in SATA 90
Sanders, Scott Russell 1945- 109
　Earlier sketch in SATA 56
Sanders, Winston P.
　See Anderson, Poul
Sanderson, Irma 1912- 66
Sanderson, Ivan T(erence) 1911-1973 6
Sanderson, Margaret Love
　See Keats, Emma
　and Sampson, Emma (Keats) Speed
Sanderson, Ruth 1951- 172
　Earlier sketches in SATA 41, 109
Sanderson, Ruth L.
　See Sanderson, Ruth
Sandin, Joan 1942- 197
　Earlier sketches in SATA 12, 94, 153
Sandison, Janet
　See Cameron, Elizabeth Jane
Sandler, Martin W. 160
Sandom, J. Gregory
　See Welsh, T.K.
Sandom, J.G.
　See Welsh, T.K.
Sandoz, Mari(e Susette) 1900-1966 5
Sanford, Agnes (White) 1897-1976 61
Sanford, Doris 1937- 69
Sanger, Marjory Bartlett 1920- 8
San Jose, Christine 1929- 167
Sankey, Alice (Ann-Susan) 1910- 27
San Souci, Daniel 192
　Earlier sketch in SATA 96

San Souci, Robert D. 1946- *158*
  Earlier sketches in SATA *40, 81, 117*
  See also CLR *43*
Santamaria, Benjamin 1955- *184*
Santat, Dan *188*
Santesson, Hans Stefan 1914(?)-1975
  Obituary *30*
Santiago, Esmeralda 1948- *129*
Santos, Helen
  See Griffiths, Helen
Santrey, Louis
  See Sabin, Louis
Santucci, Barbara 1948- *130*
Sapergia, Barbara 1943- *181*
Sapieyevski, Anne Lindbergh 1940-1993 ..... *81*
  Brief entry *32*
  Earlier sketches in SATA *35, 78*
Saport, Linda 1954- *123*
Sapp, Allen 1929- *151*
Sarac, Roger
  See Caras, Roger A(ndrew)
Sarah, Duchess of York
  See Ferguson, Sarah
Sarasin, Jennifer
  See Sachs, Judith
Sardinha, Rick *192*
Sarg, Anthony Frederick
  See Sarg, Tony
Sarg, Tony 1882-1942
  See YABC *1*
Sargent, Pamela 1948- *78*
  Earlier sketch in SATA *29*
Sargent, Robert 1933- *2*
Sargent, Sarah 1937- *44*
  Brief entry *41*
Sargent, Shirley 1927-2004 .... *11*
Sarnoff, Jane 1937- *10*
Saroyan, William 1908-1981 .... *23*
  Obituary *24*
Sarton, Eleanor May
  See Sarton, May
Sarton, May 1912-1995 .... *36*
  Obituary *86*
Sasaki, Chris *182*
Saseen, Sharon (Dillon) 1949- *59*
Sasek, Miroslav 1916-1980 .... *16*
  Obituary *23*
  See also CLR *4*
Sasso, Sandy Eisenberg 1947- *162*
  Earlier sketches in SATA *86, 116*
Sathre, Vivian 1952- *133*
  Earlier sketch in SATA *79*
Satterfield, Charles
  See del Rey, Lester
  and Pohl, Frederik
Sattgast, L. J.
  See Sattgast, Linda J.
Sattgast, Linda J. 1953- *91*
Sattler, Helen Roney 1921-1992 .... *74*
  Earlier sketch in SATA *4*
  See also CLR *24*
Sauer, Julia Lina 1891-1983 .... *32*
  Obituary *36*
Sauerwein, Leigh 1944- *155*
Saul, Carol P. 1947- *117*
  Earlier sketch in SATA *78*
Saul, John III
  See Saul, John
Saul, John 1942- *98*
Saul, John W.
  See Saul, John
Saul, John W. III
  See Saul, John
Saul, John Woodruff III
  See Saul, John
Saul, (Ellen) Wendy 1946- *42*
Saulnier, Karen Luczak 1940- *80*
Saunders, Caleb
  See Heinlein, Robert A.
Saunders, Dave 1939- *85*
Saunders, Julie 1939- *85*

Saunders, (William) Keith 1910-1994 .... *12*
Saunders, Rubie (Agnes) 1929- *21*
Saunders, Susan 1945- *96*
  Brief entry *41*
  Earlier sketch in SATA *46*
Saunders-Smith, Gail 1952- *169*
Sauvain, Philip Arthur 1933- *111*
Savadier, Elivia 1950- *164*
  Earlier sketch in SATA *79*
Savage, Alan
  See Nicole, Christopher (Robin)
Savage, Blake
  See Goodwin, Harold L(eland)
Savage, Candace 1949- *142*
Savage, Deborah 1955- *76*
Savage, Jeff 1961- *97*
Savage, Katharine James 1905-1989
  Obituary *61*
Savage, Stephen 1965- *194*
Savage, Thomas 1915-2003
  Obituary *147*
Savageau, Cheryl 1950- *96*
Savery, Constance (Winifred) 1897-1999 ..... *1*
Saville, Andrew
  See Taylor, Andrew
Saville, (Leonard) Malcolm 1901-1982 .... *23*
  Obituary *31*
Saviozzi, Adriana
  See Mazza, Adriana
Savitt, Sam 1917-2000 .... *8*
  Obituary *126*
Savitz, Harriet May 1933- *72*
  Earlier sketch in SATA *5*
  See also SAAS *26*
Sawicki, Mary 1950- *90*
Sawyer, (Frederick) Don(ald) 1947- *72*
Sawyer, Kem Knapp 1953- *84*
Sawyer, Robert J. 1960- *149*
  Earlier sketch in SATA *81*
Sawyer, Robert James
  See Sawyer, Robert J.
Sawyer, Ruth 1880-1970 .... *17*
  See also CLR *36*
Saxby, H.M.
  See Saxby, (Henry) Maurice
Saxby, (Henry) Maurice 1924- *71*
Saxon, Andrew
  See Arthur, Robert, (Jr.)
Saxon, Antonia
  See Sachs, Judith
Say, Allen 1937- *161*
  Earlier sketches in SATA *28, 69, 110*
  See also CLR *135*
Sayers, Frances Clarke 1897-1989 .... *3*
  Obituary *62*
Sayles, Elizabeth 1956- *163*
  Earlier sketch in SATA *108*
Saylor-Marchant, Linda 1963- *82*
Sayre, April Pulley 1966- *191*
  Earlier sketches in SATA *88, 131*
Sazer, Nina 1949- *13*
Scabrini, Janet 1953- *13*
Scagell, Robin 1946- *107*
Scagnetti, Jack 1924- *7*
Scamander, Newt
  See Rowling, J.K.
Scamell, Ragnhild 1940- *180*
  Earlier sketch in SATA *77*
Scanlon, Marion Stephany *11*
Scannel, John Vernon
  See Scannell, Vernon
Scannell, Vernon 1922-2007 .... *59*
  Obituary *188*
Scarborough, Elizabeth *171*
  See Scarborough, Elizabeth Ann
Scarborough, Elizabeth Ann 1947- *171*
  Earlier sketch in SATA *98*
  See Scarborough, Elizabeth
Scarf, Maggi
  See Scarf, Maggie
Scarf, Maggie 1932- *5*

Scariano, Margaret M. 1924- *86*
Scarlett, Susan
  See Streatfeild, Noel
Scarry, Huck
  See Scarry, Richard McClure, Jr.
Scarry, Patricia (Murphy) 1924- *2*
Scarry, Patsy
  See Scarry, Patricia (Murphy)
Scarry, Richard (McClure) 1919-1994 .... *75*
  Obituary *90*
  Earlier sketches in SATA *2, 35*
  See also CLR *41*
Scarry, Richard McClure, Jr. 1953- *35*
Schachner, Judith Byron 1951- *178*
  Earlier sketch in SATA *88*
Schachner, Judy
  See Schachner, Judith Byron
Schachtel, Roger 1949- *38*
Schachtel, Roger Bernard
  See Schachtel, Roger
Schade, Susan *189*
Schaedler, Sally *116*
Schaefer, Carole Lexa *173*
Schaefer, Jack (Warner) 1907-1991 .... *66*
  Obituary *65*
  Earlier sketch in SATA *3*
Schaefer, Lola M. 1950- *183*
  Earlier sketches in SATA *91, 144*
Schaeffer, Mead 1898- *21*
Schaeffer, Susan Fromberg 1941- *22*
Schaer, Brigitte 1958- *112*
Schaller, George
  See Schaller, George B.
Schaller, George B. 1933- *30*
Schaller, George Beals
  See Schaller, George B.
Schanzer, Rosalyn (Good) 1942- *138*
  Earlier sketch in SATA *77*
Schatell, Brian *66*
  Brief entry *47*
Schechter, Betty (Goodstein) 1921- *5*
Schechter, Simone
  See Elkeles, Simone
Schecter, Ellen 1944- *85*
Scheeder, Louis 1946- *141*
Scheer, Julian (Weisel) 1926-2001 .... *8*
Scheffer, Victor B(lanchard) 1906- *6*
Scheffler, Axel 1957- *180*
Scheffler, Ursel 1938- *81*
Scheffrin-Falk, Gladys 1928- *76*
Scheidl, Gerda Marie 1913- *85*
Scheier, Michael 1943- *40*
  Brief entry *36*
Schell, Mildred 1922- *41*
Schell, Orville (Hickok) 1940- *10*
Scheller, Melanie 1953- *77*
Schellie, Don 1932- *29*
Schembri, Jim 1962- *124*
Schembri, Pamela 1969- *195*
Schemm, Mildred Walker 1905-1998 .... *21*
  Obituary *103*
Schenker, Dona 1947- *133*
  Earlier sketch in SATA *68*
Scher, Paula 1948- *47*
Scherer, Jeffrey *194*
Scherf, Margaret 1908-1979 .... *10*
Schermer, Judith (Denise) 1941- *30*
Schertle, Alice 1941- *192*
  Earlier sketches in SATA *36, 90, 145*
Schick, Alice 1946- *27*
Schick, Eleanor 1942- *144*
  Earlier sketches in SATA *9, 82*
Schick, Joel 1945- *31*
  Brief entry *30*
Schields, Gretchen 1948- *75*
Schiff, Ken(neth Roy) 1942- *7*
Schiller, Andrew 1919- *21*
Schiller, Barbara (Heyman) 1928- *21*
Schiller, Pamela (Byrne) *127*
Schindel, John 1955- *115*
  Earlier sketch in SATA *77*

Schindelman, Joseph 1923- *67*
   Brief entry *32*
Schindler, S.D. 1952- *198*
   Brief entry *50*
   Earlier sketches in SATA *75, 118, 171*
Schindler, Steven D.
   See Schindler, S.D.
Schinto, Jeanne 1951- *93*
Schisgall, Oscar 1901-1984 .... *12*
   Obituary *38*
Schlaepfer, Gloria G. 1931- *154*
Schlee, Ann 1934- *44*
   Brief entry *36*
Schleichert, Elizabeth 1945- *77*
Schlein, Miriam 1926-2004 .... *130*
   Obituary *159*
   Earlier sketches in SATA *2, 87*
   See also CLR *41*
Schlesinger, Arthur M., Jr. 1917-2007 .... *61*
   Obituary *181*
   See Schlesinger, Arthur Meier
Schlesinger, Arthur Meier 1888-1965
Schlessinger, Laura (Catherine) 1947- *160*
   Earlier sketch in SATA *110*
Schlitz, Laura Amy *184*
Schloat, G. Warren, Jr. 1914-2000 .... *4*
Schmatz, Pat *197*
Schmid, Eleonore 1939- *126*
   Earlier sketches in SATA *12, 84*
Schmiderer, Dorothy 1940- *19*
Schmidt, Annie M. G. 1911-1995 .... *67*
   Obituary *91*
   See also CLR *22*
Schmidt, C.A. *196*
Schmidt, Diane 1953- *70*
Schmidt, Elizabeth 1915- *15*
Schmidt, Gary D. 1957- *193*
   Earlier sketches in SATA *93, 135*
Schmidt, James Norman 1912-1983 .... *21*
Schmidt, Karen Lee 1953- *185*
   Earlier sketch in SATA *94*
Schmidt, Lynette 1952- *76*
Schneider, Antonie 1954- *167*
   Earlier sketch in SATA *89*
Schneider, Christine M. 1972(?)- *171*
   Earlier sketch in SATA *120*
Schneider, Dick
   See Schneider, Richard H.
Schneider, Elisa
   See Kleven, Elisa
Schneider, Herman 1905-2003 .... *7*
   Obituary *148*
Schneider, Howie -2007 .... *181*
Schneider, Josh 1980- *196*
Schneider, Laurie
   See Adams, Laurie
Schneider, Nina 1913-2007 .... *2*
   Obituary *186*
Schneider, Nina Zimet
   See Schneider, Nina
Schneider, Rex 1937- *44*
Schneider, Richard H. 1922- *171*
Schneider, Richard Henry
   See Schneider, Richard H.
Schneider, Robyn 1986- *187*
Schnirel, James R. 1931- *14*
Schnitter, Jane T. 1958- *88*
Schnitzlein, Danny *134*
Schnur, Steven 1952- *144*
   Earlier sketch in SATA *95*
Schnurre, Wolfdietrich 1920-1989
   Obituary *63*
Schoberle, Cecile 1949- *80*
Schock, Pauline 1928- *45*
Schoell, William 1951- *160*
Schoen, Barbara (Taylor) 1924-1993 .... *13*
Schoenherr, Ian *177*
Schoenherr, John (Carl) 1935- *66*
   Earlier sketch in SATA *37*
   See also SAAS *13*

Schofield, Sandy
   See Rusch, Kristine Kathryn
Scholastica, Sister Mary
   See Jenkins, Marie M(agdalen)
Scholefield, A. T.
   See Scholefield, Alan
Scholefield, Alan 1931- *66*
Scholefield, Edmund O.
   See Griffin, W.E.B
Scholey, Arthur 1932- *28*
Scholz, Jackson Volney 1897-1986
   Obituary *49*
Schone, Virginia *22*
Schongut, Emanuel 1936- *184*
   Brief entry *36*
   Earlier sketch in SATA *52*
Schoonover, Frank (Earle) 1877-1972 .... *24*
Schoor, Gene 1921- *3*
Schories, Pat 1952- *164*
   Earlier sketch in SATA *116*
Schorr, Melissa 1972- *194*
Schorr, Melissa Robin
   See Schorr, Melissa
Schott, Jane A. 1946- *172*
Schotter, Roni *190*
   Earlier sketches in SATA *105, 149*
Schraff, Anne E(laine) 1939- *92*
   Earlier sketch in SATA *27*
Schram, Peninnah 1934- *119*
Schrank, Joseph 1900-1984
   Obituary *38*
Schrecengost, Maity 1938- *118*
Schrecengost, S. Maitland
   See Schrecengost, Maity
Schreck, Karen
   See Schreck, Karen Halvorsen
Schreck, Karen Halvorsen 1962- *185*
Schrecker, Judie 1954- *90*
Schreiber, Elizabeth Anne (Ferguson)
   1947- *13*
Schreiber, Ralph W(alter) 1942- *13*
Schreiner, Samuel A(gnew), Jr. 1921- *70*
Schroeder, Alan 1961- *98*
   Earlier sketch in SATA *66*
Schroeder, Binette
   See Nickl, Barbara (Elisabeth)
Schroeder, Russell (K.) 1943- *146*
Schroeder, Ted 1931(?)-1973
   Obituary *20*
Schubert, Dieter 1947- *101*
   Earlier sketch in SATA *62*
Schubert, Leda 1950(?)- *181*
Schubert-Gabrys, Ingrid 1953- *101*
   Earlier sketch in SATA *62*
Schuelein-Steel, Danielle
   See Steel, Danielle
Schuelein-Steel, Danielle Fernande
   See Steel, Danielle
Schuerger, Michele R. *110*
Schuett, Stacey 1960- *168*
   Earlier sketch in SATA *75*
Schulke, Flip Phelps Graeme 1930- *57*
Schulman, Arlene 1961- *105*
Schulman, Janet 1933- *137*
   Earlier sketch in SATA *22*
Schulman, L(ester) M(artin) 1934- *13*
Schulte, Elaine L(ouise) 1934- *36*
Schultz, Betty K(epka) 1932- *125*
Schultz, Gwendolyn *21*
Schultz, James Willard 1859-1947
   See YABC *1*
Schultz, Pearle Henriksen 1918- *21*
Schulz, Charles M. 1922-2000 .... *10*
   Obituary *118*
Schulz, Charles Monroe
   See Schulz, Charles M.
Schumacher, Julie 1958- *191*
Schumaker, Ward 1943- *96*
Schuman, Michael A. 1953- *134*
   Earlier sketch in SATA *85*

Schur, Maxine
   See Schur, Maxine Rose
Schur, Maxine Rose 1948- *135*
   Autobiography Feature *135*
   Brief entry *49*
   Earlier sketches in SATA *53, 98*
Schurfranz, Vivian 1925- *13*
Schutzer, A. I. 1922- *13*
Schuyler, Pamela R. 1948- *30*
Schwabach, Karen *185*
Schwager, Tina 1964- *110*
Schwandt, Stephen (William) 1947- *61*
Schwark, Mary Beth 1954- *51*
Schwartz, Alvin 1927-1992 .... *56*
   Obituary *71*
   Earlier sketch in SATA *4*
   See also CLR *89*
Schwartz, Amy 1954- *189*
   Brief entry *41*
   Earlier sketches in SATA *47, 83, 131*
   See also CLR *25*
   See also SAAS *18*
Schwartz, Anne Powers 1913-1987 .... *10*
Schwartz, Carol 1954- *77*
Schwartz, Charles W(alsh) 1914- *8*
Schwartz, David M. 1951- *110*
   Earlier sketch in SATA *59*
Schwartz, David Martin
   See Schwartz, David M.
Schwartz, Elizabeth Reeder 1912- *8*
Schwartz, Ellen 1949- *117*
Schwartz, Jerome L.
   See Lawrence, Jerome
Schwartz, Joel L. 1940- *54*
   Brief entry *51*
Schwartz, Joyce R. 1950- *93*
Schwartz, Julius 1907-2004 .... *45*
Schwartz, Perry 1942- *75*
Schwartz, Sheila (Ruth) 1929- *27*
Schwartz, Stephen (Lawrence) 1948- *19*
Schwartz, Virginia Frances 1950- *184*
   Earlier sketch in SATA *131*
Schwarz, (Silvia Tessa) Viviane 1977- *141*
Schweitzer, Byrd Baylor
   See Baylor, Byrd
Schweitzer, Iris *59*
   Brief entry *36*
Schweninger, Ann 1951- *168*
   Earlier sketches in SATA *29, 98*
Schwerin, Doris H(alpern) 1922- *64*
Schy, Yael *197*
Scieszka, Jon 1954- *199*
   Earlier sketches in SATA *68, 105, 160*
   See also CLR *107*
Scillian, Devin *199*
   Earlier sketch in SATA *128*
Scioscia, Mary (Hershey) 1926- *63*
Sciurba, Katie 1957- *196*
Scofield, Penrod 1933- *62*
   Obituary *78*
Scoggin, Margaret C(lara) 1905-1968 .... *47*
   Brief entry *28*
Scoltock, Jack 1942- *141*
   Earlier sketch in SATA *72*
Scoppettone, Sandra 1936- *92*
   Earlier sketch in SATA *9*
Scot, Michael
   See Rohan, Michael Scott
Scot-Bernard, P.
   See Bernard, Patricia
Scotland, Jay
   See Jakes, John
Scott, Alastair
   See Allen, Kenneth S.
Scott, Ann Herbert 1926- *140*
   Autobiography Feature *140*
   Brief entry *29*
   Earlier sketches in SATA *56, 94*
Scott, Bill
   See Scott, William N(eville)

Scott, Bill 1920(?)-1985
  Obituary 46
Scott, Cora Annett (Pipitone) 1931- 11
Scott, Dan
  See Barker, S(quire) Omar
Scott, Elaine 1940- 198
  Earlier sketches in SATA 36, 90, 164
Scott, Elizabeth 194
Scott, Jack Denton 1915-1995 83
  Earlier sketch in SATA 31
  See also CLR 20
  See also SAAS 14
Scott, Jane (Harrington) 1931- 55
Scott, Jessica
  See De Wire, Elinor
Scott, John 1912-1976 14
Scott, John Anthony 1916- 23
Scott, John M(artin) 1913- 12
Scott, Mary
  See Mattern, Joanne
Scott, Melissa 1960- 109
Scott, Richard
  See Rennert, Richard Scott
Scott, Roney
  See Gault, William Campbell
Scott, Sally 1909-1978 43
Scott, Sally 1948- 44
Scott, Sally Elisabeth
  See Scott, Sally
Scott, W. N.
  See Scott, William N(eville)
Scott, Sir Walter 1771-1832
  See YABC 2
Scott, Warwick
  See Trevor, Elleston
Scott, William N(eville) 1923- 87
Scotti, Anna
  See Coates, Anna
Scotton, Rob 1960- 177
Scribner, Charles, Jr. 1921-1995 13
  Obituary 87
Scribner, Joanne L. 1949- 33
Scribner, Kimball 1917- 63
Scrimger, Richard 1957- 164
  Earlier sketch in SATA 119
Scrimsher, Lila Gravatt 1897-1974
  Obituary 28
Scroder, Walter K. 1928- 82
Scroggs, Kirk 187
Scruggs, Sandy 1961- 89
Scudder, Brooke 1959- 154
Scudder, Mildred Lee 1908- 6
  See also SAAS 12
Scull, Marie-Louise 1943-1993 77
Scuro, Vincent 1951- 21
Seabrooke, Brenda 1941- 148
  Earlier sketches in SATA 30, 88
Seaman, Augusta Huiell 1879-1950 31
Seamands, Ruth 1916- 9
Searcy, Margaret Zehmer 1926- 54
  Brief entry 39
Searight, Mary W(illiams) 1918- 17
Searle, Kathryn Adrienne 1942- 10
Searle, Ronald (William Fordham) 1920- 70
  Earlier sketch in SATA 42
Sears, Stephen W. 1932- 4
Sebastian, Lee
  See Silverberg, Robert
Sebestyen, Igen
  See Sebestyen, Ouida
Sebestyen, Ouida 1924- 140
  Earlier sketch in SATA 39
  See also CLR 17
  See also SAAS 10
Sebrey, Mary Ann 1951- 62
Sechrist, Elizabeth Hough 1903-1991 2
Sedges, John
  See Buck, Pearl S(ydenstricker)
Sedgwick, Marcus 1968- 197
  Earlier sketch in SATA 160

Seed, Cecile Eugenie 1930- 86
  Earlier sketch in SATA 8
  See also CLR 76
Seed, Jenny
  See Seed, Cecile Eugenie
Seed, Sheila Turner 1937(?)-1979
  Obituary 23
Seeger, Elizabeth 1889-1973
  Obituary 20
Seeger, Laura Vaccaro 172
Seeger, Pete 1919- 139
  Earlier sketch in SATA 13
Seeger, Peter R.
  See Seeger, Pete
Seeley, Laura L. 1958- 71
Seever, R.
  See Reeves, Lawrence F.
Sefozo, Mary 1925- 82
Sefton, Catherine
  See Waddell, Martin
Segal, John 178
Segal, Joyce 1940- 35
Segal, Lore 1928- 163
  Earlier sketches in SATA 4, 66
  See also SAAS 11
Segal, Lore Groszmann
  See Segal, Lore
Segar, E(lzie) C(risler) 1894-1938 61
Segovia, Andres 1893(?)-1987
  Obituary 52
Seguin, Marilyn W(eymouth) 1951- 91
Seguin-Fontes, Marthe 1924- 109
Seibold, J. Otto 1960- 196
  Earlier sketches in SATA 83, 149
  See also SAAS 22
Seidel, Ross 95
Seidelman, James Edward 1926- 6
Seiden, Art(hur) 107
  Brief entry 42
Seidler, Ann (G.) 1925- 131
Seidler, Tor 1952- 149
  Brief entry 46
  Earlier sketches in SATA 52, 98
Seidman, Laurence Ivan 1925- 15
Seigel, Kalman 1917-1998 12
  Obituary 103
Seignobosc, Francoise 1897-1961 21
Seinfeld, Jerry 1954- 146
Seitz, Jacqueline 1931- 50
Seixas, Judith S. 1922- 17
Sejima, Yoshimasa 1913- 8
Selberg, Ingrid (Maria) 1950- 68
Selden, George
  See Thompson, George Selden
Selden, Neil R(oy) 1931- 61
Self, Margaret Cabell 1902-1996 24
Selfors, Suzanne 1963- 193
Selick, Henry 1952- 183
Selig, Sylvie 1942- 13
Selkirk, Jane
  See Chapman, John Stanton Higham
Sellers, Naomi
  See Flack, Naomi John White
Selman, LaRue W. 1927- 55
Selsam, Millicent E(llis) 1912-1996 29
  Obituary 92
  Earlier sketch in SATA 1
  See also CLR 1
Seltzer, Meyer 1932- 17
Seltzer, Richard 1946- 41
Seltzer, Richard Warren, Jr.
  See Seltzer, Richard
Selvadurai, Shyam 1965(?)- 171
Selway, Martina 1940- 169
  Earlier sketch in SATA 74
Selzer, Adam 1980- 192
Selznick, Brian 1966- 171
  Earlier sketches in SATA 79, 117
Semel, Nava 1954- 107
Semloh
  See Holmes, Peggy

Sendak, Jack 1924(?)-1995 28
Sendak, Maurice 1928- 165
  Earlier sketches in SATA 1, 27, 113
  See also CLR 131
Sendak, Maurice Bernard
  See Sendak, Maurice
Sender, Ruth M(insky) 1926- 62
Sengler, Johanna 1924- 18
Senisi, Ellen B. 1951- 116
Senisi, Ellen Babinec
  See Senisi, Ellen B.
Senn, J(oyce) A(nn) 1941- 115
Senn, Steve 1950- 60
  Brief entry 48
Serage, Nancy 1924- 10
Seredy, Kate 1899-1975 1
  Obituary 24
  See also CLR 10
Serfozo, Mary 1925- 194
Seroff, Victor I(ilyitch) 1902-1979 12
  Obituary 26
Serraillier, Ian (Lucien) 1912-1994 73
  Obituary 83
  Earlier sketch in SATA 1
  See also CLR 2
  See also SAAS 3
Serros, Michele 175
Serros, Michele M.
  See Serros, Michele
Servello, Joe 1932- 10
Service, Pamela F. 1945- 64
Service, Robert
  See Service, Robert W(illiam)
Service, Robert W(illiam) 1874(?)-1958 20
Serwadda, W(illiam) Moses 1931- 27
Serwer-Bernstein, Blanche L(uria)
  1910-1997 10
Sescoe, Vincent E. 1938- 123
Seth, Mary
  See Lexau, Joan M.
Seton, Anya 1904(?)-1990 3
  Obituary 66
Seton, Ernest (Evan) Thompson 1860-1946 . 18
  See also CLR 59
Seton-Thompson, Ernest
  See Seton, Ernest (Evan) Thompson
Seuling, Barbara 1937- 193
  Earlier sketches in SATA 10, 98, 145
  See also SAAS 24
Seuss, Dr.
  See Dr. Seuss
  and Geisel, Theodor Seuss
  and LeSieg, Theo.
  and Stone, Rosetta
Severn, Bill
  See Severn, William Irving
Severn, David
  See Unwin, David S(torr)
Severn, William Irving 1914- 1
Sewall, Marcia 1935- 119
  Earlier sketches in SATA 37, 69
Seward, Prudence 1926- 16
Sewell, Anna 1820-1878 100
  Earlier sketch in SATA 24
  See also CLR 17
Sewell, Helen (Moore) 1896-1957 38
Sexton, Anne (Harvey) 1928-1974 10
Seymour, Alta Halverson 10
Seymour, Jane 1951- 139
Seymour, Tres 1966- 164
  Earlier sketch in SATA 82
Sfar, Joann 1971- 182
Shachtman, Tom 1942- 49
Shackleton, C.C.
  See Aldiss, Brian W.
Shader, Rachel
  See Sofer, Barbara
Shadow, Jak
  See Sutherland, Jon
Shadyland, Sal
  See Cooper, Louise

Author Index

Shafer, Audrey *183*
Shafer, Robert E(ugene) 1925- *9*
Shaffer, Terea 1968- *79*
Shahan, Sherry 1949- *134*
  Earlier sketch in SATA 92
Shahn, Ben(jamin) 1898-1969
  Obituary *21*
Shahn, Bernarda Bryson
  See Bryson, Bernarda
Shaik, Fatima *114*
Shalant, Phyllis 1949- *150*
Shan, Darren 1972- *199*
  Earlier sketches in SATA *129, 168*
Shan, D.B.
  See Shan, Darren
Shanahan, Lisa *199*
Shanberg, Karen
  See Shragg, Karen (I.)
Shane, Harold Gray 1914-1993 .... *36*
  Obituary *76*
Shange, Ntozake 1948- *157*
Shanks, Ann Zane (Kushner) *10*
Shannon, David 1959- *152*
  Earlier sketch in SATA *107*
  See also CLR 87
Shannon, George (William Bones) 1952- ... *143*
  Earlier sketches in SATA *35, 94*
Shannon, Jacqueline *63*
Shannon, Margaret
  See Silverwood, Margaret Shannon
Shannon, Monica 1905(?)-1965 .... *28*
Shannon, Terry
  See Mercer, Jessie
Shannon, Terry Miller 1951- *148*
Shapiro, Irwin 1911-1981 .... *32*
Shapiro, Jody Fickes 1940- *193*
Shapiro, Karen Jo 1964- *186*
Shapiro, Michelle 1961- *196*
Shapiro, Milton J. 1926- *32*
Shapiro, Tricia
  See Andryszewski, Tricia
Shapp, Charles M(orris) 1906-1989
  Obituary *61*
Shapp, Martha Glauber 1910- *3*
Sharenow, Robert *193*
Sharfman, Amalie *14*
Sharma, Partap 1939- *15*
Sharma, Rashmi
  See Singh, Rashmi Sharma
Sharman, Alison
  See Leonard, Alison
Sharmat, Marjorie Weinman 1928- *133*
  Earlier sketches in SATA *4, 33, 74*
Sharmat, Mitchell 1927- *127*
  Earlier sketch in SATA *33*
Sharp, Anne Wallace 1947- *144*
Sharp, Luke
  See Alkiviades, Alkis
Sharp, Margery 1905-1991 .... *29*
  Obituary *67*
  Earlier sketch in SATA *1*
  See also CLR 27
Sharp, Zerna A. 1889-1981
  Obituary *27*
Sharpe, Jon
  See Duncan, Alice
  and Knott, William C(ecil, Jr.)
  and Messman, Jon
Sharpe, Mitchell R(aymond) 1924- *12*
Sharpe, Susan 1946- *71*
Sharratt, Nick 1962- *199*
  Earlier sketches in SATA *104, 153*
Shasha, Mark 1961- *80*
Shattuck, Roger 1923-2005 .... *64*
  Obituary *174*
Shattuck, Roger Whitney
  See Shattuck, Roger
Shaw, Arnold 1909-1989 .... *4*
  Obituary *63*
Shaw, Carolyn V. 1934- *91*
Shaw, Charles (Green) 1892-1974 .... *13*

Shaw, Evelyn S. 1927- *28*
Shaw, Flora Louisa
  See Lugard, Flora Louisa Shaw
Shaw, Janet 1937- *146*
  Earlier sketch in SATA *61*
  See also CLR 96
Shaw, Janet Beeler
  See Shaw, Janet
Shaw, Lisa
  See Rogak, Lisa
Shaw, Margret 1940- *68*
Shaw, Mary 1965- *180*
Shaw, Nancy 1946- *162*
  Earlier sketch in SATA *71*
Shaw, Ray *7*
Shaw, Richard 1923- *12*
Shawn, Frank S.
  See Goulart, Ron(ald Joseph)
Shay, Art
  See Shay, Arthur
Shay, Arthur 1922- *4*
Shay, Lacey
  See Shebar, Sharon Sigmond
Shea, Bob *188*
Shea, George 1940- *54*
  Brief entry *42*
Shea, Pegi Deitz 1960- *172*
  Earlier sketches in SATA *77, 137*
Shearer, John 1947- *43*
  Brief entry *27*
  See also CLR 34
Shearer, Ted 1919- *43*
Shearing, Leonie 1972- *184*
Sheban, Chris *182*
Shebar, Sharon Sigmond 1945- *36*
Shecter, Ben 1935- *16*
Shedd, Warner 1934- *147*
  Earlier sketch in SATA *87*
Sheedy, Alexandra Elizabeth 1962- *39*
  Earlier sketch in SATA *19*
Sheehan, Ethna 1908-2000 .... *9*
Sheehan, Patty 1945- *77*
Sheehan, Sean 1951- *154*
  Earlier sketch in SATA *86*
Sheen, Barbara 1949- *143*
Shefelman, Janice Jordan 1930- *129*
  Earlier sketch in SATA *58*
Shefelman, Tom (Whitehead) 1927- *58*
Sheffer, H. R.
  See Abels, Harriette S(heffer)
Sheffield, Charles 1935-2002 .... *109*
Sheffield, Janet N. 1926- *26*
Sheikh, Nazneen
  See Sadiq, Nazneen
Shekerjian, Regina Tor *16*
Shelby, Anne 1948- *85*
  Autobiography Feature *121*
  See also SAAS 26
Sheldon, Ann
  See Antle, Nancy
Sheldon, Ann *67*
  Earlier sketch in SATA *1*
Sheldon, Aure 1917-1976 .... *12*
Sheldon, David *185*
Sheldon, Dyan *181*
Sheldon, John
  See Bloch, Robert (Albert)
Sheldon, Muriel 1926- *45*
  Brief entry *39*
Shell, Barry 1951- *176*
Shelley, Frances
  See Wees, Frances Shelley
Shelley, Mary Wollstonecraft (Godwin)
  1797-1851 .... *29*
  See also CLR 133
Shelton, William Roy 1919-1995 .... *5*
  Obituary *129*
Shemie, Bonnie (Jean Brenner) 1949- *96*
Shemin, Margaretha (Hoeneveld) 1928- *4*
Shen, Michele 1953- *173*

Shenker, Michele
  See Shen, Michele
Shenton, Edward 1895-1977 .... *45*
Shepard, Aaron 1950- *187*
  Earlier sketches in SATA *75, 113*
Shepard, Ernest Howard 1879-1976 .... *100*
  Obituary *24*
  Earlier sketches in SATA *3, 33*
  See also CLR 27
Shepard, James R.
  See Shepard, Jim
Shepard, Jim 1956- *164*
  Earlier sketch in SATA *90*
Shepard, Mary
  See Knox, (Mary) Eleanor Jessie
Shephard, Esther 1891-1975 .... *5*
  Obituary *26*
Shepherd, Donna Walsh
  See Walsh Shepherd, Donna
Shepherd, Elizabeth *4*
Shepherd, Irana *173*
Shepherd, Roni
  See Shepherd, Irana
Sheppard, Kate *195*
Shepperson, Rob *178*
Sherburne, Zoa (Lillian Morin) 1912-1995 .... *3*
  See also SAAS 18
Sherk-Savage, Candace
  See Savage, Candace
Sherlock, Patti *71*
Sherman, D(enis) R(onald) 1934- *48*
  Brief entry *29*
Sherman, Diane (Finn) 1928- *12*
Sherman, Elizabeth
  See Friskey, Margaret (Richards)
Sherman, Harold (Morrow) 1898-1987 .... *37*
  Obituary *137*
Sherman, Josepha *163*
  Earlier sketch in SATA *75*
Sherman, Michael
  See Lowndes, Robert A(ugustine) W(ard)
Sherman, Nancy
  See Rosenberg, Nancy (Sherman)
Sherman, Pat *174*
Sherman, Peter Michael
  See Lowndes, Robert A(ugustine) W(ard)
Sherrard, Valerie (Anne) 1957- *141*
Sherrod, Jane
  See Singer, Jane Sherrod
Sherry, Clifford J. 1943- *84*
Sherry, (Dulcie) Sylvia 1932- *122*
  Earlier sketch in SATA *8*
Sherwan, Earl 1917- *3*
Sherwood, Jonathan
  See London, Jonathan (Paul)
Sheth, Kashmira *186*
Shetterly, Will 1955- *78*
  Autobiography Feature *106*
Shetterly, William Howard
  See Shetterly, Will
Shiefman, Vicky 1942- *22*
Shields, Brenda Desmond (Armstrong)
  1914- *37*
Shields, Carol Diggory *174*
Shields, Charles 1944- *10*
Shiels, Barbara
  See Adams, Barbara Johnston
Shiffman, Lena 1957- *101*
Shiina, Makoto 1944- *83*
Shimin, Symeon 1902-1984 .... *13*
Shimko, Bonnie 1941- *191*
Shine, Andrea 1955- *104*
Shine, Deborah 1932- *71*
Shinn, Everett 1876-1953 .... *21*
Shinn, Sharon 1957- *164*
  Earlier sketch in SATA *110*
Shippen, Katherine B(inney) 1892-1980 .... *1*
  Obituary *23*
  See also CLR 36
Shippey, T. A. 1943- *143*

Shippey, Thomas Alan
  See Shippey, T. A.
Shipton, Eric Earle 1907-1977 .... *10*
Shipton, Paul 1963- *196*
Shiraz, Yasmin *173*
Shirer, William L(awrence) 1904-1993 .... *45*
  Obituary *78*
Shirley, Gayle C 1955- *96*
Shirley, Gayle Corbett
  See Shirley, Gayle C
Shirley, Jean 1919- *70*
Shirreffs, Gordon D(onald) 1914-1996 .... *11*
Shirts, Morris A(lpine) 1922- *63*
Shlichta, Joe 1968- *84*
Shmurak, Carole B. 1944- *118*
Sholokhov, Mikhail (Aleksandrovich)
  1905-1984
  Obituary *36*
Shore, Diane Z. *179*
Shore, Diane ZuHone
  See Shore, Diane Z.
Shore, June Lewis *30*
Shore, Nancy 1960- *124*
Shore, Robert 1924- *39*
Short, Michael 1937- *65*
Short, Roger
  See Arkin, Alan
Shortall, Leonard W. *19*
Shortt, Tim(othy Donald) 1961- *96*
Shotwell, Louisa Rossiter 1902-1993 .... *3*
Shoup, Barbara 1947- *156*
  Earlier sketch in SATA *86*
  See also SAAS *24*
Shoveller, Herb *184*
Showalter, Jean B(reckinridge) *12*
Showell, Ellen Harvey 1934- *33*
Showers, Paul C. 1910-1999 .... *92*
  Obituary *114*
  Earlier sketch in SATA *21*
  See also CLR *6*
  See also SAAS *7*
Shpakow, Tanya 1959(?)- *94*
Shpitalnik, Vladimir 1964- *83*
Shragg, Karen (I.) 1954- *142*
Shreeve, Elizabeth 1956- *156*
Shreve, Susan
  See Shreve, Susan Richards
Shreve, Susan Richards 1939- *152*
  Brief entry *41*
  Earlier sketches in SATA *46, 95*
Shriver, Jean Adair 1932- *75*
Shriver, Maria 1955- *134*
Shriver, Maria Owings
  See Shriver, Maria
Shrode, Mary
  See Hollingsworth, Mary
Shtainmets, Leon *32*
Shub, Elizabeth 1915(?)-2004 .... *5*
Shuken, Julia 1948- *84*
Shulevitz, Uri 1935- *165*
  Earlier sketches in SATA *3, 50, 106*
  See also CLR *61*
Shulman, Alix Kates 1932- *7*
Shulman, Dee 1957- *146*
Shulman, Irving 1913-1995 .... *13*
Shulman, Mark 1962- *184*
Shulman, Max 1919-1988
  Obituary *59*
Shulman, Milton 1913-2004
  Obituary *154*
Shulman, Neil B(arnett) 1945- *89*
Shumsky, Zena
  See Collier, Zena
Shura, Mary Francis
  See Craig, Mary (Francis) Shura
Shusterman, Neal 1962- *140*
  Autobiography Feature *140*
  Earlier sketches in SATA *85, 121*
Shuter, Jane (Margaret) 1955- *151*
  Earlier sketch in SATA *90*
Shuttlesworth, Dorothy Edwards *3*

Shwartz, Susan (Martha) 1949- *94*
Shyer, Christopher 1961- *98*
Shyer, Marlene Fanta *13*
Siberell, Anne *29*
Sibley, Don 1922- *12*
Siburt, Ruth 1951- *121*
Siculan, Daniel 1922- *12*
Siddon, Barbara
  See Bradford, Barbara Taylor
Sidgwick, Ethel 1877-1970 .... *116*
Sidjakov, Nicolas 1924- *18*
Sidman, Joyce 1956- *181*
  Earlier sketch in SATA *145*
Sidney, Frank
  See Warwick, Alan R(oss)
Sidney, Margaret
  See Lothrop, Harriet Mulford Stone
Siebert, Diane 1948- *189*
Siegal, Aranka 1930- *88*
  Brief entry *37*
Siegel, Beatrice *36*
Siegel, Helen
  See Siegl, Helen
Siegel, Robert 1939- *39*
Siegel, Robert Harold
  See Siegel, Robert
Siegel, Siena Cherson 1967(?)- *185*
Siegelson, Kim L. 1962- *114*
Sieger, Ted 1958- *189*
Siegl, Helen 1924- *34*
Siepmann, Mary Aline
  See Wesley, Mary (Aline)
Sierra, Judy 1945- *195*
  Earlier sketches in SATA *104, 162*
Sieswerda, Paul L. 1942- *147*
Sievert, Terri
  See Dougherty, Terri (L.)
Silas
  See McCay, (Zenas) Winsor
Silcock, Sara Lesley 1947- *12*
Silin-Palmer, Pamela *184*
Sill, Cathryn 1953- *141*
  Earlier sketch in SATA *74*
Sill, John 1947- *140*
  Earlier sketch in SATA *74*
Sillitoe, Alan 1928- *61*
Sills, Leslie (Elka) 1948- *129*
Silly, E. S.
  See Kraus, (Herman) Robert
Silsbe, Brenda 1953- *73*
Silva, Joseph
  See Goulart, Ron(ald Joseph)
Silver, Ruth
  See Chew, Ruth
Silverberg, Robert 1935- *91*
  Autobiography Feature *104*
  Earlier sketch in SATA *13*
  See also CLR *59*
Silverman, Erica 1955- *165*
  Earlier sketches in SATA *78, 112*
Silverman, Janis L. 1946- *127*
Silverman, Mel(vin Frank) 1931-1966 .... *9*
Silverman, Robin L. 1954- *96*
Silverman, Robin Landew
  See Silverman, Robin L.
Silverstein, Alvin 1933- *124*
  Earlier sketches in SATA *8, 69*
  See also CLR *25*
Silverstein, Herma 1945- *106*
Silverstein, Robert Alan 1959- *124*
  Earlier sketch in SATA *77*
Silverstein, Shel 1932-1999 .... *92*
  Brief entry *27*
  Obituary *116*
  Earlier sketch in SATA *33*
  See also CLR *96*
Silverstein, Sheldon Allan
  See Silverstein, Shel

Silverstein, Virginia B(arbara Opshelor)
  1937- *124*
  Earlier sketches in SATA *8, 69*
  See also CLR *25*
Silverthorne, Elizabeth 1930- *35*
Silverwood, Margaret Shannon 1966- *137*
  Earlier sketch in SATA *83*
Silvey, Diane F. 1946- *135*
Sim, David 1953- *162*
Sim, Dorrith M. 1931- *96*
Simak, Clifford D(onald) 1904-1988
  Obituary *56*
Simard, Remy 1959- *168*
Simmie, Lois (Ann) 1932- *106*
Simmonds, Posy 1945- *130*
  See also CLR *23*
Simmons, Andra 1939- *141*
Simmons, Elly 1955- *134*
Simmons, Michael 1970- *185*
Simms, Laura 1947- *117*
Simner, Janni Lee *113*
Simon, Charlie May
  See Fletcher, Charlie May Hogue
Simon, Francesca 1955- *111*
Simon, Gabriel 1972- *118*
Simon, Hilda Rita 1921- *28*
  See also CLR *39*
Simon, Howard 1903-1979 .... *32*
  Obituary *21*
Simon, Joe
  See Simon, Joseph H.
Simon, Joseph H. 1913- *7*
Simon, Martin P(aul William) 1903-1969 .... *12*
Simon, Mina Lewiton
  See Lewiton, Mina
Simon, Norma (Feldstein) 1927- *129*
  Earlier sketches in SATA *3, 68*
Simon, Seymour 1931- *138*
  Earlier sketches in SATA *4, 73*
  See also CLR *63*
Simon, Shirley (Schwartz) 1921- *11*
Simon, Solomon 1895-1970 .... *40*
Simonetta, Linda 1948- *14*
Simonetta, Sam 1936- *14*
Simons, Barbara B(rooks) 1934- *41*
Simont, Marc 1915- *126*
  Earlier sketches in SATA *9, 73*
Simpson, Colin 1908-1983 .... *14*
Simpson, Harriette
  See Arnow, Harriette (Louisa) Simpson
Simpson, Jacynth Hope
  See Hope Simpson, Jacynth
Simpson, Lesley 1963- *150*
Simpson, Margaret 1943- *128*
Simpson, Myrtle L(illias) 1931- *14*
Sims, Blanche *168*
  Earlier sketch in SATA *75*
Sims, Blanche L.
  See Sims, Blanche
Simundsson, Elva 1950- *63*
Sinclair, Clover
  See Gater, Dilys
Sinclair, Emil
  See Hesse, Hermann
Sinclair, Jeff 1958- *77*
Sinclair, Olga 1923- *121*
Sinclair, Rose
  See Smith, Susan Vernon
Sinclair, Upton 1878-1968 .... *9*
Sinclair, Upton Beall
  See Sinclair, Upton
Singer, A.L.
  See Lerangis, Peter
Singer, Arthur 1917-1990 .... *64*
Singer, Isaac
  See Singer, Isaac Bashevis
Singer, Isaac Bashevis 1904-1991 .... *27*
  Obituary *68*
  Earlier sketch in SATA *3*
  See also CLR *1*

Singer, Jane Sherrod 1917-1985 .... *4*
    Obituary *42*
Singer, Julia 1917- *28*
Singer, Kurt D. 1911-2005 .... *38*
    Obituary *172*
Singer, Marilyn 1948- *158*
    Autobiography Feature *158*
    Brief entry *38*
    Earlier sketches in SATA *48, 80, 125*
    See also CLR *48*
    See also SAAS *13*
Singer, Muff 1942-2005 .... *104*
    Obituary *160*
Singer, Nicky 1956- *194*
Singer, Susan (Mahler) 1941- *9*
Singh, Rashmi Sharma 1952- *90*
Singleton, Linda Joy 1957- *166*
    Earlier sketch in SATA *88*
Singleton, L.J.
    See Singleton, Linda Joy
Sinykin, Sheri(l Terri) Cooper 1950- *142*
    Autobiography Feature *142*
    Earlier sketches in SATA *72, 133*
Sipiera, Paul P., (Jr.) 1948- *144*
    Earlier sketch in SATA *89*
Siracusa, Catherine (Jane) 1947- *82*
Sirett, Dawn (Karen) 1966- *88*
Sirimarco, Elizabeth 1966- *158*
Sirof, Harriet 1930- *94*
    Earlier sketch in SATA *37*
Sirois, Allen L. 1950- *76*
Sirvaitis (Chernyaev), Karen (Ann) 1961- ... *79*
Sis, Peter 1949- *192*
    Earlier sketch in SATA *149*
    See also CLR *110*
Sisson, Rosemary Anne 1923- *11*
Sister Mary Terese
    See Donze, Mary Terese
Sita, Lisa 1962- *87*
Sitomer, Alan Lawrence *174*
Sitomer, Harry 1903-1985 .... *31*
Sitomer, Mindel 1903-1987 .... *31*
Sittenfeld, Curtis 1975(?)- *164*
Sive, Helen R(obinson) 1951- *30*
Sivulich, Sandra (Jeanne) Stroner 1941- *9*
Siy, Alexandra *193*
Skarmeta, Antonio 1940- *57*
Skelly, James R(ichard) 1927- *17*
Skelton, Matthew 1971- *185*
Skinner, Constance Lindsay 1877-1939
    See YABC *1*
Skinner, Cornelia Otis 1901-1979 .... *2*
Skipper, G. C. 1939- *46*
    Brief entry *38*
Sklansky, Amy E(dgar) 1971- *145*
Skofield, James *95*
    Brief entry *44*
Skold, Betty Westrom 1923- *41*
Skorpen, Liesel Moak 1935- *3*
Skott, Maria
    See Nikolajeva, Maria
Skrypuch, Marsha Forchuk 1954- *134*
Skultety, Nancy Laney 1960- *175*
Skurzynski, Gloria 1930- *145*
    Autobiography Feature *145*
    Earlier sketches in SATA *8, 74, 122*
    See also SAAS *9*
Skurzynski, Gloria Joan
    See Skurzynski, Gloria
Skutch, Robert 1925- *89*
Skye, Maggie
    See Werner, Herma
Skye, Obert *170*
Slack, Michael 1969- *189*
Slackman, Charles B. 1934- *12*
Slade, Arthur G. 1967- *149*
    Earlier sketch in SATA *106*
Slade, Arthur Gregory
    See Slade, Arthur G.
Slade, Christian 1974- *193*
Slade, Richard 1910-1971 .... *9*

Slangerup, Erik Jon 1969- *130*
Slate, Joseph 1928- *174*
    Earlier sketches in SATA *38, 122*
Slate, Joseph Frank
    See Slate, Joseph
Slater, Dashka 1963- *179*
Slater, Ray
    See Lansdale, Joe R.
Slaughter, Hope 1940- *84*
Slaughter, Jean
    See Doty, Jean Slaughter
Slaughter, Tom 1955- *152*
Slavicek, Louise Chipley 1956- *144*
Slavin, Bill 1959- *199*
    Earlier sketches in SATA *76, 148*
Slaymaker, Melissa Eskridge 1958- *158*
Sleator, William 1945- *161*
    Earlier sketches in SATA *3, 68, 118*
    See also CLR *128*
Sleator, William Warner III
    See Sleator, William
Slegers, Liesbet 1975- *154*
Sleigh, Barbara 1906-1982 .... *86*
    Obituary *30*
    Earlier sketch in SATA *3*
Slepian, Jan 1921- *85*
    Brief entry *45*
    Earlier sketch in SATA *51*
    See also SAAS *8*
Slepian, Janice B.
    See Slepian, Jan
Slicer, Margaret O. 1920- *4*
Slier, Debby
    See Shine, Deborah
Sloan, Brian 1966- *172*
Sloan, Carolyn 1937- *116*
    Earlier sketch in SATA *58*
Sloan, Glenna (Davis) 1930- *120*
Sloane, Eric 1910(?)-1985 .... *52*
    Obituary *42*
Sloane, Todd 1955- *88*
Sloat, Teri 1948- *164*
    Earlier sketches in SATA *70, 106*
Slobodkin, Florence Gersh 1905-1994 .... *5*
    Obituary *107*
Slobodkin, Louis 1903-1975 .... *26*
    Earlier sketch in SATA *1*
Slobodkina, Esphyr 1908-2002 .... *1*
    Obituary *135*
    See also SAAS *8*
Sloggett, Nellie 1851-1923 .... *44*
Sloss, Lesley Lord 1965- *72*
Slote, Alfred 1926- *72*
    Earlier sketch in SATA *8*
    See also CLR *4*
    See also SAAS *21*
Slote, Elizabeth 1956- *80*
Small, David 1945- *183*
    Brief entry *46*
    Earlier sketches in SATA *50, 95, 126*
    See also CLR *53*
Small, Ernest
    See Lent, Blair
Small, Mary 1932- *165*
Small, Terry 1942- *75*
Smallcomb, Pam 1954- *159*
Smallman, Steve *197*
Smalls, Irene
    See Smalls-Hector, Irene
Smalls-Hector, Irene 1950- *146*
    Earlier sketch in SATA *73*
    See also CLR *103*
Smallwood, Norah (Evelyn) 1910(?)-1984
    Obituary *41*
Smaridge, Norah (Antoinette) 1903-1994 ...... *6*
Smath, Jerry 1933- *198*
Smee, Nicola 1948- *167*
    Earlier sketch in SATA *76*
Smiley, Virginia Kester 1923- *2*
Smit, Noelle 1972- *199*

Smith, Alexander McCall 1948- *179*
    Earlier sketch in SATA *73*
Smith, Anne Warren 1938- *41*
    Brief entry *34*
Smith, Barry (Edward Jervis) 1943- *75*
Smith, Beatrice S(chillinger) *12*
Smith, Betsy Covington 1937- *55*
    Earlier sketch in SATA *43*
Smith, Betty (Wehner) 1904-1972 .... *6*
Smith, Bradford 1909-1964 .... *5*
Smith, Brenda 1946- *82*
Smith, C. Pritchard
    See Hoyt, Edwin P(almer), Jr.
Smith, Caesar
    See Trevor, Elleston
Smith, Charles R., (Jr.) 1969- *159*
Smith, Craig 1955- *172*
    Earlier sketches in SATA *81, 117*
Smith, Cynthia Leitich 1967- *152*
Smith, Datus C(lifford), Jr. 1907-1999 .... *13*
    Obituary *116*
Smith, Debra 1955- *89*
Smith, Derek 1943- *141*
Smith, Dick King
    See King-Smith, Dick
Smith, Dodie
    See Smith, Dorothy Gladys
Smith, Doris Buchanan 1934-2002 .... *75*
    Obituary *140*
    Earlier sketch in SATA *28*
    See also SAAS *10*
Smith, Dorothy Gladys 1896-1990 .... *82*
    Obituary *65*
Smith, Dorothy Stafford 1905- *6*
Smith, E(lmer) Boyd 1860-1943
    See YABC *1*
Smith, E(dric) Brooks 1917- *40*
Smith, Emma 1923- *52*
    Brief entry *36*
Smith, (Katherine) Eunice (Young)
    1902-1993 .... *5*
Smith, Frances C(hristine) 1904-1986 .... *3*
Smith, Gary R. 1932- *14*
Smith, Geof 1969- *102*
Smith, George Harmon 1920- *5*
Smith, Gordon 1951- *184*
Smith, Greg Leitich *152*
Smith, H(arry) Allen 1907-1976
    Obituary *20*
Smith, Helene 1937- *142*
Smith, Howard E(verett), Jr. 1927- *12*
Smith, Hugh L(etcher) 1921-1968 .... *5*
Smith, Imogene Henderson 1922- *12*
Smith, Jacqueline B. 1937- *39*
Smith, Jada Pinkett 1971- *161*
Smith, James D. 1955- *176*
Smith, James Noel 1950- *193*
Smith, Janet (Buchanan) Adam
    See Adam Smith, Janet (Buchanan)
Smith, Janice Lee 1949- *155*
    Earlier sketch in SATA *54*
Smith, Jean
    See Smith, Frances C(hristine)
Smith, Jean Pajot 1945- *10*
Smith, Jeff(rey Alan) 1960- *161*
    Earlier sketch in SATA *93*
Smith, Jeff Allen
    See Smith, Jeff(rey Alan)
Smith, Jenny 1963- *90*
Smith, Jessie
    See Kunhardt, Edith
Smith, Jessie Willcox 1863-1935 .... *21*
    See also CLR *59*
Smith, Joan (Mary) 1933- *54*
    Brief entry *46*
Smith, Johnston
    See Crane, Stephen (Townley)
Smith, Jos A. 1936- *181*
    Earlier sketches in SATA *73, 120*
Smith, Joseph Arthur
    See Smith, Jos A.

Smith, Judie R. 1936- 80
Smith, Lafayette
   See Higdon, Hal
Smith, Lane 1959- 179
   Earlier sketches in SATA 76, 131
   See also CLR 47
Smith, Lee
   See Albion, Lee Smith
Smith, Lendon H(oward) 1921- 64
Smith, Lillian H(elena) 1887-1983
   Obituary 32
Smith, Linda 1949- 177
Smith, Linell Nash 1932- 2
Smith, Lucia B. 1943- 30
Smith, Maggie 1965- 190
Smith, Margaret Emily Noel Nuttall
   See Nuttall-Smith, Margaret Emily Noel
Smith, Marion Hagens 1913- 12
Smith, Marion Jaques 1899-1987 13
Smith, Mary Ellen 10
Smith, Marya 1945- 78
Smith, Mike
   See Smith, Mary Ellen
Smith, Nancy Covert 1935- 12
Smith, Norman F. 1920- 70
   Earlier sketch in SATA 5
Smith, Patricia Clark 1943- 96
Smith, Pauline C.
   See Arthur, Robert, (Jr.)
Smith, Pauline C(oggeshall) 1908-1994 27
Smith, Philip Warren 1936- 46
Smith, R. Alexander McCall
   See Smith, Alexander McCall
Smith, Rebecca 1946- 123
Smith, Robert Kimmel 1930- 77
   Earlier sketch in SATA 12
Smith, Robert Paul 1915-1977 52
   Obituary 30
Smith, Roland 1951- 193
   Earlier sketches in SATA 115, 161
Smith, Rosamond
   See Oates, Joyce Carol
Smith, Ruth Leslie 1902- 2
Smith, Samantha 1972-1985
   Obituary 45
Smith, Sandra Lee 1945- 75
Smith, Sarah Stafford
   See Smith, Dorothy Stafford
Smith, Sharon 1947- 82
Smith, Sherri L. 1971- 156
Smith, Sherwood 1951- 140
   Earlier sketch in SATA 82
Smith, Shirley Raines
   See Raines, Shirley C(arol)
Smith, Susan Carlton 1923- 12
Smith, Susan Mathias 1950- 43
   Brief entry 35
Smith, Susan Vernon 1950- 48
   Brief entry 45
Smith, Tim(othy R.) 1945- 151
Smith, Ursula 1934- 54
Smith, Vian (Crocker) 1920-1969 11
Smith, Wanda VanHoy 1926- 65
Smith, Ward
   See Goldsmith, Howard
Smith, William A. 1918- 10
Smith, William Jay 1918- 154
   Autobiography Feature 154
   Earlier sketches in SATA 2, 68
   See also SAAS 22
Smith, Winsome 1935- 45
Smith, Z.Z.
   See Westheimer, David
Smith-Ankrom, M. E. 1942- 130
Smith-Griswold, Wendy 1955- 88
Smith-Rex, Susan J. 1950- 94
Smithsen, Richard
   See Pellowski, Michael (Joseph)
Smits, Teo
   See Smits, Theodore R(ichard)

Smits, Theodore R(ichard) 1905-1996 45
   Brief entry 28
Smolinski, Dick 1932- 86
Smothers, Ethel Footman 1944- 149
   Earlier sketch in SATA 76
Smucker, Barbara 1915-2003 130
   Earlier sketches in SATA 29, 76
   See also CLR 10
   See also SAAS 11
Smucker, Barbara Claassen
   See Smucker, Barbara
Smyth, Iain 1959- 105
Snedeker, Caroline Dale (Parke) 1871-1956
   See YABC 2
Sneed, Brad 191
Sneider, Marian 1932-2005 197
Snell, Nigel (Edward Creagh) 1936- 57
   Brief entry 40
Snellgrove, L(aurence) E(rnest) 1928- 53
Snelling, Dennis (Wayne) 1958- 84
Sneve, Virginia Driving Hawk 1933- 95
   Earlier sketch in SATA 8
   See also CLR 2
Snicket, Lemony 1970- 187
   Earlier sketch in SATA 126
   See also CLR 79
Sniegoski, Thomas E. 195
Sniegoski, Tom
   See Sniegoski, Thomas E.
Snodgrass, Mary Ellen 1944- 75
Snodgrass, Quentin Curtius
   See Twain, Mark
Snodgrass, Thomas Jefferson
   See Twain, Mark
Snook, Barbara (Lillian) 1913-1976 34
Snow, Alan 1959- 190
Snow, Donald Clifford 1917-1979 16
Snow, Dorothea J(ohnston) 1909- 9
Snow, Richard F(olger) 1947- 52
   Brief entry 37
Snyder, Anne 1922-2001 4
   Obituary 125
Snyder, Bernadette McCarver 1930- 97
Snyder, Carol 1941- 35
Snyder, Gerald S(eymour) 1933- 48
   Brief entry 34
Snyder, Jerome 1916-1976
   Obituary 20
Snyder, Midori 1954- 106
Snyder, Paul A. 1946- 125
Snyder, Zilpha Keatley 1927- 163
   Autobiography Feature 163
   Earlier sketches in SATA 1, 28, 75, 110
   See also CLR 121
   See also SAAS 2
Snyderman, Reuven K. 1922- 5
So, Meilo 162
Sobel, June 1950- 149
Soble, Jennie
   See Cavin, Ruth (Brodie)
Sobol, Donald J. 1924- 132
   Earlier sketches in SATA 1, 31, 73
   See also CLR 4
Sobol, Harriet Langsam 1936- 47
   Brief entry 34
Sobol, Rose 1931- 76
Sobott-Mogwe, Gaele 1956- 97
Soderlind, Arthur E(dwin) 1920- 14
Soentpiet, Chris K. 1970- 159
   Earlier sketch in SATA 97
Soerensen, Svend Otto 1916- 67
Sofer, Barbara 1949- 109
Sofer, Rachel
   See Sofer, Barbara
Softly, Barbara Frewin 1924- 12
Soglow, Otto 1900-1975
   Obituary 30
Sohl, Frederic J(ohn) 1916- 10
Sohr, Daniel 1973- 190
Sokol, Bill
   See Sokol, William

Sokol, William 1923- 37
Sokolov, Kirill 1930- 34
Solbert, Romaine G. 1925- 2
Solbert, Ronni
   See Solbert, Romaine G.
Solheim, James 133
Solomon, Heather M. 188
Solomon, Joan 1930- 51
   Brief entry 40
Solomons, Ikey Esquir
   See Thackeray, William Makepeace
Solonevich, George 1915-2003 15
Solot, Mary Lynn 1939- 12
Somerlott, Robert 1928-2001 62
Somervill, Barbara A(nn) 1948- 140
Sommer, Angela
   See Sommer-Bodenburg, Angela
Sommer, Carl 1930- 175
   Earlier sketch in SATA 126
Sommer, Elyse 1929- 7
Sommer, Robert 1929- 12
Sommer-Bodenburg, Angela 1948- 113
   Earlier sketch in SATA 63
Sommerdorf, Norma 1926- 131
Sommerdorf, Norma Jean
   See Sommerdorf, Norma
Sommerfelt, Aimee 1892-1975 5
Son, John 160
Sones, Sonya 131
Sonneborn, Ruth (Cantor) 1899-1974 4
   Obituary 27
Sonnenblick, Jordan 1969- 185
Sonnenmark, Laura A. 1958- 73
Sopko, Eugen 1949- 58
Sorel, Edward 1929- 126
   Brief entry 37
   Earlier sketch in SATA 65
Sorensen, Henri 1950- 115
   Earlier sketch in SATA 77
Sorensen, Svend Otto
   See Soerensen, Svend Otto
Sorensen, Virginia 1912-1991 2
   Obituary 72
   See also SAAS 15
Sorenson, Jane 1926- 63
Sorenson, Margo 1946- 96
Sorley Walker, Kathrine 41
Sorra, Kristin 185
Sorrells, Walter 177
Sorrentino, Joseph N. 1937- 6
Sortor, June Elizabeth 1939- 12
Sortor, Toni
   See Sortor, June Elizabeth
Soskin, V. H.
   See Ellison, Virginia H(owell)
Soto, Gary 1952- 174
   Earlier sketches in SATA 80, 120
   See also CLR 38
Sotomayor, Antonio 1902-1985 11
Souci, Robert D. San
   See San Souci, Robert D.
Soudley, Henry
   See Wood, James Playsted
Souhami, Jessica 176
Soule, Gardner (Bosworth) 1913-2000 14
Soule, Jean Conder 1919- 10
Souster, (Holmes) Raymond 1921- 63
South, Sheri Cobb 1959- 82
Southall, Ivan 1921-2008 134
   Autobiography Feature 134
   Earlier sketches in SATA 3, 68
   See also CLR 2
   See also SAAS 3
Southall, Ivan Francis
   See Southall, Ivan
Southey, Robert 1774-1843 54
Southgate, Vera 54
Sovak, Jan 1953- 115
Sowden, Celeste
   See Walters, Celeste
Sowter, Nita 69

Spafford, Suzy 1945- *160*
Spagnoli, Cathy 1950- *134*
　Earlier sketch in SATA 79
Spain, Sahara Sunday 1991- *133*
Spain, Susan Rosson *185*
Spalding, Andrea 1944- *150*
　Earlier sketch in SATA *101*
Spalenka, Greg 1958- *198*
Spanfeller, James J(ohn) 1930- *19*
　See also SAAS 8
Spanfeller, Jim
　See Spanfeller, James J(ohn)
Spangenberg, Judith Dunn 1942- *5*
Spanyol, Jessica 1965- *137*
Spar, Jerome 1918- *10*
Sparks, Barbara 1942- *78*
Sparks, Beatrice (Mathews) 1918- *44*
　Brief entry *28*
　See also CLR *139*
Sparks, Mary W. 1920- *15*
Spaulding, Douglas
　See Bradbury, Ray
Spaulding, Leonard
　See Bradbury, Ray
Spaulding, Norma *107*
Speare, Elizabeth George 1908-1994 .... *62*
　Obituary *83*
　Earlier sketch in SATA 5
　See also CLR 8
Spearing, Judith (Mary Harlow) 1922- *9*
Spears, Rick *182*
Speck, Katie *196*
Speck, Nancy 1959- *104*
Specking, Inez 1890-1960(?) *11*
Speed, Nell
　See Keats, Emma
　and Sampson, Emma (Keats) Speed
Speed, Nell (Ewing) 1878-1913 .... *68*
Speer, Bonnie Stahlman 1929- *113*
Speer-Lyon, Tammie L. 1965- *89*
Speicher, Helen Ross S(mith) 1915- *8*
Speir, Nancy 1958- *81*
Spellman, John W(illard) 1934- *14*
Spellman, Roger G.
　See Cox, William R(obert)
Spelman, Cornelia Maude 1946- *144*
　Earlier sketch in SATA 96
Spelman, Mary 1934- *28*
Spelvin, George
　See Lerangis, Peter
　and Phillips, David Atlee
Spence, Cynthia
　See Eble, Diane
Spence, Eleanor (Rachel) 1928- *21*
　See also CLR 26
Spence, Geraldine 1931- *47*
Spencer, Ann 1918- *10*
Spencer, Cornelia
　See Yaukey, Grace S(ydenstricker)
Spencer, Donald D(ean) 1931- *41*
Spencer, Elizabeth 1921- *14*
Spencer, Leonard G.
　See Garrett, (Gordon) Randall (Phillip)
　and Silverberg, Robert
Spencer, William 1922- *9*
Spencer, Zane A(nn) 1935- *35*
Sper, Emily 1957- *142*
Speregen, Devra Newberger 1964- *84*
Sperling, Dan(iel Lee) 1949- *65*
Sperry, Armstrong W. 1897-1976 .... *1*
　Obituary *27*
Sperry, Raymond
　See Garis, Howard R(oger)
Sperry, Raymond, Jr. *1*
Spetter, Jung-Hee 1969- *134*
Spicer, Dorothy Gladys -1975 .... *32*
Spiegel, Beth *184*
Spiegelman, Art 1948- *158*
　Earlier sketch in SATA *109*
Spiegelman, Judith M. *5*
Spielberg, Steven 1947- *32*

Spier, Peter (Edward) 1927- *54*
　Earlier sketch in SATA 4
　See also CLR 5
Spilhaus, Athelstan (Frederick) 1911-1998 .. *13*
　Obituary *102*
Spilka, Arnold 1917- *6*
Spillane, Frank Morrison
　See Spillane, Mickey
Spillane, Mickey 1918-2006 .... *66*
　Obituary *176*
Spinelli, Eileen 1942- *186*
　Earlier sketches in SATA 38, *101, 150*
Spinelli, Jerry 1941- *195*
　Earlier sketches in SATA 39, 71, *110, 158*
　See also CLR 82
Spink, Reginald (William) 1905-1994 .... *11*
Spinka, Penina Keen 1945- *72*
Spinner, Stephanie 1943- *132*
　Earlier sketches in SATA 38, *91*
Spinossimus
　See White, William, Jr.
Spiotta-DiMare, Loren *173*
Spires, Ashley 1978- *183*
Spires, Elizabeth 1952- *111*
　Earlier sketch in SATA 71
Spiridellis, Gregg 1971(?)- *199*
Spirin, Gennadii
　See Spirin, Gennady
Spirin, Gennadij
　See Spirin, Gennady
Spirin, Gennady 1948- *134*
　Earlier sketch in SATA 95
　See also CLR 88
Spivak, Dawnine *101*
Spizman, Robyn Freedman *194*
Spohn, David 1948- *72*
Spohn, Kate 1962- *147*
　Earlier sketch in SATA 87
Spollen, Christopher 1952- *12*
Spooner, Michael (Tim) 1954- *92*
Spowart, Robin 1947- *177*
　Earlier sketch in SATA 82
Sprague, Gretchen 1926-2003 .... *27*
Sprengel, Artie
　See Lerangis, Peter
Sprigge, Elizabeth (Miriam Squire)
　1900-1974 .... *10*
Spring, (Robert) Howard 1889-1965 .... *28*
Springer, Margaret 1941- *78*
Springer, Marilyn Harris 1931- *47*
Springer, Nancy 1948- *172*
　Earlier sketches in SATA 65, *110*
Springstubb, Tricia 1950- *78*
　Brief entry *40*
　Earlier sketch in SATA 46
Spudvilas, Anne 1951- *199*
　Earlier sketch in SATA 94
Spurll, Barbara 1952- *78*
Spurr, Elizabeth *172*
Spykman, E(lizabeth) C(hoate) 1896-1965 .. *10*
　See also CLR 35
Spyri, Johanna (Heusser) 1827-1901 .... *100*
　Earlier sketch in SATA 19
　See also CLR 115
Squires, Phil
　See Barker, S(quire) Omar
Srba, Lynne *98*
Sreenivasan, Jyotsna 1964- *101*
S-Ringi, Kjell
　See Ringi, Kjell (Arne Soerensen)
Stacey, Cherylyn 1945- *96*
Stacy, Donald
　See Pohl, Frederik
Stadtler, Bea 1921- *17*
Stafford, Jean 1915-1979
　Obituary *22*
Stafford, Liliana 1950- *141*
Stafford, Paul 1966- *116*
Stahl, Ben(jamin) 1910-1987 .... *5*
　Obituary *54*

Stahl, Hilda 1938-1993 .... *48*
　Obituary *77*
Stahler, David, Jr. *162*
Stainton, Sue *187*
Stair, Gobin (John) 1912- *35*
Stalder, Valerie *27*
Stamaty, Mark Alan 1947- *12*
Stambler, Irwin 1924- *5*
Standiford, Natalie 1961- *169*
　Earlier sketch in SATA *81*
Stanek, Lou Willett 1931- *63*
Stang, Judit 1921-1977 .... *29*
Stang, Judy
　See Stang, Judit
Stangl, (Mary) Jean 1928- *67*
Stanhope, Eric
　See Hamilton, Charles (Harold St. John)
Stankevich, Boris 1928- *2*
Stanley, Diane 1943- *164*
　Brief entry *32*
　Earlier sketches in SATA 37, 80, *115*
　See also CLR 46
　See also SAAS 15
Stanley, George Edward 1942- *67*
　Earlier sketches in SATA 53, *111, 157, 1*
Stanley, Jerry 1941- *127*
　Earlier sketch in SATA 79
Stanley, Mandy *165*
Stanley, Robert
　See Hamilton, Charles (Harold St. John)
Stanley, Sanna 1962- *145*
Stanli, Sue
　See Meilach, Dona Z(weigoron)
Stanstead, John
　See Groom, Arthur William
Stanton, Karen 1960- *190*
Stanton, Schuyler
　See Baum, L(yman) Frank
Staples, Suzanne Fisher 1945- *151*
　Earlier sketches in SATA 70, *105*
　See also CLR 137
Stapleton, Marjorie (Winifred) 1932- *28*
Stapp, Arthur D(onald) 1906-1972 .... *4*
Starbird, Kaye 1916- *6*
　See also CLR 60
Stark, Evan 1942- *78*
Stark, James
　See Goldston, Robert (Conroy)
Stark, Ken 1943- *199*
Stark, Ulf 1944- *124*
Starke, Ruth (Elaine) 1946- *129*
Starkey, Marion L(ena) 1901-1991 .... *13*
Starr, Ward
　See Manes, Stephen
Starret, William
　See McClintock, Marshall
Starr Taylor, Bridget 1959- *99*
Stasiak, Krystyna *49*
Staub, Frank 1949- *116*
Staub, Frank Jacob
　See Staub, Frank
Staub, Wendy Corsi 1964- *114*
Stauffacher, Sue 1961- *199*
　Earlier sketch in SATA *155*
Stauffer, Don
　See Berkebile, Fred D(onovan)
Staunton, Schuyler
　See Baum, L(yman) Frank
Staunton, Ted 1956- *167*
　Earlier sketch in SATA *112*
Stead, Rebecca 1968(?)- *188*
Steadman, Ralph 1936- *123*
　Earlier sketch in SATA 32
Steadman, Ralph Idris
　See Steadman, Ralph
Stearman, Kaye 1951- *118*
Stearns, Monroe (Mather) 1913-1987 .... *5*
　Obituary *55*
Steckler, Arthur 1921-1985 .... *65*
Steding, Laurie 1953- *119*
Steel, Danielle 1947- *66*

Steel, Danielle Fernande
  See Steel, Danielle
Steele, Addison II
  See Lupoff, Richard A(llen)
Steele, Alexander 1958- 116
Steele, Henry Maxwell
  See Steele, Max
Steele, Mary 1930- 94
Steele, Mary Q(uintard Govan) 1922-1992 .. 51
  Obituary 72
  Earlier sketch in SATA 3
Steele, Max 1922-2005 168
  Earlier sketch in SATA 10
Steele, Philip 1948- 140
  Earlier sketch in SATA 81
Steele, William O(wen) 1917-1979 51
  Obituary 27
  Earlier sketch in SATA 1
Steelhammer, Ilona 1952- 98
Steelsmith, Shari 1962- 72
Stefanik, Alfred T. 1939- 55
Steffanson, Con
  See Cassiday, Bruce (Bingham)
  and Goulart, Ron(ald Joseph)
Steffens, Bradley 1955- 166
  Earlier sketch in SATA 77
Steffensmeier, Alexander 1977- 195
Stegeman, Janet Allais 1923- 49
  Brief entry 49
Steggall, Susan 1967- 182
Steig, William 1907-2003 111
  Obituary 149
  Earlier sketches in SATA 18, 70
  See also CLR 103
Steig, William H.
  See Steig, William
Stein, David Ezra 180
Stein, M(eyer) L(ewis) 1920- 6
Stein, Mathilde 1969- 195
Stein, Mini 2
Stein, R(ichard) Conrad 1937- 154
  Earlier sketches in SATA 31, 82
Stein, Wendy 1951- 77
Steinbeck, John (Ernst) 1902-1968 9
Steinberg, Alfred 1917-1995 9
Steinberg, Fannie 1899-1990 43
Steinberg, Fred J. 1933- 4
Steinberg, Phillip Orso 1921- 34
Steinberg, Rafael (Mark) 1927- 45
Steinberg, Saul 1914-1999 67
Steincrohn, Maggie
  See Davis, Maggie S.
Steiner, Barbara A(nnette) 1934- 83
  Earlier sketch in SATA 13
  See also SAAS 13
Steiner, Charlotte 1900-1981 45
Steiner, George 1929- 62
Steiner, Joan 199
  Earlier sketch in SATA 110
Steiner, Jorg
  See Steiner, Jorg
Steiner, Jorg 1930- 35
Steiner, K. Leslie
  See Delany, Samuel R., Jr.
Steiner, Stan(ley) 1925-1987 14
  Obituary 50
Steins, Richard 1942- 79
Stem, Jacqueline 1931- 110
Stemple, Jason 179
Steneman, Shep 1945- 132
Stengel, Joyce A. 1938- 158
Stephanie, Gordon
  See Gordon, Stephanie Jacob
Stephens, Alice Barber 1858-1932 66
Stephens, Casey
  See Wagner, Sharon B.
Stephens, Henrietta Henkle 1909-1993 6
Stephens, J.B.
  See Lynn, Tracy
Stephens, Mary Jo 1935- 8
Stephens, Rebecca 1961- 141

Stephens, Reed
  See Donaldson, Stephen R.
Stephens, Suzanne
  See Kirby, Susan E.
Stephens, William M(cLain) 1925- 21
Stephensen, A. M.
  See Manes, Stephen
Stephenson, Lynda 1941- 179
Stephenson, Lynda A.
  See Stephenson, Lynda
Stepp, Ann 1935- 29
Stepto, Michele 1946- 61
Steptoe, Javaka 1971- 151
Steptoe, John (Lewis) 1950-1989 63
  Earlier sketch in SATA 8
  See also CLR 12
Sterling, Brett
  See Bradbury, Ray
  and Hamilton, Edmond
  and Samachson, Joseph
Sterling, Dorothy 1913-2008 83
  Autobiography Feature 127
  Earlier sketch in SATA 1
  See also CLR 1
  See also SAAS 2
Sterling, Helen
  See Watts, Helen L. Hoke
Sterling, Philip 1907-1989 8
  Obituary 63
Sterling, Shirley (Anne) 1948- 101
Stern, Ellen Norman 1927- 26
Stern, Judith M. 1951- 75
Stern, Madeleine
  See Stern, Madeleine B.
Stern, Madeleine B. 1912-2007 14
Stern, Madeleine Bettina
  See Stern, Madeleine B.
Stern, Maggie 1953- 156
Stern, Philip Van Doren 1900-1984 13
  Obituary 39
Stern, Simon 1943- 15
Sterne, Emma Gelders 1894- 6
Steurt, Marjorie Rankin 1888-1978 10
Stevens, Bryna 1924- 65
Stevens, Carla M(cBride) 1928- 13
Stevens, Chambers 1968- 128
Stevens, Diane 1939- 94
Stevens, Franklin 1933- 6
Stevens, Greg
  See Cook, Glen
Stevens, Gwendolyn 1944- 33
Stevens, Jan Romero 1953- 95
Stevens, Janet 1953- 193
  Earlier sketches in SATA 90, 148
Stevens, Kathleen 1936- 49
Stevens, Leonard A. 1920- 67
Stevens, Lucile Vernon 1899-1994 59
Stevens, Margaret Dean
  See Aldrich, Bess Streeter
Stevens, Patricia Bunning 1931- 27
Stevens, Peter
  See Geis, Darlene Stern
Stevens, Serita 1949- 70
Stevens, Serita Deborah
  See Stevens, Serita
Stevens, Serita Mendelson
  See Stevens, Serita
Stevens, Shira
  See Stevens, Serita
Stevenson, Anna (M.) 1905- 12
Stevenson, Augusta 1869(?)-1976 2
  Obituary 26
Stevenson, Burton Egbert 1872-1962 25
Stevenson, Drew 1947- 60
Stevenson, Harvey 1960- 148
  Earlier sketch in SATA 80
Stevenson, James 1929- 195
  Brief entry 34
  Earlier sketches in SATA 42, 71, 113, 161
  See also CLR 17
Stevenson, Janet 1913- 8

Stevenson, Robert Louis (Balfour)
  1850-1894 100
  See also YABC 2
  See also CLR 107
Stevenson, Sucie
  See Stevenson, Sucie
Stevenson, Sucie 1956- 194
  Earlier sketch in SATA 104
Stewart, A(gnes) C(harlotte) 15
Stewart, Amber 181
Stewart, Chantal 1945- 173
  Earlier sketch in SATA 121
Stewart, Charles
  See Zurhorst, Charles (Stewart, Jr.)
Stewart, Eleanor
  See Porter, Eleanor H(odgman)
Stewart, Elisabeth J(ane) 1927- 93
Stewart, Elizabeth Laing 1907- 6
Stewart, Gail B. 1949- 141
Stewart, George Rippey 1895-1980 3
  Obituary 23
Stewart, Jennifer J(enkins) 1960- 128
Stewart, Joel 151
Stewart, John (William) 1920- 14
Stewart, Mary (Florence Elinor) 1916- 12
Stewart, Mary Rainbow
  See Stewart, Mary (Florence Elinor)
Stewart, Melissa 1968- 167
  Earlier sketch in SATA 111
Stewart, Paul 1955- 199
  Earlier sketches in SATA 114, 163
Stewart, Robert Neil 1891-1972 7
Stewart, Sarah 143
Stewart, Scott
  See Zaffo, George J.
Stewart, W(alter) P. 1924- 53
Stewart, Whitney 1959- 167
  Earlier sketch in SATA 92
Stewig, John Warren 1937- 162
  Earlier sketches in SATA 26, 110
Stickler, Soma Han 1942- 128
Stidworthy, John 1943- 63
Stiegemeyer, Julie 180
Stier, Catherine 198
Stiles, Martha Bennett 108
  Earlier sketch in SATA 6
Still, James 1906-2001 29
  Obituary 127
Stille, Darlene R. 1942- 170
  Earlier sketch in SATA 126
Stille, Darlene Ruth
  See Stille, Darlene R.
Stillerman, Marci 104
Stillerman, Robbie 1947- 12
Stilley, Frank 1918- 29
Stilton, Geronimo 158
Stimpson, Gerald
  See Mitchell, Adrian
Stine, Catherine 165
Stine, G(eorge) Harry 1928-1997 136
  Earlier sketch in SATA 10
Stine, Jovial Bob
  See Stine, R.L.
Stine, R.L. 1943- 194
  Earlier sketches in SATA 31, 76, 129
  See also CLR 111
Stine, Robert Lawrence
  See Stine, R.L.
Stinetorf, Louise (Allender) 1900-1992 10
Stinson, Kathy 1952- 98
Stirling, Arthur
  See Sinclair, Upton
Stirling, Ian 1941- 77
Stirling, Nora B(romley) 1900-1997 3
Stirnweis, Shannon 1931- 10
Stobbs, William 1914-2000 17
  Obituary 120
Stock, Carolmarie 1951- 75
Stock, Catherine 1952- 158
  Earlier sketches in SATA 65, 114
Stockdale, Susan 1954- 98

Stockham, Peter (Alan) 1928- 57
Stockton, Francis Richard 1834-1902 44
  Brief entry 32
Stockton, Frank R.
  See Stockton, Francis Richard
Stockwell-Moniz, Marc J. 1954- 164
Stoddard, Edward G. 1923- 10
Stoddard, Hope 1900-1987 6
Stoddard, Sandol 1927- 98
  Earlier sketch in SATA *14*
Stoehr, Shelley 1969- 107
Stoeke, Janet Morgan 1957- 136
  Earlier sketch in SATA *90*
Stohner, Anu 1952- 179
Stoiko, Michael 1919- 14
Stojic, Manya 1967- 156
Stoker, Abraham 1847-1912 29
Stoker, Bram
  See Stoker, Abraham
Stokes, Cedric
  See Beardmore, George
Stokes, Jack (Tilden) 1923- 13
Stokes, Olivia Pearl 1916- 32
Stolz, Mary 1920-2006 133
  Obituary 180
  Earlier sketches in SATA *10, 71*
  See also SAAS *3*
Stolz, Mary Slattery
  See Stolz, Mary
Stone, Alan
  See Svenson, Andrew E(dward)
Stone, David K(arl) 1922- 9
Stone, David Lee 1978- 166
Stone, Eugenia 1879-1971 7
Stone, Gene
  See Stone, Eugenia
Stone, Helen V(irginia) 6
Stone, Idella Purnell
  See Purnell, Idella
Stone, Ikey
  See Purnell, Idella
Stone, Irving 1903-1989 3
  Obituary 64
Stone, Jeff 178
Stone, Jon 1931-1997 39
  Obituary 95
Stone, Josephine Rector
  See Dixon, Jeanne
Stone, Lesley
  See Trevor, Elleston
Stone, Peter 1930-2003 65
  Obituary 143
Stone, Phoebe 134
Stone, Raymond 1
Stone, Rosetta
  See Dr. Seuss
  and Geisel, Theodor Seuss
  and LeSieg, Theo.
  and Seuss, Dr.
Stone, Tanya Lee 182
Stonehouse, Bernard 1926- 140
  Earlier sketches in SATA *13, 80*
Stones, (Cyril) Anthony 1934- 72
Stong, Phil(ip Duffield) 1899-1957 32
Stoops, Erik D(aniel) 1966- 142
  Earlier sketch in SATA *78*
Stoppelmoore, Cheryl Jean
  See Ladd, Cheryl (Jean)
Stops, Sue 1936- 86
Storace, Patricia 193
Storad, Conrad J. 1957- 119
Storey, Margaret 1926- 9
Storey, Victoria Carolyn 1945- 16
Storme, Peter
  See Stern, Philip Van Doren
Storr, Catherine (Cole) 1913-2001 87
  Obituary 122
  Earlier sketch in SATA *9*
Story, Josephine
  See Loring, Emilie (Baker)
Stotko, Mary-Ann 1960- 154

Stott, Dorothy (M.) 1958- 99
  Earlier sketch in SATA *67*
Stott, Dot
  See Stott, Dorothy (M.)
Stotter, Mike 1957- 108
Stout, William 1949- 132
Stoutenburg, Adrien (Pearl) 1916-1982 3
Stoutland, Allison 1963- 130
Stover, Allan C(arl) 1938- 14
Stover, Jill (Griffin) 1958- 82
Stover, Marjorie Filley 1914- 9
Stowe, Harriet (Elizabeth) Beecher 1811-1896
  See YABC *1*
  See also CLR *131*
Stowe, Leland 1899-1994 60
  Obituary 78
Stowe, Rosetta
  See Ogan, George F.
  and Ogan, Margaret E. (Nettles)
Stower, Adam 195
Strachan, Ian 1938- 85
Strachan, Linda 167
Strachan, Margaret Pitcairn 1908-1998 14
Strahinich, H. C.
  See Strahinich, Helen C.
Strahinich, Helen C. 1949- 78
Strait, Treva Adams 1909-2002 35
Strand, Mark 1934- 41
Strange, Philippa
  See Coury, Louise Andree
Stranger, Joyce
  See Wilson, Joyce M(uriel Judson)
Strangis, Joel 1948- 124
Strannigan, Shawn 1956- 93
Strannigan, Shawn Alyne
  See Strannigan, Shawn
Strasser, Todd 1950- 153
  Earlier sketches in SATA *41, 45, 71, 107*
  See also CLR *11*
Stratemeyer, Edward L. 1862-1930 100
  Earlier sketches in SATA *1, 67*
  See Adams, Harrison
Stratford, Philip 1927- 47
Stratton, Allan 1951- 178
Stratton, J. M.
  See Whitlock, Ralph
Stratton, Thomas
  See Coulson, Robert S(tratton)
  and DeWeese, Thomas Eugene
Stratton-Porter, Gene(va Grace) 1863-1924 . 15
  See also CLR *87*
Strauss, Gwen 1963- 77
Strauss, Joyce 1936- 53
Strauss, Linda Leopold 1942- 127
Strauss, Susan (Elizabeth) 1954- 75
Strayer, E. Ward
  See Stratemeyer, Edward L.
Streano, Vince(nt Catello) 1945- 20
Streatfeild, Mary Noel
  See Streatfeild, Noel
Streatfeild, Noel 1897(?)-1986 20
  Obituary 48
  See also CLR *83*
Street, Janet Travell 1959- 84
Street, Julia Montgomery 1898-1993 11
Streissguth, Thomas 1958- 116
Strelkoff, Tatiana 1957- 89
Stren, Patti 1949- 88
  Brief entry 41
  See also CLR *5*
Strete, Craig Kee 1950- 96
  Earlier sketch in SATA *44*
Stretton, Barbara (Humphrey) 1936- 43
  Brief entry 35
Strickland, (William) Brad(ley) 1947- 142
  Earlier sketches in SATA *83, 137*
Strickland, Craig (A.) 1956- 102
Strickland, Dorothy S(alley) 1933- 89
Strickland, Michael R. 1965- 144
  Earlier sketch in SATA *83*
Strickland, Tessa 173

Striegel, Jana 1955- 140
Striegel-Wilson, Jana
  See Striegel, Jana
Striker, Lee
  See Clark, Margaret (D.)
Striker, Susan 1942- 63
Stringer, Lauren 1957- 183
  Earlier sketch in SATA *129*
Stroeyer, Poul 1923- 13
Stromoski, Rick 1958- 111
Strong, Charles
  See Epstein, Beryl (M. Williams)
  and Epstein, Samuel
Strong, David
  See McGuire, Leslie (Sarah)
Strong, Jeremy 1949- 175
  Earlier sketches in SATA *36, 105*
Strong, J.J.
  See Strong, Jeremy
Strong, Pat
  See Hough, Richard (Alexander)
Strong, Stacie 1965- 74
Stroud, Bettye 1939- 165
  Earlier sketch in SATA *96*
Stroud, Jonathan 1970- 159
  Earlier sketch in SATA *102*
  See also CLR *134*
Stroyer, Poul
  See Stroeyer, Poul
Strug, Kerri 1977- 108
Stryer, Andrea Stenn 1938- 192
Stryker, Daniel
  See Morris, Chris(topher Crosby)
  and Stump, Jane Barr
Stuart, David
  See Hoyt, Edwin P(almer), Jr.
Stuart, Derek
  See Foster, John L(ouis)
Stuart, Forbes 1924- 13
Stuart, Ian
  See MacLean, Alistair (Stuart)
Stuart, Jesse (Hilton) 1906-1984 2
  Obituary 36
Stuart, Ruth McEnery 1849(?)-1917 116
Stuart, Sheila
  See Baker, Mary Gladys Steel
Stuart-Clark, Christopher (Anthony) 1940- .. 32
Stubis, Talivaldis 1926- 5
Stubley, Trevor (Hugh) 1932- 22
Stucky, Naomi R. 1922- 72
Stucley, Elizabeth
  See Northmore, Elizabeth Florence
Stultifer, Morton
  See Curtis, Richard (Alan)
Sture-Vasa, Mary
  See Alsop, Mary O'Hara
Sturges, Philemon 174
Sturtevant, Katherine 1950- 180
  Earlier sketch in SATA *130*
Sturton, Hugh
  See Johnston, H(ugh) A(nthony) S(tephen)
Sturtzel, Howard A(llison) 1894-1985 1
Sturtzel, Jane Levington 1903-1996 1
Stutley, D(oris) J(ean) 1959- 142
Stutson, Caroline 1940- 104
Stuve-Bodeen, Stephanie 1965- 158
  Earlier sketch in SATA *114*
Stux, Erica 1929- 140
Styles, (Frank) Showell 1908- 10
Stynes, Barbara White 133
Suba, Susanne 4
Subond, Valerie
  See Grayland, Valerie (Merle Spanner)
Sudbery, Rodie 1943- 42
Suen, Anastasia 1956(?)- 157
Sufrin, Mark 1925- 76
Sugarman, Joan G. 1917- 64
Sugarman, Tracy 1921- 37
Sugita, Yutaka 1930- 36

Suhl, Yuri (Menachem) 1908-1986 8
  Obituary 50
  See also CLR 2
  See also SAAS 1
Suhr, Joanne 129
Suid, Murray 1942- 27
Sullivan, George (Edward) 1927- 147
  Earlier sketches in SATA 4, 89
Sullivan, Jody
  See Rake, Jody
Sullivan, Kathryn A. 1954- 141
Sullivan, Mary Ann 1954- 63
Sullivan, Mary W(ilson) 1907- 13
Sullivan, Pat
  See Messmer, Otto
Sullivan, Paul 1939- 106
Sullivan, Sarah G. 1953- 179
Sullivan, Silky
  See Makowski, Silvia Ann
Sullivan, Sue
  See Sullivan, Susan E.
Sullivan, Susan E. 1962- 123
Sullivan, Thomas Joseph, Jr. 1947- 16
Sullivan, Tom
  See Sullivan, Thomas Joseph, Jr.
Sully, Tom 1959- 104
Sumichrast, Jozef 1948- 29
Sumiko
  See Davies, Sumiko
Summerforest, Ivy B.
  See Kirkup, James
Summers, Barbara 1944- 182
Summers, James L(evingston) 1910-1973 57
  Brief entry 28
Summertree, Katonah
  See Windsor, Patricia
Sun, Chyng Feng 1959- 90
Sunderlin, Sylvia (S.) 1911-1997 28
  Obituary 99
Sung, Betty Lee 26
Supeene, Shelagh Lynne 1952- 153
Supraner, Robyn 1930- 101
  Earlier sketch in SATA 20
Supree, Burt(on) 1941-1992 73
Surface, Mary Hall 1958- 126
Surge, Frank 1931- 13
Susac, Andrew 1929- 5
Susi, Geraldine Lee 1942- 98
Sussman, Cornelia Silver 1914-1999 59
Sussman, Irving 1908-1996 59
Sussman, Susan 1942- 48
Sutcliff, Rosemary 1920-1992 78
  Obituary 73
  Earlier sketches in SATA 6, 44
  See also CLR 138
Sutcliffe, Jane 1957- 138
Sutherland, Colleen 1944- 79
Sutherland, Efua (Theodora Morgue)
  1924-1996 25
Sutherland, Jon 1958- 167
Sutherland, Jonathan D.
  See Sutherland, Jon
Sutherland, Jonathan David
  See Sutherland, Jon
Sutherland, Margaret 1941- 15
Sutherland, Zena Bailey 1915-2002 37
  Obituary 137
Suttles, Shirley (Smith) 1922- 21
Sutton, Ann (Livesay) 1923- 31
Sutton, Eve(lyn Mary) 1906-1992 26
Sutton, Felix 1910(?)-1973 31
Sutton, Jane 1950- 52
  Brief entry 43
Sutton, Larry M(atthew) 1931- 29
Sutton, Margaret Beebe 1903-2001 1
  Obituary 131
Sutton, Myron Daniel 1925- 31
Sutton, Roger 1956- 93

Suzanne, Jamie
  See Hawes, Louise
  and Lantz, Francess L(in)
  and Singleton, Linda Joy
  and Zach, Cheryl (Byrd)
Suzuki, David T(akayoshi) 1936- 138
Svendsen, Mark 1962- 181
  Earlier sketch in SATA 120
Svendsen, Mark Nestor
  See Svendsen, Mark
Svenson, Andrew E(dward) 1910-1975 2
  Obituary 26
Swaab, Neil 1978- 191
Swain, Carol 1962- 172
Swain, Gwenyth 1961- 134
  Earlier sketch in SATA 84
Swain, Ruth
  See Swain, Ruth Freeman
Swain, Ruth Freeman 1951- 161
  Earlier sketch in SATA 119
Swain, Su Zan (Noguchi) 1916- 21
Swallow, Pamela Curtis 178
Swamp, Jake 1941- 98
Swan, Susan 1944- 108
  Earlier sketch in SATA 22
Swann, Brian (Stanley Frank) 1940- 116
Swann, E. L.
  See Lasky, Kathryn
Swann, Ruth Rice 1920- 84
Swanson, Helen M(cKendry) 1919- 94
Swanson, June 1931- 76
Swanson, Wayne 1942- 167
Swarthout, Glendon (Fred) 1918-1992 26
Swarthout, Kathryn 1919- 7
Swayne, Sam(uel F.) 1907- 53
Swayne, Zoa (Lourana) 1905- 53
Sweat, Lynn 1934- 168
  Earlier sketch in SATA 57
Swede, George 1940- 67
Sweeney, James B(artholomew) 1910-1999 . 21
Sweeney, Joyce 1955- 167
  Earlier sketches in SATA 65, 68, 108
Sweeney, Joyce Kay
  See Sweeney, Joyce
Sweeney, Karen O'Connor
  See O'Connor, Karen
Sweeney, Matthew (Gerard) 1952- 156
Sweet, Melissa 1956- 172
Sweet, Sarah C.
  See Jewett, (Theodora) Sarah Orne
Sweetland, Nancy A(nn) 1934- 48
Swenson, Allan A(rmstrong) 1933- 21
Swenson, May 1919-1989 15
Swentzell, Rina 1939- 79
Swiatkowska, Gabi 1971(?)- 180
Swift, Bryan
  See Knott, William C(ecil, Jr.)
Swift, David
  See Kaufmann, John
Swift, Hildegarde Hoyt 1890(?)-1977
  Obituary 20
Swift, Jonathan 1667-1745 19
  See also CLR 53
Swift, Merlin
  See Leeming, Joseph
Swiger, Elinor Porter 1927- 8
Swinburne, Laurence (Joseph) 1924- 9
Swinburne, Stephen R. 1952- 188
  Earlier sketch in SATA 150
Swinburne, Steve
  See Swinburne, Stephen R.
Swindells, Robert (Edward) 1939- 150
  Brief entry 34
  Earlier sketches in SATA 50, 80
  See also SAAS 14
Swinford, Betty (June Wells) 1927- 58
Swinford, Bob
  See Swinford, Betty (June Wells)
Swithen, John
  See King, Stephen
Switzer, Ellen 1923- 48

Swope, Sam 156
Swope, Samuel
  See Swope, Sam
Sybesma, Jetske
  See Ironside, Jetske
Sydney, Frank
  See Warwick, Alan R(oss)
Sylvester, Natalie G(abry) 1922- 22
Syme, (Neville) Ronald 1913-1992 87
  Earlier sketch in SATA 2
Symes, R. F. 77
Symes, Ruth Louise 1962- 179
Symons, (Dorothy) Geraldine 1909- 33
Symons, Stuart
  See Stanley, George Edward
Symynkywicz, Jeffrey B. 1954- 87
Symynkywicz, Jeffrey Bruce
  See Symynkywicz, Jeffrey B.
Synge, (Phyllis) Ursula 1930- 9
Sypher, Lucy Johnston 1907- 7
Szasz, Suzanne (Shorr) 1915-1997 13
  Obituary 99
Szekeres, Cyndy 1933- 157
  Autobiography Feature 157
  Earlier sketches in SATA 5, 60, 131
  See also SAAS 13
Szekessy, Tanja 98
Szpura, Beata 1961- 93
Szudek, Agnes S(usan) P(hilomena) 57
  Brief entry 49
Szulc, Tad 1926-2001 26
Szydlow, Jarl
  See Szydlowski, Mary Vigliante
Szydlowski, Mary Vigliante 1946- 94
Szymanski, Lois 1957- 91

T

Taback, Simms 1932- 170
  Brief entry 36
  Earlier sketches in SATA 40, 104
  See also CLR 100
Taber, Gladys (Bagg) 1899-1980
  Obituary 22
Tabor, Nancy Maria Grande 1949- 161
  Earlier sketch in SATA 89
Tabrah, Ruth Milander 1921- 14
Tackach, James 1953- 123
Tackach, James M.
  See Tackach, James
Tadgell, Nicole 1969- 177
Tafuri, Nancy 1946- 192
  Autobiography Feature 192
  Earlier sketches in SATA 39, 75, 130
  See also CLR 74
  See also SAAS 14
Tagg, Christine Elizabeth 1962- 138
Tagliaferro, Linda 173
Taha, Karen T(erry) 1942- 156
  Earlier sketch in SATA 71
Tai, Sharon O. 1963- 153
Tait, Douglas 1944- 12
Takabayashi, Mari 1960- 156
  Earlier sketch in SATA 115
Takahashi, Rumiko 1957- 163
Takakjian, Portia 1930- 15
Takashima, Misako
  See Misako Rocks!
Takashima, Shizuye 1928- 13
Takayama, Sandi 1962- 106
Takeda, Pete(r M.) 1964- 148
Tal, Eve 1947- 176
Talbert, Marc (Alan) 1953- 154
  Autobiography Feature 154
  Earlier sketches in SATA 68, 99
Talbot, Charlene Joy 1928- 10
Talbot, Toby 1928- 14
Talbott, Hudson 1949- 131
  Earlier sketch in SATA 84

Taliaferro, Dorothy L.
    See Martin, Del
Talifero, Gerald 1950- 75
Talker, T.
    See Rands, William Brighty
Tallarico, Tony 1933- 116
Tallcott, Emogene 10
Tallec, Olivier 1970- 197
Tallis, Robyn
    See Coville, Bruce
    and Doyle, Debra
    and Macdonald, James D.
    and Smith, Sherwood
    and Zambreno, Mary Frances
Tallon, Robert 1939- 43
    Brief entry 28
Talmadge, Marian 14
Tamar, Erika 1934- 150
    Earlier sketches in SATA 62, 101
Tamarin, Alfred H. 1913-1980 13
Tamburine, Jean 1930- 12
Tames, Richard (Lawrence) 1946- 102
    Earlier sketch in SATA 67
Tamminga, Frederick W(illiam) 1934- 66
Tammuz, Benjamin 1919-1989
    Obituary 63
Tan, Amy 1952- 75
Tan, Amy Ruth
    See Tan, Amy
Tan, Shaun 1974- 198
Tanaka, Beatrice 1932- 76
Tanaka, Shelley 136
Tang, Charles 1948- 81
Tang, Greg 172
Tang, You-Shan 1946- 53
Tania B.
    See Blixen, Karen (Christentze Dinesen)
Tankard, Jeremy 1973- 191
Tannen, Mary 1943- 37
Tannenbaum, Beulah Goldstein 1916- 3
Tannenbaum, D(onald) Leb 1948- 42
Tanner, Jane 1946- 74
Tanner, Louise S(tickney) 1922-2000 9
Tanobe, Miyuki 1937- 23
Tanselle, Eve 1933- 125
Tapio, Pat Decker
    See Kines, Pat Decker
Tapp, Kathy Kennedy 1949- 88
    Brief entry 50
Tarbescu, Edith 1939- 107
Tarkington, (Newton) Booth 1869-1946 17
Tarpley, Natasha A(nastasia) 1971- 147
Tarr, Judith 1955- 149
    Earlier sketch in SATA 64
Tarry, Ellen 1906- 16
    See also CLR 26
    See also SAAS 16
Tarshis, Jerome 1936- 9
Tarshis, Lauren 187
Tarsky, Sue 1946- 41
Taschek, Karen 1956- 185
Tashjian, Janet 1956- 151
    Earlier sketch in SATA 102
Tashjian, Virginia A. 1921-2008 3
Tasker, James 1908- 9
Tate, Don(ald E.) 159
Tate, Eleanora E. 1948- 191
    Earlier sketches in SATA 38, 94
    See also CLR 37
Tate, Eleanora Elaine
    See Tate, Eleanora E.
Tate, Ellalice
    See Hibbert, Eleanor Alice Burford
Tate, Joan 1922- 86
    Earlier sketch in SATA 9
    See also SAAS 20
Tate, Mary Anne
    See Hale, Arlene
Tate, Nikki 134
Tate, Richard
    See Masters, Anthony (Richard)

Tate, Suzanne 1930- 91
Tatham, Betty 142
Tatham, Campbell
    See Elting, Mary
Tatham, Julie
    See Tatham, Julie Campbell
Tatham, Julie Campbell 1908-1999 80
Tavares, Matt 198
    Earlier sketch in SATA 159
Tavares, Victor 1971- 176
Taves, Isabella 1915- 27
Taylor, Alastair 1959- 130
Taylor, Andrew 1951- 70
Taylor, Andrew John Robert
    See Taylor, Andrew
Taylor, Ann 1782-1866 41
    Brief entry 35
Taylor, Audilee Boyd 1931- 59
Taylor, Barbara J. 1927- 10
Taylor, Ben
    See Strachan, Ian
Taylor, Carl 1937- 14
Taylor, Cheryl Munro 1957- 96
Taylor, Cora (Lorraine) 1936- 103
    Earlier sketch in SATA 64
    See also CLR 63
Taylor, Dave 1948- 78
Taylor, David
    See Taylor, Dave
Taylor, David 1900-1965 10
Taylor, Debbie A. 1955- 169
Taylor, Elizabeth 1912-1975 13
Taylor, Florance Walton 9
Taylor, Florence M(arian Tompkins)
    1892-1983 9
Taylor, G(raham) P(eter) 1959(?)- 156
Taylor, Gage 1942-2000 87
Taylor, Graham
    See Taylor, G(raham) P(eter)
Taylor, Herb(ert Norman, Jr.) 1942-1987 22
    Obituary 54
Taylor, J. David
    See Taylor, Dave
Taylor, Jane 1783-1824 41
    Brief entry 35
Taylor, Jerry D(uncan) 1938- 47
Taylor, John Robert
    See Taylor, Andrew
Taylor, Judy
    See Hough, Judy Taylor
Taylor, Kenneth N. 1917-2005 26
Taylor, Kenneth Nathaniel
    See Taylor, Kenneth N.
Taylor, Kim 180
Taylor, L(ester) B(arbour), Jr. 1932- 27
Taylor, Lois Dwight Cole
    See Cole, Lois Dwight
Taylor, Louise Todd 1939- 47
Taylor, Margaret 1950- 106
Taylor, Mark 1927- 32
    Brief entry 28
Taylor, Mildred D. 1943- 135
    See also CLR 90
    See also SAAS 5
Taylor, Mildred Delois
    See Taylor, Mildred D.
Taylor, Paula (Wright) 1942- 48
    Brief entry 33
Taylor, Robert Lewis 1912-1998 10
Taylor, Sean 1965- 192
Taylor, Sydney (Brenner) 1904(?)-1978 28
    Obituary 26
    Earlier sketch in SATA 1
Taylor, Theodore 1921-2006 128
    Obituary 177
    Earlier sketches in SATA 5, 54, 83
    See also CLR 30
    See also SAAS 4
Taylor, William 1938- 164
    Earlier sketches in SATA 78, 113
    See also CLR 63

Tazewell, Charles 1900-1972 74
Tchana, Katrin
    See Tchana, Katrin Hyman
Tchana, Katrin H.
    See Tchana, Katrin Hyman
Tchana, Katrin Hyman 1963- 177
    Earlier sketch in SATA 125
Tchekhov, Anton
    See Chekhov, Anton (Pavlovich)
Tchen, Richard 120
Tchudi, Stephen N. 1942- 55
Teague, Bob
    See Teague, Robert
Teague, Mark 1963- 170
    Earlier sketches in SATA 68, 99
Teague, Mark Christopher
    See Teague, Mark
Teague, Robert 1929- 32
    Brief entry 31
Teal, Val 1902-1997 10
    Obituary 114
Teal, Valentine M.
    See Teal, Val
Teale, Edwin Way 1899-1980 7
    Obituary 25
Teasdale, Sara 1884-1933 32
Tebbel, John (William) 1912-2004 26
Teensma, Lynne Bertrand
    See Bertrand, Lynne
Tee-Van, Helen Damrosch 1893-1976 10
    Obituary 27
Tegner, Bruce 1928- 62
Teitelbaum, Michael 1953- 116
    Earlier sketch in SATA 59
Tejima
    See Tejima, Keizaburo
Tejima, Keizaburo 1931- 139
    See also CLR 20
Telander, Todd (G.) 1967- 88
Teleki, Geza 1943- 45
Telemaque, Eleanor Wong 1934- 43
Telescope, Tom
    See Newbery, John
Tellis, Annabel 1967- 191
Temkin, Sara Anne Schlossberg 1913-1996 . 26
Temko, Florence 13
Tempest, Margaret Mary 1892-1982
    Obituary 33
Templar, Maurice
    See Groom, Arthur William
Temple, Arthur
    See Northcott, (William) Cecil
Temple, Charles 1947- 79
Temple, Frances (Nolting) 1945-1995 85
Temple, Herbert 1919- 45
Temple, Paul
    See McConnell, James Douglas Rutherford
Temple, William F(rederick) 1914-1989 107
Tenggren, Gustaf 1896-1970 18
    Obituary 26
Tennant, Kylie
    See Rodd, Kylie Tennant
Tennant, Veronica 1947- 36
Tenneshaw, S.M.
    See Beaumont, Charles
    and Garrett, (Gordon) Randall (Phillip)
    and Silverberg, Robert
Tenniel, John 1820-1914 74
    Brief entry 27
    See also CLR 18
Tepper, Sheri S. 1929- 113
Terada, Alice M. 1928- 90
Terban, Marvin 1940- 54
    Brief entry 45
Teresi, Judith M.
    See Goldberger, Judith M.
ter Haar, Jaap 1922- 6
    See also CLR 15
Terhune, Albert Payson 1872-1942 15
Terkel, Susan N(eiburg) 1948- 103
    Earlier sketch in SATA 59

Terlouw, Jan (Cornelis) 1931- 30
Terrell, John Upton 1900-1988
  Obituary 60
Terrill, Beth 198
Terrill, Elizabeth
  See Terrill, Beth
Terris, Susan 1937- 77
  Earlier sketch in SATA 3
Terry, Luther L(eonidas) 1911-1985 11
  Obituary 42
Terry, Margaret
  See Dunnahoo, Terry Janson
Terry, Walter 1913-1982 14
Terzian, James P. 1915- 14
Tessendorf, K(enneth) C(harles) 1925-2003 . 75
  Obituary 142
Tessler, Stephanie Gordon
  See Gordon, Stephanie Jacob
Tester, Sylvia Root 1939- 64
  Brief entry 37
Tether, (Cynthia) Graham 1950- 46
  Brief entry 36
Tetzner, Lisa 1894-1963 169
Thach, James Otis 1969- 195
Thacher, Mary McGrath 1933- 9
Thackeray, William Makepeace 1811-1863 .. 23
Thaler, Michael C.
  See Thaler, Mike
Thaler, Mike 1936- 93
  Brief entry 47
  Earlier sketch in SATA 56
Thaler, Shmuel 1958- 126
  Earlier sketch in SATA 72
Thamer, Katie 1955- 42
Thane, Elswyth 1900-1984(?) 32
Tharp, Louise (Marshall) Hall 1898-1992 3
  Obituary 129
Tharp, Tim 1957- 189
Thayer, Ernest Lawrence 1863-1940 60
Thayer, Jane
  See Woolley, Catherine
Thayer, Marjorie 1908-1992 74
  Brief entry 37
Thayer, Peter
  See Wyler, Rose
Thelwell, Norman 1923-2004 14
Themerson, Stefan 1910-1988 65
Thermes, Jennifer 1966- 155
Theroux, Paul 1941- 109
  Earlier sketch in SATA 44
Theroux, Paul Edward
  See Theroux, Paul
Thesman, Jean 124
  Earlier sketch in SATA 74
The Tjong-Khing
  See Khing, T.T.
Thieda, Shirley Ann 1943- 13
Thiele, Colin 1920-2006 125
  Earlier sketches in SATA 14, 72
  See also CLR 27
  See also SAAS 2
Thiele, Colin Milton
  See Thiele, Colin
Thiesing, Lisa 1958- 159
  Earlier sketch in SATA 95
Thimmesh, Catherine 189
Thiry, Joan (Marie) 1926- 45
Thistlethwaite, Miles 1945- 12
Thollander, Earl 1922- 22
Thomas, Abigail 1941- 112
Thomas, Andrea
  See Hill, Margaret (Ohler)
Thomas, Art(hur Lawrence) 1952- 48
  Brief entry 38
Thomas, Carroll
  See Ratliff, Thomas M.
  and Shmurak, Carole B.
Thomas, Dylan (Marlais) 1914-1953 60
Thomas, Egbert S.
  See Ellis, Edward S(ylvester)
Thomas, Estelle Webb 1899-1982 26

Thomas, Frances 1943- 171
  Earlier sketch in SATA 92
Thomas, H. C.
  See Keating, Lawrence A.
Thomas, Ianthe 1951- 139
  Brief entry 42
  See also CLR 8
Thomas, Jan 1958- 197
Thomas, Jane Resh 1936- 171
  Earlier sketches in SATA 38, 90
Thomas, Jerry D. 1959- 91
Thomas, J.F.
  See Fleming, Thomas
Thomas, Joan Gale
  See Robinson, Joan (Mary) G(ale Thomas)
Thomas, Joyce Carol 1938- 137
  Autobiography Feature 137
  Earlier sketches in SATA 40, 78, 123
  See also CLR 19
  See also SAAS 7
Thomas, Lowell Jackson, Jr. 1923- 15
Thomas, Margaret
  See Thomas, Peggy
Thomas, Meredith 1963- 119
Thomas, Michael
  See Wilks, Michael Thomas
Thomas, Middy 1931- 191
Thomas, Patricia 1934- 199
  Earlier sketch in SATA 51
Thomas, Peggy 174
Thomas, Rob 1965- 97
Thomas, Scott 1959- 147
Thomas, Velma Maia 1955- 171
Thomas, Vernon (Arthur) 1934- 56
Thomas, Victoria
  See DeWeese, Thomas Eugene
  and Kugi, Constance Todd
Thomasma, Kenneth R. 1930- 90
Thomassie, Tynia 1959- 92
Thompson, Brenda 1935- 34
Thompson, Carol 1951- 189
  Earlier sketch in SATA 85
Thompson, China
  See Lewis, Mary (Christianna)
Thompson, Colin 1942- 198
  Earlier sketches in SATA 95, 163
Thompson, David H(ugh) 1941- 17
Thompson, Eileen
  See Panowski, Eileen Thompson
Thompson, George Selden 1929-1989 73
  Obituary 63
  Earlier sketch in SATA 4
  See also CLR 8
Thompson, Harlan (Howard) 1894-1987 10
  Obituary 53
Thompson, Hilary 1943- 56
  Brief entry 49
Thompson, Joanna Maxwell Pullein
  See Pullein-Thompson, Joanna Maxwell
Thompson, Julian F(rancis) 1927- 155
  Brief entry 40
  Earlier sketches in SATA 55, 99
  See also CLR 24
  See also SAAS 13
Thompson, K(athryn Carolyn) Dyble
  1952- 82
Thompson, Kay 1912(?)-1998 16
  See also CLR 22
Thompson, Lauren 1962- 174
  Earlier sketch in SATA 132
Thompson, Lauren Stevens
  See Thompson, Lauren
Thompson, Megan Lloyd
  See Lloyd, Megan
Thompson, Richard 1951- 184
Thompson, Ruth Plumly 1891-1976 66
Thompson, Sharon 1952- 119
Thompson, Sharon Elaine
  See Thompson, Sharon
Thompson, Stith 1885-1976 57
  Obituary 20

Thompson, Vivian L(aubach) 1911- 3
Thomson, Bill 1963- 187
Thomson, Celia
  See Lynn, Tracy
Thomson, David (Robert Alexander)
  1914-1988 40
  Obituary 55
Thomson, Pat 1939- 122
  Earlier sketch in SATA 77
Thomson, Peggy 1922- 31
Thomson, Sarah L. 178
Thon, Melanie Rae 1957- 132
Thong, Roseanne 174
Thorburn, John
  See Goldsmith, John Herman Thorburn
Thorn, John 1947- 59
Thorndyke, Helen Louise
  See Benson, Mildred (Augustine Wirt)
Thorne, Ian
  See May, Julian
Thorne, Jean Wright
  See May, Julian
Thornhill, Jan 1955- 148
  Earlier sketch in SATA 77
Thornton, Hall
  See Silverberg, Robert
Thornton, W. B.
  See Burgess, Thornton Waldo
Thornton, Yvonne S(hirley) 1947- 96
Thorpe, E(ustace) G(eorge) 1916- 21
Thorpe, J. K.
  See Nathanson, Laura Walther
Thorvall, Kerstin 1925- 13
Thorvall-Falk, Kerstin
  See Thorvall, Kerstin
Thrasher, Crystal (Faye) 1921- 27
Threadgall, Colin 1941- 77
Three Little Pigs
  See Lantz, Francess L(in)
Thum, Gladys 1920- 26
Thum, Marcella 28
  Earlier sketch in SATA 3
Thundercloud, Katherine
  See Witt, Shirley Hill
Thurber, James (Grover) 1894-1961 13
Thurlo, Aimee 161
Thurlo, David 161
Thurman, Judith 1946- 33
Thurman, Mark (Gordon Ian) 1948- 63
Thwaite, Ann (Barbara Harrop) 1932- 14
Tibbetts, Peggy 127
Tibbles, Jean-Paul 1958- 115
Tibo, Gilles 1951- 107
  Earlier sketch in SATA 67
Tiburzi, Bonnie 1948- 65
Ticheburn, Cheviot
  See Ainsworth, William Harrison
Tichenor, Tom 1923-1992 14
Tichnor, Richard 1959- 90
Tichy, William 1924- 31
Tickle, Jack
  See Chapman, Jane
Tiegreen, Alan F. 1935- 94
  Brief entry 36
Tierney, Frank M. 1930- 54
Tierney, Tom 1928- 113
Tiffault, Benette W. 1955- 77
Tiller, Ruth L. 1949- 83
Tilley, Debbie 190
Tilly, Nancy 1935- 62
Tilton, Madonna Elaine 1929- 41
Tilton, Rafael
  See Tilton, Madonna Elaine
Timberlake, Amy 156
Timberlake, Carolyn
  See Dresang, Eliza (Carolyn Timberlake)
Timmers, Leo 1970- 190
Timmins, William F(rederick) 10
Tinbergen, Niko(laas) 1907-1988
  Obituary 60
Tincknell, Cathy 194

Tiner, John Hudson 1944- 32
Tingle, Dolli (?)-
   See Brackett, Dolli Tingle
Tingle, Rebecca 174
Tingum, Janice 1958- 91
Tinkelman, Murray 1933- 12
Tinkham, Kelly A. 188
Tinkle, (Julien) Lon 1906-1980 36
Tinling, Marion (Rose) 1904- 140
Tipene, Tim 1972- 141
Tippett, James S(terling) 1885-1958 66
Tirone Smith, Mary-Ann 1944- 143
Titlebaum, Ellen 195
Titler, Dale M(ilton) 1926- 35
   Brief entry 28
Titmarsh, Michael Angelo
   See Thackeray, William Makepeace
Titus, Eve 1922- 2
Tjong Khing, The 1933- 76
Tobias, Katherine
   See Gottfried, Theodore Mark
Tobias, Tobi 1938- 82
   Earlier sketch in SATA 5
   See also CLR 4
Todd, Anne Ophelia
   See Dowden, Anne Ophelia Todd
Todd, Barbara 1961- 173
Todd, Barbara K(eith) 1917- 10
Todd, Chuck 195
Todd, H(erbert) E(atton) 1908-1988 84
   Earlier sketch in SATA 11
Todd, Loreto 1942- 30
Todd, Pamela 1950- 124
Todd, Peter
   See Hamilton, Charles (Harold St. John)
Toews, Miriam 1964- 165
Tofel, Richard J. 1957- 140
Toft, Kim Michelle 1960- 170
Tokunbo, Dimitrea 187
Tolan, Stephanie S. 1942- 142
   Earlier sketches in SATA 38, 78
Toland, John (Willard) 1912-2004 38
Tolbert, Steve 1944- 143
Toledo, Francisco 1940- 198
Toledo, Natalia 1967- 197
Tolkien, John Ronald Reuel
   See Tolkien, J.R.R
Tolkien, J.R.R 1892-1973 100
   Obituary 24
   Earlier sketches in SATA 2, 32
   See also CLR 56
Toll, Emily
   See Cannon, Eileen E(mily)
Toll, Nelly S. 1935- 78
Tolland, W. R.
   See Heitzmann, William Ray
Tolles, Martha 1921- 76
   Earlier sketch in SATA 8
Tolliver, Ruby C(hangos) 1922- 110
   Brief entry 41
   Earlier sketch in SATA 55
Tolmie, Kenneth Donald 1941- 15
Tolstoi, Lev
   See Tolstoy, Leo (Nikolaevich)
Tolstoy, Leo (Nikolaevich) 1828-1910 26
Tolstoy, Count Leo
   See Tolstoy, Leo (Nikolaevich)
Tomalin, Ruth 29
Tomaselli, Rosa
   See Pausacker, Jenny
Tomecek, Steve 172
Tomes, Margot (Ladd) 1917-1991 70
   Brief entry 27
   Obituary 69
   Earlier sketch in SATA 36
Tomey, Ingrid 1943- 77
Tomfool
   See Farjeon, Eleanor
Tomkins, Jasper
   See Batey, Tom

Tomline, F. Latour
   See Gilbert, W(illiam) S(chwenck)
Tomlinson, Heather 192
Tomlinson, Jill 1931-1976 3
   Obituary 24
Tomlinson, Reginald R(obert) 1885-1979(?)
   Obituary 27
Tomlinson, Theresa 1946- 165
   Earlier sketch in SATA 103
   See also CLR 60
Tompert, Ann 1918- 139
   Earlier sketches in SATA 14, 89
Toner, Raymond John 1908-1986 10
Tong, Gary S. 1942- 66
Tong, Paul 188
Took, Belladonna
   See Chapman, Vera (Ivy May)
Tooke, Louise Mathews 1950- 38
Tooke, Susan 173
Toonder, Martin
   See Groom, Arthur William
Toothaker, Roy Eugene 1928- 18
Tooze, Ruth (Anderson) 1892-1972 4
Topek, Susan Remick 1955- 78
Topping, Audrey R(onning) 1928- 14
Tor, Regina
   See Shekerjian, Regina Tor
Torbert, Floyd James 1922- 22
Torgersen, Don Arthur 1934- 55
   Brief entry 41
Torley, Luke
   See Blish, James (Benjamin)
Torres, Andres Segovia
   See Segovia, Andres
Torres, Daniel 1958- 102
Torres, John A. 1965- 163
   Earlier sketch in SATA 94
Torres, John Albert
   See Torres, John A.
Torres, Laura 1967- 146
   Earlier sketch in SATA 87
Torres, Leyla 1960- 155
Torrey, Rich
   See Torrey, Richard
Torrey, Richard 189
Torrie, Malcolm
   See Mitchell, Gladys (Maude Winifred)
Toten, Teresa 1955- 99
Totham, Mary
   See Breinburg, Petronella
Touponce, William F. 1948- 114
Tournier, Michel 1924- 23
Tournier, Michel Edouard
   See Tournier, Michel
Towle, Wendy 1963- 79
Towne, Mary
   See Spelman, Mary
Townley, Rod
   See Townley, Roderick
Townley, Roderick 1942- 177
Townsend, Brad W. 1962- 91
Townsend, John Rowe 1922- 132
   Autobiography Feature 132
   Earlier sketches in SATA 4, 68
   See also CLR 2
   See also SAAS 2
Townsend, Michael 1981- 194
Townsend, Sue
   See Townsend, Susan Lilian
Townsend, Susan Lilian 1946- 93
   Brief entry 48
   Earlier sketch in SATA 55
Townsend, Thomas L. 1944- 59
Townsend, Tom
   See Townsend, Thomas L.
Townson, Hazel 134
Toye, William Eldred 1926- 8
Traherne, Michael
   See Watkins-Pitchford, Denys James
Trahey, Jane 1923-2000 36
   Obituary 120

Trapani, Iza 1954- 116
   Earlier sketch in SATA 80
Trapp, Maria Augusta von
   See von Trapp, Maria Augusta
Travers, P(amela) L(yndon) 1899-1996 100
   Obituary 90
   Earlier sketches in SATA 4, 54
   See also CLR 93
   See also SAAS 2
Travis, Lucille 133
   Earlier sketch in SATA 88
Treadgold, Mary 1910- 49
Trease, (Robert) Geoffrey 1909-1998 60
   Obituary 101
   Earlier sketch in SATA 2
   See also CLR 42
   See also SAAS 6
Treat, Lawrence 1903-1998 59
Tredez, Alain 1926- 17
Tredez, Denise 1930- 50
Treece, Henry 1912-1966 2
   See also CLR 2
Tregarthen, Enys
   See Sloggett, Nellie
Tregaskis, Richard 1916-1973 3
   Obituary 26
Treherne, Katie Thamer 1955- 76
Trell, Max 1900-1996 14
   Obituary 108
Tremain, Ruthven 1922- 17
Trembath, Don 1963- 168
   Earlier sketch in SATA 96
Tremens, Del
   See MacDonald, Amy
Trent, Robbie 1894-1988 26
Trent, Timothy
   See Malmberg, Carl
Treseder, Terry Walton 1956- 68
Tresilian, (Cecil) Stuart 1891-(?) 40
Tresselt, Alvin 1916-2000 7
   See also CLR 30
Trevino, Elizabeth B(orton) de 1904- 29
   Earlier sketch in SATA 1
   See also SAAS 5
Trevor, Elleston 1920-1995 28
Trevor, Frances
   See Teasdale, Sara
Trevor, Glen
   See Hilton, James
Trevor, (Lucy) Meriol 1919-2000 113
   Obituary 122
   Earlier sketch in SATA 10
Trewellard, J.M. 195
Trewellard, Juliet
   See Trewellard, J.M.
Trez, Alain
   See Tredez, Alain
Trez, Denise
   See Tredez, Denise
Trezise, Percy (James) 1923-
   See CLR 41
Triggs, Tony D. 1946- 70
Trimble, Marshall I(ra) 1939- 93
Trimby, Elisa 1948- 47
   Brief entry 40
Tring, A. Stephen
   See Meynell, Laurence Walter
Tripp, Eleanor B(aldwin) 1936- 4
Tripp, Janet 1942- 108
Tripp, Jenny 188
Tripp, John
   See Moore, John Travers
Tripp, Nathaniel 1944- 101
Tripp, Paul 1916-2002 8
   Obituary 139
Tripp, Valerie 1951- 168
   Earlier sketch in SATA 78
Tripp, Wallace (Whitney) 1940- 31
Trivelpiece, Laurel 1926- 56
   Brief entry 46
Trivett, Daphne Harwood 1940- 22

Trivizas, Eugene 1946- *84*
Trnka, Jiri 1912-1969 .... *43*
  Brief entry *32*
Trollope, Anthony 1815-1882 .... *22*
Trost, Lucille W(ood) 1938- *149*
  Earlier sketch in SATA *12*
Trott, Betty 1933- *91*
Trotter, Deborah W. *184*
Trotter, Grace V(iolet) 1900-1991 .... *10*
Trottier, Maxine 1950- *175*
  Earlier sketch in SATA *131*
Troughton, Joanna (Margaret) 1947- *37*
Trout, Kilgore
  See Farmer, Philip Jose
Trout, Richard E. *123*
Trudeau, Garretson Beekman
  See Trudeau, G.B.
Trudeau, Garry
  See Trudeau, G.B.
Trudeau, Garry B.
  See Trudeau, G.B.
Trudeau, G.B. 1948- *168*
  Earlier sketch in SATA *35*
Trueit, Trudi
  See Trueit, Trudi Strain
Trueit, Trudi Strain 1963- *179*
Trueman, Matthew *183*
Trueman, Terry 1947- *178*
  Earlier sketch in SATA *132*
Truesdell, Judy
  See Mecca, Judy Truesdell
Truesdell, Sue
  See Truesdell, Susan G.
Truesdell, Susan G. *108*
  Brief entry *45*
Trumbauer, Lisa (Trutkoff) 1963- *149*
Truss, Jan 1925- *35*
Truss, Lynne 1955(?)- *194*
Tryon, Leslie *194*
  Earlier sketch in SATA *139*
Tubb, Jonathan N. 1951- *78*
Tubby, I. M.
  See Kraus, (Herman) Robert
Tucker, Caroline
  See Nolan, Jeannette Covert
Tudor, Edward
  See Browne, Anthony
Tudor, Tasha 1915-2008 .... *160*
  Earlier sketches in SATA *20, 69*
  See also CLR *13*
Tuerk, Hanne 1951- *71*
Tugeau, Jeremy *199*
Tulloch, Richard 1949- *180*
  Earlier sketch in SATA *76*
Tulloch, Richard George
  See Tulloch, Richard
Tulloch, Shirley *169*
Tully, John (Kimberley) 1923- *14*
Tumanov, Vladimir A. 1961- *138*
Tung, Angela 1972- *109*
Tunis, Edwin (Burdett) 1897-1973 .... *28*
  Obituary *24*
  Earlier sketch in SATA *1*
  See also CLR *2*
Tunis, John R(oberts) 1889-1975 .... *37*
  Brief entry *30*
Tunnell, Michael
  See Tunnell, Michael O('Grady)
Tunnell, Michael O('Grady) 1950- *157*
  Earlier sketch in SATA *103*
Tunnicliffe, C(harles) F(rederick)
  1901-1979 .... *62*
Turck, Mary C. 1950- *144*
Turk, Hanne
  See Tuerk, Hanne
Turk, Ruth 1917- *82*
Turkle, Brinton 1915- *79*
  Earlier sketch in SATA *2*
Turlington, Bayly 1919-1977 .... *5*
  Obituary *52*
Turnbull, Agnes Sligh 1888-1982 .... *14*

Turnbull, Ann 1943- *160*
  Earlier sketch in SATA *18*
Turnbull, Ann Christine
  See Turnbull, Ann
Turner, Alice K. 1940- *10*
Turner, Ann 1945- *188*
  Autobiography Feature *188*
  Earlier sketches in SATA *14, 77, 113, 178*
Turner, Ann Warren
  See Turner, Ann
Turner, Bonnie 1932- *75*
Turner, Elizabeth 1774-1846
  See YABC *2*
Turner, Glennette Tilley 1933- *183*
  Earlier sketch in SATA *71*
Turner, Josie
  See Crawford, Phyllis
Turner, Megan Whalen 1965- *174*
  Earlier sketch in SATA *94*
Turner, Philip (William) 1925- *83*
  Earlier sketch in SATA *11*
  See also CLR *89*
  See also SAAS *6*
Turner, Robyn 1947- *77*
Turner, Sheila R.
  See Seed, Sheila Turner
Turngren, Annette 1902(?)-1980
  Obituary *23*
Turngren, Ellen (?)-1964 .... *3*
Turska, Krystyna (Zofia) 1933- *31*
  Brief entry *27*
Turteltaub, H.N.
  See Turtledove, Harry
Turtledove, Harry 1949- *166*
  Earlier sketch in SATA *116*
Turtledove, Harry Norman
  See Turtledove, Harry
Tusa, Tricia 1960- *111*
  Earlier sketch in SATA *72*
Tusiani, Joseph 1924- *45*
Twain, Mark 1835-1910 .... *100*
  See also YABC *2*
  See also CLR *66*
Tweit, Susan J 1956- *94*
Tweit, Susan Joan
  See Tweit, Susan J
Tweton, D. Jerome 1933- *48*
Twinem, Neecy 1958- *92*
Twohill, Maggie
  See Angell, Judie
Tworkov, Jack 1900-1982 .... *47*
  Obituary *31*
Tyche
  See Papademetriou, Lisa
Tyers, Jenny 1969- *89*
Tyers, Kathy 1952- *82*
Tyler, Anne 1941- *173*
  Earlier sketches in SATA *7, 90*
Tyler, Linda
  See Tyler, Linda W(agner)
Tyler, Linda W(agner) 1952- *65*
Tyler, Vicki 1952- *64*
Tyne, Joel
  See Schembri, Jim
Tyrrell, Frances 1959- *107*

U

Ubell, Earl 1926-2007 .... *4*
  Obituary *182*
Uchida, Yoshiko 1921-1992 .... *53*
  Obituary *72*
  Earlier sketch in SATA *1*
  See also CLR *56*
  See also SAAS *1*
Udall, Jan Beaney 1938- *10*
Uden, (Bernard Gilbert) Grant 1910- *26*
Uderzo, Albert 1927-
  See CLR *37*

Udovic, David 1950- *189*
Udry, Janice May 1928- *152*
  Earlier sketch in SATA *4*
Uegaki, Chieri 1969- *153*
Ueno, Noriko
  See Nakae, Noriko
Ugliano, Natascia *196*
Uhlberg, Myron *174*
Uhlig, Richard 1970- *195*
Uhlig, Susan 1955- *129*
Ulam, S(tanislaw) M(arcin) 1909-1984 ...... *51*
Ullman, James Ramsey 1907-1971 .... *7*
Ulm, Robert 1934-1977 .... *17*
Ulmer, Louise 1943- *53*
Ulyatt, Kenneth 1920- *14*
Umansky, Kaye 1946- *188*
  Earlier sketch in SATA *158*
Unada
  See Gliewe, Unada (Grace)
Uncle Carter
  See Boucher, (Clarence) Carter
Uncle Eric
  See Maybury, Richard J.
Uncle Gus
  See Rey, H(ans) A(ugusto)
Uncle Mac
  See McCulloch, Derek (Ivor Breashur)
Uncle Ray
  See Coffman, Ramon Peyton
Uncle Shelby
  See Silverstein, Shel
Underhill, Alice Mertie (Waterman)
  1900-1971 .... *10*
Underhill, Liz 1948- *53*
  Brief entry *49*
Unger, Harlow G. 1931- *75*
Unger, Jim 1937- *67*
Ungerer, (Jean) Thomas 1931- *106*
  Earlier sketches in SATA *5, 33*
  See also CLR *77*
Ungerer, Tomi 1931-
  See Ungerer, (Jean) Thomas
Unkelbach, Kurt 1913-1992 .... *4*
Unnerstad, Edith (Totterman) 1900-1982 ...... *3*
  See also CLR *36*
Unobagha, Uzo *139*
Unrau, Ruth 1922- *9*
Unstead, R(obert) J(ohn) 1915-1988 .... *12*
  Obituary *56*
Unsworth, Walt(er) 1928- *4*
Untermeyer, Bryna Ivens 1909-1985 .... *61*
Untermeyer, Louis 1885-1977 .... *37*
  Obituary *26*
  Earlier sketch in SATA *2*
Unwin, David S(torr) 1918- *14*
Unwin, Nora S(picer) 1907-1982 .... *3*
  Obituary *49*
Unzner, Christa 1958- *141*
  Earlier sketch in SATA *80*
Unzner-Fischer, Christa
  See Unzner, Christa
Updale, Eleanor 1953- *175*
Updyke, Rosemary K. 1924- *103*
Upitis, Alvis *109*
Urban, Helle (Denise) 1957- *149*
Urban, Linda *199*
Urbanovic, Jackie *189*
Urbigkit, Cat 1965- *196*
Ure, Jean 1943- *192*
  Autobiography Feature *192*
  Earlier sketches in SATA *48, 78, 129*
  See also CLR *34*
  See also SAAS *14*
U'Ren, Andrea 1968- *142*
Uris, Leon 1924-2003 .... *49*
  Obituary *146*
Uris, Leon Marcus
  See Uris, Leon
Ursu, Anne *177*
Ury, Allen B. 1954- *98*
Uschan, Michael V. 1948- *129*

Usher, Margo Scegge
　See McHargue, Georgess
Uslan, Michael E. 1951- *169*
Uston, Ken(neth Senzo) 1935-1987 .... *65*
Uttley, Alice Jane (Taylor) 1884-1976 .... *88*
　Obituary *26*
　Earlier sketch in SATA *3*
Uttley, Alison
　See Uttley, Alice Jane (Taylor)
Utz, Lois (Marie) 1932-1986 .... *5*
　Obituary *50*

V

Vaeth, J. Gordon 1921- *17*
Vaeth, Joseph Gordon
　See Vaeth, J. Gordon
Vagin, Vladimir (Vasilevich) 1937- *142*
Vail, Rachel 1966- *163*
　Earlier sketch in SATA *94*
Vainio, Pirkko 1957- *123*
　Earlier sketch in SATA *76*
Valen, Nanine 1950- *21*
Valencak, Hannelore
　See Mayer, Hannelore Valencak
Valens, Amy 1946- *70*
Valens, E(vans) G(ladstone), Jr. 1920-1992 ... *1*
Valentine, Johnny *72*
Valerio, Geraldo 1970- *180*
Valgardson, W(illiam) D(empsey) 1939- *151*
　Earlier sketch in SATA *101*
Valleau, Emily 1925- *51*
Van Abbe, Salaman 1883-1955 .... *18*
Van Allsburg, Chris 1949- *156*
　Earlier sketches in SATA *37, 53, 105*
　See also CLR *113*
Van Anrooy, Francine 1924- *2*
Van Anrooy, Frans
　See Van Anrooy, Francine
Vanasse, Deb 1957- *170*
Vance, Eleanor Graham 1908-1985 .... *11*
Vance, Gerald
　See Garrett, (Gordon) Randall (Phillip)
　and Silverberg, Robert
Vance, Marguerite 1889-1965 .... *29*
VanCleave, Janice 1942- *116*
　Autobiography Feature *123*
　Earlier sketch in SATA *75*
Vandenburg, Mary Lou 1943- *17*
Vander Boom, Mae M. *14*
Vander-Els, Betty 1936- *63*
van der Heide, Iris 1970- *183*
van der Linde, Laurel 1952- *78*
van der Meer, Ron 1945- *98*
Van de Ruit, John 1975- *199*
Van der Veer, Judy 1912-1982 .... *4*
　Obituary *33*
Vanderwerff, Corrine 1939- *117*
Vander Zee, Ruth *199*
　Earlier sketch in SATA *159*
Vande Velde, Vivian 1951- *141*
　Earlier sketches in SATA *62, 95*
Vandivert, Rita (Andre) 1905-1986 .... *21*
Van Draanen, Wendelin *122*
Van Dusen, Chris *173*
Van Duyn, Janet 1910- *18*
Van Dyne, Edith
　See Baum, L(yman) Frank
　and Sampson, Emma (Keats) Speed
　and van Zantwijk, Rudolf (Alexander
　Marinus)
Vane, Mitch
　See Vane, Mitchelle
Vane, Mitchelle *176*
van Frankenhuyzen, Gijsbert 1951- *132*
Van Genechten, Guido 1957- *165*
van Haeringen, Annemarie *193*
Van Hook, Beverly H. 1941- *99*
Van Horn, William 1939- *43*

van Hout, Mies 1962- *178*
Van Iterson, S(iny) R(ose) *26*
Van Kampen, Vlasta 1943- *163*
　Earlier sketch in SATA *54*
Van Laan, Nancy 1939- *105*
van Lawick-Goodall, Jane
　See Goodall, Jane
Van Leeuwen, Jean 1937- *141*
　Autobiography Feature *141*
　Earlier sketches in SATA *6, 82, 132*
　See also SAAS *8*
van Lhin, Erik
　See del Rey, Lester
Van Loon, Hendrik Willem 1882-1944 .... *18*
van Ommen, Sylvia 1978- *186*
VanOosting, James 1951- *170*
Van Orden, M(erton) D(ick) 1921- *4*
Van Patter, Bruce *183*
Van Rensselaer, Alexander (Taylor Mason)
　1892-1962 .... *14*
Van Riper, Guernsey, Jr. 1909-1995 .... *3*
van Rossum, Heleen 1962- *174*
Van Rynbach, Iris 1952- *102*
Vansant, Rhonda Joy Edwards 1950- *92*
Van Steenwyk, Elizabeth (Ann) 1928- *89*
　Earlier sketch in SATA *34*
Van Stockum, Hilda 1908-2006 .... *5*
　Obituary *179*
van Straaten, Harmen 1961- *195*
Van Tuyl, Barbara 1940- *11*
van Vogt, A(lfred) E(lton) 1912-2000 .... *14*
　Obituary *124*
Van Woerkom, Dorothy (O'Brien)
　1924-1996 .... *21*
Van Wormer, Joe
　See Van Wormer, Joseph Edward
Van Wormer, Joseph Edward 1913-1998 ...... *35*
Van Wright, Cornelius *173*
Van Zwienen, Ilse Charlotte Koehn
　1929-1991 .... *34*
　Brief entry *28*
　Obituary *67*
Van Zyle, Jon 1942- *176*
　Earlier sketch in SATA *84*
Varela, Barry *180*
Varga, Judy
　See Stang, Judit
Varley, Dimitry V. 1906-1984 .... *10*
Varley, Susan 1961- *134*
　Earlier sketch in SATA *63*
Varon, Sara *195*
Vasileva, Tatiana
　See Wassiljewa, Tatjana
Vasiliev, Valery 1949- *80*
Vasilieva, Tatiana
　See Wassiljewa, Tatjana
Vasiliu, Mircea 1920- *2*
Vass, George 1927- *57*
　Brief entry *31*
Vaughan, Carter A.
　See Gerson, Noel Bertram
Vaughan, Harold Cecil 1923- *14*
Vaughan, Marcia (K.) 1951- *159*
　Earlier sketches in SATA *60, 95*
Vaughan, Richard 1947- *87*
Vaughan, Sam(uel) 1928- *14*
Vaughn, Ruth 1935- *14*
Vaught, Susan 1965- *195*
Vaupel, Robin *198*
Vautier, Ghislaine 1932- *53*
Vavra, Robert James 1935- *8*
Vecsey, George Spencer 1939- *9*
Vedral, Joyce L(auretta) 1943- *65*
Vega, Denise B. *174*
　See Vega, Denise
Veglahn, Nancy (Crary) 1937- *5*
Vejjajiva, Jane 1963- *189*
Velasquez, Eric *192*
Velasquez(-Trevino), Gloria (Louise)
　1949- *113*

Velasquez, Gloria (Louise) 1949-
　See Velasquez(-Trevino), Gloria (Louise)
Velthuijs, Max 1923-2005 .... *110*
　Obituary *160*
　Earlier sketch in SATA *53*
Venable, Alan (Hudson) 1944- *8*
Venezia, Mike 1945- *150*
Ventura, Anthony
　See Pellowski, Michael (Joseph)
Ventura, Piero (Luigi) 1937- *61*
　Brief entry *43*
　See also CLR *16*
Vequin, Capini
　See Quinn, Elisabeth
Verba, Joan Marie 1953- *78*
Verboven, Agnes 1951- *103*
verDorn, Bethea (Stewart) 1952- *76*
Vere, Ed *197*
Verissimo, Erico (Lopes) 1905-1975 .... *113*
Verne, Jules (Gabriel) 1828-1905 .... *21*
　See also CLR *88*
Verner, Gerald 1897(?)-1980
　Obituary *25*
Verney, John 1913-1993 .... *14*
　Obituary *75*
Verniero, Joan C. 1949- *181*
Vernon, (Elda) Louise A(nderson) 1914- *14*
Vernon, Rosemary
　See Smith, Susan Vernon
Vernor, D.
　See Casewit, Curtis W(erner)
Verr, Harry Coe
　See Kunhardt, Edith
Verral, Charles Spain 1904-1990 .... *11*
　Obituary *65*
Verrillo, Erica 1953- *199*
Verrillo, Erica F.
　See Verrillo, Erica
Verrone, Robert J. 1935(?)-1984
　Obituary *39*
Versace, Marie Teresa Rios 1917- *2*
Vertreace, Martha M(odena) 1945- *78*
Vesey, A(manda) 1939- *62*
Vesey, Mark (David) 1958- *123*
Vesey, Paul
　See Allen, Samuel W(ashington)
Vestergaard, Hope *178*
Vestly, Anne-Cath(arina) 1920- *14*
　See also CLR *99*
Vevers, (Henry) Gwynne 1916-1988 .... *45*
　Obituary *57*
Viator, Vacuus
　See Hughes, Thomas
Vicar, Henry
　See Felsen, Henry Gregor
Vick, Helen Hughes 1950- *88*
Vicker, Angus
　See Felsen, Henry Gregor
Vickers, Sheena 1960- *94*
Vickery, Kate
　See Kennedy, T.A.
Victor, Edward 1914- *3*
Victor, Joan Berg 1942- *30*
Vidrine, Beverly Barras 1938- *188*
　Earlier sketch in SATA *103*
Viereck, Ellen K. 1928- *14*
Viereck, Phillip 1925- *3*
Viertel, Janet 1915- *10*
Vigliante, Mary
　See Szydlowski, Mary Vigliante
Vigna, Judith 1936- *102*
　Earlier sketch in SATA *15*
Viguers, Ruth Hill 1903-1971 .... *6*
Villareal, Ray *187*
Villasenor, Edmundo
　See Villasenor, Victor
Villasenor, Victor 1940- *171*
Villasenor, Victor E. 1940-
　See Villasenor, Victor
Villasenor, Victor Edmundo
　See Villasenor, Victor

Villiard, Paul 1910-1974 .... *51*
    Obituary *20*
Villiers, Alan (John) 1903-1982 .... *10*
Vilott, Rhondi
    See Salsitz, Rhondi Vilott
Vincent, Eric Douglas 1953- *40*
Vincent, Erin 1969- *188*
Vincent, Felix 1946- *41*
Vincent, Gabrielle 1928-2000 .... *121*
    Earlier sketch in SATA *61*
    See also CLR *13*
Vincent, Mary Keith
    See St. John, Wylly Folk
Vincent, William R.
    See Heitzmann, William Ray
Vinegar, Tom
    See Gregg, Andrew K.
Vinest, Shaw
    See Longyear, Barry B(rookes)
Vinge, Joan (Carol) D(ennison) 1948- *113*
    Earlier sketch in SATA *36*
Vining, Elizabeth Gray 1902-1999 .... *6*
    Obituary *117*
Vinson, Kathryn 1911-1995 .... *21*
Vinton, Iris 1906(?)-1988 .... *24*
    Obituary *55*
Viola, Herman J(oseph) 1938- *126*
Viorst, Judith 1931- *172*
    Earlier sketches in SATA *7, 70, 123*
    See also CLR *90*
Vip
    See Partch, Virgil Franklin II
Vipont, Charles
    See Foulds, Elfrida Vipont
Vipont, Elfrida
    See Foulds, Elfrida Vipont
Viscott, David S(teven) 1938-1996 .... *65*
Visser, W(illem) F(rederik) H(endrik)
    1900-1968 .... *10*
Vitale, Stefano 1958- *180*
    Earlier sketch in SATA *114*
Vivas, Julie 1947- *96*
Vivelo, Jackie 1943- *63*
Vivelo, Jacqueline J.
    See Vivelo, Jackie
Vivelo, Jacqueline Jean
    See Vivelo, Jackie
Vizzini, Ned 1981- *179*
    Earlier sketch in SATA *125*
Vlahos, Olivia 1924- *31*
Vlasic, Bob
    See Hirsch, Phil
Voake, Charlotte *180*
    Earlier sketch in SATA *114*
Voake, Steve 1961- *178*
Vo-Dinh, Mai 1933- *16*
Vogel, Carole Garbuny 1951- *105*
    Earlier sketch in SATA *70*
Vogel, Ilse-Margret 1918- *14*
Vogel, John H., Jr. 1950- *18*
Vogt, Esther Loewen 1915-1999 .... *14*
Vogt, Gregory L. *94*
Vogt, Marie Bollinger 1921- *45*
Voight, Virginia Frances 1909-1989 .... *8*
Voigt, Cynthia 1942- *160*
    Brief entry *33*
    Earlier sketches in SATA *48, 79, 116*
    See also CLR *48*
Voigt, Erna 1925- *35*
Voigt-Rother, Erna
    See Voigt, Erna
Vojtech, Anna 1946- *108*
    Earlier sketch in SATA *42*
Vollstadt, Elizabeth Weiss 1942- *121*
Volponi, Paul *175*
Volting, Dr. R.E.
    See Lerangis, Peter
Von Ahnen, Katherine 1922- *93*
von Buhler, Cynthia *185*
Vondra, J. Gert
    See Vondra, Josef

Vondra, Josef 1941- *121*
Vondra, Josef Gert
    See Vondra, Josef
Von Gunden, Kenneth 1946- *113*
Von Hagen, Victor Wolfgang 1908-1985 ...... *29*
von Klopp, Vahrah
    See Malvern, Gladys
von Schmidt, Eric 1931-2007 .... *50*
    Brief entry *36*
    Obituary *181*
von Storch, Anne B. 1910- *1*
von Trapp, Maria Augusta 1905-1987 .... *16*
von Wodtke, Charlotte Buel Johnson
    1918-1982 .... *46*
von Ziegesar, Cecily 1970- *161*
Vos, Ida 1931-2006 .... *121*
    Earlier sketch in SATA *69*
    See also CLR *85*
Vosburgh, Leonard (W.) 1912- *15*
Voyle, Mary
    See Manning, Rosemary (Joy)
Vrettos, Adrienne Maria *187*
Vriens, Jacques 1946- *151*
Vugteveen, Verna Aardema
    See Aardema, Verna
Vulture, Elizabeth T.
    See Gilbert, Suzie
Vuong, Lynette Dyer 1938- *110*
    Earlier sketch in SATA *60*

W

Waas, Uli
    See Waas-Pommer, Ulrike
Waas-Pommer, Ulrike 1949- *85*
Waber, Bernard 1924- *155*
    Brief entry *40*
    Earlier sketches in SATA *47, 95*
    See also CLR *55*
Wachtel, Shirley Russak 1951- *88*
Wachter, Oralee (Roberts) 1935- *61*
    Brief entry *51*
Waddell, Evelyn Margaret 1918- *10*
Waddell, Martin 1941- *129*
    Autobiography Feature *129*
    Earlier sketches in SATA *43, 81, 127*
    See also CLR *31*
    See also SAAS *15*
Waddy, Lawrence (Heber) 1914- *91*
Wade, Mary Dodson 1930- *151*
    Earlier sketch in SATA *79*
Wade, Suzanne
    See Kirby, Susan E.
Wade, Theodore E., Jr. 1936- *37*
Wademan, Peter John 1946- *122*
Wademan, Spike
    See Wademan, Peter John
Wadsworth, Ginger 1945- *157*
    Earlier sketch in SATA *103*
Wagenheim, Kal 1935- *21*
Wagner, Michele R. 1975- *157*
Wagner, Sharon B. 1936- *4*
Wagoner, David (Russell) 1926- *14*
Wahl, Jan (Boyer) 1933- *132*
    Earlier sketches in SATA *2, 34, 73*
    See also SAAS *3*
Wahl, Mats 1945- *186*
Waide, Jan 1952- *29*
Wainscott, John Milton 1910-1981 .... *53*
Wainwright, Richard M. 1935- *91*
Wainwright, Ruth
    See Symes, Ruth Louise
Wait, Lea 1946- *137*
Waite, Judy *174*
Waite, Judy Bernard
    See Bernard, Patricia
Waite, Michael P(hillip) 1960- *101*
Waite, P(eter) B(usby) 1922- *64*
Waites, Joan C. *187*

Waitley, Douglas 1927- *30*
Wakefield, Jean L.
    See Laird, Jean E(louise)
Wakin, Daniel (Joseph) 1961- *84*
Wakin, Edward 1927- *37*
Wakiyama, Hanako 1966- *192*
Walck, Henry Z. 1908(?)-1984
    Obituary *40*
Walden, Amelia Elizabeth *3*
Walden, Mark *188*
Waldherr, Kris 1963- *76*
Waldman, Bruce 1949- *15*
Waldman, Neil 1947- *142*
    Earlier sketches in SATA *51, 94*
Waldrep, Richard *198*
Waldron, Ann Wood 1924- *16*
Waldron, Kathleen Cook *176*
Walgren, Judy 1963- *118*
Walker, Addison
    See Walker, (Addison) Mort
Walker, Alice 1944- *31*
Walker, Alice Malsenior
    See Walker, Alice
Walker, Barbara (Jeanne) K(erlin) 1921- *80*
    Earlier sketch in SATA *4*
Walker, Barbara M(uhs) 1928- *57*
Walker, (James) Braz(elton) 1934-1983 .... *45*
Walker, David 1965- *197*
Walker, David G(ordon) 1926- *60*
Walker, David Harry 1911-1992 .... *8*
    Obituary *71*
Walker, Diana 1925- *9*
Walker, Diane Marie Catherine
    See Walker, Kate
Walker, Dick
    See Pellowski, Michael (Joseph)
Walker, Frank 1931-2000 .... *36*
Walker, Holly Beth
    See Bond, Gladys Baker
Walker, Kate 1950- *165*
    Earlier sketch in SATA *82*
Walker, Kathrine Sorley
    See Sorley Walker, Kathrine
Walker, Lou Ann 1952- *66*
    Brief entry *53*
Walker, Louise Jean 1891-1976
    Obituary *35*
Walker, Mary Alexander 1927- *61*
Walker, Mildred
    See Schemm, Mildred Walker
Walker, (Addison) Mort 1923- *8*
Walker, Pamela 1948- *142*
    Earlier sketch in SATA *24*
Walker, Paul Robert 1953- *154*
Walker, Robert W(ayne) 1948- *66*
Walker, Sally M(acArt) 1954- *135*
Walker, Stephen J. 1951- *12*
Walker-Blondell, Becky 1951- *89*
Wallace, Barbara Brooks 1922- *136*
    Earlier sketches in SATA *4, 78*
    See also SAAS *17*
Wallace, Beverly Dobrin 1921- *19*
Wallace, Bill 1947- *169*
    Brief entry *47*
    Earlier sketches in SATA *53, 101*
Wallace, Daisy
    See Cuyler, Margery
Wallace, Ian 1950- *141*
    Earlier sketches in SATA *53, 56*
    See also CLR *37*
Wallace, John 1966- *155*
    Earlier sketch in SATA *105*
Wallace, John A(dam) 1915-2004 .... *3*
    Obituary *155*
Wallace, Karen 1951- *188*
    Earlier sketches in SATA *83, 139*
Wallace, Nancy Elizabeth 1948- *186*
    Earlier sketch in SATA *141*
Wallace, Nigel
    See Hamilton, Charles (Harold St. John)
Wallace, Paula S. *153*

Wallace, Rich 1957- *196*
  Earlier sketches in SATA *117, 158*
Wallace, Robert 1932-1999 .... *47*
  Brief entry *37*
Wallace, Ruby Ann 1923(?)- *77*
Wallace, William Keith
  See Wallace, Bill
Wallace-Brodeur, Ruth 1941- *169*
  Brief entry *41*
  Earlier sketches in SATA *51, 88*
Wallenta, Adam 1974- *123*
Waller, Leslie 1923-2007 .... *20*
Walley, Byron
  See Card, Orson Scott
Wallis, Diz 1949- *77*
Wallis, G. McDonald
  See Campbell, Hope
Wallner, Alexandra 1946- *156*
  Brief entry *41*
  Earlier sketches in SATA *51, 98*
Wallner, John C. 1945- *133*
  Earlier sketches in SATA *10, 51*
Wallower, Lucille *11*
Walrod, Amy 1973(?)- *182*
Walsh, Ann 1942- *176*
  Earlier sketch in SATA *62*
Walsh, Ellen Stoll 1942- *194*
  Earlier sketches in SATA *49, 99, 147*
Walsh, George Johnston 1889-1981 .... *53*
Walsh, Gillian Paton
  See Paton Walsh, Jill
Walsh, Jill Paton
  See Paton Walsh, Jill
Walsh, Joanna 1970- *182*
Walsh, Lawrence 1942- *170*
Walsh, Marissa 1972- *195*
Walsh, Mary Caswell 1949- *118*
Walsh, Mitzy
  See Walsh, Marissa
Walsh, Suella *170*
Walsh, V. L.
  See Walsh, Vivian
Walsh, Vivian 1960- *120*
Walsh Shepherd, Donna 1948- *78*
Walter, Frances V. 1923- *71*
Walter, Mildred Pitts 1922- *133*
  Brief entry *45*
  Earlier sketch in SATA *69*
  See also CLR *61*
  See also SAAS *12*
Walter, Villiam Christian
  See Andersen, Hans Christian
Walter, Virginia
  See Walter, Virginia A.
Walter, Virginia A. *134*
Walters, Audrey 1929- *18*
Walters, Celeste 1938- *126*
Walters, Eric (Robert) 1957- *155*
  Earlier sketch in SATA *99*
Walters, Helen B. (?)-1987
  Obituary *50*
Walters, Hugh
  See Hughes, Walter (Llewellyn)
Walther, Thomas A. 1950- *31*
Walther, Tom
  See Walther, Thomas A.
Waltner, Elma 1912-1987 .... *40*
Waltner, Willard H. 1909- *40*
Walton, Darwin McBeth 1926- *119*
Walton, Fiona L. M. 1959- *89*
Walton, Richard J. 1928- *4*
Walton, Rick 1957- *151*
  Earlier sketch in SATA *101*
Waltrip, Lela (Kingston) 1904-1995 .... *9*
Waltrip, Mildred 1911- *37*
Waltrip, Rufus (Charles) 1898-1988 .... *9*
Walworth, Nancy Zinsser 1917- *14*
Wangerin, Walter, Jr. 1944- *98*
  Brief entry *37*
  Earlier sketch in SATA *45*

Waniek, Marilyn Nelson 1946-
  See Nelson, Marilyn
Wannamaker, Bruce
  See Moncure, Jane Belk
Warbler, J. M.
  See Cocagnac, Augustin Maurice(-Jean)
Warburg, Sandol Stoddard
  See Stoddard, Sandol
Ward, E. D.
  See Gorey, Edward (St. John)
  and Lucas, E(dward) V(errall)
Ward, Ed
  See Stratemeyer, Edward L.
Ward, Helen 1962- *144*
  Earlier sketch in SATA *72*
Ward, Jay 1920-1989
  Obituary *63*
Ward, Jennifer 1963- *146*
Ward, John (Stanton) 1917- *42*
Ward, Jonas
  See Ard, William (Thomas)
  and Cox, William R(obert)
  and Garfield, Brian (Francis Wynne)
Ward, Lynd (Kendall) 1905-1985 .... *36*
  Obituary *42*
  Earlier sketch in SATA *2*
Ward, Martha (Eads) *5*
Ward, Melanie
  See Curtis, Richard (Alan)
  and Lynch, Marilyn
Ward, Nicholas John
  See Ward, Nick
Ward, Nick 1955- *190*
Ward, Tom
  See Stratemeyer, Edward L.
Wardell, Dean
  See Prince, J(ack) H(arvey)
Wardlaw, Lee 1955- *115*
  Earlier sketch in SATA *79*
Ware, Cheryl 1963- *101*
Ware, Chris 1967- *140*
Ware, Leon (Vernon) 1909-1976 .... *4*
Wargin, Kathy-jo 1965- *145*
Warhola, James 1955- *187*
Warner, Frank A. *67*
  Earlier sketch in SATA *1*
Warner, Gertrude Chandler 1890-1979 .... *9*
  Obituary *73*
Warner, J(ohn) F. 1929- *75*
Warner, Lucille Schulberg *30*
Warner, Matt
  See Fichter, George S.
Warner, Oliver (Martin Wilson) 1903-1976 . *29*
Warner, Sally 1946- *131*
Warner, Sunny (B.) 1931- *108*
Warnes, Tim 1971- *166*
  Earlier sketch in SATA *116*
Warnes, Timothy
  See Warnes, Tim
Warnick, Elsa 1942- *113*
Warren, Andrea 1946- *98*
Warren, Betsy
  See Warren, Elizabeth Avery
Warren, Billy
  See Warren, William Stephen
Warren, Cathy 1951- *62*
  Brief entry *46*
Warren, Elizabeth
  See Supraner, Robyn
Warren, Elizabeth Avery 1916- *46*
  Brief entry *38*
Warren, Jackie M. 1953- *135*
Warren, Joshua P(aul) 1976- *107*
Warren, Joyce W(illiams) 1935- *18*
Warren, Mary Phraner 1929- *10*
Warren, Robert Penn 1905-1989 .... *46*
  Obituary *63*
Warren, Scott S. 1957- *79*
Warren, William Stephen 1882-1968 .... *9*
Warrick, Patricia Scott 1925- *35*

Warriner, John 1907(?)-1987
  Obituary *53*
Warsh
  See Warshaw, Jerry
Warshaw, Jerry 1929- *30*
Warshaw, Mary 1931- *89*
Warshofsky, Fred 1931- *24*
Warshofsky, Isaac
  See Singer, Isaac Bashevis
Wartski, Maureen (Ann Crane) 1940- *50*
  Brief entry *37*
Warwick, Alan R(oss) 1900-1973 .... *42*
Wa-sha-quon-asin
  See Belaney, Archibald Stansfeld
Wa-Sha-Quon-Asin
  See Belaney, Archibald Stansfeld
Washburn, Bradford 1910-2007 .... *38*
  Obituary *181*
Washburn, Henry Bradford, Jr.
  See Washburn, Bradford
Washburn, Jan(ice) 1926- *63*
Washburn, Lucia *193*
Washburne, Carolyn Kott 1944- *86*
Washburne, Heluiz Chandler 1892-1970 ...... *10*
  Obituary *26*
Washington, Booker T(aliaferro)
  1856-1915 .... *28*
Washington, Donna L. 1967- *159*
  Earlier sketch in SATA *98*
Wasserstein, Wendy 1950-2006 .... *94*
  Obituary *174*
Wassiljewa, Tatjana 1928- *106*
Watanabe, Shigeo 1928- *131*
  Brief entry *32*
  Earlier sketch in SATA *39*
  See also CLR *8*
Waters, John F(rederick) 1930- *4*
Waters, Tony 1958- *75*
Waterton, Betty 1923- *99*
  Brief entry *34*
  Earlier sketch in SATA *37*
Waterton, Betty Marie
  See Waterton, Betty
Watkins, Dawn L. *126*
Watkins, Gloria Jean
  See hooks, bell
Watkins, Lois 1930- *88*
Watkins, Peter 1934- *66*
Watkins, Yoko Kawashima 1933- *93*
Watkins-Pitchford, Denys James
  1905-1990 .... *87*
  Obituary *66*
  Earlier sketch in SATA *6*
  See also SAAS *4*
Watling, James 1933- *117*
  Earlier sketch in SATA *67*
Watson, Aldren A(uld) 1917- *42*
  Brief entry *36*
Watson, Amy Zakrzewski 1965- *76*
Watson, B. S.
  See Teitelbaum, Michael
Watson, Carol 1949- *78*
Watson, C.G. *193*
Watson, Clyde 1947- *68*
  Earlier sketch in SATA *5*
  See also CLR *3*
Watson, Helen Orr 1892-1978
  Obituary *24*
Watson, James 1936- *106*
  Earlier sketch in SATA *10*
Watson, Jane Werner 1915- *54*
  Earlier sketch in SATA *3*
Watson, Jesse Joshua *199*
Watson, John H.
  See Farmer, Philip Jose
Watson, Mary 1953- *117*
Watson, N. Cameron 1955- *81*
Watson, Nancy Dingman *32*
Watson, Pauline 1925- *14*
Watson, Richard F.
  See Silverberg, Robert

Watson, Richard Jesse 1951- 62
Watson, Sally (Lou) 1924- 3
Watson, Wendy (McLeod) 1942- 142
Earlier sketches in SATA 5, 74
Watson Taylor, Elizabeth 1915- 41
Watt, Melanie 1975- 193
Earlier sketch in SATA 136
Watt, Thomas 1935- 4
Wattenberg, Jane 174
Watterson, Bill 1958- 66
Watt-Evans, Lawrence 1954- 121
Watts, (Anna) Bernadette 1942- 103
Earlier sketch in SATA 4
Watts, Ephraim
See Horne, Richard Henry Hengist
Watts, Franklin (Mowry) 1904-1978 46
Obituary 21
Watts, Helen L. Hoke 1903-1990
Obituary 65
Watts, Irene N(aemi) 1931- 111
Earlier sketch in SATA 56
Watts, Isaac 1674-1748 52
Watts, James K(ennedy) M(offitt) 1955- 59
Watts, Jeri Hanel 1957- 170
Watts, Julia 1969- 103
Watts, Leander 1956- 146
Watts, Leslie Elizabeth 1961- 168
Watts, Mabel Pizzey 1906-1994 11
Watts, Nigel 1957-1999 121
Waugh, C. C. Roessel
See Waugh, Carol-Lynn Rossel
and Waugh, Charles G(ordon)
Waugh, Carol-Lynn Rossel 1947- 41
Waugh, Dorothy -1996 11
Waugh, Sylvia 1935- 169
Waugh, Virginia
See Sorensen, Virginia
Wax, Wendy A. 1963- 163
Earlier sketch in SATA 73
Wayland, April Halprin 1954- 143
Earlier sketch in SATA 78
See also SAAS 26
Wayland, Patrick
See O'Connor, Richard
Wayne, (Anne) Jenifer 1917-1982 32
Wayne, Kyra Petrovskaya 1918- 8
Wayne, Richard
See Decker, Duane
Wayshak, Deborah Noyes
See Noyes, Deborah
Waystaff, Simon
See Swift, Jonathan
Weales, Gerald (Clifford) 1925- 11
Weary, Ogdred
See Gorey, Edward (St. John)
Weatherford, Carole Boston 1956- 181
Earlier sketch in SATA 138
Weatherly, Lee 1967- 192
Weatherly, Myra 1926- 130
Weatherly, Myra S.
See Weatherly, Myra
Weaver, Harriett E. 1908-1993 65
Weaver, John L. 1949- 42
Weaver, Robyn
See Conley-Weaver, Robyn
Weaver, Robyn M.
See Conley-Weaver, Robyn
Weaver, Tess 197
Weaver, Ward
See Mason, F(rancis) van Wyck
Weaver, Will 1950- 161
Earlier sketches in SATA 88, 109
Weaver, William Weller
See Weaver, Will
Weaver-Gelzer, Charlotte 1950- 79
Webb, Christopher
See Wibberley, Leonard (Patrick O'Connor)
Webb, Jacqueline
See Pearce, Margaret

Webb, Jacquelyn
See Pearce, Margaret
and Pearce, Margaret
Webb, Jean Francis (III) 1910-1991 35
Webb, Kaye 1914- 60
Webb, Lois Sinaiko 1922- 82
Webb, Margot 1934- 67
Webb, Sharon 1936- 41
Webb, Sophie 1958- 135
Webber, Andrew Lloyd
See Lloyd Webber, Andrew
Webber, Desiree Morrison 1956- 170
Webber, Irma E(leanor Schmidt)
1904-1995 14
Weber, Alfons 1921- 8
Weber, Bruce 1942- 120
Earlier sketch in SATA 73
Weber, Debora 1955- 58
Weber, EdNah New Rider 1919(?)- 168
Weber, Jill 1950- 127
Weber, Judith E(ichler) 1938- 64
Weber, Ken(neth J.) 1940- 90
Weber, Lenora Mattingly 1895-1971 2
Obituary 26
Weber, Michael 1945- 87
Weber, Sandra 1961- 158
Weber, William J(ohn) 1927- 14
Webster, Alice Jane Chandler 1876-1916 17
Webster, David 1930- 11
Webster, Frank V. 67
Earlier sketch in SATA 1
Webster, Gary
See Garrison, Webb B(lack)
Webster, James 1925-1981 17
Obituary 27
Webster, Jean
See Webster, Alice Jane Chandler
Wechsler, Doug 189
Wechsler, Herman J. 1904-1976
Obituary 20
Wechter, Nell (Carolyn) Wise 1913-1989 .. 127
Earlier sketch in SATA 60
Weck, Thomas L. 1942- 62
Wedd, Kate
See Gregory, Philippa
Weddle, Ethel Harshbarger 1897-1996 11
Weeks, Sarah 194
Earlier sketch in SATA 158
Weems, David B(urnola) 1922- 80
Wees, Frances Shelley 1902-1982 58
Weevers, Peter 1944- 59
Wegen, Ronald 1946-1985 99
Wegman, William (George) 1943- 135
Earlier sketches in SATA 78, 129
Wegner, Fritz 1924- 20
Weidhorn, Manfred 1931- 60
Weidt, Maryann N. 1944- 85
Weigel, Jeff 1958- 170
Weigelt, Udo 1960- 168
Weihs, Erika 1917- 107
Earlier sketch in SATA 15
Weik, Mary Hays 1898(?)-1979 3
Obituary 23
Weil, Ann Yezner 1908-1969 9
Weil, Lisl 1910- 7
Weilerstein, Sadie Rose 1894-1993 3
Obituary 75
Weill, Cynthia 1959- 167
Wein, Elizabeth E(ve) 1964- 151
Earlier sketch in SATA 82
Weinberg, Larry
See Weinberg, Lawrence (E.)
Weinberg, Lawrence (E.) 92
Brief entry 48
Weinberger, Tanya 1939- 84
Weiner, Sandra 1922- 14
Weingarten, Violet (Brown) 1915-1976 3
Obituary 27
Weingartner, Charles 1922- 5
Weinheimer, Beckie 1958- 186
Weinstein, Nina 1951- 73

Weir, Bob 1947- 76
Weir, Diana (R.) Loiewski 1958- 111
Weir, Joan S(herman) 1928- 99
Weir, LaVada 2
Weir, Rosemary (Green) 1905-1994 21
Weir, Wendy 1949- 76
Weis, Margaret 1948- 164
Earlier sketches in SATA 38, 92
Weisberger, Bernard A(llen) 1922- 21
Weiser, Marjorie P(hillis) K(atz) 1934- 33
Weisgard, Leonard (Joseph) 1916-2000 85
Obituary 122
Earlier sketches in SATA 2, 30
See also SAAS 19
Weiss, Adelle 1920- 18
Weiss, Ann E(dwards) 1943- 69
Earlier sketch in SATA 30
See also SAAS 13
Weiss, Edna
See Barth, Edna
Weiss, Ellen 1953- 44
Weiss, Harvey 1922- 76
Earlier sketches in SATA 1, 27
See also CLR 4
See also SAAS 19
Weiss, Jaqueline Shachter 1926- 65
Weiss, Malcolm E. 1928- 3
Weiss, Margaret Edith
See Weis, Margaret
Weiss, Miriam
See Schlein, Miriam
Weiss, Mitch 1951- 183
Earlier sketch in SATA 123
Weiss, Nicki 1954- 86
Earlier sketch in SATA 33
Weiss, Renee Karol 1923- 5
Weissberger, Ela 1930- 181
Weissberger, Ela Stein
See Weissberger, Ela
Weissenborn, Hellmuth 1898-1982
Obituary 31
Weitzman, David L. 1936- 172
Earlier sketch in SATA 122
Wekesser, Carol A. 1963- 76
Welber, Robert 26
Welch, Amanda (Jane) 1945- 75
Welch, D'Alte Aldridge 1907-1970
Obituary 27
Welch, Jean-Louise
See Kempton, Jean Welch
Welch, Pauline
See Bodenham, Hilda Morris
Welch, Ronald
See Felton, Ronald Oliver
Welch, Sheila Kelly 1945- 130
Welch, Willy 1952- 93
Weldin, Frauke 1969- 188
Welford, Sue 1942- 75
Weller, George 1907-2002 31
Obituary 140
Weller, George Anthony
See Weller, George
Welling, Peter J. 1947- 135
Wellington, Monica 1957- 157
Earlier sketches in SATA 67, 99
Wellman, Alice 1900-1984 51
Brief entry 36
Wellman, Manly Wade 1903-1986 6
Obituary 47
Wellman, Paul I. 1898-1966 3
Wellman, Paul Iselin
See Wellman, Paul I.
Wellman, Sam(uel) 1939- 122
Wells, H(erbert) G(eorge) 1866-1946 20
See also CLR 133
Wells, Helen
See Campbell, Hope
Wells, Helen 1910-1986 49
Earlier sketch in SATA 2
Wells, J. Wellington
See de Camp, L(yon) Sprague

Wells, June
    See Swinford, Betty (June Wells)
Wells, Robert
    See Welsch, Roger L(ee)
Wells, Robert E. 184
Wells, Rosemary 1943- 156
    Earlier sketches in SATA *18, 69, 114*
    See also CLR *69*
    See also SAAS *1*
Wells, Susan (Mary) 1951- 78
Wels, Byron G(erald) 1924-1993 9
Welsbacher, Anne 1955- 89
Welsch, Roger L(ee) 1936- 82
Welsh, David
    See Hills, C.A.R.
Welsh, Mary Flynn 1910(?)-1984
    Obituary 38
Welsh, T.K. 1956- 184
Weltner, Linda R(iverly) 1938- 38
Welton, Jude 1955- 143
    Earlier sketch in SATA *79*
Welty, S. F.
    See Welty, Susan F.
Welty, Susan F. 1905- 9
Wemmlinger, Raymond 190
Wendelin, Rudolph 1910-2000 23
Weninger, Brigitte 1960- 189
Wentworth, Robert
    See Hamilton, Edmond
Werlin, Nancy 1961- 161
    Earlier sketches in SATA *87, 119*
Werner, Elsa Jane
    See Watson, Jane Werner
Werner, Herma 1926- 47
    Brief entry 41
Werner, Jane
    See Watson, Jane Werner
Werner, K.
    See Casewit, Curtis W(erner)
Wersba, Barbara 1932- 58
    Autobiography Feature 103
    Earlier sketch in SATA *1*
    See also CLR *78*
    See also SAAS *2*
Werstein, Irving 1914(?)-1971 14
Werth, Kurt 1896-1983 20
Wesley, Alison
    See Barnes, Michael
Wesley, Kathryn
    See Rusch, Kristine Kathryn
Wesley, Mary (Aline) 1912-2002 66
Wesley, Valerie Wilson 1947- 168
    Earlier sketch in SATA *106*
West, Andrew
    See Arthur, Robert, (Jr.)
West, Anna 1938- 40
West, Barbara
    See Price, Olive
West, Betty 1921- 11
West, Bruce 1951- 63
West, C. P.
    See Wodehouse, P(elham) G(renville)
West, Dorothy
    See Benson, Mildred (Augustine Wirt)
West, Emily Govan 1919- 38
West, Emmy
    See West, Emily Govan
West, James
    See Withers, Carl A.
West, Jerry
    See Svenson, Andrew E(dward)
West, (Mary) Jessamyn 1902-1984
    Obituary 37
West, John
    See Arthur, Robert, (Jr.)
West, Owen
    See Koontz, Dean R.
West, Ward
    See Borland, Harold Glen

Westall, Robert (Atkinson) 1929-1993 69
    Obituary 75
    Earlier sketch in SATA *23*
    See also CLR *13*
    See also SAAS *2*
Westaway, Jane 1948- 121
Westcott, Nadine Bernard 1949- 130
Westera, Marleen 1962- 187
Westerberg, Christine 1950- 29
Westerduin, Anne 1945- 105
Westervelt, Virginia Veeder 1914-2005 10
Westheimer, David 1917-2005 14
    Obituary 170
Westheimer, David Kaplan
    See Westheimer, David
Westmacott, Mary
    See Christie, Agatha (Mary Clarissa)
Westman, Barbara 70
Westman, Paul (Wendell) 1956- 39
Westmoreland, William C. 1914-2005 63
Westmoreland, William Childs
    See Westmoreland, William C.
Weston, Allen
    See Hogarth, Grace (Weston Allen)
    and Norton, Andre
Weston, Carol 1956- 135
Weston, Carrie 190
Weston, John (Harrison) 1932- 21
Weston, Martha 1947- 119
    Earlier sketch in SATA *53*
Westphal, Arnold Carl 1897- 57
Westrup, Hugh 102
Westwood, Jennifer 1940-2008 10
    Obituary 192
Wexler, Jerome (LeRoy) 1923- 14
Weyland, Jack 1940- 81
Weyn, Suzanne 1955- 164
    Earlier sketches in SATA *63, 101*
Weyr, Garret
    See Freymann-Weyr, (Rhoda) Garret (Michaela)
Wezyk, Joanna 1966- 82
Whaley, Joyce Irene 1923- 61
Whalin, W. Terry 1953- 93
Wharf, Michael
    See Weller, George
Wharmby, Margot 63
Wharton, Edith (Newbold Jones) 1862-1937
    See CLR *136*
Whatley, Bruce 1954- 177
Wheatley, Arabelle 1921- 16
Wheatley, Nadia 1949- 147
Wheeler, Cindy 1955- 49
    Brief entry 40
Wheeler, Deborah 1947- 83
Wheeler, Janet D. 1
Wheeler, Jill C. 1964- 136
    Earlier sketch in SATA *86*
Wheeler, Jody 1952- 148
    Earlier sketch in SATA *84*
Wheeler, Lisa 1963- 162
Wheeler, Opal 1898- 23
Whelan, Elizabeth M(urphy) 1943- 14
Whelan, Gloria 1923- 178
    Earlier sketches in SATA *85, 128*
    See also CLR *90*
Whelan, Gloria Ann
    See Whelan, Gloria
Whipple, A(ddison) B(eecher) C(olvin)
    1918- 64
Whipple, Cal
    See Whipple, A(ddison) B(eecher) C(olvin)
Whisp, Kennilworthy
    See Rowling, J.K.
Whistler, Reginald John 1905-1944 30
Whistler, Rex
    See Whistler, Reginald John
Whitaker, Zai 183
Whitcher, Susan (Godsil) 1952- 96

Whitcomb, Jon 1906-1988 10
    Obituary 56
Whitcomb, Laura 171
White, Anne Terry 1896-1980 2
White, Bessie (Felstiner) 1892(?)-1986
    Obituary 50
White, Carolyn 1948- 130
White, Dale
    See Place, Marian T(empleton)
White, Dori 1919- 10
White, E. B. 1899-1985 100
    Obituary 44
    Earlier sketches in SATA *2, 29*
    See also CLR *107*
White, Eliza Orne 1856-1947
    See YABC *2*
White, Elwyn Brooks
    See White, E. B.
White, Florence M(eiman) 1910- 14
White, Laurence B(arton), Jr. 1935- 10
White, Lee 176
White, Martin 1943- 51
White, Nancy 1942- 126
White, Ramy Allison 67
    Earlier sketch in SATA *1*
White, Robb 1909-1990 83
    Earlier sketch in SATA *1*
    See also CLR *3*
    See also SAAS *1*
White, Ruth C. 1942- 186
    Autobiography Feature 186
    Earlier sketches in SATA *39, 117, 165*
White, T(erence) H(anbury) 1906-1964 12
    See also CLR *139*
White, Tekla N. 1934- 115
White, Timothy (Thomas Anthony)
    1952-2002 60
White, Tom 1923- 148
White, William, Jr. 1934- 16
Whitehead, Don(ald) F. 1908-1981 4
Whitehead, Jenny 1964- 191
Whitehead, Kathy 1957- 176
Whitehouse, Arch
    See Whitehouse, Arthur George Joseph
Whitehouse, Arthur George Joseph
    1895-1979 14
    Obituary 23
Whitehouse, Elizabeth S(cott) 1893-1968 35
Whitehouse, Jeanne
    See Peterson, Jeanne Whitehouse
Whitelaw, Nancy 1933- 166
    Earlier sketch in SATA *76*
Whitesel, Cheryl Aylward 162
Whitinger, R. D.
    See Place, Marian T(empleton)
Whitley, Mary Ann
    See Sebrey, Mary Ann
Whitley, Peggy 1938- 140
Whitlock, Pamela 1921(?)-1982
    Obituary 31
Whitlock, Ralph 1914-1995 35
Whitman, Alice
    See Marker, Sherry
Whitman, Sylvia (Choate) 1961- 135
    Earlier sketch in SATA *85*
Whitman, Walt(er) 1819-1892 20
Whitmore, Arvella 1922- 125
Whitney, Alex(andra) 1922- 14
Whitney, David C(harles) 1921- 48
    Brief entry 29
Whitney, Kim Ablon 162
Whitney, Phyllis A. 1903-2008 30
    Obituary 189
    Earlier sketch in SATA *1*
    See also CLR *59*
Whitney, Phyllis Ayame
    See Whitney, Phyllis A.
Whitney, Phyllis Ayame
    See Whitney, Phyllis A.
Whitney, Sharon 1937- 63

Whitney, Thomas P. 1917-2007 25
    Obituary 189
Whitney, Thomas Porter
    See Whitney, Thomas P.
Whittington, Mary K(athrine) 1941- 75
Whitworth, John 1945- 123
Whybrow, Ian 132
Whyte, Mal(colm Kenneth, Jr.) 1933- 62
Whyte, Mary 1953- 148
    Earlier sketch in SATA 94
Whyte, Ron 1942(?)-1989
    Obituary 63
Whytock, Cherry 177
Wiater, Stanley 1953- 84
Wibbelsman, Charles J(oseph) 1945- 59
Wibberley, Leonard (Patrick O'Connor)
    1915-1983 45
    Obituary 36
    Earlier sketch in SATA 2
    See also CLR 3
Wiberg, Harald (Albin) 1908- 93
    Brief entry 40
Wick, Walter 1953- 148
Wickens, Elaine 86
Wicker, Ireene 1905(?)-1987
    Obituary 55
Wickstrom, Sylvie 1960- 169
Widdemer, Mabel Cleland 1902-1964 5
Widener, Terry 1950- 105
Widerberg, Siv 1931- 10
Wiebe, Rudy 1934- 156
Wiebe, Rudy Henry
    See Wiebe, Rudy
Wieler, Diana (Jean) 1961- 109
Wiener, Lori 1956- 84
Wier, Ester (Alberti) 1910-2000 3
Wiese, Kurt 1887-1974 36
    Obituary 24
    Earlier sketch in SATA 3
    See also CLR 86
Wiesel, Elie 1928- 56
Wiesel, Eliezer
    See Wiesel, Elie
Wiesner, David 1956- 181
    Earlier sketches in SATA 72, 117, 139
    See also CLR 84
Wiesner, Portia
    See Takakjian, Portia
Wiesner, William 1899-1984 5
Wiggers, Raymond 1952- 82
Wiggin, Eric E. 1939- 167
    Earlier sketch in SATA 88
Wiggin, Eric Ellsworth 1939-
    See Wiggin, Eric E.
Wiggin (Riggs), Kate Douglas (Smith)
    1856-1923
    See YABC 1
    See also CLR 52
Wiggins, VeraLee (Chesnut) 1928-1995 89
Wight, James Alfred 1916-1995 135
    Brief entry 44
    Earlier sketch in SATA 86
    See also CLR 80
Wignell, Edel 1936- 69
Wijnberg, Ellen 85
Wikland, Ilon 1930- 93
    Brief entry 32
Wikler, Madeline 1943- 114
Wilber, Donald N(ewton) 1907-1997 35
Wilbur, C. Keith 1923- 27
Wilbur, Frances 1921- 107
Wilbur, Richard 1921- 108
    Earlier sketch in SATA 9
Wilbur, Richard Purdy
    See Wilbur, Richard
Wilburn, Kathy 1948- 68
Wilcox, Charlotte 1948- 72
Wilcox, R(uth) Turner 1888-1970 36
Wilcox, Roger
    See Collins, Paul
Wild, Jocelyn 1941- 46

Wild, Kate 1954- 192
Wild, Margaret 1948- 197
    Earlier sketch in SATA 151
Wild, Robin (Evans) 1936- 46
Wild, Robyn 1947- 117
Wilde, D. Gunther
    See Hurwood, Bernhardt J.
Wilde, Oscar 1854(?)-1900 24
    See also CLR 114
Wilde, Oscar Fingal O'Flahertie Willis
    See Wilde, Oscar
Wilder, Buck
    See Smith, Tim(othy R.)
Wilder, Laura (Elizabeth) Ingalls
    1867-1957 100
    Earlier sketches in SATA 15, 29
    See also CLR 111
Wildsmith, Brian 1930- 124
    Earlier sketches in SATA 16, 69
    See also CLR 52
    See also SAAS 5
Wiles, Deborah 171
Wilhelm, Doug 1952- 190
Wilhelm, Hans 1945- 196
    Autobiography Feature 196
    Earlier sketches in SATA 58, 135
    See also CLR 46
    See also SAAS 21
Wilkie, Katharine E(lliott) 1904-1980 31
Wilkin, Eloise 1904-1987 49
    Obituary 54
Wilkins, Frances 1923- 14
Wilkins, Kim 147
Wilkins, Marilyn (Ruth) 1926- 30
Wilkins, Marne
    See Wilkins, Marilyn (Ruth)
Wilkins, Mary Huiskamp 1926- 2
    See also CLR 42
Wilkins, Mary Huiskamp Calhoun
    See Wilkins, Mary Huiskamp
Wilkins, Rose 180
Wilkinson, (Thomas) Barry 1923- 50
    Brief entry 32
Wilkinson, Beth 1925- 80
Wilkinson, Brenda 1946- 91
    Earlier sketch in SATA 14
    See also CLR 20
Wilkinson, (John) Burke 1913-2000 4
Wilkinson, Sylvia 1940- 56
    Brief entry 39
Wilkon, Jozef 1930- 133
    Earlier sketches in SATA 31, 71
Wilkowski, Sue 193
Wilks, Michael Thomas 1947- 44
Wilks, Mike
    See Wilks, Michael Thomas
Will
    See Lipkind, William
Willard, Barbara (Mary) 1909-1994 74
    Earlier sketch in SATA 17
    See also CLR 2
    See also SAAS 5
Willard, Mildred Wilds 1911-1978 14
Willard, Nancy 1936- 191
    Brief entry 30
    Earlier sketches in SATA 37, 71, 127
    See also CLR 5
Willcox, Isobel 1907-1996 42
Willems, Mo 180
    Earlier sketch in SATA 154
    See also CLR 114
Willett, Edward (C.) 1959- 115
Willey, Bee 184
Willey, Margaret 1950- 86
Willey, Robert
    See Ley, Willy
Willhoite, Michael A. 1946- 71
William, Kate
    See Armstrong, Jennifer
Williams, Arlene 171

Williams, Barbara 1925- 107
    Earlier sketch in SATA 11
    See also CLR 48
    See also SAAS 16
Williams, Barbara 1937- 62
Williams, Beryl
    See Epstein, Beryl (M. Williams)
Williams, Brian (Peter) 1943- 54
Williams, Carol Lynch 1959- 110
Williams, Charles
    See Collier, James Lincoln
Williams, Clyde C. 1881-1974 8
    Obituary 27
Williams, Coe
    See Harrison, C(hester) William
Williams, Colleen Madonna Flood 1963- .. 156
Williams, Cynthia G. 1958- 123
Williams, Dar 1967- 168
Williams, Donna Reilly 1945- 83
Williams, Dorothy
    See Williams, Marcia
Williams, Dorothy Snowden
    See Williams, Dar
Williams, Eric (Ernest) 1911-1983 14
    Obituary 38
Williams, Ferelith Eccles
    See Eccles Williams, Ferelith
Williams, Frances B.
    See Browin, Frances Williams
Williams, Garth (Montgomery) 1912-1996 .. 66
    Obituary 90
    Earlier sketch in SATA 18
    See also CLR 57
    See also SAAS 7
Williams, Guy R(ichard) 1920- 11
Williams, Hawley
    See Heyliger, William
Williams, Helen 1948- 77
Williams, J. R.
    See Williams, Jeanne
Williams, J. Walker
    See Wodehouse, P(elham) G(renville)
Williams, Jay 1914-1978 41
    Obituary 24
    Earlier sketch in SATA 3
    See also CLR 8
Williams, Jeanne 1930- 5
Williams, Jenny 1939- 60
Williams, Karen Lynn 1952- 99
    Earlier sketch in SATA 66
Williams, Kit 1946(?)- 44
    See also CLR 4
Williams, Laura E. 180
Williams, Laura Ellen
    See Williams, Laura E.
Williams, L.E.
    See Williams, Laura Ellen
Williams, Leslie 1941- 42
Williams, Linda 1948- 59
Williams, Louise Bonino 1904(?)-1984
    Obituary 39
Williams, Lynn
    See Hale, Arlene
Williams, Marcia 1945- 159
    Earlier sketches in SATA 71, 97
Williams, Marcia Dorothy
    See Williams, Marcia
Williams, Margery
    See Bianco, Margery Williams
Williams, Mark
    See Arthur, Robert, (Jr.)
Williams, Mark London 1959- 140
Williams, Maureen 1951- 12
Williams, Michael
    See St. John, Wylly Folk
Williams, Patrick J.
    See Griffin, W.E.B
Williams, Pete
    See Faulknor, Cliff(ord Vernon)
Williams, S. P.
    See Hart, Virginia

Williams, Sam 177
Earlier sketch in SATA *124*
Williams, Selma R(uth) 1925- *14*
Williams, Sherley Anne 1944-1999 78
Obituary *116*
Williams, Sheron 1955- 77
Williams, Shirley
See Williams, Sherley Anne
Williams, Slim
See Williams, Clyde C.
Williams, Sophy 1965- 135
Williams, Susan
See Beckhorn, Susan Williams
Williams, Suzanne (Bullock) 1953- 71
Williams, Ursula Moray
See Moray Williams, Ursula
Williams, Vera B(aker) 1927- *102*
Brief entry *33*
Earlier sketch in SATA *53*
See also CLR 9
Williams-Andriani, Renee 1963- 98
Williams-Ellis, (Mary) Amabel (Nassau
Strachey) 1894-1984 29
Obituary *41*
Williams-Garcia, Rita 1957- *160*
Earlier sketch in SATA *98*
See also CLR 36
Williamson, Gwyneth 1965- 109
Williamson, Henry (William) 1895-1977 37
Obituary 30
Williamson, Joanne S(mall) 1926- 122
Earlier sketch in SATA *3*
Williamson, Melanie 196
Willis, Charles
See Clarke, Arthur C.
Willis, Connie 1945- 110
See also CLR 66
Willis, Jeanne 1959- 195
Earlier sketches in SATA *61, 123*
Willis, Jeanne Mary
See Willis, Jeanne
Willis, Meredith Sue 1946- *101*
Willis, Nancy Carol 1952- *139*
Earlier sketch in SATA *93*
Willis, Paul J. 1955- *113*
Willms, Russ 95
Willoughby, Lee Davis
See Avallone, Michael (Angelo, Jr.)
and Brandner, Gary (Phil)
and Deming, Richard
and DeAndrea, William L(ouis)
and Laymon, Richard (Carl)
and Streib, Dan(iel Thomas)
and Toombs, John
and Webb, Jean Francis (III)
Willson, Robina Beckles
See Beckles Willson, Robina (Elizabeth)
Wilma, Dana
See Faralla, Dana
Wilsdorf, Anne 1954- *191*
Wilson, April 80
Wilson, Barbara Ker
See Ker Wilson, Barbara
Wilson, Beth P(ierre) 8
Wilson, Budge 1927- 55
Brief entry 51
Wilson, Carletta 1951- 81
Wilson, Carter 1941- 6
Wilson, Charles Morrow 1905-1977 30
Wilson, Christopher B. 1910(?)-1985
Obituary 46
Wilson, Darryl B(abe) 1939- 90
Wilson, Diane Lee 172
Wilson, Dirk
See Pohl, Frederik
Wilson, Dorothy Clarke 1904-2003 .... *16*
Wilson, Edward A(rthur) 1886-1970 38
Wilson, Ellen (Janet Cameron) (?)-1976 9
Obituary 26
Wilson, Eric (H.) 1940- 34
Brief entry 32

Wilson, Erica 51
Wilson, Forrest 1918- 27
Wilson, Gahan 1930- 35
Brief entry 27
Wilson, Gina 1943- 85
Brief entry 34
Earlier sketch in SATA *36*
Wilson, (Leslie) Granville 1912- *14*
Wilson, Hazel (Hutchins) 1898-1992 3
Obituary 73
Wilson, J(erry) M. 1964- *121*
Wilson, Jacqueline 1945- 199
Brief entry 52
Earlier sketches in SATA *61, 102, 153*
Wilson, John 1922- 22
Wilson, John 1951- 182
Wilson, John Alexander
See Wilson, John
Wilson, Johnniece Marshall 1944- 75
Wilson, Jonathan 1950- 181
Wilson, Joyce M(uriel Judson) 84
Earlier sketch in SATA *21*
See also SAAS 24
Wilson, Karma 174
Wilson, Leslie 1952- 166
Wilson, Linda Miller 1936- 116
Wilson, Lionel 1924-2003 33
Brief entry 31
Obituary 144
Wilson, Marjorie
See Wilson, Budge
Wilson, Maurice (Charles John) 1914- 46
Wilson, Nancy Hope 1947- 138
Earlier sketch in SATA *81*
Wilson, Nathan D.
See Wilson, N.D.
Wilson, N.D. 1978- 194
Wilson, Nick
See Ellis, Edward S(ylvester)
Wilson, Phil 1948- 181
Wilson, Ron(ald William) 1941- 38
Wilson, Sarah 1934- 142
Earlier sketch in SATA *50*
Wilson, Tom 1931- 33
Brief entry 30
Wilson, Troy 1970- 169
Wilson, Walt(er N.) 1939- 14
Wilson-Max, Ken 1965- 170
Earlier sketch in SATA *93*
Wilton, Elizabeth 1937- 14
Wilton, Hal
See Pepper, Frank S.
Wilwerding, Walter Joseph 1891-1966 9
Wimmer, Mike 1961- 194
Earlier sketch in SATA *70*
Winborn, Marsha (Lynn) 1947- 75
Winch, John 1944- 165
Earlier sketch in SATA *117*
Winchester, James H(ugh) 1917-1985 30
Obituary 45
Winchester, Stanley
See Youd, (Christopher) Samuel
Windawi, Thura al- 1983(?)- 165
Winders, Gertrude Hecker -1987 3
Windham, Basil
See Wodehouse, P(elham) G(renville)
Windham, Kathryn T(ucker) 1918- *14*
Windham, Sophie 184
Windling, Terri 1958- 151
Windrow, Martin
See Windrow, Martin Clive
Windrow, Martin C.
See Windrow, Martin Clive
Windrow, Martin Clive 1944- 68
Windsor, Claire
See Hamerstrom, Frances
Windsor, Linda 1950- 124
Windsor, Patricia 1938- 78
Earlier sketch in SATA *30*
See also SAAS 19
Wineman-Marcus, Irene 1952- 81

Winer, Yvonne 1934- *120*
Winerip, Michael 175
Winfield, Arthur M.
See Stratemeyer, Edward L.
Winfield, Edna
See Stratemeyer, Edward L.
Winfield, Julia
See Armstrong, Jennifer
Wing, Natasha (Lazutin) 1960- 82
Winick, Judd 1970- 124
Winks, Robin William 1930-2003 61
Winn, Alison
See Wharmby, Margot
Winn, Chris 1952- 42
Winn, Janet Bruce 1928- 43
Winn, Marie 1936(?)- 38
Winnick, Karen B(eth) B(inkoff) 1946- 51
Winn-Lederer, Ilene 198
Winslow, Barbara 1947- 91
Winstead, Rosie 180
Winston, Clara 1921-1983 54
Obituary 39
Winston, Richard 1917-1979 54
Winter, Janet 1926- 126
Winter, Jeanette 1939- 184
Earlier sketch in SATA *151*
Winter, Jonah 1962- 179
Winter, Milo (Kendall) 1888-1956 21
Winter, Paula Cecelia 1929- 48
Winter, R. R.
See Winterbotham, R(ussell) R(obert)
Winter, Susan 182
Winterbotham, R(ussell) R(obert)
1904-1971 10
Winterbotham, Russ
See Winterbotham, R(ussell) R(obert)
Winterfeld, Henry 1901-1990 55
Winters, J. C.
See Cross, Gilbert B.
Winters, Jon
See Cross, Gilbert B.
Winters, Katherine 1936- 153
Earlier sketch in SATA *103*
Winters, Kay
See Winters, Katherine
Winters, Nina 1944- 62
Winters, Paul A. 1965- 106
Winterson, Jeanette 1959- 190
Winterton, Gayle
See Adams, William Taylor
Winthrop, Elizabeth
See Mahony, Elizabeth Winthrop
Winton, Ian (Kenneth) 1960- 76
Winton, Tim 1960- 98
Wintz-Litty, Julie
See Litty, Julie
Wirt, Ann
See Benson, Mildred (Augustine Wirt)
Wirt, Mildred A.
See Benson, Mildred (Augustine Wirt)
Wirtenberg, Patricia Z. 1932-2007 10
Wirtenberg, Patricia Zarrella
See Wirtenberg, Patricia Z.
Wirth, Beverly 1938- 63
Wirths, Claudine (Turner) G(ibson)
1926-2000 104
Earlier sketch in SATA *64*
Wise, Bill 1958- 191
Wise, Lenny
See Wise, Leonard
Wise, Leonard 1940- 167
Wise, Leonard A.
See Wise, Leonard
Wise, Leonard Allan
See Wise, Leonard
Wise, William 1923- 163
Earlier sketch in SATA *4*
Wise, Winifred E. 2
Wiseman, Ann (Sayre) 1926- 31
Wiseman, B(ernard) 1922-1995 4

Wiseman, David 1916- 43
  Brief entry 40
Wishinsky, Frieda 1948- 166
  Earlier sketches in SATA 70, 112
Wisler, G(ary) Clifton 1950- 103
  Brief entry 46
  Earlier sketch in SATA 58
Wismer, Donald (Richard) 1946- 59
Wisner, Bill
  See Wisner, William L.
Wisner, William L. 1914(?)-1983 42
Wisnewski, David 1953-2002
  See Wisniewski, David
Wisniewski, David 1953-2002 95
  Obituary 139
  See also CLR 51
Wister, Owen 1860-1938 62
Witham, (Phillip) Ross 1917- 37
Withers, Carl A. 1900-1970 14
Withers, Pam 1956- 182
Withrow, Sarah 1966- 199
  Earlier sketch in SATA 124
Witt, Dick 1948- 80
Witt, Shirley Hill 1934- 17
Wittanen, Etolin 1907- 55
Wittels, Harriet Joan 1938- 31
Wittig, Susan
  See Albert, Susan Wittig
Wittlinger, Ellen 1948- 189
  Autobiography Feature 128
  Earlier sketches in SATA 83, 122
Wittman, Sally (Anne Christensen) 1941- 30
Witty, Paul 1898-1976 50
  Obituary 30
Wodehouse, P(elham) G(renville)
  1881-1975 22
Wodge, Dreary
  See Gorey, Edward (St. John)
Woelfle, Gretchen 1945- 145
Wohlberg, Meg 1905-1990 41
  Obituary 66
Wohlrabe, Raymond A. 1900-1977 4
Wohnoutka, Mike 195
Wojciechowska, Maia (Teresa) 1927-2002 ... 83
  Autobiography Feature 104
  Obituary 134
  Earlier sketches in SATA 1, 28
  See also CLR 1
  See also SAAS 1
Wojciechowski, Susan 126
  Earlier sketch in SATA 78
Wojnarowski, Adrian 1970- 190
Wolcott, Patty 1929- 14
Wold, Allen L. 1943- 64
Wold, Jo Anne 1938- 30
Woldin, Beth Weiner 1955- 34
Wolf, Allan 1963- 192
Wolf, Bernard 1930- 102
  Brief entry 37
Wolf, Erica (Van Varick) 1978- 156
Wolf, Gita 1956- 101
Wolf, Janet 1957- 78
Wolf, J.M.
  See Wolf, Joan M.
Wolf, Joan M. 1966- 193
Wolf, Sallie 1950- 80
Wolfe, Art 1952- 76
Wolfe, Burton H. 1932- 5
Wolfe, Gene 1931- 165
  Earlier sketch in SATA 118
Wolfe, Gene Rodman
  See Wolfe, Gene
Wolfe, Gillian 199
Wolfe, Louis 1905-1985 8
  Obituary 133
Wolfe, Rinna (Evelyn) 1925- 38
Wolfenden, George
  See Beardmore, George
Wolfer, Dianne 1961- 167
  Autobiography Feature 117
  Earlier sketch in SATA 104

Wolff, Alexander (Nikolaus) 1957- 137
  Earlier sketch in SATA 63
Wolff, Ashley 1956- 155
  Earlier sketches in SATA 50, 81
Wolff, Diane 1945- 27
Wolff, Ferida 1946- 164
  Earlier sketch in SATA 79
Wolff, Jennifer Ashley
  See Wolff, Ashley
Wolff, Robert Jay 1905-1977 10
Wolff, Sonia
  See Levitin, Sonia
Wolff, Virginia Euwer 1937- 137
  Earlier sketch in SATA 78
  See also CLR 62
Wolfman, Judy 1933- 138
Wolfson, Evelyn 1937- 62
Wolitzer, Hilma 1930- 31
Wolkoff, Judie (Edwards) 93
  Brief entry 37
Wolkstein, Diane 1942- 138
  Earlier sketches in SATA 7, 82
Wollheim, Donald A(llen) 1914-1990
  Obituary 69
Wolny, P.
  See Janeczko, Paul B(ryan)
Wolters, Richard A. 1920-1993 35
Wondriska, William 1931- 6
Wong, Jade Snow 1922-2006 112
  Obituary 175
Wong, Janet S. 1962- 148
  Earlier sketch in SATA 98
  See also CLR 94
Wood, Anne (Savage) 1937- 64
Wood, Audrey 198
  Brief entry 44
  Earlier sketches in SATA 50, 81, 139
  See also CLR 26
Wood, Catherine
  See Etchison, Birdie L(ee)
Wood, David 1944- 87
Wood, Don 1945- 50
  Brief entry 44
  See also CLR 26
Wood, Douglas 1951- 180
  Earlier sketches in SATA 81, 132
Wood, Douglas Eric
  See Wood, Douglas
Wood, Edgar A(llardyce) 1907-1998 14
Wood, Esther
  See Brady, Esther Wood
Wood, Frances Elizabeth 34
Wood, Frances M. 1951- 97
Wood, James Playsted 1905- 1
Wood, Jenny 1955- 88
Wood, John Norris 1930- 85
Wood, June Rae 1946- 120
  Earlier sketch in SATA 79
  See also CLR 82
Wood, Kerry
  See Wood, Edgar A(llardyce)
Wood, Kim Marie 134
Wood, Laura N.
  See Roper, Laura (Newbold) Wood
Wood, Linda C(arol) 1945- 59
Wood, Marcia 1956- 80
Wood, Marcia Mae
  See Wood, Marcia
Wood, Nancy
  See Wood, Nancy C.
Wood, Nancy C. 1936- 178
  Earlier sketch in SATA 6
Wood, Nuria
  See Nobisso, Josephine
Wood, Owen 1929- 64
Wood, Phyllis Anderson 1923- 33
  Brief entry 30
Wood, Richard 1949- 110
Wood, Tim(othy William Russell) 1946- 88
Wood, Wallace 1927-1981
  Obituary 33

Woodard, Carol 1929- 14
Woodburn, John Henry 1914- 11
Woodbury, David Oakes 1896-1981 62
Woodford, Peggy 1937- 25
Woodhouse, Barbara (Blackburn)
  1910-1988 63
Woodhull, Ann Love 194
Wooding, Chris 1977- 166
Wooding, Sharon
  See Wooding, Sharon L(ouise)
Wooding, Sharon L(ouise) 1943- 66
Woodman, Allen 1954- 76
Woodrich, Mary Neville 1915- 2
Woodruff, Elvira 1951- 162
  Earlier sketches in SATA 70, 106
Woodruff, Joan Leslie 1953- 104
Woodruff, Liza 1971(?)- 182
Woodruff, Marian
  See Goudge, Eileen
Woodruff, Noah 1977- 86
Woods, George A(llan) 1926-1988 30
  Obituary 57
Woods, Geraldine 1948- 111
  Brief entry 42
  Earlier sketch in SATA 56
Woods, Harold 1945- 56
  Brief entry 42
Woods, Lawrence
  See Lowndes, Robert A(ugustine) W(ard)
Woods, Margaret 1921- 2
Woods, Nat
  See Stratemeyer, Edward L.
Woods, Titania
  See Weatherly, Lee
Woodson, Jack
  See Woodson, John Waddie Jr.
Woodson, Jacqueline 1964- 189
  Earlier sketches in SATA 94, 139
  See also CLR 49
Woodson, Jacqueline Amanda
  See Woodson, Jacqueline
Woodson, John Waddie Jr. 1913- 10
Woodtor, Dee
  See Woodtor, Delores Parmer
Woodtor, Dee Parmer 1945(?)-2002
  See Woodtor, Delores Parmer
Woodtor, Delores Parmer 1945-2002 93
Wood-Trost, Lucille
  See Trost, Lucille W(ood)
Woodward, (Landon) Cleveland 1900-1986 . 10
  Obituary 48
Woodworth, Chris 1957- 168
Woodworth, Viki 1952- 127
Woody, Regina Jones 1894-1983 3
Woodyadd, Charlotte
  See Hough, Charlotte
Woog, Adam 1953- 125
  Earlier sketch in SATA 84
Wooldridge, Connie Nordhielm 1950- 143
  Earlier sketch in SATA 92
Wooldridge, Frosty 1947- 140
Wooldridge, Rhoda 1906-1988 22
Wooley, Susan Frelick 1945- 113
Woolf, Paula 1950- 104
Woolfe, Angela 1976- 169
Woolley, Catherine 1904-2005 3
  Obituary 166
Woolman, Steven 1969-2004 163
  Earlier sketch in SATA 90
Woolsey, Janette 1904-1989 3
  Obituary 131
Worcester, Donald E(mmet) 1915- 18
Word, Reagan 1944- 103
Work, Virginia 1946- 57
  Brief entry 45
Worline, Bonnie Bess 1914- 14
Wormell, Christopher 1955- 154
  Earlier sketch in SATA 103
Wormell, Mary 1959- 96

Wormser, Richard 1933- *106*
   Autobiography Feature *118*
   See also SAAS 26
Wormser, Sophie 1897-1979 .... *22*
Worth, Richard 1945- *59*
   Brief entry *46*
Worth, Valerie 1933-1994 .... *81*
   Earlier sketches in SATA *8, 70*
   See also CLR *21*
Wortis, Avi
   See Avi
Wortis, Edward Irving
   See Avi
Wosmek, Frances 1917- *29*
Woychuk, Denis 1953- *71*
Wrede, Patricia C(ollins) 1953- *146*
   Earlier sketch in SATA *67*
Wriggins, Sally Hovey 1922- *17*
Wright, Alexandra 1979- *103*
Wright, Betty Ren 1927- *109*
   Brief entry *48*
   Earlier sketch in SATA *63*
Wright, Cliff 1963- *168*
   Earlier sketch in SATA *76*
Wright, Courtni
   See Wright, Courtni C(rump)
Wright, Courtni C(rump) 1950- *84*
Wright, Courtni Crump
   See Wright, Courtni C(rump)
Wright, Dare 1914(?)-2001 .... *21*
   Obituary *124*
Wright, David K. 1943- *112*
   Earlier sketch in SATA *73*
Wright, Elinor
   See Lyon, Elinor
Wright, Enid Meadowcroft (LaMonte)
   1898-1966 .... *3*
Wright, Esmond 1915-2003 .... *10*
Wright, Frances Fitzpatrick 1897-1982 .... *10*
Wright, J. B.
   See Barkan, Joanne
Wright, Judith 1915-2000 .... *14*
   Obituary *121*
Wright, Judith Arundell
   See Wright, Judith
Wright, Katrina
   See Gater, Dilys
Wright, Kenneth
   See del Rey, Lester
Wright, Kit 1944- *87*
Wright, Leslie B(ailey) 1959- *91*
Wright, Michael 1954- *198*
Wright, Nancy Means *38*
Wright, R(obert) H(amilton) 1906- *6*
Wright, Rachel *134*
Wright, Susan Kimmel 1950- *97*
Wrightfrierson
   See Wright-Frierson, Virginia (Marguerite)
Wright-Frierson, Virginia (Marguerite)
   1949- *110*
   Earlier sketch in SATA *58*
Wrightson, (Alice) Patricia 1921- *112*
   Earlier sketches in SATA *8, 66*
   See also CLR *14*
   See also SAAS *4*
Wroble, Lisa A. 1963- *134*
Wrongo, I.B.
   See Katz, Alan
Wronker, Lili
   See Wronker, Lili Cassel
Wronker, Lili Cassel 1924- *10*
Wryde, Dogear
   See Gorey, Edward (St. John)
Wu, Elizabeth
   See Wu, Liz
Wu, Liz *184*
Wu, Norbert 1961- *155*
   Earlier sketch in SATA *101*
Wulffson, Don 1943- *155*
   Earlier sketches in SATA *32, 88*

Wulffson, Don L.
   See Wulffson, Don
Wunderli, Stephen 1958- *79*
Wunsch, Josephine (McLean) 1914- *64*
Wuorio, Eva-Lis 1918- *34*
   Brief entry *28*
Wurts, Janny 1953- *98*
Wyatt, B. D.
   See Robinson, Spider
Wyatt, David 1968- *185*
Wyatt, Jane
   See Bradbury, Bianca (Ryley)
Wyatt, Melissa 1963- *177*
Wyeth, Betsy James 1921- *41*
Wyeth, N(ewell) C(onvers) 1882-1945 .... *17*
   See also CLR *106*
Wyler, Rose 1909-2000 .... *18*
   Obituary *121*
Wylie, Betty Jane *48*
Wylie, Laura
   See Matthews, Patricia
Wylie, Laurie
   See Matthews, Patricia
Wyllie, Stephen *86*
Wyman, Andrea *75*
Wyman, Carolyn 1956- *83*
Wymer, Norman (George) 1911- *25*
Wynard, Talbot
   See Hamilton, Charles (Harold St. John)
Wyndham, John
   See Harris, John (Wyndham Parkes Lucas)
   Beynon
Wyndham, Lee
   See Hyndman, Jane Andrews Lee
Wyndham, Robert
   See Hyndman, Robert Utley
Wynne-Jones, Tim 1948- *186*
   Autobiography Feature *136*
   Earlier sketches in SATA *67, 96, 136*
   See also CLR *58*
Wynne-Jones, Timothy
   See Wynne-Jones, Tim
Wynter, Edward (John) 1914- *14*
Wynyard, Talbot
   See Hamilton, Charles (Harold St. John)
Wyss, Johann David Von 1743-1818 .... *29*
   Brief entry *27*
   See also CLR *92*
Wyss, Thelma Hatch 1934- *140*
   Earlier sketch in SATA *10*

X

Xavier, Father
   See Hurwood, Bernhardt J.
Xuan, YongSheng 1952- *116*
   Autobiography Feature *119*

Y

Yaccarino, Dan *192*
   Earlier sketch in SATA *141*
Yadin, (Rav-Aloof) Yigael 1917-1984 .... *55*
Yaffe, Alan
   See Yorinks, Arthur
Yagher, Kevin 1962- *143*
Yakovetic, (Joseph Sandy) 1952- *59*
Yakovetic, Joe
   See Yakovetic, (Joseph Sandy)
Yamada, Utako 1963- *188*
Yamaguchi, Marianne (Illenberger) 1936- *7*
Yamaka, Sara 1978- *92*
Yamanaka, Lois-Ann 1961- *166*
Yancey, Diane 1951- *138*
   Earlier sketch in SATA *81*
Yancey, Richard *193*
Yancey, Rick
   See Yancey, Richard

Yang, Belle 1960- *170*
Yang, James 1960- *190*
Yang, Jay 1941- *12*
Yang, Mingyi 1943- *72*
Yarbrough, Camille 1938- *79*
   See also CLR *29*
Yarbrough, Ira 1910(?)-1983
   Obituary *35*
Yaroslava
   See Mills, Yaroslava Surmach
Yarrow, Peter 1938- *195*
Yashima, Taro
   See Iwamatsu, Jun Atsushi
Yates, Elizabeth 1905-2001 .... *68*
   Obituary *128*
   Earlier sketch in SATA *4*
   See also SAAS 6
Yates, Janelle K(aye) 1957- *77*
Yates, John 1939- *74*
Yates, Philip 1958- *149*
   Earlier sketch in SATA *92*
Yates, Raymond F(rancis) 1895-1966 .... *31*
Yaukey, Grace S(ydenstricker) 1899-1994 ... *80*
   Earlier sketch in SATA *5*
Ye, Ting-xing 1952- *106*
Yeahpau, Thomas M. 1975- *187*
Yeakley, Marjory Hall 1908- *21*
Yeatman, Linda 1938- *42*
Yee, Brenda Shannon *133*
Yee, Lisa 1959- *160*
Yee, Paul (R.) 1956- *143*
   Earlier sketches in SATA *67, 96*
   See also CLR *44*
Yee, Wong Herbert 1953- *172*
   Earlier sketches in SATA *78, 115*
Yeh, Chun-Chan 1914- *79*
   See Ye Junjian
Ye Junjian
   See Yeh, Chun-Chan
Yelchin, Eugene 1956- *196*
Yenawine, Philip 1942- *85*
Yensid, Retlaw
   See Disney, Walt(er Elias)
Yeo, Wilma (Lethem) 1918-1994 .... *81*
   Earlier sketch in SATA *24*
Yeoman, John 1934- *80*
   Earlier sketch in SATA *28*
   See also CLR *46*
Yep, Laurence 1948- *176*
   Earlier sketches in SATA *7, 69, 123*
   See also CLR *132*
Yep, Laurence Michael
   See Yep, Laurence
Yepsen, Roger B(ennet), Jr. 1947- *59*
Yerian, Cameron John *21*
Yerian, Margaret A. *21*
Yerxa, Leo 1947- *181*
Yetska
   See Ironside, Jetske
Yezerski, Thomas F. 1969- *190*
Yin *194*
Ylvisaker, Anne 1965(?)- *172*
Yoder, Carolyn P(atricia) 1953- *149*
Yoder, Dorothy Meenen 1921- *96*
Yoder, Dot
   See Yoder, Dorothy Meenen
Yoder, Walter D. 1933- *88*
Yolen, Jane 1939- *194*
   Autobiography Feature *111*
   Earlier sketches in SATA *4, 40, 75, 112, 158*
   See also CLR *44*
   See also SAAS *1*
Yolen, Jane Hyatt
   See Yolen, Jane
Yonezu, Yusuke *196*
Yonge, Charlotte (Mary) 1823-1901 .... *17*
Yoo, Paula 1969(?)- *174*
Yoo, Taeeun *191*
Yorinks, Adrienne 1956- *171*

Yorinks, Arthur 1953- *144*
  Earlier sketches in SATA *33, 49, 85*
  See also CLR *20*
York, Alison
  See Nicole, Christopher (Robin)
York, Andrew
  See Nicole, Christopher (Robin)
York, Carol Beach 1928- *77*
  Earlier sketch in SATA *6*
York, Rebecca
  See Buckholtz, Eileen (Garber)
  and Glick, Ruth (Burtnick)
York, Simon
  See Heinlein, Robert A.
Yoshida, Toshi 1911- *77*
Yoshikawa, Sachiko *181*
Yost, Edna 1889-1971
  Obituary *26*
Youd, C. S.
  See Youd, (Christopher) Samuel
Youd, (Christopher) Samuel 1922- *135*
  Brief entry *30*
  Earlier sketch in SATA *47*
  See also CLR *2*
  See also SAAS *6*
Young, Amy L. *185*
Young, Bob
  See Young, Robert W(illiam)
  and Young, James Robert
Young, Carol 1945- *102*
Young, Catherine
  See Olds, Helen Diehl
Young, Clarence
  See Stratemeyer, Edward L.
Young, Collier
  See Bloch, Robert (Albert)
Young, Dan 1952- *126*
Young, Dianne 1959- *88*
Young, Dorothea Bennett 1924- *31*
Young, Ed 1931- *173*
  Earlier sketches in SATA *10, 74, 122*
  See also CLR *27*
Young, Ed Tse-chun
  See Young, Ed
Young, Edward
  See Reinfeld, Fred
Young, Elaine L.
  See Schulte, Elaine L(ouise)
Young, James
  See Graham, Ian
Young, Jan
  See Young, Janet Randall
Young, Janet 1957- *188*
Young, Janet Randall 1919-1994 .... *3*
Young, Janet Ruth
  See Young, Janet
Young, Jeff C. 1948- *132*
Young, John
  See Macintosh, Brownie
Young, Judy 1956- *155*
Young, Judy (Elaine) Dockrey 1949- *72*
Young, Karen Romano 1959- *168*
  Earlier sketch in SATA *116*
Young, Ken 1956- *86*
Young, Lois Horton 1911-1981 .... *26*
Young, Louisa *161*
Young, Louise B. 1919- *64*
Young, Margaret B(uckner) 1922- *2*
Young, Mary 1940- *89*
Young, Miriam 1913-1974 .... *7*
Young, Noela 1930- *89*
Young, (Rodney Lee) Patrick (Jr.) 1937- *22*
Young, Percy M(arshall) 1912-2004 .... *31*
  Obituary *154*
Young, Richard Alan 1946- *72*
Young, Robert W(illiam) 1916-1969 .... *3*
Young, Ross B. 1955- *150*
Young, Ruth 1946- *67*
Young, Sara
  See Pennypacker, Sara
Young, Scott A. 1918-2005 .... *5*

Young, Scott Alexander
  See Young, Scott A.
Young, Vivien
  See Gater, Dilys
Younger, Barbara 1954- *108*
Youngs, Betty 1934-1985 .... *53*
  Obituary *42*
Younkin, Paula 1942- *77*
Yount, Lisa (Ann) 1944- *124*
  Earlier sketch in SATA *74*
Yourgrau, Barry *179*
Yuditskaya, Tatyana 1964- *75*
Yumoto, Kazumi 1959- *153*

Z

Zach, Cheryl (Byrd) 1947- *98*
  Brief entry *51*
  Earlier sketch in SATA *58*
  See also SAAS *24*
Zacharias, Gary L. 1946- *153*
Zaffo, George J. (?)-1984 .... *42*
Zagarenski, Pamela 1969(?)- *183*
Zagwyn, Deborah Turney 1953- *138*
  Earlier sketch in SATA *78*
Zahares, Wade *193*
Zahn, Timothy 1951- *156*
  Earlier sketch in SATA *91*
Zaid, Barry 1938- *51*
Zaidenberg, Arthur 1908(?)-1990 .... *34*
  Obituary *66*
Zalben, Jane Breskin 1950- *170*
  Earlier sketches in SATA *7, 79, 120*
  See also CLR *84*
Zallinger, Jean (Day) 1918- *115*
  Earlier sketches in SATA *14, 80*
Zallinger, Peter Franz 1943- *49*
Zambreno, Mary Frances 1954- *140*
  Earlier sketch in SATA *75*
Zanderbergen, George
  See May, Julian
Zappa, Ahmet 1974- *180*
Zappa, Ahmet Emuukha Rodan
  See Zappa, Ahmet
Zappler, Lisbeth 1930- *10*
Zarchy, Harry 1912-1987 .... *34*
Zarin, Cynthia 1959- *192*
  Earlier sketch in SATA *108*
Zaring, Jane (Thomas) 1936- *40*
Zarins, Joyce Audy
  See dos Santos, Joyce Audy
Zaslavsky, Claudia 1917- *36*
Zaugg, Sandra L. 1938- *118*
Zaugg, Sandy
  See Zaugg, Sandra L.
Zaunders, Bo 1939- *137*
Zawadzki, Marek 1958- *97*
Zebra, A.
  See Scoltock, Jack
Zebrowski, George 1945- *67*
Zebrowski, George T.
  See Zebrowski, George
Zeck, Gerald Anthony 1939- *40*
Zeck, Gerry
  See Zeck, Gerald Anthony
Zed, Dr.
  See Penrose, Gordon
Zei, Alki 1925- *24*
  See also CLR *6*
Zeier, Joan T(heresa) 1931- *81*
Zeinert, Karen 1942-2002 .... *137*
  Earlier sketch in SATA *79*
Zeises, Lara M. 1976- *184*
  Earlier sketch in SATA *145*
Zelazny, Roger 1937-1995 .... *57*
  Brief entry *39*
Zelazny, Roger Joseph
  See Zelazny, Roger

Zeldis, Malcah 1931- *146*
  Earlier sketch in SATA *86*
Zelinsky, Paul O. 1953- *154*
  Brief entry *33*
  Earlier sketches in SATA *49, 102*
  See also CLR *55*
Zellan, Audrey Penn
  See Penn, Audrey
Zemach, Harve
  See Fischtrom, Harvey
Zemach, Kaethe 1958- *149*
  Brief entry *39*
  Earlier sketch in SATA *49*
Zemach, Margot 1931-1989 .... *70*
  Obituary *59*
  Earlier sketch in SATA *21*
Zemach-Bersin, Kaethe
  See Zemach, Kaethe
Zeman, Ludmila 1947- *153*
Zephaniah, Benjamin 1958- *189*
  Earlier sketches in SATA *86, 140*
Zephaniah, Benjamin Obadiah Iqbal
  See Zephaniah, Benjamin
Zephaniah, Benjamin Pbadiah Iqubal
  See Zephaniah, Benjamin
Zephaniah, Benjamin Pbadiah Iqubal
  See Zephaniah, Benjamin
Zerman, Melvyn Bernard 1930- *46*
Zettner, Pat 1940- *70*
Zevin, Gabrielle *176*
Zhang, Christopher Zhong-Yuan 1954- *91*
Zhang, Song Nan 1942- *170*
  Earlier sketch in SATA *85*
Ziefert, Harriet 1941- *154*
  Earlier sketch in SATA *101*
Ziegler, Jack (Denmore) 1942- *60*
Ziemienski, Dennis (Theodore) 1947- *10*
Ziliox, Marc
  See Fichter, George S.
Zillah
  See Macdonald, Zillah K(atherine)
Zim, Herbert S(pencer) 1909-1994 .... *30*
  Obituary *85*
  Earlier sketch in SATA *1*
  See also CLR *2*
  See also SAAS *2*
Zim, Sonia Bleeker 1909-1971 .... *2*
  Obituary *26*
Zima, Gordon 1920- *90*
Zimelman, Nathan 1921- *65*
  Brief entry *37*
Zimmer, Dirk 1943- *147*
  Earlier sketch in SATA *65*
Zimmer, Tracie Vaughn *169*
Zimmerman, Andrea 1950- *192*
  Earlier sketch in SATA *123*
Zimmerman, Andrea Griffing
  See Zimmerman, Andrea
Zimmerman, H. Werner 1951- *101*
Zimmerman, Heinz Werner
  See Zimmerman, H. Werner
Zimmerman, Naoma 1914-2004 .... *10*
Zimmermann, Arnold E. 1909- *58*
Zimmett, Debbie
  See Becker, Deborah Zimmett
Zimmy
  See Stratemeyer, Edward L.
Zimnik, Reiner 1930- *36*
  See also CLR *3*
Zindel, Bonnie 1943- *34*
Zindel, Lizabeth *187*
Zindel, Paul 1936-2003 .... *102*
  Obituary *142*
  Earlier sketches in SATA *16, 58*
  See also CLR *85*
Ziner, Feenie
  See Ziner, Florence
Ziner, Florence 1921- *5*
Zingara, Professor
  See Leeming, Joseph

Zinger, Yitskhok
 See Singer, Isaac Bashevis
Zion, Eugene 1913-1975 .... *18*
Zion, Gene
 See Zion, Eugene
Zoehfeld, Kathleen Weidner 1954- *193*
Zohorsky, Janet R. 1958- *148*
Zolkower, Edie Stoltz *171*
Zolkowski, Cathy (A.) 1969- *121*
Zollars, Jaime *191*
Zolotow, Charlotte 1915- *138*
 Earlier sketches in SATA *1, 35, 78*
 See also CLR *77*
Zolotow, Charlotte Gertrude Shapiro
 See Zolotow, Charlotte
Zolotow, Ellen
 See Dragonwagon, Crescent

Zonderman, Jon 1957- *92*
Zonia, Dhimitri 1921- *20*
Zonta, Pat 1951- *143*
Zubrowski, Bernard 1939- *90*
 Earlier sketch in SATA *35*
Zubrowski, Bernie
 See Zubrowski, Bernard
Zucker, Miriam S.
 See Reichert, Miriam Zucker
Zuckerman, Linda *190*
Zudeck, Darryl 1961- *61*
Zupa, G. Anthony
 See Zeck, Gerald Anthony
Zupancic, Lilijana Praprotnik
 See Prap, Lila
Zurbo, Matt(hew) 1967- *98*
Zurhorst, Charles (Stewart, Jr.) 1913-1989 .. *12*

Zurlo, Tony 1941- *145*
Zuromskis, Diane
 See Stanley, Diane
Zuromskis, Diane Stanley
 See Stanley, Diane
Zusak, Markus 1975- *149*
Zwahlen, Diana 1947- *88*
Zweifel, Frances W. 1931- *14*
Zwerger, Lisbeth 1954- *194*
 Earlier sketches in SATA *66, 130*
 See also CLR *46*
 See also SAAS *13*
Zwinger, Ann (H.) 1925- *46*
Zymet, Cathy Alter 1965- *121*